PENGUIN CLASSICS

CITY OF GOD

ADVISORY EDITOR: BETTY RADICE

St Augustine of Hippo, the great Doctor of the Latin Church, was born at Thagaste in North Africa in A.D. 354. The son of a pagan father and a Christian mother, he was brought up as an aspirant to Christianity but was not baptized. At the age of sixteen he went to Carthage to finish his education. In 375 on reading Cicero's *Hortensius* he became deeply interested in philosophy. He was converted to Manicheism, some of the tenets of which he continued to hold until he went to Rome to teach rhetoric in 383. At Milan he became Master of Rhetoric and came under the influence of both Neoplatonism and the preaching of St Ambrose After agonizing inward conflict he was converted to Christianity in 386 and was baptized in 387. He then returned to Africa and formed a religious community; but in 391 he was ordained priest, against his wishes, and five years later he was chosen bishop of Hippo.

For thirty-four years St Augustine lived in community with his clergy. His written output was vast: there survive 113 books and treatises, over 200 letters, and more than 500 sermons. Two of his longest works, his *Confessions* and *City of God*, have made an abiding mark on Western theology and literature. He died in 430 as invading Vandals were besieging Hippo.

John O'Meara, an authority on St Augustine and his Neoplatonic background, was born in Eyrecourt, County Galway, Ireland, in 1915 and was educated at University College, Dublin, and Oxford University. He was Professor of Latin at University College, Dublin, from 1948 to 1984, has been a Member of the Institute for Advanced Study, Princeton, N.J., in 1956, 1963, 1968 and 1975 and held a Fellowship from Harvard University at Dumbarton Oaks Byzantine and Mediaeval Humanities Research Center in Washington, D.C., from 1979 to 1984. He was Director of Studies on Johannes Scottus Eriugena at the Royal Irish Academy from 1984 to 1989, and has been a Research Associate in Classics at Trinity College, Dublin, since 1984. Among his published works are *The Young Augustine*, *Porphyry's Philosophy from Oracles in Augustine*, *Charter of Christendom: The Significance of the City of God* and *Eriugena*.

HENRY BETTENSON was born in 1908 and educated at Bristol University and Oriel College, Oxford. After ordination and some years in parish work he went into teaching and taught Classics for twenty-five years at Charterhouse. He was afterwards rector of Purleigh in Essex, and died in 1979. His other publications are *Documents of the Christian Church*, *The Early Christian Fathers*, *The Later Christian Fathers* and *Livy: Rome and the Mediterranean* (Penguin Classics).

ST AUGUSTINE

✥

Concerning

THE CITY OF GOD

against the Pagans

✥

A NEW TRANSLATION
BY HENRY BETTENSON
WITH AN INTRODUCTION
BY JOHN O'MEARA

PENGUIN BOOKS

PENGUIN BOOKS

Published by the Penguin Group
Penguin Books Ltd, 27 Wrights Lane, London W8 5TZ, England
Penguin Books USA Inc., 375 Hudson Street, New York, New York 10014, USA
Penguin Books Australia Ltd, Ringwood, Victoria, Australia
Penguin Books Canada Ltd, 10 Alcorn Avenue, Toronto, Ontario, Canada M4V 3B2
Penguin Books (NZ) Ltd, 182–190 Wairau Road, Auckland 10, New Zealand

Penguin Books Ltd, Registered Offices: Harmondsworth, Middlesex, England

First published 1467
This translation published in Pelican Books 1972
Reprinted with a new introduction in Penguin Classics 1984
11 13 15 17 19 20 18 16 14 12

Printed in England by Clays Ltd, St Ives plc

Introduction[1]

FEW books have given rise to so much misconception as the *City of God*. By some it is thought to give a philosophy, by others a theology of history. By some it is thought to contain well-developed political theories, to be hostile to the State as such and in particular to the Roman Empire, and to outline the provinces of an established Church and Christian State. By others it is considered to be primarily a Christian reply to the charge that Rome had been sacked because it had become Christian, as identifying the city of God with the Church, and as teaching that justice does not enter into the definition of the State.

More serious still: the teaching of Augustine on predestination, never accepted in its full rigour by the Church, is, although not prominent, grim and sombre in the *City of God*. The Pelagian controversy had tended to force him into some exaggeration, at least in his expressions, in relation both to Nature and to Grace. Yet when one has studied Augustine's life and works for long, one finds it difficult to believe that he was mainly a pessimist. One comes to expect, and indeed welcome, clear evidence of a countervailing optimism in keeping with a person so vital and so unreservedly generous in the service of man.

The *City of God* is no more purely theoretical than it is purely theological. It is, of course, mainly theological; but it is at the same time founded upon Augustine's own experience. It will be seen that it is an application of the theme of his own development and conversion, as described in the burning pages of the *Confessions*, to the broader, less immediate, canvas of man's destiny. Augustine's reflection upon his experience, especially at the time of his conversion, both in outline and in surprisingly precise details, is the key to much of his characteristic teaching.

We should take warning from this: however much he might regret some of the ingredients of his past, he was happy to recognize that through these experiences Providence had brought him to where,

1. Material from my *Charter of Christendom: the Significance of the City of God*, the Saint Augustine Lecture, Villanova University, 1961, Macmillan, New York, 1961, has been incorporated here and is duly acknowledged.

humanly speaking, he felt more secure. His attitude, therefore, to these things could not be wholly negative and condemnatory. On the contrary he formed from the pattern of his life a theory of providential economy that to many might seem both too living and too tolerant. If Rome and the philosophy of the Greeks could, for all their error, not merely not prevent him from accepting Christ and the Christian revelation, but actually encourage him to do so, why should they not be equally as useful to others – to all mankind? It might seem paradoxical, for example, that the bitterest enemy of the Christians, Porphyry, should through his writing play a significant role (along with other Neoplatonists) in Augustine's conversion. This, however, happened, and Augustine was willing to take account of it in his notions of the dealings of Providence with men.

It can be said that although the scope of Augustine's writings is immense, they are animated by a few central ideas that came to him from a sensitive brooding on his own life. Thus the leading ideas of both the *Confessions* and the *City of God*, as we shall see briefly, are anticipated in his first extant works. There we can see clearly how close life and thought come in the mind of Augustine.

It is a commonplace to say that the age of Augustine was very like our own. We should remember that our view of his times is distorted by over fifteen hundred years of Christian domination, which separate his times from ours. We may not be able to see the present and the future in focus; but at least we can make some attempt to strip the past of the encumbrances which our retrospective vision imposes on it.

Some now speak of our living in post-Christian times, and seem to imply that Christianity as a force in the world can but decline. And, indeed, when one contemplates the defection from Christianity and its disunity on the one hand, and on the other the emergence of the non-Christian peoples, who are as likely to assert their independence of Christianity as they are of Western political powers, one cannot feel a firm confidence in the future of Western Christendom.

And yet, when Augustine was writing the *City of God*, his confident reading of the future cannot have seemed so justified to many of his contemporaries as it is to us now. The prospects of Christianity in the first quarter of the fifth century may have seemed bright, but we tend to forget that until that time the Church's history had been one for the most part, of bare toleration and frequent persecution. Wit in Augustine's own life there had been the pagan reaction und Julian the Apostate (361–363 A.D.). Even in the fifth century paga had not lost all countenance. Again, the decline of the powerful and closely integrated Empire of Rome, evident to all and admitted by Augustine, must have struck its citizens with a chill as great as that which affects in our day the loosely and vaguely associated West.

We should, then, note that our situation is closer to his than, perhaps, is ordinarily realized. And we should take hope from his calm confidence that, even during such a crisis, it seemed feasible to draw up in the *City of God* a charter for a Christian future, not only for Rome but for all the world. The great lesson of the *City of God* is that out of all things comes good. Augustine saw clearly that in his time both Christianity and Rome would each benefit by the good that was in the other, and by any good from wherever else it might come. For Christianity, assimilation meant acceptance that was universal in the context of his time. For Rome, it meant a new birth and an even longer future. For Greek thought, it meant transmission and development. The keynote of the *City of God* is fulfilment, not destruction.

The practical problem with which Augustine had to deal was the problem of a spiritual Church in a secular world: the city of God in the city of this world. It is of the first importance to understand that he did not condemn out of hand the city of this world. It was God's creation. It was used by God for his purposes. It was not only of practical use to the citizens of God's city but was also intended by God to give compelling example to them of what efforts they should make in their striving for something greater and something higher. Out of that world and what good it had to offer Christians should take the 'spoils of the Egyptians' and should make them their own. They should profit from secular philosophy (which in its own way was a kind of revelation); they should learn from secular history (which in its own way threw prophetic light upon the future).

Speaking absolutely, if things were to be judged only by the canon of the service and worship of the true God, what the Hebrews achieved in their temporal history, the Greeks in their academies and the Romans in the virtues of their worthies, was evil. For evil was merely not-to-do-that-service-and-give-that-worship. In this way what looked like virtue was really splendid vice. But relatively, or in our ordinary way of speaking, all these things were good and should be used by Christianity. Christianity had changed superficially, was no longer the religion of a few fishermen but was, in fact, the religion of an Empire accepting its intellectual responsibility. This superficial change, which was wrought through assimilation, absorption, reaction and, it might be, rejection, was the law of its life.

Almost the only thing that could not be accepted from Rome was her official religion, polytheism. Insofar as the *City of God* is against anything, it is radically against that. It is unfortunate that Augustine, in placing the positive part of his argument in the final twelve books and the negative in the first ten, gives the impression that he is opposed to Rome and Greek philosophy. If he had stated the basis of his positive doctrine first, it would be seen more immediately that his attitude to Rome and Greece and his general outlook is positive.

Background to the City of God

Augustine, born and reared in Roman North Africa in the second half of the fourth century, grew up in an Empire that was in evident decline. Rome's marble city, her invincible army, her wide-flung administration, her riches garnered from every corner of the world, but above all her spirit and very heart were failing. The fatal blow came quickly. On a day in August in A.D. 410, Alaric with his Chrsitian–Arian Goths sacked the great city that had not known violation by a foreign enemy for eight hundred years.

One does not need much imagination or sensibility to understand how symbolic of impending doom Rome's fall might have seemed. Even two years afterwards, St Jerome was still so affected by it that he could not dictate his commentary on Ezechiel. He had, he complained, lost the memory of his own name and could but remain silent, knowing that it was a time to weep: with Rome had perished the human race. This was the reaction of a Christian – but, it should be added, an emotional one. Another Christian, Orosius, a contemporary of the event and the chief source of information on the sack of Rome, judges soberly that the damage to the city was not great.

It is well to bear in mind that, while the sack lasted but three days and was marked by the relative clemency of the conquerors, the overthrowing of the official Roman religion, a form of polytheism, had been prolonged, bitter and serious in its consequences. From the time of Constantine onwards, there had been a succession of edicts against paganism, twenty of them in the last twenty years of the fourth century, and as many as four in the last year of that century, as if it had been determined that with the century paganism should pass from the Empire forever: idols were to be dethroned; temples to be laicized; judges were to be supervised in the enforcement of the edicts; and bishops were to report any laxity in the carrying out of these instructions.

There had, of course, been opposition to such a policy. An instance of this can be seen in the short-lived respite of the reign of Julian the Apostate already mentioned. The symbolical event, however, in this spiritual struggle is usually seen in the confrontation of Symmachus, the Prefect of Rome and the outstanding professed pagan of his day, with St Ambrose of Milan on the question of the Altar of Victory in 384.

The great goddess Victory, associated with Jupiter (Chief of the Roman gods), and with Mars (god of war), worshipped by the army (the instrument of Rome's dominion), and intimately related to the felicity of the Emperor, had been furnished with an altar, the Altar of Victory, within the Senate House of Rome itself. There she had stood, presiding over the prosperity of Rome, an earnest and an omen of continuing success. This altar had been removed by Constantius, the father of Constantine, replaced by the pagans in due course, removed again under Gratian in 382, replaced for a brief period by Eugenius (392–394), and perhaps on a final occasion by Stilicho, who died in disgrace in 408.

Of Augustine's acquaintance with one of the protagonists, St Ambrose, in the symbolical confrontation on the Altar of Victory, it will not be necessary to say anything here. On the other hand we should remember that, when Augustine came to teach rhetoric in Carthage in 374 and had some acquaintance with official circles there, Symmachus was not only in residence as Proconsul of Africa but had also been one of the most successful rhetors of his time. It is not unlikely that they met then, but in any case Symmachus knew of Augustine at least later in Rome; for it was he, the most prominent pagan of his day, who recommended Augustine for appointment to the office of Master of Rhetoric at the Imperial Court, then at Milan, the See of St Ambrose. It is well to pause and reflect on the significance that this situation, pregnant as it was to be, must have had for Augustine. Here he was in Milan, a non-Christian as yet, recommended by the champion of the pagans – perhaps for the very reason, among others, that Augustine was not a Christian – at a court subject to the influence of the champion of the Christians. Augustine arrived in Milan in the autumn of 384, only a month or two after the dispute on the Altar of Victory.

Symmachus's part in the affair was to present a petition for the restoration of the altar, removed, as we have seen, in 382. As Prefect of the city of Rome and Pontifex Maximus, he stressed the necessity for prudence: no one knew the final secret explanation of Rome's prosperity: it was therefore unwise not to preserve the institutions that had presided over her success: it was perilous to disown them for something new. He brought Rome herself forward to plead her cause: she is old; she has no desire to change her pieties; her religion has civilized the world, driven the Gauls from the Capitol and Hannibal from the city.

St Ambrose, however, was a doughty opponent, as his domination of the Arian Empress Justina in 385–386 and of the Emperor Theodosius (with the imposition of a public penance in 390) was soon to show. His argument was that the valour and virtues of the Romans were sufficient explanation of their successes. Was it not foolish to pretend to believe that the Empire depended on some 'power' that one must imagine but could not see? To restrict the future through reverence for the past was to retard progress and civilization. Christianity had, moreover, a positive contribution to make: it held truth and salvation, while polytheism led to perdition and error.

The Christian cause prevailed, and paganism was clearly and definitely, if not finally, defeated. Prudentius, the Christian poet, describes how the Senate in plenary session formally banished Jupiter and the other gods in favour of the Christian God. The senators, many of whom were known to be dissembling, yielded to mounting public approbation of Christianity and abandoned for monotheism the gods of their forefathers. They made haste to disown their ancient pride, submit to baptism, and pay reverence at the tombs of Christian martyrs.

The ordinary people were not slow to show their satisfaction, and soon the temples were mouldering in desolation. Theodosius in his time was relentless in his enforcement of the edicts against polytheism throughout the Empire, and particularly those against sacrifice to the gods. Some indeed in their zeal, fearing that shrines that were merely empty might one day be restored, hastened to destroy the temples themselves – some of them splendid edifices. A few of them were converted to Christian use, the most famous of these being the Pantheon, the temple in Rome of all the gods, which to this day stands as it ever stood.

The decrees of Theodosius, however, reached further even than destruction of the buildings. Sacrifice to idols and divination by inspection of entrails – the commonplaces of public life in Rome – were declared to be high treason and were to be punished by death. Even the most trivial trafficking in garlands and libations was suspected and became liable to fines and confiscation of property.

The collapse of polytheism was in the end sudden, universal within the Empire, and practically absolute. Its absurdity as a religious system had long been accepted by the intelligent. Now the wholesale assault on buildings and institutions, with evident impunity and no retaliation from the ousted and enfeebled gods, delivered the masses from any feelings of fear or obligation. The dismemberment of the representation of the great god Serapis at Alexandria met with no revenge in either the death of a Christian or the refusal of the Nile to grant its annual and blessed inundation. Truly the gods had lost, and Christ had won.

Augustine was by his very circumstances a close observer of this stupendous transformation. As he was torn between the loyalties he owed first to Symmachus and then to St Ambrose, so his feelings and thoughts were divided between sympathy for the Rome that was and the vision of a Christian future. Nevertheless his evident delight at the destruction of the pagan temples at Carthage by Jovius and Gaudentius, for example, and his approval, even, of punishment by death for pagan sacrificing, leave no doubt where his final loyalty lay. He was not unaware that the recent desertion *en masse* from an enervated polytheism meant that there were Christians, many Christians even, who had yielded to Christ for unworthy motives – to save their lives or canvass official support for their careers and ambitions – but for all that he felt an overflowing happiness, later perhaps to be tempered, in the visible victory of the Christians.

It is hardly surprising, then, if Augustine's distress at the sack of Rome in 410 was not only much less pronounced than that of St Jerome but was compensated for by a greater optimism. If the pagan historians Zosimus and Rutilius Namatianus, writing of the period, say not a word of the disaster – possibly because they did not find it an attractive topic – we can understand that Augustine's fondness for a theme, about which he was sometimes teased, was prompted more by its wider significance, as marking a stage in the conflict between Christianity and paganism, than by any preoccupation with the material decline and fall of Rome. The theme was with him an old one even before the sack of Rome.

The question was, however, raised for him directly by a Christian official in Africa, Marcellinus – to whom in fact the *City of God* is addressed – in a letter in the year 412. Marcellinus mentioned the view put forward by some of his friends that the miracles wrought by Apollonius and Apuleius were greater than those of Christianity. He asked how, if God had been satisfied with the type of sacrifice described in the Old Testament, He could, without changing (which in

God is impossible), be dissatisfied with it in the New? Finally there arose the problem of why it was that the Empire appeared to decline when it came to be governed by princes that had forsaken the old, tried religion and embraced a new one that inculcated precepts of tolerating offences and submitting to injury. This did not seem to go well with the interests of the Empire.

One should note carefully that, although this letter was written about two years after the sack of Rome, and purported to give the views and complaints of pagans, there is not one word about the event in question, but rather the whole emphasis is on miracles, sacrifices and religion, as causes or explanations of success in Empire or failure.

Augustine replied in a letter to a friend of Marcellinus and in a further one to Marcellinus himself. The themes of these two letters (*Letters* 137 and 138) foreshadow very clearly themes of the *City of God*, and some of them must be briefly mentioned: the Saviour came when the time was ripe for his coming; that coming was foretold not only by the prophets but also by secular philosophers and poets; the true mediator delivered man from the false mediators – the demons; Christ superseded Moses, who was greater than any pagan; the truth of Christianity is seen in its fulfilment of prophecy and its confirmation by miracles; the world is declining and is in its last age; Christians are multiplying everywhere and await the eternal happiness of the heavenly city (*Letter* 137).

Letter 138 concentrates more on the question of religion and Empire: the gods of polytheism, being by definition many, were discordant and inimical to concord, which was the constituting element of the (Roman) State; this discord issued in civil wars; the gods favour the evils that corrupt man; Christianity, on the contrary, makes men better as soldiers, better as parents, better as children, better as masters, better as slaves, better as princes, better as judges, better as taxpayers and better as tax-gatherers. In short, Christianity was the great salvation for the State; it goes, however, beyond this life below and the harmony of the State, and provides entry to eternal salvation and the heavenly and divine republic of a certain eternal people. The splendid success of the Romans, achieved without the true religion, is perfected in their becoming citizens of another city. The letter goes on to insist that the pagan gods are less powerful than even Apollonius (of Tyana, 4th *c.* B.C.) or Apuleius (of Madauros, *fl. c.* 155 A.D.); the demons caused damage to the State and aroused hostility to Christianity; prosperity with the worship of the true God was seen in the temporal history of the Hebrews, whose dispersal, even as enemies of

Christianity, aided its spread; the miracles of Christianity are incomparably superior to any others.

Augustine ends this second letter by admitting that he has not managed to treat of all the points that he would wish. If Marcellinus writes for more, he will make it his business to reply either in a letter or in a book.

In the event he wrote a book for Marcellinus. It was the *City of God*, and it deals with essentially the same topics and with the same attitudes.[2]

Anticipations of the Theme in Augustine

Of the last stages in the conflict between polytheism and Christian monotheism, Augustine could not but have been conscious, at least from the time of his being recommended by Symmachus to Milan, where he encountered St Ambrose. His conversion in 386 represented in his own regard a victory for Christianity. It would not be surprising, then, if in the earliest compositions of Augustine there were adumbrations and preliminary formulations of what was later the dominating theme of the *City of God*. Here we shall confine ourselves to a few examples from his first extant works, which reflect very strongly his own personal experiences at the time of his conversion. Our purpose is to show how the main theme of the *City of God* – salvation, attained by the worship of the one true God and the rejection of all false gods – had already taken on a special significance for him as he reflected upon the pattern of his own life. Even at that stage he had begun to think that what was true for him was true for mankind at large.

Whereas salvation in the *City of God* is represented by citizenship in a city (*ciuitas*) – an image explicitly taken from the Scriptures – it is in the earliest formulations represented as arriving in harbour (*portus*), or at the fatherland (*patria*), or being on the way (*uia*). These images are, of course, borrowed from the stock in trade of philosophy, particularly Platonic philosophy, in its eschatological aspects. Other variants used by Augustine at this time are the 'land of desire', the 'land of happiness', the 'happy land' and the 'shining home'.

The first few pages of Augustine's first extant work, the *Contra Academicos* (*Against the Academics*), written after his conversion in 386, speak of the 'harbour' of wisdom, to which Providence, making

2. Books I–III were finished by 413; IV–V by 415; VI–X by 417; XI–XIV by 418 or 419; and XV–XXII by 427.

use of misfortune, brings us. Special emphasis is laid upon the irrelevance and instability of temporal prosperity. Here Augustine alludes directly not only to the apparent misfortunes of the friend to whom the book is addressed, but to his own: prosperity had almost entrapped him, but he had been compelled by illness to give up his profession and betake himself to philosophy, which, as the work makes clear, means philosophy subject to the authority of Christ. One can suppose that Augustine's views, on the irrelevance of prosperity and the use made by Providence of misfortune, might be applied by him to the Empire as much as to mankind in general or himself and his friend.

The image of the harbour is used again in the first five sections of the *De Beata Vita* (*On Happiness*), composed at the same time as the previous work. The major image here, however, is the 'land of desire'. There are two 'ways' to this land, both across a sea. One is the way of reason, which, possible only for the few, brings men to the harbour of philosophy, which is the harbour of the land of desire. The other way is the way of Providence which uses the storms of adversity to bring men, resist and wander in ignorance and folly as they may, to the same harbour. Those who are apparently most successful in life have need of the greatest storms. Some are brought to sanity, however, by the reading of books written by the learned and the wise. And some make their way to the 'fatherland' partly by their own use of reason, and partly by providential adversity.

One great hazard threatens all who approach the harbour – a high mountain in front of the harbour itself. It is so enticing that it lures to it not only those approaching the harbour, but even some that have already been in the harbour. The people living on this mountain are full of conceit, and fear that others might share their glory; hence they impress on those approaching the difficulty, because of submerged rocks, of joining them and are happy to advise them how they can get to the land of desire. In this way they are themselves destroyed within sight of the 'shining home'.

Finally – a most important point – the harbour is wide, and one may still fail to put ashore and so not achieve one's goal.

There are significant anticipations of the *City of God* here. The term 'citizen' is used, and the phrase 'on pilgrimage from their fatherland' is one characteristically applied in the later work to the citizens of the heavenly city in their life on earth. The illusions of prosperity and the transcendent role of Providence in its use of adversity are here fully emphasized. Of particular significance, however, is the special mention of the envious and the proud, who help others to safety, but are themselves destroyed within sight of the fatherland. This, of course, must refer especially to certain Neoplatonists, who approached Christianity, helped others to become Christians, but rejected Christianity themselves. It is to be noted that not all mankind reaches the harbour, and those who are there may still be lost: so too might Christians fail to persevere.

What is of special interest for us here is Augustine's explicit relation of this theme and image to the circumstances of his own life at the time. Here indeed he gives a summary autobiography, parallel to that given in the *Contra Academicos* (Bk II, 4f.), and later to be expanded in the *Confessions*. It is clear that the theme, as set out in the *De Beata Vita*, is inspired by his own life: the providential use of illness, the effect of reading certain books (a very precise detail that he repeats and applies without hesitation to other men), his own part use of reason and part guidance by Providence, the illusions of prosperity, and the help of the proud Neoplatonists, who did not benefit from their own wisdom.

In short we have here the opportunity of seeing how the theme of the *City of God* is constructed from the details of his own conversion. To put it another way, the *City of God* is the application of the *Confessions* to the history of mankind. The inspiration of Augustine's themes is in his life.

The image of the way is found first in Augustine in, again, the *Contra Academicos* (Bk III, 34). Here we are given the story of two men travelling to the same destination, one of whom has too much and the other too little credulity. At a crossroads they meet a humble shepherd whose directions the one accepts without question and proceeds to follow. The other ridicules such credulity and does not move. By the time an elegant gentleman comes along on horseback he is finding his waiting tedious, and accordingly acts upon the directions given by the elegant gentleman, although he does not accept them as necessarily true and they conflict with those given by the shepherd. In the event he gets lost in the woods and trackless mountains – for the elegant gentleman was an impostor. Meanwhile his companion is resting at his destination.

The source of this image may have been epistemological, but Augustine explicitly refers its use here to the deeds and behaviour of men. Philosophers and those interested in religion had done so before him, and amongst those was one especially well known to him, Porphyry. Porphyry's search for a universal way to salvation, and his rejection of Christ as that way, is the high point of the tenth book of the *City of God* and, perhaps, of the work as a whole. Although Augustine's use of the image of the way is undoubtedly at a later stage influenced by Moses' leading the Children of Israel to the Promised Land and by the description of the Magi's return by another way into their own country, his treatment of it in the *Confessions* (Bk VII, 26f.) and the *De Trinitate* (*On the Trinity*) (Bk IV, 13ff.) is basically the same as here in the *Contra Academicos* and later in the *City of God* (Bk X, 32): the contrasting attitudes of the proud and the humble – the simple and credulous on the one hand, and the pretentious impostor on the other. The *Confessions* (Bk VII, 26f.) marks the point well:

> I should be able to see and understand the difference between presumption and confession, between those who see the goal that they must reach, but cannot see the road by which they are to reach it, and those who see the road to that blessed country which is meant to be no mere vision but our home . . . It is one thing to descry the land of peace from a wooded hilltop and, unable to find the way to it, struggle on through trackless wastes where traitors and runaways, captained by their prince . . . lie in wait to attack. It is another thing to follow the high road to that land of peace. (Translation by R. S. Pine-Coffin, Penguin Classics.)

Unlike those in the image of the harbour in the *De Beata Vita*, the Neoplatonists are here represented as seeking direction but being deceived. Both images complete the treatment of them in the *City of God*. The clearest and fullest anticipation is to be found in the *De Vera Religione* (*On True Religion*) (cf. 48ff.) which was begun at the same time as the works we have been discussing, but was not finished until four years later, in 390. Inasmuch as the *City of God* is a discussion of religion, both works share the same topic. The *De Moribus Ecclesiae Catholicae* (*On the Ways of the Catholic Church*), written in 388-390, has this striking passage on the 'way', which is, at the same time, a summary statement of one aspect and much of the contents of the *City of God*:

> the way which God built for us in the segregation of the Patriarchs, the bond of the Law, the foretelling of the Prophets, the sacrament of the Man assumed, the testimony of the Apostles, the blood of the martyrs and the entering into possession of the gentiles: let us heed the oracles (of Scripture) and submit our puny reasonings to divine inspiration (I. 11f.).

Here the gradual revelation of the way is emphasized. Finally the

De Catechizandis Rudibus (*On Catechizing the Unlearned*), written in 399, speaks plainly of two cities, one the devil's, the other Christ's.

What we have tried to stress is that the anticipation of the theme of the *City of God* was not so much dependent upon Alaric's sack of Rome as rooted in Augustine's own experience. This will throw light on the theme as it was later set forth. Providence had used adversity to help him, and Providence dominates the life of every man and every Empire. This might be a banal teaching of a philosophical school, but for Augustine it was also a personal realization, and so it tended to colour and affect all his thoughts and all his theories. Implicit in all of this is some regret for that prosperity from which Providence tears us; but there is compensation in the assurance afforded by the fulfilment of prophecies, the miracles of the saints, and the conversion of the multitudes. Even at the temporal level an Empire must benefit from the improved moral character of its citizens, once they had become Christians.

If, then, there is sorrow and regret for the past, there is also joy for the future; and if there is sombre pessimism, there is also hope. The thoughts and images that Augustine uses reflect the experience and life of an artist, the complicated tension of whose anxious spirit reveals to us his large humanity and ardent sensibility.

The Structure of the City of God

There are a few observations that one should make about the structure of the *City of God*. The first five books deal in the main with the polytheism of Rome, with special reference to Varro. The next five deal mainly with Greek philosophy, more particularly Platonism and especially Apuleius, and the Neoplatonists, Plotinus and Porphyry, with lengthy consideration of the views of the latter. The final twelve books deal in the main with creation, time and eternity as presented in the Bible, which is of Jewish provenance. And here we have the three great focuses of the work: Rome, Greece and Jerusalem. Augustine himself draws attention to this explicitly in one of the dramatic sections of the work (Bk XIX, 22):

> But it may be asked in reply 'Who is this God you talk of, and how is it proved that he is the only one to whom the Romans owed obedience, and that they should have worshipped no god besides him?' It shows extreme blindness to ask, at this time of day, who this God is! He is the same God whose prophets foretold the events we now see happening. He is the God from whom Abraham received

> the message, 'In your descendants all nations will be blessed.' And this promise was fulfilled in Christ, who sprang from that line by physical descent, as is acknowledged, willy nilly, even by those who have remained hostile to this name. He is the same God whose divine Spirit spoke through the lips of the men whose prophecies I have quoted in my previous books, prophecies fulfilled in the Church which we see diffused throughout the whole world. He is the God whom Varro, the greatest of Roman scholars, identifies with Jupiter; although he did not realize what he was saying. Still, I thought this worth mentioning, simply because a man of such great learning could not judge this God to be non-existent or of no worth, since he believed him to be identical with his supreme god. More important still, he is the god whom Porphyry, the most learned of philosophers, although the fiercest enemy of the Christians, acknowledges to be a great god, even on the evidence of the oracles of those whom he supposes to be gods.

The first sentence in this excerpt indicates Augustine's overall standpoint in his inquiry: the Roman world. It is not a negative attitude; on the contrary, he is concerned for that world's future. Rome was to bring together within herself the revelation in the Bible, the wisdom of Greek philosophy, and what was good in her own tradition. Augustine is fully conscious of the fusion of the elements that in fact went to make up the civilization of the West that has endured to this day. In this sense his *City of God* is a Charter of Christendom, and here lies its greatest significance.

Roman speculation on religion, Greek philosophy, the Bible, all pointed to one God: the God of the Hebrews. This God should now be accepted as the God of Rome. The prophecies in their fulfilment, and the Church in its extension, its martyrs, and its miracles, left no possible doubt about this. The aspirations of Hebrews, Greeks and Romans were to be fulfilled in a Christian Rome. The Christian Era, the *tempora Christiana*, was already a reality.

Augustine may have come to these pregnant views through reading or argument; but it is likely that once again his own personal experience influenced him. His was a life led in a Roman environment, based on Roman education, drawing importantly upon Greek philosophy at a time most critical to his development, and resting in the main after his conversion on the Christian Scriptures. His *Confessions* not merely testify to this in contents: in very form they, too, describe a Roman's background and education (Bks I–VII, 12), the contribution of Greek philosophy (Bk VII,13 –IX), and life according to the Christian revelation. In particular the last three books of the *Confessions* cover in part the same ground as is later covered in the fuller and richer canvas of the last twelve books of the *City of God*.

There are rudimentary traces of the same progress from Rome to Greece to the Scriptures in others of Augustine's works. The *Contra Academicos* proceeds from Cicero to the 'school of Plotinus', but puts the authority of Christ above that again (Bk III, 43). The preface to the *De Beata Vita*, with which we have already dealt, implies a similar progression. Its contemporary, the *De Ordine* (*On Order*) in its turn discusses more explicitly (Bk II, 25–54) a system of education based on the same lines.

In the pages that follow we shall take our cue from Augustine and consider the *City of God* from the three focuses which he indicates: the attitude to Rome; the attitude to Greek philosophy, (i.e. to Platonism, or more precisely Neoplatonism); and the interpretation of the Bible, in the context of philosophy.

Attitude to Rome

It has been declared quite roundly that the 'ultimate effect of the *City of God* is the elimination of the State';[3] or again that the book combines 'Plato's theory of ideas and his political blueprints in the *Republic*'.[4] J. N. Figgis[5] has castigated several such unfounded notions – repeated, nevertheless, at a later date – such as that Augustine's purpose in his great work was to develop a theory of Church and State as two swords; or to lay down an industrial and economic programme for the Middle Ages, which was to be discarded in due course in the rise of capitalism; or to condemn not only the institution of the State in general but the Roman Empire in particular. One can only suppose that such misunderstandings have persisted, partly at least, because of the title of the work, which to those who have not read it may well suggest a book in some way or another in line with Plato's or Cicero's *Republic*. Augustine's attitude to the institution of the State and the Roman Empire in particular, will bear some analysis.

But first it is important to realize how Roman was the attitude of Augustine and how Rome was the centre of his human interest. There has been so much discussion of Augustine the Platonist that Augustine the Romanist has been neglected.

One must recall very briefly that Augustine grew up in North

3. E. Barker, *City of God*, Everyman's Library, 1945, p. xxii.
4. J. Feibleman, *Religious Platonism*, London, 1959, p. 172.
5. *Political Aspects of Saint Augustine's City of God*, London, 1963.

Africa within a family that supported Rome, that he was educated according to Roman methods, and embarked on the characteristically Roman career of rhetor, which often led to high administrative posts within the Empire. Rhetoric marked the very soul of Rome: Rome was pragmatic, eclectic, less interested in metaphysics and eschatology than in ethics and how to achieve happiness. Even the most spiritual of the Romans recoiled from the unambiguous championing of idealism. Virgil for all his wistful mysticism has left us with many doubts as to his ultimate philosophical persuasions. Cicero is hardly more clear. And even these two are less typical than, say, Horace with his *aurea mediocritas* – his golden mean.

Great as the influence of the Neoplatonists on Augustine's mind undoubtedly was, it was the influence of Roman rhetoric which was all-pervading and can be seen in almost every paragraph that he wrote, and in many an argument that he used. He is by no means always innocent of the unrealities, exaggerations, and frigidities that characterized the profession he had espoused and practised. 'If one were asked,' he remarks in the *City of God* (Bk XXI, 14), 'either to endure death or childhood again, who would not be aghast and choose to die?' Unhappy as his experience of childhood may have been, one would hesitate to conclude that rhetorical exaggeration and unreality had no part in such a terrible declaration. We should take note also of a remarkable use of Roman rhetorical eclecticism in an argument of the gravest import and seriousness.

> Therefore Plato and Porphyry, or rather their admirers now living, agree with us in believing that even holy souls will return to bodies (as Plato says), but that they will not return to any evils (as Porphyry says). Now it follows from these premises that the soul will receive the kind of body in which it can live for ever in felicity, without any evil: and this is the teaching of the Christian faith. Then all they have to do is to add, from Varro, the doctrine that the soul returns to the same body as before; and then the whole difficulty about the resurrection of the flesh will be solved for them (Bk XXII, 28).

With regard to this very question of the eternity of the flesh, the Romans, although they might reject it for other reasons, would have had less difficulty than a true follower of Plato, for whom only non-material things could have existence. There was, indeed, a strong materialistic bias in the philosophies that most affected the Romans which would have helped in this. Moreover the Roman, when he was not a materialist, was a sceptic. Basically he was a pragmatist, and his attitude towards the doctrine of bodily immortality would be determined less by fine philosophical reasoning than by more practical considerations. Augustine, as a matter of fact, had been a materialist Manichee for the whole of his twenties and had subsequently professed himself to be a sceptic, a follower of the New Academy. It is too much to assume that his acquaintance with the Neoplatonists obliterated the attitudes of earlier and formative years; his eclecticism from Plato, Porphyry, and Varro on the question of bodily immortality is a significant reminder of how thoroughly Roman Augustine continued to be.

Augustine clearly feels no compulsion to inform the reader throughout the *City of God* that he is considering his problem from both a personal point of view and from the point of view of Rome. It is characteristic of Augustine to assume that the reader does not need to be told of what, to him, is obvious.

A simple and clear instance of this can be seen in the lack of specific reference to his sources in the *City of God*. There are hundreds of allusions to Varro's *Antiquitates*, but the title is given only once; there are frequent references to Apuleius' *De Deo Socratis*, but the title is given only once; there are over seventy references to the *Aeneid*, but the title is given only once; and there are over a dozen references to Sallust's *Catilina*, but the title is not given at all.

So it was with Rome. For his contemporaries, whose outlook on the world was bounded by the Roman Empire and its institutions, it was unnecessary, and might have been tedious, to have constant mention of what for them was the frame of reference of the argument. Rome was the background and the foreground and the whole context of the work. Even when philosophy leads him to Greece and theology to the Hebrews, his purpose is that Rome should be fulfilled in both.

Nevertheless Augustine does make the point most explicitly. We have already seen Chapter 22 of Book XIX, which gives in dramatic and sharpest outline the focuses of the whole work. There the question is asked: 'Who is this God you talk of, and how is it proved that he is the only one to whom the Romans owed obedience, and that they should have worshipped no god besides him?' The *City of God* is basically concerned with that question, and it is asked in the interest, not of the Greeks or the Jews or any other people, but of the Romans. The answer to the question, as we have seen, is that the testimony of the Hebrews, of the Greeks (represented by Porphyry), and of the Romans themselves (represented by Varro) was that the Christian God was that God.

Once again one should not fail to notice in the text just referred to the spirit of eclecticism and reverence for authority. It might be said with some justice that Augustine was aware that there might be difficulty in getting Porphyry and Varro to accept his interpretation of their positions in favour of Christianity – and he did not conceal this. Augustine's fondness for a synthesis with firm outline, however, is more in evidence here than any purely philosophical argument. Some might see in this a basic Roman scepticism allied to a fondness for action, a preference for will as against intelligence, for authority as against reason. It is not surprising, indeed, that, although Platonism was received in Rome, the Bible and the Christian Church especially became the instruments for a new glory and a longer life. That this should be so was a positive purpose of the *City of God.*

Augustine's attitude to Rome was twofold: theological and seeming historical. From the point of view of Christian theology she must stand by him condemned. She had failed to worship the true God, had thus not given Him what was His due, and therefore lacked true justice – so that if true justice was to enter into the definition of a State, Rome had never been a State. Augustine rather than accept this drastic conclusion considers the possibility that a State might be defined without reference to justice. But in fact it is quite clear that his position here is an absolute one, arising from a theological assumption involving, not simply justice between men, but *true* justice which must take account of man's duty to God. Elsewhere (Bk V, 19) he speaks of *true* virtue which cannot exist without the *true* worship of the *true* God. With it he contrasts 'the virtue which is employed in the service of human glory' which 'is not *true* virtue; still, those who are not citizens of the Eternal City . . . are of more service to the earthly city when they possess even that *sort of virtue* than if they are without it'. The very sentence which has been adduced to prove that Augustine declared that States lack justice – 'Remove justice, and what are kingdoms but gangs of criminals on a large scale?' – clearly implies that kingdoms (States) are not kingdoms unless they are founded on justice. A parallel sentence – 'take away national complacency, and what are all men but simply men?' (Bk V, 17) – again clearly implies that 'men' will be 'simply men' if they have not the specific of national complacency. Likewise a kingdom is differentiated from a gang of criminals by the specific inclusion of justice. Augustine in his 'mirror of princes' (Bk V, 24) puts as the first requirement of a prince that he should rule with justice.

Rome had not only failed to worship the true God: she had given herself, under the malign influence of demons, to the worship of many gods both to ensure, it was claimed, physical and moral well-being for the State and the person in this life, and happiness for the person hereafter. These gods, Augustine contends at length, did not save Rome from physical disasters; not only did they not promote Rome's moral well-being: they corrupted Rome through their obscene representations in the theatre and in the temple. The myths of the poets and the theatre were classified as 'mythical' theology, as the cult of the gods in the public temples was classified as 'civil' theology. Both theologies debauched Rome: 'The theology of the theatre proclaims the degradation of the people; the theology of the city makes that degradation an amenity' (Bk VI, 6). The remaining theology was called 'natural' – the theological ideas of the philosophers. According to these last, the gods were not superior to man. Hence they could do no more for man's eternal happiness than he could himself.

One may be puzzled at what seems the inordinate length of Augustine's attack upon these gods. But, as he says, 'superior intelligences . . . will have to possess themselves in patience; and I ask them, for the sake of others, not to think superfluous what for themselves they feel to be unnecessary' (Bk VII, Preface); 'we are forced very often to give an extended exposition of the obvious, as if we were not presenting it for people to look at, but for them to touch and handle with their eyes shut' (Bk II, 1). Augustine was concerned not only with superior intelligences: he was dealing with whole peoples of a vast Empire, and he was trying to break for them their long-inured association with a comforting polytheism, and substitute for it the (for them) strange concept of a single immaterial deity. The radical nature of such a change is almost impossible for us, who have inherited the concept of monotheism, to realize. But Augustine was keenly aware of it and the main burthen of the whole of the *City of God* is aimed at reinforcing that substitution.

As we have said, Augustine's attitude to Rome was also seeming historical. He accepted from Sallust the picture of Rome as having once been highly moral. The early Romans were

> greedy for praise, generous with their money, and aimed at vast renown and honourable riches. They were passionately devoted to glory; it was for this they desired to live, for this they did not hesitate to die. This unbounded passion for glory, above all else, checked their other appetites. They felt it would be shameful for their country to be enslaved, but glorious for her to have dominion and empire; and so they set their hearts first on making her free, then on making her sovereign (Bk V, 12).

Again:

> it was other causes that made them great: energy in our own land, a rule of justice outside our borders; in forming policy a mind that is free because not at the mercy of criminal passions (*ibid.*).

But such human effort and achievement does not escape the embrace of theology:

> God decided that a Western empire should arise, later in time [than the kingdoms of the East], but more renowned for the extent and grandeur of its dominion . . . He entrusted this dominion to those men, in preference to all others, who served their country for the sake of honour, praise and glory . . . (Bk V, 13). The Roman Empire . . . had this further purpose, that the citizens of that Eternal City . . . should fix their eyes steadily and soberly on those examples and observe what love they should have towards the City on high, in view of life eternal, if the earthly city had received such devotion from her citizens (Bk V, 16).

The *City of God* is not an attack on the Romans or the Roman Empire. On the contrary it sees Rome as a vehicle ordained by Providence for the benefit of Christianity in relation to which she would have a new and enduring future.

Augustine takes note of the conduct of the Christian Emperors, Constantine and Theodosius. He expects rulers who are Christians to rule with justice and 'to put their power at the service of God's majesty to extend his worship far and wide' (Bk V, 24). He does not suppose, nevertheless, that, although Theodosius was 'constrained by the discipline of the Church to do penance', and 'never relaxed in his efforts to help the Church against the ungodly by just and compassionate legislation' (Bk V, 26), he or any Christian Emperor should be the obedient servant of the institutional Church: Augustine did not prescribe a theocratic State.

Attitude to Greek Philosophy

In Books VIII–X of the *City of God* Augustine encounters those Greek philosophers who treat of theology, who admit the existence of a Divinity and of his concern for human affairs, but who consider that the worship of one unchangeable God is not sufficient for the attainment of a life of blessedness after death: they suppose that for this end many gods are to be worshipped. The philosophers he has mostly in mind are Apuleius (*c.* 124–170 A.D.), Plotinus (*c.* 205–270) and his disciple Porphyry (232–*c.* 305) – but especially Apuleius and Porphyry, the first of whom was an African who wrote in Latin, and the other the reigning philosopher of Augustine's day. Plotinus was the founder of Neoplatonism, a revival of the philosophy of Plato, and both he and Porphyry wrote in Greek and lived at Rome.

Augustine starts, however, with the threefold division of philosophy into natural, rational and moral (Physics, Logic, Ethics), a division he attributes to Plato. He expounds briefly and commends the Platonist doctrines under these heads and complements them later with a Christian gloss (Bk XI, 26–28).

But he quickly moves on to Apuleius, whose ideas on demonology were familiar to Augustine and generally current, and which receive considerable attention in the *City of God*. It is likely that he got some ideas on demons from Porphyry too. For Augustine these demons were really the fallen angels, who did their best to attract men's worship away from the one true God, were endowed with some qualities, deriving from their angelic nature, superior to those enjoyed by man, and so were capable of helping or hindering man according as he did or did not do sacrifice to them. Apuleius himself treats of their character and says that they are liable to the same emotional disturbances as human beings. They resent injury, they are mollified by flattery and by gifts, they delight in receiving honours, they enjoy all kinds of rites and ceremonies and they are annoyed at any negligence about these. Among their uses he mentions divination by means of auguries, haruspication, clairvoyance, and dreams; and he ascribes to them the remarkable feats of magicians. He gives this brief definition of demons: species, animal; soul, subject to passions; mind, rational; body, composed of air; life-span, eternal. Of those five attributes, they have the first three, says Apuleius, in common with us; the fourth is peculiar to them; the fifth they share with the gods.

Apuleius, according to Augustine, pronounces the demons worthy of divine honours. They are established 'midway between the ethereal heaven and the earth, so that since 'gods never mix with men (as Plato is reported as saying), they may carry the prayers of men to the gods and bring back to men the answers granted to their requests' (Bk VIII, 18). In their beneficent character, therefore, they were mediators, and mediation was a very popular idea at the time. Their role, however, Augustine contends, in procuring eternal felicity for men was useless: by their very nature they were as subject to passions and miseries as were men but, unlike men, their miseries were eternal. It was absurd to believe that they could achieve eternal happiness for men when they could not win it for themselves. Christ, on the other hand, was both eternal and in felicity: he was the true mediator.

The good angels, by contrast, do not seek that worship should be paid by men to themselves: they seek that it should be paid only to God.

Porphyry restricted the service that demons could render to us to the elevation of our 'spirital' soul, that is the soul by which we apprehend the images of material things – not the intellectual soul – and even about that, Augustine suggests, he was either ambiguous or unsure:

> Porphyry goes as far as to promise some sort of purification of the soul by means of theurgy, though to be sure he is reluctant to commit himself, and seems to blush with embarrassment in his argument. On the other hand he denies that this art offers to anyone a way of return to God (Bk x, 9).

(Theurgy is the art of persuading divinities to do or not to do something according to one's desire.)

Porphyry in fact was seeking some universal way for the soul's deliverance. In his *Philosophy from Oracles* he had examined the claims of Christ to be such a deliverer, such a universal way. He accepted the Hebrew–Christian god as the true god; he accepted that Christ was a good man; but he rejected the claims of the Christians. Augustine insisted that pride and his truck with demons prevented him from accepting Christ's incarnation and crucifixion. Were it not for these, Porphyry and his followers would accept the truth of Christianity.

Deliverance for the soul means not merely escape from this life: it means especially not returning to it again. Augustine agreed with Porphyry (as against Plato) in denying that in a cycle of births man's soul would return to the body of an animal. It would return to a human body. But he disagreed with Porphyry and the Platonists on whether the soul returned at all. The soul could not be happy in the after-life if it was destined to return to life again. Christianity meant the substitution of the linear for the cyclical concept of human destiny.

There is a sense in which the *City of God* can be said to centre on Porphyry and his *Philosophy from Oracles*. On the one hand this book of Porphyry's represented a serious challenge to Christianity, as is evidenced by the anxious attention it received from so many Christian apologists: Eusebius (died 339) in his *Praeparatio Evangelica*, the Africans Arnobius (*fl. c.* 300) and Lactantius (*fl. c.* 304–317), Theodoret (died *c.* 466), Claudianus Mamertus (died 474), Aeneas of Gaza (died *c.* 518), and Philoponus (died *c.* 565), as well as Augustine, in the *City of God* and elsewhere. Augustine compares the 'oracles' of the Scriptures to any others, including those of Porphyry, and avers that they are superior in every way: the 'divine oracles', expressed through the lips of the holy prophets and scattered by Augustine, as he says throughout the *City of God*, are more widely diffused, clear and frequent, summary, awesome, fearful but true; whereas the others are obscure and unknown, abstruse and rare. The comparison is made in a chapter (Bk XIX, 23) where Porphyry's *Philosophy from Oracles* is in question and is explicitly named.

But Augustine also stresses how close Porphyry came to Christian truth – he believed in the existence of a spiritual Trinity, Providence and even something like grace. Only the demons and pride prevented him from accepting Christ, of whom the *Philosophy from Oracles* spoke highly, as God.

To win Porphyry, or rather his followers in the time of Augustine, to Christianity would not only eliminate the most worthy and serious opponents of Christianity; it would also fulfil the destiny of Greek philosophy. Even the difficulty that the immaterial Platonists might have about the possibility of an immortalized body in the Resurrection was solved by the declaration in Plato's *Timaeus* that 'this was a boon granted by the supreme God to the deities created by him, the assurance that they would never die, never, that is, be separated from the bodies with which he had linked them' (Bk XIII, 16).

Interpretation of the Bible in the context of Philosophy

The concept of the City of God, or rather of the two cities – the heavenly and terrestrial cities – receives its fullest treatment in the last twelve books of Augustine's great work, of which Books XI–XIV deal with their origin, XV–XVIII with their progress from the creation to the coming of Christ, and XIX–XXII with their final destinies.

The inspiration for the idea of the city, of one kind or another, might have come from Plato's or Cicero's *Republic*, or the *Commentary on the Apocalypse* of his contemporary Tyconius, or from other sources. Augustine, however, tells us plainly that the reference of his title is to Psalm lxxxvi, 3: 'Glorious things are said of thee, O city of God.' The inspiration and character of the work is theological, not civic.

When he proceeds to describe what he means by 'city', he usually calls it 'society' or 'community': 'these two diverse and opposed communities of angels, in which we find something like the beginnings of the two communities of mankind' (Bk XI, 34). 'Society' or 'community' is, however, not the only synonym he employs for 'city'. He also uses, among others, the terms 'house' or 'temple' or 'family'.[6] The term city means little more than an association held together by some common bond:

> This is assuredly the great difference that sunders the two cities of which we are speaking: the one is a community of devout men, the other a company of the irreligious, and each has its own angels attached to it. In one city love of God has been given first place, in the other, love of self (Bk XIV, 13).

A more famous formulation has it:

> We see then that the two cities were created by two kinds of love: the earthly city was created by self-love reaching the point of contempt for God, the Heavenly City by the love of God carried as far as contempt of self (Bk XIV, 28).

In fact the cities originated in the choice of the angels to serve or not to serve God. The human component exists to make up for the angels that rebelled, and originated with Seth and Cain, the slayer of Abel. The cities, therefore, are spiritual or mystical cities.

All men are born in the earthly city but can become, if they are predestined to it, members of the heavenly city. Entry to that city is through regeneration in Christ, but people other than Christians can be members of this city. The Erythraean Sibyl,[7] for example, is thought by Augustine to belong to it because she attacked the worship of false gods. It would seem that Augustine believed that the number of men that would belong to this city would be small. The character of the earthly city can be divined from its opposition to the heavenly.

The things used in common by the two eternal and mystical cities are good (all created natures – even the Devil – are, according to Augustine, good), but limited and temporal. They do not constitute a third city, for the cities in question have to do with only the wills of men and angels. These cities existed before earthly created nature and will exist when it is no more. In this earthly period, created nature is used by citizens of both cities who can share most things,

6. *Cf.* my *Charter of Christendom*, p. 40ff.
7. *Cf.* p. 788 n. 67.

with the great exception of religion and worship: this is the great practical divide.

Ultimately, being a citizen of the city of God means salvation. Those who are still alive are on the 'way' to the fatherland; they are in the harbour whence they may pass to the fatherland itself. Here we see the persistence of Augustine's earlier ideas on man's destiny.

And what of the role of the Church in the *City of God*? In a very general way Augustine identifies the Church with the city of God on pilgrimage here below. Thus he speaks of the 'City of God, that is to say, God's Church' (Bk XIII, 16). But there were serious reservations. First there were citizens of the city of God on earth before the Church was founded, as we have seen in the case of the Sibyl. The Hebrews foreshadowed the city of God and gave it members. The Gospel parables of the cockle among the good seed, the separation of the wheat from the chaff, and the mixed collection of fish in the net, led Augustine to conclude that many existing Church members would not be found to be members of the city of God. Similarly there were some who never belonged to the Church who would be found to be members of that city.

The *City of God* is formally neither a philosophical nor a theological treatise though it is mainly theological, since it deals with man's salvation and happiness as related to the worship not of many gods but of the one true God and uses the Bible as its supreme authority. Nevertheless it treats of formal philosophical and theological matters *passim*.

Augustine's general philosophical viewpoint is Platonic (Bk VIII, 6–9 and Bk XI, 25). He accepts the traditional Platonic division of philosophy into physics, logic and ethics – in which he sees a vestige of the Trinity – but transforms it into a Theodicy in which God, 'the cause of existence, the principle of reason and the rule of life' (Bk VIII, 4), is the explanation of all.

His practical approach to physics, however, requires some explanation. Pierre Duhem judged that of all the Fathers of the Church Augustine alone did not disdain the doctrines of profane science. Galileo commended his 'circumspection' in the matter. Augustine depended for his scientific information on the works of Varro, Cicero, Pliny, Posidonius, Apuleius and the Neoplatonists. He seems to have a special acquaintance with mathematics, astronomy and medicine.[8]

8. *Cf.* my *The Creation of Man in De Genesi ad Litteram*, the Saint Augustine Lecture, Villanova University, 1977, Villanova University Press, 1980, chapter 1.

When there appeared to be a clear conflict between what he took to be the historical account of the Bible and an ascertained fact of rational science, he accepted the fact of science and understood the Bible allegorically. He was embarrassed by some fellow Christians:

> It happens often that a non-Christian too has a view about the earth, the heaven, the other elements of this world, the movement and revolution or even the size and distances of the stars . . . the natures of animals, plants, stones and such things which he derives from ineluctible reason and experience. It is too shameful and damaging and greatly to be avoided that such a one should hear a Christian talk such utter nonsense about such things, purporting to speak in accordance with Christian writings (*de Genesi ad litteram* I, XIX, 39).

On the other hand no mere *hypothesis* of science was accepted by him in preference to an account in the Bible. He believed that one could also follow the Bible as an historical account:

> Now in my opinion it is certainly a complete mistake to suppose that no narrative of events in this type of literature (i.e. the Bible) has any significance beyond the purely historical record; but it is equally rash to maintain that every single statement in those books is a complex of allegorical meanings (Bk XVII, 4).

The flood of Eastern religions into the West and the mainly spiritualist character of the dominant Neoplatonist philosophy – not to say the theurgic beliefs and practices associated with Porphyry and, especially, Iamblichus and others – had a markedly regressive effect in relation to scientific matters which Christians, including Augustine, shared with their contemporaries. Thus whereas the theory of the spherical nature of the earth put forward by Eudoxus of Cnidus (*c.* 408–337 B.C.) was accepted by Plato and Aristotle and their successors down to the second century A.D., there was a reversion in the third and fourth centuries A.D. to the earlier Homeric and Biblical theory of the earth as a flat disc surrounded by Ocean. And so whereas Plato and Cicero accepted the existence of the antipodes, Augustine demurred (Bk XVI, 9). He is careful, however, to indicate the *possibility* that the world might be a suspended sphere, and that the existence of the antipodes was simply not proved *rationally*. His reason for rejecting the theory of the antipodes was that it seemed to threaten the unity of the human race – which was the teaching of the Bible.

Augustine, therefore, found himself from time to time amongst those for whom the marvels related in Pliny the Elder's *Natural*

History were science. Hence there is a fair share of marvels, metamorphoses and monstrosities to be found in the *City of God*: they should be placed – with the demons – in the context of their times. Nevertheless his position *vis-à-vis* science was clear and acted upon:

> Whatever the [scientists] themselves can *demonstrate* by true proofs about the nature of things, we can show not to be contrary to our scriptures. But whatever they *advance* [i.e. as an hypothesis] in any of their books that is contrary to our scriptures . . . we should either indicate a solution or believe without hesitation that it is false (*De Genesi ad Litteram* I, XXI, 41).

He shared with the Roman world the belief that the end of philosophy was happiness. Happiness was possible in this life, but only by future hope rather than present reality (Bk XIX, 20). Our lives can be led in peace if we observe due order in submission:

> The peace of the body . . . is a tempering of the component parts in duly ordered proportion; the peace of the irrational soul is a duly ordered repose of the appetites; the peace of the rational soul is the duly ordered agreement of cognition and action. The peace of the body and soul is the duly ordered life and health of a living creature; peace between mortal man and God is an ordered obedience, in faith, in subjection to an everlasting law; peace between men is an ordered agreement of mind with mind; the peace of a home is the ordered agreement among those who live together about giving and obeying orders; the peace of the Heavenly City is a perfectly ordered and perfectly harmonious fellowship in the enjoyment of God, and a mutual fellowship in God; the peace of the whole universe is the tranquility of order and order is the arrangement of things equal and unequal in a pattern which assigns to each its proper position (Bk XIX, 13).[9]

Augustine's idea of philosophy is one that he attributes to Plato: 'to philosophize is to love God' (Bk VIII, 8). For him philosophy is affective – even mystical. If the end of philosophy is happiness, its agent is the will. Turning to God or turning away from God is the first and final divide. The expression of philosophy is love; its explanation likewise is love: Augustine's absorption in the idea of love must arise from his temperament which he so passionately delineates in his

9. *Cf.* R. A. Markus, *Saeculum: History and Society in the Theology of St. Augustine*, Cambridge University Press, 1970, pp. 64, 72f. This book gives an extended consideration of this and related questions and puts forward a number of original views.

Confessions. He is so insistent on the value of even human love that he refuses to follow the distinction between it, 'charity' and 'friendship' maintained by other Church Fathers (Bk XIV, 7).

Some, therefore, have concluded that Augustine was not a phlosopher in the strict sense of the word. Although he treats philosophically of problems throughout the whole range of traditional philosophy – time, space, matter, form, knowledge, problems in psychology both rational and experimental, happiness, virtue and so on – he would not have claimed to be a philosopher in the strict sense. He was more concerned to know and love God and to bring his fellowmen to do the same.

The theological content of the *City of God* is found in his handling of Scripture. He shows how the Old Testament, which he follows in the main in the Septuagint version, is one long prophecy and symbolization of Christ's coming. Its prophecies, which he repeatedly calls 'oracles', are superior in every way to the oracles of the pagans, especially to the oracles consulted by Porphyry. Its miracles and the Christian miracles since Christ's coming are likewise superior. One has to accept that Augustine felt it necessary in his apostolate to beat the pagans at their own game.

The great problems of creation, of the creation and fall of the angels, of predestination, of evil, of the last judgement, of eternal punishment, of eternal felicity, of the vision of God and many other questions come up for treatment – on the basis of the evidence of Scripture – in the parts of the *City of God* dealing with the origin (Bks XI–XIV) and the destinies (Bks XIX–XXII) of the two cities. The intervening books give a history of man's progress and development from the creation to the coming of Christ. It is based on the rather legendary *Chronicle* of Eusebius and the Bible itself, and in fact deals mainly with the Assyrian and Roman Empires.

Neither in Books XV–XVIII of the *City of God*, nor elsewhere in the work, is there any serious attempt at a philosophy of history other than his repudiation of the Platonic theory of the cycle of existences and the substitution for it of the linear progress implicit in the Christian view of the creation, fall, redemption and final destiny. More might be said for Augustine's having some kind of a theology of history, but this means little more than the view of history as given in the Scriptures, that is the prophesying of redemption and its fulfilment.[10]

In addition to the topics we have already seen, Augustine covers a

10. On the question if there is a philosophy or theology of history in the *City of God* cf. my *Charter of Christendom* pp. 54ff.

wide range of other subjects in the course of the *City of God*, including beauty, slavery, war and a discussion rather similar to Descartes's 'I think, therefore I am'. It must be added that the treatment of such topics in the *Ciy of God* is best considered alongside their treatment in other works by Augustine.

The style of the *City of God* approaches very nearly to the classical ideal as seen in Cicero. While it lacks, except on occasion, the passion and rhetoric of the shorter and more personal *Confessions*, it is on the whole in the grand manner; but for all that it shows great variation in the treatment of its different ideas. It is, perhaps, the last great prose work of classical Rome.

JOHN O'MEARA

Arrangement and Contents of the City of God

SEVERAL times in his writings Augustine tells us how the *City of God* is to be divided, and what is the leading topic of each division. A full consecutive account is to be found in a letter written in the last years of his life, accompanying the gift of a manuscript of the work, to the layman Firmus. This letter was first noted by the Benedictine scholar Dom C. Lambot, of Maredsous Abbey, Belgium, and published by him in *Revue Bénédictine*, vol. LI, nos. 2–3 (1939). In it Augustine writes as follows:

> There are XXII notebooks (*quaterniones*), too many to combine in a single volume. If you wish to make two volumes (*codices*) you must so divide them that there are ten in one and twelve in the other. If you want more than two, then you must make five volumes. The first is to contain the five first books (*libros*), in which I write against those who maintain that the worship of the gods – I would rather say, of the evil spirits (*daemones*) – leads to happiness in this life. The second is to contain the next five books, written against those who think that suchlike deities are to be worshipped by rites and sacrifices in order to secure happiness in the life to come. The three following volumes should contain four books each. This section I have arranged so that four should describe the origin of that City, four its progress, or rather its development, and the four last the ends (*sic*) in store for it.

In the *City of God* itself, the reader will find partial descriptions of the work (Bks II, 2; III, 1; IV, 1–2; VI, preface and ch. 1; XI, 1; XII, 1; XVIII, 1) as also in his *Retractations* Bk II, 43.

Within each book the topics are often so disparate as to defy broad analysis. In the translation that follows this introduction, the chapter headings (very possibly by Augustine himself) are helpful. Here an attempt has been made to pick out some salient features in each book that a reader might wish to be able to find rapidly for reference.

CITY OF GOD

Part One

BOOK I. The gods did not protect Rome. The Christians suffered with others, but disasters overtake both good and bad, and the loss of worldly goods is not always a disaster. The violation of chastity does not harm the unwilling soul. Suicide is not permissible to avoid this.

BOOK II. The pagan gods had no moral teaching to give. Examples of the obscenity of pagan rites drawn from Augustine's experience. The gods not only tolerated but even demanded obscenity on the stage. Sallust gave a picture of Rome's decadence. First appearance of Scripio's definition of a state. Cicero's judgement. Further account of obscenities in public worship.

BOOK III. The gods failed to protect Ilium or to save Rome. Rome was morally firm in Numa's day. The subsequent religious depravity.

BOOK IV. The number and futility of Roman gods. Praise of Varro.

BOOK V. The falsity of astrology. God is neither Fate nor Destiny. Roman virtue is responsible for Roman worldly success. A summary of Roman history: ambition for glory; ambition for dominion. God helps the Christian emperors.

Part Two

BOOK VI. Gods are not worshipped for their gift of eternal life. Varro and 'mythical' and 'civil' deities. 'M. Varro, you are the shrewdest of men and without doubt the most erudite' (Bk VI, 6,). The absurd small gods. They do not even help temporal life.

BOOK VII. The 'select' gods. Who are they? How chosen? Is Jupiter supreme? Is a deity the soul of the world?

BOOK VIII. 'Natural' theology. A short history of Greek philosophy. The Platonists, 'raised above the rest by the glorious reputation they so thoroughly deserve'. Platonists are near-Christians. The worship of 'demons' rejected (Apuleius – Hermes Trismegistus). The pagan cult of the dead and the Christian cult of martyrs. Pagan sacrifice and the one and only true Christian victim.

BOOK IX. More about demons. Apuleius and the Neoplatonists.

BOOK X. The true worship of God. Porphyry and the false claims of theurgy. The angels. The Christian sacrifice. Platonists refuse to acknowledge Christ, the universal way of salvation.

Part Three

BOOK XI. The Truth of the Scriptures. Creation. Time. Angels, good and apostate. Wickedness is not natural; nothing created is in itself evil. How are we sure of our own existence?

BOOK XII. Evil is non-existent. Evil has no cause – it is the turning of a limited creature from God to itself. Creation took place long ago. The Cyclic idea of history is false. The world is not eternal.

BOOK XIII. The creation of man and its problems. Death and resurrection.

BOOK XIV. The life of the spirit and the life of the flesh. Stoic 'apathy' (not human). Only the Creator can undo the results of sin. Two cities.

Part Four

BOOK XV. Early man. Abel, Cain and the patriarchs. Who were the 'giants'? Beginning of two cities. Noah and the ark.

BOOK XVI. Noah to Judah. How do we explain human monsters? There are no antipodes.

BOOK XVII. A detailed account of the preparation for Christ by prophecies throughout Scripture.

BOOK XVIII. The earthly city and the city of God down to Christ. There are two sorts of men in the Church, the predestined and the others who will be condemned. There are others besides Jews in the City of God. Job is a supreme example.

Part Five

BOOK XIX. What is man's supreme Good? Peace. Everything is directed towards peace, even war.

BOOK XX. The last judgement. Law and order. Scipio's republic again.

BOOK XXI. How is eternal punishment possible? Pain of soul or body? Does temporal punishment exist after death for some?

BOOK XXII. The creation and resurrection. Miracles still occur in the Christian Church. The Vision of God.

Bibliography

THE bibliography of Augustine is immense and there are at least three periodicals, among them the *Revue des études augustiniennes*, devoted exclusively to his work. Augustine has never been served or understood by historians better than during the past fifty years. For all save the dedicated specialist the bibliography in Peter Brown's book (below) will be sufficient for biographical and general material, and for Augustine's theology and thought the notes in Gilson's work (below) may be consulted.

BIOGRAPHY. The contemporary Life by Augustine's disciple Possidius has great value, and is available in English, translated from the edition of H. T. Weisskotten (1919), but for all strictly biographical material the work *Augustine of Hippo*, by Peter Brown (1967) is in a class by itself, including, as a bonus, chronological tables of Augustine's works and lists of English translations.

THOUGHT. Here a useful work is that of E. Gilson, *Introduction à l'étude de S. Augustin* (3rd edition, 1949), of which a shortened version can be found in Gilson's *History of Christian Philosophy in the Middle Ages* (1955), which contains biographical notes. For a 'total' view of Augustine the classic article by E. Portalié in the *Dictionnaire de théologie catholique* (1903), translated as *A Guide to the Thought of St Augustine* (1960), still retains its high value. In all the above, and in many other works, the *City of God* receives some treatment. For Plotinus the best short account is that by A. H. Armstrong in *The Cambridge History of Later Greek and Early Medieval Philosophy* (1967). S. MacKenna's translation of the *Enneads* (3rd edition, 1970, with introduction by P. Henry) is a classic.

For Manicheism, the standard work is H. Puech, *Le Manichéisme: son fondateur, sa doctrine* (1944). There is an excellent short account in the edition of the *Confessions* by Gibb and Montgomery (2nd edition, 1927). For the Donatists see W. H. C. Frend, *The Donatist Church* (1952).

Suggested Further Reading

(a short selection from an immense literature)

1. *On the General Background*

G. Boissier, *La fin du paganisme*, Paris, 1891

C. N. Cochrane, *Christianity and Classical Culture*, Oxford, 1940

S. Dill, *Roman Society in the Last Century of the Western Empire*, London, 1899

E. R. Dodds, *Pagan and Christian in an Age of Anxiety*, Oxford, 1965

P. de Labriolle, *La réaction paienne*, 10th edition, Paris, 1950

A. Momigliano (ed.), *The Conflict between Paganism and Christianity in the Fourth Century*, London, 1963

A. D. Nock, *Conversion. The Old and the New in Religion from Alexander the Great to Augustine of Hippo*, Oxford, 1933

2. *On Augustine's Life and Thought*

R. Battenhouse (ed.), *A Companion to the Study of St. Augustine*, New York, 1955 (contains a short essay on the *City of God* by E. R. Hardy)

G. Bonner, *St Augustine of Hippo. Life and Controversies*, London, 1963

J. Burnaby, *Amor Dei*, London, 1938

P. Courcelle, *Les Lettres grecques en Occident de Macrobe à Cassiodore*, Paris, 1958; *Recherches sur les 'Confessions' de S. Augustin*, Paris, 1950

R. A. Markus, *Saeculum: History and Society in the Theology of St Augustine*, London, 1970

H. Marrou, *Augustin et la fin de la culture antique*, Paris, 1938

R. O'Connell, *St Augustine's Confessions*, Harvard, 1969

J. J. O'Meara, *The Young Augustine*, London, 1954, 1980

E. Teselle, *Augustine the Theologian*, New York, 1970

F. van der Meer, *Augustine the Bishop*, London and New York, 1961

3. *On the City of God*

R. H. Barrow, *Introduction to St Augustine, The City of God*, London, 1950 (selections in Latin and English, with an analysis and a running commentary)

N. H. Baynes, *The Political Ideas of St Augustine's De Civitate Dei*, London, 1936

Bibliothèque Augustinienne, vols 33–37, *La Cité de Dieu*, Paris, 1959–60 (the most useful modern edition)

S. Burleigh, *The City of God. A Study of St Augustine's Philosophy*, London, 1950

H. A. Deane, *The Political and Social Ideas of St Augustine*, London and New York, 1963

J. N. Figgis, *The Political Aspects of St Augustine's City of God*, London (reprinted 1963)

J. C. Guy, *Unité et structure logique de la 'Cité de Dieu' de Saint Augustin*, Paris, 1961

H. I. Marrou, *Théologie de l'histoire*, Paris, 1968

J. J. O'Meara, *Charter of Christendom*, London, 1967

J. E. C. Welldon, *S. Aurelii Augustini . . . De Civitate Dei . . .*, 2 vols London, 1924 (the only annotated edition in English with full notes and a useful introduction and appendices)

Translator's Note

THE text I have used is the Teubner text of Bernard Dombart and Alphonse Kalb (fourth edition 1928–9) reprinted, with some correction, in the series *Corpus Christianorum* (Turnhout, 1955). In a very few places I have adopted a variant reading; but I have not thought it necessary to mark these places.

Quotations from Scripture are not taken from any standard version. It often happens that St Augustine's argument depends on an interpretation which differs from that of any of the existing English translations; and for this reason I have used my own versions, thus giving myself freedom to allow St Augustine to make his points, without having recourse to footnotes.

Our author is pleased, on occasion, to air his somewhat scanty knowledge of the Greek language; and where he quotes in that tongue, I have transliterated the words, with the usual indication of long vowels.

It will be observed that Augustine referring to St Paul, generally follows the convention of the Church Fathers in designating him 'the Apostle'.

H.B.

Abbreviations Used in References

A. *To Books of Scripture*

Gen.	Genesis	Zeph.	Zephaniah
Exod.	Exodus	Hagg.	Haggai
Lev.	Leviticus	Zech.	Zechariah
Num.	Numbers	Mal.	Malachi
Deut.	Deuteronomy	Esdr.	Esdras
Josh.	Joshua	Tob.	Tobit
Judg.	Judges	Wisd.	Wisdom
Sam.	Samuel	Ecclus.	Ecclesiasticus
Chron.	Chronicles	Bar.	Baruch
Ps.	Psalms	Matt.	Matthew
Prov.	Proverbs	Rom.	Romans
Eccl.	Ecclesiastes	Cor.	Corinthians
S. of S.	The Song of Songs	Gal.	Galatians
Is.	Isaiah	Eph.	Ephesians
Jer.	Jeremiah	Phil.	Philippians
Lam.	Lamentations	Col.	Colossians
Ez.	Ezekiel	Thess.	Thessalonians
Dan.	Daniel	Tim.	Timothy
Hos.	Hosea	Tit.	Titus
Am.	Amos	Hebr.	Hebrews
Obad.	Obadiah	Jas.	James
Jon.	Jonah	Pet.	Peter
Mic.	Micah	Jud.	Jude
Nah.	Nahum	Rev.	Revelation
Hab.	Habakkuk		

LXX The Septuagint: the Greek version of the Old Testament, produced in Alexandria in the second century B.C.

Vulg. The Vulgate: the Latin version of the Bible (*editio vulgata*), compiled by St Jerome; completed c. 404. St Augustine's Bible was one of the 'Old Latin Versions'. The Old Testament in this was a translation of the Septuagint, which often differs widely from the Hebrew text. Some of the notable discrepancies are indicated in the notes to this translation by the addition of (LXX) after the reference.

B. *To Secular Authors*

As a general rule references are given only by author's name when only one work of that author is extant, e.g. Plin. = Pliny, *Naturalis Historia.*

Ambr. – Ambrose of Milan (bishop and theologian, *c.* A.D. 339–*c.* 397)
  De Virg. – *De Virginibus ad Marcellinam Sororem*
  Ep. – *Epistolae*
Ammianus Marcellinus (Roman historian, *fl. c.* A.D. 390)
  Historiae
Apollod – Apollodorus (Greek mythologist, *fl. c.* 140 B.C.)
  Bibliotheca (spurious; first or second century A.D.)
Appian (Greek historian, *fl. c.* A.D. 160)
  De Bell. Civ. – *De Bello Civili*
  De Bell. Mithr. – *De Bello Mithridatico*
Apul. – Apuleius (philosophical writer, and novelist, *fl. c.* A.D. 150)
  Apol. – *Apologia Pro Se (De Magia)*
  De Deo Socr. – *De Deo Socratis*
  De Mund. – *De Mundo*
  Met. – *Metamorphoses (The Golden Ass)*
[Apul] – Pseudo-Apuleius
  Asclep. – *Asclepius*
Arist. – Aristotle (Greek philosopher, 384–322 B.C.)
  De An. – *De Anima*
  De Cael. – *De Caelo*
  Eth. Nic. – *Ethica Nicomachea*
  Met. – *Metaphysica*
Arnob. – Arnobius (Christian apologist, *fl. c.* A.D. 300)
  Adv. Gent. – *Adversus Gentes* (or *Adversus Nationes*)
Arr. – Arrian (Greek historian, *c.* A.D. 95–172)
  Anab. – *Anabasis* (of Alexander the Great)
Aug. – Augustine of Hippo (A.D. 354–430)
  Adv. Faust. Man. – *Adversus Faustum Manichaeum*
  Conf. – *Confessiones*
  De Div. Quaest. ad Simplic. – *De Diversis Quaestionibus ad Simplicanum*
  De Doctr. Christ. – *De Doctrina Christiana*
  De Gen. ad Lit. – *De Genesi ad Litteram*
  De Gen. c. Man. – *De Genesi contra Manichaeos*
  De Haer. – *De Haeresibus ad Quodvultdeum*
  De Nupt. et Conc. – *De Nuptiis et Concupiscentia*
  De Pecc. Mer. et Rem. – *De Peccatorum Meritis et Remissione (et de Baptismo Parvulorum)*
  De Spir. et Lit. – *De Spiritu et Littera*

De Trin. – *De Trinitate*
De Ver. Rel. – *De Vera Religione*
Enarr. in Ps. – *Enarrationes in Psalmos*
Ep. – *Epistolae*
Exp. ex Ep. ad Rom. – *Expositiones Quarundam Expositionum ex Epistola ad Romanos*
Quaest. in Hept. – *Quaestiones in Heptateuchum*
Retract. – *Retracttaiones*
Serm. – *Sermones*
[Aurel. Vict.] – Pseudo-Aurelius Victor
Epit. – *Epitome de Caesaribus* (wrongly assigned to Aurelius Victor, a fourth-century biographer of the emperors from Augustus to Constantine)
Cic. – Cicero (Roman orator and statesman, 106–43 B.C.)
Acad. Post. – *Academica Posteriora*
Acad. Prior. – *Academica Priora*
Ad Fam. – *Epistulae ad Familiares*
De Am. – *De Amicitia*
De Div. – *De Divinatione*
De Fat. – *De Fato*
De Fin. – *De Finibus Bonorum et Malorum*
De Har. Resp. – *De Haruspicum Responso*
De Leg. – *De Legibus*
De Nat. Deor. – *De Natura Deorum*
De Off. – *De Officiis*
De Or. – *De Oratore*
De Rep. – *De Republica*
In Cat. – *In Catilinam*
In Verr. – *In Verrem*
Philip. – *Orationes Philippicae*
Pro Lig. – *Pro Ligario*
Pro Rabir. – *Pro Rabirio*
Pro Scaur. – *Pro Scauro*
Tim. – *Timaeus* (translated or adapted from Plato)
Tusc. Disp. – *Tusculanae Disputationes*
Claudian (Roman poet, *fl. c.* A.D. 400)
Cons. Hon. III – *De Tertio Consulatu Honorii Panegyricus*
Clem. Al. – Clement of Alexandria (theologian, *c.* A.D. 150–*c.* 215)
Strom. – *Stromateis*
Curtius Rufus (Latin historian, *fl. c.* A.D. 59)
De Gest. Alex. – *De Gestis Alexandri Magni*
Cyprian of Carthage (bishop and theologian, d. A.D. 258)
Ep. – *Epistolae*
Cyr. Al. – Cyril of Alexandria (patriarch and theologian, d. A.D. 444)
C. Jul. – *Contra Julianum*

Dem. – Demosthenes (Athenian orator and statesman, 383–322 B.C.)
De Cor. – *De Corona*
Dio Cass. – Dio Cassius (Greek historian, *c.* A.D. 150–235)
Historia Romana
Diod. Sic. – Diodorus Siculus (Greek historian, *fl. c.* 40 B.C.)
Bibliotheca Historica
Diog. Laert. – Diogenes Laertius (Greek biographer and doxographer, *c.* A.D. 200–250)
De Clarorum Philosophorum Vitis . . .
Dion. Hal. – Dionysius of Halicaknassus (Greek literary critic and historian, *fl. c.* 25 B.C.)
Ant. Rom. – *Antiquitates Romanae*
Epict. – Epictetus (Greek philosopher, *c.* A.D. 60–140)
Ench. – *Enchiridion* (edited by Arrian)
Eur. – Euripides (Greek tragedian, *c.* 480–406 B.C.)
Frag. – *Fragmenta*
Ion
Iph. T. – *Iphigenia in Tauris*
Euseb. – Eusebius of Caesarea (bishop and historian, *c.* A.D. 260–*c.* 340)
Dem. Ev. – *Demonstratio Evangelica*
Praep. Ev. – *Praeparatio Evangelica*
Euseb-Hier.
Chronicon – The *Chronicle* of Eusebius, continued by Jerome
Eutrop. – Eutropius (Roman historian, *fl. c.* A.D. 370)
Breviarium ab Urbe Condita
Flor. – Florus (Roman historian, *fl. c.* A.D. 100)
Epit. – *Epitome*
Festus (Latin epitomist, second century A.D.)
De Verb. Sign. – *De Verborum Significatu* (epitome of Verrius Flaccus, grammarian in reign of Augustus)
Gell. – Aulus Gellius (Roman essayist, *fl. c.* A.D. 160)
Noctes Atticae
Hes. – Hesiod (Greek poet, probably eighth century B.C.)
Theog. – *Theogonia*
Hier. – Jerome (biblical scholar, *c.* A.D. 347–420)
Comm. in Dan. – *Commentarium in Danierem*
Comm. in Ez. – *Commentarium in Ezekielem*
Ep. – *Epistolae*
Praef. in Is. – *Praefatio in Isaiam*
Praef. in Mal. – *Praefatio in Malachiam*
Quaest. Hebr. in Gen. – *Questiones Hebraicae in Genesin*
Hom. – Homer (Greek epic poet, probably ninth century B.C.)
Il. – *Iliad*
Od. – *Odyssy*

Hor. – Horace (Roman poet, 65–8 B.C.)
Carm. – *Carmina* (*Odes*)
Ep. – *Epistulae*
Epod. – *Epodes*
Joseph. – Josephus (Jewish historian, A.D. 37–*c.* 100)
Ant. Jud. – *Antiquitates Judaicae*
Bell. Jud. – *Bella Judaica*
Jul. Obs. – Julius Obsequens (Latin epitomist, probably fourth century A.D.)
Prod. – *Liber Prodigiorum*
Justin (Latin epitomist, first or second century A.D.)
Epitome (of the *Historiae Philippicae* of Trogus Pompeius, *fl.* under Augustus)
Justin Martyr (Greek Christian apologist, A.D. 109–165)
Apol. – *Apologia contra Gentiles*
Dial. – *Dialogus cum Tryphone Judaeo*
Juv. – Juvenal (Roman satirist, *c.* A.D. 250 – *c.* 320)
Saturae
Lact. – Lactantius (Latin rhetorician and Christian apologist, *c.* A.D. 250–*c.* 320)
De Ira Dei
Div. Inst. – *Divinae Institutiones*
Liv. – Livy (Roman historian, 59 B.C.–A.D. 17)
Ab Urbe Condita (references given without title)
Epit. – *Epitome* (an abridgement of the above)
Perioch. – *Periochae* (short abstracts of each book)
(Of the 142 books of Livy's *History of Rome* only thirty-five survive. The *Epitome* of twelve books has been recovered, and we have the *Periochae* of all but two of the books.)
Luc. – Lucan (Roman epic poet, A.D. 39–65)
Phars. – *Pharsalia*
Lucr. – Lucretius (Roman philosophic poet, *c.* 99–*c.* 55 B.C.)
De Rerum Natura
Macrob. – Macrobius Theodosius (Roman philosophic writer, *fl. c.* A.D. 400)
Saturnalia
Martianus Capella (Latin allegorist, early fifth century A.D.)
De Nuptiis Mercurii et Philologiae
Minucius Felix (Christian apologist, second or third century A.D.)
Octavius
Origen (Alexandrian biblical scholar and theologian, *c.* A.D. 185–*c.* 254)
C. Cels. – *Contra Celsum*
In Gen. Hom. – *In Genesin Homiliae*
De Princ. – *De Principiis* (Περὶ Ἀρχῶν)

Oros. – Orosius (Latin historian, early fifth century A.D.)
Historiae
Ovid (Roman elegiac poet, 43 B.C.–A.D. 18)
Fast. – *Fasti*
Met. – *Metamorphoses*
Paus. – Pausanias (Greek geographer, *fl. c.* A.D. 150)
Hellados Periêgêsis (*Descriptio Graeciae*)
Pers. – Persius (Roman satirist, A.D. 34–62)
Saturae
Pind. – Pindar (Greek lyric poet, *c.* 520–*c.* 440 B.C.)
Nem. – *Nemean Odes*
Plat. – Plato (Greek philosopher, *c.* 427–348 B.C.)
Apol. – *Apologia Socratis*
Crat. – *Cratylus*
Legg. – *Leges*
Phaed. – *Phaedo*
Phaedr. – *Phaedrus*
Prot. – *Protagoras*
Rp. – *De Republica*
Symp. – *Symposium*
Tim. – *Timaeus*
Plaut. – Plautus (Roman comic playwright, *c.* 254–184 B.C.)
Amph. – *Amphitruo*
Plin. – Pliny the Elder (Roman natural historian, A.D. 23–79)
Naturalis Historia
Plot. – Plotinus (Neoplatonist philosopher, A.D. 205–270)
Enn. – *Enneades*
Plut. – Plutarch (Greek biographer and essayist, *c.* A.D. 46–*c.* 120)
Ages. – *Vitae Parallelae, Agesilaus*
Alex. – *Vitae Parallelae, Alexander*
Caes. – *Vitae Parallelae, Julius Caesar*
C. Gracch. – *Vitae Parallelae, Caius Gracchus*
Cat. – *Vitae Parallelae, Cato*
De Fort. Rom. – *De Fortuna Romanorum*
Num. – *Vitae Parallelae, Numa*
Quaest. Rom. – *Quaestiones Romanae*
Pyrrh. – *Vitae Parallelae, Pyrrhus*
Sull. – *Vitae Parallelae, Sulla*
Sall. – Sallust (Roman historian, 86–35 B.C.)
Cat. – *Catilina* (*Bellum Catilinae*)
Hist. – *Historiae Fragmenta*
Iug. – *Jugurtha* (*Bellum Iugurthinum*)
Sen. – Seneca (Roman essayist, *c.* 4 B.C.–A.D. 65)
Contr. – *Controversiae*
De Clem. – *Dialogus de Clementia*

De Ira – *Dialogus de Ira*
Ep. – *Epistulae*
Socr. – Socrates (Greek Church historian, *c.* A.D. 380–450)
Historia Ecclesiastica
Soph. – Sophocles (Greek dramatist, 496–406 B.C.).
Oed. Tyr. – *Oedipus Tyrannus*
Strab. – Strabo (Greek geographer, *c.* 64 B.C. – A.D. 10)
Geographica
Suet. – Suetonius (Roman biographer, *c.* A.D. 70–*c.* 160)
De Vita Caesarum
Tac. – Tacitus (Roman historian, *c.* A.D. 55–*c.* 115)
Hist. – *Historiae*
Ter. – Terence (Roman comic playwright, *c.* 195–159 B.C.)
Ad. – *Adelphi*
Andr. – *Andria*
Eun. – *Eunuchus*
Terentian. – Terentianus Maurus (Latin grammarian and metrist, late second century A.D.)
De Metr. – *De Litteris Syllabis et Metris Horatii*
Tert. – Tertullian (African Church Father, *c.* A.D. 160–*c.* 220)
Ad Nat. – *Ad Nationes*
Ap. – *Apologia*
De Res. Mort. – *De Resurrectione Mortuorum*
De Spect. – *De Spectaculis*
Thdt. – Theodoret (bishop, theologian, and historian, *c.* A.D. 393–*c.* 458)
H.E. – *Historia Ecclesiastica*
Val. Max. – Valerius Maximus (Latin anecdotist, *fl. c.* A.D. 30)
Factorum et Dictorum Memorabilium Libri IX
Varro (Roman polymath, 116–27 B.C.)
De Ling. Lat. – *De Lingua Latina*
De Re Rust. – *De Re Rustica*
Velleius Paterculus (Roman historian, *fl. c.* A.D. 20)
Historiae Romanae
Virg. – Virgil (Roman epic, bucolic and didactic poet, 70–19 B.C.)
Aen. – *Aeneid*
Ecl. – *Eclogae*
Georg. – *Georgica*

Facsimile of the title page of the Ludovic Vives edition, 1522, of the City of God

(The British Museum catalogue notes that the date in the colophon is misprinted MDXII)

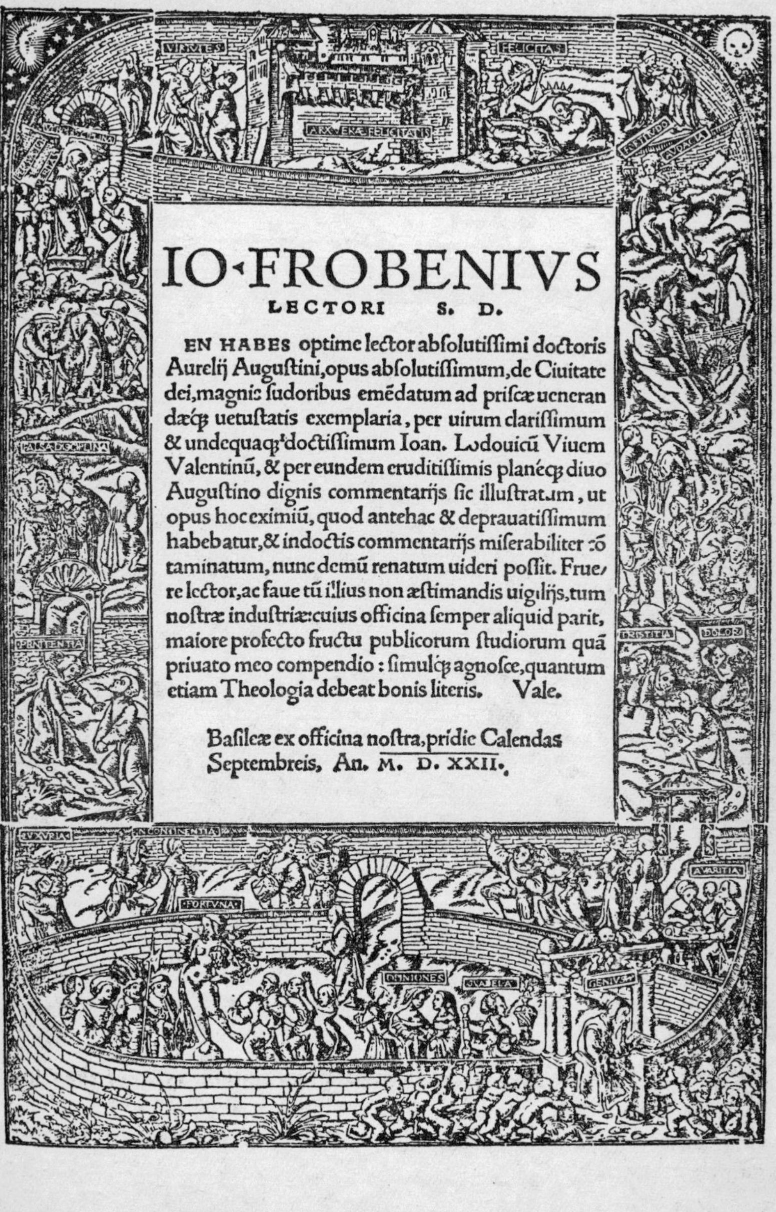

IO·FROBENIVS
LECTORI S. D.

EN HABES optime lector absolutissimi doctoris Aurelij Augustini, opus absolutissimum, de Ciuitate dei, magnis sudoribus emẽdatum ad priscæ ueneran dæq; uetustatis exemplaria, per uirum clarissimum & undequaq; doctissimum Ioan. Lodouicũ Viuem Valentinũ, & per eundem eruditissimis planéq; diuo Augustino dignis commentarijs sic illustratum, ut opus hoc eximiũ, quod antehac & deprauatissimum habebatur, & indoctis commentarijs miserabiliter cõtaminatum, nunc demũ renatum uideri possit. Fruere lector, ac faue tũ illius non æstimandis uigilijs, tum nostræ industriæ: cuius officina semper aliquid parit, maiore profecto fructu publicorum studiorum quã priuato meo compendio: simulq; agnosce, quantum etiam Theologia debeat bonis literis. Vale.

Basileæ ex officina nostra, pridie Calendas Septembreis, An. M. D. XXII.

THE PENGUIN CLASSICS

AUGUSTINE: CITY OF GOD

Part I

BOOK I

Preface. The Purpose and Argument of this work

HERE, my dear Marcellinus,[1] is the fulfilment of my promise, a book in which I have taken upon myself the task of defending the glorious City of God against those who prefer their own gods to the Founder of that City. I treat of it both as it exists in this world of time, a stranger among the ungodly, living by faith,[2] and as it stands in the security of its everlasting seat. This security it now awaits in steadfast patience, until 'justice returns to judgement';[3] but it is to attain it hereafter in virtue of its ascendancy over its enemies, when the final victory is won and peace established. The task is long and arduous; but God is our helper.[4]

I know how great is the effort needed to convince the proud of the power and excellence of humility, an excellence which makes it soar above all the summits of this world, which sway in their temporal instability, overtopping them all with an eminence not arrogated by human pride, but granted by divine grace. For the King and Founder of this City which is our subject has revealed in the Scripture of his people this statement of the divine Law, 'God resists the proud, but he gives grace to the humble.'[5] This is God's prerogative; but man's arrogant spirit in its swelling pride has claimed it as its own, and delights to hear this verse quoted in its own praise: 'To spare the conquered, and beat down the proud.'[6]

Therefore I cannot refrain from speaking about the city of this world, a city which aims at dominion, which holds nations in enslavement, but is itself dominated by that very lust of domination. I

1. *Marcellinus.* An intimate disciple of St Augustine sent by the Emperor Honorius to preside over the council summoned at Carthage to settle the dispute between Catholics and Donatists. Marcellinus was anxious to convert Volusianus, proconsul of Africa. Volusianus showed interest, but among his objections to Christianity was the charge that it had undermined the Roman Empire. Marcellinus wrote to ask for help from St Augustine (who had already corresponded with Volusianus) and this led eventually to the writing of *The City of God* (cf. Aug. *Ep.*, 135–8).

2. cf. Hab. 2, 4; Rom. 1, 17; Gal. 3, 11; Hebr. 10, 38.
3. Ps. 94, 15.
4. cf. Ps. 118, 6.
5. Jas. 4, 6.
6. Virg., *Aen.*, 6, 853.

must consider this city as far as the scheme of this work demands and as occasion serves.

1. *The enemies of Christianity were spared by the barbarians at the sack of Rome, out of respect for Christ*

From this world's city there arise enemies against whom the City of God has to be defended, though many of these correct their godless errors and become useful citizens of that City. But many are inflamed with hate against it and feel no gratitude for the benefits offered by its Redeemer. The benefits are unmistakable; those enemies would not today be able to utter a word against the City if, when fleeing from the sword of their enemy, they had not found, in the City's holy places, the safety on which they now congratulate themselves.[7] The barbarians spared them for Christ's sake; and now these Romans assail Christ's name. The sacred places of the martyrs and the basilicas of the apostles bear witness to this, for in the sack of Rome they afforded shelter to fugitives, both Christian and pagan. The bloodthirsty enemy raged thus far, but here the frenzy of butchery was checked; to these refuges the merciful among the enemy conveyed those whom they had spared outside, to save them from encountering foes who had no such pity. Even men who elsewhere raged with all the savagery an enemy can show, arrived at places where practices generally allowed by laws of war were forbidden and their monstrous passion for violence was brought to a sudden halt; their lust for taking captives was subdued.

In this way many escaped who now complain of this Christian era, and hold Christ responsible for the disasters which their city endured. But they do not make Christ responsible for the benefits they received out of respect for Christ, to which they owed their lives. They attribute their deliverance to their own destiny; whereas if they had any right judgement they ought rather to attribute the harsh cruelty they suffered at the hands of their enemies to the providence of God. For God's providence constantly uses war to correct and chasten the corrupt morals of mankind, as it also uses such afflictions to train men in a righteous and laudable way of life, removing to a better state those whose life is approved, or else keeping them in this world for further service.

7. The clemency of Alaric to those who took sanctuary in Christian shrines, and especially in the basilicas of St Peter and St Paul is attested by Orosius (7, 39) and Jerome (*Ep.* 27, 13).

Moreover, they should give credit to this Christian era for the fact that these savage barbarians showed mercy beyond the custom of war – whether they so acted in general in honour of the name of Christ, or in places specially dedicated to Christ's name, buildings of such size and capacity as to give mercy a wider range. For this clemency our detractors ought rather to give thanks to God; they should have recourse to his name in all sincerity, so as to escape the penalty of everlasting fire, seeing that so many of them assumed his name dishonestly, to escape the penalty of immediate destruction. Among those whom you see insulting Christ's servants with such wanton insolence there are very many who came unscathed through that terrible time of massacre only by passing themselves off as Christ's servants. And now with ungrateful pride and impious madness they oppose his name in the perversity of their hearts, so that they may incur the punishment of eternal darkness; but then they took refuge in that name, though with deceitful lips, so that they might continue to enjoy this transitory light.

2. *That victors should spare the vanquished out of respect for their gods, is something unexampled in history*

We have the records of many wars, both before the foundation of Rome and after its rise to power. Let our enemies read their history, and then produce instances of the capture of any city by foreign enemies when those enemies spared any whom they found taking refuge in the temples of their gods.[8] Let them quote any barbarian general who gave instructions, at the storming of a town, that no one should be treated with violence who was discovered in this temple or that. Aeneas saw Priam at the altar,

polluting with his blood
The fire which he had consecrated.[9]

And Diomedes and Ulysses

Slew all the warders of the citadel
And snatched with bloody hands the sacred image;
Nor shrank to touch the chaplets virginal
Of the dread goddess.

8. St Augustine's challenge was ill-judged. Pagans could quote the clemency of Alexander at Tyre (Arr., *Anab.*, 7, 24) and of Agesilaus after Coronea (Plut., *Ages.*, 19).

9. Virg., *Aen.*, 2, 502.

And there is no truth in the statement that comes after,

> The Grecian hopes then failed, and ebbed away.[10]

For what in fact followed was the Greek victory, the destruction of Troy by fire and sword, the slaughter of Priam at the altar.

And it was not because Troy lost Minerva that Troy perished. What loss did Minerva herself first incur, that led to her own disappearance? Was it, perhaps, the loss of her guards? There can be no doubt that their death made her removal possible – the image did not preserve the men; the men were preserving the image. Why then did they worship her, to secure her protection for their country and its citizens? She could not guard her own keepers.

3. *The folly of the Romans in confiding their safety to the household gods who had failed to protect Troy*

There you see the sort of gods to whom the Romans gladly entrusted the preservation of their city. Pitiable folly! Yet the Romans are enraged by such criticisms from us, while they are not incensed at the authors of such quotations; in fact they pay money to become acquainted with their works, and they consider that those who merely instruct them in these works merit an official salary and an honoured position in the community. Virgil certainly is held to be a great poet; in fact he is regarded as the best and the most renowned of all poets, and for that reason he is read by children at an early age – they take great draughts of his poetry into their unformed minds, so that they may not easily forget him, for, as Horace remarks,

> New vessels will for long retain the taste
> Of what is first poured into them.[11]

Now in Virgil Juno is introduced as hostile to the Trojans, and when she urges Aeolus, king of the winds, against them, she says,

> A race I hate sails the Etruscan sea
> Bringing to Italy Troy's vanquished gods,
> And Troy itself.[12]

Ought the Romans, as prudent men, to have entrusted the defence of Rome to gods unable to defend themselves? Juno no doubt spoke like a woman in anger, heedless of what she was saying. But consider what is said by Aeneas himself, who is so often called 'the pious'.

10. *Aen.*, 6, 166ff. 11. *Ep.*, 1, 2, 69f. 12. *Aen.*, 1, 67f.

Panthus, the priest of Phoebus and the citadel,
Snatching his conquered gods and his young grandson
Rushes in frenzy to the door.[13]

He does not shrink from calling the gods 'conquered', and he speaks of them as being entrusted to him, rather than the other way round, when he is told, 'To thee, Troy now entrusts her native gods.'[14]

If Virgil speaks of such gods as 'vanquished', and tells how, after their overthrow, they only succeeded in escaping because they were committed to the care of a man, what folly it is to see any wisdom in committing Rome to such guardians, and in supposing that it could not be sacked while it retained possession of them. To worship 'vanquished' gods as protectors and defenders is to rely not on divinities but on defaulters. It is not sensible to assume that Rome would have escaped this disaster had these gods not first perished; the sensible belief is that those gods would have perished long before, had not Rome made every effort to preserve them. Anyone who gives his mind to it can see that it is utter folly to count on invincibility by virtue of the possession of defenders who have been conquered and to attribute destruction to the loss of such guardian deities as these. In fact, the only possible cause of destruction was the choice of such perishable defenders. When the poets wrote and sang of 'vanquished gods', it was not because it suited their whim to lie – they were men of sense, and truth compelled them to admit the facts.

But I must deal with this subject in fuller detail in a more convenient place. For the present I will return to the ingratitude of those who blasphemously blame Christ for the disasters which their moral perversity deservedly brought upon them, and I will deal with the subject as briefly as I can. They were spared for Christ's sake, pagans though they were; yet they scorn to acknowledge this. With the madness of sacrilegious perversity they use their tongues against the name of Christ; yet with those same tongues they dishonestly claimed that name in order to save their lives, or else, in places sacred to him, they held their tongues through fear. They were kept safe and protected there where his name stood between them and the enemy's violence. And so they issue from that shelter to assail him with curses of hate.

13. *Aen.*, 2, 319f. 14. *Aen.*, 2, 203.

4. *Juno's sanctuary in Troy gave no security from the Greeks; whereas the apostolic basilicas at Rome gave protection from the barbarians*

As I said before, Troy itself, the mother of the Roman people, could not, by means of the consecrated buildings of its gods, save its citizens from the fire and sword of the Greeks, although they worshipped the same gods.

> In Juno's sanctuary
> The chosen warders, Phoenix and dread Ulysses,
> Keep safe the spoils; and there is heaped Troy's wealth:
> Plunder from burning shrines, the golden bowls,
> The tables of the gods, the captured vestments.
> And near them stand the boys and trembling matrons
> Rank upon rank.[15]

That is to say, a place consecrated to so great a goddess was chosen, not as a place from which prisoners might not lawfully be taken out, but as a place where the victors might at pleasure shut up their captives. This sanctuary was not the temple of any common god of the lower orders of deities, but that of the sister and wife of Jove himself, the queen of all the gods. Now contrast it with the memorial shrines of our apostles. To the former were taken the spoils from the burning temples and gods, not to be given to the vanquished, but to be divided among the victors; to the latter was carried, with honour and most scrupulous reverence, all that belonged to those places which was found elsewhere. There, freedom was lost; here, it was preserved. There, captives were confined; here, enslavement was forbidden. There, men were herded by foes who exercised their power by sending them into slavery; here, they were conducted by foes who showed their pity by setting them free. In short, the greedy arrogance of the contemptible Greeks chose that temple of Juno for its display; the humble clemency of the barbarians, uncouth as they were, chose those basilicas of Christ. It may be that the Greeks in their victory spared the temples of the common gods and refrained from hurting or enslaving the poor conquered Trojans who took refuge there. If so, Virgil, in the manner of poets, did not tell the truth about it. In fact he gives the familiar picture of the sack of a city by its enemies.

15. Virg., *Aen.*, 2, 761ff.

5. *Cato's description of the sack of a city, according to the custom of war*

According to Sallust, a historian renowned for his veracity, Cato,[16] in making his proposal about the conspirators, was careful to remind the senate of the usual consequences when cities are sacked.

> Maidens and boys are carried off, children are torn from parents' embrace; mothers are subjected to the pleasure of the conquerors; temples and homes are despoiled; there is fire and slaughter everywhere; the scene is crowded with fighting men, with dead bodies, with bloodshed and lamentation.[17]

If he had omitted the mention of temples, we might have supposed that it was the custom for enemies to spare the abodes of gods. Yet the Roman temples had to dread this fate, not at the hands of foreign foes, but at the hands of Catiline and his associates, that is, of Roman citizens and senators of the highest birth; but they, to be sure, were men without conscience, murderers of the land that bore them.

6. Not *even the Romans spared the conquered in the temples of captured cities*

Why should I survey in this argument the wars waged by many nations which supply no instance of mercy shown the conquered in the abodes of their gods? Let us observe the Romans themselves; let us give them further examination. It was said of them, in their particular praise, that it was their custom 'To spare the conquered and beat down the proud';[18] and that they chose 'rather to pardon than to avenge the wrongs'[19] they suffered. To extend their dominions these Romans captured, stormed or overthrew many mighty cities. Do we ever read of any privilege extended to certain temples, to ensure that any who took refuge in them should be given their freedom? Or did they act thus, even though the historians fail to mention it? These historians particularly look for points to praise. Is it likely that they would omit actions which, by their own standards, would be most convincing evidence of religious feeling?

16. *Cato Uticensis* killed himself after the battle of Thapsus (46 B.C.) and the suicide was applauded as an example of Stoic virtue. The description of war is in fact put into the mouth of Caesar in Sallust's *Catiline*.

17. *Cat.*, 51, 9.

18. Virg., *Aen.*, 6, 853, quoted above in the Preface.

19. Sall., *Cat.*, 9, 5.

That great Roman, Marcus Marcellus, who captured the splendid city of Syracuse, is said to have wept over its coming downfall and to have shed his own tears before shedding Syracusan blood.[20] He also took care to preserve the honour of his enemies, for before he ordered the invasion of the town, the victor issued an edict that no violence should be done to the person of any free citizen. And yet that city was overthrown in the usual manner of warfare, and there is no record of any proclamation by that honourable and merciful commander to order that anyone who fled to this temple or that should be immune from harm. And this would certainly not have passed unrecorded, since the records could not allow his weeping to remain unmentioned, nor his edict utterly forbidding the violation of his enemy's honour.

Fabius, who crushed Tarentum, is commended for having abstained from plundering images.[21] For when his secretary inquired what were his commands about the statues of the gods, many of which had been captured, he seasoned his moderation with a joke. He asked what sort of images they were and, on being told that many of them were of impressive size, and some were even armed, he said, 'Let us leave the Tarentines their angry gods.' Now since the Roman chroniclers could not fail to mention the tears of one and the jocularity of the other, the honourable clemency of Marcellus and the humorous moderation of Fabius, is it likely that they would omit to record it if these two had shown mercy to any man out of respect for their gods by forbidding massacre or enslavement in some temple or other?

7. *In the sack of Rome, the cruelties conformed to the conventions of war; the acts of clemency were due to the power of Christ's name*

All the devastation, the butchery, the plundering, the conflagrations, and all the anguish which accompanied the recent disaster at Rome[22] were in accordance with the general practice of warfare. But there was something which established a new custom, something which changed the whole aspect of the scene; the savagery of the barbarians took on such an aspect of gentleness that the largest basilicas were selected and set aside to be filled with people to be spared by the enemy. No one was to be violently used there, no one snatched away.

20. Liv. 25, 24, 11. In 212 B.C.

21. Liv. 27, 15f. Q. Fabius Maximus Cunctator captured Tarentum in 209 B.C.

22. Alaric entered Rome, 24 August A.D. 410; Aug. began the *City of God* in A.D. 413.

Many were to be brought there for liberation by merciful foes; none were to be taken from there into captivity even by cruel enemies. This is to be attributed to the name of Christ and the influence of Christianity. Anyone who fails to see this is blind; anyone who sees it and fails to give praise for it is thankless; anyone who tries to stop another from giving praise is a madman. Let us hope that no one with any sense will ascribe the credit for this to the brutal nature of the barbarians. Their fierce and savage minds were terrified, restrained, and miraculously controlled by him who long ago said, through his prophet, 'I will visit their iniquities with a rod, and their sins with scourges: but I will not disperse my mercy from them.'[23]

8. *Blessings and disasters often shared by good and bad*

No doubt this question will be asked, 'Why does the divine mercy extend even to the godless and ungrateful?' The only explanation is that it is the mercy of one 'who makes his sun rise on the good and on the bad, and sends rain alike on the righteous and the unrighteous'.[24] Some of the wicked are brought to penitence by considering these facts, and amend their impiety, while others, in the words of the Apostle, 'despise the riches of God's goodness and forebearance, in the hardness and impenitence of their hearts, and lay up for themselves a store of wrath in the day of God's anger and of the revelation of the just judgement of God, who will repay every man according to his actions'.[25] Yet the patience of God still invites the wicked to penitence, just as God's chastisement trains the good in patient endurance. God's mercy embraces the good for their cherishing, just as his severity chastens the wicked for their punishment. God, in his providence, decided to prepare future blessings for the righteous, which the unrighteous will not enjoy, and sorrows for the ungodly, with which the good will not be tormented. But he has willed that these temporal goods and temporal evils should befall good and bad alike, so that the good things should not be too eagerly coveted, when it is seen that the wicked also enjoy them, and that the evils should not be discreditably shunned, when it is apparent that the good are often afflicted with them.

The most important question is this: What use is made of the things thought to be blessings, and of the things reputed evil? The good man

23. Ps. 89, 33f. 24. Matt. 5, 45.
25. Rom. 2, 4ff.; 'the Apostle' refers always to St Paul in the works of the early Fathers of the Church.

is not exalted by this world's goods; nor is he overwhelmed by this world's ills. The bad man is punished by misfortune of this kind just because he is corrupted by good fortune.

However, it often happens that God shows more clearly his manner of working in the distribution of good and bad fortune. For if punishment were obviously inflicted on every wrongdoing in this life, it would be supposed that nothing was reserved for the last judgement; on the other hand, if God's power never openly punished any sin in this world, there would be an end to belief in providence. Similarly in respect of good fortune; if God did not grant it to some petitioners with manifest generosity, we should not suppose that these temporal blessings were his concern, while if he bestowed prosperity on all just for the asking we might think that God was to be served merely for the sake of those rewards, and any service of him would prove us not godly but rather greedy and covetous.

This being so, when the good and the wicked suffer alike, the identity of their sufferings does not mean that there is no difference between them. Though the sufferings are the same, the sufferers remain different. Virtue and vice are not the same, even if they undergo the same torment. The fire which makes gold shine makes chaff smoke; the same flail breaks up the straw, and clears the grain; and oil is not mistaken for lees because both are forced out by the same press. In the same way, the violence which assails good men to test them, to cleanse and purify them, effects in the wicked their condemnation, ruin, and annihilation. Thus the wicked, under pressure of affliction, execrate God and blaspheme; the good, in the same affliction, offer up prayers and praises. This shows that what matters is the nature of the sufferer, not the nature of the sufferings. Stir a cesspit, and a foul stench arises; stir a perfume, and a delightful fragrance ascends. But the movement is identical.

9. *The reasons why the good and the wicked are equally afflicted*

Thus, in this universal catastrophe, the sufferings of Christians have tended to their moral improvement, because they viewed them with the eyes of faith.

First, they consider in humility the sins which have moved God's indignation so that he has filled the world with dire calamities. And although they are free from criminal and godless wickedness, still they do not regard themselves as so far removed from such wrongdoing as not to deserve to suffer the temporal ills which are the recompense of sin. Everyone of them, however commendable his life, gives way at times to physical desires, and, while avoiding monstrous crimes, the sink of iniquity and the abomination of godlessness, is yet guilty of some sins, infrequent sins, perhaps, or more frequent because more trivial. Apart from this, it is not easy to find anyone who, when confronted with those whose fearful arrogance, lust, and greed, whose detestable wickedness and impiety, have caused God to give effect to his threats and warnings by bringing destruction on the earth – it is not, I say, easy to find anyone who regards such men as they should be regarded – who, when he meets them, treats them as they should be treated.

We tend culpably to evade our responsibility when we ought to instruct and admonish them, sometimes even with sharp reproof and censure, either because the task is irksome, or because we are afraid of giving offence; or it may be that we shrink from incurring their enmity, for fear that they may hinder and harm us in worldly matters, in respect either of what we eagerly seek to attain, or of what we weakly dread to lose. And so, although the good dislike the way of life of the wicked, and therefore do not fall into the condemnation which is in store for the wicked after this life, nevertheless, because they are tender towards damnable sins of the wicked, and thus fall into sin through fear of such people (pardonable and comparatively trivial though those sins may be), they are justly chastised with afflictions in this world, although they are spared eternal punishment; and they rightly feel this life to be bitter when they are associated with the wicked in the afflictions sent by God. But it was through love of this world's sweetness that they refused to be bitter to those sinners.

If anyone refrains from reproof and correction of ill-doers because he looks for a more suitable occasion, or because he fears that this will make them worse, or fears that they will hinder the instruction of others, who are weak, in a good and godly way of life, and that they will oppress them, and turn them away from the faith, in such a case the action seems to be prompted not by self-interest but by counsels of charity. What is culpable is when those whose life is different and who abhor the deeds of the wicked are nevertheless indulgent to the sins of others, which they ought to reprehend and reprove, because they are concerned to avoid giving offence to them, in case they should harm themselves in respect of things which may be rightly and innocently enjoyed by good men, but which they desire more than is right for those who are strangers in this world and who fix their hope on a heavenly country.

There are the weaker brothers, in the married state, who have children or look to have them, who are masters of houses and households; the Apostle addresses them in the churches, teaching them and warning them how they ought to live, wives with husbands and husbands with wives, children with parents and parents with children, servants with masters and masters with servants.[26] Such men are eager to acquire many of this world's temporal goods, and grieve to lose them, and for that reason they have not the heart to offend men whose lives of shame and crime they detest. But they are not alone.

Even those who have a higher standard of life, who are not entangled in the bonds of marriage, who are content with little food and scanty clothing, are often fearful of attacks by the wicked upon their reputation and their safety, and so refrain from reproaches. They are not so afraid of the wicked as to yield to their villainous threats to the extent of committing crimes like theirs; but though they do not commit them they too often fail to reprehend them, for although they might perhaps convert some by such rebuke they fear that, if the attempt failed, their safety and reputation might be endangered or destroyed. And this is not due to prudence, nor is it because they see their reputation and safety as essential means whereby mankind may receive the benefit of instruction; it is rather due to weakness – because they delight in flattery and popularity and because they dread the judgement of the mob, and the torture or death of the body. In fact, they are constrained by self-interest, not by the obligations of charity.

So this seems to me a major reason why the good are chastized along with the evil, when God decides to punish moral corruption with temporal calamities. Good and bad are chastised together, not because both alike live evil lives, but because both alike, though not in the same degree, love this temporal life. But the good ought to have despised it, so that the others might be reformed and corrected and might aim at life eternal; or, if they refused to be partners in this enterprise, so that they might be borne with, and loved as Christians should love their enemies, since in this life it is always uncertain whether or not they are likely to experience a change of heart.

In this matter a uniquely heavy responsibility rests on those to whom this message is given by the prophet: 'He indeed will die in his sin, but I will require his blood at the hand of the watchman.'[27] For

26. Col. 3, 18ff. 27. Ez. 33, 6.

'watchmen', that is, leaders of the people, have been appointed in the churches for this purpose, that they should be unsparing in their condemnation of sin. This does not mean that a man is entirely free from blame in this regard if, without being a 'watchman', he recognizes, but ignores, opportunities of warning and admonishing those with whom the exigencies of this life force him to associate – if he evades this duty for fear of offending them, because he is concerned for those worldly advantages, which are not in themselves discreditable, but to which he is unduly attached. There is a further reason for the infliction of temporal suffering on the good, as is seen in the case of Job – that the spirit of man may be tested, that he may learn for himself what is the degree of disinterested devotion that he offers to God.

10. *The saints lose nothing by being deprived of temporal goods*

After giving proper attention and consideration to these points, observe whether any disaster has happened to the faithful and religious which did not turn out for their good; unless we are to suppose that there is no meaning in the Apostle's statement, 'We know that God makes all things co-operate for good for those who love him.'[28] They lost all they had. Did they lose faith? Or devotion? Or the possessions of the inner man, who is 'rich in the sight of God'?[29] These are the riches of Christians, and the Apostle, who was endowed with this wealth, said,

> Devotion combined with self-sufficiency yields great profit. For we brought nothing into this world, and we cannot take anything away with us. So, if we have food and clothes, we are content with that. For those who wish to become rich fall into temptation and into a snare, and into many foolish and harmful desires, which plunge men into death and destruction. For acquisitiveness is the root of all evils; and those who have this as their aim have strayed away from the faith and have entangled themselves in many sorrows.[30]

If those who lost their earthly riches in that disaster had possessed them in the spirit thus described to them by one who was outwardly poor but inwardly rich; that is, if they had 'used the world as though not using it',[31] then they would have been able to say, with that man who was so sorely tried and yet was never overcome: 'I issued from my

28. Rom. 8, 28. 29. cf. Luke, 12, 21. 30. 1 Tim. 6, 6ff.
31. 1 Cor. 7, 31.

mother's womb in nakedness, and in nakedness I shall return to the earth. The Lord has given, the Lord has taken away. It has happened as God decided. May the Lord's name be blessed.'[32] Thus a good servant would regard the will of God as his great resource, and he would be enriched in his mind by close attendance on God's will; nor would he grieve if deprived in life of those possessions which he would soon have to leave behind at his death.

The weaker characters, who clung to their worldly goods with some degree of avarice, even if they did not prefer them to Christ, discovered, in losing them, how much they sinned in loving them. They 'entangled themselves in sorrows', as I have already quoted from the Apostle, and they suffered in proportion. They refused for so long to be taught by words, and they had to have the added teaching of experience. For when the Apostle said, 'Those who wish to become rich fall into temptation ...'[33] what he condemns in riches is the desire for them, not the opportunities they offer. This is clear from his injunction in another passage:

> I enjoin the rich of this world not to feel proud, and not to fix their eyes on the uncertainty of riches, but on the living God, who supplies us liberally with all things for our enjoyment. Let them do good; let them be rich in good works; let them be ready to give; let them share their wealth; let them store up a good foundation for the future; let them get hold of true life.[34]

Those who have done this with their riches have had great gains to compensate them for light losses, and their joy at what they assured for themselves more securely by readiness to give outweighed their sadness at the surrender of possessions they more easily lost because they clung to them fearfully. Reluctance to remove their goods from this world exposed them to the risk of loss. There were those who accepted the Lord's advice: 'Do not store your treasures on earth, where moth and rust destroy, and where thieves break in and steal. Pile up treasure in heaven, where no thief comes near and no moth destroys. For where your treasure is, your heart will be also;'[35] and such people proved in the time of tribulation how wise they were in not despising the finest of advisers and the most faithful and unconquerable guardian of treasure. For if many rejoiced at having their riches in a place which fortunately escaped the enemy's approach, with how much greater certainty and confidence could those rejoice who at the warning of their God removed themselves to a place to

32. Job 1, 21. 33. 1 Tim. 6, 9. 34. 1 Tim. 6, 17ff.
35. Matt. 6, 19ff.

which the enemy could never come. Hence our friend Paulinus,[36] bishop of Nola, deliberately reduced himself from great wealth to extreme poverty and the great riches of holiness; and when the barbarians devastated Nola, and he was in their hands, he prayed in his heart, as I learnt from him afterwards, 'Lord, let me not be tortured on account of gold and silver; for you know where all my riches are.' For he kept all his possessions in the place where he had been told to store and preserve them by him who foretold those troubles which were to come upon the world. In this way, those who obeyed their Lord's advice about where and how they ought to amass treasure, did not lose even their worldly riches in the barbarian invasions. But those who had to repent of their disobedience learnt what they should have done in this matter; if they failed to learn by wisdom before the event, at least they learned by experience after it.

It will be objected that some Christians, and good Christians, were tortured to make them hand over their goods to the enemy. But they could not hand over, nor lose, that good which was the ground of their own goodness; and if they preferred to be tortured rather than surrender 'the Mammon of unrighteousness', then they were not good. Those who suffered so much for the sake of gold should have been warned how much they should endure for the sake of Christ, so that they might learn, instead of loving gold and silver, to love him who would enrich with eternal felicity those who suffered for his sake. To suffer for the sake of wealth was pitiable, whether the wealth was concealed by telling lies, or surrendered by telling the truth. For under torture no one lost Christ by confessing him, no one preserved his gold except by denying it. In this respect we might say that torture conveyed the lesson that what is to be loved is the incorruptible good; and so torture was more useful than those possessions which tormented their owners, through the love they aroused, without bringing them any useful profit.

But there were some who were tortured even though they possessed nothing to surrender. They were tortured because they were not believed. Perhaps they desired possessions, and were not voluntarily poor through holiness. They had to be shown that the mere desire for wealth, even without the enjoyment of it, deserved such torments. As for those who had no gold and silver stored away because they had set their hearts on a better life, I am not sure that any of such people were so unfortunate as to be tortured because of their supposed wealth. But even if this did happen, those who confessed holy poverty when tor-

36. Bp. of Nola in Campania, A.D. 409–31.

tured were confessing Christ; and so anyone who confessed holy poverty, even if he did not win credence from the enemy, could not be tortured without winning a heavenly reward.

'But', they say, 'many Christians have been destroyed by prolonged starvation.' Well, the loyal and faithful turned this also to their own advantage by enduring it in fidelity to God. For when starvation killed any, it snatched them away from the evils of this life, as disease rescues men from the sufferings of the body, and if it spared their lives, it taught them to live more frugally and to fast more extensively.

11. *The end of this present life must come, whether sooner or later*

'But', they will say, 'many Christians also have been killed, and many carried off by hideous diseases of all kinds.' If one must grieve at this, it is certainly the common lot of all who have been brought into this life. I am certain of this, that no one has died who was not going to die at some time, and the end of life reduces the longest life to the same condition as the shortest. When something has once ceased to exist, there is no more question of better or worse, longer or shorter. What does it matter by what kind of death life is brought to an end? When man's life is ended he does not have to die again. Among the daily chances of this life every man on earth is threatened in the same way by innumerable deaths, and it is uncertain which of them will come to him. And so the question is whether it is better to suffer one in dying or to fear them all in living. I am well aware that a man would sooner choose to live under threat of all those deaths than by one death to be thereafter free of the fear of them. But there is a wide difference between the body's instinctive shrinking, in weakness and fear, and the mind's rational conviction, when deliberately set free from the body's influence. Death is not to be regarded as a disaster, when it follows on a good life, for the only thing that makes death an evil is what comes after death. Those who must inevitably die ought not to worry overmuch about what accident will cause their death, but about their destination after dying. Christians know that the death of a poor religious man, licked by the tongues of dogs, is far better than the death of a godless rich man, dressed in purple and linen.[37] Why then should those who have lived well be dismayed by the terrors of death in any form?

37. Luke 16, 19ff.

12. *The lack of burial does not matter to a Christian*

'But many could not even be buried, in all that welter of carnage.' Religious faith does not dread even that. We have the assurance that the ravenous beasts will not hinder the resurrection of bodies of which not a single hair of the head will perish. He who is the Truth would not say, 'Do not fear those who kill the body, but cannot kill the soul',[38] if the future life could be hindered by anything which the foe chose to do with the bodies of the slain. Unless anyone is so absurd as to contend that those who kill the body should not be dreaded before death, for fear that they should kill the body, and yet should be dreaded after death, for fear that they should not allow the corpse to be buried! In that case Christ spoke falsely about 'those who kill the body, and have nothing that they can do after that',[39] if they can do so much with the corpses. Perish the thought, that the Truth could lie! The reason for saying that they do something when they kill is that there is feeling in the body when it is killed; but after that they have nothing they can do, since there is no feeling in a body that has been killed.

And so many Christian bodies have not received a covering of earth, and yet no one has separated any of them from heaven and earth, and the whole universe is filled with the presence of him who knows from where he is to raise up what he has created. The psalm says, 'They have set out the mortal parts of thy servants as food for the birds of the sky; and the flesh of thy saints as food for the beasts of the earth. They have shed their blood like water all round Jerusalem, and there was no one to bury them.'[40] But this was said to underline the cruelty of the acts, not to stress the misfortune of the sufferers; for although their sufferings seem harsh and terrible in the eyes of men, yet 'the death of his saints is precious in the eyes of God'.[41]

Such things as a decent funeral and a proper burial, with its procession of mourners, are a consolation to the living rather than a help to the departed. If an expensive burial is any advantage to the godless, then a cheap funeral, or no funeral at all, will prove a hindrance to the poor religious man. A crowd of dependants provided the rich man in his purple with a funeral that was splendid in the eyes of men, but a funeral much more splendid in God's sight was provided for the poor

38. Matt. 10, 28. 39. Luke 12, 4. 40. Ps. 79, 2f.
41. Ps. 115, 16.

man by the ministering angels, who did not escort him to a marble tomb, but carried him up to Abraham's bosom.

This is treated with ridicule by those against whose attacks we have undertaken to defend the City of God. Yet their own philosophers have shown contempt for anxiety about burial. Whole armies, when dying for their earthly country, have often shown no concern about where they would lie, or for what beasts they would become food; and their poets could be applauded for saying,

> Who lacks an urn, is covered by the sky.[42]

By what right do they jeer at Christians because their bodies are unburied? Christians have the promise that their bodies and all their limbs will be restored and renewed, in an instant, not only from the earth, but also from the remotest hiding-places in the other elements into which their dead bodies passed in disintegration.

13. *The reason for burying the bodies of the saints*

This does not mean that the bodies of the departed are to be scorned and cast away, particularly not the bodies of the righteous and faithful, of which the Spirit has made holy use as instruments for good works of every kind. For if such things as a father's clothes, and his ring, are dear to their children in proportion to their affection for their parents, then the actual bodies are certainly not to be treated with contempt, since we wear them in a much closer and more intimate way than any clothing. A man's body is no mere adornment, or external convenience; it belongs to his very nature as a man. Hence the burials of the righteous men of antiquity were performed as acts of loyal devotion; their funeral services were thronged, arrangements made for their tombs, and they themselves during their lifetime gave instructions to their sons about the burial, or even the transference, of their bodies; and Tobit is commended, as the angel testifies, for having done good service to God by giving burial to the dead.[43] The Lord himself also, who was to rise again on the third day, proclaimed, and commanded that it should be proclaimed, that the pious woman had done 'a good deed', because she had poured costly ointment over his limbs, and had done this for his burial;[44] and it is related in the Gospel, as a praiseworthy act, that those who received his body from

42. Luc., *Phars.*, 7, 819. 43. Tob. 2, 9; 12, 12. 44. Matt. 26, 10ff.

the cross were careful to clothe it and bury it with all honour.[45]

These authorities are not instructing us that dead bodies have any feeling; they are pointing out that the providence of God, who approves such acts of duty and piety, is concerned with the bodies of the dead, so as to promote faith in the resurrection. There is a further saving lesson to be learnt here – how great a reward there may be for alms which we give to those who live and feel, if any care and service we render to men's lifeless bodies is not lost in the sight of God. There are other examples of instructions given by holy patriarchs about the disposal or the transference of their bodies, instructions which they wished to be taken as uttered in the spirit of prophecy;[46] but this is not the place to discuss them, and the examples we have given may suffice.

But if the absence of the necessities of life, such as food and clothes, although causing much misery, does not shatter the good man's courage to endure with patience, and does not banish devotion from his soul, but rather fertilizes it by exercise, still less does the absence of the usual honours of funeral and burial bring misery to those who are at peace in the hidden abodes of the devout. Therefore where those honours were not paid to the bodies of Christians in the sack of their great city, or of other towns, no fault lay with the living, who were unable to offer them, and no penalty was suffered by the dead, who could not feel their deprivation.

14. *The divine consolations of the saints in captivity*

'But many Christians have been taken into captivity.' This was certainly most pitiable if they could be taken anywhere where they did not find their God. The Bible provides great consolation for this disaster also. There were the three boys in captivity;[47] Daniel also was in captivity[48] and so were other prophets. They did not lack the consolation of God's presence; so the God who did not desert the prophet in the belly of a sea-monster,[49] did not desert his faithful followers under the domination of a people who, though barbarians, were still human. Our opponents choose rather to ridicule than to believe the tale of Jonah; and yet they believe the story, in their literature, of Arion of Methymna, that renowned minstrel, who was thrown overboard, and carried to land supported on a dolphin's

45. John 19, 38ff.
46. Gen. 49, 29; 50, 25.
47. Dan. 4.
48. Dan. 1, 6.
49. Jon. 2, 1.

back.[50] Our story about the prophet Jonah is indeed more incredible. Obviously it is more incredible because more miraculous, and more miraculous because it is evidence of greater power.

15. *The story of Regulus, an example of captivity endured for religion's sake, although a false religion*

However, our opponents have, among their most eminent heroes, a notable instance of captivity voluntarily endured for religion's sake. Marcus Regulus,[51] the Roman commander-in-chief, was a prisoner in the hands of the Carthaginians. Since the Carthaginians preferred to have their own prisoners released by the Romans, rather than keep their Roman prisoners, Regulus was the man chosen to be sent to Rome with their deputation, having first bound himself by an oath to return to Carthage if he failed to obtain the result the enemy desired. He proceeded to Rome, and in the senate he successfully urged the rejection of the proposal, since he considered that an exchange of prisoners was not to the advantage of Rome. After the success of his plea he was not forced by his countrymen to return to the enemy, but since he had taken an oath, he voluntarily fulfilled his obligation and the enemy put him to death with every refinement of dreadful torture. They shut him in a narrow box, where he was forced to stand upright, and sharp nails had been fixed on all sides of it, so that he could not lean in any direction without the most horrible suffering; thus they dispatched him by keeping him awake.

Our enemies are certainly right to praise a courage which rose superior to so dreadful a fate. And yet he had sworn by those gods, the prohibition of whose worship has led, in their opinion, to the infliction of these recent disasters on the human race. This means that they were worshipped so that they might grant prosperity in this life. Now, if they either wished or allowed such punishment to be enacted on one who kept his oath, what heavier penalty could they have imposed in their anger on an oath-breaker?

I can conclude my reasoning by two lines of argument. Regulus

50. Hdt., 1, 23; Ov., *Fast.*, 2, 113.

51. M. *Atilius Regulus* commanded the Roman forces in Africa in the First Punic War, in 256 B.C. When Carthage suggested peace talks he proposed intolerable terms; the war was renewed and Regulus was defeated and captured. After the Carthaginian defeat at Panormus in 250 Regulus was sent with an embassy to Rome. He advised the senate to continue the war; then he returned to Carthage, to be tortured to death. (Livy, *Epit.*, 16; Cic., *De Off.*, 1, 13; Hor., *Carm.*, 3, 5). Recent historians are sceptical about this hallowed tale.

venerated the gods; and the result was that because of his oath he did not stay in his own country, but went without the least hesitation, not to any place he chose, but back to his fiercest enemies. His reward was a horrible end, so that if he thought his upright conduct brought any temporal advantage he was very much mistaken. In fact he showed by his example that the gods are no help to their worshippers as far as happiness in this world goes. He was devoted to their worship; yet he was conquered and taken into captivity and because he refused to break the oath he had sworn by the gods, he was destroyed by torture of an unprecedented and excessively atrocious kind.

If, on the other hand, the worship of the gods brings happiness hereafter as a reward, why do our antagonists bring false accusations against the established Christian order, alleging that catastrophe has come upon the city just because it has left off the worship of its gods? For the most conscientious worshipper could be as unfortunate as Regulus. Surely no one is so crazy, so preternaturally blind, as to contend, in defiance of the obvious facts, that while an individual worshipper can be unfortunate, a whole worshipping community cannot? As if it were more fitting for the power of the gods to preserve large numbers rather than individuals, seeing that a multitude is made up of individuals!

Again, if they say that Marcus Regulus would have been happy in the possession of a virtuous spirit even in captivity, and during those physical torments, then let us aim at true virtue, which can bring happiness also to a community. For the source of a community's felicity is no different from that of one man, since a community is simply a united multitude of individuals. I am not at the moment discussing the nature of Regulus's virtue; it is enough for my present purpose that our opponents are compelled by this notable example to admit that the gods are not to be worshipped for the sake of physical blessings or external advantages, since Regulus preferred to be deprived of all these rather than to offend the gods by whom he had sworn.

Now how are we to cope with men who are proud to have had such a fellow-citizen, but afraid to belong to such a community? If they are not so afraid, let them admit that what happened to Regulus could have happened also to a community which worshipped the gods as conscientiously as he did and let them cease to bring false charges against the Christian order. But since the question has been raised about those Christians who also were taken prisoner, let those who shamelessly and thoughtlessly jeer at the most wholesome devotion look carefully at this example and keep silent. This most diligent worshipper of the gods was deprived of the only country he had, because he kept his oath to them, and was killed as a prisoner by a lingering death with torture of unexampled cruelty. If this was no reproach to those gods, there is much less reason to bring a charge against the Christian profession in respect of the imprisonment of its saints, who look for a heavenly country with true faith and know that even in their own homes they are no more than sojourners.

16. *Violation of chastity, without the will's consent, cannot pollute the character*

Our adversaries certainly think they have a weighty attack to make on Christians, when they make the most of their captivity by adding stories of the violation of wives, of maidens ready for marriage, and even in some cases of women in the religious life. On this point it is not our faith which is in difficulty, nor our devotion, nor is that particular virtue, the term for which is chastity, called in question. But our argument is in a way constrained and hampered, between the claims of modesty and reasoned argument. Here we are not so much concerned to answer the attacks of those outside as to administer consolation to those within our fellowship.

In the first place, it must be firmly established that virtue, the condition of right living, holds command over the parts of the body from her throne in the mind, and that the consecrated body is the instrument of the consecrated will; and if that will continues unshaken and steadfast, whatever anyone else does with the body or to the body, provided that it cannot be avoided without committing sin, involves no blame to the sufferer. But there can be committed on another's body not only acts involving pain, but also acts involving lust. And so whenever any act of the latter kind has been committed, although it does not destroy a purity which has been maintained by the utmost resolution, still it does engender a sense of shame, because it may be believed that an act, which perhaps could not have taken place without some physical pleasure, was accompanied also by a consent of the mind.

17. *The question of suicide caused by fear of punishment or disgrace*

Some women killed themselves to avoid suffering anything of the kind, and surely any man of compassion would be ready to excuse the emotions which lead them to do this. Some refused to kill themselves, because they did not want to escape another's criminal act by a misdeed of their own. And anyone who uses this as a charge against them will lay himself open to a charge of foolishness. For it is clear that if no one has a private right to kill even a guilty man (and no law allows this), then certainly anyone who kills himself is a murderer, and is the more guilty in killing himself the more innocent he is of the charge on which he has condemned himself to death. We rightly abominate the act of Judas, and the judgement of truth is that when he hanged himself he did not atone for the guilt of his detestable betrayal but rather increased it, since he despaired of God's mercy and in a fit of self-destructive remorse left himself no chance of a saving repentance. How much less right has anyone to indulge in self-slaughter when he can find in himself no fault to justify such a punishment! For when Judas killed himself, he killed a criminal, and yet he ended his life guilty not only of Christ's death, but also of his own; one crime led to another. Why then should a man, who has done no wrong, do wrong to himself? Why should he kill the innocent in putting himself to death, to prevent a guilty man from doing it? Why should he commit a sin against himself to deprive someone else of the chance?

18. *The question of violence from others, and the lust of others suffered by an unwilling mind in a ravished body*

'But', it will be said, 'there is the fear of being polluted by another's lust.' There will be no pollution, if the lust is another's; if there is pollution, the lust is not another's. Now purity is a virtue of the mind. It has courage as its companion and courage decides to endure evil rather than consent to evil. A man of purity and high principle has not the power to decide what happens to his body, but only what he will mentally accept or repudiate. What sane man will suppose that he has lost his purity if his body is seized and forced and used for the satisfaction of a lust that is not his own? For if purity is lost in this way, it follows that it is not a virtue of the mind; it is not then ranked with the qualities which make up the moral life, but is classed among physical qualities, such as strength, beauty, and health, the impairment of which does not in any way mean the impairment of the moral life. If purity is something of this sort, why do we risk physical danger to avoid its loss? But if it is a quality of the mind, it is not lost when the body is violated. Indeed, when the quality of modesty resists the indecency of carnal desires the body itself is sanctified, and therefore, when purity persists in its unshaken resolution to resist these desires, the body's holiness is not lost, because the will to employ the body in holiness endures, as does the ability, as far as in it lies.

The body is not holy just because its parts are intact, or because they have not undergone any handling. Those parts may suffer violent injury by accidents of various kinds, and sometimes doctors seeking to effect a cure may employ treatment with distressing visible effects. During a manual examination of a virgin a midwife destroyed her maidenhead, whether by malice, or clumsiness, or accident. I do not suppose that anyone would be stupid enough to imagine that the virgin lost anything of bodily chastity, even though the integrity of that part had been destroyed. Therefore while the mind's resolve endures, which gives the body its claim to chastity, the violence of another's lust cannot take away the chastity which is preserved by unwavering self-control.

Now suppose some woman, with her mind corrupted and her vowed intention to God violated, in the act of going to her seducer to be defiled. Do we say that she is chaste in body while she is on her way, when the chastity of her mind, which made the body chaste, has been lost and destroyed? Of course not! We must rather draw the inference that just as bodily chastity is lost when mental chastity has been violated, so bodily chastity is not lost, even when the body has been ravished, while the mind's chastity endures. Therefore when a woman has been ravished without her consenting, and forced by another's sin, she has no reason to punish herself by a voluntary death. Still less should she do so before the event lest she should commit certain murder while the offence, and another's offence at that, still remains uncertain.

19. *Lucretia's suicide*

We have given clear reason for our assertion that when physical violation has involved no change in the intention of chastity by any consent to the wrong, then the guilt attaches only to the ravisher, and not at all to the woman forcibly ravished without any consent on her part. We are defending the chastity not only of the minds but even of the bodies of ravished Christian women. Will our opponents dare to contradict us? They certainly heap the highest praises for modesty upon Lucretia, a noble Roman matron of antiquity.[52] When King

52. Liv. 1, 58.

Tarquin's son had lustfully gained possession of her body and had ravished her with violence, she revealed the villain's crime to her husband Collatinus and her kinsman Brutus, and constrained them to take revenge. Then she destroyed herself, unable to endure the horror of the foul indignity. What are we to say of her? Is she to be judged adulterous or chaste? Who would regard this as a matter of difficult dispute? Someone puts the truth well in a declamation on this subject: 'A paradox! There were two persons involved, and only one committed adultery.' Finely and truly said. The speaker observed in the union of two bodies the disgusting lechery of the one, the chaste intention of the other, and he saw in that act not the conjunction of their bodies but the diversity of their minds. 'There were two persons involved, and only one committed adultery.'

But how was it that she who did not commit adultery received the heavier punishment? For the adulterer was driven from his country, with his father; his victim suffered the supreme penalty. If there is no unchastity when a woman is ravished against her will, then there is no justice in the punishment of the chaste. I appeal to Roman laws and Roman judges. To execute a criminal without trial was, according to you, a punishable offence. If anyone was charged in your courts with having put to death a woman not merely uncondemned but chaste and innocent, and this charge had been proved, would you not have chastised the culprit with appropriate severity?

That is what Lucretia did. That highly extolled Lucretia also did away with the innocent, chaste, outraged Lucretia. Give your sentence. Or if you cannot do this, because the culprit is not present to receive the punishment, why do you extol with such praises the killer of the chaste and innocent? You certainly have no means of defending her before the judges of the underworld, such as are described in the verses of your poets. She would be set among those who

> Hating the light, brought death upon themselves
> Though innocent, and hurled away their souls.[53]

And if she desired to return to the world above,

> It is forbidden, the grim lake sets a bound
> With its unlovely waters.[54]

But perhaps she is not there, because in killing herself it was no innocent which she killed, but one conscious of guilt. For suppose (a thing which only she herself could know) that, although the young man

53. Virg., *Aen.*, 6, 434ff. 54. Virg., *Aen.*, 438f.

attacked her violently, she was so enticed by her own desire that she consented to the act and that when she came to punish herself she was so grieved that she thought death the only expiation. Yet not even in this case ought she to have killed herself, if she could have offered a profitable penitence to false gods.

However, if such was the case, and if it was not true that 'there were two persons involved, and only one committed adultery', but both were adulterous, the one by reason of his open assault, the other by reason of her hidden consent, then she did not kill an innocent, and her literary defenders are free to maintain that she is not in the underworld among those who 'brought death upon themselves though innocent'. But then her defence is faced with a dilemma. If her homicide is extenuated, her adultery is established; if she is cleared of adultery, the murder is abundantly proved. There is no possible way out: 'If she is adulterous, why is she praised? If chaste, why was she put to death?'

However, in the case of the noble example of that woman, it is enough for us to quote what was said in her praise: 'There were two persons involved, and only one committed adultery.' This suffices to refute those who, because any notion of chastity is alien to them, jeer at Christian women violated in captivity. They believe Lucretia to have been too good to be polluted by giving any consent to adultery. Her killing of herself because, although not adulterous, she had suffered an adulterer's embraces, was due to the weakness of shame, not to the high value she set on chastity. She was ashamed of another's foul deed committed *on* her, even though not *with* her, and as a Roman woman, excessively eager for honour, she was afraid that she should be thought, if she lived, to have willingly endured what, when she lived, she had violently suffered. Since she could not display her pure conscience to the world she thought she must exhibit her punishment before men's eyes as a proof of her state of mind. She blushed at the thought of being regarded as an accomplice in the act if she were to bear with patience what another had inflicted on her with violence.

Such has not been the behaviour of Christian women. When they were treated like this they did not take vengeance on themselves for another's crime. They would not add crime to crime by committing murder on themselves in shame because the enemy had committed rape on them in lust. They have the glory of chastity within them, the testimony of their conscience. They have this in the sight of God, and they ask for nothing more. In fact there is nothing else for them to do that is right for them to do. For they will not deviate from the authority of God's law by taking unlawful steps to avoid the suspicions of men.

20. *Christians have no authority to commit suicide in any circumstance*

It is significant that in the sacred canonical books there can nowhere be found any injunction or permission to commit suicide either to ensure immortality or to avoid or escape any evil. In fact we must understand it to be forbidden by the law 'You shall not kill',[55] particularly as there is no addition of 'your neighbour' as in the prohibition of false witness, 'You shall not bear false witness *against your neighbour.*'[56] But that does not mean that a man who gives false witness against himself is exempt from this guilt, since the rule about loving one's neighbour begins with oneself, seeing that the Scripture says, 'You shall love your neighbour as yourself.'[57]

Moreover, if anyone who gives false witness against himself is just as guilty as if he did so against a neighbour – although the prohibition forbids false witness against a neighbour and might be misunderstood as implying that there is no prohibition of false witness against oneself – then it is the more obvious that a man is not allowed to kill himself, since the text 'Thou shall not kill' has no addition and it must be taken that there is no exception, not even the one to whom the command is addressed.

Hence some people have tried to extend its scope to wild and domestic animals to make it mean that even these may never be killed. But then why not apply it to plants and to anything rooted in the earth and nourished by the earth? For although this part of creation is without feeling, it is called 'living', and is hence capable of dying and consequently of being killed, when violence is done to it. And so the Apostle, speaking of seeds of this kind, says, 'What you sow does not come to life unless it dies';[58] and it says in one of the psalms, 'He killed the vines with hail.'[59] But do we for this reason infer from 'Thou shall not kill' a divine prohibition against clearing away brushwood, and subscribe to the error of the Manicheans? That would be madness. We reject such fantasies, and when we read 'You shall not kill' we assume that this does not refer to bushes, which have no feelings, nor to irrational creatures, flying, swimming, walking, or

55. Exod. 20, 13. 56. Exod. 16. 57. Matt. 22, 39.
58. 1 Cor. 15, 36. 59. Ps. 78, 47.

crawling, since they have no rational association with us, not having been endowed with reason as we are, and hence it is by a just arrangement of the Creator that their life and death is subordinated to our needs. If this is so, it remains that we take the command 'You shall not kill' as applying to human beings, that is, other persons *and* oneself. For to kill oneself is to kill a human being.

21. *All homicide is not murder*

There are however certain exceptions to the law against killing, made by the authority of God himself. There are some whose killing God orders, either by a law, or by an express command to a particular person at a particular time. In fact one who owes a duty of obedience to the giver of the command does not himself 'kill' – he is an instrument, a sword in its user's hand. For this reason the commandment forbidding killing was not broken by those who have waged wars on the authority of God, or those who have imposed the death-penalty on criminals when representing the authority of the State in accordance with the laws of the State, the justest and most reasonable source of power. When Abraham was ready to kill his son, so far from being blamed for cruelty he was praised for his devotion; it was not an act of crime, but of obedience. One is justified in asking whether Jephtha is to be regarded as obeying a command of God in killing his daughter, when he had vowed to sacrifice to God the first thing he met when returning victorious from battle.[60] And when Samson destroyed himself, with his enemies, by the demolition of the building,[61] this can only be excused on the ground that the Spirit, which performed miracles through him, secretly ordered him to do so. With the exception of these killings prescribed generally by a just law, or specially commanded by God himself – the source of justice – anyone who kills a human being, whether himself or anyone else, is involved in a charge of murder.

22. *Is suicide ever a mark of greatness of soul?*

Those who have committed this crime against themselves are perhaps to be admired for greatness of spirit; they are not to be praised for wisdom or sanity.[62] And yet if we examine the matter more deeply

60. Judg. 11, 29ff. 61. Judg. 16, 28ff.

62. Suicide was much debated by pagan philosophers. Plato (*Legg.* 873C) and Aristotle (*Eth. Nic.*, 3, 1116A) condemned it. The Cynics approved it unre-

and logically, we shall find that greatness of spirit is not the right term to apply to one who has killed himself because he lacked strength to endure hardships, or another's wrongdoing. In fact we detect weakness in a mind which cannot bear physical oppression, or the stupid opinion of the mob; we rightly ascribe greatness to a spirit that has the strength to endure a life of misery instead of running away from it, and to despise the judgement of men – and in particular the judgement of the mob, which is so often clouded in the darkness of error – in comparison with the pure light of a good conscience. If suicide is to be taken as a mark of greatness of spirit, then Theombrotus will be a shining example of that quality. The story is that when he had read Plato's book which discusses the immortality of the soul, he hurled himself from a wall and so passed from this life to a life which he believed to be better.[63] There was no kind of misfortune, no accusation, true or false, which led him to do away with himself under an intolerable load. It was only greatness of spirit which prompted him to seek death and to 'break the pleasant bonds of life'. But Plato himself, whom he had been reading, is witness that this showed greatness rather than goodness. Plato would have been first and foremost to take this action, and would have recommended it to others, had not the same intelligence which gave him his vision of the soul's immortality enabled him to decide that this step was not to be taken – was, indeed, to be forbidden.

'But many people did away with themselves to avoid falling into the hands of the enemy.' The question is not only whether they did, but whether they ought to have done so. Sound reason is certainly to be preferred to examples. Some examples are in full harmony with sound reason, and they are the more worthy of imitation as they are more eminent in their devotion to God. Neither the patriarchs nor the prophets acted thus; nor did the apostles, since the Lord Christ himself, when he advised them to escape from one town to another in case of persecution,[64] could have advised them to take their own lives to avoid falling into the hands of their persecutors. If he did not order or advise this way of quitting this life, although he promised to prepare eternal dwellings for them after their departure,[65] it is clear that this

---

servedly (Diog. Laert. 4, 3; 6, 18; 24 etc.); the Stoics approved it, if there were honourable reasons (Cic., *Tusc. Disp.*, 1, 83; Seneca, *Ep.*, 24 etc.). The Neoplatonists generally disapproved. (Plot., *Enn.*, 1, 4, 7).

63. Cic., *Tusc. Disp.*, 1, 34, 84 (The story of Cleombrotus).

64. Matt. 10, 23. 65. John 14, 2.

course is not allowed to those who worship the one true God, whatever examples may be put forward by 'the Gentiles who have no knowledge of him'.[66]

23. *The example of Cato's suicide*

Apart from Lucretia, about whom I think I have said enough already, they will not easily find an authoritative example to appeal to, unless it is the famous Cato, who committed suicide at Utica, not because he was the only one to do so, but because he passed for a man of learning and integrity, so that one would feel justified in supposing his action could have been right then, and could be right now.

The most significant point to be made about this act is that his friends, who also were educated men, wisely endeavoured to dissuade him and considered such a course to be a mark of weakness rather than strength of mind, evidence not so much of a sense of honour seeking to avoid disgrace as of weakness unable to sustain adversity. In fact, Cato himself passed this judgement in advising his beloved son to 'place all his hopes in Caesar's kindness'. Why did he counsel such a shameful course, if it was 'shameful to live under the shadow of Caesar's victory'?[67] Why did he not compel his son to die with him? Torquatus is praised because he killed the son who engaged the enemy against his father's orders, even though his son was victorious;[68] then why did Cato, when conquered, spare his conquered son, when he did not spare himself? Was it more shameful to be a conqueror disobediently, than to endure a conqueror dishonourably? It follows that Cato judged it not at all shameful to live under the victorious Caesar; otherwise he would have released his son from this shame with a father's sword. The truth seems to be that he loved his son, for whom he hoped and wished for Caesar's pardon, as much as he grudged the praise that Caesar would win by sparing his own life. Caesar is said to have given this explanation;[69] perhaps we may put it more gently, and say that Cato would have been embarrassed at receiving Caesar's pardon.

66. 1 Thess. 4. 5.
67. Plut., *Cat.*, 65–70; Dio Cass., 10–13.
68. In the Latin War, 340 B.C. (Liv., 7, 7).
69. Plut., *Cat.*, 72; *Caes.*, 54.

24. *Regulus a nobler example of fortitude than Cato. But Christians supply much nobler instances.*

Our adversaries object to our giving preference over Cato to the holy Job or to other saints recorded in our literature – writings of supreme authority and worthy of all credence. Job would rather suffer horrible bodily distresses than free himself from all those torments by self-inflicted death; and other saints chose to endure captivity and oppression at the enemy's hands, rather than commit suicide. But in our adversaries' literature I should put Marcus Regulus above Marcus Cato. For Cato had never beaten Caesar; he was beaten by Caesar, and disdaining to submit, he chose suicide. Regulus on the other hand had already beaten the Carthaginians; as commander-in-chief of the Roman army he had won, not a victory over fellow-citizens fraught with grief for Rome, but a victory over foreign foes, crowned with glory. Afterwards he remained patient under Carthaginian domination and unmoved among Roman demonstrations of affection, not depriving his enemies of his conquered body nor his fellow-citizens of his unconquered spirit. It was not because he clung to life that he refused suicide. He proved this when, because of his oath, he returned without hesitation to the enemy, whom he had provoked more bitterly by his words in the senate than by his achievements in war. He set little store by this life; and yet when the enemy were raging against him he chose to let his life be ended by any kind of torture, rather than to die by his own hand. And by this choice he put it beyond doubt that suicide was, in his judgement, a serious crime. Among all their heroes, men worthy of honour and renowned for virtue, the Romans have none greater to produce. Here was one whom prosperity did not corrupt; for after so great a victory he remained a very poor man, one whom adversity could not shatter, for he went back without trembling to so terrible an end.

There were famous heroes who, though by the laws of war they could do violence to a conquered enemy, refused to do violence to themselves when conquered; though they had not the slightest fear of death, they chose to endure the enemy's domination rather than put themselves to death. They were fighting for their earthly country; the gods they worshipped were false; but their worship was genuine and they faithfully kept their oaths. Christians worship the true God and they yearn for a heavenly country; will they not have more reason to refrain from the crime of suicide, if God's providence subjects them for a time to their enemies for their probation or reformation? Their

God does not abandon them in that humiliation, for he came from on high so humbly for their sake; moreover, they are men who are not under an obligation, from any military authority or code of warfare, to strike a conquered foe. What is the origin of this pernicious error, that a man should kill himself because of an enemy's sin against him, or to prevent such a sin? In fact, he should not dare to kill even an enemy who did him wrong, or was about to do him wrong.

25. *One sin should not be avoided by another*

It is objected that there is a danger that the body, when subjected to another's lust, may entice the mind, by the allurements of pleasure, to consent to the sin; for fear of this, they say, one ought to commit suicide not because of one's own sin, but to forestall another's. Never! The mind which is subordinate to the wisdom of God and not to the promptings of the body will never allow itself to consent to a physical desire aroused by another's lust. If suicide is a detestable crime and a damnable sin, as the Truth plainly declares, who will be so senseless as to say, 'Let us sin now, to avoid possible sin in the future. Let us now commit murder, to avoid falling into adultery in the future'? If wickedness has such power over us that sin is chosen in preference to innocence, is not uncertain adultery in the future preferable to certain homicide in the present? Is it not preferable to do a wrong which may be cured by penitence, than an act of wickedness which leaves no chance for saving repentance?

I have made this point for the benefit of men and women who suppose that they ought to lay violent hands on themselves to prevent themselves, and not others, from sinning, for fear that their own lust might be excited by another's, and that they might consent. Let it never enter a Christian's mind that such a mind could yield to any physical pleasure so as to consent to disgrace. For a Christian mind trusts in its God, places its hope in him, and relies on his help. It is true that insubordinate desires are still to be found in our mortal bodies, acting as it were by laws of their own without reference to the law of our will. Such disobedience of the body is not to be blamed when one is asleep, still less when there is no consent.

26. *What explanation is to be given of unlawful acts committed by saints?*

'But', they say, 'in time of persecution there were holy women who escaped those who threatened their chastity by throwing themselves into rivers for the stream to whirl them away to death: and after such a death they were venerated as martyrs in the Catholic Church, and crowds thronged their tombs.'[70] I would not presume to make a hasty judgement on their case. I do not know whether divine authority convinced the church by cogent evidence that their memory should be honoured in this way; it may well be so. It may be that they acted on divine instruction and not through a human mistake – not in error, but in obedience. This is what we are bound to believe in Samson's case. When God orders, and shows without ambiguity that he orders, no one will bring an accusation against obedience. Who will lay a charge against a loyal compliance?

But if anyone decides to sacrifice his son to God, his action is not free from crime just because Abraham did this and was praised for doing it. For when a soldier kills a man in obedience to the legitimate authority under which he served, he is not chargeable with murder by the laws of his country; in fact he is chargeable with insubordination and mutiny if he refuses. But if he did it of his own accord, on his own authority, he would be liable to a charge of homicide. Thus he is punished if he did it without orders for the same reason that he will be punished if he refuses when ordered.

If that is the case when a general gives the order, how much more when the command comes from the Creator! And so one who accepts the prohibition against suicide may kill himself when commanded by one whose orders must not be slighted; only let him take care that there is no uncertainty about the divine command. We have only a hearsay acquaintance with any man's conscience; we do not claim to judge the secrets of the heart. 'No one knows what goes on inside a man except the man's spirit which is in him.'[71] What we are saying, asserting, and establishing by all means at our command is this: that no one ought deliberately to bring about his own death by way of escaping from temporal troubles, for fear that he may fall into eternal afflictions; it is wrong to commit suicide because of the sins of others, for this is to bring upon oneself a heavy burden of sin, whereas another's sin could not defile one; or because of one's past sins, for one has more need of this life on their account, so that those sins may be healed by repentance; or through longing for a better life, hoped for

70. The most famous example of martyr suicide was St Pelagia, a girl of fifteen, who, with her mother and sisters, threw herself from her house to escape outrage. St Ambrose did not share Augustine's view, and he praises Pelagia's heroism (*De Virg.*, 3, 7; *Ep.*, 37).

71. 1 Cor. 2, 11.

after death, for those guilty of their own death are not received after death into that better life.

27. *Should one commit suicide to avoid sin?*

There remains one situation in which it is supposed to be advantageous to commit suicide; I had already begun to discuss the question. It arises when the motive is to avoid falling into sin either through the allurements of pleasure or through the menaces of pain. If we agree to allow this motive we shall not be able to stop until we reach the point when people are to be encouraged to kill themselves for preference, immediately they have received forgiveness of all sins by washing in the waters of holy regeneration. For that would be the time to forestall all future sins – the moment when all past sins have been erased. If self-inflicted death is permitted, surely this is the best possible moment for it! When a person has been thus set free why should he expose himself again to all the perils of this life, when it is so easily allowed him to avoid them by doing away with himself? And the Bible says, 'A man who is fond of danger will fall into it.'[72] Why are men so fond of all these great dangers, or at any rate are willing to accept them, by remaining in this life, when they are allowed to depart from it? If a man has a duty to kill himself to avoid succumbing to sin because he is at the mercy of one man, who holds him prisoner, does he suppose that he has to go on living so as to endure the pressures of the actual world, which is full of temptations at all times, temptations such as that which is dreaded under one master, and innumerable others, which are the necessary accompaniment of this life? Has perverse silliness so warped our judgement and distracted us from facing the truth? For on this assumption, why do we spend time on those exhortations to the newly baptized. We do our best to kindle their resolve to preserve their virginal purity, or to remain continent in widowhood, or to remain faithful to their marriage vows. But there is available an excellent short cut which avoids any danger of sinning; if we can persuade them to rush to a self-inflicted death immediately upon receiving remission of sins, we shall send them to the Lord in the purest and soundest condition!

But in fact if anyone thinks that we should go in for persuasion on these lines, I should not call him silly, but quite crazy. Then how could anyone justify saying to any human being: 'Kill yourself, to avoid adding more serious sin to your small shortcomings, living, as

72. Ecclus. 3, 26.

you do, under a master with the manners and morals of a savage', if he cannot say, without being a complete criminal, 'Kill yourself, now that all your sins have been absolved, to avoid committing such sins again, or even worse, while you are living in a world full of the allurements of impure pleasures, so maddened with all its monstrous cruelties, so menacing with all its errors and terrors'? To say this would be monstrous; it follows that suicide is monstrous. If there could be a valid reason for suicide one could not find one more valid than this; and since this is not valid, a valid reason does not exist.

28. *By what judgement of God the enemy's lust was allowed to sin against the bodies of the chaste*

Therefore, faithful Christians, do not think life a burden because your enemies make a mockery of your chastity. You have a great and genuine consolation if you are sure in your conscience that you have not consented in the sins of those who have been allowed to sin against you. If you should ask why they were thus allowed, we must answer that the providence of the Creator and Governor of the universe is a profound mystery, and 'his judgements are inscrutable, and his ways cannot be traced'.[73]

And yet you should honestly examine your hearts and see if perhaps you have not plumed yourselves overmuch on the possession of your virginity, your continence, your chastity – if you have not set too much store by the praises of men and have even envied others in this respect. I make no accusations, because I do not know, nor do I hear the replies of your hearts to this examination. However, if they give an affirmative reply, do not be amazed at having lost that for which you were concerned – because it would win men's approval – while you have retained what cannot be displayed before their eyes. If you have not consented in the sin, divine aid has been added to divine grace, to prevent your losing that grace, while men's reproach has come in place of men's praise, to prevent your loving that praise. Accept this twofold consolation, you faint-hearted creatures. On the one hand there is your probation, on the other your chastisement; on one side, your justification, on the other, your correction.

Some hearts may reply that they have never prided themselves on the virtue of virginity, or widowhood, or chaste wedlock, but have rejoiced in God's gift 'with trembling',[74] and by 'sharing the outlook

73. Rom. 11, 33. 74. Ps. 2, 11.

of humble people';[75] that they have not envied the excellence of anyone of equal holiness and chastity; rather they have set little store by the praise of men (which is generally bestowed more lavishly in proportion to the rarity of the virtue which occasions it) and have rather desired that the number of such persons should be increased than that they themselves should have the distinction of scarcity.

If any such women have suffered the violence of barbarian lust, they will not blame God for allowing it, nor will they believe that God makes light of such crimes. He allows them, but no one can commit them with impunity. The truth is that in the mysterious justice of God the wickedness of desire is given rope, as it were, for the present, while its punishment is plainly being reserved for the final judgement.

It may also be that those whose conscience assures them that they have no swollen pride about the virtue of chastity had in them some latent weakness which might have swollen into arrogant complacency, if they had escaped this humiliation during the recent catastrophe. Therefore, just as some were carried off by death so that 'evil should not corrupt their mind',[76] these others were roughly deprived of a possession, so that prosperity should not tamper with their modesty. Thus there were two classes, those who boasted that their bodies had never suffered defiling contact, and those who might have boasted, if they had not been violently handled by the enemy. Neither were robbed of their chastity: both were persuaded to be humble. In one case relief was brought to a swelling already developed; in the other a threatened swelling was forestalled.

There is a further point to be made. Some of the victims might have supposed that the virtue of continence is to be classed with physical qualities and that it endures provided that the body is not defiled by anyone's lust, whereas in fact it has its seat in the strength of the will, sustained by God's help, so that both body and spirit may be holy; and it is not a treasure which can be stolen without the mind's consent. Perhaps their mistake has been corrected. For when they consider how conscientiously they have served God and realize that he cannot possibly have abandoned those who thus serve him and call upon him, and when they find it impossible to doubt how much pleasure he takes in their chastity, then they will see that it follows that he never could have allowed such a disaster to befall his saints if their purity could be destroyed in this way – a purity which he bestowed on them, and which he loves to see in them.

75. Rom. 12, 16. 76. cf. Wisd. 4, 11.

29. *The taunt of the infidels that Christ did not rescue his servants from the enemy's rage. What reply should those servants give?*

The whole family of the servants of the supreme and true God has its consolation, which never disappoints, which does not depend on hope in shifting and transitory things; and those servants have no reason to regret even this life of time, for in it they are schooled for eternity. They enjoy their earthly blessings in the manner of pilgrims and they are not attached to them, while these earthly misfortunes serve for testing and correction. But there are those who jeer at their integrity. When any temporal disaster comes upon God's servants, such people ask, 'Where is your God now?'[77] Let those scoffers tell us where *their* gods are, when the same things happen to them. After all, it is to escape from such evils that they worship their gods – or maintain that they should be worshipped.

The Christian's answer is this:

> My God is present everywhere, and wholly present everywhere. No limits confine him. He can be present without showing himself: he can depart without moving. When I am troubled with adversity, he is either testing my worth or punishing my faults. And he has an eternal reward in store for me in return for loyal endurance of temporal distress. But why should I deign to discuss your God with people like you? Still less should I speak with you about my God who 'is to be feared above all gods; since all the gods of the nations are demons; while the Lord made the heavens'.[78]

30. *Those who complain of the Christian era really wish to wallow in shameful self-indulgence*

In the terrible time of the Punic War a man of the highest character had to be chosen to introduce a cult from Phrygia, and the senate unanimously selected Scipio Nasica, who was then your pontiff.[79] If he were living now I doubt if you would dare to look him in the face, since he would certainly put a stop to your present effrontery. For why is it that you put the blame on this Christian era, when things go wrong? Is it not because you are anxious to enjoy your vices without interference, and to wallow in your corruption, untroubled and unrebuked? For if you are concerned for peace and general prosperity, it is not because you want to make decent use of these blessings, with

77. Ps. 42, 3. 78. Ps. 96, 4.
79. Liv. 29, 14. In 204 B.C. the statue of Cybele was brought to Rome.

moderation, with restraint, with self-control, with reverence. No! It is because you seek an infinite variety of pleasure with a crazy extravagance, and your prosperity produces a moral corruption far worse than all the fury of an enemy.

The great Scipio, your *pontifex maximus*, the finest character in Rome in the unanimous judgement of the senate, dreaded that this calamity might come upon you. For that reason he opposed the destruction of Carthage, Rome's imperial rival at that time, and resisted Cato's proposal for its demolition.[80] He was afraid of security, as being a danger to weak characters; he looked on the citizens as wards, and fear as a kind of suitable guardian, giving the protection they needed. And his policy was justified; the event proved him right. The abolition of Carthage certainly removed a fearful threat to the State of Rome; and the extinction of that threat was immediately followed by disasters arising from prosperity. To begin with, harmony was broken and destroyed by savage and bloody insurrections; then followed a succession of disastrous quarrels and all the slaughter of the civil wars, all the torrents of bloodshed, all the greed and monstrous seething cruelty of proscriptions and expropriations, so that the Romans, who in a period of high moral standards stood in fear of their enemies, suffered a harsher fate from their fellow-citizens when those standards collapsed. And the lust for power, which of all human vices was found in its most concentrated form in the Roman people as a whole, first established its victory in a few powerful individuals, and then crushed the rest of an exhausted country beneath the yoke of slavery.

31. *The stages of corruption by which the lust for power increased among the Romans*

For when can that lust for power in arrogant hearts come to rest until, after passing from one office to another, it arrives at sovereignty? Now there would be no occasion for this continuous progress if ambition were not all-powerful; and the essential context for ambition is a people corrupted by greed and sensuality. And greed and sensuality in a people is the result of that prosperity which the great Nasica in his wisdom maintained should be guarded against, when he opposed the removal of a great and strong and wealthy enemy state. His intention was that lust should be restrained by fear, and should not issue in debauchery, and that the check on debauchery should stop greed from running riot. With those vices kept under restraint, the morality

80. It was, in fact, his son who opposed Cato.

which supports a country flourished and increased, and permanence was given to the liberty which goes hand-in-hand with such morality.

It was the same conviction, the same patriotic forethought, which lead the same *pontifex maximus* of yours (who, as I must often repeat, was unanimously chosen by the senate of that time as the best man in Rome), to restrain the senate's project to build a theatre.[81] He deflected them from this ambitious design, and used all the weight of his authority in a speech which persuaded them not to allow Greek corruption to infiltrate into the virile morality of Rome, and to have no truck with foreign depravity which would undermine and weaken the Roman moral character. Such was the force of his authority that the senate, moved by his eloquence, had the wisdom to forbid for the future the erection of the temporary stands which the State had by now begun to provide for the spectators at the games.

What energy he would have shown in banishing from Rome the spectacles themselves, if he had dared to take a stand against the authority of those whom he supposed to be gods! He did not realize that they were harmful demons; or if he did, even he thought it better to appease than to despise them! For the nations had not yet received the revelation from heaven of the teaching which can cleanse the heart by faith and turn the interest of men in humble reverence towards things in heaven, or above the heavens, and free them from the oppressive domination of demonic powers.

32. *The establishment of stage spectacles*

Some of you do not know the facts; some of you pretend not to know, and you raise an outcry against the One who frees you from such oppressions. Well, here are the facts. The public games, those disgusting spectacles of frivolous immorality, were instituted at Rome not by the viciousness of men but by the orders of those gods of yours. It would be less offensive to decree divine honour to the great Scipio than to worship gods of this kind. Those gods were of less worth than their pontiff. Listen to me, if your minds allow you to think sensibly, after they have been drunk so long on the liquor of nonsense! The gods ordered theatrical shows to be put on in their honour to allay a plague which attacked the body,[82] while the pontiff stopped the erec-

81. St Augustine again confuses father and son. In 155 Scipio Nasica Corculum persuaded the senate to abandon the building of a stone theatre (Liv., *Perioch.*, 48). The first stone theatre was built by Pompey in 55 B.C.

82. In 364–363 B.C. (Liv., 7, 2).

tion of a theatre to prevent a plague which would infect the soul. If you have enough light in your minds to prefer the soul to the body, choose which you should worship! For if the bodily plague did come to a halt, it was not because the more sophisticated craze for theatrical shows had intruded itself into a warlike people who had hitherto been used only to circus games. The truth is that the powers of evil foresaw, in their cleverness, that the plague would soon come to its natural end, and they craftily used this opportunity to bring upon you a far more serious pestilence, which gives them greater satisfaction. For this disease attacks not the body but the character. It has blinded the minds of the sufferers with such darkness, and has so deformed and degraded them, that quite recently, when Rome was sacked, those who were infected with this plague, and who managed to reach Carthage as refugees, attend the theatres every day as raving supporters of the rival actors! I wonder if posterity will be able to believe this, when they hear of it!

33. *The vices of the Romans were not corrected by their country's overthrow*

What insanity this is! This is not error but plain madness. When, by all accounts, nations in the East were bewailing your catastrophe, when the greatest cities in the farthest parts of the earth were keeping days of public grief and mourning,[83] you were asking the way to the theatres, and going in, making full houses, in fact, behaving in a much more crazy fashion than before. It was just this corruption, this moral disease, this overthrow of all integrity and decency, that the great Scipio dreaded for you, when he stopped the building of theatres, when he saw how easily you could be corrupted and perverted by prosperity, and did not want you to be relieved from the enemy's threats. He did not think that a city is fortunate when its walls are standing, while its morals are in ruins. But the temptations of wicked demons had more effect on you than the precautions of men endowed with foresight. Thus you refuse to be held

83. The effect of Rome's fall on the Eastern world is described by Jerome (*Ep.*, 136, 2; 127, 12. *Comm. in Ez.*, 3 Pref.) 'A fearful report reached us from the West, that Rome was under siege; that the citizens were buying their safety with gold, and that when they had been despoiled they were again beset, so that they lost their lives after losing their property. My voice chokes, and sobs interrupt me as I dictate this. The city which has taken captive the entire world is itself taken captive; or rather it perished with hunger before it fell to the sword, and only a bare few remained to be taken prisoner . . .' (*Ep.*, 127, 2).

responsible for the evil that you do, while you hold the Christian era responsible for the evil which you suffer. You seek security not for the peace of your country but for your own impunity in debauchery. Prosperity depraved you; and adversity could not reform you. Scipio's desire was that you should be threatened by the enemy, to prevent you from wallowing in sensuality. But now that you have been crushed by the enemy, you have not restrained your sensuality. You have learned no salutary lesson from calamity; you have become the most wretched, and you have remained the most worthless, of mankind.

34. *The mercy of God in moderating the city's destruction*

And yet it is thanks to God's grace that you are still alive. In sparing you he warns you to amend your ways by penitence. Despite your ingratitude he gave you the means of escape from the enemy's hands either by passing as his servants or by taking refuge in the shrines of his martyrs. We are told that Romulus and Remus established a refuge, their aim being to increase the population of their city, and anyone who fled there was secure from any harm.[84] This formed a precedent for a remarkable honour done to Christ; the destroyers of Rome followed the example of its founders. Now it is not surprising that the founders should have taken this course to increase the numbers of their citizens; but the destroyers acted in the same way to preserve large numbers of their enemies.

35. *Sons of the Church lie hidden among the ungodly; and there are false Christians within the Church*

Such is the reply (which could have been amplified and extended) which the redeemed household of servants of the Lord Christ – the pilgrim City of Christ the King – may return to its enemies.

She must bear in mind that among these very enemies are hidden her future citizens; and when confronted with them she must not think it a fruitless task to bear with their hostility until she finds them confessing the faith. In the same way, while the City of God is on pilgrimage in this world, she has in her midst some who are united with her in participation in the sacraments, but who will not join with her in the eternal destiny of the saints. Some of these are hidden; some are well known, for they do not hesitate to murmur against God,

84. Liv., 1, 8.

whose sacramental sign they bear, even in the company of his acknowledged enemies. At one time they join his enemies in filling the theatres, at another they join with us in filling the churches.

But, such as they are, we have less right to despair of the reformation of some of them, when some predestined friends, as yet unknown even to themselves, are concealed among our most open enemies. In truth, those two cities are interwoven and intermixed in this era, and await separation at the last judgement. My task, as far as I shall receive divine assistance, will be to say what I think necessary in explanation of the origin, development, and appointed end of those two cities. And this I shall do to enhance the glory of the City of God, which will shine the more brightly when set in contrast with cities of other allegiance.

36. The subjects to be treated in the following discussion

But there are still certain points that have to be made against those who ascribe the disaster of the Roman State to our religion, which forbids the offering of sacrifice to Rome's gods. For we must mention the ills which that city, or the provinces belonging to its Empire, suffered before their sacrifices had been forbidden – or at least such calamities as may come to mind, or as many as seem sufficient for my purpose. They would without doubt have held us responsible for all those, if our religion had by then revealed its splendour to them, or had forbidden their sacrilegious rites.

After that we must show how the true God, in whose power are all kingdoms, deigned to assist them in attaining the moral qualities needed for the increase of their Empire, and why he did so, although those reputed gods of theirs gave them no assistance; in fact we shall show how those gods did them harm by deceiving and misleading them. Lastly we shall answer those who, in spite of being disproved and refuted by unanswerable proofs, persist in the assertion that the gods are to be worshipped not with a view to any advantage in this life but with a view to the life after death.

Unless I am much mistaken, this argument will be more difficult and will require discussion of greater subtlety. We shall have to engage with philosophers, and philosophers of no ordinary sort, but those who enjoy the most eminent reputation amongst our adversaries and who are in agreement with us on many points – on the immortality of the soul, on God's creation of the universe, and on his providence which governs his creation. But even these must be rebutted on the points on which they disagree with us; and therefore we must not fail in our duty, so that, when we have refuted their impious attacks – in so far as God gives us strength – we may establish the City of God, and true religion, and the true worship of God. For in this alone is the genuine promise of eternal bliss.

So I bring this book to an end; and after this I shall begin in my second volume to deal with the subjects thus outlined.

BOOK II

1. *The limit to be imposed on discussion of objections*

If only the weak understanding of the ordinary man did not stubbornly resist the plain evidence of logic and truth! If only it would, in its feeble condition, submit itself to the restorative medicine of sound teaching, until divine assistance, procured by devout faith, effected a cure! In that case, men of sound judgement and adequate powers of exposition would not need to engage in lengthy discussions in order to refute mistakes and fanciful conjectures. But as things are, the intelligent are infected by a gross mental disorder which makes them defend the irrational workings of their minds as if they were logic and truth itself, even when the evidence has been put before them as plainly as is humanly possible. Either they are too blind to see what is put before their face, or they are too perversely obstinate to admit what they see. The result is that we are forced very often to give an extended exposition of the obvious, as if we were not presenting it for people to look at, but for them to touch and handle with their eyes shut.

And yet, will we ever come to an end of discussion and talk if we think we must always reply to replies? For replies come from those who either cannot understand what is said to them, or are so stubborn and contentious that they refuse to give in even if they do understand. In fact, as the Bible says, 'Their conversation is unrighteousness, and they are indefatigable in folly.'[1] You can see how infinitely laborious and fruitless it would be to try to refute every objection they offer, when they have resolved never to think before they speak provided that somehow or other they contradict our arguments.

For this reason, my dear son Marcellinus, I hope that you and others, for whose benefit, in the love of Christ, I freely devote this labour of mine, will not be the kind of critics who always look for a reply when any opposition is raised to what is said in this book. I trust they will not be like the 'silly women', of whom the Apostle speaks, 'who are always being instructed, and never arrive at knowledge of the truth'.[2]

1. Ps. 94, 4. 2. 2 Tim. 3, 7.

2. *Summary of matters treated in Book I*

I began in the first book to treat of the City of God, which is the subject of the whole of this work which, with God's help, I have taken in hand. And the first duty that presented itself was to reply to those who hold the Christian religion responsible for the wars with which the whole world is now tormented, and in particular for the recent sack of Rome by the barbarians.[3] They ascribe this to the Christian prohibition of the offering of abominable sacrifices to demons, whereas they ought instead to be grateful to Christ because in his honour the established usage of war was suspended – the barbarians made available to fugitives consecrated places of vast capacity, and in many cases they respected the status of servants of Christ (whether genuine or assumed in fear) so that they held it to be unlawful to exercise on them the customary rights of war.

This question then arose: why did these divine blessings extend also to the godless and the ungrateful? And why did the hardships inflicted by the enemy fall alike on godless and godly? This question has a wide extension, for many people are continually troubled by the fact that the everyday gifts of God, as also the disasters of humanity, happen to those of good and those of evil life without distinction. The task I have set myself obliged me to attempt a solution, and this has caused some delay. In particular, I have been concerned to administer consolation to women of holy and devout chastity who have felt the pangs of shame at their treatment by the enemy, although they have not lost their resolute purity. I have urged them not to be ashamed of being alive, since they have no possible reason for being ashamed of having sinned.

Then I addressed some words to those who assail Christians in their distress with heartless insolence, and especially those who attack chaste and holy women in their humiliation and shame. Those are the most debased and cynical of mankind, utterly degenerate sons of those very Romans whose many famous exploits are praised and celebrated in history – they are in fact the sworn enemies of the glory of their ancestors. Rome was founded and extended by the labours of those men of old; their descendants made Rome more hideous while it stood than when it fell. For in the ruin of the city it was stone and timber which fell to the ground; but in the lives of those Romans we saw the collapse not of material but of moral defences, not of material but of spiritual grandeur. The lust that burned in their hearts was more deadly than the flame which consumed their dwellings.

3. A.D. 410, about 4 years before St Augustine wrote this.

With this I brought my first book to an end. My purpose now is to proceed to treat of the disasters which Rome has suffered since its foundation, whether at home or in the subject provinces, disasters which they would blame on the Christian religion, if at that time the teaching of the Gospel had rung out with its sweeping condemnation of their false and deceiving gods.

3. *A study of history will show what calamities befell the Romans when they worshipped the pagan gods before Christianity displaced them*

You must bear in mind that in mentioning these facts I am still dealing with the ignorant, the people whose stupidity has given rise to the popular proverb, 'No rain! It's all the fault of the Christians.'[4] The well-educated[5] who are fond of history are readily acquainted with these facts, but they wish to inflame the hatred of the illiterate mobs against us, and so they pretend not to know the facts, and do their best to support the vulgar notion that the disasters which are bound to fall on humanity during a given period and over a given area are to be laid at the door of Christianity, which, in opposition to their gods, is being extended everywhere with immense prestige and unexampled popularity.

So let us help them to recall the many and various disasters which overwhelmed the Roman State before Christ's incarnation – before his name became known to the nations, and received that honour which arouses their ineffectual envy. And in the face of these facts let them defend their gods if they can, assuming that the gods are worshipped in order that the worshippers may escape such calamities. For if they suffer anything of this kind now, they contend that we are to be held responsible. Why then did the gods allow the catastrophes which I am going to mention to fall upon their worshippers, before the proclamation of Christ's name offended them and before Christ's name put a stop to their sacrifices?

4. '*No rain* ...' St Augustine quotes this proverb several times; cf. Tertullian (*Ap.*, 40): 'If the Tiber comes down in flood to the walls, if the Nile fails to rise up to flood the fields, if the sky stands still, if the earth moves, if there is famine or pestilence, the cry goes up: "To the lions with the Christians!" '

5. *The well-educated*, e.g. Symmachus, prefect of the city in A.D. 384, who appealed to Gratian (382) and Valentinian (384) for the restoration of paganism, in particular for the reinstatement in the senate house of the altar of Victory, abolished by Gratian. Ambrose successfully resisted this appeal (Ambr., *Ep.*, 15, to Valentinian; *Ep.*, 17 gives the argument of Symmachus).

4. *Pagan gods had no moral teaching for their worshippers; in fact pagan rites were full of obscenities*

In the first place, why did these gods refuse to take the trouble to prevent the degeneration of morality? For the true God had a right to neglect those who did not worship him, but as for those gods of theirs – the prohibition of whose worship these utterly ungrateful men complain of – why did they give their worshippers no laws to help them to a good way of life? It would certainly have been fitting for the gods to be concerned about the conduct of those who concern themselves with their worship.

'But', it will be replied, 'a man's wickedness depends on his own free will.' Who would deny this? Nevertheless, it was the responsibility of the gods, as counsellors, not to conceal the instructions for a good life from the people who worshipped them. They should have presented and proclaimed them plainly; they should have confronted and convicted sinners by their prophets, threatening punishments to evildoers and promising rewards to those of upright life. Yet the temples of these gods never rang with any such clearly and emphatically uttered exhortations.

When I was a young man I used to go to sacrilegious shows and entertainments. I watched the antics of madmen; I listened to singing boys; I thoroughly enjoyed the most degrading spectacles put on in honour of gods and goddesses – in honour of the Heavenly Virgin, and of Berecynthia, mother of all.[6] On the yearly festival of Berecynthia's purification the lowest kind of actors sang, in front of her litter, songs unfit for the ears of even the mother of one of those mountebanks, to say nothing of the mother of any decent citizen, or of a senator; while as for the Mother of the Gods – ! For there is something in the natural respect that we have towards our parents that the extreme of infamy cannot wholly destroy; and certainly those very mountebanks would be ashamed to give a rehearsal performance in their homes, before their mothers, of those disgusting verbal and acted obscenities. Yet

6. *The Heavenly Virgin.* It is not clear whether St Augustine distinguishes her from Berecynthia (a title of Cybele, from Mt Berecynthus, centre of her worship in Phrygia) but Ch. 26 suggests the identification. The West Syrian goddess Astarte (Tanit) was specially honoured at Carthage; she was assimilated to Cybele, and both were identified with Juno. The yearly festival of her purification was originally on 4 April, the anniversary of her arrival at Rome (cf. Bk I, 30), when her image was ceremonially bathed in the Almo where it joins the Tiber near Rome (Ovid, *Fast.*, 4, 337–55). Under the Empire this *lavatio* was on 27 March, part of the ceremonies of the vernal equinox.

they performed them in the presence of the Mother of the Gods before an immense audience of spectators of both sexes. If those spectators were enticed by curiosity to gather in profusion, they ought at least to have dispersed in confusion at the insults to their modesty.

If these were sacred rites, what is meant by sacrilege? If this is purification, what is meant by pollution? And the name of the ceremony is 'the *fercula*',[7] which might suggest the giving of a dinner-party where the unclean demons could enjoy a feast to their liking. Who could fail to realize what kind of spirits they are which could enjoy such obscenities? Only a man who refused to recognize even the existence of any unclean spirits who deceive men under the title of gods, or one whose life was such that he hoped for the favour and feared the anger of such gods, rather than that of the true God.

5. *The obscenities performed in the worship of the 'Mother of the Gods'*

The last people I should choose to decide on this matter are those who are more eager to revel in the obscene practices of this depraved cult than to resist them. I should prefer the decision of Scipio Nasica,[8] the very man whom the Senate chose as their best man, whose hands received this devil's image and brought it to Rome. Let him tell us whether he would wish his mother to have deserved so well of her country that she should be accorded divine honours. For it is well known that the Greeks and the Romans, and other peoples, have decreed such honours to those whose public services they valued highly, and that such people were believed to have been made immortal and to have been received among the number of the gods.[9] No doubt he would desire such felicity for his mother, if it were possible. But let me go on to ask him whether he would like such disgusting rites as these to be included among the divine honours paid to her? Would he not cry out that he would prefer his mother to be dead, and beyond all experience, than that she should live as a goddess, to take pleasure in hearing such celebrations? It is unthinkable that a senator of Rome, of such high principles that he forbade the erection of a theatre in a city of heroes, should want his mother to be honoured as a goddess by such propitiatory rites as would have scandalized her as a

7. *Fercula* has two meanings: a) 'Litters' on which images were carried in procession, b) 'Dishes' in which the courses of a banquet were served, and so the courses themselves.

8. Bk I, 30.

9. The theory of Euhemerus; cf. Bk IV, 27n.

Roman matron. He would surely have thought it quite impossible for a respectable woman to have her modesty so corrupted by the assumption of divinity that her worshippers should call upon her with ritual invocations of this sort. These invocations contained expressions of such a kind that had they been hurled at any antagonist in a quarrel, during her life on earth, then if she had not stopped her ears and withdrawn from the company, her friends, her husband and her children would have blushed for her. In fact the 'Mother of the Gods' was such a character as even the worst of men would be ashamed to have for his mother. And when she came to take possession of the minds of the Romans she looked for the best man of the country, not so as to support him by counsel and help, but to cheat and deceive him, like the woman of whom the Bible says, 'she ensnares the precious souls of men'.[10] Her purpose was that a mind of great endowments should be puffed up by this supposedly divine testimony and should think itself truly exceptional, and therefore should cease to follow true religion and piety – without which every national ability, however remarkable, disappears in the ruin which follows on pride. And thus that goddess could seek the support of the best of men only by trickery, seeing that she requires in her worship the kind of behaviour which decent men shrink from even in their convivial moments.

6. *The pagan gods never sanctioned a doctrine of right living*

This is the reason why those divinities have no concern for the morals of the cities and peoples by whom they were worshipped. Rather they allowed the most terrible and abominable evils to have free play, to the utmost detriment, not of lands and vines, not of houses and property, not even of the body, which is the servant of the mind, but of the mind itself, the actual ruler of the flesh. They allowed this; they did not use their awful power to prevent it. Or if they did try to stop it, let us have the evidence. And we do not want to hear general assertions about whispers breathed into the ears of a chosen few, and handed down by a secret religious tradition,[11] teaching integrity and purity of life. Let the pagans show, or even mention, places consecrated for such gatherings where what happens is not the performance of spec-

10. Prov. 6, 26.

11. *Secret religious tradition.* There seems to have been a considerable revival of mystery religions, with their esoteric rites and doctrines, in the fourth century, in particular the oriental cults of Cybele and Mithras, and the Egyptian rites of Isis and Serapis (cf. Labriolle, *La Réaction Païenne*, Paris, 1934).

tacles marked by lewd utterances and gestures on the part of the actors, with a free rein to every kind of depravity – not the celebration of The Flight of the Kings[12] (which is really the flight of all decency and morality) – but where the assembled people can hear the commands of the gods about the need to restrain avarice, to curb ambition, to put a check on lust, and where wretched men may learn the lesson that Persius teaches in a voice of sharp reproach:

> Ye wretches, learn
> What we men are, and for what life were born;
> Find out your station in the race of life,
> And how to turn your corners. Learn the limit
> To be placed on wealth; and learn how much to pray for;
> The good that can be done with the crude coin;
> How much to give to country, and to friends:
> Find out the role that God would have you play,
> The part assigned you, in the scheme of things.[13]

Let us be told in what places those divine precepts are regularly proclaimed in the hearing of the people assembled for worship. We on our part can point to churches set up for this very purpose, wherever the Christian religion is spread.

7. *The conclusions of philosophers are ineffective as they lack divine authority. Man is easily corrupted; and the gods' examples influence him more than the argument of man*

But perhaps they will quote the schools of philosophers and their discussions? In the first place, these activities belong to Greece, not to Rome; and even if they belong to Rome – because Greece became a Roman province[14] – they are not the commandments of the gods, but the findings of men who were gifted with most acute intelligence and who endeavoured, by the use of reason, to discover the secrets of the physical universe, to find out what ends were to be pursued and what avoided in the sphere of human behaviour, and, in the rules of reasoning, what valid inferences could be drawn, what conclusions did not follow and what contradictions were entailed.

Some of them certainly established important points, in so far as they had divine assistance, while they went astray in so far as they

12. The *Fugalia*, on 24 February, celebrated the *regifugium*, the expulsion of the kings in 510 B.C. (Ovid, *Fast.*, 2, 68ff.)

13. *Sat.*, 3, 66ff.

14. Province of Achaia 27 B.C. Greece had been in the Roman Empire since 146.

were hindered by human weakness, especially when divine providence rightly opposed their presumption, in order to show, by contrast, the way of piety, which starts from humility and ascends to the heights. This is a matter we shall have occasion to discuss later in greater detail, if that is the will of the true God, our Lord. However, if the philosophers had reached any conclusion which could be a sufficient guide to the good life and to the attainment of ultimate felicity, it would be such men who would more rightly be accorded divine honours. How much better and more honourable would it be to have a temple to Plato where his books were read, rather than to have temples to demons where *Galli*[15] are mutilated, eunuchs are consecrated, madmen gash themselves, and every other kind of cruelty or perversion – pervertedly cruel or cruelly perverted – is regularly practised in the rites of such gods as these. How much better it would be to have the laws of the gods publicly recited and to train the younger generation in ways of righteousness than to waste empty praises on the laws and institutions of antiquity! For the worshippers of such gods direct their attention not to the teachings of Plato or the thoughts of Cato, but rather to the activities of Jupiter, so that they are whirled along by lust 'imbued', in the phrase of Persius, 'with seething venom'.[16] Thus in Terence's play, the immortal youth looks at a painting on the wall representing

> The tale of Jupiter and the golden shower
> Sent down upon the lap of Danae,[17]

and this suggests an authoritative precedent for his own shameful conduct, so that he can boast that he is following a god's example:

> And what a god to follow! He that shakes
> The vaults of heaven with thunder. And should I,
> A lowly mortal, shrink to do the like?
> Nay, thus I did, and with a right good will![18]

15. *Galli*. The eunuch priests of Cybele took their name, it was said, from the river Gallos, near Mt Berecynthus, whose waters were reputed to have intoxicating properties. A more likely derivation is from the Celtic tribes (Galli or Galatae) who settled there in the fourth century B.C. and gave their name to the neighbouring district of Galatia. These priests were said to castrate themselves in imitation of Attis; cf. Bk VI, 7.

16. *Sat.*, 3, 37. 17. *Eun.*, 584ff. 18. *Eun.*, 590f.

8. *The theatrical shows, where the gods are not offended, but propitiated, by the representation of their depravities*

Now it may be objected that these things are not taught in the rites of the gods, but in the fables of the poets. I should not like to say that the mystic ceremonies are more beastly than the theatrical performances; but I do say that those shows, in which the fictions of the poets hold sway, were introduced by the Romans into the worship of their gods, not through ignorant following of the poet's teaching, but because the gods themselves sternly commanded, indeed almost extorted, the production of such shows, demanding that they should be consecrated in their honour. History will bear this out against any who deny it; and I touched on the subject summarily in my first book.[19] For theatrical shows were first instituted at Rome by authority of the pontiffs at a time when a plague was raging. And therefore any man will surely think that in the way he lives his life he ought to follow the examples set by what is acted in plays instituted by divine authority, rather than by what is written in laws laid down by mere human wisdom. If the poets have falsely represented Jupiter as an adulterer, then the gods, chaste as they are, ought surely to have avenged themselves in anger upon mankind for introducing such abominable fictions into their shows, not for failing to present them.

There are more acceptable dramatic compositions, namely comedies and tragedies – poetical fictions designed for production in public shows. Their subject matter is often immoral, as far as action goes; but, unlike many other compositions, they are at least free from verbal obscenities, and the older generation compel the young to read and learn them as part of what is called 'a liberal education for gentlemen'.

9. *What the ancient Romans felt about the need to restrain poetic licence. The Greeks imposed no restriction*

We know what was the opinion of the older Romans on this point from the evidence of Cicero in his work *On the Commonwealth*, where Scipio argues that 'were it not for the licence of established custom, comedies would never have been able to display their depravities in the theatres'.[20] The Greeks of an earlier age certainly maintained a consistency in their reprehensible attitude, for among them the comic writer was granted the legal privilege of saying what-

19. Bk I, 32. 20. Cic., *De Rep.*, 4, 10, 11.

Grab bag

- compass
- survival kit
- face camo
- GPS
- local map
- address of friendly embassies & phone #'s
- knife - survival
- knife - pocket
- utensils
- local phone
- #'s for COP or FOB
- strobe light
- VS-17 panel
- watch band

CARDs

- Roger's Ranger's
- Ranger creed
- LRS creed
- conduct card
- Knight's Vow
- sacraments

ever he liked about whomsoever he pleased, mentioning his victim by name. And so, as Africanus says in the same work,

> Was anyone immune from the attacks, the persecutions of comedy? Was anyone spared? Oh, I agree; the irresponsible demagogues were lashed; people like Cleon, Cleophon, and Hyperbolus,[21] unpatriotic trouble-makers. Yes, that would be tolerable; although it would be better for such citizens to be reprimanded by a censor, not by a poet. But that Pericles should be abused in lines uttered on the stage, when he had led his country with supreme authority for so many years, both in war and peace; that was as inappropriate as it would have been for our own Plautus or Naevius to have chosen to malign Publius and Gnaeus Scipio, or Caecilius to libel Marcus Cato.[22]

Then a little later,

> Our Twelve Tables,[23] in contrast, though there were very few cases in which they imposed the death-penalty, decided to include among those few the crime of writing or publishing verses derogatory to anyone's reputation, or defamatory of his moral character. A very sound provision, for we should submit our lives to the judgment of magistrates and to investigation according to the laws, and not expose them to the poet's native wit. And we should not listen to attacks on individuals except on condition that they have the right to reply and judicial defence.

I have thought it best to quote these extracts from the fourth book of Cicero's *On the Commonwealth*,[24] word for word (save for certain omissions and transpositions, made to assist comprehension), for they are very relevant to the point which I shall do my utmost to establish. After some further discussion, Cicero concludes this topic by demonstrating that the ancient Romans refused to allow any living man to be either praised or maligned on the stage. Whereas, as I have said, the Greeks were more consistent, if less decent, in the licence they per-

21. Athenian demagogues attacked by Aristophanes.

22. *Plautus* was writing plays between 224–184 B.C.; Naevius was somewhat senior; Caecilius Statius died in 168. Scipio Africanus Major (234–183) defeated Hannibal at Zama in 202; Gn. Scipio was consul in 176; M. Porcius Cato ('the Censor', 239–149) was a bitter opponent of luxury and Hellenism and the persistent advocate of the extinction of Carthage (*Carthago delenda est*). Naevius certainly did not spare the Roman aristocracy, for he attacked the Metelli with great vehemence, and Aulus Gellius (33) says that he was imprisoned for 'libels in the Greek manner on the leading men of Rome'. Pericles was covertly attacked by Cratinus, the comic poet, and (after his death) by Aristophanes.

23. *Twelve Tables*: a code of laws drawn up by ten commissioners (*decemviri*) and published in 450 B.C. They prescribed clubbing to death (*fustuarium*) as the punishment for libel.

24. Cic., *De Rep.*, 4, 10, 11.

mitted. In their opinion their gods allowed and enjoyed the lampooning on the public stage not only of men but of gods themselves, whether the depravities related and acted in the theatres were the inventions of poets or genuine facts. (If only the worshippers had found them only good enough for a laugh, and not also worthy of imitation!) For it would, they thought, have been too presumptuous to show tenderness for the reputation of statesmen and citizens when the divine powers demanded no such consideration.

10. *The malicious design of the demons in allowing the enactment of their real or supposed misdeeds*

It is urged in defence that those stories to the god's discredit were not true, but lying inventions. But that is all the more detestable, if you are concerned for the interests of true religion; while if you view it from the side of the Devil's malice, what cleverer subtlety could be used to deceive mankind? For when a libel is issued against a worthy and patriotic statesman, is it not the more reprehensible the further removed it is from truth and the more inappropriate to his actual conduct? And therefore what punishment is sufficient when such criminal and unparalleled injury is offered to a god? Yet the malignant devils, which those people regard as gods, are willing that stories of enormities which they have not committed should be told about them, provided that by means of those ideas they can as it were ensnare men and drag them in their own company to their predestined punishment. It may be that in fact such enormities have been committed by men whom those devils delighted to see reckoned as gods; for they rejoice in the errors of mankind, and to further such errors put themselves forward to be worshipped by a thousand tricks designed to ruin and deceive. Or it may be that no men may truly be charged with such crimes; but the deceitful spirits are glad to allow them to be fictitiously ascribed to divinities, so that men may suppose they have sufficient authority, as it were by heaven-sent revelation, for the perpetration of abominable crimes.

The Greeks thought of themselves as the servants of such divinities; and so they thought that they should claim for themselves no special consideration from the poets among all the calumnies of the stage, either because they were eager to be likened to their gods in this way, or because they feared to provoke the gods to anger by demanding for themselves a more honourable reputation and in this way putting themselves above the divinities.

11. *Actors in Greece were admitted to political office on the ground that those who please the gods may not justly be rejected by men*

It is another mark of consistency in the Greeks that they regarded even the actors of those stories as worthy of considerable honour in the commonwealth. For example, it is related in the same book *On the Commonwealth*[25] that Aeschines[26] of Athens, a notable orator, attained success in politics, after having acted in tragedies in his youth, and that another tragic actor, Aristodemus,[27] was often sent by the Athenians as their representative to Philip of Macedon on most important matters of peace and war. For since they regarded those accomplishments and those theatrical shows as acceptable even to their gods, they thought it would be inappropriate to class the actors among outlaws and vagabonds.

Such was the practice of the Greeks. No doubt it was most improper, but it was certainly quite consonant with the character of their gods. They did not venture to exempt the behaviour of their citizens from the lash of the tongues of poets and actors, since they gave official approval to the aspersions on the behaviour of the gods, with the gods' delighted approval. And because they conceived these theatrical presentations to be welcome to the gods who were their masters, they reckoned that the men who acted in the plays, far from being despised, should be advanced to high honour in the community. For what possible reason could there be for honouring the priests on the ground that through them they offered acceptable sacrifices to the gods, while regarding actors as deserving censure? Seeing that it was through these actors that a pleasure and an honour was presented to the gods, who demanded it, and who would be angry if it were not offered – as they had been informed by a warning from the gods themselves.

Moreover, Labeo,[28] who has the reputation of being the greatest authority on the subject, distinguishes the good divinities from the

25. Cic. *De Rep.*, 4, 11.

26. *Aeschines* (born 390 B.C.) opposed the anti-Macedonian policy of Demosthenes. The latter jeers at him as a failed actor (Dem., *De Cor.*, 209; 262).

27. *Aristodemus*, with Demosthenes and Aeschines, was one of ten commissioners sent to negotiate with Philip of Macedon in 347 B.C., after the fall of Olynthus.

28. *Labeo*. Cornelius Labeo flourished probably late in the third century A.D. His work is not extant, but there are many citations in Macrobius (*fl. c.* 400) and in Augustine. He seems to have had a vast knowledge of Roman religious traditions and rituals, which he interpreted in a Neoplatonic sense.

bad by the difference between the worship given them, the bad being propitiated, he alleges, by 'murders' and 'mournful supplications', the good by 'joyful and merry observances', such as 'plays, feasts and "Banquets of the Gods"'.[29] With God's help, we shall discuss the nature of all such ceremonies in greater detail later. To keep to our present point, it may be that all these honours are to be rendered to all gods indiscriminately, on the assumption that they are all good gods (for the existence of evil gods is an improper idea, although to be sure all those 'gods' are evil, being unclean spirits); or perhaps there should be a hard and fast distinction according to the notion of Labeo, and different observances should be kept for different divinities. However this may be, the Greeks showed very good sense in paying honour both to the priests who ministered at the sacrifices and the actors who performed in the plays – to avoid either insulting all their gods, if they all take pleasure in plays, or (which would be more reprehensible) insulting those whom they regard as good, if it is only they who are addicted to such performances.

12. *The Romans granted poets licence to slander the gods, but not to libel men*

But the Romans, as Scipio boasts in the discussion *On the Commonwealth*, refused to allow character and reputation to be exposed to the calumnies and libels of poets and imposed the death penalty on anyone who dared to compose verse of this kind. This was an honourable decision as far as they themselves were concerned; but it was arrogant and irreligious in respect to their gods. For though they knew that the gods showed patience, and even pleasure, at being torn to shreds by the reproaches and defamations of the poets, they considered it more unseemly for themselves to submit to such outrages; and they even protected themselves from them by legal sanctions, while introducing those indignities into the solemn ceremonies of divine worship.

Now, Scipio, do you really praise the denial to the Roman poets of the licence to heap insults upon any Roman citizen, when you observe that these poets showed no consideration for your gods? Do you think that the reputation of your senate house is to be more highly valued than that of the Capitol, and the fair name of the single city of Rome more than that of the whole of heaven, so that poets are prevented by

29. *'Banquets of the Gods'*. In the *lectisternia* images of the gods were reclined on couches and plates of food were set before them; cf. Bk III, 17.

law from employing the tongue of slander against your citizens, while they may without a qualm hurl the greatest calumnies at your gods, without let or hindrance from senator, censor, emperor or pontiff? It would have been reprehensible, I take it, for Plautus or Naevius to insult Publius and Gnaeus Scipio, or for Caecilius to slander Marcus Castor;[30] but it was quite proper for your friend Terence to excite the base passions of young men by portraying the misdemeanours of Jupiter Most High?[31]

13. *The Romans ought to have realized that gods who demanded obscene shows in their worship deserved no divine honours*

It may be that, if he were living, Scipio would answer, 'How could we refuse to grant impunity to performances which the gods themselves wished to be held sacred? Since it was they who introduced into the Roman way of life those theatrical shows where such things are performed in speech and action; and they commanded them to be dedicated and presented among the honours paid to them.'

How is it that the inference has not rather been drawn that they themselves are not real gods, and are not in the least worthy to be accorded divine honours by the community? If we assume that it would be utterly wrong and unfitting for them to be worshipped if they demanded the performance of plays containing abuse of Roman citizens, how on earth have they been reckoned worthy of worship when they have demanded, among the honours paid them, the public presentation of their enormities? How can they be regarded as anything but abominable evil spirits, eager to deceive mankind?

Furthermore, although the Romans were at this time so much under the sway of baneful superstition that they worshipped gods whom they thought of as wishing to have theatrical obscenities devoted to their honour, they still had enough concern for their own dignity and modesty to refrain from honouring the actors of such fables in the manner of the Greeks. In fact, as Scipio says, in Cicero's book, 'They had such a low opinion of the theatre and of the acting profession that they decided not only to debar actors from normal political life, but even to remove their names from the tribal lists through the intervention of the censors.'[32]

30. cf. Bk II, ch 9.
31. cf. ch. 7; and cf. St Augustine, *Conf.*, I, 16.
32. Actors, together with charioteers and gladiators, were subject to *infamia*

Surely this was an eminently sensible decision, to be put to the credit of the Romans. But how I wish Roman good sense had consistently followed its own precedent! How right they were to refuse any chance of political life to any Roman citizen who chose a theatrical career, and besides this to disqualify him by the censor's ban from keeping his place in his tribe. Here was the genuine Roman spirit, the spirit of a community jealous for its honour. But I want an answer to this question: How can it be consistent to deprive theatrical performers of any political standing, and at the same time to admit theatrical performances as an ingredient in divine worship? Roman virtue for a long time had no acquaintance with the art of the theatre.[33] If they had cultivated that art to gratify men's search for pleasure, its introduction would have undermined morality. It was the gods who demanded those exhibitions; how then can the actor be rejected, when he is the agent of a god's worship? Can one have the face to censure those who enact a stage obscenity, when those who exact them are adored?

The Greeks and Romans are thus engaged in a dispute. The Greeks think themselves right to honour actors, because they worship gods who demand theatrical productions; the Romans do not allow stage-players to dishonour a plebeian tribe, to say nothing of the senate house. In this argument the conclusion is reached by the following line of reasoning. The Greek proposition is: 'If such gods are to be worshipped, it follows that such men are to be honoured.' The Romans put in the minor premise: 'But such men are in no way to be honoured.' The Christians draw the conclusion: 'Therefore such gods are in no way to be worshipped.'

---

at Rome, thus being deprived of the vote and debarred from political office. In 45 B.C. a law made them ineligible for municipal positions. Cf. Tertullian, *De Spect.*, 22: 'Charioteers, actors, athletes, and gladiators, popular as they are, to whom men prostitute their souls and women their bodies ... are degraded and disqualified by the Romans on the ground of those same accomplishments for which they are so highly valued.... What absurdity! The Romans are enamoured of those whom they chastise; they depreciate those whom they approve; they exalt the art, and they censure the artist!'

33. Livy (7, 2) says that plays were first performed in Rome in 364 B.C., being imported from Etruria. This would give Rome 389 years of freedom from contamination.

14. *Plato excluded poets from his well-regulated state; which proves him superior to the gods who chose to be honoured by theatrical shows*

We pass to another question. The poets who compose such fables are forbidden by the law of the Twelve Tables to injure the reputation of citizens, yet they hurl such foul insults against the gods. Why are they not considered as dishonourable as the players? On what principle is it right for the actors of poetical fictions, derogatory to the gods, to be outlawed, while the authors are honoured? Perhaps the award of victory should rather be given to Plato, the Greek; for when he was sketching his rational ideal of a perfect commonwealth, he laid it down that poets should be banished from his city as the enemies of truth.[34] He was indignant at the outrages offered to the gods, and at the same time he was concerned to prevent the infection and corruption of the minds of the citizens by such fictions.

Now contrast the humanity of Plato, who would banish poets from his city to prevent their misleading the citizens, with the divinity of the gods who demand stage plays in their honour. Though Plato did not persuade the Greeks by his argument to stop even the writing of such fictions, he still urged this course on that frivolous and irresponsible people, whereas the gods by their commands extorted the actual performance of them from the reserved and conscientious Romans. And they did not merely desire such plays to be acted, but to be dedicated and consecrated to them, and solemnly presented in their worship. Well then, who would more justly be accorded divine honours by the community – Plato, who forbade such monstrous obscenities, or the devils who delighted in the delusion of men who would not be persuaded by Plato's truth? Labeo[35] considered that Plato should be reckoned among demi-gods such as Hercules and Romulus. He puts demi-gods above heroes, though he ranks both among divinities. For my part, I have no hesitation about classing Plato, whom Labeo reckons a demi-god, above the gods themselves, to say nothing of heroes.

Now the Roman laws approximate to the arguments of Plato, since he condemns all poetical inventions, while the Romans at least deprive poets of licence to slander. Plato banished poets from residence in the city; the Romans at least banish them from any share in civic rights, and if they dared attack the gods (who demanded the performances)

34. cf. Plat., *Rp.*, 3, 398A; 8, 568B; 10, 605A; 607B.
35. cf. ch. 11.

they would remove them altogether. Thus the Romans cannot possibly receive or expect from their gods any laws for the establishment of morality or the correction of immorality, since by their own laws they reprove and correct the gods.

The gods insist on stage plays in their honour; the Romans disqualify stage-players from all honour. The gods command the presentation of insults to the gods in the fictions of poets; the Romans restrain the impudence of poets from offering insults to men. Plato, the 'demi-god', opposed the impurity of such gods, and he also showed what ought to be achieved by the Roman character, by completely forbidding poets to live in a well-ordered community, whether they published falsehoods at their own whim, or set before men, for their imitation, the most disgraceful actions of the gods.

We Christians hold Plato to be neither god nor demi-god; we do not even compare him to any holy angel of the Most High God, or to any truthful prophet, or apostle, or to one of Christ's martyrs, or any Christian man. The reason for this attitude will be explained, with God's help, in its proper place. However, since the pagans wish him to be considered a demi-god, or judge him to be superior, if not to Romulus or Hercules (although no historian or poet has recorded, or invented, a story of Plato killing his brother, or committing any crime), yet certainly to Priapus or any Cynocephalus or (to end the list) any Febris[36] – divinities some of whom the Romans received as foreign importations, some of whom they consecrated for themselves.

How then could such gods as those prevent, by their commands and laws, the corruption of character and conduct which threatened from outside, or effect a cure of corruption already implanted, since those gods were anxious that such behaviour should be made familiar to people through theatrical displays, whether as their own acts, or as resembling their acts. The result was automatically to kindle the most depraved desires in human hearts by giving them a kind of divine authority. And it was useless for Cicero to cry out against this, when he says, on the subject of poets, 'When these poets are greeted with noisy acclaim from the public, as if it were the praise of a great and

36. *Priapus*, a phallic god of fertility, especially of gardens and orchards.

Cynocephalus ('dog-head') was introduced from Egypt (cf. Bk III, 12). He is evidently the jackal-headed Anubis, the conductor of the dead to the underworld, hence identified with Hermes *psychopompus*.

Febris ('fever'): cf. Bk III, 12; IV, 15; 23. Cicero, (*De Nat Deor.*, 3, 25, 63) mentions her shrine on the Palatine.

wise master, what darkness these poets bring on, what fears they engender, what evil passions they inflame!'[37]

15. *The Romans established certain gods for flattery, not for any good reason*

Now is there any reason for choosing those false gods? Is it not rather cringing flattery? For they have not regarded Plato as deserving a simple shrine, though they repute him a demi-god, and though he laboured with all those arguments to prevent the corruption of men's morals by those perverted thoughts which are particularly to be guarded against, and when they put Romulus before many of the gods, although even he is attested as a demi-god – not a full divinity – by their more secret doctrine. For they even appointed a *flamen* for him, a type of priest so pre-eminent in Rome's religious rites that they had only three of these, distinguished by the wearing of a special mitre, appointed for three divinities, the *Flamen Dialis* of Jupiter, the *Flamen Martialis* of Mars, and the *Flamen Quirinalis* of Romulus. 'Quirinalis' was so called because Romulus was named Quirinus[38] after he had been, as they said, received into heaven through the devotion of his citizens. In this way Romulus was honoured above Neptune and Pluto, the brothers of Jupiter, and even above Saturn, their father, in that the Romans assigned to him, as a mark of greatness, the priesthood which they had created for Jupiter; and they assigned it also to Mars as his reputed father, it may be, for his sake.

16. *If the gods had been concerned for righteousness, the Romans ought to have received moral instruction from them, instead of borrowing laws*

If the Romans could have received from their gods the rules of right living, they would not have borrowed the laws of Solon from the Athenians, as they did some years after the founding of the city.[39] However, they did not keep them just as they received them, but tried to make them better and remove their flaws. Although Lycurgus pretended that he had laid down laws for the Spartans at the prompting

37. Cic., *De Rep.*, 4, 9, 9.

38. *Quirinus* was an ancient Latin deity of uncertain functions. His identification with Romulus seems to be a late development, for Cicero speaks of it as something of recent growth (*De Nat. Deor.*, 2, 62; *De Off.*, 3, 41).

39. 300 years after, in 454, according to Livy (3, 31–3). There is, however, no trace of Greek influence in the laws of the Twelve Tables of 450.

of Apollo,[40] the Romans sensibly refused to believe it and did not take over any laws from Sparta. Numa Pompilius, who succeeded Romulus on the throne, is said to have instituted some laws, though they were quite inadequate for the government of the community, and he also founded many religious ceremonies. Yet it is not related that he received these laws from heaven.

Thus though corrupt thoughts, corrupt lives and corrupt conduct are so dangerous that their most learned men assert that countries come to ruin through them, even when the cities still stand, nevertheless, their gods were not in the least concerned to protect their worshippers from such disasters. In fact, as we have argued, they were most concerned to promote this corruption.

17. *The Rape of the Sabines and other iniquities that were prevalent in the Roman society even in times that are highly praised*

Perhaps the reason why the gods did not impose laws upon the Romans was that, as Sallust says, 'Justice and morality prevailed among them by nature as much as by laws.'[41] I imagine that the Rape of the Sabines arose from this 'justice and morality'. What could be 'juster', or more 'moral', than to take other men's daughters, not by receiving them from their parents, but by luring them with a fraudulent invitation to a show, and then by carrying them off by force, in a scramble. Even if the Sabines were unfair to refuse to give their daughters on request it was surely much more unfair to take them by force after this refusal. It would have been more just to have waged war against a people that refused a request for marriage with its daughters on the part of close neighbours, than against those who asked for the restoration of daughters who had been carried off. So it would have been better if Mars had helped his son in a fight to avenge the insulting refusal of marriage, and if Romulus had thus come by the women he wished for. It might have been in accordance with some sort of law of war, had the victor justly won the women who had been unjustly refused him; it was contrary to every law of peace that he seized those who had been denied him and then waged unjust war with their indignant parents.

The outcome of this was certainly all to the good, since although

40. i.e. from the Delphic oracle. Lycurgus was the legendary legislate of Sparta. The reforms attributed to him were probably introduced *c.* 600 B.C.

41. *Cat.*, 9, 1.

the Circensian Games continued as a memorial of that shady trick, the precedent of the unpleasant business was not approved in that city and empire. And the Romans, while ready to make the mistake of consecrating Romulus as a god after that iniquitous performance, refused to allow it to be imitated either by law or custom. Another result of that 'justice and morality' was that after the expulsion of King Tarquin, whose son had violently ravished Lucretia, the consul Junius Brutus compelled Lucretia's husband, his colleague, Lucius Tarquinius Collatinus, to abdicate from office, and refused him leave to reside in the city. Though Collatinus was a good and innocent man, he was so treated just because he bore the name of Tarquin and was related to the offender; and Brutus did this with the favour and support of the people, from whom Collatinus, like Brutus himself, had received the consulship.

Another result was the treatment of Marcus Camillus. Camillus was the outstanding character of his time; he conquered the Venientines with the greatest ease, and captured their prosperous city – and that was after a ten years war[42] in which the most dangerous enemies of Rome had inflicted a series of heavy defeats on her, reducing the people to a state of terrified doubt about their prospects of survival. And after this Camillus was brought to trial because of the envy of those who disparaged his qualities and through the arrogance of the tribunes of the *plebs*; and so, feeling the ingratitude of the community which he had liberated, and convinced of his coming condemnation, Camillus went into voluntary exile, later to become once more the champion of his ungrateful country, this time against the Gauls.

I am sick of recalling the many acts of revolting injustice which have disturbed the city's history; the powerful classes did their best to subjugate the lower orders, and the lower orders resisted – the leaders of each side motivated more by ambition for victory than by any ideas of equity and morality.

18. *The Roman character as portrayed by Sallust under the pressure of fear, and in the relaxation of security*

I will therefore impose a restraint on myself, and employ the evidence of Sallust himself, whose praise of the Romans gave rise to this discussion. 'Justice and morality', he says, 'prevailed among them by nature as much as by law.'[43] He was commending the period after the expulsion of the kings, a period of enormous expansion in an incred-

42. 405–396 B.C. 43. *Cat.*, 9. 1.

ibly short space of time. In spite of this, he also admits, at the very beginning of the first book of his History, that even at the time when the government had passed from kings to consuls, after a short interval the injustices of the powerful classes led to a separation between *plebs* and *patres*,[44] and to other disputes in the city. He records the high standard of morality and the degree of concord which marked the history of Rome between the Second Punic War and the last,[45] but he ascribes as the reason for this desirable state of things not the love of justice, but the fear that peace was unreliable while Carthage still stood; and that was why Nasica resisted the annihilation of Carthage, so that wickedness should be restrained by fear, immorality checked, and the high standard of conduct preserved. And Sallust goes on to add, 'But after the destruction of Carthage there came the highest pitch of discord, greed, ambition, and all the evils which generally spring up in times of prosperity.'[46] We infer from this that those evils generally spring up and increase even before such times. Hence he continues with the reason for his statement,

> For the injustices of the powerful classes leading to separation between *plebs* and *patres* and other disputes, were found in the city right from the beginning: and the rule of equity, justice and restraint after the expulsion, that is, the ejection, of the kings lasted only as long as the threat from Tarquin and the critical war with the Etruscans continued.

Thus you observe that Sallust alleges fear to have been responsible for that brief period of 'the rule of equity, justice and moderation which followed the expulsion, that is the ejection, of the kings'. These Romans were frightened by the war which Tarquin, in alliance with Etruria, waged against them, after he had been driven from his throne and from his city. Notice how Sallust proceeds: 'After that', he says,

> the patricians reduced the plebeians to the condition of slavery; they disposed of the lives and persons of the *plebs* in the manner of kings; they drove men from their lands; and with the rest of the people disenfranchized, they alone wielded supreme power. Oppressed by such harsh treatment, and especially by the load of debt, the plebeians, after enduring the simultaneous burden of tribute and military service in continual wars, at length armed themselves, and took up a position on the Mons Sacer and the Aventine; thus they gained for themselves the tribunes of the *plebs* and other rights. The Second Punic War brought an end to the strife and rivalry between the two parties.[47]

44. The secession to the Mons Sacer, 494 B.C.
45. i.e. 202 B.C. (Zama)–146 (fall of Carthage).
46. *Hist.* fr. I, 11.   47. *Hist.* fr. I, 11.

Here is a picture of the condition of the Romans in so short a time after the expulsion of the kings. And yet Sallust says, 'Justice and morality prevailed amongst them by nature as much as by law.'

Furthermore, if this is what that period was like, when the Roman state is reported to have been at the height of excellence, what do we suppose is to be said or thought of the period following? For, to quote the words of the same historian, 'the state of the country gradually changed, from the height of excellence to the depth of depravity'.[48] This is the period, as Sallust relates, following the destruction of Carthage. In Sallust's history we can read a brief record and description of these times – how the moral deterioration, which set in during times of prosperity, continued until the Civil Wars. 'And from that time,' he says, 'the degradation of traditional morality ceased to be a gradual decline and became a torrential downhill rush. The young were so corrupted by luxury and greed that it was justly observed that a generation had arisen which could neither keep its own property or allow others to keep theirs.'[49] Sallust proceeds to dwell on the vices of Sulla, and comments on other depravities in the community. Other writers agree with him on this subject, though they are far inferior to him in style.

You see, I am sure, and anyone who pays attention cannot fail to observe, that Rome had sunk into a morass of moral degradation before the coming of our Heavenly King. For all this happened not only before Christ had begun to teach in the flesh, but even before he had been born of a virgin. Now the Romans do not dare to blame their gods for all the moral evils of these periods, either the venial sins of earlier times or the horrid and intolerable enormities that followed the fall of Carthage, though it was these gods who with malignant cunning implanted in human minds ideas which blossomed into such wickedness. Why then do they blame Christ for the present evils, when Christ by his saving doctrine forbids the worship of false and deceitful gods? Christ with divine authority denounces and condemns the offences of men, and their perverted lusts, and he gradually withdraws his family from all parts of a world which is failing and declining through those evils, so that he may establish a city whose titles of 'eternal' and 'glorious' are not given by meaningless flattery but by the judgement of truth.

48. *Cat.*, 5, 9. 49. *Hist.*, fr. 1, 16.

19. *The corruption of the Roman commonwealth before Christ abolished the worship of the gods*

There you see the Roman republic changing from the height of excellence to the depths of depravity. And this is no novel assertion of my own; I am indebted for it to Roman authorities, who far preceded the coming of Christ. After the destruction of Carthage, and before Christ's coming, 'the degradation of traditional morality ceased to be a gradual decline and became a torrential downhill rush.' I challenge these Romans to quote injunctions against luxury and greed, given by their gods to the Roman people. Would that they had merely refrained from counselling chastity and restraint, without demanding from the people acts of depravity and shame, by means of which to establish a pernicious authority through a false claim to divine power! I challenge them then to read our Scriptures, and to find, in the Prophets, in the holy Gospel, in the Acts of the Apostles, and in the Epistles, those uniquely impressive warnings against greed and self-indulgence, given everywhere to the people assembled to hear them, in a tone resembling not the chatter of philosophical debates, but the thunder of oracles from the clouds of God. Yet they do not blame their gods for the self-indulgence, the greed and the savage immorality which, before Christ's coming, brought the republic to those 'depths of depravity'. They scold the Christian religion for all the humiliations inflicted in those later times on their sophisticated self-esteem. Yet if the teachings of Christianity on justice and morality had been listened to and practised by 'kings of the earth and all peoples, princes and all judges of the world, youths and maidens, old and young together',[50] those of every age capable of reason, male and female, and even the tax-collectors and soldiers addressed by John the Baptist[51] – if all those had listened, the Roman commonwealth would now enrich all this present world with its own happiness, and would ascend to the heights of eternal life to reign in felicity. But some listened, while others rejected, and the majority found the blandishments of sin more congenial than the salutary harshness of virtue; and so Christ's servants, whether they are kings, or princes, or judges, or soldiers, or provincials, whether rich or poor, freemen or slaves, men or women, are bidden, if need be, to endure the wickedness of an utterly corrupt state, and by that endurance to win for themselves a place of glory in that holy and majestic assembly, as we call it, of the angels, in the Heavenly Commonwealth, whose law is the will of God.

50. Ps. 148, 11f. 51. Luke 3, 12f.

20. *The kind of felicity the opponents of Christianity wish to enjoy, and the morality by which they wish to live*

But the worshippers and lovers of those gods, whom they delighted to imitate in their criminal wickedness, are unconcerned about the utter corruption of their country. 'So long as it lasts,' they say, 'so long as it enjoys material prosperity, and the glory of victorious war, or, better, the security of peace, why should we worry? What concerns us is that we should get richer all the time, to have enough for extravagant spending every day, enough to keep our inferiors in their place. It is all right if the poor serve the rich, so as to get enough to eat and to enjoy a lazy life under their patronage; while the rich make use of the poor to ensure a crowd of hangers-on to minister to their pride; if the people applaud those who supply them with pleasures rather than those who offer salutary advice; if no one imposes disagreeable duties, or forbids perverted delights; if kings are interested not in the morality but the docility of their subjects; if provinces are under rulers who are regarded not as directors of conduct but as controllers of material things and providers of material satisfactions, and are treated with servile fear instead of sincere respect. The laws should punish offences against another's property, not offences against a man's own personal character. No one should be brought to trial except for an offence, or threat of offence, against another's property, house, or person; but anyone should be free to do as he likes about his own, or with his own, or with others, if they consent. There should be a plentiful supply of public prostitutes, for the benefit of all those who prefer them, and especially for those who cannot keep private mistresses. It is a good thing to have imposing houses luxuriously furnished, where lavish banquets can be held, where people can, if they like, spend night and day in debauchery, and eat and drink till they are sick: to have the din of dancing everywhere, and theatres full of fevered shouts of degenerate pleasure and of every kind of cruel and degraded indulgence. Anyone who disapproves of this kind of happiness should rank as a public enemy: anyone who attempts to change it or get rid of it should be hustled out of hearing by the freedom-loving majority: he should be kicked out, and removed from the land of the living. We should reckon the true gods to be those who see that the people get this happiness and then preserve it for them. Then let them be worshipped as they wish, let them demand what shows they like, so that they can enjoy them with their devotees or, at least, receive them from their worshippers. All the gods have to do is to ensure that there is no threat to this happiness from enemies, or plagues, or any other disasters'.

All this would suggest to a sensible man the palace of Sardanapalus rather than Imperial Rome! Sardanapalus was the king so devoted to sensuality that he had it inscribed on his tomb that his only possessions in death were the pleasures he had gulped down in indulgence during his life.[52] If these Romans had a king like that, who let them indulge in such pursuits and never opposed them by any restraint on their practices, they would be more ready to consecrate a temple and *flamen* to him than the ancient Romans were to accord such honours to Romulus.

21. *Cicero's judgement on the Roman commonwealth*

If our opponents scorn the historian's judgement that the Roman state has sunk 'to the depths of depravity', if they are not troubled about the disgusting infection of crime and immorality which rages in it, so long as that state continues to stand, then let them listen not to Sallust's description of its degradation, but to Cicero's argument that it has now utterly perished, that the republic is completely extinct.

Cicero represents Scipio, the annihilator of Carthage, as discussing the state of the country, when it was felt that it was doomed to perish through the corruption described in Sallust. This discussion is placed at the time when one of the Gracchi had been killed, an occasion from which Sallust dates the beginnings of the serious civil disturbances (Sallust records his death in this work). Now Scipio said, at the end of the second book,

> In the case of music for strings or wind, and in vocal music, there is a certain harmony to be kept between the different parts, and if this is altered or disorganized the cultivated ear finds it intolerable; and the united efforts of dissimilar voices are blended into harmony by the exercise of restraint. In the same way a community of different classes, high, low and middle, unites, like the varying sounds of music, to form a harmony of very different parts through the exercise of rational restraint; and what is called harmony in music answers to concord in a community, and it is the best and closest bond of security in a country. And this cannot possibly exist without justice.[53]

52. cf. Cic., *Tusc. Disp.*, 5, 35, 101; *De Fin.*, 2, 32, 106. Sardanapalus is the caricature drawn by classical historians of the great Assyrian king, Assur–banipal (668–626 B.C.).

53. *De Rep.*, 2, 42f.

Then after a more extended treatment of the point, describing the great advantage of justice to a community and the great loss occasioned by its absence, another of those present at the discussion, named Philus, puts in a plea for a more detailed treatment of the subject of justice because it was at that time popularly supposed that some injustice was inevitable in the government of any country. Scipio agrees that this question needed investigation and explanation. He admits in reply that, in his opinion, what they have already said about the commonwealth gives them no basis for proceeding further, unless they establish the falsity of the statement that injustice is inevitable in government, and, further, the truth of the assertion that complete justice is the supreme essential for government.[54]

The discussion of the question is then deferred to the next day, and in the third book the topic is thrashed out with the fiercest arguments. Philus undertakes to defend the position that government entails injustice, covering himself by disclaiming this as his own opinion. And he contends energetically for injustice against justice, asserting its superior utility for the country, and striving to prove his point by plausible arguments and illustrations. Then Laelius, by general request, undertakes the defence of justice, and asserts with all possible emphasis that nothing is so inimical to a community as injustice, and that a country cannot be governed, and cannot continue in being, without a high degree of justice.

When this question has, in the general opinion, been dealt with sufficiently, Scipio returns to the interrupted discussion. He starts by repeating and supporting his brief definition of a commonwealth, that it is 'the weal of the community', and he defines 'the community' as meaning not any and every association of the population, but 'an association united by a common sense of right and a community of interest'.[55] He goes on to point out the advantage of definition in argument; and from these definitions of his he derives the proposition that a commonwealth (i.e. 'the weal of the community') only exists where there is a sound and just government, whether power rests with a monarch or with a few aristocrats, or with the people as a whole. But when the king is unjust (a 'tyrant', as he calls him, in the Greek manner), or the nobles are unjust (he calls such a combination a *factio* – a caucus) or the people are unjust (and for this he finds no accepted term, unless he should call it a collective tyranny), then, he holds, the commonwealth is not corrupt, as had been argued on the previous day, but, by a logical deduction from the definition, it ceases to exist at

54. *De Rep.*, 2, 44. 55. *De Rep.*, 1, 25, 39

all – for there can be no 'weal of the community', if it is unjust, since it is not 'associated by a common sense of right and a community of interest', which was the definition of a community.

Thus when the Roman commonwealth reached the condition described by Sallust it was not by now 'in the depth of depravity', in Sallust's phrase; it had simply ceased to exist, according to the reasoning produced by the discussion of the commonwealth which engaged the leading statesmen of this time. Similarly, Cicero himself at the beginning of the fifth book speaks in his own person, and not in the person of Scipio or anyone else, when he quotes the line of Ennius:

> Ancient morality and the men of old
> Fixed firm the Roman state.[56]

and he continues,

> This verse, both by its brevity and its truth seems to me like the utterance of some oracle. For the great leaders could not have founded, or could not have so long maintained such a great state with such a vast stretch of empire, had there not been that morality in the community; nor could the morality have done so, without the leadership of such men. Thus, before our own period, the traditional moral code produced outstanding men, and these excellent men preserved the code and the practices of their forebears. Whereas our age has received the commonwealth like a magnificent picture which has almost faded away with age, and it has not only omitted to restore it with the original colours; it has not even taken trouble to preserve what one may call the general shape and the bare outlines. For what remains of that ancient morality which, according to the poet, supported the Roman state? We see that it has passed out of use into oblivion, so that far from being cultivated, it does not even enter our minds. And what about the men? The morality has passed away through lack of the men: and we are bound to be called to account for this disaster, and even, one may say, to defend ourselves on a capital charge. For we retain the name of a commonwealth, but we have lost the reality long ago: and this was not through any misfortune, but through our own misdemeanours.

Such was Cicero's admission, long after the death of Africanus, whom he represents as engaging in the discussion *On the Commonwealth*, but still some time before the coming of Christ. If those sentiments had been expressed when Christianity was spreading and gaining ground, would not all those Romans have decided that Christians were to be blamed for this state of things? If so, why did their gods show no concern to prevent the ruin and loss of that commonwealth whose loss Cicero so piteously bemoans long before Christ

56. *De Rep.*, 5, 1.

came in the flesh? Those who praise the state of Rome in the time of 'ancient morality an dthe men of old' should ask themselves whether real justice flourished in that city, or whether, it may be, it was not even then a living reality in men's behaviour, but merely a fancy picture. This, in fact, is what Cicero unconsciously admits, even when he is commending it.

But, God willing, we will look into this later on. For I intend, in the appropriate place, to examine the definitions of Cicero himself in which, through the mouth of Scipio he laid down in brief what constitutes a 'commonwealth' and what constitutes a 'community', together with the witness of many other statements in that discussion, either of his own or of his characters; and I shall do my best to demonstrate that that commonwealth never existed, because there never was real justice in the community.[57] Now it certainly was a commonwealth to some degree, according to more plausible definitions; and it was better ruled by the Romans of antiquity than by their later successors. But true justice is found only in that commonwealth whose founder and ruler is Christ; if we agree to call it a commonwealth, seeing that we cannot deny that it is the 'weal of the community'. However, if this title, so commonly used elsewhere with a different sense, may be too remote from our usual way of speaking, we may say that at least there is true justice in that City of which the holy Scripture says, 'Glorious things are said about you, City of God.'[58]

22. *The Roman gods were not concerned to prevent the destruction of the commonwealth through moral corruption*

But with regard to our present topic, however praiseworthy the pagans may say that commonwealth had been, or is, still, according to their most learned writers, it had sunk 'to the depths of degradation' long before the coming of Christ. Indeed it had perished and ceased to be because of utter moral depravity. To prevent it from perishing its guardian gods ought, above all else, to have given to their worshipping people counsels for right living and behaviour, since that people worshipped them with all those temples, all those priests and all kinds of sacrifices, with such a multiplicity of varied rites, so many annual festivals and so many attendances at lavish spectacles. Whereas in fact the demons looked after only their own interests; they did not care

57. Bk XIX 21; 24 58. Ps. 87, 5.

how their worshippers lived, or rather they were content that they should live in corruption, provided that they supplied all their wants under the compulsion of fear.

Or if they did give such laws, let the laws be produced, displayed and read, which the gods gave to that city, but which the Gracchi ignored when they started those turmoils by their seditious acts, which Marius, Cinna, and Carbo ignored when they proceeded to civil wars, undertaken for most unjust causes, and waged with a cruelty surpassed only by the cruelty in which they ended – laws that were ignored finally by Sulla himself, the description of whose life, character, and actions by Sallust and other historians would make anyone shudder in horror. Would not anyone admit that the commonwealth had perished at that time?

Can it be that because of the moral state of citizens like these our opponents will pluck up courage to quote, as usual, this statement of Virgil, in defence of their gods and in reply to us:

> The shrines and altars now were all deserted
> By all the gods through whom this realm once stood?[59]

In the first place, suppose it true; then they have no reason to complain against Christianity, or for the assertion that the gods have deserted them in disgust at that religion, because it was the behaviour of their ancestors that drove away that multitude of tiny gods like flies from the altars. But where was all that flock of divinities when, long before the corruption of ancient morality, the Gauls took Rome and set it on fire?[60] Were they there, but asleep perhaps? On that occasion the whole of the city was reduced, and only the Capitol hill remained intact; and that would have been taken if the geese had not kept watch while the gods were sleeping. As a result Rome almost fell into the superstition of the Egyptians, who worship beasts and birds, for they celebrate a yearly Feast of the Goose.[61]

But these are external disasters, affecting the body, not the mind, arising from enemy action or from some natural disaster, and I am not discussing these at the moment. I am now concerned with the poisoning of morals, which first decayed slowly and then suffered a headlong plunge. As a result such ruin came upon the commonwealth, even though buildings and walls stood unharmed, that their eminent

59. *Aen.*, 2, 351f. 60. 390 B.C.

61. *The Feast of the Goose*. Plutarch (*De Fort., Rom.*, 12) describes a procession in which a goose was conveyed in solemn state on an elaborate litter. Geese were sacred to Juno, and were kept on the Capitol at public expense.

writers have no hesitation in pronouncing the commonwealth lost. If it is true that the community had ignored the gods' instructions about the good life and about justice, then the gods were justified in departing, so that when 'the shrines and altars were all deserted', the commonwealth was lost. But, I ask you, what kind of gods were they if they refused to live with the people who worshipped them, when they had not taught that people a better way of life than the corrupt way they were following?

23. *The vicissitudes of history depend not on the favour or opposition of demons, but on the judgement of the true God*

Then what are we to think of the apparent readiness of the gods to assist the gratification of men's desires, and their obvious failure to help men to restrain them? Marius, for example, was a low-born upstart who ruthlessly caused civil wars, and ruthlessly waged them. Yet the gods helped him so effectively that he became consul seven times, and died as an old man, in his seventh consulship, so as to escape the hands of Sulla, who was soon to be victorious. If it is said that the gods did not help him to these achievements, then we have a significant admission that all this temporal felicity, which is what such men desire, can befall a man without the favour of the gods, and that men like Marius can be loaded with blessings and enjoy health and strength, riches and honours, renown and long life in spite of the anger of the gods – and also that men like Regulus can be tortured to death by captivity, slavery, want, sleeplessness and pain in spite of the favour of the gods. If they admit this, they immediately acknowledge that the gods give men no help, and that their worship is superfluous. For if the gods were eager for the people to learn all that is contrary to virtue of mind and integrity of life – whose rewards are to be hoped for after death – if they can do no harm to those they hate in regard to those transient and temporal goods, nor give any help to those whom they love, then why are they worshipped, why is their worship so earnestly insisted on? Why in these distressful and depressing times do men complain, as if the gods had taken offence and departed? And why is the Christian religion subjected to the vilest insults because of them? If the gods have power to help or to harm in these matters, why did they assist the villainous Marius and desert the exemplary Regulus? Is it not obvious that they themselves are unjust and worthless? If it is assumed that they should therefore be the more feared and worshipped, the assumption is false. For there is no evidence that Regulus worshipped less than Marius.

Nor must it be supposed that a life of wickedness should be chosen, on the assumption that the gods favoured Marius more than Regulus. For Metellus[62] was the most esteemed of the Romans; and he had five sons who became consuls, and was also happy in the enjoyment of this world's goods. But Catiline was an utter villain; and he was sunk in poverty, and was finally struck down in the war his crimes had unleashed, knowing no happiness. And the truest and surest happiness is, in general, the rich endowment of the loyal worshippers of that God who alone can bestow it.

Thus, when that commonwealth was perishing through its moral depravity, the Roman gods took no action to direct or correct morals to prevent that ruin. In fact they assisted the process of depravation and corruption, to ensure the ruin. And let them not assume an air of probity and pretend that they withdrew in disgust at the wickedness of the citizens. They were certainly there; they are shown up and convicted for what they are; they could neither help by their advice nor conceal themselves by keeping silence. I skip the fact that Marius was commended by the compassionate men of Minturnae to the protection of the goddess Marica in her sacred grove,[63] so that she might give him all success, and that from a most desperate situation he returned unharmed to Rome, at the head of an army as ruthless as its commander. And those who wish may read in the historians how bloody and barbarous his victory was, and how much more inhuman than the triumph of a foreign foe.

I pass over that, as I say; and I do not ascribe the bloodstained good luck of Marius to Marica, whoever she was, but rather to the inscrutable providence of God whose purpose is to shut the mouths of our opponents and to free from error those who are not swayed by prejudice and who carefully observe the facts. For the fact is that even if the demons have some power in these matters, their power is limited to the extent allowed them by the inscrutable decision of the Omnipotent, whose purpose is that we should not set too much store by earthly felicity, which is often granted to such scoundrels as Marius, and yet should not regard it as an evil, since we observe that many devout and upright worshippers of the one true God are also richly

62. Q. Caecilius Metellus Macedonicus, conqueror of Macedonia in 148 B.C.

63. When Sulla marched on Rome in 89 B.C. Marius took refuge in the marshes of Minturnae, but was captured. Marica is identified with Venus, or Diana, or even Circe.

blest, in spite of the demons. Nor should we suppose that those unclean spirits are to be propitiated or feared on account of those earthly goods or evils, because they, like bad men in the world, cannot do all they wish, but only as much as is allowed by the ordinance of him whose decisions no one can fully understand, and which no one has the right to criticize.

24. *The acts of Sulla, in which the demons showed themselves his supporters*

The state of things under Sulla was so appalling that the preceding period, which he was thought to have come to redress, seemed desirable by comparison. Yet according to Livy,[64] when he first advanced his army to Rome againt Marius, the entrails at his sacrifice were so favourable that Postumius the soothsayer was prepared to be kept in custody, on pain of death if Sulla did not succeed in his purpose with the help of the gods. Notice that the gods had not yet 'deserted all their shrines and altars' when they foretold the course of events without showing any concern for the moral improvement of Sulla. They promised him great good luck[65] by their presages; but they did not try, by warning threats, to break down his wicked ambitions. Later, when he was at war with Mithridates in Asia, a messenger from Jupiter was sent him by Lucius Titius, promising him victory; and so it turned out. After that, when he was using every effort to return to Rome and avenge the injuries offered to himself and to his friends with the blood of fellow-citizens, another message from Jupiter was brought by a soldier of the Sixth Legion, saying that Jupiter had previously promised him victory over Mithridates, and now promised him the chance to regain control of the country from his enemies, at the price of much bloodshed. Sulla then asked in what shape the vision had appeared, and when the soldier described it, Sulla recalled that it was the same as that described by the bringer of the message about his victory over Mithridates. It might be asked why the gods were so careful to give Sulla news of this supposed good fortune when none of them cared to admonish Sulla and reform him, though he was on the point of doing such terrible harm by a monstrous civil war – which was not only to disgrace but utterly to destroy the com-

64. Liv., 77 (one of the lost books). The story is told in Cic., *De Div.*, 1, 33, 72 and Plut., *Sull.*, 9.

65. Sulla was nicknamed Felix ('Lucky') and he assumed the epithet as a title after his triumph over Mithridates.

monwealth. What answer can be given to that question? It is of course quite clear that devils are intent on their own ends, as I have often said, as we are informed in holy Scripture, and as the facts themselves sufficiently show. Their purpose is to be reckoned and worshipped as gods, so that ceremonies may be offered in their honour which will associate the givers with the receivers in the same hopeless plight at the Judgement of God.

Then again, when Sulla reached Tarentum and sacrificed to Mars, he saw at the top of the calf's liver a shape like a golden crown. On this occasion the soothsayer Postumius interpreted it as a sign of a notable victory and ordered that Sulla alone should eat that part of the entrails. Very soon afterwards the slave of a certain Lucius Pontius cried out in a prophetic rapture, 'I bear a message from Bellona! Sulla, the victory is yours!' He added that the Capitol would be set on fire. After saying this, he left the camp immediately, and returned next day in an even more excited state, and shouted that the Capitol had been set on fire, which had in fact happened;[66] and it was easy for a demon to foresee it and bring the news with the greatest speed.

Notice carefully – and this is most relevant to our case – to what kind of deities those men wish to be subject who blaspheme the Saviour who sets free the wills of the faithful from the domination of devils. The man cried out in prophetic frenzy, 'Sulla, victory is yours!' And to ensure belief that the cry was inspired by a divine spirit, he gave notice of an event which was soon to happen, and which did happen in a place far away from his mouthpiece of the spirit. Yet he did not cry out, 'Sulla, refrain from crimes!' and Sulla committed monstrous crimes there, after he had been shown the golden crown in the calf's liver as an extraordinary sign of victory.

Now if just gods, and not impious devils, had been in the habit of granting such signs, they would surely rather have shown in the entrails the criminal acts which were to come, and which were to bring serious harm to Sulla himself. And that victory increased his glory less than it advanced his ambition to his own hurt; its effect was to remove all restraint from his appetite for conquest. Success turned his head, and his plunge into moral degradation wrought in his own character a more grievous havoc than any he inflicted on the persons of his enemies. This was the really lamentable and depressing prospect; but those gods did not foretell this by entrails or auguries or by anyone's dream or prophecy. They had more to fear from his correction than from his defeat. In fact they took pains to see that the

66. 6 July 83 B.C.

victor over his fellow-citizens should, in his moment of glory, be a captive conquered by unspeakable vices, and should thereby become more closely bound in slavery to their own demonic power.

25. *The evil spirits encourage crime by giving it the authority of their supposedly divine example*

Can anyone fail to see and understand (unless he is one of those who prefer to copy such gods than to be kept free from their society by the grace of God) what efforts these malignant spirits use, to give by their example a presumed divine authority to criminal acts? They were, indeed, seen joining battle among themselves, in a wide plain in Campania, shortly before the citizen armies fought their shameful battle in that very place. For first a terrible din was heard there, and before long many people reported that they had seen two armies fighting for several days. And when the fighting stopped men found what looked like the tracks of men and horses, such as could have been left on the ground as a result of that encounter. Thus a battle among divinities, if it really happened, gives excuse for civil wars between men – and one may notice the malice, or the misery, of gods like these. While if it was a mere pretence of a battle, the only purpose was to gloss over the crime of civil war by giving it a divine precedent. Civil war was already under way, and a number of loathsome battles had already been fought, with frightful bloodshed. Many had been touched by the tale of a soldier who stripped the spoils from one of the slain, and recognized his own brother, when the corpse was bare; moved to abhorrence of such civil strife, he killed himself on the spot, and fell on his brother's lifeless body.[67] To mitigate the disgust caused by such tragedies, and to inflame the ardour for this abominable warfare, the malign devils (whom the Romans thought of as gods, and the proper objects of worship and veneration) decided to show themselves to men as fighting among themselves, so that the natural affection between citizens should not shrink to imitate such battles, but that the gods' example might rather excuse the crimes of men.

With the same astuteness the evil spirits also commanded theatrical shows (I have already said a good deal about this[68]) to be dedicated and consecrated to them, in which the enormities of the gods were celebrated on the stage in song and in acted narrative. A man might believe or disbelieve the actual stories; but he could see that the gods were delighted to have such acts represented, and thus he would feel

67. cf. Liv., *Perioch.*, 79. 68. Bk II, 8ff.

free to imitate them. And so, to prevent the idea that whenever the poets record fighting among the gods they are libelling them by inventing discreditable stories, the gods have themselves given confirmation to the poets' songs, to deceive mankind, by displaying their battles before men's eyes not only in stage-plays but even by enacting them in person on the field of battle.

I have been forced to say this because the Roman writers have no hesitation in saying that the Roman commonwealth had been ruined by moral degradation, and had in fact ceased to exist at all, long before the coming of our Lord Christ Jesus. They did not blame their own gods for this ruin; yet they blame our Lord for the transitory disasters, which cannot bring a good man to extinction, whether he lives or dies. Yet Christ's teaching is full of instructions for the promotion of the highest morality and the reproof of wickedness, while those gods of theirs never took the trouble to impress such commands on their worshippers so as to save that commonwealth from utter ruin – in fact they were more concerned to ensure its ruin by corrupting morality through the baneful authority of their example. I do not suppose that anyone will after this have the face to assert that the commonwealth perished because those gods 'then deserted all the shrines and altars'[69] like friends of virtue, disgusted at the vices of men, since they used their efforts, by all those signs in the shape of entrails, auguries, and prophecies, to boast and commend themselves as foreseers of the future and as assistants in battle, and thus are proved to have been present. If they had absented themselves, the Romans' own ambitions would have fired them with less ardour for civil war than did the prompting of the gods.

26. *The moral instruction allegedly given in secret by demons to devotees, in contrast with the open depravity of their rites*

This, then, is the state of affairs. On certain appointed festivals, scenes of shame, accompanied with cruelty, acts of dishonour and crime, attributed (whether truly or falsely) to the divine beings, were plainly and openly represented, consecrated and dedicated to those gods at their own request and under pain of their displeasure if omitted. These acts were presented before all men's eyes for imitation, and put forward for them to gaze at. Those demons admit that they are unclean by delighting in such things. They avouch themselves as the pro-

69. Virg., *Aen.*, 2, 351.

moters of lives of crime and indecency, by their crimes and misdemeanours, real or pretended, and by the public presentation of them which is demanded from the shameless, and extorted from the modest. How is it then that, as we are told, they give to a select few of their devotees, in their shrines, in secret chambers, some salutary moral instruction? If this is true, it must be observed as a proof of the subtler malignity of these baneful spirits. For such is the power of decency and chastity that it excites the admiration of human nature all but universally, for human nature is never so perverted in its degradation as to lose all feeling for what is honourable. That is why the malignity of these demons cannot fully succeed in its deception without sometimes, as we know from our Bible, 'transforming itself into angels of light'.[70] And so, while in the streets the incessant clamour of indecent impiety rings in the ears of the public, behind closed doors the voice of pretended chastity is only just heard by the chosen few. Full publicity is given where shame would be appropriate; close secrecy is imposed where praise would be in order. Decency is veiled from sight; indecency is exposed to view. Scenes of evil attract packed audiences; good words scarcely find any listeners. It is as if purity should provoke a blush, and corruption give ground for pride. But where else should this happen but in devils' temples, in the resorts of delusion? The object is, by the one device to ensure the capture of the honourable minority, and by the other to prevent the reformation of the corrupt majority.

I do not know where or when the devotees of the Heavenly Virgin[71] heard any counsels of chastity. But we had a good view of her image standing in front of her temple; there were crowds converging from all directions, everyone taking the best position he could find, and we watched the acted shows with the closest interest. We divided our gaze between the procession of harlots on one side, and the virgin goddess on the other. I saw prayerful worship offered to her, and indecent performances enacted before her. I saw no sense of shame in the mimes, no trace of modesty in any actress – all the duly prescribed obscenities were punctiliously performed. It was well known what would please the maiden goddess; and the exhibitions would enable the matron to leave the temple for home enriched by her experiences. Some of the more modest women averted their eyes from the indecent postures of the actors, and yet by furtive glances they made themselves familiar with the techniques of vice. In the company of men they were ashamed to pluck up the courage to observe those

70. 2 Cor. 11, 14. 71. cf. ch. 4, 51.

indecorous gestures with open eyes, but they had still less courage to condemn, in the purity of their hearts, the rites offered to the deity they revered. There was teaching publicly presented at that temple which no one would have put into practice without at least first seeking out a secret room in his house: though a person of human decency (had any such been there) might have been vastly surprised that men should have any reserve in their human misconduct, when they learned of these enormities in a religious setting, and in the presence of gods who would be enraged if men neglected such exhibitions.

There is an evil spirit which drives men's minds to wickedness by a secret compulsion, which goads men on to commit adultery and finds satisfaction when they do so; it is this same evil spirit which rejoices in such rites as these. He it is who erects the images of demons in the temples, who delights in the representation of immorality in those spectacles, and who whispers in secret the words of righteousness to deceive the few decent people, while in public he makes the incitements to corruption freely available, for by these he proposes to get into his clutches the countless multitudes of the depraved.

27. *The obscene performances in propitiation of the gods had a disastrous effect on the moral standards of the republic*

Cicero was a serious-minded man and by way of being a philosopher. When he was entering on the aedileship he shouted out, in the hearing of the whole citizen body, that among the other duties of his office it fell to him to propitiate Mother Flora[72] by the holding of games; and it was usual to measure the devotion of the celebration by the obscenities of the shows. In another context[73] (when he had become consul) he says that in a time of extreme peril[74] to the country, games were put on for ten days, and nothing was omitted which might help to propitiate the gods. As if it were not better to annoy such gods by restraint than to appease them by licentiousness, and to provoke their enmity by decency than to soothe them by such infamy. Whatever the inhuman brutality of the men on whose account the propitiation was offered, the harm they were likely to inflict could not have been more serious than that inflicted by the gods themselves in being propitiated by such disgusting enormities. To ward off the dreaded assaults of the enemy upon their bodies, men tried to win the gods' favour by means which utterly overthrew virtue in their

72. Cic., 2 *Verr.*, 2, 5, 14. Flora was the goddess of crops in flower.
73. *Cat.*, 3, 8. 74. 63 B.C., the conspiracy of Catiline.

minds. For the gods would not drive off those who assailed the walls of Rome from outside unless they themselves first drove out all morality from within the city.

This form of propitiation of such gods as these – with all its lascivious impurity, its shameless, filthy corruption, and its actors whom the Romans, with a laudable, instinctive sense of honour, debarred from all political office and expelled from their tribes, marked as beneath contempt and condemned to outlawry – this disreputable propitiation of these gods, was abominable and detestable in the eyes of true religion. These scandalous and slanderous stories about the gods, those disgraceful actions attributed to them, infamous and outrageous if really committed, still more infamous and outrageous if invented, all those were presented to the eyes and ears of the public for the instruction of the whole community. Men observed that the divine beings take pleasure in such offences, and therefore believed that they should not only be displayed to the gods but also imitated by mankind. They reckoned nothing of that wholesome and decent teaching (whatever it was) which was dispensed (if at all) so secretly and to so few as to suggest a fear that it should become more known, not that it should fail to be practised.

28. *The wholesomeness of the Christian religion*

Men have been rescued, through the name of Christ, from the hellish yoke of those polluted powers and from a share in their condemnation; they have passed from the night of blasphemy and perdition into the daylight of salvation and true godliness. This fact evokes complaints and murmurs from the malicious and spiteful who are held tight in the close grip of that wicked fiend. They resent the streams of people who gather in the church in a modest assembly, where there is a decent separation of the sexes, where they can hear how they ought to live a good life on earth for a space, so that they may deserve hereafter to live a life of bliss for ever, and where the words of holy Scripture and of the teaching of righteousness are read aloud from a raised position[75] in the sight of all; those who observe the teaching hear it for their profit, and those who do not, for their condemnation. And though some come there to scoff at these instructions, all their insolence is either abandoned in a sudden change of heart, or at least suppressed by fear or shame. For nothing degrading

75. The Scriptures were read from the *ambo*, a raised platform in the Christian basilica.

or disreputable is set before them for contemplation or imitation; but there the commandments of the true God are made known, his marvellous works are related, thanks are offered for his gifts, and prayers are sent up for his favours.

29. *An exhortation to the Romans to abandon the worship of the gods*

All this should be the object of your chief desire, you people of Rome, with all your fine natural qualities, your descendants of men like Regulus, Scaevola, the Scipios, and Fabricius.[76] Observe how different all this is from the degraded folly and the malignant imposture of the demons. The admirable and excellent qualities which nature has bestowed on you can only come to purity and perfection through true godliness; ungodliness will bring them to ruin and punishment. Choose now which course to follow, so that you may receive men's praise without illusion, not for what you are in yourself but in the true God. In former times you had glory from the peoples, but, through the inscrutable decision of divine providence, the true religion was not there for you to choose. Awake! The day has come. You have already awakened in the persons of some of your people, in whose perfect virtue we Christians boast, and even in their sufferings for the true faith; they have wrestled everywhere against hostile powers, have conquered them by the courage of their deaths, and 'have won this country for us by their blood'.[77]

It is to this country that we invite you, and exhort you to add yourself to the number of our citizens. The refuge[78] we offer is the true remission of sins. Do not listen to those degenerate sons of yours who disparage Christ and the Christians, and criticize these times as an unhappy age, when the kind of period they would like is one which offers not a life of tranquility but security for their vicious pursuits. Such satisfactions have never been enough for you, even in respect of your earthly country. Now take possession of the Heavenly Country, for which you will have to endure but little hardship; and you will

76. On Regulus cf. Bk I, 15. C. Mucius Scaevola, when captured whilst attempting to kill Lars Porsenna, thrust his arm into the fire to show his contempt of death. (Liv. 2, 12). cf Bk. V, 18. Scipio Africanus Major was the victor in the Second Punic War; Scipio Africanus Minor destroyed Carthage in 146 B.C.; on Scipio Nasica and his son cf. Bk I, 30, 31. C. Luscinius Fabricius resisted the bribes of Pyrrhus in 280 B.C., and later revealed to Pyrrhus the proposal of the king's doctor to poison his master (Plut. Pyrrh, 29; Vol. Max., 2, 9, 4).

77. Virg., *Aen.*, 11, 24f.

78. cf. Bk I, 34.

reign there in truth and for ever. There you will find no Vestal hearth, no Capitoline stone,[79] but the one true God, who

> Fixes no bounds for you of space or time
> But will bestow an empire without end.[80]

You must not regret the loss of those false and deceitful gods; abandon them in contempt and spring out to genuine liberty. They are not gods, but malignant fiends, and your eternal felicity is their eternal punishment. It seems that Juno did not grudge the Trojans (from whom you derive by physical descent) their possession of the Roman citadel as much as those demons (whom up to now you have reckoned gods) grudge the human race their everlasting abode. You yourself, to a great degree, have passed judgement on such fiends, in that you have appeased them with games and decided to treat the performers in those shows as outlaws. Allow us to assert your freedom against those unclean spirits who imposed upon you, like a yoke on your neck, the duty of sanctifying and celebrating their own shame. You shut out the actors of those divine scandals from all political office; pray to the true God that he will shut out those gods who delight in their own scandals, shameful, if they are true, malicious, if they are false. You acted rightly when of your own accord you refused to allow actors and players a share in the rights of citizenship. Now become fully awake! It is impossible for the divine majesty to be propitiated by arts which cast a stain on human dignity. How can you think that gods who delight in such observances can be ranked among the holy powers of heaven, when you have decided that men who perform those ceremonies are not to be ranked as Roman citizens of any kind? The Heavenly City outshines Rome, beyond comparison. There, instead of victory, is truth; instead of high rank, holiness; instead of peace, felicity; instead of life, eternity. If you blushed to have such men as partners in your city, how could the Heavenly City admit such gods? Gods who are appeased through the performances of rogues have no right to be worshipped by honourable men. Let those gods be removed from your religion by a Christian purge, as those actors were removed from your honours by the censors' ban.

As for material satisfactions (which are all that the wicked desire to

79. The sacred fire of Vesta, goddess of the hearth, was kept perpetually burning on the altar in the temple of Vesta, tended by Vestal Virgins, and renewed at the start of each year (1 March).

The Capitoline stone was the primitive statue of Jupiter on the Capitol, called the 'Jupiter stone' (*Jupiter lapis*).

80. Virg., *Aen.*, 1, 278f.

enjoy) and material ills (which are all that they wish to avoid) those demons have not the power over these which they are thought to have – although if they had, we ought rather to despise those things than to worship the demons for their sake and, by worshipping them, to be unable to reach those blessings which they grudge us. Still, even in these things they have not the power ascribed to them by those who maintain that they should be worshipped for the sake of material benefits. This we shall see to be true in our discussion. So here we may bring this book to its close.

BOOK III

1. *The adversities that are the only dread of the wicked; the world always suffered them although it worshipped the gods*

I THINK I have now said enough about the evils which affect the character and the mind. We need to be especially on our guard against those, and I have said that the false gods had no concern to help their worshipping people to avoid being overwhelmed by their weight – rather they tried to increase this oppression as much as possible.

It is clear to me that I must now treat of those ills which are the only disasters which our adversaries dread; such things as famine, disease, war, spoliation, captivity, massacre and the like, which we have already mentioned in the first book. The only things which evil men count as evil are those which do not make men evil; and they are not ashamed that when surrounded by the 'good things' which they approve, they themselves are evil, who approve those 'goods'; and they are more disgusted by a bad house than by a bad life, as if man's highest good was to have all his possessions good – except himself.

Now those gods of theirs, when they received their unstinted adoration, never averted from them the only evils they dreaded. At different periods and in different places, before the coming of our Redeemer, the human race was oppressed by innumerable disasters, often of incredible gravity. And at that time did the world worship any other gods than those? Except, that is, for one people, the Hebrews, and some few outside that nation, wherever, by the inscrutable and most just decision of God, men were found worthy of divine grace. However, to keep my account within reasonable bounds, I will say nothing of the grievous disasters inflicted on other nations all over the world. I shall confine myself to what concerns Rome and its Empire, that is, to the city itself and its allied and subject countries, and the disasters they suffered before the coming of Christ, at a time when they formed as it were part of the body of the Roman republic.

2. *Had the gods, worshipped alike by Greeks and Romans, any reason for allowing the destruction of Ilium?*

To begin with, why was Troy (or Ilium), the source of the Roman people, conquered, captured and destroyed by the Greeks, when it possessed and worshipped the same gods as the Greeks? I have touched on this point in my first book,[1] but I must not pass it over or suppress it. 'Priam', they say, 'paid the penalty for the perjury of Laomedon, his father.'[2] It is true, then, that Apollo and Neptune were Laomedon's hired labourers?[3] For the tale is that he broke his sworn promise to pay their wages. I am astonished that Apollo, entitled 'The Foreseer', should have worked so hard on the job, in ignorance that Laomedon was going to back out of his undertaking. Apart from that, it was odd that his uncle Neptune, Jupiter's brother, the Lord of the sea, should not have known what was going to happen. For Homer, a poet who is said to have lived before the foundation of Rome, ascribes to Neptune a notable prophecy[4] about the line of Aeneas, whose descendants founded Rome. Homer tells how Neptune carried off Aeneas in a cloud, to save him from death at the hands of Achilles though (as he admits in Virgil's poem) he himself

> Was fain to batter down the ramparts
> Reared by his hands, of faithless, perjured Troy.[5]

Thus those great gods, Apollo and Neptune, did not know that Laomedon would refuse to pay. They built the walls of Troy and received neither gratuity nor gratitude. It is up to them to decide whether it is not more risky to believe in such gods than to let them down! Homer himself did not find it easy to credit this tale, since he represents Neptune as fighting against the Trojans while Apollo supports them, whereas, the story goes, they were both wronged by that breach of contract.

If our opponents believe the stories, they should blush to worship such divinities as those; if they disbelieve them, then they should not put forward the Trojan perjury as an explanation, or be astonished

1. Bk 1, 3; 4. 2. cf. Virg., *Aen.*, 4, 542; *Georg.*, 1, 502.
3. Zeus compelled Apollo and Poseidon to help Laomedon, Priam's father, in the building of Troy. When the work was finished, Laomedon refused to pay their wages, and Homer ascribes the destruction of Troy to Laomedon's breach of faith (*Il.*, 21, 441–60; cf. Hor., *Carm.* 4, 3, 18–24).
4. *Il.*, 20, 293–329. 5. *Aen.*, 5, 810f.

that the gods punished Trojan bad faith, while approving Roman perjury. For how is it that Catiline's conspiracy found in that great and corrupt city such an abundant supply of men 'who supported life by their tongues and their strong right arms, by perjury and bloodshed'?[6] Perjury, and nothing else, was the offence of the senators who were so often bribed to give their votes, or their verdicts in cases tried before their assemblies. For in the utter corruption of morality, the reason why the traditional custom of the oath was kept up was not to stop men from crime by religious fear, but to add perjury to those other misdemeanours.

3. *The gods could not have been offended at the adultery of Paris; according to the stories, adultery was common amongst the gods*

There is then no reason why the gods who are said to have maintained that empire,[7] should be represented as angry with the perjured Trojans when, as it turned out, they were conquered by the Greeks. It was not that (as some urge in their defence[8]) they were so incensed at the adultery of Paris as to abandon Troy; it is their general practice to be suggesters and counsellors of crime, not its avengers. 'The city of Rome', says Sallust, 'was first founded and inhabited, according to tradition, by Trojan refugees who were wandering with no fixed abode under the leadership of Aeneas.'[9] If the gods judged the adultery of Paris as deserving vengeance, then the Romans deserved to be punished more, or at least equally, seeing that Aeneas's mother was an adulteress. How was it then that in the case of Paris the gods hated the sin, but did not hate it in the case of their colleague Venus (not to mention others), when she sinned with Anchises and gave birth to Aeneas? Was it because Menelaus was indignant, but Vulcan complaisant? The gods, we are to suppose, are not jealous of their wives; so they are even content to share them with human beings!

Perhaps I may be thought to be laughing at those fables, and not treating so weighty a matter with proper seriousness. All right, then, let us stop believing that Aeneas was son of Venus. Very good; and, by the same token, Romulus was not the son of Mars. Why make one concession and not the other? Is it allowed for gods to have inter-

6. Sall., *Cat.*, 14. 7. Virg., *Aen.*, 2, 352. 8. Virg., *Aen.*, 2, 601ff.

9. *Cat.*, 6, 1. The tradition that Aeneas was the immediate founder of Rome is followed also by Naevius and Ennius.

course with women, but forbidden for men to mate with goddesses? This would be a harsh or rather an incredible condition, if Mars was permitted by the law of Venus a licence in love forbidden to Venus under her own law. But both stories are guaranteed by the authority of Roman tradition; and in modern times Caesar was as convinced that Venus was his ancestress as Romulus was certain that Mars was his father.

4. *Varro's opinion, that the fiction of divine descent has its uses*

Someone will ask, 'Do you yourself believe those tales?' No, I certainly do not believe them; and Varro, the most learned of the Romans,[10] almost admits their falsity, though timidly and diffidently. But he asserts that it is an advantage to communities that brave men should believe themselves to be sons of gods, even if it is not true. By this means the spirit of man, in the confidence of presumed divine descent, may be bolder in undertaking mighty enterprises, and more energetic in action, and so achieve greater success by reason of that sense of security. I have reproduced Varro's opinion in my own words, as faithfully as I can; and you notice what a wide field it offers to falsehood. This may help us to realize that many more ostensibly religious rites may have been invented in cases where lies about the gods were thought to bring advantage to the citizens.

5. *That the gods punished the adultery of Paris is improbable, since they did not punish that crime in the case of Romulus' mother*

Let us leave undecided the question whether Venus could have given birth to Aeneas after a liaison with Anchises, or Mars have become father to Romulus after an amour with Numitor's daughter. For a somewhat similar question arises from our Scriptures, where the question is whether the delinquent angels actually had intercourse with the daughters of men[11] and produced the giants – the men of great

10. M. *Terentius Varro* (116–27 B.C.): polymath and voluminous author. Of his seventy-four works in over 600 volumes only the three books on farming (*De Re Rustica*), six out of twenty-five on Latin grammar (*De Lingua Latina*) and about 600 lines of his 'Menippean Satires' survive. His great antiquarian work, the 'Antiquities', was divided into twenty-five books on 'Human Affairs' and sixteen on 'Divine Affairs'. St Augustine also has references in the *City of God* to his *De Cultu Deorum, De Gente Populi Romani,* and *De Philosophia.*

11. Gen. 6, 4.

stature and strength, who filled the earth at that period. For the present, our discussion must be confined to this dilemma. If the often-read stories about the mother of Aeneas and the father of Romulus are true, how can the gods object to men's adulteries, which they tolerate among themselves with equanimity? If they are untrue, even then the gods cannot be outraged by human adultery, seeing that they delight in false stories about their own. There is the further point that if the story about Mars is not credited and in consequence the tale about Venus is disbelieved, then the mother of Romulus cannot be defended by the plea that her liaison was with a god. Now Rhea was a priestess of Vesta, and for that reason the gods were more bound to avenge that sacrilegious sin on the Romans than they were to punish the Trojans for the adultery of Paris. For in antiquity when Vestal priestesses were caught in sexual offences the Romans used to bury them alive; as for adulterous women, they did indeed condemn them to some punishment, but they did not put them to death. For their vengeance for the profanation of their supposed divine sanctuaries was so much more severe than that for the pollution of the human marriage-bed.

6. *The gods did not avenge the fratricide of Romulus*

Yet another point: if those divinities were so indignant at men's sins, that they abandoned Troy and handed it over to fire and the sword in outrage at the action of Paris, then Romulus' murder of his brother should have stirred them more against the Romans than the fooling of a husband moved them against the Trojans. Fratricide in a community just coming into being should have troubled them more than adultery in an established kingdom. It is not relevant to our present argument whether the crime was committed at Romulus' bidding, or by his own hands. The latter possibility many brazenly deny, many honourably doubt, many sorrowfully refuse to admit. We need not waste time in minute examination of the question, carefully weighing the evidence of all the historians. One thing is agreed; the brother of Romulus was murdered, and not by enemies or strangers. Whether Romulus perpetrated or ordered this crime, he was much more the chief man of the Romans than Paris was of the Trojans. Why then did the ravisher of another's wife call down the wrath of gods upon the Trojans, while the murder of a brother attracted their protection for the Romans?[12]

12. Pagan moralists were unhappy about the story. cf. Cic., *De Off.*, 3, 40; Liv., 1, 67; Hor., *Epod.*, 7, 17f.

On the other hand, if Romulus had no part either in the committing or the ordering of the crime, it certainly should have been avenged, and therefore the whole community was guilty, because the whole community took no heed of it. And that was worse than fratricide; it was patricide. The pair were joint-founders, and the one who was put away by this crime was deprived of his right to be a ruler. There is, in my judgement, no way of showing why Troy deserved so ill that the gods abandoned her to destruction or why Rome deserved so well that the gods dwelt in her to promote her increase – unless perhaps the conquered gods escaped from Troy and took refuge with the Romans, to delude them in the same way? More likely they stayed behind to deceive in their usual manner those who afterwards settled in that country, while in Rome they practised those same techniques of deception on an even larger scale, and thus rejoiced in winning greater honours.

7. *The destruction of Troy by Fimbria, general of Marius*

However that may be, what crime had poor Ilium committed that, when the civil wars were raging, she should be destroyed by Fimbria,[13] the lowest scoundrel of the Marian party, with greater savagery and ruthlessness than she had suffered from the Greeks? For on that earlier occasion many escaped from Troy, and many were taken captive and at least preserved their lives, though in slavery. Whereas Fimbria first issued an edict that no one should be spared, and then set fire to the city and reduced the whole of it to ashes, with all its inhabitants. And Ilium won this treatment not from the Greeks whom she had provoked by her wrong-doing, but from the Romans, whom she had propagated as a result of her first disaster. While the gods whom she shared with Rome gave her no help to repel this calamity – or rather, to tell the truth, had not the power to help. Are we to say that, at this time also,

> The shrines and altars were left deserted
> By all the gods.[14]

the gods by whose favour the city had stood when rebuilt after its burning and destruction by the Greeks?

If they had withdrawn, I look into the cause; and the more merit I

13. C. *Flavius Fimbria*: a partisan of Marius in the civil war against Sulla. After Marius' death in 86 B.C. Fimbria commanded in Asia. He took Troy; but his troops mutinied, and he committed suicide in 84 B.C.

14. Virg., *Aen.*, 2, 351f.

find in the case for the townspeople, the lower the value I place on the case for the gods. For the townsfolk had shut their gates against Fimbria, so that they might keep the city intact for Sulla. It was Fimbria's anger at this that made him set fire to the city, or rather to extinguish it utterly. Up to that time Sulla had been the leader of the better of the warring factions, and so far he had been striving to restore the commonwealth by force of arms. Those good beginnings had not yet led to their disastrous consequences. So what better course could the citizens of Troy have taken, what course more honourable, more loyal, more worthy of their Roman parenthood, than to preserve their city for the better of the Roman sides and to shut their gates against the murderer of the Roman commonwealth?

But let the defenders of the gods observe how this action turned into disaster for them. The gods may have deserted the adulterers and abandoned Ilium to the flames of the Greeks, so that a purer Rome might be born from its ashes. Why did they afterwards desert that same city, so closely related to the Romans, which was not in revolt against Rome, her illustrious daughter, but was keeping unswerving and loyal faith with the party which had more justice on its side? Why did the gods abandon that city to destruction, not by Greek heroes but by the most despicable villain in Rome? Or if the gods disapproved of the cause of the party of Sulla (for those unfortunate people closed their gates to preserve the city for that side) why did they promise and foretell such good fortune for that same Sulla? Are they not here revealed as flatterers of the lucky, rather than defenders of the unfortunate?

Not even at this time was it true that Ilium was overthrown because the gods deserted her. The demons, always on the watch for a chance to deceive, did as much as they could. For when all the images were overthrown and burnt, in the destruction of the town itself, only the image of Minerva, writes Livy,[15] is said to have still stood unharmed when her temple fell in total ruin. This happened, not so that these lines could be quoted in praise of the gods:

> Gods of our fathers, whose divine protection
> Shelters great Troy,[16]

but to prevent the quotation of these words in their defence:

> The shrines and altars now were left deserted
> By all the gods.[17]

15. Liv., *Perioch.*, 83. 16. Virg., *Aen.*, 9, 247. 17. *Aen.*, 2, 351f.

For what was granted to those gods was not the ability to prove their power, but to give evidence of their presence.

8. *Should Rome have been entrusted to the gods of Troy?*

Was it really prudent to entrust the defence of Rome to the gods of Ilium, after the lesson provided by the fate of Troy itself? Perhaps I may be told that when Ilium fell to the assault of Fimbria the gods had long been settled as residents of Rome? How is it then that Minerva's image still stood? Then again, if the gods were at Rome when Fimbria destroyed Ilium, perhaps they were at Ilium when the Gauls took Rome and burned it? But so quick is their hearing and so swift their speed that they returned in a hurry at the goose's cry, so that at least they could protect the Capitol hill, which remained in Roman hands. But they received the warning to return too late to defend the rest of the city.

9. *Is the peace of Numa's reign to be credited to the gods?*

It is believed that the gods assisted Numa Pompilius, who succeeded Romulus, so that he enjoyed peace for the whole of his reign and shut the gates of Janus, which are by custom kept open in time of war. I suppose he earned this good fortune by the institution of many religious rites among the Romans.

It would be right to congratulate this person on that long period of tranquillity if he had been wise enough to employ it in salutary activities and to abandon his mischievous superstition for the quest of the true God in the spirit of true godliness. In reality, it was not those gods who granted him this tranquillity; but they would perhaps have deceived him less if they had found him less at leisure. For the less occupied they found him, the more they occupied his thoughts. Varro reveals the kind of activities he engaged in, and the techniques by which he tried to bring the gods into alliance with himself and with his city. We shall discuss this more fully in another place, if the Lord so wills. Our present topic is simply the benefits conferred by the gods.

Peace is a great benefit, but it is a benefit bestowed by the true God, often, like the sun, the rain, and other supports of life, bestowed upon the ungrateful and the worthless. But if the gods bestowed this great benefit on Rome or on Pompilius, why did they never grant it to the Roman Empire afterwards, even in its praiseworthy periods? Were the sacred rites more valuable when they were being established than when, after their establishment, they were still performed? And yet, in Numa's time these rites were not in existence. Numa brought them into the Roman religion, and so they began to exist. When they existed they were carefully preserved for the good of the community. How is it then that forty-three years (some authorities say thirty-nine) passed in that long peace of Numa's reign, while afterwards, when the rites had been established and the gods themselves, whose presence had been solicited by those rites, were now the protectors and guardians of the city, not more than one year[18] has been recorded, in all that time from the foundation of the city to the reign of Augustus, in which the Romans were able to close the Gates of War. And that was recorded as a notable miracle!

10. *Rome could have been secure and tranquil, pursuing the aims of Numa. Was it desirable that Rome's dominion should be increased by the mad pursuit of war?*

Are our opponents going to reply that the Roman Empire could not have been increased so far and wide, and Roman glory could not have spread, except by continual wars, following one upon another? What a satisfying explanation! Why must an empire be deprived of peace, in order that it may be great? In regard to men's bodies it is surely better to be of moderate size, and to be healthy, than to reach the immense stature of a giant at the cost of unending disorders – not to rest when that stature is reached, but to be troubled with greater disorders with the increasing size of the limbs. Would any evil have resulted, would not, in fact, the result have been wholly good, if that first era had persisted? Here is Sallust's brief description of those times:

> At the beginning of history the name of kings was given to the first wielders of power. Those kings differed in their inclinations: some exercised their mental powers, others their physical abilities. At that time men's life was lived without greed, and each man was content with what he had.

Was it necessary that, for the aggrandizement of empire, we should have the process deplored by Virgil, when he says,

> By slow degrees, as age succeeded age
> Life lost its beauty, and its worth declined,

18. 235 B.C. The First Punic War ended in 241. The gates of this temple of Janus, only closed in time of peace, were not shut again till after the battle of Actium in 31 B.C.

As war's fierce madness and the lust for gain
Possessed men's hearts.[19]

Now obviously the Romans had a just excuse for undertaking and carrying on those great wars. When they were subjected to unprovoked attacks by their enemies, they were forced to resist not by lust for glory in men's eyes but by the necessity to defend their life and liberty. We grant that; for, as Sallust says,

As soon as their power advanced, thanks to their laws, their moral standards, and the increase of their territory, and they were observed to be very flourishing and very powerful, then, as generally happens in human history, prosperity gave rise to envy. Neighbouring kings and people therefore made trial of them in war: only a few of their friends came to their help: the rest, paralysed with fear, kept well out of danger. But the Romans, alert both in peace and war, acted with energy, made their preparations, gave mutual encouragement, advanced to meet the enemy, and with their arms defended their liberty, their country, their parents. Then, when they had by their courage dispersed those perils, they brought help to their friends, and won friendship rather by rendering services than by receiving them.

That Rome grew great by such conduct was nothing to be ashamed of. But what was the cause of that long period of peace in Numa's reign? Was Rome being assailed by hostile attacks from her malignant enemies, when Numa came to the throne? Or was nothing of this kind happening, so that a long continuance of peace was possible? If Rome was at the time being harassed by invasions, and did not rush to oppose them by force of arms, the policy by which her foes were pacified without being defeated in battle or over-awed by any warlike initiative should have been Rome's perpetual policy; and then she would have reigned in unbroken peace and the gates of Janus would have remained closed.

If that was not possible for her it means that Rome enjoyed peace not for so long as her gods wished, but for so long as the neighbouring peoples wished, who surrounded her on all sides, and granted peace to Rome when they did not provoke her by attacking. Unless, perhaps, such gods will have the effrontery to offer for sale to men something that depends on other men's choice or refusal! The concern of their natural malignity is indeed to work on the evil dispositions of men, as far as scope is given them, by means of fear or of encouragement. But if they could always achieve their purpose, and were never thwarted by a more secret and superior power working against their designs, then peace and victory in war would always be under their control,

19. *Aen.*, 8, 326ff.

though the immediate cause of them almost always rests with the passions of human beings. Yet these things generally happen against the will of the gods, as is witnessed not only by legends (which are full of lies and give scarcely any information or hint of the truth) but by the actual history of Rome.

11. *The tears of Apollo's statue at Cumae, a portent of disaster for the Greeks*

This, and nothing else, was the reason why the famous Apollo of Cumae, as was reported, wept for four days on end,[20] during the war against the Achaeans and King Aristonicus.[21] The soothsayers were terrified by this portent and considered that the statue should be hurled in the sea. But the elders of Cumae intervened and related that a similar portent had been displayed in the same work of art during the wars with Antiochus and Perseus.[22] And they asserted that because that war had gone in Rome's favour a decree of the senate had ordered the dispatch of gifts to that Apollo of theirs. Then reputedly more accomplished soothsayers were summoned, and they gave their opinion that the weeping of Apollo was of good augury for the Romans, because Cumae was a Greek colony and the tears of Apollo signified grief and disaster for the country from which he had been brought, namely Greece itself. Soon afterwards came the news of the defeat and capture of Antiochus, a defeat which Apollo did not want and which caused him grief, as he showed by the tears shed by his image of stone.

The descriptions of the behaviour of the demons given by poets in their verses, though legendary, are not utterly incongruous; they have a semblance of truth. Thus in Virgil, Diana mourns Camilla, and Hercules weeps for Pallas as he goes to his death.[23] Hence it may be

20. Jul. Obs. *Prod.*, 87; Cic., *De Div.*, 1, 43, 98.

21. Liv., 43, 13.

22. St Augustine seems to have confused the war against the Achaean League, which ended with the capture of Corinth in 146 B.C., and that against Aristonicus of Pergamum, who tried to prevent the bequest, by his brother Eumenes, of the kingdom of Pergamum to the Roman people. Aristonicus was captured and executed in 129 B.C.

Antiochus III ('the Great'), king of Syria, came into conflict with Rome because of his activities in Asia Minor and Greece. He was defeated by Scipio Africanus Major in 190 B.C.

Perseus (or Perses), king of Macedonia, was defeated by Aemilius Paullus at Pydna in 168 B.C.

23. *Aen.*, 11, 836ff; 10, 464f.

that when Numa Pompilius was enjoying abundance of peace, without knowing or discovering to whom he owed it, he may have asked himself, in that time of tranquillity, to which gods he should entrust the safety of the Roman realm. The idea that the true, omnipotent and supreme God was concerned for the affairs of earth perhaps never entered his head; and he recalled that the Trojan gods which Aeneas had brought had not been able to preserve for long either the Trojan kingdom, or the kingdom of Lavinium founded by Aeneas himself. So he decided that other gods must be provided, to be attached to the earlier gods, who had passed over to Rome with Romulus or who were going to pass over later, after the fall of Alba, and that they should act as protectors of those refugees, or as assistants to those weaklings.

12. *The many gods added to Numa's establishment; but to no profit*

For all that, Rome disdained to content herself with the many religious institutions established by Pompilius. She had not as yet the chief temple of Jupiter; it was King Tarquin who constructed the Capitol.[24] Aesculapius came from Epidaurus[25] to solicit custom in Rome, so as to practise his profession there and to enhance his reputation by ranking as the most accomplished physician in the world's most famous city. The Mother of the Gods came from Pessinus,[26] wherever that may be; it was improper that she should be still living in some obscure retreat when her son was already presiding over the Capitoline hill. But then, if she really is the Mother of all the Gods, she not only followed some of her sons to Rome, but preceded others who were to follow her! I am truly astonished that she should have given birth to Cynocephalus, who came from Egypt so long afterwards! Whether she was the mother of the goddess Febris[27] I leave to her great-grandson Aesculapius to decide! But, whatever her birth, I do not imagine that those immigrant gods will have the insolence to despise, as low-born, a citizen goddess of Rome! Under the protection of all these gods – an innumerable multitude, indigenous and foreign, celestial and terrestrial, gods of the underworld and gods of the sea, of the springs and of the rivers, gods, according to Varro, 'certain and uncertain',[28] and, in all classes, gods distinguished, like animals, as

24. The temple of Jupiter Capitolinus. Liv., 10, 47, 7
25. 293 B.C. (Liv., 10, 47). 26. cf. Bk I, 30.
27. On Cynocephalus and Febris cf. Bk II, 14. 28. cf. Bk VII, 17.

male and female – under the protection of all these Rome should not have been troubled and afflicted by all those immense and terrible disasters, of which I shall mention only a few.

Rome had collected for her protection far too many gods, summoning them, as it were, at a given signal by the immense volume of smoke of the sacrifices. By establishing for them a supply of temples, altars, sacrifices and priests she was bound to offend the true supreme God, to whom alone those honours are rightly due. She had greater happiness when she lived with a smaller number. But it seemed that she needed a larger supply when she grew greater, as a larger ship needs a larger crew. I suppose she felt no confidence that those few gods, under whom she had enjoyed a better life (though storing up for herself a worse future), would suffice to support her increasing grandeur.

To begin with, even under the kings, except for the reign of Numa Pompilius, of whom I have already spoken, there was all the misery occasioned by the bitterness of rivalry – the rivalry which caused the murder of the brother of Romulus!

13. *How the Romans obtained their first rights of marriages*

How was it that neither Juno, who, with her husband Jupiter,

> Fostered the Romans, Lords of all the earth,
> The people of the toga,[29]

nor Venus herself was able to help the sons of Aeneas to win for themselves the rights of marriage in descent and proper form? The lack of wives issued in dire calamity. The Romans abducted their brides by means of a ruse, and soon were forced to fight with their fathers-in-law. So the unfortunate women, before they had been reconciled to their husbands after the outrage, received a dowry in their fathers' blood. True, the Romans were victorious in this encounter with their neighbours. But how much suffering, on both sides, how many deaths of such near relations and neighbours, paid the price of victory! (It was on account of one father-in-law, Caesar, and his one son-in-law, Pompey, that, on the death of Pompey's wife, Caesar's daughter,[30] Lucan was prompted by deep and justified grief to cry

> Civil war, spreading to Emathia's plains,
> And crime which claims the specious name of right,
> These form my song.[31])

29. Virg., *Aen.*, 1, 281f.
30. Julia, m. Pompey 59 B.C., d. 54.
31. *Phars.*, 1, 1f.

So the Romans were victorious, and with their hands stained with the fathers' blood they forced their embraces on the luckless daughters. The wives dared not weep for slaughtered fathers, for fear of offending victorious husbands; and while the fight was going on they did not know for whom they should offer their prayers.

It was not Venus, but Bellona, who gave the Romans marriages of this kind. Or it may be that Allecto,[32] that fury from hell, was allowed greater scope against them than when she had been aroused against Aeneas at Juno's entreaty – in spite of the fact that Juno by now was on their side. Andromache was more happy in her captivity than those Roman brides at their wedding. It is true that she suffered the embraces of Pyrrhus as his slave; but Pyrrhus afterwards did not kill any of the Trojans, whereas the Romans killed in battle the fathers of those whom they had embraced in the marriage-chamber. Andromache could only bewail the death of her dear ones; she no longer had to fear it, when she submitted to the conqueror. The Sabine women, linked as they were to the combatants, dreaded their fathers' death when their husbands left home, and mourned it when they returned, nor could they give free rein either to fear or grief. Either they suffered the torture of loyal grief at the death of their fellow-countrymen, their fathers and brothers, or they brutally rejoiced in the victory of their husbands. Furthermore, in the changes and chances of war some of them lost their husbands to the swords of their parents, some lost parents and husbands to the swords of either side.

It was no ordinary crisis that faced the Romans; they had to endure a siege, and protect themselves by closing the gates of the city. Those gates were opened by a trick; the enemy were admitted within the walls, and a battle of inhuman ferocity was joined in the forum between sons-in-law and fathers-in-law. The ravishers were actually being overcome; many of them fled to their own houses, thus sullying their previous victories, shameful and lamentable though they had been. At this point Romulus, losing all faith in the courage of his followers, called upon Jupiter to arrest the flight; and it was on this occasion that Jupiter was given the title of Stator[33] (the 'Stayer'). There would have been no end to the scene of horror, had not the ravished brides rushed out, tearing their hair, and, throwing themselves at their parents' feet, assuaged their righteous indignation not by victorious arms but by dutiful supplication. After that, Romulus was constrained to accept Titus Tatius, the Sabine king, as a partner in the Roman kingship, though he had refused to accept his own brother as a colleague.

32. cf. Virg., *Aen.*, 7, 323ff. 33. cf. Liv., 1, 12.

But how could he have put up with him for any length of time, if he could not tolerate his own brother? Hence when Tatius had been killed, Romulus held the kingship alone, so that he might become a greater god.

Strange marriage-rites, strange causes of war, strange conditions of fraternity, of affinity, of alliance, and of divinity! In short, what a strange sort of life in a city under the protection of so many gods! You see how much of importance could be said on this topic, were it not that my attention must now be directed to further questions, and that I hasten to engage in discussion on other subjects.

14. *The impiety of the war against Alba; the victory gained by lust for dominion*

What happened after Numa, in the succeeding reigns? The Albans were provoked to war, with great disaster to the Romans, as well as to Alba. No doubt they had come to undervalue the long peace of Numa's reign. There was wholesale massacre of Roman and Alban armies, and a shrinkage of both populations. Alba, the creation of Ascanius, son of Aeneas, more truly Rome's mother than Troy, was provoked to war by Tullus Hostilius, and in the ensuing conflict she inflicted and suffered heavy blows until most men were weary of a struggle which caused equal loss to both sides. Then they decided to settle the issue of the war by a combat between triplet brothers from either side. From the Roman side the three Horatii came out to battle, from the Alban side, the three Curiatii. Two of the Horatii were defeated and slain by the Curiatii, who in their turn were wiped out by the surviving Horatius. So Rome emerged as victor in that final combat – but at such disastrous cost, since only one out of six returned home. And who suffered the loss, who felt the grief, on the two sides? Who but the race of Aeneas, the descendants of Ascanius, the offspring of Venus, the grandsons of Jupiter? For here also was a case of 'civil' war spreading to something even worse,[34] when a daughter-state fought with her mother.

And there was a fearful horror to crown this battle between triplets. The two peoples had been friendly, seeing that they were both neighbours and relations; thus the sister of the Horatii had been betrothed to one of the Curiatii. When she noticed that her victorious brother was carrying the spoils taken from her betrothed, she burst into tears; and for that, he killed her. In my view this one woman had

34. cf. Luc., *Phars.*, 1, 1.

more human feeling than the whole population of Rome. She grieved for the man to whom she kept her plighted troth; maybe she also grieved for the brother who had slain the man to whom he had promised his sister. It seems to me that she was not to be blamed for her tears.

In Virgil, the 'pious Aeneas' laments over an enemy whom he destroyed by his own hand,[35] and he is to be praised for mourning. Did not Marcellus mourn with tears for the city of Syracuse,[36] when he recalled that all its pride and glory had recently fallen into sudden ruin at his hands, a thought which led him to contemplate the common condition of humanity? Surely we may demand from human feeling that it should not be thought a crime in a woman if she weeps for a betrothed whom her brother has slain, when men are praised for weeping over enemies whom they themselves have vanquished? Yet at the very time when that woman was weeping for her lover's death at the hand of her brother, Rome was rejoicing that after fighting against her mother-city with so much slaughter, she had conquered at the price of so much shedding of kindred blood, on each side.

What use is it to give as an excuse the splendid titles of 'honour' and 'victory'? Take away the screens of such senseless notions and let the crimes be seen, weighed, and judged in all their nakedness. Let the case against Alba be put, just as the crime of adultery was alleged against Troy. There is no parallel, no comparison between them. The only purpose of Tullus was

> To stir to battle his inactive folk
> And armies long with triumph unacquainted.[37]

So through that misguided design the monstrous crime of a war between allies and within families was perpetrated. Sallust glances in passing at this false step. After his brief and complimentary account of the primitive period when 'men passed their lives without lust for gain, and everyone was content with what he had', he goes on to say, 'But after Cyrus in Asia and in Greece the Spartans and Athenians had begun to subdue cities and nations, to regard the lust for domination as an adequate cause for war, to think that the highest glory lay in the widest empire ...'[38] and so on, in the same strain; the passage quoted suffices for my purpose. This 'lust for domination' brings great evils to vex and exhaust the whole human race. Rome was conquered by this lust when she triumphed over the conquest of

35. Virg., *Aen.*, 10, 821–8. 36. cf. Bk 1, 6. 37. Virg., *Aen.*, 6, 814f.
38. *Cat.*, 2, 2.

Alba, and to the popular acclaim of her crime she gave the name of 'glory', since 'the sinner', as the Bible says, 'is praised in the desires of his soul, and the man whose deeds are wicked is congratulated'.[39]

Let us strip off the deceptive veils, remove the whitewash of illusion and subject the facts to a strict inspection. Let no one tell me, 'A, or B, is a great man: he fought C, or D, and beat him.' Gladiators fight and win; and that brutality gets its reward of applause. But to my thinking it would be better to be punished for any kind of cowardice than to gain the glory of that kind of fighting. Yet if two gladiators came out to fight in the arena, and they turned out to be father and son, who could endure such a spectacle? Who would not have the match cancelled? How then could there be any glory in an armed combat between a mother-city and her daughter? Did it make any difference that the contest was not in an arena, but that a wider field of battle was filled with the bodies, not of two gladiators, but of the many slain of two peoples, that the struggle was not ringed by an amphitheatre, but presented as a blasphemous spectacle before the eyes of the whole world, the living and all posterity, as far as the report of these events extends.

However, the gods who are the patrons of the Roman empire and of such contests as these, put up with the violence involved in their chosen amusements, like spectators in the amphitheatre, until the sister of the Horatii was slain by her brother's sword, to make up three on that side to balance the three Curiatii, so that victorious Rome should have as many dead as conquered Alba. Then came the destruction of Alba, as the fruit of victory; Alba, the third place where the Trojan divinities had taken up their abode, after Ilium, destroyed by the Greeks, and Lavinium, where Aeneas had established his realm of foreign refugees. But it may be that, in their usual manner, the gods had already emigrated, and that was why Alba was destroyed? Yes, they had departed, to be sure, and

The shrines and altars now were left deserted
By all the gods through whom this realm once stood.[40]

No doubt about it, here we have the third departure, so that a fourth city, Rome, might be entrusted to their providential care. They were disgusted with Alba, where Amulius had ascended the throne after expelling his brother; but they approved of Rome, where Romulus had killed his brother to take the kingship. But, it will be said, before the destruction of Alba, the population was transferred to

39. Ps. 10, 23. 40. Virg., *Aen.*, 2, 351f.

Rome so that the two communities could be fused into one. Very good; let that be granted! It remains true that Alba, the kingdom of Ascanius and the third abode of the Trojan gods, was overthrown by her daughter-city. And the making of one people out of two by the remnants that survived the war was the pitiable coagulation of all the blood which had already been poured out by both sides. There is no need for me to recall in detail the renewal, over and over again, under the other kings, of wars which seemed to have been ended by those victories, wars which, time after time, reached a stop after colossal slaughter, and then, after treaties of peace, started again and again, between fathers-in-law and sons-in-law, their children and their posterity. A striking sign of this disastrous state of things was the fact that none of those kings closed the Gates of War.[41] That shows that none of them reigned in peace, though they were under the protection of all those gods.

15. *The lives and deaths of the kings of Rome*

And speaking of those kings, what kind of ends did they have? Take Romulus. The fulsome legend of his reception into heaven can look after itself! So can the tales of those Roman authors who allege that he was torn to pieces by the senators[42] because of his brutality, and that someone by the name of Julius Proculus was suborned to say that Romulus had appeared to him and sent a command by him to the Roman people that he should be worshipped among the divinities; by this means, they say, the people, who had begun to swell in revolt against the senate, were restrained and subdued. There followed an eclipse of the sun, attributed to the merits of Romulus by the ignorant multitude, who did not know that this was the result of the invariable laws of the sun's course. But surely the inference should have been (assuming this phenomenon to be a mark of the sun's grief) that Romulus had been murdered, and that the withdrawal of the light of day pointed to that crime: which did in fact happen when the Lord was crucified[43] through the impious brutality of the Jews. For this obscuration of the sun did not happen in the regular course of the heavenly bodies; this is shown by the fact that it was the Jewish Passover at the time, since that feast occurs annually at the full moon, while an eclipse only happens when the moon has waned.

Cicero clearly gives us to understand that the reception of Romulus

41. cf. ch. 9.　42. Liv., 1, 16; Flor., *Epit.*, 1, 1, 17f.　43. Luke 23, 44f.

among the gods is a supposition rather than a fact, when in his work *On the Commonwealth* he puts a eulogy of Romulus into the mouth of Scipio, in the course of which he says,

> It was a great achievement of Romulus that when he disappeared suddenly during an eclipse of the sun, it was supposed that he had been given a promotion in the ranks of the gods; and that is a belief which no mortal has ever succeeded in arousing except by an extraordinary reputation for exceptional qualities.[44]

When he says that Romulus 'suddenly disappeared' we are surely meant to understand either 'through the violence of the storm', or 'because he was secretly murdered', for other writers add a sudden storm to the eclipse of the sun, and that no doubt gave a chance for the crime, if it did not itself carry off Romulus.

In the same work[45] Cicero also mentions Tullus Hostilius, the third Roman king, who was himself killed by lightning; he says that in his case this death did not lead to belief in his reception among the gods, and that the reason probably was that what had been proved (or rather, generally accepted) as true of Romulus was something which the Romans did not wish to cheapen by making commonplace, and this would happen if they were ready to attribute it to another person. Cicero makes the same admission quite unmistakably in his invectives against Catiline: 'Romulus, the founder of this city, we have elevated to the ranks of the immortal gods in our affectionate tribute to his greatness',[46] thereby showing the story not to be true but a tale which was given the widest currency out of the affection inspired by the services rendered by his great qualities. In the dialogue *Hortensius*,[47] when discoursing on regular eclipses of the sun, Cicero says, '... to effect darkness, like that produced at the death of Romulus, which took place during an eclipse'. Here, at least, he was not at all afraid to speak of a human death, since he was engaged in a discussion rather than a eulogy.

The other kings of Rome, apart from Numa Pompilius and Ancus Martius, who died of illness, met frightful ends. Tullus Hostilius, conqueror and destroyer of Alba was, as I said, reduced to ashes by a thunderbolt, with the whole of his house. Tarquinius Priscus was eliminated by the sons of his predecessor. Servius Tullius was foully murdered by his son-in-law Tarquinius Superbus, who succeeded to the throne. Nor did the gods leave 'all the shrines and altars deserted'[48] on the perpetration of this abominable murder of the best

44. *De Rep.*, 2, 10, 20. 45. *De Rep.*, 2, 17. 46. *Cat.*, 3, 1.
47. Of which only fragments survive. 48. Virg., *Aen.*, 2, 351f.

of the Roman kings, though they are said to have been so upset by the adultery of Paris that they abandoned Troy, and left it to be sacked and burned to the ground by the Greeks. Far from it! Tarquin killed his father-in-law and then succeeded him. This abominable parricide gained the throne by murdering his father-in-law, and went on to find glory in many wars and victories, and to construct the Capitol out of the spoils. And the gods did not depart. They remained to watch all this in person, and to endure the sight of Jupiter, their king, presiding and reigning over them in that loftiest of the temples, which was the work of the parricide. It was not that he was still guiltless, when he built the Capitol, and was driven from Rome later for his guilty deeds; he came to his reign, during which he built the Capitol, by the perpetration of a crime of singular horror.

The guilt of the rape of Lucretia, for which the Romans deposed him from the kingship and banished him from the walls of the city, was not his, but his son's, and the crime was committed not only without his knowledge, but in his absence. He was at the time attacking Ardea, engaged in a war on behalf of the Roman people. We do not know what he would have done, if his son's outrage had been brought to his notice. Yet without waiting to find out for certain what his judgement would be, the Roman people removed him from power, recalled the army, which was ordered to desert him, shut the gates, and refused him entrance on his return. Tarquin had before this provoked the neighbouring countries to major wars which wore down the strength of Rome; now he was deserted by those on whose assistance he relied, and therefore he was not strong enough to regain his throne. And so, it is said, he lived a quiet life as a private citizen for fourteen years, in Tusculum, a town near Rome, and there grew old along with his wife. Thus he died by an end more desirable, we may think, than that of his father-in-law, who as the story goes, was foully murdered, with the full knowledge of his daughter. In spite of all this the Romans gave this Tarquin the title not of 'Cruel' or 'Criminal' but 'Proud' – perhaps because their own kind of pride could not bear his royal displays of disdain. They thought so lightly of his murder of his father-in-law, the best of their kings, that they made him king – and I wonder whether it was not a worse crime in them to give such a reward for such a crime.

Yet the gods had not 'deserted the shrines and altars',[49] unless someone is going to defend those gods by claiming that they stayed in Rome simply to be able to punish the Romans, rather than to help

49. Virg., *Aen.*, 2, 351f.

them with their favours, by seducing them with hollow victories and exhausting them with terrible wars.

Such was the life of the Romans under the kings, in the praiseworthy period of the commonwealth down to the expulsion of the kings, a period of about 243 years. All those victories, won at the price of so much blood and such heavy calamities, had scarcely extended the Roman dominion to twenty miles from the city – an area which would not stand a moment's comparison with that of any Gaetulian city of the present day!

16. *The disasters that marked the beginning of the consulship*

Let us next consider the period which, according to Sallust,[50] saw the reign of equity and just moderation, which lasted until the threat from Tarquin and the pressure of war with Etruria disappeared. So long as the Etruscans seconded the efforts of Tarquin to return to his kingdom, Rome was shaken by a formidable war. For that reason Sallust maintains that the justice and moderation shown in the government of the commonwealth was due to the pressure of foes and not to the persuasion of justice. And in that all too short period what a year of tragedy that was which saw the expulsion of the royal power and the election of consuls! Indeed, the consuls did not complete their year of office. For Junius Brutus deposed his colleague Lucius Tarquinius Collatinus from office and expelled him from Rome; and soon afterwards Brutus himself fell in battle, after inflicting wound for wound upon his enemy. He had earlier put to death his own sons and his wife's brothers, because he had discovered their conspiracy to restore Tarquin; an act which Virgil records with praise, though he follows it immediately with a shudder of compassion. He says first,

> His sons, conspiring to an armed revolt,
> He punished, in fair liberty's defence.[51]

But a little later he cries out,

> O most unhappy, howsoe'er the future
> Speak of his deed!

That is, however much future generations commend and extol the deed, the man who kills his sons is unhappy. And Virgil adds, as some consolation for his unhappiness,

50. *Hist.*, fr. 1, 11; cf. Bk II, 18. 51. *Aen.*, 6, 820 ff.

> Love of his country, and the boundless passion
> For high renown, these swayed his grim resolve.

Now Brutus slew his children; and then he could not survive the exchange of blows with Tarquin's son, but in fact was survived by Tarquin himself. Thus it seems that in him the innocence of his colleague Collatinus was vindicated. For Collatinus was a worthy citizen, and yet after the expulsion of Tarquin he suffered the same fate as that tyrant. Now it is said that Brutus was related to Tarquin; but Collatinus was ruined by a resemblance in his name – one of his names was Tarquinius. Then he should have been compelled to change his name, not his country; in fact he might simply have dropped the name, and have been known as Lucius Collatinus. The sole effect of his keeping something which he might have discarded without loss, was that one of the first consuls was ordered to be deprived of office, and the community was robbed of a worthy citizen. Is this also a glory for Junius Brutus – this detestable injustice, from which the commonwealth gained no advantage? Was it 'love of his country, and immense ambition for high renown' that led him to commit this crime? The fact remains that when Tarquinius the tyrant had been expelled, Lucius Tarquinius Collatinus, the husband of Lucretia, was elected consul, with Brutus. How right the people were to take account of a man's character, not his name! How disloyal Brutus was in this new position of chief responsibility, in depriving his colleague of office and country, when he could have deprived him merely of his name, if that gave offence!

Those wrongs were committed, and those unhappy events took place, during that period of 'equity and just restraint in the government of the commonwealth'. Besides this, Lucretius, the substitute for Brutus in the consulship, was carried off by illness before the end of the year. And so Publius Valerius, successor to Collatinus, and Marcus Horatius, brought in to fill the place of the departed Lucretius, completed that year of mourning and misery, the year which saw five consuls, and the year when the Roman commonwealth solemnly inaugurated the consulship, the new office of authority.

17. *Continued disasters in the early republic.* No *assistance given by the gods*

When the fear was a little abated – not because the fighting had ceased, but because the pressure of war was somewhat diminished – and when that epoch 'when the commonwealth was governed with equity, justice and moderation'[52] came to an end, then followed a period which Sallust thus briefly delineates:

After that, the patricians reduced the plebeians to the condition of slavery: they disposed of the lives and persons of the *plebs* in the manner of kings: they drove men from their lands: and, with the rest of the people disenfranchized, they alone wielded supreme power. Oppressed by such harsh treatment, and especially by the load of debt, the plebeians, after enduring the simultaneous burden of tribute and military service in continual wars, at length armed themselves, and took up a position on the Mons Sacer and the Aventine. Thus they gained for themselves the tribunes of the *plebs* and other rights. The Second Punic War brought an end to the strife and rivalry between the two parties.[53]

I need not waste my own time, or my reader's, on this. Sallust has given a brief sketch of the miseries of the republic in that long period, in all the years down to the Second Punic War,[54] troubled by incessant wars abroad, and at home by continued civil strife and disharmony. Even Rome's victories did not bring the substantial joys of happiness, but only the empty consolations of misery, specious allurements to tempt restless spirits to submit to more and more hardships, all of them unproductive.

I hope that no sensible Roman patriots will be incensed at me for speaking like this. And yet I know that this admonitory appeal is needless, since it is quite certain that they should be the last people to be indignant at such a statement. For I am speaking no more harshly or emphatically than Roman authors (though I have not their style – nor their leisure – at my command). And yet these Romans have taken great pains to master the works of those authorities; and they compel their children to take the same pains. I wonder if those who are indignant would have borne with me, if I had repeated the remarks of Sallust? For he says,

A great many disturbances, insurrections and, in the end, civil wars broke out. A small body of powerful men, whose influence had won them a large following, aimed at domination under the honourable name of "champions of the patricians" or "defenders of the *plebs*". Men were not entitled good or bad citizens in regard to their services to the commonwealth, in this general corruption; but any man was classed as a good citizen, in proportion as his resources increased his power to hurt, and in so far as he championed the existing state of things.[55]

52. Sall., *Hist.*, fr. 1, 11.
53. *Hist.*, 1 fr. 11; cf. Bk II, 18.
54. 218 B.C.
55. *Hist.*, 1. fr. 12.

Now those historians judged it a part of honourable freedom not to keep silence about the evils of their country, which in many places they have been constrained to praise in terms of the highest eulogy, since they have not another City which is a truer one than theirs, one whose citizens are to be chosen for eternity. What then ought we to do? For since our hope is in God, and is therefore a better hope, and more assured, our liberty of speech should be all the greater, when our opponents hold Christ to blame for these present ills, which may turn the minds of the weaker and more foolish away from that City in which alone there can be a life of eternal happiness. And nothing that we say against their gods is more shocking than the repeated statements of those Roman authors, whom they read and approve. Indeed, we have taken all our material from those authors. We would of ourselves be quite incapable of such an account, or of telling the whole tale.

The Romans thought they ought to worship their gods, to ensure the insignificant and deceptive happiness of this world. But where were the gods when the Romans, whose worship they canvassed with their cunning lies, were vexed by such calamities? Where were they, when the consul Valerius was slain in defending the Capitol, which had been set on fire by exiles and slaves?[56] It was easier for him to bring help to Jupiter's temple, than for that great mob of divinities to come to his aid, with that 'Most High and Mighty' king of theirs, whose temple Valerius had saved. Where were they when the city, exhausted by the horrors of incessant civil broils, was awaiting, in a brief interval of tranquillity, the return of envoys sent to Athens to borrow their laws,[57] and was then devastated by a severe famine and pestilence? Where were they, again, when the people, in the distress of famine, created a 'prefect of the corn supply'? Where were they when Spurius Maelius, because he distributed free corn to the hungry people as the famine increased in severity, was accused of aiming at kingship and was slain by Quintus Servilius, master of the horse, at the instance of the said prefect and at the command of the senile dictator Lucius Quintus,[58] amid a disturbance in the city of unexampled magnitude and danger? Where were they, when a fearful plague had broken out, and because the gods were of no avail the people, in the extremity of distress, decided to perform the novelty of *lectisternia*,[59] something they had never done before? Couches (*lecti*)

56. Liv., 3, 18. 57. cf. Bk II, 16.
58. Cincinnatus (aged 80) in 439 B.C.; Liv., 4, 12f.
59. 399 B.C.; Liv., 5, 13; cf. Bk II, 11.

were furnished (*sternebantur*) in honour of the gods, and hence the sacred – or, rather, sacrilegious – ceremony got its name. Where were they, when the Roman army had for ten years fought without success and without intermission at Veii,[60] had suffered a succession of disasters only relieved by the intervention of Furius Camillus – a man later condemned by his ungrateful city? Where were they, when the Gauls captured Rome,[61] sacked it, burned it, and filled it with bodies of the slain? Where were they, when the great plague claimed such a host of victims, amongst them that same Furius Camillus,[62] who had defended his ungrateful republic against Veii, and later rescued it from the Gauls? This pestilence was the occasion of the introduction of stage-shows,[63] another novel infection, attacking not the bodies of the Romans but, far more disastrously, their characters.

Where were they, when another dangerous plague broke out, started, it was believed, by poisons spread by Roman matrons, of whom an incredibly large number were revealed to be in a moral condition more dangerous than any plague?[64] Or when both consuls were trapped by the Samnites at the Caudine Forks and compelled to make a deal with the enemy that dealt dishonour, whereby six hundred Roman knights were given as hostages, and the rest of the army laid down their arms, were stripped of armour and clothing, and were sent under the enemies' yoke, clad only in a single garment?[65] Or when many in the army were killed by lightning, at a time when the general population was suffering hardships of another outbreak of pestilence?[66] Or when, in yet another intolerable outbreak, Rome was obliged to summon the aid of Aesculapius from Epidaurus,[67] as a divine physician, because, one may suppose, Jupiter, king of all the gods, so long established on the Capitol, had not learnt the art of medicine? He had been kept too busy, no doubt, by those amours for which he had abundant leisure in his youth! Or when a league of enemies was formed, of Lucanians, Bruttians, Samnites, Etruscans, Senones, and Gauls, and a massacre of Roman envoys was followed by an overwhelming defeat of the Roman army, with the loss of the praetor, seven tribunes, and thirteen thousand soldiers.[68] Or when, after a long period of serious disturbances in the city, the *plebs* finally withdrew to the Janiculum, in a secession which was in effect an act of

60. 407–396 B.C.; Liv., 5, 32; cf. Bk II, 17. 61. 390 B.C.; Liv., 5, 37–40
62. 365 B.C.; Liv., 7, 1. 63. cf. Bk I, 32n.
64. Liv., 8, 18. 65. 321 B.C.; Liv., 9,3–6.
66. Liv., 10, 31. 67. 293 B.C.; Liv., 47; cf. ch. 12.
68. 283 B.C.; Liv., *Perioch.*, 12.

war, thus producing a situation so disastrous and menacing that it led to the creation of a dictator, a step only taken in times of extreme peril.[69] This dictator, Hortensius, brought the plebeians back; but he died before the end of his term of office, a thing which had never happened to any previous dictator and which was a graver reproach to the gods, since Aesculapius was by now in attendance!

At this period the frequency of widespread wars and the consequent shortage of soldiers led to the enlistment of 'proletarians'. They had been given that name because, being too poor to bear arms, they had leisure to beget offspring (*proles*). Pyrrhus, king of Greece, a warrior of immense renown, took the field against Rome, at the invitation of Tarentum; and when he consulted Apollo about the outcome of his enterprise, the god had the wit to give a reply so ambiguous as to ensure his divine reputation in either event. What he said was, 'I tell you, Pyrrhus, you the Romans can vanquish.'[70] And so whether Pyrrhus was beaten by the Romans, or the Romans by Pyrrhus, the prophet could await either event with equanimity! And what fearful disasters befell both armies in that war. Pyrrhus, however, showed his superiority, and would have been able to extol Apollo as a divine soothsayer, from his point of view, had there not been another battle[71] shortly afterwards from which the Romans emerged victorious.

In the midst of all the carnage of this fighting, a serious epidemic broke out, affecting women, who died in pregnancy before reaching the full time for childbirth. I conceive that on this occasion Aesculapius excused himself on the ground that he claimed to be a chief physician, not a midwife! The cattle also died from the same disease, so much so that it was thought that the animal species would be wiped out.

69. The last 'secession' in 286 B.C.; Liv., *Perioch.*, 11.

70. *Proletarii.* Cicero, (*De Re.*, 2, 23) gives this etymology, when describing the constitution of Servius Tullius: 'Those whose property was less than 1,500 he called *proletarii*; so that it seemed they were expected to supply offspring (*proles*).' The word occurs in the first of the Twelve Tables (cf. note on Bk II, 9) of 450 B.C.

Pyrrhus, king of Epirus, came to the help of Tarentum against the Romans in 280 B.C. Cicero (*De Div.*, 2, 56, 116) quotes the metrical form of the oracle *aio te Aiacida Romanos vincere posse*. The ambiguity arises because either of the accusatives, *te* or *Romanos*, could be either subject or object of *vincere*. Cicero observes that (1) Apollo did not speak Latin, (2) this oracle was unknown to the Greeks, and (3) Oracles were no longer being given in verse in the third century. But the ambiguity would remain in a Greek prose version.

71. Beneventum, 275 B.C.

Besides all this there was that unforgettable winter of such incredible and monstrous severity that the snow remained piled up in the forum to a terrifying height for fourteen days, and the Tiber was frozen over. If that had happened in modern times what a great deal our opponents would have had to say about it! And think of that Great Plague! Think of how long it raged, and how many victims it claimed! When it went into a second year, with increasing violence, they consulted the Sybilline Books, since Aesculapius' attendance was of no avail. Now in the case of oracles of that kind, as Cicero remarks in his work *On Divination*,[72] it is to the interpreters that credence is given – and they make doubtful conjectures, according to their ability or inclination. On this occasion it was said that the cause of the epidemic was that a great number of sacred buildings had been seized by private persons, and remained in their possession. And so, for this time, Aesculapius was absolved of the serious accusation of incompetence or laziness. But how was it that those temples had been seized by a number of people, without opposition, unless it was that supplications had been made to that crowd of gods for so long, and all in vain, and that in consequence those places had been abandoned by worshippers, and left unused, so they could be taken over, without giving offence, in order that they might at least serve mundane purposes? At that time they were recovered and refurbished, in the hope of allaying the epidemic. But if they were not later on neglected as before, and once again taken into private possession without its being remarked, then Varro certainly should not be credited with massive erudition, since in treating of 'Sacred Edifices'[73] he records that many of them had been forgotten. But at the time, even if the plague was not eradicated, at least a plausible excuse for the gods was provided.

18. *The crushing disasters of the Punic Wars; the gods offer no protection*

In the course of the Punic Wars, when the victory remained long in doubt and hung in the balance as the two empires clashed, and two powerful peoples were engaged in massive and costly attacks on each other, how many smaller kingdoms were wiped out! How many spacious and famous towns were razed, how many communities suffered disaster or utter ruin! How many wide regions and countries endured

72. *De Div.*, 2, 54, 110 ff.
73. A section of 'Divine Affairs' in his *Antiquities*.

widespread devastation! How frequent were the interchanges of defeat and victory! What loss of life occurred among both the combatants and the civil population! What a huge total of ships was lost, either destroyed in sea-battles or sunk by storm or various kinds of bad weather! If I were to attempt to recall and relate those calamities, I should turn into just another chronicler.

It was at this time that Rome, in a panic of terror, had recourse to futile and ridiculous remedies. On the authority of the Sibylline Books the Secular Games were renewed.[74] This celebration had been instituted during the preceding century, but had been forgotten and omitted in more fortunate times, so that it had passed out of use. The pontiffs also restored the games consecrated to the infernal deities, which had likewise been abolished during the preceding happier years. No doubt when those games were restored the infernal gods were delighted to join in the celebrations, at a time when they were enriched with such a supply of dying men. For there were certainly splendid games being put on for the demons, and lavish banquets provided for the infernal gods by wretched men in their crazy wars and bloody hatreds, and in the tragic victories on either side. Surely the most heartbreaking episode in the First Punic War was when the Romans were so heavily defeated that Regulus[75] himself (whom I have mentioned in my first and second books) was taken prisoner. He was a man of unmistakable greatness, who had conquered and subdued the Carthaginians at an earlier time. And he would have brought this First Punic War to a successful end if he had not, through excessive ambition for praise and glory, sought to impose on the exhausted Carthaginians conditions too harsh for them to endure. If the utterly unexpected capture of this great man, his undeserved servitude, his complete fidelity to his oath and his most cruel death – if all these did not make those gods blush, then it is true that they are made of air, and have no blood in their veins!

Moreover, there was no lack of fearful calamities within the city's walls, during this same period. Almost all the lower parts of Rome were submerged in an unprecedented flooding of the River Tiber,[76] some buildings being knocked down by rushing torrents of water, other collapsing after a long soaking in the stagnant flood. This horror

74. *Secular Games.* St Augustine refers to the celebration of these games in 249 B.C. They were celebrated at irregular intervals: 463 (or 449), 363, 263, 249, 146, and 17 B.C.; A.D. 88 and 204.

75. cf. Bk I, 15.

76. 242 B.C.

was followed by an even more disastrous fire which swept down on all the lofty buildings round the forum and did not spare the temple of Vesta, with which it had such close connection, for there the Virgins – not so much honoured by the task as condemned to it – had continually bestowed upon fire a kind of eternal life by carefully renewing the wood as it burned away on the hearth. On this occasion the fire was not merely living in their temple; it was raging. Appalled by this flaring up the Virgins could not rescue from the fire that fateful Sacred Symbol.[77] which had already brought ruin on three cities[78] which had possessed it. And so the pontiff Metellus rushed in, without a thought for his own safety, and snatched it from the flames, being himself half burnt to death in the act.[79] The fire did not recognize the sacred object, or rather there was no divine power there; if there had been, it would not have made its escape. Thus a human being could give more effective help to Vesta's sacred emblems than those holy objects could afford to him. Now, if they could not preserve themselves from the fire, what help could they give against that flood and that conflagration? The event clearly revealed their utter impotence.

We Christians would not bring the same objections against such sacred objects, if it was said that they were appointed not for the preservation of temporal goods but to point to goods that are eternal, and therefore though those physical and visible things are fated to perish, their disappearing entails no impairment of the things which were the purpose of their appointment. They can be replaced, to fulfil the same purpose. But as it is, they think, in their astonishing blindness, that by those perishable sacred objects their earthly life and the temporal felicity of their city can be preserved imperishably. Then, when it is proved that the preservation of those objects has not in fact protected men's lives from the onset of extinction or of unhappiness, they are ashamed to change a belief which they are unable to defend.

77. *Sacred Symbol* The Palladium, an image of Pallas sent by Zeus to Dardanus (or Ilus) supposedly brought from Troy by Aeneas; it was preserved in the temple of Vesta, and concealed from profane eyes, and its safety was reputed to ensure the safety of the city which possessed it. 'The Palladium is as it were the guarantee of our safety and of our Empire, and as such it is guarded by Vesta' (Cic., *Pro Scaur.*, 48).

78. Troy, Lavinium, Alba.

79. In 241 B.C. cf. Ov. 1, *Fast.*, 6, 437–54; Liv., *Perioch.*, 19.

19. *The afflictions of the Second Punic War; both sides exhausted*

It would take too long to recall the disasters suffered in the Second Punic War by two peoples engaged in battle over such a wide area. Even the historians who set out to sing the praises of the Roman Empire, rather than to recount Rome's wars, have to admit that the victory resembled a defeat.[80] Starting from Spain, Hannibal crossed the Pyrenees, dashed across Gaul, and thrust his way through the Alps. In the course of this long circuit he increased his resources by ravaging and subduing all the countryside as he passed, before rushing through the passes of Italy like a mountain torrent. And what bloody battles were waged then! How often the Romans were defeated! How many towns defected to the enemy, how many were captured and sacked! How frightful the battles were; and how often Rome's disasters enhanced Hannibal's glory! And what am I to say about the dreadful catastrophe at Cannae, where Hannibal, for all his savagery, was sated by such wholesale slaughter of his bitterest enemies and, it is said, ordered that quarter should be given? From that battle Hannibal sent to Carthage three pecks of gold rings,[81] so that the people should realize that so many of the Roman nobility had fallen in that fight that it was easier to estimate the casualties by the peck than to count them. And from this evidence the carnage of the rest of the army – a crowd of slain who lay there without golden rings, more numerous because of lower rank – can be estimated by conjecture, not recorded in statistics. Such a shortage of soldiers followed that Rome gave impunity to convicted criminals and enlisted them, and granted freedom to slaves, and thus got together an army – for one cannot call them reinforcements. But it was no army to be proud of! And then these slaves – no, let us not insult them, those freedmen – who were to fight for the Roman republic, were in need of arms. The temples were ransacked, as if the Romans were saying to their gods, 'Give up the arms which you have possessed this long time to no purpose. It may be that our slaves may be able to make good use of them, when you divinities of ours have not been able to turn them to account.' Then there was not enough in the public treasury to pay the army, and private resources were called upon to support public expenses, so much so that individuals offered anything they had, their rings, their

80. cf. Florus, 2, 6 ('The conquering nation were more like a vanquished people'); Liv., 21, 1 ('Those who conquered were nearer to disaster.')

81. Liv., 23, 22.

lockets,[82] the pitiable emblems of rank, and even the senators had no gold left for their own use, still less the members of the other orders, or mere members of the tribes. Who would be able to bear with our opponents, if they were forced into this kind of extremity in these times? As it is, we find them almost insupportable when more money is given to actors in payment for superfluous pleasure than was at that time collected to pay the legions for the defence of the very existence of Rome.

20. *The destruction of the Saguntines. They perished because of loyal friendship to Rome; but the Roman gods gave them no help*

But in the midst of all the horrors of the Second Punic War nothing was more lamentable, nothing more deserving an outcry of compassion than the destruction of Saguntum.[83] This Spanish city, a firm friend of the Roman people, was overthrown for keeping faith with Rome. For when Hannibal broke his treaty with Rome and was seeking occasion to provoke Rome to war, he began by laying fierce siege to Saguntum. When the news reached Rome, envoys were sent to Hannibal to induce him to abandon the siege. When they were scorned, they proceeded to Carthage, lodged a complaint about the breach of treaty, and returned to Rome without achieving the object of their mission. During those delays, that unfortunate city – a flourishing community, a cherished ornament of its country and a cherished ally of Rome – was exterminated by the Carthaginians, in eight or nine months. Even to read of its end fills one with horror, to say nothing of describing it in writing. Nevertheless, I will give a brief account of it, seeing that it is very relevant to my argument. At first the community was wasted by famine, it is even said that many of them ate the dead bodies of their dear ones. Then, when they were completely exhausted, the Saguntines, intending at all costs to avoid falling captive into the hands of Hannibal, erected a huge pyre in a public place, set it on fire and, in mutual slaughter, committed themselves and their fellows to the flames.

They might surely have done something about this, those contemptible gluttons of gods, who lick their lips at the fat of the sacrifices and deceive men by the murk of their lying prophesies. They might have done something to help that city, that firm friend of the

82. *Bullae*, the golden armaments of boys of noble birth.
83. At the start of the Second Punic War, 218 B.C.

Roman people; they might have refused to allow it to perish because it kept faith.

For certainly they presided as mediators when Saguntum was linked with the Roman republic by a treaty of alliance. It was just because that city faithfully kept the compact into which it had entered by a decision taken under the presidency of the gods – a compact to which it had pledged faith and bound itself by oath – that it was besieged, overwhelmed, and annihilated by a conqueror who broke his faith. If it was those gods who later struck terror into Hannibal by storm and lightning, when he was close to the walls of Rome, and drove him far away, they might have done something of the sort on this earlier occasion. I make bold to say, indeed, that it would have been more honourable in them to have raged with their storms on behalf of those friends of theirs who were imperilling themselves rather than breaking faith, and who were then without any assistance, rather than on behalf of the Romans, who were only fighting for themselves, and who had great resources for their conflict with Hannibal.

If the gods had been the defenders of the happiness and glory of Rome they would have shielded Rome from the heavy guilt of the catastrophe that befell Saguntum. As it is, what folly to believe that Rome did not perish beneath a conquering Hannibal because of the protection of gods who had no power to save Saguntum from perishing as a reward for its friendship with Rome! If the people of Saguntum had been Christians, and had suffered any such calamity for the faith of the gospel, it would not have destroyed itself by sword and fire; but it would have suffered destruction for the gospel faith, and it would have suffered in the hope based on its faith in Christ, the hope not of a reward of a brief space of time, but of an endless eternity. We are told that the reason for the worship of those gods, the reason why their worship is demanded, is to safeguard men's felicity in respect of things perishable and impermanent. What reply will the defenders and excusers of those gods give to us in the case of the annihilation of Saguntum? They can only repeat the reply they gave concerning the destruction of Regulus. There is, to be sure, the difference that he was a single man, while Saguntum was a whole community. Still, in both cases, the cause of extinction was keeping pledged faith. It was because of this that Regulus wished to return to the enemy, and Saguntum refused to cross over to the enemy's side.

Are we to infer that keeping faith provokes the anger of the gods? Or is it that not only individuals, but entire communities can perish, even when they enjoy the favours of the gods? Let our opponents make their choice! If the gods are enraged by the keeping of faith, let them seek the worship of perjurers. Whereas if men and communities can perish, with frightful suffering, even when the gods favour them, then their worship brings no fruit of temporal happiness. Therefore those who ascribe their misfortunes to the discontinuance of sacrifice must forgo their indignation. For they could have their gods still present with them, they could even have them looking with favour on them; and yet they might not merely have their present sorry plight to grumble at, but might, after indescribable sufferings, suffer the utter destruction which in time past befell Regulus and the people of Saguntum.

21. *Rome's ingratitude to Scipio, its moral standard in its 'best period'*

The period between the Second Punic War and the last (to pass over many details, with a view to keeping within the limits of my projected task) was a time, according to Sallust, of sound morality and of a great measure of concord in Rome.[84] But that period of morality and concord witnessed the accusation of the great Scipio. He was the saviour of Rome and Italy, he won the highest renown and admiration for bringing the Second Punic War to a successful end – that war fraught with so much horror, ruin, and peril – and he conquered Hannibal and brought Carthage to its knees. We have accounts of his dedicating his life to the gods in early manhood, and of his upbringing in the temples.[85] Yet because of the accusations of his enemies he had to leave Rome, and thus deprived of his country, which he had restored to safety and freedom by his courage, he spent the rest of his life in the town of Linternum, where he ended his days. And after his glorious triumph he felt no homesickness for Rome, in fact it is said that he gave orders that even after his death no funeral service should be held for him in his ungrateful native city.[86]

Later on, Gnaeus Manlius, the proconsul, celebrated a triumph over the Gallo-Greeks;[87] and the result of this victory was the first invasion of Rome by Asiatic luxury, which was more deadly than any human enemy. It was then, we are told, that the first bronze-plated beds and expensive coverlets made their appearance; and female lu-

84. *Hist.*, fr. 1, 11; cf. Bk II, 18.
85. cf. Gellius, 7, 1.
86. Liv., 39, 6, 7.
87. The Galatians, in 189 B.C.

tanists were introduced into banquets, as were other ingredients of licence and debauchery.

But it is my intention to deal with evils which men endure and revolt against, not with the evils they delight in creating. And so the facts I mention about Scipio, his departure, under pressure from his enemies, and his death, far from the country he had saved – are the facts that are relevant to my argument. My point is that the Roman divinities, when Scipio had defended their temples from Hannibal, did not defend him in return – though the only reason for their worship is to secure that kind of temporal blessing. Since Sallust speaks of that period as a time of high moral standards, I have thought it right to make this point about Asiatic luxury so that Sallust may be understood to have made this judgement only in comparison with other epochs, when morality deteriorated in times of grave disturbances in society. In that very period, between the Second and Third Punic Wars, the law called the *Lex Voconia*[88] was passed, forbidding the appointment of a woman, even an only daughter, as heir. I cannot quote, or even imagine, a more inequitable law. All the same, this whole inter-war period was a time of less intolerable misfortune. The army suffered only the exhaustion of foreign wars, and it had the consolations of victory; while at home there were none of the savage disturbances which marked other periods. But in the last Punic War Rome's imperial rival was completely eliminated by a single sweep made by the second Scipio,[89] who won the surname Africanus by this achievement; and after that the Roman commonwealth sank under a load of accumulated disasters. Those calamities mounted in consequence of the moral corruption brought on by a state of prosperity and security, and it can be shown that the swift overthrow of Carthage, which led to this state of affairs, did more harm than her long hostility.

The next period of Roman history takes us down to Caesar Augustus. It is clear that Augustus wrested from the Romans a liberty which was no longer glorious, even in their own estimation, but productive of strife and tragedy, and by now unmistakably listless and enfeebled; he brought everything under the arbitrary rule of a monarch, and by so doing he is regarded as having restored to health and strength a commonwealth prostrated by a kind of chronic sickness. I pass over the repeated military disasters of the whole of this period,

88. In 169 B.C.

89. Africanus Minor, appointed to command 147; captured and destroyed Carthage 146 B.C.

which were due to a variety of causes. I will not dwell on the treaty with Numantia, an agreement blotted with the marks of Rome's terrible humiliation.[90] The Romans ascribe this ignominy to the fact that the sacred chickens had flown out of their cage, a sinister augury for the consul Mancinus! During all those years, in which that tiny community had inflicted heavy losses on the besieging Roman army and had even begun to strike terror into the Roman republic itself, we are doubtless to suppose that other generals had taken over command of the attack with different auspices!

22. *Mithridates' massacre of Romans in Asia*

As I said, I will not dwell on this. But I could not possibly keep silence about the massacre carried out in one day on the orders of Mithridates, king of Asia – the killing of all the Romans in that country.[91] There were an immense number of Romans engaged on business in Asia. What a pitiable sight was presented! Wherever any Roman was found, in the country, on the road, in the town, in his house, in the street, in the forum, in the temple, in bed, or at a dinner-party, he was killed without warning and without pity. The dying groaned; the spectators wept, and so perhaps did the butchers. It was a cruel compulsion, that hosts should be forced not only to behold, but even to perpetrate, such unspeakable murders in their own houses, and to remove from their faces the expressions of courteous and kind civility and pass to the achievement, in time of peace, of the purpose of an enemy; when there was an exchange of deadly blows, the assailant being smitten in his soul, as his victim was smitten in his body!

Had all those victims failed to heed the auguries? Had they no domestic or public gods worth consulting, before they set out from their homes on that journey from which there was to be no return? If so, then our opponents have no call to complain of these present times in this regard; the Romans have long despised such nonsense. While if they did consult them, then let them tell me what help they were, at a time when no laws, or at least no human laws, restricted their activities, and no one was concerned to stop them.

90. *Numantia.* C. Hostilius Mancinus, with an army of 30,000, was defeated by 4,000 Numantians in 138. The treaty he concluded with the victors was repudiated by the senate (Liv., *Perioch.*, 55; Cic., *De Or.*, 1, 40, 181).

91. 88 B.C., Liv., *Perioch.*, 78; App., *De Bell. Mithr.*, 22. Mithridates (d. 63 B.C.) was king of Pontius, but threatened to acquire much of Asia Minor, and even invaded Greece. Sulla drove him from Greece; Lucullus and Pompey defeated him in Asia.

23. *The period of internal disasters, proceeded by the prodigy of madness in domestic animals*

Let me now recall, in the briefest compass possible, the misfortunes which were the more grievous because they brought misery inside the commonwealth; civil (or rather *un*civil) discords, were no longer mere disturbances but actual wars within cities, in which so much blood was shed, in which the passions of the factions did not confine their rage to disputes in the assemblies, or to the shouting of insulting slogans, but burst into armed conflict. The Social Wars, the Servile Wars, the Civil Wars – how much Roman blood they shed, what wide devastation and depopulation they caused in Italy! For before the allies of Latium rose against Rome[92] all the animals which had been tamed to serve men's needs – dogs, horses, asses, oxen and all the other cattle which were under men's domination – suddenly turned wild, forgot the gentleness of domesticity, left their quarters and roamed at large, shunning the approach not only of strangers, but even of their owners; they threatened danger, and even death, to any who risked closing in on them to round them up.[93] If this was a portent, it was a portent of terrible calamity; if not, it was itself calamity enough! If this had happened in our times we should have had to endure from our adversaries a rage more savage than the fury of those animals.

24. *Civil disorders, aroused by the Gracchan disturbances*

The Civil Wars were ushered in by the disturbances of the Gracchi, aroused by the agrarian laws. The Gracchi wished to distribute to the people the lands which the nobles wrongly possessed. But the eradication of a long-standing injustice was a hazard of the greatest peril; in fact, as it turned out, it was fraught with utter ruin. Think of all the deaths which followed the murder of the elder Gracchus and those which attended the assassination of his brother, not long afterwards! For men, high-born and lowly alike, were put to death not by legal action, not by the due exercise of authority, but in the fighting of armed mobs. After the killing of the younger Gracchus we are told that three thousand men were put to death by Lucius Opimius, the consul, who held an inquiry to deal with the remaining supporters of the Gracchi. He had previously raised armed forces against Gracchus inside the city and overwhelmed him and his supporters. Gracchus was killed, and the consul achieved an immense slaughter of Roman

92. 90 B.C. 93. cf. Jul. Obs, *Prod*, 114; Oros. 5, 18, 9.

citizens. We can infer what colossal casualties may have been caused by the conflict of those armed mobs, when so many deaths resulted from the ostensibly regular processes of a judicial inquiry. The assassin of Gracchus himself sold the victim's head to the consul for its weight in gold, in accordance with an agreed offer made before the massacre – a massacre in which the ex-consul Marcus Fulvius was also murdered with his children.[94]

25. *The temple of Concord, on the site of riot and massacre*

There was, to be sure, a neat idea behind the senate's decree which ordered the erection of a temple of Concord[95] on the very spot where this tragic uprising happened. This ensured that the evidence of the Gracchan battle should strike the eyes and jog the memories of orators as they addressed the people. Yet it was surely nothing but a mockery of the gods, to build a temple to a goddess whose presence in the city should have prevented the community from falling into ruin, torn to pieces by internal strife. But perhaps Concord deserved to be shut up in that temple, as if in a prison, for the crime of having deserted the hearts of the citizens?

If the Romans wished for something appropriate to the events, why did they not rather construct a temple of Discord? Is there any reason why Discord should not be a goddess, as well as Concord? Then we should have a goddess of evil, and a goddess of good, according to Labeo's distinction,[96] which seems to have been suggested to him just by noticing that there was a temple set up at Rome to *Febris* (Fever),[97] as well as to *Salus* (Health). On that principle there should be a temple of Discord, as well as of Concord. It was hazardous for the Romans to decide to live under the wrath of a goddess of evil and not

94. *Tiberius Gracchus* when tribune in 133 B.C. brought forward proposals for land reform. He was killed in a riot when seeking re-election. His brother Gaius, tribune 125, and again in 122, re-enacted his brother's proposals and proceeded to further liberal measures. He was killed in 121, after the *senatus consultum ultimum* had been passed against him and his supporters. L. Opimius, consul 121, was one of the leaders of the reactionary opposition to C. Gracchus, and in 120 he was accused of the massacre of many citizens, but acquitted (Cic., *De Or.*, 2, 25, 106). Gracchus was actually killed by a faithful slave, Philocrates. His head was sold to Opimius by a certain Septimuleius, according to Plutarch (*C. Gracchus*, 17). M. Fulvius, consul 125, was a friend of the Gracchi.

95. *Concord*. There was more than one temple of Concord in Rome. The dedication of the temple by Opimius is attested by Appian, *De Bell. Civ.*, 1, 26.

96. cf. Bk II. 97. cf. Bk II, 14.

to recall that the fall of Troy had, as its first cause, the resentment of that goddess. She had not been invited with the other goddesses, and therefore devised the contention between the three goddesses by introducing the golden apple. Hence arose the quarrel of the divinities, the victory of Venus, the rape of Helen, and the annihilation of Troy. Therefore, if it be true that she set the city in turmoil with those great uprisings, in resentment at not being thought worthy of a temple among the gods in Rome, how much more violent may have been her wrath at seeing a shrine set up for her opponent on the very site of the slaughter – the site, that is, of her own achievement.

When we ridicule these absurdities, those learned philosophers are choked with rage. And yet the worshippers of gods of good and gods of evil cannot extricate themselves from this problem about Concord and Discord. Did they neglect the worship of those goddesses, and prefer to worship Febris and Bellona, for whom they built shrines in antiquity? Or is it that they did worship them also, but Concord abandoned them, and so Discord in her savagery led them on to the Civil Wars?

26. *The various wars that followed the erection of the temple of Concord*

However that may be, the Romans decided that the temple of Concord, that powerful obstacle to civil tumult, that witness to the massacre and the punishment of the Gracchi, should be set up to meet the eyes of orators as they addressed the people. The advantages that ensued are indicated by the even unhappier events that followed. From that time onwards the popular speakers used every effort, not to avoid following the example of the Gracchi, but to exceed their designs. The tribune of the plebs, Lucius Saturninus, the praetor, Gaius Servilius,[98] and, long afterwards,[99] Marcus Drusus,[100] all three of these by their revolutionary activities brought on frightful massacres to begin with, and eventually caused the conflagration of the Social Wars, which brought terrible distress to Italy and reduced

98. L. *Apuleius Saturninus*, tribune 103 and 100 B.C., and *Gn. Servilius Glaucia*, praetor 100 B.C., were extremist supporters of Marius. A *senatus consultum ultimum* declared them public enemies and they were killed in December 100 B.C.

99. Only 9 years. Perhaps the reading should be 'not long afterwards'.

100. M. *Livius Drusus*, tribune 91 B.C., proposed the enfranchisement of the Italian allies. He was assassinated; and the failure of his proposals, and his murder, lead to the *Social War* in 90 B.C.

her to an astonishing condition of devastation and depopulation. There followed the Servile War and the Civil Wars.[101]

Think of all the battles fought, all the blood poured out, so that almost all the nations of Italy, by whose help the Roman Empire wielded that overwhelming power, should be subjugated as if they were barbarous savages. The Servile War was started by a mere handful of gladiators, less than seventy, in fact, and think of the huge number finally involved, and the bitterness and ferocity of their struggle; remember the Roman generals defeated by that multitude, the cities and districts devastated – and the manner of the devastation. The adequate description of it has baffled the powers of the historians. And this was not the only Servile War. Before this the bands of slaves had depopulated the province of Macedonia; later they devastated Sicily and the maritime coast. Who could find words to match the gravity of the events – words adequate to express the horrors of their acts of brigandage at the beginning, and their wars of piracy later?[102]

27. *The civil war of Marius and Sulla*

Marius had his hands already stained with the blood of his countrymen when, after the massacre of many of the opposing factions, he was conquered and left the city in flight. The city had but the smallest breathing-space. Then (to use Cicero's words)

> Cinna, with Marius, later got the upper hand: and then with the assassination of the most eminent citizens the lamps of the city were put out. After that, Sulla took vengeance for this ruthless victory, and I need not even mention the cost of this vengeance: the grievous determination of the citizen-body, the fearful disaster to the commonwealth.[103]

Lucan also speaks of this revenge of Sulla, a greater calamity than if the crimes it punished had been left unpunished. He says:

> The remedy
> Surpassed all bounds, and followed on too far
> In chase of the disease. The guilty perished.
> Ah, yes – but only guilty men survived.[104]

101. *The Civil Wars* started with the war between Marius and Sulla 88–82 B.C.

The Servile War, led by the gladiators under Spartacus, lasted from 73–71 B.C. There were slave wars in Sicily 135–132 and 103–101 B.C.

102. The pirates were finally eradicated by Pompey in 67 B.C.

103. *Cat.*, 3, 10.

104. *Phars.*, 2, 142–4.

In the war of Marius and Sulla, quite apart from those who fell outside the city on the battlefield, the streets, the squares, forums, theatres, and temples in Rome itself were packed with corpses. It was, in fact, difficult to decide whether the victors inflicted more deaths before victory, to ensure it, or after victory, as a result of it. After the victory of Marius, when he returned from exile (to pass over the general massacre) the head of the consul Octavius was exposed on the rostrum; the Caesars were butchered by Fimbria in their homes; the two Crassi, father and son, were slaughtered before each other's eyes; Baebius and Numitorius were dragged by a hook and disembowelled, Catulus escaped his enemies' clutches by drinking poison: Merula, the *flamen* of Jupiter, cut his veins and offered to Jupiter a libation of his own blood. And those whose salutation Marius refused to acknowledge by offering his right hand were immediately struck down before the conquerer's eyes.[105]

28. *The nature of Sulla's victory, which avenged the savagery of Marius*

The subsequent victory of Sulla[106] no doubt avenged this cruelty; but after terrible bloodshed, which was the price of victory. The war was ended, but its hatreds were still very much alive; and the victory issued in a more ruthless peace. The original massacre and the later carnage of the elder Marius were followed by the even heavier slaughter carried out by his son and by Carbo,[107] who belonged to the same faction. The imminent approach of Sulla had made them despair not only of victory but of their mere survival and they had indulged in

105. In 88 B.C. the command of the war against Mithridates was given by the senate to Sulla; but the Marian party got it transferred to Marius. Sulla marched on Rome, and Marius fled. But after Sulla's departure for the East Marius returned with Cinna in 87 B.C., and proceeded to a massacre of his opponents. C. Octavius, consul in 87 B.C., was one of the first victims. L. Caesar, consul in 90 B.C., and his brother C. Caesar Strabo, a noted orator, were also put to death. P. Crassus, father of the triumvir, committed suicide in the same year, after the murder of one of his sons. Baebius and Numitorius were members of the Sullan party. Q. Lutatius Catulus is generally reported to have killed himself by inhaling the carbon monoxide from a charcoal brazier, and Merula killed himself in the temple of Jupiter Capitolinus.

Condemned criminals were sometimes dragged by hooks to be thrown into the Tiber; cf. Cic., *Philip*, 1, 2, 5; *Pro Rabir*, 5, 16, and Juvenal, 10, 66 (the treatment of the corpse of Sejanus).

106. 82 B.C.

107. The younger Marius and Gn. Papirius Carbo were consuls in 82 B.C. Carbo lead the Marian Party after Cinna's death in 84 B.C.

unrestricted massacres of their own. Besides the widespread general bloodshed, the senate was besieged, and the senators were brought from their senate house, like criminals from prison, to be executed by the sword. The pontifex, Mucius Scaevola,[108] threw his arms round the altar of Vesta, whose temple was regarded by the Romans as the most sacred sanctuary; but he was murdered there, and his blood all but extinguished that sacred flame which was kept alight by the ceaseless tendance of the Vestal Virgins. Then Sulla entered Rome as victor. In a villa belonging to the state he had slaughtered seven thousand men (it was peace, not war, that was raging then); the men had surrendered, and were of course unarmed, which saved the trouble of fighting – a mere command did the business. In the city any Sullan supporter struck down anyone as he pleased and the consequent murders were beyond all calculation, until it was suggested to Sulla that some people should be allowed to live so that the conquerors should have subjects to command.

As soon as a check was imposed on this general licence of assassination, which was spreading its fury on all sides, that notorious register of two thousand names of men from the two honourable orders of the knights and the senators, who were consigned to death and proscription, was published amid great applause. There was general grief at the number of the victims; it was some consolation that the number was not infinite. The sorrow at the multitude of the condemned was counterbalanced by the joyful feeling that the rest had nothing to fear. And yet in the case of some of those who were condemned to die the exquisite torture of their deaths won a sigh of pity even from hearts in which security had stifled all compassion. One man was torn to pieces, not with a weapon, but by the bare hands of his murderers; men treated a living human being with less humanity than animals use in dismembering a dead thing thrown to them. Another had his eyes gouged out, and his limbs cut off one by one, and was condemned to a lingering life, or rather to a lingering death, in this hideous torment. Famous cities were put up to auction as if they were country houses; one whole community was butchered by order, just as a single criminal might be brought out for execution. And all this took place in the peace which followed the war; it was not done to hasten the achievement of victory, but to ensure that the achievement should not be underrated. Peace and War had a com-

108. Q. *Mucius Scaevola*, consul in 95. A great jurist, author of an immense work (eighteen books) on civil law, he is highly praised by Cicero (*De Or.*, 1, 39, 180).

petition in cruelty; and Peace won the prize. For the men whom War cut down were bearing arms; Peace slaughtered the defenceless. The law of War was that the smitten should have the chance of smiting in return; the aim of Peace was to make sure not that the survivor should live, but that he should be killed without the chance of offering resistance.

29. *A comparison between the Gothic invasion, and the disasters of the Gallic invasion and of the Civil Wars*

Have foreign nations ever displayed a fury, or barbarians shown a savagery, to match the cruelty of this victory over fellow-countrymen? What was the foulest and most horrible spectacle ever seen in Rome? The invasion of the Gauls,[109] long ago? The recent invasion of the Goths?[110] Or the ferocity vented on those who were parts of their own body, by Marius, by Sulla and by other men of renown, the leading lights of their factions? The Gauls butchered the senators or as many of them as they could find in all the rest of the city, apart from the Capitol – the citadel which alone was defended by some means or other. But they did allow those who had taken refuge on that hill to buy their lives for gold – lives which they could have taken by the slow process of a siege, even though they were not able to do so by the swift stroke of the sword. The Goths, on the other hand, spared so many of the senators that the real surprise is that they wiped out any of them.

Sulla provides a contrast to these. While Marius was still alive Sulla took up his position as conqueror on that same Capitol which had been preserved from the Gauls, to issue decrees for massacre: and when Marius had slipped away in flight – to return with greater savagery, and a fiercer lust for blood – Sulla, in the Capitol, and by a resolution of the senate, deprived a large number of Romans of their lives and properties. Then, after Sulla's departure, there was nothing sacred, nothing that should be spared, in the judgement of the Marian faction; for when Mucius – a citizen, a senator and a pontiff – clung in his miserable plight to the altar on which, it was averred, the destiny of Rome rested, they did not spare him. Finally (to pass over countless other deaths) the last of Sulla's proscription lists contrived the slaughter of more senators than the Gauls had been able to despoil.

109. 390 B.C. 110. A.D. 410.

30. *The sequence of disastrous wars preceding the coming of Christ*

How can our opponents have the effrontery, the audacity, the impudence, the imbecility (or rather the insanity) to refuse to blame their gods for those catastrophes, while they hold Christ responsible for the disasters of modern times? The brutal Civil Wars, more bitter, on the admission of their own authors, than any wars against foreign enemies – those Civil Wars which, in the general judgement, brought on the republic not merely calamity but utter destruction – broke out long before the coming of Christ. A causal chain of criminal enormities carried the process on from the Marian and Sullan wars to the wars of Sertorius[111] and Catiline[112] (the former was one of Sulla's proscribed, the latter, one of his protégés), on to the war of Lepidus and Catulus[113] (one of whom wished to annul the acts of Sulla, the other to preserve them), on to the wars of Pompey and Caesar (Pompey had been a partisan of Sulla, whose power he equalled, and even surpassed; Caesar found Pompey's power insufferable – because he himself did not wield it – but after the defeat and death of Pompey he transcended it); and then we come to another Caesar, afterwards called Augustus. And it was in the reign of Augustus that Christ was born.

Augustus himself carried on many wars, against many enemies, during which many eminent men perished – among them Cicero, the eloquent expert on the art of government. It is true that Pompey's conqueror, Gaius Caesar, showed clemency in the exercise of power after his victory in civil war; granting his opponents their lives and allowing them to retain their rank and dignity. But certain high-born senators conspired against him on the grounds that he was ambitious for royal power, and, posing as defenders of republican liberty, they assassinated him in the actual senate-house. After this a man of very

111. Q. *Sertorius*, a leader of the popular party after Sulla's victory. Invited in 80 B.C. to lead the revolted Lusitanians, he organized a Spanish army and defied the senatorial forces until 72, when he was murdered by one of his lieutenants.

112. L. *Sergius Catilina*, an impoverished noble, gathered a band of other desperate characters in 65 B.C. intending a general massacre and revolution. This plot failing, he stood for the consulship in 64, but was defeated. In 63 came the 'second conspiracy' of Catiline, crushed by Cicero as consul. Catiline fled and was defeated and killed in battle.

113. M. *Aemilius Lepidus*, consul 78 B.C., attempted a military coup, intending to annul Sulla's measures; but he was defeated in battle near the Janiculum by the forces of the other consul, Q. *Lutatius Catulus*, the leader of the senatorial nobility.

different moral character, soiled and corrupted by all kinds of vices, seemed to be aspiring to Caesar's power. This was Antony, and Cicero vigorously opposed his efforts, again in defence of the so-called 'liberty' of the country. Then appeared on the scene another Caesar, a young man of exceptional gifts, the adopted son of Gaius Caesar. He, as I have said, was afterwards called Augustus. This young Caesar received the support of Cicero, who wanted to foster his power in opposition to Antony, hoping that, when Antony's domination had been broken down and overthrown, his hero would restore the 'liberty of the republic'. In this he showed himself quite blind and unforeseeing; for that same young man, whose position and power Cicero supported, handed over his supporter to Antony's murdering hands as a kind of condition for a pact of reconciliation and brought beneath his own sway that 'liberty of the republic' for which Cicero had been shouting so loudly.

31. *These disasters occurred when the pagan gods were still worshipped. It is sheer effrontery to ascribe the present troubles to Christ, because of the prohibition of pagan cults*

Our opponents should accuse their gods of causing all those evils, instead of being so ungrateful to our Lord Christ for all his benefits. It is certain that when those disasters were happening, 'the altars' of the divine powers 'were glowing with Arabian incense, and fragrant with fresh garlands',[114] the priesthoods were in high esteem, the shrines resplendent; sacrifices and games were going on, and prophetic frenzies in the temples, at a time when so much citizen blood was being shed on all sides, even among the very altars of the gods. Cicero did not choose a temple as his refuge; Mucius[115] had done that – to no purpose. But the Romans in modern times have taken refuge in places most particularly dedicated to Christ, or else the barbarians themselves have taken them there to preserve their lives.[116] All the less reason for their slanders against this Christian era.

One thing I am sure of, and anyone whose judgement is not warped by partisan prejudice will have no difficulty in recognizing the same fact. And the fact is this: to omit the many points I have already made, and the many instances which, I have decided, would take too long to relate, if the human race had received the Christian teaching

114. Virg., *Aen.*, 1, 416. 115. cf. ch. 28. 116. cf. Bk 1, 1.

before the Punic Wars, and then all that devastation, which exhausted Europe and Africa, had followed, none of those whose insults we now have to endure would have failed to attribute those calamities to the Christian religion. Their outcries would have been much more insupportable if (to speak of matters affecting the Romans especially) the reception and propagation of the Christian religion had preceded the invasion of the Gauls, the Tiber floods, the devastation of the fires, or the Civil Wars, the worst catastrophe of all. If the other calamities – calamities so incredible as to be classed as prodigies – had happened in the Christian era, our opponents would certainly charge the Christians with the sole responsibility. I say nothing of manifestations which were more remarkable than harmful; talking oxen, unborn infants shouting words while still in the womb, flying serpents, women turning into men, hens into cocks and so on, which are recounted not in books of fables but in historical works, and which, whether true or false, produce astonishment rather than ruin among mankind.

But when it rains earth, or chalk, or stones (and I mean real stones, not hailstones), then certainly there is a possibility of serious damage. We read in the historians that the fires of Etna ran down from the top of the mountain to the nearest shore and the sea reached such a boiling heat that the rocks were burnt and the pitch was melted in the ships. An astonishing, an incredible phenomenon, but certainly capable of causing no slight damage – if it happened. It is recorded that on another occasion a volcanic eruption of the same kind enveloped Sicily in such an enormous quantity of ash that the buildings of the city of Catana were crushed in ruins beneath the weight. And the Romans, moved by this disaster, remitted Catana's tribute for that year[117] as an expression of sympathy. There is a written account of a portentous swarm of locusts in Africa,[118] after it had become a Roman province. It is said that after devouring all the crops and the leaves of the trees they plunged into the sea in a cloud of incalculable immensity; this host of dead insects was cast up on the sea-shores and so polluted the air that a plague of great violence broke out, which caused the death, it is said, of eighty thousand men in the kingdom of Masinissa[119] alone, and many more than that in the districts nearest to the sea. At Utica at that time, we are assured, only ten thousand of the thirty thousands inhabitants survived.

The kind of folly which we have to suffer, and to which we are

117. cf. Oros., 5, 15 (Orosius says tribute was remitted for ten years).
118. Liv., *Perioch.*, 40. 119. Numidia.

forced to reply, would certainly blame each and all of those calamities on the Christian religion, if they had witnessed them in the Christian era. And yet, as it is, they do not attribute the blame to their gods; in fact they demand the restoration of the worship of those gods, to escape the lighter afflictions of these days, although the worshippers in days of old were not spared those heavier catastrophes.

BOOK IV

1. *The matters discussed in Book I*

In embarking on this treatise on the City of God, I have thought it right to begin by replying to its enemies who, in their pursuit of earthly joys and their appetite for fleeting satisfactions, blame the Christian religion – the only religion of truth and salvation – if among these pleasures they find any unhappiness; yet this unhappiness is imposed on them by God's mercy for their admonition, rather than by God's severity for their punishment. There is, among those adversaries of ours, a great mass of the uneducated, and such people suppose themselves to have the authority of the learned to foment their bitter feelings towards us. These illiterates imagine that there is something extraordinary in the mishaps of their own time and that they did not happen in other periods; those who know this idea to be false conceal their knowledge and support this delusion, to make it seem that the rest are justified in their complaints. I was therefore bound to prove that the facts were very different, from the evidence of the books in which their own authors have recorded the history of the past for the information of posterity, and bound also to demonstrate that the false gods whom they used to worship openly and still worship secretly, are really unclean spirits; they are demons so malignant and deceitful that they delight in the wickedness imputed to them, whether truly or falsely, and have wished their crimes to be publicly represented at their festivals, so that it may be impossible for human weakness to be recalled from the perpetration of such enormities, because a supposedly divine authority is given for their imitation.

We have established all this, not on the basis of our own theories, but partly on evidence still fresh in the memory, since we have seen with our own eyes such exhibitions put on in honour of such divinities,[1] and partly on evidence from writers who have left a description of these performances, not as a reproach to the gods, but in their honour. Thus Varro,[2] the greatest of Roman scholars, the weightiest authority, divided his work into books on 'human affairs' and books on 'divine affairs', arranging his subject matter under the headings

1. Bk II, 4; *Conf.*, 1, 10; 3, 2. 2. cf. Bk III, 4 n.

in proportion to the importance of the topics. And he included stage shows under the heading of 'divine affairs', not 'human affairs', though in fact if the community had consisted entirely of decent and honourable men those shows ought not to have ranked among human affairs. Varro did not make this classification on his own authority; he was born and brought up in Rome, and he found the games so classified, among divine affairs.

At the end of Book I, I briefly set out the points I intended to make in the succeeding argument. In Books II and III I have partly fulfilled that intention. I must now satisfy the expectation of my readers by completing the design.

2. *The subjects included in Books II and III*

I undertook to make some answer to those who ascribe to our religion the responsibility for the calamities of the Roman republic, and to recall (as far as they came to mind and to the extent that seemed sufficient) the disasters suffered by Rome, and by the provinces belonging to her empire, before the prohibition of their sacrifices. They would doubtless have attributed to us the blame for all these, if our religion had by then spread its light on them or had put a stop to their sacrilegious sacrifices.

If I am not mistaken, I have sufficiently dealt with these questions in previous books, treating in Book II of moral evils – which should be reckoned the only real evils, or, at least, the worst of evils – in Book III, of those evils which are the only evils dreaded by fools, namely physical and external disasters – from which even the good are not exempt. As for moral evils, those fools accept them not merely with patience, but with delight; and those are the evils which make them evil. And yet how little I have said about Rome, considered by itself, and about Rome's empire; I have not given a full account up to the time of Caesar Augustus. What if I had decided to recall and emphasize the disasters which, unlike the devastations and destructions inflicted by warring armies, are not inflicted by men upon each other, but come upon the material world by the action of the elements? Apuleius[3]

3. L. *Apuleius Afer*: (*fl. c.* A.D. 150): born in Numidia. His best known work is the satirical romance, the *Metamorphoses*, generally known as *The Golden Ass*; but he was also a professor of rhetoric and philosophy. He wrote a treatise, *De Platonis Dogmate*, and another, *De Deo Socratis*, dealing with the Platonic (or Neoplatonic) doctrine of the Deity and of the demons, the subordinate supernatural powers. This last is extensively quoted and discussed by St Augustine in the *City of God*.

briefly touches on these in his treatise *De Mundo*. He observes that all earthly things are subject to change, alteration, and annihilation. For he says that 'the ground leapt apart' (I am quoting his own words)

with the enormous tremors of the earth, and whole cities were wiped out with their inhabitants; whole districts were swamped by sudden cloud-bursts; what once were continents were changed into islands by the incursion of strange waters; islands were made accessible on foot by the withdrawal of the sea; cities were overthrown by winds and storms; in the East fire flashed from the clouds and destroyed whole districts by conflagrations: and in Western countries there were waterspouts and floods which caused equal devastation: on the summit of Etna the craters burst open and streams of flame ran down the slopes like mountain torrents: it was a conflagration kindled by the gods.[4]

If I had decided to collect such instances of historical fact from all possible sources, when could I have brought the list to an end? And these events all happened in periods before the name of Christ had suppressed any of the futilities of the pagans which destroy all genuine security.

I also promised[5] to show for what moral qualities in the Romans, and for what ends, the true God, in whose power are all kingdoms, deigned to assist the growth of the Roman Empire, and to demonstrate how utterly useless was the help of those supposed gods, whose trickery and deceit in fact did them so much harm. Hence it is clear to me that I must now enter on this topic, and treat especially of the growth of the Roman Empire. For I have dwelt already at considerable length, particularly in Book II, on the harm done by the delusions of the demons, whom the Romans worshipped as gods, and their disastrous effect on Roman morality. While throughout all the three books now completed, I have pointed out the consolations which God, even in the midst of the horrors of war, has bestowed through the name of Christ, which the barbarians hold in such respect – consolations foreign to the normal usage of war, granted to good and bad alike, in the same way as God 'makes the sun rise on good and on bad, and sends the rain on the righteous and on the unrighteous'.[6]

3. *Is the extent of dominion when acquired only by war, to be considered among the blessings of the wise or the happy?*

Let us then see on what grounds our opponents have the boldness to ascribe the immense expansion and the long duration of the Roman

4. *De Mundo*, 34 (inexactly quoted). 5. Bk I, 36.
6. Matt. 5, 45.

Empire to the credit of the gods to whom, so they claim, they offered honourable worship in the dutiful performance of degrading spectacles by the agency of degraded performers.

But I should like to preface the inquiry with a brief examination of the following question: Is it reasonable, is it sensible, to boast of the extent and grandeur of empire, when you cannot show that men lived in happiness, as they passed their lives amid the horrors of war, amid the shedding of men's blood – whether the blood of enemies or fellow-citizens – under the shadow of fear and amid the terror of ruthless ambition? The only joy to be attained had the fragile brilliance of glass, a joy outweighed by the fear that it may be shattered in a moment.

To help us to form our judgement let us refuse to be fooled by empty bombast, to let the edge of our critical faculties be blunted by high-sounding words like 'peoples', 'realms', 'provinces'. Let us set before our mind's eye two men; for the individual man is, like a single letter in a statement, an element, as it were, out of which a community or a realm is built up, however vast its territorial possessions. Let us imagine one of the two to be poor, or, better, in a middle station of life, while the other is excessively rich. But the rich man is tortured by fears, worn out with sadness, burnt up with ambition, never knowing serenity of respose, always panting and sweating in his struggles with opponents. It may be true that he enormously swells his patrimony, but at the cost of those discontents, while by this increase he heaps up a load of further anxiety and bitterness. The other man, the ordinary citizen, is content with his strictly limited resources. He is loved by family and friends; he enjoys the blessing of peace with his relations, neighbours, and friends; he is loyal, compassionate, and kind, healthy in body, temperate in habits, of unblemished character, and enjoys the serenity of a good conscience. I do not think anyone would be fool enough to hesitate about which he would prefer.

It is the same with two families, two peoples, or two realms. The same canon of judgement applies as in the case of the two men. If we apply the canon scrupulously, without allowing our judgement to be warped, we shall not have the slightest difficulty in seeing where true happiness lies, and where an empty show. And therefore it is beneficial that the good should extend their dominion far and wide, and that their reign should endure, with the worship of the true God by genuine sacrifices and upright lives. This is for the benefit of all, of the subjects even more than the rulers. For the rulers, their piety and integrity – great gifts of God – suffice for true happiness, for a good life on earth, and for eternal life hereafter. And, in this world the reign of the good is a blessing for themselves, and even more for the whole of human society. In contrast, the reign of the wicked is more harmful to those who wield the power, who bring destruction on their own souls through the greater scope thus given for their misdeeds, whereas those who are enslaved beneath them are harmed only by their own wickedness. For the evils inflicted on the righteous by their wicked masters are not punishments for crime but tests of virtue. The good man, though a slave, is free; the wicked, though he reigns, is a slave, and not the slave of a single man, but – what is far worse – the slave of as many masters as he has vices.[7] It is in reference to vices that the Scripture says, 'When a man is vanquished he becomes the bond-slave of his conqueror.'[8]

4. *Kingdoms without justice are like criminal gangs*

Remove justice, and what are kingdoms but gangs of criminals on a large scale? What are criminal gangs but petty kingdoms? A gang is a group of men under the command of a leader, bound by a compact of association, in which the plunder is divided according to an agreed convention.

If this villainy wins so many recruits from the ranks of the demoralized that it acquires territory, establishes a base, captures cities and subdues peoples, it then openly arrogates to itself the title of kingdom, which is conferred on it in the eyes of the world, not by the renouncing of aggression but by the attainment of impunity.

For it was a witty and a truthful rejoinder which was given by a captured pirate to Alexander the Great. The king asked the fellow, 'What is your idea, in infesting the sea?' And the pirate answered, with uninhibited insolence, 'The same as yours, in infesting the earth! But because I do it with a tiny craft, I'm called a pirate: because you have a mighty navy, you're called an emperor.'[9]

5. *The revolt of the gladiators, whose power had something of a royal grandeur*

I shall not discuss the question of what kind of people Romulus col-

7. *The slave of vices*: a Stoic sentiment; cf. Seneca., *Ep.*, 47, 17: 'He is a slave. Is he any the worse off for that? Show me any man who is not a slave! One man is the slave of lust, another of greed, another of ambition; and all men are the slaves of fear ... and the most degraded slavery is that which is self-imposed.'

8. 2 Pet. 2, 19.

9. Cic., *De Rep.*, 3, 14, 24.

lected; it is known that he took measures to ensure that when they were granted a share in the community after abandoning their former way of life, they should no longer have to think about the punishment to which they were liable, the fear of which had impelled them to greater crimes, so that in the future they should be less aggressive in their attitude to society.

What I want to say is that when the Roman Empire was already great, when she had subjugated many nations and was feared by all the rest, this great Empire was bitterly distressed and deeply alarmed, and had the utmost difficulty in extricating herself from the threat of overwhelming disaster, when a tiny handful of gladiators[10] in Campania escaped from the training-school and collected a large army. Under three commanders[11] they wrought cruel havoc over a wide area of Italy. Would our opponents tell us the name of the god who assisted them, so that from a small and contemptible gang of thugs they developed into a 'kingdom' inspiring fear in the Romans, for all Rome's great resources and all her strongholds? Are they going to say they did not receive divine help because they did not last long?[12] Come now, no man's life is very long! On this argument the gods never help any man to a throne, since individuals soon die; and one should not count something a benefit which vanishes like smoke in the case of each man – and so, to be sure, in all, as one individual succeeds another. What does it matter to those who worshipped the gods under Romulus, and died so long ago, that after their death the Roman Empire grew to such greatness, since they have to plead their cause in the world below? Whether their cause be good or bad is not relevant to our argument. The same consideration applies to all those who in the few days of the rapid course of their lives have wielded temporary power in the Roman Empire. However long the extension of that Empire's duration, as the generations succeed one another in their rise and fall, those individuals have passed on, taking with them the bundle of their deeds.

Now if even the benefits of the briefest space of time are to be attributed to the help of the gods, those gladiators received no inconsiderable assistance. They broke the chains of their servile condition; they escaped; they got clean away; they collected a large and formidable army; and in obedience to the plans and orders of their 'kings', they became an object of dread to the soaring might of Rome. They were more than a match for many Roman generals; they captured

10. cf. Bk III, 26. 11. Spartacus, Oenomaus, Crixus. 12. 73–71 B.C.

much booty; they gained many victories; they indulged themselves at will, following the prompting of every desire; in fact, they lived in all the grandeur of kings, until their eventual defeat, which was only achieved with the greatest difficulty.

But let us go on to matters of more importance.

6. *The ambition of King Ninus, the first ruler to extend his dominion by making war on his neighbours*

We have an account of Greek history, or rather of the history of foreign nations, from the pen of Justinus, who based his work on that of Trogus Pompeius. Both were Latin authors, but Justinus abbreviated his original; and he begins his work with these words,

> At the beginning of history the supreme power over races and nations rested with kings, who rose to that summit of authority not by canvassing popular support, but because their moderation was recognized by good men. The peoples were not under the restraint of laws: it was their custom to protect, not to extend, the frontiers of their dominion, and their realms were confined within the limits of their own country. Ninus, king of Assyria, was the first to change these ancient and, as it were, hereditary customs, through a craving for empire, which was then a novelty. He was the first to make war on his neighbours; and he extended his sway as far as the borders of Libya, over nations who were not trained to resist.

He goes on, a little later,

> Ninus established his hold on his vast acquisitions by continual occupation. Thus strengthened by the increased resources acquired by the subjugation of his neighbours he passed on to attack others. Each victory became the instrument of the next conquest; and the result was the submission of all the nations of the East.[13]

Whatever credit is to be attached to the statements of Justinus or Trogus – for other more trustworthy documents prove them guilty of inexactitude on occasion – there is general agreement among historians that the Assyrian kingdom received a wide extension under Ninus. And that kingdom lasted so long that the Roman Empire has not equalled its duration. Those who have pursued the study of chron-

13. *Justinus* (second or third century A.D.) abridged the *Universal History* of Trogus Pompeius (*fl.* under Augustus) which started with the foundation of Nineveh and came down to his own time. His source for Assyrian history was Ctesias, a Greek physician at the Persian court in the early fourth century.

Ninus is legendary, his supposed date being *c.* 2000 B.C. The foundation of Babylon was attributed to his widow, Semiramis. The rise of Assyrian power began in fact *c.* 1500.

ology ascribe to the Assyrian Empire a duration of one thousand two hundred and forty years,[14] from the first year of Ninus' reign to the time when it was taken over by the Medes.[15]

Now, to attack one's neighbours, to pass on to crush and subdue more remote peoples without provocation and solely from the thirst for dominion – what is one to call this but brigandage on the grand scale?

7. *The rise and fall of the kingdoms of the world. Are these changes due to the assistance of the gods, and their subsequent desertion?*

If this Assyrian kingdom reached such magnitude and lasted for so long, without any assistance from the gods, why are the gods given credit for the Roman Empire's wide extension in space and its long duration in time? Whatever the cause in one case, it is the same as in the other. But if our enemies maintain that the success of Assyria is to be attributed to the help of the gods, then I ask: Of what gods? For the nations which Ninus crushed and subdued did not then worship gods different from those of Assyria. Or if the Assyrians did have gods exclusively their own, more highly skilled workers as it were, in the empire-building and empire-maintaining trade, then are we to suppose that they were dead, when Assyria lost her Empire? Or that they preferred to cross over to the Medes, because they had not been paid, or, perhaps, because higher wages were offered? And then transferred to the Persians,[16] when Cyrus invited them on more favourable terms? The Persians, after the far-reaching but very short-lived Empire of Alexander,[17] have remained to this day in the possession of their dominion over no inconsiderable territory in the East. If this is so, either the gods are faithless, in deserting their own people and passing over to the enemy – a thing which Camillus[18] refused to do, when, after conquering and storming a city which was Rome's bitterest foe, he experienced the ingratitude of his own city, for which he had won that victory; he forgot this injustice and remembered only his country, when he saved her a second time from the Gauls. Or else the gods are not as strong as gods ought to be, if they can be conquered by the superior strategy or the military strength of human beings. Or again, if the gods wage war against one another, and the gods are not

14. cf. Euseb-Hier., *Chronic.*, (ed. Helm) p. 83a, 9f.
15. Fall of Nineveh, 612 B.C.
16. Capture of Babylon by Cyrus, 538 B.C.
17. 336–323 B.C.
18. cf. Bk II, 17; Bk III, 17.

conquered by men but, it may be, by other gods who belong exclusively to particular communities, we may infer that there are enmities among them, which they take up on behalf of their particular side. And it follows that a community ought to worship other gods as much as its own, to gain their help for its own side.

Finally, whatever may be the truth about this transference, or flight, or migration of the gods – or their desertion in battle – those kingdoms were lost and taken over, after immeasurable military disasters, at a time when the name of Christ had not yet been preached in that part of the world. If at the time when the Assyrian Empire was destroyed, after twelve hundred years and more, the Christian religion had already proclaimed another, an eternal, kingdom and had put an end to the sacrilegious cults of false gods, what would the fools of that race have said? Would they not have asserted that an Empire so long preserved could only have disappeared because their cults had been abandoned and the Christian religion had been accepted?

In such an absurd (but very likely) assertion our opponents should see themselves mirrored; and they should then blush, if they have any shame, to utter similar complaints. The Roman Empire has been shaken rather than transformed, and that happened to it at other periods, before the preaching of Christ's name; and it recovered. There is no need to despair of its recovery at this present time. Who knows what is God's will in this matter?

8. *The Romans could scarcely entrust a single department of life to any one god. To what gods could they ascribe the growth and preservation of their Empire?*

Next, if you will, let us inquire which gods, of all that host of gods[19] who received their worship, they believed to be specially responsible for the extension and preservation of the Roman Empire. For in a work of such nobility and sublime grandeur they do not dare to assign any part to the goddess Cloacina, or to Volupia (whose name has the same root as 'voluptuous') or to Lubentina (a name derived from *libido*), or to Vaticanus (who presides over the wails – *vagitus* – of

19. Most of those 'tiny gods' were vaguely conceived 'powers' (*numina*) invoked for various particular functions, and only a few enjoyed anything like a cult. Some of them are merely names to us, and no doubt they were little more than that to the pagans of St Augustine's time. The purpose of St Augustine's elaborate irony is to combat the sentimental nostalgia for the old days of paganism.

infants), or to Cunina (who takes care of their cradles – *cunae*). But how can I give a list, in one passage of this book, of all the names of their gods and goddesses? The Romans had difficulty in getting them into the massive volumes in which they assigned particular functions and special responsibilities to the various divine powers. They decided that responsibility for the land should not be entrusted to any one god; they put the goddess Rusina in charge of the rural countryside; they consigned the mountain ranges (*iuga*) to the care of the god Jugatinus; the hills (*colles*) to the goddess Collatina, the valleys to Vallonia. They could not even find the goddess called Segetia adequate on her own, to the responsibility for the crops (*segetes*) from start to finish. Instead, they decided that the corn when sown (*sata*) should have the goddess Seia to watch over it as long as the seeds were under ground; as soon as the shoots came above the ground and began to form the grain (*seges*), they were under the charge of the goddess Segetia; but when the corn had been reaped and stored the goddess Tutilina was set over them to keep them safe (*tuto*). Would not anyone think that Segetia should have been competent to supervise the whole process from the first green shoots to the dry ears of corn? But that was not enough for men who loved a multitude of gods – and so much so that their miserable soul disdained the pure embrace of the one true God and prostituted itself to a mob of demons. So they put Proserpina in command of germinating corn; the god Nodutus looked after the nodes and joints on the stalks; the goddess Volutina saw to the envelopes (*involumenta*) of the follicles; when the follicles opened (*patescunt*) to release the spike, the goddess Patelana took over; when the crops were evenly eared, then came the turn of the goddess Hostilina (the old word for 'make even' was *hostire*); when the crops were blooming, the goddess Flora came in; when they became milky, the god Lacturnus; when they were maturing, the goddess Matuta; when they were plucked up (*runcantur*) the goddess Runcina.

I shall not list them all; I find the whole thing disagreeable, even if the Romans do not think it disgraceful. But this very brief account is intended to make it clear that the pagans have not the impudence to allege that the Roman Empire was established, increased, and preserved by those divinities who were so clearly confined to their own particular departments that no general responsibility was entrusted to any one of them. When could Segetia have looked after the Empire, seeing that she was not allowed the simultaneous charge of crops and trees? How could Cunina have even given a thought to arms, when her authority was not permitted to range beyond cradles? How could

Nodutus help in war, when his interest was confined to the node of the stalk and did not even extend to the follicle?

Each man appoints one door-keeper for his house and that one, being a man, is enough. But the Romans appointed three gods; Forculus to guard the doors (*fores*); Cardea the hinges (*cardo*); Limentinus the threshold (*limen*).[20] So Forculus could not guard both hinges and threshold at the same time!

9. *Jupiter's worshippers consider him to be the supreme god. Is he to be held responsible for the wide extent and long duration of the Roman Empire?*

We ought then to pass over this host of tiny gods – or at least to dismiss them for a time – and to look into the functions of the greater gods, by whose activity Rome was brought to greatness and enjoyed a long period of empire over so many peoples. Here, of course, we see the work of Jupiter; it is Jupiter whom the Romans will have to be the king of all the gods and goddesses. This is the meaning of his sceptre, and of the Capitol[21] on its high hill. 'The whole universe is full of

20. *Cloacina* (*Cluacina*): a title of Venus rather than the name of a distinct deity. It derives from *cluare*, 'to purify'; but St Augustine takes it as meaning the goddess of the sewer (*cloaca*).

Volupia: personification of pleasure. Varro mentions her shrine (*De Ling. Lat.*, 5, 164).

Lubentina: personification of sensual pleasure. Cicero speaks of *Lubentina Venus* (*De Nat. Deor.*, 2, 23, 61).

Vaticanus: Augustine's derivation is, as often, fantastic; but Varro is responsible for it (Gell., 16, 17). *Cunina* is mentioned by Varro. *Rusina* is unknown.

Iugatinus is unknown: (a deity of the same name appears in ch. IV; Bk VI, 9).

Collatina, Vallonia, are unknown; *Segetia* appears as *Segesta* in Pliny; *Seia* occurs in Macrobius and Pliny; *Tutilina* is mentioned by Varro, without attribution of function.

Proserpina: her function assumes a derivation from *pro-serpere*, 'to creep forth'. Varro (*De Ling. Lat.*, 5, 68) gives another meaning to this derivation ('because, like a serpent, she sways now to the right, now to the left'). The cult of Proserpina (with Dis) was started in 249, during the first Punic War.

Nodutus, Volutina, Hostilina, Lacturnus are unknown.

Patelana is mentioned by Arnobius (Adv. Gent., 4, 7).

Flora: cf. Bk II, 27.

Matuta: cf. Bk XVII, 14. She appears in Lucretius (5, 654) as goddess of the dawn, identified with Aurora. As 'Mother Matuta' she had a festival of mothers, the *Matralia*, at Rome on 11 June (Ovid, *Fast.*, 6, 479). *Runcina* appears only here.

Forculus, Cardea (*Cardia* in Ovid, *Fast.*, 6, 101), *Limentinus* are mentioned elsewhere, but with no information about them.

21. The temple of Jupiter Capitolinus.

Jupiter.'[22] This may be a poetic utterance; but the Romans use it as the most adequate definition of the god; and Varro believes that men who worship one single God, without an idol, are really worshipping Jupiter, though under another name.[23] If that is true, why has he been so shamefully treated at Rome – and indeed among other nations – by having an idol erected to him? This action so offended Varro that, despite the pressure of perverted custom in so great a city, he had not the slightest hesitation in saying, and saying in writing, that those who set up images for the people 'have abolished reverence and introduced error'.

10. *Theories which placed different gods in charge of different parts of the universe*

Why do the pagans give Juno to Jupiter for a wife, to be called 'sister and spouse'?[24] 'The reason is', they say, 'that, by tradition, we assume Jupiter to be in the ether[25] (the upper air) and Juno in the lower air; and these two elements are joined together, the one above the other.' Then it follows that this Jupiter is not the subject of the statement, 'The whole universe is full of Jupiter', if Juno also fills some part of it. Or is it that each of them fills both elements and this married pair are at the same time in both and in each? Then why is the ether assigned to Jupiter and the air to Juno? And in any case the two of them would be enough. Why allot the sea to Neptune, and the earth to Pluto? And they must not be left wifeless, so Salacia[26] is provided for Neptune, Proserpina for Pluto. For as the lower part of the sky – the air – is, they say, occupied by Juno, so Salacia has the lower part of the sea, and Proserpina the lower parts of the earth.

They try to find ways to botch together their fables, but without success. For if their account were true their teachers of old time would have spoken of three elements, not four, so as to distribute each of the married pairs to their particular element. As it is, those teachers undoubtedly asserted that ether and air were different elements; but water, whether 'upper' or 'lower', is still just water; you may conceive some difference; but not enough to make it anything but water.

22. Virg., *Ecl.*, 3, 60. 23. cf. ch. 31. 24. Virg., *Aen.*, 1, 47.

25. *Jupiter in the ether.* The identification of Zeus with the upper air (aether), is found in two fragments of Euripides: 'This ether which extends without limit in the height of heaven, this is Zeus' (Frag. 941); 'The ether, which men call Zeus' (Frag. 877).

26. cf. Bk VII, 22.

And in spite of all imaginable differences and distinctions, 'lower' earth cannot be anything but earth.

Observe further that the whole material universe is made up of the four elements. Then where will Minerva come in? What will be her sphere? What will she fill? She was set up in the Capitol with Jupiter and Juno, although she was not the daughter of both. If they say that Minerva holds sway in the upper part of the ether and that this gave the poets occasion to invent the story of her birth from the head of Jupiter, why is she not reputed the queen of the gods on the ground that she is higher than Jupiter? Is it because it was improper to place a daughter above her father? Then why was that equity not observed in the relation between Jupiter and Saturn? Is it because Saturn was conquered? Then they fought, did they? 'Certainly not! All that is legendary gossip!' Very well. Let us not believe the fables; let us have better ideas about the gods. Then why is Jupiter's father not given at least an equal place of honour, if not a higher? 'Because Saturn represents duration of time.'[27] So they worship time when they worship Saturn! And the implication is that Jupiter, king of gods, is a child of time! Is there anything improper in calling Juno and Jupiter the children of time, if he is the sky and she is the earth? For undoubtedly sky and earth are created things; and Virgil is basing himself not on poetical fictions but on the writings of philosophers, when he says,

> The omnipotent father, ether all-supreme,
> Descends with fecund showers upon the lap
> Of his glad consort.[28]

'Upon the lap', that is, of Tellus or Terra; for here also they are determined to have some difference, and in the earth itself they distinguish Terra, Tellus, and Tellumo,[29] and all these gods are called by their special names, assigned to their own separate functions and worshipped with their own rites, at their own altars. The earth is also called the Mother of the Gods – so the fictions of the poets are more tolerable, since it is not in the poetry of the Romans but in their sacred books that Juno is found not only as 'sister and spouse' of Jupiter, but also as his mother. They make out the same earth to be Ceres and also Vesta,[30] although more often they claim that Vesta is simply fire,

27. cf. Bk VII, 19. Saturn is identified with the Greek Cronos, whose name was supposed to be derived from *chronos*, 'time'. (Cic., *De Nat. Deor.*, 2, 25, 64.)

28. *Georg.*, 2, 325ff.

29. cf. Bk VII, 23.

30. *Vesta*: Ovid, (*Fast.*, 6, 299) gives a curious etymology: 'The earth stands by its own power; Vesta gets her name because of standing with power (*vi stando*).' There seems to be no evidence for the equation Vesta = Venus; cf. Bk VII, 24n.

fire on the hearth, without which a community cannot exist; and the reason why virgins are by custom consecrated to her service is that fire, like a virgin, does not give birth. All this inanity deserved to be abolished and swept away by him who was born of a virgin.

Is it not insupportable that while they ascribe to fire so much honour and, one may say, purity, they are not ashamed sometimes to identify Vesta with Venus, thus making nonsense of the virginity which is honoured in her attendants? For if Vesta is Venus how could the virgins do her due service by abstaining from the works of Venus? Or are there two Venuses, one a virgin, the other a wife? Or, rather three! One for virgins, who is the same as Vesta; one for married women; one for harlots? This last was the goddess to whom the Phoenicians used to give a present, earned by the prostitution of their daughters, before they gave them in marriage. Which of these is the lady wife of Vulcan? Certainly not the virgin, since she has a husband. Not the harlot; perish the thought! We must not seem to insult the son of Juno, and Minerva's fellow-worker! Then we infer that Vulcan's wife was concerned with married women. I hope they will not imitate her behaviour with Mars!

'There you go! Back to the fables again.' But what kind of justice is this – to be angry with us for talking like this about their gods and not to be angry with themselves for taking such pleasure in watching the gods' depravities in the theatres? And remember (incredible though it would be, were it not proved quite incontestably) that those representations of the gods' disgrace were instituted in honour of the gods!

11. *The many gods identified by the learned with Jupiter*

So let them make what claims they like in their scientific theories and arguments. Let Jupiter be at one time the soul of this material universe, who 'fills' and 'moves the whole mass',[31] constructed and composed out of four elements – or as many elements as they please – and then let him give up to his sister and his brothers their special parts of the whole. At another time let him be the ether, so that he may from above embrace Juno, the air spread out below him, and then let him be the whole sky, air included, and fertilize, with his 'fecund showers' and seeds, the earth which is both his wife and his mother – nothing disgusting in this, in the divine context! Then (we need not discuss all

31. cf. Virg., *Ecl.* 3, 60 (ch. 9, above), and *Aen.* 6, 727. The 'world-soul' is typical teaching of Stoic Pantheism; cf. Bk VII, 6.

the possibilities) let him be the one god of whom the famous poet (as many think) is speaking when he says,

> Because God ranges all the lands of earth,
> The sea's expanse, and the vast depth of heaven.[32]

Let this one god be Jupiter in the ether, Juno in the air, Neptune in the sea, Salacia[33] in the lower depths of the sea, Pluto on earth, Proserpina in the lower depths of the earth, Vesta on the domestic hearth, Vulcan in the metal-worker's forge: in the sky, let him be the Sun, the Moon, the stars; among the seers, Apollo; in commerce, Mercury; in the person of Janus[34] let him appear as the initiator, in Terminus as the terminator. Let him be Saturn, in respect of time; in wars let him be Mars and Bellona; Liber among the vines, Ceres among the crops and Diana in the woods; and Minerva in respect of natural talents. Finally, let him also be seen in that crowd of plebian gods, as we may call them. Under the name of Liber let him be in charge of the seed of men, and in charge of the seed of women under the title of Libera;[35] let him be identified with Diespater, to bring the offspring into the light of day (*dies*), and with Mena, whom the Romans appointed to supervise the periods of women; and with Lucina,[36] who is invoked by women in childbirth. Let him bring aid (*opem*) to the newly-born by receiving them upon the lap of earth, and be called Opis; let him open the infant's mouth when the baby wails, and be called the god Vaticanus; and lift it (*levare*) from the ground as the goddess Levana; and guard the cradle as Cunina.[37] Let it be none other than he who is manifested in those goddesses, called Carmentes, who foretell the fate of the newly-born; let him be invoked as Fortuna, the presiding deity of chances. As the goddess Rumina let him give the breast to the baby (the breast was anciently called *ruma*); as Potina let him offer drink (*potio*), and as Educa serve food (*esca*) to the young. Let him be named Paventia, from the terror (*pavor*) of infants; Venilia,[38] from the advent of hope; Volupia,[39] from voluptuous delight; Agenoria, in respect of activity; from the stimulus which drives men to excessive action, let him get the title Stimula; and be the goddess Strenia,[40] in making men strenuous; and Numeria, to teach men numbers, and Camena to teach them to sin (*canere*). At the same time let him be Consus, in offering counsel, and Sentia, by inspiring sentiments; and appear as the

32. Virg., *Georg.*, 4, 221f. 33. cf. Bk VII, 22.
34. On *Janus*, and the following minor gods, see note 45.
35. cf. ch. 23; Bk VI, 9; VII, 2. 36. cf. Bk VII, 2. 37. cf. ch. 8.
38. cf. Bk VII, 22. 39. cf. ch. 8. 40. cf. ch. 16.

goddess Juventas,[41] to welcome the opening stages of youth, when the *toga praetexta* has been laid aside; and as 'Bearded Fortuna'[42] to equip the young men with beards. (The pagans refused to do these young men the honour of giving this divinity, as a male divinity of some kind or other, a masculine name, Barbatus, say – from *barba*, as Nodutus from *nodus* – or Fortunius; anything rather than the feminine Fortuna – with that beard!) In the character of Jugatinus[43] let him join couples in marriage; and let him be invoked by the name of Virginensis, when the bride's virgin girdle is untied. Let him be Mutunus, or Tutunus, whom the Greeks called Priapus.[44] If it does not embarrass our opponents, let Jupiter be all that I have mentioned – and all that I have left unsaid (for I decided to omit a great deal): let him, and him alone, be all those gods and goddesses,[45] whether, as

41. cf. ch. 23. 42. cf. ch. 19. 43. cf. Bk VI, 9. 44. cf. Bk II, 14n.

45. *Janus*: the god of beginnings. Originally one of the chief Roman gods. His temple in the forum was in the shape of an archway; cf. Bk III, 10, for the closing of the temple doors in time of peace; cf. also Bk VII, 4; 7–10; 28.

Terminus: the sacred boundary stone in the temple of Jupiter Capitolinus. Festival of Terminalia on 23 February.

Bellona. In 296 B.C., after a victory over Etruscans and Samnites, the consul Appius Claudius ('the blind') dedicated a temple to Bellona on the Campus Martius.

Liber: an old Italian fertility god, later identified with Bacchus. The festival of the *Liberalia* (March 17) was the traditional day for the assumption by young men of the *toga virilis*. Libera, his female counterpart, is identified by St Augustine with Venus (Bk VII, 2) and with Ceres (Bk VII, 3). There was a joint temple to Liber and Ceres near the Circus Maximus; cf. Bk VI, 9.

Diespiter: = Jupiter. Dies, Ju–, Jove, Zeus are all related to a Sanscrit word for the bright sky.

Mena: = Gk mên, the moon or month.

Lucina: an epithet of Juno, in her obstetric capacity, rather than a distinct deity.

Opis: apparently distinguished from Ops (personification of *ops*, 'power', 'wealth') the wife of Saturn; identified with Terra, Cybele, and other powers of fertility.

Levana. A new born child was laid on the floor. If the father acknowledged it as his, he lifted it up, thus accepting responsibility for its upbringing.

Carmentes. In classical times there was one goddess, Carmentis (Carmenta), a prophetic deity, associated with birth, and with a festival on 11 and 15 January. One of Rome's gates was the Porta Carmentalis.

Fortuna. Fors Fortuna had at least two temples in Rome, one in the Forum Boarium and one in Caesar's gardens; and three temples outside, on the right bank of the Tiber. Her festival was a river carnival, on 24 June. Fortuna Publica had three shrines on the Quirinal, and a festival there on 25 May. For Fortuna Muliebris cf. ch. 19.

some would have it, they are all aspects of Jupiter, or forces of Jupiter. The latter interpretation is advanced by those who have decided that he is the soul of the world – an opinion held by men of apparent distinction and erudition.

If this is true – and for the moment I leave aside the question of its truth – what would they lose by a wise economy in worshipping one God? Would he be in any way underrated, since he himself would be worshipped? If it should be feared that the omitted or neglected aspects of Jupiter might be angry, the inference would be that here there is not (as they would have it) one whole life of one Living Being, containing in itself all gods as its powers or members or aspects, but rather, each aspect has a life distinct from the others, if one aspect can be angry independently of another, if one can be appeased while another is irritated. If, on the other hand, it is asserted that all the aspects together, that is the whole of Jupiter himself, could have been offended if his aspects were not worshipped individually and separately, this assertion is the merest folly. None of them could have

---

Rumina. Varro tells of a shrine at the *ficus Ruminalis*, the fig-tree under which, in the legend, the wolf suckled Romulus and Remus. Ruminus was a title of Jupiter (Bk VIII, 11).

Educa appears as Edusa in Varro, *De Liberis Educandis* (quoted by the early fourth-century grammarian Nonius Marcellus). She assisted Potina and Cunina in the care of weaned infants.

Venilia. Diva Venilis was the mother of Turnus (Virg., *Aen.*, 10, 76). The Venilia of Bk VII, 22 is apparently a different goddess.

Stimula. Ovid, (*Fast.*, 6, 503) mentions a grove 'of Semele or Stimula'. It was the scene of the Bacchanalian orgies which led to the suppression of Dionysiac rites in 186 B.C.

Strenia. A shrine on the Via Sacra is recorded by Varro (*De Ling. Lat.*, 5, 47).

Numeria: the goddess of quick birth, according to Varro (quoted by Nonius Marcellus).

Camena: normally found in the plural; prophetic water nymphs, having a sacred spring outside the Porta Capena, where the Vestals drew water for their ceremonies; identified with the Greek Muses, first by Livius Andronicus (the third-century poet) who built them a temple (Ovid, *Fast.*, 3, 275).

Consus: god of fertility, and of counsel. Festival of Consualic on 21 August.

Juventas: a deified personification, identified with the Greek Hebe ('youth'). In 218 a *lectisternium* (see Bk II, 12 and n.) was offered to her, and in 191 her temple was dedicated in the Circus Maximus; cf. ch. 23 for her cult on the Capitol.

Mutunus or *Tutunus* (elsewhere Mutunus Tutunus or Mutinus): a phallic god, perhaps the Etruscan equivalent of Priapus.

Paventia, Agenoria, Sentia, Jugatinus, Virginensis, Fortuna Barbata, were presumably recorded in Varro. They are not found in extant classical literature.

been neglected while the god himself, who in himself possesses them all, was being worshipped. Out of innumerable possible examples I will content myself with this. They say that all the stars are 'aspects' of Jupiter, that they are alive and possess rational souls and are therefore indisputably gods.[46] But they do not observe how many of these gods they omit to worship, for how many they do not build temples or stars. They erect altars, while they have thought it necessary to set them up for a tiny handful of stars and to sacrifice to them individually. So if those gods are angry when they do not receive individual worship, are not the pagans afraid of living beneath the wrath of the whole heaven when they have propitiated but a few of them? While if they worship all the stars just because they exist in the Jupiter whom they worship, they could, by this economical procedure, have offered their prayers to them all, in the person of that one god, and thus none of them would have been angry, since none of them would have been neglected. This would have been better than to worship some of them and give a just cause for anger to the far greater number who were overlooked, especially when the sight presented to the stars when they shone down from their celestial abode was – Priapus, swelling in all his naked obscenity!

12. *The theory that makes God the soul of the world, the body of God*

But here is another point. And it is one which no man of quick intelligence, in fact no man at all (for there is no need here of exceptional ability) can consider unmoved. Putting aside all contentious polemics, let us note carefully that if God is the Soul of the World and the world is to him as the body to the soul, if this God is, as it were, in the bosom of nature and contains all things in himself, so that from his soul, which gives life to the whole of that mass, the life and soul of all living things is derived – according to the lot assigned at birth to each; if this is so, then nothing at all remains which is not a part of God. Can anyone fail to see the blasphemous and irreligious consequences? Anything which anyone treads underfoot would be a part of God! In the killing of any living creature, a part of God would be slaughtered! I shrink from uttering all the possibilities which come to mind; it would be impossible to mention them without shame.

46. *Stars*: The belief in the divinity of the stars was common in antiquity. It is found in Neoplatonism, and it was consonant with the Stoic equation of deity and light. St Augustine himself is not prepared to deny sentience and intelligence to the heavenly bodies; cf. Bk XIII, 16.

13. *Another theory confines the points of God to the rational animals*

But perhaps it is maintained that only rational animals, such as men, are parts of God. For my part, I cannot see how, if the whole universe is God, the lower animals can be excluded from his parts. But we need not contest the point. To confine ourselves to the rational being, man, what could be more unfortunate than the belief that when a child is smacked, God is smacked? It would follow, too, that 'parts of God' can become lustful, unjust, irreligious, and utterly worthy of condemnation. Could anyone in his right mind tolerate such a conclusion? Finally, why should God be angry with those who do not worship him, seeing that it is 'parts' of himself which deny him worship?

Our opponents are thus reduced to admitting that all the gods have their own particular lives, that each one lives for himself, that none is 'part' of any other, and that all should be worshipped who can be recognized and worshipped, since there are so many that they cannot all be recognized and worshipped.

It is because Jupiter presides over all the gods as king, that the Romans suppose him to have established and extended Rome's dominion. If Jupiter himself did not do so, what other god could they believe to have undertaken so great a task? All the other gods were fully employed in their own particular tasks and responsibilities, and none of them invades the sphere of another. Only the king of gods could have given increase and enlargement to the kingdom of men.

14. *If Victory is, as they say, a goddess, it is inconsistent to attribute the growth of empire to Jupiter*

The first question I would like to ask is: Why is not Empire itself one of those gods? Surely it should be, if Victory is a goddess?[47] Why should Jupiter himself be needed in this matter, if Victory is favourable and propitious, and always comes to those whom she wishes to be conquerors? Given her favour and sympathy, what nations would have remained unconquered, even though Jupiter had taken a holi-

47. There was a temple built for Victory on the Palatine in 294. Here was taken the image of Cybele in 204 B.C. (cf. Bk I, 30; Liv., 29, 14); and Victory's image led the procession at the Megalensia, Cybele's festival, on 4 April. In St Augustine's time occurred the removal by Gratian of the famous image of Victory from the Senate house (A.D. 382), and the pagan reaction to it, led by Symmachus (cf. Bk II, 3n.)

day, or had been otherwise employed? Surely, all kingdoms would have submitted? But perhaps honest men did not like to make war with a lack of equity too unconscionable and to enlarge their dominions by aggression against peaceful neighbours who did them no wrong? If such was their feeling, I certainly approve and applaud them.

15. *Can good men consistently desire to extend their dominion?*

I would therefore have our adversaries consider the possibility that to rejoice in the extent of empire is not a characteristic of good men. The increase of empire was assisted by the wickedness of those against whom just wars were waged. The empire would have been small indeed, if neighbouring peoples had been peaceable, had always acted with justice, and had never provoked attack by any wrong-doing. In that case, human affairs would have been in a happier state; all kingdoms would have been small and would have rejoiced in concord with their neighbours. There would have been a multitude of kingdoms in the world, as there are multitudes of homes in our cities. To make war and to extend the realm by crushing other peoples, is good fortune in the eyes of the wicked; to the good, it is stern necessity. But since it would be worse that the unjust should lord it over the just, this stern necessity may be called good fortune without impropriety. Yet there can be no shadow of doubt that it is greater good fortune to have a good neighbour and live in peace with him than to subdue a bad neighbour when he makes war. It is a wicked prayer to ask to have someone to hate or to fear, so that he may be someone to conquer.

So if it was by waging wars that were just, not impious and unjust, that the Romans were able to acquire so vast an empire, surely they should worship the Injustice of others as a kind of goddess? For we observe how much help 'she' has given towards the extension of the Empire by making others wrong-doers, so that the Romans should have enemies to fight in a just cause and so increase Rome's power. Why should not Injustice be a goddess – at least the Injustice of foreign nations – if Panic and Pallor and Fever[48] earned a place among Roman gods? With the support of those two Goddesses, 'Foreign Injustice' and Victory, the Empire grew, even when Jupiter took a holiday. Injustice stirred up causes of war; Victory brought the war to a happy conclusion.

48. cf. ch. 23; Bk II, 14, n. 36; Bk VI, 10.

As for Jupiter, what part would he have had to play, when the benefits which might have been ascribed to him were themselves considered gods, given the name of gods, worshipped as gods, and invoked to play their own parts? He would have had some part in this if he was also called Dominion, on the analogy of the goddess called Victory. While if dominion is a gift of Jupiter, why should not victory also be considered his gift? And victory certainly would have been regarded as a gift, if, instead of a stone on the Capitol,[49] the Romans had recognized and worshipped the true 'King of kings and Lord of lords'.[50]

16. *The Romans assigned a separate god to each activity. Why did they put the temple of Quies outside the gates?*

The Romans assigned particular gods to particular spheres and to almost every single movement. They had a goddess called Agenoria,[51] to arouse to action; a goddess Stimula,[51] to stimulate to extraordinary action; a goddess Murcia[52] to make a man extraordinarily inactive, that is (according to Pomponius[53]) *murcidus*, meaning slothful and inert, and a goddess Strenia,[51] to make man strenuous. They undertook to offer public sacrifices in honour of all these divinities. But although they acknowledged a goddess named Quies[54] (tranquillity) to make men tranquil and though she had a temple outside the Colline gate, they refused to adopt this temple as a national shrine. This I find very surprising. Was it a symptom of an untranquil spirit? Or did it rather mean that anyone who obstinately worshipped that mob of demons (for clearly they were not gods) could not enjoy the tranquillity to which the true Physician invites man, when he says, 'Learn from me, for I am gentle and humble in heart, and you will find rest for your souls.'[55]

49. cf. Bk II, 29, n. 79. 50. Rev. 19, 16. 51. cf. ch. 11.

52. *Murcia:* Her shrine is mentioned by Livy (1, 33). She was identified with Venus, who had the epithets Murcia, Myrcia, or Myrtea, supposedly because of her connection with the myrtle (Ovid, *Fast.*, 4, 141ff.; Plin., 15, 121; Varro, *De Ling. Lat.*, 5, 154).

53. *Pomponius*: probably Lucius Pomponius (*fl. c.* A.D. 90), a writer of *fabulae Atellanae*, a kind of farce originally acted by amateurs. In the first century A.D. they attained literary form, keeping the traditional stock characters (like those of the *commedia dell'arte*), and were acted by professionals.

54. *Quies* had a temple on the Via Laticana (Liv., 4, 41). There is no mention elsewhere of a shrine outside the Colline gate.

55. Matt. 11, 29.

17. *If Jupiter is the supreme power, is Victory also to be considered a goddess?*

They may allege that Jupiter sends Victory, and that she comes at his bidding to those of his choice in obedience to Jupiter as king of gods and takes her place on their side. This could truthfully be said not of Jupiter, who is fancifully imagined as the king of gods, but of the true King of the Ages, who sends – not Victory, who has no real existence – but his angel, and gives the conquest to whom he will. And his design may be inscrutable; it cannot be unjust.

If Victory is a goddess, why not Triumph? Why not attach Triumph to Victory, as her husband, or brother, or son? If these fancies of theirs about the gods had been invented by poets and then attacked by us, they would have answered: 'Those are poetical fictions, not to be attributed to the true divinities.' And yet they themselves did not laugh when they encountered fantastic absurdities of this sort, not when reading the poets but when worshipping in the temples. They ought then to have made all their requests to Jupiter and addressed their supplications to him alone. For if Victory is a goddess, and subject to the king of gods, she could not have dared to oppose him, wherever he had sent her, to follow her own inclination instead.

18. *If Felicitas and Fortuna are both goddesses, how are they distinguished?*

Then what of the belief that Felicity[56] also is a goddess? She has received a temple, she has earned an altar and appropriate rites are paid her. She ought to have been worshipped as a sole divinity. For when she was present what blessing could have been lacking? But what is the point of reckoning Fortune[57] also as a divinity and worshipping her as well? Is there any difference between felicity and fortune? Yes, there is: fortune may be good or bad; but felicity could not be bad, without ceasing to be felicity. But surely we ought to believe that all the gods, of either sex (if, indeed, the gods also have a sex) are good without exception! This is what Plato[58] says, and other philosophers, and the outstanding guides of the republic, and of the other peoples. How then can Fortune be sometimes good, sometimes

56. *Felicity*: a late cult, the first temple being built by L. Licinius Lucullus consul in 74 B.C., in the Velabrum. The goddess is often depicted on coins.

57. cf. n. 45 on ch. 11

58. *Rp.*, 2, 379B.

bad? Can it be that when she is bad she is no longer a divinity, but is suddenly changed into a malignant devil? How many goddesses of this kind are there? As many, to be sure, as there are fortunate men, that is, men of good fortune. Since there are other men, very many of them, enduring bad fortune simultaneously, that is at one and the same time, then Fortune – if it is the same goddess – would be simultaneously good and bad – bad for some, good for others. But is she not always good, if she is a goddess? Then she must be the same as Felicity. Why is the goddess given different names?

Well, that is allowable; the same thing is often called by different names. But why different temples, different altars, different rites? 'The reason is', they say, 'that felicity is what good men enjoy as a result of their previous merits; while fortune – what we call *good* fortune – happens to men, good and bad alike, without any weighing of their merits: it comes fortuitously; hence the name Fortune.' How can she be good if she comes, without discrimination, to good and bad? What is the point of worshipping her if she is so blind that she blunders into people at random, so that she often passes by her worshippers and attaches herself to those who disregard her? Otherwise, if her worshippers receive any advantage, if they are noticed and favoured by her, then she comes in consequence of merit and not fortuitously. So what has happened to the definition of Fortune? What about the derivation of her name from fortuitous events? If she really is fortune (i.e. luck) there is no advantage in worshipping her. If she discriminates in favour of her worshippers she is not fortune. Is it the case that Jupiter sends her at his pleasure? If so, he should be worshipped alone; Fortune cannot resist his bidding, when he sends her where he wishes. Or at least let us leave her worship to the bad, who are not inclined to acquire the merits by which the goddess Felicity could be attracted

19. *Fortuna Muliebris*

The Romans assign so much importance to the alleged divinity whom they call Fortune, that they have a traditional story that her statue, which was dedicated by the Roman women and is called 'Feminine Fortune',[59] actually spoke,[60] and said that the women had consecrated her with all proper ceremonies; and she repeated the statement on more than one occasion.

59. *Feminine Fortune.* Tradition said that a temple to Fortuna Muliebris was erected in 488 B.C. on the spot where Coriolanus turned back at the intercession of Volumnia and Veturia.

60. Val. Max., 1, 8, 4.

If the story is true, there is no call for us to be surprised. It is not so difficult for malignant demons to effect illusions; and the Romans should have been put on their guard against such cunning trickery by the fact that the goddess who spoke was one who appears fortuitously and does not come in response to merit. Fortune is represented as a chatterer, while Felicity is dumb. What can be the point of this, except to encourage men not to take pains about right living, provided that Fortuna is favourable? And she can make men fortunate, irrespective of merit. In any case, if Fortuna speaks, then it would have been better to have the 'Fortune of the Men'[61] speaking, not the 'Fortune of the Women'; for then it would not be suspected that this impressive miracle was a piece of female gossip.

20. *Virtue and Faith received divine honours; but why not other virtues?*

They also made Virtue[62] a goddess. If she really was a goddess, she certainly ought to have been preferred to many of the others. In fact, since virtue is not a divinity, but a gift of God, men should seek to gain virtue from him who alone can grant it and the whole mob of false gods should be sent packing. But why has Faith[63] been believed in as a goddess, being given a temple and an altar for herself? Anyone who has the wisdom to acknowledge Faith makes for her a dwelling in his own self. Besides, how can those people know what faith is, seeing that the first and chief function of faith is to give men belief in the true God? And why was Virtue not sufficient for their needs? Surely, where Virtue is, there Faith is also? They observed that Virtue must be divided into four species: prudence, justice, fortitude, temperance. Now each of these has its own varieties, and so faith is classed under justice and it holds the chief place with all of us who know the meaning of the statement that 'the just man lives through his faith.'[64]

What really amazes me about those who are so eager for a multitude of gods is this: if faith is a goddess, why have they insulted so many other goddesses by passing them over, when they might have

61. cf. ch. 11.

62. *Virtue* (Valour). After the capture of Syracuse, in 212 B.C., Marcellus dedicated a temple at Rome to Honour and Virtue (Valour).

63. *Faith*. There was a temple of Faith on the Capitol (Cic., *De Nat. Deor.*, 3, 24, 104) built originally, it was said, by Numa, but rebuilt in the third century B.C. The three *Flamens* (cf. Bk II, 15) were in charge of her cult (Liv., 1, 21, 4). Her image is often shown on coins.

64. Hab. 2, 4; Rom. 1, 17; Gal. 3, 11; Heb. 10, 38.

dedicated temples and altars to them in the same way? Why has temperance not been thought worthy of divinity, when it is in her name that a number of eminent Romans have won no small glory? How is it that fortitude is not divine? It was fortitude that supported Mucius,[65] when he stretched out his right hand into the flames; and Curtius,[66] when he hurled himself into a chasm, for his country's sake; and the Decii,[67] father and son, when they devoted themselves to death to save the army. (I am assuming that it was true fortitude that they exemplified; the point is not relevant at the moment.) Why have prudence and wisdom deserved no divine habitations? Is it because they are all worshipped under the general title of Virtue? By the same token, one God might be worshipped, and the other gods be accounted aspects of him. In any case, faith and modesty are included in virtue; yet Faith and Modesty[68] have been deemed worthy of altars in their special shrines, independent of Virtue.

21. *Those who did not recognize one God should at least have been content with Virtue and Felicity*

It is not truth that creates these goddesses; it is folly. These virtues are not themselves divinities; they are gifts of the true God. Furthermore, where there is virtue and felicity, what need is there to seek anything else? If men are not satisfied with these, what will suffice them? For surely, virtue includes all that ought to be done, felicity all that ought to be desired. If Jupiter is worshipped, so that he may grant those blessings – on the ground that extension and duration of empire, if they are benefits, come under the heading of felicity – why is it not recognized that they are gifts of God, not deities? While if they are

65. *Mucius Scaevola* so impressed Lars Porsenna by his fortitude that the Etruscan made peace with Rome (Liv., 2, 12).

66. *Marcus Curtius* hurled himself, on horseback and in arms, into a chasm which had opened in the Forum, because the soothsayers declared that it could be closed only if Rome's chief strength were cast into it. Rome's chief strength, said Curtius, lay in courage and arms (Liv. 7, 6; Val. Max. 5, 6).

67. *P. Decius Mus*, consul, 340 B.C., in the Latin War, secured victory for Rome by devoting himself and the enemy to destruction, and then rushing to certain death. His son and namesake repeated the feat in 295, in the Third Samnite War. This family habit was observed by his grandson in 280, during the war against Pyrrhus (Liv. 8, 9; Val. Max. 5, 6).

68. *Modesty*. There was a shrine of Pudicitia Patricia in the Forum Boarium (Liv., 10, 23). But there seems to be here a mistaken identification of the veiled statue of Fortune in her temple in that place.

reckoned as deities, there is at any rate no need to seek out all that crowd of other gods. Bearing in mind the functions of all those gods and goddesses[69] which the pagans have whimsically invented according to their fancy, let them see if they can discover anything which any god could supply to a man who possesses virtue and felicity. What teaching would he need to seek from Mercury or Minerva, since Virtue would include everything? The men of old defined virtue as 'the art of good and right living'. Thus the Latins derived the word *ars* (art) from *aretê*, the Greek word for virtue.[70] Now if this virtue (or art) could only come to one who has a certain native wit, what was the use of the god Father Catius, who was supposed to make one shrewd (*catus*), that is sharp-witted (*acutus*), since felicity, good luck, could confer this quality? To be born with this native wit is assuredly a stroke of luck – of felicity. Hence, although Felicity could not be worshipped by the unborn, she might have granted to her worshippers the boon that their children should be quick-witted. And what need was there for women in childbirth to invoke Lucina; if Felicity were at hand to help, they would not only have easy labour, but good children as well. What need to entrust the newly born to Opis, the wailing infants to Vaticanus, infants in their cots to Cunina, children at the breast to Rumina,[71] to commend them to Statilinus when standing, to Adeona when coming (*adeuntes*), to Abeona[72] when going (*abeuntes*); to the goddess Mens (Mind), for mental development, to Volumnus and Volumna[73] for a right volition; to the nuptial deities[74] for a good marriage, to the gods of the fields, and especially the goddess Fructesa,[75] for fruitful harvests; to Mars and Bellona, for courage in war; to goddess Victory, that they might be victorious; to the god Honour,[76] that honours might come

69. *Catus, Catius, Opis*: cf. ch. 11.

70. *Ars-aretê*. The two words in fact both derive from an Indo-European root *ar*, which has the sense of 'fitting'.

71. cf. ch. 11.

72. cf. Bk VII, 3.

73. *Volumnus* and *Volumna* may be a mistake for Voltumnus, Voltumnia; for Voltumnus was apparently the earlier form of Vertumnus (Vortumnus) an agricultural God (cf. Bk VII, 3).

74. *Nuptial deities*, Plutarch (*Quaest. Rom.*, 2) mentions Jupiter, Juno, Venus, Persuasion, Minerva. But the reference here is probably to the 'minute gods' described in Bk VI, 9.

75. *Fructesa, Aesculanus, Argentinus, Fessona, Pellonia, Spiniensis*, are all unknown.

76. *Honour*: see note 62 on ch. 20 for the Temple of Honour and Virtue.

to them; to the goddess Pecunia,[77] to ensure plenty of money (*pecunia*), and to the god Aesculanus and his son Argentinus for coins of brass (*aes*) and silver (*argentum*)? The reason for assuming Aesculanus as the father of Argentinus was that the first currency was bronze and silver money only came in later. What surprises me is that Argentinus did not have a son called Aurinus, because of the still later introduction of gold (*aurum*). If they had had these three gods, they might have promoted Aurinus above his father Argentinus and his grandfather Aesculanus, just as they promoted Jupiter above Saturn.

Was it really necessary to worship and invoke all that crowd of gods to obtain benefits for soul or body or external blessings? I have not mentioned all their gods, and the Romans themselves did not succeed in assigning miniature gods as specialists to deal with all benefits of human life classified in minute detail. Why all that crowd, when, with a simple and sweeping economy, Felicity could have bestowed all the benefits? Then they would have been spared the trouble of finding any other god, either to obtain blessings or to ward off disasters. Then they would not have had to call upon Fessona for the exhausted (*fessi*), or upon Pellonia to drive off (*pellere*) the enemy; and to call in Apollo or Aesculapius as a physician for their sick – or both at once, in a case of grave danger; or Spiniensis, to root out the thorns (*spinae*) from the fields; or the goddess Robigo,[78] to keep blight (*robigo*) away. With the presence and protection of the one goddess, Felicity, disasters either would not occur, or would easily be dispelled.

One final point, on the subject of the goddesses Virtue and Felicity. If felicity is the reward of virtue, felicity is not a goddess, but a gift of God. If Felicity is a goddess, why should Felicity not be said to confer virtue, since the acquisition of virtue is surely a great felicity?

22. *The knowledge of the gods to be worshipped; Varro's gifts to the Romans*

Varro boasts that he rendered his fellow-citizens an 'immense service' in not merely listing the gods whom the Romans ought to worship, but also stating the special function of each of them. What was the basis of that claim? 'It is of no purpose', he says, 'to know the name of

77. *Pecunia.* In the second century A.D. Juvenal says: 'Accursed Money (*pecunia*) does not yet live in a temple. We have erected no altars to Cash as we have to Peace, Faith, Victory, Virtue, Concord.' (1, 113ff.)

78. The festival of Robigalia (21 April) was intended to avert mildew (*robigo*) from the growing crops by means of the sacrifice of a sheep and a red puppy (Ovid, *Fast.*, 9, 907–32; Varr., *De Re Rust.*, 1, 1, 6; Plin., 18, 285).

a physician, and what he looks like, if you do not know that he is a physician. Similarly, it is no use knowing that Aesculapius is a god, without being aware that he comes to the aid of the sick. You would not know why you ought to pray to him.' He drives the point home with another parallel. 'You cannot lead a satisfactory life, in fact you cannot live at all, if you do not know who the blacksmith is, and the baker, and the plasterer, and where to go to get anything you need; and from whom to seek help, or guidance, or instruction.' In just the same way, he insists, there can be no doubt of the advantage of acquaintance with the gods, if a man knows the power, ability and competence of each god in his particular sphere. 'Thus,' he goes on, 'we shall be able to know which god we are to summon by invocation, and for what purpose. And we may avoid acting like the comedians, who apply to Liber (or Bacchus) for water, and to the Lymphae (water-goddesses) for wine.'

A great advantage, to be sure! Everyone would be grateful to Varro, if he had shown them the truth and had taught men that they should worship the true God from whom all good things come.

23. *Felicity, a late-comer to the ranks of Roman gods though she might by herself have taken the place of all the rest*

But (and this is the question before us) if the pagan books and rites are true, and Felicity is a goddess, why is it not established that she alone should be worshipped, since she could confer all blessings and, in this economical fashion, bring a man happiness? Does anyone desire anything for any other reason than to secure happiness? Then why on earth was it so long before Lucullus[79] set up a shrine for this great goddess, after so many leading men of Rome had managed without her? Surely Romulus himself was anxious to found a city that should be happy? He, of all people, should have erected a temple to her, and then he would not have addressed prayers to the other gods for anything; for if Felicity had been there, nothing would have been lacking. Why did he not? For what purpose did he establish, as gods for the Roman people, Janus, Jupiter, Picus, Faunus, Tiberinus, Hercules, and the rest?[80] Why did Titus Tatius[81] add Saturn, Ops, Sun, Moon,

79. cf. ch. 18 n. 56.

80. *Picus*: a mythical king, son of Saturn. Perhaps invented to explain a cult of the woodpecker (*picus*).

Faunus: son of Picus, a rural deity sometimes equated with Pan. According to Ovid (*Fast.*, 2, 267) he was the god of the Lupercalia (15 January). A temple to

Vulcan, Light and the rest – including even Cloacina[82] – and never think of Felicity? Why did Numa bring in so many gods and goddesses – but not Felicity? Was it that he could not find her, in all that crowd? At any rate, king Hostilius could not have introduced, as gods to be propitiated, those novel divinities, Panic and Pallor,[83] if he had known and worshipped the goddess Felicity. For if she were there, Panic and Pallor would depart without propitiation; they would be chased away in flight!

How is it that the Roman Empire was extending its power far and wide, long before anyone had started a cult of Felicity? Is that the reason why its felicity did not match its grandeur? For how could true felicity exist where there was not true religion? True religion is the worship of the true God, not the cult of false gods, who are just so many devils. In fact, the inclusion of Felicity in the ranks of the gods was followed by the terrible infelicity of the civil wars. Was it that Felicity was rightly indignant at having been summoned so late, and summoned to what was not an honour so much as an insult – in that she was associated in worship with Priapus, Cloacina, Panic, Pallor, and Fever,[84] and the rest? Such deities could not claim worship; they could only shame their worshippers.

Finally, if it was thought right that such a mighty goddess should be worshipped along with that disreputable crowd, why was she not accorded at least a worship of greater splendour than the rest? Is it not intolerable that Felicity was not ranked among the Consentes,[85] the gods who are said to be called in as Jupiter's counsellors, nor among those called 'the select gods'?[86] They might have made her a temple

---

Picus was dedicated in 194 B.C. on an island in the Tiber (Ovid, *Fast.*, 2, 193; Liv., 33, 42, 10).

Tiberinus (Father Tiber) was the object of an ancient cult, for he is mentioned in the litany of the pontiffs and the augurs' prayer (Cic., *De Nat Deor.*, 3, 20, 52). He had a sanctuary on an island in the Tiber, and games in his honour on the Campus Martius in June (Ovid, *Fast.*, 6, 237).

81. *Titus Tatius*: a legendary Sabine king, co-ruler with Romulus after the Rape of the Sabines and the union of Romans and Sabines. Varro (*De Ling. Lat.*, 5, 74) mentions his introduction of these and other deities, except Light, for whose worship we have no other evidence.

82. cf. ch. 9 n. 20. 83. cf. ch. 15. 84. cf. Bk II, 14, n. 36.

85. *Consentes*: twelve superior gods with statues in the Forum: 'Juno, Vesta, Minerva, Ceres, Diana, Venus, Mars/Mercurius, Iovi', Neptunus, Vulcanus, Apollo' (Ennius, quoted in Apul., *De Deo Socr.*, 2). The connection with *consilium* is fanciful.

86. cf. Bk VII, 2.

to stand out above the others by the elevation of its site and the excellence of its architecture. Why did they not build her something better than the temple they gave to Jupiter himself? For who but Felicity gave Jupiter his kingship – assuming, that is, that he was happy in his reign? Felicity is undeniably worth more than a kingdom. For it is certain that one could easily find a man who was afraid to become a king; but you would not find anyone who did not want to be happy. If the pagans suppose that the opinion of the gods can be obtained by auguries or by any other method, they should have been asked whether they were willing to give place to Felicity, if it should happen that temples or altars of other gods had already taken a site where a greater and loftier temple might be erected for her. Even Jupiter himself would have retired in her favour, to allow Felicity to occupy the summit of the Capitol hill, rather than himself. For no one would have resisted Felicity, except (an impossible supposition) anyone who wished to be unhappy.

Had Jupiter been consulted, it is inconceivable that he would have acted as did the three gods, Mars, Terminus, and Juventas,[87] who utterly refused to give place to their superior, in fact their king. For Roman literature has the story that when King Tarquin decided to build the Capitol, he discovered that the site which seemed most worthy and most appropriate had already been taken by other gods. He did not dare to do anything in defiance of their wishes, but he was confident that they would yield willingly to that mighty divinity, their prince; and since there were many gods installed in the place where the Capitol was set up, he inquired, through the auguries, whether they were ready to give way to Jupiter. They all agreed to do so, except for those I have mentioned: Mars, Terminus, and Juventas. And that is why the Capitol[88] was so constructed that they were included in it, though their images were so inconspicuous that the most learned men were scarcely aware of the fact. Jupiter would never have treated Felicity with the contempt that Terminus, Mars, and Juventas showed to him. And even those three, who would not give place to Jupiter, would have yielded to Felicity, who had made Jupiter their king. Or if they had not yielded, it would not have been out of contempt, but because they preferred to skulk unnoticed in the dwell-

87. *Three gods.* No other authority associates Mars with Terminus and Juventas. The altar of Juventas was allowed to remain in the new temple of Minerva; the stone of Terminus in the temple of Jupiter, close to his image (Ovid, *Fast.*, 2, 667–79; Liv., 1, 55; Dion. Hal., *Ant. Rom.*, 3, 69).

88. i.e. the temple of Jupiter Capitolinus.

ing of Felicity rather than to catch every eye in their own shrines and be parted from her.

As soon as Felicity had been thus established in a dignified and exalted setting, the citizens would have learnt where they should seek help in every prayer for blessing. The bidding of natural reason would have led them to abandon the superfluous multitude of other gods, and confine their worship to Felicity. They would have prayed to her alone; her temple alone would have been thronged with citizens who wished for happiness – and who would not? Thus felicity would have been sought from the goddess Felicity herself, instead of from all the gods as formerly. For who would wish to receive, from any god, anything other than happiness, or what, in his view, conduces to happiness? Further, if it is in the power of Felicity to choose her beneficiaries (as it must be, if she is divine), what sort of folly is it to seek happiness from another god, when one can obtain it from Felicity herself! The Romans ought therefore to have honoured this deity above the rest of the gods, and to have shown this in the splendour of her setting, as well as in other ways. We learn from Roman sources that in antiquity the Romans ascribed nocturnal lightning to a certain Summanus,[89] and they paid him more honour than Jupiter, who was responsible for lightning during the day. But when a temple of outstanding magnificence had been built for Jupiter, the crowds thronged to it, because of the impressiveness of the shrine, so that you would have difficulty in finding anyone who so much as remembers having read the name Summanus – no one ever hears it spoken.

Now if Felicity is not a goddess, because she is, in truth, a gift of God, we should seek the God who can bestow that gift and abandon the pernicious mob of false gods to which the silly mob of fools attach themselves. These fools turn the gifts of God into deities, and by the obstinacy of their insolent self-will, offend the God who confers those gifts. How can a man escape unhappiness, if he worships Felicity as divine and deserts God, the giver of felicity? Could a man escape starvation by licking the painted picture of a loaf, instead of begging real bread from someone who had it to give?

89. *Summanus* appears sometimes as Jupiter Summanus in inscriptions; he is mentioned in Cicero (*De Div.*, 1, 10, 16) and Livy (32, 29). Pliny (2, 52, 138) agrees with St Augustine about his functions, but Ovid is doubtful about him (*Fast.*, 731f. 'A temple is said to have been dedicated to Summanus, whoever he may be'). His temple, built in 278 B.C., was near the Circus Maximus.

24. *Arguments adduced in defence of the worship of the divine gifts, as well as gods*

I should like to consider the explanations put forward by our opponents. 'Are we to suppose', they say, 'that our ancestors were such idiots that they did not realize that these were the divine gifts and not themselves divinities? But they knew that these gifts were only given by the generosity of a god, and when they did not know the names of the gods concerned they called them by the name of the gifts, which, they felt, were bestowed by them. They made some modifications in the words; thus Bellona from *bellum* (war); Cunina from *cunae* (cradle); Segetia from *seges* (crop); Pomona[90] from *poma* (apples); Bubona from *bubus* (ablative of *boves*, oxen). Sometimes they were called by the actual name of their subject, as Pecunia, the goddess who gives money (*pecunia*), which does not mean that money itself is considered a divinity. In the same way, Virtue is the bestower of virtue; Honour, of honour; Concordia gives concord; Victoria gives victory. Thus when Felicity is spoken of as a goddess, the reference is not to the gift, but to the giver of happiness.'

25. *Only one God is to be worshipped. He is recognized as the giver of felicity even if his name is unknown*

This explanation will perhaps make it much easier for us to win over to our way of thinking those of our opponents whose hearts are not too hardened. Human nature in its weakness has already felt that happiness can only be given by a god; and that has been realized by men who have been worshipping many gods, including Jupiter himself, the king of the gods. Now because they did not know the name of the giver of happiness, those people decided to call him by the name of the gift for which they believed him responsible. If this is true, they have made it clear that happiness is not given by Jupiter, whom they were already worshipping, but by a deity who was, they held, to be worshipped by the name of happiness itself, the name 'Felicity'.

I put it quite bluntly. They believed that happiness is the gift of some god, unknown to them. Then let them seek him and worship him, and that is enough. Away with the hubbub of innumerable demons! The only man who would not be satisfied with this God is the man who is not satisfied with his gift. I repeat, the only man who would not be satisfied with God, the giver of happiness, as worthy of

90. *Pomona*: goddess of fruit. *Bubona* is not found elsewhere.

his worship, is the man who is not satisfied with happiness itself as worthy of his acceptance. If a man is content with happiness – and in fact man has nothing which he should desire beyond that – then let him serve the one God, the giver of happiness. And that is not the god they call Jupiter. For if they had recognized Jupiter as the giver of happiness they would not have looked for another deity, male or female, called Felicity, as its giver; nor would they have thought it right to associate the worship of Jupiter with all those slanders; for he was, according to their account, a seducer of the wives of others,[91] and a shameless lover and ravisher of a beautiful boy.[92]

26. *The theatrical shows, demanded by the gods from their worshippers*

'But this', Cicero asserts, 'is a fiction of Homer, who transferred human shortcomings to the gods. Would that he had transferred divine powers to us men.'[93] The serious-minded Cicero was justifiably displeased with a poet who imputed fictitious crimes to the deities. But those crimes are represented in speech, in song, and in action in the stage shows; and those shows are put on in honour of the gods, and are classed among 'Divine Matters' by the most learned authorities. How is this? Cicero ought on this point to cry out, not against the poet's fictions, but against the traditional institutions, established by his ancestors. But those ancestors would have cried out, in reply,

What have *we* done? It was the gods themselves who clamoured for these exhibitions in their honour, who demanded them with fearful threats, promising disaster if they were withheld, punishing any omission with the utmost harshness, and showing themselves appeased when the omission was repaired. Among the miraculous demonstrations of their power, the following story is told.[94] A Roman peasant named Titus Latinius, the father of a family, was told in a dream to inform the senate that the Roman games must be restarted, because on the first day of the games a criminal had been ordered to be led to execution before the eyes of the assembled people, and this command had displeased the gods; no doubt because the divinities looked for cheerful entertainment at those shows. The man who had received this warning dream had not courage to fulfil the order next day; and on the second night he was given the same injunction, in stricter terms. He did not obey; and so he lost his son. On the third night he was

91. e.g. Alcmena. 92. Ganymede. 93. *Tusc. Disp.*, 1, 26, 65.
94. cf. Cic., *De Div.*, 1, 26, 55; Liv. 2, 36; Val. Max., 1, 7, 4.

told that a heavier punishment awaited him, if he disobeyed. When his courage again failed him, even after this threat, he fell seriously ill with a fearful disease. Then, on the advice of his friends he did inform the magistrates, and was carried into the senate on a litter. There he recounted his dream; and immediately he was restored to health and left the senate-house on his own legs, completely cured. Astounded by this miracle, the senate voted to recommence the games, with a fourfold increase of the subsidy.

Any man in his senses could see that men who were under the sway of malignant demons – a domination from which only the grace of God, through Jesus Christ our Lord, could free them – were constrained by force to offer to such gods exhibitions which to a right judgement could only appear disgusting. Certainly in those games – which were restarted by order of the senate, under compulsion from the gods – these poetic scandals about the gods were publicly displayed. In those shows the actors portrayed Jupiter, the corrupter of innocence, in song and action; and thus they appeased him! If this was mere fiction, Jupiter would have been angry, surely? Or, if Jupiter took delight in those scandals, even though fictitious, then his worship was nothing but the service of a devil.

Was it really this Jupiter who could have founded, developed, and preserved the Roman Empire? A contemptible reprobate, in comparison with any Roman whatsoever who found such depravities revolting? Was it really a god like this who could have given happiness, who was worshipped in this miserable fashion, and who was even more miserably angry, if that worship was withheld?

27. *Three kinds of gods distinguished by Scaevola, the pontiff*

It is recorded that Scaevola,[95] a most erudite pontiff, argued that there were three kinds of gods[96] in the Roman tradition; one strand of tradition coming through the poets, another through the philosophers, the third through the statesmen. According to Scaevola, the first tradition was trivial nonsense, a collection of discreditable fictions about the gods, while the second had no value for a commonwealth, in that it introduced much that was irrelevant, and also much that was harmful for the people in general to know. The irrelevances are not important. It is a commonplace of jurisprudence that 'the irrelevant

95. cf. Bk III, 28n.

96. *Three kinds of gods.* The theory is perhaps derived from the Stoic philosopher Panaetius of Rhodes (*c.* 180–110 B.C.) who taught in Rome for some time.

is not harmful.' But what are the elements which are harmful, if divulged to the general public? 'The assertion', says Scaevola, 'that Hercules, Aesculapius, Castor and Pollux are not gods. The learned inform us that they were men,[97] and that they died, in accordance with the human condition.' And further, 'The allegation that communities do not have true images of those who really are gods, because the true God has neither sex nor age, nor has he a defined bodily form.' The pontiff did not wish the people to be aware of this; he did not think the statements were untrue. Thus he held that it was expedient for communities to be deceived in matters of religion, and Varro himself has no hesitation in saying as much, even in his books on 'Divine Affairs'.

What a splendid religion for the weak to flee to for liberation! He asks for the truth which will set him free; and it is believed that it is expedient for him to be deceived!

As for the poetic tradition, Roman literature makes it quite clear why Scaevola rejected its teaching. The poets give such a distorted picture of the gods that such deities cannot stand comparison with good men. One god is represented as a thief, another as an adulterer, and so on; all kinds of degradation and absurdity, in word and deed, are ascribed to them. Three goddesses have a beauty contest; Venus wins the prize, and the disappointed candidates overthrow Troy. Jupiter himself is changed into a bull, or a swan, to enjoy the favours of some woman or other.[98] A goddess marries a man; Saturn devours his children. Any imaginable marvel, every conceivable vice can be found in this poetic tradition, however remote from the divine nature.

Come, Scaevola, you 'supreme pontiff', suppress those spectacles – if you can! Forbid the people to offer such 'honours' to the immortal gods – shows in which men enjoy admiring the scandals of the gods and decide to imitate such behaviour, if possible. But if the people retort, 'It is you pontiffs who have introduced this among us,' ask the gods to cease demanding these exhibitions; for it was at their instigation that you ordered them to be put on. If those stories are evil, and therefore to be rejected as utterly incongruous with the majesty of the gods, then the wrong offered to the gods is the more serious because such fictions enjoy impunity.

97. *'They were men.'* The theory that the gods were deified men is called Euhemerism, after Euhemerus of Sicily, who advanced it *c.* 300 B.C. in his *Hierâ Anagraphe*, which Ennius translated into Latin. St Augustine refers to Euhemerus by name in Bk VI, 7; VII, 27.

98. Europa and Leda.

But the gods do not listen to you, Scaevola. They are, in fact, demons, who teach depravity and rejoice in degradation. Far from counting it an outrage that such fictions should be published about them, they actually take it as an intolerable outrage if such shows are not performed in their rites. Appeal against those demons to Jupiter if you will, especially as more scandals are enacted in the stage shows about him than about any other. Yet, though you pontiffs call him Jupiter the God, ruler and disposer of the whole universe, does he not suffer the greatest outrage at your hands? For you think it proper to associate his worship with those demons, and you make him out to be their king.

28. *Did the worship of the gods help the Romans in the acquisition and extension of the Empire?*

It is utterly impossible that the increase and preservation of the Roman Empire could have been due to such gods as these, gods who are appeased – or rather accused – by rites of such a kind that it would be more culpable for them to delight in such exhibitions if the stories were groundless, than if they were based on fact. If it had been in their power, the gods might have preferred to bestow this great blessing of empire upon the Greeks. For in this matter of 'divine affairs', that is, in those stage-shows, the Greeks offered a worship more honourable and more worthy of divinity. They did not withdraw themselves out of reach of the poet's biting tongue, when they saw the gods being so lacerated; they gave the poet liberty to maltreat any man at their pleasure. Nor did they condemn the actors as infamous; they considered them worthy of even the highest honours.[99]

The Romans could have had gold money without worshipping the god Aurinus, and silver and bronze, without the cult of Argentinus and his father, Aesculanus. And so on through the list, which it would be tedious to repeat. In the same way, though they could not have exercised dominion without the consent of the true God, still, if they had ignored, or despised, that multitude of false gods, and had recognized the one God, and given him the worship of sincere faith and pure lives, they would have had a better dominion – whatever its size – here on earth, and would have received hereafter an eternal kingdom, whether they had enjoyed dominion in this world or no.

99. cf. Bk II, 11.

29. *The falsity of the augury which seemed to presage the strength and stability of the Roman Empire*

I referred just now[100] to that story of the 'splendid presage', as they described it, when Mars, Terminus, and Juventas refused to yield place to Jupiter, king of the gods. What is the meaning of the tale? 'Why,' they say, 'it signifies that the race of Mars (that is, the Roman people) will never give up to anyone a place that is in their possession; that no one will ever move the Roman frontiers, thanks to the god Terminus; that the young men of Rome will yield to no one, thanks to the goddess Juventas.' It is up to our opponents to decide how they can conceive Jupiter to be the king of gods, and the giver of their Empire, when this 'presage' presents him as an adversary and makes it glorious to refuse to yield to him. And yet, granted the truth of this, they have nothing whatsoever to fear. They are not likely to admit that the gods who refused to yield to Jupiter have yielded to Christ. They have, in fact, been able to yield to Christ, without any loss of territory in the Empire; they have been able to surrender to him their established abodes, and above all the hearts of their believers. But before Christ's incarnation, before those books from which we have quoted were written, but after the event under king Tarquin that provided the 'presage', the Roman army was routed and turned to flight on a number of occasions, which showed the falsity of the 'presage'. In the 'presage' Juventas did not yield to Jupiter. And when the conquering Gauls broke through, the 'race of Mars' was crushed in Rome itself, and when many cities defected to Hannibal the frontiers of the Empire were very narrowly restricted. Thus that 'presage' lost all its 'splendour'; all that was left was the insolence shown to Jupiter, not by gods, but by demons. It is one thing not to yield; to regain what has been yielded is another. Even so, the eastern frontiers of the Roman Empire were voluntarily altered by Hadrian in later times;[101] in fact he ceded to the Persian Empire three famous provinces, Armenia, Mesopotamia, and Assyria. So it would seem that the god Terminus, who, according to the pagans, was the protector of the imperial frontiers, the god who, according to that 'splendid presage' refused to yield to Jupiter, was more afraid of a king of men than of the king of the gods. Those provinces were recovered at a later date; but later still, almost in our own times, Terminus made another cession. This was

100. ch. 23.

101. *Hadrian*, on his accession in A.D. 117, ended the war against the Parthians, started by Trajan in 114, giving up conquered territory and restoring the Euphrates as the boundary of the Roman Empire.

when Julian, in his implicit obedience to the oracles of those gods, had the reckless hardihood to order the burning of the food-ships.[102] Thus the army was cut off from supplies. Soon after, Julian himself died of wounds; the army was reduced to destitution; the enemy kept up their assaults on troops demoralized by the emperor's death; and there would have been no survivors, if a peaceful composition had not fixed the imperial frontier on the lines which remain to this day. The loss of territory was not as great as the concessions of Hadrian; the new frontier represented a compromise.

There was not much substance in that 'presage'! Terminus did not yield to Jupiter; but he yielded to Hadrian's decision, to Julian's rashness, to Jovian's[103] desperate situation. The more intelligent and thoughtful Romans saw this clearly. But they were powerless in the face of the habits of the community, which were tied up with the ceremonies of the demons. They themselves, in fact, although they realized the uselessness of such rites, believed that religious worship should be offered to the order of nature which is organized under the rule and government of the one true God. But such worship is due only to that God; and thus these Romans were, in the words of the Apostle, 'serving the created order, instead of the Creator, who is blessed for all eternity'.[104] It was the help of this true God that was needed – the God who sends men of holiness and true devotion to die for the true religion, so that false religions may be eradicated from the living.

30. *What the pagans, on their own admission, think about their gods*

Cicero, an augur himself, laughs at auguries;[105] and at men who adjust their plans of action in obedience to the cries of ravens and crows.[106] But an Academic philosopher[107] like Cicero, who main-

102. cf Bk v, 21. The story is told in Ammianus Marcellinus (24, 7, 4).

103. Elected by the army after Julian's death, A.D. 363.

104. Rom. 1, 25.

105. *'Cicero laughs at auguries'.* Cicero, who was elected augur in 53 B.C., quotes the remark of Cato the Censor, that he was amazed that one augur could meet another without bursting into laughter (*De Div.*, 2, 24).

106. *De Div.*, 2, 36–8.

107. *Academic philosophers:* Plato and his successors taught in the grove of Academus, near Athens. Arcesilaus of Pitane (*c.* 315–240) introduced the Scepticism of Pyrrhon of Elis (*c.* 365–275) into the teaching of what came to be known as the Second (or New) Academy. The denial of the possibility of certain knowledge led to controversy with the Stoics. Cicero was, in fact, a complete eclectic in philosophy.

tains that everything is uncertain, does not deserve to be treated as an authority in such matters. In the second book of his *On the Nature of the Gods*[108] Quintus Lucilius Balbus[109] is represented as taking part in a discussion; and while he himself advances some superstitions arising from the realm of physical nature – what might be called scientific or philosophical superstititions – he is indignant, for all that, at the erection of images and at fairy tales. 'Do you see', he says,

how man's reason is diverted from scientific knowledge, carefully acquired, and of practical value, towards fictitious and invented gods? And this gives rise to false notions and confused errors, to what amount to old wives' tales. And we are given information about the appearance of the gods, their age, their clothes, their ornaments; and further, about their genealogy, their marriages, their family connections: everything is translated into the resemblance of human weakness. The gods are represented as swayed by passions: we hear of their lusts and sorrows and bursts of anger. And, according to the stories, they were not exempt from wars and battles: not only, as in Homer,[110] when two armies are fighting and various gods support either side; the gods had their own wars, for instance, those against the Titans and the Giants. Those stories are told by fools and believed by fools – a mass of frivolous nonsense.

There you have the admissions of the defenders of the pagan gods! Later on, the speaker asserts that all this belongs to superstition, while his own teaching, in which he apparently follows the Stoics, belongs to religion. 'It is not only the philosophers', he says, 'who have distinguished superstition from religion. Our ancestors drew the same distinction. For those who spent whole days in prayer, and offered sacrifices, so that their children might survive them (*superstites essent*) were called 'superstitious.'[111] One cannot fail to notice that he is trying, through fear of opposing the established customs of the country, to praise the religion of his ancestors, while wishing to disentangle it from superstition. The attempt fails. For if those ancestors gave the name 'superstitious' to those who spent whole days in prayer and offered sacrifices, surely the same name applies to those who set up images (which he finds reprehensible) of gods of different ages and with distinctive clothes, and established their genealogies, marriages, and family connections. When all this is criticized as superstition, then those ancestors are immediately implicated as the founders and worshippers of such images. And Cicero himself is implicated since

108. *De Nat. Deor.*, 2, 28, 70. 109. A Stoic philosopher. 110. *Il.*, 20, 31ff.
111. An absurd etymology; but the true derivation is uncertain.

for all the eloquence with which he strives to extricate himself and free himself from the charge, he did hold that those institutions should be treated with reverence. And he would not have dared even to mutter, in a popular assembly, the opinions resonantly proclaimed by the eloquent speaker in that philosophical debate.

Let us, who are Christians, give thanks to our Lord God (not to heaven and earth, as the philosopher says in his discussion, but to him who made heaven and earth) because, through the sublime humility of Christ, through the preaching of the apostles, through the faith of the martyrs who died for the truth and live with the Truth, our God has overthrown those superstitions, which Balbus, in his stammering way (*balbutiens*), barely succeeded in criticizing; and he has overthrown them by the free servitude of his people, not only in the hearts of true believers but even in the temples of superstitition.

31. *Varro's views. He rejected popular superstition, and held that one god should be worshipped, though he did not attain the knowledge of the true God*

We regret that Varro classed stage-shows among 'Divine Matters', though this was not an expression of his own judgement. For though he assumes a pious role and exhorts men to worship the gods, as he does on many occasions, he acknowledges that he is not following his own judgement in conforming to customs which, as he points out, were established by the Roman state. Now he has no hesitation in admitting that if he had been founding that city at the beginning, he would have consecrated the gods and their names according to the rule of Nature. But he asserts that he is bound, as a member of an ancient people, to maintain the traditional story of their names and surnames as it reached him, and to make it his aim, in his writing and researches, to encourage the common people to honour the gods, not to despise them. In speaking like this he hints, with characteristic astuteness, that he is not revealing all that he knows, for much of that was not only contemptible in his eyes, but also likely to arouse contempt even in the common people if it were divulged. I should rightly be suspected of indulging in conjecture here, if Varro had not openly declared in another place, on the subject of religious rites, that there are many truths which it is not expedient for the general public to know, and, further, many falsehoods which it is good for the people to believe true, and that this is why the Greeks kept their initiation rites veiled in silence and enclosed within walls. Varro here at least reveals the whole policy of the so-called sages, by whose influence cities and peoples are governed. The malign demons rejoice exceedingly in this deceit, since they control the deluders and the deluded alike. And it is only the grace of God through Jesus Christ our Lord, that frees us from their domination.

The same shrewd and learned author also says that in his view the only people who have apprehended what God is, are those who have believed him to be the soul which governs the universe by motion and reason. In this, Varro did not attain to the whole truth; for God is not a soul, but the author and maker of the soul, as of all else. All the same, if Varro could not free himself from the prejudices of inherited custom, at least he would acknowledge, and teach, that men should worship one God, who governs the universe by motion and reason. And so the only quarrel we should still have with him concerns his assertions that God is a soul, and not, as he really is, the creator of the soul.

Varro says also that the ancient Romans worshipped the gods for a hundred and seventy years without any images. 'If that habit had been continued,' he says, 'the worship of the gods would have been conducted with greater purity.' Among the evidence for this opinion he cites the Jewish people. And he has no hesitation in concluding this passage with the assertion that those who first set up images of the gods for the people were responsible for the abolition of reverent fear in their communities and for the increase of error. He had the sense to realize that it was easy to despise the gods because of the insensibility of their images. Notice that Varro speaks of 'increase of error' not 'communication of error'. He evidently intends it to be inferred that error already existed, even without the images. And then when he says that 'the people who apprehended what God is were those who believe in him as the soul which governs the universe by motion and reason', and when he holds that 'the worship of the gods would have been conducted with greater purity' without images, one cannot fail to see how nearly he approaches to the truth. If he had had the strength to resist the power of long-established error he would assuredly have decided that the one God, whom he believed to be governor of the universe, should be worshipped without an image. And since he found himself so close to the truth, it may be that the mutability of the soul might have counselled him to the conclusion that the true God is an immutable nature, the creator of the soul, as of all else.

This being so, it follows that when such men as Varro have included in their writings all this ludicrous nonsense about the gods, they have done so because they were compelled to reveal them by the hidden working of the will of God, not because they were trying to persuade men of their truth. When we have taken our evidence from these books, we did so to refute those who refuse to see the strength and malignity of the demonic power from which we are set free by the unique sacrifice of that holy blood that was shed for us, and by the gift of the spirit which has been imparted to us.

32. *For what apparent advantage the rulers of nations wished false religions to continue among their subject peoples*

Varro says also, on the subject of the generations of the gods, that people in general are more inclined to listen to poets than to scientists, and that is why his ancestors, that is the ancient Romans, attributed sex and generation to the gods and arranged marriages for them.

We need not seek further for the reason for such beliefs than the interest of the self-styled experts and savants in misleading the people in matters of religion. In such matters they made it their business not only to worship the demons but also to imitate them; for the demons' greatest desire is to deceive. The demons can only get control of men when they have deluded and deceived them; in the same way the leaders of men (who were not men of integrity, but the human counterparts of the demons) taught men as true, under the name of religion, things they knew to be false. By this means they bound them tighter, as it were, to the citizen community, so that they might bring them under control and keep them there by the same technique. What chance had a weak and ignorant individual of escaping from the combined deceits of the statesmen and the demons?

33. *The times of all kings and kingdoms have been ordained by the counsel and power of the true God*

It is therefore this God, the author and giver of felicity, who, being the one true God, gives earthly dominion both to good men and to evil. And he does this not at random or, as one may say, fortuitously, because he is God, not Fortune. Rather he gives in accordance with the order of events in history, an order completely hidden from us, but perfectly known to God himself. Yet God is not bound in subjection to this order of events; he is himself in control, as the master of events, and arranges the order of things as a governor. As for felicity, he grants that only to the good. Men may have this happiness – or not have it – when they are slaves, or when they are rulers. But it can only be enjoyed in its fullness in that life where no one is any longer a slave. The reason why God gives worldly dominions both to the good and the evil is this: to prevent any of his worshippers who are still infants in respect of moral progress from yearning for such gifts from him as if they were of any importance.

This is the sacrament, the hidden meaning, of the Old Testament, where the New Testament lay concealed. In the Old Testament the promises and gifts are of earthly things; but even then men of spiritual perception realized, although they did not yet proclaim the fact for all to hear, that by those temporal goods eternity was signified; they understood also what were the gifts of God which constituted true felicity.

34. The kingdom of the Jews, established by the One true God, and preserved as long as they continued in the true religion

So those earthly blessings – the sole objects of breathless desire for those who can imagine nothing better – are dependent on the power of the one God, not on that of the many false gods, whom the Romans formerly believed they ought to worship. And it was so that this might be recognized that God increased his people in Egypt, starting with a very small number, and freed them from Egypt by means of miraculous signs. It was not Lucina whom those Israelite women invoked when God himself saved their new-born children from the hands of the Egyptian persecutors who intended to destroy them. God's purpose was that the children should be marvellously multiplied and that race unbelievably increased. Those children took the breast without the aid of goddess Rumina; they needed no Cunina in their cradles; they took food and drink without Educa and Potina;[112] they were reared without assistance from all those gods of childhood, married without the gods of marriage, they needed no cult of Priapus for the consummation of their marriages. Without the invocation of Neptune the sea divided and opened up a way for their crossing and brought its waters together to overwhelm their enemies in pursuit. When they received the manna from heaven they did not consecrate any goddess called Mannia, nor did they worship the Nymphs and the

112. cf. ch. 11.

Lymphs when the rock was struck and poured out water to quench their thirst. They waged war without any frenzied rites of Mars and Bellona; and if, when they won their battles, victory was with them, that meant for them a gift not of a goddess, but of their God. They did not have to thank Segetia for their crops, Bubona for their oxen, Mellona for honey, Pomona for fruits.[113] In fact, the Israelites received from the one true God all the blessings for which the Romans thought it necessary to pray to all the host of false gods, and they received them in a far happier manner. And if they had not sinned against God by turning aside to the worship of strange gods and of idols, seduced by impious superstition as if by magic arts, if they had not finally sinned by putting Christ to death, they would have continued in possession of the same realm, a realm exceeding others in happiness, if not in extent. If today they are dispersed over almost all the world, amongst almost all the nations, this is part of the providence of the one true God, whose purpose is that when in any place the images of the false gods are overthrown, with their altars, sacred groves, and temples, and when their sacrifices are forbidden, it may be proved that this was prophesied long ago; so that when this is read of in our Christian Scriptures there may be no ground for believing it a Christian invention.

The sequel of all this will be found in the next book. The present volume is already over-long, and it is time to bring it to an end.

113. cf. ch. 24. (Mellona does not appear in classical authors).

BOOK V

Preface

IT is an undisputed fact that felicity is the complete enjoyment of all that is to be desired. Felicity is not a goddess, but a gift of God; and therefore no god is to be worshipped by men except the God who can make men happy. If Felicity were in fact a goddess, then she would rightly be called the sole divinity worthy of worship. But God alone has power to bestow those blessings which can be received even by those who are not good and therefore are not happy. Let us therefore proceed to inquire why God was willing that the Roman Empire should extend so widely and last so long. We have already asserted at some length that this was not due to the multitude of false gods the Romans worshipped; and we shall have more to say on this, if occasion offers.

1. *The Roman Empire and other kingdoms were not due to mere chance, nor dependent on the position of the stars*

The cause of the greatness of the Roman Empire was neither chance nor destiny, in the sense in which those words are, somewhat arbitrarily employed, when 'chance' is used of events which have no cause, or at least no cause which depends on any rational principle, and 'destiny' of events which happen in an inevitable sequence, independent of the will of God or man. Without the slightest doubt, the kingdoms of men are established by divine providence. If anyone ascribes this to destiny, because he uses the word 'destiny' to refer to the will or power of God, then he can keep his opinion, but he should express himself more accurately. Why does he not say in the first place what he is prepared to say when asked what he meant by 'destiny'? For when people hear the word 'destiny', the established usage of the language inevitably leads them to understand by the word the influence of the position of the stars at the time of birth or conception. Some regard this influence as having no connection with the will of God, while others assert that it is dependent upon it. Those who suppose that the stars decide, quite apart from the will of God, how we shall act, and what blessings we shall enjoy or what disasters we shall suffer, are to be refused any hearing whatsoever, not only from those who hold the true religion, but even from those who choose to be worshippers of gods of any sort, however false. For can this supposition mean anything but an end to all worship, and all prayer? Our present argument is not addressed to such as these, but against those who oppose the Christian religion in defence of their supposed gods.

As for those who make the position of the stars depend on the will of God, when they in some way decide the character of each person, and what blessing and what harm is to come his way – if they think that those stars have this power deputed to them by the supreme power of God and that it is their will that decides – then they do the heavens a grave injustice in supposing that in that shining senate, as we may call it, and in that resplendent senate-house, they decreed the commission of crimes so abominable that if any earthly state had decreed them, its own destruction would have been decreed by the whole of humanity. And then, if men act under pressure of such heavenly constraint, what room is left for the judgement of God, who is the Lord of stars and of men? While if they say that the stars, having received power from God omnipotent, do not take those decisions at their own whim, but are merely fulfilling his commands when they impose those constraints, are we then to think of God himself in a way which seemed completely unworthy when we were thinking of the stars as deciding? But it may be said that the stars give notice of events and do not bring those events about, so that the position of the stars becomes a kind of statement, predicting, not producing, future happenings; and this has been an opinion held by men of respectable intelligence. Now this is not the way the astrologers normally talk. They would not say, for example, 'This position of Mars signifies murder'; they say, 'it causes murder.'

However, let us concede that they do not express themselves adequately, and that they ought to acquire from the philosophers the accepted vocabulary to communicate what they believe they find in the position of the stars. But how is it that they have never been able to explain why, in the life of twins, in their actions, in their experiences, their professions, their accomplishments, their positions – in all the other circumstances of human life, and even in death itself, there is often found such diversity that in those respects many strangers show more resemblance to them than they show to one another, even though the smallest possible interval separated their births and though they were conceived at the same moment, by a single act of intercourse.

2. *Similarity and dissimilarity in the health of twins*

Cicero[1] tells us that Hippocrates,[2] the most famous of all doctors, left it on record that in a case where two brothers fell ill at the same time and their illness grew worse simultaneously, and began to subside at the same moment, he suspected that they were twins. Now Posidonius,[3] the Stoic, who was very much given to astrology, would assert that they had been conceived and born under the same configuration of the stars. Thus the coincidence which the physician believed due to a similar constitution, the philosopher–astrologer ascribed to the configuration of the stars existing at the moment of their conception and of their birth. In a case like this the medical assumption is more acceptable and more credible from the start, since it is possible that the physical condition of parents at the moment of conception may affect the earliest beginnings of infants then conceived, so that after their initial development in the mother's body they are born with a like constitution. Thereafter they are reared in the same house, with the same food, in the same climate and situation, drinking the same water; and medical science avers that those factors have the greatest influence, for good or ill, on physical condition. Twins are also used to the same kinds of exercise. All those similarities produce the same kind of physique, and so they fall ill of the same diseases, at the same time, from the same causes. But to trace this parallelism of illness to the influence of the configuration of stars at the moment of conception and birth is an odd kind of impudence, seeing that so many conceptions and births could have been subject to the influences of the same aspect of the sky, producing beings of widely different races, vastly diverse in their actions and experiences.

Now we know quite well that twins may be very different in their behaviour; they may go to different places; they may also differ in their medical history. And, as far as I can see, Hippocrates offers the easiest explanation of this divergence in respect of illness, in ascribing it to differences in diet and in exercise, which arise not from physical temperament but from deliberate choice.

1. *De Fato* (not extant). 2. 460–357 B.C.

3. *Posidonius:* of Apamea (*c.* 135–51 B.C.), the head of the Stoic school at Rhodes; historian, scientist, philosopher, and astrologer. Varro and Cicero were among his pupils. His works are lost.

As for Posidonius and all those who assert that the stars rule human destinies, I should be surprised if they could find any answer to this, unless their object was merely to make game of the ignorant on a subject completely unknown to them. For this is what they are trying to achieve in regard to the tiny interval of time which separates the births of twins. They refer to the small section of the sky where they mark the precise hour in question – what they call the 'horoscope'. Either this interval has not sufficient importance to explain the diversity of outlook, of action, of character, of experiences, exhibited in twins, or else it is so important that it should override the identity of twins in respect of nobility or lowliness of descent; for they assign this greatest of disparities solely to the influence of the hour of birth. Thus, if the birth of the second twin follows the first so closely that the same part of the horoscope serves for both, then in that case I look for complete parity in all things – which can never in fact be found in twins. While if the slow arrival of the second twin changes the horoscope, then I expect to find different parents – which is impossible in the case of twins.

3. *Nigidius the astrologer; his argument about twins, derived from the potter's wheel*

Nothing is to be gained by bringing in the well-known parable of the potter's wheel, given by Nigidius[4] in reply to this problem, which greatly troubled him, a parable that gave him his nickname, *Figulus* ('the potter'). He revolved a potter's wheel with all the vigour he could command, and while it was spinning he made two very rapid strokes on the wheel with ink, apparently on the same spot. When the wheel stopped those marks were found to be a considerable distance apart on the edge of it. 'In the same way,' said Nigidius, 'the sky whirls round so swiftly that although twins may be born in as quick succession as my two strokes on the wheel, that corresponds to a very large tract of the sky. This would account for all the great divergences alleged in the character of twins and in the events of their lives.'

This parable is even more fragile than the pottery made on that wheel. For if a change in the constellations which cannot be observed makes such a difference in the sky that one of two twins gets ad-

4. *Nigidius:* astrologer and Pythagorean philosopher; reputedly the most learned man in Rome after Varro. He was of some service to Cicero in 63 B.C. during Catiline's conspiracy; he sided with Pompey in the Civil War, and died in exile in 45 B.C.

vantages from heredity, while the other does not, how can those astrologers have the boldness to examine the constellations, in the case of those who are not twins, and then foretell matters which depend on this unobservable mystery, and connect them with the moment of birth? Perhaps they can make those statements in the horoscopes of those who are not twins, because there we are dealing with longer intervals of time, while the few instants that may separate the births of twins are assumed to affect minor matters on which astrologers are not normally consulted. For no one is going to ask advice about when to sit down, when to take a walk, or when to have a meal! But we are certainly not here talking of minor matters. The many wide differences between twins that we are pointing out are found in their character, their actions, and the events of their lives.

4. *The twins Esau and Jacob, very different in character and actions*

In the time of our remote ancestors (to mention a very notable instance) two twins were born in such close succession that the second was holding on to the foot of the first.[5] Now there was such a difference in their lives and characters, such divergence in their actions, such disparity in the affection of their parents, that these discrepancies turned them into mutual enemies. That does not mean that when one of them was walking, the other was sitting, that the one stayed awake while the other slept, or kept silent when the other was talking, insignificant differences supposedly connected with those minute alterations in the heavens which cannot be observed by those who note the configuration of the stars under which an individual is born, and which provide the basis for astrological consultations. For one of those twins was a paid servant, the other was not; one was loved by his mother, the other was not; one lost that position which in those days was counted a great honour, while the other acquired it. And besides, what a vast difference between their wives, their sons, the whole setting of their lives! If these divergencies depend on those few instants of time which separate twins, and are not to be observed in the constellations, why are those statements made after examination of the constellations of those who are not twins? If it is said that it is because they have reference, not to mere flashes of time which defy observation, but to spaces of time which can be observed and noted, then what is the purpose of this potter's wheel except to

5. Gen. xxv, 26.

send the clay-heads spinning round until they are too giddy to notice what nonsense the astrologers talk!

5. Proofs of the falsity of astrology

Then recall the instance of the two brothers whose illness grew worse and then grew better simultaneously, which led Hippocrates, observing them professionally, to conjecture that they were twins.[6] Surely this refutes those who would attribute to the influence of the stars a similarity which arose from similarity of constitution? For why did they fall sick in the same way and at the same time, instead of one after the other, in the order of their birth – since they could not have been born simultaneously? Or, supposing that the difference in the time of their birth was not important enough to effect a difference in the time of their falling sick, why is it maintained that a difference in the time of birth is the decisive factor in all other differences? They could travel at different times, marry at different times, procreate sons at different times and so on, just because they were born at different times. Then why could they not fall sick at different times for the same reason? If the delay between the two births altered the horoscope and introduced disparity in other matters, why did the effect of simultaneous conception endure only in matters of health and sickness? If it is asserted that in regard to health one's destiny is fixed at conception, while in all other respects it is connected with the moment of birth, the astrologers ought to refrain from any predictions about health after inspection of the constellations of nativity, since the evidence for the precise time of conception is not available for their investigations. If, however, they foretell sickness without examining the horoscope of conception because the moment of birth gives sufficient evidence, how could they tell one of a pair of twins, on the evidence of the time of his birth, when he was due to fall ill, since the other, who had a different time of birth, was inevitably due to fall ill in step with his brother?

Another question: There is, we are told, such a difference between the times of birth of twins that the constellations are bound to be different for them, because their horoscopes do not match, nor do the 'cardinal points' to which such predominant influence is attached as to alter the whole destiny of the subject. But how can this be. when the moment of conception must be identical?

Or if two beings *conceived* at the same instant could have different

6. cf. ch. 2.

destinies at their birth, why should it be impossible for two who were *born* at the same instant to have different destinies for their life and their death? If the fact that both were conceived at the same moment did not prevent one from being born before the other, why should a simultaneous birth in any way prevent one from dying before the other? If simultaneous conception allows twins to have different fortunes in the womb, why should simultaneous birth prevent any creatures on earth from having diverse fortunes? Then we could sweep away all the inventions of this art – or rather of this futility. Why on earth should those *conceived* at one and the same time, at one and the same instant, under one and the same disposition of the heavenly bodies – why should they have divergent destinies, bringing them to different times of birth, while two beings *born* of two mothers in precisely similar circumstances, at the same moment, under the same celestial disposition, could not have different destinies which would impose on them, inevitably, a different course of life and a different manner of death? Is it that beings when conceived do not yet have a destiny and cannot have a destiny unless they reach birth? If so, what is the meaning of saying that if the exact time of conception could be established, the astrologers would be able to make many more inspired predictions? Hence the oft-told story of the savant who carefully chose the moment for marital intercourse, so as to beget a prodigy of a son.

The same notion is reflected in the solution given by Posidonius[7] to the problem of the two men with the simultaneous illness. The great astrologer, who was also a philosopher, suggested that the explanation was that they had been born simultaneously and been conceived at the same moment. He added 'conceived' to guard against the objection that they obviously could not have been born at exactly the same instant. No one could deny their simultaneous conception. Posidonius would not immediately attribute the parallel course of the same illness in the two men to their identical constitutions; he connected their medical history with the influence of the stars. Well, if conception has the power to ensure coincidence of destiny, then birth should not be able to alter it. Or if the destinies of twins are altered because they are born at different moments, why should we not rather infer that they were already altered to enable them to be born at different moments? Are we to suppose that the will of the living does not modify the destiny assigned by their birth, although the order of birth modifies the destiny given by conception?

7. see ch. 2n.

6. Twins of different sex

Again, seeing that twins are undoubtedly conceived at the same instant, how is it that, under the same fateful constellation, one of them may be conceived a male, the other a female? I know a pair of twins of different sex; both of them are still alive and full of vigour for their age. They resemble one another physically, as far as difference of sex allows; but they are quite dissimilar in respect of their calling and their manner of life. And I am not referring to the activities which must differ in men and women. The male twin is a staff officer; he is almost always away from home, serving abroad. His sister scarcely ever leaves her native soil, or even her own part of the country. Furthermore – and this is still more incredible if you believe in destiny fixed by stars, but in no way remarkable, if account is taken of man's free will and the gifts of God – the brother married, while the sister is a consecrated virgin. He has a large family, while she is unmarried.

'How all-powerful,' they say, 'is the influence of the horoscope!' I have already sufficiently shown that it is nothing of the kind. But whatever force this influence may be thought to have, it is at the moment of birth that it is supposed to exercise its power. Does it operate at all at the moment of conception? Conception clearly results from one act of intercourse, and the force of nature is so great that, once a woman has conceived, it is quite impossible for her to conceive again; therefore it follows inevitably that twins must be conceived at precisely the same moment. Are we to suppose either that one was changed into a male child or the other into a female while they were being born, because at birth they were under different horoscopes?

Now it could be maintained, without utter absurdity, that some influences from the stars have an effect on variations confined to the physical realm. We observe that the variation of the seasons depends on the approach and withdrawal of the sun, and the waxing and waning of the moon produces growth and diminution in certain species, such as sea-urchins and shell-fish, and also the marvellous variations of the tides. It is not conceivable that the decisions of man's will are subjected to the dispositions of the stars. Those astrologers try to bind our actions to those astral phenomena, and they challenge us to produce an instance where their system lacks coherence, merely on the physical level. Well, what could be more physical than difference of sex? Yet twins of different sexes could be conceived under the same astral disposition. So what statement or belief could be more silly than the assertion that the position of the stars, which was identical for both twins at the moment of conception, could not have prevented the sister from being of a different sex from her brother when she had the same conjunction, and that the position of the stars, at the moment of their birth, could have produced between them the vast difference between the married state and holy virginity?

7. The choice of a day for marriage, or for planting and sowing

Who could believe the notion that by selecting certain days one can in a sense create new destinies for one's own acts? It would mean that the savant in the anecdote was not born so as to be destined to beget a remarkable son, but, on the contrary, destined to beget a contemptible offspring. That is why that learned man carefully chose the time for marital intercourse. That is, he created a destiny which was not his before and as a result of his act something was fated to happen which was not destined at his birth. What an extraordinary piece of nonsense! You carefully choose the day for marriage, for fear, I imagine, of hitting on an inauspicious day, and making an unhappy match! So what has happened to what the stars decided at your birth? Can a man then alter what has been fixed for him by the choice of a day? If so, cannot what he has fixed by that choice be altered by some other power?

Then again, if it is only men who are subject to the celestial conjunctions, and not everything else under the heavens, why are days selected as specially appropriate for the planting of vines or other trees, or for sowing crops, other days for training cattle, or for their mating, so as to build up herds of oxen or mares, and so on? Suppose that the choice of days is of such importance because every body and every living being on earth is dominated by the position of the stars which varies at different moments. Then let those who believe this consider the innumerable beings which are born, or come to be, or start at any given instant of time, and have such diverse destinies, so diverse as to convince any schoolboy that those astrological observations are utterly ridiculous. Who is so bereft of his senses as to allow himself to assert that all trees, vegetables, animals, snakes, birds, fishes, worms have their individual and different 'moments of nativity'? And yet it is common for people to put the competence of astrologers to proof by bringing them the 'conjunctions' of dumb animals, whose moment of birth they note carefully at home with a view to this astrological examination. And they put into the top class those astrologers who, on inspection of the 'conjunctions', declare that they signify the birth of an animal, not a man. They even have the audacity to name the kind of animal, and whether it will be good for wool-production, or as a draught-animal, or fit for the plough, or a useful watchdog. For astrologers are consulted even about canine destinies and their replies are greeted with loud shouts of admiration. Men are such fools as to imagine that when a man is born all other births are stopped, so that not even a mouse is born at the same time and under the same tract of the heavens. For if they allowed a mouse, they would be led step by step by a process of logical reasoning to camels and elephants! They will not observe that even when they have selected a day for sowing a field, a vast number of seeds fall on the soil at the same time and germinate at the same time; then when the crop springs up, they put out shoots, come to maturity and turn golden, all at the same time; and yet, though the resultant ears are all contemporary and, to coin a word, 'congerminal', some are wiped out by blight, some are plundered by birds and some plucked off by men. They notice that these ears have very different ends; are they going to maintain that they had different 'conjunctions'? How can they? Or are they going to change their minds about selecting days for those operations, and to say that such things have no connection with the celestial decisions? Will they subject only mankind to the stars, men being the only creatures on earth on whom God has bestowed free will?

When one ponders all this, one has some justification for supposing that when astrologers give replies that are often surprisingly true, they are inspired, in some mysterious way, by spirits, but spirits of evil, whose concern is to instil and confirm in men's minds those false and baneful notions about 'astral destiny'. These true predictions do not come from any skill in the notation and inspection of horoscopes; that is a spurious art.

8. *'Fate'; a name given by some people not to the position of the stars but to a chain of causes dependent on God's will*

There are those who use the name 'destiny' to refer not to the conjunction of stars at the moment of conception, or birth, or beginning, but to the connected series of causes which is responsible for anything that happens. We need not engage in a laborious controversy with them about the use of a word. For in fact they ascribe this orderly series, this chain of causes, to the will and power of the supreme God, who is believed, most rightly and truly, to know all things before they happen and who leaves nothing unordered. From him come all powers, but not all wills. What they mean by 'destiny' is principally the will of the supreme God, whose power extends invincibly through all things. This is demonstrated by the following lines, written, if I am not mistaken, by Seneca,[8]

> Father supreme, thou sovereign of the heavens,
> Lead where thou wilt. I hasten to obey,
> Eager to do thy will. If mine be crossed,
> I'll follow, though in tears. If I be wicked
> I will endure to have that done to me
> Which, virtuous, I could choose to do myself.
> Fate leads the willing, drags the reluctant feet.[9]

It is quite evident that in the last line the poet uses 'fate', or destiny, to refer to what he had earlier called the will of the 'supreme Father'. He says that he is ready to obey, so as to be led willingly, not dragged against his will; for

> Fate leads the willing, drags the reluctant feet.

The same sentiment is expressed in the lines of Homer, turned into Latin by Cicero,

> The mind of man is governed by the light
> Which Jove dispenses on the fruitful earth.[10]

The opinions of poets should not carry weight in the present discussion. But since Cicero tells us that the Stoics generally appropriate those lines of Homer in support of their assertion of the power of destiny, we are not dealing with the ideas of the poet, but the notions of philosophers. In those lines, which they introduce into their arguments about fate, their idea of the nature of destiny is made abundantly clear. They refer to destiny under the name of Jupiter, whom they suppose to be the supreme god, and they assert that it is on him that the causal chain of every destiny depends.

8. L. *Annaeus Seneca* (4 B.C.–A.D. 65): Stoic moralist, essayist and poet. The lines are a free translation from Cleanthes (*c.* 330–231 B.C.), successor to Zeno as head of the Stoic school. The original Greek is given by Epictetus (*Ench.*, 77).

9. *Ep.*, 107.

10. *Od.*, 18, 136f. The translation was probably contained in the lost part of *De Fato*.

9. *God's foreknowledge and man's free will; a criticism of Cicero*

Cicero[11] tries hard to refute those philosophers, while realizing that he cannot make head against them without abolishing divination. He tries to get rid of it by denying the existence of knowledge of the future. He uses his best efforts to establish the utter impossibility of such knowledge and of any prediction of events, whether in man or in God. Thus he denies the foreknowledge of God, as well as trying to demolish every prophecy, even though it is clearer than daylight. He does this by spurious arguments, and by setting up as targets certain easily refutable oracles,[12] which, however, he fails to invalidate, although in his exposure of the conjectures of astrologers, his eloquence carries all before it. The fact is that such guesswork is self-destructive and self-refuting. Yet the theory that the stars decide destiny is much more tolerable than the attempt to get rid of all knowledge of the future. To acknowledge the existence of God, while denying him any prescience of events, is the most obvious madness. Cicero himself realized this, and almost ventured on the denial referred to in Scripture, 'The fool has said in his heart: God does not exist.'[13] But he did not say it in his own person; he knew that such an assertion would disturb people, and incur odium. And so he represents Cotta[14] as arguing this point against the Stoics, in the book *On the Nature of the Gods*.[15] Cicero preferred to give his vote to Lucius Balbus,[16] to whom he entrusted the defence of the Stoic position, rather than to Cotta, who denied the existence of any divine nature. However, in his book *On Divination* he comes out openly in his own name in an attack on the notion of foreknowledge. His whole purpose in this is to preserve free will by refusing to admit the existence of fate. He assumes that the admission of foreknowledge entails the acceptance of fate as a logical necessity. For our part, whatever may be the twists and turns of philosophical dispute and debate, we recognize a God who is supreme and true and therefore we confess his supreme power and foreknowledge. We are not afraid that what we do by an act of will may not be a voluntary act, because God, with his infallible prescience, knew that we should do it. This was the fear that led Cicero to oppose foreknowledge and the Stoics to deny that everything happens by necessity, although they maintained that everything happens according to fate.

11. *De Div.*, 2. 12. *De Div.*, 2, 56. 13. Ps. 14. 1.

14. C. *Aurelius Cotta*, consul 75. He is one of the disputants in Cicero's *De Oratore* and *De Natura Deorum*, representing the Academics.

15. *De Nat. Deor.*, 3. 16. cf. Bk IV, 30n.

Now what was it that Cicero so dreaded in prescience of the future, that he struggled to demolish the idea by so execrable a line of argument? He reasoned that if all events are foreknown, they will happen in the precise order of that foreknowledge; if so, the order is determined in the prescience of God. If the order of events is determined, so is the causal order; for nothing can happen unless preceded by an efficient cause. If the causal order is fixed, determining all events, then all events, he concludes, are ordered by destiny. If this is true, nothing depends on us and there is no such thing as free will. 'Once we allow this,' he says, 'all human life is overthrown. There is no point in making laws, no purpose in expressing reprimand or approbation, censure or encouragement; there is no justice in establishing rewards for the good and penalties for the evil.'[17]

It is to avoid those consequences, discreditable and absurd as they are, and perilous to human life, that Cicero refuses to allow any foreknowledge. And he constrains the religious soul to this dilemma, forcing it to choose between those propositions: either there is some scope for our will, or there is foreknowledge. He thinks that both cannot be true; to affirm one is to deny the other. If we choose foreknowledge, free will is annihilated; if we choose free will, prescience is abolished. And so, being a man of eminent learning, a counsellor of wide experience and practiced skill in matters affecting human life, Cicero chooses free will. To support this, he denies foreknowledge and thus, in seeking to make men free, he makes them irreverent. For the religious mind chooses both, foreknowledge as well as liberty; it acknowledges both, and supports both in pious faith. 'How?' asks Cicero. If there is prescience of the future, the logical consequences entailed lead to the conclusion that nothing depends on our free will. And further, if anything does so depend, then, by the converse logical process, we reach the position that there is no foreknowledge. The argument proceeds thus: if there is free will, everything does not happen by fate; if everything does not happen by fate, there is not a fixed order of all causes; if there is not a fixed order of all causes, there is not a fixed order of events for the divine prescience, for these events cannot take place unless preceded by efficient causes; if there is not a fixed order for God's prescience, everything does not happen as he has foreknown them as due to happen. Thus, he concludes, if everything does not happen as foreknown by God, then there is in him no foreknowledge of all the future.[18]

Against such profane and irreverent impudence we assert both that

17. *De Fato*, 17, 40. 18. *De Fato*, 10, 20ff.

God knows all things before they happen and that we do by our free will everything that we feel and know would not happen without our volition. We do not say that everything is fated; in fact we deny that anything happens by destiny. For we have shown that the notion of destiny, in the accepted sense, referring to conjunction of stars at the time of conception or birth, has no validity, since it asserts something which has no reality. It is not that we deny a causal order where the will of God prevails; but we do not describe it by the word 'fate', unless perhaps if we understand fate to be derived from *fari* (speak),[19] that is from the act of speaking. We cannot in fact deny that it is written in Scripture, 'God has spoken once, and I have heard those two things: that the power belongs to God; and that mercy belongs to you, Lord, and you render to each in accordance with his works.'[20] The words 'has spoken *once*' mean 'he has spoken *immovably*,' that is, unalterably, just as he knows unalterably all that is to happen and what he himself is going to do. For this reason we should be able to use the word 'fate', deriving it from *fari*, except that this word is generally used in a different sense, a sense to which we should not wish men's hearts to be directed.

Now if there is for God a fixed order of all causes, it does not follow that nothing depends on our free choice. Our wills themselves are in the order of causes, which is, for God, fixed, and is contained in his foreknowledge, since human acts of will are the causes of human activities. Therefore he who had prescience of the causes of all events certainly could not be ignorant of our decisions, which he foreknows as the causes of our actions.

Cicero's own concession[21] that nothing happens unless preceded by an efficient cause is enough to refute him in the present question. It does not help his case to assert that while no event is causeless, not every cause is the work of destiny, since there are fortuitous causes, natural, and voluntary causes. It is enough that he admits that every event must be preceded by a cause. For our part, we do not deny the existence of causes called 'fortuitous' (from the same root as the word 'fortune'); only we say that they are hidden causes and attribute them to the will, either of the true God, or of spirits of some kind. The 'natural' causes we do not detach from the will of God, the author and creator of all nature. The 'voluntary' causes come from God, or from angels, or men, or animals – if indeed one can apply the notion of will to the movements of beings devoid of reason, which carry out actions

19. The etymology is, for once, correct.
20. Ps. 61, 11f. 21. *De Fato*, 10f.

in accordance with their nature, to achieve some desire or to avoid some danger. By the wills of angels I mean both the wills of the good angels of God, as we call them, and of the evil 'angels of the devil', or even 'demons'. The same applies to the wills of men; there are those of good men, and those of evil.

This implies that the only efficient causes of events are voluntary causes, that is, they proceed from that nature which is the 'breath of life'. ('Breath' also refers to the air or the wind; but since that is corporeal, it is not the 'breath of life'.) The breath of life, which gives life to everything, and is the creator of every body and every created spirit (breath), is God himself, the uncreated spirit. In his will rests the supreme power, which assists the good wills of created spirits, sits in judgement on the evil wills, orders all wills, granting the power of achievement to some and denying it to others. Just as he is the creator of all natures, so he is the giver of all power of achievement, but not of all acts of will. Evil wills do not proceed from him because they are contrary to the nature which proceeds from him. Bodies are mostly subject to wills, some to our wills – that is to the wills of mortal beings, the wills of men rather than of animals – the others to the wills of angels. But all bodies are subject above all to the will of God, and to him all wills also are subject, because the only power they have is the power that God allows them.

Thus the cause which is cause only, and not effect, is God. But other causes are also effects, as are all created spirits and in particular the rational spirits. Corporeal causes, which are more acted upon than active, are not to be counted among efficient causes, since all they can achieve is what is achieved through them by the wills of spirits. How then does the order of causes, which is fixed in the prescience of God, result in the withdrawal of everything from dependence on our will, when our acts of will play an important part in that causal order? Let Cicero dispute with those who assert that this causal order is decided by destiny, or rather who give that order the name of destiny, or fate – a position which shocks us particularly because of that word 'fate', which is generally understood in a way which corresponds to nothing in the real world. But when Cicero denies that the order of all causes is completely fixed and perfectly known to God's foreknowledge we execrate his opinion even more than do the Stoics. For either he denies the existence of God, which indeed he has been at pains to do, in the person of a disputant in his treatise *On the Nature of the Gods*; or else, if he acknowledges God's existence while denying his foreknowledge, he is even so saying, in effect, exactly what 'the fool has said in his heart'; for he is saying, 'God does not exist.'[22] For a being who does not know all the future is certainly not God.

Thus our wills have only as much power as God has willed and foreknown; God, whose foreknowledge is infallible, has foreknown the strength of our wills and their achievements, and it is for that reason that their future strength is completely determined and their future achievements utterly assured. That is why, if I had decided to apply the term 'destiny' at all, I should be more ready to say that the destiny of the weak is the will of the stronger, who has the weak in his power, than to admit that destiny, in the Stoic sense of 'the causal order' (a use peculiar to Stoics, in conflict with the generally accepted one) does away with the free decision of our will.

10. *Are men's wills under the sway of necessity?*

There is no need, then, to dread that 'necessity', through fear of which the Stoics took such pains to distinguish between the causes of things, withdrawing some of them from the sway of necessity, subjecting others to it, and classing our wills among the causes they wished to emancipate from necessity, for fear, I suppose, that they would not be free if subject to it. Now if, in our case, 'necessity' is to be used of what is not in our control, of what achieves its purpose whether we will or no – the 'necessity' of death, for example – then it is obvious that our wills, by the exercise of which we lead a good life or a bad, are not subject to a necessity of this kind. We do a great many things which we should not have done if we had not wished to. In the first place, our willing belongs to this class of acts. If we so wish, it exists; if we do not so wish, it does not; for we should not will, if we did not so wish.

If, on the other hand, we define 'necessity' in the sense implied when we say that it is necessary a thing should be thus, or should happen thus, I see no reason to fear that this would rob us of free will. We do not subject the life and the foreknowledge of God to necessity, if we say that it is 'necessary' for God to be eternal and to have complete foreknowledge; nor is his power diminished by saying that he cannot die or make a mistake. The reason why he cannot is that, if he could, his power would certainly be less; and he is rightly called 'all-powerful', although he has not the power to die, or to be mistaken. 'All-powerful' means that he does what he wills, and does not suffer what he does not will; otherwise he would be by no means all-powerful. It is just because he is all-powerful that there are some things he

22. Ps. 14, 1.

cannot do. The same applies when we say that it is 'necessary' that when we will, we will by free choice. That statement is undisputable; and it does not mean that we are subjecting our free will to a necessity which abolishes freedom. Our wills are ours and it is our wills that affect all that we do by willing, and which would not have happened if we had not willed. But when anyone has something done to him against his will, here, again, the effective power is will, not his own will, but another's. But the power of achievement comes from God. For if there was only the will without the power of realization, that will would have been thwarted by a more powerful will. Even so, that will would have been a will, and the will not of another, but of him who willed, although it was incapable of realization. Hence, whatever happens to man against his will is to be attributed not to the wills of men, or angels, or any created spirits, but to the will of him who gives the power of realization.

It does not follow, then, that there is nothing in our will because God foreknew what was going to be in our will; for if he foreknew this, it was not nothing that he foreknew. Further, if, in foreknowing what would be in our will, he foreknew something, and not nonentity, it follows immediately that there is something in our will, even if God foreknows it. Hence we are in no way compelled either to preserve God's prescience by abolishing our free will, or to safeguard our free will by denying (blasphemously) the divine foreknowledge. We embrace both truths, and acknowledge them in faith and sincerity, the one for a right belief, the other for a right life. And yet a man's life cannot be right without a right belief about God. Therefore, let us never dream of denying his foreknowledge in the interests of our freedom; for it is with his help that we are, or shall be, free.

By the same token, it is not true that reprimands, exhortations, praise and blame are useless, because God has knowledge of them before; they are of the greatest efficacy in so far as he has foreknown that they would be effective. And prayers are effectual in obtaining all that God foreknew that he would grant in answer to them; and it is with justice that rewards are appointed for good actions and punishments for sins. The fact that God foreknew that a man would sin does not make a man sin; on the contrary, it cannot be doubted that it is the man himself who sins just because he whose prescience cannot be mistaken has foreseen that the man himself would sin. A man does not sin unless he wills to sin; and if he had willed not to sin, then God would have foreseen that refusal.

11. *God's universal providence, by whose laws the whole scheme of things is governed*

Thus God is the supreme reality, with his Word and the Holy Spirit – three who are one. He is the God omnipotent, creator and maker of every soul and every body; participation in him brings happiness to all who are happy in truth and not in illusion; he has made man a rational animal, consisting of soul and body; and when man sins he does not let him go unpunished, nor does he abandon him without pity. He has given, to good men and bad alike, the existence they share with the stones; he has given man reproductive life which he shares with the plants, the life of the senses, which he shares with the animals, and the life of the intellect, shared only with the angels. From him derives every mode of being, every species, every order, all measure, number, and weight. He is the source of all that exists in nature, whatever its kind, whatsoever its value, and of the seeds of forms, and the forms of seeds, and the motions of seeds and forms. He has given to flesh its origin, beauty, health, fertility in propagation, the arrangement of the bodily organs, and the health that comes from their harmony. He has endowed even the soul of irrational creatures with memory, sense, and appetite, but above all this, he has given to the rational soul thought, intelligence, and will. He has not abandoned even the inner parts of the smallest and lowliest creature, or the bird's feather (to say nothing of the heavens and the earth, the angels and mankind) – he has not left them without a harmony of their constituent parts, a kind of peace. It is beyond anything incredible that he should have willed the kingdoms of men, their dominations and their servitudes, to be outside the range of the laws of his providence.

12. *The moral character in the ancient Romans which earned from the true God the increase of their empire although they did not worship him*

Let us go on to examine for what moral qualities and for what reason the true God deigned to help the Romans in the extension of their empire; for in his control are all the kingdoms of the earth.

In order to discuss this question more thoroughly, I have written the previous book, which deals with this topic; and I have shown there that in this matter there is no power at all in those gods whom the Romans considered they had to worship by means of frivolous ceremonies. In the first part of the present book, up to this point, I have shown that the notion of 'destiny' must be dismissed, so that no one, once convinced that the propagation and preservation of the Roman Empire was not due to the worship of those gods, should attribute it to some 'destiny' or other, and not to the omnipotent will of God most high.

Now according to the witness of the historians, the ancient Romans – those of the earliest epoch – no doubt worshipped false gods, like the other races (except only the Hebrew people) and sacrificed victims not to God, but to demons; nevertheless they were 'greedy for praise, generous with their money, and aimed at vast renown and honourable riches'.[23] They were passionately devoted to glory; it was for this that they desired to live, for this they did not hesitate to die. This unbounded passion for glory, above all else, checked their other appetites. They felt it would be shameful for their country to be enslaved, but glorious for her to have dominion and empire; and so they set their hearts first on making her free, then on making her sovereign.

That is why, when they found the domination of kings intolerable, they 'created for themselves an annual authority in the hands of two men, who were called "consuls", from *consulere*[24] (to take counsel), not "kings" (*reges*), a word derived from *regnare* (to reign), or "lords" (*domini*), derived from *dominare* (to dominate)'.[25] (It would, in fact, seem to be more correct to derive *reges* from *regere* (to rule), *regnum* (reign) being derived from *reges*, but *reges*, as I say, from *regere*.) The Romans accounted the royal disdain to be not the strict direction of a ruler, nor the benevolent advice of a counsellor, but the arrogance of a despot. And so, after the expulsion of King Tarquin and the institution of consuls, a period followed which the same author, Sallust, ranks among the glories of the Roman people. 'When once the city had won liberty,' he says, 'the speed and extent of its development almost passes belief. So great was the passion for glory that took hold of the people.'[26] It was this greed for praise, this passion for glory, that gave rise to those marvellous achievements, which were, no doubt, praiseworthy and glorious in men's estimation.

Sallust also praises two great men of renown in his own era, Marcus Cato and Gaius Caesar.[27] He says that Rome had for a long time been deprived of any men of outstanding quality, but that in his time there had been two men of immense moral stature, though very different in character.[28] He praises Caesar, among other things, for his ambition

23. Sall., *Cat.*, 7. 6. 24. An unlikely etymology.
25. Sall., *Cat.*, 6, 7; Cic., *De Rep.*, 2, 31. 26. *Cat.*, 7, 3.
27. Cato of Utica and Julius Caesar. 28. *Cat.*, 53f.

for a great command, for an army, for a new war in which his abilities could shine. Thus the chief desire of men of eminent qualities was that Bellona should arouse wretched nations to war and drive them on with her bloody whip[29] to give an occasion for their abilities to shine. Such was the ambition aroused by their 'greed for praise' and 'passion for glory'. In early times it was the love of liberty that led to great achievements, later it was the love of domination, the greed for praise and glory. Their outstanding poet bears witness to both these motives, when he writes,

> Porsenna bade take back the exiled Tarquin,
> And pressed on Rome with overwhelming might.
> Then rushed to arms Aeneas' valiant sons,
> Defending liberty.[30]

The important thing for the men of that time was either to die bravely, or to live in freedom. But when liberty had been won, 'such a passion for glory took hold of them' that liberty alone did not satisfy – they had to acquire dominion. What mattered then was expressed by the same poet, when he makes Jupiter say,

> Only let savage Juno,
> Who wearies land and sea and heaven with dread,
> Come to a better mind, with me support
> The toga'd race, the masters of the earth.
> This is my will: as age succeeds to age
> The time will come when those of Aeneas' line
> Shall press beneath the yoke of slavery
> Phthia and famed Mycenae; yes, and Argos
> Vanquished shall feel the mastery of Rome.[31]

Virgil, of course, represents Jupiter as prophesying the future; but he is himself recalling the past and contemplating the present situation. My purpose in quoting these lines is to show that after liberty, the Romans valued dominion so highly as to place it among their greatest glories. Hence the same poet puts above the accomplishments of other races the specifically Roman arts of ruling, commanding, subduing and subjecting other nations. This is what he says,

> Others will forge the bronze that seems to breathe
> With gentler life, and chisel from the marble
> The living features. They will plead a case
> With more persuasive skill: and with the compass
> Will trace the mazes of the sky, and tell the rising

29. Virg., *Aen.*, 8, 703.   30. Virg., *Aen.*, 8, 646ff.
31. *Aen.*, 279–85.

Of all the stars. Be these thy arts, my Roman;
To hold the nations under thy dominion,
Enforcing peace till it becomes a custom;
To spare the subject, and beat down the proud.[32]

The Romans practised those 'arts' with the more skill when they were the less given to indulgence and to the enervation of soul and body by the lust to accumulate wealth – that corrupter of morality – by robbing their less fortunate fellows and by extravagant generosity to degraded stage-players.

At the time when Sallust was writing and Virgil was composing his poem, moral corruption was already general and widespread, and men thus corrupted did not seek position and glory by Virgil's 'arts', but schemed for them by trickery and deceit. Hence Sallust tells us,

> It was, at first, ambition rather than greed that worked on men's hearts; a vice closer to a virtue. The true man and the worthless wretch alike covet glory, honour and power. But the true man directs his efforts along the right way; the man who lacks the moral qualities works towards his goal by trickery and deceit.[33]

These 'moral qualities' enable a man to arrive at honour, glory, and power by merit, not by the tricks of the canvasser. The aims are shared by the true man and the worthless wretch; but 'the true man directs his efforts along the right way.' That is the way of merit; it is by this way that he strives towards his goal, towards glory, honour, and power. That this feeling was innate in the Romans is shown by the establishment of temples, very near to each other, to the gods Virtue and Honour;[34] they thought of these gifts of God as being themselves divinities. From this one can realize what they wished to be the consummation of merit, what the good man connected with merit – it was honour. Although the bad men desired honour, they did not possess it, since they tried to win it by dishonest means, by 'trickery and deceit'.

Cato is given even higher praise. Sallust says of him, 'The less he sought glory, the more it pursued him.'[35] Glory, the object of the Romans' burning ambition, is the judgement of men when they think well of others. That is why virtue is superior to glory, since it is not content with the testimony of men, without the witness of a man's own conscience. Hence the Apostle says, 'This is our glory: the testimony of our own conscience.'[36] And, in another place, 'Let each

32. *Aen.*, 6, 847–53. 33. *Cat.*, 11, 1ff. 34. cf. Bk IV, 20n.
35. *Cat.*, 54, 6. 36. 2 Cor. 1, 12.

man test his own work; and thus he will have his glory in himself, not in another.'[37] Therefore glory, honour, and power – those Roman aims, which the good men strove to attain by honourable means – must be the consequences of virtue not its antecedents. The only genuine virtue is that which tends to the end where the good of man is, which surpasses any other good. Hence Cato was not obliged to solicit the honours which he sought; it was the city's obligation to grant them to him, without his asking.

There were thus two Romans of eminent qualities at that period, Caesar and Cato. But Cato's qualities evidently approached far more nearly to the true ideal of virtue than did those of Caesar. Accordingly, if we want a picture of the condition of the commonwealth at that time, and of its previous condition, we may find it in Cato's judgement, when he says,

> Do not imagine that it was by force of arms that our ancestors made a great nation out of a small community. If that were true, we should today have a far more glorious nation. In allies, in our own citizens, in armaments, in horses, we have greater resources than they enjoyed. But it was other causes that made them great, causes that with us have ceased to exist: energy in our own land, a rule of justice outside our borders; in forming policy, a mind that is free because not at the mercy of criminal passions. Instead of these we have self-indulgence and greed, public poverty and private opulence. We praise riches: we pursue a course of sloth. No distinction is made between good men and bad: the intrigues of ambition win the prizes due to merit. No wonder, when each of you thinks only of his own private interest; when at home you are slaves to your appetites, and to money and influence in your public life. The consequence is that an attack is being launched on a republic left without defences.[38]

These words of Cato, or of Sallust, might lead one to suppose that all the Romans of antiquity, or the majority of them, resembled those of whom they speak so highly. That is not so. Otherwise the remarks of the same historian, quoted in my second book,[39] would be untrue. Sallust[40] tells us that the injustices of the powerful classes led to a secession of the plebeians from the patricians, and that from the beginning there were other domestic dissensions, and that the era of just moderation in government lasted after the expulsion of the kings only as long as the threat from Tarquin remained until the end of the major war against Etruria which Rome had engaged in because of Tarquin. But after that the plebeians were treated like slaves under

37. Gal. 6, 4. 38. Sall., *Cat.*, 52, 19ff. 39. Bk II. 18.
40. *Hist.* fr. 1. 11. The passage is quoted literally in Bk. II, 18.

the rule of the patricians, who handled them with the same violence as the kings, drove them from their lands, and wielded sole power, all others being disenfranchised. These discords, with one side aiming at domination, the other seeking to avoid slavery, were only ended by the Second Punic War, because then once again came the pressure of a serious threat, which checked their restless spirits, and distracted them from these disorders by a more urgent anxiety, and recalled them to domestic concord.

But it was by a mere handful of men, good men in their way, that the great public interests were managed; and it was thanks to the foresight of those few that those domestic ills were rendered tolerable and alleviated, and thus the country advanced to greatness.[41] Sallust adds that in reading or hearing of the many splendid exploits of the Roman people, in peace and war, on land and sea, he has been interested to observe what was the principal basis for their great achievements. He knew that on many occasions a mere handful of Romans had matched great enemy battalions and that Rome had waged war with scanty resources against opulent kings. And he declares that, after much reflection, he had reached the conclusion that all this success was due to the exceptional qualities of a small minority, and that this minority was responsible for the victory of poverty over riches – the triumph of the few over vast numbers. 'But', he continues, 'when luxury and idleness had corrupted the city, then, conversely, the greatness of the country supported the vices of generals and magistrates.'

The virtue of the few, the moral quality of those who stride towards glory, honour, and power by the right path, that is, by virtue itself – this is what Cato also praises. Hence came the energy at home, which he mentions, that brought riches to the public treasure, while private fortunes remained straitened. He contrasted this with the perverted situation after the moral corruption had set in, when we find the public purse empty and private pockets well-lined.[42]

13. *The love of praise: though a vice, it counts as a virtue because it checks greater vices*

The kingdoms of the East had enjoyed renown for a long time, when God decided that a Western empire should arise, later in time, but more renowned for the extent and grandeur of its dominion. And, to suppress the grievous evils of many nations, he entrusted this dom-

41. *Cat.*, 53, 2–5. 42. *Cat.*, 52, 21f.

inion to those men, in preference to all others, who served their country for the sake of honour, praise and glory, who looked to find that glory in their country's safety above their own and who suppressed greed for money and many other faults in favour of that one fault of theirs, the love of praise.

That the love of praise is, in fact, a fault, is recognized by the morally clear-sighted. The poet Horace did not fail to perceive this, when he wrote,

> Does lust for praise inflame you? There are rites
> Of expiation which will work a cure
> If you three times rehearse the formula
> Set in the prayer book, with a pure intent.[43]

And in one of his Odes he urges the conquest of the lust of domination when he says,

> Vaster your realm, when you subdue your passions,
> Than if you join Cadiz to far-off Libya
> Under your sway, and all the Punic Empire
> Have you for master.[44]

For all that, if men have not learnt to restrain their discreditable passions by obtaining the help of the Holy Spirit through their devout faith and their love of the Intelligible Beauty,[45] at least it is good that the desire for human praise and glory makes them, not indeed saints, but less depraved men.

Cicero himself could not disguise this fact; in his treatise *On the Commonwealth*,[46] speaking of the appointment of a chief of state, he lays it down that he must be 'nourished by glory', and goes on to recall that it was the greed for glory that inspired his ancestors to many famous and admirable achievements. Thus the Romans not only did not resist this fault; they held that it should be aroused and kindled, considering it to be in the interests of the commonwealth. And even in his philosophical writings Cicero does not disguise this pernicious doctrine; in fact he makes it as clear as daylight. For when speaking of the studies which should be pursued in the quest of the true good, rather than of the hollowness of human praise, he brings in this general and universal sentiment: 'It is honour that nourishes the arts; it is glory that kindles men to intellectual effort. All pursuits lose lustre when they fall from general favour.'[47]

43. *Ep.*, 1, 1 36f. 44. *Carm.* 2, 2, 9ff.

45. *Intelligible Beauty*: the Platonic 'idea' of beauty, apprehended by the intellect, not by the senses.

46. *De Rep.*, 5, 7, 9. 47. *Tusc. Disp.*, 1, 2, 4.

14. *Love of human praise is to be checked, because all the glory of the righteous is in God*

There can be no doubt that it is better to resist this passion than to yield to it. A man is more like God, the purer he is from this contamination. In this life it cannot wholly be rooted out from the heart, because even those souls which are making good progress are not exempt from the temptation. But at least the greed for glory should be overcome by the love of justice; and so, if things which are themselves good and right 'lose lustre' because of general disfavour, then the love of human praise itself should be ashamed, and yield place to the love of truth. For this vice is an enemy to devout faith, if the greed for glory is stronger in the heart than the fear or the love of God; so much so, that the Lord said, 'How can you believe, when you look for glory from one another, and do not seek the glory which comes from God alone?'[48] Again, the Evangelist speaks of those who believed in Christ but were afraid to confess it openly, when he says, 'They loved the glory of men rather than the glory of God.'[49]

This was not how the apostles behaved. They preached the name of Christ in places where that name was not in 'general favour', and we recall Cicero's statement: 'All pursuits lose lustre when they fall from general favour.' They preached in places where, in fact, Christ's name was held in utter detestation. They kept in mind what they had been told by their good master, the physician of souls, 'If anyone denies me before men, I will deny him in the presence of my Father in Heaven', or 'in the presence of the angels of God.'[50] Amidst curses and slanders, amidst the severest persecutions and the harshest punishments, all the clamorous hostility of men did not stop them from preaching men's salvation. The divine quality of their actions, their words and their lives, their triumphs, as one may say, over hard hearts, and their introduction of the peace of righteousness; all these brought them immense glory in the Church of Christ. And yet they did not rest on that glory, as if they had attained the goal of their own virtue. They ascribed it all to the glory of God, whose grace had made them what they were.[51] And this was a torch which kindled the fire of the love of God in the hearts of those they guided, the torch which was to make them such as the apostles were. Their master had taught the apostles not to be good in order to gain glory from men. He told them, 'Take care not to perform your righteous acts in the presence of men, so as to be seen

48. John 5, 44. 49. John 12, 43. 50. Matt. 10, 33; Luke 12, 9.
51. cf. 1 Cor. 15, 10.

by them: or you will have no reward with my Father, who is in heaven.'[52] On the other hand, so that men should not put a perverse interpretation on this injunction and reduce the influence of their goodness by concealing it, in fear of winning men's approval, the Lord explained to what purpose they ought to seek publicity. He said, 'Let your works shine in men's sight, so that they may see your acts of goodness, and glorify your Father, who is in Heaven';[53] so the purpose is not 'to be seen of them', that is, with the intention that they should be converted to *you*, because by yourselves you are nothing, but 'so that they may glorify your Father, who is in Heaven', and so that they may be converted to *him*, and become what you are.

The martyrs followed in the steps of the apostles. They did not inflict suffering on themselves, but they endured what was inflicted on them; and in so doing they surpassed the Scaevolas, the Curtii, and the Decii[54] by their true virtue, springing from true devotion, and by their countless multitude. Those Roman heroes belonged to an earthly city, and the aim set before them, in all their acts of duty for her, was the safety of their country, and a kingdom not in heaven, but on earth; not in life eternal, but in the process where the dying pass away and are succeeded by those who will die in their turn. What else was there for them to love save glory? For, through glory, they desired to have a kind of life after death on the lips of those who praised them.

15. *The temporal reward bestowed by God on Roman high qualities of character*

To such men as these God was not going to give eternal life with his angels in his own Heavenly City, the City to which true religion leads, which renders the supreme worship (the Greek word for it is *latreia*)[55] only to the one true God. If God had not granted to them the earthly glory of an empire which surpassed all others, they would have received no reward for the good qualities, the virtues, that is, by means of which they laboured to attain that great glory. When such men do anything good, their sole motive is the hope of receiving glory from their fellow-men; and the Lord refers to them when he says, 'I tell you in truth, they have received their reward in full.' They took no account of their own material interests compared with the common good, that is the commonwealth and the public purse; they resisted the temptations of avarice; they acted for their country's well-being

52. Matt. 6, 1. 53. Matt. 5, 16. 54. cf. Bk IV, 20nn. 55. cf. Bk X, 1.

with disinterested concern; they were guilty of no offence against the law; they succumbed to no sensual indulgence. By such immaculate conduct they laboured towards honours, power and glory, by what they took to be the true way. And they were honoured in almost all nations; they imposed their laws on many peoples; and today they enjoy renown in the history and literature of nearly all races. They have no reason to complain of the justice of God, the supreme and true. 'They have received their reward in full.'[56]

16. *The reward of the citizens of the Eternal City; the Roman virtues offer them useful examples*

Very different is the reward of the saints. Here below they endure obloquy for the City of God, which is hateful to the lovers of this world. That City is eternal; no one is born there, because no one dies. There is the true felicity, which is no goddess, but the gift of God. From there we have received the pledge of our faith, in that we sigh for her beauty while on our pilgrimage. In that City the sun does not rise 'on the good and on the evil';[57] the 'sun of righteousness'[58] spreads its light only on the good; there the public treasury needs no great efforts for its enrichment at the cost of private poverty; for there the common stock is the treasury of truth.

But more than this; the Roman Empire was not extended and did not attain to glory in men's eyes simply for this, that men of this stamp should be accorded this kind of reward. It had this further purpose, that the citizens of that Eternal City, in the days of their pilgrimage, should fix their eyes steadily and soberly on those examples and observe what love they should have towards the City on high, in view of life eternal, if the earthly city had received such devotion from her citizens, in their hope of glory in the sight of men.

17. *The profit the Romans gained from their wars and the benefits they conferred on the vanquished*

As for this mortal life, which ends after a few days' course, what does it matter under whose rule a man lives, being so soon to die, provided that the rulers do not force him to impious and wicked acts? Did the Romans do any harm to other nations when they subdued them and imposed the Roman laws, apart from the vast slaughter of the wars? If

56. Matt. 6, 2. 57. Matt. 5, 45. 58. Mal. 4, 2.

that result had been effected by peaceful agreement, it would have had better success; but then there would have been no glory for the conquerors. The Romans themselves lived under the same laws as they imposed on the rest. If this imposition had happened without the aid of Mars and Bellona, so that Victory had no hand in it (for there would have been no fighting and therefore no victors), the condition of the Romans and that of the other peoples would have been precisely the same – especially if they had without delay taken the step, which they took later, to win gratitude for their humanity, by associating in the commonwealth, as Roman citizens, all those who belonged to the Roman Empire; for this granted to all a privilege formerly enjoyed by a few. There was one exception to this equality: the Roman lower classes, possessing no land, lived at the public expense. The contributions to their upkeep would have been furnished with a better grace, had they been presented voluntarily through the agency of equitable administrators, after a peaceful compact, instead of being taken by extortion from conquered peoples.

As far as I can see, the distinction between victors and vanquished has not the slightest importance for security, for moral standards, or even for human dignity. It is merely a matter of the arrogance of human glory, the coin in which these men 'received their reward', who were on fire with unlimited lust for glory, and waged their wars of burning fury. Is it the case that the conqueror's lands are exempt from taxes? Have the victors access to knowledge forbidden to the others? Are there not many senators in other lands, who do not know Rome even by sight? Take away national complacency, and what are all men but simply men? If the perverse standards of the world would allow men to receive honours proportional to their deserts, even so the honour of men should not be accounted an important matter; smoke has no weight.

For all that, even in this we may profit from the goodness of our Lord God. Let us consider all the hardships these conquerors made light of, all the sufferings they endured, and the desires they suppressed to gain the glory of men. They deserved to receive that glory as a reward for such virtues. Let this thought avail to suppress pride in us. That City, in which it has been promised that we shall reign, differs from this earthly city as widely as the sky from the earth, life eternal from temporal joy, substantial glory from empty praises, the society of angels from the society of men, the light of the Maker of the sun and moon from the light of the sun and moon. Therefore the citizens of so great a country should not suppose that they have achieved anything of note if, to attain that country, they have done something good, or endured some ills, seeing that those Romans did so much and suffered so much for the earthly country they already possessed. What gives special point to this comparison is that the remission of sins, the promise which recruits the citizens for the Eternal Country, finds a kind of shadowy resemblance in that refuge of Romulus,[59] where the offer of impunity for crimes of every kind collected a multitude which was to result in the foundation of the city of Rome.

18. *Seeing that the Romans achieved so much for their earthly city, to win glory from men, Christians should shun any boasting about anything they have done for love of their Eternal Country*

This being so, is it such a great thing that one should despise, for the sake of that Eternal and Heavenly Country, all the attractions of this present life, however beguiling, if, for the sake of this temporal and earthly country, Brutus had the strength to kill his sons,[60] a thing which that other country compels no one to do? It is surely a harder thing to put one's sons to death, than to do what has to be done for that Celestial Country: to give to the poor the possessions which one had supposed should be collected and preserved for one's children, or to let them go, if a temptation should appear which made that course necessary for the sake of faith and righteousness. Happiness, whether for us or for our children, is not the result of earthly riches, which must either be lost by us in our lifetime or else must pass after our death into the possession of those we do not know or, it may be, of those whom we do not wish to have them. It is God who gives happiness; for he is the true wealth of men's souls.

As for Brutus, even the poet who praises him testifies to his ill-fortune,

His sons, conspiring to an armed revolt
He punished, in fair liberty's defence.
O most unhappy, howsoe'er the future
Speak of his deed!

Though in the next line he consoles the unhappy man,

Love of his country and the boundless passion
For high renown, these swayed his grim resolve.[61]

59. cf. Bk I, 34; Liv., 1, 8. 60. cf. Bk III, 16.
61. Virg., *Aen.*, 6, 820ff.

These were the two motives which drove the Romans to their wonderful achievements: liberty, and the passion for the praise of men. Then if a father could kill his sons for the liberty of those destined to die and because of a desire for the praises which were to be won from mortal beings, is it anything remarkable if, to gain the true liberty, which frees us from the domination of death, of iniquity and of the devil, not from desire for human praise but from the charitable longing to set men free (not from King Tarquin, but from the demons and the prince of the demons) – is it remarkable if, for the sake of all this we should be ready, not to kill our sons, but to reckon among our sons the poor people of Christ?

Another great man of Rome, surnamed Torquatus,[62] put his son to death because he had fought, not against his country but for his country, yet in defiance of the command issued by his father, his commander. The son in his youthful ardour had accepted the enemy's challenge to combat and he had conquered. Yet his father killed him, for fear that the evil of the bad example of contempt or orders would outweigh the glory of the victory over the enemy. In face of this, why should they plume themselves who, in obedience to the laws of their immortal country, despise all this world's goods, which are much less dear than sons?

Furius Camillus[63] had struck off from his country's neck the yoke of Veii, Rome's bitterest enemy, and then had been condemned by his rivals; yet he returned to rescue his ungrateful country again, this time from the Gauls. For he could find no better country where he could live with greater honour. Then why should we extol, as if for some grand accomplishment, a man who happens to have suffered grave injustice in the Church at the hands of worldly enemies by being deprived of his position; and then, instead of going over to the side of the Church's enemies, or founding some heresy against her, has preferred to use all his efforts to defend the Church against the baneful perversions of the heretics, since there is no other Church where he can find, not the chance of living gloriously in men's eyes, but the way to attain to life eternal?

When Porsenna was pressing hard on Rome in a struggle of the utmost gravity, Mucius[64] failed in an attempt to kill the Etruscan chief and by mistake killed another man instead. Thereupon he stretched out his right hand into the flame of an altar before Porsenna's eyes, saying, 'You see what kind of man I am. There are many men of the same stamp who have sworn an oath together to destroy

62. cf. Bk I, 23n. 63. cf. Bk II, 17. 64. Scaevola; cf. Bk IV, 20.

you.' Shocked by this display of fortitude, and dreading a conspiracy of such men, Porsenna made peace without delay and stopped the war. Considering this, surely no one is likely to regard his own merits as entitling him to a share in the kingdom of heaven, if for that kingdom's sake he has given to the flames not one of his hands but the whole of his body, and that not by a voluntary self-inflicted sacrifice but as the victim of another's persecution.

Then there is the case of Curtius,[65] He spurred on his horse and hurled himself, fully armed, into a gaping chasm in obedience to the oracles of his gods. They had ordered that the best possession of the Romans should be consigned to that abyss, and the Romans could only interpret this as referring to their excellence in warriors and in arms; hence it appeared that at the gods' command a fully-armed warrior must hurl himself to that death. Remembering him, will anyone claim credit for something heroic if he has encountered an enemy of his faith and then has not sent himself to such a death of his own accord, but has been sent to meet it by that enemy? And we know that he has received from his Lord, who is the king of his own country, an oracle more definite than any oracle of Rome, 'Do not fear those who kill the body, but cannot kill the soul.'

The Decii[65] devoted themselves to death, consecrating themselves in a way by sacrificial formulas, so that the anger of the gods might be appeased by the bloodshed as they fell, and the Roman army might be saved. In view of that act, the holy martyrs have no cause for boasting, as though they have done anything worthy of participation in that country where there is eternal and genuine felicity, if they have struggled in the faith of charity and the charity of faith, to the extent of shedding their blood – loving not only their brothers, for whom their blood was shed, but, in obedience to the commandment, loving even their enemies, by whom it was shed.

Marcus Pulvillus[66] was dedicating the temple of Jove, Juno, and Minerva when he received a false report of the death of his son, put about by envious rivals in the hope that he would be so distressed as to retire from the ceremony, and his colleagues would gain the glory of the dedication. But he thought so little of it that he ordered his son's body to be thrown out without burial, so completely had the passion for glory overcome the sorrow of bereavement in his heart. If Pulvillus could do that, then what of the man who was so concerned about his father's burial, to whom the Lord said, 'Follow me, and allow the dead to bury their own dead?'[67] Is he to claim that he has performed some

65. cf. Bk IV, 20n. 66. Liv., 2, 8. 67. Matt. 8, 22.

great feat for the preaching of the gospel, by which the citizens of the country on high are freed from all kinds of error and gathered into a community?

Marcus Regulus[68] refused to break his sworn promise to a ruthless enemy. He left Rome and went back to the enemy, because (as he is said to have replied to the Romans who would have kept him back) he could not hold up his head as an honourable citizen in Rome after he had been a slave to Africans. And the Carthaginians murdered him with hideous tortures, because he had acted against their interests in the Roman senate. Then surely we Christians should make light of any kind of torture in defence of the faith of that country to which faith itself guides us? Or 'what return will be given to the Lord for all the benefits which he has given,'[69] if a man has suffered, for the faith which is due to God, such torture as Regulus suffered for the faith which he owed to his pitiless foes?

How can a Christian dare to pride himself on poverty voluntarily accepted to enable him to walk less encumbered on the road that leads to his own country, where God himself is the true wealth, when he hears or reads about Lucius Valerius,[70] who died during his consulship, so poor that a public collection was made to pay for his burial? Or when he hears or reads about Quintius Cincinnatus[71] who owned two acres of land, which he cultivated with his own hands, who was taken from his plough to become dictator – an office much higher than that of consul – and who, when he had conquered the enemy and won immense glory, then continued in the same poverty as before?

And can the Christian brag of any extraordinary performance, if he has refused to be seduced from the fellowship of that Heavenly Country by any of this world's prizes, when he learns that Fabricius[72] could not be torn from his allegiance to the Roman state by the most lavish presents of Pyrrhus, king of Epirus, who offered him as much as a quarter of his kingdom? Fabricius preferred to remain in poverty as an ordinary citizen.

Those Romans had a republic richly endowed with all resources (and 'republic' means 'state of the people', 'state of the country', 'commonwealth'), while they themselves lived in poverty in their own homes. So much so that one of them,[73] who had already been consul

68. cf. Bk I, 15n.
69. Ps. 116, 2.
70. P. Valerius Publicola: Liv., 2, 16; Val. Max., 4, 4, 1.
71. Dictator, 458 B.C. Liv., 3, 26–9; Val. Max., 4, 4, 7.
72. Plut., *Pyrrh.*, 20; Eutrop., 2, 12.
73. P. Cornelius Rufinus, 275 B.C. Val. Max., 2, 9, 4; Gell., 4, 8.

twice, was dismissed from the senate by the censor's ban, because it was discovered that he had ten pounds of silver plate. Such was the poverty of men whose triumphs enriched the public treasury. It is a far nobler resolution that leads Christians to regard their riches as belonging to all, according to the principle described in the Acts of Apostles; by which everything is shared out according to individual need, no one claims anything as his private property, and everything belongs to the common stock.[74] But Christians must understand that this gives them no ground for self-conceit, since they do this to attain to the fellowship of the angels, while the Roman worthies did much the same to preserve the glory of their country.

Such instances as these (and there are many others to be found in Roman literature) would never have gained such renown, or been so often quoted, had not the Roman Empire extended far and wide, coming to greatness with so impressive a record of success. Accordingly, it was that Empire, so far-spread and so long-lasting, and given lustre and glory by the heroic quality of its great men, that gave to them the return they looked for as a recompense for their resolution, while it sets before us Christians examples whose message we cannot but heed. If we do not display, in the service of the most glorious City of God, the qualities of which the Romans, after their fashion, gave us something of a model, in their pursuit of the glory of their earthly city, then we ought to feel the prick of shame. If we do display these virtues, we must not be infected with pride, for, as the Apostle says, 'The sufferings of the present time are not worth thinking of, in view of the glory which will be manifested in us.'[75] Whereas the Romans judged their life abundantly worthwhile in view of the glory of men in the immediate present.

The Jews put Christ to death, when the New Testament revealed what was veiled in the Old Testament,[76] the knowledge that God, the one true God, is to be worshipped for the sake of eternal life and everlasting gifts and for participation in that City on high, and not for earthly and temporal blessings, which divine providence bestows on good and evil without discrimination. And for this the Jews were justly given over to the Romans, for the greater glory of Rome, so that those who had sought earthly glory and attained it by their virtue (of

74. Acts 2, 44; 4, 32. 75. Rom. 8, 18.

76. *New Testament revealed*: cf. IV, 33; XVI, 26; and the most famous statement of this relation between the Old and New Testaments in *Quaes., in Hept.*, 2, 83: *In Vetere Novum latet et in Novo Vetus patet*, 'The New Testament is latent in the Old: the Old is patent in the New.'

whatever kind), overcame those who in their perverse wickedness spurned and put to death the giver of true glory and of citizenship in the Eternal City.

19. *The difference between ambition for glory and ambition for domination*

There is a clear difference between the desire for glory before men and the desire for domination. There is, to be sure, a slippery slope from the excessive delight in the praise of men to the burning passion for domination; and yet those who long for true glory, though it be the glory of merely human praise, are anxious for the good opinion of enlightened judges. For there are many good moral qualities which are approved by many, though many do not possess them. And it is by those moral qualities that glory, power, and domination are sought by the kind of men who, as Sallust says, 'strive for them in the right way'.[77] But if anyone aims at power and domination without that kind of desire for glory which makes a man fear the disapprobation of sound judges, then he generally seeks to accomplish his heart's desire by the most barefaced crimes.

Thus the man who covets glory either 'strives by the right way' for it or 'struggles by trickery and deceit', desiring to seem a good man without being so. Therefore it is a great virtue in a virtuous man to despise glory, because this contempt is seen by God, but is not revealed to the judgement of men. If anyone acts before men's eyes with the intention of seeming to despise glory, then men may suspect that such action is designed to win greater praise, that is, greater glory; and there is no way in which he can make it apparent to perception that such suspicion is groundless. But the man who despises flattering judgement, also despises baseless suspicions; and yet, if he is a truly good man, he does not regard the salvation of his fellow-men as of no importance. For so great is the righteousness of one who has his virtues from the Spirit of God, that he loves even his enemies; and such is his love even for those who hate and disparage him, that he wishes them to be reformed so that he may have them as fellow-citizens, not of the earthly city, but of the heavenly. As for those who praise him, though he takes little account of their applause, he does not undervalue their love; he does not want to deceive those who praise him, because he would not want to play tricks on those who love him. And for that reason his ardent concern is that praise should

77. *Cat.*, 11, 2, cf. ch. 12.

rather be given to him from whom man receives whatever in him is rightly deserving of praise.

On the other hand, the man who despises glory and is eager only for domination is worse than the beasts, in his cruelty or in his self-indulgence. Some of the Romans were men of this kind, who, while caring nothing for the opinion of others, were possessed by the passion for domination. History shows that there were many such; but it was Nero Caesar who first scaled, as it were, the heights of this vice, and gained the summit. So debauched was he that one would have supposed that nothing virile was to be feared from him; such was his cruelty that one would not have suspected anything effeminate in his nature, if one had not known about it.[78] Yet even to men like this the power of domination is not given except by the providence of God, when he decides that man's condition deserves such masters. God's statement on this point is clear, when the divine Wisdom says, 'It is through me that kings rule, and through me that tyrants possess the land.'[79] It might be supposed that 'tyrants' here is used not in the sense of 'wicked and irresponsible rulers', but in the ancient meaning of 'men of power', as when Virgil says,

> To have touched the tyrant's hand will be for me
> Earnest of peace.[80]

This suggestion is precluded by an unambiguous statement in another place, that God 'makes a hypocrite to reign because of the perversity of the people'.[81]

I have now sufficiently explained, as far as I can, the reason why the one true and just God has assisted the Romans, who are good according to the standards of the earthly city, to the attainment of the glory of so great an empire. But it may be that there is another more hidden cause on account of the diverse merits of mankind, which are better known to God than to us. However, it is the conviction of all those who are truly religious, that no one can have true virtue without true piety, that is without the true worship of the true God; and that the virtue which is employed in the service of human glory is not true virtue; still, those who are not citizens of the Eternal City – which the holy Scriptures call the City of God – are of more service to the earthly city when they possess even that sort of virtue than if they are without it.

As for those who are endowed with true piety and who lead a good life, if they are skilled in the art of government, then there is no

78. cf. Suet., *Nero, passim.* 79. Prov. 8, 15. 80. *Aen.*, 7, 266.
81. Job 34, 30 (Vulg.).

happier situation for mankind than that they, by God's mercy, should wield power. Yet such men attribute to the grace of God whatever virtues they may be able to display in this present life, because God has given those virtues to them in response to their wish, their faith, and their petition. At the same time they realize how far they fall short of the perfect righteousness, such as is found in the fellowship of the angels, for which they strive to fit themselves. However much praise and public approbation is given to the virtue which is engaged in the service of human glory, it is in no way to be compared to the humblest beginnings of the saints, whose hope has been placed in the grace and mercy of the true God.

20. *For virtue to serve the end of human glory is as shameful as for her to serve the end of sensual pleasure*

The philosophers who set up virtue as the highest good for man[82] seek to induce a sense of shame in those other philosophers[83] who, while approving virtue, take physical pleasure as the end, and use that as the criterion of virtue; pleasure, in their view, is to be sought for its own sake, virtue as a means to that end. To shame them, their opponents paint a kind of picture in words,[84] representing Pleasure sitting on a royal throne like some voluptuous queen, with Virtues as her obedient servants, waiting upon her nod, to fulfil her commands. She orders Prudence to be vigilant to take all steps to ensure the untroubled reign of pleasure. She bids Justice to provide all possible benefits to secure the friendships necessary for physical well-being, and to do no wrong to anyone, lest a breach of the law should interrupt the serenity of the life of pleasure. She instructs Fortitude to see to it that in case of physical pain which is not such as to bring her to suicide, she should resolutely keep in mind her mistress, Pleasure, so as to soften the pangs of present suffering by the recollection of previous delights. She enjoins Temperance to use moderation in food, though eating may be a source of delight, for fear that indulgence may cause some upset to health, which would be a serious hindrance to pleasure, for the Epicureans regard bodily health as a prime ingredient in pleasure. Thus the virtues, with all their glory and dignity, turned out to be the slaves of Pleasure, a mistress represented as a kind of exacting and worthless baggage. Nothing could be more shameful, say the Stoics, than this picture, nothing more hideously degraded,

82. Stoics. 83. Epicureans.
84. Cic., *De Fin.*, 2, 21, 69 (after Cleanthes).

nothing more intolerable to the eyes of decent people. And they are right.

But in my view the picture would still fall short of the beauty we require, if it were painted with the virtues as the slaves of human glory. Glory may not be a female voluptuary, but she is puffed up with empty conceit; and it is most improper that the Virtues, with their solidity and strength, should be her servants. For then Prudence would exercise no foresight, Justice make no dispensations, Fortitude show no endurance, Temperance impose no moderation, except so far as to win man's approval, and to serve the ends of Glory and her inflated conceit.

And yet men must not think to free themselves from this degradation by posing as despisers of glory and paying no heed to the opinions of others, while they esteem themselves as wise men and win their own approval. For their virtue, if it exists, is dependent on the praise of man in another kind of way. For the man who wins his own approval, is still a man. But he who with genuine piety believes in God and hopes in him, is more concerned about what he finds displeasing in himself than what (if anything) is pleasing, not so much to himself as to the Truth. And he ascribes whatever there is that may be pleasing in himself entirely to the mercy of the God whom he fears to displease, offering thanks for faults amended, and pouring out prayers for the amendment of faults that still remain.

21. *The Roman Empire ordained by the true God, who is the source of all power, and by whose providence the universe is governed*

This being so, we must ascribe to the true God alone the power to grant kingdoms and empires. He it is who gives happiness in the kingdom of heaven only to the good, but grants earthly kingdoms both to the good and to the evil, in accordance with his pleasure, which can never be unjust. We have already said something on this matter, as far as he has willed to make it plain to us. But to examine the secrets of men's hearts and to decide with clear judgement on the varying merits of human kingdoms – this would be a heavy task for us men, a task indeed far beyond our powers. And for that reason the one true God, who never leaves the human race unattended by his judgement or his help, granted dominion to the Romans when he willed and in the measure that he willed. It was he who gave sovereignty to the Assyrians, and also to the Persians (who, according to the evidence of their literature, worshipped two gods only, a good god and an evil[85]) to say nothing of the Hebrew people, about whom, and about their worship of one God only and the time of their sovereignty, I have already said enough, in my judgement. It was God who gave crops to the Persians without the worship of Segetia, and the other gifts of the earth without the worship of all those gods, each of whom the Romans assigned to a particular function, sometimes appointing several gods to one duty. God himself gave dominion to the Romans without the worship of those gods to whose worship the Romans thought they owed their Empire.

This is true also in respect of individual men. The same God gave power to Marius and to Gaius Caesar, to Augustus and to Nero, to the Vespasians, father and son,[86] the most attractive emperors, as well as to Domitian, the most ruthless tyrant; and (we need not run through the whole list) the same God gave the throne to Constantine the Christian, and also to Julian the Apostate. Julian had exceptional endowments, perverted by sacrilegious and abominable superstition working through a love of domination. He gave his entire trust to the worthless oracles of superstition and, confident in the certainty of victory, he burnt the ships carrying essential food supplies. Then, pressing on feverishly with his inordinate designs he paid the just price for his rashness when he was slain, leaving his army destitute, in enemy territory.[87] And the army could not escape except by giving the lie to that 'presage' of the god Terminus[88] by the moving of the frontier of the Roman Empire. I have spoken of this in my last book. The god Terminus, who refused to give way to Jupiter, gave way to necessity.

It is clear that God, the one true God, rules and guides these events, according to his pleasure. If God's reasons are inscrutable, does that mean that they are unjust?

22. *The duration of wars and their outcome depend on the decision of God*

The same may be said of the duration of wars. It rests with the decision of God in his just judgement and mercy either to afflict or console mankind, so that some wars come to an end more speedily,

85. *Two gods*: Ormuzd (Ahura Mazda), god of light and Ahriman, god of darkness, in the teaching of Zoroaster (sixth century B.C.) given in the *Zend Avesta*.

86. Titus. 87. cf. Bk IV, 29n. 88. Bk IV, 23n.

others more slowly. The Pirate War and the Third Punic War were brought to a successful conclusion with incredible rapidity, in a very short time, the first by Pompey, the second by Scipio.[89] The war against the runaway gladiators, also, despite many defeats suffered by Roman commanders, including two consuls, and terrible destruction and devastation in Italy, was finished in two years, after heavy losses. Then the Picentines, the Massi and the Poligni, peoples of Italy, not foreigners, after serving Rome faithfully under the yoke of servitude essayed to lift up their heads and assert their liberty, although Rome had by then subdued many nations and had destroyed Carthage. In this Italian War the Romans were often defeated; two consuls perished, as did other well-known senators. Yet this horror was not long drawn-out; four years saw the end of it. The Second Punic War, on the other hand, was attended with terrible losses and disasters to the Roman state; it lasted for eighteen years, and almost drained the strength of Rome to complete exhaustion. In two battles nearly seventy thousand Romans fell.[90] The First Punic War took twenty-three years to finish; the Mithridatic War took forty. And no one should suppose that the Romans in earlier times were able, through their greater courage, to finish their wars more quickly. The Samnite War was fought in an early period highly praised for every kind of virtue; and that war was prolonged for almost fifty years, and in its course the Romans suffered a defeat of such magnitude that they had to pass under the yoke.[91] But they did not love glory for the sake of justice; they appeared to love justice only for the sake of glory; and therefore they broke the treaty of peace that had been concluded.

The reason for recalling these facts is that many people are ignorant of past history, while some others feign ignorance, and if in this Christian era any war seems somewhat unduly protracted, they seize the chance for impudent attacks on our religion, crying out that if Christianity did not exist, and the divinities were worshipped with the ancient rites, this war would by now have been brought to an end

89. Bk III, 26. 90. Lake Trasimene, 217, and Cannae, 216 B.C.

91. Pompey annihilated the pirates in six months, 67 B.C. Scipio Aemilianus (Africanus Minor) destroyed Carthage two years after taking command, 146 B.C. The Servile War of the gladiators, 73–72. The Second Punic War, 220–202. Mithridates began his aggression in 104; he was finally defeated by Pompey in 63. First Samnite War 343 B.C.; the Fourth Samnite War ended 272. St Augustine probably ignores the last war; the first three lasted 342–290. The episode of the Caudine Forks, when the Roman army had to 'pass under the yoke', happened in 321.

by that Roman valour which, with the help of Mars and Bellona, so speedily concluded so many wars in the past.

Let those who have read their history remember how long were the wars waged by Rome in times past, and with what diverse fortunes and grievous disasters they were attended; for the world is liable to be tempest-tossed by such misfortunes, like a storm-swept sea. Let them acknowledge the facts, even if it goes against the grain; and let them stop destroying themselves by crazy insults against God, and refrain from deceiving the ignorant.

23. *The war in which Radagaisus, king of the Goths, a demon-worshipper, was vanquished in one day, with his immense forces*

Our adversaries do not recall with gratitude that wonderful instance of God's merciful action in our own times, only just the other day; in fact they do their best to bury it in oblivion. If we pass it over in silence, we shall show ourselves equally ungrateful.

Radagaisus,[92] king of the Goths, had taken up a position in the vicinity of Rome, at the head of an immense army of savages, and the threat weighed heavily on Roman shoulders. But then, in a single day, he was vanquished, without one casualty to Rome, without even one wounded; more than a hundred thousand of his army were laid low, and Radagaisus himself was taken prisoner and soon paid the penalty of death he so richly deserved.

If that impious creature had entered Rome with his huge army of the ungodly, would he have given any quarter? Would he have shown any respect for the sacred sites of the martyrs?[93] Would he have feared God in the person of any man? Would he have left any blood unshed, any honour unviolated? If Radagaisus had conquered, think of the claims the pagans would have made for those gods of theirs! The insolent boasts that he had conquered, had attained such power, because he had appeased the gods, and invited their assistance, with daily sacrifices – sacrifices which the Christian religion forbade to the Romans! When he was approaching the place where he was over-

92. *Radagaisus.* At the end of A.D. 405, a barbarian host from the Danube region, consisting mainly of Ostrogoths, invaded Italy under Radagaisus. They were pagans, unlike the Vizigoths, who were Arian Christians. For six months and more they ravaged North Italy, and finally reached Florence, where they were checked, then routed, at Fiesole, by Stilicho, the Vandal general of the Western emperor, Honorius. Radagaisus was captured and executed.

93. cf. Bk I, 1 for the behaviour of Alaric.

whelmed at a mere sign from the Majesty on high, and when the report of his progress had spread over all the world, we were told in Carthage that the pagans believed and spread it abroad, even boasted, that the Gothic king enjoyed the protection and support of friendly gods, to whom, they said, he sacrificed daily, and could not conceivably be conquered by those who did not offer such rites to the Roman gods, and would not allow anyone to offer them. And those wretches do not give thanks to the great mercy of God, who after deciding to use a barbarian invasion as a chastisement for men's immorality – which deserved an even harsher punishment – tempered his wrath with such great compassion. And so, in the first place, he allowed the barbarian to be miraculously defeated, lest the glory should be given to those demons, whose help he was known to have entreated, to the overthrow of feeble minds. And, after that, he suffered Rome to be taken by barbarians[94] who, contrary to the usages of war in former times, protected those who took sanctuary in holy places out of reverence for the Christian religion, and who showed such hostility, in the name of the Christian religion, to those demons and the rites of their blasphemous sacrifices, in which the Goth had placed his trust, that they seemed to be waging a far more ruthless war with them than with men.

Thus the true Lord and Governor of the world has chastised the Romans with the scourge of his mercy, and has shown to the votaries of demons, by this incredible defeat, that those sacrifices are needless, even for the preservation of safety in this present world, so that all those who are sensible enough to face the facts, instead of engaging in obstinate debate, may not abandon true religion under pressure of the circumstances of the moment, but may adhere to it more loyally in confident expectation of eternal life.

24. *The true felicity of Christian emperors*

When we describe certain Christian emperors as 'happy', it is not because they enjoyed long reigns, or because they died a peaceful death, leaving the throne to their sons; nor is it because they subdued their country's enemies, or had the power to forestall insurrections by enemies in their own land and to suppress such insurrections if they arose. All these, and other similar rewards or consolations in this life of trouble were granted to some of the worshippers of demons, as their due; and yet those pagan rulers have no connection with the Kingdom

94. Alaric and the Vizigoths in A.D. 410.

of God, to which those Christian rulers belong. Their good fortune was due to the mercy of God; for it was God's intention that those who believe in him should not demand such blessings from him as if they represented the highest good.

We Christians call rulers happy, if they rule with justice; if amid the voices of exalted praise and the reverent salutations of excessive humility, they are not inflated with pride, but remember that they are but men; if they put their power at the service of God's majesty, to extend his worship far and wide; if they fear God, love him and worship him; if, more than their earthly kingdom, they love that realm where they do not fear to share the kingship; if they are slow to punish, but ready to pardon; if they take vengeance on wrong because of the necessity to direct and protect the state, and not to satisfy their personal animosity; if they grant pardon not to allow impunity to wrong-doing but in the hope of amendment of the wrong-doer; if, when they are obliged to take severe decisions, as must often happen, they compensate this with the gentleness of their mercy and the generosity of their benefits; if they restrain their self-indulgent appetites all the more because they are more free to gratify them, and prefer to have command over their lower desires than over any number of subject peoples; and if they do all this not for a burning desire for empty glory, but for the love of eternal blessedness; and if they do not fail to offer to their true God, as a sacrifice for their sins, the oblation of humility, compassion, and prayer.

It is Christian emperors of this kind whom we call happy; happy in hope, during this present life, and to be happy in reality hereafter, when what we wait for will have come to pass.

25. *The prosperity bestowed by God on Constantine, the Christian emperor*

God, in his goodness, did not wish that those who believed he was to be worshipped for the sake of life eternal, should suppose that no one could attain to the highest stations and the kingdoms of this world unless he made his supplications to demons, on the ground that those evil spirits have great power in this sphere. And for that reason he heaped worldly gifts such as no one would have dared to hope for, on Constantine, who made no supplication to demons, but worshipped only the true God. And God even granted him the honour of founding a city,[95] associated with the Roman Empire, the daughter, one might

95. Constantinople, A.D. 330.

say, of Rome herself, but a city which contained not a single temple or image of any demon. Constantine had a long reign,[96] and as the sole Augustus he ruled and defended the whole Roman world; he was victorious, above all others, in the wars which he directed and conducted; fortune favoured his efforts in the repression of usurpers;[97] and he died of sickness and old age after a long life, leaving the throne to his sons.[98]

On the other hand, so that no emperor should become a Christian in order to earn the good fortune of Constantine (whereas it is only with a view to life eternal that anyone should be a Christian), God removed Jovian[99] more quickly than Julian[100]; he allowed Gratian[101] to be slain by the usurper's sword – but in far less painful circumstances than attended the murder of the great Pompey, who worshipped the pretended gods of Rome. For Pompey could not be avenged by Cato,[102] whom he had, as it were, made his heir to the Civil War; while Gratian was avenged by Theodosius – although pious souls do not look for such consolation – whom Gratian had taken as a partner in his rule, although he had a young brother. Gratian was more concerned to have a trustworthy associate than to enjoy excessive power.

26. *The faith and devotion of the Emperor Theodosius*

Thus Theodosius kept faith with Gratian not only in life, but after his death. The young brother of Gratian, Valentinian, had been driven out by Maximus, his murderer. Theodosius, like a true Christian, brought him back to his part of the Empire, as his ward. He looked after him with fatherly affection. Valentinian had been deprived of all his resources; and Theodosius would have been able to remove him without trouble, if his burning passion had been the desire for an enlarged dominion rather than the love of doing good. As it was, he

96. 306–337. 97. Maxentius and Licinus.
98. Constantine, Constantius, Constans. 99. June 363–Feb. 364.
100. 361–3.
101. *Gratian*, emperor of the West and friend of St Ambrose, associated as Augustus with his father Valentinus in A.D. 367; on Valentinus' death he became practically sole emperor. But his troops deserted on the approach of Maximus and he was murdered, 383. In 379 Gratian appointed Theodosius as emperor of the East.
102. Who killed himself after the battle of Thapsus. 46 B.C.; cf. Bk I, 23.

took the boy into his care, preserved his imperial standing, and consoled him with his kindness and his favour. Later, when his great success had rendered Maximus formidable, Theodosius, for all his pressing anxieties, did not lapse into blasphemous and forbidden superstitions. He sent a message to John, who had settled as a hermit in Egypt, of whose increasing reputation he had heard, for John was regarded as a servant of God, endowed with the spirit of prophecy; and from the prophet he received a definite assurance of victory. Soon afterwards, when he had got rid of Maximus,[103] Theodosius restored the boy Valentinian, with respectful compassion, to his share in the Empire, from which he had been driven. Before long, Valentinian was destroyed, whether by an ambush, or some other plot, or by accident, and another usurper, Eugenius, was illegally put in his place. Theodosius suppressed him, in secure confidence in another prophetic reply he had received; and it was more by the power of prayer than by force of arms that he fought against the redoubtable forces of the usurper. Soldiers who took part in the battle have told us that the javelins were wrenched from their hands as they aimed them, when a violent wind blew from the side of Theodosius towards the enemy and not only whirled away with the utmost rapidity the missiles discharged against the emperor's forces, but even turned them back on to the bodies of the foe. This suggested to the poet Claudian (who was far from being a Christian) those lines in praise of Theodosius:

> O dearly loved of God, the sky fights for thee,
> And winds in league come at the trumpet's call.[104]

After victory had confirmed his confidence and his prediction, Theodosius cast down the images of Jupiter which had been supposedly consecrated against him by some kind of ceremonies and set up in the Alps. Those statues held golden thunderbolts; and when the emperor's couriers felt able, in the joy of victory, to turn those weapons into a joke, saying that they would like to be struck by thunderbolts of that kind, Theodosius was delighted and kindly gave them to the jesters as a present.

The sons of his enemies had been carried off, not by his order, but in the tumult of war; and, though they were not Christians, they took refuge in the Church. Theodosius wished them to become Christians, since the occasion thus offered; and he loved them with Christian charity. He did not deprive them of their property; in fact he heaped honours on them; and he never allowed victory to be followed by the

103. In A.D. 388. 104. *Cons. Hon.* III, 96f.; cf. Oros. 7, 35, 21.

satisfaction of private feuds. Men like Cinna, Marius, and Sulla wished the civil strife to continue when the wars were ended. Very different was Theodosius; far from wanting any harm to come to anyone after the end of civil war, he was deeply grieved that such conflicts should ever break out. Among all these anxieties Theodosius, from the beginning of his reign, never relaxed his endeavours to help the Church against the ungodly by just and compassionate legislation; and the Church at the time was in difficulties, for the heretic Valens[105] had dealt her heavy blows in his support of the Arians. Theodosius was more glad to be a member of that Church than to be ruler of the world. He ordered the demolition of pagan images, knowing that even this world's prizes are not in the gift of demons, but in the power of the true God.

But nothing could be more wonderful than the religious humility he showed after the grievous crime committed by the people of Thessalonica.[106] On the intercession of the bishops he had promised a pardon; but then the clamour of certain of his close supporters drove him to avenge the crime. But he was constrained by the discipline of the Church to do penance in such a fashion that the people of Thessalonica, as they prayed for him, wept at seeing the imperial highness thus prostrate, with an emotion stronger than their fears of the emperor's wrath at their offence. These and other good works of like nature, which it would take too long to recount, Theodosius took with him when he left the loftiest summit of power – which is nothing but a passing mist.[107] The reward of those works is eternal happiness; God is the giver; and the only recipients are the truly devout. But all the rest that this world offers, whether the peaks of power or the bare necessities of life, God dispenses freely to good and evil alike – just as he gives to all alike the world the light, the air, earth and water and the fruits of earth, and man's soul, body, senses, intelligence, and life. Among those gifts is dominion, of whatever extent; and this God bestows in accordance with his government of temporal affairs.

Our opponents have now been refuted and convicted of error by the irresistible evidence which proves that all the multitude of false gods is of no help towards the attainment of those temporal goods, which

105. Eastern Emperor, 364–78.

106. *Crime at Thessalonica.* In A.D. 390 the mob murdered the governor, Botheric, and other officials in a riot after the imprisonment of a popular charioteer. Theodosius took reprisals in a massacre by his soldiers. For this the emperor was condemned to penance by a synod at Milan under St Ambrose.

107. cf. Jas. 4, 14.

are the sole objects of desire for the fools. But I am aware that I must go on to answer those who now try to assert that the gods are to be worshipped, not with a view to advantage in this present life, but for the sake of that life which is to come after death.

I think I have given a sufficient answer, in these five books, to those who wish to worship those inanities, because of their love of this world, and who now complain, with childish indignation, that this worship is not allowed. After I had published the first three books, and they began to be widely circulated, I heard that some people were preparing to write some kind of a reply. Then I received information that this reply had been written, but the authors were looking for a suitable occasion to publish it without danger to themselves. I hereby warn them not to wish for something which is not for their own good. It is easy for anyone to imagine that he has made a reply, when he has refused to keep silence. Is anything more loquacious than folly? But it must not be supposed that folly is as powerful as truth, just because it can, if it likes, shout louder and longer than truth.

Let them consider the whole matter carefully. Perhaps if they weigh things up without partiality or prejudice, they may perceive that there are some arguments which can be attacked, but not refuted, by an impudent prattle of words, like the buffoonery of satires and mimes. If they realize this, I hope they may put a check on their frivolity, and choose to be corrected by the wise rather than win the applause of the irresponsible. If by 'looking for a suitable occasion' they mean, not the chance to tell the truth, but the freedom to slander, then may heaven shield them from the fate of the man who was called 'lucky' because he had licence to do wrong; the man of whom Cicero says, 'Unhappy man! He was given licence to sin!'[108] A man may count himself happy in having licence to slander; but he will be far happier if deprived entirely of that liberty. Then he can drop the silly pose of superiority and take the opportunity to raise what objection he likes, as one really interested in getting to know; he can ask his questions in a spirit of friendly discussion, and listen when those whom he consults do their best to give a courteous, serious, and frank reply.

108. ? *Tusc. Disp.*, 5, 19, 55.

BOOK VI

Preface

THE argument of my first five books has, I believe, given a sufficient refutation of those who suppose that many false gods are to be venerated and worshipped for advantages in this mortal life and for benefits in temporal things. They would accord them the ceremonies and the humble devotion which the Greeks call *latreia*,[1] a worship due only to the one true God. Christian truth proves those 'gods' to be useless images or unclean spirits and malignant demons, creatures at any rate, and not the Creator.

To be sure, those five books are not enough to deal with all the extravagant folly and perversity of our opponents – nor would any number of additional books suffice. That is clear to all. Stupidity glories in never yielding to the force of truth; that is how it effects the ruin of anyone who is under the dominion of this monstrous moral fault. It is a disease proof against all efforts to treat it, not through any fault in the physician, but because the patient is himself incurable. But those who understand what they read, who reflect upon it and weigh the arguments without any obstinate adherence to their old errors, or at least without excessive and exaggerated attachment to them – such people will be ready to conclude that in the five books already completed our discussion has been more, not less, than the question demanded. The ignorant try to bring odium on the Christian religion in connection with the disasters to which human life is subject, and the calamities and catastrophes that beset human affairs; and the learned not merely connive at this but even support those slanders, in defiance of their own conscience, possessed by a raging madness of blasphemy. These judicious readers cannot doubt that such attempts are utterly devoid of any clear thinking or right reasoning and are composed of nothing but irresponsible frivolity and malignant spite.

1. cf. Bk x, 1.

1. *The assertion that the gods are worshipped not for blessings in this life, but with a view to life eternal*

The scheme I have prescribed for this work demands that I should now proceed to the task of refuting and instructing those who maintain that the pagan gods, which the Christian religion does away with, are to be worshipped, not with a view to this present life, but with a view to the life which is to come after death.

I should like to take as the opening of my discussion, the truthful oracle of a holy psalm, 'Blessed is he whose hope is the Lord God, and who has not turned his attention to vain things and lying madnesses.'[2] However, on the subject of all those 'vain things' and 'lying madnesses', men are likely to give a far readier hearing to the philosophers who reject the erroneous opinions of the peoples who have set up images to the divinities, and have either invented or accepted many false and unworthy stories about the 'immortal gods', as they call them, and, having accepted them, have interwoven them into the worship and the sacred rites of those gods. Although they have not freely proclaimed their disapprobation of those practices, these philosophers have at least murmured it in their learned disputations; and so it is not inappropriate to discuss with them this question: Is it our duty to worship, with a view to the life after death, the one God, who made every spiritual and material creature; or those many gods who, according to some of the most eminent and famous of these same philosophers,[3] were created by the one God and raised by him to their exalted state?

I have mentioned in my fourth book some of the gods who are distributed among particular functions,[4] one god for each minute duty. Who could brook the suggestion, indeed the contention, that such divinities can assure eternal life to anyone? There were men of great learning and penetration, who gloried in having conferred a great benefit by giving written instructions to inform people why they should pray to each particular god, and what help should be asked for from each of them, so as to avoid the ludicrous kind of mistake which occurs in mime to raise a laugh,[5] as when Bacchus is asked for water, and the Lymphae are asked for wine. Now, if a man who prays to the immortal gods, on asking the Lymphae for wine, receives the reply, 'We only have water; apply to Liber', are those authorities likely to suggest that the correct rejoinder would be, 'If

2. Ps. 40, 4. 3. e.g. Plat., *Tim.*, 40. 4. cf. Bk IV, 11; 21. 5. cf. Bk IV, 22.

you haven't wine, at least give me eternal life?' Could anything be more monstrously absurd? If those giggling goddesses (they are always so ready for a laugh![6]) are not aiming at leading their suppliant a dance (like the demons) they would surely reply, 'My good man, why should you think we have life (*vitam*) at our disposal, when we have told you we haven't even the vine (*vitem*)?'

It is, then, a mark of the most unconscionable folly to ask or hope for eternal life from such divinities. Even supposing they are concerned with supporting and propping up this brief life of care, they watch over its particular departments, so it is asserted, in such a way that if anything belonging to one god's sphere of responsibility is sought from another god, a ridiculous anomaly arises, like some farcical situation in a mime. When those involved are actors, and know what they are doing, it gets a well-deserved laugh in the theatre; when they are fools, who do not know what they are about, it is treated with more justified scorn in the real world. That is why learned men were astute enough to determine, and put on record, which god or goddess should be entreated for what, as far as concerns the divinities established in their communities – for example, what one can obtain from Liber, or the Lymphae, or Vulcan, and the other gods, some of whom I mentioned in my fourth book, while I decided to pass over the rest. Doubtless it is an error to ask Ceres for wine, Liber for bread, Vulcan for water, the Lymphae for fire; we surely ought to realize how much more imbecile it would be to implore any of these deities for eternal life!

When we were discussing wordly dominion, and asking which gods or goddess might be believed capable of granting it, we proved, after examining every possibility, that it would be utterly remote from the truth to imagine that even the kingdoms of this world are established by any of this host of false gods. If this is true, then surely it would show the craziest impiety to suppose that any of them could grant eternal life, which is, without any doubt, incomparably to be preferred to all earthly kingdoms. The reason why such gods are incapable, in our view, of giving earthly dominion is not that they are so great and exalted and earthly power a thing so lowly and contemptible that they would not deign, in their lofty state, to be concerned with it. However great the contempt which one may rightly feel for the precarious eminences of worldly power, when one considers the frailty of man, those gods are evidently of such a character as to be quite unworthy to be entrusted with the power to grant or to preserve even

6. cf. Virg., *Ecl.*, 3, 9 ... *faciles Nymphae risere* ...

such transitory gifts. Therefore, if it be true (as the full discussion in my last two books has established) that not one of this host of gods, whether of the plebeian sort or, as one might say, the noble deities, is fit to grant mortal kingdoms to mortals, how much less could any of them turn mortals into immortals?

Furthermore, if we are now dealing with those who think that the gods are to be worshipped for the sake of the life after death and not with a view to this present life, we must conclude that it is utterly wrong to worship them even with the hope of obtaining those particular benefits which are severally assigned to the control of such gods, not on any rational grounds but by superstitious credulity. There are those who believe in the necessity of such worship, maintaining it essential for securing advantages in this mortal life; and I have refuted them, to the best of my ability, in the first five books. Accordingly, if the devotees of the goddess Juventas (Youth) enjoyed markedly greater prosperity in early life, while those who disclaimed her either deceased before maturity, or shrivelled into senile inertia while still young in years; if Bearded Fortune[7] clothed the cheeks of her votaries with a growth of notable splendour and allurement, while we observed her detractors with hairless chins or with unconvincing beards, we should even so be perfectly right in saying that those goddesses only had power within the limits somehow assigned to their particular functions, and that one should not seek eternal life from Juventas, who does not produce beards, and that no benefit after this life is to be looked for from Bearded Fortune, for even in this life she could not even give us the youthful age in which the beard first grows. In reality, the worship of those goddesses is not essential to ensure the gifts supposedly under their control. Many worshippers of Juventas have been far from flourishing in their early years; while many non-worshippers enjoy robust health in youth; many suppliants of Bearded Fortune have no beard at all, or have achieved only an unprepossessing growth, and expose themselves to the ridicule of her bearded detractors for having venerated her in the hope of hirsute adornment. Are men such fools as to think in their hearts that the worship of these gods can be of advantage for eternal life, when they realize how futile and ridiculous it is even in respect of those temporal and evanescent gifts which the divinities are said to have in their particular charge? This would be too bold a claim even for those who parcelled out those temporal responsibilities to the gods to

7. On Juventas and Bearded Fortune see Bk. IV, 11n.

ensure that they should be worshipped by the unthinking; they thought there were too many of those deities, and they did not want to have any of them sitting about with time on their hands!

2. *What was Varro's opinion of the gods? His disclosures of their nature and their rites were such that he would have shown more reverence in keeping silent*

Has anyone pursued research in this subject further than Marcus Varro?[8] Who has made more scholarly discoveries, or pondered the facts more assiduously? Who has made nicer distinctions, or written more carefully or more fully on those matters? His literary style is not particularly attractive; but he is so full of knowledge and ideas that in the kind of learning which we Christians call secular and the pagans call liberal he gives as much information to the student of history as Cicero gives pleasure to the connoisseur of style. In fact, Cicero himself gives Varro a fine testimonial in his *Academics*[9] when he says that he had engaged in discussion on the subject of that work with Marcus Varro, 'easily the most acute of intellects, and undoubtedly the most learned of men'. He does not say 'the most eloquent' or 'the most fluent'; for in truth Varro is seriously inadequate in this department. What he says is 'easily the most acute of intellects'. And in that book, the *Academics*, where his thesis is that all things should be doubted, he added 'undoubtedly the most learned of men'. He was so convinced of this that he put aside the doubt which he normally applied to everything. It seems that although he was going to argue in defence of Academic doubt, he had forgotten when speaking of Varro, but only then, that he was an Academic. In the first book he acclaims the literary works of the same author in these terms,

> We were like strangers in our own city, visitors who had lost their way. It was your books that, as it were, brought us back home, so that at last we could recognize who we were, and where we were. It was you who revealed to us the age of our country, the sequence of events, the laws of religious ceremonies and of the priesthoods, the traditional customs of private and public life, the position of geographical areas and of particular places, and the terminology of all matters, human and divine, with their various kinds, and functions, and causes.[10]

8. cf. Bk III, 4n. 9. Presumably in the lost *Acad.* III. 10. 1, 3, 9.

He was a man of pre-eminent, of unparalleled erudition, succinctly and neatly described in one line of Terentian,[11]

Varro, that man of universal science;[12]

a man who read so much that we marvel that he had any time for writing; who wrote so much that we find it hard to believe that anyone could have read it all. If this man, with all his talents and all his learning, had intended to attack and eradicate those 'divine matters' of which he wrote, and to assert that they belonged to superstition not to religion, I do not know whether he would have recorded so many elements in 'theology' which can arouse only derision, contempt, and abhorrence. In fact he worshipped those same gods and thought that they should be worshipped. So much so that in his written works he expresses the fear that the gods may perish, not through an attack of the enemy, but through the indifference of Roman citizens. It is, he says, from this disaster (as he thinks it) that he is rescuing the gods; by books of this kind he is securing and preserving for them a place in the memory of good men. This he regards as a more profitable service than the much-praised act of Metellus[13] in saving the sacred emblems of Vesta from the fire, and that of Aeneas[14] in rescuing the Penates from destruction: and yet he hands down, for the study of future generations, traditions which deserve to be rejected by the wise and the foolish alike as being, in their judgement, utterly inimical to the true religion. What ought we to think of this? Is it not that a man of acute intellect and vast erudition, but lacking the freedom given by the Holy Spirit, has succumbed to the pressure of the customs and laws of his country? At the same time he could not bring himself to keep silent about the things which troubled him, on the pretext of lending support to religion.

3. *Varro's division of his 'Antiquities' into 'Human Matters' and 'Divine Matters'*

Varro wrote forty-one books of *Antiquities*; and he divided them by subjects into 'human matters' and 'divine matters', assigning twenty-five to 'anthropology' and sixteen to 'theology'. In the anthropological section of his work he planned four parts, each of six books,

11. *Terentianus Maurus*: grammarian (*fl c.* A.D. 200). He wrote three didactic poems, on Letters, on Syllables, on Metres.

12. *De Metr.*, 2846. 13. cf. Bk III, 18. 14. cf. Virg., *Aen.*, 2, 717; 747f.

concentrating in turn on the performers of the actions, the place, the time, and the nature of the action. Thus in the first six books he writes about men, in the next six about places, in the third group about times, while the fourth and last group deals with the performances. Four sixes make twenty-four; but he leads off with a separate book, which serves as a general introduction to the whole section.

In the section on 'divine matters' the same scheme of division is kept, in regard to the rites to be performed in honour of the gods; for those rites are performed by men in certain places and at certain times. The four subjects mentioned are contained in groups of three books: the first group deals with the men involved, the second with the places, the third with the times, the fourth with the actual rites; as before, he employs the most subtle distinctions in describing the performers, the place and time of the performances, and the manner of the performances. But besides this he was bound to say – and this was what people especially looked for – to whom these ceremonies are offered. And so the three last books treat of the gods themselves; and that makes three fives, fifteen. As we have said, there are sixteen books in all, because here also he prefaces the section with a separate book to serve as an introduction.

After the end of this first book Varro goes on to subdivide the first group of three books, within his general five-part division. In this group, dealing with the men involved, the first book describes the priests, the second, the augurs, the third, the quindecimviri.[15] In the second group, dealing with the places, Book One treats of shrines, Book Two, of temples, Book Three, of sacred places. The next group, referring to feast days, contains one book about holy days; another about games in the circus, a third about stage plays. The fourth group, about the actual ceremonies, consists of a book devoted to consecrations, a book about private rites, while the last book handles public ceremonies. At the end of this kind of procession of observances the gods themselves, the recipients of the whole system of worship, bring up the rear; and they are dealt with in the remaining three books: in the first of these come the 'certain gods', in the second, the 'uncertain',[16] in the third, the last of the whole work, the 'principal and select'[17] divinities.

15. Keepers of the Sibylline Books.
16. cf. Bk III, 12. 17. cf. Bk VII, 2.

4. From Varro's account it emerges that 'Human Matters' precede 'Divine Matters' among the pagans

In the whole of this impressive sequence, with all those subtle distinctions and this precise arrangement, it is in vain to seek eternal life; it would be the height of impudence to look for it or to hope for it in this context. So much is readily apparent, from what we have already said and from what we are to go on to say, to anyone who is not his own enemy because of the obstinacy of his heart. These institutions are either the work of men, or of demons, and not of 'good demons', as the pagans call them, but, to speak frankly, of unclean spirits or undeniably malignant powers. Malignant, because with consummate spite they secretly instil into the thoughts of the impious, and at times openly suggest to their senses, pernicious notions which make the human soul more and more evanescent, and less and less able to adjust itself and attach itself to eternal truth; and they support those notions with fallacious evidence in every way they can.

Varro himself bears witness that the reason for writing about 'human matters' before 'divine matters' was that human communities first came into existence and divine institutions are afterwards established by them. Whereas it was not any terrestrial community that established true religion; it was true religion, without doubt, that established the Celestial City; and true religion is given to his true worshippers by the inspiration and teaching of the true God, the giver of eternal life.

Varro gives the following explanation of his treatment of 'human matters' before 'divine matters', on the ground that the 'divine matters' were established by men: 'The painter exists before the picture, the builder before the building: similarly, human communities precede their institutions.' But he does say that he would have written about the gods before proceeding to men, if he were treating of every aspect of the gods. Are we really to suppose that in this work he is only treating of some part of the divine nature and not of the whole: or that the divine nature, even when considered only in a particular aspect ought not to take precedence over human nature? Further, in his three last books he carefully arranges the gods into the categories of 'certain', 'uncertain' and 'select'; does it appear that he leaves any aspect unmentioned? What does he mean, then, when he says, 'If I were treating of every aspect of the gods and of men, I would have dealt with the divine before starting on the human?' Either he is writing about every aspect, or some aspects, or no aspect at all. If about every aspect, then 'divine matters' should precede 'human'; but why should they not, even if he is writing only about some? Would it be improper to make even some aspects of the divine take precedence over the whole of human nature? If it would be too much that one part of the divine should have precedence over all the human matters, would it at least be right for it to do so over merely Roman affairs? For his books on 'human affairs' treat only of Roman matters; they do not include the whole world. And yet he claims that he is justified in having given them precedence over his books on 'divine affairs', as the painter precedes the picture, the builder comes before the building. Here he plainly admits that 'divine matters' are of human institution, like pictures and buildings.

There remains the possibility that he is to be supposed to have written about no aspect of divinity at all; and that he was reluctant to admit this explicitly and left it to be inferred by the intelligent reader. For 'I have not treated of all' means, in common usage, 'I have treated of some'; but it *can* be understood as 'I have treated of none'; since 'none' is the negation of both 'all' and 'some'. Varro himself declares that if he were writing about every aspect of the divine nature it would have to precede the treatment of human affairs; but truth cries out, without need of a word from Varro, that the divine nature, even if treated only in part, should have had precedence over Roman affairs, at least. Yet it properly takes second place; therefore it is not there at all. It was not that Varro decided to rank 'human affairs' before 'divine', but to give truth the precedence over falsehood. For in his books on 'human affairs' he follows the course of history; but his account of what he calls 'divine affairs' is a collection of frivolous fantasies. And this is doubtless what he intended to signify by a subtle hint, in writing of them after the other topics, and, not content with this, in giving an explanation for taking this course. If he had said nothing in explanation, others might have defended his procedure on different grounds. But the very explanation he has given leaves others no room for arbitrary speculation and is sufficient proof that he is giving men precedence over their institutions, not ranking human nature before the divine.

Thus Varro has admitted that his books on 'divine affairs' do not deal with the truth relating to the divine nature but with the false notions which arise from error. As I have mentioned in the fourth book,[18] he states this more clearly in another place, where he acknowledges that he would have written on the principles dictated by

18. ch. 31.

nature, if he had been founding a new community; but since he found himself in a community already ancient, the only course open to him was to conform to its traditional ways.

5. *Varro's division of theology into 'mythical', 'natural', and 'civil'*

Then again, what is the significance of Varro's division of 'theology', that is the systematic theory of the gods, into the types: mythical, physical and civil?[19] We should have called the first type 'fabular', if Latin usage had permitted. Let us call it 'fabulous', since the name 'mythical' is derived from *mythos*, the Greek word for fable. Usage allows us to call the second type 'natural' (*physis* being the Greek for 'nature'). The third category, 'civil', Varro himself designated by a Latin word.

He goes on to say, 'The name "mythical" applies to the theology used chiefly by the poets, "physical" to that of the philosophers, "civil" to that of the general public. The first type contains a great deal of fiction which is in conflict with the dignity and nature of the immortals. It is in this category that we find one god born from the head, another from the thigh, a third from drops of blood;[20] we find stories about thefts and adulteries committed by gods, and gods enslaved to human beings.[21] In fact we find attributed to gods not only the accidents that happen to humanity in general, but even those which can befall the most contemptible of mankind.' In this passage he has the courage to take the chance, when he thinks he can do it with impunity, of casting off all obscurity and ambiguity, and making it quite clear what injustice is done to the nature of the gods by these lying fables. For he is talking, not about 'natural', or 'civil' theology but about 'fabulous' theology, which he thinks he has the right to criticize quite candidly.

Let us see what he says about the second type:

> The second type which I have pointed out, is one on which the philosophers have left a number of works, in which they discuss who the gods are, where they are, of what kind and of what character they are: whether they came into being at a certain time, or have always existed: whether they derive their being from fire (the belief of Heraclitus) or from numbers

19. Scaevola's distinction; Bk IV, 27.
20. Minerva, Bacchus, and ? Pegasus (the winged horse from the blood of Medusa).
21. e.g. Mercury, Jupiter, Apollo (slave to Admetus).

(as Pythagoras thought) or from atoms (as Epicurus alleges).[22] And there are other like questions all of which men's ears can more readily tolerate within the walls of a lecture-room than in the market-place outside.

He has no fault to find with this 'physical' theology, which is the special preserve of philosophers, except for a mention of the philosophical controversies, which have given rise to a multitude of dissident sects. All the same, he removes the subject from the market-place, that is, from the general public, and shuts it up between the walls of a lecture-room. But he has not removed the first type – the mythical – with all its lies and filth. What sensitive ears ordinary people have, including the Roman people, in matters of religion! They cannot tolerate the discussions of philosophers about the immortal gods. Yet they not merely tolerate, they listen with pleasure to fictions, sung by poets and acted by players, which offend against the dignity and the nature of the gods, because such adventures are appropriate to human nature, or rather to human nature at its most contemptible. More than this, they have decided that such stories are pleasing to the gods, and must be employed to obtain their favour.

Now perhaps someone is going to say, 'Let us make the same distinction as Varro himself makes between the "mythical' and "physical" ("fabulous" and "natural") and the "civil" variety of theology. We are now discussing "civil" theology; let us see how Varro describes it.' I do indeed see why Varro had to distinguish the fabulous type; because it is false, degraded, and unworthy. But to wish to separate natural theology from civil, is surely tantamount to an admission that civil theology itself is false. If 'natural' theology is really natural, what is found wrong with it, to cause its exclusion from the city? While if so-called 'civil' theology is not natural, what merit has it to cause its admission? This is, we may suppose, the reason why Varro treated 'human affairs' before 'divine affairs' – in 'divine affairs' he was dealing not with something in nature but with purely human institutions.

Let us inspect this 'civil theology'. 'The third variety,' says Varro, 'is that which the citizens in the towns, and especially the priests, ought to know and put into practice. It contains information about

22. *Heraclitus* of Ephesus (*c.* 500 B.C.) attributed the origin of all things to fire, an immaterial substance.

Pythagoras of Samos settled in Magna Graecia in the second half of the sixth century B.C. He found the explanation of all things in numbers and their relations.

Epicurus of Samos (341–270 B.C.) settled in Athens in 306. His physical speculations developed the atomic theory of Leucippus and Democritus.

the gods which should be worshipped officially and the rites and sacrifices which should be offered to each of them.' We should pay special attention to the statement which follows. Varro says, 'The first type of theology is particularly suited to the theatre; the second is particularly concerned with the world; the special relevance of the third is to the city.' It is easy to see to which he gives the first prize. Obviously it is the second type, the theology, as he said earlier, of the philosophers. He claims that this is concerned with the world, and, in the opinion of the philosophers,[23] the world is the most important of all existing things. As for the two other theologies, the first (that of the theatre) and the second (that of the city), does he separate them or associate them? For what belongs to a city is not necessarily connected with the world, although a city is in the world. It may happen that cults are practised in a city, and beliefs held, which are based on mistaken ideas which correspond to no reality in the world or outside it. But a theatre must of necessity be in a city; for only a city community establishes a theatre. And the sole object of a theatre is the presentation of stage shows. And stage shows can only be classed among 'divine affairs', which are treated with such subtlety in these books of Varro's.

6. *Criticism of Varro's treatment of 'mythical' and 'civil' theology*

Marcus Varro, you are the shrewdest of men, and, without a shadow of doubt, the most erudite. You are only a man, for all that; you are not God, and you have not been borne aloft by the Spirit of God into truth and liberty so that you could see things divine and bring news of them to men. You do indeed discern how important it is to separate divine matters from the follies and falsehoods of men. But you are afraid of falling foul of pernicious popular notions and traditional practices in state-established superstitions. You yourself feel, when you consider them in all their aspects, that they are utterly alien from the nature of the gods, even of those gods which the human mind, in its weakness, suspects to exist in the elements of this world; and the whole of your literature is loud in condemnation of them. And yet how does your native talent – which, for all its pre-eminence, is merely human – acquit itself at this point? What support do you derive, in this quandary, from your learning – which is also merely human, however manifold and immense? You desire to worship 'natu-

23. The Stoics. cf. Cic., *De Nat. Deor.*, 2, 7; 2, 14, 37ff.

ral' gods; you are compelled to worship the 'gods of the city'. You have found other gods, those of the fables, and you can be less reserved in loosing off your feelings about *them*. But, whether you like it or not, some of your shots land on the 'civil' gods as well. You say, to be sure, that the 'fabulous' gods are appropriate to the theatre, the 'natural' gods are relevant to the world, the 'civil' deities to the city. But, surely, the world is a divine work, while cities and theatres are works of men? And the gods who are laughed at in the theatres are the same as those adored in the temples, and the deities to whom you offer sacrifices are identical with those for whom you put on games. You would have shown much more candour and percipience in your division if you had distinguished between 'natural gods' on one side and 'gods of human institution' on the other, observing that the writings of poets on the latter display a different attitude from the teaching of the priests, but that poetry and priestcraft are allied in a fellowship of deception, and so are equally acceptable to the demons, whose enemy is the teaching of truth.

Leaving on one side, for later discussion, the so-called 'natural theology', we may ask whether we are really prepared to ask or hope for eternal life from the gods of poetry and the theatre, the gods of the games and the plays? A thousand times, no! The God of truth forbids that we should entertain such monstrous, blasphemous insanity. What! Are we to seek eternal life from gods who are pleased and appeased by shows at which scandalous stories about them are enacted for all to see? No one, I conceive, has reached this degree of insanity, this bottomless pit of blasphemous delirium. It is agreed, then, that no one attains to everlasting life by means either of 'fabulous' or 'civil' theology. The former sows a crop of shame by inventing foul stories about the gods; the latter by supporting them, reaps the harvest. The one scatters lies: the other collects them. The one slanders 'divine matters' with false reports: the other includes among 'divine matters' the shows in which the slanders are presented. The one chants in verse the unspeakable fictions of human imagination about the gods; the other consecrates those fictions in the festivals of the gods. The one sings the crimes and shames of the deities; the other views them with complacence. The one reveals, or else invents them; the other either attests them as true, or enjoys them, even if false. Both 'theologies' are disgusting, both deserve condemnation. The theology of the theatre proclaims the degradation of the people; the theology of the city makes that degradation into an amenity. Can eternal life be looked for from a source of corruption to this short life of time? Or are we to suppose that while association with evil men corrupts our life, if they insinuate themselves into our affections and secure our approval, the society of demons has no such effect, although those outrageous tales form part of their cult? If the tales are true, how degraded are the gods! If false, how degraded the worship!

In saying this we may give the impression to one who had but scant acquaintance with the subject, that it is only in the songs of the poets and in performances on the stage that these fables, so insulting to the divine majesty, so ludicrous and detestable, are presented to the public in honour of gods of this kind, while the sacred rites, which are conducted by priests, not by actors, are pure from any disgrace and unconnected with any such pollution. If this were true, no one would ever decide that obscenities should be presented on the stage in honour of the gods, and the gods themselves would never have ordered such exhibitions for themselves. In fact, it is just because this kind of thing goes on in the temples that there is no shame about putting on similar performances in the theatre.

It comes to this; that our authority, in attempting to distinguish 'civil theology' as a third category separate from 'fabulous' and 'natural' theology, really meant it to be regarded as a mixture of the two others, rather than distinct from them. For he distinctly states that what the poets write is inadequate to serve as a model for the people to follow, while the writings of philosophers are too demanding for the common folk to find profit from their study. 'These two theologies,' says Varro, 'are incompatible; and yet quite a number of ingredients have been taken from them to help to form the principles of "civil" theology. For that reason, where elements in "civil theology" coincide with elements in the other categories, we shall enter them under "civil theology". But we ought to cultivate the society of the philosophers more than that of the poets.' This implies that we should not utterly shun the society of the poets. Besides, in another passage, dealing with the 'generation of the gods', he says that people in general are more inclined to believe the poets than the 'naturalists'.[24] In the former passage he is talking about what *ought* to happen, in the second about what actually does happen. He says that the 'naturalists' have written with a view to edification; the poets to give pleasure. Thus the poets have written about the scandalous conduct of the gods, which gives pleasure to the general public – and to the gods; but they do not offer models for the people to imitate. As he says, poets write to give

24. i.e. the philosophers.

pleasure, not for edification. All the same, they write the kind of things the gods ask for and that the people present to them.

7. *The similarity and agreement of 'mythical' and 'civil' theology*

The truth is, then, that 'fabulous' theology – the theology of theatre and stage, with all its abundant degradation and obscenity, is brought into 'civil' theology. And all that theology which is rightly judged worthy of condemnation and rejection, is part of the theology which it is considered right to foster and put into practice. Clearly it is not a discrepant part, as I have undertaken to prove; not a part alien from the whole of the rest of the body, tacked on to it as an incongruous pendant; it is completely consonant with it, and is joined to it with perfect compatibility, like a component part of the same organism.

This is made plain by those images which show the shape, the age, the sex, and the clothing of the gods. The poets have their 'bearded Jupiter' and 'beardless Mercury'; so do the pontiffs. It is not only the mimes who give Priapus an enormous phallus; the priests do the same. He stands there in his sacred places to claim men's adoration in just the same guise as when he comes on the stage to provoke laughter. The old man Saturn and Apollo the stripling are not merely actors' parts; they are also statues in temples. Why is it that Forculus, who is in charge of doors (*fores*), and Limentinus, who looks after the threshold (*limen*), are masculine; while Cardea,[25] who comes between them – she watches over the hinge (*cardo*) – is feminine? Do we not find details, in the books on 'divine matters', which the serious poets judged unworthy of their verses? Is it true that only on the stage does Diana carry arms, while in the city she is shown simply as a maiden? Is it true that Apollo is a lute-player only in the theatre, while at Delphi he has no connection with that accomplishment?

But these details are quite respectable compared with the disgusting character of some of the others. What conception of Jupiter was in the minds of those who placed his nurse[26] in the Capitol? Have they not given support to the theory of Euhemerus,[27] who, writing as a careful researcher, not as a purveyor of legendary chatter, maintained that all those gods were originally men, mere mortals? And what of those banqueting gods, Jupiter's parasites?[28] Surely those who set them

25. On these three 'deities', cf. Bk. IV, 8.
26. The goat Amalthea (Ovid, *Fast.*, 5, 115–128). 27. cf. Bk IV, 27n.
28. *Banqueting gods: epulones deos.* Epulones is the name of *priests* in

round Jupiter's table intended to turn the ceremonies into scenes of farce! For if a mime had talked of Jupiter's parasites, admitted to his banquet, he would be taken to be asking for a laugh. It was, in fact, Varro who spoke of them. And he was not meaning to make fun of the gods, but to win them respect; this is witnessed by the fact that he wrote this in his books on 'divine affairs' not in those on 'human affairs'; not in the place where he describes the theatrical shows, but where he reveals the solemnities of the Capitol. In the end the evidence constrains him to admit that the Romans, having made gods in human form, believed them to take delight in human sensual pleasures.

The fact is that the malignant spirits did not fail in their proper task, which was to confirm these pernicious opinions by deluding men's minds. Hence such stories as the one about a guardian of the temple of Hercules, who had a day off with nothing to do and played dice by himself. He threw first with one hand for Hercules, then with the other for himself: the rule of the game being that if he won he would get himself a dinner at the temple's expense and pay for a mistress, while, if the game went to Hercules, he should supply the god with the same pleasures at his own expense. Then, being beaten by himself, representing Hercules, he provided for the god the dinner he owed him and the well-known courtesan Larentina. She went to sleep in the temple and had a dream in which Hercules lay with her, and told her that the first young man she met on leaving the temple would pay her a fee which she was to take as being her payment from Hercules. Now the first young man she met on her departure was the extremely wealthy Tarutius. He fell in love with her, and kept her as his mistress for many years; then he died, and left her as his heiress. Thus she came into a very handsome fortune and, not wishing to seem ungrateful for the divine payment, she did what she supposed would be most acceptable to the divine powers, in making the Roman people her heir. She disappeared, but her will was found; and for this benefit, so the story goes, she was accorded divine honours.[29]

---

charge of sacrificial banquets offered to gods, and it is occasionally found in inscriptions referring to the gods to whom such banquets are offered. We have no other evidence for the banquets implied by St Augustine, where Zeus entertains other deities. The closest resemblance seems to be the *epulum Jovis* during the *ludi Romani* in September, repeated at the 'Plebeian Games' in November. This was a religious banquet on the Capitol, attended by the senate and magistrates, at which the statue of Jupiter reclined, while those of Juno and Minerva sat on chairs (Val. Max., 2, 12).

29. cf. Plut., *Quaest. Rom.*, 36; Gell., 6, 7.

If the poets had invented this story, and if the mimes had acted it on the stage, it would, without any doubt, have been assigned to 'fabulous' theology, and the decision would have been that it should be separated from the respectable category of 'civil' theology. But such disgraceful stories are presented by so learned an authority as belonging not to the poets, but to the people; not to the mimes, but to the rites of religion; not to theatres, but to temples; in fact, not to 'fabulous' but to 'civil' theology. And that is why it is not idle for the actors to use their arts to represent the complete degradation of the gods; but it is utterly idle for the priests to try, by their supposed sacred rites, to invest the gods with an honour to which they have no claim whatsoever.

There are rites of Juno, celebrated in her favourite island of Samos,[30] in which she is given in marriage to Jupiter. There are rites of Ceres, in which she searches for Proserpina, carried off by Pluto. Venus has her rites, in which she mourns the death of her beloved Adonis, a lovely youth, killed by the tusk of a boar. The Mother of the Gods[31] has her rites, in which the beautiful youth Attis, whom she loved and castrated in feminine jealousy, is lamented by those called *Galli*, who themselves suffer the same misfortune.[32] Such performances are more disgusting than any obscenity on the stage. What then is the point of ostensibly taking pains to separate the fabulous fictions of the poets about the gods, which belong to the theatre, from 'civil' theology, which is, in theory, appropriate for the city, this being represented as a separation of what is honourable and decent from what is disgusting and dishonourable? In fact, we ought here to be grateful to the actors, who have had consideration for men's eyes, and have not unveiled in their shows everything that is concealed within the walls of sacred temples.

How can we think any good of the rites which are shrouded in darkness, when such abominations are produced in the light of day? Certainly, the practices performed in secret by those castrated perverts is their affair. But it has not been possible to keep out of sight those unfortunates, so foully unmanned and corrupted. The pagans should try to convince anyone that they perform any holy action through the ministry of such men, for they cannot deny that such men have an appointed role and activity among their ceremonies. We do not know the nature of the performances: we do know the nature of the ministers. In contrast, we do know what happens on the stage; we know

30. cf. Virg., *Aen.*, 1, 15f. 31. Cybele; cf. Bk II, 4n.
32. cf. Ovid, *Fast.*, 4, 223–30; Bk II, 7n; Bk VII, 25n.

that no eunuch or pervert finds a place there, even in a chorus of harlots. Yet the actors are regarded as degraded and outside the pale; and it would be wrong for respectable citizens to act such parts. Then what kind of sacred rites are these, seeing that holiness chooses as ministers the kind of men whom the stage, for all its obscenity, has refused to admit!

8. *The naturalistic explanations of the gods suggested by pagan scholars*

'But all these phenomena', we are told, 'have what one may call "physiological" explanations, explanations, that is, in terms of natural science.' This is to assume that it is 'physiology' we are looking for in this discussion and not theology, that is, the science of nature, not the science of God. Doubtless, the true God is God by nature, not in idea, but that does not mean that all nature is God; for there is a nature of man, of beast, of tree, of stone; and God is none of these. However, if the main point in this line of interpretation, when applied to the rites of the Mother of Gods, is that she is certainly the earth, do we need to look further and to examine other explanations? There could be no clearer support for the theory which alleges that all those gods were once mere men. They are 'sons of earth', and so earth is their mother. But according to the true theology, the earth is the work of God, not his mother.

Besides, in whatever way the rites of the Mother of Gods may be interpreted in reference to the facts of nature, it remains true that for men to be treated as women is not in accordance with nature; it is contrary to nature. This disease, this scandal, this disgrace, is openly professed in these religious ceremonies; whereas it is reluctantly confessed, under torture, by men of corrupted morals. Then again, if those rites, which are proved to be more disgusting than the obscenities of the theatre, are excused and made pure by the interpretation which makes them symbolical of natural phenomena, why then does not the same excuse and purification affect the fictions of poets? Many interpreters have in fact explained them in the same way. Even the myth of Saturn devouring his children, regarded as the most brutal and shocking of all legends, is interpreted by a number of exegetes in this way; the name Saturn signifies the long passage of time,[33] which consumes all that it brings into existence; or, according to Varro's notion, Saturn refers to the seeds which issue from the

33. cf. Bk IV, 10n.

ground and then fall back to the ground again. There are other similar interpretations of this legend, and of the other myths.

But still there is talk of 'fabulous' theology; it is criticized, rejected, and scorned with all its interpretations of this kind; and it is distinguished, as rightly to be repudiated, not merely from the 'natural' theology of the philosophers, but also from the 'civil' theology, which we are now discussing; and it is rejected, on the ground that it has invented unworthy stories about the gods. The intention underlying this distinction is obvious. The men of acute intelligence and profound erudition who have written treatises on this subject realized that both 'fabulous' and 'civil' theology merit reprobation. Now they had the courage to find fault with the former, but not with the latter. They exposed the one for criticism; they put up the other, so like it, for comparison. It was not that they wanted 'civil' theology to be chosen in preference to the other; they hoped that it would be realized that both ought equally to be cast aside. Thus, they thought, the contempt of both these theologies would give an opening for 'natural' theology to establish itself in superior minds, and that without any risk to those who were afraid to criticize 'civil' theology. For both 'civil' and 'fabulous' theologies are alike fabulous and civil. Anyone who intelligently examines the futile obscenities of both will conclude that both are fabulous; anyone who observes that stage shows closely related to 'fabulous' theology are included in the festivals of the gods of the city and in the civic religious cult, will recognize that both theologies are, in fact, civil.

How is it, then, that the power of giving eternal life is ascribed to any of those gods, when their images and their ceremonies show quite unmistakably that they are precisely the same as those openly rejected 'fabulous' divinities in respect of their physical form, their age, sex, clothing, their marriages, their children and their rites? All this makes it clear that they were originally human beings in whose honour rites and ceremonies were established in response to some special circumstance in their life or death and that this error has crept in with the encouragement of the demons who insinuated it, or at least through the activity of an unclean spirit, seizing any chance to delude the minds of men.

9. *The functions of individual gods*

Then what about those functions assigned to the gods, portioned out in minute penny packets, with instructions that each of those divinities should be supplicated for his special responsibility? I have said a good deal about this already, though not all that could be said. But is it not all more appropriate to the buffoonery of farce than to the divine dignity? If anyone engaged two nurses for a child, one to give him solid food only, the other to give him nothing but drink, we should think him a clown, putting on a kind of farcical performance in his own home. But the Romans employ two divinities for these purposes, Educa and Potina![34] They want to derive the name Liber from *liberamentum* (deliverance),[35] on the ground that through his assistance males are 'delivered' from semen in coition – and they will have it that Libera (whom they identify with Venus) renders the same service to women, because their story is that she ensures the emission. For this reason they prescribe the offering of the male part of the body to Liber, in his temple, and of the female to Libera. Besides this they have women, as well as wine, assigned to Liber, with a view to provoking sexual desire, and in this way the Bacchanalia were celebrated with all their limitless insanity; Varro himself admits that the Bacchants could not have performed their feats if their minds had not been deranged. However, these rites later incurred the displeasure of the senate when it came to its senses and ordered their abolition.[36] It may be that here at any rate the Romans realized what power those unclean spirits, whom they took for gods, could exercise over men's minds. One thing is certain; such performances would never have taken place in the theatre; they had entertainment there, not raving madness. And yet to have gods who delight in such entertainments is a similar kind of lunacy.

Varro certainly lays down the distinction between a religious and a superstitious man. The superstitious, he says, is afraid of the gods. The religious man respects them as he respects his parents; he does not fear them as enemies, and when he calls them good, he means that they are more ready to spare the guilty than to harm one innocent person. And yet Varro records that three divinities are brought in as guards for a woman after childbirth to prevent Silvanus from entering and tormenting her; and, to symbolize the three guards, three men make the rounds of the doorways of the house at night. They strike the

34. cf. Bk IV, 11.

35. *Liberamentum*. The word is not found elsewhere. Liber is generally a vine god (cf. Bk IV, 11n.) and the name is perhaps from the same root as 'libation'. Cicero (*De Nat. Deor.*, 2, 24, 62) distinguishes the sexual from the alcoholic Liber, and connects the former with *liberi*, 'children'.

36. In 186 B.C.; Liv., 39, 18.

threshold first with an axe, then with a pestle, and afterwards they sweep it with besoms, these emblems of agriculture being used to prevent the entrance of Silvanus. They are agricultural emblems because axes are necessary for the polling or lopping of trees, pestles for the making of flour, besoms for the piling up of corn. The three gods get their names from those activities: Intercidona from the incision (*intercisio*) made by the axe, Pilumnus from *pilum* (pestle), Deverra from the besoms used in sweeping (*deverrere*). By these guardian deities the woman is protected after childbirth from the violence of the god Silvanus.[37] Thus good gods could not offer strong enough protection against the savagery of a harmful deity unless they outnumbered him by three to one and opposed this rough, terrible, and uncouth god (he was, remember, the god of the forest) with the symbols of agriculture, as being contrary to him. Does this show the harmlessness of the gods? And their concord? Are those the protecting deities of cities – more laughable than the comic turns of the theatre?

The god Jugatinus[38] is brought in when a man and a woman are united in the 'yoke' (*iugum*) of marriage. So far, so good. But the bride has to be escorted home. The god Domiducus is employed to 'lead her home' (*domum ducere*). To install her in the house, the god Domitius sees to her 'going home' (*domum ire*). The goddess Manturna is called in as well, to see that she will 'remain' (*manere*) with her husband.[39] What else is needed? Should we not show consideration for human modesty, and let the sexual desire of flesh and blood achieve the rest, without violation of the secrets of modesty? Why fill the bridal chamber with a mob of divinities, when even the bridal escort retires? And what is the purpose of so crowding it? That the thought of the presence of the gods should make the couple more concerned to preserve decency? Not at all. It is to ensure that with their cooperation, there shall be no difficulty in ravishing the virginity of a girl who feels

37. *Silvanus*: generally an agricultural deity. These post-natal precautions are not mentioned elsewhere.

Pilumnus: mentioned in Virgil, *Aen.*, 10, 76, where the note of Servius, citing Varro, says that a bed was made up for Pilumnus and Pitumnus in the *atrium* of a house where a child had been born.

Intercidona, Deverra: unknown elsewhere.

38. cf. Bk IV, 11.

39. *Domiducus* appears in Martianus Capella (fifth century), *De Nuptiis Mercurii et Philologiae*, 2, 149. *Domiduca* occurs as an epithet of Juno (cf. Bk VII, 3).

Domitius Manturna Virginensis (cf. Bk IV, 11), *Subigus* are all unknown.

the weakness of her sex and is terrified by the strangeness of her situation. For here are the goddess Virginensis, and Father Subigus (to subdue – *subigere*) and Mother Prema (to press – *premere*) and the goddess Pertunda (to pierce – *pertundere*) as well as Venus and Priapus.[40] What does all this mean? If the husband finds the job altogether too much for him and needs divine assistance, would not one god, or one goddess be enough? Do you mean to tell me that Venus alone would not be adequate? She is, they say, so called (among other reasons) because 'not without violence' (*vi non sine*) can a woman be robbed of her virginity! If there is any modesty in human beings (there seems to be none in the gods!), I feel sure that the belief in the presence of so many divinities of both sexes to urge on the business in hand would so embarrass the couple as to quench the enthusiasm of the one and stiffen the reluctance of the other! And then, if Virginensis is among those present, to see to the untying of the virgin girdle, and Subigus, to see that the bride is subdued to her husband, and Prema, to make sure that, when subdued, she is pressed tight, to prevent her moving – if they are there, what is the function of the goddess Pertunda? She should blush for shame and take herself off! Let the bridegroom have something to do for himself! It would be most improper for anyone but the husband to do what her name implies. But it may be that she is tolerated just because she is a goddess, not a god. If she were supposed to be masculine, with the name Pertundus, the husband would demand greater protection against him, in defence of his wife's honour, than the newly-delivered mother seeks, in order to ward off Silvanus. But what am I talking about? Priapus is there as well, that all-too-male divinity. And the newly wedded bride used to be told to sit on his phallus, that monstrous obscenity, following the most honourable and most religious custom of Roman matrons.

So let our friends go and try (and good luck to them!) to use all their subtlety to make a distinction between 'civil' and 'fabulous' theology, between the city and the theatre, the temple and the stage, priestly ceremonies and poets' verses – a supposed distinction between decency and obscenity, truth and falsehood, solemnity and frivolity, the serious and the farcical, between what is to be desired and what is to be rejected. We understand what they are up to. They know that the theology of the theatre and of fable depends on their 'civil' theology,

40. *Prema* is mentioned in Tertullian (*Ad Nat.*, 2, 11).
Priapus: cf. Bk II, 14n. *Pertunda*: her function is described in Arnobius (*Adv. Gent.*, 3, 10).

which is reflected in the verses of the poets as in a mirror. They have not the courage to condemn 'civil' theology, but they give a detailed exposition of it, and then criticize its reflection in terms of reprobation. The purpose of this is that those who perceive their intention may repudiate the original also, of which this is the image. As for the gods, they look at themselves in the same mirror, and are so enamoured of what they see, that they can be more clearly recognized, in both image and original, for who they are and what they are.

This is why the gods have compelled their worshippers, by commandments backed by fearful threats, to dedicate to them the indecencies of 'fabulous' theology, to include them in their festivals, to class them under 'divine matters'. In so doing they have made it all the more obvious that they themselves are unclean spirits; and at the same time, they have made this rejected and condemned theology, that of the theatre, a component part of 'civil' theology, which is regarded as chosen and approved. The whole of this 'theology' is a mass of lies and delusions; yet we find part of it in the priestly books, the other part in the verses of poets.

Whether one could discover still more divisions is another question. For the present I have followed the distinctions made by Varro, and I believe that I have sufficiently shown that both the theology of the city and the theology of the theatre belong to one division, namely, 'civil' theology. Hence, since they are both alike in their indecency, their absurdity, their unworthiness, their falsity, heaven forbid that any man of genuine religion should hope for life eternal from either of them.

Varro himself begins his enumeration of the gods with the moment of a man's conception and starts with Janus. Then he traces the sequence up to the moment of the death of a decrepit old man, and brings to an end the list of gods concerned with man himself with the goddess Nenia,[41] who is invoked in song at the funerals of the aged. He then passes to a record of the gods who are concerned, not with man himself, but with the necessities of man's life, food, clothing, and the rest. And in every case he indicates the function of each god and the purpose for which prayer should be directed to each. Yet in the whole of this careful examination he never mentions or names any gods from whom eternal life is to be asked; and it is, strictly speaking, for the sake of eternal life alone that we are Christians.

Who is so slow-witted as to fail to realize that in expounding and

41. *Nenia* means 'dirge'. Arnobius (*Adv. Gent.*, 4, 7) calls her the protector of those *in extremis*.

exposing 'civil' theology with such care, in showing its resemblance to the shameful and infamous 'fabulous' theology, and in demonstrating quite clearly that it is part of the former – that, in this Varro is really making every effort to prepare a place in men's minds for 'natural' theology, which, according to him, is the concern of the philosophers? He employs great subtlety in criticizing 'fabulous' theology, without daring to criticize 'civil', but demonstrating the reprehensible character of the latter by his manner of exposition. Thus, in his intention, both those theologies will be condemned by the judgement of intelligent readers, and only 'natural' theology will remain for them to adopt. We shall treat of this theology more thoroughly in the appropriate place, with the help of God.

10. *Seneca's frankness in criticizing 'civil' theology more vigorously than Varro denounced the 'mythical'*

Varro lacked the frankness and courage to criticize the theology of the city with the same freedom he showed towards the theology of the theatre, which resembled it so closely. Annaeus Seneca had those qualities in some degree, if not in full measure. That is he had them in his writing; but he failed to display them in his life.

Seneca (who I suppose, on good evidence, to have been at the height of his fame in the time of our apostles)[42] wrote a book *Against Superstitions.*[43] In it he attacked this 'civil' theology, the theology of the city, in much greater detail, and with much greater vehemence than Varro had used against the 'fabulous' theology of the theatre. Thus, on the subject of images, he writes,

> They dedicate images representing sacred, immortal, inviolable beings in base, inert matter; they give them the shapes of men, of wild beasts, or of fishes; some make bi-sexual gods, having bodies with incongruous characteristics. And they give the name of divinities to those images, though they would be classed as monsters if they suddenly came to life.

Somewhat later, he speaks in praise of 'natural' theology, and sets out the opinions of some of the philosophers. He then confronts him-

42. *Seneca* (cf. Bk v, 8n.) was certainly contemporary with the apostles; his elder brother, Gallio, encountered St Paul in Corinth in A.D. 52 (Acts 18, 12). An apocryphal correspondence (of unutterable banality) between Seneca and Paul is extant (trans. in M. R. James, *Apocryphal New Test.*); and, as we know from Jerome (*De Vir. Ill.*, 12) and from St Augustine himself (*Ep.*, 153, 14) it was accepted as authentic, and widely read, in the fourth century. Many others besides Jerome believed that Seneca was at least sympathetic to Christianity.

43. Not extant.

self with a question. 'At this point,' he says, 'someone asks, "Am I to believe that the sky and the earth are gods? And that some gods live above the moon and some below? Am I to bear patiently with Plato, who proposed a god without a body; or Strato,[44] the Peripatetic, who suggested a god without a soul?"' Seneca then replies, 'Do you really suppose that the dreams of Titus Tatius, or Romulus, or Tullus Hostilius, were nearer to the truth? Tatius dedicated a statue to the goddess Cloacina;[45] Romulus to Picus and Tiberinus. Hostilius made divinities of Panic and Pallor,[46] the most unpleasant conditions of human beings; the one being the emotion of a terrified mind, the other not even a disease, but merely a change of complexion. Are you more inclined to believe in these deities, and to give them a place in heaven?'

Seneca was quite outspoken about the cruel obscenity of some of the ceremonies:

> One man cuts off his male organs: another gashes his arms. If this is the way they earn the favour of the gods, what happens when they fear their anger? The gods do not deserve any kind of worship, if this is the worship they desire. So extreme is the frenzy of a mind disturbed and toppled from its throne, that the gods are appeased by rites which surpass the savagery of the foulest of mankind, whose cruelty has passed into legend. Tyrants have sometimes lacerated men's limbs: they have never ordered men to lacerate themselves. Men have been gelded to serve a monarch's lustful pleasure; but no one has ever unmanned himself with his own hands, at the bidding of his master. Men gash themselves in the temples, and offer their wounds and their blood as a supplication. If anyone had the time to notice what those people do and what they have done to them, he would discover things so unbecoming for men of honour, so unworthy of freemen, so incongruous for men of sane mind, that no one would hesitate to call them mad, if there were not so many sharing the same frenzy. As it is, their title to sanity rests on the multitude of the apparently insane.

He goes on to recount the ceremonies habitually observed in the Capitol itself, and he exposes them without the slightest reserve. No one would believe, he implies, that those were performed by any but lunatics – unless it were in a spirit of mockery. He himself speaks in

44. *Strato* 'was called Physicus because he held that all divine power was situated in nature, which possesses the causes of birth, growth, and diminution, while it lacks any shape or sensibility' (Cic., *De Nat. Deor.*, 1, 13, 35). Strato succeeded Theophrastus as head of the Peripatetic school in 288 B.C.

45. cf. Bk IV, 8n.

46. *Picus, Tiberinus*: cf. Bk IV, 23n.; *Panic, Pallor*: cf. Bk IV, 15.

derision of the mourning for Osiris[47] in the Egyptian mysteries, followed soon by the joy at his finding, since both the loss and the discovery are fictitious, and yet the grief, and the joy, are expressed with every appearance of genuine emotion by people who have neither lost nor found anything. Seneca adds,

> But at least this delirium has a limited period; it is allowable to go mad once a year. If you go to the Capitol, you will be ashamed at the demented performances presented to the public, which frivolous lunacy looks upon in the light of a duty. Jupiter has someone to announce the names of his callers; another to tell him the time; he has an attendant to wash him, another to oil him, and this one merely goes through the motions with his hands. There are women to do the hair of Juno and Minerva; these stand at a distance not only from the statues, but from the temple, and move their fingers like hairdressers, while others hold up a looking-glass. You find people praying the gods to stand bail for them; others handing them their writs and explaining their law cases. A leading pantomime actor of great experience, grown old and decrepit, used to put on his act every day on the Capitol, as if the gods still took pleasure in his performance now that human beings had abandoned him. Craftsmen of all kinds hang about the place waiting to do some work for the immortal gods.

Soon afterwards, Seneca adds,

> At least the services they offer are not indecent or dishonourable, though they may be superfluous. But there are some women who haunt the Capitol in the belief that Jupiter is in love with them: and they are not deterred by the thought of Juno's jealous anger, which (if one is to believe the poets) can be formidable!

Here we have a freedom of speech such as Varro did not display. He could only bring himself to criticize poetic theology; he did not dare find fault with 'civil', which Seneca cut to pieces. Yet, if we really want the truth, the temples where those rites go on are worse than the theatres where those fictions are enacted. Hence, in the rites of 'civil' theology the role chosen by Seneca for the wise man is to simulate conformity in act while having no religious attachment. This is what he says: 'The wise man will observe all these customs as being ordered by law, not as acceptable to the gods.' And, a little later,

47. *Osiris.* The Egyptian myth described him as a king who brought civilization to his people; but he was murdered and his body dissected by his wicked brother Set. Isis, his sister and wife, collected his remains and buried them, and then, with her son Horus, took revenge on Set. Osiris becomes the god of the dead, and through Horus (identified with the Sun) the source of new life. Osiris' incarnation in the bull Apis suggests that he essentially represents the male generative power.

And what of the marriages we arrange among the gods, including the blasphemy of unions between brothers and sisters? We give Bellona to Mars, Venus to Vulcan, Salacia[48] to Neptune. We leave some of the gods as bachelors, for lack, one assumes, of suitable matches. There are, to be sure, some unattached females available, such as Populonia, Fulgora,[49] and Rumina;[50] but it is not surprising that no suitors were forthcoming for them. All that undistinguished mob of gods which long-standing superstition has amassed over the centuries, will receive our worship; but we shall bear in mind that their cult is a matter of custom, having little connection with truth.

Thus, what the laws and custom established in 'civil' theology is not what was acceptable to the gods, nor anything related to reality. But Seneca, who had been, as it were, emancipated by the philosophers, but who was also an illustrious senator of the Roman people, worshipped what he criticized, performed acts which he reprehended, venerated what he condemned. Doubtless philosophy had taught him an important lesson, that he should not be superstitious in his conception of the physical universe; but, because of the laws of the country and the accepted customs, he also learnt that without playing an actor's part in theatrical fictions, he should imitate such a performance in the temple. This was to take a line the more reprehensible in that he acted this insincere part in such a way as to lead people to believe him sincere. The stage-player on the other hand, only aims at giving pleasure by his performance; he has no desire to mislead or deceive his audience.

11. *Seneca's opinion of the Jews*

Besides criticizing the superstitions of 'civil' theology, Seneca attacks the rites of the Jews, and the Sabbath in particular. He maintains that the Sabbath is a harmful institution, since by the interposition of this one day in seven they practically lose a seventh part of their life in inactivity, and they suffer by having to put off urgent tasks. As for the Christians, who were at that time already bitterly opposed to the Jews, he did not dare to mention them for good or ill – not wishing to praise them in defiance of the ancient traditions of his country, nor to criticize them against (it may be) his personal feelings. It is in speaking

48. cf. Bk IV, 11.

49. *Populonia* occurs as an epithet of Juno, as protectress against devastation (*populari* = 'to devastate'). Perhaps *Fulgora* describes her as guarding against lightning (*fulgor*).

50. cf. Bk IV, 11n.

of the Jews that he says: 'The customs of this detestable race have become so prevalent that they have been adopted in almost all the world. The vanquished have imposed their laws on the conquerors.' He expresses his surprise when he says this, and he shows his ignorance of the ways of God's working in adding a remark in which he reveals what he thought about the Jewish ritual system: 'At least they know the origins of their ceremonies: the greater part of our people have no idea of the reason for the things they do.'

The questions that arise about the Jewish religious practices, why, and to what extent, they have been established by divine authority, and afterwards taken over, with divine approval, by the people of God, to whom the mystery of eternal life has been revealed – these questions I have treated in other places, and in particular in my books against the Manicheans.[51] And I shall have more to say on this topic at a more convenient moment in this present work.

12. *The falsity of the pagan gods has been exposed; they can give no help in respect of temporal life; they certainly cannot bestow life eternal*

Here then are three theologies: the Greeks call them 'mythical', 'physical', and 'political', and in Latin they can be called 'fabulous', 'natural', and 'civil'. Men can look to neither the first nor the third of these for eternal life: not to 'fabulous' theology, which the pagans themselves criticize with extreme candour, although they are worshippers of many false gods, nor to 'civil' theology, for that has been proved to be a subdivision of the 'fabulous', closely resembling it, or even morally inferior to it. If what I have said in this book is not enough to convince every reader, I would refer to the ample discussions in the previous volumes, and especially in the fourth, on God as the giver of felicity. For to whom should men consecrate themselves, with a view to eternal life, save to felicity alone, if felicity were a goddess?[52] But felicity is not a goddess, but the gift of God. To what God then should we consecrate ourselves except to the giver of felicity, if we fix our devout affection on eternal life, where there is the true fulfilment of felicity?

After what has been already said, I do not imagine that anyone is likely to suppose that any of the pagan gods is the giver of felicity. Their worship has so much that is disgraceful in it, and even more

51. *Adv. Faust. Man.*, ch. 6; 7.   52. cf. Bk IV, 18.

disgraceful is their indignation if such worship is withheld; it is that which betrays them for the unclean spirits they are. Then how can one who does not give felicity be capable of giving eternal life? For what we mean by eternal life is the condition of unending felicity. If the soul lives in the eternal pains with which the unclean spirits themselves will be tormented, that is not eternal life, but eternal death. The greatest and worst of all deaths is where death does not die. Now since the soul, being created immortal, cannot be deprived of every kind of life, the supreme death of the soul is alienation from the life of God in an eternity of punishment. Therefore life eternal, that is, life of unending felicity, is the gift of him alone who gives true felicity. It has been proved that the gods worshipped by 'civil' theology cannot give it. They are not to be worshipped, even with a view to temporal and earthly goods; we have demonstrated that in the five preceding books. Much less are they to be honoured with a view to eternal life, the life after death; that is the point we have made in this present book, with the support of the arguments in the previous discussions.

But inveterate custom has the strength derived from very deep roots: and some readers may think that my arguments have not adequately established the need to reject and to shun this 'civil' theology. I would ask any such readers to give their attention to the next volume, which, with God's help, is to follow.

BOOK VII

Preface

I AM using my most earnest endeavours to destroy and eradicate the baneful and long-held notions which are the enemies of true religion, and which have been fixed in the darkened minds of mankind through centuries of error, putting out deep and tenacious roots. I am co-operating, in my small measure, with the grace of the true God, relying on the help of him who alone can accomplish this design. No doubt the argument of my previous books is more than sufficient to achieve this object for livelier and superior intelligences; but they will have to possess themselves in patience; and I ask them, for the sake of others, not to think superfluous what for themselves they feel to be unnecessary.

The task before us is a matter of supreme importance: to establish that the true and truly holy Divinity is to be sought and worshipped not with a view to this mortal life, which passes away like smoke[1] (although we do receive from the Divinity the help needed for our present frailty), but for the sake of the life of blessedness, which must needs be the life of eternity.

1. *Since it is agreed that no divinity is to be found in 'civil' theology, are we to believe that it is to be found in the 'select' gods?*

This Divinity, or, as I may call it, this Deity – for our Christian writers have no reluctance about using this word, as a more accurate translation of the Greek *theotês*[2] – this Divinity, or Deity, is not to be found in the 'civil' theology which Marius Varro has expounded in sixteen books: that is to say, it is impossible to attain to the felicity of eternal life by means of the worship of such gods as have been established in the cities, together with the ritual of their worship. Any

1. cf. Ps. 102, 3; Jas. 4, 14.

2. Neither the Greek *theotês* nor the Latin *deitas* are found in classical authors. *Divinitas* is a classical Latin word. Christian writers do not establish any firm distinction between *deitas* and *divinitas*, but there is a tendency to use *deitas* of the nature of God, the Godhead, and *divinitas* of his attributes.

reader who has not been convinced by my sixth book, just completed, will no doubt find, after reading the present book, that he needs no further elucidation of the subject.

It may be, in fact, that someone will imagine that at any rate the 'select' and 'principal' gods, which Varro has treated of in his last book, and about which I have as yet said all too little, ought to be worshipped with a view to a life of happiness, which can only mean eternal life. On this subject I am not going to echo what Tertullian said, perhaps with more wit than truth, 'If gods are "selected" like onions, then the others are rejected as worthless.'[3] I am not saying that; for I see that even among a select few, a further selection is made for some task of exceptional importance. For instance, in an army, when recruits have been selected, a choice is made from these for some important military operation; and when a choice is made of leaders in the Church, it does not mean that the rest are rejected, since all the truly faithful are rightly called 'elect'. 'Corner stones'[4] are 'selected' for a building, but that does not imply the 'rejection' of the rest, which are appointed to a place in other parts of the structure. Grapes are 'selected' for eating, but the others, which are reserved for drink, are not 'rejected'. There is no need to labour an obvious point. We can take it that the mere fact that certain gods have been selected out of a large number is not a reason for attacking the author, or the worshippers of the gods, or the gods themselves. Our task is rather to examine who those gods are and for what purpose they have, apparently, been 'selected'.

2. *Who are these 'select' gods? Are they excused the duties of the less considerable gods?*

At all events, here are the gods to whom Varro, in the course of one book, gives the testimonial of 'select': Janus, Jupiter, Saturn, Genius,[5] Mercury, Apollo, Mars, Vulcan, Neptune, the Sun, Orcus, Father Liber,[6] Earth, Ceres, Juno, the Moon,[7] Diana, Minerva, Venus, Vesta – twenty in all, twelve males, eight females. Are these divinities called 'select' because of their more important responsibilities in the universe or because they are better known to the people in general and because a higher degree of worship is offered to them? If it is because of their more responsible functions in the universe, we should not expect to find them among what we may call the plebeian multitude of div-

3. Tert., *Ad Nat.*, 2, 9. 4. cf. Ps. 118, 22. 5. cf. ch. 13n.
6. cf. Bk IV, 11n; VI, 9. 7. Generally identified with Diana.

inities which are assigned to tiny tasks. In fact, to start with Janus himself, at the moment of conception – for that is where they start, all these tasks minutely distributed among those minute divinities – at that moment it is Janus who opens the door for the reception of the seed. Saturn is there too, in charge of the actual seed; Liber is there, for he liberates the male by the emission of the seed; Libera is there (some identify her with Venus) who performs the same good office for the female, to give her liberation by the emission of the seed. All these belong to the class of 'select' gods. But the goddess Mena[8] is there as well, and she looks after the menstrual flux – an obscure divinity, although the daughter of Jupiter. Varro, in his book about 'select' gods, assigns this department of menstruation to Juno herself, who is queen even among the 'select' gods, and, in her capacity as Juno Lucina she presides over this haemorrhage in company with her step-daughter, Mena. Among those present there, there are a couple of very obscure divinities of some sort, Vitumnus and Sentinus:[9] the first gives vitality to the foetus, the latter bestows sensibility. And in spite of their utter obscurity those two perform a much more important office than all those noble and 'select' gods. For surely, without life and sense, what is it that a woman carries in her womb? Merely a lump of worthless matter, of the same order as dust and mud.

3. *There is no discoverable principle in the selection of certain gods, since more important responsibilities are assigned to many inferior deities*

What drove all those 'select' gods to undertake these lowly tasks, where Vitumnus and Sentinus, who 'are wrapped in complete obscurity',[10] are superior to them in gifts allotted for their bestowal? It is the 'select' Janus who gives access – opens the door (*janua*) as it were – for the seed; the 'select' Saturn confers the actual seed; the 'select' Liber procures for men the emission of the seed; Libera (or Ceres, or Venus) does the same for women; the 'select' Juno provides the menses for the growth of the foetus when conceived – and she does this not alone, but with the help of Mena, daughter of Jupiter. And it is the obscure and unknown Vitumnus who gives life, the obscure and unknown Sen-

8. *Libera* and *Mena*: cf. Bk IV, 11n.

9. *Lucina*: cf. Bk IV, 11n. *Vitumnus* is perhaps *Vertumnus*; cf. Bk IV, 21n. *Sentinus* occurs elsewhere only in Tert., *Ad. Nat.* 2, 11.

10. Virg., *Aen.*, 5, 302.

tinus gives sensibility; and those are more important gifts than the others, in proportion as they themselves are inferior to intellect and reason. For just as beings endowed with reason and intelligence are by that very fact superior to those without those faculties, whose life is merely that of sense, so in the same way beings equipped with life and sense are rightly ranked above those which have neither life nor sensibility. Thus Vitumnus, giver of life, and Sentinus, giver of sense, have a better claim to a place among 'select' gods than Janus, the admitter of seed, Saturn, giver or sower of seed, and Liber and Libera, movers or emitters of seeds – seeds which are not worthy of consideration until they have reached the stage of life and sensibility ; and life and sense are 'select' gifts which are not in the gift of 'select' gods but of unknown gods, gods regarded as negligible in comparison with the high rank of those others.

The reply may be that Janus is the authority concerned with all beginnings, and for that reason the opening made for conception is rightly assigned to him; and that Saturn is in charge of all seeds, and therefore the seeding of man cannot be separated from his operation; that Liber and Libera are in charge of the emission of all seeds, and must in consequence be concerned with the emission of seeds which are connected with the formation of men; that Juno presides over all purifications and all parturition, and therefore cannot fail to be present at the purification of women and the births of men. If so, let our antagonists decide what to reply about Vitumnus and Sentinus. Do they wish *them* to be the authorities over all living and sentient beings? If the answer is Yes, then they should give thought to the question of giving them a loftier position. For to be born by means of seed is to be born on earth and from earth, while to live and to feel are, in their view, attributes of the heavenly gods. If they say, on the other hand, that Vitumnus and Sentinus are only given responsibility for beings which live in the flesh and with the aid of senses, why does not their great god, who makes all things live and feel, confer life and sensibility on the flesh also, and, as part of his universal operation, bestow this gift on creatures at their birth? What need is there for Vitumnus and Sentinus? Let us imagine that the Supreme Being, who presides over life and sensibility in general, has entrusted to those whom we may call his servants the oversight of things of the flesh as being utterly remote from him and too lowly for his immediate attention. But are we to suppose that those 'select' gods are so deprived of domestic staff that they cannot themselves entrust those tasks to servants, but are compelled, for all their renown (which leads to their being selected), to share such tasks with obscure deities? Juno is a 'select' goddess; she is queen, the 'sister and consort of Jupiter', yet she is Iterduca for children, and shares her task with those most obscure goddesses, Abeona and Adeona.[11] In the same sphere they placed another goddess, called Mens[12] (Mind), to give to children a good intelligence; and yet that divinity is not ranked among the 'select' deities – as if this gift were not the most valuable that could be given. Yet Juno is ranked as 'select', because she is Iterduca and Domiduca – as if it were the slightest use 'to find one's way' (*iter ducere*) or 'to be brought back home' (*domum duci*), if one has not a good intelligence (*mens*).[13] And yet the selectors never thought of entering the giver of this blessing among their 'select' divinities. But surely she (Mens) ought to have been preferred even to Minerva, who was made responsible for the memory of children in this allocation of detailed functions. For it can hardly be doubted that a good intelligence is a more valuable possession than a memory however vast. No one who has a good mind can be a bad man; whereas there are complete villains with remarkable memories, who are all the worse because they cannot forget their evil thoughts. For all that, Minerva is among the 'select' deities while Mens is lost to sight among the common herd. And what am I to say of Virtue? Or of Felicity? I have already said a good deal about them in my fourth book.[14] Although our pagans consider them gods, they have refused them any place among the 'select', while giving places to Mars and Orcus, of whom the first ensures death, the second receives the dead.

We observe that in these tiny duties which are distributed in tiny fragments to a plurality of gods these 'select' deities themselves operate on a footing of equality, like a senate in conjunction with the plebs; and we find that some of the gods who have not been considered at all worthy of selection are in charge of more important and dignified functions than those performed by gods entitled 'select'. We are left with the conclusion that the titles 'select' and 'principal' are not bestowed on account of more eminent responsibilities in the universe, but simply because those divinities have succeeded in winning greater renown among the general public. That is why Varro himself says that some father gods and some mother goddesses have received obscurity as their fate – just as it happens to human beings.

11. cf. Bk IV, 21. 12. cf. Bk IV, 21.

13. *Iterduca, Domiduca* appear as epithetis of Juno as goddess of marriage in Martianus Capella (De Nuptiis Mercurii et Philologiae, 2, 149); cf. Bk VI, 9.

14. ch. 21; 23.

Now it may be that Felicity was not bound to find a place among the 'select', just because this dignified position is attained not by merit but by mere chance. But Fortune at least should have been ranked among them, or rather before them; for, they say, this goddess grants favours to each person not by any rational principle of distribution but by the random luck of the draw. She ought by rights to occupy the highest eminence among the 'select' gods, since it is there that she shows her power at its highest; for we see that they are selected, not for exceptional virtues, not in accordance with any rational principle of felicity, but by the random operation of the power of Fortune, or so their worshippers believe. It may be that the eloquent Sallust had those very gods in mind when he said, 'But fortune, without doubt, is the dominant power in all that happens; it is fortune that brings fame or obscurity, according to her whim rather than on the basis of true desert.'[15] For no one can find a reason why Venus should be held in honour and Virtue be hid in obscurity, although both are canonized deities, and their merits are very different.

Perhaps this honoured position is earned by the enthusiasm of devotees? Venus, to be sure, has more votaries than Virtue. But then why is Minerva so illustrious, and the goddess Pecunia (money) so obscure?[16] Humanity in general finds wealth more alluring than artistic skill. Even among the practitioners of an art you would be hard put to it to find a man who does not regard his art as a means to pecuniary reward; and the end is invariably more highly valued than the means. If then the choice of 'select' gods depends on the judgement of the ignorant multitude, why is the goddess Pecunia not preferred to Minerva, seeing that artists in general practise their art for monetary gain? If, on the other hand, we owe this distinction of 'select' deities to a few philosophers, then why is Virtue not ranked higher than Venus, since reason should prefer Virtue by a long way?

At any rate, if that Fortune, who in the opinion (as I have said) of those who attach most importance to her, 'is the dominant power in all that happens, and brings fame or obscurity according to her whim rather than on the basis of true desert', if Fortune has such power even over the gods, that she brings fame or obscurity at her pleasure, according to her random decision, then she ought to hold an eminent place among the 'select' gods, seeing that she wields such eminent power over the gods themselves. Are we to suppose that Fortune herself had only ill-fortune in this case, so that she was unable to gain that position?

15. *Cat.*, 8, 1. 16. cf. Bk IV, 21.

Then she has been her own adversary; for she has given to others a renown which she herself does not enjoy.

4. *The inferior gods are better treated than the select deities: They are not dishonoured by slanders, while the infamies of their superiors are widely publicized*

Those whose main aim is renown and glory would congratulate those 'select' gods and call them fortunate, if they failed to see that they were selected more for insult than for honour. The mob of deities of the common sort are sheltered by their very obscurity, so that no slanders are heaped on them. No doubt we smile when we see them distributed, in the fantasies of human imagination, to the various tasks allotted to them, like sub-collectors of taxes, or like craftsmen in Silver Street, where one small piece of plate passes through many hands to achieve the final result, although it could be finished by one thoroughly competent craftsman. But this was thought to be the only way to suit the interests of the large number of craftsmen, by letting each individual acquire skill in a single part of the craft, which could be done quickly and easily, so as to obviate the long and painful process required to make them all masters of the whole art. For all that, it would be hard to find one of the unselected gods whose reputation has been smirched by any scandal, while it would be equally difficult to find a single 'select' god who has not suffered the stigma of some outrageous insult. The superior deities have descended to the lowly tasks of their inferiors; the inferiors have not reached the exalted level of the scandals of the greater gods.

I must confess that nothing immediately occurs to me to the discredit of Janus; and perhaps he was that kind of a character, living in innocence and remote from crimes and sins. He gave a kind welcome to Saturn, the refugee; he divided his kingdom with his guest, so that they each founded a community, that of Janus being Janiculum, that of Saturn, Saturnia.[17] But the pagans, whose aim is to introduce unpleasantness into the cult of the gods, finding nothing dishonourable in the life of Janus, have dishonoured him by images of monstrous deformity, representing him sometimes with two faces, sometimes with four – a kind of twin.[18] Perhaps their intention was that since

17. cf. Virg., *Aen.*, 8, 355–9; Ovid, *Fast.*, 1, 235–46.

18. *Janus–two faces*: cf. ch. 8, *four faces*. There was an image of *Janus Quadrifrons* in the Forum Transitorium in a shrine with four gates (Servius on Virg., *Aen.*, 7, 607).

the majority of the 'select' gods had lost face by the shameful acts they perpetrated, Janus should have an extra supply of face to match his innocence!

5. *Concerning the more esoteric teaching of the pagans and their naturalistic interpretations*

But let us rather listen to the 'natural' interpretations given by the pagans themselves, the explanations by which they try to disguise the squalor of their wretched superstition under a pretentious show of profundity in doctrine.

To begin with, Varro supports those interpretations by saying that the men of antiquity invented images of gods, and their attributes and ornaments, so that those who had been initiated into the mysteries of the teaching could fix their eyes on them, and then apprehend with their mind the true gods, namely the Soul of the World and its manifestations. He explains that those who made images in human form seem to have followed the principle that the spirit of man, which is in the human body, most nearly resembles the Immortal Spirit. It is as if vessels were placed to signify gods, and in the temple of Libera a wine-jar were set up to signify wine, the contents being represented by the container. Thus, the rational soul is signified by the statue of human form, because that kind of 'vessel' generally contains that which they hold to be the constitutive nature of God, or the gods.

These are the mysteries of doctrine which that most learned of men had penetrated, so that he could bring them to light. But Varro, you are one of the shrewdest of mankind, and I would like to ask you a question. In treating of those 'mysteries of doctrine', have you by any chance lost that insight which enabled you to see, in sober truth, that those who first set up images for the people banished reverent fear from their fellow-citizens and introduced error, and that the Romans in the remote past offered a purer worship, without images? It was the evidence of the ancient Romans that gave you the courage to criticize the Romans of later times. For if the Romans in times long past had set up images you might well have kept a timid silence, and suppressed your conviction, well-grounded though it is, that images ought not to be erected; and on the subject of pernicious and futile inventions of this kind you would have held forth in a loftier strain, with a more copious flow, about those 'mysteries of doctrine'. However, that soul of yours, for all your learning and your great talents (and this is why we are so grieved for you) could never arrive, by way of those 'mysteries of doctrine', at its God; at the God, that is, *by* whom the soul was created, not *with* whom it was made – the God of whom it is a creature, not a part, who is not the 'Soul of all things', but the God who created every soul, the God by whose illumination the soul attains blessedness, if it is not ungrateful for his grace.

The subsequent discussion will reveal what these 'mysteries of doctrine' are, and what they are worth. Meanwhile, we observe that the learned Varro declares that the Soul of the World and its manifestations are the true gods. It follows that the whole of his theology, the 'natural' theology, that is, to which he attaches the highest importance, could extend only as far as to the nature of rational soul. Varro treats very briefly of 'natural' theology at the beginning of his last book, which is devoted to the 'select' gods. We shall see here whether, by means of 'physiological' explanations, he can bring 'civil' theology under this 'natural' theology. If so, then all theology will be 'natural'; and what was the point of taking such trouble to distinguish 'civil' theology? While if the distinction was based on a real difference then, since 'natural' theology, which Varro approves, is not true (for it only reaches as far as the soul, and does not arrive at the true God, the maker of the soul) how much more worthless and false is 'civil' theology! For 'civil' theology is mainly concerned with material nature. This will be shown by the interpretations which Varro himself has worked out and clarified with the greatest industry. Some of those I shall have to quote.

6. *Concerning Varro's notion, that God is the Soul of the World; but the world has many souls in its different parts, and their nature is divine*

In Varro's preliminary remarks about 'natural' theology he declares that, in his belief, God is the Soul of the World, or as the Greeks say, the *cosmos*, and that this world itself is God. But just as a wise man, although he consists of body and soul, is called 'wise' in virtue of his soul; so the world is called 'God' in virtue of its soul, although consisting both of soul and body. Here Varro seems in some manner to be acknowledging the unity of God. But in order to introduce a plurality of gods also, he adds that the world is divided into two parts, the sky and the earth, and the sky is subdivided into ether and air, and the earth into water and land, and of these ether is the highest element, next comes air, below that water, and at the bottom, earth. All these four parts[19] are full of souls, immortal souls in ether and air, mortal souls in water and earth. Between the highest circumference of the sky and the circle of the moon there are ethereal souls, the planets and stars; and they appear as gods not only to the mind but to the eyes. Between the moon's sphere and the summits of the clouds and winds there are aerial souls, but these are visible only to the mind, not to the eyes; and they are called 'heroes', *lares*, and *genii*.

Such is the account, a brief account, to be sure, of 'natural' theology given in Varro's prefatory remarks; and it is this theology which has commended itself not only to Varro, but to many philosophers. I shall have to discuss it in greater detail when, with God's help, I have finished what remains to be said about 'civil' theology as far as it is concerned with the 'select' gods.

7. *Was it reasonable to separate Janus and Terminus as two divinities?*

Varro begins with Janus. I ask, 'Who is Janus?' I get the reply, 'He is the world.' A succinct answer, to be sure, and a plain one. Then why are we told that he has to do with the beginnings of things while their endings are looked after by someone else, called Terminus? For they inform us that because of beginnings and endings two months are dedicated to these two gods in addition to the ten months leading off with March and going on to December; January being sacred to Janus, February to Terminus. That, they assure us, is why the *Terminalia* are celebrated in the month of February,[20] when the sacred purification, called *Februm*, takes place; and that gives the month its name. Are we to take it that the beginnings of things are the concern of the world (which is Janus), while their endings are not? And so another god has to be put in charge of them? But surely they admit that everything which begins in this world also has its ending in the world. What nonsense it is to give Janus a double face in his image, and to halve his exercise of power!

Would it not give a far more intelligent interpretation of the two-faced god to identify Janus and Terminus, and assign one face to beginnings, the other to endings? For one who engages in an activity

19. *Four parts*. The notion of the four elements, and their local distribution, goes back to Aristotle. It was developed by Pythagoreans and Stoics; Varro appears to have identified the ether with fire, which Aristotle and the Stoics regarded as the highest element.

20. 23 Feb.; Ovid, *Fast.*, 2, 639–84.

ought to keep both beginning and end in view; anyone who does not look back to the beginning throughout a course of action, does not look forward to the end. Hence it necessarily follows that an intention which looks ahead depends on a recollection which looks back; and a man who forgets what he has begun will not discover how to finish. But if they had thought that the life of blessedness is begun in this world, yet is completed outside this world, and for that reason limited the power of Janus to beginnings, then surely they would have ranked Terminus above him and would not have excluded him from the 'select' gods. Yet, even as it is, when the beginnings and endings of merely temporal things are allotted to these two gods, greater honour ought to be paid to Terminus. For there is the greater joy when a matter is brought to a successful end; enterprises are beset with anxiety until they are carried to their conclusion. When anyone begins an undertaking, it is on the end that he fixes his desires, his thoughts, his hopes, and his prayers; and he only feels exultation when the enterprise is crowned with achievement.

8. *Why the worshippers of Janus invented a two-faced image of the god*

We may now examine the interpretation of the two-faced image. It is said that the god has two faces, one in front and one behind, because when we open our mouth the cavity has a certain resemblance to the world; hence the Greeks call the palate *ouranos*, and several Latin poets, according to Varro, call the sky, 'the palate';[21] and he points out that this oral cavity has two exits, one leading outwards, in the direction of the teeth, the other inwards, towards the throat. See to what a state the world has been reduced, on account of the Greek word for 'palate', or the poetical meaning of 'palate'! What has this to do with the soul, or with eternal life? This god is to be worshipped because of salivation and for nothing else, for the provision of the two openings under the 'sky of the palate', one for swallowing, the other for spitting. But could anything be more absurd? It is impossible to find in the actual world two openings on opposite sides through which it can admit anything from outside or emit anything from inside; and yet we are asked to imagine, on the basis of our mouth and throat (which the world does not in the least resemble), a represen-

21. *Latin poets.* Cicero (*De Nat. Deor.*, 2, 18, 29) quotes *caeli palatum* from Ennius, 'the palate of the sky' meaning 'the vault of heaven', the converse of the Greek use of *ouranos* for 'the palate'.

tation of the world in the person of Janus, solely because of the palate (which Janus does not in the least resemble).

Now when they make Janus four-faced and call him the double Janus, this is interpreted in relation to the four parts of the world, as if the world looked at anything outside itself as Janus looks out with all his four faces. Then, if Janus is the world and the world consists of four parts, the image of two-faced Janus is false. Or if it is justified by the fact that the expression 'the East and the West' is generally understood as meaning 'the whole world', are we to take it that when we name the two other parts, North and South, someone is going to talk about a 'double world', in the same way as they call the four-faced god the 'double Janus'? In the case of the two-faced Janus the interpreters found an explanation in reference to the human mouth, regarded as a representation of the world. They have no similar explanation of any kind to offer in the case of the four doors (*januae*) open for entrance and exit. Neptune, to be sure, might come to their aid and supply them with a fish, which has, besides the openings of mouth and throat, the two apertures of the gills on left and right. And yet no soul can escape from futility by any of those numerous doors except the soul that has heard the Truth saying, 'I am the door.'[22]

9. *Concerning the power of Jupiter, and his relation to Janus*

And now I should like our friends to explain what interpretation they want to be put on Jove, who is also called Jupiter.[23] 'He is the god', they say, 'who has power over the causes which effect all that happens in the world.' There is a famous line of Virgil which attests the importance of this responsibility,

> I call him happy
> Who could discern the causes of all things.[24]

But why is Janus placed in front of him? Let us have the reply of the learned and shrewd Varro: 'The reason is that the start of things rests with Janus, but the fulfilment with Jupiter, who is therefore rightly

22. John 10, 9.

23. *Jove-Jupiter.* The root *Iov* for all cases of Jupiter other than the nominative implies a nominative *Iovis*, which occurs in chs. 14, 15 (twice) and ch. 16. It is perhaps significant that in ch. 15 and ch. 16 this form is found where God is identified with the world, which may suggest a traditional formula. *Iovis* (nominative) occurs in lines of Ennius quoted in Apuleius (*De Deo Socr.*, 2, 112) in a list of the 'great gods'. It is used by Apuleius himself in two places (*De Mund.*, 37, 370 and *Met.*, 1, 33, 311).

24. *Georg.*, 2, 490.

held to be the sovereign power. For the fulfilment surpasses the beginning; the beginning has precedence in time, but the fulfilment is superior in dignity.' This would be a sound observation, if the beginnings of processes had been kept distinct from their fulfilment. To set out is a start; to arrive is a fulfilment. To begin a course of study is a start; to understand the teaching is the fulfilment. Similarly, in all spheres, the commencement is the start, the achievement is the fulfilment. We have already dealt with this matter in reference to Janus and Terminus. But the causes which are assigned to Jupiter are efficient causes, not effects; and, in the temporal order, it is utterly impossible that the effects or the start of the effects should precede the cause. What produces an effect always precedes the effect produced. It follows that if the start of processes belongs to Janus, that does not mean that the beginnings are prior to the efficient causes, which are attributed to Jupiter. In fact nothing happens, nothing begins to happen without a precedent efficient cause.

If it is this God – the God who controls all the causes of events, and of all substances, and of all things in nature – whom the people call Jupiter and whom they worship with all those insults and outrageous slanders, they are guilty of greater blasphemy than if they believed in no god at all. Hence it would have been much better for them to have given the name of Jupiter to some other person, someone deserving those degraded and scandalous honours, substituting an idle fiction to be the object of their blasphemies (as a stone, so it is said, was substituted as an offering to Saturn, for him to devour instead of his son). This would have been far better than to represent Jupiter as both the thunderer and an adulterer, the ruler of the universe and an abandoned debauchee, controlling the highest causes of all substances and all things in nature, but not having good motives for his own actions.

Next I ask what place among the gods they assign to this Jupiter, if Janus is the world. Varro has laid it down that the true gods are the Soul of the World and its parts or manifestations. According to this definition nothing else can be a genuine god, in the theory of this school of thinkers. Are they then ready to say that Jupiter is the Soul of the World while Janus is its body, that is, the visible world? If this is what they say, they cannot possibly claim that Janus is a god, since, in their thoughts, it is not the world that is a god, but the Soul of the World and its parts. Varro says quite explicitly that, for him, God is the Soul of the World, and the world itself is God: but just as a wise man, though constituted of body and soul, is called 'wise' in virtue of his soul, so the world is called 'God' because of its soul, although it consists of body and soul. Thus the body of the world, by itself, is not God, but either its soul, or its body and soul taken together (bearing in mind that it is God in virtue of its mind, not of its body). Then if Janus is the world, and Janus is God, is it going to be said that Jupiter, so that he can be God, is some part of Janus? It is more usual to attribute the whole universe to Jupiter; hence the poet says,

> The whole universe
> Is filled with Jupiter.[25]

And so if Jupiter is to be a god and, above all, if he is to be the king of gods, we are bound to identify him with the world, so that he may reign over the other gods who are, according to this theory, parts of himself. It is in this sense that Varro, in the separate book which he wrote *On the Worship of the Gods*, explains some lines of Valerius Soranus.[26] These lines are,

> Almighty Jupiter
> Sovereign of all things, and of all the gods;
> Father and mother of the gods; himself
> The only god and, in himself, all gods.

This is the explanation given in the book. By the male we mean the emitter of the seed, the female being the recipient; so Jupiter is the world, emitting all seeds and receiving them in himself. 'Soranus was right', says Varro, 'in calling Jupiter "father and mother", equally right in calling him "one" and "all". For the world is one, and that one world contains in itself all things.'

10. *The distinction between Janus and Jupiter*

If Janus, then, is the world and Jupiter is the world,[27] and there is only one world, how is it that Janus and Jupiter are two gods? Why do they have separate temples, separate altars, different ceremonies, and dissimilar images? Is it because there is a difference between the principle of origins and the principle of causes, and Janus is the former, Jupiter the latter? Is it then suggested that, if a man has two different powers and accomplishments in two different spheres, it follows from

25. Virg., *Ecl.*, 3, 60.

26. Q. *Valerius Soranus* of Sora, tribune in 82 B.C. was a friend of Varro and Cicero, and the writer of works on philosophy and philology, of which only a few fragments remain.

27. cf. ch. 7; 9.

the diversity of the particular abilities that we should speak of two judges or two craftsmen? Similarly, the one God has power over origins and causes; but are we therefore bound to suppose the existence of two gods, because origins and causes are two different things? If this reasoning is considered sound, then they must say that Jupiter himself is as many gods as they have given him names corresponding to his many powers, since all those many functions which justify those names are distinct. I will enumerate some of them.

11. *The titles of Jupiter, which all refer to one God*

Jupiter is entitled Victor, Invictus, Opitulus, Impulsor, Stator,[28] Centumpeda, Supinalis, Tigillus, Almus, Ruminus – it would be tedious to go through the whole list. These titles have been bestowed on one god for various causes on account of different powers. The existence of many activities in Jupiter does not compel him to turn into an equal number of gods; he is Victor because he always conquers; because he is never conquered he is Invictus. Because he brings help to the needy he is Opitulus; as Impulsor he has power to drive on; as Stator, to halt; as Centumpeda to give stability; as Supinalis, to throw down. Because he holds up and supports the world like a beam of timber he is Tigillus; because he nourishes all things he is Almus. And he is called Ruminus because, by means of *ruma*, the mother's breast, he nourishes all living creatures. Among those functions, we observe, some are important, some trivial; yet one god is reputed to be responsible for both kinds. It seems to me that there is a closer resemblance between causes and beginnings than between supporting the world and giving the breast to animals; yet the difference between cause and beginning was the reason why one world should produce two gods, Janus and Jupiter. For all that, no compulsion was felt to postulate two gods for functions so different in importance and value as the support of the universe and the feeding of animals: the same Jupiter was entitled Tigillus because of the one function, Ruminus on account of the other.

I have no wish to suggest that to offer the breast to sucking animals would be more proper for Juno than for Jupiter, especially because a goddess called Rumina also exists to offer assistance and service in this task. For I am aware that the reply could be that Juno herself is

28. cf. Bk III, 13. The other epithets are not found as titles of Jupiter in classical literature.

identical with Jupiter, according to those lines of Valerius Soranus,[29]

Almighty Jupiter ...
Father and mother of the gods.

Why then is he also called Ruminus, seeing that more diligent inquirers might perhaps discover that he is also identical with this goddess Rumina? It appeared unworthy of the majesty of the gods that in the same ear of grain one divinity should look after the node, another be in charge of the follicle.[30] If this judgement was sound, then how much more unworthy that one of the lowlier activities, the suckling of animals, should engage the attention of two deities, one of them being Jupiter, the universal sovereign, and he has to perform this office with the help not of his wife but of some obscure goddess called Rumina. It must be that he is himself identical with Rumina; perhaps he is Ruminus when concerned with male sucklings, Rumina when in charge of females. I should certainly have said that they would not have wished to give Jupiter a feminine name, had it not been that he is called 'father and mother' in the lines I have quoted, and that I have read that among his other titles he is called Pecunia, and she is a goddess whom we discovered among the diminutive gods, those whom I mentioned in my fourth book.[31] But since both men and women have money, why is he not called Pecunia and Pecunius, on the analogy of Rumina and Ruminus? There is something for them to think about!

12. *Jupiter-Pecunia*

What a brilliant explanation they give for this name! 'He is called Pecunia', says Varro, 'because all things belong to him.' What an exquisite reason for a divine name! It is in fact a degrading insult to give the title of Pecunia (money) to the Being to whom all things belong. For what are all the possessions of men, all man's property or money, in comparison with all things contained in heaven and earth? It is clear that it is avarice which imposed this name on Jupiter, so that the lover of money might imagine that the object of his adoration was no ordinary deity but the sovereign of the universe himself.

Now it would be quite another matter, if he had been called Riches;

29. cf. ch. 9n.
30. *Nodutus* and *Volutina*: cf. Bk IV, 8. *Rumina* occurs in Bk IV, 21.
31. Bk IV, 21; 24.

for riches and money are very different things. We speak of the 'riches' of the wise, the just, the virtuous; they are richer than others because of their virtues, thanks to which they are content with what they have, even when their material resources are straitened. We speak of the 'poverty' of the avaricious who are always yearning for more and always in want; they can have all the money possible, and yet in their abundance they cannot help being in want. And we call the true God himself 'rich', not rich in money, but in his omnipotence. Moneyed men, of course, are called rich; but they are needy in their hearts, if they are greedy: the moneyless are called poor; but if they are wise, they are rich in their hearts.

How ought this theology to stand in the estimation of a wise man, when the king of gods receives the name of something 'which no wise man has ever desired'?[32] If this teaching had any salutary instruction to impart in connection with eternal life, the god who rules the world would much more appropriately be called Wisdom, not Pecunia. For the love of wisdom purifies from the stain of avarice, that is, from the love of money.

13. *The accounts of Saturn and Genius show that both are identified with Jupiter*

But we need say no more about Jupiter, if it is true that the rest of the gods are to be reduced to him: which means that belief in a multiplicity of gods would be left a mere delusion, since Jupiter in himself is all gods, and they are regarded as parts or powers of Jupiter; or else the spiritual force, which Varro and his like suppose to be diffused through all the universe, has received the names of many gods from the different elements which go to make up the mass of the visible world and from the multiple forms of the operations of nature.

What, for example, is Saturn? Varro says, 'He is one of the principal gods, who has dominion over all sowing of seeds.' But according to his exposition of those lines of Valerius Soranus,[33] Jupiter is the world, and he emits all seeds from himself, and receives them into himself. It follows that Jupiter must have dominion over the sowing of seeds.

And what is Genius?[34] 'A god', says Varro, 'who is put in charge

32. Sall., *Cat.*, 11, 3. 33. cf. ch. 9.

34. *Genius*: the spirit presiding over man's birth, and also dwelling with him, like a guardian angel, or in him, giving him the power of generation; hence the

of the generation of things, and has the power of generation'. But do they believe that this power belongs to anyone else except the world, which is addressed with the words, 'Jupiter, father and mother'? Now in another passage Varro says that *genius* is the reasonable soul of the individual, and thus each one has a personal genius, while the corresponding function in respect of the world is fulfilled by the World-Soul, which is God. Here he comes back to the same point; the Soul of the World is believed to be the Universal *Genius*. This is the god whom they call Jupiter. For if every *genius* is God, and the soul of every man is a *genius*,[35] if follows that the soul of every man is God. If they are forced to recoil from such an absurdity, it remains for them to give the name Genius, in this singular and pre-eminent sense, to the god whom they call the Soul of the World, that is, to Jupiter.

14. *The functions of Mercury and Mars*

As for Mercury and Mars, these thinkers have not discovered any way of connecting them with any part of the world, or any of the works of God in the material elements. For that reason they have given them responsibility for the works of men, putting them in charge of speech and of war. But if Mercury has authority over the speech of the gods, then he has dominion over the king of the gods as well, seeing that Jupiter must speak in accordance with the will of Mercury; or at least he has received from him the faculty of speech, which is obviously absurd. If, on the other hand, we are told that it is only the authority over human speech that is attributed to Mercury, it is impossible to believe that Jupiter was willing to condescend to the oversight of the suckling not only of children but even the animals (hence his title Ruminus), while refusing to be concerned with human speech, the faculty which raises men above the level of animals. Thus Jove must be identified with Mercury.

Now it may be said that it is language itself that is Mercury. This is suggested by the interpretation they give of him; for they derive the name Mercury from *medius currens*, 'running in between', because speech 'runs between' men. His name in Greek is Hermes, be-

---

marriage bed is the *lectus genialis*. The notion is somewhat vague and elastic, and St Augustine in ch. 23 seems to identify a man's genius with his soul, or spirit. The *genius* of the Roman Empire was the focus of emperor-worship. A place could have a *genius loci*; and we find mention of the *genius urbis Romae*. The Genius included among the 'select' gods in ch. 2 is perhaps the *genius populi Romani*.

35. cf. Apul., *De Deo Socr.*, 14.

cause speech, or rather, interpretation – which is clearly connected with speech – is called *hermeneia*.[36] The reason why Mercury presides over commerce is that speech is the means of communication between sellers and buyers. The wings on his head and feet symbolize the swift flight of speech through the air; he is called a messenger because it is through speech that thoughts are conveyed. If this is so, and Mercury is language itself, then these interpreters themselves acknowledge that he is not a god. But while they make gods of beings who are not even demons, the prayers they offer to unclean spirits put them into the possession of those who are not gods but demons.

In the same way they failed to discover any element or part of the world for Mars, to be his sphere of operations in nature; and so they appointed him god of war, which is a human activity and not a desirable one. And if Felicity had granted perpetual peace, Mars would be out of employment. Perhaps, on the other hand, Mars is simply identical with war, as Mercury is identical with language. Then it is manifest that he is not a god; and would to heaven it were equally manifest that there could be no such thing as war, to be called, even falsely, a god!

15. *Concerning certain stars, to which the pagans gave the names of their divinities*

It may be that those gods are to be identified with the stars to which their names were given; for there is a star called Mercury, and another called Mars. But there is also a star in the sky called Jupiter; and yet, in their view, Jupiter is the world. There is also a star called Saturn; and yet they assign to Saturn an important responsibility, the charge of all seeds. There is another star, and that the most brilliant of them all, to which they give the name of Venus; and yet they insist that Venus is also the moon. However, this glittering planet is, like the famous golden apple, a subject of contention between Juno and Venus. Some ascribe the morning star to Venus, others to Juno. But, as usual, Venus wins. For the overwhelming majority give the star to Venus, and holders of the contrary opinion are hard to find. How can one help laughing, when they call Jupiter the king of all things, seeing

36. *Mercury*. St Augustine's (or Varro's) derivation is, as usual, fantastic. The name is almost certainly connected with *merx*, *merces*, 'merchandise', as the Augustan philologist, Verrius Flaccus, thought (Festus – epitomata of Verrius Flaccus – *De Verb. Sign.*, 11). *Hermeneia* is of course derived from Hermes.

that his planet is so far outshone in brilliance by that of Venus? For Jupiter's star ought to be as much more brilliant than the others as Jupiter himself is more powerful than the other gods. They reply that this appearance is due to the fact that the star which is reputed less bright is in fact higher and much further away from the earth. But then, if higher rank earns a higher position in the sky, how is it that Saturn is higher than Jupiter? Perhaps the idle fable, which makes Jupiter a king, was not able to reach as far as the stars? And so Saturn has been allowed to keep his royal position in heaven, even though he had not the strength to retain it in his own kingdom, or on the Capitol?[37] Again, why has Janus not received a star? Is it because he is the world, and the world contains all the stars? But Jove also is the world; yet he has a star. Or is is that Janus made the best compromise he could achieve, and settled for all those faces on earth in compensation for not having one star among the constellations?

Furthermore, we assume that it is just because they have stars that Mercury and Mars are considered to be parts of the world, and so can be reckoned as gods – since it is obvious that speech and war are human activities, not parts of the world. Why is it that the Ram, the Bull, the Crab, the Scorpion, and the rest of them, which are counted as celestial signs, consisting not of single stars but each of them made up of a cluster, and which are placed above the planets in the height of heaven where a more regular motion provides the stars with an unvarying course – why is it that they have had no altars established for them, no rites, no temples? Why is it that they have not been given a place, if not among the 'select' gods, at least among what we may call the plebeian deities?

16. *Concerning Apollo, Diana, and the other 'select' gods, reckoned to be parts of the world*

Apollo is held to be the prophet and the healer; yet the pagans were determined to locate him in some part of the world, and so they said that he was the sun. And his sister Diana was the moon and the goddess in charge of roads[38] – hence they insisted that she was a virgin, because a road is unproductive. The reason why these two carry arrows is that those two stars extend their rays from the sky to

37. *Saturn on the Capitol.* Legend said that Saturn was driven out of Crete by Jupiter, and settled on the hill Saturnia, which was later called the Capitol when Jupiter took it over; cf. Bk IV, 23.

38. As *Trivia.*

the earth. Vulcan is supposed to be the fire of the world, Neptune its waters, while Dis pater, that is, Orcus, is the lower, terrestrial part of the world. Liber and Ceres[39] are responsible for seeds, the former in charge of the male, the latter of the female seeds; or else Liber is in command of the liquid part, Ceres of the dry element, in the seeds. And all this evidently refers to the world, that is, to Jupiter, who is called 'father and mother' just because he emits all seeds from himself and receives them all into himself. Sometimes they want to identify Ceres with the Great Mother, and they say that she is nothing other than the earth; and they say the same of Juno, and for that reason they assign to her the secondary causes. Yet it is Jupiter who is called 'father and mother of the gods', because, in their theory, Jove is himself the whole of the world. As for Minerva, they have given her the responsibility for the arts of mankind; but they have not found a star to be her habitation, and so they have identified her with the upper region of the ether, or even with the moon. Vesta also has been considered the greatest of the goddesses, simply because she is the earth,[40] although they believed that they should attribute to her the lighter fire of the world – the fire which is readily available for the use of mankind – and not the violent element, which is the kind of fire which belongs to Vulcan.

Thus the contention is that all those 'select' gods are in fact the world; some represent the whole universe, some the parts of it. Jupiter, for example, is the whole; while Genius, the Great Mother, the Sun and Moon (or rather Apollo and Diana), are parts. Sometimes one god is identified with a number of things, sometimes one thing is represented by a number of gods. Jupiter is an instance of one god standing for a number of things; according to their way of thinking and their way of talking, the whole world is Jupiter, and the sky by itself is Jupiter, and one star by itself is Jupiter. Similarly, Juno is the mistress of secondary causes, and Juno is the air,[41] Juno is the earth, and, if she had triumphed over Venus, Juno would be a star. In the same way, Minerva is the highest region of the ether, and Minerva is also the moon, which is regarded as situated on the lower boundary of the ether. Examples of a number of gods standing for one thing are found in the representation of the world by both Janus and Jupiter, and of the earth by Juno, by the Great Mother, and by Ceres.

39. cf. Bk IV, 11.
40. *Ceres, Vesta*: cf. Bk IV, 10n. *The Great Mother*: cf. Bk VI, 7; Bk II, 4n.
41. cf. Bk IV, 10.

17. *The ambiguities in Varro's theories about the gods*

The examples of interpretation which I have given produce confusion rather than enlightenment. Under the compulsion of their extravagant superstition, these interpreters dart hither and thither; they advance and then retreat – so much so that Varro himself prefers to suspend judgement on every case, rather than make any firm statement. After completing the first of his three last books, which is devoted to the 'certain' gods, he begins the second, on the 'uncertain' gods, with these words:

> I ought not to be blamed for having advanced hesitating opinions about the gods in this book. Anyone who thinks that a clear decision is desirable and possible will make that decision for himself, after hearing what I have to say. For my part, I could more readily be induced to call in doubt what I have said in the first book, than to bring to any firm conclusion what I am going to write in this volume.

Thus he brings uncertainty not only into his book on 'uncertain' gods, but even into that on 'certain' deities.

In the third of these books on 'select' gods he begins with a preface on 'natural' theology, making such points as he thinks necessary, before entering upon the follies and crazy falsehoods of 'civil' theology, where, so far from being guided by the actual truth, he writes under the pressure of tradition. 'In this book', he says,

> I shall be writing about the official divinities of the Roman people, the gods to whom they have dedicated temples, and whom they have distinguished by setting up numerous statues in their honour. But I shall be writing, in the manner of Xenophanes[42] of Colophon, an account of my opinions, not my convictions. For on these subjects men have ideas; only God has knowledge.

And so, as he approaches the subject of religious practices of human institution, all that Varro promises, and that with trepidation, is a discourse on matters where there is neither comprehension nor firm belief – where only doubt and surmise are possible. He was sure of the existence of the world, of the sky and the earth – the sky brilliant with stars, the earth fertile with seeds – and of other things of this kind; he believed, with unshaken intellectual conviction, that all this vast structure of nature is ruled and directed by some invisible force.

42. *Xenophanes* (sixth century) wrote a philosophic poem on Nature of which only fragments survive. He attacked polytheism and anthropomorphic conceptions of deity, and ridiculed those who professed knowledge about divine matters.

But he could have no such confidence in asserting that Janus is identical with the world, or in discovering in what sense Saturn is the father of Jupiter, and at the same time subject to Jupiter's kingly rule, or in making pronouncements on other similar questions.

18. *The most probable reason for the spread of pagan superstition*

The most plausible explanation of all this is the suggestion that the gods were once human beings[43] who received adulation from men who wished to have them as gods. Those men instituted rites and ceremonies in honour of each of their heroes, based on their personalities, their characters, their achievements, and their adventures. These observances gradually won a hold on men's souls (which resemble the demons in their avidity for frivolous entertainment) and attained wide popularity, tricked out as they were by the fictions of the poets and helped by the seductive arts of the deceitful spirits. The supposition that an unfilial son, or a son who was afraid of being killed by his father, had driven his father from the throne is more credible than Varro's interpretation of the story of Saturn – that the explanation of Jupiter's conquest of his father is that the cause (represented by Jupiter) is anterior to the seed (represented by Saturn). If that were the case, Saturn would not have preceded Jupiter; nor would he have been his father. For the cause always precedes the seed; it is never engendered by it. In fact, the attempts to dignify these stories (which are either nonsensical fables or tales of human exploits) by pretended interpretations in terms of natural phenomena, reduce the interpreters to such straits, for all their ingenuity, that we cannot help grieving at the nonsense they also convey.

19. *The rationalizing explanations of the cult of Saturn*

'We are told', says Varro, 'that Saturn had the habit of devouring his offspring. This is because the seed returns to the place from which it is produced. The story that a clod of earth was given to him to devour as a substitute for Jupiter, symbolizes the fact that before the invention of ploughing, the seedlings, after sowing, were covered with soil by hand.' According to that, Saturn ought to be called the earth, not the seed; for it is the earth which, in a way, devours what it has en-

43. Euhemerism, cf. Bk IV, 27n.

gendered, since the seeds are produced from the earth and return to the earth to be taken into it. As for the story of the substitution of a clod of earth, what has that to do with the fact that the seed used to be covered with soil by hand? How can this covering with soil mean that it is not devoured like the others? The explanation assumes that the man who put on the soil removed the seed (as in the fable Saturn was offered the clod, and then Jupiter was removed), whereas in fact the covering of the seed by the soil results in its being devoured more thoroughly. And again, on this showing, Jupiter is the seed, not the cause of the seed, as I said just now. But what can one expect? How can a sensible interpretation be found for such nonsense?

'Saturn has a hook', says Varro, 'on account of agriculture.' To be sure, in Saturn's reign agriculture did not yet exist; and the reason for the ascription of a very early period to Saturn, according to Varro's own interpretation of the stories, is just that primitive man lived on the seeds which the earth produced spontaneously. Perhaps Saturn received his hook after losing his sceptre? In that case he would have been in early times a king with nothing to do, becoming a hard-working labourer in the reign of his son!

Varro goes on to tell us that some peoples used to sacrifice children to Saturn, as did the Carthaginians; others, like the Gauls, used to sacrifice adults. The reason for this practice was that of all seeds the human race is the best. There is no need to waste words on such barbarous folly. Let us instead observe this fact, and take it to heart: that these interpretations have nothing to do with the true God, the living, incorporeal, unchangeable being from whom we must beg the life of eternal happiness; their concern is limited to things material, temporal, subject to change and dissolution.

'The myth of the castration of Heaven (Uranus) by his son, Saturn, stands for the fact that the divine seed belongs to Saturn, not to Heaven.' Varro's interpretation, in so far as it is intelligible at all, depends on the fact that nothing in the sky is produced from seeds. But notice, if Saturn is the son of Heaven, then he is the son of Jupiter; for we have innumerable earnest assurances that Jupiter is identical with the sky. That is the way those theories which do not spring from truth destroy themselves without any help from outside.

Varro says that Saturn was called *Chronos*,[44] a Greek word meaning 'time'; for 'without the passage of time', he says, 'the seed cannot be productive.' Many other things are said about Saturn and they all

44. cf. Bk IV, 10.

have reference to seed. And surely Saturn, with all that power of his, should have been competent to deal with seeds by himself. Then why were other deities brought in, especially Liber and Libera (that is, Ceres)? And when Varro comes to deal with these divinities, he says so much about seeds that he might never have mentioned Saturn.

20. *On the ceremonies of Ceres of Eleusis*

Among the rites of Ceres, the Eleusinian cult[45] is widely known, for it was the most notable religious ceremony held at Athens. Varro offers no interpretation of it, except for a reference to the discovery of corn by Ceres, and to her loss of Proserpina, when Orcus carried her off. He asserts that Proserpina represents the fertility of seeds. When this fertility had failed on one occasion, and the earth was in a mournful state of sterility, the idea grew up that the daughter of Ceres, namely fertility (Proserpina being derived from *proserpere*[46] – 'to come forth'), had been carried off by Orcus and detained in the underworld. This event was solemnized by national mourning. Then fertility was restored; there was an outbreak of rejoicing at the 'return of Proserpina'; and this led to the establishment of these ceremonies. Varro adds that there are many traditional rites in the mysteries of Ceres, all of them relating to the discovery of grain.

21. *The obscenities of the rites of Liber*

Liber[47] is the god whom they have put in command of liquid seeds – not only the liquors derived from fruits, among which wine holds, one may say, the primacy, but also the seeds of animals. The depth of obscenity reached in his ceremonies would take so long to tell that one would be reluctant to embark on the task; but in the face of the arrogant stupidity of the pagans the reluctance can be overcome.

There are so many points that I must omit most of them. But I have

45. *The Eleusinian cult.* The mysteries of Demeter and Persephone seem to have arisen from a local fertility rite connected with the autumn sowing at Eleusis in Attica some twelve miles from Athens. After the union of Eleusis with Athens (about 600 B.C.) this rite somehow developed into a ceremony of initiation, the principal features of which were a procession from Athens to Eleusis, a ceremonial bath of purification in the sea, and some kind of performance in a darkened hall, consisting of 'doings, sayings, and showings'.

46. cf. Bk IV, 8n. 47. cf. Bk IV, 11n; Bk VI, 9.

to mention that Varro tells us about some of the rites of Liber which were celebrated at the crossroads in Italy with such obscene licence that the male organs were made the objects of worship in honour of this divinity. And this was not done in secret, so that some degree of modesty might be retained; it was performed as a public display in an exultation of debauchery. During the festival of Liber this obscene organ was mounted, with great honour, on carts, and exhibited first at the crossroads in the country, and afterwards conveyed to the city. In the town of Lavinium a whole month was consecrated to Liber, during which time everyone used the most indecent language, until the time when that organ was conveyed across the forum and brought to its final resting-place. It was obligatory for the most respected mother of a family to place a crown on this disreputable organ in full view of the public. This was how Liber had to be placated to ensure successful germination of seeds; this was how evil spells had to be averted from the fields. A matron had to be compelled to perform an act in public, which even a harlot ought not to have been allowed to perform in the theatre if there were matrons in the audience.

This was why Saturn was not thought to have sufficient power by himself to look after seeds; it was so that the impure soul might find occasions for multiplying deities, and, being abandoned by the one true God as a just punishment for impurity, and prostituted to numerous false gods in its avidity for even greater impurity, might give the name of sacred rites to those blasphemies and offer itself to crowds of filthy demons for defilement and pollution.

22. *Concerning Neptune, Salacia, and Venilia*

Neptune, we know, had a wife called Salacia,[48] representing, they say, the lower waters of the sea. But why was Venilia[49] added unless it was to multiply the invitations offered to demons by the gratuitous invention of unnecessary ceremonies at the whim of a corrupted soul?

But let us examine the interpretation offered by this splendid theology. It is intended to give an explanation to silence our criticism. 'Venilia', says Varro, 'is the water which comes (*venit*) to the shore: Salacia is the water which returns to the open sea (*salum*).' Why then are there two goddesses? It is the same water which comes up and then

48. cf. Bk IV, 11.

49. Unknown. *Venilia* in Bk IV, 11 appears to be a different deity (cf. n. there).

returns. Here we have again that whimsical lunacy which boils up into a vapour of numerous divinities. The water which comes in and goes back is not duplicated; and yet the human soul makes this idle excuse to invite two demons for its greater defilement. And it is the soul that goes away; and it does not return.

Now I appeal to you, Varro, and to you readers of these works of those great scholars, who plume yourselves on receiving such valuable instruction. Please give your explanation of this point about those two goddesses. I do not ask for an explanation in terms of that eternal and immutable Being who is the only God; merely an explanation in reference to the Soul of the World and its parts, for they, in your eyes, are the true gods. That part of the World-Soul which permeates the sea, you have made into the god Neptune. That, to be sure, is a comparatively tolerable error. But what of the tide which comes in shorewards, and goes out seawards? Are they, on this theory, two parts of the world, or two parts of the Soul of the World? Are any of you so foolish as to think that this makes sense? Why then have they become two goddesses for you? Unless it is that your wise ancestors made arrangements, not that you should be ruled by a plurality of gods, but that you should be possessed by a plurality of those demons who love this kind of nonsense and falsehood? Besides this, how is it that Salacia has lost, according to this explanation, the lower part of the sea, where she was placed under her husband? For just now, in identifying her with the retreating waves, you have put her on the surface. Was she angry when her husband took Venilia as a paramour? Did she therefore exclude him from the upper waters of the sea?

23. *Concerning the earth, which Varro holds to be a deity*

There is, to be sure, only one earth; and we observe it to be full of its own living creatures; but at the same time we see that in itself it is a great body among the natural elements and the lowest part of the universe. Why do they make it out to be a goddess? Because of its fecundity? In that case, have not men a better title to divinity, seeing that they increase its fecundity? And they do this not by a cult, but by cultivation. But, they say, the earth is made divine by a part of the World-Soul which permeates it. But surely the presence of a soul is more obvious in human beings? No one, in fact, questions its presence. Yet men are not held to be gods. Indeed (and here is the pity of it) under the compulsion of an astonishing and miserable deception men are brought beneath the sway of beings who are not gods, who are inferior in worth to human beings; and men are constrained to worship and adore them. Varro himself, in the same treatise on the 'select' gods, asserts that there are three degrees of soul[50] in the whole universe of nature. The first is that which penetrates all living parts of a body; this does not confer sensibility but simply supplies the condition requisite for life; and this power, says Varro, is diffused in our bones, our nails, and our hair, in the same way that in the world in general the trees are nourished and grow, and are, in a certain sense, alive, though without having sensibility. The second degree of soul brings with it sensibility; this power extends to our eyes, our ears, our nostrils, our touch. The third and highest degree of soul is also called mind, and in this intelligence holds pre-eminent place; and intelligence is a faculty denied to all mortal beings except man. It is this part of the World-Soul which, according to Varro, is God; in man he calls it the *genius*.[51] The stones and the earth which we see in the world, which are not permeated by sensibility, are as it were the bones and nails of God, while the sun, the moon, and the stars which we perceive by our senses and which are his means of sensibility, these represent God's senses; the ether is his mind, and its power extends to the stars to make them deities; and the goddess Tellus (Earth) is constituted by that influence which penetrates to the earth through the mediation of the stars; and that which reaches to the sea and the ocean forms the god Neptune.

Such is Varro's account. But now let him leave this reputedly 'natural' theology, to which he turned aside for a rest when wearied by all those circuitous detours. Let him come away, I say, and return to that 'civil' theology. I still want to hold him to this, and this is what I am concerned with all the time. I could argue that if earth and stones are like our bones and nails, then, like them, they are without intelligence, just as they are devoid of sensibility; or, if our bones and nails are alleged to possess intelligence, just because they are part of man who is endowed with intellect even so it is as absurd to speak of those parts of the universe as gods as to speak of our bones and nails as men. But perhaps these are matters for discussion with the philosophers. For the moment I am still concerned with Varro the politician. It may well be that although he gives the impression of having wanted to raise his head for a little while into the freedom, as it were, of 'natural'

50. *The three degrees of the soul* are first distinguished in Aristotle's *De Anima*.

51. cf. ch. 13n.

theology, nevertheless, while still engaged on this book, and supposing himself to be concentrating on it, he has given a backward glance to the previous topic of 'civil' theology, and has made this statement to avert the suspicion that the Romans of old, or other peoples, had no rational justification for the worship of Tellus and Neptune.

What I do say is this: there is only one world; why then does Varro not make one divinity of the part of the World-Soul which permeates the earth, the goddess he calls Tellus? But in that case what will happen to Orcus, the brother of Jupiter and Neptune, who is called Dis Pater? And where will Proserpina be? For she, according to another belief put forward in the same books, represents not the fertility of the earth but the earth's lower part. Now, if they say that a part of the World-Soul, when it permeates the upper part of the earth, makes Dis Pater a god, while it makes Proserpina a deity in penetrating the lower level, what will happen to Tellus? For the whole of what Tellus represented has now been divided into two parts, and assigned to two deities, leaving Tellus as a third, for whom neither a function nor a place can be found. A possible suggestion is that the two gods, Orcus and Proserpina, are together identical with one deity, namely Tellus; and thus there are not three of them, but either the one, or the two others. Yes, but it is three deities that are spoken of, three deities are thought of, three deities are worshipped with their own separate altars, ceremonies, images and priests; and by means of all this, their own deceitful demons join in defiling the prostituted soul.

May we be told what part of the earth is permeated by part of the World-Soul to produce the god Tellumo?[52] 'It is not like that,' says Varro:

> The fact is that one and the same earth possesses a double quality, a masculine and a feminine property. The masculine property produces the seeds; the feminine receives and nurtures them. Thus the name Tellus derives from the feminine property; the name Tellumo from the masculine.

Why then do the pontiffs, as Varro himself informs us, add two further deities and perform divine ceremonies in honour of four gods, Tellus, Tellumo, Altor, and Rusor?[53] We have already touched on the first two. But why the sacrifices to Altor? 'Because', says Varro, 'all that comes to birth is nourished (*aluntur*) from the earth.' And

52. cf. Bk IV, 10.

53. *Altor* and *Rusor* are unknown elsewhere.

Rusor? 'Because', he says, 'everything comes back again (*rursus*) to the same place.'

24. *The titles of the god Tellus, and their meanings*

Since the earth is one entity, this fourfold property should have given rise to four titles, not to four gods. This is what happened to Jupiter and Juno. They have many epithets, but remain single deities, since all those titles describe the multifarious properties connected with a single god or goddess, and the multiplicity of names does not constitute a multiplicity of deities.

The fact is that there comes a time when the vilest of women grow tired of the crowds of lovers they have acquired to gratify their sensuality; and in the same way the debauched soul which has prostituted itself to filthy spirits takes the greatest delight in the multiplication of gods before whom to fall and offer itself for defilement; but in the end comes disgust – Varro himself seems ashamed of this collection of divinities, and would like to have Tellus as a single goddess. 'The Great Mother', he says,

> is another name for the same goddess. She carries a tambour, signifying that she is the earth's disc: and she has towers on her head, to represent the towns; and she is portrayed seated, to show that she remains motionless, while all things move round her. The appointment of *Galli*[54] as her attendants tells us that those who are without seed should devote themselves to the earth, since all seeds are to be found there. Those *Galli* hurl themselves about in her presence: and the lesson of this is that those who cultivate the land should not sit still; there is always something for them to do. The noise of their cymbals stands for the rattling of implements in vigorous use, and for all the noise of agricultural activity: and the cymbals are made of bronze, because that metal was used in ancient agriculture, before the invention of iron. The addition of a lion, unchained and tame, is meant to show that no kind of land is so remote, or so utterly wild, as to be incapable of being brought under cultivation.

Varro goes on to add that the numerous titles and epithets attached to Mother Tellus have lead to the belief in a plurality of deities. 'They think of Tellus', he says, 'under the name of Ops, because the land (*tellus*) is improved by work (*opus*); as Mother, because she is so productive; as Great, because she produces food; as Proserpina, because the crops come forth (*proserpant*)[55] from her; as Vesta because of her

54. cf. Bk II, 7n. 55. cf. Bk IV, 8n.

vestment of vegetation.[56] In this way other goddesses are, with good reason, reduced to Tellus.' If, then, she is a single deity (but, to be sure, she is no such thing, if we have regard for the truth) why go on to make many of her? One goddess may enjoy a number of divine powers; but those are names, not deities. However, Varro is weighed down by the authority of ancient tradition, which causes him to have qualms after uttering this opinion. In fact he adds, 'My theory is not at variance with the traditional view of those goddesses, which considers them a plurality.' How can it help being at variance? There is a vast difference between a single goddess with many titles and a plurality of goddesses. 'But', says Varro, 'it is possible for a thing to be a unity, and yet contain a plurality.' I agree that one man contains a multiplicity; but that does not mean that there is in him a plurality of men. Similarly, a goddess may contain a multiplicity, but that does not entail a plurality of deities. But let them have all they want, in the way of divisions, conflations, multiplications, reduplications and complications.

Such are the noble mysteries of Tellus and the Great Mother, in which everything has reference to mortal seeds and to the pursuit of agriculture. Such is the reference and the purpose of the tambour, the towers, the *Galli*, the frenzied gesticulations, the clashing cymbals, and the fantasy of the lions. Is there any promise here of life eternal? The Great Mother has for servants the mutilated *Galli*, to signify that those who lack seed should devote themselves to the earth. Is that so? Was it not rather the devotion to her service that robbed them of seed? Do they acquire seed by attending on this goddess because they lack it? Or do they rather lose the seed they have by reason of that attendance? Is this interpretation? Or is it deprecation? It is not observed how great is the ascendancy gained by the malign demons. They did not venture to make any great promises in return for those ceremonies; but they were able to exact such cruel sacrifices. If the earth had not been a goddess, men would have laid hands on her in their labour to get seed from her; they would not have laid violent hands on themselves, to rob themselves of seed for her sake. Had she not been a goddess, she would have been made fertile by the hands of others; she would not have compelled men to make themselves sterile by their own hands. In the rites of Liber a respectable matron used to crown the male genitals in front of a crowd of spectators, among whom her husband would be blushing and sweating as he stood there, if there is

56. *Vesta* = Gk. *Hestias*, the hearth, from an Indo-European root *vas* = burn; cf. Bk IV, 10n.

any modesty in men. At marriage celebrations the new bride was bidden to sit on the tool of Priapus. But those are negligible and trivial indecencies compared with that other savage depravity, or depraved savagery. In those devils' rites both sexes were treated with mockery; but neither sex was destroyed by a self-inflicted wound. In the one kind of ceremony there was the fear of an evil spell on the land; in the other the mutilation of the body was no cause for dread. In the one ceremony the modesty of the new bride was dishonoured, but there was no loss of fecundity, or even of virginity; while in the other there was amputation of virility, and the sufferer was neither changed into a woman nor allowed to remain a man.

25. *The explanation of the mutilation of Attis, according to Greek thinkers*

Gallus mutilated himself for love of Attis. But no mention is made of Attis by Varro, nor is any explanation supplied.[57] However, the Greek savants and scholars have by no means kept silence about his wonderful and holy story and its explanation. The renowned philosopher Porphyry[58] tells us that the tale refers to the aspect of the earth in the spring, the loveliest of the seasons. Attis represents the flowers; and the reason for his mutilation is that the flower falls before the fruit. It is thus not the man himself, or the semblance of a man called Attis, but his male parts which were compared to the flower. For when they fell Attis was still alive; or rather they did not fall, nor were they plucked; they were mangled. And the loss of the flower was not followed by any fruit but by sterility. What about the rest of him, all that remained after the mutilation? What is that said to symbolize? What reference is found for it, what interpretation is offered? Perhaps by their vain efforts to find explanations they convince us that the best thing is simply to accept the traditional tale of a castrated man, which has received literary form. Varro had good reason to shrink from such a conclusion, and preferred not to mention the story. He could not have been ignorant of it with all his learning.

57. *Attis* (cf. Bk VI, 7n.) was a foreign divinity (a Phrygian god associated with Cybele) and Varro had no reason to treat of him in his *Roman Antiquities*.

58. *Porphyry* of Tyre (A.D. 233–*c.* 300): a pupil of Plotinus and a leading exponent of Neoplatonism. He wrote an attack on Christianity, *Against the Christians*, which is often mentioned by the Christian Fathers.

26. *The obscene rites of the Great Mother*

The same applies to the effeminates consecrated to the Great Mother, who violate every canon of decency in men and women. They were to be seen until just the other day in the streets and squares of Carthage with their pomaded hair and powdered faces, gliding along with womanish languor, and demanding from the shopkeepers the means of their depraved existence. Varro did not like to make any comment on them; and I do not remember having read anything anywhere about the creatures. Interpretation failed; reason blushed; speech was reduced to silence.

The Great Mother surpassed all the gods, her sons, not by reason of the greatness of her divine power but in the enormity of her wickedness. Even the monstrosity of Janus is nothing to this monster. Janus was merely hideous in his images; the Great Mother displayed hideous cruelty in her ceremonies. He had stone effigies with added members; she had living men with their organs mutilated. This was a degradation which outdid all the carnal excesses of Jupiter himself. He was a great seducer of women; but he only once disgraced heaven with a Ganymede, whereas all those professed and public perverts of hers were a defilement to the earth and an insult to heaven. In this kind of obscene cruelty we might perhaps find Saturn a match for her, or even her superior; for he, the story says, castrated his father. But in the rites of Saturn men could be slain by the hands of others:[59] they were not gelded by their own hands. The poets tell us that Saturn ate his sons (and the 'naturalists' have their chosen interpretation of the myth); history relates that he killed them. But the Romans did not take over the Carthaginian custom of sacrificing their own sons to this god. In contrast, the Great Mother of the gods introduced eunuchs even in the temples of Rome. And she kept up this savage custom, since it was supposed that she increased the virility of the Romans by depriving these men of their manhood.

Compared with this horror, what are the thefts of Mercury, the lechery of Venus, the dissipations and depravities of the rest? We would quote the evidence for these scandals from books, were it not that they are daily rehearsed in song and dance in the theatres. All this fades into nothing compared with this horror, the greatness of which was appropriate only to the Great Mother. This is emphasized by the fact that these stories are alleged to be the fantasies of poets – as

59. cf. ch. 19.

if the poets also invented the idea that they were pleasant and acceptable to the gods! Even supposing that these stories were sung or written as a result of the wanton effrontery of poets, it remains true that their inclusion among divine ceremonies in honour of the gods, at the express bidding and demand of those same divinities, must certainly be charged against the gods; or rather we may say that in this the demons acknowledge themselves for what they are, and impose their deceptions on the unfortunate. However this may be, the notion that the Mother of the gods deserved to be worshipped with the consecration of eunuchs was no invention of the poets. They preferred to shrink from this in horror, rather than make it a subject of their verse.

Is it to these 'select' gods that anyone should be consecrated with a view to a life of blessedness after death? No one consecrated to them could live an honourable life before death, being the victim of such foul superstitions and under the sway of filthy demons. 'But all these myths and ceremonies', says Varro, 'have reference to the world of nature.' He should make sure that they are not related less to natural science than to unnatural vice.[60] But surely anything that can be shown to exist in the world can be referred to the world? As for us, what we are looking for is a soul which puts its trust in true religion and does not worship the world as god, but praises the world as the work of God and for the sake of God. Such a soul, when purified from worldly stains, may come in purity to the God who created the world.

27. *The fantasies of the 'naturalists'. They do not worship true divinity, nor employ the worship appropriate to true divinity*

The 'select' gods certainly gained more renown than the others; but we observe that the result was rather to keep their scandals in view than to shed lustres on their merits. This makes more plausible the supposition that they started as human beings, a tradition found among the historians as well as among the poets. Virgil says,

> Saturn came first, from the Olympian heights
> Etherial, fleeing the assault of Jove,
> A banished exile, throne and kingdom lost.[61]

60. There is here a play on the Latin noun *mundus* (the world) and the adjective *immundus* (impure).

61. *Aen.*, 8, 319f.; cf. ch. 15.

These lines and the following passage are concerned with the same subject, a story which Euhemerus[62] has described in full; and Ennius has translated him into Latin. But this position has been abundantly developed by previous writers in Greek and Latin who have attacked errors of this kind, and I have decided to spend no more time on it.

When I consider the 'naturalistic' explanations by which learned and shrewd scholars attempt to turn these human affairs into divine activities, I see nothing which cannot be referred to temporal activities in this world, to an entity which is material, invisible perhaps, but subject to change. This cannot be the true God. All the same, if the symbolical interpretations employed were at least congruous with the spirit of religion these would be some consolation in the absence of depraved practices and corrupting commandments, even though we would certainly have to regret that such teaching did not proclaim the true God or make him known. But in fact, since it is blasphemy to worship anything, whether material or spiritual, in place of the true God, who alone can bring happiness to the soul in which he dwells, how much more wicked is it to adore such objects of worship in such a way as cannot bring material or spiritual salvation to the worshipper, or win him honour on the human level.

For this reason, if any element of the world, or any created spirit, even if it is neither unclean nor evil, is worshipped with temple, priest, and sacrifice, which are due only to the true God, that is an evil thing – not evil because the vehicles of the worship are evil, but because such vehicles should be employed only in the worship of him to whom such worship and service are due. On the other hand, if anyone should maintain that by means of senseless or even monstrous images, by human sacrifices, by the garlanding of genitals, by the commerce of prostitution, by the amputation and mutilation of sexual organs, by the consecration of effeminates, by the celebration of festivals with spectacles of degraded obscenity – if anyone should maintain that by such means he was worshipping the one true God, the creator of every soul and every material thing; then his sin would consist not in worshipping an unworthy object, but in worshipping the proper object of worship by improper means. As for the man who uses such degraded and infamous means not to worship the true God, the creator of soul and body, but to worship a creature, not necessarily an evil creature but still a creature, whether it be a soul or a material body, or a combination of both, such a man commits a double sin against God; in the first place, he worships, in place of God, a being who is other than

62. cf. Bk IV, 27n.

God; in the second place, his instruments of worship are such as should not be employed in the worship either of God or of any other being.

There is no difficulty in discovering the methods of pagan worship; we can easily see its infamy and degradation. But it would be hard to discover what, or whom, they worship if their own historians did not bear witness that the performances, which they admit to be foully obscene, were offered to powers who demanded such worship with terrible menaces. Hence it is clear, without any ambiguity, that this 'civil' theology has invited wicked demons and unclean spirits to take up residence in those senseless images and by this means to gain possession of the hearts of the stupid.

28. *The inconsistency of Varro's theology*

What success attends the effort of Varro, that shrewdest of scholars, to reduce those gods, by would-be subtle arguments, to the sky and the earth, and give that reference to them all? The attempt is impossible. The gods wriggle out of his clutch; they jump from his hands, slip away, and tumble to the ground. Before speaking of the females, the goddesses that is, he says,

> As I have already said in the first book about places, there are two recognized sources of origin for the gods, the sky and the earth. Hence some gods are called celestial, others terrestrial. I started, earlier on, with the sky, in speaking about Janus whom some have identified with the sky, others with the world.[63] So now I will begin to treat of feminine deities by speaking about Tellus.

I understand the difficulty experienced by an intelligence of such range and quality. A plausible line of argument leads him to see the sky as an active principle, the earth as passive. And so he attributes masculine energy to the former, feminine to the latter; and he fails to realize that the activity in both spheres is the activity of him who created both. Varro uses the same line of interpretation in his previous book, in dealing with the celebrated mysteries of Samothrace.[64]

63. cf. ch. 7; 10.

64. *Samothrace*. The mysteries of the Cabiri, non-Hellenic deities, were probably (like Dionysus) from Phyrgia. The centre of their worship was Samothrace, where rites of initiation were performed at the festival of Cabiria, but their cult was observed on other islands and on the mainland, and it became widespread in the Hellenistic age. Primarily gods of fertility, they were often called the 'Great Gods'; but they also extended their protection to sailors and in later times they were assimilated with the Dioscuri because their functions overlapped in this regard.

He starts by making a solemn undertaking (adopting a kind of religious tone of voice) that he will explain those teachings in writing and convey their meaning to the Samothracians themselves, who do not understand their purport. He says, in fact, that a study of the evidence in Samothrace leads to the conclusion that one of their images represented the sky, another the earth, another the archetypes which Plato called 'ideas'. He urges that Jupiter should be understood as the sky, Juno as the earth, Minerva as the 'ideas'; the sky being the maker, the earth the material, the 'ideas' providing the patterns for creation. I pass over the fact that Plato ascribes such importance to his 'ideas' that, according to him, the sky does not create anything, using them as patterns; in fact it is itself so created. What I want to observe is that, in this book on the 'select' gods, Varro has abandoned his scheme of the three divinities whom he took as embracing the totality of existence. He ascribed masculine deities to the sky, feminine deities to the earth; but among the goddesses he has placed Minerva, whereas earlier he had given her a rank above heaven itself. Furthermore, Neptune, a masculine divinity, is in the sea, which belongs to the earth rather than to the sky, and finally Dis Pater, called *Pluto* in Greek, is a male deity, brother of the other two,[65] and he is traditionally a god of the earth, while he has his wife, Proserpina, in the lower regions. How then can Varro attempt to refer the gods to the sky, the goddesses to the earth? Is there any stability or consistency, any sobriety or precision, in such a line of argument?

This goddess Tellus is then the original goddess, the Great Mother in whose presence rises the obscene, crazy din of those effeminates – those mutilated creatures, gashing themselves and performing their antics.[66] What is the point of calling Janus the head of the gods, and Tellus the head of the goddesses? Superstition makes Janus many-headed, and frenzy makes Tellus addle-pated! Why all this effort to refer all this to the world? Even if the attempt succeeded, no truly religious person worships the world in place of the true God. Anyhow, the facts prove beyond all doubt that the attempt is impossible. They should rather refer all this to dead men and evil demons; and that would be the end of the question.

65. sc. Jupiter and Neptune. 66. cf. ch. 24.

29. *All the attributes ascribed to the world and its parts by 'naturalists' should have been ascribed to the one true God*

In fact, all that is attributed to the world by the theology of those 'select' gods, employing ostensibly 'natural' principles of interpretation, should rather be ascribed, without the slightest trace of blasphemy, to the true God, who made the world, who is the creator of every soul and every material substance. We may put it this way: we worship God, not the sky and the earth, which are the two elements of which this world consists; we do not worship a soul, or souls, diffused through all living beings; we worship God, who made the sky and the earth and everything that exists in them, who made every soul, the souls which simply exist in some manner, without sensibility or reason, and sentient souls as well, and those endowed with intelligence.

30. *The true religion which distinguishes Creator from creature, to avoid worshipping many gods representing the many works of the one source of all*

And now to make a start at running over the works of the one true God. It is those works that have given occasion for the pagans to fashion a multitude of false gods, in attempting to give an ostensibly honourable explanation for their obscene and abominable ceremonies. The God of our worship is he who has created all beings, and ordered the beginning and the end of their existence and their motion. He has in his hands the causes of all that exists; and all those causes are within his knowledge and at his disposition. From him comes the vital force of seeds; he has bestowed the rational soul (or mind) on such living beings as he pleased, and he has given to mankind the faculty and the use of speech. He has imparted the gift of foretelling the future to certain spirits of his choice, and he himself prophesies the future through those whom he chooses; and he uses men at his pleasure to drive away sickness. He also controls the beginning, the progress, and the end even of wars, when mankind needs to be corrected and chastized by such means.

He has created, and he directs, the universal fire, so fierce and violent, to ensure the equilibrium of the natural order in all its vastness. He is creator and regulator of all the waters; he made the sun, the brightest of all material means of light, and gave to it the requisite force and movement. He does not withhold his lordship and power even from the underworld itself. He supplies seed and nourishment, whether dry or liquid, to all living creatures, distributing what is appropriate to the needs of each. He gives to the earth its stability and fertility; he lavishes its fruits upon animals and men. He knows and orders all causes, primary and secondary alike. He determines for the moon the order of its course, and provides the paths, in the sky and on the earth, for changes of position. He has granted to human intelligences, created by himself, the knowledge of the various arts designed to help man to live and to develop his possibilities. He instituted the union of male and female to ensure the propagation of children; he has conferred on human societies the blessing of terrestrial fire, to make life easier for man, giving him the advantages of heat and light.

These are without doubt the works which Varro, shrewdest of scholars, has endeavoured to parcel out among his select gods, by some kind of 'natural' interpretation, whether he took over the principle from elsewhere, or conjured it up from his own imagination. But it is the one true God who is active and operative in all those things, but always acting as God, that is, present everywhere in his totality, free from all spatial confinement, completely untrammelled, absolutely indivisible, utterly unchangeable, and filling heaven and earth with his ubiquitous power which is independent of anything in the natural order. He directs the whole of his creation, while allowing to his creatures the freedom to initiate and accomplish activities which are their own; for although their being completely depends on him, they have a certain independence. He often acts through the medium of his angels, but he is himself the sole source of the angels' blessedness. And so, although he sends angels to men for various purposes, it is from him, not from the angels, that blessings come to men, as they come also to the angels. It is from this one true God that we hope for eternal life.

31. *The special blessings, apart from God's general bounty, enjoyed by the followers of the truth*

Besides the benefits which God lavishes on good and bad alike in accordance with his government of the natural order, about which I have already said something, he has given us a striking proof of his great love, a proof which is the special privilege of the good. We can, to be sure, never give him adequate thanks for our existence, our life, our sight of sky and earth, or our possession of intelligence and reason, which enable us to search for him who created all these things. But there is more than this. When we were overwhelmed by the load of our sins, when we had turned away from the contemplation of his light and been blinded by our love of darkness, that is, of wickedness, even then he did not abandon us. He sent to us his Word, who is his only Son, who was born and who suffered in the flesh which he assumed for our sake – so that we might know the value God placed on mankind, and might be purified from all our sins by that unique sacrifice, and so that, when love has been diffused in our hearts by his Spirit, and when all difficulties have been surmounted, we may come to eternal rest and to the ineffable sweetness of the contemplation of God. In view of all that, what heart or what tongue would claim to be competent to give him thanks?

32. *The mystery of Christ's redemption was not absent in any previous era, but it was made known under different symbols*

This mystery of eternal life has been made known by the ministry of angels from the very beginning of the human race. It was revealed to those who were fit to receive the knowledge by means of signs and symbols appropriate to the times. Later, the Hebrew people was gathered and united in a kind of community designed to perform this sacred function of revelation. In that people the future course of events, from the coming of Christ to the present day, and even beyond, was prophesied through the agency of some who realized, and some who did not realize, what they were doing. In the course of time, this people was scattered among the nations to bear witness to the Scriptures, which foretold the coming salvation in Christ. For not only all the prophesies contained in words, not only all the precepts for the conduct of life which shape men's character and their piety and are contained in the Scriptures, but also the ceremonies, the priesthoods, the tabernacle or the temple, the altars, the sacrifices, the sacred rites, the festal days, and everything which is concerned with the homage due to God (the Greeks call it *latreia*)[67] – all these were symbols and predictions that find their fulfilment in Christ, so as to give eternal life to those who believe. We believe that they have been fulfilled; we observe that they are being fulfilled; we are convinced that they will go on being fulfilled.

67. cf. Bk v, 15 and Bk x, 1.

33. *Only the Christian religion could have exposed the deceit of the malignant spirits*

This religion, the one true religion, had the power to prove that the gods of the nations are unclean demons. Those demons seized the chance offered by the souls of the dead, or disguised themselves as creatures of this world, in their desire to be reputed gods; in their arrogance and impurity they took delight in supposed divine honours, a medley of infamy and obscenity, and were full of resentment when human souls were converted to the true God. Man is set free from their monstrous and blasphemous domination when he believes in him who achieved his resurrection by the example of a humility as great as the pride which brought about the fall of the demons.

In this category are found not only those gods about whom we have already said a great deal, and many other similar deities of other nations and other lands, but also those of whom we have been treating recently, the 'select' divinities, chosen to form a kind of senate of the gods. In sober truth they are selected rather for the notoriety of their scandals than for the eminence of their virtues! Varro does his best to explain their ceremonies by supposing a reference to the system of nature, in an effort to lend respectability to obscene activities. But he fails to find a way to square his theory with the facts and give it any consistency. The truth is that the actual motives for these ceremonies are not what he thinks them to be – or rather what he would like them to be thought to be. If there had been motives of this kind, or any similar reasons, then in spite of their having no connection with the true God or with eternal life (which is the essential aim in religion), they might have allowed some kind of explanation relating to the natural order, which would have mitigated the offensiveness of obscenities and absurdities in religious rites whose meaning was misunderstood. Varro has made a similar attempt in the case of some of the fables performed in the theatre, and some of the mysteries enacted in the temples. But the result has been not to justify the theatre by showing its resemblance to the temple, but to condemn the temple by comparing it with the theatre. All the same, he has tried his hardest to offer a supposed explanation from the natural order and so to soothe feelings which had been scandalized by those abominations.

34. *The burning of Numa's books, at the senate's order, to prevent the divulging of the reasons for pagan rites*

In contrast we find (as the learned Varro himself revealed) that the reason for the ceremonies advanced in the books of Numa Pompilius proved quite intolerable. Not merely were they considered unfit to be divulged by being read to the devout; it was even thought improper to preserve them in the obscurity of a written text. I am now going to reveal what I promised, in the third volume of this work,[68] to mention in the appropriate place. Here is a passage, again from Varro, in his book *On the Worship of the Gods:*

> A man named Terentius had a farm near the Janiculum. His ploughman was driving his plough near the tomb of Numa Pompilius when he turned up the books of that author which dealt with the reasons for the established ceremonies of religion. He took them to the city and handed them to the praetor. The praetor took a look at the opening passages, and then reported the find to the senate, as a matter of great importance. When the leading senators had read some of the reasons given by Numa for various religious practices, the senate approved the action of the deceased king, and, as pious conscript fathers, decreed that the praetor should burn those books.[69]

Anyone is entitled to his own opinion; equally, any distinguished defender of such terrible impiety is entitled to say whatever a wrong-headed love of argument may put into his head. For my part, I am content to point out that explanations of the religious ceremonies offered by King Pompilius, the founder of the Roman rites, were not fit to be divulged to the Roman people, or the senate, or even to the priests, and that Numa Pompilius himself, led on by an unlawful curiosity, had discovered certain secrets of the demons which he himself committed to writing to assist his memory. But, although he was king and had no reason to fear any man, he did not venture to pass on the information to anyone; and yet he could not bring himself to suppress it by erasing or destroying the manuscript in some way. He did not want anyone to know, for he shrank from passing on a lesson in corruption; yet he dreaded laying violent hands upon the document for fear of incurring the demons' wrath. And so he buried the books in what he thought would be a safe spot, never imagining that a plough could come so near his tomb. The senate, for its part, recoiled from the prospect of condemning their ancestral religion, and therefore felt obliged to approve of Numa's action; but the fathers decided that the books were so dangerous that they could not order them to be re-interred; for they feared that human curiosity would be all the more keen to search for something of which a glimpse had now been afforded. And so they ordered the outrageous documents to be consigned to the flames, for they believed it essential that those cere-

68. Bk III, 9.   69. Liv., 40, 29; Plut., *Num.*, 22; Plin., 13, 13, 84ff.

monies should continue, and they deemed it more tolerable that the community should remain deluded, in ignorance of the reasons for those ceremonies, than that it should be distressed by learning the truth about them.

35. *How Numa was fooled by hydromancy and a vision of demons*

None of God's prophets, or of his holy angels, was ever sent to Numa. But he was constrained to indulge in hydromancy, in order to see reflected in water the forms of the gods, or rather the conjuring tricks of demons, and to learn from them what he ought to establish and observe in the way of religious ceremonies. Our friend Varro alleges that this type of divination was imported from Persia and he mentions that Numa himself employed it, as the philosopher Pythagoras also did at a later date. Varro also tells us that if blood is used one may also consult the dwellers in the underworld, and that the Greek term for this is *necromancy*. Whether it be called hydromancy or necromancy, the practice has the same object: to obtain a supposed divination from the dead; and by what arts this end is achieved is their own affair. I am not concerned to assert that even before the coming of our Saviour those practices were generally forbidden by law even in pagan communities and were punished with the greatest severity. I am not concerned to assert this; it may well be that such practices were permitted at that time.[70] However that may be, it was by these arts that Numa learnt about those ceremonies, the practices of which he divulged while burying the theory, being himself so afraid of what he had discovered. And when the books giving the theoretical explanations came to light the senate had them burnt. Why then does Varro offer us other explanations of some sort or other, supposedly taken from nature? If it had been explanations of this kind that were contained in those books, they certainly would not have put them to the flames. Otherwise the conscript fathers would have burned the books which Varro published and dedicated to Caesar, the pontiff.

It was the fact that Numa had to draw off (*egerere*), or convey some water for the conduct of his hydromantic operations, that led to the story of his marriage to the nymph *Egeria*, as Varro explains in the afore-mentioned book. This is the way that facts are turned into fables

70. *Such practices were permitted.* We have no record of legislation against magical practices as such until the time of Diocletian, whose laws were reinforced by edicts of Constantine forbidding all nocturnal ceremonies and all forms of divination concerned with individuals.

by the addition of a sprinkling of untruth. Thus it was by means of hydromancy that this king of Rome, with his insatiable curiosity, received the information both about the rites, which is contained in the books of the pontiffs, and about their causes; but this latter he wished to keep to himself. And so he wrote about the causes separately, and in a way put them to death when he died, taking care that they should be withdrawn from men's knowledge and buried.

Therefore it must have been either that the passions of demons described in the book were so bestial and degraded that their revelation would make the whole of 'civil' theology abominable in the eyes of such men as had undertaken so many shameful practices in the conduct of religious rites, or else that those 'gods' were shown up as being merely dead men, and that in the course of ages a belief had grown up among almost all people that they were immortal gods. For the demons delighted in such ceremonies and, by supplying the evidence of illusory miracles, they ensured belief in the 'divinity' of the dead men and then substituted themselves as the objects of worship. But the inscrutable providence of the true God ensured that the demons should be won over by those hydromantic arts and should be allowed to reveal those secrets to their friend Pompilius, and yet that they should not be allowed to warn him to burn the evidence – and not to bury it – when at the point of death. They were not able to prevent the knowledge coming to light either by stopping the plough, which turned up the books, or by stopping Varro's pen, the instrument by which the whole story has been transmitted to this present age. For they can only act within the limits allowed them; and they are given liberty of action by the profound and just judgement of God most high, in accordance with the deserts of men, some of whom rightly endure affliction, but no more, at the hands of those demons, while others are, with justice, deluded by them, and brought under their sway. How dangerous those writings were judged to be, and how remote from the worship of genuine divinity, can be realized from the fact that the senate chose to burn what Pompilius had hidden rather than to be prompted by the fear which prevented him from daring to take this step.

Anyone may seek life eternal by means of such rites if he has no desire for a life of true religion even in this present world. But if a man spurns any association with malignant demons, he must not let himself be frightened by the superstitions with which they are worshipped; let him acknowledge the true religion, by which the demons are unmasked and overcome.

BOOK VIII

1. *'Natural' theology is to be discussed with the most eminent philosophers*

OUR present subject demands much more concentrated attention than was needed for the solution and explanation of the questions raised in the earlier books. We shall be treating of 'natural' theology, which is a different matter from 'fabulous' or from 'civil' theology, the theology of the theatre and that of the city; the former of those makes great play with the scandals of the gods, while the latter reveals their even more scandalous desires, showing them to be malignant demons rather than gods. But in discussing 'natural' theology we shall have to cross swords not with the man in the street, but with philosophers; and that name means that they profess to be 'lovers of wisdom'.

Now if wisdom is identical with God, by whom all things were made, as we are assured by divine authority[1] and divine truth, then the true philosopher is the lover of God. But the thing designated by the name is not found in all those who boast of the name. Because men call themselves philosophers it does not follow that they are lovers of true wisdom. In fact we have to choose some, from those whose opinions we have been able to discover from their writings, with whom we may discuss the subject on a reasonable level.

It is not my aim, in this present work, to refute all the baseless opinions of all the philosophers, but only those appertaining to theology – and I take this Greek word to signify reasoning or discussion about the Divinity. And I shall not deal with all the theological speculation of philosophers, but confine myself to those thinkers who, while admitting the existence of a Divinity and his concern for human affairs, do not consider that the worship of one unchangeable God is sufficient for the attainment of a life of blessedness even after death, but suppose that for this end many gods are to be worshipped, gods who were created and established by him. Such philosophers certainly go far beyond Varro's ideas and come much nearer to the truth. For Varro could extend his 'natural' theology as far as the visible world, or the World-Soul, but no further. But these thinkers acknow-

1. cf. Wisd., 7, 24ff.

ledge a God who transcends any kind of soul, being the maker not only of this visible world – heaven and earth, in the familiar phrase – but also of every soul whatsoever, a God who gives blessedness to the rational and intelligent soul – the class to which the human soul belongs – by giving it a share in his unchangeable and immaterial light. Those philosophers are called Platonists, a name derived from their master Plato, as is well known to those who have even a superficial acquaintance with these ideas. I shall touch briefly on Plato, saying as much as I think essential for the present discussion. But first I shall mention those who preceded him in this branch of study.

2. *The Italian and Ionian schools of philosophy and their founders*

As far as Greek literature is concerned (and the Greek language has the highest international reputation) there is a tradition of two types of philosophy: the Italian, deriving from the part of Italy which used to be called Magna Graecia, and the Ionian, which flourished in the countries still called by the name of Greece. The Italian school had as its founder Pythagoras of Samos,[2] who is credited with the coinage of the actual name of 'philosophy'. Before his time the title of 'sages' was given to those who stood out from the rest of mankind by reason of some kind of quality of life which merited praise. But when Pythagoras was asked about his profession, he replied that he was a 'philosopher', that is, a devotee, or lover of wisdom; it seemed to him to be most presumptuous to claim to be a 'sage'. The originator of the Ionian school was Thales of Miletus.[3] He was one of the 'Seven Sages'; but the other six were distinguished merely by their kind of life and by certain practical rules designed to promote the good life; Thales, for his part, took steps to ensure a succession of disciples, and after his researches into natural science he committed his findings to writing, and thus won renown. His most admired achievement was

2. cf. Bk VI, 5n.

3. *Thales*, born *c.* 624 B.C. As a statesman he helped to organize Ionian resistance to Persia. He is reputed to have foretold the solar eclipse of 23 May 585, the day of the battle of the Halys, and to have introduced to Greece Egyptian mensuration. His cosmological speculations make him the father of natural science. Water, in his theory, is the fundamental and eternal substance from which all things are derived, and to which they return. His works are not extant.

the ability to predict solar and lunar eclipses, thanks to his grasp of astronomical calculations. His theory was that water is the origin of all things, and out of water issued all the elements of the world and the world itself and all that is produced in it. But he did not ascribe the oversight of this work of creation, which strikes us with wonder when we contemplate the universe, to any operation of a Divine Intelligence.

Thales was succeeded by Anaximander,[4] one of his pupils, and he changed his master's conception of the physical universe. He did not derive everything from a single element as Thales had derived everything from water; Anaximander held that each thing has its own special source. These individual sources he believed to be infinite in number, and they give rise to an infinity of worlds with all that is produced in them. In his theory those worlds alternately disintegrate and are reborn after as long a duration as each is able to attain. Anaximander, like his master, gave no place to a Divine Intelligence in those operations of nature.

He left behind him a successor in the person of his disciple Anaximenes,[5] who ascribed the causes of all things to the infinite air. He did not deny the existence of gods, nor did he refrain from speaking of them; yet he did not believe that they created the air, but that they themselves derived their origin from it. His pupil, Anaxagoras,[6] asserted his belief that the author of all the visible world is a Divine Mind working on an infinite matter, which consists of the mutually similar particles, which make up the whole universe, the individual

4. *Anaximander* of Miletus (b. 610 B.C.), author of the first Greek prose treatise. In his theory the source of all things is 'the Infinite', an indefinite and unlimited substance capable of modification into the various forms of matter. St Augustine seems to have misunderstood this, perhaps by a confusion with Anaxagoras (see n. 6) but he is right about Anaximander's teachings of innumerable worlds. Anaximander seems to have been the first to hold that the earth is spherical, thus revolutionizing astronomy. He is also credited with the introduction of the sundial into Greece, and with the drawing of the first map of the world.

5. *Anaximenes* of Miletus (*fl. c.* 500 B.C.), taught that air is rarefied into fire, condensed into cloud, water, earth, stone. The earth is flat (a retrogression in astronomy) and the heavenly bodies are flakes of fire exhaled from the earth.

6. *Anaxagoras* of Clazomenae (*c.* 500–*c.* 430 B.C.), teacher and friend of Pericles. Accounts of his teaching vary, but St Augustine seems right on the fundamental point, a radical pluralism of an infinitely complex matter, derived from an infinity of 'seeds', homogeneous for each distinct substance. The universe is controlled by a Supreme Intelligence, independent of matter, and in this he is perhaps the originator of the mind-matter dualism. Another 'flat-earther'.

things being constituted by their own special particles, but through the creative activity of the Divine Mind. Another pupil of Anaximines was Diogenes.[7] He also maintained that air is the primal matter, from which all things are created. But he believed that the air participates in Divine Reason, without which nothing could issue from it.

The successor to Anaxagoras was his disciple Archelaus.[8] He also held that the universe is constituted by mutually similar particles which make up all the particular things; but he asserted the presence of a Divine Intelligence in them, believing that this intelligence is the active force in the universe, operating by conjoining and separating the 'eternal bodies', that is, the particles.

Socrates is alleged to have been a disciple of Archelaus; and this brief recapitulation is designed to lead up to him.

3. *The teaching of Socrates*

Socrates is recorded as the first to turn the whole of philosophy towards the improvement and regulation of morality. All his predecessors had concentrated their attention on the study of physics, that is, on natural science. It is, in my view, impossible to decide for certain whether Socrates was led to take this course by the boredom induced by obscure and inconclusive subjects, which suggested that he should turn his attention to an inquiry offering greater clarity and certainty – the question of the necessary conditions for happiness, the goal of sleepless and laborious efforts of all philosophers – or whether, according to the more favourable interpretation of some expositors, he did not wish men's minds to seek to invade the sphere of the divine, when they were polluted by earthly passions.

He saw that man had been trying to discover the causes of the universe, and he believed that the universe had its first and supreme cause in nothing but the will of the one supreme God; hence he thought that the causation of the universe could be grasped only by a purified intelligence. That is why he thought it essential to insist on the need to cleanse one's life by accepting a high moral standard, so

7. *Diogenes* of Appollonia (*fl. c.* 440 B.C.) revived the teaching of Anaximenes (he can hardly have been a pupil) about air and its rarefaction and condensation. He made important contributions to physiology. In astronomy he followed Anaximenes and Anaxagoras.

8. *Archelaus* (*fl.* fifth century) seems to have combined the 'seeds' of Anaxagoras with the 'air' of Anaximenes and Diogenes.

that the soul should be relieved of the weight of the lust that held it down, and then by its natural vigour should rise up to the sphere of the eternal and behold, thanks to its pure intelligence, the essence of the immaterial and unchangeable light where dwell the causes of all created things in undisturbed stability. There is no doubt about the remarkable charm and the shrewd urbanity with which he examined and exposed the ignorant stupidity of those who fancied they possessed some knowledge about ethical questions – to which he had applied his whole mental effort, although confessing his ignorance, or concealing his knowledge of the subject. The result was that he aroused a great deal of enmity, and was condemned to death on a trumped-up charge. But the same Athenian community which had publicly condemned him later honoured him with official mourning. The public indignation was so turned against his two accusers that one of them fell a victim to the violence of the mob, while the other only escaped a similar fate by a voluntary and perpetual exile.

Thanks to the renown of his life and his death, Socrates left behind him a large body of followers of his philosophy, who rivalled each other in their enthusiastic application to discussions of ethical questions which give rise to the problem of the Highest Good, the necessary condition of human happiness. The nature of this *Summum Bonum* did not emerge clearly from the discussions of Socrates, his method being to sift every question by advancing hypotheses and then overthrowing them. And so everyone took from him what he fancied, and set up whatever agreed with his own ideas as the Final Good (the Final Good meaning that whose attainment ensures man's happiness). Such were the differences of opinion about the Final Good held by the Socratics that (though it is scarcely credible, in the disciples of a single master), some, like Aristippus, held that pleasure is the *Summum Bonum*; others, like Antisthenes, found it in virtue;[9] others had their varying opinions, and it would be tedious to enumerate them.

9. *Aristippus* of Cyrene, founder of the Cyrenaic school, was probably *not* the companion of Socrates, but the grandson of that Aristippus. He taught that immediate pleasure was the only end of action; but he seems to have distinguished between pleasures, since some ultimately cause pain. Man must be selective about his pleasures; and since this involves self-control, we find an approach here to the teaching of Epicurus (cf. Bk XIV, 2n.). *Antisthenes* (*fl* 400 B.C.); pupil of Socrates. The reputed founder of the Cynic school (cf. Bk XIV, 20n.), he taught that virtue, and resulting happiness, depended on freedom from wants and desires.

4. *Plato, the chief disciple of Socrates. His division of philosophy into three parts*

Among the disciples of Socrates it was Plato who deservedly achieved the most outstanding reputation; and he quite overshadowed all the rest. Plato was an Athenian, born in a family which stood high in the community. He far out-distanced his fellow-students in his remarkable natural gifts; yet he decided that his own ability, aided by the teaching of Socrates, was not enough to bring his philosophy to perfection. And so he travelled far and wide, wherever he was drawn by any teacher's reputation for philosophical insight. Thus it was that he went to Egypt to acquire all the highly prized teaching given there, and from thence passed on to that part of Italy where the Pythagoreans were in great renown. There he attended the lectures of the most eminent teachers and readily attained a grasp of the philosophy which was then enjoying its heyday in Italy.

He was devoted to his master Socrates with singular affection, and therefore even put into his mouth in almost all his discourses the ideas he himself had learnt from others, or those which he owed to his own intelligent perception, tempering them with Socrates' charm and moral earnestness. The study of philosophy is conducted along two lines, one concerned with action, the other with pure thought – hence they may be called practical and speculative philosophy, the former dealing with the conduct of life and the establishment of moral standards, the latter concerned with the theory of causation and the nature of absolute truth. Socrates is the type of excellence in practical wisdom, while Pythagoras concentrated on the contemplative, for which he was equipped by his intellectual power. It was Plato's great claim to fame that he brought philosophy to its perfection by joining together these two strands. He then divided philosophy into three parts: moral philosophy, which particularly relates to action; natural philosophy, devoted to speculation; and rational philosophy, which distinguishes truth from falsehood. This last is essential to both the others; but it is speculation which has a special claim to insight into the truth. Thus it is that this threefold division is not inconsistent with the distinction which recognizes the whole field of philosophical inquiry as consisting of active and speculative reasoning. However, Plato's own thought in and about these three separate divisions; that is, how he defined (by process of knowledge or by the intuition of faith), the end of all action, where he located the cause of all phenomena, and where he found the illumination of all reasoning processes;

these are matters which, in my judgement, it would take too long to discuss in detail, and I do not think one ought to make any unsubstantiated allegations on the subject. The fact is that Plato makes a point of preserving the manner of his master Socrates, whom he introduces as a disputant in his books. It is well known that Socrates was in the habit of concealing his knowledge, or his beliefs; and Plato approved of that habit. The result is that it is not easy to discover his own opinion, even on important matters. For all that, there are some points met with in reading Plato's works, whether his own statements, or the remarks of others recorded by him, which I ought to mention and to include in this work. Sometimes these quotations support the true religion, which our faith has received and now defends; sometimes they seem to show him in opposition to it. They are passages concerning the question of the divine unity or plurality with reference to the life after death, which is the life of true blessedness.

There are thinkers who have rightly recognized Plato's pre-eminence over the pagan philosophers and have won praise for the penetration and accuracy of their judgement, and enjoy a widespread reputation as his followers. It may be that they have some such conception of God as to find in him the cause of existence, the principle of reason, and the rule of life. Those three things, it will be seen, correspond to the three divisions of philosophy: natural, rational, and moral. For if man has been so created as to attain, through the special excellence in man's being, to that excellence which is superior to all other things, that is, to the one true God of supreme goodness, without whom no being exists, no teaching instructs, no experience profits, then we should seek him in whom for us all things are held together, we should find him in whom for us all things are certain, we should love him, in whom is found all goodness.

5. *Theological questions are to be discussed with the Platonists rather than with any other philosophers, whose opinions must be counted inferior*

If Plato says that the wise man is the man who imitates, knows and loves this God, and that participation in this God brings man happiness, what need is there to examine the other philosophers? There are none who come nearer to us than the Platonists.[10] Platonism

10. *None nearer to us than the Platonists*: cf. *De Ver. Rel.*, 7, 'If these men (viz. the Platonists) could have had this life over again with us.... They would have become Christians, with the change of a few words and statements.' Min-

must take pride of place over 'fabulous' theology, with its titillation of impious minds by rehearsing the scandals of the gods, and over 'civil' theology, where unclean demons, posing as gods, have seduced the crowds who are wedded to earthly joys, and have desired to make human errors serve as divine honours for themselves; where those demons arouse in their worshippers an interest in degraded filth, to stimulate them to watch the representation of their scandals on the stage, as if it were an act of worship; and where the spectators present a spectacle even more delightful for those false gods; where any respectable performance in the temples is defiled by its connection with the obscenities of the theatre, and all the depravities in the theatre seem praiseworthy by comparison with the infamies conducted in the temples.

Platonism must be held superior to the interpretations produced by Varro, in which he tried to refer those ceremonies to sky and earth and the seeds and activities of life in this world; those rites have no such significance as he tried to read into them and the facts lent no support to his attempt; and even had the explanations been true, the rational soul could not find it right to worship as its God anything which is below itself in the order of nature, or to put above itself, as gods, things which the true God has put below it.

The same is true of the genuine revelations about the meaning of those cults which Numa Pompilius took care to conceal by having them buried with him,[11] which were turned up by a plough, and then were burnt by order of the senate. To this class also belong (and this has to be said to prevent any harsh suspicions about Numa) the revelations which Alexander of Macedon, writing to his mother, says that he received from a high priest of the Egyptian religion, named Leo.[12] According to this, not only Picus, Faunus, Aeneas, and Romulus, not only Hercules, Aesculapius, Liber (son of Semele), the two sons of Tyndarus, and other deified mortals, but even 'the gods of the great nations' to whom Cicero seems to be alluding (without mentioning names) in his *Tusculans*,[13] namely, Jupiter, Juno, Saturn, Vulcan, Vesta, and all those others, whom Varro tries to identify with the parts, or elements, of the universe – all these, according to

---

ucius Felix says much the same in *Octavius*, ch. 21; and Clement of Alexandria (*Strom.*, 1, 21) quotes Numenius of Apamea: 'What, after all, is Plato but Moses in Attic Greek?'

11. cf. Bk VII, 34. 12. cf. ch. 27; Bk XII, 11; Plut., *Alex.*, 27.

13. *Tusc. Disp.*, 1, 13, 29.

this revelation, were originally human beings. The high priest was so afraid at having revealed those 'mysteries' that he begged Alexander to make sure that the letter to his mother, conveying this information, should be burnt to ashes.

The teaching of both these theologies, the 'fabulous' and the 'civil', must yield place to the doctrine of the Platonists; for the Platonists assert that the true God is the author of the universe, the source of the light of truth, and the bestower of happiness. And the other philosophers also must yield to those great men who recognize so great a God – I mean those other philosophers whose minds were so subservient to the body they conceived only of corporeal origins for all natural phenomena, Thales finding it in water, Anaximenes in air, the Stoics in fire, Epicurus in the atoms, that is, in infinitesimal material particles, indivisible and imperceptible;[14] and there are all the other thinkers, whom it is unnecessary to enumerate, who have maintained that the cause and origin of the universe is to be found in material bodies, simple or compound, inanimate or animate, but still material bodies. Some of them believed, like the Epicureans, that living things could be produced by inanimate things. Others supposed that a living being is the source both of living things and of things without life; but still they held that bodies have their origin in a material body. The Stoics, for example, believed that fire, one of the four elements which constitute the visible universe, is endowed with life and wisdom, and is the creator of the universe and of all its contents; that fire, in fact, is actually God.

These thinkers and their like could not conceive of anything beyond the fantasies suggested by imagination, circumscribed by the bodily senses. They had, to be sure, something within themselves which they did not see; they formed a mental picture of what they had seen outside themselves, even when they did not see it any longer but merely thought of it. Now when a material thing is thus seen in the mind's eye, it is no longer a material object but the likeness of such an object; and the faculty which perceives this likeness in the mind is neither a material body, nor the likeness of a physical object; and the faculty which judges its beauty or ugliness is certainly superior to the image on which it passes judgement. This faculty is the human intellect, the rational constituent in the soul of man, and that, without

14. *Epicurus* (341–270 B.C.) accepted the atomic theory of Leucippus and Democritus (*fl. c.* 420 B.C.).

Stoics held that the universe, at the end of each cycle (the series of which is infinite) is dissolved into the divine fire.

any doubt, is not a material object, if it is true that the image of the object, when it is seen and judged in the mind of a thinking man, is not a material object. Then it cannot be earth, or water, or air, or fire; not one of the four elements, as they are called, of which the visible material world is constituted. But if our mind is not a material object, how can God, the creator of the mind, be himself a material thing?

So, then, those thinkers must rank below the Platonists, as we have said. And so must those who would blush to assert that God is material, but suppose him to be of the same nature as the mind of man. They are not worried by the excessive mutability of the human soul, a mutability which it would be blasphemous to ascribe to the divine nature. They retort, 'It is the body that changes the nature of the soul; in itself the soul is immutable.' They might as well say, 'It is an external material object which wounds the flesh: in itself the flesh is invulnerable.' Nothing at all can change the immutable; what can be changed by an external object is susceptible of change, and cannot properly be called immutable.

6. The Platonist conception of natural philosophy

These philosophers, as we have seen, have been raised above the rest by a glorious reputation they so thoroughly deserve; and they recognized that no material object can be God; for that reason they raised their eyes above all material objects in their search for God. They realized that nothing changeable can be the supreme God; and therefore in their search for the supreme God, they raised their eyes above all mutable souls and spirits. They saw also that in every mutable being the form which determines its being, its mode of being and its nature, can only come from him who truly *is*, because he exists immutably. It follows that the whole material universe, its shapes, qualities, its ordered motions, its elements disposed throughout its whole extent, stretching from heaven to earth, together with all the bodies contained within them; and all life, whether that which merely nourishes and maintains existence, as in the trees, or that which has sensibility as well, as in the animals; or that which has all this, and intelligence besides, as in human beings; or that life which needs no support in the way of nourishment, but maintains existence, and has feeling and intelligence, as in the case of angels – all these alike could come into being only through him who simply *is*. For him existence is not something different from life, as if he could exist without living; nor is life something other than intelligence, as if he could live without understanding; nor understanding something other than happiness, as if he could understand without being happy. For him, to exist is the same as to live, to understand, to be happy.

It is because of this immutability and this simplicity that the Platonists realized that God is the creator from whom all other beings derive, while he is himself uncreated and underivative. They observed that whatever exists is either matter or life, and that life is superior to matter, that the form of matter is accessible to sense, that the form of life is accessible to intelligence. They therefore preferred the 'intelligible' to the 'sensible'. By 'sensible' we mean that which can be apprehended by bodily sight and touch, by 'intelligible' that which can be recognized by the mind's eye. Physical beauty, whether of an immobile object – for instance, the outline of a shape – or of movement – as in the case of a melody – can be appreciated only by the mind. This would be quite impossible, if this 'idea' of beauty were not found in the mind in a more perfect form, without volume or mass, without vocal sound, and independent of space and time. But even here, if this 'idea' of beauty were not subject to change, one person would not be a better judge of sensible beauty than another; the more intelligent would not be better than the slower, nor the experienced and skilled than the novice and the untrained; and the same person could not make progress towards better judgement than before. And it is obvious that anything which admits of increase or decrease is changeable.

This consideration has readily persuaded men of ability and learning, trained in the philosophical discipline, that the original 'idea' is not to be found in this sphere, where it is shown to be subject to change. In their view both body and mind might be more or less endowed with form (or 'idea'), and if they could be deprived of form altogether they would be utterly non-existent. And so they saw that there must be some being in which the original form resides, unchangeable, and therefore incomparable. And they rightly believed that it is there that the origin of all things is to be found, in the uncreated, which is the source of all creation.

Thus 'what is known of God is what he himself has revealed to them. For his invisible realities have been made visible to the intelligence, through his created works, as well as his eternal power and divinity.'[15] It is by him that the visible and temporal things have been created.

So much for that section of philosophy which they call physical, or natural.

15. Rom. 1, 19f.

7. *The pre-eminence of the Platonists in rational philosophy, or logic*

As for the teaching which is comprised in the second division of philosophy, which the Platonists call logic, or rational philosophy, heaven forbid that I should think to compare them with those who have placed the criterion of truth in the bodily senses and have decided that all that belongs to the realm of learning is to be measured by such unreliable and misleading standards. Such are the Epicureans, and other philosophers of that type; and even the Stoics, who are so violently attached to the subtle art of disputation, which they call 'dialectic', hold that the art is to be derived from the bodily senses.[16] They assert that it is from this source that the mind draws its concepts (*ennoiai*, in their vocabulary) of the things which they explain by means of definition. This is taken as the starting-point of their whole connected system of learning and teaching.

Here I always wonder what bodily senses they use to see that beauty which they say is found only in the wise. With what physical eyes have they beheld the beauty and grace of wisdom? On the other hand, those philosophers whom we deservedly prefer to all the rest, have distinguished between the things discerned by the mind and those attained by the senses, without either detracting from the proper powers of the senses, or ascribing to them powers beyond their competence, while they have declared that God himself, the creator of all things, is the light of the mind, which makes possible every acquisition of knowledge.

8. *The Platonists' superiority in moral philosophy*

There remains the moral section of philosophy ('ethics' in Greek), which discusses the question of the *Summum Bonum*, to which we refer all our actions, which we seek for its own sake, not for any ulterior end, and the attainment of which leaves us nothing more to seek for our happiness. For this reason it is called the 'end'; everything else we desire for the sake of this, this we desire for itself alone.

This Good, which conveys blessedness, is said by some to depend on

16. *Epicurus* held that 'the criteria of truth were the feelings, the preconceptions and the experiences' (Diog. Laert. 10, 20, 31). In *Stoic* theory perceptions arise from impressions; their repetition produces experience, and from experience concepts are formed.

man's body, by others to derive from his mind; while yet others have located it in both mind and body. They observed, of course, that man himself consists of mind and body, and therefore they believed that the one *or* the other of the two constituents, or the one *and* the other, could be the source of his well-being – the source of that Good which is an end in itself, the guarantee of happiness, the standard of reference for all action, beyond which there is no further standard to be looked for. Thus those who are said to have added a third 'extrinsic' kind of good – honour, glory, money, or the like – have not introduced it as the 'Final' Good, to be sought for its own sake, but as a good relative to some other end. A good of this kind they held to be a good for the good, but an evil for the evil. And so those who looked to find man's good in his mind, or in his body, or in both together, did not believe that it should be looked for anywhere but in man himself. Those who looked for it in the body were seeking its source in the lower element in man's nature; those who derived it from the mind traced its origin to man's nobler part; those who expected it from mind and body together required it from man's whole being. But whether it was one part or both that they looked to, they did not go outside of man. Those three different principles did not result in three divergent schools of philosophy; they produced many more sects with widely different conceptions of the good of the body, the good of the mind, and the good of both.

All those schools must be ranked below those philosophers who have found man's true Good not in the enjoyment of the body or the mind, but in the enjoyment of God. This is not like the mind's enjoyment of the body, or of itself; nor is it like the enjoyment of friend by friend; it is like the eye's enjoyment of light – or rather that is the closest analogy possible. With God's help, I will explain the point to the best of my ability in another place. For the present, it suffices to mention that Plato defined the Sovereign Good as the life in accordance with virtue;[17] and he declared that this was possible only for one who had the knowledge of God and who strove to imitate him; this was the sole condition of happiness. Therefore Plato has no hesitation in asserting that to be a philosopher is to love God, whose nature is immaterial. It immediately follows that the seeker after wisdom (which is the meaning of 'philo-soph-er') will only attain to happiness when he has begun to enjoy God. To be sure, it does not automatically follow that a man is happy, just because he enjoys what he has set his heart on; many are miserable because they are in love

17. cf. *Gorg.*, 470D; 508B.

with things that should not be loved, and they become even more miserable when they enjoy them. But it remains true that no one is happy without the enjoyment of what he loves. Even those who set their heart on the wrong things do not suppose their happiness to consist in the loving, but in the enjoyment. If anyone then enjoys what he loves, and loves the true Supreme Good, only the most miserable would deny his happiness. Now this Sovereign Good, according to Plato, is God. And that is why he will have it that the true philosopher is the lover of God, since the aim of philosophy is happiness, and he who has set his heart on God will be happy in the enjoyment of him.

9. *The philosophy that approximates most nearly to Christianity*

Thus there are philosophers who have conceived of God, the supreme and true God, as the author of all created things, the light of knowledge, the Final Good of all activity, and who have recognized him as being for us the origin of existence, the truth of doctrine and the blessedness of life. They may be called, most suitably, Platonists; or they may give some other title to their school. It may be that it was only the leading members of the Ionian school who held the same opinions as Plato, and who understood him thoroughly; on the other hand, the same concepts may have been held also by Italian philosophers, because of Pythagoras and the Pythagoreans, and perhaps by some others of the same way of thinking and from the same part of the world. There may be others to be found who perceived and taught this truth among those who were esteemed as sages or philosophers in other nations: Libyans of Atlas, Egyptians, Indians, Persians, Chaldeans, Scythians, Gauls, Spaniards.[18] Whoever they may have been, we rank such thinkers above all others and acknowledge them as representing the closest approximation to our Christian position.

10. *Christianity and philosophy*

A Christian whose education has been confined to the study of the Church's literature may be quite unfamiliar with the name of Pla-

18. Diogenes Laertius (1, 122) describes the diffusion of philosophy among the Magi of Asia Minor, 'the gymnosophists' of India (cf. Bk X, 32; XIV, 17; XV 20), the Celts, the Galatians, the Druids, and in North Africa.

tonist, and may not know of the existence of two types of Greek-speaking philosophy, the Ionian and the Italian. For all that, he is not so out of touch with life in general as to be unaware that philosophers profess the pursuit of wisdom, or even the possession of it. But he is wary of those whose philosophy is 'based on the elements of this world', and not on God, the world's creator. That is because he is put on his guard by the Apostle's injunction, and gives an attentive hearing to those words: 'Take care that no one leads you astray by philosophy and useless misleading teaching, based on the elements of the world.'[19] However, he is prevented from regarding all thinkers as belonging to this class, when he listens to the Apostle's remarks about some of them. 'What can be known of God has been revealed among them. God in fact has revealed it to them. For his invisible realities, from the foundation of the world, have been made visible to the intelligence through his created works, as well as his eternal power and divinity.'[20] And in his speech to the Athenians, after uttering that great saying about God, a saying which only a few can understand, 'It is in him that we have our life, our movement, and our being,' Paul goes on to say, 'as some of your own writers have also said.'[21] The Christian knows, to be sure, that he must be on his guard against their errors. For while the Apostle says that through his created works God has revealed to them his invisible qualities by making them visible to the intelligence, he says at the same time that they have not offered the right sort of worship to God himself, because they have transferred the divine honours, due to God alone, to other objects, which have no right to them.

> Though having some acquaintance with God, they have not glorified him as God, nor have they given thanks to him; but they have dwindled into futility in their thinking and their stupid heart is shrouded in darkness. In claiming to be wise they have become fools and have exchanged the glory of the incorruptible God for images representing corruptible man, or birds, beasts or snakes.[22]

In this passage Paul intends us to understand a reference to the Romans, the Greeks and the Egyptians, who were proud of their reputation for wisdom. We shall later on engage in argument with them on this subject. But they agree with us in the conception of one God, who is the author of this whole universe, who is not only above all

19. Col. 2, 8. 20. Rom. 1, 19f.

21. Acts 17, 28, referring to Cleanthes' *Hymn to Zeus* and the *Phaenomena* of Aratus.

22. Rom. 1, 21f.

material things, as immaterial, but also, as incorruptible, above all souls, who is, in fact, our source, our light, our good; and in respect of this we rank them above all the others.

A Christian may be unacquainted with the writings of the philosophers; he may not employ in debate words which he has never learnt; he may not apply the Latin term 'natural' or the Greek term 'physical' to the division of philosophy which deals with the study of nature, or the term 'rational', or 'logical', to the division which discusses how we can reach the truth; or 'moral' or 'ethical' to the part which treats of morality, of the good ends which are to be pursued and the evil ends to be avoided. It does not follow that he fails to realize that we derive from the one true God of all goodness the nature with which we were created in his image. It does not mean that he is ignorant of the teaching thanks to which we acquire knowledge of God and of ourselves, nor that he is ignorant of the grace through which we are united to him and thus attain our happiness.

This is why we rate the Platonists above the rest of the philosophers. The others have employed their talents and concentrated their interests on the investigation of the causes of things, of the method of acquiring knowledge, and the rules of the moral life, while the Platonists, coming to a knowledge of God, have found the cause of the organized universe, the light by which truth is perceived, and the spring which offers the drink of felicity. All philosophers who have this conception of God are in agreement with our idea of him, whether they are Platonists or philosophers of any other kind, of any nation. The reason why I have decided to concentrate on the Platonists is that their writings are more generally known. For one thing, the Greeks, whose language enjoys a pre-eminent position internationally, have given the Platonists the widest publicity; for another, the Latins, struck by their excellence, or by their renown, have studied their writings in preference to others, and by translating them into our language have made them better known and more highly regarded.

11. *How Plato may have acquired the insight which brought him so close to Christianity*

Some of those who are united in fellowship with us in the grace of Christ are amazed when they hear or read that Plato had a conception of God which they recognize as agreeing in many respects with the truth of our religion. This has given rise to the suggestion that, at the time of his journey to Egypt, Plato listened to the prophet Jeremiah, or else that during the same foreign tour he read the prophetical Scriptures. I have put forward this suggestion in some of my books.[23] But a careful calculation of the dates, which are to be found in the chronicles, shows that Plato was born about a century after the period of Jeremiah's prophetic activity. Plato lived to be eighty-one, and it was, we find, a full sixty years after his death when Ptolemy, king of Egypt, ordered from Judaea a copy of the prophetic writings of the Hebrew people and had them translated into Greek for his use by seventy Jews who were familiar with the Greek language. This means that Plato could not have seen Jeremiah when on his travels, since the prophet had been dead for so long; nor could he have read his writings, since they had not yet been translated into Greek, the language in which Plato was such a master, unless perhaps, in his eager thirst for knowledge, he gained acquaintance with them – as he did with Egyptian books – with the help of an interpreter. There is no suggestion of a written translation which he could take away with him (that was reserved for Ptolemy, who, as the story goes, earned the privilege by an act of great generosity,[24] though he may also have feared for his royal power). It may have been that he learnt by word of mouth as much as he could understand of the contents of the Scriptures.

There seems to be some evidence in support of this suggestion. Thus, the book of Genesis begins with these words: 'In the beginning God made heaven and earth. But the earth was invisible and unformed, and there was darkness over the abyss, and the spirit of God soared above the water.'[25] Now in the *Timaeus*, the book in which he writes about the creation of the world, Plato says that God in that work first brought together earth and fire;[26] and it is obvious that for Plato fire takes the place of the sky, so that this statement has a certain resemblance to the one just quoted: 'In the beginning God made heaven and earth.' Plato goes on to say that water and air were the two intermediaries whose interposition effected the junction of those two extremes.[27] This is supposed to be his interpretation of the biblical statement: 'The spirit of God soared above the water.' Now the

23. *In some of my books: De Doctr. Christ.*, 2, 43. St Augustines revokes the idea in *Retract.*, 2, 4. For Plato's supposed acquaintance with Scripture, cf. Justin Martyr (*Apol.*, 1, 60), Origen (*C. Cels.*, 4, 39), Eusebius (*Praep. Ev.*, 11, 9, 2), Cyril of Alexandria (*C. Jul.*, 29), Clement of Alexandria (*Strom.*, 1, 22).

24. Jeremiah was called to a prophetic ministry *c.* 626 B.C. (Jer. 1, 2); Plato lived 428–347. 'About a century' is something of an understatement on St Augustine's part. For the translation of the Septuagint see Bk XV, 13.

25. Gen. 1, 1f. 26. *Tim.*, 31B. 27. *Tim.*, 32B.

air is also called 'spirit' (in the sense of 'breath'); and so it might be thought that Plato failed to notice the normal use of the title 'the Spirit of God' in Scripture, and assumed that the four elements are mentioned in this passage. Then there is Plato's assertion that the philosopher is 'the lover of God'. Nothing shines out from the pages of Scripture more clearly than this. But what impresses me most, and almost brings me to agree that Plato cannot have been unacquainted with the sacred books, is that when the angel gave Moses the message from God, and Moses asked the name of him who gave the command to go and free the Hebrew people from Egypt, he received this reply, 'I am HE WHO IS, and you will say to the sons of Israel, "HE WHO IS has sent me to you." '[28] This implies that in comparison with him who really *is*, because he is unchangeable, the things created changeable have no real existence. This truth Plato vigorously maintained and diligently taught.[29] And I do not know whether it can be found anywhere in the works of Plato's predecessors, except in that book which has the statement, 'I am HE WHO IS; and you will say to them: "HE WHO IS has sent me to you." '

12. *Despite their true concept of one God, the Platonists countenance polytheism*

We do not know the source of Plato's knowledge of this teaching, whether it came from previous books of ancient writers, or whether, as the Apostle says, 'what can be known about God has been revealed among them: in fact, God himself has revealed it. For his invisible realities have from the creation of the world, been made visible to the understanding through his created works; as well as his eternal power and divinity.' But however this may be, I think I have shown myself justified in selecting the Platonists as my respondents in the present debate on natural theology; the question at issue being this: With a view to future blessedness after death, is it right to worship one God, or many?

The reason for my choice of the Platonists, in preference to all others, is that the reputation and prestige they enjoy above the rest is in proportion to the superiority of their concept of one God, the creator of heaven and earth. The judgement of posterity has rated them far above other philosophers; how far is shown by the sequel. Aristotle (a disciple of Plato and a man of commanding genius, no

28. Exod. 3, 14. 29. cf. e.g., *Rp.*, 2, 380D–381C.

match for Plato in literary style, but still far above the general run), founded a school called the 'Peripatetics' (the name being derived from his habit of walking about while discussing) and, thanks to his brilliant reputation, attracted to his sect a large number of disciples, even in the lifetime of his teacher. After Plato's death, his nephew Speusippus and his favourite disciple Xenocrates succeeded him in his school, which was called the Academy, and they and their successors were hence called the 'Academics'.[30] In spite of this, the most notable philosophers of recent times have rejected the title of 'Peripatetics' or 'Academics', and have elected to be called 'Platonists'.[31]

Among these modern philosophers the most highly esteemed of the Greeks are Plotinus, Iamblichus, and Porphyry;[32] while Apuleius[33] of Africa stands out as a notable Platonist, writing in both Greek and Latin.

Yet all those philosophers, and others of the same way of thinking, and even Plato himself,[34] thought it right to render worship to a plurality of Gods.

13 *By Plato's definition all the gods are morally good*

There are, to be sure, many other important points on which the Platonists differ from us. But I am particularly concerned with one point, which I have already mentioned; it is a matter of no small moment, and it is the topic of our present discussion. My first question is this: To what gods do they think this worship should be rendered? To the good, or the bad, or to both alike? Now we have the opinion of Plato[35] that all gods are good, and that there is no such thing as a bad god. It follows that worship is offered to good gods. For only then is it offered to gods, seeing that they will not be gods at all, if they are

30. cf. Bk IV 30n. 31. They are usually called 'Neoplatonists'.

32, *Plotinus* (*c.* A.D. 205–*c.* 270): born in Egypt, and settled in Rome in 244; the chief Neoplatonist teacher. Reality, in his doctrine, is to be found in the spiritual world accessible to reason; the material world is in comparison unreal, created by the soul through the imposition of 'forms'. The ascending degrees of reality are: matter – soul – reason – God (who is pure existence). The moral aim for man is to achieve purification through discipline, and thus to ascend to the spiritual world through love of the Divine.

Iamblichus (d. *c.* A.D. 325): Syrian mystic, pupil of Porphyry. Part of his account of Pythagoreanism survives; cf. Bk VII, 25n.

33. cf. Bk IV, 2n. 34. cf. *Legg.*, 4, 716D–717B; 8, 828A–D.

35. cf. *Rp.*, 2, 379A.

not good. If this be true – and how could we rightly think otherwise of the gods? – it immediately makes nonsense of the idea, held by a good many people, that the bad gods are to be mollified by sacrifice to prevent them from doing harm, while the good are to be invoked to induce them to give help. For bad gods do not exist; therefore it is to the good gods that the honour of these rites is to be offered, as, allegedly, their due.

But then, who are the gods who like the stage shows and demand that those spectacles should be included in the divine ceremonies and exhibited among the honours paid to them? The power wielded by those gods proves their existence; their taste in entertainment unmistakably reveals their wickedness. Plato's opinion on stage shows is well known.[36] His decision is that poets should be banished from the community for having composed poetical fictions so dishonourable to the majesty and the goodness of the gods. Then who are these gods who are at odds with Plato himself on this subject of stage performances? Plato would not suffer the gods to be slandered by false accusations, while the gods demanded that those slanders should be performed in their honour. In fact, when the gods prescribed the establishment of those shows, they added active malignity to their demand for obscenity. They robbed Titus Latinius[37] of his son, and inflicted sickness on him for his disobedience to their orders; and they restored him to health when he had fulfilled their requirements. Plato, for his part, does not consider that gods so evil should be feared, and he maintains his firm decision with the greatest resolution, and shows no hesitation in removing from a well-ordered people all the blasphemous frivolities of the poets, in which those gods delighted to find companionship in impurity. As I mentioned in my second book, Labeo[38] classes Plato among the demi-gods. And yet Labeo holds that the evil deities should be placated by the blood of victims, and by supplications of the same kind, while the good divinities are to be propitiated by games and other ceremonies supposedly connected with joy. How is it then that the 'demi-god' Plato has the steadfast courage to deprive not demi-gods but gods, and, what is more, good gods, of the diversions which he regards as obscene? These gods certainly refute Labeo's opinion, since in the case of Latinius they showed themselves not merely playful and pleasure-loving, but savage and terrible. And so I should like the Platonists to explain this problem. They follow the opinion of their master in thinking that all the gods are good and honourable, sharing with the sages a fellowship in

36. cf. Bk II, 14. 37. cf. Bk IV, 26. 38. cf. Bk II, 11.

virtue; and they hold it blasphemous to entertain any other opinion about any of the gods.

'Here', they say, 'is our explanation.' Very good. Let us give it an attentive hearing.

14. *The notion of three kinds of rational souls: in the gods of heaven, in the demons in the air, in men on earth*

There is, they say, a threefold division of all beings possessed of a rational soul; there are gods, men, and demons. The gods occupy the most exalted situation; mankind has the most lowly; and the demons are in between. For the gods have their abode in heaven; mankind lives on earth; demons dwell in the air.[39] And their natures are graded to correspond to their different elevations. The gods are superior to men and demons, while men are set below gods and demons in respect of difference of merit as well as in the order of the physical elements. The demons are in a middle position; they are inferior to the gods and dwell below them, but superior to men, having their abode above them. In common with the gods, they have immortality of body; in common with men, they have the passions of the soul. Therefore it is not remarkable, the Platonists tell us, that they delight in the obscenities of the shows and the fantasies of the poets, seeing that they are subject to human desires, which are remote from the gods, and altogether alien to them. It follows then that in his detestation of poetry and his prohibition of poetical fictions, it is not the gods, who are all of them good and sublime, that Plato has deprived of the pleasures of stage shows; it is the demons.

These ideas can be found in many writers; but the Platonist Apuleius[40] of Madaura has devoted a whole book to the subject, under the title, *The God of Socrates*. In this book he discusses and explains to what class of divinities that power belonged which was attached to Socrates in a kind of friendly companionship.[41] The story is that he constantly received warnings from this divinity to abandon some line of action when the contemplated enterprise was not destined to be successful. Apuleius says quite frankly that this power was not a god but a demon and supports his contention with a wealth of argument, in the course of which he takes the statement of Plato about the sublime situation of the gods, the lowly state of man and the intermediate position of the demons, and subjects it to a thorough exam-

39. cf. Eph. 2, 2. 40. cf. Bk IV, 2. 41. cf. Plat., *Apol.*, 31D.

ination. Now if this represents Plato's belief, how did he have the audacity to expel the poets from his city, and thus to deprive of their theatrical pleasures, if not the gods (for he withdrew them from any contact with mankind), at any rate the demons? Perhaps it was because he intended to advise the spirit of man (situated though it is in a bodily frame which is destined for death) to treat with contempt the corrupt commands of the demons and to abhor their obscenities in order to preserve an unsullied integrity. For it was in a spirit of the highest integrity that Plato condemned and prohibited these diversions; it follows that it was utterly infamous in the demons to demand and prescribe them.

Then either Apuleius is mistaken and the supernatural companion of Socrates did not come from this category of spiritual powers; or Plato is inconsistent in showing honour to demons at one moment, and at another banishing their enjoyments from a well-conducted city; or else Socrates is not to be felicitated on his friendship with a demon. Apuleius himself felt some embarrassment about the point. In fact he was prepared to give his book the title, *The God of Socrates*, whereas in line with his own discussion, in which he makes a carefully and copiously argued distinction between gods and demons, he ought to have called it *The Demon of Socrates*. However, he has preferred to make this point in the actual discussion rather than in its title. The fact is that as a result of the healthy doctrine which has shone upon the world of men, mankind in general has conceived a horror of the very name of demon, so that anyone reading the title, *The Demon of Socrates*, before studying the discussion in which Apuleius seeks to establish the excellence of demons, would conclude that Socrates was by no means a normal human being.

But what is it that Apuleius himself has found to praise in demons, apart from the subtlety and stability of their bodies and the elevation of their abode? As for their morality, in the general remarks he makes about demons as a whole, he has nothing good to say of them but a great deal of ill. In fact, when one has read the book, one can no longer be astonished that these demons wished the obscenities of the stage to have a place among divine ceremonies, and that while eager to be accounted gods, they could find pleasure in the scandals of the deities, and that everything in the sacred rites which arouses laughter or disgust by reason of its celebration of obscenity or its degraded barbarity is very much to their taste.

15. *Neither the airy composition of their bodies nor the elevation of their abodes confers on the demons any superiority over mankind*

In view of all this, heaven forbid that any truly religious spirit, a subject of the true God, should imagine that the demons are superior to itself simply because they enjoy a superiority in respect of their bodies. In that case many animals would be superior to human beings since they surpass us in the keenness of their senses, in facility and speed of movement, in muscular strength, and in vigorous longevity. Can any man equal the long sight of an eagle or a vulture? Or match a dog in sense of smell? Or rival the speed of a hare, a stag, or any of the birds? Or the strength of a lion or an elephant? Or the longevity of a serpent, who, they say, puts off old age when he puts off his skin, and thus has his youth restored? But just as we are superior to the beasts by reason of our powers of reason and intelligence, so our superiority to the demons should appear in a life of goodness and integrity. If divine providence has bestowed certain physical advantages on beings which are unquestionably our inferiors, the purpose of this is to encourage us to be more careful to cultivate the faculties in which we surpass the beasts than to develop the body, and to teach us to take no account of the physical superiority which, as we realize, the demons enjoy, in comparison with moral goodness, which gives us pre-eminence over the demons. For we also are destined for bodily immortality – not the immortality which is to endure the torment of eternal punishment, but the immortality for which purity of heart is the preparation.

Furthermore, it is utterly absurd to allow ourselves to be so impressed by spatial elevation, by the fact that the demons live in the air while we live on the earth, as to suppose that this means that they are to be considered our betters. On this showing we should regard all flying creatures as our betters! But, we shall be told, when the birds are tired with flying or when they have to take nourishment, they come down to earth for rest or food; the demons do not. Are our friends disposed to conclude that the birds rank above us, while the demons rank above the birds? If this is a crazy notion, there is no reason why we should suppose that because the demons inhabit an element above ours we ought to abase ourselves before them with a religious reverence. It does not follow that the birds of the air are to be rated above us inhabitants of earth; in fact they are subordinate to us because of the value of the rational soul, which we possess. Similarly, though the demons belong more to the air than we do, they are not superior to us just because the air is higher than the earth; in fact, human beings are to be ranked above them for this reason: that there is no possible comparison between the devout man's hope and the demon's despair.

The system by which Plato connects and disposes the four elements in a symmetrical order[42] interposes the two intermediary elements of air and water between the two extremes, fire, the most mobile element, and the motionless earth, in such a way that water is as far above earth as air is above water and fire above air. This arrangement may serve tc warn us not to estimate the merits of living beings in proportion to the grades of the elements. Apuleius himself agrees with others in calling man a terrestrial animal[43] and yet he is ranked far above the aquatic animals, although Plato sets water above earth. Thus we may see that in the question of the merits of souls, we must not keep to the order which is observed in the grading of material things. An inferior material body may well be the habitation of a superior soul, and an inferior soul may dwell in a superior body.

16. *The views of Apuleius on the character and activities of the demons*

Apuleius the Platonist also treats of the character of the demons, and says that they are liable to the same emotional disturbances as human beings. They resent injury, they are mollified by flattery and by gifts, they delight in receiving honours, they enjoy all kinds of rites and ceremonies and they are annoyed at any negligence about these.[44] Among their functions he mentions divination by means of auguries, haruspication, clairvoyance, and dreams; and he ascribes to them the remarkable feats of magicians.[45] He gives this brief definition of demons: species, animal; soul, subject to passions; mind, rational; body, composed of air; life-span, eternal. Now, of those five attributes, they have the first three, says Apuleius, in common with us; the fourth is peculiar to them; the fifth they share with the gods.[46] But I observe that of the first three, which they have in common with us, they share two with the gods. For Apuleius asserts that the gods are themselves animals (i.e. living beings); when he assigns each species to its own element he places us among the terrestrial animals with all the

42. *Tim.*, 32B; cf. ch. 11.
43. *De Deo Socr.*, 3.
44. *De Deo Socr.*, 12; 14.
45. *De Deo Socr.*, 6.
46. *De Deo Socr.*, 13.

other beings on the earth which have life and sensibility; among the aquatic animals he puts the fish and other swimming creatures; among the animals of the air he sets the demons; and the gods among etherial animals.[47] Consequently, if the demons belong to the animal species, they have that attribute in common with the gods and the beasts, as well as with mankind. Their rational mind they share with the gods and with mankind. Their eternity they share only with the gods; their liability to passions, only with men, while their body of air is their own peculiarity.

Thus it is no special distinction for the demons to belong to the animal species; so do the beasts. The possession of a rational mind does not raise them above our level; we also have it. What advantage is it to be eternal, if it does not mean eternal happiness? Temporal felicity is preferable to an eternity of wretchedness. Liability to passions gives them no superiority to us; we also are so liable – and this is because of our misfortune. And what value are we to put on that airy body, seeing that a soul is to be esteemed above any kind of body, whatever its nature is? And that is why religious worship, the homage due from the soul, cannot be due to something which is inferior to the soul. If Apuleius had included the qualities of virtue, wisdom and felicity among the attributes of demons, and if he had told us that the demons possessed these for eternity, in common with the gods, then he would have been speaking of something to be envied, something to be highly prized.

Yet even so it would not have been right for us to worship them on this account as God is worshipped; it would have been our duty rather to worship God as the being from whom, as we knew, they had received those attributes. As it is, how much less right have they to divine honours, these animals of air, who only have reason so that they may be capable of wretchedness, and passions so that they may in fact be wretched, and eternity so that their wretchedness can have no end.

17. *It is wrong for men to worship demons. We should free ourselves from their vices*

Putting aside all other points, I want to limit my consideration to the matter of the passions of the soul which, according to Apuleius, the demons share with us. If the four elements are full of the living beings which belong to each of them, fire and air filled with immortal beings,

47. *De Deo Socr.*, 7; 8

water and earth with mortals, I would like to know why the souls of the demons are disturbed by the storms and tempests of the passions. For 'disturbance' represents the Greek *pathos* (passion), and that is what Apuleius means by calling the demons 'subject to passions' (*passiva*), since the word 'passion' (*pathos* in Greek) signifies an irrational motion of the soul. Why then do we find these 'passions' in the souls of demons and not in the beasts? Because if anything similar is apparent in the beasts, it is not a 'disturbance', in that it is not contrary to reason,[48] which they do not possess. In men these disturbances are possible as a result of either stupidity or wretchedness. For we are not yet in that happy condition of perfect wisdom which is promised us in the end, when we have been set free from this mortal state. The gods are said to be exempt from those disturbances just because they are not only immortal but also happy. We know that the gods themselves are said to have rational souls; but these are souls completely pure from all taint or infection. If then the gods do not suffer such disturbances, as they are blessed beings (*animalia*), knowing no unhappiness, and if the beasts are free from such disturbances, as they are beings incapable either of blessedness or of misery, it remains that the demons must be liable to such disturbances just as men are, as they are beings (*animalia*) who are not blessed, but wretched.

What folly it is then, or rather what madness, for us to subject ourselves to demons by any kind of worship, when the true religion sets us free from the vicious tendencies in which we resemble them! Apuleius is very tender towards the demons – he even pronounces them worthy of divine honours; and yet he is forced to admit that the demons are prompted by anger.[49] But we, on the contrary, are bidden by the true religion not to allow ourselves to be prompted by anger, but rather to resist it. The demons are influenced by gifts; but we are bidden by the true religion not to show favour to anyone in consideration of gifts received. The demons are mollified by honours; but we are bidden by the true religion not to be influenced in any way by such things. The demons hate some men and love others – not as a result of a calmly considered decision, but because their soul, in the phrase of Apuleius, is 'subject to passions';[50] as for us, we have the instruction of the true religion that we should love even our enemies. Lastly, the true religion bids us abjure all those movements of the

48. *Contrary to reason.* According to Cicero (*Tusc. Disp.*, 4, 6, 11), Zeno defined a disturbance (a *pathos*, as he termed it) as something opposed to right reason, contrary to the nature of the mind that is affected by it.

49. *De Deo Socr.*, 13.

50. *De Deo Socr.*, 12.

heart, all those agitations of the mind, all those storms and tempests of the soul which in the demons make a raging sea of passion. It is nothing but folly, nothing but pitiable aberration, to humble yourself before a being whom you would hate to resemble in the conduct of your life and to worship one whom you would refuse to imitate. For surely the supremely important thing in religion is to model oneself on the object of one's worship.

18. *Demons are incapable of mediating between mankind and the God*

It is therefore in vain that Apuleius and those of his way of thinking ascribe an honourable function to those demons by establishing them in the air, midway between the ethereal heaven and the earth, so that, since 'gods never mix with men' (as Plato is reported as saying),[51] they may convey the prayers of men to the gods and bring back to men the answers granted to their requests. Those who thought in this way counted it improper that men and gods should be in direct contact, but quite proper for demons to be in contact with both men and gods, so that they may deliver petitions from mankind and return with the favours granted by the gods. The notion was, I suppose, that a man of probity, a stranger to the black arts of magic, should employ the good offices of such advocates to ensure that the gods should listen to his requests. And yet those advocates have a liking for those black arts, whereas his own aversion from such practices would give him a better claim to a ready and favourable hearing from the gods. Those demons have a liking, we know, for the obscenities of the theatre which modesty abhors; for the 'thousand ways of doing ill'[52] found in the malpractices of the sorcerers, which innocence detests. We are to suppose then, that if modesty and honesty seek anything from the gods, they cannot obtain it on their merits, but only by the intercession of their enemies! There is no point in striving, as Apuleius strives, to justify the poetical fictions and buffooneries of the theatre. We have on our side, in opposition to those practices, the master of their philosophical school, and their great authority, Plato himself – even if human modesty is so untrue to itself as to delight in obscenity, and, what is worse, to account it pleasing to the divine nature.

51. Plat., *Symp.*, 203A; cf. Apul., *De Deo Socr.*, 4; 6.
52. Virg., *Aen.*, 7, 338.

19. *The blasphemy of magic, which employs the services of demons*

In addition to this, I can quote the testimony of public feeling against those magic arts which some people – as unfortunate as they are blasphemous – are pleased to boast of. If these practices are the work of powers worthy of adoration, why are they so sternly chastised by the law? Are we to be told that it was the Christians who established the laws making sorcery a punishable offence? But what about these lines of the most illustrious of poets:

> I call to witness, sister dear, the gods
> And your beloved self, that if I seek
> To arm myself with power of magic art
> 'Tis much against my will?[53]

Can this have any other meaning than that these malpractices are undoubtedly dangerous for mankind?

And here is another passage relating to these practices:

> I've seen the crops removed from field to field,[54]

which is an allusion to that pernicious and abominable science by which, as the tale goes, one man's crops could be transferred to another's land. Cicero, it will be remembered, mentions that this practice was listed as a crime in the Twelve Tables, the most ancient order of Roman law, and that severe punishment was laid down for anyone who committed it.[55]

Moreover, was it before Christian judges that Apuleius himself was accused of magical practices? If he had been convinced that the acts laid to his charge were truly religious and devout and in harmony with the operations of the divine powers, he ought not merely to have confessed to them but to have professed his pride in them. He should have laid the blame on the laws which prohibited such practices and held them worthy of condemnation, when in fact they ought to be considered worthy of admiration and reverence. Then either he would have won the judges to his opinion or else the judges would have conformed to the unjust law and inflicted the death penalty on him for his laudatory testimonial to magic, and the demons would have given a recompense appropriate to the soul of a man who did not fear to sacrifice his human life for his testimony in praise of their activities. It was in this way that our Christian martyrs acted, when charged with the crime of professing Christianity, a crime which, as

53. Virg., *Aen.*, 4, 492f.
54. Virg., *Ecl.*, 8, 98.
55. Cic., *De Leg.*; Plin., 28, 2, 17.

they knew, brought them salvation and eternal glory; they did not choose to escape temporal punishment by denying their faith they preferred to confess it, to proclaim it, to preach it; they endured all their suffering for their religion with fidelity and fortitude, and they died with a devout serenity. It was such conduct that brought shame upon the laws forbidding Christianity and brought about their alteration.

There is extant an elaborate and eloquent oration of Apuleius,[56] in which he defends himself against the charge of magic on the ground that he had nothing to do with it, saying that the only way he wished to show his innocence was by the denial of actions which no innocent man could commit. He was right in considering the sorcerers deserving of condemnation. But seeing that all the marvels of sorcery are achieved by means of the science taught by the demons and by their operations, Apuleius should have asked himself why he judged them worthy of honour, alleging them indispensable for the delivery of our prayers to the gods – when it is their activities that we ought to shun if we want our prayers to reach the true God.

Next, I would like to ask Apuleius what kind of prayers they are which he supposes that the demons convey to the good gods. Are they magical prayers, or permitted prayers? If magical, the gods do not want that kind of prayer. If permitted, they do not want to receive them from such messengers. If a penitent sinner pours out his prayers, and especially if he has committed the offence of sorcery, is it likely that he receives pardon at the intercession of those who have encouraged and impelled him to fall into the sin which he now laments? Or do we imagine that the demons themselves first make an act of penitence for their deception, so that they may be able to win indulgence for the penitents? No one has ever alleged this about the demons. If this were the case and they longed to attain to the grace of absolution by their penitence, they would never have dared to claim divine honour for themselves. For this claim is a piece of detestable arrogance; but penitence displays a humility deserving of compassion.

20. *Is it credible that the God would rather have contact with demons than with men?*

'But there is a pressing, urgent reason which demands the mediation of demons between gods and men, to present requests from men and to convey the desired boons from the gods.'

56. *Apologia* (*De Magia*).

'And what, pray, is that reason, that pressing necessity?'

'The fact that a god never has direct contact with a human being.'[57]

What a glorious notion of the holiness of God! He has no contact with a suppliant human being; but he has contact with an arrogant demon! He has no dealings with a man who repents; yet he has dealings with a demon who deceives. He has no contact with a man who flees to the Divinity for refuge; but contact with a demon who has pretensions to divinity. He has no contact with a man who craves his pardon; but contact with a demon who eggs man on to wickedness. God holds aloof from the man who, in his philosophical works, is for outlawing the poets from a well-constituted city, but not from the demons who demand from the civic authorities and the pontiffs the presentation in the theatre of the buffooneries of the poets. He holds aloof from men who forbid the invention of scandals about the gods, but not from the demons who delight in such calumnies. He shuns men who punish the crimes of sorcerers under just laws, but not the demons who teach the arts of magic and ensure their results. He shuns men who take care not to imitate the demons, but not the demons who are always on the look-out to deceive mankind.

21. *Do the Gods employ demons as messengers?*

'But of course there is an imperative necessity for this absurdity, this indignity! The gods, we must remember, dwell in the ether: they are concerned about human affairs, but they would not know what is happening in the world of men, if the demons of the air did not keep them informed. For the ether is far away from the earth, high aloft; while the air is in contact with the earth.'

What a wonderful sample of wisdom! This is a fair summary of their conception of the gods. They insist on their goodness; they hold that they are concerned with human affairs – otherwise they would appear unworthy of worship; but because of the distance between the elements the gods are ignorant of those affairs. And so demons are believed to be indispensable, to enable the gods to learn what is going on in the world of men and to know when they ought to give men help. And that is why it is thought that the demons themselves should be worshipped.

If this is true, then demons are better known to those gods, by reason of physical proximity, than is man, by reason of the goodness

57. cf. Plat., *Symp.*, 203A, quoted in ch. 18.

of his heart. What a deplorable necessity! Or rather, what ridiculous and outrageous futility – designed to preserve the gods from futility! For if the gods, with their spirit unencumbered by any material obstacle, can see our spirit, they do not need demon-messengers for this purpose; while if it is through their own body that the gods of the ether perceive the outward expressions of the spirit, such as speech, facial expression and gesture, and receive the news from the demons in the same way, then they can be misled by the lies of the demons. While if the divine nature of the gods precludes the possibility of their deception by the demons, then the same divine nature should preclude the possibility of their ignorance of the affairs of us men.

I should like those philosophers to let me know whether the demons told the gods about Plato's dislike of the fictions put about by the poets concerning the scandals of the gods and concealed the fact that they themselves enjoyed them. Or did they keep both facts from the gods, preferring them to be in total ignorance of the situation? Or did they disclose both Plato's religious prudence in regard to the gods and the demons' flippant outrages against them? Or did they prefer the gods to be unaware of the decision of Plato, his refusal to let the gods be slandered by false accusations of crime at the impious caprice of poets, while they had no shame or fear about admitting their own wickedness, their enjoyment of the stage shows in which the infamies of the gods are presented to the public? Will the Platonists kindly make their choice among the four possibilities I have put before them in these questions? And then will they please observe, whatever their choice, how bad is the opinion they hold about these 'good gods'.

If they select the first hypothesis, they will be acknowledging that it was not allowable for the gods to be on terms with the good Plato, who forbade the outrages against them, and yet that they were on terms with the evil demons, who rejoiced in those outrages. For the 'good gods' would not have been able to know about that good man, who was situated so far away from them, except through the evil demons; and they would not have known the demons very well, for all their proximity.

Perhaps they choose the second, confessing that the demons concealed the facts and left the gods in complete ignorance both of Plato's most religious law and their own sacrilegious pleasure? Then what useful knowledge could the gods obtain through the agency of those demon-messengers, when they know nothing of the reverent decisions that good men make for the honour of the 'good gods' and in restraint of the licentiousness of evil demons?

Or they may choose the third possibility, and reply that the gods were informed by the agency of the demons, not only about Plato's prohibition of outrages against the gods, but also about the demons' wicked exultation in those outrages. Would this be a report, or an insult? And did the gods listen to this information, and learn both these items of news, without banishing from their presence those malignant demons whose desires and actions were utterly at variance with the honour of the gods and the reverent attitude of Plato? What is more, did they employ those wicked neighbours to convey their gifts to the good Plato in his remote abode? It looks as if they are so linked up in this chain of the elements, that they can be in connection with their slanderers, but not with their defenders. They knew both these facts, but they had no power to alter the weights of air and earth.

There only remains the fourth suggestion, which is the worst of them all. It would surely be insupportable to imagine that the demons told the gods all about the slanderous fantasies of the poets concerning the immortal gods, and the dishonourable buffooneries of the theatre; and about their own avidity for such productions and the exquisite pleasure they afforded them, while they said nothing about the philosophical seriousness which led Plato to decree the removal of all such performances from his ideal republic. This would mean that the gods have no choice but to rely on such messengers for information about the iniquities of the worst characters – the iniquities of these same messengers – while they are not allowed to learn of the virtues of the philosophers – and that, too, though the aim of the former is to do them outrage, of the latter, to do them honour!

22. *The worship of demons is to be rejected*

Thus we see that none of these four suggestions is a possible choice, since any one of them would imply an intolerable conception of the gods. The only remaining possibility is to refuse any credence to the teaching of Apuleius and the other philosophers of his way of thinking. Apuleius is at great pains to persuade us that the demons are situated midway between gods and men to serve in some way as messengers and go-betweens, to carry our petitions to the gods and to convey to us the gods' assistance. We must realize that they are in reality spirits whose only desire is to do harm, who are completely alien from any kind of justice, swollen with arrogance, livid with envy, and full of crafty deception. They do indeed dwell in the air, because they have been cast down from the upper heights of heaven as a reward for their irremediable transgression and condemned to inhabit this region as a kind of prison appropriate to their nature. But the fact that their dwelling-place is above the earth and the water does not mean that they are superior to mankind in worth, for men far surpass them, in spite of having terrestrial bodies, by virtue of the reverent attitude of mind which leads them to choose God for their support.

In spite of that, the demons clearly hold sway over many men, who are unworthy to participate in the true religion, and they treat them as prisoners and subjects; and they have persuaded the greater part of them to accept the demons as gods, by means of impressive but deceitful miracles, whether miracles of action or of prediction. But there are others who have observed the viciousness of these demons with rather more careful attention. The demons have failed to persuade them of their divinity; and so they have pretended that they are intermediaries between gods and men, securing for mankind the benefits of the gods. And yet when men have decided that not even this honourable position is to be accorded to the demons, because, seeing their wickedness, they did not believe them to be gods (since they would have it that all gods are good), even so men could not bring themselves to declare that demons were altogether unworthy of any divine honour, especially because they were afraid of shocking the general public. For they saw that people in general were enslaved to those demons by the superstitious beliefs to which they were inured, thanks to all those ceremonies, and all those temples.

23. *Hermes Trismegistus on the worship of idols*

Hermes the Egyptian (called Trismegistus)[58] expressed very different opinions about those demons. Apuleius, to be sure, denies that they are gods. But, for all that, in asserting that they are engaged in a kind of mediatory activity between gods and men, so that they appear to be indispensable to men in their relations with the gods, he does not distinguish their cult from the worship of the gods on high. The Egyptian, by contrast, distinguishes between gods created by the supreme God, and gods made by men.

Put like that, the statement sounds as if it referred to images which

58. *Hermes Trismegistus*: a legendary figure, to whom various religio-philosophical works (*Hermetica*) were attributed in the second century. A Latin version of one of them, *Asclepius*, was wrongly ascribed to Apuleius.

are 'the work of men's hands'; but Hermes asserts that the visible and tangible idols are in some way the bodies of gods; certain spirits have been induced to take up their abode in them, and they have the power either to do harm, or to satisfy many of the wants of those who offer them divine honours and obedient worship. When Hermes talks of gods being made by men, he refers to a kind of technique of attaching invisible spirits to material bodies, so that the images dedicated and subjected to those spirits become, as it were, animated bodies. This, he says, is the great, the marvellous power of creating gods, which has been given to men.

Here are the actual words of the Egyptian, as given in a Latin translation,

> Since the subject of our discussion is the relationship and the fellowship between men and gods, observe, Asclepius, the power and force of man. As the Lord, the Father, that is (to give him his full title) God, is the creator of the gods of heaven, so man is the maker of the gods who are content to dwell in temples, in close contact with human beings.[59]

And, a little later,

> Humanity, while remaining mindful of its nature and origin, perseveres in this imitation of the divinity. That is, just as the Father and Lord has created the eternal gods, to be like himself, so humanity has fashioned gods after the likeness of its own appearance.[60]

At this point Asclepius, his chief interlocutor, responds with the question, 'Are you talking about statues, Trismegistus?' To which he replies,

> Statues? My dear Asclepius, what an infidel you are! Statues endowed with souls, fully equipped with sensibility and spirit; statues which perform such great and wonderful works; statues which foreknow the future, and foretell it by means of the lot, by means of seers and dreams and many other methods; which send diseases upon men and also cure them, bestowing sadness or joy, according to deserts. Are you aware, my friend, that Egypt is the image of heaven? Or, more precisely, that in Egypt we have the transference, the descent to earth, of all that goes on in heaven, under the guidance of God? And, to tell the whole truth, our land is the temple of the universe. Yet for all that (since it is right that a wise man should have foreknowledge of all the future) it must not be that you should remain in ignorance of this fact: there will come a time when it will be apparent that it is in vain that the Egyptians have kept up the worship of the gods with reverent piety and attentive devotion.[61]

59. *Asclep.*, 23. 60. *Asclep.*, 23. 61. *Asclep.*, 24.

Hermes goes on to treat of this topic at great length; and it appears that he is predicting the present time when the Christian religion has overthrown all these deceitful images with an irresistible finality corresponding to its truth and holiness, so that the grace of the true Saviour may set man free from these man-made gods, and subject him to God, man's creator. But, in predicting this, Hermes speaks as if amicably disposed towards these mockeries of the demons, and he makes no express mention of Christianity by name. He tells of the future suppression and abolition of the worship, the observance of which safeguarded the resemblance to heaven in the land of Egypt; and his prophecy adopts the tone of mourning and lamentation. He was one of those of whom the Apostle is speaking when he says,

> Though they have some acquaintance with God they have not glorified him as God, nor have they given him thanks: but they have dwindled into futility in their thinking and their stupid heart is shrouded in darkness. In claiming to be wise they have become fools; and have exchanged the glory of the incorruptible God for images representing corruptible man.[62]

– and so on; it would take too long to give the whole passage.

Certainly Trismegistus had much to say in this strain about the one true God, the creator of the world – much that corresponds to the teaching of the truth. And yet in some way because of that 'darkening of the heart' he sank low enough to wish men to remain forever subject to gods who, on his own showing, are the creations of men, and to bewail the prospect of their extirpation at some future time, as if there were any unhappier situation than that of a man under the domination of his own inventions. It is easier for a man to cease to be a man, by worshipping as gods things of his own creation, than it is for things of man's own creation to become gods as a result of his worship. It is more likely that 'man who is in a position of honour and who does not realize it', should become 'comparable to the beasts',[63] than that the work of man's hands should be ranked above a work of God, created in God's image – that is, man himself. So it is just that man should be sundered from him who made him, when he puts above himself that which he has created.

Hermes of Egypt grieved because he knew the time was coming when all those futile delusions and those pernicious blasphemies would be done away with. But the impudence of his grief matched the imprudence of his knowledge. For it was not the Holy Spirit that had revealed this to him, as he revealed it to the holy prophets, who fore-

62. Rom. 1, 21ff. 63. Ps. 49, 20.

saw it and expressed their joy in such words as these: 'Suppose man makes gods for himself. Why, they are not gods at all!'[64] and in another place: 'The day will come, says the Lord, when I will extirpate from the land the names of the idols, and there will not be the memory of them';[65] and (appropriately to our present subject) Isaiah speaks of Egypt in particular: 'The works of men's hands will be removed from before his face; and their heart will be overcome in them',[66] and so on.

To the same class of seers belong those who rejoiced at the coming of what they had known would come, such seers as Simeon and Anna, who recognized Christ soon after his birth, and Elizabeth, who acknowledged him, by inspiration of the Spirit, soon after his conception;[67] such as Peter, who said, when the Father revealed it to him, 'You are the Christ, the son of the living God.'[68] Whereas it was the spirits who informed this Egyptian about the coming of the time for their destruction, those spirits who cried out in terror to the Lord, when he was present in the flesh, 'Why have you come to destroy us before the time?'[69] Perhaps they said this because it happened so suddenly to them – they knew it was bound to come, but they thought it would be slower in coming; perhaps what they meant by their destruction was the fact that they were recognized and despised, and this happened 'before the time', that is before the time of judgement, when they are to be punished with eternal damnation together with all the men who have continued in their fellowship. This is what we are told by the religion which never deceives and is never deceived, unlike the teaching of Hermes, who is 'blown from side to side by every wind of teaching';[70] who gives a mixture of truth and falsehood, and who grieves at the thought of the destruction of a religion which he later confesses to be false.

24. *Hermes acknowledges the falseness of Egyptian religion, while lamenting its coming destruction*

After a lengthy digression, Hermes returns to his starting-point, the man-made gods, and says,

That is enough on this subject. Let us return to the subject of man and his reason, the divine gift which justifies man's title of 'rational being'. What has been said about man is marvellous, but there is something still

64. Jer. 16, 20. 65. Zech. 13, 2. 66. Is. 19, 1.
67. Luke 2, 25; 36–38; 1, 41ff. 68. Matt.16, 16.
69. Matt. 8, 29, (cf. Bk IX, 21). 70. Eph., 4, 14.

more wonderful. For the miracle of all miracles is that man has been able to discover the divine nature and to bring it into being. Thus, because our ancestors went far astray in their conception of the gods, on account of their lack of faith and their neglect of divine worship and true religion, they invented the art of creating gods. They also brought in a power derived from the nature of the universe as a supplement to this technique, suitable for their purpose, and by this adidtion (since they could not create souls) they called up the souls of angels or demons and made them inhere in sacred images and in divine mysteries, so that by their means the idols could have the power of doing good or inflicting harm.[71]

I doubt if the demons themselves, if conjured, would confess as much as Hermes admitted. He says, 'It is because our ancestors went far astray in their conception of the gods, on account of their lack of faith and their neglect of divine worship and true religion, that they invented the art of creating gods.' There was no question of his ascribing the invention of this art of creating gods to any trivial error. It was not enough for him to say 'they went astray'; he had to go further than that; 'they went *far* astray'. It was a serious error, a failure of belief and a neglect of worship and religion that led to the invention of the art. And yet the sage laments the abolition of this manufacture of gods, discovered as a result of serious error and infidelity and the neglect of religion; he laments the coming disappearance of this at an appointed time, as if it were the end of true religion. One is bound to ask whether it was not the power of God which inspired him to disclose the past errors of his ancestors and the power of the Devil which constrained him to lament the future punishment of the demons. If the ancestors of the Egyptians discovered the art of making gods because of their grievous errors about the nature of the gods, their lack of faith, and their neglect of worship and religion, it should not cause astonishment if the products of this abominable art – the direct opposite of true religion – are abolished by the true religion, seeing that the truth corrects error, faith refutes infidelity, and conversion remedies opposition.

Even if Hermes had merely stated that his forebears had discovered the art of making gods without mentioning the causes, it would have been up to us, if we had any feeling of justice and piety, to realize that they would never have arrived at that art of making gods, if they had not strayed from the truth – if they had had a worthy conception of God and if they had been attentive to divine worship and religion. Now if this had been *our* discovery, if *we* had alleged the causes of this

71. *Asclep.*, 37.

art to be the grievous error of men, their lack of faith, and the estrangement from true religion of a mistaken and unbelieving attitude of mind, then the impudence of the opponents of truth would be in some degree tolerable. But when Hermes himself, while regarding the mastery of this technique of god-making as the supreme marvel of man, grieves that the time is coming when even the laws will enforce the abolition of all these invented divinities established by man, when in the same breath he expressly acknowledges the causes which brought the Egyptians to this pass, and tells us that his ancestors discovered the technique of god-making by reason of their grievous error, their lack of faith, their carelessness about divine worship and religion, what, in view of this, ought we to say – or rather, what ought we to do, except to offer all possible thanks to the Lord our God who has stopped these practices by means of causes quite opposite to those which lead to their establishment? What was established by multitudinous error was removed by the way of truth; what was established by infidelity was removed by faith; what was established by opposition to true religion was removed by conversion to the one true and holy God.

The lament of Hermes was concerned only with Egypt; but the change was not confined to that country. It has happened throughout the world, and the whole earth sings a new song to the Lord, as was truly prophesied in the Scriptures and in the writings of the prophets, where we read, 'Sing to the Lord a new song; sing to the Lord, all the earth.'[72] And this is the title of the psalm just quoted: *When the house was being built, after the captivity*. Indeed this house, the City of God, which is the holy Church, is now being built in the whole world after the captivity in which the demons held captive those men who, on believing in God, have become like 'living stones' of which the house is being built.[73] For the fact that man was the maker of his gods did not mean that he was not possessed by what he had made, for by worshipping them he was drawn into fellowship with them, and I do not mean fellowship with senseless idols, but with crafty demons. For what are idols but the things of which Scripture says, 'They have eyes, but they do not see,'[74] and all the rest that can be said of material things, bereft of life and sense, however skilfully fashioned? But the unclean spirits, bound to these images by this wicked art, had brought the souls of their worshippers into a wretched captivity, by forcing them into their fellowship. Hence the Apostle says, 'We know that an idol is nothing; when the gentiles offer sacrifice, it is to demons

72. Ps. 96, 1. 73. cf. 1 Pet. 2, 5. 74. Ps. 115, 5.

that they sacrifice, not to God. I do not want you to enter into fellowship with demons.'[75] It is after this captivity, in which men were kept prisoner by malignant demons, that God's house is being built in all the earth. Hence comes the title of the psalm, which has these words:

Sing to the Lord a new song; sing to the Lord, all the earth. Sing to the Lord, bless his name, give the good news of his salvation, day by day. Proclaim his glory among the nations, his wonderful acts among all peoples: for the Lord is great, and worthy of all praise; he is to be feared above all gods. Because all the gods of the nations are demons; but the Lord has created the heavens.[76]

Thus, in lamenting that the time was to come, when the worship of idols would be abolished and with it the domination of demons over their worshippers, Hermes was inspired by an evil spirit to desire the perpetual continuance of that captivity, whose passing was the occasion for the psalm which sings of the building of God's house in all the earth. Hermes made his prophecy with lamentation; the prophet announced his vision with joy. But since the victory is with the Spirit, who sang of these triumphs through the mouth of the holy prophets, even Hermes was in a miraculous way constrained to admit that the institutions whose abolition he contemplated with revulsion and lamentation were the work not of the wise, the faithful, and the devout, but of those in error, of unbelievers, and of those estranged from the worship of true religion. He gives these creations the name of gods, but then he declares they are the creation of men whom he certainly ought not to resemble. By admitting this he shows, whether he will or no, that these 'gods' are not to be worshipped by those who do not resemble those who created them – not to be worshipped, that is, by the wise, the faithful, and the devout. He also demonstrates that the men who created them imposed on themselves the burden of having 'gods' who were not gods. How true is the prophetic saying, 'Suppose man makes gods for himself. Why, they are not gods at all.'[77]

Hermes then, gives the title of 'man-made gods' to the 'gods' of this kind, the gods of men of this kind, manufactured by men of this kind, that is, to demons which some strange art has attached to idols by means of the fetters of their own passions. For all that, he has not assigned to them the role conferred on them by Apuleius the Platonist (whose absurd inconsistencies we have already sufficiently exposed); he has not assigned them the role of intermediaries and intercessors

75. 1 Cor. 10, 20. 76. Ps. 96, 1ff. 77. Jer. 16, 20.

between the gods created by God and men – who also are God's creation – to convey men's prayers to the gods and to bring back divine gifts to men. It is the height of folly to believe that gods made by man could have more influence with gods created by God than men themselves – whom God himself created. The demon attached to an image by an impious art has been made a god by man, but a god for this particular kind of man, not for all mankind. What sort of a god then is this who could only be made by a man who is in error, who lacks faith, who is estranged from the true God? Furthermore, if the demons who are worshipped in the temples and made to inhere in images (that is, in visible statues), through some strange art, by men who made them gods by means of this art because they were estranged from true religious worship – if such beings are not intermediaries and messengers between gods and men, both because of their corrupt and degraded characters, and also because men, however much in error, however faithless and estranged from true religious worship, are nevertheless better than those whom they have made into gods by their art – if this is true, it remains that what power they have is the power they have as demons. Either they make pretence of procuring benefits for men, and so do the greater harm, in so far as the deception is the greater, or they do evil without disguise. And yet they can only work in either way when they are permitted by the deep and inscrutable providence of God. But it is never as intermediaries between men and gods because of their friendship with the gods that they have power in the world of men. For they cannot conceivably be friends of the 'good gods' – whom we Christians call holy angels (rational creatures who have their holy abode in heaven) or Thrones, Dominations, Principalities, Powers.[78] The demons are as remote from them as vice from virtue, wickedness from goodness.

25. *The community between the holy angels and good men*

We must therefore never dream of canvassing the goodwill or the generosity of the 'good gods' – or rather of the good angels – through the supposed mediation of demons. We can only do this in virtue of a resemblance to them in goodness of will; for it is by such goodness that we share with them our being, our life and our worship of the God whom they worship, even though we cannot see him with our bodily eyes, while in so far as we are in misery by reason of the dissimilarity of our will and our frailty and weakness, we are remote from

78. cf. Col. 1, 16.

them – but remote in quality of life, not in physical situation. If we are not united with them, it is not because we dwell on earth under the conditions of fleshly existence; it is because in the impurity of our heart we have a taste for earthly things.[79] When we are restored to health and so become like the angels, we come near to them even now by faith, if we believe that we receive our happiness with their support, from him who has already given them theirs.

26. Pagan religion was bound up with the cult of the dead

We should pay particular attention to what this Egyptian says in the course of his lament over the coming time when those institutions will be abolished in Egypt, which, on his own admission, were the work of men grievously astray, and faithless, and estranged from true religious worship. His words are: 'At that time, this land, the holy abode of shrines and temples, will be full of tombs and of dead men.'[80] This suggests that, if these rites were not abolished, men would not be destined to die, or else that the dead were going to be put somewhere else than in the earth! Of course, as time goes on the number of tombs increases, because of the greater number of the dead.

It seems that what Hermes was really lamenting was that the pagan temples and shrines would be succeeded by the memorials of our Christian martyrs. To be sure, those who read these words in a perverse spirit of hostility to Christianity, suppose that the pagans used to worship gods in their temples, while we worship dead men in their tombs. Men are so blind in their impiety that, as it were, they bump into mountains and refuse to see what hits them in the eye. And so they fail to observe that in the whole of pagan literature no gods, or scarcely any gods, are to be found who were not originally human beings who have been accorded divine honours after their death. I pass over the statement of Varro that all the dead were regarded by the pagans as the gods called Manes. Varro proves this by the rites which are performed for almost all the dead, mentioning especially the funeral games as being the most impressive proof of divinity, since the custom is to hold games only in honour of divine powers.

Hermes himself, with whom we are at the moment concerned, testifies that the gods of Egypt are dead men. He does this in the very same book in which, when he purports to foretell the future, he says in lamentation, 'Then this land, the holy abode of shrines and temples,

79. cf. Phil. 3, 19; Col. 3, 2. 80. *Asclep.*, 24; cf. ch. 23.

will be full of tombs and dead men.' After saying that his ancestors had 'gone far astray in their conception of the gods, on account of their lack of faith, and their neglect of divine worship and true religion; and so they discovered the art of making gods', he goes on to say,

> They also brought in a power derived from the nature of the universe, as a supplement to this technique, suitable for their purpose, and by this addition (since they could not create souls) they called up the souls of angels or demons and made them inhere in sacred images and in divine mysteries, so that by their means the idols could have the power of doing good or inflicting harm.

He then proceeds as if he intended to prove this by examples,

> In fact, your grandfather, my dear Asclepius, the first inventor of medicine, has a temple dedicated to him on a mountain in Libya, in which his terrestrial being, his body, lies. The rest of him, or rather the whole of him, if we assume that the whole person consists of life and feeling, has returned to heaven in a better state of being; and now, by his divine power, he provides the sick with all the help which he used to afford them in virtue of his medical skill.[81]

You see that Hermes declares that a dead man was worshipped as a god in the place where he had his sepulchre. In saying that he 'returned to heaven' Hermes is at once deceived and deceiving.

After that he adds, 'My grandfather Hermes, whose name I bear, resides, as you know, in his own city, which is called after him, and there he gives help to those who come from all parts of the world, and preserves them from danger.' The story is that the elder Hermes, or Mercury, whom Trismegistus claims as his ancestor, lives in Hermopolis, the city called by his name. Now we have two gods, Asclepius and Hermes, who, by his account, were once men. Greeks and Latins agree in this opinion about Asclepius; as for Mercury, many people do not think that he started as a mortal, although our Hermes attests that he is his grandfather. It may be suggested that there were two different characters called Hermes. I am not much concerned to argue the question whether Hermes the god is distinct from Hermes the grandfather. The point is that according to the testimony of his grandson, a man of high repute among his own people, Hermes, like Asclepius, started as a man and became a god.

Trismegistus proceeds, 'We know how many benefits Isis, wife of Osiris,[82] bestows on us when she is favourable; how much harm she

81. *Asclep.*, 37. 82. cf. Bk VI, 10n.

does to us, in her wrath!' And he is concerned to point out that the gods created by men by means of the art previously mentioned belong to the class of capricious divinities. He thus gives us to understand that, in his opinion, the demons derived their existence from the souls of the dead – the demons who were installed in images by means of the art discovered by men with erroneous notions, without faith, and without true religion, because the makers of these gods were, of course, unable to make souls. After his above-mentioned remark about Isis ('we know how much harm she does, in her wrath'), he continues, 'The fact is, that the gods of the earth and of the world are easily irritated, being made and compounded of both natures by men.' By 'both natures' he means soul and body, the demon being the soul, the image, the body. 'And that', he says, 'is why those beings are called by the Egyptians "holy animals (creatures with souls)" and in their various cities worship is rendered to the souls of men, which were consecrated during their lifetime. The Egyptians in those cities obey the laws of those gods and adopt their names.'

What has become of that apparent cry of lamentation, when Hermes grieves that the land of Egypt, 'the holy abode of shrines and temples', is doomed to be 'full of tombs and of dead men'? To be sure, the deceiving spirit, at whose inspiration Hermes uttered those words, was constrained to admit, through Hermes' own mouth, that that country was even then 'full of tombs and of dead men', whom the people worshipped as gods. It was the grief of the demons that found expression in his words. They bewailed the punishment that was in store for them in the future at the memorial shrines of the Christian martyrs. For in many such places they are tormented, and acknowledge themselves for what they are, and are expelled from the bodies of the men they have possessed.

27. *The Christian cult of martyrs*

For all that, we Christians do not assign to the martyrs temples, priests, ceremonies and sacrifices. They are not gods for us; their God is our God. We certainly honour the memory of our martyrs, as holy men of God, who have contended for the truth as far as the death of their bodies, so that the true religion might be made known and fiction and falsehood convicted. There may have been some in previous times who thought as they did, but, if so, fear kept them silent.

But has any of the faithful ever heard the priest say, in his prayers as he stands at the altar, even if that altar has been erected for the glory and worship of God over the body of a holy martyr, 'I offer sacrifice to you, Peter, or Paul, or Cyprian'?[83] He has not. For at the memorials of martyrs the sacrifice is offered to God who made them men and made them martyrs, and has brought them into fellowship with his holy angels in the glory of heaven. And so in this solemn celebration we offer thanks to the true God for their victories, and by renewing their memory we encourage ourselves to emulate their crowns and palms of victory, calling upon God to help us. Thus all the acts of reverence which the devout perform at the shrines of the martyrs are acts of respect to their memory. They are not ceremonies or sacrifices offered to the dead as to gods.

There are some Christians who bring banquets to the memorials.[84] This is not the custom of the better-instructed, and in most parts of the world the practice is unknown. But even those who do this first lay the food at the tomb, then say their prayers and then remove the viands, which they either eat themselves, or distribute to the poor. Their intention is that the food should be sanctified through the merits of the martyrs in the name of the Lord of the martyrs. That this is not a sacrifice to the martyrs is well known to anyone who knows of the one and only Christian sacrifice, which is offered there also.

Thus we honour our martyrs neither with divine worship nor with human slanders as the pagans worship their gods. We neither offer sacrifice to them, nor turn their disgraces into religious ceremonies.

Consider the stories of Isis,[85] the Egyptian goddess, wife of Osiris, and their ancestors, who, according to Egyptian literature, were all kings. (When Isis was offering sacrifice to these ancestors, she found a crop of barley, and showed the ears to the king, her husband, and to his counsellor, Mercury; that is why she is identified with Ceres.) There are full accounts of the misdeeds of this family not in the poets, but in the books of the Egyptian mysteries; and Alexander wrote about them in a letter to his mother,[86] after the revelations of Leo, the priest. Those who have the inclination and the ability to read about them should do so, and should think over what they have read. Then they should ask themselves what kind of human beings these were, for whom religious rites were established after their death, and

83. Cyprian, bishop of Carthage, martyred A.D. 258.

84. cf. *Conf.*, 6, 2. By the second century the Christian *agape*, a holy meal of fellowship, seems to have become a funeral feast, like the pagan *silicernium*, or a memorial supper at the tomb of a departed Christian.

85. cf. Bk VI, 10n.

86. cf. ch. 5; Bk XII, 11.

what kind of actions were the basis of these ceremonies. Let them not, in heaven's name, have the audacity to compare them in any way with our holy martyrs, although they hold them to be gods, whereas we Christians do not deify our martyrs. We have not established priests in their honour, nor do we offer sacrifice to them; that would be unfitting, improper, and forbidden, since sacrifice is due only to God. Nor do we divert them with scandals about them, or with disgusting shows like those in which the pagans celebrate the offences of their gods, whether those which they have committed, when they were human beings, or those which have been invented for the delight of noxious demons, if these 'gods' did not start as men.

Socrates certainly would not have taken one of this category of demons as his god, if it is true that he had a private god. But it may be that this upright man, so innocent of the art of manufacturing gods, had a god of this kind foisted on him by those who aspired to excel in that art.

Need I say more? That these spirits are not to be worshipped with a view to the attainment of a life of blessedness after death, is something which no one, of even average intelligence, could doubt. But it may be that we shall be told that while all the *gods* are good, some of the demons are evil, others good, and that it is to the good ones that we should render worship with a view to eternal blessedness.

We must see, in the next book, if this notion has any value.

BOOK IX

1. *The upshot of the previous discussion*

SOME people believe in the existence both of good and of bad gods. Others take a better view of the gods, and ascribe to them so much praise and honour that they cannot bring themselves to believe that there can be such a thing as a bad god. Now those who have asserted the existence of good gods and bad gods,[1] have applied the name of gods to demons also, while sometimes, though more rarely, speaking of gods as 'demons'. In fact they admit that Jupiter himself, the king and leader of the gods, in their view, was called 'demon' by Homer.[2]

As for those who assert that there can only be good gods, whose goodness far excels anything that is called goodness in man, they are rightly disturbed by the actions of the demons, which they cannot deny, and consider it impossible that such things could be done by gods, whom they hold to be good. So they are forced to postulate a difference between gods and demons. All that they disapprove of, with good reason, whether in the evil activities or in the degraded passions where the hidden spirits display their power – all this they attribute to the demons, not to the gods. On the other hand, they hold that 'gods never have direct contact with men'[3] and therefore suppose that these demons are established midway between men and gods, to carry men's requests to the gods and to bring back the benefits the gods have granted. This is the view of the Platonists, the most eminent and celebrated of the philosophers. And it is with them, because of their superiority to all the other thinkers, that we decided to discuss the question whether the worship of a plurality of gods is of any value for the attainment of blessedness in the life after death. Thus in the preceding book we observed that demons rejoice in such things as are detested and condemned by men of virtue and wisdom, in the blasphemous, outrageous, criminal fictions of the poets, invented not

1. cf. Lact., *Div. Inst.*, 2, 14, 6; 4, 27, 14f.

2. *Il.*, 1, 222. But δαίμων means 'divine power' and can be used of any divine or semi-divine being. The pejorative sense of 'demon' comes in with Christian writers.

3. Apul., *De Deo Socr.*, 4 (cf. Plat., *Symp.*, 203A).

about any mere human being but about the gods themselves, and in the abominable and legally punishable violence of magic arts. And we asked how it could be that such demons should be able, as being reputedly closer to the gods and more friendly with them, to bring good men into the favour of the 'good gods'. And our finding was that this was utterly impossible.

2. *Are there any good demons who might assist the human soul to attain felicity?*

This present volume will have to fulfil the promise given at the end of the last book, and contain a discussion of the distinction (if any is admitted to exist) between different kinds of demons. We shall not treat of any distinction between gods, since the Platonists insist that all gods are good, nor of the distinction between gods and demons. There is, according to them, a vast interval separating men from gods, while the demons are situated in between the two. We shall be concerned with the distinction among the demons, as far as is relevant to the question before us. Now it is with many people a commonplace that there are good demons and bad demons. And whether this opinion is also held by the Platonists, or whether by any other philosophical school, we must certainly not omit to discuss it. We should not let anyone imagine that so-called 'good demons' are to be courted, on the assumption that their mediation can assure him that reconciliation with the gods (all of whom he believes to be good) on which he has set his heart. Such a man might suppose that he would be able to enter into fellowship with the gods after death; but in fact he would find himself in the toils of malignant spirits, the victim of their deception, far astray from the true God, with whom alone, in whom alone, and through whom alone, the soul of man, the rational and intelligent soul, can attain to felicity.

3. *Apuleius attributes reason, but not goodness, to the demons*

What then is the distinction between good demons and bad? Apuleius the Platonist describes the demons in general, and writes at length about their bodies of air. But he has nothing to say about the virtues of their character, with which they would have been endowed, if they had been good. Thus he was silent about the essential condition of felicity; but he could not suppress the proof of their wretchedness, since he admits that their mind, which in his account made them rational beings, far from being steeped in virtue and thus protected against any surrender to irrational passions of the soul, was itself in some measure liable to disturbances, agitations, and storms of passion, the normal condition of foolish minds. These are his words on the subject:

It is from this collection of demons that the poets generally select their characters when, without departing much from the truth, they give a fictitious picture of the gods as haters or lovers of particular men: when they represent them as raising some people to prosperity and bringing to others frustration and affliction. Hence the gods are shown feeling pity and indignation, anguish, joy and every facet of human emotion; being subject, like men, to such agitation of the heart and turmoil in the mind they are tossed about on the stormy waters of their imaginations. All these squalls and tempests banish them far away from the tranquillity of the gods of heaven.[4]

There is no uncertainty in those words. It is not any of the lower parts of the souls of the demons that Apuleius describes as agitated as if by raging seas and storms of passion; it is their mind, the faculty that makes them rational beings. And therefore they are not worthy of comparison with wise men who, even under the conditions of their present life, offer the resistance of an undisturbed mind to those disturbances of the soul from which human weakness cannot be exempt, and do not allow themselves either to command or to commit any act which strays from the path of wisdom or transgresses the law of justice. It is the foolish and the lawless among mortals that these demons resemble, not in their bodies but in their characters. I might say that they are worse than such men, inasmuch as they are older in wickedness, and incapable of being reformed by the punishment they deserve. And so they are tossed about on what Apuleius calls the raging sea of their minds. Only truth and virtue can offer a centre of resistance against turbulent and degraded passions. And there is no truth or virtue in the constitution of their souls.

4. *The opinions of Peripatetics and Stoics about the passions*

Two opinions are found among the philosophers concerning these agitations of the soul, which the Greeks call *pathê*, while some of our Latin authors, Cicero for example,[5] describe them as disturbances, others as affections or affects, or again as passions, the word used by

4. *De Deo Socr.*, 12. 5. cf. Bk VIII, 17.

Apuleius, which is closer to the meaning of the Greek term. Now these disturbances (or affections or passions), according to some philosophers, befall even a wise man, though with him they are restrained and subjected to reason, and the predominant intellect as it were imposes laws on the passions, which keep them within strict bounds. This opinion is held by the Platonists and the Aristotelians – Aristotle being a disciple of Plato who founded the Peripatetic school. Others, the Stoics among them, refuse to admit that passions of this kind can conceivably befall a wise man. Now Cicero, in his work *On the Ends of Good and Evil*, proves that the opposition between Stoics and Platonists (or Peripatetics) is really a quarrel about words rather than things. For example, the Stoics refuse to give the name 'goods' to what they call material and external 'advantages'. According to them there is no 'good' for man except virtue, meaning the art of the good life, which exists only in the soul. The other side called them quite simply 'goods', in conformity with the normal usage, but they regarded them as goods of small or infinitesimal value in comparison with virtue, the practice of the good life. The result is that both sides attach the same value to 'goods' or 'advantages', in spite of the different terminology; the Stoics are only indulging in the pleasure of linguistic innovation on this point. And it seems to me that in the question whether passions of the soul can befall the wise man, the dispute is a matter of words rather than of things. In my opinion, the Stoic view of the matter is identical with that of Platonists and Peripatetics, in respect of the objective reference of their statements, as opposed to the sound of their words.

To dispense with the tedium of a detailed demonstration, I shall confine myself to one most cogent piece of evidence. In his work entitled *Attic Nights*, Aulus Gellius,[6] a writer of polished eloquence and multifarious erudition, tells the following anecdote.[7] He once found himself on a sea voyage in the company of a well-known Stoic. When the ship began to pitch dangerously on a stormy sea beneath a lowering sky (I am condensing the detailed and copious narrative of Gellius) the philosopher turned pale with fright. This was noticed by those present, who were curious to observe, even when death was imminent, whether a philosopher would be disturbed in soul or not.

6. *Aulus Gellius*. After spending his youth in Rome, Gellius went to Athens *c.* 140, where he studied philosophy and compiled his *Noctes Atticae*, a kind of 'commonplace book', a collection of brief essays and miscellaneous pieces of information.

7. 19, 1.

Once the storm had passed, and restored confidence afforded the opportunity for conversation, and even raillery, one of the other passengers, a rich and self-indulgent Asiatic, hailed the philosopher with a jibe at his terror and pallor, in contrast with the speaker's own unshaken intrepidity in the face of impending destruction. The Stoic replied with the retort given in a similar situation by Aristippus[8] the Socratic to a man of the same type who had made the same remark: 'You were quite right not to be worried about the life of a contemptible scoundrel: but I was bound to be afraid for the life of Aristippus.' This reply put the rich man in his place. But later on Gellius asked the philosopher, with no intention of criticizing him, but simply for information, what really was the reason for his panic. The Stoic was ready to instruct a man who betrayed such an ardent thirst for knowledge, and he immediately produced from his baggage a work of Epictetus[9] the Stoic, an exposition of doctrines in harmony with the principles laid down by Zeno and Chrysippus, whom we know as the originators of Stoicism.[10] Gellius tells us that he read in that book that the Stoics had concluded that there are certain mental phenomena, to which they give the name of 'fantasies', which we cannot control. We cannot decide whether they will happen, or when they will happen. When these are brought on by circumstances of overwhelming terror they are bound to disturb even the mind of a philosopher, so that, for a moment, he experiences the panic of terror or the anguish of grief. It is as if these passions are too quick for the functioning of his intellect and reason. This does not mean that his intellect forms any judgement on the evil, or that his reason approves those reactions or consents to them. It is this consent, they insist, that is under our control, and this, according to the Stoics, is the difference between the attitude of a wise man and a fool. The soul of the fool gives way to these passions and accords them the consent of his mind, while the wise man's soul, although it cannot help experiencing these emotions, still keeps its mind unshaken and holds firmly to its right decision about what aims it ought, in reason, to pursue, and what it should reject.

Such is the teaching which Gellius read, according to his own ac-

8. cf. Bk VIII, 3.

9. *Epictetus* (*c.* A.D. 60–140). His doctrines are recorded by Arrian in the *Diatribae* and the *Enchiridion*.

10. *Zeno* of Citium (*fl. c.* 300 B.C.) founded the Stoic school; cf. n. on Bk XIV, 2. *Chrysippus* (*c.* 280–204 B.C.) was the third head of the Stoics. He completed and systematized their teachings.

count, in the book of Epictetus, where the author expresses ideas based on the principles of Stoicism. I have expounded the teaching to the best of my power, less attractively, no doubt, than Gellius, but more succinctly, and, I fancy, with greater clarity.

On this showing there is little or no difference between the opinions of Stoics and of other philosophers on the subject of the disturbances – or passions – of the soul. Both sides champion the mind and the reason against the tyranny of the passions. And the meaning of the Stoic assertion that passions do not touch a wise man is probably that passions in no way cloud with error that wisdom in virtue of which he is wise, nor can they undermine and overthrow it. However, they do happen to his soul, but that is because of circumstances which the Stoics call 'advantageous' or 'disadvantageous', being unwilling to describe them as 'good' or 'evil'. For, to be sure, if the philosopher in the anecdote had attached no importance to all that he felt he was going to lose in the shipwreck, including his life, and his material existence, he would not have dreaded the danger to the point of betraying his fear by turning pale. Yet it was possible for him to experience that emotion, while retaining in his mind the fixed conviction that life and material existence, which were threatened by the violence of the storm, are not 'goods' of the same order as justice; they cannot determine the goodness of their possessor.

The Stoic insistence that such things are not to be called 'good', but 'advantageous', should be regarded as a quibble about words, not a question of the realities they signify. What does it matter whether they are more properly called 'goods', or 'advantages', seeing that Stoic and Peripatetic alike turn pale with dread at the prospect of their loss? There is a difference of terminology, but an identical judgement of value. Both schools certainly maintain that if they were urged to any disgraceful or criminal act by a threatened danger to these 'goods' or 'advantages' as the only way to ensure their retention, they would prefer to lose all that guarantees the life and health of the physical body rather than commit any violation of justice. Thus the mind in which this principle is fixed does not allow any of those disturbances to prevail in it against reason, even though they may occur in the lower parts of the soul. On the contrary, the mind exercises dominion over them. Far from consenting to them, it resists, and by that resistance establishes the reign of virtue. Virgil describes Aeneas as such a man when he says

> Unmoved his mind: the tears roll down in vain.[11]

11. *Aen.*, 4, 449 ('the tears' are Dido's).

5. *For Christians, the passions offer a training in virtue, not an inducement to sin*

It is not at this point necessary to expound in copious detail what is taught about these passions in the divine Scriptures, which contain the syllabus of instruction for Christians. Scripture subjects the mind to God for his direction and assistance, and subjects the passions to the mind for their restraint and control so that they may be turned into the instruments of justice. In fact, in our discipline, the question is not *whether* the devout soul is angry, but *why*; not whether it is sad, but what causes its sadness; not whether it is afraid, but what is the object of its fear.

To be indignant with the sinner with a view to his correction, to feel sorrow for the afflicted with a view to his release from suffering, to be afraid for one in danger so as to prevent his death – those are emotions which, as far as I can see, no sane judgement could reprove. The Stoics, to be sure, are in the habit of extending their condemnation to compassion;[12] but how much more honourable would it have been in the Stoic of our anecdote to have been 'disturbed' by compassion so as to rescue someone, rather than by the fear of being shipwrecked! Far more creditable, more humane, and more in harmony with the feelings of true religion was the sentiment expressed in Cicero's praise of Caesar, 'Of all your virtues, none was more admirable, none more attractive, than your compassion.'[13] What is compassion but a kind of fellow-feeling in our hearts for another's misery, which compels us to come to his help by every means in our power? Now this emotion is the servant of reason, when compassion is shown without detriment to justice, when it is a matter of giving to the needy or of pardoning the repentant. Cicero, with his unique mastery of words, did not hesitate to call compassion a virtue, while the Stoics did not scruple to class it as a vice. Yet, on the evidence of the book of that notable Stoic, Epictetus (a book based on the principles of Zeno and Chrysippus, the founders of that sect) even the Stoics admit passions of this kind into the soul of a wise man, while insisting that such a man is free from every vice. From this one must conclude that they do not regard them as vices when they occur in a wise man in such a way as to have no power against his strength of mind and his reason. The Stoic position would then be identical with that of the Peripatetics and even the Platonists; and, as Cicero says, 'It is high

12. cf. Seneca (*De Clem.*, 2, 5): 'Compassion is the vice of a feeble soul.'
13. *Pro Lig.*, 12, 37.

time that these linguistic disputes were left to torment those poor little Greeks who are more devoted to controversy than to truth.'[14]

There is another question which merits examination. Are we to suppose that our experience of such emotions, even in the practice of good works, is one of the disabilities involved in this present life? Do we then assume that the holy angels feel no anger when they punish those who are consigned to them for punishment by God's eternal law? That they come to the help of the wretched without feeling compassion for their wretchedness, and have no fear for those whom they love when they rescue them from danger? Certainly, we follow the conventions of human language in applying to the angels the words denoting these passions, but this is perhaps because of the analogy between their actions and those of men, not because they are subject to the infirmity of our passions. In the same way, God is described in Scripture as showing anger though in fact he is not troubled by any passion. The word 'anger' signifies that his vengeance is effected; it does not mean he is himself affected by any storm of emotion.

6. *Demons are at the mercy of passions*

Let us postpone the question of the holy angels for the time being and notice how, according to the Platonists, these demons, located midway between gods and men, are tossed about on the waves of the passions. If they experienced these emotions while their minds remained free from their influence, and exerted mastery over the passions, Apuleius would not have spoken of them as 'tossed about on the stormy waters of their imaginations, subject, like men, to such agitation of the heart and turmoil in the mind'.[15] It follows that it is their mind that is affected, the superior part of the soul, the faculty that makes them rational beings, the place where virtue and wisdom, if they have any, exercises mastery over the turbulent passions of the lower parts of the soul by directing and controlling them. It is their mind, which, on the admission of this Platonist, is 'tossed on those stormy waters'. Thus the mind of the demons is in subjection to the passions of desire, of fear, of anger, and the rest. Then is there any part of them free and capable of wisdom, which can make them acceptable to the gods, and of service to man by offering an example of morality? How can there be, if their mind is subdued under the oppressive tyranny of vicious passions, and employs for seduction and deception all the rational

14. *De Or.*, 1, 11, 47. 15. cf. ch. 3.

power that it has by nature, with all the more eagerness as the lust for doing harm gains increasing mastery?

7. *According to the Platonists, the poets' slanders of the gods refer to the demons*

It may be objected that it is not the whole class of demons, but only the evil kind, to which this applies; that it is from this class that the poets have taken their characters, when, without straying far from the truth, they give a fictitious picture of gods as haters and lovers of men (these being the 'gods' who, in the words of Apuleius, 'are tossed about on the stormy waters of their imaginations'). What are we to make of this? For when Apuleius made this remark he was describing the intermediate situation between gods and men held, in virtue of their bodies of air, by *all* the demons, not just by some of them, the evil kind.

According to Apuleius the effect of the poets' fictions was to make some of these demons into gods, to give them the names of gods, and to distribute them to men as friends or foes, quite capriciously, thanks to the unrestricted licence of poetical fiction; whereas the gods, he maintains, are worlds apart from such demon morality in virtue of their situation in the heavens and their abundant felicity. Thus it is mere poetic fiction to give the names of gods to those who are not gods, and to portray them in mutual conflict on account of men for whom they feel the affection or dislike of partisanship. For all that, Apuleius declares that this fiction is not far from the truth, seeing that though they are given names of gods, to which they are not entitled, it is demons who are being presented in their real characters. In fact Apuleius asserts that Minerva, as Homer presents her, belongs to this class 'when she intervenes to restrain Achilles in the midst of the Greek assemblies'.[16] It was, he insists, a poetical fiction to say that she was Minerva; for he considers Minerva to be a goddess and sets her among the gods, whom he believes to be all of them good and happy in their ethereal abode on high, far from any intercourse with mortals. But he agrees that there was some demon supporting the Greeks against the Trojans and another demon helping the Trojans against the Greeks, whom the poet calls Venus, or Mars, using the names of gods whom Apuleius locates in heavenly abodes, taking no part in such activities, and that those demons fought among themselves in support of those whom they loved, and in opposition to those

16. *De Deo Socr.*, 10; cf. Hom. *Il.*, 1, 195ff.

whom they hated. All this he admitted to be not far from the truth in the poet's narrative. For these accounts were concerned with beings who were, on his showing, 'subject, like men, to such agitation of the heart and turmoil in the mind, tossed about on the stormy waters of their imaginations', so that their loves or hates could prompt them to act in favour of some and in opposition to others, without regard to justice, but at the bidding of partisan feeling, just as the members of the populace, who are the image of them, support their favourite wild beast fighters and charioteers. The chief anxiety of our Platonist was that the activities described by the poets should be attributed to these intermediary demons, and not to the gods whose names the poets misapplied.

8. *Gods, demons, and men, as defined by Apuleius*

But we must not too lightly pass over the actual definition of demons, given by Apuleius – a definition intended to include them all. The demons, he says, are animals in respect of species; in respect of soul, liable to passions; in mind, capable of reason; in body, composed of air; in life-span, eternal.[17] Now in all these five attributes thus listed, he has mentioned nothing at all which would suggest that the demons have something in common with good men which is not found in the bad. For he gives a somewhat extended description of man, to embrace him in a definition; he treats of him in his turn as being a creature made of earth on the lowest scale of existence, when he had previously treated of the gods of heaven, and so after allocating these two divisions of the universe, the highest and the lowest, he goes on to speak in the third and last place about the demons, who occupy the intermediate situation. These are his words:

> And so we come to men, rejoicing in reason, endowed with the great power of speech; with immortal souls, but with physical frames destined for death; with minds unstable and unquiet, and bodies clumsy and vulnerable; diverse in character, but alike in error, persistent in daring, pertinacious in hope, ineffectual in their striving, dogged by ill-luck; individually mortal, yet perpetual as a whole species, one generation taking the place of another in continual exchange; their life a fleeting span, their wisdom slow in coming, but their death swift; their life full of complaining. Such are the inhabitants of the earth.

While saying so many things, which apply to most men, he certainly did not omit to mention something which he knew to apply to only a

17. *De Deo Socr.*, 13; cf. Bk VIII, 17.

few. He mentioned this in speaking of 'wisdom', which is 'slow in coming'. Had he omitted this element, he would have failed to give a complete description of the human race, for all his care and thoroughness. On the other hand, when he is concerned to emphasize the pre-eminence of the gods, it is felicity that he asserts as their pre-eminent quality; the felicity which they wish men to attain through wisdom.

Accordingly, if he had wished it to be understood that there are some good demons, he would have put into his description of them some characteristic which would suggest that the demons shared some portion of felicity with the gods, or some kind of wisdom with men. But in fact he mentions no good quality in them by which the good might be distinguished from the evil. Doubtless he was chary of expressing himself frankly about their wickedness, for fear, not so much of offending the demons themselves, as of offending their worshippers, who formed his audience; nevertheless he made clear, to the thoughtful readers, what they ought to think about the demons. For he made the gods, (who, he insisted, must all be understood to be good) completely aloof from the passions and, as he put it, the 'storms', which affect the demons. He united gods and demons only in respect of the eternity of their bodies, while expressly driving home the point that in soul the demons resemble men, and not the gods; and they resemble men not in the good quality of wisdom, of which men can have a share, but in the turbulent passions, which gain the mastery over the foolish and the wicked, but are controlled by the wise and the good – though they would prefer not to have them rather than to gain the victory over them. Now if he had wished it to be understood that the eternity which the demons share with the gods is an eternity of souls, not of bodies, he would not have excluded men from a share in it, because there can be no shadow of doubt that, as a Platonist, he believed the soul of man to be eternal. That is why, in describing this species of living beings, he ascribes to man 'an immortal soul, but a physical frame destined for death'. It follows that if it is the mortality of their bodies that debars man from sharing the eternity of the gods, it must be the immortality of their bodies that entitles the demons to share it.

9. *Can men receive the friendship of the gods through the mediation of demons?*

What kind of beings are these mediators between gods and men through whom men are to canvass the friendly offices of the gods?

They share man's inferiority in respect of the better part of a living being, the soul; they share the superiority of the gods in respect of the lower part of a living being, the body. Now every living being, or 'animal', consists of a soul and a body. Of these two constituents the soul is certainly better than the body, however faulty and weak it may be, better even than the healthiest and strongest body, because its nature is more excellent, and the blemishes of vice cannot make it inferior to the body – just as gold, even if dirty, is valued above silver or lead, however pure. And these 'mediators' between gods and men, through whose intervention the human is joined to the divine, have an eternal body in common with the gods, but a corrupted soul in common with men – as if religion, by which men aspire to be united with the gods by the mediation of demons, were located in the body, not in the soul. What a wicked thing to do, to hang those spurious and deceptive mediators upside down! Or perhaps it was a punishment? Anyhow, they have their body, the lower part of their being, in the company of the higher powers, while their higher part, the soul, is with the lower creatures; united with the gods of heaven in virtue of their subordinate part, they are united in misery with men on earth in respect of the part which should command. For the body is undoubtedly a servant; as Sallust says, 'Our soul is appointed to command, our body to obey.'[18] And he adds, 'One element in us we share with the gods, the other with the beasts,' for he is speaking about man, who, like the beasts, has a mortal body. On the other hand, these demons, whom the philosophers have provided for us as mediators between ourselves and the gods, can indeed say of their soul and body, 'One element in us we share with the gods, the other with men.' But, as I have said, they have been tied up and suspended as it were topsy-turvy, with their body, the servant, in the company of the blessed gods, and their soul, the master, in the company of wretched men; exalted in the lower part of their being, they are abased in their upper part. Hence even if one supposes that the demons share eternity with the gods, because their souls are never sundered from the body by death, as happens with terrestrial creatures, one should not think of their body as the eternal instrument of beings advanced to honour, but as the eternal chain that binds the damned.

18. *Cat.*, 1, 2.

10. *The opinion of Plotinus that men are less wretched in their mortal bodies than demons in their eternal bodies*

Plotinus is accorded the praise of having understood Plato more thoroughly than anyone else, at any rate in modern times. And when speaking of the human soul, he says, 'The Father in his compassion made these fetters mortal.'[19] That is, he considered that the very fact of man's corporal mortality is due to the compassion of God, who would not have us kept for ever in the misery of this life. The wickedness of the demons was not judged worthy of this compassion, and in the misery of their condition, with a soul subject to passions, they have not been granted the mortal body, which man has received, but an eternal body. They would certainly have been happier than man, if they had shared man's mortal body and the blessed soul of the gods. They would have been on an equality with man, if they had been counted worthy to share man's wretched soul, but, at the same time, his mortal body – provided that they could have acquired some measure of piety, so that they might at least in death have rest from their sorrows. As it is, not only does the wretchedness of their soul prevent them from being happier than men; they are even more miserable than men because they are chained to the body for all eternity. For our Platonist did not want it to be supposed that demons could make progress in the practice of piety and wisdom and so turn into gods. He declared in unmistakeable terms that they are demons in perpetuity.

11. *The notion of the Platonists that the souls of men, released from the body, become demons*

Apuleius says also that the souls of men are demons.[20] On leaving human bodies they become *lares* if they have shown themselves good, if evil, *lemures* or *larvae*, while they are called *di manes*, if it is not certain to which class they belong. Surely anyone can see, on a moment's reflection, what an abyss of moral degradation is opened by this notion. It means that however wicked men have been, they will suppose that they are on the way to becoming *larvae*, or *di manes*, and they will become worse in proportion to their desire to do evil, believing that after their death some sort of sacrifice will be offered them, like the honours paid to the gods, to invite them to continue their evil

19. *Enn.*, 4, 3, 12. 20. *De Deo Socr.*, 15.

work. According to Apuleius, *larvae* are malignant demons created out of men; but that raises another question. He also says that this is the reason why the blessed are called in Greek *eudaimones*;[21] it is because their souls, that is to say their *demons*, are good, which proves, he thinks, that the souls of men are demons.

12. *The distinctive marks of demons and men, according to the Platonists*

Our present concern is with those demons whose special characteristics have been listed by Apuleius, situated between gods and men, belonging to the 'animal' species, with a rational mind, a soul subject to passions, a body made of air, a life-span of eternity.[22] Having located the gods in the heights of heaven and men on the earth, the lowest level of the universe, he concludes with these words:

> You now have two classes of 'animals': the gods are vastly different from man in respect of their lofty abode, the perpetuity of their life, the perfection of their nature: there is no direct intercourse between gods and men, because of the immensity of the gulf which yawns between the highest and the lowest dwelling-places; and the life there above is eternal and unfailing, while here below it is fleeting and unreliable; and natures there are lifted up to felicity, while here they are forced down to sorrows.[23]

I find quoted here three pairs of contraries distinguishing the two extremes of being, the highest and the lowest. In other words, our author has repeated the three excellencies which he had already ascribed to the gods, to contrast them with three characteristics of mankind. The three attributes of the gods are these: the sublimity of their abode, the eternity of their life, the perfection of their nature. He has repeated these, in different words, so as to oppose to them three contrasting attributes of mankind. Previously he had said, 'the sublimity of their abode', now he speaks of 'the immensity of the gulf which yawns between the highest and lowest habitations'. He had said, 'eternity of life'; now we have, 'the life there above is eternal and unfailing, while here below it is fleeting and unreliable.' And for 'perfection of their nature' we read, 'natures there are lifted up to felicity, while here they are forced down to sorrows.' Thus he attributes to the gods three characteristics: a sublime abode, eternity, and felicity, and he attributes to men three contraries: a lowly abode, mortality, and misery.

21. *De Deo Socr.*, 22. 22. cf. ch. 8. 23. *De Deo Socr.*, 4.

13. *If the demons are not happy like the gods or wretched like men, how can they act as intermediaries?*

Apuleius gave the demons an intermediate position between gods and men in respect of these three pairs of contrary attributes. About their location in the universe there is no dispute. They are assigned a most appropriate place, midway between the heights and the depths. There remain the other two pairs, and here more careful attention is required, both to show that neither attribute is inapplicable to the demons, and then to assign them to the demons in such a way as their intermediate situation appears to demand.

Now it is impossible that neither attribute should apply. We can speak of an intermediate location as being neither the highest nor the lowest; but we cannot rightly say that the demons, being rational 'animals', are neither happy nor wretched like the plants which lack sensibility, or the beasts who lack reason. Beings whose minds are possessed of reason are of necessity either happy or unhappy. Again, we cannot rightly say that the demons are neither mortal nor immortal; for all living things either live for ever, or bring their span of life to an end in death. Besides, our philosopher has said that the demons have a 'life-span of eternity'.

We must conclude that these intermediate beings have one of the two superior attributes and one of the two inferior. For if they had both of the superior, or both of the inferior, they would not be intermediate; they would either rise up to the higher position, or sink down to the lower. Now since, as has been shown, one of the opposed attributes of these two pairs must apply to them, they will preserve their intermediate station by receiving one from the higher extreme and one from the lower. Accordingly, since they cannot have their eternity from below, where it is not to be found, that is the attribute they take from the higher side; and thus the only attribute they can have from the lower side to make sure of their intermediate state is misery.

Thus, according to the Platonists, the gods, who dwell on high, have the attributes of blessed eternity or eternal blessedness; men, who inhabit the lowest level of the universe, are characterized by mortal misery, or miserable mortality; the intermediate demons by miserable eternity, or eternal misery. As for those five distinctive marks[24] in his definition of the demons, Apuleius has not used them to fulfil his promise to demonstrate the intermediate state of the demons. He

24. cf. ch. 8.

states that they share three attributes with us men: membership of the animal species, possession of reason, susceptibility to passions; one attribute they share with the gods: eternal life; and one, the body of air, is their peculiar possession. How then could they be intermediate, if they have one attribute in common with the superior beings, but share three with the inferior sort? Is it not obvious that, in this case, they have abandoned their middle situation, and are forced down to the lower level?

But it is clear that they could be shown to be in a middle situation, even so, in that they have one peculiar attribute, their body of air – as at the two extremes, the gods have their ethereal bodies and men their terrestrial bodies, as their unique distinction; while two attributes are common to all three, namely, membership of the class of 'animals', and rationality. For Apuleius himself says, 'You have two classes of "animals",' meaning gods and men, and the Platonists always represent the gods as endowed with reason. Two characteristics are left: the soul susceptible to passion, and eternal existence. The demons share the former with the lower beings, the latter with the higher, so that their middle state is equally balanced and is not lifted up to the higher level or pushed down to the lower. And this it is that constitutes the miserable eternity, or eternal misery, of the demons. The philosopher speaks of 'a soul susceptible to passions'; he would have added 'and wretched', had he not been embarrassed by the thought of their worshippers. Furthermore, since the world is directed, as these philosophers themselves admit, by the providence of God and not by random chance, the misery of the demons would never have been eternal, had not their wickedness been great.

Therefore, if happy people are correctly called *eudaimones*,[25] the demons, whom these philosophers have situated midway between gods and men, are not *eudaimones*. Then what place can be found for the 'good demons', so that, being stationed above men and below the gods they may afford help to the former and perform service for the latter? For if they are good and eternal, they are of necessity happy also. But eternal felicity precludes an intermediate state, because it brings them so close to the gods and separates them so far from men. So the philosophers will strive in vain to show how 'good demons', if they are immortal and happy, can really be established midway between immortal and blessed gods and mortal and miserable men. Since they have both felicity and immortality in common with the gods, and no community in those respects with men, who are both wretched

25. cf. ch. 11.

and mortal, how can they help being far removed from men, and closely connected with the gods, rather than established midway between the two? In fact they could only be midway between them if they themselves, instead of sharing two attributes with one of the other classes, had one attribute in common with each of them. Thus man is an intermediate being, but intermediate between beasts and angels. A beast is irrational and mortal, while an angel is rational and immortal. Man is intermediate, inferior to the angels, and superior to the beasts; he is a rational and mortal animal, sharing mortality with the beasts, and rationality with the angels. And that is why, when we look for a mean between blessed immortals and wretched mortals, we have to find a being who combines happiness with mortality, or wretchedness with immortality.

14. *Can man have genuine felicity, though mortal?*

Whether man can be both mortal and happy is a vexed question. Some have formed a low opinion of man's condition, denying that man is capable of felicity in this mortal life. Others[26] have held a more exalted view of the human state, and have dared to say that those who are possessed of wisdom can be happy, though mortal. If that is true, why are such men not established as mediators between wretched mortals and blessed immortals, sharing felicity with blessed immortals and mortality with miserable mortals? For it is certain that if they are happy, they envy no one (for is anything more wretched than envy?) and, therefore, they will give to unhappy mortals all the aid in their power, to help them to attain happiness so that they may also be able to be immortal after death and join the company of immortal and blessed angels.

15. *'The Mediator between God and man, the man Christ Jesus'*

The more credible and probable position is that all men, as long as they are mortals, must needs be also wretched. If this is so, we must look for a mediator who is not only human but also divine, so that men may be brought from mortal misery to blessed immortality by the intervention of the blessed mortality of this mediator. It was necessary that he should not fail to become mortal, equally necessary that he should not remain mortal. He was in truth made mortal, not

26. The Stoics.

by the weakening of the godhead of the Word but by the assumption of the weakness of the flesh. But he did not remain mortal in that flesh which he raised from the dead. For the fruit of his mediation is just this: that those for whose liberation he was made a mediator, should not themselves remain for ever in death, even the death of the flesh. Thus it was necessary that the mediator between God and man should have a transient mortality, and a permanent blessedness, so that through that which is transient he might be conformed to the condition of those who are doomed to die, and might bring them back from the dead to that which is permanent. So it is that good angels cannot mediate between wretched mortals and blessed immortals, because they also are both blessed and immortal. On the other hand, bad angels could mediate, because they are immortals, like the gods, and wretched, like men. Utterly different from them is the good Mediator who, in contrast with the immortality and misery of the bad angels, was willing to be mortal for a time, and was able to remain in blessedness for eternity. Those immortals, in their pride, those wretches, in their wickedness, sought to seduce men into misery by their boast of immortality; to prevent this, the good Mediator by the humility of his death and the kindness of his blessedness has destroyed their power over those whose hearts he has purified, through their faith, and delivered from the filthy tyranny of those demons.

So here is man, in his mortality and misery, so far removed from the immortals in their felicity. What kind of mediation is he to choose to unite him to immortality and felicity? What he could find to delight him in the immortality of the demons is in fact nothing but misery; what he might have recoiled from in the mortality of Christ no longer exists. With the demons, everlasting misery is to be dreaded; with Christ, death is not to be feared, for death could not be everlasting, and the felicity which is to be welcomed is everlasting. For the being who is immortal and wretched intervenes simply to prevent one passing to a blessed immortality, since the obstacle that stands in the way, that is, the misery itself, always persists. But the one who is mortal and blessed interposed in order to make an end of mortality, and give immortality to those who were dead – as he showed by his resurrection – and to give to the wretched the happiness from which he himself had never departed.

Thus there is such a thing as a bad intermediary, who separates friends; very different is a good intermediary, who reconciles enemies. And the reason why there are many intermediaries who separate, is that the multitude of the blessed is made blessed by participation in the one God, and the multitude of evil angels – wretched because deprived of participation in him – rather opposes our approach to blessedness than interposes to help us thither, and even by its very multitude makes a kind of uproar, designed to make it impossible for man to reach that one good which can bring us happiness – that good for which we needed not many mediators, but the one Mediator who could lead us to it. And that Mediator in whom we can participate, and by participation reach our felicity, is the uncreated Word of God, by whom all things were created. And yet he is not the Mediator in that he is the Word; for the Word, being pre-eminently immortal and blessed, is far removed from wretched mortals. He is the Mediator in that he is man, by his very manhood making it plain that for the attainment of that good, which is not only blessed but beatific also, we have not to look for other mediators, through whom, as we may think, we can achieve the approach to happiness. God himself, the blessed God who is the giver of blessedness, became partaker of our human nature and thus offered us a short cut to participation in his own divine nature. For in liberating us from mortality and misery it is not to the immortal and blessed angels that he brings us, so that by participation in their nature we also may be immortal and blessed; it is to that Trinity, in which the angels participate, and so achieve their felicity. For that reason, when he 'took the form of a servant',[27] so as to be a mediator, and was willing to be 'below the angels',[28] he remained 'in the form of God'[29] above the angels. In the lower world he was the Way of life, as in the world above he is the Life itself.

16. *The Platonists' denial of contact between men and gods*

There is no truth in the statement, ascribed to Plato by Apuleius,[30] that 'the gods have no direct dealing with men', with the addition that the principal mark of their sublimity is that they are not defiled by any contact with humanity. This amounts to an admission that demons are thus contaminated; it follows that demons cannot purify those by whom they are contaminated, and both parties become equally impure, the demons by contact with men, men by contact with demons. Otherwise, if demons can have contact and intercourse with men without incurring defilement, they are proved to be superior to gods, since the gods would be contaminated by this intercourse. For this is alleged as the principal mark of divinity, that the

27. Phil. 2, 7. 28. Heb. 2, 7 (Ps. 8, 5). 29. Phil. 2, 6.
30. *De Deo Socr.*, 4 (cf. Plat., *Symp.*, 203A).

gods, in their sublimity, are aloof from human contact and cannot be contaminated by it.

Our philosopher assures us that when Plato spoke of the supreme God,[31] the creator of all things, whom we Christians call the true God, his teaching was that God is the sole being who cannot be even remotely defined in words because of the poverty of human language. Yet it is just possible for men of wisdom, when, through a strenuous effort of the soul, they have withdrawn themselves from the body as far as may be, to receive an apprehension of this God, and for this illumination to shine on them at intervals, like a sudden flash of dazzling light in the depth of darkness.[32] Then if God, who is truly supreme over all things, presents himself to the minds of wise men, when they have withdrawn themselves, as far as may be, from the body, revealing himself to the intellect in an ineffable manner (even if this happens only at intervals, and resembles a sudden flash of dazzling light) and if he can so present himself without possibility of contamination, why should they say that those other gods are established in a lofty dwelling, to prevent their pollution by human contact? Surely it would be enough merely to look at the stars whose light gives the earth illumination sufficient for its needs! The stars, according to our philosopher, are so many visible gods,[33] and they are not contaminated by being seen; and the demons are not contaminated when men behold them, although they are seen from close at hand.

But perhaps it is by men's voices that the gods might be contaminated, although not polluted by the glances of their eyes? Perhaps that is the reason why they employ the demons as intermediaries, so that they may have men's words conveyed to them, while they remain far removed from men, completely sheltered from contamination? Is there anything to say of the other senses? The gods could not be contaminated through the sense of smell. If they were in the company of men, they could not be polluted by smelling the effluvia of living human bodies – any more than the demons, who are present, can be so polluted – if they are not contaminated by the stench of all those corpses in their sacrifices. As for the sense of taste, the gods have no need to restore mortal substance, so they are not likely to be driven by hunger to ask food from men. On the other hand, touching depends on them. For though, when we speak of contact, it seems as if it is touching that we have particularly in mind, the gods could, if they wished, have dealings with men only so far as seeing and being seen,

31. cf. *Tim.*, 28C. 32. Apul., *De Deo Socr.*, 3.
33. Apul., *De Deo Socr.*, 3, 33

hearing and being heard are concerned. What need of touching? Men would not dare to desire it, when they were enjoying the sight of the gods – or of good demons – and conversation with them. And even if their curiosity went so far as to wish for physical contact, how could any man touch a god – or a demon – against his will, seeing that he cannot touch a sparrow until he has caught it?

The gods, then, could have bodily contact with men by seeing and offering themselves to be seen, by speaking and listening. If, on the other hand, the demons have dealings with men, as I said above, without contamination, while the gods would be contaminated by such intercourse, that would imply that the demons are exempt from pollution and the gods are not. If, on the contrary, the demons also incur pollution, how can they help men to attain a blessed life after death? If they are contaminated themselves, they cannot purify men so as to bring them into fellowship with the unpolluted gods, between whom and men they have been set as intermediaries. Or if they do not confer this benefit, what use to man is their friendly mediation? Is it so that after death men may not pass over to the gods, by the aid of the demons, but may live in the company of the demons, equally polluted and equally deprived of happiness? Perhaps it may be suggested that demons act like sponges or something of that kind. They cleanse their friends, and in the process become as much dirtier themselves as men become cleaner by their 'washing'. If so, then the gods have dealing with demons, more polluted creatures, while they have shunned the proximity of men to avoid contamination! Or is it that the gods are able to purify the demons, polluted by men, without incurring pollution, and yet could not do the same for men?

Who could entertain such notions unless he were misled by the most deceitful of the demons? At this rate, if to see, or to be seen, brings defilement, there are gods who are seen by men – those gods whom Apuleius calls 'visible',[34] the 'shining lights of the world'[35] and the other stars, while the demons are better protected than the gods from this contamination, since they cannot be seen, unless they wish it. Or if it is by seeing, not by being seen, that pollution is incurred, the Platonists have to deny that men are seen by those 'shining lights of the world' (whom they hold to be gods) although they extend their rays as far as the earth. And yet those rays are not polluted, although diffused over all those impurities. And would the gods be contaminated, if they were in contact with men, even if this contact were essential for bringing help to men? For the rays of the

34. *De Deo Socr.*, 2. 35. Virg., *Georg.*, 1, 5f.

sun and the moon touch the earth, without any contamination of their light.

17. *Christ the only sufficient mediator*

It amazes me that such learned men, who have decided that all material things, discerned by the senses, are inferior in value to spiritual things accessible only to the intellect, should make any mention of physical contact, when the question concerns the life of felicity. What has become of that saying of Plotinus, 'We must flee to our beloved country. There the Father is, and there is everything. Where shall we take ship? How can we flee? By becoming like God.'[36] If man comes near to God in proportion as he grows more like him, then unlikeness to God is the only separation from him, and the soul of man is estranged from that immaterial, eternal and unchangeable being in proportion as it craves for things that are temporal and changeable.

For the cure of this condition we need a mediator, since there can be no direct meeting between the immortal purity on high and the mortal and unclean things below. But our need is not for a mediator with an immortal body, like the bodies on high, but with a diseased soul, like those below – for that disease would make him envious of our possible cure, and by no means ready to assist us towards health. We need a mediator linked with us in our lowliness by reason of the mortal nature of his body, and yet able to render us truly divine assistance for our purification and liberation, through the immortal justice of his spirit in virtue of which he has remained in his dwelling on high – not by spatial remoteness from us, but by his unique resemblance to God. It is unthinkable that God, who is incapable of defilement, should be afraid of contamination by the human nature in which he was clothed. For by his incarnation he showed us, for our salvation, two truths of the greatest importance: that the true divine nature cannot be polluted by the flesh, and that demons are not to be reckoned our superiors because they are not creatures of flesh. This mediator is, as the holy Scripture proclaims, 'the mediator between God and mankind, the man Christ Jesus'.[37] In respect of his divinity he is always equal to the Father, and by his humanity he became like us. But this is not the place to attempt (as far as our powers would allow) an adequate discussion of this doctrine.

36. *Enn.*, 1, 6, 8; 1, 2, 3 (conflated and freely rendered).
37. 1 Tim. 2, 5.

18. *The deceitful promises of the demons*

Those pretended and deceitful mediators, the demons (whose misery and malignity – the result of the impurity of their spirit – is clearly shown by their achievements) use every effort to distract us and divert us from spiritual progress, helped in their deceit by the distances of material space and by the lightness of their bodies of air. They do not help us on the way to God; they prevent us from keeping to the way. This supposed 'road to God' through physical space is utterly mistaken; it leads men completely astray. It is not the road taken by righteousness, since it is not by physical elevation, but by spiritual – that is incorporeal – likeness to God that we must ascend to God. It is a road designed by the friends of the demons, which mounts through the levels of the elements, the demons of air being set midway between gods of the ether and men of earth. And these philosophers suppose that the chief advantage afforded the gods by this 'road' is that of being shielded from polluting contact with mankind by the distance that separates them.

Thus they believe that demons are contaminated by men rather than that men are purified by demons and that the gods themselves might be contaminated, were they not protected by the elevation of their abode. Who is unfortunate enough to believe that he can attain purification by this road, where we are told that men contaminate, demons are contaminated, and gods capable of contamination? Who would not choose that way where demons who contaminate are avoided, and where the God who cannot be polluted purifies men from pollution so that they may enter into fellowship with unpolluted angels?

19. *The title 'demon' no longer has a good significance*

But we should not like to appear to be disputing about words; and since some of these demonolators (to coin a word), including Labeo,[38] claim that those whom they call 'demons' are identical with those called 'angels' by others, I see that I must say something about the good angels. Our opponents do not deny their existence, but they prefer to call them 'demons', rather than 'angels'.

For our part, we abide by the language of Scripture, which is the basis of our Christian belief. And there we read of good and bad angels, but never of good demons. In fact, wherever this name is found

38. cf. Bk II, 11.

in the books of the Bible, whether in the form *daemones* or in the form *daemonia*, it always refers to malignant spirits. And this way of speaking has been so generally adopted, that even among those who are called pagans, who maintain that it is right to worship many gods and demons, scarcely anyone would be so literary and pedantic as to bring himself to say, even to his slave, by way of a compliment, 'You are possessed of a demon.' He would know, without a shadow of a doubt, that if he decided to say this to anyone it would inevitably be taken as a deliberate insult. Then why should we feel compelled to start by offending the ears of so many of our hearers, in fact almost all of them (who normally understand the term only in a bad sense), and then to go on to explain our meaning? By using the word 'angel' we can avoid the shock which the word 'demon' is likely to produce.

20. *The meaning of the word 'demon'*

However, the actual derivation of the word 'demon', if we consult the divine Scriptures, teaches us something very well worth learning. The word 'demons' is Greek; and demons are so called because of their knowledge.[39] Now the Apostle, under the inspiration of the Holy Spirit, says, 'Knowledge inflates: but love edifies.'[40] The only correct interpretation of this saying is that knowledge is valuable when charity informs it. Without charity, knowledge inflates; that is, it exalts man to an arrogance which is nothing but a kind of windy emptiness. There is in the demons knowledge without charity, and so they are inflated; that is to say, they are so arrogant that they have done their best to obtain for themselves the divine honours and the devout service which they know to be due to the true God. They still pursue this aim as much as they can and wherever they can. Against this arrogance of the demons, to which mankind was enslaved as a deserved punishment, is set the humility of God, revealed in Christ. But the power of humility is unknown to men whose souls are inflated with the impurity of inflated pride. They resemble the demons in arrogance, but not in knowledge.

21. *How God willed to be made known to the demons*

The demons have also the knowledge which made them say, 'What business have you with us, Jesus the Nazarene? Have you come to

39. cf. Plat., *Crat.*, 398B (deriving *daimôn* from daêmôn, 'knowing').
40. 1 Cor. 8,1.

destroy us?'[41] Those words show clearly that they had so much knowledge, but lacked charity. They dreaded receiving their punishment from him; they did not love the righteousness that was in him. He made himself known to them to the extent he willed; and he willed to be made known to the extent that was fitting. But he was not made known to them as he is known to the holy angels; for the angels enjoy the participation in his eternity, in that he is the Word of God; to the demons he is known as he had to be made known to strike terror into them, for his purpose was to free from their tyrannical power (as we may call it) those who were predestined for his kingdom and glory, which is eternally true and truly eternal.

Therefore, he did not make himself known to the demons as the life eternal, and the unchangeable light which illuminates his true worshippers, whose hearts are purified by faith in him so that they see that light; he was known to the demons through certain temporal effects of his power, the signs of his hidden presence, which could be more evident to angelic senses, even those of malignant spirits, than to the weak perception of men. It is true that when he decided that those signs of power should be restrained, and when he concealed his real person more completely, the prince of the demons had doubts about him, and tested him to see if he were the Christ – in so far as he allowed himself to be tempted so that, under his control, the human nature which he wore might present an example for our imitation. But after that temptation, as the Scripture says, angels ministered to him[42] – good and holy angels, of course, and therefore striking fear and trembling into the impure spirits; and after that his greatness was increasingly made known to the demons, so that none of them dared to resist his commands, even though the weakness of his flesh might seem contemptible.

22. *The difference between the knowledge of angels and the knowledge of demons*

The good angels hold cheap all the knowledge of material and temporal matters, which inflates the demons with pride. It is not that they are ignorant of such things: it is because the love of God, by which they are sanctified, is dear. His beauty is not only immaterial, but immutable also and ineffable, and it inflames them with a holy love. In comparison with that beauty, they despise everything that is below it, everything that is other than that beauty; they despise even them-

41. Mark 1, 24; Matt. 8, 29. 42. Matt. 4, 11.

selves, so that they may enjoy, to the full extent of their goodness, that good from which their goodness comes. And they have a surer knowledge even of those temporal and changeable things, just because they see their first causes in the Word of God, through whom the world was made. By those causes all things are ordained, though some of these things are approved, and some are reprobated.

In contrast, the demons do not behold the eternal causes of temporal events, the cardinal causes, so to speak, in the Wisdom of God, but they have much more knowledge of the future than men can have, by their greater acquaintance with certain signs which are hidden from us; sometimes they also foretell their own intentions. It is true that they are often deceived, while the angels are never deceived. It is one thing to conjecture temporal matters from temporal evidence, mutable things from mutable evidence, and then to interfere in events in a temporal and mutable fashion by the exercise of will and power; this is, in a restricted measure, permitted to the demons. It is a very different thing to foresee the changes of the temporal order in the eternal and unchanging laws of God, which live eternally in his wisdom, and, by participation in the Spirit of God, to know the will of God, which is supremely certain and supremely powerful; this privilege is granted, by a just distinction, to the holy angels. Thus they are blessed, as well as eternal. The good, which renders them blessed, is God, by whom they were created; and the participation in his life and the contemplation of his beauty is their never-failing joy.

23. *The ascription of the title 'gods'*

The Platonists may prefer to call those good angels 'gods' rather than 'demons', and to include them among those whom Plato, their founder and master, writes of as having been created by the supreme God.[43] They may do as they like; there is no need for us to engage in a tiresome dispute about words. If they mean that they are immortal, but, at the same time, created by the supreme God and that they are blessed, not by themselves, but through adhering to him who made them, then their meaning is the same as ours, whatever title they use. That this is the opinion of the Platonists, or at least of the better Platonists, can be proved from their writings. As for the actual title, the fact that they give the name 'gods' to creatures who are immortal and blessed in the above sense, there is here no dispute between us, simply because one can find in our sacred Scriptures such quotations as

43. *Tim.* 40.

'The Lord, the lord of gods, has spoken,'[44] and, in another place: 'Give thanks to the God of gods,'[45] and 'a great king above all gods'.[46] The passage where it says, 'He is terrible above all gods',[47] is explained by what immediately follows, 'Since all the gods of the nations are demons; but the Lord made the heavens'.[48] The psalmist says 'above all *gods*'; but he adds '*of the nations*', meaning those whom the nations regard as gods, who are really 'demons': 'terrible' refers to the terror which made the demons say to the Lord, 'Have you come to destroy us?'[49] But 'God of gods' cannot be understood as meaning 'God of demons'; and it is unthinkable that 'a great king above all gods' should mean 'a great king above all demons'. The Scriptures also use the name 'gods' to describe men who belong to the people of God. 'I have said, "You are gods, and all of you are sons of the Highest." '[50] Thus it is possible to take 'God of gods' as referring to 'gods' in this sense, and to interpret 'a great king above all gods' in the same way.

But it may be asked: If men are called 'gods', because they belong to the people of God – that people with whom God talks by the agency of either angels or men – are not the immortal beings much more worthy of that name? For they now enjoy that blessedness which men long to reach in their worship of God. The only reply is that it is not for nothing that in the holy Scriptures men are given the title of 'gods' more expressly than are those immortal and blessed beings, to whom, as we are promised, we shall become equal in the resurrection. Presumably the intention was to guard against the possibility that man, in his feebleness, might become unfaithful to God and presume to set up one of those angels as a god for us. There was less risk of this in the case of a man. And it was essential that men who belonged to God's people should be called 'gods' with greater emphasis, so that they might have sure confidence that he was their God, who was entitled 'God of gods'. For although the name 'gods' is applied to those blessed immortals who are in the heavens, they are not called 'gods of gods', that is, gods of men who have been given a place among the people of God, the men to whom it was said, 'I have said, "You are gods, and all of you are sons of the Highest".' Hence the saying of the Apostle,

> Although there are those who are called gods, whether in heaven or on earth, there being many 'gods' and many 'lords'; nevertheless for us there is one God, the Father, from whom all things come, and in whom we have our being; and one Lord, Jesus Christ, through whom all things come into being, through whom we came to be.[51]

44. Ps. 50, 1. 45. Ps. 136, 2. 46. Ps. 95, 3. 47. Ps. 96, 4.
48. Ps. 96, 4. 49. Mark 1, 24. 50. Ps. 82, 6. 51. 1 Cor. 8, 5f.

There is no need, then, of a long discussion about the name, since the facts are clear beyond any shadow of doubt. But there is another matter. We Christians say that it is from the company of these blessed immortals that angels have been sent to announce the will of God to men. The philosophers will not have it so. They ascribe this ministry not to those beings whom they call 'gods', that is, to beings who are both immortal and blessed, but to demons who are immortal, but whom they do not venture to call blessed – or at least, if they are both immortal and blessed, they are still good *demons*, and not gods, since gods (for them) have their dwelling on high, far removed from human contact. Here we may seem to have a dispute about names. But the name 'demons' is so detestable that we are bound to repudiate utterly its application to the holy angels.

And so we may end this book with this assertion. We know that immortal and blessed beings, by whatever name they are called, who for all that, are created beings, do not act as intermediaries, to bring to immortal blessedness wretched mortals, from whom they are separated by a twofold difference. On the other hand, those who are in an intermediate position, by sharing immortality with those above them and misery with those below, are more likely to grudge us happiness than to procure it for us, since their own misery is the due reward of their malice. Hence the supporters of the demons cannot put forward any sound reason why we should worship those demons as our helpers, seeing that we ought rather to shun them as deceivers. As for those good beings, who, because of their goodness, are happy as well as immortal, these philosophers reckon that they should be given the title of 'gods', and worshipped with sacred rites and sacrifices, in order that we may attain to a life of blessedness after death. But, whatever be the nature of those beings, and whatever be the name they deserve, they themselves do not wish that such devout homage should be offered in worship to any being other than the one God, by whom they were created, the God who imparts to them their happiness by granting them a share in his own being. This is a matter we shall, God helping us, discuss in detail in the next book.

BOOK X

1. *The Platonists say that true blessedness is conferred only by God. The question now arises: do those beings, whom they suppose that men should worship for the attainment of blessedness, desire that men should sacrifice to them, or to God alone?*

THAT all men desire happiness is a truism for all who are in any degree able to use their reason. But mortals, in their weakness, ask, 'Who is happy? And how is happiness gained?' And those questions have stirred up many disputes of importance which have consumed the energy and the leisure of philosophers. It would be tedious to bring them up and discuss them, and it is also unnecessary. The line we followed in the eighth book was to select the philosophers with whom we should debate the question about the life of happiness which follows death, the question whether we can attain this life by offering the homage of devotion and worship to the one true God, who is also the creator of the gods, or to a multitude of gods. If the reader remembers this, he will not be expecting us to go over the same ground again: especially because, if he happens to have forgotten the details, he can turn back to refresh his memory.

Now we selected the Platonists as being deservedly the best known of all philosophers, because they have been able to realize that the soul of man, though immortal and rational (or intellectual), cannot attain happiness except by participation in the light of God, the creator of the soul and of the whole world. They also assert that no one can attain this life of blessedness, the object of all mankind's desire, unless he has adhered, with the purity of chaste love, to that unique and supreme Good, which is the changeless God. And yet those philosophers themselves have either yielded to the futile errors of people in general or, in the Apostle's words, 'have dwindled into futility in their thinking',[1] in that they have supposed (or were willing that it should be supposed) that many gods are to be worshipped. Some, in fact, have gone so far as to lay it down that the divine honours of ceremonies and sacrifices are to be rendered even to demons. But I

1. Rom. 1, 21.

have already replied to this at some considerable length. Our present task concerns those immortal and blessed beings, established in heavenly abodes, in 'dominations, principalities and powers',[2] the beings whom the philosophers call 'gods', and give to some of them the name of 'demons', or 'angels' – the word used by Christians. The question we must consider and discuss, as far as God grants us strength, is this: What kind of observances of religion and devotion are we to believe that they wish to see in us? Or, to put it more plainly: Is it their desire that we should offer ceremony and sacrifice, or consecrate with solemn ritual either our possessions or ourselves, to their God, who is also our God, and to him alone? Or do they claim those honours also for themselves?

For this is the kind of worship which we owe to the Divinity, or, more precisely, the Deity. I cannot think of a suitable Latin term to express it in one word, and so I shall be inserting, where necessary, a Greek word to convey my meaning. *Latreia* is the word represented in our translations by 'service', wherever it is found in the Scriptures. But the service due to man, the service referred to by the Apostle when he says that servants should be obedient to their masters,[3] is called by a different word in Greek, whereas *latreia*, according to the usage of the writers who preserve for us the words of God, is always, or almost always, the word employed for the service which concerns the worship of God. The word 'cult' (*cultus*) by itself would not imply something due only to God. For we are said to 'cultivate' (*colere*) men when we continually pay respect to them either in our memory or by our presence. And this word is employed not only in respect of things which in a spirit of devout humility we regard as above us, but even of some things which are below us. For from the same word are derived *agricolae* (cultivators), *coloni* (farmers) and *incolae* (inhabitants); and the gods themselves are called *caelicolae* simply because they dwell in (*colunt*) heaven (*caelum*) – the verb here meaning, of course, 'inhabit', not 'worship'; they are, as it were, 'colonists' of heaven. They are not *coloni* in the sense in which the word is used of those whose lives are bound up with their native soil, which they cultivate under the authority of a land-owner, but in the sense in which one of the great Latin authors used it in the line,

> An ancient town there was, the dwelling-place
> Of *colonists* from Tyre.[4]

He speaks of 'colonists' because they inhabited (*ab incolendo*), not

2. cf. Col. 1, 16. 3. Eph. 6, 5. 4. Virg., *Aen.*, 1, 12.

because they cultivated the place (*ab agricultura*). Hence also the name 'colonies' is given to settlements founded by larger communities as a result of a kind of swarming of the population. Thus although it is quite true that 'cult', in the special use of the term, is due only to God, still the word *cultus* is used in other significations, and for that reason there is no one word in Latin to denote the 'cult' which is due to God.

The word 'religion' would seem, to be sure, to signify more particularly the 'cult' offered to God, rather than 'cult' in general; and that is why our translators have used it to render the Greek word *thrêskeia*. However, in Latin usage (and by that I do not mean in the speech of the illiterate, but even in the language of the highly educated) 'religion' is something which is displayed in human relationships, in the family (in the narrower and the wider sense) and between friends; and so the use of the word does not avoid ambiguity when the worship of God is in question. We have no right to affirm with confidence that 'religion' is confined to the worship of God, since it seems that this word has been detached from its normal meaning, in which it refers to an attitude of respect in relations between a man and his neighbour.

The word 'piety' (*eusebeia* in Greek) is generally understood as referring particularly to the worship of God. But this word also is used of a dutiful attitude towards parents; while in popular speech it is constantly used in connection with acts of compassion – the reason for this being, in my opinion, that God especially commands the performance of such acts, and bears witness that they please him as much as sacrifices or even more than sacrifices. From this familiar usage comes the application of the epithet *pius* to God himself;[5] although the Greeks never call God *eusebês*, in their language, in spite of the fact that *eusebeia* is in common use as a synonym for compassion. Hence in some passages of Scripture, to make the precise meaning clear, the word *theo-sebeia* (God-worship) is preferred to *eu-sebeia* (good worship). We have no one word in Latin to express either of these Greek words.

There is, then, an attitude which is called in Greek *latreia* and is translated by the Latin *servitus*, meaning the service of the worship of God; or it may be called *thrêskeia* in Greek, but in Latin *religio*, the religion which 'binds' us to God;[6] or the Greeks may call it *theosebeia*, which, in default of one equivalent word we may call 'worship of God'. What is expressed by those words is the worship we hold to

5. cf. 2 Chron. 30, 9; Ecclus. 2, 13; Judith 7, 20. 6. cf. ch. 3.

be due only to him who is the true God, who transforms his worshippers into gods. Therefore those immortal and blessed beings, whoever they are, who dwell in heavenly habitations, certainly have no claim to our worship, if they do not love us and do not desire our happiness. On the other hand, if they love us and desire our happiness, then they must want that happiness to come from whence theirs is derived. Can our happiness have a different source from theirs?

2. *Plotinus on illumination from on high*

There is no conflict on this subject between us and those eminent philosphers. For they saw, and in their writings proclaimed, with abundant emphasis and in all kinds of ways, that those beings received their happiness from the same source as we do, by a kind of light which is shed on them, a light apprehended by the intellect. This light for them is God. It is something other than themselves: it brings them illumination, so that they are full of light, and, by participation in this light, exist in a state of perfection and bliss.

Plotinus often stresses, in expounding Plato's views, that even the being whom they hold to be the 'Soul of the Universe' receives its blessedness from the source of our soul's felicity; and that source is the light, distinct from the Soul itself, by which it was created and by whose intelligible illumination it shines with intelligible light. Plotinus finds a comparison for these immaterial realities in the great material bodies in heaven which are visible to our sight, God being the sun, and the soul the moon, for it is supposed that the moon is illuminated by the light cast on her by the sun.

The great Platonist holds that the souls of the immortal and blessed beings who, he is certain, dwell in celestial abodes, belong to the class of rational (perhaps the better term would be 'intellectual') souls. The rational (or intellectual) soul, he writes, has nothing above it in the scale of being except God, who fashioned the world, the God by whom the soul itself was created; and those supernal beings receive the life of bliss and the light of the understanding of the truth from no other source than that from which they are given to us. Thus he agrees with the Gospel, where we read these words, 'There was a man sent from God, and his name was John. He came as a witness, to bear witness to the light, so that all men should believe through him. He was not the light, but he had to bear witness to the light. The true light was that which illuminates every man coming into the world.'[7] This dis-

7. John 1, 6ff.

tinction clearly shows that the rational (or intellectual) soul, like the soul of John, cannot be light to itself, and that it shines only by participation in the true light of another. John himself admits this when, in bearing witness to that light, he says, 'We have all received from his plenitude.'[8]

3. *The true worship of God, and the Platonic deviation in the cult of angels*

This being so, if the Platonists, or any others who shared those opinions, had acquaintance with God, had glorified him as God and given thanks to him and had not 'dwindled into futility in their thinking',[9] and had not sometimes sponsored the errors of the people in general, and sometimes failed in courage to resist them, then they would straightway have admitted that there was one object of worship both for the immortal and blessed beings, and for us, in our mortal and wretched condition, so that we may attain to immortality and bliss. Both alike must worship the one God of gods, who is the angels' God, as he is ours.

To this God we owe our service – what in Greek is called *latreia* – whether in the various sacraments or in ourselves. For we are his temple, collectively, and as individuals.[10] For he condescends to dwell in the union of all and in each person. He is as great in the individual as he is in the whole body of his worshippers, for he cannot be increased in bulk or diminished by partition. When we lift up our hearts to him, our heart is his altar. We propitiate him by our priest, his only-begotten Son. We sacrifice blood-stained victims to him when we fight for truth 'as far as shedding our blood'.[11] We burn the sweetest incense for him, when we are in his sight on fire with devout and holy love. We vow to him and offer to him the gifts he has given us, and the gift of ourselves. And we have annual festivals and fixed days appointed and consecrated for the remembrance of his benefits, lest ingratitude and forgetfulness should creep in as the years roll by. We offer to him, on the altar of the heart, the sacrifice of humility and praise,[12] and the flame on the altar is the buring fire of charity. To see him as he can be seen and to cleave to him, we purify ourselves from every stain of sin and evil desire and we consecrate ourselves in his name. For he himself is the source of our bliss, he himself is the goal of all our striving. By our election of him as our goal – or rather

8. John 1,16. 9. Rom. 1, 21. 10. cf. 1 Cor. 3, 16f.
11. cf. Hebr. 12, 4. 12. cf. Ps. 116, 15.

by our re-election (for we had lost him by our neglect); by our re-election (and we are told that the word 'religion' comes from *relegere*, 'to re-elect'[13]), we direct our course towards him with love (*dilectio*), so that in reaching him we may find our rest, and attain our happiness because we have achieved our fulfilment in him. For our Good, that Final Good about which the philosophers dispute, is nothing else but to cleave to him whose spiritual embrace, if one may so express it, fills the intellectual soul and makes it fertile with true virtues.

We are commanded to love this Good with all our heart, with all our soul, with all our strength; and to this Good we must be led by those who love us, and to it we must lead those whom we love. Thus are fulfilled those two commands on which 'all the Law and the prophets depend': 'Thou shalt love the Lord thy God with all thy heart, with all thy soul, and with all thy mind', and, 'Thou shalt love thy neighbour as thyself.'[14] For in order that a man may know how to love himself an end has been established for him to which he is to refer all his action, so that he may attain to bliss. For if a man loves himself, his one wish is to achieve blessedness. Now this end is 'to cling to God'.[15] Thus, if a man knows how to love himself, the commandment to love his neighbour bids him to do all he can to bring his neighbour to love God. This is the worship of God; this is true religion; this is the right kind of devotion; this is the service which is owed to God alone.

Therefore every immortal Power, however great its importance, will have no other wish, if it loves us as itself, than that we, for our happiness, should be subjected to God, seeing that it is such subjection that gives that Power its blessedness. If it does not worship God, it is wretched, because deprived of God; if it worships God, it will not wish itself to be worshipped in the place of God. Far from that, it will subscribe to the statement in Scripture, 'He who sacrifices to gods, and not to the Lord alone, will be extirpated.'[16] This saying it will approve with all the strength of its love.

4. *Sacrifice due only to God*

For, to say nothing of other acts of religious obedience performed in the worship of God, at least no one would dare to assert that sacrifice is

13. cf. *Retract.*, 2, 13, 19, where St Augustine prefers a derivation from *religare*, 'to bind'. cf. ch. 1.

14. Matt. 22, 37f. 15. 'cf.' Ps. 73, 28. 16. Exod. 22, 20.

due to any other being than God. There are in fact many ingredients in the worship of God which are also found in the honour paid to human beings, in a spirit either of humility or of noisome flattery; but even when men are said to be worthy of homage and veneration, and even, in extreme cases, of adoration, it is remembered that they are still human beings. But who has ever thought it right to offer sacrifice, except to a being known, or supposed, or imagined to be God? The antiquity of the worship of God by means of sacrifice is sufficiently proved by the story of Cain and Abel, the two brothers, where God rejected the sacrifice of the elder, and viewed with favour that of the younger brother.[17]

5. God does not require sacrifices, but he wishes them to be offered as symbols of what he does require

Could anyone be such a fool as to suppose that the sacrificial offerings are necessary to God – that they are of any use to him? There are many passages in holy Scripture to witness this point; but it will be enough to cut a long story short by quoting a short extract from one of the psalms: 'I said to the Lord, "You are my God, for you have no need of my possessions."'[18] Thus, far from needing any cattle, or any other corruptible and earthly thing, we must believe that God does not need even the righteousness of man; and that it is man, not God, who is benefited by all the worship which is rightly offered to God. For no one is going to say that he does any service to a spring by drinking from it, or to the light by beholding it. If in times gone by our ancestors offered other sacrifices to God, in the shape of animal victims (sacrifices which the people of God now read about, but do not perform) we are to understand that the significance of those acts was precisely the same as that of those now performed amongst us – the intention of which is that we may cleave to God and seek the good of our neighbour for the same end. Thus the visible sacrifice is the sacrament, the sacred sign, of the invisible sacrifice. That is why the penitent in the prophet's book, if it was not the prophet himself, seeks God's forgiveness for his sins with these words, 'If you had wished for sacrifice, I would certainly have given it: but you will not delight in holocausts. The sacrifice offered to God is a broken spirit; God will not despise a heart that is broken and humbled.'[19]

Observe how he says that God does not want sacrifice, and how in the same place, he shows that God does desire sacrifice. God does not

17. Gen. 4, 4f. 18. Ps. 16, 2. 19. Ps. 51, 18f.

want the sacrifice of a slaughtered animal, but he desires the sacrifice of a broken heart. That offering which, he says, God does not want, signifies the offering which, he adds, God does desire. When he says that God does not want sacrifices he means that he does not want them in the way supposed by the fools, namely for his own gratification. For if he had not wished the sacrifices he desires (and there is only one, the heart bruised and humbled in the sorrow of penitence) to be signified by those sacrifices which he was supposed to long for as if they gave him pleasure, then he would certainly not have prescribed their offering in the old Law. And the reason why they had to be changed, at the fitting and predestined time, was to prevent the belief that those things were objects of desire to God himself, or at least were acceptable gifts from us to him, and to make us realize that what God required was that which they signified. This is the message of another passage, from another psalm: 'If I am hungry, I shall not tell you: for the whole earth, and all that is in it, belongs to me. Am I likely to eat the flesh of bulls, or to drink the blood of goats?'[20] God is saying, in effect, 'Had I needed such things, I certainly would not have applied to you for them, seeing that I have them in my power.' The psalmist goes on to explain the meaning of sacrifice by adding, 'Offer to God the sacrifice of praise, and fulfil your vows to the Most High. And call upon me in the day of tribulation and I shall rescue you; and you will glorify me.'

And there is another passage, in another prophet:

> By what means shall I reach God, or take hold of my God, the most high? Shall I reach him with holocausts, with year-old calves? Will God be satisfied with thousands of rams or ten thousands of fat goats? What if I give the first-born of my impiety, the fruit of my belly for the sin of my soul? Have you been told, O man, what is good? Or what does the Lord require from you, except to practise justice, and to love mercy, and to be prepared to go with the Lord your God?[21]

In the words of this prophet the two things are distinguished, and it is made quite plain that God does not require, for their own sake, the sacrifices which signify the sacrifices that God does demand. In the epistle entitled *To the Hebrews* we read, 'Do not forget to do good and to give to others: for it is with such sacrifices that God is pleased.'[22] Hence the meaning of the text, 'I desire mercy rather than sacrifice,'[23] is simply that one sacrifice is preferred to another; for what is generally called sacrifice is really a sign of the true sacrifice.

20. Ps. 50, 12f. 21. Mic. 6, 6f. 22. Hebr. 13, 16.
23. Hos. 6, 6.

Mercy is, in fact, the true sacrifice; hence the text I have just quoted: 'It is by such sacrifices that God is pleased.'

The instructions about the multifarious sacrifices in the service of the Tabernacle or the Temple are recorded in Scripture as divine commands. We see now that they are to be interpreted as symbolizing the love of God and the love of one's neighbour. For 'on these two commands the whole Law depends, and the Prophets.'[24]

6. *The true and perfect sacrifice*

Thus the true sacrifice is offered in every act which is designed to unite us to God in a holy fellowship, every act, that is, which is directed to that final Good which makes possible our true felicity. For that reason even an act of compassion itself is not a sacrifice, if it is not done for the sake of God. For sacrifice is a 'divine matter', in the phrase of the old Latin authors, even if it is performed or offered by man. Hence a man consecrated in the name of God, and vowed to God, is in himself a sacrifice inasmuch as he 'dies to the world' so that he may 'live for God'.[25] For this also is related to compassion, the compassion a man shows towards himself. Hence the text, 'Have compassion on your own soul by making yourself acceptable to God.'[26]

Our body also is a sacrifice when we discipline it by temperance, provided that we do this as we ought for the sake of God, so that we may not offer our bodily powers to the service of sin as the instruments of iniquity, but to the service of God as the instruments of righteousness.[27] The Apostle exhorts us to this, when he says, 'I entreat you, brothers, by the compassion of God, to offer your bodies as a living sacrifice, holy and acceptable to God, as the reasonable homage you owe him.'[28] If then the body, which the soul employs as a subordinate, like a servant or a tool, is a sacrifice, when it is offered to God for good and right employment, how much more does the soul itself become a sacrifice when it offers itself to God, so that it may be kindled by the fire of love and may lose the 'form' of worldly desire, and may be 're-formed' by submission to God as to the unchangeable 'form', thus becoming acceptable to God because of what it has received from his beauty. This is what the Apostle says, when he adds, 'And do not be "con-formed" to this age, but be "re-formed" in newness of mind, so that you may prove what is the will of God,

24. Matt. 22, 40. 25. cf. Rom. 6, 11. 26. Ecclus. 30, 23.
27. cf. Rom. 6, 16f. 28. Rom. 12, 1.

namely, what is good, what is acceptable to God, what is perfect.'

So then, the true sacrifices are acts of compassion, whether towards ourselves or towards our neighbours, when they are directed towards God; and acts of compassion are intended to free us from misery and thus to bring us to happiness – which is only attained by that good of which it has been said, 'As for me, my true good is to cling to God.'[29] This being so, it immediately follows that the whole redeemed community, that is to say, the congregation and fellowship of the saints, is offered to God as a universal sacrifice, through the great Priest who offered himself in his suffering for us – so that we might be the body of so great a head – under 'the form of a servant'.[30] For it was this form he offered, and in this form he was offered, because it is under this form that he is the Mediator, in this form he is the Priest, in this form he is the Sacrifice. Thus the Apostle first exhorts us to offer our bodies as a living sacrifice, holy, acceptable to God, as the reasonable homage we owe him, and not to be 'con-formed' to this age, but to be 're-formed' in newness of mind to prove what is the will of God – namely what is good what is acceptable to God, what is perfect, because we ourselves are that whole sacrifice. And after this exhortation, he continues,

> Through the grace of God which has been given to me, I say this to all of you: Do not have greater notions of yourselves than you ought to have, but keep your notions under control, according to the measure of faith which God has imparted to each. For just as we have many members in one body, and all the members have not the same functions; so we are many, but we make up one body in Christ; and individually we are members of one another, possessing gifts differing according to the grace which has been given us.[31]

This is the sacrifice of Christians, who are 'many, making up one body in Christ'. This is the sacrifice which the Church continually celebrates in the sacrament of the altar, a sacrament well-known to the faithful where it is shown to the Church that she herself is offered in the offering which she presents to God.

7. *The holy angels, in their love for us, wish us to worship only the true God, not themselves*

Those immortal and blessed beings, who are established in dwellings in heaven, rejoice together in participation in their creator, and find in

29. Ps. 73, 28. 30. Phil. 2, 7. 31. Rom. 12, 3f.

his eternity their stability, in his truth their assurance, and from his bounty derive their holiness. They have such a compassionate love for us wretched mortals that their aim is for our immortality and blessedness; and therefore they wish us not to sacrifice to themselves, but to God; for they know that they themselves, together with us, are his sacrifice. For with us they make one City of God, which is addressed in the words of the psalm, 'Most glorious things have been said about you, City of God.'[32] Part of this City, the part which consists of us, is on pilgrimage; part of it, the part which consists of the angels, helps us on our way. It is from that City on high where the will of God is intelligible and unchangeable Law, it is from that supernal court (*curia*), so to speak, which has concern (*cura*) for us, it is from that community that the holy Scripture descended, brought to us by the ministry of angels,[33] the Scripture in which we find the saying, 'The man who sacrifices to gods, and not to the Lord only, will be extirpated.'[34]

This Scripture, this Law, the precepts of this kind, have been attested by such great miracles that it is abundantly clear to whom these immortal and blessed beings would have us offer sacrifice, these beings who wish for us the same blessings as for themselves.

8. *The miracles performed through the ministry of angels to confirm the faith of God's people*

No doubt I shall be thought to be going too far back into the remote past if I recall the miracles which proved the truth of the promises which God made to Abraham thousands of years before, when he foretold that in Abraham's seed all nations were to obtain a blessing. No one could fail to marvel that Abraham should have had a son born to him of a barren wife who had already reached an age when even a fertile woman would not be able to have any more children, and that in the sacrifice offered by Abraham a flame came from heaven and ran between the divided victims.[35] Nor could they fail to marvel that to Abraham also was foretold by angels the burning of Sodom by fire sent from heaven, and that these angels, appearing in the likeness of men, were welcomed as guests by Abraham, who received from them the promises of God about the coming birth of a son, and that when the burning of Sodom was imminent, Lot, Abraham's brother's son,

32. Ps. 87, 3. 33. cf. Gal. 3, 19. 34. Exod. 22, 20.

35. Gen. 15, 17; cf. *Retract.*, 2, 69, 3. St Augustine corrects himself; this was a vision, not a miracle.

was miraculously rescued from the city by the same angels, and his wife was suddenly turned into salt when she looked back on the road – thus giving, in symbolic form, a warning that no one, having started on the way to liberation, should look back with regret at his past life.

Then there were all those tremendous miracles performed in Egypt through Moses, in the liberation of God's people from the yoke of servitude, when the magicians of Pharaoh, the king of Egypt, who was oppressing that people under his tyranny, were allowed to perform some miracles so that they might be overcome in an even more marvellous fashion! The magicians achieved their effects by the use of enchantments and magical spells, the specialities of evil angels, that is, of demons; but Moses wielded a power that was as much greater as his cause was more just, and he easily prevailed over them in the name of God, the creator of heaven and earth, with the assistance of the angels. In the end the magicians gave up the struggle at the third plague, and the plagues reached the final number of ten, in an ordered sequence of events, full of hidden meanings,[36] carried out through the hand of Moses; and by those plagues the hard hearts of Pharaoh and the Egyptians were forced to yield and to allow God's people to go free. They soon regretted this permission, and tried to catch up with the departing Hebrews; and then the sea divided to afford a dry crossing for the fugitives, but flowed back from each side to engulf and overwhelm their pursuers.

What am I to say of the repeated displays of the stupendous power of God in the miracles that accompanied the people's passage through the desert? Water which had been undrinkable lost its bitterness when, at God's instruction, a log of wood was flung into it; and it quenched the thirst of the parched Hebrews. Manna came from heaven when they were hungry; a limit was fixed for the amount to be collected, and any excess turned bad and produced maggots, though on the day before the Sabbath a double supply was collected, since collection was forbidden on the Sabbath, and none of that suffered any putrefaction. When the people longed for a meal of meat, and it seemed quite impossible to supply such a large multitude, their camp was filled with birds, and the ardour of their appetite was quenched by satiety and consequent disgust. When the enemy tried to oppose their passage, and gave battle, Moses prayed, with his arms stretched out in the form of a cross;[37] and the enemy was crushed,

36. cf. *Serm.*, 8; *Enarr. in Ps.*, 77, 27.
37. cf. *Adv. Faust. Man.*, 12, 30.

without the loss of a single Hebrew. When a revolt broke out in the people of God, and some insurgents separated themselves from the divinely ordained community, the earth opened and swallowed them up alive – a visible token of invisible punishment. A rock, struck by a rod, poured out running water in abundance for so great a multitude. The fatal bites of snakes (a just punishment for the people's sins) were cured by the sight of a brazen serpent erected on a wooden pole, and not only was relief brought to the afflicted people, but the destruction of death by a death was also signified by the image of crucified death. This serpent was preserved as a memorial of the miracle; but in later times the people went astray and began to worship it as an idol. And so King Hezekiah made devout use of his royal power in the service of God, and destroyed the image,[38] thus winning great praise for his piety.

9. *The unlawful practices of demon-worship, and the inconsistency of Porphyry, the Platonist*

Those miracles and many others of the same kind – it would take too long to mention them all – were intended to support the worship of the one true God, and to prevent the cult of many false deities. They were achieved by simple faith and devout confidence, not by spells and charms composed according to the rules of criminal superstition, the craft which is called magic, or sorcery – a name of detestation – or by the more honourable title of 'theurgy'.[39] For people attempt to make some sort of a distinction between practitioners of illicit arts, who are to be condemned, classing these as 'sorcerers' (the popular name for this kind of thing is 'black magic') and others whom they are prepared to regard as praiseworthy, attributing to them the practice of 'theurgy'. In fact, both types are engaged in the fraudulent rites of demons, wrongly called angels.

Porphyry[40] goes so far as to promise some sort of purification of the soul by means of theurgy, though to be sure he is reluctant to commit himself, and seems to blush with embarrassment in his argument. On the other hand, he denies that this art offers to anyone a way of return to God; and so one can observe him maintaining two

38. 2 Kings 18, 4.

39. *Theurgy*: divination bringing man into contact with deity either by raising the visionary in an ecstasy, or by bringing down the divinity by means of magical arts.

40. cf. Bk VII, 25n.

contradictory positions, and wavering between a superstition which amounts to the sin of blasphemy, and a philosophical standpoint. For at one moment he is warning us to beware of such practices as fraudulent, fraught with danger in their performance, and prohibited by law,[41] and the next minute he seems to be surrendering to the supporters of magic,[42] saying that the art is useful for the purification of one part of the soul. This is not the 'intellectual' element by which is perceived the truth of intelligible realities which have no resemblance to material substances; it is the 'spiritual' part of the soul, by which it apprehends the images of material things. Porphyry declares that by means of certain 'theurgic consecrations', which are called *teletae*, this spiritual element of the soul is put into a proper condition, capable of welcoming spirits and angels, and of seeing the gods. But he admits at the same time that those 'theurgic rites' do not effect any purification of the intellectual soul which would fit it to see its God and to apprehend the true realities.[43] From this one can gather what kind of gods and what kind of vision he is talking about in those 'theurgic consecrations'; it is not a vision of the true realities. In fact, he says that the rational soul (or, as he prefers, the 'intellectual' soul) can escape into its own sphere, even without any purification of the spiritual element by means of 'theurgic art', and further, that the purification of the spiritual part by theurgy does not go so far as to assure its attainment of immortality and eternity.

Now Porphyry distinguishes between angels and demons, explaining that the demons inhabit the lower air, while the ether, or empyrean, is the abode of the angels, and he recommends us to cultivate the friendship of some demon, by whose assistance a man may be raised just a little above the earth after death – though he gives us to understand that it is by another way that one reaches the heavenly company of angels. For all that, he makes what one may call an explicit admission that warns men to beware of the society of demons. This is in the passage where he says that the soul, in the expiation which follows death, is horrified at the worship of demons who used to beset it. And although he recommends theurgy as being a means of

41. cf. Bk VII, 35n.

42. *Magic* secured indirect revelation, in which the divinity appeared in some material object (e.g. a flame, in 'lychnomancy'), or through a medium in a trance. *Sorcery* (*goetia*) secured indirect revelation by the use of material things, without the divinity being present in them. cf. A. J. Festugière, *La Révélation d'Hermès Trismégiste*. Paris, second edition, 1950, I, p. 283f.

43. cf. ch. 28.

conciliation between men and angels or gods, he cannot deny that it is concerned with such powers as grudge the soul's purification, or support the machinations of those who grudge it. He quotes the complaints of some Chaldean astrologer on this matter, 'A good man in Chaldea complains that his energetic efforts to purify a soul have been frustrated, because a powerful practitioner of the same art had been led by envy to conjure the powers with sacred spells and had bound them, to prevent their granting his requests. And so', says Porphyry, 'what the one had bound, the other could not undo.' On this evidence, as he admits, theurgy is a science capable of achieving good or evil, whether among men or among gods. It also follows that the gods are susceptible to those disturbances and emotions which Apuleius ascribes to demons and men as their common condition, although Porphyry separates the gods from mankind by the elevation of their dwelling in the ether, and quotes the teaching of Plato in support of this distinction.

10. *The false claims of theurgy*

Porphyry is regarded as a greater authority than Apuleius. Yet here we find him, another Platonist, saying that even the gods themselves can be constrained by emotional disturbances through the power of the theurgic art, since they could be conjured by sacred spells, and prevented from effecting the purgation of a soul; and they were so terrified by the practitioner who demanded an evil result, that the other, who asked for a good result, was not able to release them from their fear by the same theurgic art, and to set them free to grant a benefit.

That this is all the invention of lying demons must be clear to anyone who is not their wretched slave, and a stranger to the grace of the true liberator. For if this business was concerned with 'good gods', the good man who undertook to purify a soul would undoubtedly have prevailed over his malevolent opponent. Or if the truth was that in the eyes of just gods the subject of the action did not deserve this purification, then they certainly should not have been terrified by the envious opponent, or prevented, as Porphyry says, by fear inspired by a greater power; they should have refused to grant the boon by an act of free judgement. The amazing thing is that the benevolent astrologer, who desired to purify a soul by theurgic rites, did not find some superior divinity capable either of inspiring greater terror and of compelling the terrified gods to perform a good work, or of restraining the author of their terror, thus leaving them free to do good – unless perhaps the benevolent theurgist was not equipped with a ritual to purify (as a preliminary measure) the gods whom he invoked to purify a soul from the infection of terror? How is it then that a more powerful god could be engaged to terrify, but not to purify? Are we to suppose that a god can be found to hear the appeal of the envious and strike terror into other gods to prevent their doing good, but that one cannot be found to hear the appeal of the benevolent, and deliver the gods from their fear, so that they can perform a good work?

What a wonderful art is this 'theurgy'! What a marvellous way of purifying the soul, where foul envy has more success in demanding than pure benevolence has in obtaining a result! The whole thing is in fact an imposture of malignant spirits. We must beware of it; we must abhor it; we must listen to the teaching of salvation. Porphyry relates that those who engage in those polluted rites of purification, with their blasphemous ceremonies, have some marvellously beautiful visions, whether of angels or of gods, after the supposed purification. But even if they do in fact see anything of the sort, it is just as the Apostle says: 'Satan transforms himself to look like an angel of light.'[44] For it is from the Devil that these phantoms come. The Devil longs to ensnare men's wretched souls in the fraudulent ceremonies of all those false gods, and to seduce them from the true worship of the true God, by whom alone they are purified and healed. And so, as is said of Proteus,

he turns himself into all shapes,[45]

sometimes appearing as a ruthless persecutor, sometimes as a fraudulent helper; in either case he seeks man's hurt.

11. *The letter of Porphyry to Anebo of Egypt*

Porphyry showed better sense in his letter to Anebo of Egypt,[46] in which, while appearing to ask for advice and information, he exposes this blasphemous art of magic and overthrows it. In this letter he attacks all the demons, declaring that they are so foolish as to be attracted by damp vapour, and for that reason they do not live in the ether, but in the air under the moon, and on the sphere of the moon itself. And yet he cannot bring himself to attribute to all the demons

44. 2 Cor. 11, 14. 45. Virg., *Georg.*, 4, 411.

46. Anebo, an Egyptian priest, mentioned by Eusebius (*Praep. Ev.*, 5, 7). A reply to Porphyry (*De Mysteriis*) is attributed to Iamblichus.

all the impostures, the malignities, the absurdities which excite his just indignation. In fact he follows the general convention of calling some of them 'good demons', even while admitting stupidity to be their general characteristic.

He also expresses astonishment that the gods are not only enticed by sacrificial victims, but even constrained and compelled to do what men want. And, assuming that gods are distinguished from demons by the fact that they are immaterial, whereas demons have material bodies, he wonders how the sun, the moon, and the other visible heavenly bodies (which are, he is quite sure, material bodies) are to be thought of as gods. And if they are gods, how is it that some are said to be beneficent, others malign, and how, being material, can they be united with immaterial beings?

He also asks, as if he were really in doubt, whether in the case of diviners and miracle-workers their powers are due to passions of the human soul, or to spirits of some kind coming from outside. He is inclined to favour the second suggestion, on the ground that it is by the employment of stones and herbs that they cast spells on people, open closed doors, and perform other miraculous feats of this kind. Hence, he says, some people have come to the conclusion that there is a class of beings whose characteristic property is to listen to man's commands; they are by nature deceitful; they can take all shapes and forms, appearing as gods, or demons, or departed spirits. These are the beings who effect all these marvels, some of which appear to be good, some evil. As for such manifestations as are really good, those beings give no assistance to them; in fact they know nothing about them, and all they do is to suggest and impute evil; and very often they hinder those who are most eager in the pursuit of virtue. They are full of blind folly and arrogance; they delight in foul stenches; they are at the mercy of flattery – and so on. All this description of this class of fraudulent and malignant spirits, who come into the soul from outside and delude the senses of men, asleep or awake, Porphyry records, but not as his own conviction. It is for him a faint suspicion, a tentative suggestion, and so he puts it forward as the opinion of others.

It was, no doubt, difficult for so great a philosopher either to acknowledge all this society of demons or to censure them with confidence, whereas any Christian old woman would have no hesitation about the fact of their existence, and no reserve about denouncing them. Was it, perhaps, because Porphyry was afraid of offending his correspondent, seeing that Anebo was an eminent priest of such rites, and of offending others who were impressed by such performances, assuming them to be divine works, closely connected with the worship of the gods?

However that may be, Porphyry pursues the subject, and, under colour of asking for information, he mentions facts which on sober consideration would only be attributed to malicious deceitful powers. He asks how it is that when powers have been invoked as being utterly good, the commands given to them assume that they are completely evil, when they are bidden to fulfil the unjust instructions of mankind. Why do these powers refuse to listen to the supplication of one who is contaminated by the 'work of Venus', while they have no hesitation about leading anyone to illicit unions? Why do they insist that their priests should abstain from eating meat, no doubt to guard themselves from the danger of pollution by their bodily exhalations, while they themselves are attracted by smells, and especially by the stench of sacrificial victims? Why has the initiate in the mysteries to avoid any contact with dead bodies, when the celebration of the mysteries themselves generally involves dead bodies? How is it that a human being addicted to any kind of vice can direct his threats, not just to any demon, or to a departed spirit, but even to the sun itself, or to the moon, or any of the heavenly bodies and terrify them with his lies so as to extort true service from them? For men threaten to batter the heavens, and to perform other feats beyond human competence, so that the gods may be terrified by false and absurd menaces, like silly children, and induced to fulfil men's commands. Porphyry also quotes an author called Chaeremon,[47] who was well versed in such rites – or rather blasphemies – as saying that the mysteries of Isis and her husband Osiris,[48] which are in such repute in Egypt, have the greatest power to force the gods to do what they are bidden, if the man who seeks to constrain the gods with spells threatens to reveal or indeed to abolish those mysteries – if, that is, he cries out in a terrible voice that he will scatter the members of Osiris, unless the gods are prompt to carry out his orders.

There is every reason for Porphyry's astonishment at the thought that a human being should utter such futile and crazy threats against the gods (and not against any ordinary gods, but the gods of the heavens, shining with the light of the stars) and that such threats should not be without result, but that their violence should have power to inspire such terror as to induce the gods to perform the service required. The truth is that under pretence of expressing astonishment

47. A Stoic writer of the first century A.D. No works extant.
48. cf. Bk VI, 10.

and asking for explanations of these facts, Porphyry is really giving us to understand that all these manifestations are the work of spirits of the kind he has previously described when ostensibly giving the opinion of others; these spirits are deceitful, not by nature, as he put it, but by their own viciousness. They disguise themselves as gods or as ghosts; but they do not *pretend* to be demons as Porphyry says, for that is what they clearly are.

Then there is the magic by means of herbs and stones and animals, by certain prescribed sounds and phrases, by the use of figures and models, or again by the observation of certain movements of the stars in the changing face of heaven. Porphyry supposes that by such methods men contrive for themselves on earth the forces capable of achieving their various designs. But all this again is connected with those same demons who delude the souls of those who submit to their control, and provide for themselves delightful entertainments arising from the follies of mankind.

Porphyry is really puzzled and is asking for information on these matters; and yet he mentions the facts which could prove the falsity and demonstrate the wickedness of such practices, which are obviously connected not with the powers which help us to the attainment of felicity, but with the demons of delusion. Or else, to take a more favourable view of the philosopher, he knows that the Egyptian is addicted to those errors, and has a high opinion of the importance of his science, and so he wants to avoid offending him by what might seem an arrogant assumption of a teacher's authority, and not to upset him by frankly opposing him in argument; and so he adopts the humility of an enquirer who seeks to know the truth, in the hope of leading his correspondent to reflect on those practices, and thus of showing him how contemptible they are, and how much they are to be shunned.

Finally, almost at the end of the letter, he asks for instruction about the way to happiness, according to the wisdom of Egypt. As for those whose dealings with the gods get no further than to trouble the Divine Intelligence about the finding of a runaway slave, or the acquisition of a piece of property, or on the subject of a marriage, or a business deal, and that sort of thing, such people, he says, have evidently cultivated that wisdom to little purpose. And the divine powers, with whom they have had dealings, may have given true predictions about all other matters; but in spite of that, since they have not given any sensible or useful advice on the subject of happiness, they cannot be gods, or even good demons: they are either identical with that being who is called the Deceiver, or else they are nothing but a figment of the human imagination.

12. *The miracles of God performed through the ministry of angels*

However, since effects are achieved by those arts which surpass the limits of all the power of mankind, the only sensible course is to realize the true nature of those marvels, in the way of predictions or events which seem to be examples of divine power, and yet have no connection with the worship of the one God. It is to this God that man must cleave in all sincerity, if he is to attain the only Good which brings true happiness. The Platonists themselves admit this, by a multitude of testimonies. And so all these marvels are to be seen as mockeries, seductions, and hindrances, contrived by malicious demons – things from which true piety must protect us.

Contrasted with these are all the miracles which are effected by divine power, whether by means of angels or in any other manner, so as to commend to us the worship and religion of the one God, in whom alone is the life of blessedness. All these we must believe to be done either by the action of those who love us according to truth and piety, or through their agency, God himself being at work in them. For we must not listen to those who say that God does not work visible miracles, since, according to their own admission, it is God who made the world, and they cannot deny that the world is a visible work. And whatever miracle happens in this world, it is certainly a lesser marvel than the whole world, that is to say, the heavens and the earth and all that is in them, which God undoubtedly made. But the manner of its making is as hidden from man and as incomprehensible to man as is he who made it. And so although the miracles of the visible world of nature have lost their value for us because we see them continually, still, if we observe them wisely they will be found to be greater miracles than the most extraordinary and unusual events. For man is a greater miracle than any miracle effected by man's agency.

And therefore God who made the visible marvels of heaven and earth does not disdain to work visible miracles in heaven and earth, by which he arouses the soul, hitherto preoccupied with visible things, to the worship of himself, the invisible God. But where and when he does this is a secret of his unchanging counsel, in whose plan all future events are already present. For he moves events in time, while himself remains unmoved by time. He knows what is to happen as already having happened. To him there is no difference between seeing us about to pray and listening to our prayers, for even when his angels listen, it is he himself who listens in them, being in them as in his true temple, not made with hands, as he is in his saints on earth; and his commands, which are eternal when viewed in reference to his everlasting Law, are fulfilled in time.

13. *The invisible God makes himself visible, according to the capacity of the beholders*

We ought not to be disturbed by the fact that, although he is invisible, God is reported as having often shown himself in visible form to our ancestors. Just as the uttered sound which makes audible the thought that has its existence in the silence of the understanding, is not the same as that thought, so the visible form in which God – who exists in his invisible substance – became visible was not identical with God himself. For all that, he was seen in that material form, just as the thought is heard in the sound of the voice. And those patriarchs were well aware that they were seeing the invisible God in a material form, though God himself was not material. For God spoke to Moses, and Moses spoke to him in reply; and yet Moses said to him, 'If I have found favour in your sight, show me yourself, so that I may see you and know you.'[49]

Now it was necessary that the Law of God should be given, under the form of decrees proclaimed by angels,[50] in awe-inspiring circumstances, and given not to one man, not to a few sages, but to the whole nation, an immense people; and therefore great portents happened on the mountain in the sight of that people; and there the Law was given through the agency of one man, while the multitude beheld the fearful and terrible happenings. For the belief of the people of Israel in Moses was something quite different from the Spartans' belief in Lycurgus,[51] when he told them that he had received from Jupiter or from Apollo the laws which he laid down. When the Hebrew people received the Law that prescribed the worship of one God, marvellous signs and commotions of nature occurred in the sight of the people, to the extent which divine providence judged sufficient, which made it apparent that for the giving of that Law the creation was serving the purpose of the Creator.

49. Exod. 33, 13. 50. cf. Acts 7, 53; Gal. 3, 19.

51. Legendary law-giver of Sparta to whom were ascribed the reforms which changed the character of that state *c.* 600 B.C.

14. *God is to be worshipped as well for temporal as for eternal benefits*

The experience of mankind in general, as far as God's people is concerned, is comparable to the experience of the individual man. There is a process of education, through the epochs of a people's history, as through the successive stages of a man's life, designed to raise them from the temporal and the visible to an apprehension of the eternal and the invisible. But even at the time when visible rewards were promised by divine revelation, man was commanded to worship one God, lest, even for the sake of the earthly benefits of this transient life, man should subject his mind to any being other than the Creator and Master of his soul. For all things which men can receive at the hands of either angels or men, are in the power of the one Omnipotent: and anyone who does not admit this is insane.

Plotinus the Platonist has a discussion about providence,[52] in which he proves, by the beauty of flowers and leaves, that providence extends from the supreme God, whose beauty is intelligible and ineffable, as far as those lowly things of earth. All those castaways, so to speak, doomed to perish so swiftly, could not, he maintains, display such perfection of graceful harmony in their shapes, were it not that they received their form from the eternal abode of the intelligible and changeless 'form'[53] which contains them all together in itself. This is what the Lord Jesus tells us in the passage where he says,

> Consider the lilies of the field: they do not work, or spin. Yet I tell you, Solomon in all his splendour was not clothed like one of those. Now if this is how God dresses the grass of the countryside, which is here today and tomorrow is put in the stove; how much more will he clothe you, you men of small faith?[54]

Now the soul of man is still weak because of its earthly desires, and in this temporal existence it craves for those inferior goods of this world which, although essential for this transitory life, are to be despised in comparison with the eternal blessings of that other life. Even so, it is altogether right that the soul should learn to look for those temporal blessings from God, and from him alone, so that even in longing for them it should not withdraw from the worship of that God, whom it only reaches by despising them and turning away from them.

52. *Enn.* 3, 2, 13. 53. The Platonic 'idea'. 54. Matt. 6, 28f.

15. *The ministry of the holy angels as instruments of God's providence*

Thus it pleased divine providence to arrange the course of the ages in such a way that, as I have said, and as we read in the *Acts of the Apostles*, the Law concerning the worship of the one true God was given in decrees communicated by angels.[55] God's own substance always remains invisible to corruptible eyes: and yet in those edicts the person of God himself became manifest by unmistakable signs, through the medium of created things in subjection to the Creator. God, in his own nature, so to say, neither begins nor ceases to speak; he speaks not temporally, but eternally; not corporally but spiritually; not to the senses but to the understanding. Yet through his created beings he spoke in successive syllables, following one another in transitory intervals of time. His ministers and messengers enjoy his unchanging truth in their immortal blessedness, and they hear his language in its purity, with the ear of the mind, not of the body; and when what they hear demands to be put into action and to be brought into the sphere of the visible and the sensible, then they put it into effect without delay or difficulty.

Now in this arrangement of the successive ages, the Law was given so as to offer, to begin with, the promise of the good things of this world. But these good things were intended to stand for the eternal blessings; and this was the meaning of the outward and visible rites which were celebrated by all the people, but understood by few. For all the words of that Law and all the acts enjoined by it united in the clearest testimony to teach the worship of one God – not one of a host of gods, but the one God who made heaven and earth, and every soul and every spirit which exists outside himself. He is the creator, and all the rest are created, and for their being, and for their well-being, they have need of him by whom they have been created.

16. *For the attainment of happiness we should listen to the angels who teach that worship should be offered only to the one God*

Which angels are we then to believe, in the matter of the life of blessedness and eternity? What is our decision? Is it to be those who wish to receive for themselves the worship of religious ceremonies, and demand from mortals the performance of rites and sacrifices in

55. cf. Acts. 7, 53.

their honour? Or those who say that all this worship is due to God, the sole creator of all things, and who teach with true piety that it is to be rendered to him, the contemplation of whom gives them the happiness which they promise it will bring to us in the future? For this vision of God is a vision of such beauty and altogether deserving of such a love, that Plotinus says without hesitation that a man who fails of it is altogether unfortunate, no matter how richly endowed he may be with any other kind of goods.[56] Thus by various signs and wonders we are invited by angels of one sort to devote our worship in the highest sense of the word to this one God, by angels of another sort to devote that worship to themselves – with this difference, that the former forbid the worship of the second while the latter sort do not dare to forbid the worship of God. Which sort are we to believe? Let us have an answer from the Platonists, from the philosophers of all the schools, from the theurgists (though 'periurgists' – 'superstitious meddlers' – would be a more appropriate term for them), and let us have an answer also from ordinary men, if any sense of their nature, as created capable of reason, remains alive in them in any degree. Let them tell us, I say, if we should sacrifice to those gods or angels who demand sacrifices for themselves, or to him alone to whom sacrifice is to be offered, according to the commands of those who forbid the offering of sacrifice to themselves or to the other angels.

If neither the one sort nor the other had performed any miracles, but had only given instructions, the one prescribing sacrifice to themselves, the other forbidding those sacrifices, but insisting that they should be offered only to the one God; even so, piety by itself should have sufficed to decide which of those commands derived from arrogant pride, and which from true religion. I would go further; if it had been only those who demand sacrifices for themselves who had astonished the souls of men by their miraculous feats, while those who forbid such sacrifices and order that they should be reserved for God alone, had not deigned to perform any visible miracles; even so, the authority of the latter certainly ought to have carried the day, not by the verdict of the bodily senses but in the judgement of the reasoning mind. But in fact God has decided to support the oracles of his truth by performing miracles through those immortal messengers who proclaim not their own arrogance but the majesty of God; and their miracles are greater, more certain, more impressive than all the others. The purpose of those wonders was to prevent those angels who demand sacrifices for themselves from finding it easy to persuade men

56. *Enn.*, 1, 6, 7.

of unstable piety to a false religion just by making a prodigious display to their senses. In view of those miracles, surely no one would like to be such a fool as not to choose to recognize the truth that he should follow, where he finds more to excite his wonder?

When I speak of the miracles of the gods of the Gentiles, which history vouches for, I am not referring to accidental prodigies which occur at long intervals by the interplay of mysterious causes at work in this world, causes which nevertheless are fixed and ordained under the rule of divine providence – such things, I mean, as the birth of extraordinary animals, unusual phenomena in the sky and on the earth, whether merely frightening or harmful as well, all of which, according to the claim put out by the crafty deceit of the demons. can be conjured up or controlled by demonic rites. What I am talking about are the phenomena which are quite evidently the result of the force and power of demons: like the story that the images of the Penates, carried from Troy by Aeneas in his flight, removed themselves from one place to another;[57] the feat of Tarquinius in cutting a whetstone with a razor;[58] the serpent from Epidaurus accompanying Aesculapius on his voyage to Rome;[59] the ship which conveyed the image of the Phyrgian Mother, which stuck fast and resisted all the efforts of men and oxen, but was set in motion and drawn along by one mere woman, with her girdle attached to it – a testimony to her chastity;[60] the Vestal Virgin, under suspicion of violation of her vows, who put an end to the question by filling a sieve with water from the Tiber without losing any.[61] Such miracles as those are in no way comparable in power and grandeur with those performed, as we read, among the people of God. How much less comparable are the performances prohibited and punished by the laws of the nations who worshipped gods of this kind, I mean the feats of magic or theurgy! Most of those are mere appearance, deceiving men's senses by extravagant illusions: such things as 'bringing down the moon'

> Until she flings her foam upon the grass
> That spreads below her,

as Lucan says.[62]

It is true that some of those miracles may seem in externals to equal many of those performed among true worshippers; the distinction lies

57. Val. Max., 1, 8, 7. 58. Liv., 1, 36. 59. Val. Max., 1, 8, 2.
60. Ovid., *Fast.*, 4, 305f. 61. Val. Max., 8, 1, 5.
62. *Phars.*, 6, 506, cf. Virg., *Ecl.*, 8, 69.

in the difference of the end, and here our miracles show incomparable superiority. For the former give us added reason for refusing sacrifice to those multiple gods, with a resolution proportional to the insistence of their demands; the latter bear witness to the one God, who has no need of such rites, as he shows by the evidence of his Scriptures, as also by the later abolition of the same sacrifices.

And so, if any angels claim sacrifice for themselves, we must prefer to them those who claim it not for themselves but for the God whom they serve, the creator of all things. In this way they show the sincerity of their love for us, since by such sacrifice they wish to subject us not to themselves, but to him. For they find their own happiness in the contemplation of him, from whom they have never departed; and they desire that we also should come to him. If, on the other hand, there are angels who desire that sacrifice should be offered to many gods, and not only to one, while not asking sacrifice for themselves but for those gods whose angels they are, even so we ought to hold them inferior to those who are the angels of the one God of gods, and who command sacrifice to be offered to him, while forbidding its offering to any other, since none of these other angels forbids sacrifice to the God whose angels command sacrifice to him alone. And if angels show, by their arrogance and deceit, that they are not good angels, nor angels of good gods, but evil demons, whose aim is that sacrificial worship should be offered to themselves and not to the one supreme God, what more potent defence against them can we choose than that of the one God, whom the good angels serve? And the good angels command us to offer the service of sacrifice not to themselves but to him to whom we owe the sacrifice of ourselves.

17. *The Ark of the Testimony and the miracles performed to support the authority of the Law and the promise*

The Law of God was given in decrees conveyed by angels,[63] and it prescribed the worship of the one God of gods in religious rites, and forbade the offering of such worship to any other beings. This Law was placed in an ark (a chest), which was called the Ark of the Testimony. The meaning of this title is quite evident. It is not that God, who was worshipped in all those ceremonies, was habitually confined and enclosed in a place, although his replies were given from the place where the Ark was and certain miracles were there presented to

63. cf. Acts 7, 23; Gal. 3, 19.

human senses; but the testimonies of his will were said to come from there, because the Law itself was inscribed on tablets of stone and deposited, as I said, in this Ark. During the period of wandering in the desert the priests carried the Ark with all proper reverence, together with the tent which was similarly entitled the Tent of the Testimony. There was also a sign, a cloud which appeared in the daytime and glowed like a fire by night. When this cloud began to move, they struck camp; when it halted, they pitched camp.[64]

Great miracles gave testimony to the Law, apart from those I have spoken of, and apart from the utterances which issued from the place of the Ark. When the Hebrews were entering the promised land and the Ark started to cross over, the river Jordan stopped its flow on the upstream side and flowed away downstream, thus affording a dry passage for the Ark and the people. After that, when they met with the first resistance from a city, which followed the custom of the Gentiles in worshipping a plurality of gods, the Ark was carried round the city seven times and the walls suddenly collapsed, without any physical assault or any use of the battering-ram.[65] Thereafter, when the Hebrews were by now within the promised land, and the Ark had been captured by the enemy because of the sins of the people, its captors set it in a place of honour in the temple of the god whom they honoured above all the rest, and shut the temple when they went out. Next day, when they opened the temple, they found the image to which they offered their prayers fallen to the ground and broken, a sorry sight. Under the stress of such prodigies, and after even more unpleasant punishment, the enemy restored the Ark of God's Testimony to the people from whom they had captured it. And what circumstances attended that restoration! They loaded the Ark on a cart, to which they harnessed cattle from whom they had taken their sucking calves. Then they let the cattle go where they liked, wishing even here to test the divine power. The cattle, without any man to guide or steer them, resolutely made their way to the Hebrews, without turning back in response to the lowing of their hungry calves; and thus they restored the sacred object to those who revered it.[66]

Such miracles are small things for God, but important for mortals, to inspire in them a salutary fear and to give them instruction. Now the philosophers, and in particular the Platonists, have won praise for wisdom superior to the rest of mankind, as I said a little earlier, for having taught that divine providence controls even the lowest things

64. Exod. 13, 21; 40, 34f. 65. Josh. 3, 16f. 66. 1 Sam. 46.

on the earth, producing as evidence all the thousands of beauties found not only in the bodies of living creatures but even in blades of grass.[67] If this is so, how much clearer is the witness to divine power in the miracles which take place at the moment when the religion is presented to men which forbids sacrifice to any being in heaven, on earth, or in the underworld, and prescribes sacrifice solely to the one God, who alone gives us happiness by his love for us and our love for him. He defines in advance the periods in which these sacrifices are demanded; he foretells that these sacrifices will be changed for something better through the action of a better priest, and by this he makes it clear that he does not himself desire such sacrifices but uses them to point to things of greater worth. His purpose is not that he should be glorified by those honours, but that we should be inflamed by the fire of his love and aroused to worship him and unite ourselves to him; and that is a good for us, not for him.

18. *Against those who deny the credibility of the Church's books in the matter of the miracles by which God's people were instructed*

Is anyone going to say that those miracles are false; that they never happened, but were lies invented by writers of Scripture? Anyone who says this, and asserts that in these matters no reliance is to be placed on any written evidence, can go on to say that none of the gods has any concern for the affairs of mortals. It was, in fact, only by the performance of miracles that the pagan gods persuaded men that they should offer them worship; and the evidence for those miracles is found also in history, the history of the pagan world; and these gods were able to show their power as wonder-workers, even though they could not point to any service they rendered to mankind. Hence, in this present work (on the tenth book of which we are now engaged) we have not undertaken to refute those who claim that there is no such thing as divine power, or maintain that it has no concern for human affairs.[68] Our argument is with those who prefer their own gods to our God, the founder of the Holy and Most Glorious City. Such men do not know that he is the invisible and unchanging founder of this visible and changing world, the true giver of the life of blessedness, the source of which is not to be found in his creatures but in himself.

For it is God's prophet who says, with complete truth, 'As for me,

67. cf. ch. 14. 68. Epicureans.

my true good is to cling to God.'[69] The question of the Supreme Good, to the attainment of which all duties are to be referred, is a matter of debate among philosophers. Our prophet did not say, 'For me the good is the possession of abundant wealth', or, 'to enjoy the distinction of the purple robe and the glory of sceptre or crown'; nor (as some philosophers[70] have not blushed to say), 'My good is bodily pleasure'; nor (following what seems to have been the better conception of those whom I take to be better philosophers),[71] 'My good is the virtue of my soul.' What he said was, 'As for me, my true good is to cling to God.' He had received this teaching from him to whom alone sacrifice should be offered, according to the instructions of the holy angels, borne out by the witness of miracles. Thus the prophet himself became a sacrifice to him whose immaterial fire set him ablaze with rapture, and a holy desire hurried him into the ineffable and spiritual embrace of God.

Now the worshippers of many gods (whatever may be their conception of the character of those gods) believe, one assumes, that miracles have been effected by them, accepting the records of their national history, or their magic books or (more respectably, as they think) their 'theurgic documents'. Then why do they refuse credence to the record of such events in those writings which should be held more trustworthy in proportion as the God for whom they reserve all sacrificial worship[72] is great above all others?

19. *The reason for visible sacrifice, which is only to be offered to the one true and invisible God*

There are some who suppose that these visible sacrifices are suitable for other gods, but that for the one God, as he is invisible, greatest and best, only the invisible, the greatest, and the best sacrifices are proper; and such sacrifices are the services of a pure mind and a good will. But such people evidently do not realize that the visible sacrifices are symbols of the invisible offerings, just as spoken words are the symbols of things. Therefore in our prayers and praises we address significant sounds to him, as we render to him in our hearts the realities thus signified. In the same way, in offering our sacrifices we shall be aware that visible sacrifice must be offered only to him, to whom we ourselves ought to be an invisible sacrifice in our hearts. It is

69. Ps. 73, 28. 70. Cyrenaics. 71. Stoics.
72. cf. Ps. 103, 20.

then that the angels and the higher powers and all who 'excel in strength'[73] by reason of their very goodness and piety, support us and rejoice with us and assist us in this enterprise with all their might.

But if we wish to render this worship to them, they are not glad to receive it; and when they are sent to men in such a form that their presence is detected by the senses, they directly forbid such worship. There are instances of this in the Scriptures. There have been some who thought that angels should be rendered the honour of adoration and sacrifice which is due to God; and they were forbidden to do so by the angels' warning, and ordered to render it to him to whom alone, as the angels know, it could be offered without blasphemy.[74] The example of the angels was copied by holy men of God. In Lycaonia, Paul and Barnabas performed a miracle of healing and in consequence were taken for gods; and the Lycaonians wanted to sacrifice victims to them. But in humble piety the apostles declined this worship; and they proclaimed to the people the God in whom they should believe.[75]

But the reason why those deceitful angels arrogantly claim this honour for themselves is simply that they know that it is the due of the true God. The notion, entertained by Porphyry and a number of others,[76] that those angels enjoy the smell of dead bodies, is false. It is divine honours that really delight them. They have a plentiful supply of smells everywhere; and if they want more, they can produce them for themselves. So the spirits who arrogate to themselves divinity, do not find their pleasure in the smoke of any burning body, but in the soul of a suppliant, deluded and subjected to their domination. They bar the way to the true God, so that a man may not become a sacrifice to him, so long as he sacrifices to any other being.

20. *The supreme and true sacrifice of the Mediator between God and man*

Hence it is that the true Mediator (in so far as he 'took the form of a servant'[77] and was thus made 'the mediator between God and mankind, the man Christ Jesus'[78]) receives the sacrifice 'in the form of God', in union with the Father, with whom he is one God. And yet 'in the form of a servant' he preferred to be himself the sacrifice than to receive it, to prevent anyone from supposing that sacrifice, even in

73. Ps. 103, 20.
74. cf. Exod. 22, 20; Judg. 13, 16; Rev. 19, 20; 22, 8f.
75. Acts 14, 7ff.
76. cf. ch. 11.
77. Phil. 2, 6f.
78. 1 Tim. 2, 5.

this circumstance, should be offered to any created being. Thus he is both the priest, himself making the offering, and the oblation. This is the reality, and he intended the daily sacrifice of the Church to be the sacramental symbol of this; for the Church, being the body of which he is the head, learns to offer itself through him. This is the true sacrifice; and the sacrifices of the saints in earlier times were many different symbols of it. This one sacrifice was prefigured by many rites, just as many words are used to refer to one thing, to emphasize a point without inducing boredom. This was the supreme sacrifice, and the true sacrifice, and all the false sacrifices yielded place to it.

21. *Power given to demons for the glorification of the saints through their steadfast endurance of sufferings*

It is true that power was allowed to the demons, for a limited period, fixed in advance; a power which enabled them to egg on those whom they controlled, and so to exercise their hatred against the City of God in the manner of tyrants. Not only could they receive sacrifices from those who readily offered them and demand them from their willing subjects: they could extort them by the violence of persecution from those who refused. But this persecution, far from being the ruin of the Church, in fact turned out to its advantage, by filling up the number of the martyrs.[79] The City of God regards these martyrs as citizens so much the more glorious and the more honoured the more bravely they struggled against the sin of impiety and resisted it, up to the point of shedding their blood.[80]

If it were not contrary to the usage of the Church, we might call those martyrs our 'heroes', a much more fitting name. 'Hero' is said to be derived from the name of Juno. The Greek name for Juno is Hera, and that is why one or other of her sons was called Heros, according to Greek legend. This myth evidently signifies, though in cryptic fashion, that Juno is assigned the power over the air;[81] and the meaning is that the heroes dwell with the demons, the name 'heroes' denoting the souls of the departed who have rendered some exceptional service. Our martyrs, in contrast, would be called 'heroes', if (as I said) the usage of the Church allowed it, not because of any association with the demons in the air, but as the conquerors of those demons, that is, of the 'powers of the air',[82] and of Juno herself among them,

79. cf. Rev. 6, 11. 80. cf. Hebr. 12, 4.

81. 'Hero' and Hera are unconnected. Heros is unknown. St Augustine evidently connects Hera with *aêr*('air').

82. cf. Eph. 2, 2.

whatever we take to be the meaning of the name. For the poets were not altogether off the mark in representing her as the enemy of virtue, jealous of brave men who strove to attain to heaven. But observe how once again Virgil, most unfortunately, gives her best and yields to her power. Although he makes Juno say,

> Conquered am I by Aeneas,[83]

he represents Helenus, ostensibly the religious adviser, as warning Aeneas himself in these words:

> Offer your prayers to Juno of goodwill,
> And win the powerful queen with suppliant gifts.[84]

There is a notion mentioned by Porphyry, not as his own opinion but as one held by others. According to this a good spirit, god, or demon, cannot enter into a man unless the evil spirit has first been appeased. It seems that, according to the philosophers, the evil powers are stronger than the good, seeing that the evil spirits prevent the good from giving aid unless they are appeased and give place to them, while the good spirits cannot assist us against the will of the evil powers; whereas the evil spirits can do harm, while the good have no power to resist them. This is not the way of the true and truly holy religion. It is not in this manner that our martyrs overcome Juno, that is to say, the powers of the air who envy the virtues of the saints. Our 'heroes' (if usage would allow the title) overcome Hera by divine virtues, not at all by 'suppliant gifts'. There is no doubt that Scipio was rightly called Africanus for having conquered Africa by his soldierly qualities; he would have had less claim to the title if he had appeased the enemy by gifts to secure their mercy.

22. *The source of the power of the saints, and of their purification*

It is by true piety that the men of God cast out this power of the air, the enemy and adversary of piety; it is by exorcizing, not by appeasing them, and they triumph over all temptations of that hostile power not by praying to the enemy but by praying to their God against the enemy. For the hostile power cannot vanquish or subdue a man unless that man becomes associated with the enemy in sin. And so the power is conquered in the name of him who assumed human nature and whose life was without sin, so that in him, who was both priest and sacrifice, remission of sins might be effected, that is, through the

83. *Aen.*, 7, 310. 84. *Aen.*, 3, 438f.

'mediator between God and mankind, the man Christ Jesus',[85] through whom we are purified from our sins and reconciled to God. For it is only sins that separate men from God; and in this life purification from sins is not effected by our merit, but by the compassion of God, through his indulgence, not through our power; for even that poor little virtue which we call ours has itself been granted to us by his bounty. Yet we should have a high opinion of ourselves, in this life in the flesh, were it not that, right up to the time of our departure, we live under pardon. And that is why grace has been bestowed on us through the intervention of a mediator, so that when we had been polluted by the sinful flesh we might be purified by 'the likeness of sinful flesh'.[86] By this grace of God, the evidence of his great mercy, we are guided in this life by faith, and after this life are brought to complete fulfilment by the vision of the unchanging truth.

23. *The 'principles' of the Platonic theory of spiritual purgation*

Porphyry also says that, according to the reply of the divine oracles, the initiatory rites of the sun and of the moon cannot purify us. The purpose of this reply, he says, is to make it clear that a man cannot be purified by the initiatory rites of any god. For where is the god whose rites can effect our purification, if those of the sun and the moon are of no avail? For they are regarded as the chief divinities among the gods of heaven. Porphyry's main point is that the same oracle made it clear that purification is effected by the 'principles'. This was to prevent the belief in the efficiency of the rites of any other god, among the crowd of divinities, after it had been stated that the rites of the sun and the moon were of no avail for this purpose.

We know what Porphyry, as a Platonist, means by the 'principles'.[87] He refers to God the Father, and God the Son, whom he calls in Greek the Intellect or Mind of the Father. About the Holy Spirit he says nothing, or at least nothing clear; although I do not understand what other being he refers to as holding the middle position between these two. If, like Plotinus in his discussion of the three

85. 1 Tim. 2, 5. 86. Rom. 8, 3.

87. *Principles* or 'beginnings' (Gk. *archai*). The Trinity of Neoplatonism is thus described by Cyril of Alexandria (*c. Jul.*, 8): 'Plato said that the substance of God issues in three subsistences (*hypostaseis*, 'persons'): the supreme God being the Good; after him, in the second place, the Creator (the Demiurge); then, in the third place, the Soul of the World.'

'principal substances',[88] he had intended it to be inferred that this third entity is the natural substance of the soul, he would certainly not have said that this held the middle place between the two others, the Father and the Son. Plotinus certainly regards the nature of the soul as inferior to the Intellect of the Father;[89] whereas Porphyry, in speaking of an entity in the middle position, places it between, not below, the two others. Doubtless he meant what we mean when we speak of the Holy Spirit, who is not the spirit of the Father only or of the Son only, but of both; and he described him to the best of his power, or according to his inclination. For the philosophers are free in their choice of expressions, and are not afraid of offending the ears of the religious when treating of subjects very hard to understand, while we Christians are in solemn duty bound to speak in accordance with a fixed rule,[90] for fear that a looseness of language might give rise to a blasphemous opinion about the realities to which the words refer.

24. *The one true 'principle' of purification and regeneration*

Thus when we speak about God we do not talk about two or three 'principles', any more than we are allowed to speak of two or three gods, although in talking of each person, whether the Father, the Son, or the Holy Spirit, we acknowledge that each of them is God. But we do not, like the Sabellian heretics,[91] identify the Father with the Son, and the Holy Spirit with both Father and Son. What we say is that the Father is Father of the Son, the Son is Son of the Father, the Holy Spirit is the Spirit of both Father and Son, but he is not identical with either. Thus the true statement is that man is only purified by 'the principle', although these philosophers have spoken of 'principles' in the plural.

But since Porphyry was in subjection to those envious powers, and was at the same time ashamed of his subjection and yet afraid to contradict them openly, he refused to recognize that the Lord Christ is the 'principle', and that by his incarnation we are purified. The fact is that he despised Christ as he appeared in flesh, in that very flesh which he assumed in order to effect the sacrifice of our purification. It was of course his pride which blinded Porphyry to this great mystery, that pride which our true and gracious Mediator has overthrown by

88. cf. *Enn.*, 45, 1. 89. *Enn.*, 45, 6.

90. The Rule of Faith, cf. Bk XV, ch. 7n.

91. The 'Modalist Monarchians' of the third century, who explained the three Persons as successive modes of divine activity.

his humility, in showing himself to mortals in the condition of mortality. It was because they were free from that mortal condition that the false and malignant 'mediators' vaunted their superiority, and deluded unhappy men by false promises of assistance, as immortals coming to the aid of mortals. And so the good and true Mediator has shown that it is sin which is evil, not the substance or nature of flesh, since that substance could be assumed, with a human soul, and preserved free from sin, and could be laid aside in death, and changed into something better by resurrection. He has shown that death itself, although it is the punishment for sin (a punishment which he paid for us, though being himself without sin), is not to be avoided by sinning but rather, if occasion offers, to be endured for the cause of right. For it is just because he died, and his death was not the penalty of sin, that he was able by dying to pay the price of our sins.

But this Platonist failed to see that Christ was the 'principle'; for then he would have recognized him as the means of purification. The fact is that it is not the flesh which is the 'principle', nor the human soul in Christ, but the Word, 'through whom everything came into existence'.[92] And therefore the flesh does not purify by itself, but through the Word by which it was assumed, when 'the Word became flesh, and dwelt among us'.[93] When Christ spoke in a mystical sense about 'eating his flesh' some of his uncomprehending hearers were shocked, and they said, as they went away, 'This kind of talk is intolerable! Who can endure to listen to it?' And Jesus said to those who stayed behind, 'It is the spirit which gives life: but the flesh is of no help to anyone.'[94] The 'principle', then, having assumed a soul and flesh, purifies the soul and the flesh of believers. Hence, when the Jews asked him who he was, Christ replied that he was the 'principle' (or beginning).[95] We should certainly have been utterly unable to understand this, carnal as we are, and weak, liable to sin, and shrouded in the darkness of ignorance, had we not been purified and healed by Christ, by means of what we were and what we were not. For we were men, but we were not righteous, while in his incarnation there was the human nature, but it was righteous and sinless. This was the mediation, the stretching out of a hand to those who lay

92. John 1, 3. 93. John 1, 14. 94. John, 6, 57; 61; 64.

95. *Christ ... the 'principle'*: Christ's answer to the question, 'Who are you?' is ambiguous in the Greek of John 8, 25. It could mean either 'What I told you at the beginning' or 'Why do I speak to you at all?' The Vulgate introduces another ambiguity, since *principium* (translating *tên archên*, 'at the start' or 'at all') could be nominative, as St Augustine takes it, making the reply 'I am the beginning (principle).'

fallen; this is the 'seed (of Abraham)' which was prepared for, through the ministry of those angels, whose edicts gave man the Law[96] which prescribed the worship of one God and promised the coming of this Mediator.

25. *The saints in earlier ages under the Law were all justified by the mystery of Christ's incarnation and through faith in him*

It was through faith in this mystery that the righteous men of antiquity were able to be purified by living piously, not only before the Law was given to the Hebrew people – for God never failed to instruct them, nor did the angels – but also in the period of the Law; although in its foreshadowing of spiritual realities, the Law seems to offer promises of material rewards, and that is the reason why it is called the *Old* Testament.

For there were then the prophets, through whom, as through the angels, the same promise was announced, and among them was the author of that great and inspired saying about the supreme good of man which I quoted just now, 'As for me, my true good is to cling to God.'[97] This psalm marks the clear distinction between the two Testaments, the Old and the New. For the prophet observed that the promises of material and earthly blessings were abundantly granted to the wicked, and he says that his feet had almost stumbled, and his steps had nearly slipped. It seemed that he had served God to no purpose since he saw those who despised God flourishing in the happiness which he had looked to receive from him. He says that he wearied himself in his efforts to solve the problem why this should happen, until he went into the sanctuary of God and reflected on the end of those men who had seemed to him, mistakenly, to be happy. Then he understood that in their exaltation of themselves they have been, in his words, 'cast down, and have disappeared because of their wickedness', and all that height of temporal felicity has become for them 'like a dream from which a man wakes' and finds himself suddenly robbed of those illusory delights of which he has dreamed. And because in this world, in this earthly city, they felt themselves to be of great importance, 'in your City, Lord, you will reduce their phantom to nothing.'

96. cf. Acts 7, 53; Gal. 3, 19.

97. Ps. 73, 28. St Augustine goes on to paraphrase and expound verses 17 to 28 of this psalm.

For all that, the psalmist makes it plain that he has profited from seeking even worldly benefits only from the one true God who has all things in his power. He says, 'I have become like a beast in your presence'; and by 'like a beast' he obviously means 'without understanding'.

I ought to have desired to receive from you the things which I cannot share with the wicked. But when I saw the wicked abundantly supplied with these goods, I thought that I had served you to no purpose, seeing that those goods were enjoyed even by those who refused to serve you. And yet 'I am always with you'; for even in my search for those benefits I have not applied to any other gods.

Thus he goes on to say, 'You have taken hold of my right hand: you have guided me according to your will, and have taken me to yourself in glory.' He implies that all those advantages which he saw the wicked enjoying in abundance – a sight which brought him almost to collapse – all those belong to the *left* hand. 'What do I possess in heaven?' he asks; 'and what have I wished to receive from you on earth?' He is reproaching himself and is ashamed of himself with good reason because, having (as he afterwards realized) such a treasure in heaven, he sought from his God such transient benefits on earth such a fragile and shabby felicity. 'My heart and my flesh', he says, 'have failed, God of my heart'; but this is a happy failure, a desertion of the lower level, to gain the heights. Hence, in another psalm, 'My soul longs, and faints with desire for the courts of the Lord.'[98] And again, in another psalm, 'My soul has fainted with desire for your salvation.'[99] And yet, though he has spoken of the failure of both heart and flesh, he does not add, 'God of my heart and flesh', but 'God of my heart'. For it is clearly by means of the heart that the flesh is purified. Thus the Lord says, 'Clean what is inside, and then the outside will be clean.'[100]

The psalmist goes on to say that his 'possession' is God himself, and not something which comes from God. 'God of my heart', he says, 'and God my possession for all the ages', because out of all the possible choices offered to men, he has decided to choose God himself. 'For look,' he says, 'those who remove themselves far away from you will perish: you have destroyed everyone who deserts you to play the harlot', that is, everyone who chooses to prostitute himself to a multitude of gods. Then follows the statement which led me to quote the

98. Ps. 84, 3. 99. Ps. 119, 81. 100. Matt. 23, 26.

other verse of the psalm, 'As for me, my true good is to cling to God, not to depart from him; not to indulge in the promiscuity of a harlot. Now this 'cleaving to God' will only be perfect when all that has to be set free has gained its freedom.

Meanwhile, now is the time, as he goes on to say, 'to place my hope in God'. For, as the Apostle says, 'To experience what one hopes for is no longer to hope; for why should anyone hope for what he already experiences? But if we hope for something we do not experience, it is with patient endurance that we await it.'[101] Now since we are established in this hope, let us put into practice the next verse of the psalm, and be ourselves, to the best of our poor ability, the angels – that is the heralds – of God, proclaiming his will, praising his glory and his grace. 'To place my hope in God', says the psalmist, and he proceeds, 'so that I may proclaim all your praises in the gates of the Daughter of Sion.'[102] 'The Daughter of Sion' is the most glorious City of God, which knows and worships one God. It is proclaimed by holy angels, who have invited us into the society of that City, and have desired us to become their fellow-citizens in it. They have no wish that we should honour them as our gods. Their desire is that we should join with them in the worship of him who is their God and ours, not that we should sacrifice to them, but that we should be, with them, a sacrifice to God.

No one who considers these facts without malice or prejudice can have any hesitation in concluding that the blessed immortals feel no jealousy towards us – and indeed jealousy would prevent their blessedness – but rather that they all extend their love to us, that their purpose is that we should join them in their blessedness, and that they offer us more support and more assistance when we, with them, worship one God, Father, Son, and Holy Spirit, than they would give us if we worshipped those immortal spirits themselves by our sacrifices.

26. *The inconsistency of Porphyry, in his hesitation between the true God and demon-worship*

It seems to me that Porphyry feels some embarrassment in his attitude to his friends the theurgists. For his own belief corresponded more or less to what we hold, but he did not defend his opinions without reserve against the worship of many gods. He alleged, in fact, that there are two classes of angels: the one sort come down from above and reveal divine prophecies to men who practice theurgy, while the

101. Rom. 8, 24f. 102. Ps. 73, 26f.

others are those who make known on earth the truth about the Father, his height and his depth.

Are we to believe that those angels, whose task is to declare the will of the Father, wish us to be in subjection to any other being than him whose will they convey to us? Thus our Platonist himself very rightly advises us to imitate them rather than to invoke them. And so we have no need to fear that we shall offend those blessed and immortal beings by failing to offer sacrifice to them. For they know that such worship is due only to the one true God, and their blessedness is derived from their adherence to him. Can it then be doubted that they would not wish such worship to be offered to them either figuratively, or in the reality which is represented by the symbols? To claim such honour is the arrogance of the proud and wretched demons; far different is the piety of those beings who are subject to God, and who derive their happiness from adherence to him, and from no other source. They are bound to support us with sincere goodwill towards the attainment of the same blessing. They could not arrogate to themselves a worship which would bring us into subjection to them; they must needs proclaim him under whom we may enjoy peace in fellowship with them.

Why do you still tremble, my dear philosopher, to raise your voice without restraint against the powers who are envious of genuine virtue and of the gifts of the true God? You have already distinguished between the angels who announce the will of the Father, and those who come down to the theurgists, attracted by magical art of some kind. Why do you still do these latter the honour of stating that they reveal divine prophecies? What divine prophecies can they reveal, seeing that they do not reveal the will of the Father? No doubt these are the spirits which were bound by that envious magician by means of sacred spells, to prevent them from effecting the purification of a soul.[103] You tell us that the good magician who was anxious to effect the purification was unable to release those spirits from their bondage and restore their freedom of action. Do you still doubt that they are malignant demons? Or is it perhaps that you pretend ignorance for fear of offending the theurgists, who have taken advantage of your superstition to seduce you into accepting the pernicious nonsense of their teaching as if it were some great benefit? Here is a malicious power – or rather a plague – holding sway over malicious men – or rather, according to your own account, acting as their humble servant. Have you the audacity to exalt this power above the

103. cf. ch. 9.

air and establish it in heaven among your gods, even among your gods of the stars, or even to dishonour the stars themselves with these disgraceful slanders?

27. *Porphyry's impiety is worse than the errors of Apuleius*

Your fellow-Platonist, Apuleius, went wrong in a more civilized and acceptable fashion. It was only to the demons that he attributed unhealthy passions and perturbations of the mind;[104] and they were stationed beneath the moon. He venerated them; but, for all that, he had to admit that such was their condition, whether he liked it or not. But when it came to the higher gods, who belong to the ethereal spaces, the visible gods, whom he saw shining for all to see, like the sun, the moon, and the other lights in the same sphere, as well as the invisible deities, whose existence he imagined, he used every possible argument to isolate them from the taint of such disturbances.

You did not get this doctrine from Plato. It was your Chaldean teachers who persuaded you to bring human weakness up into the exalted heights of the universe, into the ether and the empyrean, up to the heavenly firmaments, so that your gods might be able to give supernatural revelations to the theurgists. Yet you consider yourself superior to such supernatural knowledge, in virtue of your intellectual life. You, of course, feel that, as a philosopher, you have not the slightest need of the purifications of theurgic art. Yet as a kind of repayment of your debt to those masters of yours, you prescribe such purgations for others. You inveigle those who are incapable of becoming philosophers to indulge in practices which, on your own showing, are of no use to you, because you are capable of higher things. Thus all those who cannot approach to philosophic virtue (a lofty ideal to which only a few attain) have your authority to seek out theurgists, in order to receive at their hands the purgation of the 'spiritual' soul at least, though not of the 'intellectual'. The result is, naturally, that since the vast majority have no taste for philosophy, you collect far more clients for those secret and illegal masters of yours than candidates for the Platonic schools. You have made yourself the preacher and the angel of those unclean spirits who pretend to be gods of the ether; and they have promised you that those who have been purified in their 'spiritual' soul, by theurgic art, although they cannot, indeed, return to the Father, will have their dwelling among the gods of the ether, above the levels of the air.

104. cf. Bk IX, 8; *De Deo Socr.*, 12.

Such teaching gets no hearing from that vast multitude whom Christ came to set free from the domination of the demons. For it is in him that they find a purification full of compassion, the purification of mind, spirit, and body. For he took upon himself entire humanity, though without sin, for this precise purpose, that he might cure all the constituents of human nature of the plague of sins. Would that you had recognized him and had entrusted yourself to him for your healing, instead of relying either on your own virtue, fragile and insecure as human virtue is, or on disastrous superstition! That would have been safer, for he would not have deceived you. Even your own oracles, as you yourself say, acknowledged him as holy and immortal; and the most renowned of poets also spoke of him, in a poetical manner certainly, for Christ is represented by an imaginary portrait of another person, but with complete truth, if the picture is referred to Christ.[105] This is what Virgil says:

> With you for guide, whatever trace remains
> Of our past crimes, shall all be done away;
> The world shall then be freed from endless fear.[106]

He means that even in those who are far advanced in righteousness and virtue there may remain, because of the weakness of our mortal life, if not the crimes at least the traces of crimes; and they can only be healed by that Saviour, whom this verse expressly describes. It is quite clear that Virgil did not say this on his own. This is shown by the fourth verse of the same eclogue,

> Now comes the last age in the prophecy
> Of Cumae's oracle.

It is immediately apparent that this passage was derived from the Sibyl of Cumae.[107]

But those theurgists, or rather the demons who disguise themselves by appearing in the form of gods, cannot purify the human spirit; rather they defile it by their fantastic illusions, by the deceptive apparitions through which they make game of their victims. For how could they purify a man's spirit, when their own spirit is unclean? If it were

105. *Christ is represented:* The fourth Eclogue of Virgil, addressed to the consul Pollio, predicts a golden age of peace under a new-born child who will have the virtues of his father. Christian writers supposed that Virgil had been inspired to speak of the birth of Christ and the coming of the Christian era. Virgil was probably thinking of the expected child of Octavian and Scribonia.

106. *Ecl.* 4, 13f.

107. *The Sibyl of Cumae:* see Bk XVIII, 23n.

not, they could not possibly have been bound by the spells of a malicious man, and terrified into withholding that worthless boon which, it was supposed, they intended to convey; nor would they have refused it because of a like malice in themselves.[108] It is enough for our purpose that you admit that theurgic purification cannot purify the 'intellectual' soul – that is, our mind; and that while you assert that it can purify the 'spiritual' soul – that is, the part of the soul inferior to the reason – you confess that theurgic art cannot make it immortal and eternal. Whereas Christ promises eternal life; and therefore the world flocks to him. You and your like are indignant at this, but dumbfounded in amazement as well.

You have not been able to deny that men are led astray by the practices of theurgy, that large numbers are deceived by its confused and nonsensical doctrines, that the most certain of all false steps is to betake oneself to those 'principalities' and 'angels' with sacrifices and supplications. But to what avail is this acknowledgement, if you go back on it (as if to assure yourself that all this learning has not been a waste of time) by sending men to theurgists, so that those practitioners may purify the 'spiritual' soul of those who do not live the life of the 'intellectual' soul?

28. *The blindness of Porphyry to the true wisdom, which is Christ*

And so you send men on the most certainly mistaken path; and you are not ashamed of doing so great a wrong, although you profess to be a lover of virtue and wisdom. If you were a genuine and faithful lover, you would have recognized 'Christ, the Power of God and the Wisdom of God',[109] instead of shying away[110] from his saving humility, inflated with the swollen pride of useless learning.

You admit, however, that even the 'spiritual' soul can be purified by the virtue of self-control, without the aid of theurgic arts or of initiations, which you have been at such unprofitable pains to learn about. Sometimes you go as far as to say that initiations do not lift up the soul after death, so that it now seems that they are of no value after the end of this life even for what you call the 'spiritual' soul. And yet you keep on discussing them in various aspects; you return to them again and again, your only object being, as far as I can see, to

108. cf. ch. 9. 109. 1 Cor. 1, 24.

110. According to an old tradition Porphyry was a renegade Christian (Socr., 3, 23).

give the appearance of being an expert in those matters also, and to ingratiate yourself with those who hanker after such illicit practices, or else to arouse a curious interest in them on your own account. But I give you a good mark for admitting that this is a dangerous art, both by reason of the perils of the law[111] and of the risk involved in the actual performance. I trust that the unfortunates will attend at least to these warnings and will retreat from these arts, or never approach them at all, to avoid being sucked into the gulf.

You do say, to be sure, that ignorance, and the many faults that arise from ignorance, cannot be purified by any initiatory rites. That can only be done through the *patrikos nous*, that is, the Mind or Intellect of the Father, which is acquainted with the Father's will. But you do not believe that this is what Christ is. In fact, you despise him on account of the body which he received from a woman, and because of the shame of the cross; you are of course, the kind of thinker to reject such lowness with disdain, and to cull your exalted wisdom on the heights. While Christ fulfils the true prophecy of the holy prophets when they said of him, 'I will destroy the wisdom of the wise men, and I will reprove the prudence of the prudent.'[112] It is not his own wisdom, the wisdom which he has given them, which he destroys and reproves in them; it is the wisdom which they arrogate to themselves, when they have not the wisdom which comes from him. This is why the Apostle, after quoting the witness of the prophet, goes on to say,

> Where is the wise man now? Where is the learned scholar? Where is your worldly-wiseman? Has not God turned worldly wisdom into foolishness? For according to God's wise design the world did not find God by its worldly wisdom: and therefore God decided to save those who believe by means of the folly of the preaching of the gospel. The Jews demanded miracles, the Greeks look for wisdom. But what we preach is a crucified Christ, which is shocking to the Jews, and ludicrous to the Greeks; but for those who have been called, Jews and Greeks alike, he is the Power of God and the Wisdom of God. For God's piece of folly is wiser than men, and God's show of weakness is stronger than men.[113]

This is rejected, as folly and weakness, by those who think themselves wise and strong by their own virtue. But this in fact is grace, which heals the weakness of those who do not proudly boast of their delusive happiness, but instead make a humble admission of their genuine misery.

111. cf. Bk VII, 35. 112. Is. 29, 14, cited 1 Cor. 1, 19.
113. 1 Cor. 1. 20–25.

29. *The Platonists in their impiety are ashamed to acknowledge Christ's incarnation*

You assert the Father and his Son, whom you call the Intellect or Mind of the Father; you also speak of a being who is between the two, and we imagine that you are referring to the Holy Spirit. And it is your habit to call them three gods.[114] In spite of your irregular terminology you Platonists have here some kind of an intuition of the goal to which we must strive, however dimly seen through the obscurities of a subtle imagination. And yet you refuse to recognize the incarnation of the unchanging Son of God, which brings us salvation, so that we can arrive at those realities in which we believe, and which we can in some small measure comprehend. Thus you see, to some extent, though from afar off and with clouded vision, the country in which we must find our home; but you do not keep to the road along which we must travel.

For all this, Porphyry, you acknowledge the existence of grace, when you say that it is granted only to few to reach God by virtue of their intelligence. For you do not say, 'Only few have decided', or, 'Few have had the wish'; you speak of its being 'granted'. And this is an undoubted confession of the grace of God and the insufficiency of man. You even use the word 'grace' itself quite openly in the passage where, following Plato,[115] you assert without hesitation that man cannot by any means reach the perfection of wisdom in this life, but that, after this life, all those who live the life of the intellect receive all that is needed for their fulfilment from the providence and grace of God.

If only you had recognized the grace of God through Jesus Christ our Lord! If only you had been able to see his incarnation, in which he took a human soul and body, as the supreme instance of grace! But what can I do? I know that it is to no avail that I speak to a dead man, to no avail, that is, as far as you are concerned. But there are people who hold you in high regard, who are attached to you by reason of some kind of a love of wisdom, or a superstitious interest in those magic arts which you should never have studied, and they are the audience to whom my colloquy with you is really directed, and it may be that for them it is not in vain. The grace of God could not be commended in a way more likely to evoke a grateful response, than the way by which the only Son of God, while remaining unchangeably in his own proper being, clothed himself in humanity and

114. cf. ch. 24. 115. cf. e.g. *Phaed.*, 66–7B.

gave to men the spirit of his love by the mediation of a man, so that by this love men might come to him who formerly was so far away from them, far from mortals in his immortality, from the changeable in his changelessness, from the wicked in his righteousness, from the wretched in his blessedness. And because he has implanted in our nature the desire for blessedness and immortality he has now taken on himself mortality, while continuing in his blessedness, so that he might confer on us what our hearts desire; and by his sufferings he has taught us to make light of what we dread.

But humility was the necessary condition for submission to this truth; and it is no easy task to persuade the proud necks of you philosophers to accept this yoke. For what is there incredible – especially for you who hold certain opinions which should encourage you to believe – what is there incredible in the assertion that God has assumed a human soul and body? You Platonists have, at any rate, so lofty a conception of the 'intellectual' soul (which must be identified with the human soul) that you assert that it is capable of becoming consubstantial with the Mind of the Father, which is, on your admission, the Son of God. Why then is it incredible that one 'intellectual' soul should have been assumed, for the salvation of many, in some unique and ineffable manner? That the body is united with the soul, so that man may be entire and complete, is a fact we recognize on the evidence of our own nature. If it had not been a fact of familiar experience, we should certainly have found it even more incredible; for it should be easier for faith to accept the union of spirit with spirit even though it is the union of human and divine, changeable with changeless, or, to use the terms employed by you Platonists, corporeal with incorporeal, than that of a body with an incorporeal entity.

Perhaps you were put off by the unexampled birth of his body from a virgin? But this should not have presented a difficulty. The fact that a wonderful being was born in a wonderful way ought rather to induce you to accept our religion. But the difficulty may be the fact that this body was laid aside in death, and then transformed by his resurrection, and that when it had thus become incorruptible and immortal he carried it up into the realms above. It may be that you refuse to believe this, since you are well aware that in these same books from which I have so often quoted, which treat of the *Return of the Soul*, Porphyry so often lays it down that one must escape from any kind of body in order that the soul may dwell with God in blessedness. It is in fact Porphyry himself who needs correction in respect of this opinion, especially in view of the incredible notions which you Platonists share with him on the subject of the Soul of this visible world, of this vast corporeal mass. For you allege, on the authority of Plato,[116] that the world is a living being, and a being of utter blessedness, and this being you hold to be eternal. How then can it enjoy unceasing happiness, without being ever released from its body, if it is true that escape from the body is necessary for the happiness of the soul?

Besides this you admit in your books that this sun of ours and all the other stars are bodies, and all mankind has no hesitation in joining you in observing this and acknowledging the fact. But you go further, and give it out, on the basis of what you suppose to be a profounder knowledge, that these are living beings of utter blessedness, eternal in these corporeal forms. Why is it, then, that when the Christian faith is urged upon you, you straightway forget, or pretend to have no knowledge of, your customary arguments and doctrines? What reason is there for your refusal to become Christians on account of opinions which are your own, though you yourselves attack them? It can only be that Christ came in humility, and you are proud. What will be the nature of the bodies of the saints in the resurrection is a question for discussion in much more detail among those who are specially qualified in knowledge of the Christian Scriptures. Of this we have no doubt: the resurrected body will be eternal, and its nature will be like that example which Christ showed us in his resurrection. But whatever may be its nature, the fact is that while the Christian teaching is that this body will be incorruptible and immortal and will present no obstacle to that contemplation by which the soul is fixed on God, you also say that in the celestial sphere there are immortal bodies of beings whose blessedness is immortal. Then what basis is there for your notion that escape from any kind of body is an essential condition for our happiness, a notion that makes you feel that you have rational justification for your rejection of Christianity? The only reason, I repeat, is that Christ is humble, and you are proud.

Now perhaps you are ashamed to have your errors corrected? Here again is a fault which is only found in the proud. No doubt it seems disgraceful for learned men to desert their master Plato to become disciples of Christ, who by his Spirit taught a fisherman wisdom, so that he could say,

> The Word was in the beginning of all things, and the Word was with God, and the Word was God. He was with God at the beginning. All things

116. *Tim.* 30f.

came into being through him, and nothing that came into being came into being without him. In him was life, and that life was the life of men. The light shines in the darkness, and the darkness has not overwhelmed it.

This is the beginning of the holy Gospel which we call the *Gospel According to John.*

There is a story I often heard recounted by a holy old man called Simplicianus,[117] who later became head of the Church in Milan, as its bishop. He told us that a certain Platonic philosopher used to say that this passage should be inscribed in letters of gold and set up in the most prominent place in every church. But God, the great teacher, became of no account in the eyes of the proud simply because 'the Word became flesh, and dwelt among us'.[118] And so it was not enough for the unfortunate that they should be sick, they must needs glory in their sickness, and be ashamed to take the medicine which could cure them. Now the result of this is not to exalt them, but to ensure for them a more disastrous fall.

30. *Porphyry's refutation and correction of Platonic teaching*

If it is considered improper to correct Plato on any point, why did Porphyry himself offer a number of important corrections? For it is an established fact that Plato wrote that after death the souls of men return to earth, and even enter into the bodies of beasts. The same belief was held also by Plotinus, the teacher of Porphyry.[119] Nevertheless, Porphyry refused to accept it, quite rightly.[120] His theory was that human souls return, but into men's bodies, not the bodies which they have left, but into others, into new bodies. One supposes that he was ashamed to hold the Platonic theory, for fear that a mother might come back as a mule and be ridden by her son! Yet it caused him no embarrassment to hold a belief which would admit the risk of a mother's returning as a girl and marrying her own son. How much more honourable is the belief taught by the holy and truthful

117. *Simplicianus:* d. A.D. 400. He prepared Ambrose for baptism in 373; and he was an important influence in the conversion of St Augustine when he recounted the story of the conversion of the Neoplatonist, Victorinus (cf. *Conf.* VIII, 2; and cf. Bk X, 29). Simplicianus became Bishop of Milan in 397.

118. John 1, 14.

119. cf. Plat., *Phaed.*, 81E; *Phaedr.*, 249B; *Rp.*, 10, 619D–620B; *Tim.* 42C; Plot., *Enn.*, 3, 4, 2.

120. cf. Bk XIII, 19.

angels, spoken of by the prophets under the guidance of the Spirit of God, and by him whose coming as Saviour was foretold by heralds sent in advance, and by the apostles who were sent out and who filled the whole world with the teaching of the gospel. The belief that souls return once for all to their own bodies is far more honourable than that they return time after time to different bodies. For all that, Porphyry, as I have said, is right to an important extent in his opinion, in that at least he held that it is only into men that human souls can be thrust; and had no hesitation at all in abolishing their animal prisons.

Porphyry also says that God has put the soul into the world for this purpose, that the soul might realize the evils of the material world and so hurry back to the Father, and never again be held back by the polluting contact of such evils. Certainly his theory on this subject is to some degree inconsistent with the facts. The soul is given to the body in order to do good, for it would not recognize evil if it did not do good. Nevertheless he did correct the opinion of other Platonists on this point, and he did so on an important question. For he admitted that when the soul has been purified from all evil and established with the Father it will never afterwards suffer the evils of this world. By this belief he did away with the theory which is regarded as a principal feature of Platonism, the theory that just as the dead came from the living so the living always come from the dead.[121] And he shows the falsity of the statement of Virgil (apparently following Plato) that the souls who are dispatched, after their purification, to the Elysian Fields (which seems to be a poetical description of the joys of the blessed) are summoned to the river of Lethe, that is, to forgetfulness of the past,

> So that, forgetful, they may seek again
> The vault of heaven, and once more desire
> To take a mortal body.[122]

Porphyry was entirely justified in rejecting this teaching; since it is really absurd to believe that in that other life, which could not be completely blessed if there were not complete assurance of its eternity, souls yearn for the taint of corruptible bodies and desire to return from thence to those bodies; as if the effect of the final purification were a longing for renewed defilement. For if the result of perfect cleansing is the forgetfulness of all ills, and the forgetfulness of ills produces a longing for bodies, in which the souls will again be involved in ills, it follows that the supreme felicity will be the cause of

121. cf. *Phaed.*, 70cf. 122. *Aen.*, 6, 750f.

misery, the perfection of wisdom the cause of folly, and perfect cleansing the cause of uncleanness. And the happiness of the soul will not be based on truth, however long it is to continue, in a state where it must be deceived, if it is to be happy. For it will not be happy without a sense of security; and to have a sense of security it must believe that its happiness will be everlasting, which is a false belief, since in time it will come to misery. How can it then rejoice in truth, when its joy depends on a false belief? Porphyry saw this, and for this reason he asserted that the soul after purification returns to the Father so that it may never be held back by the polluting contact of evil. Therefore the belief held by certain Platonists is false, that there is a kind of inevitable cycle of departure from evil followed by return. Even if this were true, what advantage would be gained by the knowledge of it? Unless perhaps the Platonists would venture to claim superiority to us on the ground that we in this life have already attained that ignorance which they are going to reach in another and better life, after complete purification and the acquisition of supreme wisdom, so that they may enjoy happiness by believing a falsehood!

Now if such a suggestion is utterly absurd and ridiculous, we are clearly bound to prefer the opinion of Porphyry to that of the thinkers who have imagined a circular movement of souls, in which they alternate for ever between bliss and misery. If so, we have here a Platonist departing from Plato, for the better. Here we have one who saw what his master failed to see; and though he was a disciple of a teacher of such eminence and authority, he did not shrink from correcting his teacher, because he preferred the truth to the man.[123]

31. *Against the argument of the Platonists, that the human soul is co-eternal with God*

Since these are questions which are beyond the competence of human wit to sift to the bottom, why do we not trust instead in the divine power which tells us that the soul itself is, like other things, created out of non-existence? The Platonists are evidently satisfied with justifying their refusal to believe this by the argument that nothing can have an eternal future which has not had an eternal past. And yet, when treating of the universe, and the gods which, he says, God has created in the universe, Plato distinctly affirms that they come into being and have a beginning; yet he declares that they will not have an end, but will continue for ever, thanks to the mighty will of their

123. cf. 'Plato is my friend; but truth is still more my friend.' Cic., *Tusc. Disp.*, 1, 17, 39.

creator.[124] Nevertheless the Platonists have discovered a way of interpreting this statement, by asserting that this refers not to a beginning in time, but to a relation of dependence. 'If a foot', they say, 'had been from all eternity planted on dust, the print of it would always be underneath; but for all that no one would doubt that the footprint was made by the pressure of the foot: and yet there would be no temporal priority, although one was made by the other. Similarly', they say, 'the universe and the created gods in it have always existed, while their maker always exists; and yet they have been made.'

Yes, but if the soul has always existed, are we to say that its misery also has always existed? If not, then if there is anything in the soul which has not existed from eternity but has come into being in time, why could it not be that the soul itself has a temporal beginning, without having had a previous existence? Furthermore, its blessedness also, as Porphyry admits, will be more secure after the experience of evils, and will endure without end. Then evidently this blessedness has a beginning in time; and yet it will exist for ever, without having had a previous existence.

Thus the whole argument falls to the ground, since it purported to establish that nothing could be without an end in time unless it did not have a beginning in time. For it has been shown that the beatitude of the soul has had a beginning in time, but will not have an end in time. And so let human weakness yield to divine authority. And on the subject of the true religion let us believe those blessed and immortal beings who do not claim for themselves the honour which they know to be due to their God, who is also our God, who do not bid us to sacrifice to any but him to whom we, with them, owe the sacrifice of ourselves. As I have often said, and as cannot be said too often, this is a sacrifice offered through that priest who, in the manhood which he assumed and through which he willed to be also a priest, has deigned to become a sacrifice for us, even as far as death.[125]

32. *The way of salvation for all, which Porphyry failed to discover*

This is the religion which contains the universal way for the liberation of the soul, since no soul can be freed by any other way. For this is, one may say, the royal road, which alone leads to that kingdom whose glory is not the tottering grandeur of the temporal, but the secure stability of the eternal.

124. *Tim.*, 41B. 125. cf. Phil. 2, 8.

Now Porphyry says – towards the end of his first book *On the Return of the Soul* – that no doctrine has yet been established to form the teaching of a philosophical sect, which offers a universal way for the liberation of the soul; no such way has been produced by any philosophy (in the truest sense of the word), or by the moral teaching and disciplines of the Indians,[126] or by the magical spells of the Chaldeans, or in any other way, and that this universal way had never been brought to his knowledge in his study of history. He admits without any doubt that such a way exists, but confesses that it had never come to his notice. Thus he was not satisfied with all that he had taken such pains to learn on the subject of the liberation of the soul, the knowledge and the beliefs which he convinced himself – or rather convinced others – that he possessed. For he felt that he had failed to obtain any supreme authority which he was bound to follow on such an important subject. Now he states that he has never become acquainted with any philosophical sect, even among the genuine philosophies, which would offer a universal way for the liberation of the soul. And in saying this he makes it clear, as it seems to me, that the kind of philosophy in which he was engaged was not a genuine philosophy, or, if it was, that it did not offer such a way of liberation. And yet how could it be a genuine philosophy, if it did not offer this way? For what is a universal way for the liberation of the soul, if it is not a way by which all souls are liberated, and therefore the only way for any soul? And when he goes on to say, 'or by the moral teaching and discipline of the Indians, the magical spells of the Chaldeans, or any other way' he testifies quite explicitly that this way is not afforded by the teaching he had learnt from the Indians and the Chaldeans: and he certainly could not keep quiet about his borrowing of 'divine oracles' from the Chaldeans, those oracles which he refers to so continually.

What then does Porphyry mean to be understood by this 'universal way of liberation for the soul'? He says that it has not been obtained either from any of the genuine philosophies, or from the teaching of those nations which were regarded as great authorities in so-called 'divine matters', because those nations were especially influenced by a superstitious interest in the doctrine and the cult of angels of various kinds. What then does he mean by this cult which has never come to his notice in his historical inquiries? What in fact is this universal way, unless it is one which is not the exclusive property of a particular nation but has been divinely imparted to be the common property of all the nations? That such a way exists is not doubted by a man so

126. The 'gymnosophists'; cf. Bk VIII, 9n.; XIV, 17; XV, 20.

exceptionally talented as Porphyry. He does not believe that divine providence could have left mankind without such a universal way for the liberation of the soul. For what he says is not that the way does not exist, but only that this great boon, this great assistance, has not come to his notice. No wonder in that. For Porphyry was active at a time when the universal way for the liberation of the soul, which is simply the Christian religion, was, by divine permission, under attack[127] from the demon-worshippers and the kings of the earth, in order to make up the number of consecrated martyrs, that is, of the witnesses to the truth, whose purpose was to show that all bodily sufferings must be endured in loyalty to true religion and for the commendation of the truth. Porphyry saw what was happening; and he supposed that persecutions of this kind would soon lead to the disappearance of this way, and that therefore it was not the universal way for the soul's liberation. He did not realize that this persecution which so influenced him, and which he was afraid of suffering if he chose to follow that way, in fact tended to strengthen Christianity and to commend it more forcefully.

This then is the universal way for the soul's liberation; universal because it is granted to all nations by the divine compassion. But wherever the knowledge of this way has already come, and wherever it will come in the future, no one has, or will have, the right to ask, 'Why just now?' or 'Why so late?' for the design of him who offers it is inscrutable to natural human understanding. Porphyry himself understood this when he said that this gift of God had not yet been obtained and had not yet come to his knowledge. For he did not decide that it was not a reality just because he had not yet accepted it as his belief, or because it had not come to his knowledge.

This is, I repeat, the universal way for the liberation of believers. The faithful Abraham received this divine message about it: 'In your seed all nations will be blessed.'[128] Now Abraham was by birth a Chaldean, but he was bidden to leave his country, his family, and his father's house, so that he might receive this promise, and that from him might issue the 'seed prepared for by the ministry of angels, the mediator offering his hand';[129] so that in this mediator should be found that universal way for the soul's liberation, the way made available for all nations. Then when he had first been liberated from the superstitions of the Chaldeans, Abraham worshipped and followed the one true God, and believed with complete trust in his promises.

127. Porphyry 233–301; persecution of Decius 249–51, of Valerian 257–60.
128. Gen. 22, 18. 129. cf. Gal. 3, 19.

This is the universal way of which the holy prophet speaks, when he says, 'May God have mercy on us and give us his blessing. May he make his face to shine on us; that we may know your way on the earth, and your salvation in all nations.'[130] Hence, so long afterwards, the Saviour, who took flesh from 'the seed of Abraham', said of himself, 'I am the way, the truth, and the life.'[131]

This is the universal way about which the prophecy was made so long before,

> In the last days there will appear in full view the mountain of the Lord, prepared on the summit of the mountains, and lifted up above the hills; and all the nations will come to it, and many nations will enter and say: 'Come, let us go up to the mountain of God, and go into the house of the God of Jacob: and he will announce to us his way, and we will start upon it'. For the Law will issue out of Sion, and the Word of the Lord from Jerusalem.[132]

This means that the way does not belong to one people, but is for all nations; and the Law and the Word of God did not stay in Sion and Jerusalem but went out from there so that it might spread through the whole world. Hence the Mediator himself, after his resurrection, said to his trembling disciples, 'What was written about me in the Law, the Prophets, and the Psalms, had to be fulfilled.' Then

> he opened their understanding, so that they comprehended the meaning of the Scriptures: and he told them that Christ was bound to suffer and to rise from the dead on the third day; and that penitence and remission of sins was to be proclaimed in his name throughout all the nations, beginning at Jerusalem.[133]

So this is the universal way of liberation for the soul which the holy angels and the holy prophets foretold. They revealed it in former times among a small number of men, where they could find a hearing, among men who enjoyed the favour of God, and in particular among the Hebrew people, whose political community was in a manner consecrated for the purposes of prophesying and announcing the City of God which was to be assembled out of all nations. The angels and saints pointed to this way by means of the tabernacle, the temple, the priesthood, and the sacrifices; and they spoke of it sometimes by explicit statements, more often in the language of mystic symbolism. But in the end the Mediator himself came in flesh, and he and his blessed apostles now revealed the grace of the new covenant and disclosed openly what in previous ages had been indicated by veiled

130. Ps. 67, 2f. 131. John 14, 6. 132. Is. 2, 2. 133. Luke 24, 44f.

allusions, when hints were given in accordance with the stages of mankind's development, following the plan decided upon by God, in his wisdom.

This revelation had the supporting testimony of the signs of God's miraculous works, of which I have already given some few examples.[134] Such signs appeared not only in the form of visions of angels, and the resounding utterances of celestial ministers. There were also men of God who used the word of simple piety to drive out unclean spirits from the bodies and minds of men; and by this means bodily sickness and infirmities were cured, savage beasts on land and sea, the winged creatures of the sky, the woods, the elements, and the stars were made obedient to the divine commands, the infernal powers retreated, the dead came back to life. And this is to leave on one side the miracles which belong to the Saviour, and to him alone; above all, the miracles of his birth and resurrection. In the former we are presented simply with the mystery of a virgin motherhood, whereas in the latter he has shown us the pattern which is to be reproduced in those who will rise again at the last day.

This is the way which purifies the whole man and prepares his mortal being for immortality, in all the elements which constitute a man. We have not to seek one purification for that element which Porphyry calls the 'intellectual' soul, another for the 'spiritual', and yet another for the body itself. It was to avoid such quests that our Purifier and Saviour, the true Purifier and the all-powerful Saviour, took upon himself the man in his entirety. This way has never been withheld from mankind, either when those events were foretold as destined in the future, or when the news was brought of their accomplishment. And apart from this way no one has been set free, no one is being set free, no one will be set free.

Porphyry, however, says that the universal way for the soul's liberation has never come to his knowledge in his study of history. Yet what could be found more striking than this historical record, which has taken possession of the whole world by its towering authority; or what more worthy of belief, seeing that in this record the events of the past are so narrated as to be also prophecies of the future? Many of those prophecies we see to have been fulfilled, and we confidently expect the fulfilment of the rest. Neither Porphyry nor any other Platonist can brush aside the revelations of the future and the predictions encountered in this way, on the grounds that they are concerned merely with worldly matters and with this present life – a

134. cf. e.g. ch. 8.

criticism justly levelled by the philosophers against soothsaying and the divination of other sects, carried on by all manner of methods and techniques. They say that predictions of this kind are never practised by men of standing, that they are of little value; and this judgement is soundly based. Such foreknowledge either derives from the anticipatory perception of secondary causes, in the same way as medical skill can foresee, by antecedent indications, many future conditions affecting bodily health; or else it comes from unclean demons. For they give forewarning of events which result from their designs, and in some measure assert their claim to be the lawful controllers of events by directing the thoughts and desires of the wicked towards any facts which suit those thoughts and desires, and by appealing to the lowest elements in human frailty.

It was not such prophecies as these that were the concern of the holy men who walked on that way of universal liberation for souls. They did not attach importance to such things: although such matters did not escape them, and such predictions were often made by them, to serve as credentials for prophecies of things which could not be apprehended by the senses, and which could not be swiftly and readily brought to a test. But there were other matters, of high importance, matters truly relating to God, which they foretold in the future according to such knowledge as was granted to them by the will of God. These matters were the future coming of Christ in the flesh, and all the wonders which were accomplished in him and which were effected in his name; the repentance of men, the conversion of men's wills to God, the remission of sins, the grace of justification; the faith of the devout, and the multitude of men all over the world who believe in the true doctrine of God; the abolition of the worship of idols and demons; and the training to resist temptation, the purification of those who persevere and their liberation from all evil; the day of judgement, the resurrection of the dead, the eternal condemnation of the society of the wicked, and the eternal dominion of the glorious City of God in the deathless enjoyment of the vision of God. All this was foretold and promised in the Scriptures. We see the fulfilment of so many of these promises that we look for the fulfilment of the rest with the confidence of a devotion rightly directed. This is the right road which leads to the vision of God and to eternal union with him; it is proclaimed and asserted in the truth of the holy Scriptures. And all those who do not believe in it, and therefore fail to understand it, may attack it; they cannot overthrow it.

Thus in the ten books now completed we have refuted the objections of the wicked, who prefer their own gods to the founder of that Holy City which is the subject of this undertaking; and although the refutation may not be all that some eagerly expected of us, still it has met the wishes of some, through the help that our true God and Lord has deigned to give us. The first five books have been written against those who imagine that the gods are to be worshipped for the sake of the good things of this life, the latter five against those who think that the cult of the gods should be kept up with a view to the future life after death. I shall now proceed to fulfil the promise made in the first book, and, in so far as I receive assistance from on high, I shall put forward what I think ought to be said about the two cities, which are, as I have pointed out, intermixed with one another in this present world; and I shall treat of their origin, their development, and their destined ends.

Part II

BOOK XI

1. *The subject of the second part: The origins and ends of the two cities*

THE City of God of which we are treating is vouched for by those Scriptures whose supremacy over every product of human genius does not depend on the chance impulses of the minds of men, but is manifestly due to the guiding power of God's supreme providence, and exercises sovereign authority over the literature of all mankind. Now in this Scripture we find these words, 'Glorious things have been said of you, City of God', and in another psalm, 'The Lord is great, and to be highly praised in the City of our God, in his holy mountain, spreading joy over the whole earth.' And soon afterwards in the same psalm, 'As we have heard, so have we seen, in the City of the Lord of Powers, in the City of our God: God has founded that City for eternity.' Again, in yet another psalm, 'The swift stream of the river brings gladness to the City of God: the Most High has sanctified his tabernacle; God in her midst will not be shaken.'[1]

From such testimonies as these – and it would take too long to quote them all – we have learnt that there is a City of God: and we have longed to become citizens of that City, with a love inspired by its founder. But the citizens of the earthly city prefer their own gods to the founder of this Holy City, not knowing that he is the God of gods; not, that is, the God of the false gods, the impious and arrogant gods who are deprived of his changeless light which is shed upon all alike, and are therefore reduced to a poverty-stricken kind of power, and engage in a kind of scramble for their lost dominions and claim divine honours from their deluded subjects. He is the God of the good and holy gods,[2] who would rather have themselves in subjection to the one God than have many subjects for themselves. Their delight is to worship God rather than to be worshipped instead of God.

But we have already replied to the enemies of this Holy City, in the first ten books, to the best of our ability, with the assistance of our Lord and King. And now, knowing what is expected of me, and not forgetting my obligation, I will approach my task, relying always on

1. Ps. 87, 3; 48, 1, 2, 8; 46, 4f. 2. sc. angels; cf. Bk IX, 23; X, 1.

the help of the same Lord and King. My task is to discuss, to the best of my power, the rise, the development and the destined ends of the two cities, the earthly and the heavenly, the cities which we find, as I have said, interwoven, as it were, in this present transitory world, and mingled with one another. And first I shall explain how the beginnings of those two cities arose from the difference between two classes of angels.

2. *Of the knowledge of God, attainable only through the one Mediator*

It is a great achievement, and no everyday matter, that man in his speculation should go beyond the created universe, having examined it, both in its material and immaterial aspects, and found it mutable, and arrive at the immutable being of God; and then should learn from him that everything which exists, apart from God himself, is the creation of God, and of him alone. For when God speaks to man in this way, he does not need the medium of any material created thing. He does not make sounds audible to bodily ears; nor does he use the kind of 'spiritual' intermediary which takes on a bodily shape, as happens in dreams or similar phenomena – for in such cases he speaks as it were to bodily ears, because he speaks, we may say, through the medium of a body, and, in a way, over a distance of physical space; indeed such visions have much in common with physical bodies. But when God speaks in the way we are talking of, he speaks by the direct impact of the truth, to anyone who is capable of hearing with the mind instead of with the ears of the body. He speaks to the highest of man's constituent elements, the element to which only God himself is superior. For man is rightly understood – or, if this passes understanding, is believed – to be made 'in the image of God'. And his nearness to God who is above him is certainly found in that part of man in which he rises superior to the lower parts of his nature, which he shares with the brute creation. And yet the mind of man, the natural seat of his reason and understanding, is itself weakened by long-standing faults which darken it. It is too weak to cleave to that changeless light and to enjoy it; it is too weak even to endure that light. It must first be renewed and healed day after day so as to become capable of such felicity. And so the mind had to be trained and purified by faith; and in order to give man's mind greater confidence in its journey towards the truth along the way of faith, God the Son of God, who is himself the Truth, took manhood without abandoning his godhead, and thus established and founded this faith, so that man might have a path to man's God through the man who was God. For this is 'the mediator between God and men, the man Christ Jesus.'[3] As man he is our Mediator; as man he is our way. For there is hope to attain a journey's end when there is a path which stretches between the traveller and his goal. But if there is no path, or if a man does not know which way to go, there is little use in knowing the destination. As it is, there is one road, and one only, well secured against all possibility of going astray; and this road is provided by one who is himself both God and man. As God, he is the goal; as man, he is the way.

3. *The authority of the canonical Scriptures*

This Mediator spoke in former times through the prophets and later through his own mouth, and after that through the apostles, telling man all that he decided was enough for man. He also instituted the Scriptures, those which we call canonical. These are the writings of outstanding authority in which we put our trust concerning those things which we need to know for our good, and yet are incapable of discovering by ourselves. Now we ourselves are our own witnesses for the knowledge of things which are within reach of our senses, whether interior or exterior – hence they are said to be 'present', because, as we say, they are 'before our senses' (*prae sensibus*), as things accessible to sight are 'before our eyes'. And so we clearly need other witnesses for things which are out of reach of our senses, since we cannot base our knowledge on our own evidence; and we trust the witnesses of those who, we believe, have, or have had, those things within reach of their senses. Thus, in the case of visible things which we ourselves have not seen, we believe those who have seen them, and similarly with respect to things related to the various senses. There are other matters which are perceived by the mind and the reason: and such perception is rightly described as a kind of sense; and that is why the term *sententia* denotes a mental process. Hence, in respect of invisible things which are out of reach of our own interior perception, we ought likewise to put our trust in witnesses who have learnt of those things, when they have been once presented to them in that immaterial light, or who behold them continually so displayed.

3. 1 Tim. 2, 5.

4. *The creation of the world; not outside of time, yet not the result of any change in God's design*

Of all visible things the greatest is the world; of all invisible things the greatest is God. But the existence of the world is a matter of observation: the existence of God is a matter of belief. For the belief that God made the world we can have no more trustworthy witness than God himself. Where do we hear this witness? Nowhere, up to the present time, more clearly than in the holy Scriptures, where his prophet said: 'In the beginning God made heaven and earth.' Are we to suppose that the prophet was there, when God made them? No: but the Wisdom of God was there, and it was through that Wisdom that all things were made; and that Wisdom 'passes also into holy souls and makes them friends of God and prophets',[4] and tells them, inwardly and soundlessly, the story of God's works. The angels of God also speak to them, the angels who 'always see the face of the Father',[5] and announce his will to those who are fit to know it. One such was the prophet who said and wrote, 'In the beginning God made heaven and earth.' He was so suitable a witness to produce belief in God that by inspiration of the same Spirit of God, through whom he learnt these truths revealed to him, he foretold even our faith, which was then so far off in the future.[6]

But why did the eternal God decide to make heaven and earth at that particular time, and not before?[7] If the motive for this question is to make it appear that the world is eternal without beginning, and therefore not the creation of God, then the questioners are far away from the truth, and affected by the deadly madness of impiety. For, leaving aside the utterances of the prophets, we have the evidence of the world itself in all its ordered change and movement and in all the beauty it presents to our sight, a world which bears a kind of silent testimony to the fact of its creation, and proclaims that its maker could have been none other than God, the ineffably and invisibly great, the ineffably and invisibly beautiful.

There are some who admit that the world is created by God, but refuse to allow it a beginning in time, only allowing it a beginning in the sense of its being created, so that creation becomes an eternal process. There is force in this contention, in that such people conceive

4. Wisd. 7, 27; Prov. 8, 27. 5. Matt. 18, 10.

6. sc. in the 'Protevangelium', Gen. 3, 15.

7. A question posed by Epicureans (Cic., *De Nat. Deor.*, 1, 9, 21) and by Manicheans (Aug., *De Gen. C. Manich.*, 1, 3, 4).

themselves to be defending God against the notion of a kind of random, fortuitous act; to prevent the supposition that the idea of creating the world suddenly came into his mind, as an idea which had never before occurred to him, that he happened to take a new decision, whereas in fact he is utterly insusceptible of change. But I cannot see how their reasoning will stand up in application to other things, and especially if applied to the soul. If they maintain that the soul is co-eternal with God, how can it experience a change to unhappiness, to a condition from which it has been exempt for all eternity? This is something they will never be able to explain. For if they say there has been a perpetual alternation of the soul between misery and felicity, then they are forced to say that this alternation will continue for ever. And this leads them to this absurdity, that the soul is said to be happy, which is obviously impossible if it foresees its coming misery and degradation, while if it does not foresee this, but thinks that it will always enjoy happiness, its felicity is based on a mistake; and you could not have a more nonsensical proposition than that. If, on the other hand, they suppose that the soul has always alternated between felicity and misery throughout the infinity of past ages, but from now onwards, after its liberation, it will not return to a state of misery, they still lose the argument. They are saying that the soul was never truly happy in the past, but then begins to enjoy a kind of novel and genuine felicity, which is to admit that the soul has a new experience, something which had never before happened to it in all its eternity; and this new experience is something of remarkable importance! If they are going to deny that the production of this novelty has no part in God's eternal plan, they will be saying at the same time that God is not the author of felicity, which is intolerable blasphemy. While if they say that even God himself decided on an alteration in his design, to give the soul felicity for all future eternity, how are they to show him to be exempt from the mutability which they also refuse to ascribe to God?[8]

If then they admit that the soul is created in time, and yet will never perish in the time to come (just as number has beginning but no end) and that therefore when it has been freed from the miseries which it has once experienced, it will never thereafter be unhappy, they will agree without demur that this happens without altering the immutability of the God's design. In the same way let them believe that the world could have been created in time, and yet that would not

8. cf. Bk X 31.

mean that in the act of creation God made any change in his eternal purpose and design.

5. *We are not to think about infinite time before the world, any more than about infinite space outside it. As there was no time before it, so there is no space outside it*

These philosophers agree that the world was created by God, but they go on to ask us how we reply to questions about the date of creation. So let us now find out what they themselves would reply to questions about the position of the creation. For the question, 'Why at this time and not previously?' is on the same footing as, 'Why in this place rather than that?' For if they imagine that there were infinite stretches of time before the world existed, an infinity in which they cannot conceive of God's being inactive, they will, on the same showing, imagine infinite stretches of space; and if anyone says that the Omnipotent could have been inoperative anywhere in that infinity, it will follow that they are compelled to share the Epicurean fantasy of innumerable worlds.[9] The only difference would be that while Epicurus asserts that these worlds come into being and then disintegrate through the fortuitous movements of atoms, the Platonists will say that they are created by the action of God. This infinite number of worlds must follow, if they refuse to allow God to be inactive throughout the boundless immensity of space which stretches everywhere around the world, and if they hold that nothing can cause the destruction of those worlds, which is what they believe about this world of ours.

For we are now disputing with those who agree with us in believing that God is an immaterial being, the creator of all things other than himself. It would not be worth while to admit other pagans to this discussion on matters of religion, for this reason in particular; that among those who consider that the honours of worship should be paid to many gods, those Platonist philosophers excel all others in reputation and authority, just because they are nearer to the truth than the rest, even though they are a long way from it.

Now those thinkers have a right conception of God in that they do not confine his being to any place, nor set bounds to it, nor extend it spatially: they acknowledge that God's being is everywhere entire, in his immaterial presence. Are they going to say that his being is absent from those immense tracts of space outside the world? That he is

9. cf. Lucr. 2, 1048 f.

enclosed in this one space in which the world is situated, so tiny a space, compared with that infinity? I do not suppose that they will go in for such nonsense as this.

They say that this one world, for all its material vastness, is finite and bounded by its own space, and that it was created by the action of God. If they have an answer about the infinite spaces outside this world, if they can answer the question why God 'ceases from his work' in that infinity, then they can answer their own question about the infinity of time before the world, and why God was inactive then. It does not follow that it was by mere chance rather than by divine reason that God has established this world where it is and not elsewhere, since this space could be chosen among the infinite spaces available everywhere, with no differences of eligibility, even though the divine reason which determined the choice is beyond human comprehension. In the same way it does not follow that we conceive of anything fortuitous in God's action in creating the world at that particular time rather than earlier, since the previous ages had passed without any difference which might make one time preferable to another.

Now if they assert that it is idle for men's imagination to conceive of infinite tracts of space, since there is no space beyond this world, then the reply is: it is idle for men to imagine previous ages of God's inactivity, since there is no time before the world began.

6. The beginning of the world and the beginning of time are the same

If we are right in finding the distinction between eternity and time in the fact that without motion and change there is no time, while in eternity there is no change, who can fail to see that there would have been no time, if there had been no creation to bring in movement and change, and that time depends on this motion and change, and is measured by the longer or shorter intervals by which things that cannot happen simultaneously succeed one another? Since God, in whose eternity there is no change at all, is the creator and director of time, I cannot see how it can be said that he created the world after a lapse of ages, unless it is asserted that there was some creation before this world existed, whose movements would make possible the course of time.

The Bible says (and the Bible never lies): 'In the beginning God made heaven and earth.' It must be inferred that God had created nothing before that; 'in the beginning' must refer to whatever he made before all his other works. Thus there can be no doubt that the world was not created *in* time but *with* time. An event in time happens after one time and before another, after the past and before the future. But at the time of creation there could have been no past, because there was nothing created to provide the change and movement which is the condition of time.

The world was in fact made *with* time, if at the time of its creation change and motion came into existence. This is clearly the situation in the order of the first six or seven days, in which morning and evening are named, until God's creation was finished on the sixth day, and on the seventh day God's rest is emphasized as something conveying a mystic meaning. What kind of days these are is difficult or even impossible for us to imagine, to say nothing of describing them.

7. *Of the nature of the days when there was 'morning and evening' before the creation of the sun*

In our experience, of course, the days with which we are familiar only have an evening because the sun sets, and a morning because the sun rises; whereas those first three days passed without the sun, which was made, we are told, on the fourth day. The narrative does indeed tell us that light was created by God, and that God separated that light from the darkness, and gave to the light the name of 'day', and to the darkness the name of 'night'. But what kind of light that was, and with what alternating movement the distinction was made, and what was the nature of this evening and this morning; these are questions beyond the scope of our sensible experience. We cannot understand what happened as it is presented to us; and yet we must believe it without hesitation.

For either there was some material light, whether in the upper regions of the universe, far removed from our sight, or in the regions from which the sun later derived its light; or else the word 'light' here means the Holy City which consists of the holy angels and the blessed spirits, the City of which the Apostle speaks, 'Jerusalem which is above, our mother, eternal in the heavens.'[10] He certainly says in another place, 'You are all the sons of light, sons of day: you do not belong to night and darkness.'[11] But this latter interpretation depends on our being able to discover some appropriate meaning for 'the evening and the morning' of this day.

10. Gal. 4, 26. 11. 1 Thess. 5, 5.

Now the knowledge of the creature is a kind of twilight, compared with the knowledge of the Creator; and then comes the daylight and the morning, when that knowledge is linked with the praise and love of the Creator; and it never declines into night, so long as the Creator is not deprived of his creature's love. And in fact Scripture never interposes the word 'night', in the enumeration of those days one after another. Scripture never says, 'Night came'; but, 'Evening came and morning came; one day.' Similarly on the second day and on all the rest. The creature's knowledge, left to itself, is, we might say, in faded colours, compared with the knowledge that comes when it is known in the Wisdom of God, in that art, as it were, by which it was created. For that reason it can more appropriately be described as evening than as night. And yet that evening turns again to morning, as I have said, when it is turned to the praise and love of the Creator.

When the created light so acts in coming to the knowledge of itself, there is one day; when it comes to the knowledge of the firmament called heaven, between the lower and upper waters, there is the second day; when it comes to the knowledge of the earth and sea, and of all growing things, whose roots stretch into the ground, there is the third day; when to the knowledge of the luminaries, the greater and the lesser, and of all the stars, there is the fourth day; when to the knowledge of all the living things that come from the waters, creatures that swim and those that fly, there is the fifth day; when to knowledge of all land animals and of man himself, there is the sixth day.

8. *How God's rest on the seventh day is to be understood*

When 'God rested on the seventh day from all his works, and sanctified that day', this is not to be understood in any childish way, as if God had toiled at his work, seeing that 'he spoke and they were made'[12] by a word which was intelligible and eternal, not vocal and temporal. No, the 'rest of God' means the rest of those who find their rest in him, just as 'the joy of a house' means the joy of those who rejoice in that house – even if it is not the house itself but something else which is responsible for the joy. How much more appropriate it would be if in fact the house itself were to make the inhabitants glad by reason of its beauty. In that case the house would be called joyful not by the figure of speech in which the container stands for the contents (as in 'the theatre applauds', when it is the audience that applauds, or 'the pastures are lowing', when it is the cattle that are

12. Ps. 148, 5; 33, 9.

calling) but by the figure in which the efficient cause stands for the effect – as in 'a glad letter', meaning a letter which makes the readers glad.

And so it is most appropriate that when God is said, on the authority of the prophetic narrative, to have 'rested', what is meant is the rest of those who find their rest in him, and to whom he gives rest. The prophecy promises this to men also, for it speaks to men, and was in fact written for men's benefit. It promises them that they also, after the good works which God performs in them and through them, will have eternal rest in him, if they have already in some measure drawn near to him already in this life, through faith. For this promise is prefigured also by the Sabbath cessation from work in God's ancient people, in obedience to the instructions of the Law. But I think that I must discuss this more fully in its own place.[13]

9. *The scriptural evidence about angels*

I have undertaken to treat of the origin of the Holy City, and I have decided that I must first deal with the subject of the holy angels. They form the greater part of that City, and the more blessed part, in that they have never been on pilgrimage in a strange land; and I shall be at pains to explain, with God's aid, the information given on this subject in the inspired testimonies of Scripture, as far as shall seem sufficient. When the sacred writings tell of the making of the world, there is no explicit statement about whether the angels were created, or in what order they were created. But if they were not passed over in the narrative, they were referred to either under the name of 'heaven', when it is said that 'in the beginning God created heaven and earth', or, more probably, under the name of the 'light', about which I have been speaking.

I do not think that the angels were passed over, for this reason: that the Scripture says that God rested on the seventh day from all the works that he had done, while the whole book starts with the statement, 'In the beginning God made heaven and earth.' He began with heaven and earth, and the earth itself, which he made first, was, according to the next statement in Scripture, 'invisible and disordered' and, because light had not yet been created, 'darkness was over the abyss', that is, over a kind of confused and indistinct mass of land and water – since there must needs be darkness where light does not exist; then all things were set in order by God's creative act, all the things

13. cf. Bk XXII, 30.

which, in the narrative, were completed in the course of the six days. How, then, could the angels have been passed over, as though they were not among those works, from which God rested on the seventh day?

Now although the fact that angels are a work of God is not passed over in this narrative, it is not explicitly stated: but in other places the holy Scripture testifies to the fact with the utmost clarity. For the hymn of the three men in the furnace starts with the words, 'Bless the Lord, all you works of the Lord';[14] and in the enumeration of his works the angels are included. And in one of the psalms there are these verses:

> Praise the Lord from the heavens, praise him in the heights. Praise him, all his angels: praise him, all his powers. Praise him, sun and moon: praise him, all stars and light. Praise him heaven of heavens; and the waters which are above the heavens, let them praise the Lord. For he spoke, and things were made: he gave the command, and they were created.[15]

Will anyone now venture to suppose that the angels were created after all those things which were enumerated in the six days? However, if anyone is silly enough for this, he is refuted by another passage in Scripture, of equal authority, where God says, 'When the stars were made, all my angels praised me with a loud voice.'[16] That shows that angels already existed when the stars were made. Now the stars were created on the fourth day. Are we then to say that the angels were made on the third day? Most certainly not. For it is quite plain what was made on that day; the land was separated from the waters, and each of the two elements took on its characteristic and distinct appearance; and the dry land produced all that has its roots in it. On the second day, then? No, indeed. For then the firmament was made between the upper and lower waters, and was called 'heaven'; this is the firmament in which the stars were made on the fourth day. The obvious conclusion is that if the angels are among the works of God of those days, they are that light which received the name of 'day'. And the unity of that day is underlined by its not being called 'the first day', but 'one day'. Thus the second day, and the third, and the rest are not different days; the same 'one day' was repeated to complete the number of six or seven, to represent the seven stages of knowledge, the six stages comprehending the created works, and the seventh stage embracing God's rest.

For when God said, 'Let there be light', and light was created, then,

14. Dan. 3, 57. 15. Ps. 148, 1ff. 16. Job 38, 7.

if we are right in interpreting this as including the creation of the angels, they immediately become partakers of the eternal light, which is the unchanging Wisdom of God, the agent of God's whole creation; and this Wisdom we call the only begotten Son of God. Thus the angels, illuminated by that light by which they were created, themselves became light, and are called 'day', by participation in the changeless light and day, which is the Word of God, through whom they themselves and all other things were made. This is 'the true light, which illuminates every man as he comes into this world';[17] and this light illuminates every pure angel, so that he is not light in himself, but in God. If an angel turns away from God he becomes impure: and such are all those who are called 'impure spirits'. They are no longer 'light in the Lord';[18] they have become in themselves darkness, deprived of participation in the eternal light. For evil is not a positive substance: the loss of good has been given the name of 'evil'.[19]

10. *In the Trinity quality and substance are the same*

There is then one sole Good, which is simple, and therefore unchangeable; and that is God. By this Good all good things were created; but they are not simple, and for that reason they are changeable. They are, I say, *created*, that is to say, they are made, not begotten. For what is begotten by the simple Good is itself equally simple, identical in nature with its begetter: and these two, the begetter and the begotten, we call the Father and the Son; and these two, with their Spirit, are one God; and this Spirit is called, in holy Scripture, the 'Holy Spirit' of the Father and the Son, 'Holy' being used with special significance, as a kind of proper name. Now the Spirit is other than the Father and the Son, since he is not the Father or the Son; but I said 'other', not 'another thing', because this Good also is equally simple, equally changeless, and co-eternal. This Trinity is one God; the fact that it is a Trinity does not mean that it is not simple. For when we speak of this Good as being by nature simple, we do not mean that it consists solely of the Father, or solely of the Son, or solely of the Holy Spirit, or that there is really only a nominal Trinity, without subsistent Persons; that is the notion of the Sabellian heretics.[20] What is

17. John 1, 9. There is an irreproducible pun here (as in Bk VII, 26) on *mundus* (world) and the adjective *mundus* (pure) with its opposite, *immundus*.
18. Eph. 5, 8.
19. cf. Plot., *Enn.*, 3, 2, 5. 'Evil is to be defined as the lack of good'; cf. also ch. 22, and *Enchir.* 4, 'What is called evil is really the privation of good.'
20. cf. Bk X, 24n.

meant by 'simple' is that its being is identical with its attributes, apart from the relation in which each person is said to stand to each other. For the Father of course has the Son; and yet he himself is not the Son; and the Son has the Father; and yet he himself is not the Father. But when each is regarded in himself, not in relation to the other, his being is identical with his attributes. Thus each in himself is said to be living, because he *has* life; and at the same time he himself *is* life.

The reason why a nature is called simple is that it cannot lose any attribute it possesses, that there is no difference between what it *is* and what it *has*, as there is, for example, between a vessel and the liquid it contains, a body and its colour, the atmosphere and its light or heat, the soul and its wisdom. None of these *is* what it contains; the vessel is not the liquid, nor the body the colour, nor the atmosphere the light or heat; nor is the soul the same as its wisdom. Hence things of this sort may be deprived of what they have, and adopt other qualities and different attributes; the full vessel may be emptied of its liquid, the body lose its colour, the atmosphere become dark or cold, the soul become stupid. And even if a body is incorruptible, such a body as is promised to the saints at the resurrection, still, although this quality of incorruptibility is something which cannot be lost, the body is not identical with this incorruptibility, since the corporal substance remains. For this quality is entire in all the different parts of the body; it does not differ in intensity from one part to another, no part is more incorruptible than any other; although some parts of the body are bigger than others, they are not more incorruptible. Thus the body, which is not in each of its parts the entire body, is different from its incorruptibility, which is everywhere entire, because each part of the incorruptible body is equally incorruptible, in spite of inequality in other respects. For example, a finger is smaller than the whole hand: but that does not mean that the hand is more incorruptible than a finger; hand and finger may be unequal, but their incorruptibility is the same.

It follows that although incorruptibility is a quality inseparable from an incorruptible body, the substance in virtue of which it is called a body is other than the quality from which it derives the epithet incorruptible. And so even in this case, *being* and *attribute* are not the same. Further, the soul itself, even though it may be always wise – as it will be, when it is set free for all eternity – will be wise through participation in the changeless Wisdom, which is other than itself. For even if the atmosphere were never bereft of the light which is shed on it, there would still be the difference between its being and the light by which it is illuminated. (Now I do not mean by this to give the impression that the soul is air,[21] as has been the notion of some thinkers, who could not conceive of an immaterial substance. But there is a certain similarity between the two, in spite of a great disparity, which makes it quite appropriate to speak of the illumination of the immaterial soul by the immaterial light of the simple Wisdom of God, in terms of the illumination of the material atmosphere by the material light. For the darkness of the atmosphere is due to loss of light – for when we talk of the darkness of any locality in the material world we are in fact referring to atmosphere deprived of light – and so we naturally speak of the 'darkening' of the soul when it is deprived of the light of Wisdom.)

Accordingly, the epithet 'simple' applies to things which are in the fullest and truest sense divine, because in them there is no difference between substance and quality, and their divinity, wisdom and blessedness is not acquired by participation in that of others. On the other hand, it is said in the holy Scriptures that the Spirit of Wisdom is 'multiple',[22] in that it has many qualities in itself; but the Spirit's being is identical with its qualities, and all those qualities are one Person. For there are not many wisdoms, but one Wisdom, the storehouse, we may say, of things intelligible, of the riches which are infinite and yet confined to that Wisdom. And in that storehouse are contained all the invisible and unchanging causes of things visible and changing, which were created by the operation of Wisdom. Now God created nothing in ignorance, in fact the same could be truly said of any human craftsman. Then it is evident that if God created knowingly, he created things which he already knew. This suggests a thought which is surprising, but true; that this world could not be known to us, if it did not exist, whereas it could not have existed, if it had not been known to God.

11. *Did the apostate spirits share the bliss of the holy angels at the beginning?*

If this is so, the spirits whom we call angels can never have been darkness during any period in the past; as soon as they were created, they were made light. Yet they were not created merely to exist and live in any sort of way; they were given illumination so as to live in

21. The view of Diogenes of Apollonia (cf. Bk VIII, 2n.) according to Aristotle (*De An.*, 1, 2, 15). The same notion is attributed to some Stoics.

22. Wisd. 7, 22.

wisdom and bliss. But there were some angels who turned away from this illumination, and so did not attain to the excellence of a life of wisdom and bliss, which must of necessity be eternal, and certainly assured of its eternity. These angels have a life of reason, though not of wisdom, and they cannot lose this, even if they wish. Who can say with certainty how far they were partakers of that Wisdom, before their fall? How can we say that they were on an equality with those angels who truly enjoy the fullness of bliss, because they are thoroughly assured of the eternity of their blessedness? How can we say this, when if they had had an equal share in that Wisdom those fallen spirits would have continued in that eternity, equally blessed, because equally assured of bliss? For life, however long it may last, cannot truly be called eternal, if it is going to have an end. It is called life because of the fact of living, but the epithet 'eternal' is given by reason of its having no end. For this reason, although it is not true that everything eternal is necessarily blessed (for the fire of punishment is said to be eternal), nevertheless, if life cannot be truly and completely blessed unless it is eternal, then the life of those spirits was not of this kind, since it was destined to come to an end, and therefore could not be eternal. And so their life could not be truly blessed, whether they knew that it must end, or in their ignorance imagined otherwise. In neither case could they enjoy felicity because fear would prevent it, if they knew their end, while if they did not know it, bliss would not be compatible with error. And if their ignorance meant that they placed no trust in deceptions and uncertainties, but hovered uncertainly between the expectation of an end to their good and the hope of its eternity, without reaching a firm conviction, that situation would preclude the full enjoyment of bliss which we believe to be the lot of the holy angels. For we do not confine the word 'beatitude' within such narrow limits of connotation as to ascribe it only to God, although he is so truly blessed that no greater beatitude is possible. In comparison with the beatitude of God, what is the quality or extent of the bliss of the angels, though they reach the summit of the felicity which is possible to angels?

12. *The blessedness of the just (before their reward) compared with the primal happiness before the Fall*

It is not only the angels, among the rational or intellectual creation, that are to be called blessed, or so we suppose. For no one, surely, would be bold enough to deny that the first human beings were happy in paradise, before their sin, although they had no certainty how long their bliss would last, or whether it would continue for ever – as it would have continued, if they had not sinned. Even today we need not be ashamed to call those people happy whom we see living a life of righteousness and piety, with the hope of future immortality, without guilt to work havoc in their conscience, as they receive the ready forgiveness of God for the offences that arise from human frailty. Now although such people are assured of a reward for perseverance, they are not found to be certain of their perseverance. Can any man be sure that he will persevere to the end in the practice of righteousness, making progress in it? No one can, unless he is assured by some revelation from him who, according to his just but secret decision, instructs only a few, but deceives no one.

And so the first man was more blessed in paradise than any righteous man in this state of mortal frailty, as far as concerns the enjoyment of present good. But as for the hope of the future, any man in the extreme of bodily suffering is happier than the first-created. For it has been revealed to man with the certainty of truth – it is no mere opinion – that, free from all distresses, he will share with the angels the endless enjoyment of God Most High, whereas that first man, in all that bliss of paradise, had no certainty about his future.

13. *Did the angels, in their original bliss, know their future, their fall or perseverance?*

Anyone can now easily gather that the blessedness which the intellectual being desires with unswerving resolution is the product of two causes working in conjunction, the untroubled enjoyment of the changeless Good, which is God, together with the certainty of remaining in him for eternity, a certainty that admits of no doubt or hesitation, no mistake or disappointment. Such, we devoutly believe, is the felicity enjoyed by the angels of light. But by the same reasoning we conclude that the offending angels, who were deprived of that light by their own wickedness, did not have this bliss, even before their fall. We must certainly believe that they had some bliss, if they had any life before their sin, even though that bliss was not endowed with foreknowledge. Now it may be intolerable to believe that when the angels were created, some were created without being given foreknowledge of their perseverance or fall, while others were given full and genuine assurance of the eternity of their bliss; and perhaps in fact all were created at the beginning with equal felicity, and remained in that state until those angels who are now evil fell, by their own choice, from that light of goodness. But without any shadow of doubt it would be much more intolerable to suppose that the holy angels are now uncertain of their bliss, and that they themselves are left in ignorance about their future, while we have been able to know about it from the holy Scriptures. Every Catholic Christian knows that no new Devil will ever come in the future from the ranks of the good angels, just as he knows that the Devil will never return to the fellowship of the good angels. He who is Truth has promised in the Gospel that his faithful saints will be 'equal to the angels of God'.[23] They also have the promise that they will 'go into life eternal'.[24] But, if we are assured that we will never fall from that immortal felicity, then we shall be in a better state than the angels, not merely equal to them, if the angels have not the same assurance. But the truth cannot possibly deceive, and therefore we shall be equal to the angels. It must then follow that the good angels are themselves assured of their eternal felicity. The other angels had not that assurance, since their bliss was destined to have an end, and there was no eternity of bliss for them to be assured of. It remains that either the angels were unequal, or, if they were equal, the good angels received the certainty of eternal felicity after the ruin of the others.

Now perhaps someone will quote what the Lord says in the Gospel about the Devil: 'He was a murderer from the beginning and did not stand fast in the truth';[25] and he will suggest that this is to be interpreted as meaning not merely that the Devil was a murderer from the beginning of the human race, from the time of the creation of man, whom the Devil could deceive and bring to death, but that even from the beginning of his own creation the Devil did not stand fast in the truth, and for that reason he never enjoyed felicity with the holy angels, because he refused to be subject to his creator, and in his arrogance supposed that he wielded power as his own private possession and rejoiced in that power. And thus he was both deceived and deceiving, because no one can escape the power of the Omnipotent. He has refused to accept reality and in his arrogant pride presumes to counterfeit an unreality. And so this is the meaning of the saying of blessed John, 'the Devil sins from the beginning.'[26] That is, from the moment of his creation the Devil refused righteousness, which can only be possessed by a will that is reverently subjected to God.

To assent to this suggestion is not to fall in with the heresy of the

23. Matt. 22, 30. 24. Matt. 25, 46.
25. John 8, 44. 26. 1 John 3, 8.

Manichees,[27] or any similar baneful teaching; the notion that the Devil has evil as the essential principle of his being, that his nature derives from some hostile First Principle. Such people are so far gone in folly that they do not listen to what the Lord has said, although they agree with us in recognizing the authority of the words of the Gospel. The Lord did not say, 'the Devil was by nature unconnected with the truth,' but, 'he did not stand fast in the truth'. He meant us to understand that the Devil has fallen from the truth. If he had stood fast in the truth he would clearly have shared in the truth with the holy angels, would have shared their felicity, and would have continued in that state.

14. *The meaning of the text: 'The Devil did not stand fast in the truth, because there is no truth in him'*

As if in answer to a question from us, the Lord added an indication of the reason why the Devil did not 'hold fast to the truth'. He says, 'because there is no truth in him'. Now there would be truth in him, if he had stood fast to it. But the expression is unusual in form. It says, on the surface, 'He did not hold fast to the truth, because there is no truth in him.' Which seems to be saying that the absence of truth in him was the cause of his failure to stand fast, whereas the fact is that his failure to stand fast is the cause of the absence of truth. We find the same way of speaking in one of the psalms, 'I cried out because you, Lord, have listened to me';[28] where it seems that the psalmist should have said, 'You have listened to me, Lord, because I cried out.' In saying 'I cried out' he appears to be answering the question, 'Why did you cry out?' But, in fact, the verse shows the affecting character of his cry by its effect in winning the attention of God. It is tantamount to saying, 'I prove that I cried out by the fact that you listened to me.'

15. *The meaning of the text: 'The Devil sins from the beginning'*

As for John's statement about the Devil, that 'he is a sinner from the beginning', the Manichees do not realize that if the Devil is a sinner *by nature*, there can really be no question of sin in his case. But what

27. Followers of the teaching of Manes (*c.* 215–75) of Persia, who taught a radical dualism, with two ultimate realities of Good and Evil (Light and Darkness).

28. Ps. 17, 6.

are they to make of the witness of the prophets; either what Isaiah says when he denotes the Devil in the figurative person of the Babylonian emperor, 'What a fall was that, when Lucifer fell, who rose in the early morning!'[29] or the passage in Ezekiel, 'You have been among the delights of God's paradise: you have been decked with every kind of precious stone'?[30] The inference is that the Devil was once without sin. In fact this is made more explicit when he is told, a little later, 'You behaved faultlessly in your time.' If this is the most natural interpretation of those passages, we are bound to take the saying, 'He did not stand fast in the truth', as meaning that he *was* in the truth, but did not continue in it. 'The Devil sins from the beginning' will then mean, not that we are to think that he sinned from the first moment of his creation, but from the first beginning of sin, because sin first came into existence as a result of the Devil's pride.

Then there is the passage in the Book of Job, when the Devil is under discussion, 'This is the beginning of the Lord's handiwork, and he made him to be mocked by angels'[31] (which seems to be echoed by the psalm, 'This is the dragon, whom you fashioned for him to mock at'[32]). This is not to be taken as implying that we should imagine that he was created at the start as a fit object for angelic mockery, but that he was consigned to this punishment after his sin. To start with, then, the Devil is the Lord's handiwork. For there is nothing in nature, even among the last and least of the little creatures, which is not brought into being by him, from whom comes all form, all shape, all order; and without those definitions nothing can be found in nature or imagined in the mind. How much more must the angelic creation derive from him; for the angels take precedence, in natural worth, over all the works of God.

16. *The distinctions among created things; and their different ranking by the scales of utility and logic*

Now among those things which exist in any mode of being, and are distinct from God who made them, living things are ranked above inanimate objects; those which have the power of reproduction, or even the urge towards it, are superior to those who lack that impulse. Among living things, the sentient rank above the insensitive, and animals above trees. Among the sentient, the intelligent take precedence over the unthinking – men over cattle. Among the intelli-

29. Is. 14, 12. 30. Ez. 28, 13f.
31. Job 40, 14. 32. Ps. 104, 26 (LXX).

gent, immortal beings are higher than mortals, angels being higher than men.

This is the scale according to the order of nature; but there is another gradation which employs utility as the criterion of value. On this other scale we would put some inanimate things above some creatures of sense – so much so that if we had the power, we should be ready to remove these creatures from the world of nature, whether in ignorance of the place they occupy in it, or, though knowing that, still subordinating them to our own convenience. For instance, would not anyone prefer to have food in his house, rather than mice, or money rather than fleas? There is nothing surprising in this; for we find the same criterion operating in the value we place on human beings, for all the undoubted worth of a human creature. A higher price is often paid for a horse than for a slave, for a jewel than for a maidservant.

Thus there is a very wide difference between a rational consideration, in its free judgement, and the constraint of need, or the attraction of desire. Rational consideration decides on the position of each thing in the scale of importance, on its own merits, whereas need only thinks of its own interests. Reason looks for the truth as it is revealed to enlightened intelligence; desire has an eye for what allures by the promise of sensual enjoyment.

Now in establishing the order of rational beings, such weight is attached to the qualities of freedom and love, that although angels are superior to men in the order of nature, good men rank above the evil angels according to the criterion of righteousness.

17. *Wickedness is not natural, sin being due to an act of will, not to nature as created*

Thus the text, 'This is the beginning of God's handiwork'[33] refers, on the correct interpretation, to the nature of the Devil, not to his wickedness. There can be no doubt that the fault of wickedness supervenes upon a faultless natural state. Evil is contrary to nature; in fact it can only do harm to nature; and it would not be a fault to withdraw from God were it not that it is more natural to adhere to him. It is that fact which makes the withdrawal a fault. That is why the *choice* of evil is an impressive proof that the *nature* is good.

But God, who is supremely good in his creation of natures that are good, is also completely just in his employment of evil choices in his design, so that whereas such evil choices make a wrong use of good

33. Job 40, 14.

natures, God turns evil choices to good use. Thus when the Devil, who was good as God created him, became bad by his own choice, God caused him to be cast down to a lower station and to become a derision to the angels of God; and this means that the Devil's temptations prove to be for the benefit of God's saints, though the Devil longs to injure them thereby. Now God, when he created the Devil, was without doubt well aware of his future wickedness, and had foreseen the good that he himself would bring out of that evil. That is why the psalm says, 'This is the dragon which you fashioned for him to mock at.'[34] In the very creation of the Devil, though by God's goodness he was made in a state of good, God had already, in virtue of his foreknowledge, laid plans for making good use of him even in his evil state; and this is the message of the passage in the psalm.

18. *The beauty of the universe, made richer by God's providence, through the opposition of contraries*

For God would never have created a man, let alone an angel, in the foreknowledge of his future evil state, if he had not known at the same time how he would put such creatures to good use, and thus enrich the course of the world history by the kind of antithesis which gives beauty to a poem. 'Antithesis' provides the most attractive figures in literary composition: the Latin equivalent is 'opposition', or, more accurately, 'contra-position'. The Apostle Paul makes elegant use of antithesis in developing a passage in the Second Epistle to the Corinthians,

> By means of the arms of righteousness on right hand and left; through glory and ignominy, through infamy and high renown; as deceivers and yet truthful; as unknown and well-known; as dying, and here we are, alive; as punished, and yet not put to death; as full of grief, but always joyful; as in poverty, and yet enriching many others; as having nothing, while possessing everything.[35]

The opposition of such contraries gives an added beauty to speech; and in the same way there is beauty in the composition of the world's history arising from the antithesis of contraries – a kind of eloquence in events, instead of in words. This point is made very clearly in the book Ecclesiasticus, 'Good confronts evil, life confronts death: so the sinner confronts the devout. And in this way you should observe all the works of the Most High; two by two; one confronting the other.'[36]

34. Ps. 17, 6. 35. 2 Cor. 6, 7ff. 36. Ecclus. 33, 14f.

19. *The meaning of the text: 'God made a division between light and darkness'*

There is something to be gained from the obscurity of the inspired discourses of Scripture. The differing interpretations produce many truths and bring them to the light of knowledge; and the meaning of an obscure passage may be established either by the plain evidence of the facts, or by other passages of less difficulty. Sometimes the variety of suggestions leads to the discovery of the meaning of the writer; sometimes this meaning remains obscure, but the discussion of the difficulties is the occasion for the statement of some other truths. Although this is true, I do not think it would be out of harmony with the ways of God's working to suggest that, assuming the creation of the first light to refer to the creation of the angels,[37] the distinction between the holy and the unclean angels is described in the passage, 'And God divided the light from the darkness: and God called the light "Day"; and he called the darkness "Night".'[38] It was certainly only God who could have made the distinction; for he alone could foresee that some angels would fall, before that fall happened, and that they would be deprived of the light of truth and would remain in the darkness of their pride.

As for the day and night with which we are so familiar, the light and darkness of this world, God commanded that they should be distinguished by the visible lights of our everyday experience. 'Let there be lights in the firmament of heaven, to give light on the earth, and to divide the day and the night.' And a little later, 'And God made two great lights, the larger light to shine to rule the day, the smaller to shine to rule the night. He also made the stars. And God placed those in the firmament of the sky to give light on the earth and to be in charge of day and night, and to divide light from darkness.[39]

Between that light (which is the holy fellowship of the angels, shining with the intelligible illumination of truth) and the contrasted darkness (which stands for the depraved minds of the evil angels who have rejected the light of righteousness) God could make the division; for the evil, though in the future, could not be hidden from him. He knew it with certainty, though it was an evil arising not from nature but from choice.

37. cf. ch. 7. 38. Gen. 1, 4f. 39. Gen. 1, 14–18.

20. *The significance of the statement after that division: 'And God saw that the light was good'*

Now we must not omit to point out that the statement, 'God said: "Let there be light"; and light was created', is immediately followed by, 'And God saw that the light was good.' This is not said after he had separated the light from the darkness, calling the light 'Day' and the darkness 'Night'. For in that case it might have seemed that he gave a testimony of approval to the darkness as well as the light. But where darkness is blameless, that darkness which is distinguished by the lights of heaven from the light which is seen by our bodily eyes, then the phrase, 'God saw that it was good', follows the division, instead of preceding it. 'God set them in the firmament of the sky, to shine on the earth, to be in charge of day and night, and to separate light and darkness. And God saw that it was good.' Both the light and the darkness were here approved, because both were sinless. In contrast, when God said, "Let there be light", and light was created', then 'God saw that the light was good.' After that follows the passage, 'God divided the light from the darkness: and God called the light "Day", and the darkness "Night".' But this is not followed by, 'And God saw that it was good.' The omission was designed to avoid the attachment of the epithet 'good' to both, because one of them was evil, not by nature, but through its own fault. Therefore it was only the light which won the Creator's approval, whereas the darkness of the angels, although it had been a fitting part of the divine plan, was not a fit enough subject for the divine approbation.

21. *The eternal and unchanging knowledge and will of God in his creation*

'God saw that it was good.' This statement, applied to all his works, can only signify the approval of work done with the true artist's skill, which here is the Wisdom of God. It is not that God *discovered* that it was good, after it had been made. Far from it. Not one of those works would have been done, if he had not known it beforehand. It could not have come into being if he had not seen it already; and so when he 'sees that it is good' he is not discovering that fact, but communicating it. Plato indeed is bold enough to go further, and to say that God was actually delighted when the whole scheme of things was finished, and rejoiced in the created world.[40] He was not such a fool as to suppose

40. *Tim.* 37C.

that God's happiness was increased by the novelty of his own creation.[41] What he wanted to express was the fact that the finished work met with the artist's approval, as he had before approved it as something for his art to make. It is not that God's knowledge varies in any way, that the future, the present, and the past affect that knowledge in three different ways. It is not with God as it is with us. He does not look ahead to the future, look directly at the present, look back to the past. He sees in some other manner, utterly remote from anything we experience or could imagine. He does not see things by turning his attention from one thing to another. He sees all without any kind of change. Things which happen under the condition of time are in the future, not yet in being, or in the present, already existing, or in the past, no longer in being. But God comprehends all these in a stable and eternal present. And with him there is no difference between seeing with the eyes and 'seeing' with the mind, for he does not consist of mind and body. Nor is there any difference between his present, past, and future knowledge. His knowledge is not like ours, which has three tenses: present, past, and future. God's knowledge has no change or variation. 'With him there is no alteration, or shadow of movement.'[42]

Nor does his attention pass from one thought to another; all things which he knows are present at the same time to his incorporeal vision. He knows events in time without any temporal acts of knowledge, just as he moves events in time, without any temporal motions in himself. And so he saw that what he had made was good when he saw that it was good that he should make it. In seeing it when he made it he did not duplicate his knowledge, nor did he increase his knowledge in any way; that would imply that his knowledge was less before he made something for him to see. In fact God could not have produced works in such perfection, without having such perfect knowledge that no addition could be made to it as a result of those works.

For this reason, if we were merely being asked, 'Who made the light?' it would be enough to answer, 'God.' If the question were not just who made the light, but also how he made it, it would be enough to quote the statement, 'And God said: "Let there be light": and light was created.' And thus we know not only that God created the light, but also that he created it through the Word. But there are three things above all which we need to know about a created thing, three things which we should be told: who made it, how he made it, and why he made it. That is why the Scripture says, 'God said: "Let there

41. cf. Plot., *Enn.*, 5, 8, 8. 42. Jas. 1, 17.

be light": and light was created. And God saw that the light was good.' So the answer to our question 'Who?' is 'God.' To the question 'How?' the answer is, 'He said: "Let it be"; and it was created.' And to 'Why?' we get the reply, 'It was good.' There can be no better author than God, no more effective skill than his word, no better cause than that a good product should be created by God, who is good. This was given by Plato as the most valid reason for the creation of the world – that good works should be effected by a good God.[43] Plato may have read this passage of Scripture or have learnt of it from those who had read it; or it may be that with the intuition of genius he observed 'the invisible realities of God' presented to the mind by means of his creation,[44] or learned about them from those who had thus observed them.

22. *The apparent evil in the universe*

Thus we find a valid and appropriate explanation of creation in the goodness of God leading to the creation of good. When carefully considered and devoutly meditated it is an explanation which gives a final answer to all queries about the origin of the world. And yet there are heretics who fail to see this, because there are so many things which do not suit the inadequacy and frailty of our mortal flesh, which has already come under deserved punishment, many things which cause distress, like fire, cold, wild animals, and so on. They do not observe the value of those things in their own sphere and in their own nature, their position in the splendour of the providential order and the contribution they make by their own special beauty to the whole material scheme, as to a universal commonwealth. They even fail to see how much those same things contribute to our benefit, if we make wise and appropriate use of them. Even poisons, which are disastrous when improperly used, are turned into wholesome medicines by their proper application. By contrast, things which give pleasure, like food and drink, and even light itself, are experienced as harmful when used without restraint and in improper ways.

Divine providence thus warns us not to indulge in silly complaints about the state of affairs, but to take pains to inquire what useful purposes are served by things. And when we fail to find the answer, either through deficiency of insight or of staying power, we should believe that the purpose is hidden from us, as it was in many cases where we had great difficulty in discovering it. There is a useful pur-

43. *Tim.* 30. 44. Rom. 1, 20.

pose in the obscurity of the purpose; it may serve to exercise our humility or to undermine our pride. There is no such entity in nature as 'evil'; 'evil' is merely a name for the privation of good.[45] There is a scale of value stretching from earthly to heavenly realities, from the visible to the invisible; and the inequality between these goods makes possible the existence of them all.

Now God is the great artificer in the great things; but that does not mean that he is an inferior artist in the small. For those small things are not to be measured by their size, which is next to nothing, but by the wisdom of their artificer. Take the case of a man's visible appearance. An eyebrow is virtually nothing compared with the whole body; but shave it off and what an immense loss to his beauty! For beauty does not depend on mere size, but on the symmetry and proportion of the component parts.

It is surely little cause for wonder that those who imagine that there is some evil in nature, which is derived and produced from a supposed 'adverse first cause' of its own, refuse to accept that the reason for the creation of the universe was God's good purpose to create good. They believe instead that God was compelled to the creation of the vast structure of this universe by the utter necessity of repelling the evil which fought against him, that he had to mingle the nature of his creating, which was good, with the evil, which is to be suppressed and overcome, and that this good nature was thus so foully polluted, so savagely taken captive and oppressed that it was only with the greatest toil that he can cleanse it and set it free. And even then he cannot rescue all of it, and the part which cannot be purified from that defilement is to serve as the prison to enclose the Enemy after his overthrow.

This was the silly talk, or rather the delirious raving, of the Manicheans. They would not have babbled like this if they had believed in the truth, that the nature of God is unchangeable and completely incorruptible, and that nothing can do it harm; and if they had held, according to sound Christian teaching, that the soul, which could change for the worse through free choice, and could be corrupted by sin, is not a part of God, nor of the same nature as God, but is created by him, and is far inferior to its creator.

23. *The mistake of Origen*

What is much more remarkable is that there are some who agree with us that there is one 'First Principle' of all things, and that God must be

45. cf. ch. 9.

the creator of all things outside himself; and yet they refuse to accept the good and simple belief in the good and simple reason for the making of the world, namely that God in his goodness created good things, and that all things which do not belong to God's own being, though inferior to God, are nevertheless good, and the creation of God's goodness. They allege that souls are not indeed parts of God, but were created by him, and that these souls sinned in withdrawing from God. Then by various stages, in proportion to their various sins, they came down to the earth and incurred the penalty of imprisonment in various bodies. Hence this world came into being; and the reason for the world's creation was to restrain evil, not to establish good.

Hence arises the just reproach against Origen; for this is the notion he set out in his book entitled *Peri Archôn, Concerning First Principles*.[46] I cannot express my astonishment that so learned and experienced a theologian should have failed to notice in the first place that such a theory is contrary to the meaning of the highly authoritative passage of Scripture, where, after each of God's works, is added, 'And God saw that it was good', and after the completion of the whole series we have, 'And God saw all that he had made, and, behold, it was very good.' The meaning of this is that there is only one cause for the creation of the world – the purpose of God's goodness in the creation of good.

If no one had sinned in the world, the world would have been furnished and fitted only with things naturally good. And the fact that sin has happened does not mean that the whole universe is full of sin, since by far the greater number of celestial beings preserve the order of their nature; and the evil will that refused to keep to the order of its nature did not for that reason escape the laws of God who orders all things well. A picture may be beautiful when it has touches of black in appropriate places; in the same way the whole universe is

46. *De Princ.*, 1, 6. *Origen:* b. *c.* A.D. 185 in Egypt; he studied theology at Alexandria under Clement, whom he succeeded as head of the Catechetical School; he later studied philosophy under Ammonius Saccas, the Neoplatonist; he was imprisoned and tortured during the Decian persecution (250) and died soon after. A prolific author, his writings had wide influence, but some of his speculations became suspect, perhaps because they were misunderstood. He was accused of heresy in Trinitarian doctrine, of erroneous notions about the soul, of teaching metempsychosis ('migration of souls'), and of treating Scripture as mere allegory. The controversy over 'Origenism' had flared up shortly before St Augustine started the *City of God*, and in A.D. 400 a council at Alexandria condemned certain doctrines ascribed to Origen. There was further controversy during the sixth century, and 'Origenism' was finally repudiated at the Second (Oecumenical) Council of Constantinople in 543.

beautiful, if one could see it as a whole, even with its sinners, though their ugliness is disgusting when they are viewed in themselves.

Again, Origen (and all who think with him) should have seen that if there were truth in the idea that the purpose of the world's creation was that souls should be enclosed in bodies, as in prisons, in accordance with their just deserts, the minor offenders receiving higher and lighter bodies, the greater sinners lower and heavier, then the demons, as the worst characters, ought to have the lowest and heaviest bodies, earthly bodies, that is. Whereas in fact such bodies are the lot of men, even of good men. But as it is, so that we may realize that the worth of a soul is not to be measured by the quality of its body, the worst of the demons has been given a body of air, while man has a body of clay, and man, though evil, is guilty of wickedness far less serious than the Devil's; and besides, he had that body even before he sinned. But could there be a more stupid assertion than that this sun of ours was not created by God the artificer, as the sole sun of a single universe to be a source of beauty and also of health for bodily creatures, but that the sun was created because a single soul had sinned in such a way as to deserve to be shut up in such a body? According to this theory, if the same sin, or its equivalent, had been committed not by one soul, but by two, or even by ten or a hundred souls, would the universe have as many as a hundred suns? That this did not happen was not due to the miraculous providence of the Maker in his concern for the health and beauty of his corporal creation; it merely chanced that only one soul advanced so far in sin as to deserve a body of this kind!

It is quite clear where restraint should rightly be applied: not on those souls about which these people talk such nonsense, but on their own, seeing that their notions stray so far from the truth.

As I suggested above, there are three questions to be asked in respect of any created being: 'Who made it?', 'How?', and 'Why?' I put forward the answers: 'God', 'Through his word', 'Because it is good.' Now whether this formula is to be regarded as a mystical revelation of the Trinity, the Father, the Son, and the Holy Spirit, or whether there is anything which prevents this interpretation of the passage in Scripture, is a question meriting extended discussion; and we are not to be forced to unravel every question in a single volume.

24. *The divine Trinity in creation*

We believe, hold, and faithfully proclaim that the Father has begotten the Word, that is, the Wisdom by which all things have been made, his only-begotten Son, one begotten of one, eternal of eternal, Supreme Good of Supreme Good. And we believe that the Holy Spirit is at the same time the Spirit of the Father and of the Son, himself consubstantial and co-eternal with both, and that this totality is a Trinity in respect of the distinctive character of the persons, and is also one God in respect of the inseparable divinity, just as it is one Omnipotent in respect of the inseparable omnipotence; but with this provision, that when the question is asked about each individual the reply is that each is God and Omnipotent, whereas when the question is about all at the same time they are not three Gods or three Omnipotents, but one God omnipotent. Such is the inseparable unity in persons; and this is how that Unity wills to be proclaimed.

As for the question whether the Holy Spirit of the good Father and the good Son can rightly be called the goodness of both, as being common to both, I should not dare to hazard a rash judgement about that. I should however be more ready to risk the statement that he is the holiness of them both, not as a mere quality, but being himself a subsistent being – a substance – and the third person in the Trinity. What lends probability to this suggestion is the fact that although the Father is spirit, and the Son is spirit, and Father and Son are both holy, it remains true that holiness is the distinguishing attribute of the Spirit, which suggests that he is the holiness of both, in substantial and consubstantial form. Now if the divine goodness is identical with the divine holiness, it is evidently not a rash presumption but a reasonable inference to find a hint of the Trinity in the description of God's creative works, expressed somewhat enigmatically, so as to exercise our speculations. This hint we may find when we ask the questions, Who? How? and Why?

It was, of course, the Father of the Word who said, 'Let it be made.' And since creation was effected by his speaking, there can be no doubt that it was done by means of the Word. And the statement, 'God saw that it was good' makes it quite plain that God did not create under stress of any compulsion, or because he lacked something for his own needs; his only motive was goodness; he created because his creation was good. And the assertion of the goodness of the created work follows the act of creation in order to emphasize that the work corresponded with the goodness which was the reason for its creation.

Now if this goodness is rightly interpreted as the Holy Spirit, then the whole united Trinity is revealed to us in its works. Hence comes the origin, the enlightenment, and the felicity of the Holy City constituted by the holy angels on high. If we ask whence it arises, God founded it; if whence comes its wisdom, it receives light from God; if whence comes its bliss, it rejoices in God. It receives its mode of being by subsisting in God, its enlightenment by beholding him, its joy from cleaving to him. It exists; it sees; it loves. It is strong with God's eternity; it shines with God's truth; it rejoices in God's goodness.

25. *The tripartite division of philosophy*

As far as I can understand, it was on this account that philosophers decided on a tripartite division of philosophical division, or rather it was for this reason that they were able to see that philosophy was in fact threefold, for they did not establish this division but found it already there. One part is called physics, the second logic, the third ethics. The names now in common use among Latin authors are natural, rational, and moral philosophy, and I have briefly touched on these in the eighth book. Not that it follows that these philosophers had any idea of a trinity in the nature of God in these three divisions, although Plato is said to have been the first to discover and to give currency to this division,[47] and in his view God alone was the author of all nature, the giver of all reason, the inspirer of the love which is the condition of a good and happy life.

There are many different opinions about the nature of the universe, about principles for establishing truth, and about the Ultimate Good to which all our actions are to be referred. Yet all philosophical speculation falls under those three main heads of discussion. And so, although in each subject there is a wide variety of opinions entertained by individual thinkers, there is no doubt in anyone's mind on three points: that there is some cause underlying nature, some form of knowledge, some supreme principle of life. There are also three things looked for in any artist: natural ability, training, and the use to which he puts them. Those are needed for any real achievement; and his ability is judged by his talent, his training by his knowledge, his use of them by the enjoyment of the fruits of his labours.

I am well aware that 'fruit' and 'enjoyment' are properly used with reference to one who enjoys, and 'use' with reference to a user, the difference clearly being that we are said to enjoy something which gives us pleasure in itself, without reference to anything else, whereas we 'use' something when we seek it for some other purpose. Hence we should use temporal things, rather than enjoy them, so that we may be fit to enjoy eternal blessings, unlike the wicked, who want to enjoy

47. cf. Bk VIII, 4.

money, but to make use of God, not spending money for God, but worshipping God for money. In spite of this distinction, the accepted conventions of language allow us to 'make use' of 'fruits' and to 'enjoy' the 'use' of things; for 'fruits' are also properly the 'fruits of the earth', and we all 'make use' of them in this temporal life.

It was this common meaning of 'use' that I had in mind when I remarked that we should look for three things in assessing a man's value: nature, training, and use. Those three elements are the basis of the threefold division devised by philosophers for the attainment of happiness in life: natural science, which is concerned with nature; rational science (or logic), concerned with training; moral science, concerned with use. Now if our nature derived from ourselves we should clearly have produced our own wisdom; we should not be at pains to acquire it by training, which means learning it from some other source. And our love would start from ourselves and be related to ourselves; and thus we should not need any other good to enjoy. But as it is, our nature has God as its author; and so without doubt we must have him as our teacher, if we are to attain true wisdom; and for our happiness we require him as the bestower of the delight in our hearts which only he can give.

26. The partial image of the Trinity in human nature

We do indeed recognize in ourselves an image of God, that is of the Supreme Trinity. It is not an adequate image, but a very distant parallel. It is not co-eternal and, in brief, it is not of the same substance as God. For all that, there is nothing in the whole of God's creation so near to him in nature; but the image now needs to be refashioned and brought to perfection, so to become close to him in resemblance. We resemble the divine Trinity in that we exist; we know that we exist, and we are glad of this existence and this knowledge. In those three things there is no plausible deception to trouble us. For we do not apprehend those truths by the bodily senses by which we are in contact with the world outside us – perceiving colour by sight, sound by hearing, odour by the sense of smell, flavours by the taste, hardness and softness by touch. We can also summon up in thought the immaterial images which closely resemble those material things apprehended by sense; we retain them in our memory; and through those images we are aroused to desire the things they represent. But the certainty that I exist, that I know it, and that I am glad of it, is independent of any imaginary and deceptive fantasies.

In respect of those truths I have no fear of the arguments of the Academics.[48] They say, 'Suppose you are mistaken?' I reply, 'If I am mistaken, I exist.' A non-existent being cannot be mistaken; therefore I must exist, if I am mistaken.[49] Then since my being mistaken proves that I exist, how can I be mistaken in thinking that I exist, seeing that my mistake establishes my existence? Since therefore I must exist in order to be mistaken, then even if I am mistaken, there can be no doubt that I am not mistaken in my knowledge that I exist. It follows that I am not mistaken in knowing that I know. For just as I know that I exist, I also know that I know. And when I am glad of those two facts, I can add the fact of that gladness to the things I know, as a fact of equal worth. For I am not mistaken about the fact of my gladness, since I am not mistaken about the things which I love. Even if they were illusory, it would still be a fact that I love the illusions. For how could I be rightly blamed and forbidden to love illusions, if it were an illusion that I loved them? But since in fact their truth is established, who can doubt that, when they are loved, that love is an established truth? Moreover, it is as certain that no one would wish himself not to exist as it is that no one would wish himself not to be happy. For existence is a necessary condition for happiness.

27. *Existence, knowledge, and the love of both*

Mere existence is desirable in virtue of a kind of natural property. So much so that even those who are wretched are for this very reason unwilling to die; and even when they are aware of their misery they do not wish to be removed from this world. Instead of this, they want their wretchedness taken away. This is true even of those who appear utterly wretched to themselves and who clearly are so, and of those whom the wise account wretched because of their folly, and also of those whose poverty and beggary makes them wretched in the judgement of men who regard themselves as happy. If those wretches were offered immortality, on the condition that their misery would be undying, with the alternative that if they refused to live for ever in the same misery they would cease to have any existence at all, and would

48. The philosophers of the 'Second Academy' who followed Arcesilaus of Pitane (*c.* 315–240 B.C.) in adopting the scepticism of Pyrrhon of Elis; cf. Bk IV, 30n.

49. cf. the argument of Descartes, *Cogito ergo sum*, 'I think, therefore I exist.'

perish utterly, then they would certainly be overjoyed to choose perpetual misery in preference to complete annihilation.

This reaction is the most uncontrovertible evidence for the fact we are examining. For why should men fear to die, and prefer to live in such distress than to end it by dying? The only reason is the obvious natural revulsion from annihilation. And that is the reason why men, although they know that they are destined to die, long for this mercy to be granted them, as a great boon, the mercy, that is, of an extension of life in this pitiable state, and the deferment of their death. This shows without any shadow of doubt that they would grasp at the offer of immortality, with the greatest delight, even an immortality which would offer no end to their beggarly condition.

Why, even the irrational animals, from the immense dragons down to the tiniest worms, who are not endowed with the capacity to think on those matters, show that they wish to exist and to avoid extinction. They show this by taking every possible action to escape destruction. And then there are the trees and shrubs. They have no perception to enable them to avoid danger by any immediately visible movement; but they send up one shoot into the air to form their crown, and to safeguard this they fix another shoot into the earth to form their root, so that they may draw their nourishment thereby, and thus in some way preserve their existence. Even material objects which are not only bereft of sense-perception, but lack even reproductive life, shoot up aloft or sink down to the depths or hang suspended in between, so as to secure their existence in the situation to which they are by nature adapted.

Furthermore, the strength of man's love of knowledge and of human nature's dislike of being deceived can be realized from the fact that anyone would rather keep his wits and be sorrowful than lose his reason and be joyful. This great and marvellous power of the mind belongs to no mortal being but man. Some other creatures may have much sharper vision than we have for seeing in the light of the sun; but they cannot attain to that immaterial light which casts as it were its rays upon our minds, to enable us to come to a right judgement about all these other creatures. For this we can do, in proportion as we receive this light.

Nevertheless, although there is no kind of real knowledge in the senses of irrational creatures, there is at least something parallel to knowledge, whereas all other material things are called 'sensible', not because they have senses, but because they are perceived by the senses. In the case of trees and plants there is something like sensitivity in their powers of taking nutriment and of reproduction. Yet these and all other material things have their causes hidden in nature; but they offer their forms to the perception of our senses, those forms which give loveliness to the structure of this visible world. It almost seems as if they long to be known, just because they cannot know themselves. We apprehend them by our bodily senses, but it is not by our bodily senses that we form a judgement on them. For we have another sense, far more important than any bodily sense, the sense of the inner man, by which we apprehend what is just and what is unjust, the just by means of the 'idea' which is presented to the intellect, the unjust by the absence of it. The working of this sense has nothing to do with the mechanism of eye, ear, smell, taste or touch. It is through this sense that I am assured of my existence; and through this I love both existence and knowledge, and am sure that I love them.

28. *Whether we should approximate more nearly to the image of the divine Trinity by loving our love of our existence and our knowledge*

Now we have said enough, to satisfy the apparent demands of this present work, on the subject of existence and knowledge, and how much we love them in ourselves, and how far some resemblance to them, though with great difference, is found in the lower creation. But we have not dealt with the question whether the love with which they are loved is itself the object of love. The answer is Yes; and the proof is that in all cases where love is rightly bestowed, that love is itself loved even more. For we are justified in calling a man good not because he merely knows what is good, but because he loves the Good. Therefore why should we not feel in ourselves that we love that love with which we love what is good? There is indeed a love which is given to what should not be loved, and that love is hated in himself by one who loves the love which is given to a proper object of love. For these can both exist in the same man; and it is good for man that what makes for right living should increase in him, and what makes for evil should die away until he is made perfectly sound, and all his life is changed into good. If we were mere beasts, we should love the life of sensuality and all that relates to it; this would be our sufficient good, and when this was satisfied, we should seek nothing further. If we were trees, we should not indeed be able to love anything with any sensual emotion; yet we would seem to have a kind of desire for increased fertility and more abundant fruitfulness. If we were stones, waves, wind or flame, or anything of that kind, lacking sense and life, we would still show something like a desire for our own place and order. For the specific gravity of a body is, in a manner, its love, whether a body tends downwards by reason of its heaviness or strives upwards because of its lightness. A material body is borne along by its weight in a particular direction, as a soul is by its love.[50]

Now we are human beings, created in our Creator's image, whose eternity is true, whose truth is eternal, whose love is eternal and true, who is a Trinity of eternity, truth and love, without confusion or separation; and the constituents of the world which are inferior to us could not exist at all, could not have shape or form, could not aspire to any ordered pattern, or keep that pattern, had they not been created by him who supremely exists, and who is supremely wise and supremely Good. Therefore let us run over all these things which he created in such wonderful stability, to collect the scattered traces of his being, more distinct in some places than in others. And let us gaze at his image in ourselves, and, 'returning to ourselves', like the younger son in the Gospel story,[51] let us rise up and go back to him from whom we have departed in our sinning. There our existence will have no death, our knowledge no error, our love no obstacle. Yet in our present state, although we are sure in our grasp of those three realities, although we do not believe in them on the witness of others, but are conscious of them ourselves as present in our experience, and discern them unerringly with our inner gaze, we still cannot know by ourselves how long they will last, or whether they will last for ever, or what will be their final destination if they are well directed, and if they are wrongly employed. Hence we search for other witnesses or we have them already to hand. This is not the place for detailed discussion about the credibility of this testimony, and why we should have no doubt of it; that will come on a later occasion.

But now we will proceed, to the best of our power and with the help of God, with the discussion we have started in this present book. We are speaking of the City of God which is not on pilgrimage in this mortal life, but is eternally immortal in heaven, consisting of the holy angels who cleave to God, who have never deserted nor ever will desert him. And we have already described how God at the beginning made a division between these holy angels and those who were made darkness by deserting the eternal light.

50. cf. Donne, *Nocturnal on St Lucy's Day*, 33f., 'Yea plants, yea stones detest,/And love . . .'

51. cf. Luke 15, 17.

29. *The angel's knowledge of the Trinity*

These holy angels, to be sure, do not learn about God by spoken words, but by the actual presence of the unchanging Truth, that is by his only-begotten Word, by the Father himself, and by his Holy Spirit. They know that this is the inseparable Trinity, and that the three Persons in it are substantial beings, and yet are not three Gods. They know this with more certainty than we know ourselves. And they have better knowledge of the created world there, in God's wisdom, in the art by which it was made, than in the created world itself, and consequently in that wisdom they know themselves better than in themselves, although they have that knowledge in themselves as well. For they were made, and they are different from their Creator; and therefore they know themselves in him by a daylight knowledge; and in themselves, as we said,[52] by a kind of twilight recognition. For there is a wide difference between knowing something in the cause of its creation, and knowing it as it is in itself. Compare, for example, the conception of a straight line, or any figure as truly apprehended by the mind, with the representation of it drawn in the dust; or the concept of justice in its changeless truth, and its manifestation in the soul of a just man. The same applies to the whole of creation; the firmament between the upper and lower waters, which we call the sky; the gathering of the waters on earth below; the uncovering of the dry land, and the establishment of plants and trees; the setting up of sun, moon, and stars; the creation of the living creatures from the waters, the flying things, the fishes, and the swimming beasts; of things that walk and creep on the earth; and of man himself, excelling all the rest of the creatures on earth. These are all known by the angels in the word[53] of God, where they have the causes and reasons for their creation, fixed and unchanging; and they are known there in a different fashion than in themselves. In the word they are known by a clearer perception than in themselves – the difference between the knowledge of the art and the knowledge of the works of that art. Yet when all these works are referred to the praise and worship of the Creator, then

52. cf. ch. 7.

53. i.e. the *logos* ('word' or 'reason', cf. 'wisdom' in the preceding paragraph). The Stoics, from who the Logos doctrine of the Christian Fathers was, in part, derived, distinguished the λόγος ἐνδιάθετος, immanent in God, from the λόγος προφορικός, externalized as the agent of creation. It is the latter which is generally designated the personal 'Word', the Second Person of the Trinity, while the denotation of the former shifts between the personal *Logos* and the *logos* as an attribute of God.

there is the light as of morning sunshine in the minds of those who contemplate them.

30. *The perfection of the number six*

The works of Creation are described as being completed in six days, the same formula for a day being repeated six times. The reason for this is that six is the number of perfection. It is not that God was constrained by the intervals of time, as if he could not have created all things simultaneously, and have made them afterwards conform to temporal succession by appropriate movements. No, the reason was that the completion or perfection of the works is expressed by the number six. For six is the first number which is the sum of its parts, that is of its fractions, the sixth, the third and the half; for one, two and three added together make six. By 'parts' of a number, in this sense, we mean what may be called its quotients, half, third, fourth and so on as fractions with different denominators. For example, four is a part of nine, being contained in it, but it is not a part in the sense of a fraction; but one is, being a ninth, and so is three, being a third. But these two parts, one and three, are far from making the total of nine. Again, four is a part of ten, but it cannot be called a fraction of it. But one is a fraction, a tenth; and two is a fifth, and five a half. But these three parts, the tenth, the fifth and the half, that is one, two, and five, do not make ten if added together, but eight. On the other hand, the sum of the fractions of twelve exceeds that number, being the twelfth the sixth, the fourth, the third and the half – one, two, three, four and six, making a total of sixteen. This point seemed worthy of a brief mention to show the perfection of the number six, as the first number, as I have said, which is made up by the sum of its parts, and in this number God brought his works to complete perfection. Hence the theory of number is not to be lightly regarded, since it is made quite clear, in many passages of the holy Scriptures, how highly it is to be valued. It was not for nothing that it was said in praise of God, 'You have ordered all things in measure, number and weight.'[54]

31. *The seventh day, of completeness and rest*

The number seven is also perfect, for a different reason; and it was on the seventh day, that is on the seventh repetition of the same day's pattern, that the rest of God is emphasized, and in this rest we hear

54. Wisd. 11, 21. On the significance of numbers cf. Bk XV, 20; XVII, 4; XX, 5; 7.

the first mention of 'sanctification'. Thus God did not wish to sanctify that day by the performance of any of his works, but by his rest, which has no evening. For that rest is no created thing, to make itself known in two different ways, in the Word of God, the 'daylight knowledge' as we may call it, and in itself, the 'twilight knowledge'.[55]

There is a great deal that could be said about the perfection of the number seven; but this book is prolix enough already, and I am afraid of seeming to seize an occasion for showing off my trifles of knowledge, for idle effect rather than for any advantage to the reader. And so I must be careful to observe moderation and show proper seriousness, or I may be judged to neglect 'measure and weight' in indulging in talk about 'number'. Suffice it to point out that three is the first odd whole number, and four the first whole even number, and seven is made up of these two. That is why seven often stands for an unlimited number, as in, 'The righteous will fall seven times, and rise again,'[56] which means, 'However many times he falls, he will not perish' – which is to be understood as referring not to the falls of wickedness, but to tribulations, which lead to humility. Similarly, 'Seven times a day I will praise you', expresses the same thought as, 'His praise is always on my lips.'[57] And there are many other passages of the kind in the Scriptures of divine authority, in which the number seven is habitually used, as I have said, to indicate any conceivable number of anything.

For this reason the Holy Spirit is often referred to by this same number; and the Lord says of the Spirit, 'He will teach you all the truth.'[58] Here is God's rest, in which we rest in God. In this whole, in this complete perfection, is rest, whereas in the part is labour. Therefore we labour, as long as we 'know in part; but when perfection is reached, what is partial will vanish.'[59] Hence it is that even our probing of the Scriptures is laborious.

But the holy angels, for whose society and fellowship we sigh as we travel on this laborious pilgrimage, enjoy an ease of knowledge and a felicity of rest which correspond to their eternity and permanence. And they help us, we may be sure, without difficulty, since their motions are spiritual, pure and free, and therefore unlaborious.

32. *The notion that angels were created before the world*

Now someone may oppose this with the assertion that the passage in Scripture, ' "Let there be light"; and light was created' does not refer to

55. cf. ch. 7. 56. Prov. 24, 16. 57. Ps. 119, 164; 34, 2.
58. Is. 11, 2; John 16, 13. 59. 1 Cor. 13, 9f.

the holy angels. He may be inclined to suppose, or he may even lay it down that it was some kind of material light that was then first created, and that the angels were created not only before the firmament between the two waters which is called the sky, but even before the event described in the words, 'In the beginning God created heaven and earth.' This interpretation would take 'in the beginning' as meaning not that this was the start of creation (since the angels were already created) but that he made all things 'in his Wisdom'. For this Wisdom is the same as his Word, who is called 'the beginning' in Scripture; for instance. the Word himself in the Gospel replied to the Jews who asked who he was by saying that he was 'the beginning'.[60] I would not attempt to refute this position, especially because I am delighted with the idea that the Trinity is emphasized even in the very first chapter of the sacred book of Genesis. For first we have the statement: 'In the beginning God created heaven and earth', by which it can be understood that the Father created 'in the Son', an interpretation which is supported by one of the psalms, where we read, 'How glorified are your works, Lord: you have made all things *in Wisdom*.'[61] Then shortly afterwards we find a most appropriate mention of the Holy Spirit. For there is the description of the condition of the earth as first created by God, or rather of the mass of raw material for the future construction of the universe, material to which the writer gives the name of 'heaven and earth'. This is described in the words which follow: 'But the earth was invisible and unformed, and darkness was over the abyss.' Then, to complete the mention of the Trinity, the writer goes on immediately: 'And the Spirit of God soared above the water.'

Each reader may take it as he likes. The matter is so profound that it may give rise to many interpretations which are not in conflict with the Rule of Faith, to exercise the minds of readers, provided that no one has any uncertainty about the fact that the holy angels are established in the realms on high, not co-eternal with God, but still assured and certain of their eternal and true felicity. Our Lord teaches us that his little ones belong to the fellowship of these angels when he says, 'They will be on the same footing as the angels of God.'[62] He goes further than that, when he shows us the contemplation enjoyed by the angels, in saying, 'Take care not to despise one of these little children: for I tell you that their angels in heaven always see the face of my Father, who is in heaven.'[63]

60. John 8, 25; cf. Bk x, 24 and n. 61. Ps. 104, 24.
62. Matt. 22, 30. 63. Matt., 18, 10.

33. *The two different companies of angels, appropriately called 'Light' and 'Darkness'*

We know that some angels sinned and were thrust into the lowest parts of this world, which is a kind of prison for them, where they are confined until the condemnation which is to come in the day of judgement. We know this on the authority of the apostle Peter, who makes the fact plain in these words, 'God did not spare the angels who sinned. He thrust them into the prison of the darkness below, and handed them over to be kept for punishment at the judgement.'[64] Can anyone doubt that God separated these angels from the others in his foreknowledge and by his creative act? Who could deny that the good angels are rightly called 'Light'? Even we men, while still living in faith, still hoping for equality with the angels, not yet attaining it, even we are already called 'Light' by the Apostle. 'You were', he says 'Darkness in the past; but now, in the Lord, you are Light.'[65]

And that 'Darkness' is a most apt name for those apostates will readily be appreciated by all those who realize or believe that the rebellious angels are worse than unbelieving men. It may be that a different kind of light is to be taken as the meaning in the passage of Genesis, where we read, 'God said: "Let there be light"; and light was created'; and another sort of darkness is meant in the passage, 'God divided the light from the darkness.' But for the reasons stated, we think that the two companies of angels are also meant by the terms 'Light' and 'Darkness'. One of these companies enjoys God, the other swells with pride; to one is said, 'Adore him, all you angels of his';[66] while the chief of the other company says, 'I will give you all these things, if you bow down and worship me.'[67] The one company burns with holy love of God; the other smoulders with the foul desire for its own exaltation; and since 'God resists the proud, while he gives his favour to the humble',[68] the one dwells in the heaven of heavens, the other is cast down in confusion to inhabit this air, the lowest region of the sky. The one enjoys tranquillity in the bright radiance of devotion; the other rages in the dark shadows of desire. The one brings merciful aid, or just punishment, in obedience to God's bidding; the other seethes with the lust to subdue and to injure, at the behest of its own arrogance. The one serves the good purposes of God, striving to give full effect to the desire to help; the other is restrained by God's power, to prevent their fulfilling the desire to harm. The good angels

64. 2 Pet. 2, 4. 65. Eph. 5, 8. 66. Ps. 97, 7.
67. Matt. 4, 9. 68. Jas. 4, 6; 1 Pet. 5, 5.

hold the others in derision,[69] because by their persecutions they unwillingly benefit the faithful; the evil angels envy the good, as they gather the pilgrims into their fellowship.

These are the two societies of angels, contrasted and opposed; the one good by nature and rightly directed by choice, the other good by nature but perverted by choice. This contrast is plainly indicated by unmistakable evidence in other parts of Scripture; and we think that those two companies are meant by 'Light' and 'Darkness' in this book of Genesis. It may indeed be that the writer here had something else in mind; but even so the discussion of this obscure passage is not unprofitable. For even if it is impossible to make sure of the meaning of the author of the book, we have at least not departed from the Rule of Faith, which is well enough known to the faithful by reason of other passages which convey the same authority of Scripture.

For even if it is the material works of God that are described here, they have undoubtedly a considerable parallel to spiritual realities, for the Apostle uses the same comparison when he says, 'You are all sons of light, and sons of the day; we do not belong to night and darkness.'[70] But if this comparison was in fact in the mind of the writer of Genesis, then our inquiry has reached a more satisfying conclusion. For the result is that we may believe that this man of God, inspired with such supernatural wisdom, or rather the Holy Spirit working through him, did not leave out the angels in describing the works of God as being all brought to completion on the sixth day. Whether 'in the beginning' means that this was the first act of creation, or (which is more appropriate) that creation was effected through the only-begotten Word,[71] we know that 'in the beginning God created heaven and earth'; and 'heaven and earth' means the whole of creation, spiritual and material. This, at least, is the more probable interpretation; but 'heaven and earth' may mean the two chief divisions of the physical universe, which together comprise all created things. On this latter interpretation the author gives the whole picture to begin with; and after that he describes the sequence of the component parts according to the mystic number of days.

34. *Another suggestion, which connects the angels with the 'waters'*

There have been those, however, who thought that in some way the two communities of angels were referred to under the name of

69. cf. Job 40, 14; ch. 15. 70. 1 Thess. 5, 5. 71. cf. ch. 32.

'waters' and that the words, 'Let a firmament be made between the waters' are to be taken as meaning by the upper waters the angels, and by the lower waters perhaps the actual waters of the visible world, or else the multitude of evil angels, or even the nations of mankind. If this is right, there is no evidence in this passage for the creation of angels, only for their separation. While there are some who say, with perverse and senseless blasphemy, that God did not create the waters; on the ground that the Scripture nowhere says, 'God said: "Let waters be made".' With equal foolishness they could say the same about the earth; for we are not told that 'God said: "Let earth be made".' But, they reply, it says, 'In the beginning God created heaven and earth.' Well then, water is to be understood as included, for the word 'earth' covers both; for, as the psalm says, 'To him belongs the sea, and it was he who made it; and his hands fashioned the dry land.'[72]

But those who want 'the waters above the heavens' to be taken as meaning the angels, are influenced by the question of the specific gravity of the elements. They think it impossible that water should be established in the upper regions of the universe, because it is by nature a fluid and heavy substance. According to this line of reasoning these men, if they could make a human being, would not put *pituita* (what the Greeks call *phlegma*) into the head, since this phlegm takes the place of water in the elements of the body. For the head is in fact the seat of the phlegm; appropriately, according to the creative work of God, but absurdly, according to the theory of these thinkers. So much so that if we had been ignorant of this fact, and it had been recorded in the book of Genesis that God has placed this fluid, cold, and consequently heavy moisture in the uppermost part of man's body, those element-weighers would utterly have refused to believe it; and if they had submitted to Scriptural authority, they would have decided that some other meaning would have to be given to the passage.

But the thorough scrutiny and discussion of all the points raised by the narrative of creation in the inspired book would entail a long digression from the subject of this present work. And so it seems to me that we have sufficiently examined these two diverse and opposed communities of angels, in which we find something like the beginnings of the two communities of mankind. My purpose is now to describe these two latter communities; and so now at last I bring this book to a close.

72. Ps. 95, 5.

BOOK XII

1. *Good and bad angels have the same nature*

I AM going to discuss the creation of man; for it will be apparent that the two cities took their origin from that creation, as far as they are concerned with beings who are both rational and mortal. But, as I showed in my last book,[1] the beginning of the two cities had already been seen in the angels; and so I see that I must say something about them first. I hope to demonstrate, if I can, that there is no absurdity or incongruity in asserting a fellowship between men and angels. So that there is no need to suppose four cities, two of angels and two of men. We may speak of two cities, or communities, one consisting of the good, angels as well as men, and the other of the evil.

The contrasted aims of the good and the evil angels did not arise from any difference in nature or origin. It would be utterly wrong to have any doubt about that, since God created both, and he is good in his creation and fashioning of all substances. We must believe that the difference had its origin in their wills and desires, the one sort persisting resolutely in that Good which is common to all – which for them is God himself – and in his eternity, truth, and love, while the others were delighted rather with their own power, as though they themselves were their own Good. Thus they have fallen away from that Supreme Good which is common to all, which brings felicity, and they have devoted themselves to their own ends. They have chosen pride in their own elevation in exchange for the true exaltation of eternity; empty cleverness in exchange for the certainty of truth; the spirit of faction instead of unity in love; and so they have become arrogant, deceitful, and envious. The cause of the bliss of the others is their adherence to God; and so the cause of the misery of the apostates must be taken to be the exact contrary, their failure to adhere to him. Therefore the correct reply to the question, 'Why are the one sort happy?' is 'Because they cling to God'; and to 'Why are those others wretched?' the reply is, 'Because they do not cleave to him.' It follows that there is only one Good which will bring happiness to a rational or intellectual creature; and that Good is God. And so although felicity is

1. cf. Bk XI, 9; 33; 34.

not possible for all creatures (for such things as beasts, trees, and stones are incapable of enjoying this blessing), yet those creatures which are capable of it, do not attain it by themselves, being created out of nothing, but receive it from him who created them. In attaining this Good they find their happiness; in losing it they are sunk in misery. But a being whose felicity springs from his own goodness, instead of from another's, cannot be wretched, because he cannot lose himself.

Thus we say that there is only one unchanging Good; and that is the one, true, and blessed God. The things he made are good because they were made by him; but they are subject to change, because they were made not out of his being but out of nothing. Therefore although they are not supreme goods, since God is a greater good than they, still those mutable goods are of great value, because they can adhere to the immutable Good, and so attain happiness; and this is so truly their Good, that without it the creatures cannot but be wretched. Yet the other things in the created universe are not in a better condition because they are incapable of misery; for the other members of our body are not to be called better than our eyes, just because they cannot be blind. A sentient nature, when suffering, is better than a stone which is quite incapable of suffering; and in the same way the rational nature, even in wretchedness, is superior to the nature which is bereft both of reason and sense and therefore cannot be the victim of misery.

This being so, the failure to adhere to God must be a perversion in this rational nature. For it is created in such a privileged position that, though it is itself changeable, it can yet obtain blessedness by adhering to the unchangeable Good, that is, to the supreme God; and, as we can see, it cannot satisfy its need except by attaining that bliss which only God can supply. Moreover, any perversion does harm to nature, which means that it is contrary to nature. Therefore it is not by nature but by a perversion that the rebellious creation differs from the good, which adheres to God; yet even this perversion shows how great and honourable is the nature itself. For if we are right to condemn the perversion, that shows without doubt that the nature is honourable, since what justifies the condemnation of the perversion is that the perversion disgraces a nature which deserves honour. We call blindness a fault in the eyes, and that shows that it is of the nature of eyes to see; we call deafness a fault in the ears, which shows that it is of the nature of ears to hear. In the same way, when we say that it was fault, or perversion, in the angelic creation not to adhere to God, it shows quite plainly that adherence to him belonged to their nature. How great a glory it is to cleave to God, so as to live for him, to gain wisdom from him, to rejoice in him, and to enjoy so great a Good without death, without distraction or hindrance – this is beyond our power to imagine or describe. And thus the perversion of the evil angels in not adhering to God is a proof (since all perversion is contrary to nature) that God created their nature so good that it is harmful for it to be separated from him.

2. *No existence is contrary to God. Non-existence is contrary to him, who is supreme existence*

The reason for saying all this is to prevent anyone from thinking, when we are talking of the apostate angels, that they could have had another kind of nature derived from some other First Principle, and that God was not the author of their nature. The quickest and easiest way for anyone to divest himself of that erroneous and blasphemous notion is to understand clearly what God said by the mouth of his angel when sending Moses to the children of Israel: God said, 'I am HE WHO IS.'[2] For God is existence in a supreme degree – he supremely *is* – and he is therefore immutable. Hence he gave existence to the creatures he made out of nothing; but it was not his own supreme existence. To some he gave existence in a higher degree, to some in a lower, and thus he arranged a scale of existences of various natures. Now 'existence' (*essentia*) is derived from the verb 'to be' or 'to exist' (*esse*), in the same way as 'wisdom' (*sapientia*) from the verb 'to be wise' (*sapere*). It is a new word, not employed by ancient Latin writers, but it has come into general use in modern times to supply the need for a Latin word to express what the Greeks call *ousia*, of which *essentia* is a literal translation.

Thus to this highest existence, from which all things that are derive their existence, the only contrary nature is the non-existent. Non-existence is obviously contrary to the existent. It follows that no existence is contrary to God, that is to the supreme existence and the author of all existence whatsoever.

3. *Enmity to God arises not from nature but from choice, in violation of a nature essentially good*

Scripture speaks of 'enemies of God'; but these enemies oppose God's sovereignty not by nature but by their perversion, and they have

2. Exod. 3, 14.

power only to hurt themselves; they cannot harm God. They are his enemies because of their will to resist him, not because of their power to hurt him. For God is utterly incapable of any change or injury; and therefore the perversion which makes these 'enemies of God' resist him does harm to themselves, not to God, and it harms them simply because it does injury to the goodness of their nature. No nature is contrary to God; but a perversion, being evil, is contrary to good.

Now, can anyone deny that God is supremely good? It follows then that any perversion is contrary to God, as evil to good. Further, the nature which it injures is also a good, and therefore the perversion must be contrary to this good also. It is contrary to God only as evil is opposed to good; but to the nature that it perverts it is not merely evil but harmful. It goes without saying that no evil can harm God; but evils can harm natural substances liable to change and injury, although the very fact that perversions are perversions is a proof that such natures are in themselves good; if they were not good these faults would not harm them. What, in fact, is the harm effected by such faults? It can only be the loss of integrity, beauty, health or virtue, or of any goodness in a nature that is, as a general rule, liable to destruction or diminution through perversion. If there is no good there at all, there is nothing for perversion to destroy; and if no harm can be done, there can be no perversion. The conclusion is that although a fault cannot hurt unchangeable good, it cannot hurt anything except a good of some kind, since it only exists where it does harm. It may be put in this way: a fault cannot exist in the Highest Good, but it cannot exist except in some kind of good.

Therefore good may exist on its own, but evil cannot. The natures which have been perverted as a result of the initiative of an evil choice, are evil in so far as they are vitiated, but in so far as they are natures, they are good. And when this vitiated nature is punished there is, apart from the good that is there because it is a nature, the further good that it does not go unpunished; for the punishment is just, and what is just is undoubtedly good. It is just, in that no one is punished for faults of nature but for faults of will; and even the wickedness which has become habitual, and has developed and hardened into 'second nature', had its origin in an act of choice. At the moment, of course, we are speaking of the perversions of that nature in which there is a mind capable of the intellectual light, by which we distinguish between right and wrong.

4. *Irrational and inanimate natures; their place in the beauty of the universe*

It would be ridiculous, on the other hand, to regard the defects of beasts, trees and other mutable and mortal things which lack intelligence, sense, or life, as deserving condemnation. Such defects do indeed effect the decay of their nature, which is liable to dissolution; but these creatures have received their mode of being by the will of their Creator, whose purpose is that they should bring to perfection the beauty of the lower parts of the universe by their alternation and succession in the passage of the seasons; and this is a beauty in its own kind, finding its place among the constituent parts of this world. Not that such things of earth were meant to be comparable with heavenly realities. Yet the fact that those other realities are of higher value does not mean that these lower creatures should have been excluded from the whole scheme of things.

Consequently, in those areas of the universe where such creatures have their proper being, we see a constant succession, as some things pass away and others arise, as the weaker succumb to the stronger, and those that are overwhelmed change into the qualities of their conquerors; and thus we have a pattern of a world of continual transience. We, for our part, can see no beauty in this pattern to give us delight; and the reason is that we are involved in a section of it, under our condition of mortality, and so we cannot observe the whole design, in which these small parts, which are to us so disagreeable, fit together to make a scheme of ordered beauty. Hence the right course for us, when faced with things in which we are ill-equipped to contemplate God's providential design, is to obey the command to believe in the Creator's providence. We must not, in the rashness of human folly, allow ourselves to find fault, in any particular, with the work of that great Artificer who created all things.

As for those defects, in things of this earth, which are neither voluntary nor punishable; if we observe them closely we shall find that, on the same principle as before, they attest the goodness of the natures themselves, every one of which has God as its sole author and creator. For in their case also we are displeased when a defect takes away the pleasure we find in their original nature, although it is true that men are often displeased by the natural state or behaviour of things, when they experience discomfort from them, and so think only of how they affect them personally, not of those natural properties in themselves. An example would be those animals, whose excessive abundance plagued the pride of the Egyptians.[3] But by the same token men might find fault with the sun, because offenders against the law, or defaulting debtors, are sometimes exposed to the sun by order of the magistrates.

Therefore it is the nature of things considered in itself, without regard to our convenience or inconvenience, that gives glory to the Creator. Thus the nature of the eternal fire is without doubt a subject for praise, although to the wicked after their condemnation it will be the fire of punishment. For what is more beautiful than a fire, with all the vigour of its flames and the splendours of its light? And what more useful, with its heat, its comfort, and its help in cooking? And yet nothing can cause more distress than the burns inflicted by fire. Thus a thing which is dangerous and destructive in some situations proves to be of the greatest utility when properly employed. Who could give a complete account of all the useful functions of fire in the whole universe?

So we must not give a hearing to those who praise the fire's light and find fault with its heat, because they are not thinking of its natural properties, but are judging it by the standard of their own convenience or inconvenience. They like to see the fire; but they do not like being burned. They fail to notice that even the light, which they certainly enjoy, does harm to weak eyes, because it does not suit them; while many animals live and flourish in the heat[4] which these critics dislike, because it happens to suit their nature.

5. *The Creator is to be praised in respect of every kind and mode of being in nature*

And so all nature's substances are good, because they exist and therefore have their own mode and kind of being, and, in their fashion, a peace and harmony among themselves.[5] And when they are in that situation where they ought to be in the orderly scheme of nature, they preserve the full existence they have been given. Those which have not been given an eternal existence obey the laws of the Creator in changing for the better or the worse in accordance with the lines of development he has laid down for them in the scheme of things; and all tend, in God's plan, to that end which is included in the whole design for the government of the universe. But it is ensured that the process of destruction, which results in the disappearance of mutable

3. cf. Exod. 8–10.
4. e.g. the salamander; cf. Bk XXI, 4.
5. cf. Bk XIX, 12; 13.

and mortal natures, brings what existed to non-existence in such a way as to allow the consequent production of what is destined to come into being.

Now God supremely exists, and therefore he is the author of every existence which does not exist in this supreme degree. No existence which came from nothing can claim to be equal to him; nothing could exist in any way, if it had not been created by him. Therefore God is not to be blamed for any fault or defect which offends us; he is to be praised, when we contemplate everything that exists in nature.

6. *The cause of the bliss of the good angels and of the misery of the bad*

The true cause therefore of the bliss of the good angels is their adherence to him who supremely *is*. When we ask the cause of the evil angels' misery, we find that it is the just result of their turning away from him who supremely is, and their turning towards themselves, who do not exist in that supreme degree. What other name is there for this fault than pride? 'The beginning of all sin is pride.'[6] Thus they refused to 'keep watch for him who is their strength'.[7] They would have existed in a higher degree, if they had adhered to him who exists in the highest degree; but in preferring themselves to him they chose a lower degree of existence.

This was the first defect, the first impoverishment, the first fault of that nature, which was so created that it did not exist in the supreme degree; yet it was capable of attaining blessedness in the enjoyment of him who supremely exists. Even when it turned away from him it did not become nothing; but it sank to a lower state of being, and therefore came to misery. If you try to find the efficient cause of this evil choice, there is none to be found. For nothing causes an evil will, since it is the evil will itself which causes the evil act; and that means that the evil choice is the efficient cause of an evil act, whereas there is no efficient cause of an evil choice; since if anything exists, it either has, or has not, a will. If it has, that will is either good or bad; and if it is good, will anyone be fool enough to say that a good will causes an evil will? If it does, it follows that a good will is the cause of sin; and a more absurd conclusion cannot be imagined. Now if whatever is supposed to cause the evil will itself had an evil will, then I go on to ask what caused *that* evil will, and thus, to set a limit to these questions, I look for the cause of the first evil will. An evil will which is caused by

6. Ecclus. 10, 13. 7. cf. Ps. 59, 9.

an evil will is not the first; the first is that which has no cause, since cause precedes effect.

If it is replied that it had no cause, and therefore always existed, I ask whether it existed in any nature. If it was not in any nature, then it did not exist at all. If it existed in some nature, it vitiated that nature and corrupted it; it was harmful to it and therefore deprived it of good. Therefore a bad will cannot exist in a bad nature, but in a good but mutable nature, which this fault could harm. For if it did no harm, it obviously was not a fault, and if not a fault it could not rightly be called an *evil* will. And if it did harm, it must have done harm by destroying or diminishing good. Therefore an evil will could not be eternal in anything. For there would have to be a preceding goodness of nature for the evil will to harm and destroy. Then if that evil will was not eternally there, who created it?

The only possible answer is: Something which had no will. Was this, then, superior, inferior, or equal to it? If superior, it must be better. How then could it have no will? Must it not have a good will? The same applies if it is equal. When two things are equally good in will, the one cannot cause an evil will in the other. It remains that an inferior thing, without will, caused an evil will in the angelic nature, which first sinned.

But any existing thing which is inferior, even to the lowest depth of earth, is a nature and an existence, and therefore it is undoubtedly good, having its own mode and form in its own kind and order. How then can a good thing be the efficient cause of evil choice? How, I repeat, can good be the cause of evil? For when the will leaves the higher and turns to the lower, it becomes bad not because the thing to which it turns is bad, but because the turning is itself perverse. It follows that it is not the inferior thing which causes the evil choice; it is the will itself, because it is created, that desires the inferior thing in a perverted and inordinate manner.

Suppose that two men, of precisely similar disposition in mind and body, see the beauty of the same woman's body, and the sight stirs one of them to enjoy her unlawfully, while the other continues unmoved in his decision of chastity. What do we suppose to be the cause of an evil choice in the one and not in the other? What produced that evil will? It was not the beauty of the woman; for it did not have that effect in both of them, although both had precisely the same view of her. Was it the flesh of the beholder? Then why did it affect one and not the other? The mind? Why not the mind of both? For we assumed them to be alike in both mind and body. Are we to say that one of them was tempted by an unseen suggestion from a malignant spirit, which would imply that he did not of his own will fall in with the suggestion, or whatever sort of persuasion it was?

It is just this consent, this evil choice which responded to the evil suggestion for which we are trying to find the efficient cause. Now if both experienced the same temptation, and one succumbed and consented to it, while the other remained unmoved, the only way to solve the difficulty is evidently to say that one refused and the other agreed to lose his chastity. What other reason could there be than this personal decision, given that their dispositions were precisely the same, in body and mind? The woman's beauty was seen by the eyes of both of them, the same beauty, in the same way. The unseen temptation was equally present in both of them. And so, if anyone tries to discover a cause which produced the evil choice in one of the pair, if he scrutinizes the situation carefully, no cause suggests itself.

Suppose we say that the man himself caused it? But before that evil choice he was simply a good nature, created by God, who is the immutable Good. Now we have assumed that these two men both had the same chance of seeing the beautiful body, and both were alike in mind and body, before the sight of the woman brought temptation; yet the one yielded to the persuasion of the Tempter to enjoy her unlawfully; the other resisted it. And so if anyone asserts that the man himself caused the evil choice, though before that evil choice he was undoubtedly good, he must go on to ask *why* he caused it. Was it because he is a natural being, or because his natural being is created from nothing? It will then be found that the evil choice takes its origin not from the fact that the man is a natural being, but from the fact that his natural being is created from nothing. For if nature is the cause of the evil will, can we help saying that evil is derived from good, and that good is the cause of evil? This must be so, if the evil will derives from a nature which is good. But how can this be? How can a nature which is good, however changeable, before it has an evil will, be the cause of any evil, the cause, that is, of that evil will itself?

7. *We must not look for any efficient cause of the evil act of will*

The truth is that one should not try to find an efficient cause for a wrong choice. It is not a matter of efficiency, but of deficiency; the evil will itself is not effective but defective. For to defect from him who is the Supreme Existence, to something of less reality, this is to begin to have an evil will. To try to discover the causes of such defection – deficient, not efficient causes – is like trying to see darkness or to hear silence. Yet we are familiar with darkness and silence, and we can only be aware of them by means of eyes and ears, but this is not by perception but by absence of perception.

No one therefore must try to get to know from me what I know that I do not know, unless, it may be, in order to learn not to know what must be known to be incapable of being known! For of course when we know things not by perception but by its absence, we know them, in a sense, but not-knowing, so that they are not-known by being known – if that is a possible or intelligible statement! For when with our bodily eyes, our glance travels over material forms, as they are presented to perception, we never see darkness except when we stop seeing. And we can only perceive silence by means of our ears, and through no other sense, and yet silence can only be perceived by not hearing. In the same way, the 'ideas' presented to the intellect are observed by our mind in understanding them. And yet when these 'ideas' are absent, the mind acquires knowledge by not-knowing. For 'who can observe things that are lacking?'[8]

8. *The perverse affection whereby the will defects from the immutable to the mutable good*

This I do know; that the nature of God cannot be deficient, at any time, anywhere, in any respect, while things which were made from nothing are capable of deficiency. And such things have efficient causes, the higher their degree of reality, the greater their activity in good, for it is then that they are really active; but in so far as they fail, and consequently act wrongly, their activity must be futile, and they have deficient causes. I likewise know that when an evil choice happens in any being, then what happens is dependent on the will of that being; the failure is voluntary, not necessary, and the punishment that follows is just. For this failure does not consist in defection to things which are evil in themselves; it is the defection in itself that is evil. That is, it is not a falling away to evil natures; the defection is evil in itself, as a defection from him who supremely exists to something of a lower degree of reality; and this is contrary to the order of nature.

Greed, for example, is not something wrong with gold; the fault is in a man who perversely loves gold and for its sake abandons justice,

8. Ps. 19, 12 ('Who can detect his failings?).

which ought to be put beyond comparison above gold. Lust is not something wrong in a beautiful and attractive body; the fault is in a soul which perversely delights in sensual pleasures, to the neglect of that self-control by which we are made fit for spiritual realities far more beautiful, with a loveliness which cannot fade. Boasting is not something wrong with the praise of men; the fault is in a soul which perversely loves the praise of others and cares nothing for the 'witness of conscience'.[9] Pride is not something wrong in the one who loves power, or in the power itself; the fault is in the soul which perversely loves its own power, and has no thought for the justice of the Omnipotent. By the same token, anyone who perversely loves the goodness of any nature whatsoever, even if he obtains the enjoyment of it, becomes evil in the enjoyment of the good, and wretched in being deprived of a higher good.

9. *Whether the Creator is the author of the good will of the holy angels*

There is then no efficient natural or (if we may so call it) 'essential' cause of evil choice, since the evil of mutable spirits arises from the evil choice itself, and that evil diminishes and corrupts the goodness of nature. And this evil choice consists solely in falling away from God and deserting him, a defection whose cause is deficient, in the sense of being wanting – for there is no cause. Now if we draw the conclusion that a good will also has no efficient cause we must beware of giving the idea that the good will of the good angels is uncaused in the sense of being co-eternal with God. In fact, since the angels were themselves created, it follows that their will must also be created. Now if their will was created, was it created together with them, or did they first exist without it? If with them, obviously it was created by him who created them: and as soon as they were created they adhered to their Creator with that love with which they were created. And the rebellious angels were separated from fellowship with the good, because the latter continued in that good will, while the others were changed by falling away from it, by an act of will which was evil in the very fact that they fell away from that good will; and they would not have fallen away, had they not willed to do so.

If, on the other hand, the good angels were at first without this good will, and produced it by themselves without the operation of God, then they themselves improved upon God's original creation, which is un-

9. cf. 2 Cor. 1, 12.

thinkable. Indeed. without a good will they could not but be evil. Or if they were not evil, because there was no evil will in them, and they had not fallen away from something which they had never begun to possess, at any rate they were not as good as they began to be when they had a good will. But if they could not by themselves have improved upon the work of the best possible Creator, then clearly they could only have gained possession of a good will, by which they would be improved, by the assistance of the Creator's activity. And the effect of their good will was to turn them not to themselves who were inferior in being, but to him who supremely exists, so that by adhering to him they might advance in being and live in wisdom and felicity by participation in him. And so they demonstrate just this: that any good will would have been impoverished, remaining in the state of longing, had it not been that he who made, out of nothing, a nature that was good and capable of enjoying him, made it better by fulfilling that desire, first having excited it to greater eagerness for that fulfilment.

There is another point to be discussed. If the angels themselves created this good will in themselves, did they do this by some act of will? If there was no act of will, they could not have created it. That needs no saying. Then, if there was some act of will, was it a bad or a good act of will? If the former, how could a bad will produce a good? If the latter, then they had a good will already. And who had produced that will but the one who created them with a good will, that is with pure love, the love with which they could adhere to him, the one who showered grace on them at the same time as he formed their nature? Hence we must believe that the holy angels were never without good will, never that is, without the love of God.

Those other angels were created good but have become evil by their own bad will; and this bad will did not originate from their nature, which was good. It came through a voluntary falling away from the good, so that evil is caused not by good, but by falling away from good. Either they received less grace of the divine love than did the others, who continued in that grace; or, if both were created equally good, the one sort fell through their evil will, while the others had greater help to enable them to attain to the fullness of bliss with the complete assurance that they will never fall away – a point we have already made, in the previous book.[10]

Therefore we must acknowledge, giving due praise to the Creator, that 'the love of God diffused by the Holy Spirit who has been given'[11] does not refer merely to holy men, but is applicable also to

10. cf. Bk XI, 13. 11. Rom 5, 5.

the holy angels; that when the Scripture says, 'As for me, my true good is to cling to God'[12] it refers not only to the good for mankind, but first and foremost, to the good of the holy angels. Those who share in this good have holy fellowship with him to whom they adhere, and also among themselves; and they are one City of God, and at the same time they are his living sacrifice[13] and his living temple.[14] Part of this community, which is an assembly formed of mortal men destined to be united with the immortal angels, is now on pilgrimage on earth, under the condition of change, or else is at rest, in the persons of those who have passed from this life, in the secret resting-places of the souls of the departed.[15] I see that I must go on to describe how this part of the community originated with God as its creator, as I have already described the origin of the angels.

Now the whole human race took its beginning from the one man, whom God first created. This we believe on the authority of the holy Scriptures, an authority which is held, and rightly, in unique respect in all the world, and among all nations.[16] In fact, among the other true predictions given in the Scripture, by divine inspiration, is the prophecy that all those nations would believe its testimony.[17]

10. *Of the opinion that the human race, like the world itself, has always existed*

We may pass over the speculations about the nature and origin of the human race that have been put forward by men who do not know what they are talking about. Some have supposed that the world itself always existed,[18] and they have expressed the same belief about mankind. Thus Apuleius describes this class of living creatures in these words: 'Mortal as individuals; but eternal as a whole species'.[19] Now we may put this question to the theorists: 'If the world has always existed, how can the statements in your histories be true, when they ascribe various inventions to various people, and name those responsible for the first establishment of liberal education and of other arts, or the first inhabitants of different regions of the world and of the various islands?' And we get this answer: 'At periodic intervals the world, or rather the greater part of it, is so devastated by floods and conflagrations, that mankind is reduced to a meagre few, and the original population is restored by the progeny of that remnant. And

12. Ps. 73, 28.
13. cf. Rom. 12, 1; Bk X, 16.
14. cf. Eph. 2, 19–22.
15. cf. Bk XIII, 8.
16. cf. Mark 14, 9.
17. cf. Bk XII, 11.
18. cf. Bk XI, 4.
19. *De Deo Socr.*, 4.

so things are discovered and started time after time, and it seems as if each time is the first beginning; whereas in fact these "beginnings" are restorations of what has been interrupted and extinguished by these colossal devastations. Man can come into existence only from man.'[20] Now such statements are based on mere supposition, not on knowledge.

11. *The falsity of such history as ascribes to the world a past of many thousand years*

Those who hold such opinions are also led astray by some utterly spurious documents which, they say, give a historical record of many thousand years, whereas we reckon, from the evidence of the holy Scriptures, that fewer than 6,000 years have passed since man's first origin.[21] To avoid any long argument in refutation of the nonsense of the writings which allege many more thousands of years, and to show how utterly inadequate is their authority on this subject, I need only refer to the well-known letter of Alexander the Great to his mother Olympias.[22] This incorporates the narrative of an Egyptian priest, which he produced from writings considered sacred by the Egyptians. This document records, among other empires, the monarchies which are also known to Greek historical sources. In Alexander's letter the Assyrian monarchy is represented as lasting more than 5,000 years, while in the Greek records it covered only 1,300 years, from the reign of Belus, who appears as the first king in the Egyptian's story as well as in the Greek.[23] The Egyptian alleged a duration of more than 8,000 years for the Persian and Macedonian Empires down to the time of Alexander, to whom he was speaking. But in the Greek account the Macedonian monarchy is found to have lasted only 485 years up to the death of Alexander,[24] while the Persian Empire, according to this reckoning, was brought to an end by Alexander's conquest after 233 years of power.[25] The Greek figures are thus much smaller than the Egyptian. In fact they would not equal them,

20. cf. Plat., *Tim.*, 22c, 23c; Cic., *De Nat. Deor.*, 2, 118 (the Stoic doctrine).

21. St Augustine is probably following Eusebius, whose *Chronicle* gives 5,611 years from the creation to Alaric's capture of Rome.

22. cf. Bk VIII, 5; 27.

23. cf. Bk IV, 6 (1,240 years – following Euseb. *Chron.*); Bk XVIII, 21 (1,305 years – including Belus).

24. So Velleius Paterculus (1, 6); Justin, (33, 2) gives 924 years.

25. Curtius (*De Gest. Alex.*, 4, 14, 20) and Jerome (*Com. in Dan.*, 9) both give 230 years.

even if multiplied by three. Now it is said that the Egyptians at one time had short years, lasting only four months, so that one real year, a full year, like the modern Egyptian year (which is the same as ours) would contain three of those old Egyptian years.[26] But even so, as I said, Greek records would not coincide with the Egyptian in chronology. And there is good reason for regarding the Greek account as more worthy of credence, in that it does not exceed the true statement of the number of years, as presented in our Scriptures, which are truly sacred. Moreover if this well-known letter of Alexander is so widely discrepant from the trustworthy record of the facts in respect of chronology, how much less credence should be given to those writings, packed with fairy-tales about reputed antiquity, which our opponents may decide to produce in attempts to controvert the authority of our sacred books, whose inspiration is so generally acknowledged. This is the authority which foretold that the whole world would believe in it; and the belief of the whole world has answered to that prophecy.[27] The fulfilment in reality of those prophecies of the future guarantees the truth of the biblical narrative of the past.

12. *The theory of the periodic disintegration and renewal of innumerable worlds, or of one*

There are others who hold that this world is not eternal. They suppose an infinite series of dissolutions and restorations at fixed periods in the course of ages; some of them believing that this happens to the one world,[28] which is the only one, while others believe in an infinite number of worlds.[29] These theorists are forced to admit that the human race existed first, before men were begotten. They cannot suppose that when the whole world is destroyed any representatives of humanity could remain, as happened according to the other theory of periodic inundations and conflagrations. For according to that contention, these disasters did not affect the whole earth, and so a few human beings remained on each occasion, and from them the original population could be restored.[30] But this present theory supposes that the world itself is rebuilt from its own material, and so it also holds that mankind is produced again out of its elements, and then from

26. cf. Bk xv, 12. 27. cf. ch. 9. 28. Heraclitus and the Stoics.
29. Anaximander, Democritus, Epicurus. cf. Lucr. 2, 1023–1174.
30. cf. ch. 10.

those first parents comes the teeming progeny of mortals, and that the same happens in the other animals.

13. *The reply to the argument against the recent creation of man*

Some people raise the question why an infinity of ages passed without man's being created, why his creation was so late that less than 6,000 years, according to scriptural evidence, have passed since he first came into existence. Our answer to this is the same as that we offered to the similar objection about the origin of the world,[31] raised by those who refused to believe, not that the world has always existed, but that it had a beginning (as Plato clearly admits,[32] although some[33] believe that he was not expressing his real opinion). If the idea of so short a time upsets them, and the years since man's creation, as recorded in our authorities, seem so few, they should consider that nothing which has a limit is of enormous duration, and that all the finite spaces of the ages, when compared with endless eternity, are to be counted not as very little, but as nothing at all. Therefore even if we speak of not just 5,000 or 6,000 years, but even 60,000 or 600,000 or 6,000,000 or 60,000,000 or 600,000,000, and go on squaring the numbers until we reach a number to which we cannot give a name, and make that the time since man's creation, the question could still be asked: 'Why not earlier?'

For God's pause before the creation of man was eternal and without beginning, so that compared with it an inexpressibly great number of centuries, which must still have an end and a defined extent, is not so much as the smallest drop of water compared with all the oceans of the world: for in this comparison, though one is tiny and the other incomparably huge, still both terms are finite. But any space of time which starts from a beginning and is brought to an end, however vast its extent, must be reckoned when compared with that which has no beginning, as minimal, or rather as nothing at all. For if you take from it the shortest moments one by one, beginning from the end, however great the number may be, even if it is too great to have a name, it will still decrease as you go back, until the process of subtraction brings you to the beginning. It is like subtracting the days of a man's life working back from the present until you reach his birthday. But if you take what has no beginning, and work backwards, not

31. cf. Bk XI, 5. 32. cf. Plat., *Tim.*, 28B.
33. The Neoplatonists, e.g. Plotinus.

subtracting moments one by one, or hours, or days, or months, or years, but intervals equal to that number of years which exceeds all possible computation and yet can be wiped out by the subtraction of moments one by one, and if you subtract those immense spaces of time not once or twice or any number of times, but without limit, it is all to no avail; you never reach the beginning, because there is no beginning at all. Therefore the question which we now ask after 5,000 years or more, posterity could as well ask, with the same curiosity, after 600,000 years, if the mortal state of humanity, with its succession of birth and death, should last so long, and our frailty, with all its ignorance, should endure. And our predecessors might have raised the same question soon after the creation of man. In fact the first man himself might have asked, on the day after he was made, or even on the very day of his creation, why he had not been made sooner. And whenever he had been made, no matter how much earlier, this objection about the beginning of temporal things would have had precisely the same force then as now – or at any other time.

14. *The cyclical theory of the world's history*

The Physicists, for their part, considered that there was only one possible and credible way of solving this difficulty; and that was by the postulate of periodic cycles.[34] They asserted that by those cycles all things in the universe have been continually renewed and repeated, in the same form, and thus there will be hereafter an unceasing sequence of ages, passing away and coming again in revolution. These cycles may take place in one continuing world, or it may be that at certain periods the world disappears and reappears, showing the same features, which appear as new, but which in fact have been in the past and will return in the future. And they are utterly unable to rescue the immortal soul from this merry-go-round, even when it has attained wisdom; it must proceed on an unremitting alternation between false bliss and genuine misery. For how can there be true bliss, without any certainty of its eternal continuance, when the soul in its ignorance does not know of the misery to come, or else unhappily fears its coming in the midst of its blessedness? But if the soul goes from misery to happiness, nevermore to return, then there is some new state of affairs in time, which will never have an end in time. If so, why cannot the same be true of the world? And of man, created in the world? And so we may escape from these false circuitous courses,

34. e.g. the Platonic 'Great Year'; cf. *Tim.*, 39D; Cic., *De Nat. Deor.*, 2, 51f.

whatever they may be, which have been devised by these misled and misleading sages, by keeping to the straight path in the right direction under the guidance of sound teaching.

Now there are some[35] who quote the passage in the book of Solomon called Ecclesiastes, 'What is what has been? The same as what will be. What is what has been done? The same as what will be done. There is nothing new under the sun. If anyone says: "Look, here is something new"; it has already happened in the ages before our time.'[36] And they want this to be taken as referring to those circular movements, returning to the same state as before, and bringing all things back to the same condition. But in fact the writer is speaking of what he has just been mentioning: the successive generations, departing and arriving, the paths of the sun, the streams that flow past. Or else he is speaking generally of all things which come to be and pass away: for there were men before us, there are men contemporary with us, and there will be men after us; and the same holds good for all living creatures, and for trees and plants. Even the very monsters, the strange creatures which are born, although different one from another, and even though we are told that some of them are unique, still, regarded as a class of wonders and monsters, it is true of them that they have been before and they will be again, and there is nothing novel or fresh in the fact of a monster being born under the sun.

Some interpreters, to be sure, have taken the passage quoted to mean that all things have already happened in God's predestination, and that is why there is 'nothing new under the sun'. They think this is what the wise man intended to convey. However this may be, heaven forbid that correct faith should believe that those words of Solomon refer to those periodic revolutions of the Physicists, by which, on their theory, the same ages and the same temporal events recur in rotation. According to this theory, just as Plato, for example, taught his disciples at Athens in the fourth century, in the school called the Academy, so in innumerable centuries of the past, separated by immensely wide and yet finite intervals, the same Plato, the same city, the same school, the same disciples have appeared time after time, and are to reappear time after time in innumerable centuries in the future.

Heaven forbid, I repeat, that we should believe this. For 'Christ died once for all for our sins'; and 'in rising from the dead he is never

35. e.g. Origen; cf. *De Princ.*, 3, 5, 3.

36. Eccl. 1, 9f.

to die again: he is no longer under the sway of death.[37] And after the resurrection 'we shall be with the Lord for ever';[38] and even now we say to the Lord, as the holy psalm reminds us to say, 'Lord, you will preserve us and guard us from this generation for ever.'[39] The following verse I think suits our theorists very neatly, 'The ungodly will walk in a circle';[40] not because their life is going to come round again in the course of those revolutions which they believe in, but because the way of their error, the way of false doctrine, goes round in circles.

15. *God's creation of mankind in time involved no change of purpose*

It is no wonder that those theorists wander in a circuitous maze finding neither entrance nor exit, for they do not know how the human race, and this mortal condition of ours, first started, nor with what end it will be brought to a close. They cannot penetrate 'the depth of God',[41] the deep counsel by which, being himself eternal and without beginning, he started time and man from a beginning, and made man in time, as a new act of creation, and yet with no sudden change of purpose but in accordance with his unchanging and eternal plan. Who could plumb this unplumbable depth of God's counsel, and scrutinize his inscrutable design? This is the design by which God made man as a being in time, when no man had existed before him, making him in time with no change of purpose, and multiplying the whole human race from that one man.

For when the psalmist has said, 'Lord, you will preserve us and guard us from this generation for ever',[42] he then goes on to hit back at those whose foolish and godless teaching allows no room for the eternal liberation and felicity of the soul, when he adds, 'The ungodly will walk in a circle.' It is as if he had been asked: 'What then do *you* believe? What do you think? How do you understand it? Are we really to imagine that God suddenly decided to make man, whom he had not made in all that previous infinite eternity, remembering that nothing new can happen to God, and there is no possibility of change in him?' And the psalmist immediately replies by addressing God him-

37. Rom. 6, 9. 38. 1 Thess. 4, 17. 39. Ps. 12, 7.
40. Ps. 12, 9. (In the Latin versions derived from the Septuagint. The Hebrew reads: 'The wicked prowl on every side.')
41. 1 Cor. 2, 10. 42. Ps. 12, 7.

self: 'According to your deep design you multiplied the sons of men.'[43] He says, in effect, 'Let men form their opinions from their own imaginations: let them theorize and argue as they please, but "according to your deep design you multiplied the sons of men" – that deep design which no human being can discover.' For it is certainly a profound mystery that God existed always and yet willed to create the first man, as a new act of creation, at some particular time, without any alteration in his purpose and design.

16. *Does God's eternal sovereignty imply an eternal creation for its exercise?*

I certainly would not dare to deny that God is eternally sovereign Lord; yet at the same time I must not doubt that man was first created at a certain time, before which he did not exist. But when I ponder the question what was the eternal subject of God's eternal sovereignty, if creation did not always exist, I am afraid to give any positive answer, because I examine myself, and remember what the Scripture says, 'What human being can know the design of God? Who will be able to think what God intends? For the thoughts of mortals are timorous, and our speculations uncertain. For the corruptible body weighs down the soul, and the earthly habitation depresses the mind as it ponders many thoughts.'[44]

There are many thoughts which I ponder while in this earthly habitation – many, just because I cannot find one thought, among those I ponder, or any thought beyond them which happens not to be among my thoughts, which is certainly true. Suppose I say that creation has always existed, for God to be its sovereign (since God always is sovereign, and always has been) but that one creation followed another in the passage of ages – to avoid saying that any creation is co-eternal with God, an idea condemned alike by faith and sound reason. Then we must beware of the absurdity (an absurdity remote from the light of truth) of supposing that the mortal creation has existed from the beginning, though changing through the ages, with the departure of one creation and the succession of another, and saying at the same time that the immortal creation did not come into being until this age of ours was reached, when the angels also were created. (I am assuming that we are right in taking

43. Ps. 12, 8. (In the Latin versions. The Hebrew reads: 'baseness is exalted among men.')

44. Wisd. 9, 13ff.

'first created light' as referring to them, or, more probably, in so interpreting 'heaven' in the statement, 'In the beginning God created heaven and earth.')[45] For the angels did not exist before they were made; otherwise these eternal beings would be thought to be co-eternal with God, if they are said to have existed always.

On the other hand, if I say that the angels were not created in time, but existed before all time was for God to be sovereign over them, since he has always been sovereign, then I shall be asked whether beings who were created could exist always – if it is true that they were made before time was. Perhaps the reply should be: 'Why should they not exist always, seeing that what exists for all time may appropriately be said to exist always? They have existed for all time: so much so that they were created before all measured time, if we accept it that measured time began with the creation of the sky, and they existed before that. But time, we suppose, did not begin with the sky, but existed before it; though not indeed in hours, days, months and years. For these measurements of temporal spaces, which are by usage properly called "times", evidently took their beginning from the motion of the stars; hence God said, in creating them, "Let them serve for signs and times and days and years."[46] Time, we suppose, existed before this in some changing movement, in which there was succession of before and after, in which everything could not be simultaneous. If then before the creation of the sky there was something of this sort in the angelic motions, and therefore time already existed and the angels moved in time from the moment of their creation, even so they have existed for all time, seeing that time began when they began. Will anyone assert that what has existed for all time has not existed always?'

But if I make this reply, I shall be asked, 'Surely then they must be co-eternal with the Creator, if they, as he, have always existed? How can they be said to be created, if we take it that they have always existed?' What answer is there to this? Are we to say that they have always existed, in that they were made together with time, or that measured time began with them, and so they have existed for all time; but that nevertheless they were created? For we shall not deny that 'times' were created, although no one doubts that time has existed for all time.

For if time has not existed for all time, it would follow that there was a time when there was no time. And the most complete fool would not say that! We can correctly say, 'There was a time when

45. cf. Bk XI, 9. 46. cf. *Conf.*, 11, 23.

Rome did not exist: there was a time when Jerusalem, or Abraham, or man, or anything of this kind, did not exist.' We can in fact say, 'There was a time when the world did not exist', if it is true that the world was created not at the beginning of time, but some time after. But to say, 'There was a time when time did not exist', is as nonsensical as to say, 'There was a man when no man existed', or, 'This world existed when this world was not.' If we are referring to different individuals, we can rightly say, 'There was a man when that man did not exist', and so we can say, 'There was a time when this time did not exist'; but to say, 'There was a time when there was no time' is beyond the capability of the veriest idiot.

And so, since we say that time was created, while it is said to have existed always, because time has existed for all time, the fact that the angels have existed always does not entail that they were not created. They are said to have existed always because they have been for all time; and they have existed for all time because without them periods of time could not exist. For when there was no created thing whose change and movement could be the condition of time's passage, time could not exist. Thus although the angels always existed, they were created, and the fact that they always existed does not make them co-eternal with the Creator. For he has always existed in changeless eternity; whereas they were created. But they are said to have existed always because they have existed for all time, and without them no time could exist.

However, since time is changing and transitory, it cannot be co-eternal with changeless eternity.[47] Now the immortality of the angels is not transitory or temporal; it is not in the past, as if it no longer existed, nor in the future, as though it had still to come into existence; and yet their movements, which condition the passage of time, pass from the future into the past, and therefore they cannot be co-eternal with the Creator. For in the movement of the Creator there is no question of a past which no longer exists or a future which is yet to be.

Hence, if God has always been sovereign, he has always had a creation subject to his sovereignty, not begotten from him, but made by him out of nothing, and not co-eternal with him. He existed before his creation, although not in any time before it; he preceded it not by a transitory interval of time but in his abiding perpetuity.[48]

This is my answer to those who ask how the Creator was always Creator and always sovereign Lord if created beings did not always

47. cf. Bk XI, 6. 48. cf. *Conf.*, 11, 13–16.

exist to serve him: but, if I make this reply, I am afraid I shall readily incur the criticism that this is an affirmation of ignorance, not the communication of knowledge. And so I return to what our Creator wished us to know. What he has allowed wiser heads to know in this life, or has reserved for the knowledge of those who have reached their fulfilment in the other life, that I confess to be beyond my powers. But I thought I should discuss this question, without reaching any positive conclusion, so that my readers may see what questions they should refrain from tackling, as dangerous, and to discourage them from thinking themselves capable of understanding everything. Instead they should realize that they ought to submit to the wholesome instruction of the Apostle, when he says, 'In virtue of the authority given to me by God's grace I say this to all in your company: do not be wiser than you ought to be: but be wise in moderation, in proportion to the faith which God has allotted to each of you.'[49] For if a child's upbringing is adjusted to his strength, he will grow, and become capable of further progress, but if he is strained beyond his capacity he will fade away before he has the chance to grow up.

17. *The meaning of God's promise to man of eternal life, before eternity*

I confess my ignorance about the ages which passed before the creation of mankind, yet I am certain that no creature is co-eternal with the Creator. The Apostle also talks of eternal times not as in the future but, what is more surprising, in the past. He says, 'In the hope of eternal life, which God, who never lies, promised before eternal times; but at his own appointed times he manifested his word.'[50] You see how he speaks of 'eternal times' as being in the past, but not as co-eternal with God; seeing that, 'before eternal times', he not only existed, but also promised eternal life, which he 'manifested at his own appointed times', that is, at fitting times. What else is this than his Word? For this is life eternal. But in what sense did he 'promise' it, since it was clearly to men that he made the promise, and men did not exist before eternal times? It can only mean that what was to happen at his appropriate time was already fixed, by his predestination, in his eternity and in this co-eternal Word.

49. Rom. 12, 3. (But the Greek word translated as 'be wiser' means 'think more highly of yourself'.

50. Tit. 1, 2f. (But the Greek means 'ages ago' rather than 'before eternal times'.)

18. *God's immutable purpose defended against cyclical theories*

I am quite certain that no man existed before the creation of the first man; there were no repeated appearances of the same man, coming round again goodness knows how often in the course of goodness knows what cyclical revolutions;[51] nor had there there ever been any other being like him in nature. And the arguments of philosophers cannot drive me from this conviction. The most effective of those arguments, in their opinion, is that 'infinite things are beyond the comprehension of any knowledge.'[52] Therefore, they say, God himself has finite conceptions in his mind of all the finite things he creates. And yet, they say, his goodness cannot be thought of as ever inactive, for otherwise his activity would be temporary, with an eternity of rest before it; and it would seem as if he repented of his former everlasting leisure, and that was why he began to set to work.

Hence, they say, there must be this continual sequence in which the same events happen repeatedly, and things pass away only to reappear, while the world either persists, though in a state of continual change, and this world has always existed, and yet is created, though without a beginning in time; or else the world comes to be and passes away in these cyclical revolutions, coming to be as a repetition of what was before, and passing away only to be brought back again. Otherwise, if we ascribe to God's works a beginning in time, we obviously suggest the idea that in some way he disapproved of his own previous eternal inactivity, and condemned it as sloth and idleness, and therefore changed his ways!

Let us suppose, in contrast, that God is regarded as having been always engaged in the creation of temporal things, but as creating different things in succession, eventually arriving at the making of man, as a novel creation. Then he would appear to have effected all his creation not with knowledge (for our philosophers maintain that knowledge cannot embrace an infinity of things) but on the spur of the moment, as it were, just as it occurred to his mind, with haphazard capriciousness, as we might call it. But, they say, if we admit these revolutions which bring back the same temporal things and events time after time, we can either assume one continuing world, or suppose that the world itself provides its own dissolution and restoration in the course of these cycles. Then, in either case, we are no longer attributing to God the laziness of inactivity during all that

51. cf. ch. 14. 52. e.g. Arist., *Met.*, 14; cf. ch. 19.

length of eternity without beginning; and we acquit him of rashness in the creation of the unforeseen. For if the same things are not repeated, then there is an infinite range of possible variations, and that could not be embraced within God's knowledge or foreknowledge.

Such are the arguments with which the ungodly try to turn our simple piety from the straight road, and to make us join them in 'walking in circles'.[53] But faith ought to laugh at these theories, even if reason could not refute them. In fact we can do more than that. With the help of the Lord our God, reason, and cogent reason, breaks up those revolving circles which speculative theory has devised. This is the chief source of the error of those theorists; they would rather walk in a mistaken circle than keep to the straight and right path, because they measure the utterly unchangeable mind of God, which can embrace any kind of infinity and numbers all the innumerable possibilities without passing them in sequence before its thought – they measure this mind by the standard of their own human intellect, with its mutability and narrow finitude. The Apostle describes what happens to them; 'They measure themselves by their own standard, and fail to understand.'[54] When it occurs to their minds to do something new, they change their plans in so acting; for their minds are subject to change. Thus it is not really God whom they are thinking of, in this argument; they find that impossible, and instead they imagine themselves in God's place. And so they do not measure him by his own standard, but themselves by their own standard.

As for us, we are forbidden to suppose that God is in a different condition when he is at rest than when he is at work. In fact it is improper to speak of God's 'condition', which would imply that some novel element might come into his nature, something that was not there before. When we speak of 'condition', we suggest something influenced or 'conditioned' from outside, and that implies a liability to change. So we must not think of God's inactivity as involving sloth, or idleness, or laziness, any more than of his work as involving toil, effort, and industry. God knows how to be active while at rest, and at rest in his activity. He can apply to a new work not a new design but an eternal plan; and it is not because he repented of his previous inactivity that he began to do something he had not done before.

Even if he rested first and started work later (and I do not know how man can understand this) this 'first' and 'later' refer, without doubt, to things which first did not exist and later came into existence. But in God there was no new decision which altered or cancelled a previous

53. Ps. 12, 8; cf. ch. 14. 54. 2 Cor. 10, 12.

intention; instead, it was with one and the same eternal and unchanging design that he effected his creation. So long as things did not exist it was his decree that prevented their existence at first, and when they came into being it was his will which brought them into existence later. In this way perhaps he shows, in a wonderful manner, to those who can see such things, that he did not stand in need of his creation, but produced his creatures out of pure disinterested goodness, since he had continued in no less felicity without them from all eternity without beginning.

19. *The answer to the allegation that even God's knowledge cannot embrace an infinity of things*

Then there is the assertion that even God's knowledge cannot embrace things which are infinite. If men can say this, it only remains for them to plunge into the depths of blasphemy by daring to allege that God does not know all numbers. It is certainly true that numbers are infinite. If you think to make an end with any number, then that number can be increased by the addition of one. More than that, however large it is, however great the quantity it expresses, it can be doubled; in fact it can be multiplied by any number, according to the very principle and science of numbers.

Every number is defined by its own unique character, so that no number is equal to any other. They are all unequal to one another and different, and the individual numbers are finite but as a class they are infinite. Does that mean that God does not know all numbers, because of their infinity? Does God's knowledge extend as far as a certain sum, and end there? No one could be insane enough to say that.

Now those philosophers who revere the authority of Plato will not dare to despise numbers and say that they are irrelevant to God's knowledge. For Plato emphasizes that God constructed the world by the use of numbers,[55] while we have the authority of Scripture, where God is thus addressed, 'You have set in order all things by measure, number, and weight.'[56] And the prophet says of God, 'He produces the world according to number';[57] and the Saviour says in the Gospel, 'Your hairs are all numbered.'[58]

Never let us doubt, then, that every number is known to him 'whose understanding cannot be numbered'.[59] Although the infinite

55. cf. *Tim.*, 35f. 56. Wisd. 11, 20. 57. Is. 40, 26 (LXX).
58. Matt. 10, 30. 59. Ps. 147, 5.

series of numbers cannot be numbered, this infinity of numbers is not outside the comprehension of him 'whose understanding cannot be numbered'. And so, if what is comprehended in knowledge is bounded within the embrace of that knowledge, and thus is finite, it must follow that every infinity is, in a way we cannot express, made finite to God, because it cannot be beyond the embrace of his knowledge.

Therefore if the infinity of numbers cannot be infinite to the knowledge of God, in which it is embraced, who are we mere men to presume to set limits to his knowledge, by saying that if temporal things and events are not repeated in periodic cycles, God cannot foreknow all things which he makes, with a view to creating them, or know them all after he has created them? In fact his wisdom is multiple in its simplicity, and multiform in uniformity. It comprehends all incomprehensible things with such incomprehensible comprehension that if he wished always to create new things of every possible kind, each of them unlike its predecessor, none of them could be for him undesigned and unforeseen, nor would it be that he foresaw each just before it came into being; God's wisdom would contain each and all of them in his eternal prescience.

20. *'World without end'*

Whether in fact this is what God does, whether, that is, there is a continuously connected series of what are called 'ages of ages', running on one after the other in an ordered diversity, with only those souls which are set free from misery remaining in their immortality of felicity without end; or whether the expression 'ages of ages' is to be taken as meaning that the ages continue with undisturbed stability in the wisdom of God, as the efficient causes of the transient ages of temporal history – these are questions to which I would not venture a definite answer. It is quite possible that there is no difference in meaning between the plural and the singular, that 'age of age' and 'ages of ages' are interchangeable, as are 'heaven of heaven' and 'heavens of heavens'. For God gives the name 'heaven' to the firmament above which are the waters; and yet the psalm says, 'And let the waters, which are above the *heavens*, praise the name of the Lord.'[60]

Which of those two suggestions is correct, or whether the phrase 'ages of ages' can have some other meaning, besides these two, is a very deep question; and it is no hindrance to our present discusion to leave the matter unresolved for the present. We might be able to reach

60. Ps. 148, 4. The Hebrew word for 'heaven' is plural in form.

some conclusion; or a more thorough examination might only make us more cautious about venturing a rash judgement on so obscure a problem. In any case, our present concern is to combat the theory of cycles, which are alleged to effect the inevitable repetition of things and events at periodic intervals. And whatever be the true interpretation of 'ages of ages', it has no reference to those cycles. For if 'ages of ages' means not the repetition of the same ages, but an ordered series of connected ages running on one after the other, while the felicity of the souls set free remains permanent and assured, without any return to misery, or if the 'ages of ages' are the eternal ages which hold sway over the temporal ages, as over subjects; in either case these cyclical revolutions have no place. The eternal life of the saints[61] refutes them completely.

21. *The blasphemous notion of cyclical returns to misery of the souls in bliss*

It is intolerable for devout ears to hear the opinion expressed that after passing through this life with all its great calamities (if indeed it is to be called life, when it is really a death,[62] a death so grievous that for love of this death we shrink from the death which frees us from it), that after all these heavy and fearful ills have at last been expiated and ended by true religion and wisdom and we have arrived at the sight of God and reached our bliss in the contemplation of immaterial light through participation in his changeless immortality, which we long to attain, with burning desire – that we reach this bliss only to be compelled to abandon it, to be cast down from that eternity, that truth, that felicity, to be involved again in hellish mortality, in shameful stupidity, in detestable miseries, where God is lost, where truth is hated, where happiness is sought in unclean wickedness; and to hear that this is to happen again and again, as it has happened before, endlessly, at periodic intervals, as the ages pass in succession; and to hear that the reason for this is so that God may be able to know his own works by means of those finite cycles with their continual departure and return, bringing with them our false felicities and genuine miseries, which come in alternation, but are everlasting in this incessant round. For this theory assumes that God can neither rest from his creative activity, nor grasp within his knowledge an infinity of things.

Who could give a hearing to such a notion? Who could believe it,

61. cf. Matt. 25, 46. 62. cf. Bk XIII, 10.

or tolerate it? If it were true it would be more prudent to suppress the truth, nay, wiser to be in ignorance – I am trying to find words to express what I feel. For if our happiness in the other life will depend upon our forgetfulness of these facts, why should we aggravate our wretchedness in this life by knowing them? If, on the other hand, we shall of necessity know them there, let us at least be ignorant here, that we may have greater felicity here in the expectation of the Supreme Good than there in the attainment of it, seeing that here we look for the achievement of eternal life, while there that life is known as blessed but not eternal, since it is at some time to be lost.

If, however, they say that no one can reach that bliss unless he has learnt by instruction in this life about those cycles in which bliss and misery alternate, what becomes of their assertion that the more one loves God the easier is the approach to bliss, when their own teaching must make that love grow cold? For surely anyone's love will grow feebler and cooler towards one whom, as he supposes, he will have to leave, whose truth and wisdom he will have to reject, and that after he has come to the full knowledge of them, according to his capacity, in the perfection of felicity. No one can love a human friend with loyalty, if he knows that in the future he will be his enemy.[63] But God forbid that what the philosophers threaten should be true, that our genuine misery is never to have an end, but is only to be interrupted time and time again, throughout eternity, by intervals of false happiness. In fact, nothing could be falser or more deceptive than a happiness in which we shall be ignorant of our coming wretchedness, even while we are in that light of truth; or else we shall dread it even while we are at the summit of felicity. If in the other life we are going to be ignorant of the coming calamity, our misery here on earth is wiser, for in it we know of our coming happiness, while if the imminent disaster will not be hidden from us there, the soul passes these periods of wretchedness in a happiness greater than that of its periods of bliss. For after the periods of misery have passed, the soul will be lifted up to felicity; whereas after the passing of the times of felicity the turning circle will bring the soul to misery once more. And so our expectation in our unhappiness is happy, and the prospect before us in our felicity is miserable. In consequence, because here we suffer present ills, and there we dread them as imminent, it would be nearer the truth to say that we are likely to be wretched all the time than that we may sometimes enjoy felicity.

But piety cries out against this, and truth convicts it of falsehood. It

63. cf. Cic., *De Am.*, 6, 59.

is a true felicity which is truly promised us; we shall keep it always, in assured security, and no unhappiness can interrupt it. So let us keep to our straight way, which is Christ,[64] let us take him as our guide and saviour, and turn our minds from the absurd futility of this circular route of the impious,[65] and keep instead to the way of faith. Porphyry the Platonist refused to follow the opinion of his fellows of that sect in the matter of those cycles, those incessant and alternate comings and goings of souls. This was either because the absurdity of the very idea repelled him, or because he was impressed by the Christian dispensation, and (as I mentioned in my tenth book[66]) preferred to say that the soul is sent into the world to recognize evil for what it is, so that it may be cleansed and purified from it and come back to the Father, and experience no evil thereafter. If Porphyry so decided, how much more ought we to detest and shun this false teaching as the enemy of the Christian faith!

Now that we have done away with these cycles and consigned them to oblivion, there is nothing to compel us to suppose that the human race had no beginning, no start in time, because there is no reason to believe in those strange cycles which prevent the appearance of anything new, since everything has already existed in the past and will exist in the future and at certain intervals of time. For if a soul is set free, and will never return again to misery, just as it has never before been set free, then something has come into being which has never been before, and something of great importance, namely the eternal felicity of a soul, a felicity which will know no end.

Now if this happens in an immortal nature, something new, something not repeated and not to be repeated by any cyclic revolution – why is it argued that this cannot happen in mortal things? If they assert that bliss is no novelty to a soul, since the soul is returning to the bliss which before it always enjoyed, still the freedom is certainly a novelty, since the soul is set free from the misery which it never suffered before, and that misery itself is also a novelty, the production in the soul of something which had not existed before. If this novelty does not come about in the ordered course of God's providential government of events, but by mere chance, then what has happened to those measured and regulated cycles, in which there is no novelty, but the repetition of the same things which have been already? If, however, this novelty is not excluded from the providential ordering, then novelties are possible, things which have not happened before and yet are not at variance with the ordering of the world. This holds

64. cf. John 14, 6. 65. cf. ch. 14. 66. ch. 30.

true, whether the soul was consigned to the body by God or fell by its fault into this new condition.[67] And if the soul through folly could make a new wretchedness for itself, and the divine providence foresaw this so that God included this also in his ordering of events, and, in his foresight, set the soul free from that misery, then how can we have the temerity, in our human folly, to venture to deny that the divine power can create things which are new, not to itself, but to the world, things which God never made before, though to him they were never unforeseen?

Now suppose they admit that souls are set free from misery, never to return to wretchedness, but contend that this introduces no novelty in events, since souls have continually been liberated, are being liberated, and will be liberated. Then at least they concede that new souls are created for them to have new misery and to be newly set free. If they say that these are not new souls, but souls existing from of old, from all eternity, and that with those souls new men come into being, from whose bodies the souls, if they have lived wisely, are set free so as never to return to misery; if they say this, they must go on to say that the souls are infinite in number. For however great had been the number of souls, if it was a finite number it could never be enough for all those infinite ages of the past to supply souls for all the men who came into being, if the souls were always to be set free from that mortality, never to return to it. And then they will be unable to explain how there could be an infinite number of souls when they insist that things must be finite in number, if God is to have knowledge of them.

Therefore, seeing that those cycles of theirs have been hissed off the stage, those cycles by which the soul was supposed inevitably to return to the same misery as before, the only possibility left which is agreeable to true religion is to believe that it is not impossible for God to make something new, something he has not made before, and at the same time, because of his unimaginable foreknowledge, never to change his design. The question whether the number of the liberated souls who are never to return to their misery can be continually increased, we leave to those who engage in subtle argument about the limit which is to be set to the infinity of things!

For our part, we will end this philosophical disputation with a dilemma. If that number can be increased, what reason is there for denying that something can be created which has never been created before, seeing that the number of freed souls, which never existed

67. These two possibilities were debated by the Neoplatonists.

before, was not just created once for all, but will be continually created? On the other hand, if there must be a fixed number of freed souls, which never return to misery, a number which is never increased, then that number itself, whatever it may be, certainly did not exist before; and it cannot increase and reach its final sum without starting from a beginning; and that beginning did not exist before. And so to provide that beginning, a man was created, before whom no man ever existed.

22. *The creation of man*

I have done my best to elucidate this very difficult question about God's creation of new things without any innovation in his design, in view of his eternity. And now it is not hard to see that it was far better that he should have started, as he did, with one man, whom he created as the first man, and should have multiplied the human race from him, instead of starting with many. For while he created some living creatures of a solitary habit, who walk alone and love solitude, such as eagles, kites, lions, wolves, and the like, he made others gregarious, preferring to live in flocks and herds, such as doves, starlings, deer, fallow-deer, and so on. Yet neither of these classes did he produce by starting with individuals of the species; he commanded many to come into existence at once.

But he created man's nature as a kind of mean between angels and beasts, so that if he submitted to his Creator, as to his true sovereign Lord, and observed his instructions with dutiful obedience, he should pass over into the fellowship of the angels, attaining an immortality of endless felicity, without an intervening death;[68] but if he used his free will in arrogance and disobedience, and thus offended God, his Lord, he should live like the beasts, under sentence of death, should be the slave of his desires, and destined after death for eternal punishment. God created man as one individual; but that did not mean that he was to remain alone, bereft of human society. God's intention was that in this way the unity of human society and the bonds of human sympathy be more emphatically brought home to man, if men were bound together not merely by likeness in nature but also by the feeling of kinship.[69] And to this end, when he created the woman who was to be joined with the man he decided not to create her in the

68. cf. Bk XIII, 1; 3. In opposition to the Pelagians, who taught that death is natural to man, and not the result of sin.

69. cf. Bk XIV, 1.

same way as he created man himself. Instead he made her out of the man,[70] so that the whole human race should spread out from the one original man.

23. *God's foreknowledge of man's sin and of the salvation of the elect*

God was well aware that man would sin and so, becoming liable to death, would then produce a progeny destined to die. He knew also that mortals would reach such a pitch of boundless iniquity, that brute beasts, deprived of rational will, would live in greater security and peace among their own kind – although their teeming multitudes took their origin from the waters and the earth – than men, whose race was derived from a single ancestor, a fact which was intended to foster harmony among them. Yet not even lions or serpents have ever carried on among themselves the kind of warfare in which men engage.[71]

But God also foresaw that by his grace a community of godly men was to be called to adoption as his sons,[72] and these men, with their sins forgiven, were to be justified by the Holy Spirit and then to enter into fellowship with the holy angels in eternal peace, when the 'last enemy', death, had been destroyed.[73] And this company of the godly was to benefit from consideration of this truth, that God started the human race from one man to show to mankind how pleasing to him is unity in plurality.[74]

24. *Man's soul, created in God's image*

Thus God made man in his own image,[75] by creating for him a soul of such a kind that because of it he surpassed all living creatures, on earth, in the sea, and in the sky, in virtue of reason and intelligence; for no other creature had a mind like that. God fashioned man out of the dust of the earth[76] and gave him a soul of the kind I have described. This he did either by implanting in him, by breathing on him, a soul which he had already made, or rather by willing that the actual breath which he produced when he breathed on him should be

70. cf. Gen. 2, 22.

71. A commonplace of classical authors; cf. Hor., *Epod.*, 7, 11f; Plin., 7, 1, 5; Juvenal 15, 159ff; Sen., *De Clem.*, 1, 26; *Ep.*, 95, 31.

72. cf. Rom. 8, 15; Gal. 4, 5.

73. 1 Cor. 15, 26.

74. cf. Ps. 133, 1.

75. cf. Gen. 1, 26f.

76. cf. Gen. 2, 7.

the soul of the man. For to breathe is to produce a breath. He then took a bone from his side and made a wife[77] to help him to beget children.

This he did as God. For we must not imagine this operation in the physical terms of our experience, where we see artisans working up material from the earth into the shape of human limbs, with the ability of skilled craftsmanship. God's 'hand' is his power, and God achieves even visible results by invisible means. But some people use the standards of their own daily experience to measure the power and wisdom of God, by which he has the knowledge and the ability to make seeds even without seeds. And so they regard the account of man's creation as fable, not fact; and because the first created works are beyond their experience, they adopt a sceptical attitude. They do not realize that the facts of human conception and parturition, which fall within their experience, could seem even more incredible if told to those who were unacquainted with them. And yet some attribute even these phenomena to the working of natural physical causation and not to the operation of the divine purpose.

25. *Angels are not creators*

We have nothing to do, in this work, with those who hold that the divine mind does not create, and has no interest in this world.[78] But there are others who follow their master Plato in asserting that all mortal creatures (among whom man holds the chief place, close to the gods themselves) were not made by the supreme God who fashioned the world, but by other gods, by lesser gods whom he created, though they did this with his permission or at his command.[79] Now if these philosophers could rid themselves of the superstition which leads them to look for reasons to justify their offering of worship and sacrifice to their reputed creators, they would soon also free themselves from this misguided belief.

For it is out of the question to hold and assert that any creature, however small and mortal, has any other creator than God, even before anything can be known about him. Certainly the angels (the Platonists prefer to call them gods) have their part to play, at God's command, or by God's permission, in relation to the creatures which are born in the world. But we do not call them creators of living beings any more than we call farmers the creators of crops and trees.

77. Gen., 2, 21f. 78. The Epicurean doctrine. 79. cf. Plat., *Tim.*, 41C.

26. God the sole creator of every nature and form

Forms are of two kinds. There is one sort of form given *externally* to material substances; potters, for instance, woodworkers, and craftsmen of that kind, fashion and paint forms resembling the bodies of living creatures in the pursuit of their art. There is another kind of form which operates *internally*; this form supplies the efficient causes, and it derives from a secret and hidden decision of a living and intelligent nature, which, being itself uncreated, is responsible for the creation not only of the natural, physical forms, but also of the souls of living creatures. The first kind of form may be ascribed to the artist or craftsman concerned; the second belongs to God alone, who alone is artist, maker and creator. He needed no material from the world, nor help from angels, when he made the world itself, and created the angels.

By his divine power, by what we may call his 'effective' power, which cannot be made, but can only make, the round sky and the round sun received that form, when the world was made; and from the same 'effective' power of God, which cannot be made but can only make, came the roundness of the eye and the apple, and the other natural shapes which we observe as given to all things in nature, not externally, but by the power of the Creator working within, the power of the Creator who said, 'I fill the sky and the earth',[80] and whose 'Wisdom reaches from one end to the other in its strength and orders all things with grace.'[81]

Hence I do not know what kind of service the angels, who were made first, afforded to the Creator in the rest of his creation. I will not take the risk of ascribing to them more than may be in their power, and it would be wrong to detract from what they have the power to do. But I attribute the creation and establishment of all natures, that which makes them exist as natures at all, to God. And I do this with the approval of the angels themselves, for they know, and thankfully acknowledge, that it is to that same God that they owe their existence.

We do not call farmers 'creators' of crops, since we are told, 'The planter does not matter, nor does the waterer. It is God who matters, for it is he who makes things grow.'[82] We do not even ascribe creative power to the earth, although it is clearly the fruitful mother of growing things, promoting their growth as they burst out into shoots, and holding them safely by their roots; for we are also told, 'God gives

80. Jer. 23, 24. 81. Wisd. 8, 1. 82. 1 Cor. 3, 7.

to the seed a body of his choosing, its own body to each seed.'[83] We must not attribute to a woman the creation of her child, but instead to him who said to his servant, 'I knew you, before I formed you in the womb.'[84] The mother's consciousness can induce some special characteristics in the unborn child, by being in some particular state; it was on this principle that Jacob ensured the birth of parti-coloured sheep by the device of parti-coloured rods.[85] But even so, the mother has not made the nature that is produced, any more than she has made herself.

And so, whatever the physical or seminal causes that play their part in the production of living things, by the activities of angels or of men, or by the intercourse of male and female in animals or human beings, whatever effect the longings or emotions in the mother's consciousness may have on the child in her womb, in its susceptible state, leaving some traces in its features or complexion, it remains true that only God most high can create the actual natures which are thus affected in different ways, each in its own kind. His hidden power, penetrating all things by its presence, yet free from contamination, gives existence to whatever in any way exists, in so far as it exists at all. For the absence of God's creative activity would not merely mean that a thing would be different in some particular way; it simply could not exist.

In respect of the form which artists impose upon material things from outside, we speak of Romulus as the founder of Rome, and Alexander of Alexandria, ascribing the foundation of those cities not to the architects and builders, but to the kings at whose will and by whose design and command they were built. How much more are we bound to call God the founder of natures; for he does not create from material which he himself did not make, nor does he employ any workmen, except those of his own creation. And if he were to withdraw what we may call his 'constructive power' from existing things, they would cease to exist, just as they did not exist before they were made. When I say 'before', I mean in eternity, not in time. For the creator of time is none other than he who made the things whose change and movement is the condition of time's course.[86]

83. 1 Cor. 15, 38.
84. Jer. 1, 5.
85. cf. Gen. 30, 37f.
86. cf. Bk XI, 6; XII, 16.

27. *The Platonic theory that the angels were created, but were creators of men's bodies*

Plato, to be sure, held that the lesser gods, created by the supreme God, are the makers of the other living beings; but the immortal part they took from God himself, while they themselves fashioned the mortal frame.[87] Thus he refused to make them the creators of our souls; but they made our bodies, on his theory. Porphyry holds that the soul must escape from any kind of material body to achieve purification,[88] and agrees with Plato and other Platonists that those who have lived undisciplined and dishonourable lives return to mortal bodies as a punishment – though Porphyry limits this return to the bodies of men, while Plato includes those of animals.[89] Hence it follows that these thinkers are asserting that those gods of theirs, whom they want us to worship as our parents and creators, are simply the forgers of our fetters, the builders of our prisons; they are not our makers but our jailers, who lock us up in miserable prisons and lead us with heavy chains. Therefore the Platonists should either cease to threaten us with punishment for our souls in the shape of these bodies of ours, or else leave off proclaiming that we should worship their gods, while urging us by all possible means to escape from our involvement in their handiwork.

In fact, both of these positions are entirely false; for it is not true that souls are returned to this earthly life for punishment; and the one and only Creator of all living things in heaven and earth is the Creator by whom heaven and earth were made. In fact, if the only cause for our living in this body is that we should pay our punishment, how is it that Plato himself says that the world could only have reached the highest beauty and worth by being filled with living beings of all kinds, that is, with immortal and mortal beings?[90]

If, then, our creation, although we were made mortal, is the gift of God, how can it be a punishment to return to bodies which are God's blessings? And Plato repeatedly insists that God's eternal understanding contains the form of the whole universe and also the forms of all living creatures.[91] Surely, then, he must be the Creator of them all? Are we to imagine that he would have refused to be the artificer of some of them, when the art that could produce them was in his mind, that mind which is beyond our telling and whose praise is more than our words can express?

87. cf. ch. 25. 88. cf. Bk x, 29; xxii, 12; xxii, 26–8.
89. cf. Bk x, 30; xiii, 19. 90. cf. *Tim.*, 30D; 92C.
91. cf. *Tim.*, 30B–D; *Rp.*, 597 B; C.

28. *In the first man is the beginning of all mankind, and of the two cities*

True religion therefore rightly acknowledges and proclaims that the Creator of the universe is also the Creator of all living creatures whatsoever, the Creator, that is, of both souls and bodies. Among those creatures of earth man is pre-eminent, being made in the likeness of God. And, for the reason I have mentioned (though it may be that there are other and weightier reasons that are hidden from us) man was created as one individual; but he was not left alone. For the human race is, more than any other species, at once social by nature and quarrelsome by perversion. And the most salutory warning against this perversion or disharmony is given by the facts of human nature. We are warned to guard against the emergence of this fault, or to remedy it when once it has appeared, by remembering that first parent of ours, who was created by God as one individual with this intention: that from that one individual a multitude might be propagated, and that this fact should teach mankind to preserve a harmonious unity in plurality. Furthermore, the fact that a woman was made for the first man from his own side shows us clearly how affectionate should be the union of man and wife.[92]

These first works of God are, of course, unparalleled just because they are the first. Those who refuse to believe in them ought to refuse credence to any extraordinary phenomena. But in fact these events would not be classed as extraordinary, if they had occurred in the normal course of nature. For no event is to no purpose under the all-embracing government of God's providence, even if the reason for it is hidden from us. One of the sacred psalms contains these words, 'Come and see the works of the Lord, the wonders he has placed on the earth.'[93] I shall discuss in another place,[94] God helping me, the reason for woman's creation from the side of her husband, and what was prefigured by this 'prodigy', if we should so call it.

But now I must bring this book to its close, with this thought: that in this first-created man we find something like the beginning, in the human race, of the two cities; their beginnings, that is, in the foreknowledge of God, though not in observable fact. For from that man were to come all men, some of them to join the company of the evil angels in their punishment, others to be admitted to the company of the good angels in their reward. This was God's decision; a just decree,

92. cf. Gen. 2, 22ff; Matt. 19, 5; Eph. 4, 28; 31; cf. ch. 22; 23.
93. Ps. 46, 8 94. cf. Bk XXII, 17.

however inscrutable to us. For Scripture says, 'All the Lord's ways are mercy and truth',[95] and his grace cannot be unjust; nor can his justice be unkind.

95. Ps. 25, 10.

BOOK XIII

1. *The Fall of Man and his consequent mortality*

WE have disposed of some very difficult questions about the beginning of the world and the start of the human race. Next on the list of subjects to be treated is the fall of the first man, or rather of the first human beings, and the origin and propagation of human mortality. For God did not create men in the same condition as the angels, completely incapable of death, even if they sinned. The condition of human beings was such that if they continued in perfect obedience they would be granted the immortality of the angels and an eternity of bliss, without the interposition of death, whereas if disobedient they would be justly condemned to the punishment of death. I have already made this point in the previous book.[1]

2. *The death of the soul and the death of the body*

It is clear to me that I must explain more carefully the kind of death I am talking about. For though the human soul is rightly described as immortal, it has nevertheless a kind of death of its own. It is said to be immortal for this reason, that it never entirely ceases to live and to feel, even if only in the slightest degree. The body, on the other hand, is mortal in that it can be completely bereft of life, and by itself it has no life of any sort. Thus the death of the soul results when God abandons it, the death of the body when the soul departs. Therefore the death of the whole man, of both these elements, comes when the soul, abandoned by God, leaves the body. For then the soul no longer derives life from God, nor does the body receive life from the soul. This death of the whole man is followed by what is called, on the authority of the divine oracles, 'the second death'.[2] And this is what the Saviour meant when he said, 'Fear him, who has power to destroy both body and soul in Gehenna.'[3]

Now since this cannot happen until soul and body have been so combined that they cannot be sundered or separated, it may seem strange that the body is said to be killed by a death in which it is not

1. cf. Bk XII, 22. 2. cf. Rev. 2, 11; 20, 6; 20, 14; 21, 8. 3. Matt. 10, 28.

abandoned by the soul, but remains possessed of soul and feeling, and endures torment in this condition. For in that final and everlasting punishment (about which we shall have to speak in greater detail in the appropriate place)[4] we correctly talk of the 'death of the soul', because it no longer derives life from God. But how can we talk in this case of the death of the body, since it is deriving life from the soul? For otherwise it cannot feel the bodily torments which are to follow the resurrection. Is it because life of any kind is a good thing, while pain is an evil, and for that reason the body cannot be said to be alive, when the purpose of the soul is not the body's life, but the body's pain?

The soul therefore derives life from God, when its life is good – for its life cannot be good except when God is active in it to produce what is good – while the body derives life from the soul when the soul is alive in the body, whether the soul derives its life from God or not. For the life of the bodies of the ungodly is not the life of their souls but of their bodies, a life which souls can confer even when those souls are dead, that is, when God abandons them; for their own life, in virtue of which they are immortal, still persists, in however low a degree.

But in that last condemnation, although a man does not cease to feel, his feeling is not that of pleasure and delight, nor that of health and tranquillity. What he feels is the anguish of punishment, and so his condition is rightly called death rather than life. The second death is so called because it follows the first, in which there is a separation of natures which cohere together, either God and the soul, or the soul and the body. It can therefore be said of the first death that it is good for the good, bad for the bad; but the second death does not happen to any of the good, and without doubt it is not good for anyone.

3. *Death has passed to all mankind through the sin of the first human beings. Is it the punishment of sin in the case of the saints?*

A question now arises which must not be suppressed. Is death, which separates soul and body, really a good thing for the good? If so, how can it be maintained that death is itself the penalty of sin? For the first human beings would certainly not have suffered it, if they had not sinned. Now if death could only have happened to the bad, how could it be good for the good? In fact, if it could only have happened to the bad, so far from being good for the good, it ought not to have hap-

4. cf. Bk XIX, 28.

pened to them at all. Why should there have been any punishment where there were no sins to be punished?

We must therefore admit that the first human beings were created under this condition, that they would not have experienced any kind of death, if they had not sinned; and yet those first sinners were sentenced to death, with the provision that whatever sprang from their stock should incur the same punishment. For whatever was born from them could not have been different from what they themselves had been. In fact, because of the magnitude of that offence, the condemnation changed human nature for the worse; so that what first happened as a matter of punishment in the case of the first human beings, continued in their posterity as something natural and congenital.

This is because the descent of man from man is not like the derivation of man from the dust. Dust was the raw material for the making of man; but in the begetting of a human being man is a parent. Hence, although flesh was made out of earth, flesh is not the same as earth, whereas the human parent is the same kind of thing as the human offspring. Therefore the whole human race was in the first man, and it was to pass from him through the woman into his progeny, when the married pair had received the divine sentence of condemnation. And it was not man as first made, but what man became after his sin and punishment, that was thus begotten, as far as concerns the origin of sin and death.

For the first man was not reduced by his sin, or by its punishment, to the state of infantile torpor and weakness of mind and body which we observe in little children. Such was to be the early state of children, like the early state of young animals, according to the decision of God, who had cast down their parents to a life and death like that of animals. As Scripture says, 'Man was in a place of honour, but did not realize it: he has been brought to the level of the animals without understanding and been made like them.'[5] Though in fact we observe that infants are weaker than the most vulnerable of the young of other animals in the control of their limbs, and in their instincts of appetition and defence; this seems designed to enhance man's superiority over other living things, on the analogy of an arrow whose impetus increases in proportion to the backward extension of the bow.

Thus the result of the first man's lawless presumption and his just condemnation was not a relapse – or a repulse – into the rudimentary

5. Ps. 49, 12; 20.

condition of infancy. But human nature in him was vitiated and altered, so that he experienced the rebellion and disobedience of desire in his body, and was bound by the necessity of dying; and he produced offspring in the same condition to which his fault and its punishment had reduced him, that is, liable to sin and death. But if infants are released from the bonds of this sin through the grace of Christ the Mediator, they can only suffer the death which separates soul from body; they do not pass on to that second death of unending punishment, since they have been freed from the entanglement of sin.

4. *Why absolution from sin does not entail deliverance from death, sin's punishment*

If anyone is troubled by the question why those whose guilt is removed through grace should suffer the death which is the penalty of sin, this problem has been treated, and its solution given, in another book of mine, *On the Baptism of Infants*.[6] There it is suggested that the experience of the separation of soul from body remains, although its connection with guilt is removed, because if the immortality of the body followed immediately upon the sacrament of regeneration, faith itself would be weakened, since faith is only faith when what is not yet seen in reality is awaited in hope.[7]

Futhermore, it was by the strength of faith and in the conflict of faith that even the fear of death admitted of being conquered, at any rate in the earlier ages; and this was seen pre-eminently in the holy martyrs. This conflict would have had no victory, no glory, since there could have been no conflict at all, if after the 'washing of regeneration'[8] the saints were straightway exempt from bodily death. If this were so, surely everyone would rush to the grace of Christ, with the children to be baptized, just to avoid being released from the body. And faith would not be tested by the fact that its reward was unseen; indeed, it would not be faith any longer, since the reward of the act of faith would be demanded and taken immediately.

But as it is, the punishment of sin has been turned by the great and wonderful grace of our Saviour to a good use, to the promotion of righteousness. It was then said to man, 'You will die if you sin.' Now it is said to the martyr, 'Die, rather than sin.' It was then said, 'If you

6. Published in 412. The full title is *De Peccatorum Meritis et Remissione et de Baptismo Parvulorum*.

7. cf. *De Pecc. Mer. et Rem.*, 3, 31; 34; cf. Rom. 8, 24; Heb. 11, 1.

8. Tit. 3, 5.

break the commandment you will certainly die.' Now it is said, 'If you shrink from death, you will break the commandment.' What was then an object of fear, to prevent man from sinning, is now something to be chosen, to avoid sinning.

So by the ineffable mercy of God even the penalty of man's offence is turned into an instrument of virtue, and the punishment of the sinner becomes the merit of the righteous. Then death was purchased by sinning; now righteousness is fulfilled by dying. This is true of the holy martyrs, who are presented by their persecutors with this choice; either to abandon the faith, or to suffer death. The righteous prefer to endure for their belief what the first sinners suffered for their unbelief. For if those sinners had not sinned, they would not have died; the martyrs would sin, if they did not die. And so the former died because they sinned; the latter do not sin, because they die. The effect of the fault was to bring the offenders under punishment; the effect of their punishment is now to prevent the incurring of guilt. It is not that death has turned into a good thing, when it was formerly an evil. What has happened is that God has granted to faith so great a gift of grace that death, which all agree to be the contrary of life, has become the means by which men pass into life.

5. *The wicked turn a good, the law, to bad account: the good turn death, an evil, to good*

When the Apostle wanted to show sin's power to do harm when grace was not there to help, he did not shrink from saying that the law, which forbids sin, is itself the strength of sin. 'The sting of death is sin; and the strength of sin is the law.'[9] This is very true; for the prohibition increases the desire to commit the unlawful act, when the love of righteousness is not strong enough to overcome the sinful desire by the delight it affords. And genuine righteousness is never so beloved, never gives such delight, without the help of God's grace. But the Apostle is concerned that the law should not be considered an evil because it is called 'the strength of sin'; and so he says, in another place, when dealing with the same problem,

> And so the law is holy, and the commandment is holy, just and good. Does this mean that something which is good has turned into death for me? Perish the thought! What has happened is that sin was made to show its true character: it used a good thing to effect my death, so that sin should

9. 1 Cor. 15, 56.

appear for what it is, and sinner or sin should go beyond all bounds, because of the commandment.[10]

'Beyond all bounds', because violation of the law is added, when the law itself is despised by the increased lust for sinning.

Why have we thought this worth mentioning? Because, just as the law is not an evil thing when it increases the evil desire of the sinner, so death is not itself a good thing when it enhances the glory of the sufferer; when the law is abandoned for wickedness and thus produces law-breakers, or when death is accepted for truth's sake and so produces martyrs. It follows that the law is good, because it is the prohibition of sin, while death is evil, because it is the reward of sin.[11] But as unrighteousness puts all things, good and evil alike, to a bad use, so righteousness puts all things, evil as well as good, to good employment. Thus it is that the evil make bad use of the law, though it is a good thing, and the good die a good death, although death itself is an evil.

6. *Death, the severing of soul from body, is, in general, an evil*

For this reason, the death of the body, the separation of the soul from the body, is not good for anyone, as it is experienced by those who are, as we say, dying. This violent sundering of the two elements, which are conjoined and interwoven in a living being, is bound to be a harsh and unnatural experience as long as it lasts, until the departure of all feeling, which depended on this interconnection of soul and body. All this unpleasantness is sometimes cut short by one sudden physical blow, or by the sudden snatching away of the soul, where the speed of the stroke outruns sensation and does not allow death to be felt. But whatever it is which in dying men takes away sensation with such a distressing sensation, it increases the merit of patience if it is endured with devout faith, though it does not cancel the term 'punishment'. And so, although death is perpetuated by propagation from the first man, and is without doubt the penalty of all who are born, yet it becomes the glory of those who are reborn, if it is the price paid for piety and righteousness; and death, the recompense of sin, sometimes ensures that there is no sin to be recompensed.

10. Rom 7, 12f. 11. cf. Rom. 6, 23.

7. *Some who are not reborn in baptism undergo death for the confession of Christ*

For whenever men die for confessing Christ, even though they have not yet been reborn in baptism, their death is of the same value for the remission of their sins as if they had been washed in the sacred font of baptism. It is true that Christ said, 'No one will enter into the kingdom of heaven if he has not been reborn from water and the spirit;'[12] but in another statement he made an exception in favour of those to whom I am referring. For he said, with the same generality, 'Anyone who acknowledges me before men, I shall acknowledge before my Father in heaven';[13] and in another passage, 'Anyone who loses his life for me will find it.'[14]

Hence the text, 'Precious in the Lord's sight is the death of his saints.'[15] For what is more precious than a death which ensures that all offences are forgiven and the store of merits abundantly increased? Those who have been baptized when they could not postpone their death and have departed from this life with all their sins wiped out, have won less merit than those who could have deferred their death but did not, because they chose to end their life by confessing Christ, rather than by denying him to arrive at his baptism. Even if they had denied him, this also would have been forgiven in that sacramental washing, because that denial was prompted by the fear of death. For in that sacrament forgiveness was given even to the appalling crime of those who killed Christ. But how could they have loved Christ so dearly as to be unable to deny him in the ultimate crisis, when offered the hope of official pardon? How, except by the abundant grace of the Spirit which 'inspires where he wills'?[16]

Therefore the death of the saints is precious, the saints for whom the death of Christ was the price already paid in advance. And such grace came from Christ's death that to gain him they did not hesitate to pay the price of their own death, the death which showed that what had been imposed as the penalty for sin had been turned to such good use that it brought to birth a richer harvest of righteousness. Death therefore ought not to be regarded as a good thing because it has been turned to such great advantage. For this happened not in virtue of any quality of its own, but by the help of God; so that death, which was put forward as a fearful warning against sin, is now set before men as something to be accepted when that acceptance means the avoidance

12. John 3, 5. 13. Matt. 10, 32. 14. Matt., 16, 25.
15. Ps. 116, 15. 16. John 3, 8.

of sin and the cancellation of sins committed, and the award of the palm of victory as the just reward of righteousness.

8. *The acceptance of the first death in the cause of truth abolishes the second death*

Careful consideration shows that the very act of dying faithfully and laudably for the truth's sake is a precaution against death. A partial death is certainly accepted, but that is so that total death may not come, so that the second death may not supervene, that death which has no end. For the separation of soul from body is accepted, so that the soul may not be separated from God and then severed from the body, and thus when the first death of the whole man was past, the second death, the eternal death, should follow.

For this reason, as I have said, death as it is experienced by the dying, death as the cause of that condition, is not good in itself for anyone, but it is endured (and this is praiseworthy) for the attainment and possession of a good. But when men are in the state of death, when they are called 'the dead', then death is evil for the evil, but good for the good. This may be said without absurdity. For the souls of the faithful, when separated from the body, are at rest, while the souls of the wicked are paying their penalty, until the bodies of the righteous come to life again for eternal life, and the bodies of the wicked rise to be consigned to the eternal, the second, death.

9. *Problems about the meaning of 'death', 'dying', 'dead'*

There is a problem about the period when the souls separated from the body exist either in a state of good or in a state of evil. Are we to say that this period is *after* death or *in* death? If it is after death, then it is not the actual death, which is by now past and gone, which is good or bad, but the present life of the soul after death. Death was evil for them, certainly at the time when it was present, that is, when they were experiencing it in the act of dying, since it entailed a heavy burden of suffering – though the good make good use of that evil. But now that death is past, how can it be good or evil, since it no longer exists?

Again, a more careful consideration will make it clear that the heavy burden of suffering we spoke of as experienced by the dying, is not in fact death. For as long as men feel, they are obviously still alive; and if so, they should be said to be 'before death', not 'in death'. For death, when it comes, takes away all feeling from the body, including the feeling of anguish at death's approach. Thus it is difficult to explain how we can describe people as dying, when they are not yet dead, but are struggling in the last mortal pangs at the imminence of death; and yet they are rightly called 'dying men', because when the impending death has arrived they are said to be dead, not dying.

Therefore a man who is dying must be living; for when he is in the last extremity, 'giving up the ghost (that is, the soul)' as we say, he is evidently still alive, because his soul has not yet left him. So he is at once dying and living; but he is approaching death and leaving life. He is still in life because the soul is still in his body; he is not yet in death, because the soul has not yet departed. But when the soul has departed, he will not be *in* death, but after it. Then can anyone say precisely when one is *in* death? No dying man can be, assuming that no one can be dying and living at the same time. As long as the soul is in the body we clearly cannot say a man is not living. Or, if a person should be said to be dying, when in his body the process is going on which ends in death, and if no one can be simultaneously living and dying – then I do not know when anyone is living.

10. *The life of mortals: should it be called death?*

In fact, from the moment a man begins to exist in this body which is destined to die, he is involved all the time in a process whose end is death. For this is the end to which the life of continual change is all the time directed, if indeed we can give the name of life to this passage towards death. There is no one, it goes without saying, who is not nearer to death this year than he was last year, nearer tomorrow than today, today than yesterday, who will not by and by be nearer than he is at the moment, or is not nearer at the present time than he was a little while ago. Any space of time that we live through leaves us with so much less time to live, and the remainder decreases with every passing day; so that the whole of our lifetime is nothing but a race towards death, in which no one is allowed the slightest pause or any slackening of the pace. All are driven on at the same speed, and hurried along the same road to the same goal. The man whose life was short passed his days as swiftly as the longer-lived; moments of equal length rushed by for both of them at equal speed, though one was farther than the other from the goal to which both were hastening at the same rate. There is a difference between a longer journey and a slower pace of walking. If a man passes through a more extended period of time on this road to death, his progress is no slower; he merely has a longer journey.

Now if each man begins to die, that is to be 'in death', from the moment when death – that is, the taking away of life – begins to happen in him (and we may assume this, since when this taking away is completed he will not be in death, but after death) then everyone is in death from the moment that he begins his bodily existence. For what else is going on, every day, every hour, every minute, but this process of death? And when that comes to fulfilment, and death has completed its work, then the period after death follows the period in death, when life was being taken away. And so, if one cannot be in death and in life at the same time, man can never be in life, from the moment that he begins to exist in a body which is dying rather than living. Or is he really in life and in death at the same time? In life, that is, because he is alive until life is wholly taken away; but in death, because he is dying all the time that life is being taken from him. For if he is not in life, what is it that is being taken away, until the process of diminution is completed? While if he is not in death, what is this taking away of life? When all the life has been taken from the body, we use the phrase 'after death',which would be meaningless, were it not that death was the time when life was being taken away. For if a man is not 'in death' but 'after death' when life has been taken away, when will he be 'in death', if not while life is being diminished?

11. *Can one be living and dead at the same time?*

Now it may seem absurd to say that a man is in death before he arrives at death; for how can he be approaching death as he passes through the periods of his life, if he is already there? In particular, it seems extremely odd to say that a man is living and dying simultaneously, when he cannot be waking and sleeping at one and the same time. If so, we must try to discover when a man is dying. Now before death comes, he is not dying, but living; and when death has come, he is dead, not dying. Thus there is a period which is still before death, another which is already after death.

So when is he 'in death'? For it is then that he is dying; and so there are three situations: 'before death', 'in death', and 'after death', and three corresponding adjectives: 'living', 'dying', and 'dead'. This makes it very hard to define when he is dying, that is 'in death'; a state in which he is neither living (which is the state *before* death) or dead (which is *after* death), but dying, or 'in death'. It is evident that as long as the soul is in the body, especially if sensibility remains, a man is alive, his constituent parts being soul and body. Consequently he must be described as being still 'before death', not 'in death'. But when the soul has departed and has withdrawn all bodily sensation, a man is said to be 'after death', and dead.

Thus between these two situations the period in which a man is dying or 'in death' disappears. For if he is still alive, he is 'before death'; if he has stopped living, he is by now 'after death'. Therefore he is never detected in the situation of dying, or 'in death'. The same thing happens in the passage of time; we try to find the present moment, but without success, because the future changes into the past without interval.

We must evidently then beware of using this argument to assert that there is no such thing as the death of the body. For (we might say) if there is such a thing, *when* is it? It cannot be in anyone; nor can anyone be in it. If a man is alive, there is as yet no death, because this is the period before death, not in death. Whereas if life has ceased, then there is no death any more, because it is now after death, not in death. On the other hand, if there is no such thing as death, what is meant by 'before death' and 'after death'? Before or after what? For these phrases also are meaningless if there is no such thing as death. Would that we had ensured, by living rightly in paradise, that there really was no death! But as it is, death is a reality; and so troublesome a reality that it cannot be explained by any verbal formula, nor got rid of by any rational argument.

We had better conform to normal usage, as indeed we are bound to do, and use the phrase 'before death' to mean before death occurs, as in the scriptural text: 'Do not praise any man before his death.'[17] And after death has happened we should say, 'This or that occurred after the death of so and so.' And when we are using the present participle we must do the best we can with such statements as, 'He made his will when dying' and, 'When dying he made this and that bequest to so and so', although he could have done no such thing unless he had been living – and in fact it was before death, not 'in death' that he did it.

And we may use the same expressions as we find in holy Scripture. For the Bible has no hesitation about referring to the dead as being 'in death', not 'after death'. Hence we get the statement, 'Because there is no one who remembers you in death.'[18] For until they come to life

17. Ecclus. 11, 28; cf. Hdt., 1, 32, 7 (Solon to Croesus); the final line of Soph., *Oed. Tyr.*; Juv. 10, 274f. 18. Ps. 6, 5.

again, they are correctly spoken of as 'in death', just as a person is said to be 'in sleep' until he wakes. And yet, although we say that those who 'in a deep sleep' are sleeping, we cannot say, by analogy, that those who are dead are dying. For those who are separated from their bodies are not still dying. (I am referring, it will be understood, to that death of the body, which is our present subject.)

But this is what I said could not be explained by any verbal formula. How can the dying be spoken of as living, or those who are already dead be said, after death, to be still 'in death'? For how can they be 'after death' if they are still 'in death'; especially as we do not say that they are dying, as we say that those in sleep are 'sleeping' and those in a faint are 'fainting', those in sorrow are certainly 'sorrowing', and those in life are 'living'? And yet the dead, until they rise again, are said to be 'in death', although they cannot be called 'the dying'.

Hence I find it significant and appropriate – though it happened not by human design, but perhaps by divine decision – that the grammarians have not been able to decline (or conjugate) the Latin verb *moritur* ('he dies') by the same rule as other verbs of this form. For from *oritur* ('he arises') comes the past tense *ortus est* ('he has arisen'), and all similar verbs are declined in the perfect with the perfect participle. But if we ask the perfect of *moritur*, the invariable answer is *mortuus est* ('he has died' *or* 'he is dead'), with the doubling of the *u*. Now *mortuus* is a word of the same form as *fatuus* ('silly'), *arduus* ('steep'), *conspicuus* ('visible') and others, with no reference to past time; they are adjectives, and as such are declined without any temporal implications. The adjective *mortuus*, however, is used instead of a perfect participle as if to give a conjugation for an impossible tense. And so, most appropriately, the verb cannot be declined in speech, just as the reality which it signifies cannot be declined (that is, avoided) by any action.

Nevertheless with the help of the grace of our Redeemer we may be enabled to decline (or avoid)[19] that second death. For that death, which means not the separation of soul from body but the union of both for eternal punishment, is the more grievous death; it is the worst of all evils. There, by contrast, men will not be in the situations of 'before death' and 'after death', but always 'in death', and for this reason they will never be living, never dead, but dying for all eternity.

In fact, man will never be 'in death' in a more horrible sense than in that state where death itself will be deathless.

19. St Augustine puns on two meanings of *declinare*, 'to decline (inflect)' and 'to refuse', or 'avoid'.

12. *The meaning of the death with which God threatened the first human beings*

Now it may be asked what sort of death God threatened to the first human beings if they broke the commandment he had given and did not maintain obedience. Was it the death of the soul? Or of the body? Or of the whole person? Or was it what is called the second death? Our reply to the question is, 'All of these deaths.' For the first death consists of two; total death consists of all of them. Just as the whole earth consists of many lands, and the whole Church of many churches, so total death consists of all the deaths.

This is because the first death consists of two, the death of the soul and the death of the body; so that the first death is the death of the whole person, when the soul is without God and without a body, and undergoes punishment for a time. The second death, on the other hand, is when the soul is without God, but undergoes punishment with the body. Thus, when God spoke about the forbidden food to the man whom he had placed in the garden, he said, 'On whatever day you eat of it, you will surely die';[20] and the threat embraced not only the first part of the first death, when the soul is bereft of God, nor only the second part, in which the body is bereft of the soul; it comprised every kind of death, down to the last or second death, which has no other death to follow it.

13. *The first punishment of the first offence*

For after their disobedience to God's instructions, the first human beings were deprived of God's favour; and immediately they were embarrassed by the nakedness of their bodies. They even used fig leaves, which were perhaps the first things they could lay hands on in their confusion, to cover their *pudenda*, the 'organs of shame'.[21] These organs were the same as they were before, but previously there was no shame attaching to them. Thus they felt a novel disturbance in their disobedient flesh, as a punishment which answered to their own disobedience.

The soul, in fact, rejoiced in its own freedom to act perversely and disdained to be God's servant; and so it was deprived of the obedient service which its body had at first rendered. At its own pleasure the soul deserted its superior and master; and so it no longer retained its inferior and servant obedient to its will. It did not keep its own flesh

20. Gen. 2, 17. 21. Gen. 3, 7ff.

subject to it in all respects, as it could have kept it for ever if it had itself continued in subjection to God. This then was the time when the flesh began to 'lust in opposition to the spirit',[22] which is the conflict that attends us from our birth. We bring with us, at our birth, the beginning of our death, and with the vitiation of our nature our body is the scene of death's assault, or rather of his victory, as the result of that first disobedience.

14. *Man as he was created, and man's condition after his Fall*

God created man aright, for God is the author of natures, though he is certainly not responsible for their defects. But man was willingly perverted and justly condemned, and so begot perverted and condemned offspring. For we were all in that one man, seeing that we all *were* that one man who fell into sin through the woman who was made from him before the first sin. We did not yet possess forms individually created and assigned to us for us to live in them as individuals; but there already existed the seminal nature from which we were to be begotten. And of course, when this was vitiated through sin, and bound with death's fetters in its just condemnation, man could not be born of man in any other condition. Hence from the misuse of free will there started a chain of disasters: mankind is led from that original perversion, a kind of corruption at the root, right up to the disaster of the second death, which has no end. Only those who are set free through God's grace escape from this calamitous sequence.

15. *The first death of the soul. Adam forsook God, and was then forsaken by God*

Now the words of the threat, 'You will certainly die', are literally, 'You will die *by the death.*' It does not say 'by the deaths', in the plural; and so we may take it as meaning only the death which happens when the soul is forsaken by its own life; and this, for the soul, is God. The soul, we note, was not first forsaken by God, so that it forsook him as a result; it first forsook, and as a result it was forsaken. For the evil of the soul, its own will takes the initiative; but for its good, the will of its Creator makes the first move, whether to make the soul which did not yet exist, or to recreate it when it had perished through its fall. We may therefore take it that this was the

22. Gal. 5, 17.

death God meant when he gave the warning, 'On the day that you eat from that tree you will die by the death', this being tantamount to saying, 'On the day that you forsake me in disobedience, I shall forsake you with justice.' But even so, he certainly gave warning, in this death, of the other deaths also, which without doubt were destined to follow.

For in that unruly disturbance that arose in the flesh of the unruly soul, which caused our first parents to cover their *pudenda*, there was experienced one death, the death in which God forsook the soul. This death was indicated by the words addressed to the man, who was hiding himself, out of his wits with fear, when God said, 'Where are you, Adam?'[23] Obviously God was not asking for information; he was rebuking Adam; and by the form of the rebuke he was warning him to take notice where he was, in that God was not with him.

But when the soul itself forsook the body, worn out with the passage of time and exhausted with the weight of years, another death came into man's experience, the death about which God had spoken to him, when still pronouncing punishment on his sin saying, 'You are earth, and into earth you will go.'[24] And so by those two deaths the first death was completed, the death of the whole man. This is followed in the end by the second death, unless a man is set free by grace. In fact, even the body, which is made of earth, would not return into the earth, except through its own death, which comes to it when its own life, the soul, forsakes it. Hence all Christians who truly hold the Catholic faith[25] are agreed that even the death of the body was not inflicted on us by the law of our nature, since God did not create any death for man in his nature, but it was imposed as a just punishment for sin. For it was when God was taking vengeance on sin that he said to the man, in whom we all existed at that time, 'You are earth, and into earth you will go.'

16. *The philosophers who do not regard the separation of body and soul as penal. Plato's evidence on the other side*

Now the philosophers against whose attacks we are defending the City of God, that is to say, God's Church, think that they show their wisdom in laughing at our assertion that the separation of soul from body is to be reckoned among the soul's punishments. Their reason for this is that, in their view, the perfect bliss of the soul comes only when

23. Gen. 3, 9. 24. Gen. 3, 19.
25. In contrast to the Manicheans; cf. Bk XI, 13n.; XI, 22.

it has been completely stripped of the body and returns to God, simple and alone, and, as one may say, naked.

On this point, if I had found nothing in their own writings to refute this notion, I should have to engage in a more laborious argument to prove that it is not the body as such, but the corruptible body, that is a burden to the soul. Hence the scriptural statement which we quoted in the last book, 'The corruptible body weighs down the soul.'[26] The addition of 'corruptible' shows that the writer meant that the soul was weighed down, not by any kind of body but by the body as it became as a result of sin and the punishment that followed. Even if he had not added this epithet, we ought still to have given this meaning to the statement, as the only correct interpretation. But in fact Plato teaches quite plainly that the gods who were made by the supreme God have immortal bodies; and he represents God himself, their creator, as promising them, as a great boon, that they will remain for ever with their bodies and will never be parted from them by any death. In the face of this, why is it that these philosophers, in their desire to rail at the Christian faith, pretend not to know what they know very well; or even choose to quarrel with themselves, and to argue against themselves, provided that they never stop their attacks on us.

Here then are the actual words of Plato,[27] in Cicero's Latin translation, in which he represents the supreme God as addressing the divinities he created in these words,

> You who are sprung from the seed of the gods, listen to this. The works of which I am parent and maker cannot suffer dissolution against my will, although everything that is composite can be dissolved; but it is in no way good to seek to undo what has been bound together by reason. Now since you had a beginning, you of yourselves cannot be immortal and indissoluble. Yet you will certainly not be dissolved, nor will any doom of death destroy you, or be more powerful than my design, which is a stronger bond for your perpetuity than those bonds by which you were joined together at the time when you were brought to birth.[28]

Notice that Plato says both that the deities are mortal because of the linking of body and soul,[29] and yet immortal by reason of the will and design of God, who made them.

Now if it is a punishment for the soul to be bound to any sort of body, why is it that God addresses the gods as though they were worried by the fear that they might die, that is, be severed from the

26. Wisd. 9, 15; cf. Bk XII, 16. 27. *Tim.*, 41A; B.
28. Cic., *Tim.*, 11 (inexactly quoted).
29. Plato makes no explicit mention of bodies.

body? Why does he give them the assurance of their immortality? And this assurance does not depend upon their nature, which is composite not simple, but on his own irresistible will, which gives him the power to ensure that things which have a beginning shall not die, things joined together shall not be sundered, but shall continue without impairment.

It is another question whether what Plato says about the stars[30] is true or not. We do not need to grant him, out of hand, that those globes of light or small discs that shine on the world with physical light by day or night are alive in virtue of souls of their own, and that these souls are endowed with intelligence and possessed of happiness. This is an assertion he also makes, with emphasis, about the whole universe, speaking as if it were a single immense living being, including in itself all other living things.[31] But this, as I said, is another question, and I do not propose to discuss it at the moment.

I have made the only point I want to make. I thought it right to bring it up against those who pride themselves on being called, or on being, Platonists, and whose arrogance about that title makes them ashamed to be Christians. They are afraid that if they share an appellation with ordinary people it will cheapen the scarcity value of the wearers of the *pallium*,[32] a value inflated in proportion to their rarity. They are trying to find something to criticize in Christian doctrine, and so they attack the immortality of the body, as if there were a contradiction in seeking the felicity of the soul and at the same time wishing it to exist for ever in the body, bound to the body by what they conceive as a burdensome connection. And yet Plato, their own founder and master, asserts that this was a boon granted by the supreme God to the deities created by him, the assurance that they would never die, never, that is, be separated from the bodies with which he had linked them.

17. *Against the assertion that earthly bodies cannot become immortal*

These philsophers also contend that earthly bodies cannot be eternal, although they have no doubt that the whole earth is itself a constituent part of their god, situated in the centre and everlasting – this god being not the supreme God but the great god who is the whole universe.[33] Now, that supreme God created for them another being

30. cf. *Tim.*, 41D–42A. 31. *Tim.* 30C–D; 92C.
32. The Greek cloak which became the conventional garb of philosophers.
33. cf. *Tim.* 34A—B.

whom they regard as a god, that is, this universe of ours, and this divinity is to be ranked above all the others, who are below him. They suppose also that this god is animate, that is, he has a soul, according to them, a rational or intelligent soul enclosed within all this physical mass which is his body.[34] Moreover the supreme God established the four elements, the constituent parts, as it were, of that same body, arranged and distributed in their own places; and to ensure that this great god of theirs shall never die, they insist that the conjunction of these elements is indissoluble and everlasting.[35] On this asumption if the earth, the so-called 'central member', in the body of this larger living being, is eternal, is there any reason why the bodies of other living beings of the earth should not be everlasting, if God willed this as he willed the other?

But, they say, the earth from which the earthly bodies of living creatures are derived, has to be returned to the earth; and this, according to them, is why those bodies must inevitably disintegrate and perish, and in this way be restored to the enduring and everlasting earth from which they were taken. Now suppose someone made the same assertion about fire, and said that the bodies taken from the universal fire for the creation of heavenly beings must be returned to it. Then surely, if this were admitted, the immortality which Plato,[36] speaking as the mouthpiece of the supreme God, promised to such deities would fall a victim, as it were, to the violence of this argument. Or does this not apply in this case, just because God does not so will; and God's will, as Plato says, no force can conquer? If, so, what prevents God from having the power to affect the same result in respect of earthly bodies also, seeing that Plato admits that God is able to ensure that things which have a beginning should not perish, things which have been bound together should not be sundered, that what has been derived from the elements should not be returned to them, and that souls established in bodies should never forsake them, but should with them enjoy immortality and everlasting bliss?[37]

Then why should God not be able to ensure that terrestrial bodies also should not die? Are we to suppose that his power does not extend as far as Christians believe, but only as far as the Platonists are ready to allow? Those philosophers, to be sure, were able to know God's purpose and power, but the prophets could not! In fact the contrary is true. The prophets were taught by God's Spirit, so that they could make known his purpose, as far as he deigned to reveal it; whereas the

34. cf. *Tim.*, 30B.
35. cf. *Tim.*, 32 A–C.
36. cf. *Tim.*, 41A.
37. cf. *Tim.*, 32C–33D.

philosophers were misled by human speculation when they tried to learn the divine intention.

But they ought not to have been so far misled either by ignorance, or a combination of ignorance and wrong-headedness, as to contest their own position. They assert with great force of argument that the soul, if it is to be capable of bliss, must get away not only from an earthly body but from any kind of body; on the other hand, they say that the gods have souls which are utterly blessed, and yet are bound to eternal bodies – celestial souls bound to bodies of fire;[38] while the soul of Jupiter himself, whom they hold to be the universe, is wholly enclosed in all the material elements which compose the massive structure which rises up from earth to heaven.[39]

Plato's theory is that this soul is diffused and extended by harmonic proportions from the middle point in the heart of the earth, from what the geometers call the centre, through all its parts as far as the highest and furthest zones of heaven.[40] And so this universe is a living being, of the greatest size and the utmost felicity, and it is everlasting: its soul enjoys continually the perfect bliss of wisdom, and it does not abandon its own body, while that body derives its life from this soul for all eternity, and, although it is not simple but composed of so many bodies of great size, it cannot deaden or benumb the soul.

These philosophers certainly give free rein to their guesswork. Why then are they so unwilling to believe that by God's will and power earthly bodies can be made immortal, and souls can live in those bodies everlastingly and in felicity, not separated from them by any death, nor weighed down by their burden? They are quite ready to maintain that this is possible for their deities in fiery bodies, and for Jupiter himself in all the material elements. For if a soul must avoid any kind of body in order to attain bliss, then their deities should escape from the starry globes, and Jupiter should get away from sky and earth. Or if they cannot, they should be accounted miserable.

But these philosophers refuse either of those alternatives. They cannot bring themselves to ascribe to their deities either a separation from their bodies, for fear of seeming to worship mortal gods, or a deprivation of felicity, for fear of admitting that their gods are unhappy.

The conclusion is that it is not necessary for the achievement of bliss to avoid every kind of body, but only bodies which are corruptible, burdensome, oppressive, and in a dying state; not such bodies

38. cf. *Tim.*, 40A. 39. cf. *Tim.*, 34A–B. 40. cf. *Tim.*, 35B–36B.

as the goodness of God created for the first human beings,[41] but bodies in the condition which the punishment for sin forced upon them.

18. *The contention that earthly bodies cannot exist in the heavenly regions*

These philosophers object that earthly bodies must inevitably be held down on the earth or forced down to the earth by their natural weight; and therefore they cannot exist in heaven.[42] Those first human beings did indeed live on earth, in a wooded and fruitful land which was given the name 'paradise'. Now we must reply to this objection, in view of the body with which Christ ascended into heaven, and the sort of body that the saints are to have at the resurrection. And so I should like them to give a closer examination to this question of earthly weights in themselves.

Now human skill makes possible the construction, by certain methods, of vessels capable of floating, even out of metals which immediately sink when placed in water. How much more credible is it that God should operate more effectively in some unexplained way! Plato tells us that God's almighty will prevents the disappearance of things which had a beginning and the disintegration of things that were bound together;[43] and immaterial things are much more wonderfully linked with material things than bodies are with bodies of any kind. Then surely God's mysterious operation can ensure that earthly masses should not be pressed down to the lowest regions by any weight and, more than that, can allow the souls themselves, enjoying the highest perfection of bliss, to put their bodies (which though earthly are also incorruptible) wherever they wish, and to move them wherever they wish, thus enjoying complete facility of position or movement.

Well then, if angels can do this, and can carry off any earthly creatures from wherever they please and deposit them wherever they please,[44] are we to suppose that they cannot do so without feeling the weight? Then why should we not believe that the spirits of the saints made perfect and happy by God's bounty can without any difficulty convey their bodies wherever they wish and place them wherever they wish? Now the weight of earthly bodies is in direct proportion to their size, like the weight of burdens we normally feel in carrying

41. cf. Bk XII, 22; XIII, 1; 3. 42. cf. also Bk XXII, 11. 43. cf. ch. 16.
44. As the angel transplanted Habbakuk (*Bel and the Dragon*, 33–9).

them; and the heavier the weight the more oppressive the burden. And yet the soul finds the limbs of its own body lighter to carry when they are in health and therefore robust than when they are emaciated with weakness; and though a strong and healthy man is heavier for others to carry than a thin and sickly person, still the man himself can move and carry his body more briskly when he is in good health and has more weight to carry than when disease or want of food has left him very little strength. Thus even when we are dealing with earthly bodies, though still liable to corruption and death, it is not their size and weight that matters but their state of health. And words cannot express the immense difference between what we call health in our present condition and the immortality which is to be ours in the future.

Thus our belief is not refuted by the objections of those philosophers about the weights of bodies. And I will refrain from asking them why they do not believe that an earthly body can exist in heaven, although the whole earth is 'balanced on nothing'.[45] It may be, indeed, that an even more plausible argument may be based on the fact of a centre of the universe on which all heavier bodies converge. What I do say is this: Plato entrusted the lesser divinities with the task of creating man, as well as the other animals on earth;[46] and they had the power, according to him, to remove from fire the property of burning, while leaving the property of illumination to flash through the eyes.[47] And Plato allowed the will of the supreme God to have the power to ensure that things which had a beginning should not perish, and to preserve from any possibility of disintegration and dissolution the connection of material and immaterial substances, for all their diversity and dissimilarity. Shall we then hesitate to allow him to remove the possibility of corruption from the flesh of a man to whom he grants immortality, while leaving its nature unaltered, and to keep the symmetry of its outline and limbs, while getting rid of the inertia of its weight?

But I shall have to discuss in more detail our belief in the resurrection of the dead and their immortal bodies at the end of this work, if God wills.[48]

45. cf. Job 26, 7.
46. cf. *Tim.*, 41C–D.
47. cf. *Tim.*, 45B–C.
48. cf. Bk XXII, 12–21; 25–30.

19. *Against the doctrine that the first human beings would not have been immortal had they not sinned and the contention that the eternal life of souls is bodiless*

Let us continue our discussion about the bodies of the first human beings. They could not have suffered even that death which is said to be good for the good, and which is known not merely to the few who have understanding or faith but to all, if it had not been the merited consequence of sin. This is the death which brings the separation of soul from body, and which certainly brings it about that the body of a living being, which was demonstrably alive, demonstrably dies. And although we must never for a moment doubt that the souls of the righteous and devout live in a state of rest after their departure from this life, yet they would be in a better state if they were living in conjunction with their bodies in perfect health. So true is this that even those who think that to be disembodied is the height of felicity, disprove this theory of theirs by a conflicting opinion.

For none of them will venture to rank wise men, whether already dead or still to die (that is, men who are already bodiless or who are going to abandon their bodies) above the immortal deities to whom, according to Plato, the supreme God promises, as an inestimable privilege, an indissoluble life, that is, an everlasting union with their bodies.[49] On the other hand, Plato also thinks that men receive the best possible treatment, assuming that they have passed their lives on earth in piety and justice, when they are separated from their bodies and received into the bosom of the gods – those gods who never forsake their own bodies,[50]

> So that, forgetful, they may seek again
> The vault of heaven, and once more desire
> To take a mortal body.[51]

as Virgil says, expressing Plato's teaching admirably.

Thus Plato certainly does not believe that the souls of mortals can always exist in their bodies. He holds that they are set free by the inevitability of death. Yet he does not believe that they continue for ever without bodies; there is, he thinks, a ceaseless alternation, in which men pass from life to death and from death to life. But there is a difference, apparently, between the destiny of the wise and that of the rest. The wise, on this theory, are borne aloft after death to the stars,

49. cf. ch. 16.
50. cf. *Phaed.*, 108C; *Phaedr.*, 248C.
51. *Aen.*, 6, 750f.

where each of them rests for a considerably longer time on the star appropriate to him; and from there, after he has forgotten his earlier misery and thus has given way to desire for the possession of a body, he returns again to the trials and troubles of mortal men. While those who have lived a life of folly are almost immediately brought back again to inhabit bodies suitable to their deserts, whether bodies of men or of animals.[52]

This then is the excessively harsh condition which Plato has imposed even on good and wise souls; for they were not assigned bodies with which they could live for ever in immortality. Consequently they could neither continue in their bodies, nor live without them in eternal purity. I have already mentioned in an earlier book[53] that Porphyry, in the Christian era, was embarrassed about this Platonic dogma; and I have shown how he refused to allow the union of animal bodies and human souls, and how he went further, in holding that the souls of the wise are so thoroughly released from connection with the body that they shun a body of any kind and are kept in the Father's presence in endless bliss. Thus to avoid appearing to be surpassed by Christ, with his promise of eternal life for his saints, Porphyry also established purified souls in a state of everlasting felicity, without any return to their former miseries. And he carried on his opposition to Christ by denying the resurrection of imperishable bodies, asserting that souls would live for all eternity not only without earthly bodies but without bodies of any sort.[54]

And yet in proposing this theory, for what it was worth, Porphyry stopped short of teaching that those souls should not submit themselves in religious homage to the embodied deities. Why was this, unless it was because he did not believe that those souls, although not associated with a body, were superior to those deities? Therefore, if those philosophers will not venture (and I do not think they will) to rate human souls above gods who are in the height of bliss and yet incorporated in eternal bodies, why does it seem to them ridiculous that the Christian faith should proclaim that the first human beings were so created that, if they had not sinned, no death would have sundered them from their bodies? In fact, that faith declares that as a reward for preserving obedience, they would have received the gift of immortality and would have lived for ever, united with those bodies; and that at the resurrection the saints will inhabit the actual bodies in which they suffered the hardships of this life on earth; yet these bodies will be such that no trace of corruption or frustration will affect their

52. cf. *Phaedr.*, 248A–249D. 53. Bk X, 30. 54. cf. Bk XXII, 27.

flesh, nor will any sorrow or mischance interfere with their felicity.

20. *The flesh of saints, now resting in hope, will be restored to a better state than that of our first parents before their sin*

In the same way, the souls of departed saints do not find death grievous, when it has separated them from their bodies; and for this reason, that their flesh 'rests in hope',[55] whatever the insults that flesh may seem to have received after it has been bereft of sensation. It is not, as Plato imagined,[56] through forgetfulness that they long to have their bodies again. In fact it is just because they remember the promise of him who never lets anyone down, who gave them the assurance that even the hairs would remain intact;[57] remembering this, they look for the resurrection of their bodies with patient longing, for though they suffered much hardship in those bodies, they will experience nothing of the kind hereafter.

To be sure, if they did not hate their own flesh[58] when in its weakness it resisted their mental resolve, when they had to discipline it by the law of the spirit, how much more do they love it now, when it too is to become spiritual! For just as the spirit is quite appropriately called carnal when it is the servant of the flesh, the flesh will with equal propriety be called spiritual, when it serves the spirit. This is not because the flesh will be converted into spirit (a notion which some people derive from the scriptural text: 'It is sown as an animal body: it will arise as a spiritual body')[59] but because it will submit to the spirit with a ready obedience, an obedience so wonderfully complete that the body will fulfil the will of the spirit in such a way as to bring perfect assurance of indissoluble immortality, free from any feeling of distress, and relieved of any possibility of corruption, any trace of reluctance.

Not only will the body be different from the body as it is now even when in perfect health; it will not even be such as it was in the first human beings, before their sin. For though they would not have been destined to die, if they had not sinned, still, as human beings, they took nourishment, since the bodies they bore were not yet spiritual but animal, still bodies of earth. Those bodies were not indeed growing old and senile, so as to be brought in the end to an inevitable death. This condition was granted to them by the wonderful grace of God, and was

55. cf. Ps. 16, 9. 56. cf. ch. 19. 57. cf. Luke 21, 18.
58. cf. Eph. 5, 29. 59. 1 Cor. 15, 44.

derived from the tree of life which was in the middle of paradise, together with the forbidden tree. For all that, they took other kinds of food, except from that one tree which had been banned, not because it was an evil in itself, but in order to emphasize the good of pure and simple obedience which is the great virtue of a rational creature set under the authority of the Lord his creator. For where nothing evil was touched it is obvious that, if something forbidden was touched, the sin consisted solely in the disobedience.

Thus the purpose of the other foods was to prevent their animal bodies from experiencing any distress through hunger or thirst, whereas the reason for their tasting of the tree of life was to prevent death that might come on them unawares from any source, or the death that would come in extreme old age after their lives had run full course. It could be said that other foods served as nourishment, but that from the tree of life was a kind of sacrament. On this interpretation the tree of life in the material paradise is analogous to the wisdom of God in the spiritual or intelligible paradise; for Scripture says of wisdom, 'It is the tree of life to those who embrace it.'[60]

21. *The spiritual interpretation of the paradise of Eden does not conflict with its historical truth*

Hence a number of interpreters give a symbolic meaning to the whole of that paradise, in which dwelt the first parents of mankind, according to the truthful narrative of holy Scripture. They give a spiritual reference to those fruit-bearing trees, and the others, turning them into symbols of virtues and moral qualities. They take it for granted that those were not visible and material objects, but were thus described in speech or writing to stand for spiritual and moral truths.

It is, however, arbitrary to suppose that there could not have been a material paradise, just because it can be understood also in a spiritual significance; it is like the assumption that there were not two wives of Abraham, named Hagar and Sarah, who bore two sons, one a slave's son, the other the son of a free woman, just because the Apostle finds in them the prefiguration of the two covenants;[61] or that there was no rock from which water flowed when Moses struck it, just because it can be interpreted in a symbolic sense, as prefiguring Christ; which is how the same Apostle takes it when he says, 'Now the rock was Christ.'[62]

60. Prov. 3, 18. 61. cf. Gal. 4, 22ff; Gen. 16, 4; 21, 2.
62. cf. 1 Cor. 10, 4; Exod. 17, 6; Num. 20, 11.

And so no one can stop us from interpreting paradise symbolically as the life of the blessed; its four rivers as the four virtues, prudence, courage, temperance, and justice; its trees as all the beneficial disciplines; the fruit of the trees as the character of the righteous; the tree of life as wisdom, the mother of all good things; and the tree of the knowledge of good and evil as the experience of disobedience to a commandment. For it was certainly a good thing, because it was just, that God should have imposed a punishment for sinners; but it is not a good thing for man himself that he experiences it.

We can also interpret the details of paradise with reference to the Church, which gives them a better significance as prophetic indications of things to come in the future. Thus paradise stands for the Church itself, as described in the *Song of Songs*,[63] the four rivers represent the four Gospels; the fruit trees, the saints; and the fruit, their achievements; the tree of life, the Holy of Holies, must be Christ himself; while the tree of knowledge of good and evil symbolizes the personal decision of man's free will.

For it is certain that if man ignores God's will he can only employ his own powers to his own destruction; and thus he learns what a difference it makes whether he gives his adherence to the good that is shared by all, or finds pleasure only in his own selfish good. In fact, if he loves himself, a man is given over to himself so that when as a result he has had his fill of fears and griefs he may use the words of the psalm (if, that is, he is aware of his evil plight) and sing, 'My soul is troubled within me',[64] and then, when he is set right, he may then say, 'I shall keep watch for you, my strength.'[65]

This is the kind of thing that can be said by way of allegorical interpretation of paradise; and there may be other more valuable lines of interpretation. There is no prohibition against such exegesis, provided that we also believe in the truth of the story as a faithful record of historical fact.

22. *The post-resurrection bodies of the saints will be spiritual, but without the conversion of flesh into spirit*

The bodies of the righteous, after the resurrection, will not need any tree to preserve them against death from disease or from extreme old age, nor any material nourishment to prevent any kind of distress from hunger or thirst. This is because they will be endowed with the gift of assured and inviolable immortality, and so they will eat only if

63. cf. 4, 12ff. 64. Ps. 42, 6. 65. Ps. 59, 9.

they wish to eat; eating will be for them a possibility, not a necessity. This is what the angels also did, when they appeared in visible and tangible form. They ate, not because they needed food, but because they were able to eat, and they wanted to do so, to fit in with men's ways by displaying some human characteristics in the performance of their ministry. For we ought not to suppose that the angels ate only in illusory appearance when they were entertained by human beings.[66] Though it seemed to their hosts, who did not know whether they were angels, that they partook of food because, like us, they needed nourishment. That is why the angel in the book of Tobias says, 'You saw me eating, but it was in your own vision that you saw me',[67] which means, 'You supposed that I took food, as you do, because of the need to restore the body's losses.'

Well, it is possible that a more credible suggestion might be put forward on the subject of the angels. However that may be, the Christian faith has no doubts about the Saviour himself. Christians believe that even after his resurrection, when he was now appearing in spiritual, though still real, flesh, he took food and drink in the company of his disciples.[68] For it is not the ability, it is the need to eat and drink that will be taken away from bodies like this. They will be spiritual, not by ceasing to be bodies, but by being supported in their existence by a life-giving spirit.[69]

23. *The meaning of 'animal' body and 'spiritual' body; and of 'all die in Adam' and 'all are brought to life in Christ'*

Bodies which have a living soul, but not yet a life-giving spirit, are called 'animal' bodies (that is, bodies with *anima* – 'life' or 'soul'; and yet they are not souls, but bodies). In the same way, those other bodies are called 'spiritual'. Yet we must not allow ourselves to believe that they will be spirits; we must think of them as bodies having the substance of flesh, though never having to experience corruption or lethargy, being preserved from such a fate by the life-giving spirit. Then man will no longer be earthly, but heavenly, not because his body, made of earth, will not be the same, but because the heavenly gift will fit it for living in heaven itself, not by a loss of its natural substance, but by a change in its quality.

The first man, however, was 'of the earth, earthly', and he was made as a 'living soul', not a 'life-giving spirit';[70] that condition was

66. cf. Gen. 18, 8; 19, 3; Tob. 11, 20.
67. Tob. 12, 19.
68. cf. Luke 24, 43; Acts 10, 41.
69. cf. 1 Cor. 15, 45.
70. cf. 1 Cor. 15, 47; 45.

reserved for him after he had merited it by obedience. There is no doubt that his body was animal, not spiritual; this is shown by the fact that it needed food and drink to prevent its suffering from hunger and thirst; and it was preserved from the inevitability of death and kept in the flower of youth, not by that ultimate immortality, which is absolute and indissoluble, but by the tree of life. Yet that first man would certainly not have died had he not, by his offence, fallen under the sentence of God who had given him ample warning in advance. Then, though he was not denied nourishment, outside paradise, he was banned from the tree of life and handed over to time and old age, for them to make an end of him, in respect of that life, at least, which he might have enjoyed perpetually in paradise, had he not sinned, though he would have been in an animal body, until that body became spiritual as a reward for obedience.

Therefore, even if we were to suppose that when God said, 'On the day you eat of it, you will die by the death,'[71] he referred to that obvious death in which the soul is separated from the body; still we need not see any inconsistency in the fact that the offenders were not immediately severed from the body on the actual day when they took the forbidden and mortal food. It was in fact on that day that their natural condition changed for the worse; there was a taint on that nature, and they were barred from the tree of life as the just punishment of their offence. The result was that they became subject to the inevitable death of the body; and we are born under the same necessity. That is why the Apostle does not say, 'The body will die because of sin,' but, 'The body is dead because of sin: but the spirit is life because of righteousness.' And then he adds, 'Then, if the Spirit of him who raised up Christ from the dead is living in you, he who raised Christ from the dead will bring to life your mortal bodies also, through the indwelling of his Spirit in you.'[72]

The body will thus be related to the life-giving spirit as it is now to the living soul. Nevertheless, the Apostle calls it dead because it is in the grip of inevitable death. Yet originally it was related to a living soul, though not to a life-giving spirit, in such a way that it could not rightly be called dead, since it could not be faced with death, as an inevitability, except in consequence of a sin committed.

But when God asked, 'Where are you, Adam?'[73] he signified the death of the soul, which came about when he forsook it; and when he said, 'You are earth, and into earth you will go,'[74] he signified the

71. Gen. 2, 17. 72. Rom. 8, 10f.
73. Gen. 3, 9. 74. Gen. 3, 19.

death of the body, which comes about when the soul forsakes it. We must believe that he said nothing about the second death because he wished to keep it from men's knowledge with a view to the revelation of his purpose in the New Testament, where the second death is proclaimed in unmistakable terms.[75] Thus it would first be made clear that the first death, which is the common lot of mankind, resulted from that sin which in one man became an act in which all mankind shared. Whereas the second death is certainly not the common lot of all men because those are exempt 'who have been called in fulfilment of his purpose', those whom he previously 'foreknew and predestined', as the Apostle says, 'to be fashioned in the likeness of his Son, so that he might be the first-born in a family of many brothers'.[76] They have been rescued from the second death by God's grace, through the action of the Mediator.

Thus it was in an animal body, the Apostle says, that the first man was created. For when he is concerned to distinguish the present animal body from the spiritual body which is to come at the resurrection, the Apostle says, 'It is sown in corruption: it will rise in incorruption; it is sown in humiliation: it will rise in glory; it is sown in weakness: it will rise in power; it is sown as an animal body: it will rise as a spiritual body.' Then he adds, to support this, 'If there is such a thing as an animal body, there is also a spiritual body.' And to show what is meant by an animal body, he says, 'This is the sense in which Scripture says: "The first man was made into a living soul." '[77] His intention in speaking in this way was to show what an animal body is, although in the account of the first man, named Adam, and the creation of his soul by the breath of God, the Scripture does not say, 'And man was made in an animal body', but, 'Man was made into a living soul.'[78] Thus in this scriptural statement, 'The first man was made into a living soul', the Apostle intended us to understand a reference to man's animal body.

On the other hand, he shows how the spiritual body is to be understood by adding, 'The last Adam was made into a life-giving spirit.'[79] Here undoubtedly he means Christ, who has already risen from the dead so as to be thereafter utterly insusceptible of death. He then goes on to say, 'But the spiritual does not come first: first comes the animal body, and the spiritual afterwards.' Here he makes it much clearer that he finds a reference to the animal body in the scriptural statement that the first man was made into a living soul, and intends a

75. cf. Rev. 2, 11; 20, 6; 20, 14; 21, 8.
76. Rom. 8, 28f.
77. 1 Cor. 15, 42–45.
78. Gen. 2, 7.
79. 1 Cor. 15, 45.

reference to the spiritual body in his own statement that 'the last Adam was made into a life-giving spirit.'

For the animal body comes first, a body like that of the first Adam, although that would not have died, if Adam had not sinned. Such is the body that we also have, with its nature as much changed and marred as it was in Adam, after his sin, with the result that death became inevitable for him. Christ also condescended to take such a body at first, not of necessity, but as an act of power. But afterwards will come the spiritual body, like that which has gone ahead of us in the person of Christ, who is our head;[80] this spiritual body will follow, in the person of those who are 'members of Christ'[81] at the final resurrection of the dead.

The Apostle then adds a very striking difference between those two men. He says, 'The first man is from the earth, earthly: the second man is from heaven. Those who are earthly are like the man of earth; those who are heavenly are like the man of heaven. And as we have put on the likeness of the man of earth, let us also put on the likeness of the man who is from heaven.'[82] The Apostle put it in this way so that the sacrament of rebirth may even now have its effect in us; as he says in another place, 'All of you who have been baptized in Christ have put on Christ,'[83] although this process will not be completed in reality until what is animal in us, because of our birth, has become spiritual because of our resurrection. For, to use his own words again, 'It is *in hope* that we have been saved.'[84]

Now we *have* put on the likeness of the man of earth by the physical inheritance of sin and death, conveyed to us by birth; but we *shall* put on the likeness of the heavenly man, by the gracious gift of pardon and of perpetual life. This gift we receive by rebirth, but it comes only through 'the mediator between God and men, the man Christ Jesus'.[85] It is Christ whom the Apostle means to be understood by 'the heavenly man', because he came from heaven to be clothed in a body of earthly mortality, so that he might clothe it in heavenly immortality. The reason why he uses the epithet 'heavenly' of the others also is that they become, through grace, 'members of Christ', so that with them Christ forms a unity like that of head and body.[86]

The Apostle puts this in more striking terms in the same letter: 'It was by a man that death came; and by a man came the resurrection of

80. cf. Eph. 4, 15. 81. cf. 1 Cor. 12, 27. 82. 1 Cor., 15, 47ff.
83. Gal. 3, 27. 84. Rom. 8, 24. 85. 1 Tim. 2, 5.
86. cf. Rom. 12, 5; 1 Cor. 12, 27; Eph. 5, 30.

the dead. For as it is in Adam that all die, so also it is in Christ that all will be brought to life'[87] – 'brought to life', undoubtedly, in a spiritual body which will exist in relation to a life-giving spirit. But it does not mean that all who die in Adam will be members of Christ, for the great majority of them will be punished with the second death, which is for ever. What the Apostle means by using 'all' in both parts of the statement is that no one dies in his animal body except 'in Adam'; and in the same way no one is brought to life in a spiritual body except 'in Christ'.

It follows then that we must certainly not suppose that at the resurrection we shall have the kind of body that the first man possessed before his sin. And the saying, 'Those who are earthly are like the man of earth', should not be taken as referring to the condition that resulted from his sin. We are not to imagine that the first man had a spiritual body before he sinned, and that it was changed into an animal body as the reward of that sin. To suppose this is to pay too little attention to the actual words of the great teacher. Paul says, 'If there is such a thing as an animal body, there is also a spiritual body. As the Scripture also says, "The first man, Adam, was made into a living soul."' We cannot think that this happened after Adam had sinned, since it is the original condition of man; for the blessed Paul quotes this evidence from the Law[88] about that condition, to show what is meant by the animal body.

24. *The meaning of God's breathing into the first man, and the Lord's breathing on the disciples*

There is another passage which has been thoughtlessly explained by some interpreters. This is the passage where we read, 'God breathed into his face the breath (*spiritus*) of life, and man was made into a living soul.'[89] They assume this to mean not that man was then first given his soul (*anima*), but that the soul was already in him, and now it was brought to life by the Holy Spirit (*Spiritus*).[90] They are influenced by the fact that, after the Lord Jesus had risen from the dead, he breathed on his disciples and said, 'Receive the Holy Spirit.'[91] Hence they imagine that something of the sort happened on the first occasion, as if the evangelist had gone on to say here also, 'and they were made into a living soul.' If indeed this had been said,

87. 1 Cor. 15, 21f. 88. i.e. Gen. 2, 7. 89. Gen. 2, 7.
90. A Manichean doctrine. cf. Aug., *De Gen. c. Man.*, 2, 8, 11.
91. John 20, 22.

we should have taken it to mean that the Spirit of God is, in a sense, the life of souls, and without that Spirit rational souls are to be reckoned as dead, although their presence gives to bodies the semblance of life. But this was not what happened when man was created, as is clearly shown by the biblical evidence, in these words, 'And God fashioned dust from the earth into a man.'[92]

Some interpreters have thought that this passage needed clearer explanation and have therefore put it thus: 'And God devised a man from the mud of the earth.' For the preceding passage was, 'But a spring went up from the earth and watered the whole surface of the ground',[93] and they imagined that this implied mud, that being a mixture of earth and water. For the very next statement is, 'And God fashioned dust from the earth into a man.' This is the reading of the Greek manuscripts, of which the Latin Bible is a translation. It is of no importance whether the translation 'fashioned' (*formavit*) or 'devised' (*finxit*) is preferred, to represent the Greek *eplasen*; though 'devised' is a more literal rendering. But those who preferred 'fashioned' had decided that it was desirable to avoid the ambiguity of 'devised', since that word is employed in general Latin usage to describe the composition of something false with intent to deceive.

And so this man, formed from the dust of the earth or from mud (for the dust was moistened) – or, to use the express words of Scripture, this 'dust from the earth' – became an animal body, according to the Apostle's teaching, when he received a soul. 'And this man was made into a living soul', that is, this dust, when fashioned, was then made into a living soul.

But, they say, he already had a soul. Otherwise, he would not have been called a man, since man is not merely a body or merely a soul, but a being constituted by body and soul together. This is indeed true, for the soul is not the whole man; it is the better part of man, and the body is not the whole man; it is the lower part of him. It is the conjunction of the two parts that is entitled to the name of 'man'; and yet those parts taken separately are not deprived of that appellation even when we speak of them by themselves. For there is no law (as we may call it) of ordinary speech to prohibit such a statement as, 'The man has died, and is now at rest, or under punishment', when in fact this can be said only of his soul; or, 'The man is buried in such and such a place', although this can only be understood as meaning his body.

They may, perhaps, be ready with the retort that this is not the

92. Gen. 2, 7. 93. Gen., 2, 6.

normal form of expression in holy Scripture. But the truth is that Scripture supports our contention on this point, to the extent of employing the term 'man' to designate the separate constituents, even during a man's life, when the two elements are conjoined. That is to say, it calls the soul 'the inner man' and the body 'the outer man',[94] as if there were two men, whereas the two elements together make up one man. We must, in fact, understand what is meant by speaking of 'man made in the likeness of God', and 'man who is earth, and destined to return into earth'. The former refers to the rational soul, as God implanted it in man (in his body, that is) by breathing on him – 'by inspiration' might be a more suitable phrase. While the latter statement applies to man's body, as devised by God out of dust, the thing which was given a soul so that it should become an animal body, that man should be made into a living soul.

Hence, by the act in which the Lord breathed on the disciples and said, 'Receive the Holy Spirit',[95] he surely intended it to be understood that the Holy Spirit is the spirit (or breath) not only of the Father but also of the only-begotten Son himself. The Spirit of the Father and the Son is one and the same, and with the Spirit, the Father and the Son form the Trinity, the Holy Spirit being not created but creator. For that material breath which came from the physical mouth of Christ was not the substance and natural being of the Holy Spirit; rather it was a sign to enable us to understand, as I said, that the Holy Spirit is common to the Father and the Son, because they have not separate spirits, but one spirit belongs to both.

The spirit is always designated in the holy Scriptures by the Greek word *pneuma*, which is also the term used by Jesus in this passage, when he symbolized it by the breath of his physical mouth, in giving the Spirit to the disciples. But in the passage where it says, 'And God fashioned dust from the earth into a man and breathed (or inspired) into his face the spirit (or breath) of life', the Greek version does not use *pneuma*, the usual term for the Holy Spirit, but *pnoê*, a word which appears more often in relation to the created world than in connection with the Creator. Hence, to mark the distinction, some Latin versions also have preferred to translate the word by *flatus* (breath) instead of *spiritus* (spirit). This word *flatus* also occurs in the passage of Isaiah where God says, 'I have made every breath',[96] which undoubtedly means 'every soul'.

Thus the Greek *pnoê* is sometimes rendered into Latin by *flatus* (breath), sometimes by *spiritus* (spirit), *inspiratio* (breathing into, in-

94. cf. 2 Cor. 4, 16. 95. John 20, 22. 96. Is. 57, 16 (LXX).

spiration), or *aspiratio* (breathing on), even when used of God's action. Whereas *pneuma* is invariably represented by *spiritus*. This holds good whether it is used of man (the Apostle says, 'Among mankind, who knows the truth about a man except the spirit of the man within him?'[97]), or of an animal (for example, in the book of Solomon, 'Who knows whether the spirit of man goes upward into heaven, and the spirit of the animal goes downward into the earth?'[98]), or of the physical phenomenon which is also called wind (for this term is used in the verse of the psalm, 'Fire, hail, snow, ice, spirit of the storm'[99]), or, lastly, of the Spirit which is not created but Creator. This last is the reference in the Lord's saying in the Gospel, 'Receive the Holy Spirit',[100] with the symbolism of the breath from his physical mouth; and when he says, 'Go and baptize all nations in the name of the Father, the Son, and the Holy Spirit',[101] a passage where the Trinity is emphasized with a clarity unparalleled elsewhere; and in the place where we read, 'God is spirit',[102] and in very many other places in holy Scripture.

Now in all these scriptural references we observe that, in the Greek text, the word is not *pnoê* but *pneuma*, and in the Latin, *spiritus* instead of *flatus*. Therefore, in the statement, 'He *inspired*' – or, to put it more accurately, 'he breathed' – 'into his face the spirit of life', even if the Greek had *pneuma* here, instead of *pnoê* (the actual reading), it would not have followed that we were forced to refer it to the Creator Spirit, who is properly called, in the Trinity, the Holy Spirit, seeing that it is established that *pneuma* is frequently used of the created as well as of the creator.

But, these interpreters allege, when the author said 'spirit' (*spiritus*) he would not have added 'of life', if he had not intended the Holy Spirit to be understood, and when he said 'Man was made into a soul', he would not have put in the epithet 'living' if he had not meant the life of the soul which is divinely imparted to it by the gift of the Spirit of God. For, they argue, since the soul lives in a manner appropriate to its own life, what was the need to add 'living', except to ensure that it would be understood as meaning that life which is given to the soul through the Holy Spirit? It would not have entailed much effort for them, without going to any great lengths, to read, slightly earlier in the same book, 'Let the earth produce the living soul',[103] at the time when the terrestrial animals were all created. It would not

97. 1 Cor. 2, 11. 98. Eccl. 3, 21. 99. Ps. 148, 8.
100. John 20, 22. 101. Matt. 28, 19. 102. John 4, 24.
103. Gen. 1, 24.

have cost them much to notice, a few chapters later, but still in the same book, these words: 'And all things which have the spirit of life, and everyone who was on the dry land died'[104] – which means that all things that lived on the earth perished in the Flood.

So we find both a 'living soul' and a 'spirit of life' even in the animals, according to the normal usage in divine Scripture. In this passage also, in the phrase, 'all things which have the spirit of life', the Greek word is *pnoê*, not *pneuma*. Then why do we not ask, 'What need was there to add "living", since the soul cannot exist without being alive? And what need to add "of life" after saying "spirit"?' But we take it that Scripture, as usual, speaks of 'living soul' and 'spirit of life' because it intends us to take the meaning as 'animals', in the sense of animate bodies, obviously possessed of the bodily sense perception which comes through the possession of a soul. But when we think of the creation of man we forget the normal usage of Scripture. And yet Scripture here kept strictly to its customary language to make the point that man did indeed receive a rational soul, which (the Bible intends us to realize) was not produced from water or earth, like the soul of the other physical creatures, but created by the breath of God; but that man was nevertheless created to live in an animal body, which comes into life when a soul begins to live in it. For Scripture says of the animals in general, 'Let the earth produce the living soul'; and it also speaks of them as having 'the spirit of life'. In this latter phrase also the Greek word is *pnoê*, not *pneuma*; and it is obvious that the noun signifies not the Holy Spirit but the soul of the animals.

But in fact, comes the reply, the breath of God is to be taken as having issued from God's mouth, and if we suppose it to be the soul, it follows that we must admit that it is of the same substance as God's Wisdom, on an equality with that Wisdom which says, 'I came out of the mouth of the Most High.'[105] Yes, but Wisdom did not say that it had been 'breathed' out of God's mouth, but that it 'came out'. Besides, when we breathe out, we can expel our breath without taking from our own natural substance, the substance that makes us human beings; we breathe by taking from the surrounding air, drawing it in and letting it out by inhaling and exhaling. Almighty God equally has the ability to produce a breath which was taken neither from his own natural substance nor from anything in his subject creation; he could produce it from nothing. And to say that he 'inspired' or 'breathed' this breath when he implanted it into man's body is the

104. Gen., 7, 27 (LXX). 105. Ecclus. 24, 3.

suitable way of expressing God's action; for he is immaterial, as was the breath, but the breath was mutable, and he is immutable, the uncreated producing a created breath. And apart from this, I should like these people, who are ready to hold forth about Scripture without observing the linguistic usages of Scripture, to know that it is not only something of equal and identical nature with God that is said to come out of his mouth; and so I should like them to listen to, or to read, this passage in Scripture, where God is speaking, 'Because you are lukewarm, and neither hot nor cold, I shall go on to spit you out of my mouth.'[106]

So there is no reason to withhold assent from the clear statement of the Apostle on this point. He is distinguishing the animal body from the spiritual, the body in which we are now from the body in which we shall be in the future; and he says,

> It is sown as an animal body: it will rise as a spiritual body. If there is such a thing as an animal body, there is also a spiritual body. This is the testimony of Scripture: 'The first man, Adam, was made into a living soul: the last Adam into a life-giving Spirit'. But the spiritual does not come first: the animal body is first, the spiritual comes later. The first man is of the earth, earthly: the second man is from heaven. Those who are earthly are like the man of earth: those who are heavenly are like the man from heaven. And just as we have put on the likeness of the earthly man, we shall also put on the likeness of the man who is from heaven.

We have already discussed these words of the Apostle.[107]

Thus the animal body, with which, the Apostle says, the first man Adam was made, was not made so as to be incapable of dying, but so as not to die, if the man had not sinned. For the body which will be incapable of death is that which will be spiritual and immortal in virtue of the presence of a life-giving spirit. In this it will be like the soul, which was created immortal. The soul, it is true, may be spoken of as dead because of sin, in that it loses one kind of life, namely the Spirit of God, which would have enabled it to live in wisdom and felicity. Still, it does not cease to live with a kind of life of its own, however wretched, since it is created immortal. The same holds good of the apostate angels; they have, in a fashion, died by sinning, because they forsook the fountain of life which is God; by drinking from that fountain they might have lived in wisdom and felicity. However, they could not die in the sense of ceasing altogether to live and feel, since they were created immortal. And so, after the last judgement, when they will be hurled into the second death, that will not mean

106. Rev. 3, 16. 107. 1 Cor. 15, 44–9; cf. ch. 23.

that they will even there be deprived of life, seeing that they will not be deprived of feeling, when they are in pain.

But men who are in the sphere of God's grace, who are fellow-citizens of the holy angels who live in continual bliss, will be equipped with spiritual bodies in such a way that they will sin no more, nor will they die. The immortality with which they are clothed will be like that of the angels, an immortality which cannot be taken away by sin; and though the natural substance of flesh will continue, no slightest trace of carnal corruptibility or lethargy will remain.

A question then arises which demands discussion and resolution, with the help of the Lord God of Truth. If sensual desire arose in the disobedient bodies of the first human beings as a result of the sin of disobedience, when they had been forsaken by divine grace, if, in the consequence, they opened their eyes to their own nakedness, that is, they observed it with anxious curiosity, and if they covered up their shameful parts because an excitement, which resisted voluntary control, made them ashamed – if this is true, how would they have produced children if they had remained without sin, in the state in which they were created?

But this book must now come to its close; and in any case this is too important a question to be discussed in a constricted space. I shall therefore postpone it for more adequate treatment in the next book.

BOOK XIV

1. *The disobedience of the first man would have involved all mankind in the second, everlasting, death, had not God's grace rescued many*

I HAVE already stated in the foregoing books[1] that God chose to make a single individual the starting-point of all mankind, and that his purpose in this was that the human race should not merely be united in a society by natural likeness, but should also be bound together by a kind of tie of kinship to form a harmonious unity, linked together by the 'bond of peace'. And this race would not have been destined for death, in respect of its individual members, had not the two first human beings (of whom one was created from no one, and the other from him) incurred death as the reward of disobedience: and so heinous was their sin that man's nature suffered a change for the worse; and bondage to sin and inevitable death was the legacy handed on to their posterity.

Now the reign of death has held mankind in such utter subjection that they would all be driven headlong into that second death, which has no ending, as their well-deserved punishment, if some were not rescued from it by the undeserved grace of God. The result is that although there are many great peoples throughout the world, living under different customs in religion and morality and distinguished by a complex variety of languages, arms, and dress, it is still true that there have come into being only two main divisions, as we may call them, in human society: and we are justified in following the lead of our Scriptures[2] and calling them two cities. There is, in fact, one city of men who choose to live by the standard of the flesh, another of those who choose to live by the standard of the spirit. The citizens of each of these desire their own kind of peace, and when they achieve their aim, that is the kind of peace in which they live.

1. Bk XII, 22; 28. 2. cf. Eph. 2, 19; Phil. 3, 20.

2. *The carnal life depends on defects of the mind as much as of the body*

We need to examine first what is meant by living 'by the rule of the flesh' and 'by the rule of the spirit'. For a superficial inspection of my statement may lead to misconception, if it is not carefully borne in mind how the holy Scriptures use the expressions. It may be thought that the Epicurean[3] philosophers certainly live 'by the rule of the flesh', since they place the Highest Good of man in physical pleasure,[4] and that the same is true of other philosophers who have in various ways held that the good of the body is man's Highest Good; and that it is also true of people in general, who are not attached to any philosophical doctrine, who hold no sort of theory, but, having a natural propensity towards sensuality, have no acquaintance with any delight except that derived from the pleasure they experience in physical sensations. On the other hand, it may be supposed that the Stoics[5] live 'by the rule of the spirit', because they place man's highest good in the mind;[6] and what is man's mind, but spirit? But in fact both of these groups live 'by the rule of the flesh', as divine Scripture uses the expression.

For Scripture does not confine the application of the term 'flesh' to the body of an earthly and mortal living being, as it is used, for example, in, 'All flesh is not the same; there is one kind belonging to man, another to animals, another to birds, another to fish.'[7] There are, in fact, many other ways in which it uses the noun, to describe different things; and among these different usages is its employment to denote man himself, that is, the essential nature of man, an example of the figure of speech known as 'part for whole'. For example, 'All flesh will not be justified by the works of the Law.'[8] Obviously this can only be intended to mean 'every man'. This is

3. *Epicureans:* Epicurus (341–270 B.C.) taught that pleasure (or absence of pain) is the sole good; and that the highest pleasure is to be found in a life of simplicity and virtue. He was no advocate of sensuality.

4. cf. Cic., *De Fin.*, 1; 2.

5. *Stoics:* the followers of Zeno of Citium (*fl.* 300 B.C.) who taught in the *Stoa Poikilê* at Athens. He held that the true aim of life was harmony with nature. Happiness was to be obtained through right conduct. Although the Stoics preached the brotherhood of mankind and the duty of universal benevolence, the desired state of indifference to outward circumstances ('apathy') demanded a detachment from the world.

6. Cic., *De Fin.*, 3; 4. 7. 1 Cor. 15, 39. 8. Rom. 3, 20.

made explicit a little later, 'No man is justified by the Law',[9] and in the epistle to the Galatians, 'Knowing, however, that a man is not justified as a result of works of the Law.'[10]

It is on these lines that we interpret this passage, 'And the Word became flesh'.[11] that is, 'became man'. Some people have misunderstood it and therefore have supposed that Christ had no human soul. But we have the part implied by the whole in the passage in the Gospel where Mary Magdalen's words are quoted, 'They have taken away my Lord, and I do not know where they have laid him',[12] for she was speaking only about the flesh of Christ, which, she thought, had been taken from the tomb where it was buried; and similarly we have the 'whole from part' figure when 'flesh' is mentioned, and 'man' is meant, as in the text quoted above.

Thus the inspired Scripture uses the term 'flesh' in many ways, and it would be tedious to collect and scrutinize them all. Our present purpose is to track down the meaning of 'living by the rule of the flesh' (which is clearly a bad thing, though the natural substance of flesh is not an evil in itself); and to enable us to achieve this purpose, let us carefully examine the passage in St Paul's Epistle to the Galatians where he says,

> It is obvious what the works of the flesh are: such things as fornication, impurity, lust, idolatry, sorcery, enmity, quarrelsomeness, jealousy, animosity, dissension, party intrigue, envy, drunkenness, drunken orgies, and so on. I warned you before, and I warn you again, that those who behave in such ways will never have a place in God's kingdom.[13]

A consideration of this whole passage of Paul's letter sufficient for the requirements of the present topic will enable us to answer the question of what is meant by 'living by the rule of the flesh'. For among the 'works of the flesh' which he said were obvious, and which he listed and condemned, we find not only those concerned with sensual pleasure, like fornication, impurity, lust, drunkenness and drunken orgies, but also those which show faults of the mind, which have nothing to do with sensual indulgence. For anyone can see that devotion to idols, sorcery, enmity, quarrelsomeness, jealousy, animosity, party intrigue, envy – all these are faults of the mind, not of the body. Indeed, it may happen that a man refrains from sensual

9. Gal. 3, 11. (St. Augustine mistakenly attributes it to Rom.)

10. Gal., 2, 16.

11. A doctrine attributed to Apollinarian and Arian heretics (cf. Aug. *De Haer.*, 49; 55).

12. John 20, 13. 13. Gal. 5, 19–21.

indulgence because of devotion to an idol, or because of the erroneous teaching of some sect; and yet even then, though such a man seems to restrain and suppress his carnal desires, he is convicted, on the authority of the Apostle, of living by the rule of the flesh; and it is the very fact of his abstention from fleshly indulgence that proves that he is engaged in 'the works of the flesh'.

Can anyone feel enmity except in the mind? Would anyone, speaking to an enemy, real or supposed, express himself by saying, 'Your flesh is set against me', rather than 'Your mind'? Finally, if anyone heard of 'carnalities' (if there is such a word) he would undoubtedly attribute them to the carnal nature; and by the same token, no one doubts that animosities are concerned with the *animus*, with the mind. It follows that the reason why 'the teacher of the Gentiles in faith and truth'[14] gives the name of 'works of the flesh' to those and similar failings is simply that he intends the word 'flesh' to be taken as meaning 'man' by the 'part for whole' figure of speech.

3. *The cause of sin arises in the soul, not in the flesh; and the corruption resulting from sin is not a sin but a punishment*

Now it may be asserted that the flesh is the cause of every kind of moral failing, on the ground that the bad behaviour of the soul is due to the influence of the flesh. But this contention shows a failure to consider man's nature carefully and in its entirety. For 'the corruptible body weighs down the soul.'[15] Hence also the Apostle, when treating of this corruptible body, first says, 'Our outer man is decaying,'[16] and later goes on thus:

> We know that if the earthly house we inhabit disintegrates, we have a building given by God, a house not made by human hands, eternal, in heaven. For in this body we do indeed sigh – as we long for our heavenly dwelling to be put on over it, hoping that when we have put it on, we shall not find ourselves naked. For we, who are in this present dwelling, feel its weight, and sigh; not that we desire to be stripped of our body; rather we desire to have the other clothing put on over it, so that what is mortal may be absorbed by life.[17]

And so we are weighed down by the corruptible body; and yet we know that the cause of our being weighed down is not the true nature and substance of our body but its corruption; and therefore we do not

14. cf. Tim. 2, 7. 15. Wisd. 9, 15. 16. 2 Cor. 4, 16.
17. 2 Cor. 5, 1–4.

wish to be stripped of it, but to be clothed with the immortality of the body. For then there will still be a body, but it will not be corruptible, and therefore not a burden. Consequently, in this present life, 'the corruptible body weighs down the soul, and the earthly habitation depresses the mind as it meditates on many questions.' However, those who imagine that all the ills of the soul derive from the body are mistaken.

True, Virgil is apparently expounding Platonic teaching[18] in glorious poetry when he says,

> Of those seeds heaven is the source, and fiery
> The energy within them, did not bodies
> Hamper and thwart them, and these earthly limbs
> And dying members dull them.[19]

And he will have it that the body is to be taken as the source of all four of the most familiar emotional disturbances of the mind: desire and fear, joy and grief, which may be called the origins of all sins and moral failings.[20] Thus he adds these lines,

> Hence come desire and fear, gladness and sorrow;
> They look not up to heaven, but are confined
> In darkness, in the sightless dungeon's gloom.

However, our belief is something very different. For the corruption of the body, which weighs down the soul, is not the cause of the first sin, but its punishment. And it was not the corruptible flesh that made the soul sinful; it was the sinful soul that made the flesh corruptible.

No doubt this corruption of the flesh results in some incitements to wrongdoing and in actual vicious longings; yet we must not attribute to the flesh all the faults of a wicked life, which would mean that we absolve the Devil of all those faults, since he has no flesh. Certainly, we cannot accuse the Devil of fornication or drunkenness or any other such wickedness connected with carnal indulgence, although he is the hidden persuader and instigator of such sins. Nevertheless, he is proud and envious in the highest degree; and this moral corruption has so mastered him that he is destined because of it to eternal punishment in the prison of this murky air of ours.

Now those vices, which are predominant in the Devil, are attributed to the flesh by the Apostle, although it is certain that the Devil is without flesh. For St Paul says that enmity, quarrelsomeness, jeal-

18. cf. *Phaedr.*, 245E–250E. 19. *Aen.*, 6, 730ff.
20. cf. Cic., *Tusc. Disp.*, 3, 11, 24; 4, 6, 11; 12.

ousy, animosity, and envy are 'works of the flesh';[21] and the fountain-head of all these evils is pride; and pride reigns in the Devil, although he is without flesh. For who is a greater enemy than he is to the saints? Who is found to quarrel with them more bitterly, to show more animosity, jealousy, and envy towards them? Yet he displays all these faults, without having flesh. So how can they be 'the works of the flesh' except in that they are the works of man, to whom, as I have said, the Apostle applies the term 'flesh'?

It is in fact not by the possession of flesh, which the Devil does not possess, that man has become like the Devil: it is by living by the rule of self, that is by the rule of man. For the Devil chose to live by the rule of self when he did not stand fast in the truth, so that the lie that he told was his own lie, not God's. The Devil is not only a liar; he is 'the father of lies'.[22] He was, as we know, the first to lie, and falsehood, like sin, had its start from him.

4. *The meaning of living 'by the standard of man' and 'by the standard of God'*

Thus, when man lives 'by the standard of man' and not 'by the standard of God', he is like the Devil; because even an angel should not have lived by the angel's standard, but by God's, so as to stand firm in the truth and speak the truth that comes from God's truth, not the lie that derives from his own falsehood. For the Apostle has this to say about man also, in another passage, 'But if the truth of God has been abundantly displayed through my falsehood'.[23] The point is that the falsehood is ours, but the truth is God's.

So when man lives by the standard of truth he lives not by his own standard, but by God's. For it is God who has said, 'I am the truth.'[24] By contrast, when he lives by his own standard, that is by man's and not by God's standard, then inevitably he lives by the standard of falsehood. Not that man himself is falsehood, since his author and creator is God, who is certainly not the author and creator of falsehood. The fact is that man was created right, on condition that he should live by the standard of his creator, not by his own, carrying out not his own will, but his creator's. Falsehood consists in not living in the way for which he was created.

Man has undoubtedly the will to be happy, even when he pursues

21. cf. Gal. 5, 19ff.
22. John 8, 44.
23. Rom. 3, 7.
24. John 14, 6.

happiness by living in a way which makes it impossible of attainment. What could be more of a falsehood than a will like that? Hence we can say with meaning that every sin is a falsehood. For sin only happens by an act of will; and our will is for our own welfare, or for the avoidance of misfortune. And hence the falsehood: we commit sin to promote our welfare, and it results instead in our misfortune; or we sin to increase our welfare, and the result is rather to increase our misfortune. What is the reason for this, except that well-being can only come to man from God, not from himself? And he forsakes God by sinning, and he sins by living by his own standard.

I have already said that two cities, different and mutually opposed, owe their existence to the fact that some men live by the standard of the flesh, others by the standard of the spirit. It can now be seen that we may also put it in this way: that some live by man's standard, others by God's. St Paul puts it very plainly when he says to the Corinthians, 'For since there is jealousy and quarrelling among you, are you not of the flesh, following human standards in your behaviour?'[25] Therefore, to behave according to human standards is the same as to be 'of the flesh', because by 'the flesh', a part of man, man himself is meant.

In fact, St Paul had previously employed the term 'animal' to the same people whom he here calls 'carnal'. This is what he said,

> For what man on earth knows the truth about a man except the spirit of the man which is in him? Similarly, no one knows the truth about God except the Spirit of God. Now we have not received the spirit of this world, but the spirit which is the gift of God, so that we may understand the gifts which God has granted us. We speak of those gifts in words which we have been taught, not by human wisdom, but by the Spirit, interpreting spiritual truths to men possessed by God's Spirit. The 'animal' man does not grasp what belongs to the Spirit of God; it is all folly to him.[26]

It is then to such men, that is, to 'animal' men, that he says, somewhat later, 'Now I, my brothers, could not speak to you as I should to men possessed by the Spirit; I could only speak as to men of the flesh.'[27] Both these terms, 'animal' and 'carnal', are examples of the 'part for whole' figure of speech. For *anima* (the soul) and *caro* (the flesh) are parts of a man, and can stand for man in his entirety. And thus the 'animal' man is not something different from the 'carnal' man: they are identical, that is, man living by human standards. In the same way, the reference is simply to men when we read 'No flesh

25. 1 Cor. 3, 3. 26. 1 Cor. 2, 11ff. 27. 1 Cor. 3, 1.

will be justified as a result of the works of the law',[28] and also when Scripture says, 'Seventy-five souls went down to Egypt with Jacob.'[29] In the first case 'no flesh' means 'no man', and in the second, 'seventy-five souls' means 'seventy-five men'.

Further, in the phrase, 'in words taught not by human wisdom', 'carnal wisdom' could be substituted; and in 'you follow human standards in your behaviour', 'carnal standards' would express the same meaning. This comes out more clearly in the words that follow, 'For when a man says, "I belong to Paul", and another, "I belong to Apollos", are you not merely men?'[30] Paul said earlier, 'You are "animal" ', and, 'You are carnal.' Now he makes his meaning plainer by saying, 'You are men.' That is, 'You live by man's standards, not God's. If you lived by his standards, you would be gods.'

5. *The Platonic theory of body and soul; more tolerable than the Manichean view, but to be rejected because it makes the nature of the flesh responsible for all moral faults*

There is no need then, in the matter of our sins and faults, to do our Creator the injustice of laying the blame on the nature of the flesh which is good, in its own kind and on its own level. But it is not good to forsake the good Creator and live by the standard of a created good, whether a man chooses the standard of the flesh, or of the soul, or of the entire man, who consists of soul and flesh and hence can be denoted by either term, soul or flesh, by itself. For anyone who exalts the soul as the Supreme Good, and censures the nature of flesh as something evil, is in fact carnal alike in his cult of the soul and in his revulsion from the flesh, since this attitude is prompted by human folly, not by divine truth.

The Platonists, to be sure, do not show quite the folly of the Manicheans.[31] They do not go so far as to execrate earthly bodies as the natural substance of evil, since all the elements which compose the structure of this visible and tangible world, and their qualities, are attributed by the Platonists to God the artificer. All the same, they hold that souls are so influenced by 'earthly limbs and dying members' that they derive from them their morbid desires and fears, joy and sadness. And those four 'disturbances' (to employ Cicero's word[32]) or

28. Rom. 3, 20. 29. Gen. 46, 27. 30. 1 Cor. 3, 4.

31. Who ascribed the creation of flesh to an evil power, opposed to God, and co-eternal with him (Aug., *De Haer.*, 46); cf. Bk XI, 13n.

32. *Tusc. Disp.*, 4, 6, 11.

'passions' (which is a literal translation of the Greek, and is the term in common use), cover the whole range of moral failure in human behaviour.[33]

But if this is true, how is it that, in Virgil, when Aeneas is told by his father in the world below that souls will return again to bodies, he is amazed at this notion, and cries out,

> Father, can we believe that souls return
> To dwell beneath the sky, again to assume
> The body's lethargy? Oh, what dread lust
> For life under the sun holds them in misery?[34]

Must we really suppose that this 'dread lust', deriving from 'earthly limbs and dying members', still finds a place in that purity of souls which we hear so much about? Does not Virgil assert that souls have been purified from all such 'bodily infections' (as he calls them)? Yet, after that, they begin to feel the desire 'again to assume their bodies'.

Hence, even if it were true (it is in fact an utterly baseless assumption) that souls pass through a ceaseless alternation of cleansing and defilement as they depart and return, we must infer that there can have been no truth in the claim that all their culpable and perverted emotions that arise in them are derived from their earthly bodies. For we see that, on the admission of the Platonists themselves, this 'dread lust', as their renowned spokesman puts it, is so far from deriving from the body that of its own accord it urges the soul towards a bodily existence, even when the soul has been purified from all bodily infection, and has been placed in a situation outside any kind of body. Thus on their own confession, it is not only from the influence of the flesh that the soul experiences desire and fear, joy and distress; it can also be disturbed by those emotions from a source within itself.

6. *The character of the human will determines the quality of the emotions*

The important factor in those emotions is the character of a man's will. If the will is wrongly directed, the emotions will be wrong; if the will is right, the emotions will be not only blameless, but praiseworthy. The will is engaged in all of them; in fact they are all essentially acts of will. For what is desire or joy but an act of will in agreement with what we wish for? And what is fear or grief but an act

33. cf. Bk VIII, 17. 34. *Aen.*, 6, 719ff.

of will in disagreement with what we reject? We use the term desire when this agreement takes the form of the pursuit of what we wish for, while joy describes our satisfaction in the attainment. In the same way, when we disagree with something we do not wish to happen, such an act of will is fear; but when we disagree with something which happens against our will, that act of will is grief. And in general, as a man's will is attracted or repelled in accordance with the varied character of different objects which are pursued or shunned, so it changes and turns into feelings of various kinds.

For this reason, the man who lives by God's standards, and not by man's, must needs be a lover of the good, and it follows that he must hate what is evil. Further, since no one is evil by nature, but anyone who is evil is evil because of a perversion of nature, the man who lives by God's standards has a duty of 'perfect hatred'[35] towards those who are evil; that is to say, he should not hate the person because of the fault, nor should he love the fault because of the person. He should hate the fault, but love the man. And when the fault has been cured there will remain only what he ought to love, nothing that he should hate.

7. *The scriptural terms for love*

When a man's resolve is to love God, and to love his neighbour as himself, not according to man's standards but according to God's, he is undoubtedly said to be a man of good will, because of this love. This attitude is more commonly called 'charity' (*caritas*) in holy Scripture; but it appears in the same sacred writings under the appellation 'love' (*amor*). For instance, when the Apostle is giving instructions about the choice of a man to rule God's people, he says that such a man should be a lover (*amator*) of the good.[36] And when the Lord himself had asked the apostle Peter, 'Are you more fond (*diligis*) of me than those?' Peter replied 'Lord, you know that I love (*amo*) you.'[37] Then the Lord repeated his question, asking, not whether Peter loved him, but whether he was fond of him; and Peter again replied, 'Lord, you know that I love you.' However, when Jesus asked for the third time, he himself said, 'Do you love me?' instead of, 'Are you fond of me?' And then the evangelist goes on, 'Peter was grieved because the Lord said to him, for the third time: "Do you love me?"' Whereas in fact it was not the third time; the Lord said, 'Do you love me?' only once, but he had twice asked, 'Are you fond of me?' From this we infer that

35. Ps. 139, 22. 36. cf. Tit. 1, 8. 37. John 21, 15ff.

when the Lord said, 'Are you fond of me?' he meant precisely the same as when he asked, 'Do you love me?' Peter, in contrast, did not change the word used to express the same meaning, when he replied the third time, 'Lord, you know everything. You know that I love you.'

The reason why I thought I should mention this is that quite a number of people imagine that fondness and charity are something different from love. They say, in fact, that 'fondness' is to be taken in a good sense, 'love' in a bad sense. It is, however, well established that this was not the usage even of authors of secular literature. But the philosophers will have to decide whether they make this distinction, and on what principle. Certainly their books are sufficient evidence of the high value they place on love, when it is concerned with good things and directed towards God himself. My task, however, was to make the point that the Scriptures of our religion, whose authority we rank above all other writings, do not distinguish between 'love' and 'fondness' or 'charity'. For I have shown that 'love' also is used in a good sense.

But I should not like anyone to suppose that while 'love' can be employed both in a bad and a good sense, 'fondness' can have only a good connotation. I would draw attention to a passage in one of the psalms, 'The man that is fond of wickedness hates his own soul';[38] and to a statement of the apostle John, 'If anyone has become fond of the world, there is no fondness in him for the Father.'[39] Notice that in this one text we find 'fondness' used both in a good sense and in a bad. As for 'love', I have already shown its use in a good sense; and in case anyone should demand an example of its employment with a bad connotation, here is a quotation from Scripture: 'For men will be lovers of themselves, lovers of money.'[40]

And so a rightly directed will is love in a good sense and a perverted will is love in a bad sense. Therefore a love which strains after the possession of the loved object is desire; and the love which possesses and enjoys that object is joy. The love that shuns what opposes it is fear, while the love that feels that opposition when it happens is grief. Consequently, these feelings are bad, if the love is bad, and good if the love is good.

Let me prove this statement from Scripture. The Apostle 'desires to depart and to be with Christ';[41] and, 'My soul has desired to long for your judgements',[42] or (to put it more appropriately), 'My soul has longed to desire your judgements'; and, 'The desire for wisdom leads to

38. Ps. 11, 5. 39. John 2, 15. 40. 2 Tim. 3, 2.
41. cf. Phil. 1, 23. 42. Ps. 119, 20.

sovereignty.'[43] All the same, it is the established usage that when we use 'desire' (*cupiditas* or *concupiscentia*) without specifying its object, it can only be understood in a bad sense. 'Joy' has a good connotation: 'Have joy in the Lord, and exult, you righteous ones',[44] and 'You have put joy into my heart';[45] and 'You will fill me with joy by your countenance.'[46] 'Fear' has a good sense in the place where the Apostle says, 'With fear and trembling work out your own salvation';[47] and, 'Do not think highly of yourself, but fear',[48] and 'I fear, however, that as the serpent seduced Eve by his craftiness, so your minds will be enticed away from the purity which is in Christ.'[49] As for 'grief', it is a nice question whether any instance can be found of its use in a good sense. Cicero tends to use the word 'distress' (*aegritudo*)[50] for this feeling, while Virgil prefers 'pain' (*dolor*), as in the passage, 'They feel pain and gladness.'[51] The reason why I prefer 'grief' is that 'distress' and 'pain' are more generally employed of physical sensations.

8. *The three emotions of the wise, according to the Stoics*

The Stoics wished to find in the mind of the wise man three dispositions, called in Greek *eupatheiai*, and by Cicero, in Latin, *constantiae*, 'constant states'.[52] These were to replace three mental disorders; there would be will instead of desire, gladness instead of joy, caution instead of fear. But they denied the possibility of any emotion in the wise man's mind answering to distress or pain, which I have preferred to call 'grief', to avoid ambiguity.

The will, say the Stoics, undoubtedly pursues the good, and this is what the wise man does; gladness is felt in the attainment of the good, which the wise man attains in every situation; caution avoids evil, and that is what the wise man ought to avoid. Furthermore, grief is occasioned by evil which has already happened; and since they think that no evil can happen to a wise man, they have asserted that there can be no corresponding emotion in a wise man's mind. What they are saying then comes to this – that only a wise man can have will, gladness, and caution, while a fool can only experience desire, joy, fear, and grief, the three former being 'constant states', while the latter four are disorders, called 'perturbations' in Cicero, but 'passions'

43. Wisd. 6, 20. 44. Ps. 32, 11. 45. Ps. 4, 7.
46. Ps. 16, 11. 47. Phil. 2, 12. 48. Rom. 11, 20.
49. 2 Cor. 11, 3. 50. *Tusc. Disp.*, 3, 10. 51. *Aen.*, 6, 733.
52. *Tusc Disp.*, 4, 6, 11ff: cf Diog. Laert. 7, 116.

in the majority of authors. While in Greek, as I have already said, the three former states are called *eupatheiai*, while the four latter are known as *pathê*.

When I was examining, as carefully as I could, the question whether this usage agreed with the practice of holy Scripture, I found this text in one of the prophets, 'There is no gladness for the wicked, says the Lord.'[53] This implies that the wicked can feel joy, rather than gladness, because gladness properly belongs to the good and the devout. Again, the text in the Gospel, 'Whatever you will that men should do to you, do that also to them',[54] seems to imply that no one can *will* anything in an evil or dishonourable way; he can only so *desire*. In fact, because of this linguistic convention a number of translators have added the words 'good things' in their translation, rendering the passage thus: 'Whatever good things you will that man should do to you.' This was because they imagined it advisable to guard against the chance of anyone's wishing to have dishonourable things done for him by others – the provision of extravagant banquets, for example, to say nothing of more discreditable possibilities. Such a one might suppose that he would be fulfilling this instruction, if he did the same for others. But in the Greek Gospel, of which the Latin is a translation, 'good things' is not in the text, which says, 'Whatever you will that men should do to you, do that also to them.' The reason being, I suppose, that the use of 'you *will*', is intended in itself to imply 'good things'. For the text avoids saying 'you *desire*'.

For all that, we are not obliged always to curb our use of language by such niceties of interpretation; they are, however, to be employed occasionally. And when we are reading those writers whose authority we cannot reject without sin, these precisions of meaning are to be understood in places where the straightforward sense can find no other way out; for example in the illustrations I quoted above, from the prophet and from the Gospel. For everyone knows that the ungodly exult with joy, and yet, 'There is no gladness for the wicked, says the Lord.' This can only make sense because 'gladness' has a special meaning when it is used in a precise and prescribed sense. Again, no one would deny that it is wrong for men to be told to do to others what they desire to have done to themselves by others, in case they should gratify each other in disgraceful and forbidden indulgences. And yet the most wholesome and the truest of all injunctions is this: 'Whatever you will that men should do to you, do that also to them.' And this is because in this context 'will' is used in a precise

53. Is. 57, 21 (LXX). 54. Matt. 7, 12.

sense, and cannot be given a bad connotation. On the other hand if there were not also such a thing as an evil will, there would not be the more familiar usage, very frequently employed in ordinary speech, which produces the command, 'Let it not be your will to tell any lie.'[55] And a distinction is made between the depravity of an evil will and the will of which the angels spoke when they proclaimed 'Peace on earth to men of good will.'[56] The addition of 'good' was otiose if will can only be good. Again, there would have been no great commendation of charity in the Apostle's statement that 'charity feels no gladness in wickedness'[57] were it not that malignity does feel gladness in it.

A similarly indiscriminate use of these terms is seen also in secular authors. Cicero, for example a most resourceful speaker, says, 'I desire, conscript fathers, to be merciful.'[58] He used the word 'desire' in a good sense; and no one would be so pedantic as to maintain that he should have said, 'My will is,' instead of 'I desire.' Again, in Terence's play, there is an immoral young man who is crazed with the heat of his desire; and he says,

My will is set on naught but Philumena.[59]

But his 'will' was in fact his lust: and this is made quite evident by the retort of his slave – more sensible than his master – which is put in at this point. The slave says to his owner,

Better would it be for you
If you'd brace yourself to put this love completely from your mind,
Instead of idly talking, to inflame your lust in vain.

Then again we have evidence for the use of 'gladness' in a bad sense in that very verse of Virgil's which includes the four disorders, concisely enumerated,

Hence come desire and fear, gladness, and sorrow.[60]

The same author also says,

The evil gladness of the mind.[61]

This shows that will, caution, and gladness are felt by good and bad alike; and (to make the same statement in other words) desire, fear, and joy are emotions common to both good and bad. But the good feel these emotions in a good way, the bad feel them in a bad way, just as an act of will may be rightly or wrongly directed. Even 'grief' – and

55. Ecclus. 7, 13. 56. Luke 2, 14. 57. 1 Cor. 13,6.
58. *Cat.*, 1, 2, 4. 59. *Andr.* 306ff. 60. *Aen.*, 6, 733.
61. *Aen.*, 6, 278f.

the Stoics imagined nothing could be found in the mind of a wise man to correspond to this emotion – even 'grief' is discovered used in a good sense, especially in our Christian authors. The Apostle, for example, praises the Corinthians for having felt a grief 'in God's way'. However, someone may say that the Apostle congratulated his readers on feeling grief in repentance, a grief such as can only belong to those who have sinned. This, in fact, is what the Apostle says:

> I see that the letter grieved you, if only for the moment. And so I am glad, not because you were grieved, but because your grief led to repentance. For you felt a grief pleasing to God, and so you suffered no hurt from us. For the grief that is according to God's will produces a repentance which brings salvation, a repentance not to be repented of: this world's grief produces death. Your grief was according to God's will; and see what serious intention it has brought about in you![62]

This gives the Stoics a chance of replying, in defence of their point of view, that grief does no doubt appear to serve a useful purpose when it engenders penitence for sin; but, they say, it cannot exist in the mind of a wise man, just because sin is not for him a possible contingency, with the chance of grief and penitence; no more is any other evil, to bring him grief in the enduring or the feeling of it. Now there is a story told of Alcibiades – that was the name, if my memory serves me. He was happy, they say, in his own estimation; but when Socrates in an argument proved to him how miserable he was, because he was foolish, he burst into tears.[63] Thus for him foolishness was the cause of this salutary and desirable grief, the grief of one who laments that he is not what he ought to be. And yet it is the wise man, according to the Stoics, not the fool, who is incapable of grief.

9. *The agitations of the mind, which appear as right feelings in the lives of the righteous*

As far as this question of mental disturbances is concerned, I have already given my reply to these philosophers in the ninth book of this work.[64] I have shown that they are dealing in words rather than in realities, and are more eager for controversy than for truth. Among us Christians, on the other hand, the citizens of the Holy City of God, as they live by God's standards in the pilgrimage of this present life, f[illegible] fear and desire, pain and gladness in conformity with the holy Scriptures and sound doctrine; and because their love is right, all these feelings are right in them.

62. 2 Cor. 7, 8–11. 63. Cic., *Tusc. Disp.*, 3, 22. 64. Bk IX, 4; 5.

They fear eternal punishment and desire eternal life. They feel pain in their actual situation, because they are still 'groaning inwardly as they wait for adoption, for the ransoming of their bodies';[65] they rejoice in the hope that 'the saying, "Death has been swallowed up in victory", will become a reality'.[66] Again, they fear to sin, and they desire to persevere. They feel pain about their sins, and they feel gladness in good works. To make them fear to sin, they are told, 'Because wickedness will abound, the love of many will grow cold.'[67] To make them desire to persevere, the Scripture tells them, 'The man who perseveres up to the end is the man who will be saved.'[68] To make them feel pain about sins they are told, 'If we say that there is no sin in us, we are fooling ourselves, and we are remote from the truth.'[69] To make them feel gladness in good works, they are told, 'God loves a cheerful giver.'[70]

Similarly, they fear or desire to be tempted, they feel pain or gladness in temptations, according to their weakness or strength of character. To prompt them to fear temptations, they are told, 'If anyone is caught doing something wrong, you who are guided by the Spirit must set him right in a spirit of kindness. Look to yourself, each one of you, for fear you too may be tempted.'[71] By way of contrast, to encourage them to desire temptation, they hear a valiant citizen of God's City saying, 'Prove me, Lord, and try me: test my heart and mind in the fire.'[72] So that they may feel pain in temptations, they have the sight of Peter weeping;[73] so that they may feel gladness in temptations, they hear the voice of James, saying, 'Consider it nothing but gladness, my brothers, when you come upon temptations of all kinds.'[74]

Besides this, it is not only on their own account that the citizens are moved by these feelings; they also feel them on account of those whose liberation they desire, while they fear that they may perish; they feel pain if they do perish, and feel gladness if they are set free. Those of us who have come into the Church of Christ from the Gentile world should remind ourselves above all of that 'teacher of the Gentiles in faith and truth'.[75] He was a man of outstanding virtue and courage who boasted of his own weaknesses,[76] who toiled more than all his fellow-apostles,[77] and in many epistles instructed the peoples of God, not only those who were seen by him at the time, but

65. Rom. 8, 23. 66. 1 Cor. 15, 54. 67. Matt. 24, 12. 68. Matt. 10, 22.
69. 1 John 1, 8 70. 2 Cor. 9, 8. 71 Gal. 6, 1. 72. Ps. 26, 2.
73. cf. Matt. 26, 75. 74. Jas. 1, 2. 75. 1 Tim. 2, 7. 76. 2 Cor. 12, 5; 12, 9f.
77. 1 Cor. 15, 10

also those who were foreseen as yet to be. He was Christ's athlete, taught by Christ, anointed by him, crucified with him;[78] he gloried in Christ, and in the theatre of this world, for which he was made a spectacle in the sight of angels as well as men,[79] he fought a great fight and kept the rules[80] and pressed on ahead for the prize of the calling to the realms above.[81] The citizens of God's City are happy to gaze at this hero with the eyes of faith. They see him rejoicing with those who rejoice, and weeping with those who weep,[82] troubled by fighting outside and fears within,[83] desiring to depart and be with Christ.[84] They see him longing to see the Romans so that he may enjoy a harvest among them also, as among other nations,[85] being jealous for the Corinthians, and in that jealousy fearing that their minds may be seduced from the purity which is in Christ.[86] They watch him feeling deep grief and ceaseless pain in his heart for the Israelites,[87] because, in ignorance of the righteousness that God bestows, and wishing to establish their own, they did not submit to God's righteousness.[88] They watch him as he makes known not only his pain but his mourning for certain persons who had sinned before and had shown no repentance for their impurity and their acts of fornication.[89]

If these emotions and feelings, that spring from love of the good and from holy charity, are to be called faults, then let us allow that real faults should be called virtues. But since these feelings are the consequence of right reason when they are exhibited in the proper situation, who would then venture to call them morbid or disordered passions? Hence, when the Lord himself condescended to live a human life in the form of a servant,[90] though completely free from sin, he displayed these feelings in situations where he decided that they should be shown. For human emotion was not illusory in him who had a truly human body and a truly human mind. And so, when these feelings are ascribed to him in the Gospel, there is certainly no falsehood in the ascription; when we are told, for instance, that he felt an angry grief at the Jews' hardness of heart,[91] that he said 'I am glad for your sake, so that you may believe',[92] that he even shed tears when he was about to awaken Lazarus,[93] that he yearned to eat the passover with his disciples,[94] that at the approach of his passion, his

78. Gal. 1, 12; 2; Cor. 1, 21; Gal. 2, 20.
79. 1 Cor. 4, 9.
80. 2 Tim. 2, 5.
81. Phil. 3, 14.
82. Rom. 12, 15.
83. 2 Cor. 7, 5.
84. Phil. 1, 23.
85. Rom. 1, 11ff.
86. 2 Cor. 11 2f.
87. Rom. 9, 2.
88. Rom. 10, 3.
89. 2 Cor. 12, 21.
90. Phil. 2, 7.
91. Mark 3, 5.
92. John 11, 15.
93. ibid., 11, 35.
94. Luke 22, 15.

soul was grieved.[95] In fact, he accepted those emotions in his human mind for the sake of his fixed providential design, when he so decided, just as he was made man when he so willed.

At the same time, we have to admit that the emotions we experience, even when they are right and as God would have them, belong to this life, not to the life we hope for in the future; and often we yield to them even against our will. Thus we sometimes weep, even when we do not want to, though we may be moved not by any blameworthy desire but by praiseworthy charity. That implies that we have these emotions as a result of the weakness of our human condition; but this was not true of the Lord Jesus, whose weakness resulted from his power. Yet if we felt none of those emotions at all, while we are subject to the weakness of this life, there would really be something wrong with our life. For the Apostle censured and denounced certain people who, he said, were even devoid of natural feeling.[96] One of the sacred psalms also blames those about whom it says, 'I waited for someone to share my grief; but there was no one.'[97] In fact, complete exemption from pain, while we are in this place of misery, is certainly as one of the literary men of this world expressed it, 'a piece of luck that one has to pay a high price for; the price of inhumanity of mind and insensitivity of body'.[98]

At this point, we may examine that condition which in Greek is called *apatheia*,[99] which might be translated in Latin by *impassibilitas* (impassibility) if such a word existed. Now, bearing in mind that the reference is to a mental, not a physical condition, if we are to understand it as meaning a life without the emotions which occur in defiance of reason and which disturb the thoughts, it is clearly a good and desirable state; but it does not belong to this present life. For it is not the voice of men of any and every sort, but the voice of the most godly, of those advanced in righteousness and holiness, which says, 'If we say that there is no sun in us, we are fooling ourselves, and we are remote from the truth.'[100] And since this state of *apatheia* will not come until there is no sin in man, it will not come in this present life.

At present, however, we do well if our life is free from external blame. But anyone who thinks that his life is without sin does not succeed in avoiding sin, but rather in forfeiting pardon. Moreover, if

95. Matt. 26, 38. 96. Rom. 1, 31. 97. Ps. 69, 20.
98. Cic., *Tusc. Disp.*, 3, 6, 12.
99. The Stoic moral principle; cf. ch. 2.
100. 1 John 1, 8.

apatheia is the name of the state in which the mind cannot be touched by any emotion whatsoever, who would not judge this insensitivity to be the worst of all moral defects? There is therefore nothing absurd in the assertion that the final complete happiness will be exempt from the spasms of fear and from any kind of grief; but only a man utterly cut off from truth would say that love and gladness will have no place there. Then if *apatheia* describes a condition in which there is no fear to terrify, no pain to torment, then it is a condition to be shunned in this life, if we wish to lead the right kind of life, the life that is, according to God's will. But in that life of bliss which, it is promised, will be everlasting, it is clearly right that we should hope for this condition.

Now one kind of fear is that which the apostle John has in mind when he says, 'There is no fear in love; in fact perfect love sends fear packing; because fear brings punishment. Anyone who is afraid has not reached the perfection of love.'[101] This fear is not of the same kind as that felt by the apostle Paul when he was afraid that the Corinthians might be seduced by the craftiness of the serpent.[102] This latter is the fear which love feels, which, in truth, only love can feel. But the fear that is not prompted by love is the other kind of fear, the kind the apostle Paul means when he says, 'You did not receive the spirit of slavery, bringing you back to a state of fear.'[103] That fear which 'is pure, enduring for ever',[104] if it will exist in the world to come (and how else can it be understood to endure for ever?) is not the fear that frightens someone away from an evil which may befall him, but the fear that keeps him in a good which cannot be lost.

For in a situation where the love of a good thing attained is changeless, there certainly the fear of an evil to be avoided is a serene fear – if that is a possible expression! The phrase 'fear that is pure' signifies without doubt the act of will which makes it inevitable that we shall refuse to sin and that we shall be on our guard against sin, not with the anxiety of weakness, in fear of sinning, but with a tranquillity based on love. Or, if no kind of fear whatsoever can exist in that assured serenity, with the certainty of unending and blissful gladness, then the saying, 'The fear of the Lord is pure, enduring for ever', is analogous to, 'The patience of the poor will not perish eternally.'[105] For patience itself will not be eternal, since it is only necessary where evils are to be endured; it is the destination reached through patience that will be eternal. So perhaps 'pure fear' is said to

101. 1 John 4, 18. 102. 2 Cor. 11, 3. 103. Rom. 8, 15.
104. Ps. 19, 9. 105. Ps. 9, 18.

endure for ever in the sense that the destination to which the fear itself leads will be permanent.

It comes to this then: we must lead a right life to reach the goal of a life of felicity; and this right kind of life exhibits all those emotions in the right way, and a misdirected life in a misdirected way. But the life of felicity, which is also the life of eternity, will show a love and a gladness that are not only right but also assured, while it will show no fear or pain at all. Hence it is clear what must be the quality of the citizens of God's City during their earthly pilgrimage. They must live a life according to the spirit and not according to the flesh, that is, they must live by God's standards, not man's. And it is also apparent what will be their quality in that immortality towards which they are making their way.

In contrast, the city, that is the society, of the ungodly consists of those who live by the standards not of God but of man; of those who follow the doctrines of men or demons in their worship of false divinity and their contempt for the true Godhead. This city is shaken by these emotions as by diseases and upheavals. And if it has any citizens who give an appearance of controlling and in some way checking these emotions, they are so arrogant and pretentious in their irreligion that the swelling of their pride increases in exact proportion as their feeling of pain decreases. Some of those people may display an empty complacency, the more monstrous for being so rare, which makes them so charmed with this achievement in themselves that they are not stirred or excited by any emotions at all, not swayed or influenced by any feelings. If so, they rather lose every shred of humanity than achieve a true tranquillity. For hardness does not necessarily imply rectitude, and insensibility is not a guarantee of health.

10. *The emotions of the first human beings before their sin*

What of the first human being? Or rather, what of the first human beings, since there was a married couple? We have every reason to ask whether they experienced these emotions in their animal bodies before they sinned – the kind of emotions which we shall not feel in our spiritual bodies, when all sin has been washed away and ended. For if they did feel them, how could they have been happy in that ever-memorable place of bliss called paradise? Can anyone really be described as happy if he is exposed to fear or pain? Moreover, was there anything for them to fear where there was such abundance of all good things, where there was no threat of death or any bodily sickness, and there was nothing lacking that a good will would seek to obtain, nor was anything present that could spoil man's life of felicity, either in body or mind?

The pair lived in a partnership of unalloyed felicity; their love for God and for each other was undisturbed. This love was the source of immense gladness, since the beloved object was always at hand for their enjoyment. There was a serene avoidance of sin; and as long as this continued, there was no encroachment of any kind of evil, from any quarter, to bring them sadness. Or could it have been that they desired to lay hands on the forbidden tree, so as to eat its fruit, but that they were afraid of dying? In that case both desire and fear was already disturbing them, even in that place. But never let us imagine that this should have happened where there was no sin of any kind. For it must be a sin to desire what the Law of God forbids, and to abstain merely from fear of punishment and not for love of righteousness. Never let us suppose, I repeat, that before all sin there already existed such a sin, the same sin, committed in respect of that tree, which the Lord spoke of in respect of a woman, when he said, 'If anyone looks at a woman with the eyes of lust, he has already committed adultery with her in his heart.'[106]

How fortunate, then, were the first human beings! They were not distressed by any agitations of the mind, nor pained by any disorders of the body. And equally fortunate would be the whole united fellowship of mankind if our first parents had not committed an evil deed whose effect was to be passed on to their posterity, and if none of their descendants had sown in wickedness a crop that they were to reap in condemnation. Moreover, this felicity would have continued until, thanks to the blessing pronounced in the words, 'Increase and multiply,'[107] the number of the predestined saints was made up; and then another and a greater happiness would have been granted, the happiness which has been given to the blessed angels. In this state of bliss there would have been the serene assurance that no one would sin and no one would die, and the life of the saints, without any previous experience of toil, or pain, or death, would have been already what it is now destined to become after all these experiences, when our bodies are restored to incorruptibility at the resurrection of the dead.

106. Matt. 5, 28. 107. Gen. 1, 28.

11. *The natural state of man, created good and spoilt by sin, can only be restored by its Creator*

Now God foreknew everything, and therefore could not have been unaware that man would sin. It follows that all our assertions about the Holy City must take into account God's foreknowledge and his providential design; we must not advance theories which could not have become matters of knowledge for us, because they had no place in God's plan. Man could not upset the divine purpose by his sin, in the sense of compelling God to alter his decision. For God in his foreknowledge anticipated both results: he knew beforehand how evil the man would become whom God himself had created good; he also knew what good, even so, he would bring out of man's evil.

It is true that God is said to alter his decisions; and so we are told in Scripture, by a metaphorical way of speaking, that God even 'repented'.[108] But such assertions are made from the standpoint of human expectation, or the prospect suggested by the normal procedure of natural causation; they do not take into account the Almighty's foreknowledge of what he is going to do. Thus, as the Bible says, 'God made man upright,'[109] and therefore possessed of a good will – for he would not have been upright, had he not possessed a good will. Good will then is the work of God, since man was created with it by God.

But the first evil act of will, since it preceded all evil deeds in man, was rather a falling away from the work of God to its own works, rather than any substantive act. And the consequent deeds were evil because they followed the will's own line, and not God's. And so the will itself was, as it were, the evil tree which bore evil fruit,[110] in the shape of those evil deeds; or rather it was the man himself who was that tree, in so far as his will was evil. Moreover, though an evil will is not natural but unnatural because it is a defect, still it belongs to the nature of which it is a defect, for it cannot exist except in a nature. But it can only exist in a nature which God created out of nothing, not in that nature which the Creator begot out of himself, as he begot the Word through whom all things were made.[111] For, although God fashioned man from the dust of the earth,[112] the earth itself and all earthly matter are derived from nothing at all; and when man was made, God gave to his body a soul which was created out of nothing.

108. Gen. 6, 6; Exod. 32, 14; 1 Sam. 15, 11; 15, 35; 2 Sam. 24, 16.
109. Eccles. 7, 29. 110. cf. Matt. 7. 17f. 111. cf. John 1, 3.
112. cf. Gen. 2, 7.

But in spite of man's sin, the good things overcome the evil; so much so that although evil things are allowed to exist in order to show how the righteousness and foreknowledge of the Creator can turn even those very evils to good account, nevertheless good things can exist without the evil, just as the true and supreme God, as also all the celestial creation, visible and invisible, exists above this murky air of ours. In contrast, evil things cannot exist without the good, since the natural entities in which evil exists are certainly good, in so far as they are natural. Furthermore, an evil is eradicated not by the removal of some natural substance which had accrued to the original, or by the removal of any part of it, but by the healing and restoration of the original which had been corrupted and debased.

The choice of the will, then, is genuinely free only when it is not subservient to faults and sins. God gave it that true freedom, and now that it has been lost, through its own fault, it can be restored only by him who had the power to give it at the beginning. Hence the Truth says, 'If the Son sets you free, then you will be truly free.'[113] This is the same as saying, 'If the Son saves you, you will be truly saved.' For he is our Saviour for the same reason that he is our liberator.

We know that the first man lived according to God's will in a paradise both material and spiritual. It was not merely a material paradise – that is, it did not provide merely material blessings, while failing to be a spiritual paradise, because it did not yield the blessings for a man's spirit. And yet it was not merely spiritual – a paradise which man could enjoy through his inward senses, without being a material paradise, to satisfy man's outward perceptions. It was clearly both, to satisfy both. But after that, the arrogant angel came, envious because of that pride of his, who had for the same reason turned away from God to follow his own leading. With the proud disdain of a tyrant he chose to rejoice over his subjects rather than to be a subject himself; and so he fell from the spiritual paradise. I have discussed his fall, to the best of my ability, in the eleventh and twelfth books of this work,[114] and the fall of his confederates, who, from being angels of God, were turned into angels of this new chief. After his fall, his ambition was to worm his way, by seductive craftiness, into the consciousness of man, whose unfallen condition he envied, now that he himself had fallen. To this end he selected as his mouthpiece a serpent in the material paradise where the other terrestrial animals lived, tame and harmless, with those two human beings, male and female. This animal, to be sure, was suitable for the rebel angel's work, with his

113. John 8, 36. 114. Bk XI, 13; XII, 1.

slippery body, moving along in tortuous twists and turns The rebel, in virtue of his angelic prestige and his superior nature subdued the serpent to his will in spiritual wickedness, and by misusing it as his instrument he had deceitful conversation with the woman – no doubt starting with the inferior of the human pair so as to arrive at the whole by stages, supposing that the man would not be so easily gullible, and could not be trapped by a false move on his own part, but only if he yielded to another's mistake.

That is what happened to Aaron. He was not persuaded by argument to agree with the erring people to erect an idol; he yielded to constraint.[115] And it is unbelievable that Solomon mistakenly supposed that he ought to serve idols; he was induced to such acts of sacrilege by feminine cajolery.[116] It was the same with that first man and his wife. They were alone together, two human beings, a married pair; and we cannot believe that the man was led astray to transgress God's law because he believed that the woman spoke the truth, but that he fell in with her suggestions because they were so closely bound in partnership. In fact, the Apostle was not off the mark when he said, 'It was not Adam, but Eve, who was seduced,'[117] for what he meant was that Eve accepted the serpent's statement as the truth, while Adam refused to be separated from his only companion, even if it involved sharing her sin. That does not mean that he was less guilty, if he sinned knowingly and deliberately. Hence the Apostle does not say, 'He did not sin,' but, 'He was not seduced.' For he certainly refers to the man when he says, 'It was through one man that sin came into the world,'[118] and when he says more explicitly, a little later, 'by reproducing the transgression of Adam'.[119]

The Apostle intended us to take 'the seduced' as meaning those who do not think that what they do is sin. But Adam knew; otherwise how would it be true that 'Adam was not seduced'? However, he was unacquainted with the strictness of God, and he might have been mistaken in that he supposed it to be a pardonable offence he had committed. In consequence, while he was not seduced in the same sense as the woman, it remains true that he was mistaken about the kind of judgement that would be passed upon his allegation that 'The woman you gave me as companion, she gave it to me, and I ate.'[120] Need I say more? They were not both deceived by credulity; but both were taken captive by their sin and entangled in the snares of the Devil.

115. Exod. 32, 3ff. 116. 1 Kings 11, 4. 117. 1 Tim. 2, 14.
118. Rom. 5, 12. 119. Rom. 5, 14. 120. Gen. 3, 12.

12. *The nature of the first sin*

Someone may be worried about the question why other sins do not alter human nature in the same way as it was changed by the transgression of the two first human beings. The effect of that sin was to subject human nature to all the process of decay which we see and feel, and consequently to death also. And man was distracted and tossed about by violent and conflicting emotions, a very different being from what he was in paradise before his sin, though even then he lived in an animal body. Anyone who is worried about this question ought not to regard the offence as unimportant and trivial just because it was concerned with food – a food not evil or harmful except in that it was forbidden. For God would not have created or planted anything evil in such a place of felicity.

But God's instructions demanded obedience, and obedience is in a way the mother and guardian of all the other virtues in a rational creature, seeing that the rational creation has been so made that it is to man's advantage to be in subjection to God, and it is calamitous for him to act according to his own will, and not to obey the will of his Creator. The injunction forbidding the eating of one kind of food, where such an abundant supply of other foods was available, was so easy to observe, so brief to remember; above all, it was given at a time when desire was not yet in opposition to the will. That opposition came later as a result of the punishment of the transgression. Therefore the unrighteousness of violating the prohibition was so much the greater, in proportion to the ease with which it could have been observed and fulfilled.

13. *In Adam's transgression the evil will preceded the evil act*

It was in secret that the first human beings began to be evil; and the result was that they slipped into open disobedience. For they would not have arrived at the evil act if an evil will had not preceded it. Now, could anything but pride have been the start of the evil will? For 'pride is the start of every kind of sin.'[121] And what is pride except a longing for a perverse kind of exaltation? For it is a perverse kind of exaltation to abandon the basis on which the mind should be firmly fixed, and to become, as it were, based on oneself, and so remain. This happens when a man is too pleased with himself: and a man is self-complacent when he deserts that changeless Good in which, rather

121. Ecclus. 10, 13; cf. Bk XII, 6.

than in himself, he ought to have found his satisfaction. This desertion is voluntary, for if the will had remained unshaken in its love of the higher changeless Good, which shed on it light to see and kindled in it fire to love, it would not have been diverted from this love to follow its own pleasure; and the will would not have been so darkened and chilled in consequence as to let the woman believe that the serpent had spoken the truth and the man to put his wife's will above God's commandment, and to suppose that his was a venial transgression when he refused to desert his life's companion even though the refusal entailed companionship in sin.

Thus the evil act, the transgression of eating the forbidden fruit, was committed only when those who did it were already evil; that bad fruit could only have come from a bad tree.[122] Further, the badness of the tree came about contrary to nature, because without a fault in the will, which is against nature, it certainly could not have happened. But only a nature created out of nothing could have been distorted by a fault. Consequently, although the will derives its existence, as a nature, from its creation by God, its falling away from its true being is due to its creation out of nothing.

Yet man did not fall away to the extent of losing all being; but when he had turned towards himself his being was less real than when he adhered to him who exists in a supreme degree. And so, to abandon God and to exist in oneself, that is to please oneself, is not immediately to lose all being; but it is to come nearer to nothingness. That is why the proud are given another name in holy Scripture; they are called 'self-pleasers'.[123] Now it is good to 'lift up your heart', and to exalt your thoughts, yet not in the self-worship of pride, but in the worship of God. This is a sign of obedience, and obedience can belong only to the humble.

Thus, in a surprising way, there is something in humility to exalt the mind, and something in exaltation to abase it.[124] It certainly appears somewhat paradoxical that exaltation abases and humility exalts. But devout humility makes the mind subject to what is superior. Nothing is superior to God; and that is why humility exalts the mind by making it subject to God. Exaltation, in contrast, derives from a fault in character, and spurns subjection for that very reason. Hence it falls away from him who has no superior, and falls lower in consequence. Thus the scriptural saying is fulfilled, 'You have thrown them down when they were being lifted up.'[125] It does not say,

122. Matt. 7, 18.
123. 2 Pet. 2, 10.
124. cf. Matt. 23, 12; etc.
125. Ps. 73, 118.

'When they had been lifted up', that is, that they were first lifted up and then thrown down; they were thrown down in the very act of being exalted. The exaltation itself is in fact already an overthrow.

That is why humility is highly prized in the City of God and especially enjoined on the City of God during the time of its pilgrimage in this world; and it receives particular emphasis in the character of Christ, the king of that City.[126] We are also taught by the sacred Scriptures that the fault of exaltation, the contrary of humility, exercises supreme dominion in Christ's adversary, the Devil. This is assuredly the great difference that sunders the two cities of which we are speaking: the one is a community of devout men, the other a company of the irreligious, and each has its own angels attached to it. In one city love of God has been given first place, in the other, love of self.

We can see then that the Devil would not have entrapped man by the obvious and open sin of doing what God had forbidden, had not man already started to please himself. That is why he was delighted also with the statement, 'You will be like gods.'[127] In fact they would have been better able to be like gods if they had in obedience adhered to the supreme and real ground of their being, if they had not in pride made themselves their own ground. For created gods are gods not in their own true nature but by participation in the true God. By aiming at more, a man is diminished, when he elects to be self-sufficient and defects from the one who is really sufficient for him.

This then is the original evil: man regards himself as his own light, and turns away from that light which would make man himself a light if he would set his heart on it. This evil came first, in secret, and the result was the other evil, which was committed in the open. For what the Bible says is true: 'Before a fall the mind is exalted: before honour it is humbled.'[128] The fall that happens in secret inevitably precedes the fall that occurs in broad daylight, though the former is not recognized as a fall. Does anyone think of exaltation as a fall, even though the falling away was already there, in the desertion of the Most High? On the other hand, no one could fail to see that there is a fall when there is an obvious and unmistakable transgression of a commandment.

This was the reason why God forbade an act which could not be defended, after it had been committed, by any fantasy of justification. And I venture to say that it is of service to the proud that they should fall into some open and obvious sin, which can make

126. cf. Phil. 2, 8–11. 127. Gen. 3, 5. 128. Prov. 18, 12.

them dissatisfied with themselves, after they have already fallen through self-complacency. Peter's dissatisfaction with himself, when he wept, was healthier than his complacency when he was over-confident.[129] We find the same thought in a verse of a holy psalm: 'Fill their faces with shame, and they will seek your name, Lord',[130] which means, 'They set their heart on themselves in seeking their own name; let them set their heart on you, by seeking yours.'

14. *The pride of the transgressor was worse than the sin itself*

Even worse, and more deserving of condemnation, is the pride shown in the search for an excuse, even when the sins are clear as daylight. This was shown in the first human beings, when the woman said, 'The serpent led me astray, and I ate'; and the man said, 'The woman whom you gave me as a companion, she gave me fruit from the tree, and I ate.'[131] There is not a whisper anywhere here of a plea for pardon, nor of any entreaty for healing. True, they did not deny their sin, as Cain did,[132] and yet their pride seeks to pin the wrong act on another; the woman's pride blames the serpent, the man's pride blames the woman. But in the case of so obvious a transgression of the divine command, to talk like this is really to accuse rather than to excuse oneself. For the fact that the woman committed the offence on the serpent's suggestion, and the man because of the woman's offer, did not mean that it was not their own act – as if anything should have priority over God in a claim for credence or obedience!

15. *The justice of the retribution*

Man took no heed of the command of God who had created him, who had made him in his own image, who had set him above the other animals, who had established him in paradise, who had supplied him with abundance of all things for his well-being, who had not burdened him with a large number of oppressive and difficult rules, but had given him one very short and easy commandment to support him in healthy obedience. God's intention in this command was to impress upon this created being that he was the Lord; and that free service was in that creature's own interest. Therefore it was a just punishment that followed, and the condemnation was of such a kind that man

129. Matt. 26, 33; 26, 75.
130. Ps. 83, 16.
131. Gen. 3, 12f.
132. cf. Gen. 4, 9.

who would have become spiritual even in his flesh, by observing the command, became carnal even in his mind; and he who in his pride had pleased himself was by God's justice handed over to himself. But the result of this was not that he was in every way under his own control, but that he was at odds with himself, and lived a life of harsh and pitiable slavery, instead of the freedom he so ardently desired, a slavery under him with whom he entered into agreement in his sinning. So he was dead in spirit, of his own will; but doomed, against his will, to die in body; forsaking eternal life, he was condemned also to eternal death, unless he should be set free by grace. Anyone who considers this sort of condemnation to be excessive or unjust certainly does not know how to measure the immensity of the wickedness in sinning when it was so immensely easy to avoid the sin.

Abraham's obedience is renowned in story as a great thing, and rightly so, because he was ordered to do an act of enormous difficulty, namely, to kill his own son.[133] By the same token, the disobedience in paradise was all the greater inasmuch as the command was one of no difficulty at all. The obedience of the second man is the more worthy of renown in that 'he became obedient unto death.'[134] By the same token, the disobedience of the first man was the more abominable in that he became disobedient unto death. For where the penalty set for disobedience is great, and it is an easy thing which has been ordered by the Creator, who can adequately describe the enormity of the evil in a refusal to obey in a matter so easy, when the command comes from so great a power, and the punishment that threatens is so grave?

In fact, to put it briefly, in the punishment of that sin the retribution for disobedience is simply disobedience itself. For man's wretchedness is nothing but his own disobedience to himself, so that because he would not do what he could, he now wills to do what he cannot. For in paradise, before his sin, man could not, it is true, do everything; but he could do whatever he wished, just because he did not want to do whatever he could not do. Now, however, as we observe in the offspring of the first man, and as the Bible witnesses, 'man has become like nothingness.'[135] For who can list all the multitude of things that a man wishes to do and cannot, while he is disobedient to himself, that is, while his very mind and even his lower element, his flesh, do not submit to his will? Even against his volition his mind is often troubled; and his flesh experiences pain, grows old, and dies, and endures all manner of suffering. We should not endure all this against

133. Gen. 22, 2. 134. Phil. 2, 8. 135. Ps. 144, 4.

our volition if our natural being were in every way and in every part obedient to our will.

It may be objected that the flesh is in such a state that it cannot serve our will. But what difference does it make how this situation comes about? The important point is that through the justice of God, who is our Lord and master and whom we refused to serve as his subjects, our flesh, which had been subject to us, now gives us trouble through its non-compliance, whereas we by our defiance of God have only succeeded in becoming a nuisance to ourselves, and not to God. For he does not need our service as we need the service of our body, so that what we receive is punishment for ourselves, while what we have done is no punishment for him. Moreover, the so-called pains of the flesh are really pains of the soul, experienced in the flesh and from the flesh. The flesh can surely feel no desire or pain by itself, apart from the soul.

When the flesh is said to desire or to suffer pain, it is in fact the man himself who has this experience – as I have maintained[136] – or else some part of the soul which is affected by the experience of the flesh, whether a harsh experience producing pain, or a gentle experience, producing pleasure. Bodily pain is really nothing but a distress of the soul arising from the body, and a kind of disagreement with what happens to the body, in the same way as mental pain, which is called grief, is a disagreement with what has happened to us against our will. And grief is usually preceded by apprehension, which is also something in the soul, not in the body. Whereas bodily pain is not preceded by anything that we may call bodily apprehension, felt in the physical organism before the pain. Pleasure, on the other hand, is preceded by a kind of craving which is felt in the body as its own desire – hunger, for instance, and thirst, and the feeling normally called lust, when it is concerned with the sexual organs, though lust is the general name for desire of every kind.

Even anger was defined in antiquity as being simply the lust for revenge,[137] although very often a man is angry even with inanimate objects where the vengeance cannot be felt, and in a rage he smashes his stylus when it writes badly, or he breaks his reed pen. But even this, irrational as it is, is a kind of lust for revenge and, in a strange way, a shadow, so to speak, of the notion of retribution, the principle that those who do evil should suffer evil. Thus we have the lust for vengeance, called anger; the lust for possession of money, called greed; the lust for victory at any price, called obstinacy; the lust for boasting,

136. cf. ch. 2. 137. Cic., *Tusc Disp.*, 3, 5, 11; 4, 9, 21.

called vanity. There are many different kinds of lust, and some of them even have their special titles, while others have not. For instance, one would have difficulty in giving a name to the lust for domination, though the evidence of civil wars shows how powerful is its influence on the minds of tyrants.

16. *The evil of lust, in the specifically sexual meaning*

We see then that there are lusts for many things, and yet when lust is mentioned without the specification of its object the only thing that normally occurs to the mind is the lust that excites the indecent parts of the body. This lust assumes power not only over the whole body, and not only from the outside, but also internally; it disturbs the whole man, when the mental emotion combines and mingles with the physical craving, resulting in a pleasure surpassing all physical delights. So intense is the pleasure that when it reaches its climax there is an almost total extinction of mental alertness; the intellectual sentries, as it were, are overwhelmed. Now surely any friend of wisdom and holy joys who lives a married life but knows, in the words of the Apostle's warning, 'how to possess his bodily instrument in holiness and honour, not in the sickness of desire, like the Gentiles who have no knowledge of God'[138] – surely such a man would prefer, if possible, to beget children without lust of this kind. For then the parts created for this task would be the servants of his mind, even in their function of procreation, just as the other members are its servants in the various tasks to which they are assigned. They would begin their activity at the bidding of the will, instead of being stirred up by the ferment of lust.

In fact, not even the lovers of this kind of pleasure are moved, either to conjugal intercourse or to the impure indulgences of vice, just when they have so willed. Sometimes the impulse is an unwanted intruder, sometimes it abandons the eager lover, and desire cools off in the body while it is at boiling heat in the mind. Thus strangely does lust refuse to be a servant not only to the will to beget but even to the lust for lascivious indulgence; and although on the whole it is totally opposed to the mind's control, it is quite often divided against itself. It arouses the mind, but does not follow its own lead by arousing the body.

138. 1 Thess. 4, 4f.

17. *The nakedness of the first human beings, and the feeling of shame after their sin*

It is right, therefore, to be ashamed of this lust, and it is right that the members which it moves or fails to move by its own right, so to speak, and not in complete conformity to our decision, should be called *pudenda* ('parts of shame'), which they were not called before man's sin; for, as Scripture tells us, 'they were naked, and yet they felt no embarrassment.'[139] This was not because they had not noticed their nakedness, but because nakedness was not yet disgraceful, because lust did not yet arouse those members independently of their decision. The flesh did not yet, in a fashion, give proof of man's disobedience by a disobedience of its own.

It was not that the first human beings had been created blind, as is commonly believed among the uneducated, since Adam saw the animals to which he gave names,[140] while of Eve we are told, 'The woman saw that the tree was good for food, and was pleasant for the eyes to look at.'[141] It follows that their eyes were open, but not wide enough open, that is to say, not attentive enough to recognize what a blessing they were given in the garment of grace, inasmuch as their members did not know how to rebel against their will. When this grace was taken away, and in consequence their disobedience was chastised by a corresponding punishment, there appeared in the movements of their body a certain indecent novelty, which made nakedness shameful. It made them self-conscious and embarrassed.

That is why Scripture says of them, after they had violated God's command by an overt transgression, 'The eyes of both of them were opened and they recognized that they were naked. And they sewed together fig leaves and made aprons for themselves.'[142] 'The eyes of both', it says, 'were opened', not to enable them to see (they could see already) but to enable them to distinguish the good which they had lost and the evil into which they had fallen. Hence the tree itself, which was to make this distinction for them if they laid hands on it to eat the fruit in defiance of the prohibition, got its name from that event, and was called 'the tree of the knowledge of good and evil'. For experience of the distresses of sickness reveals the joys of health in a clearer light.

And so 'they recognized that they were naked' – stripped, that is, of the grace that prevented their bodily nakedness from causing them any embarrassment, as it did when the law of sin made war against

139. Gen. 2, 25. 140. cf. Gen. 2, 20. 141. Gen. 3, 6. 142. Gen. 3, 7.

their mind.[143] Thus they gained a knowledge where ignorance would have been a greater bliss if they had trusted in God and obeyed him and thus had refrained from an action which would force them to learn by experience the harm that disloyalty and disobedience would do. The consequence was that they were embarrassed by the insubordination of their flesh, the punishment which was a kind of evidence of their disobedience, and 'they sewed together fig leaves and made aprons (*campestria*) for themselves.' (*Campestria* means 'loincloths', and that is the word used in some translations. The Latin word *campestria* is derived from the custom of the young men who covered their pudenda when they stripped for exercise on the playing-field, the *campus*. Hence those who are so girdled are called *campestrati*.)

Thus modesty, from a sense of shame, covered what was excited to disobedience by lust, in defiance of a will which had been condemned for the guilt of disobedience; and from then onwards the practice of concealing the pudenda has become a deep-rooted habit in all peoples, since they all derive from the same stock. Some barbarians even go so far as to refrain from exposing those parts even in the baths, and they keep their covering on when they wash. And in the darkened solitudes of India, those who practise philosophy in nakedness[144] (and are hence called 'gymnosophists') nevertheless have coverings on their genitals, although they have none on the rest of the body.

18. *The sense of shame in sexual intercourse*

The sexual act itself, which is performed with such lust, seeks privacy. This is true not only in respect of the various kinds of debauchery for which secret hiding-places are needed to avoid the sentence of human law courts, but also in the practice of fornication, which the earthly city has made a legalized depravity. This practice is not punishable by any law of that city, and yet this permitted lust, which carries no penalty, shuns the public gaze. A natural sense of shame ensures that even brothels make provision for secrecy; and it was easier for immorality to dispense with the fetters of prohibition than for shamelessness to abolish the furtive dens of this degradation.

Fornication, in fact, is called a depravity even by those who are depraved themselves; and, fond as they are of it, they dare not display it in public. But what of conjugal intercourse, whose purpose is, according to the prescriptions of the marriage contract, the procreation of children? It is lawful and respectable certainly; but does it not require a private room and the absence of witnesses? Does not the

143. cf. Rom. 7, 23. 144. cf. Bk VIII, 9n; X, 32; XV, 20.

bridegroom, before he begins even to caress the bride, show the door to all the attendants, and even his groomsmen, and all the others who had been permitted to enter because of some tie of kinship? Now, a certain 'author supreme of Roman eloquence' asserts that all right actions desire to be set in the full daylight,[145] that is to say, they long to get themselves known. So this right action longs to become known; and yet it blushes to be seen. For everyone knows what act is performed by the married pair for the procreation of children. All the ceremony that attends the marriage of wives is designed towards the fulfilment of that act. Nevertheless, when this act is being performed, with a view to the birth of children, not even the children who have already been born as the result of such an act are permitted to witness it. This right action craves for recognition in the light of the mind's understanding, but it is equally concerned to escape the light of the eyes's vision. What can be the reason for this, if it is not that something by nature right and proper is effected in such a way as to be accompanied by a feeling of shame, by way of punishment?

19. *Anger and lust were not part of man's healthy state before his sin*

This explains why the Platonists, who approached the truth more nearly than other philosophers, acknowledged that anger and lust are perverted elements in man's character, or soul, on the ground that they are disturbed and undisciplined emotions, leading to acts which wisdom forbids, and therefore they need the control of intelligence and reason. This third rational division of the soul is located by them in a kind of citadel, to rule the other elements, so that with the rational element in command and the others subordinate, justice may be preserved in the relation between all the parts of man's soul.[146]

These philosophers therefore admit that the two divisions of the soul are perverted, even in a wise and disciplined man. Consequently, the mind by repression and restraint bridles them and recalls them from courses they are wrongly moved to follow, while it allows them to follow any line of action permitted by the law of wisdom. Anger, for example, is allowed for the purpose of imposing compulsion, when that is justified, and lust is permitted for the duty of procreation. But in paradise before man's sin these elements did not exist in their perverted state. For then they were not set in motion, in defiance of a

145. Luc., *Phars.*, 7, 62, describing Cicero. Cic., *Tusc. Disp.* 2, 26, 64.
146. cf. Plat., *Rp.*, 586 D-E.

right will, to pursue any course which made it necessary to hold them back with the guiding reins, so to speak, of reason.

The situation now is that these passions are set in motion in this fashion, and are brought under control by those who live disciplined, just, and devout lives, sometimes with comparative ease, sometimes with difficulty. But this control entails coercion and struggle, and the situation does not represent a state of health in accordance with nature, but an enfeebled condition arising from guilt. Again, we observe that modesty does not hide the acts of anger and of the other emotions in the same way as it conceals the acts of lust, which are performed by the sexual organs; but this is simply because in the effects of other emotions the members of the body are not set in motion by the feelings themselves but by the will, after it has decided to co-operate with them, for the will has sovereign power in the employment of those members. Anyone who utters a word in anger, anyone who goes so far as to strike another person, could not do so if his tongue or hand were not put in motion at the command, as one may say, of his will; and those members are set in motion by the same will even when there is no anger. But the genital organs have become as it were the private property of lust, which has brought them so completely under its sway that they have no power of movement if this passion fails, if it has not arisen spontaneously or in response to a stimulus. It is this that arouses shame; it is this that makes us shun the eyes of beholders in embarrassment. A man would be less put out by a crowd of spectators watching him visiting his anger unjustly upon another man than by one person observing him when he is having lawful intercourse with his wife.

20. *The ridiculous indecency of the cynics*

The Cynics,[147] those canine philosophers, failed to observe this fact

147. *Cynics.* Some authorities derive this school from Antisthenes (*fl.* 400 B.C.), a pupil of Socrates, who taught in a gymnasium at Cynosarges, a suburb of Athens; and they derive the name 'Cynic' from this place-name. The more probable derivation of the sect, and the name, is from Diogenes of Sinope, a fourth-century disciple of Antisthenes, who was nicknamed *kuôn* ('dog') because of his rejection of the conventions of civilization and his determination to live on nothing – and in a tub. The Cynic ideal was freedom from wants, desires, and all involvements. There was a great revival of Cynicism in the first three centuries of the Christian era, manifested on two levels: there were educated philosophers, such as Dio Chrysostom (first century A.D.); and there were the beggar-philosophers who ostentatiously rejected conventional standards, reproducing the 'shamelessness' (*anaideia*) of Diogenes.

when they put forward an opinion directly opposed to human modesty, an opinion truly canine, that is to say, filthy and indecent. They hold that since the sexual act is lawful between husband and wife, one should not be ashamed to engage in it in public and to have marital intercourse in any street or square. However, a natural sense of decency has prevailed over this mistaken idea. It is true that there is a story that Diogenes once made an exhibition of himself by putting this theory into practice,[148] because he imagined that his school of philosophy would gain more publicity if its indecency were more startlingly impressed on the memory of mankind. However, the Cynics did not continue this practice, and modesty, which makes men feel shame before their fellows, prevailed over error – the mistaken idea that men should make it their ambition to resemble dogs.

Hence I am inclined to think that even Diogenes himself, and the others about whom this story is told, merely went through the motions of lying together before the eyes of men who had no means of knowing what was really going on under the philosopher's cloak. I doubt whether the pleasure of that act could have been successfully achieved with spectators crowding round, for those philosophers did not blush to appear willing to lie together in a place where lust itself would have blushed to put in an appearance. Even now we see that there are still Cynic philosophers about. They are the people who not only wear the philosopher's cloak but also carry a club.[149] However, none of them dares to act like Diogenes. If any of them were to venture to do so they would be overwhelmed, if not with a hail of stones, at any rate with a shower of spittle from the disgusted public.

Human nature then is, without any doubt, ashamed about lust, and rightly ashamed. For in its disobedience, which subjected the sexual organs solely to its own impulses and snatched them from the will's authority, we see a proof of the retribution imposed on man for that first disobedience. And it was entirely fitting that this retribution should show itself in that part which effects the procreation of the very nature that was changed for the worse through that first great sin. This offence was committed when all mankind existed in one man, and it brought universal ruin on mankind; and no one can be rescued from the toils of that offence, which was punished by God's justice, unless the sin is expiated in each man singly by the grace of God.

148. Diog. Laert. 6, 69.

149. The attribute of *Heracles*, who represented the Cynic ideal of self-sufficiency.

21. *The blessing of fertility not forfeited by sin, but associated with morbid lust*

We must never allow ourselves to believe that God's blessing, 'Increase and multiply and fill the earth'[150] would have been fulfilled through this lust by the pair who were set in paradise. It was, in fact, after the sin that this lust arose. It was after the sin that man's nature felt, noticed, blushed at, and concealed this lust; for man's nature retained a sense of decency, although it had lost the authority to which the body had been subordinate in every part. But the nuptial blessing, bidding the married couple to increase and multiply and fill the earth, still stood, although they were offenders; yet it had been given before the offence, so that it might be realized that the procreation of children belonged to the glory of marriage and not to the punishment of sin.

There are, however, men at the present time who are evidently unaware of the bliss that existed in paradise. They suppose that children could not have been begotten except by the means with which they are familiar, namely, by means of lust, which, as we observe, brings a sense of shame even in the honourable state of matrimony. Some of them[151] utterly reject the holy Scriptures, and even scoff at them in their unbelief, in the passage where we are told that after their sin our first parents were ashamed of their nakedness and that they covered their parts of shame – their pudenda. Others of them, in contrast, accept and honour the Scriptures; but while so doing they maintain that the words 'increase and multiply' should not be interpreted as referring to carnal fertility, on the grounds that a somewhat similar remark is made with reference to the soul, 'You will multiply me with strength (or virtue) in my soul.'[152] And so they interpret the words that follow in Genesis, 'Fill the earth and hold sway over it', in this way: 'earth' they take to mean the flesh, which the soul 'fills' with its own presence and over which it 'holds sway' when it is 'multiplied in strength (virtue)'. Carnal offspring, in their opinion, could not then have been born, any more than they can be born now, without the lust which arose after sin, the lust which was noticed, caused embarrassment, and was concealed. They assert that children would not have been born in paradise, but outside it, which is what in fact happened. For it was after the pair had been sent away from paradise that they came together to beget children, and did beget them.

150. Gen. 1, 28. 151. sc. the Manicheans; cf. Bk XI, 13n. 152. Ps. 138, 3.

22. *Marriage as originally instituted and blessed by God*

For myself, however, I have no shadow of doubt that to increase and multiply and fill the earth in accordance with God's blessing is a gift of marriage, and that God instituted marriage from the beginning, before man's Fall, in creating male and female: the difference in sex is quite evident in the physical structure. And the actual blessing was obviously attached to this work of God, for the words, 'he created them male and female', are immediately followed, in the scriptural account, by this statement: 'And God blessed them, saying, "Increase and multiply, and fill the earth and hold sway over it"', and so on.[153]

Now it is true that we can quite properly give this a spiritual meaning; however, we cannot interpret 'male' and 'female' allegorically, by finding an analogy in the individual, namely a distinction between the ruling element and the ruled. There is no denying the obvious evidence of bodies of different sex, which shows that it would be a manifest absurdity to deny the fact that male and female were created for the purpose of begetting children, so as to increase and multiply and fill the earth. And when the Lord was asked whether it was allowed to dismiss a wife for any cause whatever (since Moses allowed the giving of a bill of divorce because of the hardness of heart of the Israelites) his reply had nothing to do with the spirit which commands and flesh which obeys, or the rational mind which rules and the irrational desire which submits to rule, or the contemplative virtue which is pre-eminent and the active virtue which is subject to it, or the intellectual power of the mind and the body's perception. The Lord's answer explicitly concerned the marriage bond which binds the two sexes to one another. He said,

> Have you not read that the Creator made the male and female from the start? And that he said: 'This is why a man will say goodbye to his father and mother, and will be joined to his wife, and they will be two in one flesh'? So they are no longer two, but one flesh. Therefore, what God joined together, man must not separate.[154]

It is certain then that at the beginning male and female were constituted just as two human beings of different sex are now, in our observation and knowledge, and that they are said to be 'one' either on account of their being joined together in marriage, or because of

153. Gen. 1, 27f. 154. Matt. 19, 4ff.

woman's origin, since she was created from the man's side. For the Apostle appeals to this latter fact as an illustration, a precedent instituted by God, when he admonishes husbands, telling them that each one of them should love his wife.[155]

23. *Would procreation have taken place in paradise, if no one had sinned?*

If anyone says that there would have been no intercourse or procreation if the first human beings had not sinned, he is asserting, in effect, that man's sin was necessary to complete the number of the saints. For if they would have remained in solitude by refraining from sin, because, as some imagine, they could not have bred if they had not sinned, it follows that sin was essential if there were to be a number of righteous people, instead of a single pair. But if that is absurd beyond belief, we must believe instead that even if no one had sinned there would have come into being a number of saints sufficient to complete the muster of that Blessed City, as large a number as is now being assembled, through God's grace, from the multitude of sinners, so long as the 'children of this world' beget and are begotten.[156]

It follows that, if there had been no sin, marriage would have been worthy of the happiness of paradise, and would have given birth to children to be loved, and yet would not have given rise to any lust to be ashamed of; but, as it is, we have no example to show how this could have come about. Yet that does not mean that it should seem incredible that the one part of the body could have been subject to the will, without the familiar lust, seeing that so many other parts are now in subjection to it. We move our hands and feet to perform their special functions, when we so will; this involves no reluctance on their part, and the movements are performed with all the ease we observe in our own case and in that of others. And we observe it particularly in craftsmen engaged in all kinds of physical tasks, where natural powers which lack strength and speed are developed by active training. Then why should we not believe that the sexual organs could have been the obedient servants of mankind, at the bidding of the will, in the same way as the other, if there had been no lust, which came in as the retribution for the sin of disobedience?

155. Eph. 5, 25; Col. 3, 19. 156. Luke 20, 34.

In Cicero's discussion of the different types of government, in his book *On the Commonwealth*,[157] the author takes an analogy from human nature. He says, it will be remembered, that the members of the body are governed like children, because of their ready obedience, while the perverted elements of the soul are coerced like slaves under a harsher régime. Now in the order of nature the soul is unquestionably ranked above the body; and yet the soul itself finds it easier to rule the body than to rule itself. In fact, this lust we are now examining is something to be the more ashamed of because the soul, when dealing with it, neither has command of itself so as to be entirely free from lust, nor does it rule the body so completely that the organs of shame are moved by the will instead of by lust. Indeed if they were so ruled they would not be *pudenda* – parts of shame.

As it is, the soul is ashamed of its body's resistance when the body is subordinate to it by reason of its inferior nature. When the soul is in opposition to itself in respect of the other emotions, it feels less shame just because it is conquered by itself, and thus is itself the victor. No doubt this victory is disordered and perverse, because it is due to elements which ought to be subject to reason, yet it is a victory won by the soul's elements, and therefore, I repeat, the soul is conquered by itself. For when the soul defends itself in an orderly fashion, so that the irrational impulses are subordinated to the reason and the intellect, that is a laudable and virtuous victory, provided that the reason is itself subjected to God. Nevertheless, the soul is less ashamed when it is divided against itself by the disobedience of its perverted elements than when the body does not yield to its will and obey its command; for the body is something different from it, inferior to it, and the body's natural substance has no life without the soul.

But when restraint is imposed by the will's control on the other members, without whose assistance the organs that are excited by lust in defiance of the will cannot satisfy their appetite, then decency is preserved, not because the pleasure of sin has been foregone but because it has been forestalled. Without doubt, the marriage in paradise would not have known this opposition, this resistance, this tussle between lust and will, or at least the contrast between the insatiability of lust and the self-sufficiency of the will, had there not been that guilt of disobedience which was followed by disobedience as a punishment. Instead of this, the will would have received the obedience of all the members, including the organs of sex.

Then the instrument created for the task would have sown the seed

157. *De Rep.*, 3, 25, 37.

on 'the field of generation'[158] as the hand now sows seed on the earth, and there would be no cause for modesty to object when I wish to discuss this subject in detail, no reason for decency to insist on my asking pardon, with an apology to pure ears. Discussion could then have free scope, without any fear of obscenity, to treat of any idea that might come to mind when thinking about bodily organs of this kind. Nor would there be any reason for calling the actual words obscene; in fact whatever was said on this subject could be as respectable as any talk about other parts of the body. Accordingly, if anyone has indecent thoughts in approaching what I am now writing, it is his own guilt that he should beware of, not the facts of nature. He should censure the actions prompted by his own depravity, not the words imposed on me by necessity. The modest and religious reader or hearer will readily excuse my use of such words, provided that I refute the infidelity which bases its argument not on a faith in things outside our experience but on its perception of the facts of our experience. What I am saying will not shock the reader who is not horrified at the Apostle's attack on the horrible vices of the women who 'instead of natural practices have changed to practices contrary to nature',[159] especially as, unlike the Apostle, I am not now mentioning and condemning abominable obscenities. Nevertheless, in explaining, to the best of my powers, the processes of human generation, I must endeavour, like him, to avoid obscene words.

24. *The power of the will over the body*

Then (had there been no sin) the man would have sowed the seed and the woman would have conceived the child when their sexual organs had been aroused by the will, at the appropriate time and in the necessary degree, and had not been excited by lust. For we set in motion, at our command, not only those members which are fitted with bones and joints, like the hands, feet and fingers, but also those which are loosely constructed of pliant tissues and muscles, which we can move, when we choose, by shaking, which we extend by stretching, which we twist and flex, contract and harden – such parts, I mean, as those of the mouth and face, which the will moves, as far as it can. In fact, even the lungs, which are the softest of all the internal organs and for that reason are protected in the cavity of the chest, are controlled by the will for the purpose of drawing breath and expelling it, and for producing and modulating the vocal sounds. In the same way as

158. Virg., *Georg.*, 3, 136. 159. Rom. 1, 26.

bellows serve the purpose of smiths and of organists, the lungs are obedient to the will of a man when he breathes out or breathes in, or speaks or shouts or sings.

I pass over the fact that some animals are endowed with a natural power of moving the covering which clothes their whole body; if they feel anything in any part which needs to be driven away, they can move their hide at the spot, and only there, where they feel the irritation, and thus they can by this quiver shake off not only flies but even spears that are sticking into them. Man has not this ability; but surely that does not mean that the Creator could not have bestowed it, at his pleasure, on any animate creatures? Then man himself also may have once received from his lower members an obedience which he lost by his own disobedience. It would not have been difficult for God to fashion him in such a way that even what is now set in motion in his flesh only by lust should have been moved only by his will.

We do in fact find among human beings some individuals with natural abilities very different from the rest of mankind and remarkable by their very rarity. Such people can do some things with their body which are for others utterly impossible and well-nigh incredible when they are reported. Some people can even move their ears, either one at a time or both together. Others without moving the head can bring the whole scalp – all the part covered with hair – down towards the forehead and bring it back again at will. Some can swallow an incredible number of various articles and then with a slight contraction of the diaphragm, can produce, as if out of a bag, any article they please, in perfect condition. There are others who imitate the cries of birds and beasts and the voices of any other men, reproducing them so accurately as to be quite indistinguishable from the originals, unless they are seen. A number of people produce at will such musical sounds from their behind (without any stink) that they seem to be singing from that region. I know from my own experience of a man who used to sweat whenever he chose; and it is a well-known fact that some people can weep at will and shed floods of tears.

Far more incredible is the phenomenon which a great many of our brothers witnessed in recent times. There was a presbyter in the diocese of Calama, named Restitutus. Whenever he pleased (and he was often asked to perform the feat by people who desired to have first-hand experience of so remarkable a phenomenon) he would withdraw himself from all sensations, to the accompaniment of cries like those of someone making lamentation, and would then lie immobile, exactly like a corpse. When pinched and pricked he felt nothing whatsoever;

and even when he was burned by the application of fire he was quite insensible to pain, except later on from the resulting burn. That this immobility was not achieved by an effort of endurance, but through loss of sensitivity is proved by the fact that no trace of breathing was observed in him, as in a dead man. However, he related that he heard people talking, if they spoke with particular clarity, though they sounded as if a long way off.

We observe then that the body, even under present conditions, is an obedient servant to some people in a remarkable fashion beyond the normal limitations of nature; this is shown in many kinds of movements and feelings, and it happens even in men who are living this present troubled life in the corruptible flesh. If this is so, is there any reason why we should not believe that before the sin of disobedience and its punishment of corruptibility, the members of a man's body could have been the servants of man's will without any lust, for the procreation of children? It was because man forsook God by pleasing himself that he was handed over to himself, and because he did not obey God he could not obey himself. Hence came the more obvious misery where man does not live as he wishes to live. If he lived as he wished, he would consider himself happy; yet even so he would not be really happy if he lived in degradation.

25. *True happiness, which is unattainable in our present life*

In fact, a closer examination will show that no man lives as he wishes, unless he is happy; and no man is happy, unless he is righteous. But even the righteous man himself will not live the life he wishes unless he reaches that state where he is wholly exempt from death, deception and distress, and has the assurance that he will for ever be exempt. This is what our nature craves, and it will never be fully and finally happy unless it attains what it craves. In our present state, what human being can live the life he wishes, when the actual living is not in his control? He wishes to live; he is compelled to die. In what sense does he live as he wishes when he does not live as long as he wishes? Even if he should wish to die, how can he live as he wishes, when he does not wish to live? And if the reason why he wishes to die is not that he does not wish to live, but so that he may have a better life after death, then he does not yet live as he wishes, but will do so when by dying he has reached the object of his wish.

Come then, let us behold him living as he wishes, since he has put the screw on himself and ordered himself not to wish for what is beyond his power, but to wish for what he can get; in the words of Terence,

> Since what you wish is not within your power
> Direct your wish to what you can achieve.[160]

Now is this man happy, just because he is patient in his misery? Of course not! If a man does not love the happy life he certainly does not possess it. And besides, if he does love it and possess it, he must needs love it more dearly than all other things, since everything else that he loves must be loved for the sake of the happy life. Again, if it is loved as much as it deserves to be loved (and a man cannot be happy unless he loves that life as it deserves) the man who so loves it must inevitably wish it to be eternal. Therefore life will only be truly happy when it is eternal.

26. *Generation in paradise would have occurred without the shame of lust*

We conclude then that man lived in paradise as long as his wish was at one with God's command. He lived in the enjoyment of God, and derived his own goodness from God's goodness. He lived without any want, and had it in his power to live like this for ever. Food was available to prevent hunger, drink to prevent thirst, and the tree of life was there to guard against old age and dissolution. There was no trace of decay in the body, or arising from the body, to bring any distress to any of his senses. There was no risk of disease from within or of injury from without. Man enjoyed perfect health in the body, entire tranquillity in the soul.

Just as in paradise there was no extreme of heat or of cold, so in its inhabitant no desire or fear intervened to hamper his good will. There was no sadness at all, nor any frivolous jollity. But true joy flowed perpetually from God, and towards God there was a blaze of 'love from a pure heart, a good conscience, and a faith that was no pretence'.[161] Between man and wife there was a faithful partnership based on love and mutual respect; there was a harmony and a liveliness of mind and body, and an effortless observance of the commandment. Man was at leisure, and tiredness never wearied him, and sleep never weighed him down against his will.

160. *Andr.*, 305f. 161. 1 Tim. 1, 5.

When mankind was in such a state of ease and plenty, blest with such felicity, let us never imagine that it was impossible for the seed of children to be sown without the morbid condition of lust. Instead, the sexual organs would have been brought into activity by the same bidding of the will as controlled the other organs. Then, without feeling the allurement of passion goading him on, the husband would have relaxed on his wife's bosom in tranquillity of mind and with no impairment of his body's integrity. Moreover, although we cannot prove this in experience, it does not therefore follow that we should not believe that when those parts of the body were not activated by the turbulent heat of passion but brought into service by deliberate use of power when the need arose, the male seed could have been dispatched into the womb, with no loss of the wife's integrity, just as the menstrual flux can now be produced from the womb of a virgin without loss of maidenhead. For the seed could be injected through the same passage by which the flux is ejected. Now just as the female womb might have been opened for parturition by a natural impulse when the time was ripe, instead of by the groans of travail, so the two sexes might have been united for impregnation and conception by an act of will, instead of by a lustful craving.

The activities I am discussing are bound to induce a feeling of shame, under present conditions. And although I am doing my best to imagine the state of affairs before these activities were shameful, nevertheless, in present circumstances, my discussion must be held in check by the restraining appeal of modesty instead of being furthered by such little eloquence as I command. The possibility that I am speaking of was not in fact experienced by those for whom it was available, because their sin happened first, and they incurred the penalty of exile from paradise before they could unite in the task of propagation as a deliberate act undisturbed by passion. The result is that the mention of this subject now suggests to the mind only the turbulent lust which we experience, not the calm act of will imagined in my speculation.

This is the reason why a sense of shame inhibits my speech, though reason supplies abundant material for thought. But despite what has happened, God almighty, the supreme and supremely good creator of all beings, who assists and rewards good wills, while he abandons and condemns the bad (and yet he controls both good and bad) surely did not fail to have a plan whereby he might complete the fixed number of citizens predestined in his wisdom, even out of the condemned human race. He does not now choose them for their merits, seeing that the whole mass of mankind has been condemned as it were in its infected root; he selects them by grace and shows the extent of his generosity to those who have been set free not only in his dealings with them but also in his treatment of those who have not been freed. For each person can recognize that his deliverance from evils is due to an act of kindness freely granted, not owed to him by right, when he is exempted from sharing the final destiny of those whose just punishment he had shared. Then is there any reason why God should not have created men in the foreknowledge that they would sin? For that made it possible for him to show in them and through them what their guilt deserved and what his grace could give; and with God as creator and disposer of all things, the perverse disorder of transgressors did not pervert the right ordering of the universe.

27. *The perversity of sinners does not disturb God's providential design*

It follows that the actions of sinners, whether angels or men, cannot obstruct the 'great works of God, carefully designed to fulfil all his decisions',[162] since in his providence and omnipotence he assigns to each his own gifts and knows how to turn to good account the good and the evil alike. Hence the evil angel had been so condemned and so hardened in evil, as the fitting retribution for his first evil will, that he could no longer have a good will; but nothing prevented God from turning him to good use and allowing him to tempt the first man, who had been created upright, that is, with a good will. For the fact is that man had been so designed that if he had trusted in God's help as a good human being he would have overcome the evil angels, whereas if in pride and self-pleasing he deserted God, his creator and helper, he would be overcome. Thus he would win a good reward with a rightly directed will that was divinely helped, but an evil retribution with a perverted will that deserted God.

Now man could not even trust in the help of God without God's help; but this did not mean that he did not have it in his power to withdraw from the benefits of divine grace by self-pleasing. For just as it is not in our power to live in this physical frame without the support of food, and yet it is in our power not to live in it at all (which is what happens to suicides), so it was not in man's power, even in paradise, to live a good life without the help of God, yet it was in his power to live an evil life; but then his happiness would not continue and a most just punishment would follow. Therefore, since God was

162. Ps. 111, 2.

well aware that man would fall as he did, was there any reason why he should not have allowed him to be tempted by the malice of the jealous angel? God was perfectly certain that man would be defeated, but he foresaw with equal certainty that this same Devil was to be overcome by the man's seed,[163] helped by God's own grace, to the greater glory of the saints.

Thus it came about that God was not unaware of any event in the future, and yet he did not, by his foreknowledge, compel anyone to sin; and by the consequent experience he showed to angels and men, the rational part of creation, what a difference there was between the individual's own self-confidence and God's divine protection. Who would dare to believe or assert that it was not in God's power to ensure that neither angel nor man should fall? But God preferred not to withdraw this issue from their power, and thus to show the magnitude of their pride's power for evil and of God's grace for good.

28. *The character of the two cities*

We see then that the two cities were created by two kinds of love: the earthly city was created by self-love reaching the point of contempt for God, the Heavenly City by the love of God carried as far as contempt of self. In fact, the earthly city glories in itself, the Heavenly City glories in the Lord.[164] The former looks for glory from men, the latter finds its highest glory in God, the witness of a good conscience. The earthly lifts up its head in its own glory, the Heavenly City says to its God: 'My glory; you lift up my head.'[165] In the former, the lust for domination lords it over its princes as over the nations it subjugates; in the other both those put in authority and those subject to them serve one another in love, the rulers by their counsel, the subjects by obedience. The one city loves its own strength shown in its powerful leaders; the other says to its God, 'I will love you, my Lord, my strength.'[166]

Consequently, in the earthly city its wise men who live by men's standards have pursued the goods of the body or of their own mind, or of both. Or those of them who were able to know God 'did not honour him as God, nor did they give thanks to him, but they dwindled into futility in their thoughts, and their senseless heart was darkened: in asserting their wisdom' – that is, exalting themselves in their wisdom, under the domination of pride – 'they became foolish, and changed

163. cf. Gen. 3, 15 (the 'Protevangelium'). 164. 2 Cor. 10, 17.
165. Ps. 3, 3. 166. Ps. 18, 1.

the glory of the imperishable God into an image representing a perishable man, or birds or beasts or reptiles' – for in the adoration of idols of this kind they were either leaders or followers of the general public – 'and they worshipped and served created things instead of the Creator, who is blessed for ever.'[167] In the Heavenly City, on the other hand, man's only wisdom is the devotion which rightly worships the true God, and looks for its reward in the fellowship of the saints, not only holy men but also holy angels, 'so that God may be all in all'.[168]

167. Rom. 1, 21ff. 168. 1 Cor. 15, 28.

BOOK XV

1. *The two lines of descent of the human race, advancing from the start towards different ends*

CONCERNING the happiness of paradise and paradise itself, and concerning the life there of the first human beings and their sin, with its punishment, many opinions have been held by different people, many notions have been expressed in speech, or committed to writing. I myself have had a good deal to say on those subjects in previous books,[1] basing my statements on holy Scripture; what I said there was either what I found stated in Scripture or what I could infer from scriptural statements, always keeping in conformity with the authority of the Bible. A more searching discussion of the subject would produce a great number and a great variety of arguments which would require for their deployment a greater number of volumes than the present work demands and my time permits. The time at my disposal does not allow me to linger on all the questions that may be raised by men with time on their hands and with a curiosity for finer points – the kind of people who are more ready to ask questions than capable of understanding the answers.

All the same, I think that I have already discharged my obligation to the important and knotty problems about the beginning of the world, and of the soul, and of the human race itself. I classify the human race into two branches: the one consists of those who live by human standards, the other of those who live according to God's will. I also call these two classes the two cities, speaking allegorically. By two cities I mean two societies of human beings, one of which is predestined to reign with God for all eternity, the other doomed to undergo eternal punishment with the Devil. But this is their final destiny, and I shall have to speak of that later on.[2] At present, since I have said enough about the origins of these societies, whether in the angels, whose number is unknown to us, or in the two first human beings, it seems to me that I should undertake to describe their development from the time when that first pair began to produce offspring up to the time when mankind will cease to reproduce itself. For the development of these two societies which form my subject

1. Especially Bk XIV. 2. In Bks XIX–XXII.

lasts throughout this whole stretch of time, or era, in which the dying yield place to the newly-born who succeed them.

Now Cain was the first son born to those two parents of mankind, and he belonged to the city of man; the later son, Abel, belonged to the City of God.[3] It is our own experience that in the individual man, to use the words of the Apostle, 'it is not the spiritual element which comes first, but the animal; and afterwards comes the spiritual',[4] and so it is that everyone, since he takes his origin from a condemned stock, is inevitably evil and carnal to begin with, by derivation from Adam; but if he is reborn into Christ, and makes progress, he will afterwards be good and spiritual. The same holds true of the whole human race. When those two cities started on their course through the succession of birth and death, the first to be born was a citizen of this world, and later appeared one who was a pilgrim and stranger in the world, belonging as he did to the City of God. He was predestined by grace, and chosen by grace, by grace a pilgrim below, and by grace a citizen above. As far as he himself is concerned he has his origin from the same lump which was condemned, as a whole lump, at the beginning. But God like a potter (the analogy introduced by the Apostle is not impertinent but very pertinent) made 'out of the same lump one vessel destined for honour, and another for dishonour'.[5] But the first one made was the vessel for dishonour, and afterwards came the vessel for honour. For in the individual man, as I have said, the base condition comes first, and we have to start with that; but we are not bound to stop at that, and later comes the noble state towards which we may make progress, and in which we may abide, when we have arrived at it. Hence it is not the case that every bad man will become good, but no one will be good who was not bad originally. Yet the sooner a man changes for the better the more quickly will he secure for himself the title belonging to his attainment and will hide his earlier appellation under the later name.

Scripture tells us that Cain founded a city,[6] whereas Abel, as a pilgrim, did not found one. For the City of the saints is up above, although it produces citizens here below, and in their persons the City is on pilgrimage until the time of its kingdom comes. At that time it will assemble all those citizens as they rise again in their bodies; and then they will be given the promised kingdom, where with their Prince, 'the king of ages',[7] they will reign, world without end.

3. cf. Gen. 4, 1f. 4. 1 Cor. 5, 46. 5. Rom. 9, 21.
6. cf. Gen. 4, 17. 7. cf. 1 Tim. 1, 17.

2. *The children of the flesh and the children of the promise*

There was certainly a kind of shadow and prophetic image of this City which served rather to point towards it than to reproduce it on earth at the time when it was due to be displayed. This image was also called the holy city, in virtue of its pointing to that other City, not as being the express likeness of the reality which is yet to be. Concerning this image, in its status as a servant, and that free City to which it points, the Apostle says, when writing to the Galatians,

Now tell me, you who want to be under law; have you not listened to what the Law says? We are told in Scripture that Abraham had two sons, one by a slave-woman, one by his free-born wife. The slave-woman's son was born in the course of nature, the free woman's as a result of a promise. These facts are allegorical. For the two women stand for two covenants. The one bearing children for slavery is the covenant from Mount Sinai; this is Hagar. Now Sinai is a mountain in Arabia and it stands for the present Jerusalem; for she is in slavery with her children. But the Jerusalem above is free; and she is our mother. For Scripture says: 'Rejoice, you barren woman who bear no child: break into a cry of joy, you who are not in labour; for the deserted woman has many sons, more than the woman who has a husband'.[8] Now we, my brothers, are sons of the promise, as Isaac was. But just as at that time the son who was born in the course of nature persecuted the son who was spiritually born, so it is now. But what does Scripture say? 'Send away the slave woman and her son; for the son of the slave shall not be joint-heir with the son of the free woman'.[9] Thus you see, brothers, that we are not the sons of a slave-woman, but of the free woman, by reason of the freedom brought us by Christ's liberation.[10]

This manner of interpretation, which comes down to us with apostolic authority, reveals to us how we are to understand the Scriptures of the two covenants, the old and the new. One part of the earthly city has been made into an image of the Heavenly City, by symbolizing something other than itself, namely that other City; and for that reason it is a servant. For it was established not for its own sake but in order to symbolize another City; and since it was signified by an antecedent symbol, the foreshadowing symbol was itself foreshadowed.[11] Hagar, the servant of Sarah, represented, with her son, the image of this image. But the shadows were to pass away with the coming of the light, and Sarah, the free woman, stood for the free city

8. Is. 54, 1. 9. Gen. 21, 10. 10. Gal. 4, 21–5, 1.

11. Hagar prefigures the earthly Jerusalem which is a symbol of the Heavenly City. She was a slave and Jerusalem was enslaved, and therefore *serves* as a prophecy of the Heavenly Jerusalem, the free city, symbolized by the free Sarah.

which the shadow, Hagar, for her part served to point to in another way. And that is why Sarah said, 'Send away the slave-woman and her son; for the son of the slave shall not be joint-heir with my son Isaac,' or as the Apostle puts it, 'with the son of the free woman'.

Thus we find in the earthly city a double significance: in one respect it displays its own presence, and in the other it serves by its presence to signify the Heavenly City. But the citizens of the earthly city are produced by a nature which is vitiated by sin, while the citizens of the Heavenly City are brought forth by grace, which sets nature free from sin. That is why the former are called 'vessels of wrath', the latter 'vessels of mercy'.[12] This difference is also symbolized in Abraham's two sons: the one, Ishmael, son of the slave named Hagar, was born in the course of nature, whereas the other, Isaac, son of Sarah, the free woman, was born in fulfilment of a promise. Both sons, it is true, were born of Abraham's seed; but one was begotten by the normal procedure, a demonstration of nature's way, while the other was given by a promise, a symbol of God's grace. In one case we are shown man's customary behaviour, in the other we are given a revelation of the goodness of God.

3. *The barrenness of Sarah, made fertile by the grace of God*

Sarah, as we know, was barren, and, despairing of her chances of children, she was eager at least to have from her slave-girl what she realized she could not have from herself; and so she gave her slave to her husband to be made pregnant by him.[13] She had wished to have children by him, but it had proved impossible. Thus she exacted her due from her husband even so, by availing herself of her rights in respect of another's womb. Thus Ishmael was born, as men in general are born, as a result of sexual intercourse, following the established laws of nature. Hence the expression, 'according to the flesh' for 'in the course of nature'. It does not mean that such bounties do not come from God, or that those operations are not part of God's activity, whose craftsman, Wisdom, 'reaches', according to Scripture, 'from one end to another in its power, and orders all things delightfully.'[14] But when there was a need to point out that a gift was being bestowed by God of his free grace, and not as a matter of obligation, then a son had to be given in a way that was independent of the ordinary processes of nature. For nature denies children to the kind of sexual intercourse that was possible to Abraham and Sarah at the age they had

12. Rom. 9, 22f. 13. cf. Gen. 16, 1ff. 14. Wisd. 8, 1.

reached. And, apart from that, Sarah had hitherto been barren, and unable to produce a child even when she was the right age. Even then she failed in fertility, and by now she was the wrong age.

The fact that a nature in this condition had no right to any fruit of posterity signifies that human nature corrupted by sin, and therefore rightly condemned, did not deserve any true happiness for the future. Isaac therefore, who was born as a result of a promise, is rightly interpreted as symbolizing the children of grace, the citizens of the free city, the sharers in eternal peace, who form a community where there is no love of a will that is personal and, as we may say, private, but a love that rejoices in a good that is at once shared by all and unchanging – a love that makes 'one heart' out of many,[15] a love that is the whole-hearted and harmonious obedience of mutual affection.

4. *Conflict and peace in the earthly city*

The earthly city will not be everlasting; for when it is condemned to the final punishment it will no longer be a city. It has its good in this world, and rejoices to participate in it with such gladness as can be derived from things of such a kind. And since this is not the kind of good that causes no frustrations to those enamoured of it, the earthly city is generally divided against itself by litigation, by wars, by battles, by the pursuit of victories that bring death with them or at best are doomed to death. For if any section of that city has risen up in war against another part, it seeks to be victorious over other nations, though it is itself the slave of base passions; and if, when victorious, it is exalted in its arrogance, that victory brings death in its train. Whereas if it considers the human condition and the changes and chances common to mankind, and is more tormented by possible misfortunes than puffed up by its present success, then its victory is only doomed to death. For it will not be able to lord it permanently over those whom it has been able to subdue victoriously.

However, it would be incorrect to say that the goods which this city desires are not goods, since even that city is better, in its own human way, by their possession. For example, that city desires an earthly peace, for the sake of the lowest goods; and it is that peace which it longs to attain by making war. For if it wins the war and no one survives to resist, then there will be peace, which the warring sections did not enjoy when they contended in their unhappy poverty for the

15. cf. Acts 4, 32.

things which they could not both possess at the same time. This peace is the aim of wars, with all their hardships; it is this peace that glorious victory (so called) achieves.

Now when the victory goes to those who were fighting for the juster cause, can anyone doubt that the victory is a matter for rejoicing and the resulting peace is something to be desired? These things are goods and undoubtedly they are gifts of God. But if the higher goods are neglected, which belong to the City on high, where victory will be serene in the enjoyment of eternal and perfect peace[16] – if these goods are neglected and those other goods are so desired as to be considered the only goods, or are loved more than the goods which are believed to be higher, the inevitable consequence is fresh misery, and an increase of the wretchedness already there.

5. *Of the first founder of the earthly city, whose fratricide was reproduced by the founder of Rome*

The first founder of the earthly city was, as we have seen, a fratricide; for, overcome by envy, he slew his own brother, a citizen of the Eternal City, on pilgrimage in this world. Hence it is no wonder that long afterwards this first precedent – what the Greeks call an *archetype* – was answered by a kind of reflection, by an event of the same kind at the founding of the city which was to be the capital of the earthly city of which we are speaking, and was to rule over so many peoples. For there also, as one of their poets says when he mentions the crime,

> Those walls were dripping with a brother's blood.[17]

For this is how Rome was founded, when Remus, as Roman history witnesses, was slain by his brother Romulus. The difference from the primal crime was that both brothers were citizens of the earthly city. Both sought the glory of establishing the Roman state, but a joint foundation would not bring to each the glory that a single founder would enjoy. Anyone whose aim was to glory in the exercise of power would obviously enjoy less power if his sovereignty was diminished by a living partner. Therefore, in order that the sole power should be wielded by one person, the partner was eliminated; and what would have been kept smaller and better by innocence grew through crime into something bigger and worse.

In contrast, the earlier brothers, Cain and Abel, did not both entertain the same ambition for earthly gains; and the one who slew his

16. cf. Bk XIX, 17. 17. Luc. 1, 95.

brother was not jealous of him because his power would be more restricted if both wielded the sovereignty; for Abel did not aim at power in the city which his brother was founding. But Cain's was the diabolical envy that the wicked feel for the good simply because they are good, while they themselves are evil. A man's possession of goodness is in no way diminished by the arrival, or the continuance, of a sharer in it; indeed, goodness is a possession enjoyed more widely by the united affection of partners in that possession in proportion to the harmony that exists among them. In fact, anyone who refuses to enjoy this possession in partnership will not enjoy it at all; and he will find that he possesses it in ampler measure in proportion to his ability to love his partner in it.

Thus the quarrel that arose between Remus and Romulus demonstrated the division of the earthly city against itself; while the conflict between Cain and Abel displayed the hostility between the two cities themselves, the City of God and the city of men. Thus the wicked fight among themselves; and likewise the wicked fight against the good and the good against the wicked. But the good, if they have reached perfect goodness, cannot fight among themselves. However, while they are on their way towards the perfection they have not yet attained, there may be fighting among them inasmuch as any good man may fight against another as a result of that part of him which makes him also fight against himself. And in the individual it is true that 'the flesh has desires which resist the spirit, and the spirit has desires which resist the flesh'.[18] Accordingly, spiritual desire can fight against the carnal desire of another person, or carnal desire against another's spiritual desire, just as the good and the wicked fight against one another. Or even the carnal desires of two good men (who have obviously not yet attained perfection) may fight, just as the wicked fight among themselves, until those who are on the way to recovery are finally brought to triumphant health.

6. *On the weaknesses from which even the citizens of the City of God suffer as punishment for sin during their life's pilgrimage, and for which they are cured by God's healing*

Now this kind of weakness, the disobedience, that is, which we discussed in the fourteenth book,[19] is, of course, the punishment for the primal disobedience. Consequently, it is not part of nature, but a

18. Gal. 5. 17. 19. cf. Bk XIV, 1; 11 etc.

defect in nature. Hence the admonition given to the good who are making progress and who are living by faith during this pilgrimage: 'Carry each other's loads, and in this way you will fulfil the Law of Christ.'[20] And in another place, 'Correct the unruly, encourage the faint-hearted, support the feeble, be patient with all men. Take care that none of you returns evil for evil.'[21] And in yet another place, 'If a man has been caught in any offence, you who are spiritual must instruct such a person in a kindly spirit. Keep an eye on yourself, in case you may be tempted.'[22] And elsewhere, 'Do not let the sun set on your anger.'[23] And in the Gospel, 'If your brother sins against you correct him, just between the two of you.'[24] Similarly, on the subject of sins, as a precaution against the bad effect on others, the Apostle says, 'As for sinners, rebuke them publicly, so as to instil fear in the rest.'[25]

This is why so many precepts are given about mutual forgiveness and the great care needed for the maintenance of peace, without which no one will be able to see God.[26] Hence the terrifying sentence on the slave when he was ordered to repay a debt of ten thousand talents, which had been forgiven, because he did not forgive his fellow slave a debt of a hundred denarii. And when the Lord Jesus had told this parable, he added, 'This is what your Heavenly Father will do to you, if you do not, every one of you, forgive your brother from your heart.'[27] This is how the citizens of the City of God are restored to health while on pilgrimage on this earth, as they sigh for their Heavenly Country. At the same time the Holy Spirit is at work internally to make effective the medicine which is externally applied. Otherwise, even if God makes use of a creature subject to him to speak to human senses in some human form, whether to the bodily senses or those closely resembling them that we possess when we are asleep, and does not rule and guide our minds with his inward grace, no preaching of the truth is of any help to man.

In fact, this is what God does, distinguishing the vessels of wrath from the vessels of mercy, by the deeply hidden yet just dispensation, known only to himself.[28] He certainly helps in wonderful and secret ways; and when the sin (or rather the punishment of sin) which dwells in our members no longer, to use the words of the Apostle's precept, 'reigns in our mortal bodies inducing obedience to the body's desires', and when we no longer 'place our bodily parts at sin's dis-

20. Gal. 6, 2.
21. 1 Thess. 5, 14f.
22. Gal. 6, 1.
23. Eph. 4, 26.
24. Matt. 18, 15.
25. 1 Tim. 5, 20.
26. cf. Hebr. 12, 14.
27. cf. Matt. 18, 23–35.
28. cf. Rom. 9, 22f.

posal, to be instruments of wickedness',[29] there is a change in us, so that man's mind, under the rule of God, does not conspire with man to do evil, but man finds in this changed mind a ruler that brings a greater tranquillity, here and now; and hereafter, when he has attained perfect health and achieved immortality, man will reign, without sin, in eternal peace.

7. *The cause of Cain's crime, and his headstrong resolution*

But in this matter of God's speech with man, which I have described above, to the best of my power, what good was it to Cain when God spoke to him in the way in which he conversed with the first human beings, through the medium of a creature subject to him, taking on an appropriate form, as if he were a fellow-creature? Did he not carry out the planned crime in killing his brother, even after God had spoken a word of warning? God, we remember, had distinguished between the sacrifice of the two brothers, showing approval of the offering of the one, and disapproval of that of the other; and we must suppose that this distinction could be recognized by the evidence of some visible sign. The reason for God's action must have been that Cain's activities were evil, and his brother's were good. But the result was that Cain turned sullen, and his face fell. For Scripture says, 'And the Lord said to Cain: "Why have you become sullen? Why has your face fallen? If your sacrifice is rightly offered, but not rightly divided, have you not sinned? Calm yourself; for there is to be a return of it to you, and you will have the mastery over it." '[30]

In this admonition or warning which God offered to Cain, it is not clear what is the reason or ground for the saying, 'If your sacrifice is rightly offered, but not rightly divided, have you not sinned?' And the obscurity of it has produced a number of interpretations, in which each commentator on the holy Scriptures tries to explain the words in accordance with the Rule of Faith.[31] A sacrifice, to be sure, is rightly offered when it is offered to the true God, to whom alone sacrifice is due. But it is not 'rightly divided' when there is not a right distinction of the places or times of sacrifice, or the material of the sacrifice or its recipient, or those to whom the victim is distributed for eating. This is to interpret 'division' as here meaning 'distinction'. An

29. cf. Rom. 6, 12f.
30. Gen. 4, 6f. (LXX). The passage is obscure in the Hebrew.
31. The traditional orthodoxy governing the interpretation of Scripture. It is not identical with any accepted formula.

offering may be at the wrong place, or the object offered may be inadmissible there, though appropriate elsewhere; it may be at the wrong time, inadmissible on that occasion, but appropriate at another time; or it may be an offering that is utterly improper at any time or place. Or it may be that a man keeps back for himself the choicer portions of the kind of things which he offers to God; or else the sacrifice is shared by a profane person, or anyone else who may not lawfully partake of it.

Now it is not easy to find out in which of these respects Cain displeased God. The apostle John, when speaking of those brothers, said, 'Do not be like Cain, who was on the side of the evil one and slew his brother. And for what reason? Because his deeds were of evil intention, and his brother's were righteous.'[32] This gives us to understand that God did not approve his gift, because it was wrongly 'divided' in this point, that he gave to God something belonging to him, but gave himself to himself. This is what is done by all those who follow their own will, and not the will of God; that is, those who live with a perverted instead of an upright heart, and yet offer a gift to God. They suppose that with this gift God is being bought over to help them, not in curing their depraved desires, but in fulfilling them. And this is the characteristic of the earthly city – to worship a god or gods so that with their assistance it may reign in the enjoyment of victories and an earthly peace, not with a loving concern for others, but with lust for domination over them. For the good make use of this world in order to enjoy God, whereas the evil want to make use of God in order to enjoy the world – those of them, that is, who still believe in the existence of God, or in his concern for human affairs; those who do not believe even this are in a much worse case. And so when Cain discovered that God had approved his brother's sacrifice but not his own, he ought surely to have changed his ways and imitated his good brother, instead of showing pride and jealousy. In fact, Cain turned sullen, and his face fell. This is a sin which God particularly rebukes, namely, sulkiness about another's goodness, and a brother's goodness at that. And it was this that God was rebuking when he asked, 'Why have you turned sullen? Why has your face fallen?' Because God saw that Cain envied his brother, and that was what God rebuked.

Now from the point of view of human beings, from whom the heart of another person is hidden, it might be doubtful, in fact completely uncertain, whether Cain's sullenness was due to remorse for his own evil intent, which, as he had learned, made him displeasing to God, or

32. John 3, 12.

to annoyance at his brother's goodness, which pleased God, as was shown when God approved Abel's sacrifice. But God gave the reason why he refused to accept Cain's sacrifice, so that he should be rightly displeased with himself, instead of being wrongly displeased with his brother. Thus God showed that although Cain was unrighteous in not 'dividing' rightly, that is in not living rightly, and so did not deserve to have his offering approved, he was much more unrighteous in hating his righteous brother without a cause. However, God did not send Cain away without giving him a command which was holy, righteous and good. For he said, 'Calm yourself; for there is to be a return of it to you, and you will have the mastery over it.' Did it mean 'over *him*', that is, his brother? Heaven forbid! Over what, then? It can only be 'over sin'. For God had said, 'You have sinned'; and he went on, 'Calm yourself; for there is to be a return of it to you, and you will have the mastery over it.' The saying that there is bound to be a return of sin to the man himself can certainly be interpreted as meaning that he should know that his sin should be ascribed to his own fault and not blamed on another.

For this is a health-giving medicine of repentance and a petition for pardon which is suitable to the case. Thus, when God says, 'For (there is to be) a return of it to you', the verb to be understood is 'should be' rather than 'will be'; it is said by way of prescription rather than prediction. For a man will have the mastery over his sin if he does not put it in command of himself by defending it, but subjects it to himself by repenting of it. Otherwise, he will also be its slave, and it will have the mastery, if he affords it encouragement when it occurs.

But sin can also be taken to mean carnal desire itself. Thus the Apostle says, 'The desires of the flesh oppose the spirit',[33] and among the 'fruits of the flesh' he includes envy; and it was certainly envy which goaded and inflamed Cain to his brother's destruction. On that interpretation the verb to be understood is 'will be', and the passage will run thus: 'There will be a return of it to you, and you will have the mastery over it.' This is what may happen after the carnal element of man has been aroused. The Apostle gives this element the name of 'sin', in the passage where he says, 'It is not my own action, but the action of sin which dwells in me.'[34] (There are also philosophers who say that this element in the soul is perverted, and that it ought not to drag the mind after it, but should be under orders from the mind, and restrained by reason from unlawful acts.) Thus, when this element has been aroused to commit some wrongful act, if we then calm our-

33. Gal. 5, 17. 34. Rom. 7, 17.

selves and obey the Apostle's instructions not to 'place your bodily parts at sin's disposal, to be the instruments of wickedness',[35] then that element 'returns', subdued and conquered, to the mind and accepts the mastery of reason.

This was God's instruction to Cain, who was inflamed with the fires of jealousy against his brother, and longed to have him destroyed, when he ought to have imitated his example. 'Calm yourself', God said, 'restrain your hands from crime, and do not let sin reign in your mortal body so that you obey its desires,[36] and do not place your bodily parts at sin's disposal, as the instruments of wickedness. "For there will be a return of it to you" provided that you do not encourage it by slackening your control but bridle it by keeping calm "and you will have the mastery over it". Thus, so long as it is not allowed to be active outwardly, it will become accustomed to remain quiet inwardly as well, under the control of the mind's benevolent sovereignty.'

Something of this sort was said in the same inspired book about the woman also, when God asked questions and gave judgement after the sin. The sinners received the sentences of condemnation, the Devil in the person of the serpent, the woman and her husband in their own persons. God said to the woman, 'I shall many times multiply your sorrows and your groaning, and in sorrows you will produce children;' and then he added, 'And your turning will be to your husband, and he will have the mastery over you.'[37] What was said to Cain about sin, or the perverted desire of the flesh, is said in this passage about the sinful woman, and here is to be taken as meaning that man, in ruling his wife, should resemble the mind which rules the flesh. For that reason the Apostle says, 'A man who loves his wife is loving himself. For no one ever hated his own flesh.'[38]

We should then look for a cure of those sins, as being our own, instead of condemning them as if they did not belong to us. But Cain received that instruction from God like a lawbreaker. For the fault of jealousy grew stronger, and he planned and carried out his brother's murder. Such was the man who founded the earthly city. He also symbolizes the Jews by whom Christ was slain, the shepherd of the flock of men, who was prefigured in Abel, the shepherd of the flock of sheep. But this is a matter of prophetic allegory, and so I shall refrain from explaining it here. Besides, I recall having said something on this point in my book *Against Faustus the Manichean*.[39]

35. Rom. 6, 13. 36. cf. Rom. 6, 12. 37. cf. Gen. 3, 16 (LXX).
38. Eph. 5, 28f. 39. *Adv. Faust. Man.*, 12, 9.

8. *The reason why Cain founded a city among the first beginnings of the human race*

My present duty, as it seems to me, is to defend the historical truth of the scriptural account, in case it may seem incredible that a city should have been built by one man at a time when there were apparently only four men in existence on the earth – or rather three men, after Cain had killed his brother. These three were the first man, the father of all, Cain himself, and Cain's son Enoch, after whose name the city itself was called. But those who are worried by this have given too little consideration to the fact that the writer of this sacred history had no need to mention by name all the people who may then have existed. He only needed to give the names of those who were demanded by the plan of the work he had undertaken. For the intention of the writer, through whom the Holy Spirit was achieving his purpose, was to arrive at Abraham through the clearly defined succession of generations descended from one man; and then to pass from the line of Abraham to the people of God, which was kept distinct from all other nations and in which were prefigured and foretold all things which were foreseen, by inspiration of the Spirit, as destined to come, the things, that is, relating to the City whose kingdom will be eternal, and to Christ, its king and founder. And in this account the other society of men was not ignored, the society which we call the earthly city. It was mentioned as far as was necessary to enable the City of God to shine out in contrast with its opposite.

Now when holy Scripture mentions the number of years which those early men lived it concludes the account by saying of the man spoken about, 'And he begat sons and daughters, and all the days' that this or that man lived 'were' so many years 'and he died.'[40] But the omission of the names of those sons and daughters, does not forbid the inference that during all those years that people lived in that first age of the world, large numbers of men could have been born and large numbers of cities also could have been founded by their association. But those narratives were written under the inspiration of God; and God's purpose was to direct and distinguish, from the start, those two societies in their different lines of descent. And so on one side the generations of men, that is, of those who live by human standards, and on the other side the generations of the sons of God, that is, of those who live by God's standards, were interwoven down to the Flood, where the discrimination and the combination of the two so-

40. cf. e.g. Gen. 5, 4f.

cieties is described. The discrimination is described in that the genealogies of the two societies are recorded separately, one deriving from Cain the fratricide, the other from the brother called Seth (for he was another son of Adam, taking the place of the one murdered by his brother). At the same time, their combination is described in that, as the good deteriorated, they all became bad enough to be wiped out by the Flood, except for one righteous man named Noah, his wife, his three sons and three daughters-in-law. These eight human beings deserved to escape in the ark from that destruction of all mortal beings.

About the first city the Scripture says, 'And Cain knew his wife, and she conceived, and gave birth to Enoch: and Cain built a city in the name of Enoch, his son.'[41] But it does not follow that we are to suppose Enoch to have been his first son. For this is not to be inferred from the fact that he is said to have known his wife, as if that meant that this was the first sexual intercourse he had with her. For the same expression is used of Adam himself, the father of all, not only at the time of Cain's conception (and Cain appears to have been his first-born) but also later on, where the same Scripture says, 'Adam knew Eve, his wife, and she conceived and gave birth to a son, and called his name Seth.'[42] From this we see that this is the normal, though not the invariable, usage of Scripture, when we are told of the conception of men; but the expression is not confined to the first act of intercourse. And the fact that the city was called after Enoch's name is not cogent proof that Enoch was his father's first-born. It is not impossible that his father, although he had other sons, loved Enoch more than the rest for some reason. Judah, for example, was not a first-born son, and yet Judaea and the Jews get their names from him.

But even if Enoch was in fact the first-born of the founder of that city, we are not therefore to assume that it was founded by Cain and given Enoch's name at the time of his birth. For a city, which is nothing but a number of people bound together by some tie of fellowship, could not have been established at that time by one man. However, when that man's household grew to such a number as to reach the size of a population, then it was certainly possible for him to establish a city and give the name of his first-born to the city thus established. It must be remembered that the lives of men in that period were so long that of those mentioned in the narrative whose years are disclosed, the shortest-lived, before the Flood, attained the total of 753

41. Gen. 4, 17. 42. Gen. 4, 25.

years.[43] In fact, several passed the 900 years mark, although no one reached a thousand.

Then can one doubt that it was possible for the human race to multiply to such an extent during one man's lifetime that there would be material for the founding of not one but many cities? We can very easily draw this conclusion from the case of Abraham. For from that one man the Hebrew people reproduced itself in such numbers in little more than 400 years[44] that there were, according to the account, 600,000 young warriors in the exodus of that people from Egypt.[45] And this is to leave out the nation of the Idumaeans, which does not belong to the people of Israel, being descended from Israel's brother Esau, Abraham's grandson,[46] and the other nations derived from the seed of Abraham himself, but not through his wife Sarah.[47]

9. *The long life and the great stature of antediluvian man*

For this reason no intelligent student of history could doubt that Cain could have founded not only some sort of a city but even a large one, at a time when the lives of mortals were prolonged to so great an age. But it may be that some unbeliever or other will start a dispute with us about the immense number of years which, in the record of our authorities, the men of that period lived; he may assert that this tradition is incredible. Similarly, as we know, some people do not believe that human bodies were then of much greater size than they are now. Now the most distinguished pagan poet, Virgil, has something on this point. He is describing a huge stone set as a boundary mark on the land; a mighty warrior snatches it up in battle, runs on, then swings it round and hurls it. And Virgil says,

> That stone twice six picked men could scarce upheave
> With bodies such as the earth now produces.[48]

He means it to be understood that in those days the earth normally produced larger bodies than now. How much more then in the days when the world was newer, before that renowned and far-famed Flood!

Now in the matter of the size of bodies the incredulous are usually convinced by the tombs uncovered by the action of time, or by the violence of storms or various other accidents. Bones of incredible size have come to light in them, or have fallen out of them.[49] On the

43. cf. Gen. 5, 31 (LXX). 44. cf. Exod. 12, 40. 45. cf. Exod. 12, 37.
46 cf. Gen. 36. 47. cf. Gen. 25, 1–4; 12–15. 48. *Aen.*, 12, 899f.
49. cf. Virg., *Georg.*, 1, 4, 93–7.

shore at Utica I myself saw – and I was not alone but in the company of several others – a human molar so immense that if it had been cut up into pieces the size of our teeth it would, as it seemed to us, have made a hundred. But that tooth I should imagine, belonged to some giant. For not only were the bodies of men in general much larger at that time than ours are now, but the giants far exceeded all the rest, just as thereafter, and in our own times, there have been bodies which have far surpassed the size of the others. They have indeed been rare, but scarcely any period has been without them. Pliny the Elder, a man of profound learning, testifies that as the centuries pass and the world gets older and older, the bodies produced by nature become smaller and smaller.[50] He mentions that Homer often lamented this fact in his poems,[51] and Pliny does not laugh at these complaints as being poetic fictions; in his capacity as a recorder of the marvels of nature, he takes them as reliable statements of historical fact. However, as I have said, the magnitude of bodies of antiquity is witnessed even to much later ages by the frequent discovery of bones, since bones are very durable.

On the other hand, the longevity of individuals in that period cannot be put to the proof of such material evidence. Nevertheless we should not for that reason call in question the reliability of the sacred narrative. Our impudence in doubting the scriptural record is measured by the certainty of the fulfilment of its prophecies, which we see before our eyes. Apart from this, Pliny also states that there is to this day a nation where men live for two hundred years.[52] And so, if it is believed that places unknown to us provide examples, at the present time, of a longevity which is outside our experience, why should we not believe the same of the unknown past? Are we to say that it is credible that something which does not happen here does happen somewhere, but incredible that something which does not happen now did happen at some other time?

10. *The apparent discrepancy between the Hebrew version of the Scriptures and our own translation, on the precise ages of men of old*

On this point, it is true, we observe a considerable discrepancy between the Hebrew text and our version[53] in regard to the precise

50. cf. Plin. 7, 16.
51. cf. *Il.* 5, 302ff; 12, 378ff; 445ff.
52. cf. Plin. 7, 48.
53. i.e. the Old Latin Version, a translation of LXX. St Augustine knew

number of years. I do not know the reason for this; but in any case the difference is not enough to cause any disagreement about the fact of the great longevity of the men of that period. For instance, we find in our texts that Adam, the first man, was 230 years old before he begot the son called Seth, whereas in the Hebrew he is said to have been 130. On the other hand, we read in our version that Adam lived another 700 years after the birth of Seth, while the Hebrew gives 800 years.[54] Thus both texts agree about the total.

Thereafter, in subsequent generations, we find the age of the father at the birth of those whose birth is mentioned, given in the Hebrew as a hundred years less than in our version; but the rest of his life, after the birth of the son, is a hundred years less in our text than in the Hebrew. Thus the sum of the two numbers agrees, in both versions. In the sixth generation, however, there is no discrepancy at all in the two texts. But in the seventh (in which the narrative records that Enoch was born and, instead of dying, was translated, because he pleased God[55]) there is the same discrepancy of a hundred years before the birth of the son there mentioned, and the same agreement in the total. For he was 365 years old before translation, according to both texts.

The eighth generation certainly shows a certain discrepancy, but it is smaller than the others and of a different kind. For according to the Hebrew text, Methuselah, son of Enoch, was twenty years older than in our version, before he begot the son who comes next in the list, instead of a hundred years younger,[56] but, once again, these years are found added in our text after the birth of his son, and so the total coincides in both versions. The only discrepancy in the total sum appears in the ninth generation, in the age of Lamech, son of Methuselah and father of Noah; but the difference is not very large.[57] For we find that in the Hebrew version he lived twenty-four years longer than in our text. Before the birth of his son named Noah he is six years younger in the Hebrew than in our version; but after Noah's birth he lived thirty years longer in the Hebrew text than in ours. Thus, with the subtraction of those six years the remainder, as I said, is twenty-four.

Jerome's Latin translation of the Hebrew, for Jerome's version of the Bible (the Vulgate) was completed some ten years before St Augustine began the *City of God* in 413.

54. Gen. 5, 3f. 55. Gen. 5, 21ff.
56. cf. Gen. 5, 25ff. 57. Gen. 5, 28ff.

11. *The age of Methuselah, whose life apparently extends fourteen years beyond the Flood*

From this discrepancy between the Hebrew text and ours arises that notorious problem about the fourteen years that Methuselah, by our reckoning, lived after the Flood. Now according to the scriptural account only eight persons, of all those who were then on earth, escaped destruction by the Flood in the ark, and Methuselah was not one of them. According to our text, Methuselah was 167 years old before the birth of the son whom he named Lamech;[58] and then Lamech was 188 years old before Noah was born to him.[59] These two figures together make 355. Add to these the 600 years of Noah, which was his age at the time of the Flood,[60] and the total is 955,[61] and this is the period from the birth of Methuselah down to the year of the Flood.

But all the years of Methuselah's life are reckoned as 969; for he was 167 years old at the time of the birth of his son called Lamech, and he lived on for 802 years after that,[62] which gives, as I said, the total of 969. If we subtract the 955 years from Methuselah's birth to the Flood it leaves fourteen years; so we assume that he lived for fourteen years after the Flood. For this reason there are some who think that he was alive, though not on the earth, where, it is agreed, all flesh which nature does not allow to live in water was destroyed. They suppose that he was for some time with his father, who had been translated, and that he lived there until the Flood had passed. For they refuse to question the reliability of the text which is accepted by the Church and is thus given a wider authority; and they believe that it is the version of the Jews and not the other text which contains inaccuracies.

These people will not allow that it is more likely that we have here a mistake on the part of the translators, than that there should be a false statement in the language from which the Scriptures themselves were translated, through the Greek version, into our tongue. They assert that it is unbelievable that seventy translators who made their translation at one and the same time and produced one and the same meaning, could have made a mistake, or should have deliberately uttered a falsehood on a point of no importance to them. But they maintain that the Jews, in their jealousy at the transference to us, through translation, of the Law and the prophets, altered some passages in their own texts to diminish the authority of our version.

58. cf. Gen. 5, 25 (Vulg., 187). 59. cf. Gen. 5, 28 (Vulg., 182). 60. cf. Gen. 7, 6. 61. Vulg. 969. 62. cf. Gen. 5, 26 (Vulg. 782).

Anyone may accept this idea, or suspicion, as he thinks fit. One thing remains certain: Methuselah did not live on after the Flood; he ended his life in the same year, if the information is true which is found in the Hebrew text about the number of his years. As for the seventy translators, I must insert a more detailed statement of my opinions about them in the appropriate place, when, with God's assistance, I come to deal with that period as far as the subject of this work demands.[63] For the present discussion it is enough that according to both versions the longevity of human beings at that period was such that it was possible for the human race to multiply sufficiently even to establish a city in the lifetime of one man, who was the first child born to the parents who were then the sole inhabitants of the earth.

12. *Concerning the opinion of those who refuse to believe in the longevity of the human beings in the early ages, as recorded in Scripture*

Not the slightest attention should be given to those who fancy that years were differently reckoned in those times, that is, that they were of such short duration that one of our years should be assumed to include ten of theirs. Therefore, they maintain, when anyone hears or reads that someone lived for 900 years he should interpret this as ninety, since ten of their years equal one of ours, and ten of ours make a hundred of theirs. According to this reckoning, Adam was twenty-three when he became the father of Seth, and Seth for his part was twenty years and six months old when Enos was born to him. Scripture, to be sure, ascribes to Seth 205 years; but on the speculative theory we are examining one year such as we now have was then divided into ten, and each of those divisions was called a year. Each of those parts contains the square of six, because God completed his works in six days so that he might rest on the seventh day (I have discussed this topic, to the best of my ability, in Book XI).[64] Six times six, the square of six, is thirty-six days; and that multiplied by ten comes to 365 days, that is, twelve lunar months. That leaves five days to be supplied to complete the solar year, plus a quarter of a day (hence the introduction, every fourth year, of one day, called *bissextus*);[65] and that is the reason why, in antiquity, days were later added to

63. cf. Bk XVIII, 42–4. 64. Bk XI, 8.

65. In the Roman calendar Feb. 24 (a.d. VI Kal. Mart., the 6th day before March 1) was duplicated every fourth year. Hence the extra day was called 'the twice sixth', *bissextus*.

make the number of years tally. These are the days called by the Romans 'intercalary'.

On this assumption Enos, the son of Seth, was nineteen years old when his son Cainan was born, though Scripture gives his age as a hundred and ninety.[66] And after that through all the generations, among the men whose ages are mentioned before the Flood, no case is found in our version of a man's having a son when he was a hundred years old or less, or even 120 or a little more. In fact the earliest age of any father is recorded as 160 or more. For no one can beget children (as those who hold this theory maintain) at the age of ten, or, as those people would call it, a hundred. Puberty is fully developed and capable of procreating children by the age of sixteen, which in antiquity was called 160.

To reduce the incredibility of the supposition that the year was differently reckoned in those days, those theorists adduce evidence from a number of historians that the Egyptians had a year of four months,[67] the Acarnianians of six, and the Lavinians of thirteen. Pliny the Elder mentions reports in written documents that one man lived 152 years, another for ten years more than that, others for 300 years, while some attained the age of 500, 600, or even 800 years.[68] But he decides that these reports were based on ignorance of chronology. 'For some people', he says, 'used to treat summer as a complete year, and winter as another, while others treated each of the four seasons as a whole year, like the Arcadians, who had years of three months.' He adds that the Egyptians (whose short year of four months I have mentioned above) sometimes ended the year with the final phase of each moon; 'and so', he says, 'we have reports among the Egyptians of people who lived a thousand years.'

Some people advance these as being plausible arguments, seeking not to undermine the credibility of this sacred narrative but doing their best to support it, and to reduce the difficulty of believing the tradition of the longevity of men in antiquity. Thus they have persuaded themselves, and consider that they need not be ashamed to try to persuade others, that what was then called a year was so short a time that ten of those years were equal to one of ours, and ten of ours the same as a hundred of theirs. That this theory is utterly erroneous can be proved by the clearest evidence.[69] But before I do so, I think that I should not pass over a suggestion which may be more worthy of credence.

66. cf. Gen. 5, 9 (LXX). 67. cf. Bk XII, 11.
68. Plin. 7, 48. 69. cf. ch. 14.

We could certainly have refuted and overthrown this contention by the evidence of the Hebrew text, where Adam is found to have been 130, instead of 230 years of age at the time when he became the father of his third son.[70] If this means thirteen of our years, he was undoubtedly little more than eleven years, at most, when his first son was begotten. But can anyone become a father at that age, according to the established laws of nature with which we are so familiar?

But let us pass over Adam. It may well be that he could have procreated children at the time of his creation, for we cannot suppose that when he was made he was as small as our infants are. His son Seth was not 205, as we find in our version, but 105 when he became the father of Enos.[71] This means that he was not yet eleven, on the theory we are examining. And what of his son Cainan? Although he appears as 170 in our version, the reading of the Hebrew is that he was seventy when he became the father of Mahalaleel.[72] But – if we assume that 'seventy years' meant at that time 'seven years' – who can become a father at the age of seven?

13. *Whether we should follow the authority of the Hebrew text rather than that of the Septuagint, in the reckoning of the years*

But when I have said this, the response will be that this is a falsehood of the Jews – a point which I have sufficiently dealt with above.[73] The assertion is that the seventy translators, men of well deserved renown, could not have lied. Now let us suppose these two possibilities: either the Jewish people, scattered so far and wide, were able to unite in a planned conspiracy to write this false account and thus deprive themselves of the truth because they grudged others a share in the authority of their Scriptures, or else it was the seventy men who grudged foreign nations a share in this scriptural truth and carried out their purpose by following an agreed plan. Now these seventy (who were themselves Jews) had been assembled in one place, because Ptolemy, king of Egypt, had appointed them to this task.[74] If I should

70. cf. Gen. 5, 3.
71. cf. Gen. 5, 6.
72. cf. Gen. 5, 12.
73. cf. ch. 11.
74. The *Septuagint* (LXX). According to Jewish tradition Ptolemy Philadelphus (285–246 B.C.) engaged seventy-two translators to prepare a Greek version of the Hebrew Law (the Pentateuch) for his library at Alexandria. Later the story was extended to include the whole Old Testament. In fact the version was probably the work of a number of Alexandrian Jews and was gradually completed. The preface of Ecclesiasticus suggests that most of the work had been done by *c.* 132 B.C.; cf. Bk XVIII, 43.

ask which is the more credible alternative, could anyone fail to see which can more easily and readily be believed?

But in fact it is unthinkable that any sensible person should suppose either that the Jews, whatever their perversity and malice, could have achieved such a feat in so many texts, so widely dispersed; or that those seventy men of renown should have united in a common plan to deprive the Gentiles of the truth, because of jealousy. It would be more plausible, therefore, to suggest that when the text began to be transcribed for the first time from the copy in Ptolemy's library, some inaccuracy of this sort might have happened in one copy. Now if that was the original transcription it might have been the source of widespread error, starting with a simple mistake on the part of a scribe. There is no implausibility in this supposition in respect of the problem raised by Methuselah's life, or in the other instance[75] where the totals do not agree, and show an excess of twenty-four years. But in some places the identical error is displayed time after time, with a hundred extra years appearing in the one version, before the birth of a son who is included in the list, while after the birth the same number of years is subtracted in that version, to make the total agree with the other text. This happens in the first, second, third, fourth, fifth, and seventh generations. Here the error seems to have, if I may so put it, a certain consistency which smacks of design rather than accident.

In these instances, then, we find that a century subtracted is balanced by the subsequent addition of a hundred years, and the procedure occurs in a number of successive generations. In the other cases, the divergence of the numbers given in the Latin and Greek versions from those appearing in the Hebrew, should not be ascribed either to Jewish malice or to a carefully thought-out plan on the part of the seventy translators. It should be put down to the mistake of the scribe who first received the text from the library of the aforesaid King Ptolemy to transcribe. For even in these days, numbers are carelessly copied and even more carelessly checked when they do not direct the reader's attention to something which can be easily understood, or which is evidently useful to learn. Would anyone consider that he ought to learn how many thousand men each of the Israelite tribes might have had? It is not thought that such knowledge offers any advantage, and few people see in it any practical importance or deep significance.

But we have a different problem when in successive generations one text gives a hundred years which are missing in the other version, and

75. viz. Lamech; cf. ch. 10.

then after the birth of the son next to be mentioned we find the missing hundred years added in the one, and the excess subtracted from the other, so that the totals agree. No doubt the discrepancy is due to someone who wanted to establish the point that the reputed longevity of men in antiquity was based on the extreme brevity of 'years'. He also sought to support this theory with regard to the development of puberty necessary for procreation; that was why he thought that the incredulous should be informed that ten of our years equalled a hundred of the ancient years, so that they should be willing to believe those reports of great longevity. Thus he added a hundred years where he did not find the age suitable for begetting children, and subtracted the same number after the birth of the sons, to make the totals agree. For his purpose was to make the ages credible and appropriate for procreation, without defrauding the individuals of the total number of years of their lives.

The fact that he did not do this in the sixth generation is in itself a further indication that he did it when it was demanded by the situation I have suggested, since he did not do it when it was not so demanded. For he found in that generation, according to the Hebrew,[76] that Jared was a hundred and sixty-two when he became the father of Enoch; and this age, on this short-year theory, becomes sixteen and something under two months. Now that age is already suitable for procreation, and therefore there was no need to add a hundred short years, to make his age twenty-six in our years, or to subtract them after the birth of Enoch, since he had not added them before his birth. So it came about that there was no divergence here in the two texts.

But to return to the problem of the eighth generation. What is puzzling is that before Lamech was born, his father Methuselah was 182 years old, according to the reading of the Hebrew text;[77] whereas in our version, instead of the usual addition of a hundred years, we find twenty years less.[78] These are put back after Lamech's birth to complete the total, which is the same in both texts. Now if our short-year advocate intended us to interpret 170 years as meaning seventeen, to give the necessary sexual development, there was no need for any addition or subtraction, because he was presented with an age suitable for procreation, which was the reason for his addition of a hundred years in places where he did not find the age suitable. To

76. cf. Gen. 5, 18.
77. cf. Gen. 5, 25 (the Hebrew text gives 187, which agrees with what follows).
78. LXX gives 167 years.

be sure, we might be justified in supposing that the twenty years were the result of an accidental mistake, if it were not that he took pains to restore the subtraction afterwards, so that the total sum should agree with the other version. But should we perhaps think that there was a more cunning purpose here? He may have intended to conceal his practice of first adding and then subtracting a hundred years by following the same procedure in a case where it was not necessary. It is true that in this case it was not a matter of a hundred years; but still a number of years, however small, was first subtracted and then restored.

However, it matters little what line of interpretation is adopted. The main point is that whether my explanation is believed or not, whether, in fact, this is the truth of the matter or not, I should certainly not be justified in doubting that when some difference occurs in the two versions, where it is impossible for both to be a true record of historical fact, then greater reliance should be placed on the original language from which a version was made by translators into another tongue. There are, in point of fact, three Greek texts, one Latin, and one Syriac, which agree in showing Methuselah as having departed this life six years before the Flood.[79]

14. *The years in the early periods were of the same length as they are now*

Let us now observe how it can be conclusively demonstrated that the years reckoned in the immensely long lives of those men of antiquity were not so short that one of our years would be equal to ten of them, but that they were in fact of the same length as those we now have, which are, as we know, completed by the revolution of the sun. Now Scripture records that the Flood happened in the six hundredth year of Noah's life. And we are told, 'The water of the Flood came on the earth in the 600th year of the life of Noah, in the second month, on the twenty-seventh day of the month.'[80] Now why are we told this, if that tiny year, one tenth of our year, had only thirty-six days? Surely so small a year (if it was given that name in the usage of antiquity) either has no months, or – if it is to have twelve of them – has three-day months. So how could it be said here, 'In the six hundredth year, in the second month, on the twenty-seventh day of the month', unless the months were even then such as they are now? How could it be said otherwise that the Flood started on the twenty-seventh day of the

79. cf. Aug., *Quaest. in Hept.*, 1, 2. 80. Gen. 8, 4f.

second month? And then later on, at the end of the Flood, we read, 'In the seventh month, on the twenty-seventh day of the month, the ark grounded on the mountains of Ararat. And the water subsided until the eleventh month. And in the eleventh month, on the first day of the month, the tops of the mountains came into sight.'[81]

If then the months were like ours, we may assume that the years were the same as we now have. Certainly those three-day months could not have had twenty-seven days. Or if we are to reduce everything in proportion, and a thirtieth part of three days was then called a day, the great Flood which is reported to have taken forty days and nights[81] did not take a whole four days, in our calendar. But who could endure such empty nonsense? Let us sweep away this error which seeks to support the reliability of Scripture by false conjecture, at the expense of overthrowing it elsewhere. The day was even then precisely as long as it is now, completed by twenty-four hours in the course of a day and a night. The month was as long as it is now, being the period defined by the waxing and waning of the moon. The year was as long as it is now, being made up of twelve lunar months, with the addition of five and a quarter days to bring it in line with the sun's course. And this was the length of the 600th year of Noah's life in the second month of which, on the twenty-seventh day of the month, the Flood began. In this Flood immense falls of rains are recorded for forty days without remission; and these days consisted not of a little over two hours but twenty-four hours, comprising a day and a night. It follows that the years of the men of antiquity who lived lives in excess of 900, were as long as those of Abraham who lived to the age of 170[82] and after him of his son Isaac, who reached 180[83] and of Isaac's son Jacob, who lived to nearly 150,[84] and, after a considerable interval, of Moses, who attained 120,[85] and of people at this day who live to seventy or eighty, or not much more – and it is said of these ages that 'more than these years is toil and sorrow.'[86]

Indeed, the difference in numbers found in the Hebrew text and our own does not entail a disagreement about the longevity of the men of ancient times; and if the divergence is such as to preclude the possibility that both versions are true, the historical truth must be looked for in the language from which our version was translated. Although this opportunity is open to any who wish to take it, anywhere in the world, it is not without significance that no one has ventured to amend, from the Hebrew text, the very many places where the

81. cf. Gen. 7, 12. 82. cf. Gen. 25, 7. 83. cf. Gen. 35, 28.
84. cf. Gen. 47, 28. 85. cf. Deut. 34, 7. 86. Ps. 90, 10.

seventy translators seem to say something different. In fact, this divergence was not regarded as corruption of the text, and for my part I do not think it should be so regarded. Instead, where it is not a question of an error of transcription, and where the sense would be in harmony with the truth and would proclaim the truth, we should believe that under the influence of the divine Spirit the seventy chose to express the meaning differently, not in fulfilment of their task as translators but in the exercise of their liberty as prophets

Hence it is found that apostolic authority, when adducing evidence from Scripture, makes use of the Septuagint as well as the Hebrew text. But I have promised,[87] with God's help, to discuss this point in greater detail at a more appropriate place.[88] At the moment I shall confine my discussion to the present question. The point I am making is that it is not to be doubted that at a time when men were so long-lived it was possible for a city to be established by the man who was the first son of the first man I am speaking, of course, of an earthly city, not of that City which is called the City of God It was in order to write about that City that I took in hand the labour involved in this immense work.

15. *Whether it is credible that men of the first era abstained from intercourse until the age at which they are recorded as having begotten sons*

Now someone is going to ask, 'Are we then to believe that a man who intended to have children, and had not formed a resolution of continence, abstained from sexual intercourse for a hundred years and more, or (if we follow the Hebrew text) not much less, that is, for eighty, seventy, or sixty years; or if he did not abstain, was quite incapable of procreation?' This problem can be solved in two ways. Either sexual development was then later, in proportion to the greater length of the whole life, or (and this, in my view, is more probable) it is not the first-born children who are mentioned here, but those needed for the order of succession to arrive at Noah. Then, as we see, the line of descent stretches from Noah on to Abraham, and from Abraham down to a fixed point of time, as far as was necessary to indicate, by the record of generations, the course of the most glorious City which is on pilgrimage in this world and looks for a native land on high.

Now it cannot be denied that Cain was the first to be born from the

87. cf. ch. 11. 88. cf. Bk XVIII, 42–4.

union of man and woman. For Adam is recorded to have said at Cain's birth, 'I have acquired a man, through God's help';[89] and he would not have said this, if Cain had not been the first one added by birth to the original pair. Abel followed Cain, and he was killed by his elder brother, thus being the first to display a kind of foreshadowing of the pilgrim City of God; showing that it was to suffer unjust persecution at the hands of wicked and, in a sense, earth-born men, that is, men who delight in their earthly origin and rejoice in the earthly felicity of the earthly city. But it is not made clear at what age Adam became the father of these sons.

After that, the generations divide into the line of Cain and the line of descent from the son whom Adam begot to take the place of the one slain by his brother. Adam called him Seth, saying, according to Scripture, 'For God has raised up for me another seed, in place of Abel whom Cain murdered.'[90] Thus there are two lines of descent, one from Seth and the other from Cain; and their separate lists convey the notion of the two cities, the Heavenly City on pilgrimage in this world, and the earthly city, which longs for earthly joys, or clings to them, as though they were the only joys. However, although Cain's progeny is enumerated in detail, starting from Adam, down to the eighth generation, there is nowhere any statement of the precise age at which anyone became the father of the person next mentioned. For the Spirit of God preferred not to mark the chronology before the Flood by the generations of the earthly city, but instead by those of the Heavenly City, as being, by implication, more worthy of record.

Further, when Seth was born, his father's age was not indeed omitted,[91] but Adam had already had other children, and who would be so bold as to say for certain whether Cain and Abel were the only ones or not? We are not justified in taking for granted that they were the only children of Adam at that time, just because they are the only children named in order to preserve the genealogies which had to be recorded. For we are told that Adam had had sons and daughters born to him, although the names of all the others are veiled in silence. Would anyone take upon himself to state (assuming that he wants to avoid the charge of presumption) the number of children here referred to?

It is certainly possible that Adam was moved by divine inspiration to say, after the birth of Seth, 'For God has raised up for me another seed, in place of Abel', because Seth was to prove to be the son to carry on

89. Gen. 4, 1. 90. cf. Gen. 4, 25.
91. cf. Gen. 5, 3 (Vulg., 130; LXX, 230).

his brother's holiness, and not because he was the first in point of time to be born after Abel. And when Scripture says afterwards, 'Now Seth lived 205 years (105 years in the Hebrew text) and became the father of Enos,'[92] only an unthinking reader could assert that Enos must have been the first-born. This assumption gives rise to astonishment, and we are justified in asking how it could be that he eschewed intercourse for so many years without any intention of permanent continence, or if he did have sexual relations, why he did not have children, for we are also told about him that 'he had sons and daughters, and all the days of Seth were 912 years, and he died.'[93]

The same applies to all those whose ages are recorded thereafter, with the additional information that they had sons and daughters. The conclusion is that it is by no means clear whether the child mentioned by name is in fact the first-born. Indeed it is beyond credibility that those fathers were immature for so long a period of their life, or that they were without wives or offspring; and so it is incredible that those sons were their first-born. It was in fact the intention of the writer of the sacred history to mark the chronology through successive generations until he reached the birth and life of Noah, in whose time the Flood happened. Thus the children he mentioned were clearly those which came in the line of descent, rather than those first born to their parents.

I will give an example, to make my point clearer, which will put it beyond doubt that what I am suggesting may well have happened. The evangelist Matthew wished to put on record the descent of the Lord, according to the flesh, through a series of ancestors. He begins with father Abraham and, with the intention of arriving first at David, he says, 'Abraham was the father of Isaac.' Why did he not say 'of Ishmael', who was his first-born? He goes on, 'Isaac was the father of Jacob.' Why did he not say 'of Esau', who was Isaac's first son? The reason is, of course, that he could not arrive at David by way of those other sons. Matthew proceeds, 'Jacob was the father of Judah and his brothers.' Does that mean that Judah was his first-born? Then he says, 'Judah was the father of Phares and Zara.' But neither of these twin brothers was Judah's first-born; he had already had three children before them. Thus Matthew kept in the genealogical tree only those which would bring him down to David, and eventually to his destination. We can infer from this that those early men before the Flood were not mentioned as being the first-born, but as those through whom the line of descent could be traced through

92. Gen. 5, 6. 93. Gen. 5, 7f.

successive generations down to Noah, the patriarch. So we do not have to weary ourselves with the obscure and unnecessary problem of the retarded development of the men of antiquity.

16. *The early law of marriage differed from that of later times*

After the first sexual union between the man, created from dust, and his wife, created from the man's side, the human race needed, for its reproduction and increase, the conjunction of males and females, and the only human beings in existence were those who had been born from those two parents. Therefore, men took their sisters as wives. This was, of course, a completely decent procedure under the pressure of necessity; it became as completely reprehensible in later times, when it was forbidden by religion. For affection was given its right importance so that men, for whom social harmony would be advantageous and honourable, should be bound together by ties of various relationships. The aim was that one man should not combine many relationships in his one self, but that those connections should be separated and spread among individuals, and that in this way they should help to bind social life more effectively by involving in their plurality a plurality of persons. 'Father' and 'father-in-law', for instance, are names denoting two different relationships. Thus affection stretches over a greater number when each person has one man for father and another for father-in-law. Adam was compelled to be, in his one self, both father and father-in-law to his sons and daughters, since brothers and sisters were joined in marriage. In the same way, his wife Eve was both mother-in-law and mother to her children of both sexes. If two women had been involved, one as mother and the other as mother-in-law, social sympathy would have been a binding force over a wider area. Finally, a sister also, because she became a wife as well, united in herself two relationships, whereas if these had been separated, and each had involved a different woman, one being a sister, and the other a wife, the number of people bound by intimate ties would have been increased.

But there was no way in which this could happen at a time when the only human beings were brothers and sisters, the children of the first human pair. The necessary change had to be made when it became possible; and so, as soon as there came to be a supply of possible wives, who were not already their sisters, men had to choose their spouses from their number. Not only was there no necessity for unions between brother and sister; such unions henceforth were banned. For if the grandchildren also of the first human beings, who by then could have taken their cousins as wives, were joined in marriage to their sisters, then there would no longer be two but three relationships comprised in one person; and those relationships ought to have been separated and distributed among different individuals so as to link together a greater number in the affection of kinship. For marriage of brothers with sisters would at this stage mean that one man would be father, father-in-law and uncle to his own children. Similarly, his wife would be mother, aunt and mother-in-law to the children she shared with her husband. And the children of the couple would be to each other not only brothers and sisters and spouses, but also cousins, as being the children of brothers and sisters.

On the other hand, if those relationships were distributed singly to different persons they would have connected nine people, instead of three, to each of these persons. For then one man would have one person as his sister, another as his wife, another as his cousin, another as his father, another as his uncle, another as his father-in-law, another as his mother, another as his aunt, another as his mother-in-law. Thus the social tie would not be confined to a small group but would extend more widely to connect a large number with the multiplying links of kinship.

With the growth and multiplication of the human race this rule is observed, we notice, even among the impious worshippers of many false gods, in that their corrupt laws may permit the marriage of brother and sister, but their actual practice is better than their laws, and they tend to abhor this licence. It was indeed generally allowed that brothers and sisters should marry in the earliest ages of the human race; but the practice is now so utterly repudiated that it might seem that it could never have been permitted. For custom is the most effective agent in soothing or shocking human sensibilities. And in this case custom acts as a deterrent to unbridled lust, and therefore men are right in judging it criminal to cancel or transgress the custom. For if it is wicked to go beyond the boundary of one's lands in the greed for increasing possession, how much more wicked is it to remove a moral boundary in the lust for sexual pleasure! It has also been our experience that even in our own days marriages between cousins were of rare occurrence because of moral scruples, although they were permitted by law; and that was because of the degree of kinship involved, only one step removed from that of brother and sister. Yet such unions were not prohibited by divine Law, and they had not yet been forbidden by the law of man.[94] Nevertheless, an aversion was felt from an act which, though lawful, bordered on illegality, and union with a cousin was felt to be almost the same as union with a sister – for even among themselves cousins are called brothers and sisters because of their close relationship, and they are in fact the next thing to full brothers and sisters.

The ancient fathers, for their part, were concerned that the ties of kinship itself should not be loosened as generation succeeded generation, should not diverge too far, so that they finally ceased to be ties at all. And so for them it was a matter of religion to restore the bond of kinship by means of the marriage tie before kinship became too remote – to call kinship back, as it were, as it disappeared into the distance. That is why, when the world was already full of people, they did not indeed like to marry half-sisters or full sisters, but they certainly liked to marry wives from their own family. Yet no one doubts that the modern prohibition of marriage between cousins is an advance in civilized standards. And this not only because of the point I have already made, namely that the ties of kinship are thereby multiplied, in that one person cannot stand in a double relationship, when this can be divided between two persons, and so the scope of kinship may be enlarged. There is another reason. There is in human conscience a certain mysterious and inherent sense of decency, which is natural and also admirable, which ensures that if kinship gives a woman a claim to honour and respect, she is shielded from the lust (and lust it is, although it results in procreation) which, as we know, brings blushes even to the chastity of marriage.

Now the intercourse of male and female is the seedbed, as it were, of a city, as far as the race of mortals is concerned. But the earthly city needs only generation, whereas the Heavenly City needs regeneration also, to escape the guilt connected with generation. As for the question whether there was any bodily and visible sign of regeneration before the Flood, like the circumcision which was afterwards demanded of Abraham,[95] and if there was, what form it took, on this the sacred narrative is silent. The account does tell us, however, that those human beings of the earliest times offered sacrifices to God, as is made clear by the story of the first two brothers;[96] and we read that Noah offered victims to God after the Flood, when he had emerged from the ark.[97] I have already dealt with this subject in previous

94. They were forbidden by Theodosius ([Aurel. Vict.] *Epit.*, 48; Ambr. *Ep.*, 60, 5).

95. cf. Gen. 17, 10ff. 96. cf. Gen. 4, 3f. 97. cf. Gen. 8, 20.

books, where I pointed out that the demons, who arrogate divinity to themselves and desire to be regarded as gods, claim sacrifices for themselves and rejoice in such honours simply because they know that true sacrifice is due only to the true God.[98]

17. *The two fathers and leaders both begotten by the same parent*

Adam was therefore the father of both lines of descent, that is, of the line whose successive members belong to the earthly city, and of the line whose members are attached to the City in heaven. But after the murder of Abel (with the wonderful hidden meaning his killing conveyed[99]) there were two fathers appointed, one for each of those lines of descent. Those fathers were Cain and Seth; and in their sons, whose names had to be recorded, indications of these two cities began to appear with increasing clarity in the race of mortals.

Cain, we know, became the father of Enoch, and founded a city in his name. This was the earthly city, of course, the city which is not just a pilgrim in this world, but rests satisfied with its temporal peace and felicity. Now the name Cain is translated 'possession',[100] which is why either his father or his mother said at his birth, 'I have acquired a man, through God's help.'[101] Enoch, on the other hand, means 'dedication';[102] for the earthly city is dedicated here, where it is founded, since it has here the end of its purpose and aspiration. Moreover, the name Seth means 'resurrection',[103] and the name of his son, Enos, means 'man'[104] but not in the same sense as Adam. For although Adam means 'man', we are told that in Hebrew it is common to male and female; thus Scripture says, 'He created them male and female, and blessed them, and named them Adam.'[105] This makes it clear that although the woman was called Eve, and that was her personal name, the name Adam, which means 'man', belonged to them both. Enos, on the other hand, means 'man' in the sense which makes it impossible for it to be used as a woman's name, or so Hebrew scholars assure us. The name Enos, then, suggests 'son of the resurrection', and in the resurrection 'they will neither be given in marriage nor will

98. cf. Bk x, 4–6; 26. 99. cf. ch. 7.
100. An assonance (*Kayin* – *kānāh*, 'to get'). 101. Gen. 4, 1.
102. A possible meaning. 103. Impossible. 104. In Hebrew poetry.
105. Gen. 5, 2. It is true that *ādām* in Hebrew usually means 'human being'; but *ēnōsh* has the same generic sense.

they marry.'[106] For in the resurrection there will be no generation, when regeneration has brought them to that state.

In this connection it is not irrelevant, I think, to point out that among the generations derived from the man called Seth, although the birth of sons and daughters is recorded, no woman is expressly mentioned by name in that line. In contrast, among those descended from Cain, at the very end of the whole list, the last woman to be born is named. For we read,

> Methusael was the father of Lamech. And Lamech took two wives, one called Adah, the other called Zillah. Adah gave birth to Jabal; he was the father of those who live in tents, keepers of cattle. His brother's name was Jubal; it was he who introduced men to the harp and the lyre. Zillah for her part, gave birth to Tubal: he was a metal-worker, a forger of bronze and iron. The sister of Tubal was Naamah.[107]

This is the final extent of the generations descended from Cain. Starting from Adam they come to eight in all (including Adam); that is, there are seven generations down to Lamech, who was the husband of two wives, and the eighth generation consists of his children, among whom a woman is recorded. This is a neat way of suggesting that the earthly city, right up to its end, will have carnal births, resulting from the union of male and female. That is why the wives of this man (who is the last father to be named in the passage) are expressly mentioned under their personal names, which is not found in any other case (except for Eve) in the narrative before the Flood. Now Cain (whose name means 'possession') is the founder of the earthly city, and Enoch ('dedication') is the son in whose name the city was founded. This indicates that this city has its beginning and end on this earth, where there is no hope of anything beyond what can be seen in this world. In contrast with him is Seth, whose name means 'resurrection'. He is the father of generations which are separately listed; and we must now examine what this sacred narrative says about his son.

18. *The symbolism of Abel, Seth, and Enos, with reference to Christ and the Church*

The Scripture says, 'A son was born to Seth, and he called his name Enos. This son hoped to call on the name of the Lord God.'[108] Here

106. Luke 20, 35. 107. Gen. 4, 18–22. 108. Gen. 4, 26 (LXX).

certainly we have a testimony which shouts the truth aloud. It is in hope, therefore, that a man lives, as the 'son of the resurrection'; it is in hope that the City of God lives, during its pilgrimage on earth, that City which is brought into being by faith in Christ's resurrection. For Abel's name means 'lamentation',[109] and the name of Seth, his brother, means 'resurrection'. And so in those two men the death of Christ and his life from among the dead, are prefigured. As a result of this faith the City of God comes into being here on earth in the person of a man who 'hoped to call on the name of the Lord God'.

'For it is in hope that we have been saved', says the Apostle. 'Now hope that is seen is no longer hope. For how can a man hope for what he already sees? But if we hope for what we do not see, then we wait for it with patience.'[110] Could anyone fail to see that we have here a symbolism full of profound significance? For did not Abel hope to call upon the name of the Lord God, to whom, as Scripture records, his sacrifice was so acceptable? Did not Seth also hope to call on the name of the Lord God? And the Bible says, referring to Seth, 'God has raised up for me another seed, in place of Abel.'[111]

Then why should something which is taken to be true of all devout men alike be ascribed to Enos in particular? It can only be because he is recorded as the first offspring of the father who started the line which is marked out for a better destiny, that is for participation in the Heavenly City. And it was appropriate that in him should be prefigured the man, that is, the society of men, that lives not by the standards of men, in the present enjoyment of earthly happiness, but by God's standards, in the hope of eternal felicity. Notice that Scripture does not say, 'He hoped in the Lord God', or, 'He called on the name of the Lord God', but 'He hoped to call on the name of the Lord God.' The meaning of 'he hoped to call' can only be prophetic. It indicates that a people would arise which being 'chosen by grace'[112] would call on the name of the Lord God. There is a message conveyed by another prophet which is taken by the Apostle as referring to this people, the community which belongs to God's grace. The prophet says, 'And it will come about that everyone who calls on the name of the Lord will be saved.'[113]

Now the words in our present passage, 'and he called his name Enos ('man')' and the next statement, 'he hoped to call on the name of the Lord God', indicate quite clearly that man is not to rest his hope on himself. For we read in another place: 'Cursed is everyone who rests

109. *Hebel* in Hebrew='breath'.
110. Rom. 8, 24f.
111. Gen. 4, 25.
112. cf. Rom. 11, 5.
113. Joel 2, 32; cf. Rom. 10, 13.

his hope in man';[114] and accordingly a man must not hope in himself in order that he may become a citizen of that other City, which is not dedicated in this present age, after the fashion of Cain's son, not, that is, in the transient course of this mortal world, but in that immortality of everlasting bliss.

19. *The symbolic meaning of Enoch's translation*

The line of descent that begins with Seth has the name that means 'dedication', as well as the other. It appears in the generation which is seventh from Adam, if we include Adam himself; for Enoch means 'dedication', and that was the name of the seventh in descent from Adam. Now Enoch is the man who was 'translated because he won God's approval';[115] and his number in the order of descent, the seventh from Adam, is the significant number which made the Sabbath a consecrated day. He is also the sixth from Seth, the father of the line which is distinguished from the descendants of Cain; and it was on the sixth day that man was created and God brought his works to completion. The translation of Enoch thus prefigures the deferment of our own dedication.

This dedication is an accomplished fact in the person of Christ, our head, who rose again, never to die thereafter, being himself translated. The other dedication yet remains to be accomplished, the dedication of the whole house of which Christ himself is the foundation.[116] This dedication is deferred until the end, when there will be the resurrection of those who are to die no more. Whether we call it the 'House of God' or the 'Temple of God', or the 'City of God', it is the same thing, and all those titles conform to Latin usage. Virgil, for example, uses the name 'the house of Assaracus' for the great city of the Empire, meaning the Romans, who trace their origin, through the Trojans, from Assaracus. He also calls the Romans 'the house of Aeneas' because Rome was founded by Trojans who had come to Italy under the leadership of Aeneas.[117] In this idiom the famous poet followed the example of holy Scripture, in which the Hebrew people, even when it had increased to immense size, is called 'the house of Jacob'.

114. Jer. 17, 5.
115. cf. Gen. 5, 24; Heb. 11, 5f.
116. cf. Eph. 2, 20.
117. cf. *Aen.*, 1,284; 3, 97.

20. *Why Cain's line ends at the eighth generation, while Noah belongs to the tenth*

Now someone is going to say, 'Let us suppose that the purpose of the writer of this narrative, in recording the line of Adam through his son Seth, was to arrive at Noah, in whose time the Flood happened, and thereafter to give a connected account of the line of descent as far as Abraham, with whom the evangelist Matthew starts his list of the generations which ends in Christ, the eternal king of the City of God. But, granted that, what was his intention in recording the line of descent from Cain? To what termination did he want to bring this genealogy?' The answer will be, 'To the time of the Flood, in which the whole race of the earthly city was annihilated; though it was afterwards restored from Noah's descendants.' In fact, this earthly city, this society of men who live by man's standards, cannot vanish until the end of this world, about which the Lord says, 'The children of this world generate and are generated.'[118] The City of God, in contrast, is on pilgrimage in this world, and it is by regeneration that it is brought to another world, whose children neither generate nor are generated.

Thus in this world generation is common to both communities alike, although the City of God has even in this world many thousands of citizens who abstain from the act of procreation. And the other city also has those who imitate their abstinence, although they are in error. For there are among those who belong to this earthly city people who have strayed from the faith of the other City and have founded various heresies; they live of course by man's standards, not by God's. The Indian 'gymnosophists'[119] also, who are said to wear no clothes as they pursue their philosophy in remote places of India, are citizens of the earthly city; and yet they refrain from procreation. This abstinence is only good when it is connected with faith in the Highest Good, which is God. Nevertheless we find no one who practised it before the Flood; in fact even Enoch himself, the seventh in descent from Adam, who is reported to have been translated instead of dying, was the father of sons and daughters before his translation. Among those children was Methuselah, through whom passed the line of descent which was to be recorded.

Why then do we find so few generations recorded in the descent from Cain, assuming that the line had to be brought down as far as the Flood, and that the men in this line were not such a long time in

118. cf. Luke 20, 34. 119. cf. Bk VIII, 9n.; X, 32; XIV, 17.

reaching puberty that they were without offspring for a hundred years or more? Now in respect of the line of descent from the seed of Seth the author of Genesis aimed at reaching Noah, and then he was to resume the list in the necessary sequence. But if he had no such aim in respect of the descent of Cain, no person to whom he had to bring down the line, what need had he to pass over the first-born sons in order to reach Lamech, with whose children the end of the connected series is reached, that is, in the eighth generation from Adam, and the seventh from Cain? It looks as if there were going to be a connection added after that to bring the list down either to the people of Israel, in whom the earthly Jerusalem also displayed a prophetic foreshadowing of the Heavenly City,[120] or to Christ 'according to the flesh, who is over all things, God blessed for ever',[121] the builder and ruler of the Jerusalem on high. But this could not be, since the whole of Cain's progeny was wiped out by the Flood.

This being so, we may suppose that first-born sons were recorded in this line of descent. Then why are they so few? There could not have been, in fact, so small a number of first-born down to the time of the Flood, for the fathers were not exempt from the duty of procreation until they reached maturity at the age of a hundred – if we assume that puberty was not at that period late in developing, to correspond with the longevity of the time. Supposing that they were on average thirty years of age when they began to have children, then if we multiply thirty by eight (there being eight generations if we include Adam and Lamech's children) we have 240 years. Are we to imagine that they had no children during the whole interval from that time to the time of the Flood?

What possible reason could the writer have had for refusing to record the subsequent generations? For according to our version 2,262 years are reckoned from Adam down to the Flood, while the Hebrew text gives 1,656. If we take the lower number to be more correct, let us subtract 240 years from 1,656. Is it really credible that for 1,400 years or so – the interval down to the Flood – Cain's offspring could have failed to produce children?

Now if anyone is puzzled about this, he should remember that when I was discussing how we could believe that the men of antiquity could have refrained from begetting children for all those years, I put forward two ways of solving the problem: either they were late in coming to puberty, to correspond with their longevity, or else the sons recorded in the lineage were not the first-born, but those through

120. cf. ch. 2. 121. Rom. 4, 5.

whom the author of Genesis could arrive at the person whom he intended to reach, as in the line from Seth the goal was Noah. Accordingly, if no one presents himself in the line of Cain as the one on whom the author had fixed as the necessary goal to be reached through the persons recorded, the only alternative is the theory of delayed puberty. And if the descent was traced through the first-born and accounts for so large a number of years to reach the time of the Flood, we must assume that men took rather more than a hundred years to attain puberty and to become capable of procreation.

All the same, it is possible that, for some more obscure reason which escapes me, this city which we call the earthly city was described until the genealogy reached Lamech and his children, and the author of Genesis then ceased to record the other generations that may have existed down to the Flood. It is possible, however, that there was another reason why the line of descent was not traced through the first-born sons, and this would obviate the need to suppose that puberty was so long delayed in the men of that time. It may be that the city founded by Cain and named after Enoch, his son, extended its sway far and wide, and yet did not have a number of kings ruling simultaneously, but only one king in each period, and that each king was succeeded by one of his sons. The first of those kings may have been Cain; the second, his son Enoch, in whose name the city was founded as the royal capital; the third, Gaidad, son of Enoch; the fourth Mevia, son of Gaidad; the fifth, Mathusael, son of Mevia, the sixth Lamech, son of Mathusael, the seventh in descent from Adam through Cain. Now it would not follow that fathers were succeeded in the kingship by their first-born sons; the successor may have been chosen in virtue of qualities useful to an earthly city which qualified him for the throne, or by some kind of lot. Alternatively, the succession might have fallen to the son who was singled out from the rest as the particular object of his father's affection, who thus gained a kind of right of inheritance.

Thus the Flood may have happened while Lamech was still alive and on the throne, and so the Flood may have found him there to be destroyed along with all the rest of mankind, except for those who were in the ark. And really there is nothing remarkable in the fact that the two lines of descent do not show an equal number of generations, considering the variation in length of life in the long period that elapsed between the time of Adam and the Flood. In fact, the line of Cain had seven generations, and Seth's line had ten, for Lamech, as I have already remarked, was the seventh from Adam, while Noah was the tenth. And the reason why Lamech has a number of sons recorded[122] (instead of only one, as in the case of all those before him) is that it was uncertain which of them would have succeeded him on his death if there had remained time for another reign between Lamech and the Flood.

However this may be, whether the line from Cain passes through the first-born or through the kings, I do not think it would be at all right for me to pass over in silence the fact that when Lamech had been shown to be the seventh from Adam, so many of his sons were listed as to bring the number to eleven, which signifies sin. For three sons and one daughter are added. (The wives, for their part, may have some other significance, but not the meaning which, as it seems to me, now calls for remark – for I am now discussing descent, and we are told nothing about the origin of these wives.)

Now the Law is clearly indicated by the number ten (hence the never-to-be-forgotten 'decalogue') and therefore the number eleven undoubtedly symbolizes the transgression of the Law, since it oversteps ten; and so it is the symbol of sin. Hence the instruction for the making of eleven curtains of goats' hair for the tabernacle of the testimony,[123] which was a kind of portable temple for the people of God while they were on their journey. (In the goats' hair there was a reminder of sin, because goats are destined to be placed on the left;[124] and when we confess our sins we prostrate ourselves in cloth of goats' hair as if we were saying, in the words of the psalmist, 'My sin is always before me.'[125])

The line of descent then from Adam through Cain the criminal ends with the number eleven, symbolizing sin. And it is a woman who makes up this number, because the female sex began the sin which is responsible for the death of us all. More than this, another result of the sin is physical pleasure with its resistance to the spirit,[126] and Lamech's daughter was called Naamah, which means 'pleasure'.[127] In contrast, the line from Adam to Noah through Seth gives us the significant number ten, the number of the Law. To this the three sons of Noah are added; but one of these fell into sin, and two received their father's blessing, so that with the removal of the rejected son, and the addition of the sons who were approved, we are presented with the

122. Gen. 4, 19ff.; 5, 28ff.
123. cf. Exod. 26, 7. On significant numbers cf. Bk XI, 30f; XVII, 4; XX, 5, 7.
124. cf. Matt. 25, 33.
125. Ps. 51, 3. The hair shirt was from early times the garb of penitence.
126. cf. Gal. 5, 17.
127. *Na'âmāh* in Hebrew means 'pleasant', 'gracious'.

number twelve. This number is significant as being the number of the patriarchs and of the apostles, because it is the product of the two parts of seven – that is, three multiplied by four, or four multiplied by three, makes twelve.

This being so, it is clear to me that I must proceed to examine and record how those two posterities, which by their distinct lines of descent suggest the two cities, one the community of the earth-born, the other the community of the reborn, became afterwards so mingled and confused that the entire human race, except for eight persons, deserved to be destroyed by the Flood.

21. *Why, after the mention of Cain's son, Enoch, the whole line is recorded continuously as far as the Flood, while after the mention of Enos, son of Seth, there is a return to man's first creation*

The first question that needs examination is the different treatment of the two genealogies. For when the generations from Cain are listed, the one in whose name the city was founded, that is, Enoch, is mentioned before the other descendants, and after that we have a catalogue of the rest until we reach the end of which I have spoken, namely the extinction of that line, and the whole of Cain's posterity, in the Flood. In the other line, however, we have the mention of one son of Seth, namely Enos, and then the interposition of the following section, 'This is the book of the birth of mankind. On the day that God made Adam, he made him in the image of God. He made them male and female; and he blessed them and gave them the name Adam on the day that he made them.'[128]

It seems to me that this was inserted in order at this point to make another beginning of the chronological account, starting with Adam himself. The writer did not wish to do this in respect of the earthly city, to give the impression that God included it in the record but not in the reckoning. But why does he go back to the recapitulation at this point, after the mention of the son of Seth, the man who 'hoped to call on the name of the Lord God'?[129] It can only be that this gave an appropriate picture of the two cities, one represented by a line starting with a murderer and ending with a murderer (for Lamech also confesses to his two wives that he has committed homicide[130]), the other represented by a man who hoped to call upon the name of the Lord God. For this calling upon God is the supreme business, the whole

128. Gen. 5, 1f. 129. cf. Gen. 4, 26; ch. 18. 130. cf. Gen. 4, 23.

business in this mortal life, of the City of God while on pilgrimage in this world; and this had to be emphasized in the person of one man who was certainly the son of the 'resurrection' of a murdered man. This one man, in fact, stands for the unity of the whole City on High, which indeed is not yet accomplished; but it is to be fulfilled, and it is anticipated in this prophetic foreshadowing

And so the son of Cain, the son, that is, of 'possession' (and it must mean 'earthly possession') must have a name in the earthly city, because it was founded in his name. For it is of people like this that the psalmist sings, 'They will call upon their names in their own lands';[131] and that is why they are overtaken by the fate described in another psalm, 'Lord, in your city you will bring their image to nothing.'[132] As for the son of Seth, that is, the 'son of the resurrection', let him hope to call upon the name of the Lord God. He in fact prefigures that society of men which says, 'I for my part have hoped in the mercy of God, like a fruitful olive tree in the House of God.'[133] But let him not look for the empty glory of a famous name on earth, for 'Blessed is the man whose hope is the name of the Lord, the man who has no regard for vanities and crazy lies.'[134]

Here then the two cities are presented, one existing in actuality, in this world, the other existing in hope which rests on God. They come out, we may say, from the same door of mortality, a door which was opened in Adam, so that they may go forward and onward along their courses to their own distinct and appropriate ends. Then begins the chronological account, in which, after a recapitulation from Adam, other generations are added; and from this origin in Adam, this condemned beginning, God makes both 'vessels of wrath destined for dishonour', and also 'vessels of mercy designed for honour',[135] as if out of a single lump consigned to well-merited condemnation. To the former he gives their due, by way of punishment; on the latter he bestows the undeserved gift of grace. And this he does so that the Celestial City, on pilgrimage in this world, may learn, through this very comparison with the vessels of wrath, that it should not trust in its own free will, but should 'hope to call upon the name of the Lord God'.[136] For man's nature was created good by God, who is good; but it was made changeable by him who is changeless, since it was created from nothing. And so the will in that nature can turn away from good to do evil – and this through its own free choice; and it can

131. Ps. 49, 11. 132. Ps. 73, 20. 133. Ps. 52, 8.
134. Ps. 40, 4. 135. Rom. 9, 22f. 136. cf. Gen. 4, 26.

also turn from evil to do good – but this can only be with the divine assistance.

22. *The fall of the sons of God and the consequent destruction by the Flood*

It was this free choice of the will that produced the mingling of the two cities, as the human race progressed and increased. These cities became associated in wickedness, and the result was a kind of amalgam of the two communities. This evil owed its origin, once again, to the female sex, but not in the same way as the evil at the beginning of the world, for these women were not seduced by cunning so as to persuade their husbands to sin. What happened was that the women who had been depraved in morals in the earthly city, that is, in the community of the earth-born, were loved for their physical beauty by the sons of God,[137] that is, the citizens of the other City, on pilgrimage in this world. Such beauty is certainly a good, a gift of God; but he bestows it on the evil as well as on the good for this reason, for fear that the good may consider it an important good.

Hence the abandonment of a greater good, one that is confined to good people, led to a fall towards a good of little importance, one that is not confined to good people, but common to good and bad alike. Thus the sons of God were captivated by love for the daughters of men, and in order to enjoy them as wives, they abandoned the godly behaviour they had maintained in the holy community and lapsed into the morality of the earth-born society. Now physical beauty, to be sure, is a good created by God, but it is a temporal, carnal good, very low in the scale of goods; and if it is loved in preference to God, the eternal, internal and sempiternal Good, that love is as wrong as the miser's love of gold, with the abandonment of justice, though the fault is in the man, not in the gold. This is true of everything created; though it is good, it can be loved in the right way or in the wrong way – in the right way, that is, when the proper order is kept, in the wrong way when that order is upset. This is how I put the same thought in some verses in praise of the paschal candle:[138]

137. cf. Gen. 6, 2.

138. *Paschal candle.* St Augustine says 'verses in praises of a (the) candle' and the reference may be to a votive candle offered as a prayer or a thanksgiving; and that might suit the words better, which have no particular reference to the candle blessed by the deacon in the solemnities of Holy Saturday. The chant for that ceremony in the Missal, the *Exsultet*, has been ascribed to St Augustine without good reason. It is just possible that the ascription may be due to this passage.

These are thy gifts; they are good, for thou in thy
goodness has made them.
Nothing in them is from us, save for sin when,
neglectful of order,
We fix our love on the creature, instead of on thee,
the Creator.[139]

But if the Creator is truly loved, that is, if he himself is loved, and not something else in his stead, then he cannot be wrongly loved. We must, in fact, observe the right order even in our love for the very love with which we love what is deserving of love, so that there may be in us the virtue which is the condition of the good life. Hence, as it seems to me, a brief and true definition of virtue is 'rightly ordered love'. That is why in the holy *Song of Songs* Christ's bride, the City of God, sings, 'Set love in order in me.'[140] Thus it was because the order of love (that is of attachment and affection) was disturbed, that the sons of God defected from God in their affection for the daughters of men.

These two descriptions are sufficient to show the difference between the two cities. It is not that 'the sons of God' were not sons of men by nature; but they began to have another name by virtue of grace. Indeed, in the same scriptural passage, where the sons of God are said to have fallen in love with the daughters of men, they are also called 'angels of God'.[141] For this reason many people suppose that they were not men but angels.

23. *Are we to believe that angels mated with women, and that the giants resulted from these unions?*

In the third book of this work we mentioned in passing the question whether angels, being spirits, could have physical connection with women, and we left the problem unresolved.[142] Now Scripture says, 'He makes spirits his angels,'[143] that is, those who are by nature spirits he makes into his angels, by imposing on them the duty of carrying messages. For the Greek *angelos*, which becomes *angelus* in the Latin derivative, means *nuntius*, a 'messenger', in the Latin

139. The three lines quoted appear (with certain variations) as the opening of a poem *De Anima*, of fifty-three hexameters, attributed to St Augustine (text in *Anthologia Latina*, ed. Buecheler, Lommatzsch, Reise, 1, 2, 43).

140. 2, 4 (LXX).

141. cf. Gen. 6, 2 ('angels' is given in one MS. of LXX). 'Sons of God' elsewhere denotes 'angels'; cf. Job 1, 6; 28, 7; Ps. 29, 1.

142. cf. Bk III, 5.

143. Ps. 104, 4.

language. But it is uncertain whether the writer refers to their bodies when he goes on to say, 'and he makes a flaming fire his ministers', or whether he means that his ministers ought to burn with love as with a spiritual fire.

Nevertheless it is the testimony of Scripture (which tells us nothing but the truth) that angels appeared to men in bodies of such a kind that they could not only be seen but also touched.[144] Besides this, it is widely reported that Silvani and Pans,[145] commonly called *incubi*, have often behaved improperly towards women, lusting after them and achieving intercourse with them. These reports are confirmed by many people, either from their own experience or from the accounts of the experience of others, whose reliability there is no occasion to doubt. Then there is the story that certain demons, whom the Gauls call Dusii, constantly and successfully attempt this indecency. This is asserted by so many witnesses of such a character that it would seem an impertinence to deny it. Hence I would not venture a conclusive statement on the question whether some spirits with bodies of air (an element which even when set in motion by a fan is felt by the bodily sense of touch) can also experience this lust and so can mate, in whatever way they can, with women, who feel their embraces.

In spite of this, I cannot possibly believe that the holy angels of God could thus have fallen at that time, or that it is to them that the apostle Peter refers when he says, 'For if God did not spare the sinful angels, but thrust them into the dungeons of the darkness of hell, and handed them over to be kept for punishment at the judgement.'[146] I should rather suppose that he is speaking of those who revolted from God and fell with the devil, their leader, who in envy brought the first man to his fall by the deceit of the serpent. Now the holy Scripture gives abundant witness that men of God were often entitled 'angels'. For example, Scripture says of John, 'Behold, I am sending my angel ahead of you, and he will prepare your way';[147] and the prophet Malachi is called an 'angel' in virtue of a particular grace, that is, a grace particularly imparted to him.[148]

Some people, however, are worried by the statement in the Bible that the mating of those who are called 'sons of God' with the women

144. cf. e.g. Gen. 19, 1–22; Judg. 6, 12–22.

145. *Silvanus*: cf. Bk VI, 9n. *Pan*: pastoral god of Arcadia, identified with the Italian god Faunus.

146. 2 Pet. 2, 4; cf. Jude 6. This, the oldest interpretation, appears in the apocryphal books of Enoch (4, 2ff.) and Jubilees (5, 1).

147. Mark 1, 2. 148. cf. Mal. 2, 7.

they loved resulted in offspring who were not like men of our own kind; they were giants. These critics seem to ignore the fact that even in our own time men have been born whose bodies far exceed the normal stature of men today; a fact that I have already mentioned.[149] Was there not in Rome a few years ago, when the destruction of the city by the Goths was drawing near, a woman, living with her father and mother, who towered far above all other inhabitants with a stature which could be called gigantic? An amazing crowd rushed to see her, wherever she went. And what excited special wonder was the fact that both her parents were not even as tall as the tallest people that we see in our everyday experience.

Thus it is possible that giants were born even before the sons of God (also called 'angels of God') mated with the daughters of men, which means daughters of those who live by man's standards – that is to say, before the sons of Seth married the daughters of Cain. In fact, this is what the canonical Scripture says in the book which gives this account. The passage runs as follows,

> And it happened that after human beings had begun to multiply on the earth, and daughters were born to them, that angels of God saw that the daughters of men were good, and so they took wives for themselves from all those whom they chose. And the Lord said: 'My spirit will not stay in those men for ever, because they are flesh; however, their days will be a hundred and twenty years.' Now the giants were on the earth in those days, and afterwards, when the sons of God mated with the daughters of men and begot children for themselves. Those were the giants in the days of old, men of renown.[150]

Those words of the inspired book are sufficient indication that there had been giants on the earth when the sons of God took as wives the daughters of men, since they loved them because they were 'good', that is, beautiful; for it is customary in Scripture to apply the term 'good' also to those who are physically attractive. It is true that giants were also born after this happened; for the Scripture says, 'Now the giants were on the earth in those days, and afterwards, when the sons of God mated with the daughters of men.' Thus there were giants both before and after that time.

Then when Scripture says, 'And they begot children for themselves', it shows quite clearly that previously before the sons of God fell in this way, they begot children for God, not for themselves; that means that lust for coition was not their master, but it was a servant, subordinate to duty of procreation. They did not procreate children to

149. cf. ch. 9. 150. Gen. 6, 1–4.

found a family to minister to their pride but to produce citizens for the City of God, so that they, as angels of God, could give their children this message: that they must put their hope in God, like the son of Seth, the 'son of the resurrection', who 'hoped to call on the name of the Lord God'. And in virtue of this hope they, with their posterity, would be co-heirs of eternal blessings, and brothers of their sons, under God the Father.

Now these sons of God were not angels of God in such a way that they were not also human beings as some people suppose. Scripture itself declares without any ambiguity that they were human; there can be no doubt about this. For after the statement that 'the angels of God saw that the daughters of men were good, and they took wives for themselves from all those whom they chose', it goes on immediately to say, 'Then the Lord God said: "My spirit will not stay in those men for ever, because they are flesh."' It was indeed through God's spirit that they had been made angels of God and sons of God, but in sinking to a lower level they are called 'men', a name denoting their nature, not God's grace. They are also called 'flesh', because they deserted the spirit, and, in deserting, were themselves deserted.

In the Septuagint also they are certainly called 'angels of God' and 'sons of God'; though it is true that this reading is not offered in all the texts, for some of them read only 'sons of God'. While Aquila,[151] whose translation the Jews prefer to all the others, gives neither 'angels of God' nor 'sons of God'; his version gives 'sons of gods'. In fact both renderings are correct. For they were sons of God, under whose fatherhood they were also brothers of their own fathers; they were sons of gods as being the offspring of gods, and together with them they themselves were gods, according to the passage in the psalm where it says 'I said: "You are gods, and all of you sons of the Most High."'[152] We are justified in supposing that the seventy translators received the spirit of prophecy; and so, if they altered anything by its authority and used expressions in their translation different from those of the original, we should not doubt that these expressions also were inspired by God.[153] Although in fact it is said that the expression is ambiguous in the Hebrew, and admits of either 'sons of God' or 'sons of gods' as a translation.

We may then pass over the tales contained in the scriptures which are called 'Apocrypha' because their origin is obscure and was not

151. He produced, c. A.D. 140, an extravagantly literal Greek version of the Old Testament.

152. Ps. 82, 6.

153. cf. Bk XVIII, 43.

clear to the fathers, from whom the authority of the true Scriptures has come down to us by a well-defined and well-known line of succession. There is indeed some truth to be found in these Apocrypha; but they have no canonical authority on account of the many falsehoods they contain. Certainly, we cannot deny that Enoch (the seventh in descent from Adam) wrote a number of things by divine inspiration, since the apostle Jude says as much in a canonical epistle.[154] But there was good reason for the exclusion of these writings from the canon of the Scriptures, which was preserved in the temple of the Hebrew people by the careful custody of the priestly succession. The reason was that these books were judged of doubtful reliability because of their antiquity; and it was impossible to discover whether they were what Enoch had written, since those who put them forward are not found to have preserved them with the due formality, that is, through an appointed succession. That is why responsible judges have decided that we should reject the attribution to Enoch of the documents put forward under his name, containing stories about giants who are said not to have had human fathers. Many other writings are similarly put forward under the names of other prophets, and more recent productions under the names of apostles. All these have been excluded from canonical authority as a result of careful examination, and are classed as Apocrypha.

Thus according to the canonical Scriptures, Hebrew and Christian, there is no doubt that many giants existed before the Flood, and that these were citizens of the earth-born society of men, whereas the sons of God, who by physical descent belonged to Seth's lineage, sank down into this society, after abandoning righteousness. And it is not to be wondered at that their children also could be giants – not that all of them were in fact giants, but there were certainly more giants at that time than in all succeeding periods since the Flood. The Creator decided to create them for a specific purpose: to demonstrate in this way, as in others, that the wise man should not attach much importance either to physical beauty or to physical size and strength; for the wise man is blessed with the possession of goods far better and more lasting than these, spiritual and immortal goods, which are not the common property of the good and the bad alike, but the exclusive property of the good. This fact is underlined by another prophet when he says, 'There were those renowned giants, who from the beginning were men of great stature, experts in war. It was not those whom the Lord chose, nor did he give them the way of knowledge. In fact they per-

154. cf Jude 14; cf. n. 146.

ished because they had no wisdom; they disappeared through their lack of thought.'[155]

24. *The meaning of the Lord's saying, 'their days will be a hundred and twenty years'*

To pass to God's saying that 'their days will be a hundred and twenty years';[156] this is not to be taken as foretelling that after this men would not exceed 120 years, since we find that after the Flood, as well as before, men surpassed even 500 years. We must realize that God said this when Noah had nearly completed 500 years, that is, he was in his 480th year, which is called the 500th year in Scripture, in accordance with its general practice of using round numbers for a total only slightly less. Now we know the Flood happened in the 600th year of Noah's life,[157] in the second month, and thus the prediction meant that men who were going to perish would live a hundred and twenty years more, and at the end of that period they would be wiped out by the Flood.

It is a well-founded belief that the Flood happened at a time when there were no longer to be found on earth any beings who did not deserve such a death as served to punish the wicked. Not that a death of this kind can affect good men – who are destined to die at some time – in any way that could harm them after death; nevertheless none of those who, according to the scriptural account, were descended from the seed of Seth, did in fact perish in the Flood. For the divinely inspired narrative gives the cause of the Flood as follows:

> The Lord God saw that the wickedness of mankind had multiplied on the earth, and that everyone was carefully planning evil in his heart throughout his life. And God considered his creation of man on the earth: and he reconsidered, and said: 'I will wipe off man, whom I created, from the face of the earth, and all creatures, from man to beast, from creeping things to birds of the air; because I am angry at having created them.'[158]

25. *God's anger does not disturb his changeless tranquillity*

Now God's anger is not an agitation of his mind; it is a judgement by which punishment is inflicted on sin. And his consideration and reconsideration are his unchanging plan applied to things subject to change. For God does not repent of any action of his,[159] as man does,

155. Bar. 3, 26ff. 156. Gen. 6, 3. 157. cf. Gen. 7, 11.
158. Gen. 6, 5ff. 159. cf. Num. 23, 19.

and his decision on any matter whatsoever is as fixed as his foreknowledge is sure. But if Scripture did not employ such words, it would not strike home so closely, as it were, to all mankind. For Scripture is concerned for man, and it uses such language to terrify the proud, to arouse the careless, to exercise the inquirer, and to nourish the intelligent; and it would not have this effect if it did not first bend down and, as we may say, descend to the level of those on the ground. When it goes on to announce the annihilation of all living creatures on earth and in the air, it is proclaiming the magnitude of the coming disaster. It is not threatening the destruction of creatures bereft of reason, as if they too had sinned.

26. *Noah's ark as a symbol of Christ and the Church*

We now pass on to Noah. He was a righteous man and, according to the truthful witness of Scripture, he was 'perfect in his generation'.[160] That is, he was perfect, not as the citizens of the City of God are to be made perfect in the immortal condition in which they will become equal to the angels of God, but as they can be perfect during their pilgrimage on earth. It was to Noah that God gave instructions to make an ark in which he was to be rescued from the devastation of the Flood, together with his family, that is, his wife, his sons and daughters-in-law, and also the animals that went into the ark in accordance with God's directions. Without doubt this is a symbol of the City of God on pilgrimage in this world, of the Church which is saved through the wood on which was suspended 'the mediator between God and men, the man Christ Jesus'.[161]

The actual measurements of the ark, its length, height and breadth, symbolize the human body, in the reality of which Christ was to come, and did come, to mankind. For the length of the human body from the top of the head to the sole of the foot is six times its breadth from side to side, and ten times its depth, measured on the side from back to belly. I mean that if you have a man lying on his back or on his face, and measure him, his length from head to foot is six times his breadth from right to left, or from left to right, and ten times his altitude from the ground. That is why the ark was made 300 cubits in length, fifty cubits in breadth, and thirty in height. And the door which it was given in its side surely represents the wound made when the side of the crucified was pierced with the spear.[162] This, as we know, is the way of entrance for those who come to him, because from

160. Gen. 6, 9. 161. 1 Tim. 2, 5. 162. cf. John 19, 34.

that wound flowed the sacraments with which believers are initiated. And the order for squared beams in the ark's construction refers symbolically to the life of the saints which is stable on every side; for in whatever direction you turn a squared object, it will remain stable. All the other details mentioned in the construction of the ark are symbols of realities found in the Church.

But it would be tedious to work all this out in detail; and, in any case, I have done this already in my work *Against Faustus the Manichean*,[163] who denied that anything was prophesied about Christ in the books of the Hebrews. Besides, there is certainly a possibility that someone may explain these points more adequately than I can, or one man than another. That does not matter, provided that all that is said has reference to the City of God, which is our subject, the City which is on pilgrimage in this wicked world as though in a flood. This reference must be observed, if the commentator does not wish to stray widely from the sense intended by the writer of this narrative.

It may be, for example, that someone will prefer a different interpretation to the one that I have given in the above-mentioned work of this passage, 'You will make it with lower, second, and third storeys.'[164] I suggested[165] that the Church is said to have two storeys because it is assembled from all nations, having two classes of men, the circumcised and the uncircumcised, or, as the Apostle puts it in another way, Jews and Greeks;[166] and that it is called three-storeyed because all nations were re-established after the Flood from the three sons of Noah. But my critic must suggest some other interpretation which is not at variance with the Rule of Faith.[167] For instance, God wanted the ark to have living-quarters not only on the lowest level but on the higher level (which he called the second storey) and on the level above that (the third storey) so that a dwelling-place should rise up, the third from the bottom upwards. Now this could be interpreted as illustrating the three virtues extolled by the Apostle: faith, hope, and charity.[168] Again, three storeys could be much more appropriately explained as standing for the three abundant harvests in the Gospel, 'thirty fold, sixty fold, and a hundred fold'.[169] Married chastity, on this interpretation, would inhabit the lowest level, widowed chastity the floor above, and virginal purity the top storey. And there may be other explanations and better ones, that could be advanced, which would be in harmony with the faith of this City. I would be

163. 12, 14. 164. Gen. 6, 16. 165. *Adv. Faust. Man.*, 12, 16.
166. cf. Rom. 1, 16; 3, 9; Gal. 3, 28. 167. cf. ch. 7, n31. 168. 1 Cor. 13, 13.
169. cf. Matt. 13, 8.

prepared to say the same about all the other interpretations which can be put forward on this topic. Different suggestions may be made; but they must be checked by the standard of the harmonious unity of the Catholic faith.

27. *The account of the Flood is neither merely historical nor purely allegorical*

No one ought to imagine, however, that this account was written for no purpose, or that we are to look here solely for a reliable historical record without any allegorical meaning, or, conversely, that those events are entirely unhistorical, and the language purely symbolical, or that, whatever may be the nature of the story it has no connection with prophecy about the Church. Surely it is only a twisted mind that would maintain that books which have been so scrupulously preserved for thousands of years, which have been safeguarded by such a concern for so well-ordered a transmission, that such books were written without serious purpose, or that we should consult them simply for historical facts? For, to take one point only, if it was the large number of animals that compelled the building of an ark of such great size, why was it necessary to embark two of each unclean species, and seven of each clean kind? Both clean and unclean could have been preserved by the same number. Or are we really to suppose that God, who ordered their preservation so as to renew their species, had not the power to re-create them in the same way as he had first created them?

Now there are those who maintain that the account of the Flood is not historical, but is simply a collection of symbols and allegories. They maintain, in the first place, that it is impossible for so vast a flood to have happened that the water rose to the level of fifteen cubits above the highest mountains, their evidence being the alleged fact that clouds cannot gather above the top of Mount Olympus, because the atmosphere there is already so high that the denser air is lacking, in which winds, clouds, and rains originate. It escapes their notice that earth, the densest of all elements, could exist there. Or are they going to deny that the summit of a mountain is formed of earth? If not, why do they admit that earth is allowed to reach such high levels in the atmosphere, and yet maintain that the same possibility is not open to the waters? And yet those who measure and weigh the elements inform us that water rises higher and weighs less than earth. What rational argument then do they put forward to explain why earth, a heavier and lower element, should have intruded into the region of the serener atmosphere during the revolutions of so many years, if water, a lighter and higher element, has not been permitted to do so even for an inconsiderable time?

It is also said that an ark of the dimensions described could not have contained so many species of animals of both sexes, two of each species of the unclean, and seven of each of the clean. They appear to reckon only 300 cubits in length, and fifty in width, without taking into account that there is an equal amount of space on the higher and on the highest level, so that the measurements are multiplied by three, making 900 cubits by 150. We may also bear in mind the clever suggestion contributed by Origen. He points out[170] that Moses, 'the man of God', was, according to the Scriptures, 'versed in all the learning of the Egyptians',[171] who were addicted to geometry, and therefore Moses may have meant geometrical cubits, one of which is alleged to equal six of ours. If that suggestion were adopted it would be clear to anyone that an ark of such size would have an immense capacity.

As for the argument that an ark of such enormous size could not have been constructed, this is a misrepresentation, and a most unconvincing one. For they know that immense cities have been built, and they fail to notice the hundred years that were spent in the fabrication of that ark. Now if it is possible for stones to adhere together, cemented merely by lime, to make an encircling wall so many miles long, are we to suppose it impossible that timbers should be joined together by pegs, bolts, nails and bituminous glue, to frame an ark extending in length and breadth in straight, not curved lines? This ark would not require launching into the sea by human effort, but would be raised by the water, when it arrived, owing to the natural difference in specific gravity; and it would be steered by divine providence when it was afloat, instead of by human vigilance, to keep it from shipwreck wherever it went.

Then there is a problem constantly suggested by excessively minute criticism. It concerns the tiniest creatures, not only such creatures as mice and newts, but also such as locusts, beetles, and even flies and fleas; and the question raised is whether they could not have been present in the ark in greater numbers than the limit set when God gave the command. We must begin by pointing out to those who are puzzled on this point that the words, 'the things which crawl on the earth'[172] are to be taken as meaning that it was not necessary to

170. *In Gen. Hom.*, 2, 2. 171. Acts 7, 22. 172. Gen. 6, 20.

preserve in the ark the creatures able to live in the waters; and this would include besides the fishes and other submerged creatures, those that swim on the surface, for instance, many of the birds. Again, the words, 'they shall be male and female'[173] are surely to be understood as referring to the need to renew the species, and so it was not necessary to have in the ark those creatures which can be produced without sexual intercourse from various substances, or from the decomposition of substances. Or if they were there in the ark, as they are generally present in houses, they could have been there without the fixing of a definite number. On the other hand, a mystery of the highest solemnity was being enacted here, a symbolic presentation of a reality of the greatest importance; and it may be that it could not be adequately conveyed by the historical event unless all the creatures which were unable, through natural limitations, to maintain life in the waters, were there in the ark in that fixed number. If so, this was not the responsibility of any particular man or men, but of God. In fact, Noah did not catch the animals and then put them in, he let them in as they came and entered. That is the force of the words 'they will come in to you';[174] not, to be sure, through man's driving, but at God's bidding. But there is this exception: we are surely not to suppose that sexless creatures were included, since it was definitely laid down that 'they shall be male and female.'

There are, we know, some animals which are produced from various substances without sexual intercourse, but afterwards reproduce by intercourse; flies are an example of this. There are others, such as bees, which have no distinction of male and female. Then again, there are animals which show sexual characteristics without producing offspring, such as male and female mules. It would be surprising if they were in the ark. Instead, it would be enough to have their parents there, that is, the species of horse and ass. And the same is true of any other animals which produce some different kind of creature by interbreeding. But if such hybrids had anything to contribute to the allegorical meaning of the ark, then they were included, for such a species also has male and female.

Some people are puzzled about the kinds of food that would have been available in the ark for animals which are supposed to be purely carnivorous. They speculate whether there were animals taken on in excess of the prescribed number, without transgressing the command, since their inclusion would have been compelled by the need to feed the others, or whether (and this is the more plausible solution) there

173. Gen. 6, 19. 174. Gen. 6, 20.

could have been some foodstuffs other than meat which were suitable for all animals. We know, in fact, that many carnivorous animals feed on vegetables and fruit, especially figs and chestnuts. Thus it would not be surprising if that wise and righteous man was also instructed by God about the appropriate food for each species and prepared a store of meatless food adapted for the various animals.

Is there anything which we would refuse to eat under the compulsion of hunger? Is there anything that God could not render agreeable and wholesome? He could indeed have endowed these creatures with the ability to live without food – this would have been easy for his divine power – had it not been that their eating played its part in completing the allegorical representation of so great a mystery. In fact, only a love of disputation would allow anyone to contend that the elaborate details of the historical narrative are not symbols designed to give a prophetic picture of the Church. For nations have already filled the Church, and the clean and the unclean are contained as it were in the framework of the Church's unity, until the appointed end is reached. The meaning is so abundantly clear on this particular point, that we must never think of doubting that the other details have their own meanings, although the language is rather more obscure and the references less easy to recognize.

This being so, no one, however stubborn, will venture to imagine that this narrative was written without an ulterior purpose; and it could not plausibly be said that the events, though historical, have no symbolic meaning, or that the account is not factual, but merely symbolical, or that the symbolism has nothing to do with the Church. No; we must believe that the writing of this historical record had a wise purpose, that the events are historical, that they have a symbolic meaning, and that this meaning gives a prophetic picture of the Church.

Now that this book has arrived at this point, I must bring it to a close. My next task will be to examine the development of both cities, that is, of the earthly city, which lives by man's standards, and of the Heavenly City, which lives according to God's will, in the period following the Flood, and thereafter in the following periods of history.

BOOK XVI

1. *Whether any families are to be found in the period from Noah to Abraham whose members lived according to God's will*

IF it is asked whether the progress of the holy City can be traced in a continuous line after the Flood, or was so interrupted by intervening periods of irreligion that there are times when not one man emerges as a worshipper of the one true God, it is difficult to find an answer to the question from any clear statement of Scripture. In fact from the time of Noah, who with his wife and his three sons and their wives was found worthy to be rescued from the devastation of the Flood by means of the ark, we do not find, until the time of Abraham, anyone whose devotion is proclaimed by any statement in the inspired Scriptures – except for the fact that Noah commends his sons Shem and Japheth in his prophetic benediction, since he knew, by prophetic insight, what was to happen in the far-distant future. Hence it was that he also cursed his middle son, that is the one younger than the first-born and older than the last, because he had sinned against his father. He did not curse him in his own person, but in the person of his son, Noah's grandson; and he used those words: 'A curse on Canaan! He shall be a slave, a servant to his brothers.'[1] Now Canaan was the son of Ham, who had not covered the nakedness of his sleeping father, but instead had called attention to it. This is also why Noah went on to add a blessing on his two sons, the eldest and the youngest, saying, 'Blessed be the Lord God of Shem, and Canaan shall be his slave; may God enlarge Japheth, and may he dwell in the houses of Shem.'[2] In the same way the vineyard planted by Noah, the drunkenness resulting from its fruit, the nakedness of the sleeping Noah, and all the other events recorded in this story, were laden with prophetic meanings and covered with prophetic veils.[3]

1. Gen. 9, 25. 2. Gen. 9, 27.

3. *Noah.* The allegorical interpretation of Noah's drunkenness as prophetic of Christ's passion appears first in Cyprian, *De Doctr. Christ.*, 3, 21.

2. *The prophetic symbolism of Noah's sons*

But now that the historical fulfilment of these prophecies has come about in the posterity of these sons, the things which were concealed have been abundantly revealed. For no careful and intelligent observer can fail to recognize their fulfilment in Christ. The name Shem, as we know, means 'named'; and it was of Shem's line that Christ was born in the flesh. And what 'name' is of more renown than the name of Christ, the name that by now is fragrant everywhere, so much so that in the Song of Songs it is compared, in prophetic anticipation, with ointment poured out?[4] The name Japheth means 'enlargement'; and 'in the houses' of Christ, that is, in the churches, the 'enlargement' of the nations dwells. Again, the name Ham means 'hot';[5] and Noah's middle son, separating himself, as it were, from both the others, and keeping his position between them, is included neither in the first-fruits of Israel nor in the full harvest of the Gentiles, and he can only stand for the hot breed of heretics. They are hot, because they are on fire not with the spirit of wisdom, but with the spirit of impatience; for that is the characteristic fervour in the hearts of heretics; that is what makes them disturb the peace of the saints. And yet the effect of their activities is to assist the progress of the faithful, in accordance with the saying of the Apostle, 'Heresies are necessary, to show which of you are in a sound condition.'[6] The same idea is expressed in the scriptural statement that 'the well-instructed son will be wise; he will employ the fool as his servant.'[7] For we can see that many matters of importance to the Catholic faith are canvassed by the feverish restlessness of heretics, and the result is that they are more carefully examined, more clearly understood, and more earnestly propounded, with a view to defending them against heretical attack, and thus an argument aroused by an adversary turns out to be an opportunity for instruction. Nevertheless it is possible and reasonable to regard Noah's middle son as typifying not only those in open schism from the Church, but also those who boast the name of Christian and yet live scandalous lives. For it is certain that such people proclaim Christ's passion, symbolized by Noah's nakedness, in their professions, while they dis-

4. S. of S. 1, 3.

5. The name *Shem* was naturally associated with the Hebrew *sem*, 'name' or 'fame'; *Japheth* suggested a derivation from *pāthāh*, 'to open'; the derivation of *Ham* from *ham*, 'hot' is probable; *Canaan* (who was evidently the villainous brother in one version of the story) is perhaps rightly connected with a root *kanā*, meaning 'low'.

6. 1 Cor. 11, 19.

7. Prov. 10, 5 (LXX).

honour it by their evil actions. It was of such people that we read in Scripture, 'You will recognize them by their fruits.'[8]

That is why Ham was cursed in the person of his son, in his fruit, as it were, that is, in his activities. Hence it is suitable that the son's name, Canaan, means 'their movement',[9] which is surely the same as 'their activities'. In contrast, Shem and Japheth, representing circumcision and uncircumcision, or Jews and Greeks, in the Apostle's terminology (but with reference only to those called and justified) when they somehow learned of their father's nakedness (symbolizing the Saviour's passion) took a garment, held it over their backs, and entered, facing the other way, and hid their father's nakedness without looking on what they reverently covered.[10] Now in the passion of Christ we may be said to honour what was done on our behalf while at the same time we turn our backs on the crime of the Jews. The garment stands for a mystery; the backs symbolize the memory of past events; for this, we may be sure, is now the time when 'Japheth lives in the houses of Shem' and the wicked brother lives between them,[11] and the Church now celebrates Christ's passion as an accomplished fact, and no longer looks for it in the future.

The evil brother, however, in the person of his son – that is, through his actions – is the slave, the servant, of the good brothers, when the good make skilful use of the wicked for their own training in endurance or for their own development in wisdom. For as the Apostle bears witness, there are those who preach Christ with impure motives; but, he says, 'whether speciously or genuinely, let Christ be preached.'[12] Now Christ himself planted a vineyard about which the prophet says, 'The vineyard of the Lord of Hosts is the house of Israel,'[13] and he drinks of its wine. And the wine may be interpreted with reference to that cup which he speaks of when he says, 'Are you able to drink the cup which I am going to drink?'[14] and, 'Father, if it is possible, let this cup pass me by',[15] where it obviously means his passion. Or, since wine is the product of the vineyard, we may prefer this meaning, that from the vineyard itself, that is, from the race of the Israelites, was derived the flesh which he assumed for our sake, and the blood, so that he might suffer his passion. 'He was drunk' – that is, he suffered – and 'he was naked'; for then his weakness was laid bare,

8. Matt. 7, 20.
9. St Augustine's derivation of Canaan is unexplained.
10. Gen. 9, 23.
11. Sc. Gentiles and Jews in the Church, with heretics in their midst.
12. Phil. 1, 18.
13. Is. 5, 7.
14. Matt. 20, 22.
15. Matt. 26, 39.

that is, was made evident. As the Apostle says, 'He was crucified through his weakness.'[16] And that is why he also says, 'The weakness of God is stronger than men and the foolishness of God is wiser than men.'[17] Moreover, after saying 'he was naked' the Scripture adds 'in his own house',[18] thus ingeniously indicating that Christ was destined to endure the cross, and death, at the hands of a people of his own flesh and blood, members of his own family, namely the Jews.

It is only externally, only by the sounds they utter, that wicked men preach this passion of Christ; for they do not understand what they are preaching, whereas the upright have this great mystery in their inner selves, and inwardly in their heart they honour the weakness and foolishness of God, because it is stronger and wiser than men. This is the reality symbolized by the fact that Ham went out and published his father's nakedness outside, while Shem and Japheth came in to veil it, that is, to honour it – which means that their action had a more inward character.

These hidden meanings of inspired Scripture we track down as best we can, with varying degrees of success; and yet we all hold confidently to the firm belief that these historical events and the narrative of them have always some foreshadowing of things to come, and are always to be interpreted with reference to Christ and his Church, which is the City of God. It has never failed to be foretold in prophecy from the beginning of the human race, and we now see the prophecy being fulfilled in all that happens.

Thus, after two of Noah's sons had been blessed, and the middle son cursed, from then onwards down to Abraham, the record is silent about any righteous men who worshipped God with true devotion; and that covers a period of more than a thousand years.[19] I am not inclined to suppose that such people did not exist, but if they were all mentioned the narrative would become tedious, and would be more notable for historical accuracy than for prophetic foresight. Accordingly, the writer of these holy Scriptures (or rather the Spirit of God through his agency) is concerned with those events which not only constitute a narrative of past history but also give a prophecy of things to come, though only those things which concern the City of God. For everything that is here said about those human beings who are not citizens of that City is said with this purpose, that the City

16. 2 Cor. 13, 4. 17. 1 Cor. 1, 25. 18. Gen. 9, 21.

19. According to the LXX and the Old Latin Versions. The Vulgate (and the Hebrew) give 290 years; cf. Bk XV, 10–13.

may show up to advantage, may be thrown into relief, by contrast with its opposite. To be sure, we must not suppose that all the events in the narrative are symbolical; but those which have no symbolism are interwoven in the story for the sake of those which have this further significance. For it is only the share of the plough that cuts through the earth; but the other parts of the plough are essential to make this operation possible. It is only the strings of the lyre, and of other similar musical instruments, that are designed to produce the music; but to effect the result the other components are included in the framework of the instruments. These parts are not struck by the player, but the parts which resonate when struck are connected with them. Similarly, in the prophetic history some things are recorded which have no prophetic significance in themselves; but they are there for the significant events to be attached to them, moored to them, as we might say.

3. *The lines of descent from Noah's three sons*

We have next to examine the lines of descent from the three sons of Noah, taking what seem to be the important observations and weaving them into this work, in which is displayed the development in history of the two cities, the earthly and the heavenly. The record starts with the youngest son, called Japheth; his eight sons are named, together with seven grandsons by two of them, three by one and four by the other, which gives a total of fifteen. Then follow the four sons of Ham, Noah's middle son, with five grandsons from one of them, and two great-grandsons from one grandson, eleven in all. After these have been listed, we are taken back to the beginning in these words:

> And Cush had a son called Nimrod; he began to be a giant on the earth. He was a gigantic hunter against[20] the Lord God. Hence the saying: 'Like Nimrod, a gigantic hunter against the Lord.' And the beginning was made of his kingdom, Babylon, Erech, Accad and Calneh in the land of Shinar. Out of that land Assur departed and built Nineveh and the city of Rehoboth, and Calah, and Dasem, midway between Nineveh and Calah; this is a great city.[21]

Now this Cush, father of the giant Nimrod, was named first among the sons of Ham; and his five sons and two grandsons had been re-

20. A mistranslation by the Old Latin Version. The Hebrew means 'in the sight of'; cf. ch. 4.

21. cf. Gen. 10, 8ff. (LXX). In St Augustine's text Nimrod appears as 'Nabroth', the Greek form of the name taken from LXX by the Old Latin Version.

corded already. Then either this giant was born to him after the birth of his grandsons, or (more credibly) the Scripture mentions him separately because of his eminence. For in fact his kingdom is recorded, whose beginning was the world-famed city of Babylon, and also the cities or districts which are recorded along with Babylon. But Assur's departure from that land (the land of Shinar, which was part of Nimrod's kingdom) and his building of Nineveh and the other cities which he attached to Nineveh, belong to a much later period, though they are mentioned here. The writer took this occasion to mention them in passing because of the fame of the Assyrian Empire, which received a remarkable extension under Ninus,[22] son of Belus, the founder of the great city of Nineveh; the name of which was derived from its founder, Nineveh being named after Ninus. Assur, on the other hand, from whom sprang the Assyrians, was not one of the sons of Ham, Noah's middle son; he is found among the sons of Shem, Noah's eldest son. Hence it is apparent that it was men sprung from the line of Shem who later gained control of the realm of that giant, and went on from there to found other cities, the first of which was called Nineveh, after Ninus.

After that, the narrative goes back to Ham's second son, Mizraim; and his descendants are recorded, not as individuals but as seven nations. From the sixth nation, from the sixth son, as it were, it is recorded that a nation arose called the Philistines, thus bringing the number to eight. Then we return to Canaan, the son in whose person Ham was cursed, and eleven of his progeny are named; the extent of their territory is mentioned, and some of their cities are given. Thus when sons and grandsons are reckoned in, the list of the line of Ham contains thirty-one descendants.

It remains to record the progeny of Shem, Noah's eldest son; in fact, the narrative of these generations has arrived at him by steps, starting with the youngest son. However, there is a certain obscurity in the passage where the record of Shem's descendants begins, and we must clear this up by an explanation, since it is very relevant to the subject of our inquiry. The passage reads, 'And to Shem, even to Shem himself, the father of all his sons, Heber was born, the son of the elder brother of Japheth.'[23] The logical order of the sentence is: 'And to Shem was born Heber, even to himself, that is to Shem himself, was born Heber, and this Shem is the father of all his sons.' The narrator therefore intended Shem to be understood as the patriarch of all who

22. cf Bk IV, 6.
23. Gen. 10, 21 (in the obscurity of the Old Latin Version).

sprang from his stock, who were to be included in his list, whether they were sons, grandsons, or great-grandsons, or those of his later posterity. For Shem himself was certainly not the father of Heber; in fact, he is found among Heber's ancestors, in the fifth generation before him. Shem was the father of Arphaxad, among other sons; Arphaxad was the father of Cainan; Cainan of Salah; Salah of Heber.

There is therefore a special point in naming Heber before all the rest of the line of descent from Shem, and giving him preference even over Shem's sons, although in fact his place is in the fifth generation. It assumes the truth of the tradition that the Hebrews were called after him, being *Heberaei*, as it were. There is, indeed, another possible theory, that they were named after Abraham, and supposedly called *Abrahaei*. But it is doubtless true that they were named *Heberaei*, after Heber, and later, with the omission of one letter, *Hebraei*, Hebrews.[24] The Hebrew language is the exclusive property of the people of Israel; and it is in that people that the City of God has been on pilgrimage, as well as in the persons of the saints, besides having a shadowy representation, in a symbolical form, in all mankind.

Accordingly, six sons of Shem are first named; then from one of them four grandsons were born. Another of Shem's sons also produced a grandson for him, and to this grandson in turn was born a great-grandson and to him a great-great-grandson, and this was Heber. Then Heber had two sons, one of whom he named Peleg, which means 'divider';[25] and Scripture adds a note to explain the reason for the name, 'For in his time the earth was divided.'[26] What this refers to will become clear later.[27] Another of Heber's sons had twelve sons; and thus the descendants of Shem amount in all to twenty-seven. Thus the grand total of the progeny of Noah's three sons is seventy-three, fifteen from Japheth, thirty-one from Ham, twenty-seven from Shem. The Scripture then goes on to say, 'These are the sons of Shem in their tribes, according to their languages, in their regions and their nations'; and then similarly about all Noah's line we are told, 'These are the tribes of the sons of Noah according to their generations and their nations. From these the islands of nations were dispersed on the earth after the Flood.' Hence we gather that there were at that time seventy-three nations (or rather, as will be shown later, seventy-two) not seventy-three men. The list of Japheth's sons, given earlier, also concluded with these words: 'From these the islands of nations were

24. cf. ch. 11.
25. A possible interpretation.
26. Gen. 10, 25.
27. cf. ch. 10.

separated, each in its own land, everyone according to language, with their own tribes and in their own nations.'

The nations had already been more clearly recorded in a passage about the sons of Ham, as I have pointed out above. 'Mizraim was the father of those who are called Ludim', and the rest are similarly listed, making up seven nations. After enumerating all these the writer says in conclusion, 'These are the sons of Ham, in their tribes, according to their languages, in their regions and in their nations.' No sons are recorded for many of these, the reason being that they were added to existing nations at their birth and could not found nations of their own. For that can be the only reason why eight sons of Japheth are listed, but only the sons of two of them are mentioned; and that while four sons of Ham are named, the sons of only three are added to the list; and that although six sons of Shem are named the descendants of only two of these are attached. We are surely not to suppose that the others remained childless. That would be absurd. It is obvious that they did not qualify for mention in virtue of having founded nations, because at birth they were enrolled in existing nations.

4. *The diversity of languages and the beginning of Babylon*

Now those nations, according to the narrative, possessed 'their own languages'. But despite that statement the narrator goes back to the time when all men had the same language; and then he explains how the diversity of languages arose. 'The whole earth,' he says,

had one language and all men had the same way of speaking. Then it happened that, as they migrated from the East, they found a plain in the land of Shinar and settled there. And one man said to the next man: 'Come, let us make bricks and bake them in the fire.' And so bricks were used for stone, and they had bitumen for mortar; and they said: 'Come, let us build a city for ourselves, and a tower, whose top will reach to the sky; and let us make a name for ourselves, before we are scattered over the face of all the earth.' And the Lord came down to see the city and the tower which the sons of men had built. And the Lord God said, 'Behold, the people are one race, and all of them have one language; and they have begun to build, and from now on they will not fail to achieve anything they may try to do. Come, let us go down and bring confusion in their speech, so that no one may understand what the next man says.' Then the Lord dispersed them from there over the face of all the earth, and they left off building the city and the tower. That is why the name 'Confusion' was given to the city; because it was here that the Lord confused the languages of all the earth.

And the Lord God dispersed them from there over the face of all the earth.[28]

This city which was called 'Confusion' is none other than Babylon, whose marvellous construction is praised also by pagan historians. The name 'Babylon' means, in fact, 'confusion'.[29] Hence it may be inferred that Nimrod 'the giant' was its founder, as was briefly suggested earlier. For when the Scripture mentions him, it says that 'the beginning of his empire was Babylon', that is, Babylon was the city which had the pre-eminence over all the others, where the king's dwelling was, in the metropolis, so to speak; although it was not finished on the great scale which their arrogant impiety had in mind. For their plan provided for an enormous height, to 'reach to the sky', as was said; whether this referred to a single tower, which was designed as the principal structure among others, or to all the towers, denoted by the collective singular (as 'the soldier' is used, to mean thousands of soldiers, and 'the frog' or 'the locust' to designate a multitude of frogs or locusts in the plagues with which Moses smote the Egyptians[30]).

But what could the empty presumption of man have achieved, no matter how vast the structure it contrived, whatever the height to which that building towered into the sky in its challenge to God? What though it should overtop the mountains and escape beyond the region of this cloudy atmosphere? When all is said, what harm could be done to God by any spiritual self-exaltation or material elevation however high it soared? The safe and genuine highway to heaven is constructed by humility, which lifts up its heart to the Lord, not against the Lord, as did that giant who is called 'a hunter against the Lord'. Some interpreters have misunderstood this phrase, being deceived by an ambiguity in the Greek, and consequently translating it as 'before the Lord', instead of 'against the Lord'.[31] It is true that the Greek *enantion* means 'before' as well as 'against'. For example, we find the word in one of the psalms: 'Let us lament before (*ante*) the Lord who made us';[32] and also in the Book of Job, where it says, 'You have burst into fury against (*ante*) the Lord.'[33] It is in the latter sense that we must take it in the description of Nimrod; that giant was 'a

28. Gen. 11, 1–10.

29. Hebrew, *balal*, 'to confuse'. Babylon, in fact, means 'Gate of God' (*Bâb-Il*).

30. The collective singular is common in Latin.

31. Gen. 10, 9; cf. ch. 3n. 32. Ps. 95, 6. 33. Job 15, 13.

hunter against the Lord'. For the word 'hunter' can only suggest a deceiver, oppressor and destroyer of earth-born creatures. Thus he, with his subject peoples, began to erect a tower against the Lord, which symbolizes his impious pride. Now it is right that an evilly affected plan should be punished, even when it is not successfully effected. And what kind of punishment was in fact imposed? Since a ruler's power of domination is wielded by his tongue, it was in that organ that his pride was condemned to punishment. And the consequence was that he who refused to understand God's bidding so as to obey it, was himself not understood when he gave orders to men. Thus that conspiracy of his was broken up, since each man separated from anyone whom he did not understand, and only associated with those to whom he could talk. And so the nations were divided by languages, and were scattered over the earth. Such was God's design; and he achieved it by ways that are to us inscrutable and incomprehensible.

5. *The Lord's descent to confuse the language of those who were building the tower*[34]

Let us consider the statement, 'And the Lord came down to see the city and the tower built by the sons of men' – not, be it noted, by the sons of God, but by that society which lives by man's standards, the society we call 'the earthly city'. Now God is present everywhere in his entirety, and so does not move from one place to another; but he is said to 'come down' when he performs an action which is miraculous in being contrary to the ordinary course of nature, and thus in some way points to his presence. Again, he can never be unaware of anything; and so he does not learn the facts by seeing them at a particular time. But he is said to 'see' and to discover' at a particular time anything which he causes to be seen and discovered. Thus the city had not so far been seen in the way in which God caused it to be seen when he made it clear how much it displeased him. On the other hand, God can be understood as coming down to the city in the sense that his angels, in whom he dwells, did so descend. And so the next passage, where it says, 'And the Lord God said: "Behold the people are one race, and they all have the same language" ', and so on; and the following words, 'Come, let us go down and bring confusion in their speech', are a recapitulation[35] which shows how the action described by 'the

34. A commentary on Gen. 11, 5–7.
35. i.e., a return to an earlier point in the narrative; cf. ch. 15.

Lord came down' was effected. If, in fact, he had already come down, what is the point of the words, 'Come, let us go down and bring confusion' (which is taken as said to the angels) except that he was present in the angels when they descended and thus came down himself through his agents? And it is appropriate that he does not say, 'Come, go down and bring confusion' but, 'Come, let us bring confusion on their speech'; for in this way he shows that he works through his servants, so that they themselves are also God's fellow-workers; as the Apostle says, 'we are fellow-workers with God.'[36]

6. *The mode of God's speech with the angels*

There is another passage which might have been interpreted with reference to the angels; it is the place where, at the creation of man, God said, 'Let us make man',[37] instead of 'Let me make man.' However, since this is followed by 'in our image', and since it is unthinkable that we should believe man to have been made in the image of the angels, or that the angels and God have the same image, the plural here is correctly understood to refer to the Trinity. Nevertheless, the Trinity is one God, and therefore even after the words 'Let us make' the narrative proceeds: 'And God made man in the image of God.' It does not say, 'The gods made' or, 'in the image of the gods'.

Now the passage we are discussing might also be understood as referring to the Trinity, as if the Father said to the Son and the Holy Spirit, 'Come, let us go down and bring confusion on their speech', if there had been anything to prevent our understanding this in reference to the angels. But it is more appropriate that the angels should 'come' to God with holy movements, that is to say, with reverent thoughts; for it is with reverent thoughts that they consult the changeless Truth, as the law which is established eternally in that heavenly court of theirs. For they themselves are not the truth for themselves; they are partakers of the creative Truth, and move towards it, as to the fountain of life,[38] to receive from it what they do not possess of themselves. And this movement of theirs is a stable movement, by which they approach without withdrawing.

And God does not speak to the angels in the same way as we speak to one another, or to God, or to the angels, or as the angels speak to us. He speaks in his own fashion, which is beyond our describing. But his speech is explained to us in our fashion. God's speech, to be sure, is on a higher plane; it precedes his action as the changeless reason of the

36. 1 Cor. 3, 9. 37. Gen. 1, 26. 38. cf. Ps. 36, 9.

action itself; and his speaking has no sound, no transitory noise; it has a power that persists for eternity and operates in time. It is with this speech that he addresses the holy angels, whereas he speaks to us, who are situated far off, in a different way. And yet, when we also grasp something of this kind of speech with our inward ears, we come close to the angels. Therefore I do not have to be continually explaining about God's acts of speaking in this present work. For unchanging Truth either speaks by itself, in a way we cannot explain, to the minds of rational creatures, or it speaks through a mutable creature, either to our spirit by spiritual images, or to our physical sense by physical voices.

Certainly the words, 'And from now on they will not fail to achieve anything they try to do',[39] were not put as an assertion but as a question. This is frequently the way men express a threat, as when a speaker says,

> Shall they not take up arms and then pursue
> From the whole city?[40]

Accordingly, the passage quoted must be interpreted as if God said, Will not they fail to achieve everything they try to do?' The quotation as given would not in itself suggest a threat. But I have added the particle *-ne*, for the benefit of the slow-witted, to read *nonne*, since a tone of voice cannot be indicated in writing.

We now see that from those three men, Noah's sons, seventy-three nations – or rather seventy-two, as a calculation will show – and as many languages came into being on the earth, and by their increase they filled even the islands. However, the number of nations increased at a greater rate than the languages. For even in Africa we know of many barbarous nations using only one language.

7. *Whether the remotest island received all kinds of animals from those preserved in the ark*

There can be no doubt that men could have crossed over by boat to inhabit the islands, after the human race had multiplied. But there is a problem about beasts of all kinds which are not looked after by human beings, and are not, like frogs, brought into life from the earth,[41] but only as a result of the intercourse of male and female, such as wolves

39. Gen. 11, 6. (St Augustine's argument here is unconvincing in Latin, and impossible to reproduce in English, which is incapable of the ambiguity.)

40. Virg., *Aen.*, 4, 592.

41. cf. Bk XV, 27 (spontaneous generation of bees and flies).

and the other animals of that kind. How could they have existed on the islands, as well as on the mainland, after the Flood in which all creatures were wiped out, except for those in the ark? For we have to assume that they could be restored only from those whose species was preserved, in both sexes, in the ark. It is credible, to be sure, that they crossed to the islands by swimming, but that could only be true of the nearest islands; and there are some islands situated so far from the mainlands that it is clearly impossible for any beasts to have swum to them. But if we assume that men captured beasts and took them with them, and in this way established the species where they lived, because they were interested in hunting, this could give a credible explanation of the facts. On the other hand, it would be wrong to rule out the possibility that they were transported by activity of angels, either at God's command or with his permission. If, however, they sprang from the earth, as at their first origin, when God said, 'Let the earth produce the living soul',[42] then it becomes much more apparent that all species were in the ark not so much for the purpose of restoring the animal population as with a view to typifying the various nations, thus presenting a symbol of the Church. This must be the explanation, if the earth produced many animals on islands to which they could not cross.

8. *The origin of recorded monstrosities*

There are accounts in pagan history[43] of certain monstrous races of men. If these are to be believed, the question arises whether we are to suppose that they descended from the sons of Noah, or rather from that one man from whom they themselves derived. Some of those monsters are said to have only one eye, in the middle of their forehead;[44] others have the soles of their feet turned backwards behind their legs;[45] others have the characteristics of both sexes,[46] the right breast being male and the left female, and in their intercourse they alternate between begetting and conceiving. Then there are men without mouths,[47] who live only by inhaling through their nostrils; there are others whose height is only a cubit – the Greeks call them

42. Gen. 1, 24.
43. St Augustine's chief authority is Pliny's *Natural History*, esp. 7, 2.
44. *Arimaspi*; cf. Hdt., 4, 13.
45. *Abarimonians*.
46. *Androgyni*.
47. The *Astomi* of India.

'Pygmies',[48] from their word for a cubit. We are told in another place that there are females who conceive at the age of five and do not live beyond their eighth year.[49] There is also a story of a race who have a single leg attached to their feet;[50] they cannot bend their knee, and yet have a remarkable turn of speed. They are called *Sciopods* ('shadow-feet') because in hot weather they lie on their backs on the ground and take shelter in the shade of their feet. There are some men without necks, and with their eyes in their shoulders; and other kinds of men or quasi-men portrayed in mosaic on the marine parade at Carthage, taken from books of 'curiosities', as we may call them.

What am I to say of the *Cynocephali*,[51] whose dog's head and actual barking prove them to be animals rather than men? Now we are not bound to believe in the existence of all the types of men which are described. But no faithful Christian should doubt that anyone who is born anywhere as a man – that is, a rational and mortal being – derives from that one first-created human being. And this is true, however extraordinary such a creature may appear to our senses in bodily shape, in colour, or motion, or utterance, or in any natural endowment, or part, or quality. However, it is clear what constitutes the persistent norm of nature in the majority and what, by its very rarity, constitutes a marvel.

Moreover, the explanation given for monstrous human births among us can also be applied to some of those monstrous races. For God is the creator of all, and he himself knows where and when any creature should be created or should have been created. He has the wisdom to weave the beauty of the whole design out of the constituent parts, in their likeness and diversity. The observer who cannot view the whole is offended by what seems the deformity of a part, since he does not know how it fits in, or how it is related to the rest. We know of cases of human beings born with more than five fingers or five toes. This is a comparatively trivial abnormality; and yet it would be utterly wrong for anyone to be fool enough to imagine that the Creator made a mistake in the number of human fingers, although he may not know why the Creator so acted. So, even if a greater divergence from the norm should appear, he whose operations no one has the right to criticize knows what he is about.

48. cf. Hom., *Il.*, 3, 3ff; Hdt., 3, 32. πυγμή, 'cubit'; πυγμαῖοι, 'cubit – length men', Pygmies.

49. *Calingi.* 50. *Monocoli.*

51. cf. Hdt., 4, 191; Gell., 9, 4.

At Hippo Zaritus[52] there is a man with feet shaped like a crescent, with only two toes on each, and his hands are similarly shaped. If there were any race with those characteristics it would be listed among the marvels of nature. But are we therefore going to deny that this man is descended from that one man who was first created?

As for *Androgynes*, also called Hermaphrodites, they are certainly very rare, and yet it is difficult to find periods when there are no examples of human beings possessing the characteristics of both sexes, in such a way that it is a matter of doubt how they should be classified. However, the prevalent usage has called them masculine, assigning them to the superior sex; for no one has ever used the feminine names, *androgynaecae* or *hermaphroditae*.

Some years ago, but certainly in my time, a man was born in the East with a double set of upper parts, but a single set of the lower limbs. That is, he had two heads, two chests, and four arms, but only one belly and two feet, as if he were one man. And he lived long enough for the news of his case to attract many sightseers.

In fact, it would be impossible to list all the human infants very unlike those who, without any doubt, were their parents. Now it cannot be denied that these derive ultimately from that one man; and therefore the same is true of all those races which are reported to have deviated as it were, by their divergence in bodily structure, from the normal course of nature followed by the majority, or practically the whole of mankind. If these races are included in the definition of 'human', that is, if they are rational and mortal animals, it must be admitted that they trace their lineage from that same one man, the first father of all mankind. This assumes, of course, the truth of the stories about the divergent features of those races, and their great difference from one another and from us. The definition is important; for if we did not know that monkeys, long-tailed apes and chimpanzees are not men but animals, those natural historians who plume themselves on their collection of curiosities might pass them off on us as races of men, and get away with such nonsense. But if we assume that the subjects of those remarkable accounts are in fact men, it may be suggested that God decided to create some races in this way, so that we should not suppose that the wisdom with which he fashions the physical being of men has gone astray in the case of the monsters which are bound to be born among us of human parents; for that would be to regard the works of God's wisdom as the products of an

52. Now Bizerta, Tunis; Hippo Regius, St Augustine's bishopric, is now Bone, Algeria, some 100 miles to the west.

imperfectly skilled craftsman. If so, it ought not to seem incongruous that, just as there are some monstrosities within the various races of mankind, so within the whole human race there should be certain monstrous peoples.

I must therefore finish the discussion of this question with my tentative and cautious answer. The accounts of some of these races may be completely worthless; but if such peoples exist, then either they are not human; or, if human, they are descended from Adam.

9. *The story of the 'antipodes'*

As for the fabled 'antipodes', men, that is, who live on the other side of the earth, where the sun rises when it sets for us, men who plant their footsteps opposite ours, there is no rational ground for such a belief.[53] The upholders of this notion do not assert that they have discovered it from scientific evidence; they base their conjecture on a kind of *a priori* reasoning. They argue that the earth is suspended within the sphere of the heavens, so that the lowest point and the middle point of the world are identical; and this leads them to suppose that the other half of the world which lies below this part cannot be devoid of human inhabitants. They ignore the fact that even if the world is supposed to be a spherical mass, or if some rational proof should be offered for the supposition, it does not follow that the land on that side is not covered by 'the gathering together of the waters'.[54] Again, even if the land were uncovered, it does not immediately follow that it has human beings on it. For there is no untruth of any kind in the Scripture, whose reliability in the account of past events is attested by the fulfilment of its prophecies for the future; and it would be too ridiculous to suggest that some men might have sailed from our side of the earth to the other, arriving there after crossing the vast expanse of ocean, so that the human race should be established there also by the descendants of the one first man.

Let us therefore search among those early peoples of mankind who were, we gather, divided into seventy-two nations and as many languages, to see if we can find among them the City of God on

53. *The Antipodes.* The Pythagoreans assumed another world on the opposite side, to which they gave the name of the 'Antiworld' (Ar., *De Cael.*, 2, 13). The word 'antipodes' appears first in Cic., *Acad. Post.*, 2, 39, 123. By the third century A.D. the picture of the earth as a flat disc had displaced the spherical theory of the earlier Greeks (cf. Bk VIII, 2nn.), and Lactantius (*fl. c.* 290) ridiculed the theory, together with the supposition of the antipodes (*Inst. Div.*, 3, 24).

54. Gen. 1, 10.

pilgrimage here on earth. We have brought its story down to the Flood and the ark, and have shown its continuance in the sons of Noah through his blessings on those sons, especially in the eldest of them, who was called Shem; for Japheth was blessed only in respect of his dwelling in the habitations of his brother Shem.

10. *The progress of the City of God towards Abraham, by way of Shem's descendants*

Thus the line of descent must be followed from Shem himself, to show us the City of God after the Flood, in the same way as the line from the man called Seth showed it before the Flood. This is the reason why the inspired Scripture, after showing the earthly city in Babylon, that is, in 'confusion', goes back to the patriarch Shem, to make a fresh start; and from that point it begins the list of generations down to Abraham, mentioning also the number of years that passed before each man named became the father of the son belonging to this line, and the length of each man's life. And here we must recognize the explanation of the passage which I promised earlier to explain;[55] we can see why it was said of the sons of Heber, 'The name of one of them was Peleg, because in his time the earth was divided.'[56] For the statement that the earth was divided can only refer to its division by the diversity of languages.

The record omits the rest of Shem's sons, who are irrelevant to the purpose, and gives the series of generations to bring us down to Abraham, just as before the Flood we were given only the list which led directly to Noah in the line of descent from the son of Adam whose name was Seth. Thus the list of generations begins, 'These are the generations of Shem. Shem, the son of Noah, was a hundred years old when he became the father of Arphaxad, in the second year after the Flood. And Shem lived five hundred years after the birth of Arphaxad, and he had other sons and daughters, and then he died.'[57] The narrative goes on to mention the others in the same fashion, giving the age at which each became the father of the son belonging to the line leading to Abraham, and stating how many years he lived after that, and noting that he had other sons and daughters. The purpose of this last information is to let us know the sources from which the population was able to increase; for otherwise, if our attention was limited to the few names that are listed, we might be held up by the childish question about how such vast extents of lands and kingdoms could have

55. cf. ch. 3. 56. Gen. 10, 25. 57. Gen. 11, 10f.

been stocked by Shem's posterity, especially when we think of the Assyrian Empire. For it was from Assyria that Ninus, the great conqueror of the nations throughout the East, ruled in vast prosperity, and handed down to his successor an empire of enormous extent and extreme stability, which was to endure for a very long time.[58]

For our part, to avoid lingering on this period unnecessarily, we are not putting down the number of years of each man's life in these successive generations; we note only the age at which each had his son, the purpose of the record being to calculate the number of years from the end of the Flood down to the time of Abraham; and any other points that compel our attention will be briefly touched on in passing.

Well, then, in the second year after the Flood Shem became the father of Arphaxad. Arphaxad, in his turn, had a son called Cainan, at the age of 135. Cainan, when 130 years old, became the father of Salah; and Salah himself was the same age when his son Heber was born. Heber was 134 at the birth of his son Peleg, 'in whose time the earth was divided'. Now Peleg lived 130 years, and then had a son called Reu; and Reu lived 132 years and became the father of Serug. Serug lived 130 years and begot Nahor. Nahor lived seventy-nine years and begot Terah. Terah lived seventy years and begot Abram whose name God changed, calling him Abraham.[59] And so the years from the Flood to Abraham make a total of 1,072 according to the standard version, that is, the Septuagint. But we are told that a much smaller total of years is found in the Hebrew texts; and for this discrepancy there is offered either no explanation or one very difficult to follow.[60]

Thus when we look for the City of God among those seventy-two tribes, we cannot say with certainty that at that time, when men had one tongue, that is, one way of speaking, the human race had been already so estranged from the worship of the true God that true religion continued only in those generations which were descended from the line of Shem through Arphaxad, leading to Abraham. Yet, as a result of the arrogance shown in building a tower to reach into the sky, the city, that is, the society, of the ungodly became apparent. It may be that this city had not existed before that time, or it may have existed in concealment; or perhaps both cities were there all the time, the godly city continuing in the two sons of Noah who received the blessing, and in their posterity, the ungodly in the son who was

58. cf. Bk IV, 6. 59. Gen. 11, 10ff. 60. cf. ch. 2.

cursed, and in his descendants, among whom arose that 'giant hunter against the Lord'.[61] It is not easy to decide among these possibilities.

For it is possible (and this is the most plausible suggestion) that there were already, among the descendants of the two good sons, men who treated God with contempt, even before the building of Babylon started, while there were also those who worshipped God among the descendants of Ham. However this may be, we are bound to believe that the world was never devoid of men of both these kinds. In fact, even when the Scripture says, 'All men have gone astray; all alike have become useless: there is no one who does good, not a single one', in both the psalms which contain these words we also read, 'Will none of them understand, these workers of wickedness, who devour my people in the bread they eat?' And so the inference is that even at that time the people of God existed. Hence the words, 'there is no one who does good' refer to the sons of men, not to the sons of God. For the previous verse reads, 'God looked down from heaven on the sons of men, to see if there was anyone who understood or looked for God.'[62] After that are added the words which show the rejection of all the 'sons of men', that is, those who belong to the city which lives by the standards of men, instead of the standards of God.

11. *Hebrew was the original language, named after Heber*

Accordingly, just as when all men had one language, that did not mean that the 'sons of pestilence'[63] were not to be found – for there was only one language before the Flood, and yet all men deserved to be wiped out by the Flood, except for the one family of the righteous Noah – so also when the nations received the merited punishment for their impious presumption and were divided by diversity of languages, and the city of the ungodly received the name 'Confusion', that is, was called Babylon,[64] even then there existed one family, the family of Heber, in which the language which was formerly that of all mankind could continue. This is the reason why, as I mentioned above,[65] Heber is given prominence as the first in the list of those sons of Shem who were the ancestors of individual nations, although Heber was Shem's great-great-grandson, that is, he is found to be fifth

61. Gen. 10, 9; cf. ch. 3; 4.

62. Ps. 14, 2ff; 53, 2ff.

63. Presumably St Augustine's version of 'sons of Belial'; cf. e.g. Judg. 19, 22; 1 Sam. 2, 12.

64. cf. ch. 4 and n.

65. cf. ch. 3.

in descent from Shem. The same language continued to be used in his family when the other nations were divided by different languages, and there is good reason for believing that this was the language common to all mankind in previous ages. This explains why this language was thenceforward called Hebrew. For at that point it had to be distinguished from the other tongues by a proper name, just as the others were given their proper names; but when there was only one language it had no other name than 'the human tongue' or 'human speech', since it was the only language spoken by mankind.

It may be objected that if it was in the time of Peleg, son of Heber, that the earth was divided by different languages – that is, the languages spoken by men on the earth at that time – the language common to all men up to that time should have been called after the name of Peleg rather than that of Heber. But we must assume that Heber gave his son that name of Peleg – which means 'division' – just because he was born to him at the time when the earth was divided on the basis of languages – that is, at that particular time, to correspond with the statement that 'in his time the earth was divided.'[66] For if Heber had not still been alive when the multitude of languages came into being, the language which succeeded in persisting in his family would not have received its name from him. For that reason we are to believe that this was the first language, shared by all, since the multiplication and change of languages came by way of punishment, and doubtless the people of God had to be outside the scope of this penalty.

It is not without significance that Hebrew was the language used by Abraham, and that he could not hand it on to all his descendants but only to those who were derived from him through Jacob, and by uniting to form the people of God in the most evident and conspicuous fashion, were able to keep the covenants and to preserve the stock from which Christ came. And Heber himself did not bequeath that language to all his posterity, but only to the line whose generations can be followed down to Abraham. For this reason, although we have no direct statement that there was any godly race of men at the time when Babylon was being founded by the ungodly, the effect of the obscurity on this point is not to baffle the interest of an inquirer but rather to give it exercise. For we read that in the first ages there was one language common to all men; and Heber is selected for mention before all the sons of Shem, although he is the fifth in descent from him; and Hebrew is the name of the language preserved by the

66. Gen. 10, 25; cf. ch. 3.

authority of patriarchs and prophets not only in their speech but also in the sacred writings. And so when the question is raised, on the subject of the division of languages, where that language could have persisted which was the common language of earlier days – and there can be no doubt that the punishment in the form of a change of language did not take effect where that language survived – the only answer that suggests itself is that it persisted in the family of the man from whom the language took its name. And there is an impressive indication of the righteousness of that nation in the fact that when other nations were chastised by the change of languages, this punishment did not extend to that people.

But now another problem is put forward. How could Heber and his son Peleg have each started nations, if the same language persisted in both of them? And it is true that the Hebrew people derived in one line of descent from Heber to Abraham, and after that through Abraham until Israel became a great nation. How was it, then, that all the recorded descendants of Noah's sons started separate nations, if Heber and Peleg did not? Surely the most likely explanation is that the giant Nimrod also started a nation of his own; but he is mentioned separately to call attention to his exceptional power and outstanding physique. His founding of a nation thus safeguards the number of seventy-two nations and languages. On the other hand the reason for the mention of Peleg is not that he founded a people – for his people was the Hebrew nation itself, and his language was Hebrew – it was to call attention to an important epoch, because in his time the earth was divided.

We should not be worried by the question how the giant Nimrod could have been alive at the time when Babylon was founded, and the confusion of languages came about, resulting in the division of the nations. For the fact that Heber is sixth in descent from Noah, while Nimrod is fourth, does not mean that their lives could not have coincided in point of time. This kind of thing happens where there are fewer generations and longer lives, and shorter lives in more generations, or when men are born later, in cases of fewer generations, and earlier in cases of more. We must certainly take it that when the earth was divided not only had the other descendants of Noah's son been born – those who are listed as the fathers of nations – but they had also reached an age when they could have had large families, worthy of the name of 'nations'. Hence we must on no account suppose that they were necessarily born in the order in which they are recorded. Otherwise, how could the twelve sons of Joktan, another of Heber's sons, have already founded nations, if the fact that Joktan is recorded after his brother Peleg means that he was born after him? For we know that it was at the time when the earth was divided that Peleg was born. It follows that we must understand that Peleg was indeed put before Joktan in the list, but was born long after his brother, whose twelve sons already had such substantial families that they could be divided into 'nations' with their distinctive languages. For the son who was later in respect of birth might be mentioned earlier just as happened with the descendants of Noah's three sons. Those descended from Japheth, the youngest, are given first, then those descended from Ham, the second son, and last those from Shem, who was the first and eldest.

We observe that the names of some of those nations have persisted with so little change that even today their derivation is obvious. For example, 'Assyrians' derives from Assur, and 'Hebrews' from Heber. Some names, however, have been so changed in the passage of ages that the most learned scholars who examine the records of remote antiquity have not been able to discover the origins of all of them, but only those of some of them. The Egyptians, for example, are said to owe their origin to a son of Ham called Mizraim; but there is here no trace of the sound of the original name. The same is true of the Ethiopians, who, we are told, belong by descent to the son of Ham who was called Cush. All in all, it is evident that the names which have been changed outnumber those which have survived unaltered.

12. *The new era that begins with Abraham*

Let us now go on to observe the development of the City of God from the epoch marked by Father Abraham. From that time onwards our knowledge of that City becomes clearer and we find more evident promises from God which we now see fulfilled in Christ. Now, as we have learned from the evidence of holy Scripture, Abraham was born 'in the territory of the Chaldeans'[67] a land which formed part of the Assyrian Empire;[68] and even at that time impious superstitions were rife among the Chaldeans, as among other nations. So there was only one family in which the worship of the one true God persisted and that was the family of Terah, the father of Abraham, and it is reasonable to suppose that the Hebrew language was preserved there only. And yet Terah himself, according to the account of Joshua,[69] served

67. Gen. 11, 28 (LXX and Old Latin Version; Heb. 'in Ur of the Chaldeans').
68. Not until more than 1,000 years after Abraham.
69. Josh. 24, 2.

the gods of other peoples in Mesopotamia just as God's people did in Egypt, when they were more clearly marked out as God's people. Meanwhile, the other descendants of Heber were gradually absorbed in other nations and languages.

From that time only Terah's family remained, to preserve a seedbed for the City of God, amid the flood of all the superstitions that covered the world, just as only the family of Noah survived the Flood of waters, to effect the restoration of the human race. It is significant that in one case the statement, 'These are the generations of Noah,'[70] follows the record of the generations down to Noah, together with numbers of years, and the explanation of the cause of the Flood, and comes before God begins to speak to Noah about the building of the ark; and in the present case, correspondingly, after the list of the generations of Noah's son called Shem down to Abraham, a new epoch is emphasized by these words:

> These are the generations of Terah. Terah was the father of Abram, Nahor and Haran; and Haran was the father of Lot. Haran died in the home of his father Terah in the country where he was born, in the territory of the Chaldeans. Now Abram and Nahor married wives, the name of Abram's wife being Sarah, while Nahor's wife was Milcah, daughter of Haran.[71]

This Haran was the father of Milcah and Iscah, and Iscah is believed to be identical with Sarah, Abraham's wife.

13. *The reason for the omission of Nahor in the account of the migration*

The narrative then describes how Terah and his family left the territory of the Chaldeans, came to Mesopotamia, and made their home in Haran. But it is silent about one of Terah's sons, called Nahor, giving the impression that he did not take him with him. For the narrative says, 'Then Terah took his son Abraham, and his grandson Lot, Haran's son, and Sarah his daughter-in-law, and led them out of the territory of the Chaldeans, on the way to the land of Canaan. And he came into Haran and made his home there.'[72] There is no mention anywhere in the passage of Nahor and his wife Milcah. But later, when Abraham sent his servant to get a wife for his son Isaac, we find this account: 'Then the slave took with him ten of his master's camels, and a part of all his master's property, and he set out for Mesopotamia and the city of Nahor.'[73]

70. Gen. 6, 9. 71. Gen. 11, 27ff.
72. Gen. 11, 31. 73. Gen. 24, 10.

This passage, as well as other evidence in this sacred narrative, shows that Abraham's brother Nahor also left the Chaldean territory and established himself in Mesopotamia where Abraham had made his home with his father Terah. Then why did the Scripture not mention him when Terah set out from the Chaldean people with his family, and made his home in Mesopotamia? For it mentions not only Abraham his son, but also Sarah his daughter-in-law, and Lot his grandson. We can only suppose that Nahor split off from the religion of his father and brother and attached himself to the superstition of the Chaldeans, and that later on he also emigrated either because he repented of his desertion or because he suffered persecution when he fell under suspicion.

For in the book entitled Judith, when Holophernes, the enemy of the Israelites, inquired what that nation was, and whether he ought to make war on them, Achior, leader of the Ammonites, answered,

> Let our lord listen to a word from the mouth of his servant and I will tell you the truth about the people who live near you in this hill country, and no lie will pass the lips of your servant. Now these people are descendants of the Chaldeans, and their former home was in Mesopotamia because they refused to follow the gods of their fathers, who were men of renown in the land of the Chaldeans. They turned off from the way of their parents and adored the God of heaven, whom they had come to know. And the Chaldeans cast them out from the presence of their gods; and they fled to Mesopotamia, and had their home there for many days. Then their God told them to leave their home and go into the land of Canaan; and they made their home there,

and so on, as the narrative of Achior the Ammonite proceeds.[74] This makes it evident that the family of Terah had suffered persecution from the Chaldeans for the true religion, in which they worshipped the one true God.

14. *The age of Terah, who ended his life in Haran*

Now when Terah died in Mesopotamia, where he is said to have reached the age of 205 years, God's promises made to Abraham were already beginning to be revealed. The Scripture says, 'Now the days of Terah in Haran were 205 years; and Terah died in Haran.'[75] But we are not to take this as meaning that he spent all his time there, but only that he completed all the days of his life in Haran, and they came to 205 years. Otherwise it would not be known how many years

74. Judith 5, 5ff. 75. Gen. 11, 32.

Terah lived, since it is not recorded how old he was when he came to Haran. It would be ridiculous to imagine that in the list of generations, where the number of years of each man's life is carefully recorded, it is only the total of years of this man's life which is not put on record. It is true that there are some men recorded in Scripture without any mention of their ages; but that is because they are not in the line in which the chronology is set out according to succeeding generations – whereas the line which leads directly from Adam to Noah, and then from Noah to Abraham does not include anyone without a statement of the number of years he lived.

15. *The time of Abraham's departure from Haran, on God's instructions*

After recording the death of Terah, Abraham's father, the story continues, 'Then the Lord said to Abraham: "Leave your country and your kindred, and your father's house" '[76] and so on. But it is not to be supposed that because this immediately follows Terah's death in the narrative as written, it must therefore have done so in the order of events. In fact, if this were so, an insoluble problem would present itself. For after those words of God to Abraham the Scripture says, 'And Abram departed, as the Lord had bidden him, and Lot went away with him. Now Abram was seventy-five years old when he left Haran.'[77] But how could this be true, if he left Haran after his father's death? For it was when Terah was seventy, as was mentioned above, that he became the father of Abraham: and if we add seventy-five, which was Abraham's age when he left Haran, we get a total of 145 years. This, then, was Terah's age when Abraham left that city of Mesopotamia; for Abraham was then in his seventy-fifth year, and thus his father, who had begotten him in his seventieth year, was, as I have said, 145 years old. It follows that he did not depart *after* his father's death, that is, after his father's lifetime of 205 years; in fact, the year of his departure, since it was the seventy-fifth year of his own life, is found by reckoning to be, without any shadow of doubt, the 145th year of his father's, who had begotten him in his seventieth year.

So we must realize that Scripture is here, as so often, going back to a point that the narrative had already passed; similarly in the earlier passage, after recording Noah's sons, it states that they were, 'according to languages and nations',[78] and yet later, as if this followed in

76. Gen. 12, 1. 77. Gen. 12, 4. 78. Gen. 10, 31.

chronological order, it says, 'and all the earth had one tongue, and there was one speech for all men.'[79] How then could they have been classified 'according to their nations and languages', if there was 'one speech for all men'? It can only be that the narrative goes back to a point it had already passed to make a fresh start.[80] Similarly, then, in this passage Scripture says first, 'The days of Terah in Haran were 205 years, and Terah died in Haran';[81] and then it returns to a point that had been omitted, the omission being due to the desire first to complete that story of Terah which had been begun. 'Then the Lord', it says, 'said to Abram, "Leave your country" ',[82] and so on. And these words of God are followed by, 'And Abram departed, as the Lord had bidden him, and Lot went away with him. Now Abram was seventy-five years old when he left Haran.'[83] This happened, then, when his father was in his hundred and forty-fifth year; for Abraham was then in his seventy-fifth year. The problem can be solved in another way, by assuming that the seventy-five years of Abraham when he left Haran were reckoned from the time of his escape from the 'fire of the Chaldeans',[84] instead of from his birth, as if this escape is to be regarded as his real birthday.

However, the blessed Stephen, when he recounted these events in the Acts of the Apostles, said, 'The God of glory appeared to our father Abraham, when he was in Mesopotamia, before he made his home in Haran, and said to him: "Leave your country and your kindred and the home of your father, and come into the country which I shall show you." '[85] According to these words of Stephen it was not after his father's death that God spoke to Abraham – for Terah died in Haran, where his son Abraham also lived with him – but it was before Abraham made his home in Haran, although he was already in Mesopotamia. Thus he had by now left the Chaldeans. For when Stephen adds, 'Then Abraham departed from the land of the Chaldeans and made his home in Haran', the statement does not refer to what happened after God had spoken to him – for he did not depart from the land of the Chaldeans *after* God's bidding, since Stephen says that God spoke to him when he was in Mesopotamia; it refers to the whole period, 'then' meaning 'after the time when'. Stephen is saying.' After

79. Gen. 11, 1; cf. ch. 4. 80. cf. ch. 5. 81. Gen. 11, 32.
82. Gen. 12, 1. 83. Gen. 12, 4.
84. '*The fire of the Chaldeans*'. There was a Jewish legend, related by Jerome (*Quaest. Hebr. in Gen.*, 19) that Abraham was put in a fire for refusing to worship the Chaldean fire-god. 'Ur of the Chaldeans' becomes, for this story, 'the fire of the Chaldeans'.
85. Acts 7, 2ff.

the time when he departed from the Chaldeans and made his home in Haran'. Similarly, the following statement, 'Then, after his father died, God settled him in this land, where you now live [and where your fathers lived][86] does not mean 'after his father died, he left Haran', but 'after his father died, then God settled him here.'

Thus we are to understand that God had spoken to Abraham when he was in Mesopotamia, before he lived in Haran, but that Abraham had arrived at Haran with his father, in obedience to God's instructions, and had left Haran in his seventy-fifth year, the 145th year of his father's life. We are told that his settling in the country of Canaan, not his leaving Haran, took place after his father's death, since his father was already dead when Abraham bought the land in Canaan of which he then, and not till then, became proprietor. As for the words which God spoke to him when he was already established in Mesopotamia, that is, when he had already left the country of the Chaldeans, 'Leave your land and kindred and your father's home'; this was not a command to remove his body from there – he had done that already – but to tear his mind away from it. For he had not left the place in spirit, if he was still in the grip of the hope and the longing to return; and the tie of this hope and longing needed to be severed, according to God's command and with God's help, and by his own obedience. There is certainly nothing improbable in the supposition that it was when Nahor subsequently followed his father into Haran that Abraham fulfilled the Lord's instructions to leave Haran, taking with him his wife Sarah and his nephew Lot.

16. *The order and nature of God's promises to Abraham*

We now have to consider God's promises to Abraham; for in these the oracles of our God, that is, of the true God, begin to become more evident. These oracles concern the people of his genuine worshippers, which had been foretold by the authority of the prophets. Now the first of these promises is contained in this passage,

> The Lord said to Abram: 'Leave your land and kindred and your father's home and go into the land which I shall show you; and I shall make you into a great nation, and I shall bless you and give you a great name, and you will be blessed; and I shall bless those who bless you and curse those who curse you, and in you all the tribes of the earth will be blessed.[87]

Eusebius decides that this promise was made in Abraham's seventy-

86. The bracketed clause is not in the text of Acts.

87. Gen. 12, 1ff.

fifth year, assuming that Abraham left Haran soon after it had been made, since the Scripture cannot be contradicted, and in Scripture we read, 'Abram was seventy-five years old when he left Haran.' Now if the promise was made in that year, Abraham was evidently already staying with his father in Haran; for he could not have left Haran without having lived there first. Now is this in contradiction to what Stephen says? His words are, 'The God of glory appeared to our father Abraham when he was in Mesopotamia, before he made his home in Haran.' It is not; for we must take it that all these events happened in the same year: God's promise before Abraham made his home in Haran, Abraham's settlement in Haran, and his departure from Haran. And this is not only because Eusebius in his *Chronicle* reckons from the year of this promise and shows that the Exodus from Egypt, when the Law was given, took place 430 years later,[88] but also because the apostle Paul mentions it.[89]

17. *The three outstanding Gentile empires. Assyria already a great power when Abraham was born*

At this period there were three outstanding Gentile empires, in which the city of the earthborn, that is, the society of men who live by man's standards, achieved a notable predominance under the sway of the apostate angels. These three realms were those of Sicyon, Egypt, and Assyria.[90] But the Assyrian Empire was by far the most powerful and exalted of the three. For the famous King Ninus,[91] son of Bel, had subjugated the peoples of the whole of Asia, with the exception of India. When I say 'Asia' here I do not refer to that part which is only one province[92] of greater Asia, but what is called 'the whole of Asia'. Some people[93] have reckoned this as one of the two divisions of the world, though the majority count it as the third part of the whole, which, according to them, consists of Asia, Europe, and Africa. This does not make an equal division. For the part called Asia reaches from the south, through the east, to the north, Europe from the north to the west, and then Africa begins and stretches from the west to the south. Hence the divisions, Europe and Africa, are seen to contain half the world, while Asia by itself contains the other half. The reason why

88. The *Chronicle* of Eusebius (translated and continued by Jerome) gives 505 years from Abraham's birth to the Fxodus, and Abraham's age as seventy-five when the promise was given – hence St Augustine's 430 years.

89. Gal. 3, 17. 90. cf. Bk XVIII, 2ff. 91. cf. Bk IV, 6.

92. i.e. the Roman province of Asia. 93. e.g. Sallust (*Jug.*, 17, 3).

Europe and Africa are treated as two separate parts is that between them the water enters from the Ocean to form the intervening sea, our Great Sea. Therefore, if you divide the world into two parts, the East and the West, Asia will be in one, and both Europe and Africa in the other. That is why the Sicyon realm, of the three outstanding powers of the time, was not subject to the Assyrians, because it was in Europe. Whereas Egypt inevitably came under the power of those who held all Asia, with the sole exception, it is said, of India.

Thus in Assyria the ungodly city exercised predominant power. Its capital was that Babylon whose name, 'Confusion', is most apt for the earthborn city. Ninus was reigning there at this time, after the death of his father Bel, who was the first king there, reigning for sixty-five years. Now his son Ninus, who succeeded to the throne on the death of his father, reigned fifty-two years; and he had been on the throne for forty-three years when Abraham was born. This was about 1,200 years before the foundation of Rome, the second Babylonia, as it were, the Babylonia of the West.

18. *God's second promise: the land of Canaan*

And so Abraham departed from Haran in his seventy-fifth year, when his father was 145. With Lot, his nephew, and his wife Sarah, he reached the land of Canaan, and arrived eventually at Shechem, where he again received an oracle from God, which is thus described: 'Then the Lord appeared to Abram, and said to him: "I shall give this land to your seed." '[94] There is nothing said here about that seed in respect of which he became the father of all nations; the only seed mentioned is that by which he is the father of the one nation of Israel; for it was this seed that took possession of that land.

19. *Sarah's chastity safeguarded by God in Egypt*

Then Abraham built an altar there and called upon the name of the Lord. After that he left the place and lived in the desert; and from there he was compelled by stress of famine to go into Egypt. In Egypt he called his wife his sister;[95] and this was no lie, for she was that also, because she was closely related by blood. In the same way Lot, who was similarly related, being his brother's son, was called his brother. And so Abraham said nothing of her being his wife; he did not deny it. Thus he entrusted his wife's chastity to God, and, as a

94. Gen. 12, 7. 95. Gen. 12, 10–20.

man, took precautions against man's treachery; since if he had not taken all possible precautions against danger he could have been testing God, rather than putting his hope in him. But on this subject I have said all that needs saying in rebutting the false criticisms of Faustus the Manichean.[96] In fact Abraham's trust in God was confirmed by the event. For Pharaoh, king of Egypt, who had taken her as his wife, was grievously afflicted and restored her to her husband. In this connection it would be utterly wrong for us to suppose that she had been polluted by intercourse with another; for it is much more probable that Pharaoh was prevented by his great affliction from such intercourse.

20. *The separation of Lot and Abraham by amicable agreement*

On the return of Abraham from Egypt to the place from which he had come, his nephew Lot left him to go into the land of Sodom, without any breach of affection. In fact they had become rich, and had begun to have many herdsmen for their flocks. These men quarrelled among themselves, and Abraham and Lot took this course to avoid disputes and fighting between their households. For in the way of human nature this might have given rise to quarrels between themselves also. These are the words which Abraham then addressed to Lot to obviate this unpleasantness: 'Let there not be any quarrel between you and me, and between my herdsmen and yours, for we are kinsmen. Look, is not the whole land in front of you? Leave me. If you go to the left, I shall go to the right; if you go to the right, I shall go to the left.'[97] This was perhaps the start of the peaceable custom among men whereby when any landed property is to be shared, the elder makes the division and the younger has the choice.

21. *God's third promise: the land of Canaan in perpetuity*

Thus Abraham and Lot parted company and settled in separate homes, not because of a quarrel – that would have been a disgrace – but because of the need to support their households. Abraham was now in the land of Canaan, while Lot was living among the men of Sodom; and now God spoke to Abraham in his third oracle,

Lift your eyes and from the place where you are now look towards the

96. *Adv. Faust. Man.*, 22, 36. 97. Gen. 13, 8f.

north and the south and the east, and towards the sea; for all the land which you see I shall give to you and your seed for ever, and I will make your seed like the sands of the earth. If any man can number the sands, your seed also will be numbered. Arise and walk through the length and breadth of the land, because I shall give it to you.[98]

It is not clearly disclosed whether this promise includes also the promise by which Abraham became the father of all nations. For the words, 'I shall make your seed like the sands of the earth', might seem to connect it with the former promise. But we have here an instance of the figure of speech called 'hyperbole' by the Greeks; it is surely a figurative rather than a literal statement. Indeed, no student of Scripture can have any doubt that Scripture often employs this figure, as it does the other tropes. Now this trope, or figure of speech, occurs when what is said is far in excess of the facts referred to in the statement. No one could fail to see how incomparably greater is the number of the sands than the number of all human beings can possibly be, from Adam himself to the end of the world. How much more numerous, then, are they than the seed of Abraham, meaning not only that posterity of his which belongs to the race of Israel, but also those who are and will be his descendants, by following the example of his faith, in all nations throughout the whole world! This seed is certainly represented by a mere few, in comparison with the multitude of the ungodly; and yet these few make up an innumerable multitude of their own, and this is expressed, in hyperbole, by 'the sands of the earth'. This multitude, to be sure, which is promised to Abraham is innumerable to men, but not to God; for to God not even the sands of the earth are beyond counting.

Since it is not only the nation of Israel to whom this promise is made, but the whole seed of Abraham, referring rather to spiritual than physical descendants, then these are more fittingly compared to the multitude of the sands, and so we can understand that the promise of both these posterities is given in this passage. But the reason for my statement that there is some ambiguity here is that the nation physically descended from Abraham through his grandson Jacob increased to such a multitude that it has filled almost all parts of the world. Because of this it would have been possible for this nation itself to be compared, in hyperbole, to the multitudes of the sands, since even this race, by itself, is beyond man's reckoning.

At any rate, no one doubts that the only land referred to here is the country called Canaan. Yet the statement, 'I shall give it to you and to

98. Gen. 13, 14ff.

your seed for ever', may puzzle some people, if they take 'for ever' (*usque in saeculum*) to mean 'for eternity'.[99] If, on the other hand, they accept the word *saeculum* here in accordance with our confident belief that the beginning of the future era (*saeculum*) starts with the end of the present era, there will be nothing to puzzle them. For even though the Israelites have been expelled from Jerusalem, they still remain in other cities of the land of Canaan, and they will remain there to the end. And the whole land, being inhabited by Christians, is itself the seed of Abraham.

22. *Abraham's victory over the enemies of Sodom; the rescue of Lot; and the blessing of Melchizedek*

On receiving this promise Abraham moved on and stayed in another place in the same land, Hebron, near the Oak of Mamre.[100] After that, there was the war of five kings against four, when the enemy attacked the men of Sodom. Sodom was defeated and Lot was among those captured by the enemy. Then Abraham procured his release, bringing with him to the battle 318 men, his own household dependants, and winning a victory for the kings of Sodom. He refused to take off any of the spoils when the king for whom he had won the victory, offered them to him.[101] But he received at that time a public blessing from Melchizedek, who was the priest of the Most High God. Many important things are written about Melchizedek in the epistle entitled To the Hebrews,[102] which the majority attribute to apostle Paul, though some deny the attribution. Here we certainly see the first manifestation of the sacrifice which is now offered to God by Christians in the whole world, in which is fulfilled what was said in prophecy, long after this event, to Christ who was yet to come in the flesh: 'You are a priest for all eternity, in the line of Melchizedek.'[103] Not, it is to be observed, in the line of Aaron, for that line was to be abolished when the events prefigured by these shadows came to the light of day.

99. cf. ch. 26. 100. Gen. 13, 18. 101. Gen. 14.

102. Hebr. 7. The Pauline authorship of the epistle was generally accepted in the East by the third century, though Origen doubted it. The West in general rejected the attribution, and in North Africa Barnabas was said to be the author.

103. Ps. 110, 4.

23. *The promise that Abraham's posterity would equal the number of the stars; Abraham's faith, and his consequent justification, before circumcision*

It was at this time that the word of the Lord came to Abraham in a vision. The Lord promised him protection and an exceedingly great reward; and then Abraham, concerned about his posterity, said that a man called Eliezer, a servant born in his household, was likely to be his heir. Straightway an heir was promised him, not that house-slave, but one who was to come from Abraham himself; and once again he was promised an innumerable seed, not like the sands of the earth, but like the stars of heaven.[104] And here it seems that the promise is of a posterity exalted in heavenly felicity; for in respect of mere number, the stars will not bear comparison with the sands of the earth. Although it might be maintained that this comparison is similar to the other, in that the stars also cannot be numbered, because we have to believe that not all of them can be seen by us. For the keener the observer's sight, the more stars he sees; and so we are justified in supposing that some stars are invisible even to the keenest eyes, quite apart from those stars which, we are assured, rise and set in another part of the world far removed from us. While as for all those who boast that they have made a comprehensive list of the whole number of the stars, Aratus,[105] for example, and Eudoxus,[106] and any others, the authority of this book treats them with contempt.

This, it should be noticed, is the context of the statement which the Apostle recalls for the purpose of emphasizing the grace of God: 'Abraham believed in God, and this was accounted to him for righteousness.'[107] Paul's intention was to prevent the circumcised from boasting, and from refusing to admit the uncircumcised peoples to faith in Christ. For at the time when this happened, when Abraham's faith was accounted to him for righteousness, Abraham had not yet been circumcised.

24. *The meaning of Abraham's sacrifice*

In the same vision, when God was speaking to Abraham, he said this also to him: 'I am your God, who brought you from the land of the Chaldeans, to give you this land so that you may inherit it.'[108] Then

104. Gen. 15, 1–5. 105. Astronomer-poet, of third century B.C.
106. Astronomer of fourth century B.C. 107. Gen. 15, 6; Gal. 3, 6; Rom. 4, 3.
108. Gen. 15, 7.

Abraham asked God by what token he should know that he would inherit it; and God replied, ' "Take a heifer of three years old, and a she-goat and a ram of three years old, and a dove and a pigeon." Then he took all these and divided them in half, and put the halves facing each other: but he did not divide the birds. 'And', as the Scripture says,

> birds came down on the carcasses which had been divided; and Abraham sat there by them. Now about sunset a horror assailed Abraham, and, behold, a dark and mighty dread fell upon him. And he was told: 'You will know for a certainty that your seed will be strangers in a land not their own, and men will reduce them to slavery and afflict them for four hundred years. But I shall judge the nation to which they are enslaved; and after that they will depart with many possessions. You, for your part, will go to your fathers, nourished in peace in a great old age. But in the fourth generation they will return to this place. For the sins of the Amorites are not yet completed, up to the present time.' Now when the sun was about to set, a flame appeared, and behold, a smoking furnace and burning torches, which passed along between the divided carcasses. On that day the Lord God arranged a covenant with Abram, saying: 'To your seed I shall give this land, from the river of Egypt, as far as the great river, the river Euphrates, the Kenites, the Kenizzites, the Kadmonites, the Hittites, the Perizzites, the Rephaims, the Amorites, the Canaanites, the Girgashites and the Jebusites.'[109]

All these things were done and said in a vision sent by God. Now it would be tedious to discuss every detail and explain every meaning, and it would go beyond the purpose of this work. Therefore we need to understand only what suffices for our inquiry. After the statement that Abraham believed in God and it was accounted to him for righteousness, we observe that he did not fail in his faith in saying, 'Lord God, by what token shall I know that I shall inherit it?' – referring, of course, to the promised inheritance of the land. For he did not say, 'How am I to know?', implying that he did not yet believe. He said, 'By what token shall I know?' in the hope that he might be given some representation of what he already believed, by which he could realize in what way it was to be effected. In the same way there is no suggestion of lack of faith in the Virgin Mary when she says, 'How will this happen, since I do not know a man?'[110] She was convinced that it would happen, but she asked in what way it was to be effected; and when she asked this, she was told. Thus on this occasion also a symbolic representation was presented in the form of the

109. Gen. 15, 18ff. (The Old Latin, translating LXX). 110. Luke 1, 34.

animals, the heifer, the she-goat, the ram, and the two birds, the dove and the pigeon, so that he might know that the event about whose future happening he had no doubt, would come about in a way suggested by those symbols.

Thus the heifer may have symbolized the people placed under the yoke of the Law, and the she-goat the same people in their future state of sin, the ram the same people as destined to reign. Those animals are specified as three years old because the important eras are from Adam to Noah, from Noah to Abraham, from Abraham to David, who, after Saul's rejection, was the first man established on the throne of Israel by the will of the Lord.[111] Hence it was in this third period, extending from Abraham to David, that the people attained adult status, in what may be called the third stage of its life. Or there may be some other more suitable application of the symbolism of these animals. However that may be, I have no shadow of doubt that Abraham's spiritual offspring are foreshadowed by the addition of the dove and the pigeon.

The reason for the statement that 'he did not divide the birds' is that carnal beings are divided among themselves, whereas spiritual beings are not divided in any way, whether, like the turtle-dove, they keep away from the busy world of human affairs, or, like the pigeon, pass their time in the midst of those activities. Both those birds, however, are without guile and harmless, thus signifying that in the people of Israel, to which that land was to be given, there would be individual sons of the promise and heirs of the kingdom, destined to continue in eternal felicity. As for the birds descending on the divided carcasses, they do not stand for anything good; they represent the spirits of this lower air, looking for their own special food, as it were, in this division of carnal creatures. Further, the fact that Abraham sat by them symbolizes that even amidst those divisions of carnal creatures the truly faithful will persevere to the end. And the horror that assailed Abraham at sunset and the dark and mighty dread signify that about the end of this era there will be great distress and tribulation coming on the faithful. In the Gospel the Lord says about this, 'For there will be great tribulation at that time, such tribulation as there has not been since the beginning.'[112]

Then there are the words spoken to Abraham: 'You will know for a certainty that your seed will be strangers in a land not their own, and men will reduce them to slavery, and afflict them for four hundred years.'[113] This was a clear prophecy about the people of

111. cf. 1 Sam. 15. 112. Matt. 24, 21. 113. Gen. 11, 32.

Israel who were to be slaves in Egypt; not that they were to spend 400 years in the same state of servitude under the Egyptians, enduring affliction at their hands. The prophecy was rather that this would happen in the course of 400 years. For the Scripture says of Terah, Abraham's father, 'The days of Terah in Haran were 205 years', not because all those years were spent in Haran, but because they were completed there; and in the same way in this passage the introduction of the statement, 'and they will reduce them to slavery, and will afflict them for 400 years', means that this period of years was completed in that affliction, not that the whole of it was passed in that situation. 400 years, in fact, is given as a round figure, whereas the actual period was somewhat longer, whether it is reckoned from the time of those promises to Abraham, or from the birth of Isaac, because he was the 'seed of Abraham', about which these predictions are made. For, as I said above, 430 years are reckoned from Abraham's seventy-fifth year, when the first promise was given, down to the departure of Israel from Egypt. And in recalling those events the Apostle says, 'Now this is what I am saying; that the law, made 430 years later, does not invalidate the covenant confirmed by God, so as to make the promise void.'[114] This shows that those 430 years could at that time be called 400, because they were not much more than that. How much more naturally could they be so called when a considerable number of them had already gone by at the time when this demonstration and these words were given to Abraham in a vision, or when Isaac was born to his father, now a hundred years old, twenty-five years after the first promise, when of those 430 years only 405 were left, which God chose to call 400. As for the rest of the substance of God's prediction, no one can doubt that it all refers to the Israelite people.

But then follows this description: 'Now when the sun was about to set, a flame appeared, and behold, a smoking furnace and burning torches, which passed along between the divided carcasses.' For the affliction of the City of God, such an affliction as has never happened before, which is to be expected in the future under the power of Antichrist, is symbolized by Abraham's 'dark and mighty dread' just before sunset, that is when the end of the world is approaching. In the same way at sunset, that is, at the very end, this fire symbolizes the day of judgement as it separates the carnal men who are to be saved by fire from those who are to be condemned to punishment in the fire.[115]

There follows the covenant made with Abraham: and this clearly

114. Gal. 3, 17. 115. cf. 1 Cor. 3, 12–15; and cf. Bk XXI, 26.

specifies the land of Canaan, naming eleven rivers there, from the river of Egypt to the great river Euphrates. We can see that this does not mean from the great river of Egypt, the Nile, but from the small river which divides Egypt from Palestine, where there is a town called Rhinocorura.[116]

25. *Hagar, Sarah's maidservant, chosen by Sarah as Abraham's concubine*

Then follows the period of Abraham's sons, one by Hagar the maidservant, and the other by Sarah the free woman. I have already spoken about these in the last book.[117] Now in view of the facts of the case Abraham is in no way to be branded with guilt in the matter of this concubine.[118] For he made use of her for the procreation of offspring, not for the satisfaction of lust: not to insult his wife, but rather to obey her; for she believed it would be a consolation for her own barrenness if she made her maidservant's fertile womb her own, by her own choice, since she could not do so by nature. Thus as a wife she availed herself of that right referred to by the Apostle when he says, 'In the same way also the man has no authority over his body, but the woman has',[119] in order to produce a child from another when she could not do so from herself. There is here no lascivious desire, nothing degraded or shameful. The maidservant is handed over to the husband by the wife for the sake of offspring, and she is received by the husband for the sake of offspring. The aim of both of them is not guilty self-indulgence but the natural fruit of the union. Finally, when the pregnant servant flouted her barren mistress, and Sarah, in feminine jealousy, chose to blame her husband, even in that situation Abraham showed that he had been not a slavish lover but a free parent, and that in respect of Hagar he had safeguarded the reputation of his wife Sarah, having acted not to gratify his own sensuality but to carry out his wife's decision. He had not sought Hagar but had taken her; he had come to her, but he had not become attached to her; he had given her his seed, but not his love. For he said, 'Look, your maid is at your disposal; employ her as you wish.'[120] What a true man he was, treating women like a true man; treating his wife temperately, her maid obediently, treating no woman intemperately.

116. The modern El Arish.
117. cf. Bk.XV, 2.
118. As the Manicheans alleged; cf. *Adv. Faust. Man.*, 22, 30.
119. 1 Cor. 7, 4.
120. Gen. 16, 6.

26. *The promise of a son to Sarah, to be father of nations, the promise sealed by circumcision*

After this, Ishmael was born of Hagar; and Abraham might have supposed that in him there was the fulfilment of the promise given when he had decided to adopt his house-born slave, and God said, 'This man will not be your heir; but he who will issue from you, he will be your heir.'[121] Therefore, to prevent the supposition that this promise had been fulfilled in the maid-servant's son, when he was already ninety-nine years old, the Lord appeared to him and said to him: 'I am God; be pleasing in my sight, and be without blame, and I shall establish my covenant between me and you, and I shall increase you exceedingly.' And Abram fell on his face. Then God spoke to him and said: 'As for me, here is my covenant with you, and you will be the father of a multitude of nations. And your name will no longer be Abram, but Abraham,[122] because I have appointed you as the father of many nations. And I shall increase you most exceedingly, and make you into nations, and kings will issue from you. And I shall establish my covenant between me and you and your seed after you, for their generations, to be an eternal covenant, so that I shall be your God, and the God of your descendants after you. And to you and to your descendants after you I shall give the land in which you are dwelling, all the land of Canaan for an eternal possession; and I shall be their God.' Then God said to Abraham: 'As for you, you will keep my covenant, you and your seed after you in their descendants. Now this is the covenant which you will keep between me and you and your descendants after you in their generations: Every male of yours shall be circumcised; and you shall be circumcised in the flesh of your foreskin, and this will be a token of the covenant between me and you. The boy of eight days shall be circumcised, every male in your generations. The slave born in your house and the slave bought from anyone of another nation, who is not of your seed, shall be circumcised, the house-slave and the bought slave; and my covenant will be in your flesh, to be an eternal covenant. And the male child who is not circumcised, who is not circumcised in the flesh of his foreskin on the eighth day, his soul will perish from his people, because he has broken my covenant.'

And God said to Abraham: 'As for Sarai your wife, her name will not be called Sarai, but Sarah will be her name.[123] Moreover, I shall bless her and give you a son by her, and I shall bless him, and he shall become nations, and kings of nations will issue from him.' Then Abraham bowed down to the ground; and he laughed and said in his heart: 'Will a child be born to

121. Gen. 15, 4.

122. *Abram*='the Father is exalted'; *Abraham* is meaningless, but explained here by assonance with *hāmōn*='multitude'.

123. *Sarah* = 'princess': *Sarai* is obscure.

me, at the age of a hundred years? And will Sarah bear a child, at the age of ninety?' Then Abraham said to God: 'Let Ishmael here live in your sight!' But God said: 'It is true. Sarah your wife will bear you a son, and you will call his name Isaac. And I shall establish my covenant for him as an eternal covenant, to be his God and the God of his descendants after him. While as for Ishmael, see, I have listened to you; see, I have blessed him, and I shall increase him and multiply him greatly. He will be the father of twelve nations, and I shall make him into a great nation. But I shall establish my covenant with Isaac, the son that Sarah will bear to you at this time next year.'[124]

Here are more explicit promises about the calling of the Gentiles in Isaac, that is, in the son of the promise, in whom grace, rather than nature, is symbolized, because he is promised as the son of an old man and a barren old woman. For though God is also at work in the natural process of procreation, nevertheless, where God's operation is manifest, in a case where nature is decayed and failing, there his grace is more clearly recognizable. And since this was going to happen not by way of generation but by regeneration, that is why circumcision was commanded at this time, when a son was promised from Sarah. As for the fact that God orders the circumcision not only of all the sons, but of the house-born slaves and the purchased slaves as well, this is evidence that this grace pertains to all men. For what does circumcision symbolize but the renewal of nature by the sloughing off of old age? And what does the eighth day symbolize but Christ, who rose again after the completion of seven days, that is, after the Sabbath? The names of the parents are also changed. 'Newness' is the note struck in every detail; and the new covenant is presented, in a veiled manner, in the old. For what is the 'Old Testament' but a concealed form of the new? And what is the 'New Testament' but the revelation of the old? Abraham's laughter is the exultation of the thankfulness, not the derision of incredulity. As for the words which he said in his heart, 'Is a son to be born to me, at the age of a hundred years? And is Sarah to bear a child, at the age of ninety?', these are not expressions of doubt, but of wonder.

If anyone is worried by the statement, 'And to you and your seed after you I shall give the land in which you are dwelling, all the land of Canaan for an eternal possession', and is puzzled about how this may be taken as being fulfilled, or whether its fulfilment is still to be awaited, since no earthly possession whatsoever can be eternal for any nation whatsoever; he should know that 'eternal' is used by our trans-

124. Gen. 17, 1–21.

lators to represent the Greek *aiônios*, which comes from the Greek word for 'age', *aiōn* being the Greek equivalent of the Latin *saeculum*. But the Latin translators have not ventured to render it by 'secular', for fear of conveying a very different meaning. Many things, in fact, are called 'secular' which take place in this age (*saeculum*) in such a manner that they pass away even in a brief time. Whereas when a thing is called *aiônios* it means either that it has no end or that it lasts to the end of this age.

27. *The perishing of the male child, if not circumcised on the eighth day*

Another question may cause perplexity. How are we to interpret the statement in this passage that 'the male child who is not circumcised in the flesh of the foreskin on the eighth day, his soul will perish from his people, because he has broken my covenant'?[125] Now this is in no way the fault of the infant whose soul is said to be doomed to perish; and it is not the infant himself who has broken the covenant of God; it is his elders, who have not taken care to circumcise him. That is, unless it is because even infants have broken the covenant, not in consequence of any particular act in their own life but in consequence of the origin which is common to all mankind, since all have broken God's covenant in that one man in whom all sinned.[126] Now it is true that many covenants are called God's covenants, apart from the two principal ones, the Old and New, which anyone may get to know by reading them. But the first covenant, made with the first man, is certainly this: 'On the day you eat, you will surely die.'[127] Hence the statement in the book called Ecclesiasticus. 'All flesh grows old like a garment. For the covenant from the beginning is, "You will surely die." '[128] Now, seeing that a more explicit law was given later, and the Apostle says, 'Where there is no law, there is no law-breaking',[129] how can the psalm be true, where we read, 'I have counted all sinners on earth as law-breakers'?[130] It can only be true on the assumption that those who are held bound by any sin are guilty of a breach of some law.

Therefore if even infants, as the true faith holds, are born sinners,

125. Gen. 17, 14.

126. cf. Rom. 5, 12. (The Latin versions give *in quo* ('in whom') for the Greek ἐφ' ᾧ. The English versions interpret it as 'in that', which is almost certainly correct.)

127. Gen. 2, 17. 128. Ecclus. 14, 17. 129. Rom. 4, 15. 130. Ps. 119, 119.

not on their own account, but in virtue of their origin (and hence we acknowledge the necessity for them of the grace of remission of sins), then it follows that just as they are sinners, they are recognized as breakers of the Law which was given in paradise. And so both passages in Scripture are true, 'I have counted all sinners on earth as lawbreakers', and 'Where there is no law, there is no law-breaking.' Thus the process of birth rightly brings perdition on the infant because of the original sin by which God's covenant was first broken, unless the rebirth sets him free; and circumcision was instituted as a sign of rebirth. Therefore, those divine words must be interpreted as saying, in effect, 'He who has not been reborn, his soul will perish from his people, because he broke God's covenant' when, in Adam, he himself also sinned, along with all the rest of mankind.

For if God had said 'because he had broken *this* covenant of mine' we should be forced to take it as referring exclusively to circumcision. As it is, since he did not explicitly say what sort of covenant the infant has broken, we are free to take it as referring to that covenant whose infringement could be connected with the child. If, on the other hand, anyone maintains that the saying applies exclusively to circumcision, on the ground that it was in the failure to be circumcised that the infant broke the covenant of God, he will have to find some way of stating it which could be interpreted, without absurdity, as meaning that the child has broken the covenant because it has been broken in his case, though not broken by him. Yet even so it must be observed that it would be unjust that the soul of an infant should perish, when the child itself was not responsible for the neglect of circumcision, if it were not that the child was under the bondage of the original sin.

28. *The change of names of Abraham and Sarah; the fertility granted to them*

Now after this great promise, so clearly expressed, had been made to Abraham, the pair are thereafter no longer called Abram and Sarai in the Scriptures, as before, but Abraham and Sarah, as we have called them from the start, since these are the names in universal use. The promise was in these explicit terms, 'I have appointed you as the father of many nations; and I shall increase you most exceedingly and make you into nations, and kings will come from you. And I will give you a son by Sarah, and I will bless him, and he will become nations, and kings of nations will issue from him.'[131] This is a promise we

131. Gen. 17, 5f.; 16.

now see fulfilled in Christ. The reason for the change of Abraham's name is thus given, 'Because I have appointed you as the father of many nations.' This must then be taken to be the meaning of Abraham, whereas Abram, his former name, is translated 'exalted father'.[132] No reason, however, is given for the change of Sarah's name, but according to the statement of the writers who have recorded the meanings of the Hebrew names contained in the sacred writings Sarai means 'my princess', while Sarah means 'strength'. Hence the statement in the Epistle to the Hebrews, 'By faith also Sarah herself received strength to deliver an offspring.'[133]

For both of them had reached old age, on the evidence of Scripture, while Sarah was also sterile, and her menstruation had ceased, so that she was no longer capable of childbirth even if she had not been sterile. Moreover, even if a woman is advanced in years, so long as her normal menstruation continues, she can bear a child to a young man, but not to an old man; while the older man is still capable of begetting a child, but only by a young woman, as Abraham was able to have children by Keturah, after the death of Sarah, because he found her still in the vigour of youth. This, then, is what the Apostle emphasizes as miraculous, and this is why he says Abraham's body was already 'dead',[134] because by that time he was not capable of begetting a child from any and every woman who still had some final period of fertility left. For we must understand that his body was 'dead' in a particular respect, not in every way. For if it was dead in all respects it would not be the elderly body of a living man, but the corpse of a dead man. Although the problem is usually solved by the assumption that Abraham ('dead' as he was) had children by Keturah because the gift of procreation which he received from the Lord remained after the death of his wife. Nevertheless, the solution of the difficulty which I have adopted seems to me preferable for this reason: that although an old man, a centenarian, certainly cannot have a child by any woman in these days, this was not true at that period, when men were still living so long that a hundred years did not reduce a man to the decrepitude of senility.

132. cf. ch. 26n.

133. Heb. 11, 11. St Augustine's impossible explanation of *Sarah* seems to be an inference from this text; cf. 20n.

134. Rom. 4, 19; cf. Hebr. 11, 12.

29. *The appearance of the Lord to Abraham in the shape of three men, or angels, at the Oak of Mamre*

God appeared again to Abraham by the Oak of Mamre in the shape of three men, who, without doubt, were angels, although some people suppose that one of them was the Lord Christ – maintaining that he had been visible even before he clothed himself in flesh. It is, to be sure, within the capacity of divine and invisible power, of incorporeal and immutable nature to appear to mortal sight, without any change in itself, not appearing in its own being, but by means of something subordinate to itself – and what is not subordinate? Now the reason for the assertion that one of those three was Christ is that Abraham, seeing three men, addressed the Lord in the singular (for the narrative says, 'And behold three men stood by him, and seeing them he ran forward from the door of his tent to meet them, and he prostrated himself and said: "Lord if I have found favour in your sight ..." ')[135] But if this is so, why do they not observe this point also, that two of those men had gone to effect the destruction of the men of Sodom, while Abraham was still speaking to one of them, calling him Lord, and begging him not to destroy the just man along with the wicked in Sodom?

Moreover, Lot received those men in the same way, and he also called them Lord, in the singular, when he talked with them. For he first addressed them in the plural, when he said, 'Look, my lords, turn aside into your servant's house';[136] and so he does in the rest of the conversation in this passage. And yet later on the narrative continues,

> And the angels took his hand, and the hand of his wife, and the hands of his two daughters, because the Lord was going to spare them. And it happened that, as soon as they had brought him out of doors, they said: 'Save your life, do not look back, and do not stop anywhere in this district; go for safety on the mountains so that you may not be caught.' Then Lot answered: 'Lord, I beseech you, since your servant has found mercy in your sight ...'[137]

Then after these words the Lord uses the singular in his reply, although he was in the two angels, when he said, 'Behold, I have marvelled at your face ...'[138] Hence it is much more likely that Abraham recognized the Lord in the persons of the three men, as also did Lot in the two, and that they spoke to him in the singular, even

135. Gen. 18, 2f.
136. Gen. 19, 2.
137. Gen. 19, 16ff.
138. Gen. 19, 21 (LXX).

though they thought their visitors to be merely men. And their only reason for taking them in was to minister to their wants on the assumption that they were mortals in need of refreshment. But there was, we may be sure, something extraordinary about them, so that although they appeared as men, those who offered them hospitality could not doubt that the Lord was in them, as he is wont to be in the prophets. And this explains why their hosts sometimes addressed them in the plural and sometimes in the singular, to address the Lord in their persons. That they were angels is the testimony of Scripture not only in this book of Genesis where these events are described, but also in the Epistle to the Hebrews, which says, when praising hospitality: 'By this some men have entertained angels unawares.'[139]

Thus the promise of a son, Isaac, to be born of Sarah, was again conveyed to Abraham by these three men; and the divine assurance was also given him in these words: 'Abraham will become a great and populous nation, and all the nations of the earth will be blessed in him.'[140] Here were the two promises in the briefest and yet the amplest terms: the promise of Israel according to the flesh, and the promise of all nations according to faith.

30. *Lot's escape from Sodom: Abimelech and the chastity of Sarah*

After the giving of this promise, when Lot had escaped from Sodom, a fiery storm came down from heaven and the whole territory of that ungodly city was reduced to ashes. It was a place where sexual promiscuity among males had grown into a custom so prevalent that it received the kind of sanction generally afforded by law to other activities. But the punishment of the men of Sodom was a foretaste of the divine judgement to come. And there is a special significance in the fact that those who were being rescued by the angels were forbidden to look back. Does it not tell us that we must not return in thought to the old life, which is sloughed off when a man is reborn by grace, if we look to escape the final judgement? Furthermore, Lot's wife was rooted to the spot where she looked back; and by being turned into salt she supplied a kind of seasoning for the faithful – a seasoning of wisdom to make them beware of following her example.[141]

After this Abraham again used the device in respect of his wife that he had employed in Egypt; this time it was at Gerar, in relation to Abimelech, the king of that city; and once more Sarah was restored to

139. Hebr. 13, 2. 140. Gen. 18, 8. 141. Gen. 19, 24ff.

him inviolate. And here indeed when the king reproached him, and asked why he had concealed the fact that she was his wife, and had called her his sister, Abraham revealed the nature of his fears, and added, 'She is in fact my sister through her father, though not through her mother',[142] because she was Abraham's sister by his father, through whom she was in this close relation. We observe that her beauty was such that even at that age she was found attractive.

31. *The birth of Isaac, and the meaning of his name*

After this a son was born to Abraham from Sarah, in fulfilment of the promise; and he gave him the name Isaac, which means 'laughter'.[143] This was because when this son was promised to him, his father had laughed in wonderment and joy;[144] and when the promise was repeated by the three men, his mother too had laughed in joy that was mixed with incredulity. However, when the angel reproached her because her laughter, though it showed joy, did not show complete faith, she was afterwards strengthened in faith by the same angel. This is how the boy received his name. And indeed, when Isaac was born and was given that name, Sarah showed that her laughter had no suggestion of scorn or derision but was rather a joyful expression of gladness, for she said, 'The Lord has provided laughter for me; for anyone who hears of it will rejoice with me.'[145] But after a very short time the maidservant was expelled from the house with her son, and according to the Apostle the two covenants, the old and the new, are symbolized here, where Sarah figures as the heavenly Jerusalem, that is, the City of God.[146]

32. *Abraham's obedience and faith tested. The death of Sarah*

It would be too tedious to give a detailed narrative of all these events; but in the course of them Abraham was tempted in the matter of the sacrifice of his beloved son Isaac, so that his dutiful obedience might be put to the proof, and be brought to the knowledge, not of God, but of future ages. It is to be observed that temptation does not always imply anything blameworthy, since the testing that brings approval is a matter for rejoicing. And as a general rule, there is no other way in which the human spirit can acquire self-knowledge except by trying its own strength in answering, not in word but in deed, what may be

142. Gen. 20, 12. 143. *Isaac* in Hebrew means 'he laughs'.
144. Gen. 17, 16. 145. Gen. 21, 6. 146. cf. Gal. 4, 22–6.

called the interrogation of temptation. And then, if God acknowledges the task performed, there is an example of a spirit truly devoted to God, with the solidity given by the strength of grace, instead of the inflation of the empty boast.

Abraham, we can be sure, could never have believed that God delights in human victims; and yet the thunder of a divine command must be obeyed without argument. However, Abraham is to be praised in that he believed, without hesitation, that his son would rise again when he had been sacrificed. For when he had refused to accede to his wife's wish that the maidservant and her son should be turned out of the house, God had said to him, 'Through Isaac your descendants will carry on your name.' Now it is true that this is followed by the statement, 'And I will make of the son of the maidservant a mighty nation, because he is your son.' What then is the meaning of the words, 'Through Isaac your descendants will carry on your name', seeing that God also called Ishmael Abraham's seed? The Apostle explains the force of 'Through Isaac your descendants will carry on your name' in this way: 'It does not mean that the sons of the flesh are the sons of God: it is the sons of the promise who are counted as his descendants.'[147] Consequently, the sons of the promise are called in Isaac to be the descendants of Abraham, that is they are called by grace and gathered together in Christ. The devout father therefore clung to this promise faithfully, and since it had to be fulfilled through the son whom God ordered to be slain, he did not doubt that a son who could be granted to him when he had ceased to hope could also be restored to him after he had been sacrificed.

This is the interpretation we find in the Epistle to the Hebrews, and it is explained as follows: 'By faith Abraham, when tested, went before Isaac and offered his only son, who received the promises, to whom it was said: "In Isaac your seed will be called", considering that God is able to raise men from the dead.' Then he went on, 'Hence he brought him also to serve as a type.'[148] A type of whom? It can only be of him of whom the Apostle says, 'He did not spare his own son, but handed him over for us all.'[149] This is why, as the Lord carried his cross, so Isaac himself carried to the place of sacrifice the wood on which he too was to be placed. Moreover, after the father had been prevented from striking his son, since it was not right that Isaac should be slain, who was the ram whose immolation completed the sacrifice by blood of symbolic significance? Bear in mind that when

147. Rom. 9, 8. 148. Hebr. 11, 17ff. (in a variant version).
149. Rom. 8, 32.

Abraham saw the ram it was caught by the horns in a thicket. Who, then, was symbolized by that ram but Jesus, crowned with Jewish thorns[150] before he was offered in sacrifice?

But now let us turn our attention to the divine words spoken by the angel. For the Scripture says,

> And Abraham stretched out his hand to take the knife to slay his son. Then the angel of the Lord called to him from heaven and said: 'Abraham.' And he said: 'Here I am.' And the angel said: 'Do not lay your hand on the boy, nor do anything to him; for now I have the assurance that you fear your God, and you have not spared your beloved son, for my sake.'[151]

'Now I have the assurance' means 'Now I have made it known', for God was not in ignorance before this happened. After that, when the ram had been sacrificed instead of his son Isaac, 'Abraham', we are told, 'called the name of the place "The Lord saw", so that people say today: "The Lord appeared on the mountain." '[152] Just as 'Now I have the assurance' stood for 'Now I have made it known', here 'The Lord saw' stands for 'The Lord appeared', that is, he made himself visible.

> Then the angel of the Lord called to Abraham from heaven a second time, saying: 'I have sworn by myself' says the Lord 'because you have carried out this bidding and have not spared your beloved son for my sake, that I shall certainly bless you, and I shall assuredly multiply your posterity like the stars of the sky, and like the sand that stretches by the lip of the sea. And your posterity will possess by inheritance the cities of your enemies, and all the nations of the earth will be blessed in your descendants, because you have obeyed my voice.'[153]

In this way the promise of the calling of the nations in Abraham's descendants, after the whole burnt-offering, by which Christ is symbolized, was confirmed also by an oath given by God. For he had often given promises, but never before had he taken an oath. Now what is the oath of the true and truthful God but the confirmation of his promise, and a kind of rebuke to the unbelieving?

After this, Sarah died, in the 127th year of her life, and the 137th year of the life of her husband. For he was ten years her senior in age, as he himself declared when he was promised a son by her, when he said, 'Is a son to be born to me, at the age of a hundred years? And is Sarah to bear a child at the age of ninety?'[154] Then Abraham bought a piece of land, in which he buried his wife. It was then, according to

150. But the crown of thorns was the work of Roman soldiers; cf. Mark 15. 16f.; John 19, 1.

151. Gen. 22, 10ff.

152. Gen. 22, 14.

153. Gen. 22, 15ff.

154. Gen. 17, 17.

Stephen's narrative,[155] that Abraham was settled in that land, since he now began to be a landowner there – that is, after the death of his father, who is reckoned to have passed away two years previously.

33. *Isaac marries Rebecca*

After that, when Isaac was forty years old, he married Rebecca, the granddaughter of his uncle Nahor; this, as we see, was when his father was 140, and when his mother had been dead for three years. Now when the servant was sent by Isaac's father into Mesopotamia to fetch Rebecca, Abraham said to him, 'Put your hand under my thigh, and I shall put you on oath, by the Lord God of heaven and the Lord of the earth, not to take a wife for my son Isaac from the daughters of the Canaanites.'[156] This was nothing but a sign that the Lord God of heaven and the Lord of the earth was destined to come in the flesh which was derived from that thigh. These are no trivial proofs of the foretelling of the reality which we now see fulfilled in Christ.

34. *The meaning of Abraham's marriage to Keturah*

But what is the meaning of Abraham's taking Keturah as a wife after the death of Sarah? We must never imagine that this was a case of incontinence, especially at his age, and considering the holiness of his faith. Are we to suppose that he was still looking to procreate children, even though God's promise assured him, by a pledge of utter reliability, that Isaac's children would be multiplied to the number of the stars of the sky and the sands of the earth? But if Hagar and Ishmael, as the Apostle teaches,[157] symbolized the carnal people of the old covenant, there is obviously no reason why Keturah and her sons should not stand for the carnal people who suppose themselves to belong to the new covenant. For both Hagar and Keturah are called concubines of Abraham as well as wives, whereas Sarah is never spoken of as a concubine. For when Hagar was given to Abraham, the Scripture says, 'Then Sarah, Abram's wife, took Hagar, her Egyptian maidservant, after Abraham had been living in the land of Canaan for ten years, and gave her as a wife to Abram her husband.'[158] While the passage about Keturah, whom Abraham received after Sarah's death, runs thus: 'Furthermore, Abraham took another wife, whose name was Keturah.' Here we see both of them called wives; but they

155. Acts 7, 4. 156. Gen. 24, 2f.
157. Gal. 4, 24. 158. Gen. 16, 3.

are both also found to have been concubines, for the Scripture goes on to say, 'Now Abraham gave all his property to his son Isaac; and to the sons of his concubines Abraham gave presents, and sent them away from his son Isaac, in his own lifetime, to the east, to the eastern lands.'[159]

Thus the sons of the concubines have some gifts, but they do not come to the promised kingdom – neither the heretics nor the Jews by physical descent – because there is no heir except Isaac, and 'it is not those who are sons of the flesh that are the sons of God, but the sons of the promise are reckoned as his descendants', about whom the Scripture says, 'It is through Isaac that your descendants will carry on your name.' For I can see no reason why Keturah, who was married to Abraham after his wife's death, should be called a concubine, unless it was for the sake of this hidden meaning. But anyone who refuses to take the passage in this sense must not make false accusations against Abraham. For it may be that this episode was designed to provide a refutation of the heretics who were to condemn second marriages;[160] that a second marriage after the death of a wife is not a sin is shown by the example of the father of many nations.

Then Abraham died, at the age of 175. Thus he left behind him his son Isaac, now seventy-five, who was born to him when he was a hundred years old.

35. *The divine prophecy about Rebecca's twins*

We must now observe the historical progress of the City of God through Abraham's descendants. In the period between the first year of Isaac's life and his sixtieth year, in which his sons were born, this fact is noteworthy; that when he asked God that his wife, who was barren, might bear a child, God had granted his request, and his wife had already conceived, and the twins, shut in her womb, were already struggling. Then in the anguish of this distress she asked the Lord about it, and this was the reply, 'Two nations are in your womb, and two peoples will derive their separate existence from your belly. One of those peoples will overcome the other, and the elder will be servant to the younger.'[161] The apostle Paul wishes this to be understood as

159. Gen. 25, 1ff.

160. The Montanists, apocalyptic enthusiasts of the late second century. They developed sternly ascetic traits, especially in Roman Africa. cf. Aug., *De Haer.*, 26.

161. Gen. 25, 23.

an important proof of God's grace, because when they were not yet born, and were engaged in no activity, good or bad, the younger was chosen, without any question of merit, while the elder was rejected.[162] At the time, both were on the same footing, without a shadow of doubt, in respect of original sin, while in respect of personal sin neither of them had any guilt.

But the scheme of the work on which I am engaged does not allow of a wider discussion of this subject at the present moment; and I have treated the matter at length in other works.[163] As for the statement 'The elder will be servant to the younger', hardly anyone of our people has taken it as meaning anything else but that the older people of the Jews was destined to serve the younger people, the Christians. Now it is true that this prophecy might seem to have been fulfilled in the nation of the Idumaeans, which was derived from the elder son (who had two names, being called Esau and also Edom,[164] which is the source of 'Idumaeans') for the Idumaeans were later to be overcome by the people descended from the younger son, that is, by the Israelites. But in fact it is more appropriate to believe that the prophetic statement, 'One of these peoples will overcome the other, and the elder will be servant to the younger', was intended to convey some more important meaning. And what can this meaning be except a prophecy which is now being clearly fulfilled in the Jews and the Christians?

36. *The oracle and blessing of Abraham repeated to Isaac*

Isaac also received an oracle of the same kind as his father had received several times. The Scripture gives this account of it:

> Now a famine came upon the land, besides the earlier famine that occurred in the time of Abraham. And Isaac went away to Abimelech the king of the Philistines in Gerar. Then the Lord appeared to him and said, 'Do not go down to Egypt; but live in the land which I shall tell you of, and settle in this land; and I shall be with you and I shall bless you. For I shall give all this land to you and your posterity, and I shall confirm my oath which I swore to your father Abraham: and I shall multiply your descendants like the stars of the sky, and I shall give your descendants all this land, and all the nations of the earth will be blessed in your descendants, because your father Abraham obeyed my bidding and kept my precepts, my commandments, my statutes, and my laws.'[165]

162. Rom. 9, 11ff.
163. e.g. *Exp. ex. Ep. ad Rom.; De Div. Quaest. ad Simplic.; Quaest. in Hept.*
164. cf. Gen. 25, 30.
165. Gen. 26, 1–5.

This patriarch had no other wife, nor any concubine, but he was content with his posterity of the two twins produced from one act of intercourse. He also, to be sure, was afraid of danger arising from the beauty of his wife, when he was living among foreigners, and he did what his father had done, calling her his sister and concealing the fact that she was his wife. She was, in fact, closely related to him in blood both on the father's side and the mother's. But she too remained inviolate at the hands of foreigners, when it became known that she was his wife. For all that, we should not put Isaac on a higher level than his father just because he did not have relations with any woman except his one wife. In fact, there can be no doubt that the merits of his father's faith and obedience were superior to his own, so much so that God says that the blessings he bestowed on Isaac were granted him for his father's sake. 'All the nations of the earth will be blessed in your descendants, because your father Abraham obeyed my bidding, and kept my precepts, my commandments, my statutes, and my laws.' Further, he says in another oracle, 'I am the God of your father Abraham. Do not be afraid; for I am with you, and I have blessed you, and I will multiply your descendants for the sake of your father Abraham.'[166]

Thus we may realize how chastely Abraham behaved in a matter where he is thought to have acted under the influence of lust; for that is the opinion of men without decency who seek authority for their own wickedness in the holy Scriptures. And we may go on to learn this lesson; that we should not make comparison between men on the basis of particular good qualities; instead, we should observe the whole pattern of each man's life. For it may be that one man has some quality in his life and behaviour in which he surpasses another, and this excellence far outweighs some other quality in which he is surpassed by that other man. According to this method of judgement (which is the sound and true method) even though continence is ranked above marriage, still a married man who has faith in God is superior to the man who is continent but faithless. Indeed, the faithless man is not merely less praiseworthy; he is utterly detestable. Let us assume that both are good men; even so the married man who is completely faithful and completely obedient to God is better than a continent man of less faith and less obedience. Whereas if other things were equal, who would hesitate to rank the continent above the married man?

166. Gen. 26, 24.

37. *The hidden prophecies in Esau and Jacob*

Isaac's two sons, Esau and Jacob, thus grew up together. The primacy of the elder is transferred to the younger as the result of a compact and agreement between them, because the elder had an inordinate craving for the dish of lentils which the younger brother had prepared for his meal, and he sold his first-born's portion to his brother for this price, after he had pledged his oath.[167] Hence we learn that in the matter of eating it is not the kind of food he craves that brings blame upon a man, but his unrestrained greed. Isaac is growing old and he is losing his eyesight through advancing years. He intends to bless his older son and without knowing it he blesses his younger son, instead of the elder brother, who was a hairy man; for the younger brother put himself beneath his father's hands, with the kidskins attached to himself, as if bearing the sins of another. To prevent us from supposing that this trick of Jacob's was a fraudulent deceit, and from failing to look for a hidden meaning of great significance, the Scripture made this statement earlier: 'Now Esau was a man skilled in hunting, a man of the open country; Jacob, on the other hand, was a simple man, living at home.'[168]

Some of our scholars have translated this as 'without deceit' (instead of 'simple'). But whether it is rendered 'without deceit' or 'simple' or (better) 'without pretence' – the Greek word is *aplastos* – what deceit is there in the obtaining of a blessing by a man 'without deceit'? What kind of deceit can be shown by a simple man? What kind of pretence by a man who tells no lies, unless we have here a hidden meaning conveying a profound truth? And then, what was the nature of the blessing? 'Behold', says Isaac,

> the smell of my son is like the smell of a plentiful field, which the Lord has blessed. And may God give you of the dew of heaven and of the richness of the soil, and abundance of corn and wine, and may nations serve you and princes do reverence to you. Become lord over your brother, and your father's sons will do reverence to you. Whoever curses you, let him be cursed; and whoever blesses you, let him be blessed.[169]

Thus the blessing of Jacob is the proclamation of Christ among all nations. This is happening; this is actively going on.

Isaac is the Law and the Prophets; and Christ is blessed by the Law

167. Gen. 25, 29–34.
168. Gen. 25, 27. 'Simple' here probably means 'settled', 'quiet', in contrast with the restless hunter.
169. Gen. 27, 27ff.

and the Prophets, even by the lips of Jews, as by someone who does not know what he is doing, because the Law and the Prophets are themselves not understood. The world is filled like a field with the fragrance of the name of Christ; and his is the blessing of the dew of heaven, that is, of the showers of divine words, of the richness of the soil, that is of the gathering of the peoples. His is the abundance of corn and wine, that is, the multitude which the corn and wine gather together in the sacrament of his body and blood. It is Christ whom the nations serve, and to whom the princes do reverence. He is lord over his brother, since his people have dominion over the Jews. He it is to whom the sons of his father do reverence, that is, the sons of Abraham according to faith; for he himself is also a son of Abraham according to physical descent. He who has cursed him is accursed; he who has blessed him is blessed. Our Christ, I repeat, is blessed, that is, he is truly spoken of, even by the lips of Jews who, although in error, still chant the Law and the Prophets: and they suppose that another is being blessed, the Messiah who is still awaited by them, in their error.

Look at Isaac! He is horror-stricken when his elder son asks for the promised blessing, and he realizes that he has blessed another in his place. He is amazed, and asks who this other can be; and yet he does not complain that he has been deceived. Quite the contrary. The great mystery[170] is straightway revealed to him, in the depths of his heart, and he eschews indignation and confirms his blessing. 'Who then', he says, 'hunted game for me and brought it in to me? And I ate of all of it, before you arrived! Well, I have blessed him; so let him be blessed.'[171] One would surely expect at this point the curse of an angry man, if all this happened in the ordinary course of events, instead of by inspiration from above. Historical events, these, but events with prophetic meaning! Events on earth, but directed from heaven! The actions of men, but the operation of God!

If all the details that are so pregnant with hidden meanings of great importance were closely sifted, the results would fill many volumes. But a limit has to be set to this work, to keep it to a reasonable size; and this compels us to hurry on to other topics.

170. *Sacramentum*, an event with an allegorical significance, forming part of the divine plan.

171. Gen. 27, 33.

38. *Jacob goes to get a wife; his dream on the journey; and his four women*

Jacob is now sent by his parents into Mesopotamia, to marry a wife there. When his father sent him off, he said to him,

> You must not take one of the daughters of the Canaanites for your wife. Make haste, and be on your way to Mesopotamia to the home of Bethuel, your mother's father, and take a wife for yourself from there, one of the daughters of Laban, your mother's brother. And may my God bless you, increase and multiply you; and you will become a group of nations. And may God give you the blessing of your father Abraham, to you and to your descendants after you, so that you may inhabit the land where you settle, which God gave to Abraham.[172]

Here we already understand that Jacob's descendants are separated from those other descendants of Isaac, who are derived through Esau. For the saying, 'Through Isaac your descendants will carry on your name', refers clearly to the descendants belonging to the City of God, and the other descendants of Abraham, represented by the son of the maidservant, and later to be represented also by the sons of Keturah, were distinguished from them. But there was still a doubt about the twin sons of Isaac, whether the blessing belonged to them both, or to only one of them, and if to one, which of them it was. The question has now been cleared up, when Jacob is prophetically blessed by his father, with these words: 'And you will become a group of nations. And may God give you the blessing of your father Abraham.'

Now while Jacob was on his way into Mesopotamia he received an oracle in his sleep. The account of it runs as follows:

> Now Jacob left 'the well of the oath',[173] and set out for Haran; and he came to a place and slept there, for the sun had set. And he took one of the stones of the place and put it under his head and fell asleep in that place; and he had a dream. And behold, a ladder was set up on the earth, whose top reached to heaven; and the angels of God were ascending and descending on it. And the Lord leant over it and said: 'I am the God of Abraham your father, and the God of Isaac. Do not be afraid. The land on which you are sleeping I shall give to you and your descendants. And your descendants will be like the sands of the earth, and will spread over the sea and into Africa, and to the north and the east. And all the tribes of the earth will be blessed in you and your descendants. And look, I am with you, guarding you in every way along which you will go; and I shall bring you back to this land; because I shall not leave you, until I have achieved all that I have spoken of to you.'
>
> Then Jacob arose from his sleep, and said: 'Why, the Lord is in this place,

172. Gen. 28, 1ff. 173. *Beer-sheba.*

and I did not know it!' And he was afraid, and said: 'How terrible is this place: this is nothing else than the house of God;[174] and this is the gate of heaven!' Then Jacob rose up; and he took the stone, which he had put under his head, and set it up as a monument, and poured oil on its top. And Jacob named that place 'the House of God'.[175]

This has a prophetic reference. For when Jacob poured oil over the stone he was not following an idolatrous practice, as if making it into a god; for he did not worship the stone, or sacrifice to it. It was because the name 'Christ' has the same derivation as 'chrism', which means anointing; and thus without doubt we have here a symbolic act which points to a hidden meaning of great significance. As for the ladder, we are aware that the Saviour himself recalls this in the Gospel. For he first said of Nathaniel, 'Here is an Israelite in the true sense, and there is no deceit in him' (because it was Israel – who is Jacob – who saw that vision); and then, in the same passage, he says, 'Mark my words! I tell you that you will see heaven opened, and the angels of God ascending and descending above the Son of Man.'[176]

Jacob then proceeded to Mesopotamia, to get a wife there. In fact, as it turned out, he had four women from there, and holy Scripture tells us how this happened. By these women he had twelve sons and one daughter, and yet he felt no unlawful lust for any of them. He had in fact come there to get one wife; but when another sister had been foisted on him instead of the one intended, he did not reject her, after he had unwittingly had intercourse with her in the night, for fear of appearing to treat her with contempt. Now at that time there was no legal prohibition of polygamy, to ensure the multiplication of descendants; and so Jacob took the other sister also, to whom alone he had pledged himself for future marriage. When she proved barren, she gave her maidservant to her husband, so that she might take over her children. The elder sister also followed the same course, although she had borne children, because she wished to increase the number of her offspring. We are not told that Jacob tried to get any other women but the one, nor that he had intercourse with any except with a view to procreation. And he kept his marriage vow, in that he would not have acted as he did, if his wives had not insisted on this course of action – and wives had legitimate control of their husband's person.[177] Thus Jacob became the father, by four women, of twelve sons and one daughter. He then went into Egypt, thanks to his son Joseph, who was

174. *Beth-el.*
175. Gen. 28, 10–19.
176. John 1, 47; 51.
177. cf. 1 Cor. 7, 4.

sold by his envious brothers and taken into that country, where he rose to a position of eminence.

39. *The reason for the surname 'Israel'*

Now, as I said just now, Jacob was also called Israel, which was the name generally borne by the people descended from him. This name was given him by the angel who wrestled with him when he was on his way back from Mesopotamia. This angel obviously presents a type of Christ. For the fact that Jacob 'prevailed over' him (the angel, of course, being a willing loser to symbolize the hidden meaning) represents the passion of Christ, in which the Jews seemed to prevail over him. And yet Jacob obtained a blessing from the very angel whom he had defeated; thus the giving of the name was the blessing. Now 'Israel' means 'seeing God';[178] and the vision of God will be the reward of all the saints at the end of the world. Moreover, the angel also touched the apparent victor on the broad part of his thigh, and thus made him lame. And so the same man, Jacob, was at the same time blessed and lame – blessed in those who among this same people of Israel have believed in Christ, and crippled in respect of those who do not believe. For the broad part of the thigh represents the general mass of the race. For in fact it is to the majority of that stock that the prophetic statement applies, 'They have limped away from their paths.'[179]

40 *The meaning of the statement that Jacob entered Egypt 'with seventy-five souls'*

The narrative tells us that seventy-five people entered Egypt in company with Jacob himself – Jacob being reckoned in, together with his children. In this number only two women are mentioned, one a daughter, the other a granddaughter.[180] But a careful examination of the facts does not reveal that Jacob's offspring amounted to that number in the day or year when he entered Egypt. In fact even the great-grandsons of Jacob are recorded among the number, and those could not possibly have been alive at that time, seeing that Jacob was

178. *Israel* probably means 'God perseveres'; but in Gen. 32, 28, it is interpreted as 'One who perseveres with God'. St Augustine here adopts a popular etymology deriving the name from *'īsh*, 'man', *rā'āh*, 'see', and *'el*, 'God'.

179. Ps. 18, 45 (LXX).

180. Gen. 46, 26 (66 persons); 27 (LXX) (9 descendants of Jacob); cf. Acts, 7, 14.

then 130 years old, while his son Joseph was thirty-nine. Since it is established that Joseph married his wife in his thirtieth year, or later, how could he have had great-grandsons within nine years from the sons he had by that wife? Since Joseph's sons, Ephraim and Manasseh, did not then have sons (in fact Jacob found them as boys of less than nine years old when he entered Egypt) how is it that not only their sons, but even their grandsons, are counted among the seventy-five persons who entered into Egypt at that time with Jacob? For Machir is mentioned there, the son of Manasseh, and Joseph's grandson, and Machir's son Galaad, Manasseh's grandson and Joseph's great-grandson. Included also is the son of Ephraim, Joseph's second son, that is Utalaam, Joseph's grandson, and Edom, son of this Utalaam; and he was Ephraim's grandson and Joseph's great-grandson. They could not conceivably have been born by the time when Jacob went to Egypt, and found Joseph's sons, his own grandsons, who were the grandfathers of the above-named, as boys of less than nine years old.[181]

No doubt the entry of Jacob into Egypt, which the scriptural narrative describes as the entry of a company of seventy-five people, is not a matter of one day or one year; it includes the whole period of the life of Joseph, who was responsible for that entry. For the same Scripture says, speaking of Joseph himself, 'Now Joseph lived in Egypt, with his brothers and all his father's household; and he lived 110 years. And Joseph saw the sons of Ephraim as far as the third generation.' The third generation from Ephraim is Joseph's great-grandson, the third generation undoubtedly referring to son, grandson, and great-grandson. Then the account continues, 'And the sons of Machir, son of Manasseh, were born on Joseph's knees.' Now this is the son of Manasseh, and the great-grandson of Joseph. (The plural is here used in the common scriptural idiom, just as Jacob's only daughter is called 'the daughters'; similarly Latin idiom speaks of 'sons' even if there is no more than one child.)

Thus, when the felicity of Joseph himself is emphasized, in the fact that he was able to see his great-grandsons, we must by no means suppose that those were already in existence in the thirty-ninth year of their great-grandfather Joseph, at the time when his father Jacob came to him in Egypt. Now this is a point which is missed by those who do not examine the facts carefully, since the Scripture says, 'Now these are the names of the children of Israel, who entered Egypt together with their father Jacob.' The ground for this statement is that seventy-

181. The problem arises from the LXX (and therefore also the Old Latin Version), not from the Hebrew text.

five people, including Jacob, are reckoned, not that they were all together at the time when Jacob entered Egypt. But, as I said, this entry is taken to cover the whole lifetime of Joseph, who is regarded as responsible for that entry.

41. *The blessing promised by Jacob to his son Judah*

Thus when we are studying the people of Christ, in whom the City of God is on pilgrimage in this world, if we look for the physical ancestry of Christ in the descendants of Abraham, we discount the sons of his concubines, and Isaac presents himself. If we look in the descendants of Isaac, we set aside Esau, who is also Edom, and Jacob presents himself, who is also Israel. If we examine the descendants of Israel himself, we set aside the others, and Judah presents himself, because it was from the tribe of Judah that Christ was born. And for this reason we should attend to the prophetic blessing invoked on Judah by Israel when he blessed his sons in Egypt just before his death.

'Judah', he said,

your brothers will praise you. Your hands will be laid on the back of your enemies: the sons of your father will do reverence to you. Judah is a lion's whelp; you have arisen, my son, from the shoot; you have lain down and slept, like a lion, and a lion's whelp; who will rouse him up? A prince shall not be lacking from Jacob, nor a leader from his loins, until three things come which have been laid up for him; and he himself is the expectation of the nations. Binding his foal to the vine and his ass's foal with the tendril, he will wash his garment in wine, and his clothing in the blood of the grape. His eyes are dark with wine, and his teeth whiter than milk.[182]

I have explained these points in my argument against Faustus the Manichean,[183] and the true meaning of this prophecy shines out, I think, clearly enough. Here is foretold the death of Christ, in the mention of sleeping; and also, in the title, 'lion', power, not compulsion, is foretold in his death. He himself emphasizes this power in the Gospel, when he says, 'I have the power to lay down my life, and I have power to take it up again. No one takes it away from me; but I lay it down of my own accord, and I take it up again.'[184] This is how the lion roared, this is how he fulfilled what he said. For there is another reference to this power in the following words about his resurrection: 'Who will rouse him up?' It means that no man will do so, except himself, for he said, about his own body, 'Destroy this temple,

182. Gen. 49, 8–12 183. *Adv. Faust. Man.*, 12, 42. 184. John 10, 18.

and in three days I will raise it up again.'[185] While the manner of his death, that is the exaltation of the cross, is implied by one word, when he goes on, 'You have arisen.' The words which follow, 'You have lain down and slept', are explained by the evangelist, when he says, 'Then he bowed his head, and gave up his spirit.'[186] Or if not, it certainly refers to his burial, for he lay down in the grave and slept; and no human being aroused him from that grave, as the prophets aroused some persons, or as he himself aroused others. He arose of himself, as if from sleep.

Moreover, the robe which he washes in wine means that he washes away sins in his blood, for the baptized experience the sacrament of that blood. Hence Israel adds, 'and his clothing in the blood of the grape'. What is this clothing but the Church? And 'his eyes are dark with wine' means the spiritual men who are made drunk with his cup, the cup about which the psalm sings, 'And your cup which makes me drunk, how wonderful it is.'[187] 'And his teeth are whiter than milk'; this is the milk that the infants drink – as the Apostle says – meaning nourishing words when they are not yet capable of solid food.[188] Thus it is Christ himself in whom the promises made to Judah 'have been laid up'; and 'until these things come' to fulfilment princes from that stock – that is, kings of Israel – have never been lacking. 'And he himself is the expectation of the nations.' This is a saying which is clearer at first sight than it can be made by any explanation.

42. *The two sons of Joseph, whom Jacob blessed by a prophetic crossing of hands*

We have seen that Isaac's two sons, Esau and Jacob, presented a symbol of the two peoples, the Jews and the Christians – although in respect of physical descent it is not the Jews, but the Idumaeans who are descended from Esau; and it is not the Christian Gentiles, but the Jews, who are descended from Jacob; for the symbol only held good as far as the words 'the elder shall be servant to the younger.'[189] Now the same thing happened in the case of Joseph's two sons – for the elder typifies the Jews, the younger the Christians. When Jacob blessed them, putting his right hand on the younger, whom he had on his left side, and his left hand on the younger, whom he had on the right, it seemed a serious matter to their father, and he warned his

185. John 2, 19. 186. John 19, 30. 187. Ps. 23, 5 (LXX).
188. Cor. 3, 2; cf. Pet. 2, 21. 189. Gen. 25, 23.

father, thinking to correct his mistake and to show him which of them really was the elder. But his father refused to change his hands, and said, 'I know, my son, I know. This one also will become a prophet, and he will be exalted; but his younger brother will be greater than he, and his descendants will become a multitude of nations.'[190] What could be more evident than that in those two promises the people of Israel and the whole world are included in Abraham's descendants, the former in respect of physical descent, the latter in respect of faith?

43. *The period of Moses, Joshua, the judges and the kings. Saul the first king; but David the most important, both for his achievements, and as a symbol.*

After the death of Jacob and of Joseph, for the remaining 144 years until their exodus from the land of Egypt, the race increased in an incredible fashion, even though they were worn down by such great persecutions, which went as far as the massacre at one time of the male children born to them, because the excessive increase of the people aroused amazement and alarm in the Egyptians.[191] On this occasion Moses was secretly extricated from the hands of those who were butchering the infants, and taken to the royal palace, since God was planning immense achievements for him. He was reared and adopted by the daughter of Pharaoh (the name Pharaoh was borne by all the Egyptian kings) and he grew into such a great man that he rescued that race, so miraculously multiplied, from the cruel and burdensome yoke of slavery – or rather God rescued them through his agency, thus fulfilling his promise to Abraham. Moses, it is true, had formerly fled from the land, because in defending an Israelite he had killed an Egyptian,[192] and was panic-stricken. But later he was sent on a divine mission, and in the power of God's spirit he overcame Pharaoh's magicians who opposed him. Then through his agency ten memorable plagues were inflicted on the Egyptians, since they refused to release God's people; water turned to blood, frogs, lice, dog-flies, cattle murrain, ulcers, hail, locusts, darkness, death of the first-born. Finally, when the Egyptians had been broken down by all those great plagues and at last had released the Israelites, they were wiped out in the Red Sea when they were pursuing the fugitives. For the sea had divided and offered a path for the departing Israelites; but as the Egyp-

190. Gen. 48, 19. 191. Exod. 1. 192. Exod. 2, 1–15.

tians followed after them the water came together again and overwhelmed them.[193]

Thereafter God's people were led through the desert for forty years, under the command of Moses. During this time the 'tabernacle of the testimony' was given this name, the place where God was worshipped with sacrifices which foretold future events. This, we observe, was after the Law had been given on the mountain, with everything to inspire awe, for the divine power and presence was attested by the clearest evidence of miraculous signs and voices. This happened soon after the departure from Egypt, at the start of the period when the people lived in the desert, on the fiftieth day after the Paschal Feast had been celebrated by the sacrifice of a lamb.[194] This lamb is so accurate a symbol of Christ, foretelling that through the sacrifice offered in his passion he would pass over from this world to the Father – 'Pascha', as is well known, is the Hebrew for 'pass over' – that when the new covenant was revealed after 'Christ our Passover was sacrificed', it was on the fiftieth day that the Holy Spirit came down from heaven. The Spirit is called in the Gospel 'the finger of God'[195] to bring to our minds the remembrance of that original symbolic event, since we are told that the tables of the Law also were written by the finger of God.[196]

After the death of Moses, Joshua led the people, and brought them into the land of promise and divided it among the people. Wars were waged, with marvellous success, by these two marvellous leaders. But God bears witness that these victories came to them not on account of the merits of the Hebrew people, but because of the sins of the nations whom they defeated. After those two leaders there were a number of 'judges', when the people were by now settled in the land of promise; and so the first promise to Abraham began to be fulfilled at this time, as far as it concerned one people, the Hebrew nation, and the land of Canaan, but not yet as it referred to all nations and to the whole world. This was to be fulfilled by the coming of Christ in the flesh, and not by the keeping of the old Law, but by the faith of the Gospel. This was symbolized in the fact that the people were led into the land of promise not by Moses, who had received the Law for the people on Mount Sinai, but by Joshua whose name had even been changed at God's bidding, so that he should be called Jesus.[197]

193. Exod. 7–12; 14. 194. Exod. 12, 1–11. 195. Luke 11, 20.
196. Exod. 31, 18.
197. *Jesus* is the Greek equivalent of the Hebrew *Joshua*, used in LXX and simply transliterated in St Augustine's Old Latin Version, the Old Testament

Then, in the period of the judges, there was alternation of success and failure in war, according to the sins of the people and the mercy of God. After this comes the period of the kings, Saul being the first to exercise the royal power. When he was rejected by God and fell in a military disaster and his line was abandoned, so that it should not be the source of kings, David succeeded to the throne; and 'Son of David' is the chief title of Christ. David marks the beginning of an epoch, and with him there is what may be called the start of the manhood of God's people, since we may regard the period from Abraham to David as the adolescence of this race. And there is a special significance in the fact that the evangelist Matthew records the generations in such a way as to attribute fourteen generations to this first stage, that is, the period from Abraham to David. For it is at adolescence that a man becomes capable of procreation; and that is why the list of generations starts with Abraham, who was also marked out as the 'father of nations' when he received his change of name.[198] Before that time there was, as it were, the boyhood of this race of God's people from Noah down to Abraham himself; and that is why this boyhood is found to have a language, namely Hebrew. For it is at boyhood that man begins to talk, after he leaves infancy – which is so called because it has not the power of speech.[199] And this first age of infancy is sunk in oblivion, as the first age of mankind was wiped out by the Flood. For there are very few men who have any recollection of their infancy.

Thus the previous book covers one age, the first, in the development of the City of God, and this present book deals with the second and third. In this third age, as symbolized by the heifer, goat, and ram – all three years old – the yoke of the Law was imposed, a multitude of sinners came on the scene, and the earthly kingdom entered its first stage. Yet at the same time there were not lacking spiritual men who were prophetically indicated by the symbol of the dove and the pigeon.[200]

Joshua being called *Jesus Nave* ('son of Nun') to distinguish him from the Jesus of the New Testament.

198. cf. ch. 28.

199. *Infans* in Latin means literally 'not speaking'.

200. cf. ch. 24.

BOOK XVII

1. *The era of the prophets*

WE have learned that it is from the line of Abraham that the Israelite race derives its origin, in respect of physical descent; while, in respect of faith, all nations have issued from him; and this is according to God's promise. And the history of the City of God, as it develops through succeeding periods, will show how the promises made to Abraham are being fulfilled. My previous book brought the story as far as David's reign; and now we touch on the events which followed that reign, in so far as seems sufficient for the task in hand.

The next period extends from the time when the holy Samuel began to prophesy down to the deportation of the Israelite people to captivity in Babylon, and from then on to the restoration of the House of God, fulfilling the prophecy of the holy Jeremiah,[1] after the return of the Israelites, seventy years later. This whole period is the era of the prophets. It is true that we can quite rightly give the title of prophet to Noah himself, in whose time the whole earth was wiped out by the Deluge; and also to others, before and after him, down to the time when kings first arose among God's people. They have a right to this title because through them certain future events connected with the City of God and the kingdom of heaven were in some fashion symbolized or foretold. This is particularly true of some of these men, Abraham and Moses, for example, of whom we read that they were expressly given this appellation. For all that, 'the days of the prophets' is a name given chiefly and especially to the era beginning with the prophetic activity of Samuel, who at God's bidding first anointed Saul and then, when Saul proved unsatisfactory, David himself, from whose stock the whole succession of kings derived, so long as this succession was permitted.

Now it would develop into an immense undertaking if I were to try to record all the predictions about Christ uttered by the prophets while the City of God was running its course during this era, as generation succeeded generation. For, in the first place, the scriptural narrative itself gives an account of the succession of kings and their

1. Jer. 25, 11.

achievements and the events of their reigns; and yet a careful examination of the narrative, with the help of God's spirit, reveals it to be more concerned – or at least not less concerned – with foretelling the future than with recording the past. And no one who gives the slightest thought to the matter can fail to realize what a laborious and boundless task it would be to track down all those points, by a minute scrutiny of the record, and then to discuss them so as to show their relevance. It would, in fact, require many volumes. Moreover, even the matters which are unambiguously prophetic in character refer in so many cases to Christ and the kingdom of heaven, which is the City of God, that merely to broach the subject would entail a more elaborate disquisition than the scope of this work demands. From now on, therefore, I shall do my best to control my pen so as neither to include anything superfluous, nor to omit anything necessary for the accomplishment of this undertaking, according to God's will.

2. *The fulfilment of God's promise about the land of Canaan: Israel 'according' to the flesh obtained possession of it*

In the previous book I have said that two things were promised to Abraham from the beginning. One was that his descendants would possess the land of Canaan; and this is signified in the passage which says, 'Go into the land which I shall show you; and I will make of you a great nation'.[2] The other, far more important, related not to his physical descendants but to his spiritual posterity, through whom he is the father not of the one nation of Israel, but of all nations which follow in the footsteps of his faith. This promise begins with these words: 'And all the tribes of the earth will be blessed in you.'[3] And I have shown that these two promises were repeated thereafter, according to the evidence of a large number of passages. Thus Abraham's descendants, in the physical sense, that is, the people of Israel, were already in the land of promise and had already started their kingdom there, not only in the sense of holding in possession the cities of their enemies, but also by having kings. Thus God's promises about this people had already been fulfilled in large measure, not only the promise which had been made to the three patriarchs, Abraham, Isaac, and Jacob, and others made in their period, but also those given through Moses, by whom this people was set free from slavery in Egypt, and through whom all the events of the past were revealed, when he led the people through the desert.

2. Gen. 12, 1f. 3. Gen. 12, 3.

However, the promise of God about the land of Canaan was not fulfilled through the great leader Joshua, by whom the people was brought into the land of promise. What Joshua did was to conquer and dispossess the nations of the land, and divide the country, as God had bidden, among the twelve tribes. Then he died; and the promise was not fulfilled in the whole period of the judges which followed his death. For the promise spoke of the land of Canaan stretching from a certain river of Egypt to the great River Euphrates.[4] But this was by now no longer a prophecy for the distant future: its immediate fulfilment was awaited; and the fulfilment came through David and his son Solomon, whose dominion was extended over the whole area mentioned in the promise. For they subdued all those peoples and made them tributary nations.[5] Thus under those kings the descendants of Abraham had been established in the land of promise, in the physical sense, that is, in the land of Canaan; and this meant that nothing further remained for the fulfilment of that promise which concerned worldly territory, except that the Hebrew people should continue in the same land in undisturbed stability, as far as temporal prosperity is concerned, through the successive ages of posterity right down to the end of this mortal age, provided that they obeyed the laws of the Lord their God. But since God knew that they would not do so, he also imposed on them temporal punishments, for the training of the few faithful men in that nation, and for a warning to those who were to come in future times among all nations, a warning needed by those in whom he was to fulfil his second promise by the revelation of the new covenant through the incarnation of Christ.

3. *The threefold meanings of the prophets, referring sometimes to the earthly Jerusalem, sometimes to the Heavenly City, sometimes to both at once*

Now the divine oracles given to Abraham, Isaac, and Jacob, and all the other prophetic signs or words found in previous sacred writings, refer partly to the nation physically derived from Abraham, but partly to those descendants of his in whom all nations are blessed as coheirs of Christ through the new covenant, so as to obtain possession of eternal life and the kingdom of heaven. The same is true of the rest of the prophecies, from this period of the kings. Thus the prophecies refer in part to the maidservant whose children are born into slavery, that is, the earthly Jerusalem, who is in slavery, as are also her sons;

4. Gen. 15, 18. 5. cf. 1 Kings 4, 21.

but in part they refer to the free City of God, the true Jerusalem, eternal in heaven, whose sons are the men who live according to God's will in their pilgrimage on earth. There are, however, some prophecies which are understood as referring to both; literally to the bondmaid, symbolically to the free woman.[6]

Thus the utterances of the prophets are found to have a threefold meaning, in that some have in view the earthly Jerusalem, others the heavenly, and others refer to both. It is clear to me that I ought to prove my point by examples. Nathan the prophet was sent to convict King David of a grave sin and to predict the coming misfortunes, misfortunes which in fact followed.[7] Can anyone doubt that these statements and others of the same tenor had reference to the earthly city, whether they were public pronouncements, that is, uttered for the welfare and betterment of the people, or private communications, when an individual earned the privilege of divinely inspired utterances for his own benefit, imparting some knowledge of the future to his advantage in his temporal life? On the other hand we have such a passage as,

> Behold, the days are coming, says the Lord, when I shall ratify a new covenant with the house of Israel, and with the house of Judah. It will not be in the terms of the covenant that I drew up for their fathers at the time when I took them by the hand to lead them out of the land of Egypt; for they did not keep to my covenant, and I have abandoned them, says the Lord. Now this is the covenant that I establish for the house of Israel after those days, says the Lord. I shall establish it by putting my laws in their minds; and I shall write them on their hearts, and I shall look on them. And I shall become their God; and they will become my people.[8]

This is, without doubt, a prophecy of the Jerusalem above, whose 'reward'[9] is God himself; and to possess him, and to be his possession, is the Highest Good, and the Entire Good, in that City.

But the fact that Jerusalem is called the city of God has a double reference, combined as it is with the prophecy of the future house of God in that city. This prophecy seems to have its fulfilment when King Solomon builds that renowned temple. But this was not only an event in the history of the earthly Jerusalem; it was also a symbol of the Jerusalem in heaven. Now this class of prophecy, in which there is a compounding and commingling, as it were, of both references, is of the greatest importance in the ancient canonical books, which contain historical narratives; and it has exercised and still exercises the wits of

6. cf. Gal. 4, 21–31.
7. 2 Sam. 12, 1–15.
8. Jer. 31, 31ff.
9. cf. Gen. 15, 1.

those who examine the sacred literature. And so, when we read of prophecy and fulfilment in the story of Abraham's physical descendants, we also look for an allegorical meaning which is to be fulfilled in those descended from Abraham in respect of faith. So much so that some interpreters have decided that everything prophesied and accomplished in those books, or accomplished without being prophesied, has, without exception, some meaning which is to be referred by symbolical application to the City of God in heaven, and the sons of that City who are pilgrims in this life. On this theory the utterances of the prophets will be of two types only, not three – or rather, this will be true of all those scriptures which are classed under the title of the Old Testament. For there will be nothing there which relates only to the earthly Jerusalem, if whatever is said there, and accomplished, either about that city or in connection with that city, has a reference, by prophetic allegory, to the Heavenly Jerusalem. So there will be only two kinds of prophecy; one concerned with the 'free' Jerusalem, and the other with both cities.

Now in my opinion it is certainly a complete mistake to suppose that no narrative of events in this type of literature has any significance beyond the purely historical record; but it is equally rash to maintain that every single statement in those books is a complex of allegorical meanings. That is why I have spoken of a triple, instead of a double classification; for this is my own considered judgement. In spite of that, I do not censure those who have succeeded in carving out a spiritual meaning from each and every event in the narrative, always provided that they have maintained its original basis of historical truth. There are also statements which cannot be made to apply to events either past or future, whether brought about by human or divine activity; and no believing man would doubt that those were uttered from some good purpose. Such a man would certainly attach a spiritual sense to them, if he could; or at least he would acknowledge that they should be so interpreted by anyone who is able to do so.

4. *The change in the Israelite kingship, and its prophetic significance. The prophecies of Hannah, Samuel's mother, who personifies the Church*

The City of God thus developed down to the period of the kings, to the time when Saul was rejected and David first ascended the throne, so that his descendants thereafter reigned in the earthly Jerusalem in a succession which lasted a long time. This change was symbolic; it was an event which pointed prophetically to the future, and its significance must not be passed over in silence. It betokened the change which was to come in the future in respect of the two covenants, the old and the new, and the transformation of priesthood and monarchy by the new and eternal priest-king, who is Christ Jesus. For when Eli the priest had been rejected, and Samuel was substituted for him in the service of God, and performed the double function of priest and judge, and when Saul was put aside and King David was established in the royal power, those events prophetically symbolized the change which I have mentioned.

Besides this, Hannah, Samuel's mother, who had formerly been barren and was now gladdened with fertility, is shown as prophesying exactly the same transformation, when in exaltation she pours out her thanksgiving to the Lord, when she gives back to God the same child, after he had been born and weaned, with the same devotion with which she had made her vow. For she says,

My heart is strengthened in the Lord; my horn is exalted in my God. My mouth is enlarged over my enemies; I have rejoiced in your salvation. For there is none who is holy as the Lord is holy; there is none who is just as our God is just; there is none holy besides you. Do not boast; do not speak lofty words; let no bragging talk come from your lips. For the Lord is the God of all knowledge, and a God who prepares his own designs. He has made weak the bow of the mighty ones; and the weak have girded themselves with strength. Those who were full of bread have been reduced to want; and the hungry have passed over the earth. Because the barren woman has given birth to seven children while she who has many sons is enfeebled. The Lord brings death, and he brings life; he leads men down to the grave and leads them back again. The Lord makes men poor, and he enriches them; he humbles them, and he exalts them. He raises up the poor man from the earth, and lifts up the needy from the dunghill, that he may station them with the men of power among the people, giving them also the seat of glory as their inheritance, granting fulfilment to the man who makes a vow; and he has blessed the years of the righteous, since man is not powerful in his own strength. The Lord will make weak his adversary; the Lord is holy. Let the prudent man not glory in his prudence, nor the powerful glory in his power, nor the rich man glory in his riches. He who glories, let him glory in this: to understand and know the Lord, and to perform justice and righteousness in the midst of the earth. The Lord has ascended into the heavens and has thundered; he himself will judge the ends of the earth, because he is just; and he gives strength to our kings, and will exalt the horn of his anointed.[10]

10. 1 Sam. 2, 1–10.

Are these words going to be regarded as simply the words of one mere woman giving thanks for the birth of her son? Are men's minds so turned away from the light of truth that they do not feel that the words poured out by this woman transcend the limit of her own thoughts? In truth, anyone who is appropriately moved by the events whose fulfilment has already begun, even in this earthly pilgrimage, cannot but attend to these words, and observe and recognize that through this woman (whose very name, Hannah, means 'God's grace'[11]), there speaks, by the spirit of prophecy, the Christian religion itself, the City of God itself, whose king and founder is Christ; there speaks, in fact, the grace of God itself, from which the proud are estranged so that they fall, with which the humble are filled so that they rise up, which was in fact, the chief theme that rang out in her hymn of praise. Now it may be that someone will be ready to say that the woman gave voice to no prophecy, but merely praised God in an outburst of exultation for the son who was granted in answer to her prayer. If so, what is the meaning of this passage, 'He has made weak the bow of the mighty ones, and the weak have girded themselves with strength. Those who were full of bread have been reduced to want, and the hungry have passed over the earth. Because the barren woman has given birth to seven, while she who has many children has become weak.' Had Hannah herself really borne seven children, although she was barren? She had only one son when she spoke these words; and even afterwards she did not give birth to seven, or to six, which would have made Samuel the seventh. She had in fact three male and two female children. And then observe her concluding words, spoken among that people at a time when no one had yet been king over them: 'He gives strength to our kings, and will exalt the horn of his anointed.' How is it that she said this, if she was not uttering a prophecy?

Therefore, let the Church of Christ speak, the 'City of the great king',[12] the Church that is 'full of grace',[13] fruitful in children; let her speak the words that she recognizes as spoken prophetically about herself, so long ago, by the lips of this devout mother, 'My heart is strengthened in the Lord; my horn is exalted in my God.' Her heart is truly strengthened and her horn truly exalted, because it is 'in the Lord her God' not in herself that she finds strength and exaltation. 'My mouth is enlarged over my enemies'; because even in the straits of oppression 'the word of God is not bound',[14] not even when its

11. *hannāh* = 'graciousness'.
12. Ps. 48, 2.
13. Luke 1, 28.
14. cf. 2 Tim. 2, 9.

heralds are bound. 'I have rejoiced', she says, 'in your salvation.' This salvation is Christ Jesus; for we read in the Gospel that Simeon took him in his arms, an old man embracing a little child and recognizing his greatness, and he said, 'Lord, you are now discharging your servant in peace; for my eyes have seen your salvation.'[15] And so let the Church say, 'I have rejoiced in your salvation. For there is none who is holy as the Lord is holy; there is none who is just as our God is just'; for he is holy – and he makes men holy; he is just – and he makes men just. 'There is none holy besides you.' For no one is made holy except by you. Then there follow these words: 'Do not boast; do not speak lofty words; let no bragging talk come from your lips. For God is the God of all knowledge.' He himself knows you, even where no one knows, since 'he who thinks himself to be something important, when he is nothing, is fooling himself.'[16]

These words are directed to the adversaries of the City of God, who belong to Babylonia, who presume on their own strength, and glory in themselves, instead of in God. Among them are also the Israelites by physical descent, the earth-born citizens of the earthly Jerusalem, who, in the words of the Apostle, 'know nothing of God's righteousness'[17] – that is, the righteousness which God gives, who alone is righteous and makes men righteous – 'and desire to establish their own righteousness' – that is, they suppose it to be something gained by themselves, instead of given by God and so they have not submitted to God's righteousness. Arrogant as they are, they think that by their own righteousness, not God's, they can please God, who is 'the God of all knowledge' and therefore also the judge of men's inner thoughts; for in them he sees men's imaginations, knowing them to be futile,[18] if they are only men's, and do not come from him.

'God', says Hannah, 'prepares his own designs.' What do we suppose these designs are, except that the proud should fall and the humble arise? For no doubt she is elaborating these designs when she says, 'The bow of the mighty ones has been weakened, and the weak have girded themselves with strength.' The bow has been weakened – that is, the intention of those who seem to themselves so powerful that without the gift of God and without his aid they can fulfil the divine commands in human self-reliance. And men gird themselves with strength when their inner voice says, 'Have mercy on me, Lord, for I am weak.'[19]

15. Luke 2, 29f. 16. Gal. 6, 3. 17. Rom. 10, 3.
18. cf. Ps. 94, 11. 19. Ps. 6, 2.

'Those who were full of bread', says Hannah, 'have been reduced to want; and the hungry have passed over the earth.' Who are to be understood by those who were full of bread, except those supposedly 'powerful ones', that is, the Israelites, to whom the utterances of God were entrusted? But among that people the sons of the maidservant[20] were 'reduced'. Now the verb *minorati sunt* ('have been reduced') is not a good Latin expression; but it expresses the meaning well, since they were reduced from major to minor importance. They were reduced, because while possessed of this bread, that is, the divine utterances, which the Israelites, alone of all the nations at that time, had received, they had a taste only for earthly things. On the other hand, nations to whom that Law had not been given, after they came to the knowledge of these utterances through the new covenant, passed over the earth in great hunger, since in these words it was the heavenly meaning, not the earthly, that they savoured. And Hannah seems to be looking for an explanation of how this happened, when she says, 'For the barren woman has given birth to seven; while she who has many children is enfeebled.' Here the whole of the prophecy becomes illuminated for those who recognize the significance of the number seven; for by that number the perfection of the universal Church is symbolized. This is the reason why the apostle John writes to seven churches;[21] it is his way of showing that he is writing to the entirety of the one Church. In the Proverbs of Solomon also Wisdom prefigured this Church long before, when she 'built her house and supported it on seven columns.'[22] For the City of God was barren in all nations before the birth of the offspring we now behold. We also behold the enfeeblement of the earthly Jerusalem, who had many children; for her strength lay in whatever sons of the free woman were in that city. But now only the letter is there and not the spirit;[23] and so her strength has been lost, and she has been enfeebled.

'The Lord brings death, and he brings life.' He brought death to her who had many sons; he brought life to the barren woman who gave birth to seven children. However, this might more suitably be understood to mean that he brings life to the same persons to whom he has brought death. For it looks as if she is repeating this statement when she adds, 'He leads men down to the grave, and leads them back again.' Now the Apostle says, 'If you are dead with Christ, seek the realms on high, where Christ is seated on God's right hand':[24] and

20. cf. Gal. 4, 21–31.
21. cf. Rev. 1, 4. On seven as a 'perfect number' cf. Bk XI, 30f.; XV, 20; XX, 5.
22. Prov. 9, 1.
23. cf. 2 Cor. 3, 6–16.
24. Col. 3, 1; cf. Rom. 6, 8.

those to whom this is addressed are certainly brought to death by God for their own well-being. And he adds these words to them, 'Savour the things on high, not the things on earth'; so that these are the same persons who 'have passed over the earth in hunger'.

For St Paul says, 'You are dead.' But see how healthfully God brings men to death! He goes on to say, 'and your life is hidden with Christ in God.'[25] See how God brings life to these same men! But is it true that those whom he has brought to the realm of the dead and those he has brought back again are the same people? Indeed it is, since there is, for believers, no disputing that we see both these actions fulfilled in him (and, remember, he is 'our head') 'with whom', as the Apostle says, 'our life is hidden in God'. For he 'who did not spare his own son, but delivered him up on behalf of us all',[26] surely brought him to death in so doing; and in raising him from the dead, he brought him to life again. And since his voice is recognized in the prophecy, 'You will not leave my soul in the underworld',[27] it was the same person whom he brought down to the realm of the dead and brought back again. By this poverty of his we have been enriched;[28] for 'the Lord makes men poor, and enriches them.' Now to understand what this means, we must listen to what follows: 'He humbles, and he exalts'; which clearly means that he humbles the arrogant and exalts the humble. For elsewhere we find those words: 'God resists the proud, while he gives grace to the humble';[29] and this is the message of the whole discourse of Hannah, whose name means his 'grace'.

As for the words that follow, 'He raises up the poor from the earth', I can find no better application of them than to him who 'became poor for our sake, though he was rich, so that by his poverty' – as I said just now – 'we might be enriched.'[30] For God raised him up from the earth so quickly that his flesh did not 'see corruption'.[31] And I shall not withdraw from him the application of what follows: 'And he lifts up the needy from the dunghill.' 'The needy' is certainly identical with 'the poor'; and the dung from which he is raised is most correctly understood of the Jewish persecutors, among whom the Apostle counted himself, as having persecuted the Church, when he used these words: 'The things which were my assets I have written off as losses for the sake of Christ; in fact I have counted them not only as drawbacks, but even as so much dung, so that I might have Christ as

25. Col. 3, 3. 26. Rom. 8, 21. 27. Ps. 16, 10.
28. cf. 2 Cor. 8, 9. 29. Jas. 4, 6. 30. 2 Cor. 8, 6.
31. Ps. 16, 10.

my assets.'[32] Thus that poor man was raised up from the earth above all the rich, so as to sit 'with the men of power among the people' to whom he says, 'You will sit on twelve thrones.'[33] 'Giving them also the seat of glory as their inheritance' – for those 'men of power' had said, 'Look, we have abandoned everything and have become your followers.' This vow they had made with the utmost power. But whence did they derive the ability to do so, unless from him of whom Hannah's song immediately goes on to say that he 'grants fulfilment to him who makes a vow'? For no one could ever make a rightful vow to the Lord without receiving from him the fulfilment of his prayer.

The words that follow, 'and he has blessed the years of the righteous', mean, we can be sure, that the righteous will live without end with him to whom it was said, 'Your years will never come to an end.'[34] For there the years stand still, whereas here they pass by; in fact, they perish. For before they come they do not exist, and when they have come, they will exist no more, because when they come they bring with them their own end. Now of the two statements, 'granting fulfilment to one who makes a vow' and 'he has blessed the years of the righteous', one refers to something we do, the other to something we get. But the second is not acquired through God's generosity, unless the former has been accomplished with his assistance. For 'man is not powerful in his own strength; the Lord will make weak his adversary', which means, of course, one who in malice resists the man who makes a vow, so that he may be incapable of fulfilling his vow. But there is an ambiguity in the Greek, and it may be taken as 'his own adversary'. For as soon as God has begun to possess us, then straightway he who was our adversary becomes God's adversary, and will be conquered by us, but not by our own powers, 'because a man is not powerful in his own strength'. Thus 'the Lord will make weak his own adversary; the Lord is holy'; so that the adversary is overcome by holy men, sanctified by the holy Lord of holy people.

And for this reason 'let the prudent man not glory in his prudence, nor the powerful glory in his power, nor the rich man glory in his riches. He who glories, let him glory in this: to understand and know the Lord, and to perform justice and righteousness in the midst of the earth.' It is in no trivial measure that a man understands and knows God, when he understands and knows that this knowledge and understanding is itself the gift of God. 'For what do you possess', says the Apostle, 'which you have not received? Then, if you have received it,

32. Phil. 3, 7f. 33. Matt. 19, 28.
34. Ps. 102, 27; Hebr. 1, 12.

why do you boast, as if you had not received it?'[35] That is, why do you behave as if the ground of your boasting came from your own achievement? Now the man who lives rightly 'performs justice and righteousness'; and that man is he who obeys God's bidding. And 'the end of the commandment', that is the object to which it is directed, 'is the love that springs from a pure heart, a good conscience, and a faith that is without pretence'.[36] Moreover, as the apostle John testifies, 'this love comes from God.'[37] Thus the ability to 'perform justice and righteousness' comes from God.

But what is the meaning of 'in the midst of the earth'? It is certainly not that those who live at the ends of the earth are exempt from the duty of doing justice and righteousness. Would anyone say this? Why, then, the addition of the words, 'in the midst of the earth'? Without the addition, the remaining words, 'to perform justice and righteousness' would make the command applicable to both classes: those who live in the midst of the earth, and those on the shores of the ocean. My belief is that the words were added to preclude the notion that after the end of the life lived in this mortal body a period remains for the performance of justice and righteousness, which a man has failed to achieve while in the flesh, and so there is a chance of escaping the divine judgement. The words therefore mean, in my view, 'while each man lives in the body'. Certainly in this life each man carries his 'earth' around him, and the common earth receives it when he dies, to restore it, as we know, when the man rises again. It follows that 'in the midst of the earth', that is, as long as our soul is enclosed in this earthly body, we must 'perform justice and righteousness' for our benefit in the future when 'everyone receives either good or bad, according to his actions done through the body.'[38] Here we can see that by 'through the body' the Apostle means 'throughout the time when he lived in the body'. For it is not implied that anyone who blasphemes against God, the wickedness being in his mind and the impiety in his thoughts, without his bodily organs being involved, is exempt from judgement simply because there was no bodily activity in this behaviour; for he behaved in this way during the time when he inhabited the body. We can appropriately apply the same line of interpretation to a passage in the psalms, where it says, 'Now God our king before the ages has achieved salvation *in the midst of the earth*.'[39] We may take 'our God' to mean the Lord Jesus, who is before the ages (since the ages were created by him); for he 'achieved

35. 1 Cor. 4, 7. 36. 1 Tim. 1, 5. 37. 1 John 4, 7.
38. 2 Cor. 5, 10. 39. Ps. 74, 12.

salvation in the midst of the earth' when the Word was made flesh and dwelt in a human body.

These words in Hannah's prophecy describe how a man who glories ought to glory, not in himself, of course, but in the Lord. Hannah next alludes to the retribution which is to come on the day of judgement. 'The Lord has ascended into the heavens and has thundered; he himself will judge the ends of the earth, because he is just.' Here she kept precisely to the order of the confession of the faithful,[40] 'The Lord ascended into heaven, and thence he will come to judge the living and the dead.' For, as the Apostle says, 'Who ascended, except him who also descended into the lower parts of the earth? He who descended is the same person as he who ascended above all the heavens, so that he might fulfil all things.'[41] Thus it was through his own clouds that he thundered, the clouds which he filled with the Holy Spirit when he ascended. It was concerning these clouds that he speaks to Jerusalem the maidservant (the 'ungrateful vine'), in the book of Isaiah, threatening that the clouds would not send rain upon it.[42] Now to say 'he himself will judge the ends of the earth' is as much as to say '*even* to the ends of the earth'. For it is not that he will fail to judge the other parts of the world; he will, without a shadow of doubt, judge all men. But it is better to take 'the ends of the earth' to mean 'the latter end of man'. For the judgement will not be passed on situations which change for better or worse in the intermediate period. The judgement will be on the final state in which the man who will be judged is found. That is why it is said that 'the man who perseveres to the end is the man who will be saved.'[43] Therefore the man who perseveres in the performance of justice and righteousness 'in the midst of the earth' will not be condemned when 'the ends of the earth' are judged.

'He gives strength to our kings', she says. The purpose of this is that he may not condemn them in his judgement. He gives them strength by which they may, like kings, rule over the flesh, and overcome the world in the power of him who shed his blood for them. 'And he will exalt the horn of his anointed.' In what way will Christ exalt the horn of his anointed? For it was said earlier of him, 'The Lord has ascended into the heavens', and this was taken to mean 'the Lord Christ'. It is Christ himself, as is said here, who 'will exalt the horn of his anointed'. Who then is the anointed (*christus*) of Christ? Does it mean that he will exalt the horn of every faithful follower of his, just as Hannah herself says at the start of her hymn, 'My horn is exalted in my God'?

40. The Apostles' Creed. 41. Eph. 4, 9.
42. cf. Is. 5, 6. 43. Matt. 10, 22.

Certainly we can properly apply the name 'anointed' (*christus*) to all who have been anointed with his chrism; and yet it is the whole body, with its head, which is the one Christ.

This was what Hannah prophesied; and she was the mother of Samuel, a holy man, a man highly praised. In him indeed the transformation of the ancient priesthood was then symbolically represented, a transformation which has now been fulfilled, when she who had many sons has become feeble, with the result that the barren woman who has borne seven children has received a new priesthood in Christ.

5. *The meaning of the prophecy addressed to Eli by the 'man of God'; the supersession of the Aaronic priesthood*

This change in the priesthood is more explicitly stated by the 'man of God' who was sent to Eli the priest himself. His name, to be sure, is not revealed, but the nature of his office and ministry puts it beyond doubt that he was a prophet. The account runs like this:

Now a man of God came to Eli and said: 'This is what the Lord says: "I revealed myself clearly to your father's house, when they were in the land of Egypt as slaves in the house of Pharaoh; and I chose your father's house out of all the sceptres of Israel to perform the priestly office for me, to go up to my altar, and to burn incense and to wear the ephod. And I gave to your father's house for their food all that was offered as burnt sacrifice by the sons of Israel. Why have you looked upon my incense and my sacrifice with disrespectful eyes, and have honoured your sons above me, so that they bless the first fruits of every sacrifice in my sight?" Therefore, the Lord God says this: "I have said: 'Your house and your father's house will pass by in my presence for ever.' " But now the Lord says: "This will not be so; but I shall honour those who honour me, and those who spurn me will be spurned. Behold, the days are coming when I shall banish your seed and the seed of your father's house, and you will not have an elder in my house all your days, and I will banish all the men of your family from my altar, so that their eyes will fail and their spirit will fade away. Every one of your family that survives, they all will fall by the sword of men. And this will be a sign for you, that will come upon those two sons of yours, Ophni and Phineas: they will both die on one day. Then I shall raise up a faithful priest for me, who will do all that is in my heart and in my soul. I shall build him a faithful house, and he will pass by in the presence of my anointed all his days. And it will happen that any who survives in your family will come to do him obeisance for a piece of silver, and will say: 'Thrust me into some part of your priestly office, so that I may have bread to eat.' " '[44]

44. 1 Sam. 2, 27–36.

This is a prophecy of a change in the ancient priesthood, announced in quite unmistakable terms; but there is no reason for maintaining that it was finally fulfilled in Samuel. It was in a degree fulfilled: for although Samuel was not of a different tribe from the one which had been appointed by the Lord to serve the altar, still he was not among the sons of Aaron, whose descendants had been granted the privilege of supplying the priesthood.[45] And in this way the transformation that was to come about through Jesus Christ was hinted at; and the prophecy contained in the event, not the prophecy expressed in the words, was concerned directly with the old covenant; but it had a figurative application to the new. In the event, what was said to Eli the priest in words through the mouth of the prophet had reference to the new covenant. However, there were in later times priests of the stock of Aaron, Zadok, for example, and Abiathar in the reign of David, and others thereafter, until the time came when the prophecies about the transformation of the priesthood, uttered so long before, were destined to be brought to effect in Christ. No one who looks at these prophecies with the eye of faith could fail to see that they have been fulfilled. For now, to be sure, no tabernacle has been left to the Jews, no temple, no altar, no sacrifice and, it follows, no priesthood; although the Jews had once been commanded by God's law to have a priesthood established belonging to the line of Aaron.

This was indeed mentioned in the passage, where the prophet says, 'This is what the Lord says: "I have said: 'Your house and your father's house will go to and fro before me for ever.' " But now the Lord says: "This will not be so; but I shall honour those who honour me, and those who spurn me will be spurned." ' The prophet speaks of 'your father's house'; but he does not mean his immediate father, but the great Aaron who was ordained as the first priest, from whose

45. St Augustine corrects himself on this point in *Retract.*, 11, 69. 'The statement that "Samuel was not among the sons of Aaron" should rather have been put in this way: "Samuel was not the son of a priest." The regular custom was for priests to be succeeded by their sons. Samuel's father is in fact listed among the sons of Aaron, but in the same way as all the people are called 'sons of Israel.' The present passage is somewhat opaque, but St Augustine's argument goes like this: The prophecy to Eli remained unfulfilled in its direct application, inasmuch as the Aaronic priesthood continued. But it had a temporary fulfilment in Samuel's succession to the priesthood, since he was not 'a son of Aaron' (or, rather, not a son of a priest). This event was itself a prophecy of the supersession of the Jewish priesthood by the Christian; and so in this event, concerned with the old covenant, the words of the prophet pointed to the new covenant.

descendants all other priests were to follow in succession. This is shown by his previous words, where he says, 'I revealed myself to your father's house, when they were in the land of Egypt as slaves in the house of Pharaoh; and I chose your father's house out of all the sceptres of Israel, to perform the priestly office for me.' Which of his fathers was in that slavery in Egypt, and was elected to the priesthood after the liberation? Only Aaron. It follows that it was of Aaron's stock that the prophet was speaking in this passage, when he said that the time would come when they would no longer be priests. We now see this prophecy fulfilled. Let faith be on the alert! The reality is before our eyes; the facts are observed and laid to heart; they are thrust upon the notice even of those who have no wish to see them. 'Behold, the days are coming', he says, 'when I shall banish your seed, and the seed of your father's house, and you will not have an elder in my house all your days; and I shall banish all the men of your family from my altar, so that their eyes will fail and their spirit fade away.'

Look, the days which were foretold have now arrived. There is no priest in the line of Aaron; and any man who belongs to his line sees the Christian sacrifice prevailing all over the world, while that great honour has been taken from him; and seeing this, his 'eyes fail and his spirit fades away', wasted with grief.

Now the following statement applies directly to the house of Eli, to whom it was spoken, 'Everyone of your house that survives, they all will fall by the sword of men. And this will be a sign for you, that will come upon those two sons of yours, Ophni and Phineas: they will both die on one day.' This, therefore, happened as a sign of the transference of the priesthood from this man's family; and by this sign it was indicated that the priesthood of Aaron's house was to be changed. It is plain that the death of this man's sons did not signify the death of individuals, but the death of the priesthood itself in the line of Aaron. Again, the following words refer to that priest who was prefigured by Samuel, in succeeding Eli. Hence the statement that follows was spoken about Christ Jesus, the true priest of the new covenant: 'Then I shall raise up a faithful priest for me, who will do all that is in my heart and in my soul. I shall build him a faithful house, and he shall go to and fro in the presence of my anointed all his days.' By 'he shall go to and fro' (the word is *transibit*) he means 'he shall live with me'; just as he had previously said, about the house of Aaron, 'I have said: "Your house and your father's house will pass by in my presence for ever."' Now the statement, 'he will pass by in the presence of my anointed' must certainly be understood to refer to the house itself, not to that priest who is himself the anointed Christ, the mediator and saviour. His house, then, will 'pass by' before the Christ. But 'will pass by' (*transibit*) can also be interpreted of the passing from death to life in 'all his days' the days in which life is spent in this mortal condition, up to the end of this world. We may also observe that when God says, 'he will do all that is in my heart and in my soul', this should not suggest to us that God has a soul, since he is the creator of the soul. It is, in fact, said of God in a metaphorical sense, not literally, in the same way as we speak of the hands of God, or his feet, or other parts of the body. And to prevent our supposing, on account of such statements, that man is made in God's image in respect of his physical appearance, we have the addition of wings also, and man certainly does not possess these. Statements such as, 'Under the shadow of your wings you will protect me',[46] are intended to make men realize that such descriptions of God's ineffable nature are employing words not in a literal but in a transferred application.

To pass to the next statement: 'And it will happen that anyone who survives in your family will come to do him obeisance.' This is not said directly about the family of Eli, but about that of Aaron, of which there were individual survivors up to the time of the coming of Jesus Christ; and even now the line has not died out. For it had earlier been said, about that family of Eli, that 'everyone of your family that survives, they will all fall by the sword of men.' Then how could it be truly said in this verse, 'And it will happen that anyone who survives in your family will come to do him obeisance', if it was true that none of them would survive the avenging sword? This latter statement could only be true if the prophet meant it to be understood of those who belong to the same stock, in the sense of the whole priesthood in the line of Aaron. We may assume, then, that this refers to the predestined remnant, of whom another prophet says, 'A remnant will be saved',[47] and the Apostle says, 'In the same way a remnant has come into being at the present time through God's gracious choice.'[48] Therefore, since it is well understood that the man described as 'the survivor in your family's is one of this remnant, then without doubt, that man believes in Christ, in the same way as in the time of the apostles very many of that race believed; and even now there is not a complete absence of believers from among them, though they are few and far between. In this we see the fulfilment of the next prophecy of the man of God, 'He will come to do him obeisance for a piece of silver.' Obeisance to whom? It can only be to that high priest who is also God. For

46. Ps. 17, 8. 47. Is. 10, 22. 48. Rom. 11, 5.

not even in that priesthood following Aaron's line did men come to the temple or the altar of God in order to do obeisance to the priest. And then, what is the meaning of 'a piece of silver'? It must be the short statement of the faith; for in reference to this the Apostle quotes this saying, 'The Lord will make his statement on the earth final and short.'[49] And evidence for the use of 'silver' for 'utterance' is given by a verse of one of the psalms, 'The utterances of the Lord are pure, they are silver tested in the fire.'[50]

Then what is this man saying when he comes to do obeisance to the priest of God, and to the priest who is God? ' "Thrust me into some part of your priestly office, so that I may have bread to eat." I do not desire to be established in the honoured rank of my ancestors: that has now vanished. Thrust me into some part of *your* priesthood. For "I have chosen to be a menial servant in the house of God"[51] I long to be a member of your priesthood, in however lowly a capacity.' Doubtless by 'priesthood' he means the people itself, the people whose priest is 'the mediator between God and men, the man Christ Jesus'.[52] This is the people whom the apostle Peter calls 'a holy people, a royal priesthood'.[53] It is true that some translators give the rendering 'your sacrifice, not following the line of Aaron, but the line of Melchizedek, same Christian people. That is why the apostle Paul says, 'We are many, but we are one loaf, one body.'[54] And so the addition of 'to have bread to eat' neatly describes the kind of sacrifice referred to; for the priest himself says of this sacrifice, 'The bread that I shall give you is my flesh, given for the life of the world.'[55] This is the sacrifice, not following the line of Aaron, but the line of Melchizedek, 'let the reader understand this.'[56] Here, then, we have a short confession of faith, a confession of salutary humility, in these words: 'Thrust me into some part of your priestly office, so that I may have some bread to eat.' This confession is itself the 'piece of silver'; it is short, and it is the utterance of God, dwelling in the heart of the believer. God had said earlier that he had given portions of food to the family of Aaron, from the sacrificial victims of the old covenant. That was when he said, 'I gave your father's house all the burnt-sacrifices of the children of Israel, for their food'; and those were, of course, the sacrifices of the Jews. Accordingly, the man of God at this point used the words 'to eat bread'; for that, in the new covenant, is the sacrifice of the Christians.

49. cf Rom. 9, 28; Is. 10, 23. 50. Ps. 12, 6. 51. Ps. 84, 10.
52. 1 Tim. 2, 5. 53. 1 Pet. 2, 9. 54. 1 Cor. 10, 17.
55. John 6, 51. 56. Matt. 24, 15.

6. *The Jewish priesthood and kingdom, said to have been established for ever, no longer exist. The promised eternity must be interpreted as applying to others*

These prophecies were uttered at that time in such an elevated strain, and are now revealed with such clarity; and yet someone may be puzzled, not without justification, and may ask, 'How can we be confident that all the things prophesied in these books as due to happen in the future will in fact happen, if a particular statement, made there by divine inspiration was not capable of fulfilment? This is the statement: "Your house and your father's house will pass by in my presence for ever." Now we observe that that priesthood has been superseded and that the promise made to that house has no hope of fulfilment at any time; because the priesthood which succeeded, on the rejection and supersession of the old order, is proclaimed as eternal in its stead.' This questioner does not yet understand, or does not recall, that the priesthood of Aaron's line was itself set up as a kind of shadow of the eternal priesthood that was to be. It follows that when eternity was promised to it, it was not promised for the shadow, the prefigurement, but for what was foreshadowed and prefigured by it. We were not intended to suppose that the shadow itself was to continue; and for that reason its supersession had to be foretold.

In the same way, the kingdom of Saul himself, who was certainly rejected and cast aside, was a shadow of the future kingdom which was to continue for ever. Undoubtedly the oil with which he was anointed – and because of that chrism he was called the anointed (*christus*) – is to be taken in a mystical sense and interpreted as a great sacrament.[57] In fact, David himself had such reverence for this sacrament in the person of Saul that he was smitten to the heart and shaken with dread when, after hiding in the dark cave which Saul had entered, under the compulsion of a call of nature, he secretly cut off a tiny piece of Saul's robe from behind, so as to have a proof of how he had spared him when he could have taken his life. David's purpose was to remove from Saul's mind the suspicions that led him to pursue the holy David with violence, supposing him to be his enemy. But David was filled with terror in consequence, for fear that he should be guilty of violating so great a sacrament in the person of Saul, simply because he had so treated even his clothing. The scriptural narrative says, 'Now David's heart smote him, because he took away the tail of Saul's cloak.' Furthermore, when the men who were with him were

57. i.e. an event or action with an ulterior meaning; cf. Bk XVI, 37n.

urging him to make away with Saul, now that he was delivered into their hands, David said to them, 'May the Lord preserve me from doing what you suggest, to my lord, the Lord's anointed, that I should lay hands on him, for he is the Lord's anointed.'[58] So great, we see, was the reverence displayed to this shadow of what was to come, not on its own account, but for the sake of what it foreshadowed.

The same consideration applies to what Samuel said to Saul,

> 'You have not observed my command, an order given to you by the Lord; and therefore, just as the Lord had once designed that your kingdom over Israel should be everlasting, so now your kingdom will not endure for you. The Lord will look for a man after his own heart, and the Lord will command him to be the ruler over his people, because you have not kept the commands of the Lord.'[59]

We must not take this to mean that God had designed that Saul himself should reign for ever, and then refused to carry out his design when Saul sinned, for God was not unaware that Saul would sin. No; the meaning is that God had designed his kingship to be a prefigurement of the eternal kingship. That is why Samuel added, 'and now your kingdom will not endure *for you*.' Thus what was symbolized in that kingdom endured, and will endure; but the kingship 'will not endure' for Saul, since he was not destined to reign for ever, nor was his line – for in that case, with his posterity succeeding one after the other, the promise of an 'everlasting' kingdom would have seemed, in that sense, to have been fulfilled. But Samuel goes on to say, 'The Lord will look for a man'; and this means either David or the Mediator of the new covenant[60] himself, who was prefigured also in the chrism with which David and his descendants were anointed. Now when God 'looks for' a man for himself, it does not mean that God does not know where that man is. The truth is that when God speaks through the mouth of a man he speaks in human fashion; for he uses the same way of speaking when he 'seeks' us. The only-begotten Son came 'to seek what was lost',[61] although we were already so well-known to him, as well as to God the Father, that we were 'chosen in him before the foundation of the world'.[62] Thus in saying 'he will look for', Samuel means 'he will have as his own.' Hence in Latin this verb *quaerere*, 'to seek', receives a preposition and becomes *ad-quirere*, 'to acquire'; and the meaning then is quite clear. And yet even without the prefix the simple verb can mean 'acquire'; in fact, from this simple verb is derived the noun *questus*, meaning 'profit'.

58. 1 Sam. 24, 1–6. 59. 1 Sam. 13, 13f. 60. Hebr. 12, 24.
61. Luke 19, 10. 62. Eph. 1, 4.

7. *The disruption of the Israelite kingdom, prefiguring the perpetual separation of spiritual from carnal Israel*

Saul sinned again through disobedience, and again Samuel said to him, speaking the word of the Lord, 'Because you have spurned the word of the Lord, the Lord has spurned you, so that you will not be king over Israel.' And again, for the same sin, when Saul confessed and prayed for pardon, and besought Samuel to return with him to make his peace with God, Samuel said,

> 'I shall not return with you, because you have spurned the word of the Lord and he has spurned you, so that you will not be king over Israel.' Then Samuel turned his face away, to leave Saul; and Saul held on to the tail of his robe, and tore it. And Samuel said to him: 'The Lord has torn the kingdom from Israel, out of your hand, today: and he will give it to a neighbour of yours, who is a better man than you, and Israel will be divided in two. The Lord will not go back on his word, nor will he change his mind; for he is not like a man, so as to change his mind. A mere man threatens, and does not stand by this threats.'[63]

Thus Saul was told, 'The Lord will spurn you, so that you will not be king over Israel', and, 'The Lord has torn the kingdom from Israel, out of your hand, today.' And yet he reigned over Israel for forty years, in fact the same length of time as David himself; and he heard this prophecy in the early part of his reign. So the purpose of the prophecy is that we may realize that none of his line was destined to reign, and may turn our attention to the stock of David, from which sprang, by physical descent, 'the mediator between God and men, the man Christ Jesus'.[64]

Now the Scripture does not snow the reading found in most Latin texts: 'The Lord has torn the kingdom *of* Israel out of your hand', but the reading we have followed, which is found in the Greek version: 'The Lord has torn the kingdom *from* Israel, out of your hand.' The purpose of this reading is to make it plain that 'out of your hand' means the same as 'from Israel'. Thus the man Saul figuratively personified Israel, the people which was to lose its kingdom when Christ Jesus our Lord should take the kingship under the new covenant, a spiritual instead of a physical kingship. When it is said of him, 'And he will give it to a neighbour of yours', the reference is to physical kinship; for Christ was descended from Israel by physical descent, just as Saul was. Now the following phrase, *bono super te*, can be rendered

63. 1 Sam. 15, 23–9. The last sentence is not in the Hebrew, nor in LXX.
64. 1 Tim. 2, 5.

'a better man than you', and that is how some interpreters have translated it. But it is better to take it as meaning 'good, *above* you', indicating that his superiority is based on his goodness. This would fit in with the prophetic saying, 'until I put all your enemies under your feet'.[65] Israel is one of these enemies, and Christ has taken away the kingdom from Israel, his persecutor. And yet there was even there an Israel 'in whom there was no trickery',[66] like some grain among that chaff. For the apostles, as we know, came from Israel, as did all those martyrs, of whom Stephen was the first; and so did all those churches, which the apostle Paul mentions as giving glory to God for his conversion.[67]

I have no doubt that the next words are to be interpreted along these lines. 'And Israel will be divided into two' must mean, into Israel the enemy of Christ, and Israel which attaches itself to Christ – the Israel connected with the maidservant, and the Israel connected with the free woman.[68] For these two kinds of Israel were at first together, just as Abraham was still attached to the maidservant until the barren wife, made fertile by the grace of Christ, exclaimed, 'Throw out the maidservant and her son.'[69] We know, of course, that because of Solomon's sin Israel was divided into two in the reign of his son Rehoboam, and that it continued so divided, each part having its own king, until that whole nation was overthrown with enormous devastation and deported by the Chaldeans. But what has this to do with Saul? If any such threat had to be uttered, it should have been levelled at David, rather than Saul, for Solomon was David's son. And then again, the Hebrew race at the present time is not divided, but dispersed indiscriminately throughout the world, though united by association in the same error. But that division with which God threatened this same kingdom and people in the person of Saul, who personified that kingdom and people, was shown to be eternal and unchangeable by the words which follow: 'The Lord will not go back on his word, nor will he change his mind; for he is not like a man, so as to change his mind. A mere man threatens, and does not stand by his threats.' That is, a man threatens and does not stand by his threats, unlike God, who does not change his mind, as a man does. For when we are told that God changes his mind, or repents, this signifies an alteration in the course of history, though the divine prescience remains unchanged. Thus when it is said that God does not change his mind the meaning is that there is no alteration in him.

65. Ps. 110, 1. 66. John 1, 47. 67. cf. Gal. 1, 24.
68. cf. Gal. 4, 21–31. 69. Gen. 21, 10.

We see that by these words an utterly irrevocable sentence was divinely proclaimed concerning this division of the people of Israel, a sentence absolutely perpetual. For all those who have passed over from that people to Christ, or who are now passing over, or who will pass over, were not of that people according to God's foreknowledge, nor by reason of the one common nature of the human race. Moreover, all those of the Israelites who attach themselves to Christ and continue steadfastly in his fellowship will never be associated with those Israelites who persist in their hostility to him to the end of his life; in fact, they will continue for ever in that state of separation which is prophesied here. For the old covenant from Mount Sinai which 'has children destined for slavery'[70] is of no value except in so far as it bears witness to the new covenant. Otherwise, as long as 'Moses' is read, 'a veil is laid on their hearts'; on the other hand, whenever anyone passes over from that people to Christ, the veil will be taken away.[71] For we may be sure that the very aim of those who pass over is transformed from the old to the new, so that the aim of each is no longer the attainment of material felicity, but spiritual happiness. That explains the action of the great prophet Samuel himself, before he had anointed King Saul.

Samuel cried out to the Lord on behalf of Israel, and God heard him; and when he offered a whole burnt-offering, and the foreigners approached to do battle with the people of God, the Lord thundered over them and they were thrown into confusion and panic as they faced Israel, and so they were overcome. Then Samuel took a stone and set it up between the old and the new Mizpah, and gave it the name Ebenezer, which means 'the stone of the helper'. And he said: 'So far the Lord has helped us.'[72]

Now Mizpah means 'aim'.[73] That 'stone of the helper' is the mediation of the Saviour, through whom we must pass over from the old Mizpah to the new, that is from the aim which looked for material bliss – a false bliss, in a material kingdom – to the aim which looks for spiritual bliss – the really true bliss, in the kingdom of heaven. And since there is nothing better than this, God helps us 'so far'.

70. Gal. 4, 24. 71. cf. 2 Cor. 3, 15f.

72. 1 Sam. 7, 9–12. (LXX. 'Old and new Mizpah' is in the Hebrew 'Mizpah and Shen'.)

73. The Hebrew word means 'watch-tower'.

8. *God's promises to David about his son; in no way fulfilled in Solomon, but abundantly fulfilled in Christ*

It is clear to me that my next task is to explain the promises given by God to David himself, who succeeded Saul on the throne. This transference of the royal power was a symbol of that final transference, and all these things were said and recorded by divine inspiration with reference to that change; and these promises are relevant to our present subject. After King David had met with much prosperity, he contemplated the building of a house for God. What he had in mind was that world-famous Temple which was afterwards erected by King Solomon, his son. While David was contemplating this prospect the word of the Lord came to Nathan the prophet, for him to convey it to the king. The first part of God's message was that his house would not be built by David himself, and that he had never given orders to any member of his people, during all that length of time, that a house of cedar should be constructed for him. He then went on to say,

'And now you will say this to my servant David: "This is the message of the Lord omnipotent: 'I took you from the sheepfold so that you should become the leader over my people, over Israel; and I was with you in your every enterprise. I have banished all your enemies from before your face; and I have given you a title borne by all the great ones who are on the earth. I shall provide a place for my people Israel, and I shall plant them there, and they will dwell by themselves; and they will be troubled no longer. The son of wickedness will not continue to oppose them, as he has done from the beginning from the time when I established judges over my people Israel; and I will give you rest from all your enemies, and the Lord will give you news that you will build a house for him. What will happen is that when your days are ended, and you are at rest with your ancestors, I shall raise up your offspring after you, the issue of your body, and I shall prepare his kingdom. He will build me a house for my name, and I shall direct his throne for all eternity. I shall be a father to him, and he shall be a son to me. If any wickedness appears in him, I shall chastise him with the rod that men use, with the touches that human beings inflict. Yet I shall not withdraw my mercy from him, as I did from those whom I banished from my presence. His house will be faithful, and his sovereignty will be secure for ever in my presence, and this throne will stand for all eternity.' " '[74]

It is a great mistake to pay attention only to the words 'he will build me a house', and, because Solomon erected that famous Temple, to imagine that this magnificent promise was fulfilled in Solomon, overlooking the statement that 'his house will be faithful to me and his

74. 2 Sam. 7, 8–16.

sovereignty will be secure for ever in my presence.' Anyone who supposes this should turn his attention to Solomon's household, and consider the state of things there; for his house was full of foreign women who worshipped false gods; and the king himself, who had been a man of wisdom, was seduced and degraded to the same idolatry. Such a reader must not dare to imagine that God made this promise untruthfully, nor to suppose that God could not foresee that Solomon and his house would be like this. We ought not, in fact, to have any doubt about this even if we did not see these prophecies now fulfilled in Christ our Lord, who was born of the line of David by physical descent. This would prevent us from vainly and foolishly looking for someone else, as the 'Jews after the flesh' still look. For they realize that the son promised, as they read in this passage, to King David, was not Solomon; but so amazing is their blindness that they go on to profess their hope for another, even when the promised son has been so clearly manifested.

No doubt a partial reflection of the future reality was shown even in Solomon, in that he did build the Temple, and that he enjoyed the peace that fits his name – for 'Solomon' means 'peacemaker'.[75] And at the start of his reign he was remarkably praiseworthy. Even so, Solomon himself in his own person merely gave notice of the coming of Christ, by a foreshadowing of the future; he did not show men the Lord Christ himself. Hence some things are written about him as if they were predictions of Solomon himself, while in fact holy Scripture, which prophesies by historical events also, sketches, as it were, in him a pattern of the future. For besides the books of sacred history in which the events of his reign were recorded, the seventy-first psalm also has his name inscribed in its title. In this psalm there are many sayings which cannot conceivably apply to Solomon, but are appropriate – nothing could be clearer – to the Lord Christ. So much so that there is no mistaking the fact that in Solomon there is a kind of shadowy sketch, while in Christ the reality itself is presented to us. For the limits bounding Solomon's kingdom are well known; yet we read in this psalm, to mention only one point, 'His sway will extend from sea to sea, and from the river as far as the bounds of the earth.'[76] It is in Christ that we see the fulfilment of these words. It was certainly from the river that he began his lordship; for there, after his baptism by John, he began to be recognized, at John's prompting,

75. A popular etymology; the Hebrew word *shalôm*='*peace*'.
76. Ps. 72, 8.

by his disciples. And they called him not only 'Master' but also 'Lord'.

Moreover, the reason why Solomon began to reign while his father David was still alive (a thing which did not happen to any other of their kings) was simply to make it sufficiently obvious, in this way as well as in others, that he himself was not the man designated by that prophecy which was addressed to his father. For the prophecy said, 'What will happen is that when your days are ended, and you are at rest with your ancestors, I shall raise up your offspring after you, the issue of your body, and I shall prepare his kingdom.' How can it be supposed that this is a prophecy about Solomon, just because of the following statement: 'He will build me a house'? Instead, we should notice what precedes: 'When your days are ended, and you are at rest with your ancestors, I shall raise up your offspring after you', and infer from this that another 'peacemaker' is promised, who is to be raised up, according to the prediction, after David's death, not, like Solomon, before it. It may be that there was a long interval before the coming of Jesus Christ, but certainly it was after the death of King David, to whom the promise was made, that he was to come who would build God a house, not of wood and stone, but of human beings, the kind of house that he makes us glad by building. It is to this house, that is, to all Christ's faithful believers, that the Apostle addresses the words, 'For the temple of God is holy; and you are that temple.'[77]

9. *The prophecy of Christ in the eighty-ninth psalm compared with Nathan's prophecy*

For the same reason God's promises to King David are also recorded in the eighty-eighth psalm, which has the title 'For the understanding of Ethan the Israelite'. Some of the things said in the psalm are similar to those set down in the book of Kingdoms;[78] for example, 'I have sworn to David my servant: "I shall establish your offspring for ever."'[79] Again,

> Then you spoke in a vision to your sons, and you said: 'I have conferred help on a mighty man, I have exalted a man chosen from my people. I have found David my servant; I have anointed him with my holy oil. For my hand will help him, and my arm will support him. The enemy will not get the better of him, and the son of wickedness will not hurt him. I shall strike

77. 1 Cor. 3, 17.
78. The LXX title for the books of Samuel and Kings.
79. Ps. 89 (LXX 88), 3f; cf. n.124.

down his enemies from before his face, and I shall put to flight those who hate him. My truth and mercy will be with him, and in my name his prosperity will be exalted. I shall give him authority over the sea and supreme power over the rivers. He will invoke me thus: "You are my father, my God, and the upholder of my safety": and I shall make him my firstborn, exalted among the kings of the earth. I shall keep my mercy for him for ever, and my covenant will be faithfully kept for him. I shall establish his line to last for ever and ever, and his throne to endure as long as the heavens.'[80]

All these prophecies, when rightly interpreted, are referred to the Lord Jesus, under the name of David because of the 'form of a servant'[81] which that same mediator took from the virgin, from the line of David.

There follows immediately a mention of the sins of his son, very similar to that found in the book of Kingdoms. This is too easily assumed to apply to Solomon. For here, in the book of Kingdoms, the Lord says, 'If any wickedness appears in him, I shall chastise him with the rod that men use, with the touches that human beings inflict. Yet I shall not withdraw my mercy from him.'[82] 'Touches' means here the strokes of correction. Hence the saying, 'Do not touch my anointed ones',[83] which can only mean 'Do not injure them.' Now in the psalm, when ostensibly dealing with David, the Lord's intention is to say something of the same sort there also; and so he says, 'If his sons desert my Law and cease to live according to my rulings; if they violate my statutes and do not keep my commandments, I shall punish their wickedness with the rod and their sins with the scourge; yet I shall not sweep away my mercy from him.'[84] He did not say 'from *them*', although he was speaking of his sons, not of David himself. He said 'from *him*', which, if correctly interpreted, has exactly the same force. For no sins could be found in Christ himself, who is the head of the Church, which would need to be disciplined by human correction, while the divine mercy continued unchanged. Such sins could only be found in his body and limbs, that is, in his people. Now in the book of Kingdoms '*his* iniquity' is spoken of, whereas in the psalm we find 'the iniquity *of his sons*'. The purpose of this is to make us realize that what is said about his body is in some measure spoken of himself. (For the same reason he himself also spoke from heaven, when Saul was persecuting his body, that is, his faithful followers, and his words were: 'Saul, Saul, why are you persecuting *me*?'[85]) Then in the fol-

80. Ps. 89, 19–29. 81. cf. Phil. 12, 7. 82. 2 Sam. 7, 14f.
83. Ps. 105, 15. 84. Ps. 89, 30ff. 85. Acts 9, 4.

lowing verses of the psalm he says, 'I shall not do injury to my truth, nor shall I violate my covenant; and I shall not revoke the words that issue from my lips. I have sworn once by my holiness, if I prove a liar to David – ' that is, I shall in no way prove a liar to David, this being a common idiom in Scripture. Now as to the subject on which he will not prove a liar, he adds this when he says, 'His line endures for ever, and his throne in my sight is like the sun, like the moon that is established for ever, the faithful witness in the sky.'[86]

10. *The contrast between God's promises and the actual history of the earthly Jerusalem teaches us that the promise refers to the glory of the other king and the other kingdom*

After these solid guarantees of such an important promise the psalmist prevents us from supposing that the prophecies were fulfilled in Solomon, for he suggests that these things were hoped for, and not found in actuality, by adding, 'But you have cast him aside and reduced him to nothing, O Lord.' This is certainly what happened to the kingdom of Solomon under his successors, whose history culminated in the overthrow of the earthly Jerusalem itself, which was the seat of that kingdom, and, above all, in the destruction of the very Temple which had been erected by Solomon. But we are not allowed to suppose that God acted in contradiction of his promise, for the psalm immediately continues, 'You have deferred your anointed.'[87] It follows that, if the anointed of the Lord was deferred, the anointed is not Solomon, nor even David himself. It is true that all kings consecrated with that mystic chrism were called 'the Lord's anointed', not only in David's time, and subsequently, but even in the time of Saul, who was first anointed king over that people. David himself, as we know, called Saul 'the Lord's anointed'. For all that, there was just one true anointed, the one whom these kings represented symbolically in virtue of an anointing which was prophetic. In relation to the general assumption that 'the anointed' was to be identified with David or Solomon, the coming of the true anointed was long deferred; but in respect of God's design, his future coming, in God's own time, was already in preparation.

The psalm then continues with an account of what happened to the

86. Ps. 89, 33–7.
87. Ps. 89, 38 (LXX; Hebrew: 'You have been enraged with your anointed.')

kingdom of the earthly Jerusalem, where it was certainly expected that Christ would reign, while his coming was deferred.

> You have overthrown the covenant of your servant, you have dishonoured his sanctity and cast it to the ground. You have destroyed all his walls, you have brought dread upon his defences. All the wayfarers have looted him; he has become an object of scorn to his neighbours. You have given his enemies the upper hand over him; you have gladdened the hearts of all his foes. You have turned aside the sword that should have helped him; you have not supported him in war. You have stripped him of his immaculate attire; you have dashed his throne to the ground. You have diminished the length of his sovereignty; you have covered him with confusion.[88]

All this came upon Jerusalem the maidservant, in which there reigned also some sons of the free woman,[89] holding that kingdom on a temporary lease, while possessing, by true faith, the kingdom of the Heavenly Jerusalem, whose sons they were, and placing their hope in the true Christ. How these things happened to that kingdom is revealed in the historical records to those who care to read them.

11. *The substance of the people of God, in Christ in virtue of his incarnation*

After these prophecies, the prophet turns to address supplications to God; but the prayer is itself also an act of prophecy. 'How long, Lord, do you turn away, to the end?'[90] We must supply 'your face', on the analogy of another passage, 'How long do you turn away your face from me?'[91] That is why some texts read here 'are you turned away', instead of 'do you turn away'. Still, a possible interpretation is, '... do you turn away your mercy, which you promised to David?' Then what is the meaning of 'to the end'? It must be 'right up to the end'; and 'the end' is to be understood as the last time, when even that nation is destined to believe in Christ Jesus.[92] Before that end those distressing events were bound to happen which the psalmist had lamented previously. This is the reason for the next words, 'Your anger blazes out like fire; remember what my substance is.'[93] The best way of taking this is to refer it to Jesus as the substance of that people from whom he derived his physical nature.

88. Ps. 89, 39–45. 89. cf. Gal. 4. 90. Ps. 89, 46.
91. Ps. 13, 1. 92. cf Bk XX, 29.
93. Ps. 89, 46f. (*substantia*; LXX, *hypostasis*, taken by St Augustine as 'essential being').

The psalm continues, 'For you have not created all the sons of men for nothing.' The truth is that all the sons of men *would* have been created for nothing, had there not been one Son of Man who was the 'substance' of Israel, a Son of Man through whom many sons of men would be set free. For at this time all mankind had fallen from the truth into futility through the sin of the first man; that is why another psalm says, 'Man has become like a thing of futility; his life passes away like a shadow.'[94] And yet God did not create all the sons of men for nothing, seeing that he sets many free from this futility through Jesus the Mediator; while as for those who, in his foreknowledge, were not to be set free, he created them for the advantage of those who were to be liberated, and to mark the contrast between the two mutually opposed cities. Thus we may be sure that their creation was not in vain; it was included in a design of supreme beauty and justice, a design for the whole rational creation.

Then follows this passage: 'What man is there who will live and not see death? Who will rescue his own soul from the clutches of hell?' What man indeed, unless it is that 'substance' of Israel, the descendant of David, Christ Jesus. For it is of him that the Apostle says, 'in rising from the dead he dies no more; and death will no more hold sway over him.'[95] For he will live and will not see death, though on this condition: that he will first have died, but will have rescued his soul from the clutches of hell, where he descended in order to undo the bonds of hell from some of the dead. Moreover, he will have rescued his soul in virtue of that power he speaks of in the Gospel: 'I have the power to lay down my life; and I have the power to resume it again.'[96]

12. *Who are represented in this psalm as appealing for God's 'ancient mercies'?*

The rest of the psalm runs like this: 'Lord, where are your mercies of ancient times, which you promised to David, swearing an oath on your truth? Remember, Lord, the insult offered to your servants, the insult of many peoples that I took to heart, the insult whereby your enemies, Lord, have taunted you, whereby they have taunted the transformation of your anointed.' Now the question can justly be raised whether this represents the complaint of those Israelites who longed to receive the fulfilment of the promise made to David; or is it rather the appeal of the Christians, who are Israelites not by physical

94. Ps. 144, 4. 95. Rom. 6, 9. 96. John 10, 18.

descent but by spiritual kinship? Now these words, as we know, were said or written in the time of Ethan, from whose name the psalm received its title; and this was the time of David's reign. It follows that it would not have been put in this form, 'Lord, where are your mercies of ancient times, which you promised to David, swearing an oath on your truth?' unless this prophecy assumed the person of those who were to come long afterwards, for whom the period when those promises were given to David would be 'ancient times'. It can, indeed, be taken as meaning that many nations, when they were persecuting the Christians, taunted them with the passion of Christ, which the Scripture calls his 'transformation', because by dying he became immortal. The 'transformation' of Christ can also be taken, on this line of interpretation, as a reproach to the Israelites; for Christ was expected to come as their saviour, but in fact he became the saviour of the Gentiles, and many nations who have believed in him through the new covenant make this a reproach to the Israelites, who continued in the old. This would give point to the words, 'Remember, Lord, the insult offered to your servants', since if God does not forget those servants, but takes pity on them instead, they themselves will come to believe, after this reproach.

Still, the first interpretation I suggested seems the more appropriate. For the cry, 'Remember, Lord, the insult offered to your servants', is incongruous if it is put into the mouths of Christ's enemies, suffering reproach because Christ has abandoned them and gone over to the Gentiles; for such Jews are not to be called 'servants of God'. On the other hand, these words are fitting for those who, when they endured oppressive persecutions for Christ's name, could recall that a kingdom on high had been promised to David's line, and in their longing for it could make their appeal, not despairing, but seeking, searching, and knocking. in these words: 'Lord, where are your mercies of ancient times, which you promised to David, swearing an oath on your truth? Remember, Lord, the insult offered to your servants, the insult of many peoples that I took to heart' – that is, which I patiently endured in my inner being – 'the insult whereby your enemies, Lord, have taunted you, whereby they have taunted the transformation of your anointed' – supposing it to be a destruction rather than a transformation. Then what does 'Remember, Lord' mean except this: 'Remember to have mercy, and in return for the humiliation patiently endured, repay me with the exaltation which you promised to David, swearing by your truth'?

On the other hand, we may assign these words to the Jews, since an appeal could have been made by those 'servants of God' who, after the sack of the earthly Jerusalem, before the birth of Jesus Christ in human form, were taken into captivity. We should then interpret 'the transformation of the anointed' in this sense, that it was not an earthly, material happening, such as was seen during the few years of Solomon's reign, that was to be awaited with faith, but a heavenly, spiritual felicity. The heathen nations had no idea of such happiness at that time, when they were exulting over God's people and taunting them in their captivity. But what else were they insulting but 'the transformation of the anointed', reviling, in their ignorance, those who knew the truth? That is the reason for the concluding words of the psalm, which follow this verse: 'The blessing of the Lord for ever. So be it! So be it!' These words are eminently suitable for the whole people of God who belong to the Heavenly Jerusalem, whether among those who were hidden in the time of the old covenant, before the revelation of the new, or among those who, after its revelation, are clearly manifested as belonging to Christ. And we may be sure that 'the blessing of the Lord' on David's line is not something to be hoped for a limited period, like that which was seen in the days of Solomon; it is something to be expected to last for all eternity; and in the supreme certainty of that hope we have the words, 'So be it! So be it!'

This repeated phrase is a confirmation of that hope. David, then, understands this, when he says, in the second book of Kingdoms, from which we have digressed to deal with this psalm, 'You have spoken on behalf of your servant's house for a distant future.' Again, when he says, a little farther on, 'Now begin, and bless the house of your servant for all eternity ...'[97] the reason is that he was then about to have a son through whom his posterity would be traced down to Christ, and thanks to Christ his house was destined to become eternal, and to be the house of God. It is the house of David because of its descent from him; but it is also the house of God because it is God's temple, built not of stones, but of human beings, for the people to dwell there for ever with their God and in their God, and for God to dwell there with his people and in his people. Thus God will fill his people and the people will be full of their God, when God will be all in all,[98] being himself our prize in peace, as he is our strength in war. For this reason Nathan's words, 'the Lord will bring you news that you will build him a house', were afterwards repeated in David's state-

97. 2 Sam. 7, 19; 29.
98. cf. Eph. 2, 20; 1 Pet. 3, 5; Rev. 21, 3; 1 Cor. 15, 28.

ment: 'For you, Lord omnipotent, the God of Israel, have made a revelation to your servant, saying that I shall build you a house.'[99] Now we build this house by living good lives, and God also builds it by helping us so to live. For 'unless the Lord builds a house, those who build it have laboured to no purpose.'[100] When the final dedication of this house arrives, then will come the fulfilment of what God said to Nathan in this passage, 'Then I shall establish a place for my people Israel; and I shall set them there, and they will dwell by themselves, and shall be disturbed no more. And the son of wickedness will not continue to humiliate them as he has done from the start, from the time when I set up judges over my people Israel.'[101]

13. *Can we suppose that the promised peace became a reality in the time of Solomon?*

Anyone who hopes for so great a blessing in this world and on this earth has the wisdom of a fool. Can anyone really imagine that this blessing was fully granted in the peace of Solomon's reign? No doubt the Scripture paints a glowing picture of that peace by way of a prophecy of an ideal, a foreshadowing of what was to be. Yet Scripture is careful to forestall the question of fulfilment under Solomon. It does this in the passage where, after the statement that 'the son of wickedness will not continue to humiliate them', those words are immediately added, 'as he has done from the start, from the time when I set up judges over my people Israel'. Now before the beginning of the rule of kings, judges had been appointed over that people from the time when they received the land of promise. The 'son of wickedness', namely the foreign enemy, certainly humiliated them, during those periods in which we are told that intervals of peace alternated with times of war. And yet during that era we find periods of peace more prolonged than the peace which Solomon enjoyed during the forty years of his reign. For example, under the judge named Ehud there were eighty years of peace.[102] So we must never imagine that it was Solomon's time that was predicted in this promise, not to speak of the reign of any other king; for none of the other kings reigned in such peace as Solomon. Yet that people never possessed the kingdom so securely as not to fear subjugation by their enemies; in fact, such is the instability of human affairs that no people has ever been allowed such a degree of tranquillity as to remove all dread of hostile attacks

99. 2 Sam. 7, 11; 27.
100. Ps. 127, 1.
101. 2 Sam. 7, 10f.
102. Judg. 3, 30.

on their life in this world. That place, then, which is promised as a dwelling of such peace and security is eternal, and is reserved for eternal beings, in 'the mother, the Jerusalem which is free'.[103] There they will be in truth the people of Israel; for the name 'Israel' means 'seeing God'.[104] It is in the longing for this reward that we must lead devout lives, guided by faith, during this troublesome pilgrimage.

14. *David's careful arrangement of the psalms to give a mystical significance*

In the course of the temporal history of the City of God, David at first reigned in the earthly Jerusalem, which was a shadow of what was to come. Now David was a man highly skilled in songs, a man who loved the harmony of music. But David was not the ordinary man for whom music is merely for pleasure; for him it served the purpose of his faith. He used it in the service of his God, the true God, by giving a mystical prefiguration of a matter of high importance. For the concord of different sounds, controlled in due proportion, suggests the unity of a well-ordered city, welded together in harmonious variety. Indeed, almost all his prophecy is in the psalms, and the book called Psalms contains a hundred and fifty of them. Some people have it that only those of the psalms which are inscribed with David's name were composed by him. Others suppose that none were his work except those which are headed '*Of* David himself'; while those who have in their titles the note '*For* David himself' were composed by others in a manner appropriate to David's personality. But this suggestion is refuted by the statement of the Saviour himself in the Gospel, where he says that David, inspired by the Spirit, said that Christ was his Lord, since the 109th psalm begins thus: 'The Lord said to my Lord: "Sit at my right hand, till I put your enemies as a stool for your feet."'[105] And this psalm certainly does not have '*Of* David himself' in its title. Like the majority of the psalms it has '*For* David himself'.

For my part, I find more credible the judgement of those who attribute all the 150 psalms to David's authorship, and consider that he also supplied the prefatory notes to some of them, giving the names of other men who stood for something relevant to the subject, whereas he decided that the others should not have the name of any man in their titles. Similarly, it was at the inspiration of the Lord that he made his arrangement of diverse material, an arrangement which is

103. cf. Gal. 4, 26. 104. cf. Bk XVI, 39 and n.
105. Ps. 110 (LXX 109); Matt. 22, 43.

not without purpose, obscure though the purpose may be. No one should be led to reject this hypothesis by the fact that we find inscribed above some of the psalms in this book the names of some prophets who lived a long time after the reign of David,[106] and that the contents of these psalms give the appearance of having been uttered by them. For the prophetic spirit was not incapable of revealing to King David, when he was prophesying, those names of prophets to come, and of ensuring that something appropriate to their personalities should be sung prophetically. In the same way the birth and reign of King Josiah, which was then more than 300 years in the future, was revealed together with his name, to a prophet, who also predicted his future achievements.[107]

15. *This book cannot include all the prophecies of Christ and his Church in the psalms*

I am aware that what is now expected from me in this part of my book is an explanation of David's prophecies in the psalms about Jesus Christ and his Church. In fact, although I have done this in respect of one psalm, I am prevented from meeting the apparent demands of this expectation by the abundance of matter rather than the lack of it. For I am prevented from including everything by my intention to shun prolixity; on the other hand, I am afraid that if I select a limited number of points, I may seem to many who are versed in the subject to have omitted more essential matter. Again, the evidence adduced needs to be corroborated by the context of the whole psalm, at least to the extent of showing that there is nothing there to refute it, even if every detail does not support it. Otherwise I might seem to be collecting short excerpts suitable to a chosen theme, using the method of a *cento*, where selections are taken from a long poem not written on the subject in hand, but about something else, something very different.[108] Now to be able to demonstrate this in every psalm, the whole of it has to be explained; and this is no small task, as can be seen from the works of other authors and from my own, in which I have done just this. Anyone who has the wish and the capacity may read those books; he will discover the large number and the

106. Haggai and Zechariah in the LXX version of Psalms.
107. 1 Kings 13, 2.
108. Christian *centos* ('patchworks') were constructed from the classical works; e.g. an epic on the life of Christ composed of material from Virgil's *Aeneid* in the fourth century.

great importance of the prophecies uttered by David, who was both king and prophet, about Christ and his Church, that is, about the king and the community which he founded.

16. *The witness, direct and allegorical, to Christ and his Church in Psalm 45*

Though there may be direct and clear prophetic statements on any subject, allegorical statements are inevitably intermingled with them, and it is those especially that force upon scholars the laborious business of discussion and exposition for the benefit of the more slow-witted. However, some of these point to Christ and his Church at first glance, as soon as they are uttered, although some details are less easily intelligible and are reserved for exposition at leisure. An example can be taken from the same book of Psalms:

> My heart has given vent to a noble subject; I am addressing my composition to the king. My tongue is the pen of a swift writer. You are more handsome than all the sons of men; grace has been poured on your lips, because God has blessed you for ever. Gird your sword on your thigh, most mighty one, in your majesty and beauty; arise and advance in prosperity and reign in the cause of truth, kindness and justice; and your right hand will lead you marvellously. Your arrows are sharp, most mighty one – peoples will fall beneath your sway – against the hearts of the king's enemies. Your throne, O God, is for ever and ever, the sceptre of your rule is a sceptre of uprightness. You have loved justice and hated unrighteousness: therefore God, your God, has anointed you with the oil of exultation, in preference to your fellows. Myrrh, aloes, and cassia give fragrance from your garments, from palaces of ivory, from which the king's daughters have given you delight, in your honour.[109]

No one, however slow of wit, could fail to recognize in this passage the Christ whom we proclaim and in whom we believe, when he hears of 'God, whose throne is for ever and ever', and to recognize God's anointed, anointed, be it understood, as God anoints – not with the visible oil but with the spiritual and intelligible chrism. For is there anyone so uninformed about our religion, or so deaf to its widespread renown, that he does not know that the name Christ is derived from 'chrism', that is from anointing? But as soon as he has recognized Christ as the king, let him subject himself to the king who reigns in the cause of truth, kindness, and justice, and let him inquire at leisure into all the allegorical descriptions of this psalm. Let him discover how

109. Ps. 45, 1–9.

Christ's beauty excels all the sons of men, with a kind of loveliness that calls forth the more love and admiration for not being mere physical grace, and let him find the meaning of his sword, his arrows and all the other details which are given for their allegorical meaning, not as literal description.

Then let him turn his attention to Christ's Church, wedded to so great a husband by a spiritual marriage and a divine love, the Church which is described in the following verses:

> The queen has taken her place at your right hand, in a garment of cloth of gold, swathed in a many-coloured robe. Listen, daughter; see, and incline your ear: forget your people and your father's home. For the king has desired your beauty, because he himself is your God. And the daughters of Tyre will do you reverence with gifts; the rich among the people will beg for your regard. All the glory of that king's daughter is within, swathed in a many-coloured robe with golden fringes. Her maidens will be brought to the king after her, her companions will be brought to you. They will be brought with joy and exultation; they will be led into the king's temple. In place of your fathers there are sons born to you; you will make them princes over all the earth. They will remember your name in every succeeding generation. Therefore the nations will acknowledge your praise for ever and ever.[110]

I do not imagine that anyone is such a fool as to think that some mere woman is here praised and described, as the wife, that is, of one who is thus addressed: 'Your throne, O God, is for ever and ever; the sceptre of your kingdom is a sceptre of uprightness. You have loved justice and hated unrighteousness; therefore God, your God, has anointed you with the oil of gladness, in preference to your fellows.'[111] Obviously, this is Christ, anointed above his Christian followers. For they are his followers, from whose unity and concord in all nations that queen comes into being, who in another psalm is described as 'the city of the great king'.[112]

This queen is Sion, in the spiritual sense. The name Sion means 'contemplation';[113] for she contemplates the great blessing of the age to come, since all her striving is directed to that end. She is also Jerusalem, in the same spiritual sense, which is a point on which I have already said a great deal. Her enemy is Babylon, the city of the Devil, whose name means 'confusion'.[114] However, this queen among the nations is set free from that Babylon by rebirth, and passes over

110. Ps. 45, 10–17. 111. Ps. 48, 2. 112. Ps. 18, 43f.
113. Impossible. Probably 'stronghold', or 'dry place'.
114. cf. Gen. 11, 10; Bk XVI, 4.

from the worst to the best of kings, that is, from the Devil to Christ. That is why she is told to 'forget your people and your father's home.' Those who are Israelites only by physical descent, and not by faith, are a part of that godless city; they are also enemies of this great king himself, and of his queen. For Christ came to them; but he was slain by them; and so he became instead the Christ of other men, men whom he did not see in his incarnate life. Hence he himself, our king, says in prophecy in one of the psalms. 'You will rescue me from the attacks of the people; you will set me at the head of the nations. A people I did not know has become my servant; when they heard with their ears they obeyed me.'[115] Thus the people of the Gentiles, whom Christ did not know in his bodily presence, believed in him, nevertheless, when he was announced to them. So it was justly said of them that 'when they heard with their ears they obeyed me', because 'faith results from hearing'.[116] This people, I say, added to those who are true Israelites both by descent and by faith, constitute the City of God, the City which also gave birth to Christ himself in the flesh, when it consisted solely of those Israelites. For the Virgin Mary, as we know, was of that race, and in her Christ assumed the flesh, so as to become man.

Another psalm speaks of this City in these terms: ' "Mother Sion", a man will say, and, "a man was born in her, and the Most High founded her." '[117] Who is this 'Most High' but God? This means that Christ, who is God before he became man by Mary in that City, himself founded the City in the persons of the patriarchs and prophets. Thus what we now see fulfilled was said in prophecy so long before to this queen, 'In place of your fathers there are sons born to you; you will make them princes over all the earth'; for it is true that from her sons throughout all the earth come her leaders and fathers, since the people acknowledge her pre-eminence, as they flock together to confess her everlasting praise for all time to come. There can be no doubt then that whatever is said in this passage, though somewhat obscurely, in allegorical fashion, whatever the precise line of interpretation, must be consistent with those very obvious facts.

17. *Christ's priesthood described in Psalm 110, and his passion in Psalm 22.*

In the psalm we have been examining Christ is proclaimed as king. Similarly, in another psalm he is set forth as priest. The pro-

115. Ps. 17, 44ff. 116. Rom. 10, 17. 117. Ps. 87; 5.

nouncement is made in the clearest terms: 'The Lord said to my Lord: "Sit on my right hand, until I put your enemies as a stool for your feet." '[118] That Christ is at the right hand of the Father is a matter of belief, not of sight; and it is not yet obvious that his enemies are put under his feet. But this is what is happening, and it will be obvious in the end; so here we have something else which is now a matter of belief and will later be a matter of sight. As for the following statement: 'The Lord will send out of Sion the rod of your strength; rule amidst your enemies!' this is so plain that its denial would show not only the loss of faith and of happiness but even the failure of conscience. For even our enemies acknowledge that the law of Christ, which we call the gospel, was issued out of Sion, and in it we recognize the 'rod of his strength'. While the fact that he 'rules amidst his enemies' is witnessed by the very men among whom he rules, as they gnash their teeth and waste away[119] and are powerless against him.

A little later we have these words: 'The Lord has taken an oath, and he will not change his mind', and this statement indicates the unchangeable nature of the following pronouncement: 'You are a priest for ever, in the line of Melchizedech.' Now who could take leave to doubt of whom these words are spoken, given the fact that there is at this time nowhere a priesthood or sacrifice in the line of Aaron, and that under Christ's priesthood there is offered everywhere the oblation presented by Melchizedech, when he blessed Abraham?[120] So we see that matters which are somewhat obscurely expressed in this psalm are, when rightly taken, referred to these obvious facts. I have already so related them in my sermons to the people.

We find the same thing in the psalm where Christ in a prophecy gives an eloquent description of the humiliation of his passion, in those words: 'They have pierced my hands and feet; they have counted all my bones. Yes, they have looked me over and stared at me.'[121] In this description, we may be sure, he points to his body stretched out on the cross, with his hands and feet pierced and fastened by the nails driven through them, and the spectacle he thus provided for those who looked him over and stared at him. He also adds, 'They have divided my clothing among them and have cast lots for my garment', and the gospel account records how this prophecy was fulfilled. Then there are other sayings in the psalm which are less explicit in their

118. Ps. 110, 1f. 119. cf. Ps. 112, 10. 120. cf. Gen. 14, 18.
121. Ps. 22, 16f; cf. Matt. 27, 35; John 19, 24.

reference; but there can be no question that they are rightly taken when the interpretation is consistent with the passages where the meaning is so patent, so luminously clear. We have the best of reasons for this conviction in that other events, not events of the past which we believe but of the present time which we behold, events which are now presented to observation over the whole world, answer precisely to the predictions we read in this same psalm, uttered so long ago. For example, these words occur a little later in the psalm: 'All the ends of the earth will remember, and they will turn back to the Lord: all the families of the nations will offer worship in his sight. For the sovereignty belongs to the Lord, and he will hold sway over the nations.'[122]

18. *The death and resurrection of the Lord prophesied in Psalms 3, 41, 16 and 69*

Moreover, the oracles of the psalms are by no means silent about the Lord's resurrection. For what else is meant by the song which he is represented as singing in the third psalm, 'I went to bed and fell asleep; I arose from sleep, for the Lord upheld me'?[123] Or is there anyone silly enough to believe that the prophet wanted to let us know, as an important piece of information, that he slept and got up again? That sleep must stand for death, and that awakening for resurrection; and the psalmist had to prophesy about Christ's death and resurrection in this way.

This appears much more obviously in the fortieth psalm.[124] There, in the usual manner, prophecies of the future are put into the mouth of the Mediator himself, in the form of a narrative of past events, because coming events had already, in a sense, happened, in the predestination and foreknowledge of God. 'My enemies,' he says,

> spoke maliciously of me, saying: 'When will he die, and his name perish?' And if anyone came in to see me, his heart spoke empty words, and he heaped up wickedness for himself. They went out of doors and spoke all together with one intent. All my enemies whispered against me, they planned evil against me. They put about an evil saying against me: 'Will not he who sleeps go on to rise up again?'[125]

122. Ps. 22, 27f. 123. Ps. 3, 5.
124. Ps. 40 in LXX and hence in St Augustine's text; Ps. 41 in the Hebrew Bible and English Versions.
125. Ps. 41, 5ff.

This is surely so phrased here as to suggest the same meaning as if he had said: 'Will not he who sleeps go on to come to life again?' The earlier words prove that his enemies planned and arranged his death, and this was carried out by the agency of someone who came in to see him and went out to betray him. Here, inevitably, there comes to mind the disciple who turned traitor – Judas.

Thus because they were going to accomplish their designs, that is, they were about to kill him, he shows that they would kill him to no purpose in their futile malice, since he would rise again. He makes this plain by adding the verse, in which he says in effect, 'You futile men, what are you achieving? What is a crime in you will be sleep for me. Will not he who sleeps go on to rise again?' Nevertheless, he points out that they will not commit so grievous a crime with impunity, by saying, in the following verses: 'Indeed, the man of my peace, in whom I placed my hope, who used to eat my bread, has enlarged his heel over me', that is, he has trodden me down. 'But Lord', he says, 'have mercy on me, and revive me, and I shall pay them back.'[126] Who would now reject this interpretation, when he sees that the Jews, after the passion and resurrection of Christ, have been extirpated, root and branch, from their homes by the slaughter and destruction of war? For after the Lord had been killed by them he rose again and repaid them, in the meanwhile, with temporal discipline, which is temporal only if we discount the recompense reserved for those who have not amended, when he comes to judge the living and the dead.

For the Lord Jesus himself pointed out to his apostles that this Judas was his betrayer by handing him the bread; and in so doing he recalled this verse of our psalm and said that it was fulfilled in himself: 'He who used to eat my bread has enlarged his heel over me.'[127] But the words 'in whom I placed my hope' are appropriate not to the head but to the body. What I mean is that the Saviour himself was not ignorant of the character of the man of whom he had said earlier, 'One of you will betray me', and 'One of you is a devil.'[128] But it is his habit to transfer to himself the role of his members, and to attribute to himself what belongs to them, because Christ is at one and the same time both the head and the body. This explains the Gospel saying, 'I was hungry and you gave me food to eat', which he explains by saying, 'When you did it for one of the least of my people, you did it for me.'[129] So in this passage he ascribes to himself the hopes that

126. Ps. 41, 9.
127. John 13, 18; 26.
128. John 6, 70f.
129. Matt. 25, 35; 40.

the disciples had placed in Judas when he was included in the number of the apostles.

Now the Jews do not expect that the Messiah ('the Anointed', the *Christ*) whom they hope for, will die. For that reason they do not think that the one whom the Law and the Prophets announced is our Christ, but some kind of Messiah of their own, a fiction of their imagination, a being remote from the suffering of death. This explains why with amazing stupidity and blindness, they maintain that the words we have quoted do not signify death and resurrection, but simply sleep and awakening.

But the fifteenth psalm[130] also cries aloud, 'For this cause my heart was glad and my tongue exulted; my body, too, will rest in hope. For you will not abandon my soul in hell, nor will you allow your holy one to see corruption.' Who would claim that his body had rested in hope, with the result that his soul was not abandoned in hell, but the soul quickly returned to his body and came to life again, so that his body should not suffer corruption as corpses normally do? No one, surely, but he who rose again on the third day. The Jews certainly cannot make this claim for their prophet and king, David.

The sixty-seventh[131] psalm also cries out, 'Our God is the God who brings men salvation, and to the Lord belongs the way of escape of death.'[132] What clearer statement could there be? For 'the God who brings men salvation' is the Lord Jesus, whose name means 'saviour', or 'saving'. In fact the reason for his name was given when before his birth from the Virgin these words were said, 'She will bear a son, and you will call his name Jesus; for he will save his people from their sins.'[133] Now since his blood was shed for the remission of those sins, it was, we can see, inevitable that he had no other 'way of escape' from this life, but only the way of death. Therefore after the statement that 'our God is the God who brings men salvation' we have the immediate addition of 'and to the Lord belongs the way of escape of death', to make it plain that it was by dying that he would bring salvation. But the words 'and to the Lord belongs' were said in a tone of wonder. They amount to saying, 'Such is this mortal life that the Lord himself could not leave it except by the way of death.'

130. Ps. 16 (LXX 15), 19f. 131. Ps. 68 (LXX 67), 20.

132. The Latin is ambiguous; 'escape of' or 'escape from'.

133. Matt. 1, 21. *Jesus* is the Greek form of *Joshua*, which in Hebrew (*Yehōshûa'*, *Yeshûa'*) means, probably, 'Yahweh is salvation.'

19. *Psalm 69 exposes the unbelief and obstinacy of the Jews*

However, the Jews refuse to yield an inch in the face of such clear evidence as that of this prophecy, even when events have brought it so plainly and certainly to fulfilment; and therefore the words of the next psalm are, without question, fulfilled in them. For in that psalm also when the events connected with Christ's passion are being prophetically described, with Christ represented as the speaker, a detail is recorded whose meaning is revealed in the Gospel story, 'They gave me gall to eat, and in my thirst they gave me vinegar to drink.'[134] Then after such a feast, as it were, and such a banquet had been offered him, he went on to say, 'Let their table become a trap before them, and a retribution and a snare. May their eyes be dimmed so that they may not see, and their backs always bowed ...'[135] This was not said by way of a wish; it was a prophetic prediction in the form of a wish. Is it any wonder, then, if those whose eyes were dimmed to prevent their seeing fail to observe these obvious facts? Is it any wonder if those whose backs are always bowed so that they bend down towards things of earth, fail to look upwards towards things in heaven? For these bodily metaphors refer to spiritual failings.

But this discussion must be kept within bounds, and so let this suffice for my treatment of the psalms, that is of the prophecy of King David. I hope that my readers who are familiar with the whole subject will forgive me, and will not complain if they know or suppose that I have passed over passages which perhaps provide stronger evidence.

20. *The reign and achievements of David and Solomon: the prophecies of Christ in the writings of Solomon, and in associated books*

Thus David reigned in the earthly Jerusalem, a son of the Heavenly Jerusalem, highly praised by the testimony of inspired writings, because even his sins were overcome by such great devotion, shown in a penitence of healthy humility, that he is certainly among those of whom he himself says, 'Blessed are those whose wickedness is pardoned, whose sins are covered.'[136] After him there reigned over that whole people his son Solomon who, as was stated above,[137] began to reign while his father was still alive. He made a good start, but

134. Ps. 69 (LXX 68) 21; cf. Matt. 27, 34; 48.
135. Ps. 69, 22f. 136. Ps. 32, 1. 137. ch. 8.

finished badly. Prosperity, in fact, which 'wearies the resolution of the wise',[138] did him more damage than his wisdom brought him profit, that wisdom which even now is memorable and will be remembered in the future, which in his own time also earned such widespread renown. He, too, is found to have uttered prophecies in his books, three of which have been included in the authorized canon, namely, Proverbs, Ecclesiastes, and the Song of Songs. There are, indeed, two others, one entitled Wisdom and the other Ecclesiasticus, which are, by general custom, ascribed to Solomon on the ground of a considerable resemblance to his literary style; however, the weightier authorities have no hesitation in rejecting the attribution. Nevertheless, the Church, and in particular the Western Church, has from early times accepted them as canonical.

In one of these books, called the Wisdom of Solomon, Christ's passion is most expressly prophesied. For without question it is his godless murderers who are recorded as saying,

> 'Let us lie in wait for the righteous man, because he is displeasing to us and opposed to our activities, and accuses us of offences against the Law, and blames us for sins against our upbringing. He claims to have knowledge of God, and calls himself God's son. He has become a reproach to our way of thinking. The very sight of him depresses us, because his manner of life is different from that of other men, and his paths are unchanged. In his opinion we are men of no account, and he holds aloof from our ways as though from filth. He holds in honour the latter end of the righteous, and boasts of having God for his father. Let us see then if what he says is true; let us test what will happen to him, and we shall know what his latter end will be. For if the righteous man is God's son, God will uphold him and set him free from the clutches of his adversaries. Let us examine him with insult and torture, so that we may explore the extent of his devotion, and put his endurance to the proof. Let us condemn him to the most degrading death, since, on the evidence of his own words, he will be well looked after.' This is how they reasoned, but they were misled; for they were blinded by their own malice.[139]

Moreover, in Ecclesiasticus the future faith of the nations is predicted thus:

> Have mercy on us, God, the ruler of all, and send the fear of yourself upon all nations. Raise your hand over the foreign nations and let them see your power. As you have been sanctified in us in their sight, so prove yourself great in them in our sight; and let them recognize you just as we have recognized you, that there is no God besides you, Lord.[140]

138. Sall. *Cat*, 11, 8. 139. Wisd. 2, 12–21. 140. Ecclus. 36, 1–5.

This prophecy, in the form of a wish and a prayer, we see fulfilled through Jesus Christ. However, the writings not included in the Jewish canon do not carry as much weight as the canonical books when put forward as evidence against the opposition.

On the other hand, when we turn to the three books universally accepted as Solomon's and taken as canonical by the Jews, laborious discussion is essential if we are to prove that anything of this kind found in those books is relevant to Christ and his Church; and the undertaking would be an unnecessary digression. However, we find these words put into the mouth of the ungodly in the book of Proverbs: 'Let us hide the righteous man in the earth unrighteously; let us act the part of hell and swallow him up alive, and let us sweep away his memory from the earth, and get hold of his valuable property';[141] and this is not so obscure that it cannot be understood to refer to Christ and his property, the Church. This needs no laborious explanation. It is something of this sort, to be sure, that the Lord Jesus himself represents the wicked tenants as saying, in the Gospel parable, 'Here is the heir! Come on, let us kill him, and we shall get his inheritance.'[142]

There is another passage in the same book which we touched on earlier, when we were concerned with the barren woman who bore seven children.[143] This is generally understood, even at first hearing, to refer simply and solely to Christ and his Church; understood, that is, by those who have come to know that Christ is the Wisdom of God. The passage runs thus:

> Wisdom has built herself a house, supported on seven columns. She has sacrificed her victims, has mixed her wine in the bowl and laid her table. She has sent her slaves, summoning guests to the bowl with a proclamation from the heights, saying: 'Who is foolish? Let him put up at my house.' And to those lacking wit she has said: 'Come and eat my bread and drink the wine that I have mixed for you.'[144]

Here we recognize with certainty the Wisdom of God, that is, the Word, co-eternal with the Father, who built, as a house for himself, a human body, in the virgin's womb, and united the Church to it, as limbs are united to the head; who sacrificed the martyrs as her victims; who set his table with wine and bread, the table at which also appears the priesthood in the line of Melchizedek; and who has invited foolish men, men lacking in wit, because, in the words of the Apostle he 'has

141. Prov. 1, 11ff.
142. Matt. 21, 38.
143. 1 Sam. 2, 5. cf. ch. 4.
144. Prov. 9, 1–5.

chosen weak things, by the world's standards, to put to shame the strong.'[145] But to those weak objects he goes on to say, 'Abandon folly so that you may live; acquire discretion so that you may have life.'[146] Now to become a guest at that table is to begin to have life.

There is also a text in another book, called Ecclesiastes, where it says, 'The only good for man is in eating and drinking';[147] and surely the most plausible interpretation of this saying is that it refers to partaking of this table which the priest himself, the mediator of the new covenant, provides, in the line of Melchizedech, the table furnished with his body and blood. For that is the sacrifice which superseded all the sacrifices of the old covenant, which were offered as a foreshadowing of what was to come. That is why we also recognize in the thirty-ninth psalm the voice of the same mediator, speaking in prophecy, when he says, 'Sacrifice and oblation you have refused; but you have perfected a body for me.'[148] We recognize the speaker, because in place of all those sacrifices and oblations his body is offered and served to the participants. For our 'preacher' (*ecclesiastes*) is not thinking of feasts of bodily indulgence, in his saying, often repeated and underlined, about eating and drinking. This is made plain enough when he says, 'It is better to go into a house of mourning than into a house of drinking'; and, a little later, 'The heart of the wise is in the house of mourning: the heart of fools is in the house of feasting.'[149]

Even more worth quoting is the following passage in the same book. It is concerned with the two cities, that of the Devil, and that of Christ, and with their kings, the Devil and Christ. It says, 'You are in sorry case, a land whose king is a mere boy, whose leaders feast in the morning. Happy the land whose king is nobly born, whose leaders feast at a decent time, to give them strength, not to bring them shame.'[150] He calls the Devil 'a mere boy' because of his stupidity, his pride, his rashness, his indiscipline, and the other faults which are generally found in profusion at that age. Whereas he calls Christ 'nobly born', as being the descendant of the holy patriarchs, who belong to the free city, whose offspring he was, in the body of his incarnation. The leaders of the other city 'feast in the morning', that is before the appropriate hour, because they do not wait for the felicity which comes at the right time, the true felicity in the age to come, but are in a hurry in their desire to be made happy with the renown of this present age. The leaders of Christ's City, for their part, patiently await the time of that happiness which does not disappoint.

145. 1 Cor. 1, 27. 146. Prov. 9, 6. 147. Eccl. 8, 15.
148. Ps. 40 (LXX 39) 6. 149. Eccl. 7, 2; 4. 150. Eccl. 10, 16f.

The preacher says that they feast 'to give them strength, not to bring them shame', because they are not disappointed in their hope; in the Apostle's words, 'Hope does not put men to shame.'[151] There is also a saying in one of the psalms, 'Those who await you will not be put to shame.'[152]

Then again, the Song of Songs voices a kind of spiritual delight felt by holy minds in the marriage of the king and queen of that city, namely, Christ and his Church. But this delight is wrapped up in allegorical draperies, so that it may be more eagerly longed for, and that its uncovering may afford more pleasure, and that the bridegroom may be revealed to whom it is said, in the same song, 'Righteousness has loved you',[153] and the bride also, who is told 'Love is among your delights.'[154] There are many points we pass over without mention, in our anxiety to reach the end of the work.

21. *The kings after Solomon, both in Judah and in Israel*

The other kings of the Hebrews, after Solomon, are found to have uttered scarcely any prophecies, by means of hidden meanings in their words or actions, with reference to Christ and his Church. This is true both of the kings of Judah and of those of Israel. Those were the names given to the two divisions of that people, from the time when it was divided, when God punished them for Solomon's offences, in the time of his son Rehoboam, who succeeded to his father's throne. From that time onwards the ten tribes taken over by Jeroboam, Solomon's servant, who was set up as their king in Samaria, were called Israel, this name being restricted to them, though it had been the title of the whole nation. While the name Judah was given to two tribes, Judah and Benjamin, which had remained subject to the city of Jerusalem for David's sake, so that the kingdom of his stock should not be completely uprooted. They took the name of Judah because this was David's own tribe. Benjamin was, as I have said, the other tribe attached to this kingdom; it was the tribe of Saul, the king before David. But the two tribes together were called Judah, as I said, and by this name they were distinguished from Israel, which was the special title of the ten tribes, who had their own king. We observe that Levi, as the priestly tribe, bound to the service of God instead of that of the kings, was counted as the thirteenth tribe. Joseph, as we know, one of the twelve sons of Jacob, did not found one tribe, as did each of the other sons; he founded two tribes, Ephraim and Manasseh. Never-

151: Rom. 5, 5. 152. Ps. 25, 3.
153. 1, 4 (LXX). 154. 7, 7.

theless, the tribe of Levi had also a closer connection with the kingdom of Jerusalem, since the Temple of God, which they served, was situated there.

Now after the division of the people, Rehoboam, king of Judah, Solomon's son, was the first to reign in Jerusalem, while the first to reign in Samaria was Jeroboam, king of Israel, Solomon's servant. And when Rehoboam decided to engage in war against him as a usurper over that part of the divided kingdom, the people were prevented from fighting against their brothers by God's pronouncement, through the mouth of a prophet, that he was responsible for the division. Thus it was made clear that in this matter there had been no sin on the part of the king or the people of Israel; God's decision to punish had been fulfilled. On learning this both sides were pacified, and preserved a mutual peace; for it was not their religion that had suffered division, but only the kingdom.

22. *Jeroboam's idolatry; its effects reduced by prophets under God's inspiration*

Now Jeroboam, king of Israel, had had proof that God was true to his word, since he had promised him the kingdom, and had given it to him. Yet in the perversity of his heart he refused to put his faith in God. He was afraid that if his people visited the Temple of God in Jerusalem, to which the whole nation was bound to go to offer sacrifice, according to the divine Law, they would be seduced from his allegiance and restored to the line of David, as being the royal stock. That is why he established idolatry in his kingdom, and led God's people astray with his detestable apostasy, so that with him the people were addicted to the worship of images. Yet God did not cease to employ his prophets to reprove, by every means, not only that king, but his successors who imitated his apostasy, and the people themselves. For in that kingdom there emerged those great prophets of renown, who also performed many marvels, namely Elijah and his disciple Elisha. It was there also that Elijah said, 'Lord, they have killed your prophets, they have demolished your altars; and I am left alone, and they are after my life', and he received the reply that there were in that kingdom seven thousand men who had not bent their knees before Baal.[155]

155. 1 Kings 19, 10; 14; 17.

23. *The varying fortunes of the kingdoms till their captivity. The restoration of Judah, and its final transference to the Roman Empire*

We find the same situation in the kingdom of Judah, which was attached to Jerusalem. There too there was no lack of prophets even in the times of the kings who succeeded David. They appeared as it pleased God to send them, either to make some necessary prediction, or to rebuke sins and to demand righteousness. For there also, although to a much lesser extent than in Israel, kings did arise who grievously offended God by their impieties, and who had to be chastised, along with the people who resembled them, with punishment in proportion to their faults. There were, it is true, pious kings in Judah, and their not inconsiderable merits receive praise, whereas we are told that in Israel all the kings were reprobate, though some more than others. Thus both parts, according to the command or with the permission of God's providence, experienced vicissitudes of fortune, now being lifted up by times of prosperity, now depressed by periods of adversity; and they were so afflicted, not only by foreign wars but even by civil strife among themselves, that it became clear that God was acting in mercy or in wrath when particular causes arose. Finally, as his indignation increased, the whole nation was not only crushed and overthrown by the Chaldeans in its own homeland, but was also for the most part transferred to the territory of the Assyrians; first that division called Israel, with its ten tribes, and later Judah also, after the destruction of Jerusalem and its world-famed Temple. In those lands the Judeans lived in peaceful captivity for seventy years. After that period they were allowed to return, and they restored the Temple which had been demolished; and although very many of them still lived in foreign lands, they did not thereafter have a kingdom divided in two, with separate kings for each part. There was now only one prince over them in Jerusalem; and all of them all over the world, wherever they were, used to come back at fixed times to the Temple of God, which was in Jerusalem, if they could travel there from their homes. But even then they did not lack enemies from other nations, and conquerors, for Christ found them in his time tributaries of the Romans.[156]

156. Capture of Samaria by Sargon II of Assyria, 721 B.C.; end of the Kingdom of Israel. First deportation of Judeans to Babylon by Nebuchadnezzar, 596 B.C. Fall of Jerusalem and second deportation, 586 B.C. Capture of Babylon by Cyrus of Persia, 538 B.C.; Jews allowed to return. The return from Exile began in 537 B.C.; the building of the second Temple 520–516. Jerusalem was captured

24. *The prophets mentioned in the gospel narrative*

Now in the whole period following the return of the Jews from Babylonia, after Malachi, Haggai, and Zechariah, who prophesied at the time of the return, and after Ezra, the Jews had no prophets up to the time of the Saviour's coming, except the other Zechariah, the father of John, and his wife Elizabeth, when Christ's birth was near, and, after his birth, the old man Simeon, and Anna, a widow by then advanced in years, and, last of all, John himself. John, it is true, did not foretell the coming of Christ, for by that time Christ and he were both young men; still, he did recognize, by prophetic inspiration, the Christ who was yet unrecognized, and he pointed him out. This is why the Lord himself says, 'The Law and the Prophets down to John.'[157] Now the prophetic utterances of these five people are known to us from the Gospel, in which the Virgin herself, the Lord's mother, is also represented as prophesying, before John. But the rejected Jews do not accept the utterances of those prophets; however, the innumerable individuals from among them who have believed in the gospel do accept them. For at that time Israel was truly divided into two parts, by that division which was fore-announced to King Saul through Samuel the prophet, as an unalterable division. As for Malachi, Haggai, Zechariah, and Ezra, even the rejected Jews accept them, as the last authors to be added to the list of inspired Scripture. For writings by these prophets are extant, as are those of others, who wrote books which were to enjoy canonical authority. But they form but a small proportion of the great host of prophets. It is clear to me that some of their predictions referring to Christ and his Church must be included in this work. It will be more convenient to fulfil this obligation, with God's help, in the next book, to avoid adding further to the burden of this volume, which is already so protracted.

---

by the Romans under Pompey, 63 B.C. Judea became part of the Roman province of Syria.

157. Matt. 11, 13.

BOOK XVIII

1. *The course of history down to the era of the Saviour, as discussed in seventeen books*[1]

I PROMISED that (given God's gracious help) I would first refute the enemies of the City of God, who honour their own gods above Christ, the founder of that City, and display a bitter hatred of the Christians, with a rancour most ruinous to themselves. This task I achieved in my first ten books. I undertook after that to write about the origin, the development, and the destined ends of the two cities. One of these is the City of God, the other the city of this world; and God's City lives in this world's city, as far as its human element is concerned; but it lives there as an alien sojourner. The promise I have just mentioned was in three parts; and in the four books following my tenth I gave a summary of the *origin* of both these cities. Then in one book, the fifteenth of this work, I sketched their *progress* from the first man down to the Flood. After that the two cities proceeded on their course in our narrative, just as they did in history, down to the time of Abraham. But from the time of father Abraham down to the time of the kings of Israel (where the sixteenth book finished), and from then to the coming of the incarnate Saviour (the point reached in Book XVII), it is evident that my pen has been devoted solely to the progress of the City of God. And yet this City did not proceed on its course in this world in isolation; in fact, as we well know, just as both the cities started together, as they exist together among mankind, so in human history they have together experienced in their progress the vicissitudes of time. It was however, with set purpose that I followed this plan. My intention was first to bring out more distinctly the development of the City of God by describing its course, without interruption from its contrary, that other city, from the time when God's promises began to be more explicit, down to his birth from the Virgin, in which the original promises were fulfilled. This is in spite of the fact that the City of God developed not in the light, but in the shadow. Now, therefore, I am conscious that I must make good my

1. Augustine depends largely on the *Chronicle* of Eusebius, translated and continued by Jerome (ed. R. Helm C.G.S., 47) The obelus symbol (†) indicates this dependence in the account of the early empires and their kings.

omission, by outlining the progress of that other city from the time of Abraham, giving it what seems adequate treatment, so that my readers may observe both cities and mark the contrast between them.

2. *The earthly city; its kings and dates, corresponding to the dates of the saints, from the birth of Abraham*

Well then, the society of mortal men spread everywhere over the earth; and amid all the varieties of geographical situation it still was linked together by a kind of fellowship based on a common nature, although each group pursued its own advantages and sought the gratification of its own desires. In such pursuits not everyone, perhaps no one, achieves complete satisfaction, because men have conflicting aims. Hence human society is generally divided against itself, and one part of it oppresses another, when it finds itself the stronger. For the conquered part submits to the conqueror, naturally choosing peace and survival at any price – so much so that it has always provoked astonishment when men have preferred death to slavery. For in almost all nations the voice of nature, as we might say, has pealed out the message that those who have suffered the misfortune of defeat should prefer subjugation at the hands of the victors to total destruction by the devastation of war. The result has been – though under the providence of God, in whose power it rests to order conquest or subjugation in each case – that some nations have been entrusted with empire, while others have been subdued to alien domination. Now the society whose common aim is worldly advantage or the satisfaction of desire, the community which we call by the general name of 'the city of this world' has been divided into a great number of empires; and among these we observe that two empires have won a renown far exceeding that of all the rest. First comes the Assyrian Empire; later came that of the Romans. These two powers present a kind of pattern of contrast, both historically and geographically. For Assyria rose to power in earlier times; Rome's emergence was later. Assyria arose in the East, Rome in the West. And, to complete the pattern, the beginning of the one followed hard on the end of the other. All the other kingdoms and kings I should describe as something like appendages of those empires.

Ninus,[2] then, was already on the throne as the second king of

2. cf. Bk IV, 6; XVI, 17. It would be tedious to attempt a detailed annotation of St Augustine's sketch of ancient history. His sources show the vagueness of

Assyria, in succession to Belus his father, the first ruler of that kingdom, when Abraham was born in the territory of the Chaldeans. There was also at that time the empire of the Sicyonians, quite a small power; but Marcus Varro, an unrivalled authority in all fields of learning, begins his work *On the Race of the Roman People* with an account of the Sicyonian kingdom,[3] on the grounds of its antiquity. For he starts with the kings of Sicyon and proceeds to the Athenians, passing from them to the Latins, and then to the Romans. But such powers as he records before the foundation of Rome are inconsiderable in comparison with the Assyrian Empire. Yet even the Roman historian Sallust admits that the Athenians attained the highest renown in Greece, more, however, by prestige than in virtue of their real power. For he describes them in these words: 'The achievements of the Athenians, in my judgement, were great and impressive enough; and yet their importance was a good deal less than their reputation. But because writers of remarkable genius emerged in that city, the Athenian exploits are extolled throughout the world as incomparable. So true is it that the qualities of men of action are assumed to be in proportion to the ability of writers of outstanding genius to sing their praises.'[4] Besides this, the city of Athens won no small glory from her literature and her philosophers, because such pursuits flourished there in a pre-eminent degree. But in fact, as far as empire is concerned, there was no power greater in early times than that of Assyria – none so widely extended; for, according to tradition, King Ninus, son of Belus, subdued the whole of Asia as far as the frontiers

---

antiquity about the great empires of the East; Assyria and Babylon are generally – and understandably – confused. But a few dates may be of service.

The First Babylonian Empire began towards the end of the third millenium B.C., and, for nearly a thousand years, the centre of power was in the South of Mesopotamia. By 1000 B.C. this power was crumbling; Egypt was dominant, and in the North of Mesopotamia the Assyrians (racially indistinguishable from the Babylonians) were asserting themselves, with their capital at Nineveh. By the middle of the ninth century the Mesopotamian Empire had its political centre in the North. This Assyrian Empire collapsed before the New Babylonian Empire founded by Nabopalassar in 625 B.C., and Nineveh fell in 612. In 538 Babylon in its turn fell to Cyrus, the Persian, who had started the Persian rise to empire with the overthrow of the Medes (northern allies of Babylon) in 549.

3. Sicyon was never a great power; in early times it was dependent on Argos. It attained independence and international importance under a series of 'tyrants' in the seventh and sixth centuries B.C., and its list of ancient monarchs seems to have acquired for Sicyon some of the renown properly belonging to Mycenae and Argos in the Heroic Age; and its reputation was enhanced by its prominence in the Achaean League of the third century.

4. Sall., *Cat.*, 8, 7ff.

of Lydia, and Asia is said to be a third of the entire world, though in fact it proves to be as much as half the area of the earth.[5] Actually, the only people of the East that he did not bring under his dominion were the Indians; and even the Indians were attacked, after his death, by Semiramis, his wife. Thus it came about that all the peoples and rulers in all those countries accepted the sway of the throne of Assyria and carried out all the commands laid upon them.

Abraham, then, was born in that Empire, among the Chaldeans, in the time of Ninus. But Greek history is much more familiar to us than Assyrian, and those who have explored the ancient origins of the Roman people have traced a chronological sequence through the Greeks to the Latins, and from them to the Romans, who are themselves also Latins. For this reason we are obliged to give the names of Assyrian kings, where necessary, to make it clear how Babylonia, the first Rome, as it were, proceeds on its course side by side with the City of God, on pilgrimage in this world. However, the points which we must insert into this work, with a view to contrasting the two cities, that is, the earthly city and the heavenly, must be taken for preference from Greek and Latin sources, in which Rome appears in the role of a second Babylon.

Well then, when Abraham was born, the second kings in the two lines were on the throne, Ninus in Assyria, Europs in Sicyon – the first kings being Belus in the former and Aegialeus in the latter line.† But when God promised Abraham, who had now left Babylonia, that a great nation would derive from him and that a blessing would come to all nations in his descendants, the Assyrians at that time were under their fourth king, the Sicyonians under their fifth. For the son of Ninus ascended the Assyrian throne after his mother Semiramis. It is said that she was killed by her son, because she, his mother, had dared to defile him by incestuous intercourse. Some people think that it was Semiramis who founded Babylon; and she may, indeed, have rebuilt the city. But I have stated in the sixteenth book when and how it was founded.[6] We also note that the son of Ninus and Semiramis,

5. cf. Bk XVI, 17.

6. cf. Bk XVI, ch. 4. Justinus (1, 2) ad Diodorus Siculus (2, 7) attribute the building of Babylon to Semiramis. The Greek fables about Semiramis, representing her as the Assyrian equivalent of Catherine of Russia, came from Diodorus, who based this account on Ctesias, the Greek historian of Persia (fourth century B.C.). The historical Semiramis was probably a Babylonian princess, Sammuramat, wife of the Assyrian king Shamshi-Adad V, and queen-regent 810–805 B.C. for her son Adad-Niram III. It appears that she introduced the worship of Nebo into Nineveh.

who succeeded his mother on the throne, is himself also called Ninus by some authorities, while others call him Ninyas, a name derived from that of his father. The throne of Sicyon was at that time occupied by Telxion,† whose reign was a time of such undisturbed happiness that after his decease his people worshipped him as a god, offering sacrifices to him and celebrating games which they say were originally established in his honour.

3. *The kings on the throne of Assyria and Sicyon at the time of Isaac's birth, and of the birth of Esau and Jacob*

The reign of Telxion was also the time of the birth of Isaac to his centenarian father, in fulfilment of God's promise; he was the son of Abraham by his wife Sarah, who was barren and old, and by that time had abandoned all hope of children. The king of Assyria then was Arrius, the fifth on the throne.† Now to Isaac himself, at the age of sixty, twins were born, Esau and Jacob. Isaac's wife Rebecca bore those sons to him, while their grandfather Abraham was still alive, now in his 160th year. Abraham died after completing 175 years, at a time when the elder Xerxes, who is also called Baleus, was on the throne of Assyria, and Thuriacus (some authorities write Thurimachus) reigned in Sicyon; they were the seventh kings. Now the kingdom of the Argives started at the time of the birth of Abraham's grandsons. Varro tells us that the Sicyonians were also accustomed to sacrifice at the tomb of their seventh king, Thuriacus, and this is certainly a piece of information that should not be omitted. Then, during the reigns of the eighth kings of Assyria and Sicyon, Armamitres† and Leucippus† respectively, God spoke to Isaac and gave him the same two promises which he had given to his father, namely, the land of Canaan for his descendants, and a blessing for all nations in his descendants. The very same promises were also given to his son, Abraham's grandson, who was first called Jacob, and afterwards Israel, at the time when Belacus, the ninth king, was reigning over Assyria,† and Phoroneus, son of Inachus, was the second king of Argos,† while Leucippus still remained on the throne of Sicyon.

It was during this period that Greece increased in renown under Phoroneus king of Argolis, owing to the institution of certain laws and law-courts.[7] Yet it was at the tomb of Phegous, younger brother of Phoroneus, that a temple was erected, after his death, in which he was to be worshipped as a god, and cattle were to be sacrificed in his

7. Pausanias (2, 19, 5) says that he was credited with the invention of fire.

honour. I imagine that they counted him worthy of this high honour because in his part of the kingdom (his father, I should observe, had assigned territories to both his sons, for them to rule over in his lifetime) he had established shrines for the worship of the gods, and had taught his people to mark the passage of time by months and years, instructing them what to take as units of measurement and what number of them to count for larger divisions. In amazement at these novelties of his, men who were still primitive believed, or at least decreed, that at his death he had become a god. For there is also a story that Io was the daughter of Inachus, and she was afterwards called Isis, and was worshipped in Egypt as a great goddess. Other writers, however, say that she came to Egypt from Ethiopia as queen, and that because her rule was both widespread and just, and because she established many useful practices, especially the art of reading and writing, divine honours were accorded her in that country after her death.[8] In fact, so great was the honour in which she was held that anyone who asserted that she was a mere human being was liable to a capital charge.

4. *The times of Jacob and Joseph*

During the reigns of Baleus, tenth king of Assyria, and Messapus, ninth king of Sicyon,† who is called Cephisus by some authorities (that is, if the two names belong to one man, and it is not a case of confusion between one man and another) and when Apis† was the third king of Argos, Isaac died at the age of 180, leaving twin sons who were 120 years old. The younger twin, Jacob, belonged to the City of God, which is our subject, while the elder son had been rejected. Jacob had twelve sons, one of whom, called Joseph, was sold by his brothers to merchants who were travelling to Egypt. This happened in the lifetime of Isaac, their grandfather. But in his thirtieth year Joseph was lifted up to a lofty position from this humiliation which he had endured, and he took his place before Pharoah. This was because by divine inspiration he had interpreted the king's dreams and foretold from them that there would be seven years of plenty, whose abundance would be consumed by the seven years following, years of infertility. For this reason the king had set him free from prison and put him in control of Egypt. It was his inviolate chastity that had thrown him into prison; for he bravely guarded that chastity when he refused to consent to adultery with his mistress. She had conceived a

8. Eusebius identifies Io and Isis.

wicked love for him, and she was to tell a wicked lie to his credulous master; but he escaped from her, even leaving his garment behind in her hands, as she tried to drag him towards her. Now in the second of the seven infertile years, Jacob joined his son in Egypt, with all his household. He was then a hundred and thirty years old, as he himself declared in answer to the king's question.[9] Joseph at the time was thirty-nine years of age, that is to say there had been seven years of plenty and two of famine added to the thirty years, which was his age when he was advanced by the king to a position of honour.

5. *Apis, king of Argos; worshipped by the Egyptians under the name of Serapis*

This was the time when Apis, the Argive king, sailed across to Egypt with his ships; and when he died in that country he became Serapis, the greatest of all the Egyptian gods.† Varro gives a very simple explanation of this change of names after his death, from Apis to Serapis. The suggestion is that the coffin in which a dead man is put, which is now called a sarcophagus, is called *soros* in Greek, and that people started to worship Apis when he had been buried in his coffin, before his temple was built, and thus he was first called Sorapis, a combination of *soros* and Apis, and then by the alteration of one letter – the kind of thing that often happens – his name became Serapis.[10] And in his case also a decree was passed that anyone who asserted him to have been a mere human being should incur capital punishment. This, in Varro's opinion, is also the significance of the image, which was found in nearly all the temples where Isis and Serapis were worshipped, which had a finger pressed to its lips, apparently enjoining silence, thus indicating that not a word should be said of their having been human. On the other hand, that bull which Egypt, infatuated by a strange delusion, nourished with abundant delicacies in his honour, was called Apis, not Serapis, because the Egyptians worshipped it alive, without a sarcophagus. When this bull died, a calf of the same colouring was sought, that is, one similarly marked with special white patches; and it was always found. Therefore they supposed it to be some kind of miracle, divinely provided for them. It was, in fact, no great task for demons, bent on deceiving them, to

9. Gen. 47, 9.

10. The name Serapis is probably a combination of Osiris and Apis; cf. Bk VI, 10; VIII, 26; 27. Serapis was a syncretistic deity, combining Egyptian and Greek elements and his worship was introduced by Ptolemy I, to unite the mixed population, especially in Alexandria.

display to a cow which had conceived and was pregnant a phantom of a bull, which the cow alone could see, so that the mother's desire should from that stimulus induce the marks which would then appear in her young. This was how Jacob ensured the birth of parti-coloured lambs and goats by the use of variegated rods.[11] Doubtless what men can achieve, by means of material things and colours, demons have no difficulty in effecting, by displaying unreal shapes to animals at the time of conception.

6. *The kings of Argos and Assyria at the time of Jacob's death in Egypt*

Apis then died in Egypt, though he was king of the Argives, not of the Egyptians. He was succeeded on the throne by his son Argus;† and it was from Argus that the people were called Argi, and by a development from this name, Argives. For under the previous kings neither the land nor the people bore this name. It was during the reign of Argus over the Argives, and of Erato in Sicyon,† and while Baleus was still on the Assyrian throne, that Jacob died in Egypt at the age of 147. When death was approaching he had blessed his sons, and his grandsons by Joseph; and in this benediction he had made a prophecy of Christ in the clearest terms. For in blessing Judah he said, 'There shall not be lacking a ruler from Judah, and a leader from his loins, until those things that are in store for him shall come to fulfilment; and he will be the expectation of the nations.'[12] It was in the reign of Argus that Greece began to make use of cereal crops, and to keep cornfields in cultivation, having imported seed from foreign parts. Argus was another ruler who began to be considered a god after his death, and a temple and sacrifices were established in his honour. This honour had in fact been given before this, during his reign, to a private individual who was struck by lightning; this was a man called Homogyrus, and the reason for the cult was that he was the first to yoke oxen to the plough.

7. *The kings reigning at the time of Joseph's death*

It was during the reign of Mamythus,[13] the twelfth king, in Assyria, and of Plemmeus,† the eleventh king, in Sicyon, and while Argus was still on the Argive throne, that Joseph died in Egypt, at the age of 110.

11. Gen. 30, 37ff. 12. Gen. 49, 10.
13. Mamylus, according to Eusebius.

After his death God's people stayed in Egypt for 145 years, and increased remarkably. At first they lived in tranquillity, until the death of those Egyptians to whom Joseph was well-known. After that their increasing numbers aroused enmity and they were viewed with suspicion. Thus they suffered oppression in the form of persecutions and the hardships of intolerable slavery, until their liberation from that country; and yet amid all these sufferings they were made fertile by God's grace, and their numbers went on increasing. Meanwhile, in Assyria and Greece the same kings continued on the throne.

8. *The kings at the time of Moses' birth; and the gods whose cult arose at that time*

Now when the fourteenth king, Saphrus,[14] was reigning in Assyria, and the twelfth king, Orthopolis, was on the throne of Sicyon, and Criasus was ruling as the fifth king of Argus,† Moses was born in Egypt. It was through him that the people of God were set free from slavery in Egypt, a slavery which was a necessary discipline for them, to induce a longing for the help of their creator. Some authorities believe that Prometheus lived in the reigns of the kings above mentioned. The story[15] that he fashioned men out of mud derives from his reputation as an outstanding teacher of wisdom; and yet we are not informed who were the wise men living in his times. His brother Atlas is said to have been a great astrologer;[16] and this is what gave rise to the legendary story that he carries the sky.[17] There is, however, a mountain bearing his name whose height seems a more likely cause of the popular belief that he supports the heavens. Many other legendary stories were first made up in the Greece of those days; in fact, down to the reign of Cecrops at Athens,[18] which was when the city was given its name, and when God led his people from Egypt through the agency of Moses, the Greeks enrolled a number of departed human beings among the number of the gods. Such was their blind superstition and their characteristic folly.

Among these deified mortals were Melantomice, wife of King Criasus, and Phorbas their son, who succeeded his father as the sixth king of Argos;† also Iasos, son of the seventh king, Triopas,† and the

14. Sphaenis, according to Eusebius.
15. Paus., 10, 4, 4; cf. Hor., *Carm.*, 1, 16, 13ff.
16. Plin. 7, 56, 283. 17. Hes., *Theog.*, 517ff; 746.
18. Mythical first king; civilizer and benefactor. cf. Eur., *Ion*, 116 3f; Apollod., 3, 177ff.; Paus., 1, 5, 3.

ninth king, Sthenelas, or Stheneleus, or Sthenelus – various forms of the name are given in different authorities. There is a story that Mercury also lived at this time. He was the grandson of Atlas through the latter's daughter Maia, and this story is made much of even in popular writings. Mercury was renowned as an expert in many accomplishments, and he also imparted them to mankind.[19] In return for this service men wished him, after his death, to be a god – perhaps they even believed that he really was divine. Hercules is said to have been later than Mercury, though still belonging to the Argive era. Some authorities, it is true, put him before Mercury in time, but I think they are mistaken. All the same, whatever the time of the birth of those two, serious historians, who have committed those old tales to writing, are agreed that they both were originally human beings,[20] and that they won divine honours from men because they conferred on mortals many benefits to make this life a more comfortable experience.

Minerva, however, belonged to far more ancient times than they; for the tale is that she made her appearance as a young girl in the time of Ogygus,† near the lake called Tritonis[21] – hence she is also called Tritonia. She was doubtless the inventor of many crafts and was the more easily believed to be a goddess because so little was known about her origin. For the romantic tale of her birth from the head of Jove must be classed with poetical fantasies, not reckoned among facts of history. And yet there is no consensus among historians about the date of Ogygus himself, in whose time there also occurred a great deluge. It was not that greatest of all floods, unknown to pagan history whether Greek or Roman, from which no human beings escaped, except those who were privileged to be in the ark. But it was a greater deluge than the flood which occurred afterwards, in the time of Deucalion. For Varro begins his book, which I mentioned earlier,[22] with the reign of Ogygus, and he gives himself no earlier point from which to arrive at the history of Rome than the flood of Ogygus,† I mean the flood that happened during his reign. But our Christian writers of chronicles, first Eusebius, and afterwards Jerome, record that the flood of Ogygus occurred more than 300 years later, when Phoroneus, the second king of Argos, was already on the throne; and we may be sure that they based their belief on some previous historians. However that may be, whatever the date of Ogygus, Minerva was already receiving

19. Especially the lyre, and the literary accomplishments in general.
20. The theory known as Euhemerism; cf Bk IV, 27n.
21. In Libya.
22. cf. Bk IV, 3; 4; 5.

worship as a goddess when Cecrops was reigning at Athens; and it was during his reign, we are told, that the city was either rebuilt or founded.

9. *Varro's explanation of the name of Athens*

Now the name of Athens is certainly derived from Minerva, who is called Athene in Greek. Varro gives the following explanation of the reason why the city was so called. An olive tree suddenly appeared and in another spot water gushed out, and these portents so alarmed the king that he sent to Delphic Apollo to inquire their meanings and to ask what action he should take.[23] Apollo answered that the olive signified Minerva and the water stood for Neptune, and that it rested with the citizens to decide from which of the two deities thus symbolized their city should, for preference, take its name. On receipt of this oracle, Cecrops called an assembly of all the citizens, male and female, to vote on the question; for at that time and in that part of the world the custom was that women as well as men should take part in deliberations on matters of state. Now when the matter was put before the multitude, the men voted for Neptune, the women for Minerva; and, as it happened, the women outnumbered the men by one; and so the victory went to Minerva.

Then Neptune was furious, and devastated the Athenian territory by floods of sea-water – for it is quite easy for demons to spread waters about on any scale at their pleasure. To appease his wrath, according to the same authority, the women suffered a threefold punishment: they were never to have the vote again; their children were never to take their mother's name; and no one was ever to call them 'Athenian women'. And so that great city, the mother or nurse of liberal studies and of so many great philosophers, the greatest glory and renown of Greece, was fooled by the demons, and received its name of Athens as the result of a dispute between two of its deities, a male and a female, and from the victory of the female through the female vote. Then, when it was afflicted by the defeated male, that city was compelled to arrange the victory of the female conqueror, being in greater dread of Neptune's waters than of Minerva's arms. In fact, the victorious Minerva was vanquished in the persons of the women who were punished in this way; and the goddess did not come to the aid of the women who had voted for her. Though they had lost their voting rights and their sons were debarred from taking their mother's name,

23. cf. Apollod., 3, 14, 1. This account says that Zeus entrusted the verdict to a jury, of twelve gods; cf. also *Hdt.*, 8, 55; Ovid, *Met.*, 6, 70ff.

Minerva could at least have ensured them the right to be called 'Athenian women', and to be rewarded by bearing the name of the goddess to whom their votes had brought victory over the male divinity. What a great deal could be said on this subject, were it not that my discourse is hastening to other topics!

10. *Varro's account of the naming of the Areopagus, and of Deucalion's flood*

Marcus Varro, however, refuses to give credence to fantastic fables which dishonour the gods, for fear of entertaining an opinion unworthy of their majesty. That is why he will not have it that the Areopagus, where the apostle Paul disputed with the Athenians,[24] the place from which the councillors of that city derived their name of 'Areopagites', was so called because Mars – who in Greek is called Ares – stood trial for homicide[25] on that hill before a jury of twelve gods, and was acquitted by six votes. For when the voting was equal, the custom was that acquittal had precedence over condemnation. In opposition to this notion, which is the one most widely accepted, Varro attempts to construct another explanation of this name, derived from his recondite literary knowledge. He would not have it supposed that the Athenians named the Areopagus from *Ares* and *pagus*, as if it were 'the hill of Mars'. That would obviously be an insult to the gods, for, in his opinion, lawsuits and trials are alien to them. He maintains that this story about Mars is as false as the tale told about the three goddesses, Juno, Minerva, and Venus, who are related to have engaged in a beauty competition, with Paris as judge, for the prize of the golden apple – a story which is performed in song and dance, amid the applause of the theatre, when the intention is to appease, by such exhibitions, the gods who take delight in the misdeeds with which they are charged, whether they be fact or fiction.[26]

Varro does not believe such tales, being unwilling to credit anything incongruous with the nature or character of the gods. And yet while he offers an explanation of the name of Athens which is historical instead of mythical, he includes in his writings that great lawsuit of Neptune against Minerva, by whose name, in preference to Neptune's, that city was called. The story goes that those two competed with a display of prodigies and Apollo, when appealed to, could

24. Acts 17, 19ff.
25. For the murder of Halirrhothius, cf. Appollod., 3, 14. 2.
26. cf. Bk II, 10.

not bring himself to decide between them. But, to put an end to this quarrel between divinities, Apollo referred their case to human beings, in the same way as Jupiter sent the goddesses just mentioned to Paris for his verdict. In that trial Minerva won by the votes, but was defeated in the punishment of the women who voted for her. She was able to exercise power over Athens in the persons of the men, who were her opponents, and yet she could not secure for her friends the title of 'Athenian women'. In these times, writes Varro, when Cranaus, successor to Cecrops, was on the Athenian throne (or, according to our Christian authorities, Eusebius and Jerome, while Cecrops was still king) there occurred a deluge which is known as 'Deucalion's flood', because Deucalion ruled in those parts[27] of the world which suffered most. This deluge, however, certainly did not reach Egypt and its adjacent lands.

11. *The date of the Exodus; the kings reigning at the death of Joshua*

Moses led God's people out of Egypt at the very end of the reign of Cecrops, king of Athens, when Ascatades was on the Assyrian throne, Marathus was king of Sicyon, and Triopas king of Argos.† It was when the people had been led out that Moses conveyed to them the Law which he had received from God on Mount Sinai. This Law is called the 'old covenant' because it offers earthly promises, whereas the new covenant was to come into being through Jesus Christ, and in this the kingdom of heaven was to be promised. This order had to be kept, just as it has to be observed in the case of the individual, so that, in the Apostle's words, 'It is not the spiritual that comes first, but the animal: the spiritual comes later.' For it is true, as he says, that 'the first man is from the earth, is by nature earthy: the second man is from heaven.'[28] Now Moses ruled the people in the desert for forty years, and died at the age of 120 after having himself also prophesied of Christ by the symbols of material observances in the tabernacle and the priestly ministry, in sacrifices and other ordinances rich in mystical significance. Joshua succeeded Moses. He led the people into the land of promise and settled them there by God's authorization, after he had crushed the nations who were then in possession of that part of the

27. Phthiotis, in Thessaly. Strab., 8, 7, 1. The story of the Flood is told in Ovid, *Met.*, 1, 262–437.
28. 1 Cor. 15, 46f.

world. He ruled the people for twenty-seven years after the death of Moses, and then he also died. This was when Amyntas was on the throne of Assyria, as the eighteenth king, while Corax was reigning as the sixteenth king of Sicyon, Danaus as the tenth king of Argos, and Erichthonius as the fourth king of Athens.†

12. *The cult of false gods introduced in Greece in this period*

During this period, that is from the departure of Israel from Egypt down to the death of Joshua, through whose agency that people were given the land of promise, ceremonies in honour of false gods were established by the kings of Greece. These cults recalled the memory of the deluge and the liberation of mankind from it, as well as the troubles of life at that time, when men first migrated to high ground and then returned to the plains. That, indeed, is the interpretation put upon the ascent and descent of the Luperci along the Sacred Way.[29] It is said that they symbolize the men who made for the mountain tops because of the floods of water, and again returned to the lowlands when the floods subsided. It is in this period, as the story goes, that Dionysus (also called Father Liber)[30], who was regarded as a god after his death, introduced the vine to his host in the land of Attica.[31] At the same time, musical festivals were instituted in honour of Delphic Apollo, to appease his anger, because they imagined that the regions of Greece had been punished with sterility by him in his wrath because they had not defended his temple when it was set on fire by King Danaus during his invasion of those parts.[32] They were indeed advised by Apollo's oracle to institute those festivals. In Attica, however, it was King Erichthonius who was the first to institute festivals in honour of Apollo,[33] and not only for him, but

29. At the Feast of Lupercalia on 15 February, goats and a dog were sacrificed to Lupercus (identified, it seems, with Faunus) in a cave below the Palatine called the Lupercal. Two youths belonging to the college of Luperci, chosen from certain noble families, were smeared with the sacrificial blood and ran naked (or clad in the skins of the goats) round the Palatine 'beating the bounds' of the original city with thongs (*februa*) cut from the skins of the goats. This was a purificatory ceremony (*februa*='means of purification') and from this is derived the name of the month. It was also a fertility rite, in which women desiring children tried to incur blows from the *februa*. cf. Ovid, *Fast*., 2, 267–428; and Shakespeare, *Julius Caesar*, I, ii.

30. cf. Bk VI, 9; VII, 2; VII, 16.

31. Apollod. 3, 14, 7.

32. The authority for this has not been traced.

33. Erichthonius (Erechtheus) traditionally founded the temple of Apollo at Delos.

also for Minerva.[34] At these latter celebrations olive oil was the prize offered for the winners, because their tradition said that Minerva discovered the olive, as Liber introduced the vine.

During these years, so runs the tale, Europa[35] was carried off by Xanthus, king of Crete – though we find his name differently given by some authorities[36] – and the result was the birth of Rhadamanthus, Sarpedon, and Minos – though the more generally accepted story makes them the sons of Jupiter by the same woman. However, the worshippers of such gods reckon the story we have given about the Cretan king to be the historical truth, whereas they class as empty fable the tale about Jupiter which is such a theme for the poets, such a success in the theatre, such a favourite with the public. It gives a popular subject for those shows designed to appease the deities by tales – even false tales – of their own misdeeds.

During the same period Hercules was held in renown in Syria. This was no doubt a different person from the Hercules of whom we have spoken earlier. In fact, in the more recondite history it is said that there was more than one Father Liber, and more than one Hercules.[37] It was certainly this Hercules of whom the twelve colossal achievements are recounted; but the slaying of Antaeus[38] of Africa was not one of them, since that exploit belongs to the other Hercules. These authorities in their writings tell the story of the suicide of Hercules on Mount Oeta, where he set himself on fire, because a disease was sapping his strength, and he was not able to endure it with the courage he had shown in his many conquests.

It was at that time that the king – or rather the tyrant – Busiris[39] used to sacrifice his guests to his divinities. According to tradition, he was the son of Neptune by Libya, daughter of Epathus.† But we must

34. The Panathenaic festival of Athena. Apollod., 3, 14, 6.

35. The standard myth told how Europa, daughter of Agenor of Tyre, was carried off to Crete by Zeus in the form of a bull (or by a bull sent by Zeus). There she bore to Zeus the three sons mentioned, and afterwards married Asterius, king of Crete. Apollod., 3, 1, 1; Ovid, *Met.*, 2, 836–875; *Fast.* 5, 603ff.

36. Asterius, in Diod. Sic. 4, 60.

37. According to Diodorus Siculus (3, 82) one tradition spoke of three Dionysi, Herodotus (2, 44) mentions two Heracles, a god and a hero; Diodorus (3, 73) says that there were three, Cicero (*De Nat. Deor.*, 3, 16, 42) six. Servius (on Virg. *Aen.*, 8, 564) quotes Varro as saying that Hercules was a title given to mighty heroes in general, and that hence we find the Tirynthian, the Argive, the Theban and the Libyan Hercules.

38. Apollod., 2, 5, 10—supplementary to the Twelve Labours.

39. Busiris, king of Egypt, used to sacrifice strangers to Zeus in order to avert drought. He was killed by Heracles. Apollod., 2, 5, 11; Diod. Sic., 4, 18; Ovid. *Met.*, 9, 182f.; *Ars Amat.*, 1, 647–52.

never believe that Neptune perpetrated so immoral an act; the gods must not be accused! Such themes should be assigned to the poets and the theatres, as material for the propitiation of the gods! The parents of King Erichthonius are said to have been Vulcan and Minerva;[40] and the death of Joshua, as the evidence shows, fell within the last years of his reign. However, because they insist that Minerva was a virgin, we have the story that while the pair were struggling, Vulcan in his excitement discharged his seed on the ground, and that the man born as a result was given his name for that reason, for in Greek *eris* means struggle, and *chthôn* means earth, and the name Erichthonius is a compound of the two.

Still, it has to be admitted that the better authorities vigorously defend their gods against such allegations. They hold that this fantastic idea arose from the discovery of an abandoned child in the temple shared by Vulcan and Minerva at Athens.[41] The infant was wrapped in the coils of a serpent, betokening his future greatness; and because the temple belonged jointly to Neptune and Minerva, and because the child's parents were unknown, he was said to be the son of the two deities. For all that, it is the legend rather than the historical account that explains the origin of the name. But does that concern us? The latter account, in reliable books, may serve for the instruction of the religious; the other story may give pleasure to the foul demons in the shows, whose intent is to deceive. And yet it is these demons that receive divine worship from those religious pagans, and although they may deny those stories about them, they cannot clear their deities of all guilt, seeing that it is the gods who demand the holding of those shows wherein the myths, ostensibly rejected with such wisdom are enacted with such obscenity. And the gods are propitiated with such falsehoods, with such indecencies as these! The plays sing of the misdeeds of the gods. These may, it is true, be false charges; nevertheless, to find entertainment in a fictitious crime is itself a real crime.

13. *The fables that arose in the pagan world at the beginning of the period of the judges*

After Joshua's death the people of God had judges as their rulers, and in that period they experienced alternations of humiliating hardship

40. Apollod., 3, 14, 6; cf. Eur., *Ion*, 20ff; 266ff.

41. There was a temple of Hephaestus above the Ceramicus, and an image of Athena nearby. Paus., 1, 14, 5.

in retribution for their sins and encouraging prosperity, thanks to the mercy of God. It was in those times that fantastic tales were made up about Triptolemus; how at the bidding of Ceres, he was borne by winged serpents and bestowed grain, as he flew, on needy countries;[42] tales about the minotaur, that a beast was shut up in the Labyrinth, and that when men entered the building they could not get out, but wandered 'in a maze inextricable';[43] stories of Centaurs, that they were beings compounded of horse and man; about Cerberus, the three-headed dog of the underworld; about Phryxus and his sister Helle, and how they flew on the back of a ram; about the Gorgon, who had serpent locks, and turned to stone those who looked upon her; about Bellerophon, and how he rode on a flying horse with wings, called Pegasus; about Amphion, who by the sweet music of his lyre charmed the stones and drew them to him; about the craftsman Daedalus and Icarus his son, and how they fitted themselves with wings, and flew; about Oedipus, the story that he compelled a monster, called the Sphynx, a quadruped with a human face, to hurl herself to death, by solving a riddle which she used to pose, supposing it insoluble; about Antaeus who was slain by Hercules, the tale that he was son of the earth, and therefore when he fell to the earth he always rose up stronger. There are other tales, perhaps, which I have omitted.

Down to the time of the Trojan War, which is where Marcus Varro ends the second book of his *On the Race of the Roman People*, these mythical stories were made up by the ingenuity of men, taking the opportunities offered by historical records which contain true accounts of actual events, but without linking them with slanders on the divinities. After that, however, we get the story of Ganymede, the beautiful boy snatched away to be Jupiter's catamite – a foul crime committed by King Tantalus and ascribed by legend to Jupiter – and the tale that Jupiter sought entrance to Danae's bed in the form of a shower of gold – meaning that a woman's purity was corrupted by gold. Whoever were the inventors of such tales, whether fact or fiction, or facts concerning others and fictitiously attributed to Jove, words fail to express what a low opinion these fable-mongers must have formed of human nature to assume that men could endure such lies with patience. And yet men gave them a delighted welcome. One would have thought that the more devotion men felt in their worship

42. The winged dragons are mentioned in Paus. 8, 18, 2; cf. Ovid, *Met.*, 5, 642ff. Triptolemus, a fertility god, was associated with Demeter in the Eleusinian mysteries.

43. Virg., *Aen.*, 6, 14–30; Ovid, *Met.* 8, 152ff.

of Jupiter, the greater should have been their severity in punishing those who dared to tell such tales about him. But in fact, far from being angry with those who invented these fictions, men were even induced to enact those inventions in the theatre by their fear of incurring the anger of the gods.

It was in this period that Latona gave birth to Apollo, not the Apollo we were speaking of earlier, whose oracles were generally consulted, but the one who, with Hercules,† was a servant to Admetus.[44] In spite of that, so strong is the belief in his divinity that the majority, in fact almost all men, suppose the two to be identical. At that time also Father Liber engaged in wars in India.[45] He had many women in his army, who were called Bacchae, more renowned for their madness than for their valour. Some accounts, indeed, say that Liber was conquered and bound; others that he was slain in battle by Perseus,† going as far as to record his place of burial. Nevertheless, Bacchanalian sacred rites – or rather sacrileges – were instituted in his name, as if in the name of a god, by impure demons, and many years afterwards the senate was so ashamed of the frenzied obscenity of those observances that they prohibited their performance in Rome.[46] During the same period, after the death of Perseus and his wife Andromeda there was such a general conviction that they had been taken up into heaven, that men traced their likenesses in the stars, and gave their name to constellations, and felt neither shame nor fear in so doing.

14. *The 'theological' poets*

During the same period there emerged poets who were also called 'theologians',[47] because they wrote poems about the gods, but such gods as were only men, albeit great men; or else they are elements of this world which the true God created, or were set up in principalities and powers in accordance with their Creator's will and their own deserts. These poets may have had something to say about the one true God, among all their frivolous lies; but they did not rightly serve him, we may be sure, in worshipping him together with those others who are not gods, and offering to them the service which is due only to the one God. And even they could not refrain from those

44. In the story of Alcestis. Cicero (*De Nat. Deor.*, 3, 25, 57) says that there were four distinct Apollos.

45. Diod. Sic., 4, 3. For Liber cf. ch. 12n.

46. In 186 B.C. (Liv., 39, 18; cf. Bk VI, ch. 9).

47. Herodotus (2, 53) so describes Homer and Hesiod.

legends which bring shame on their deities – I am thinking of the poets Orpheus, Musaeus, and Linus.[48] It is true that those 'theologians' worshipped the gods; they were not worshipped in the place of gods, and yet somehow or other the city of the ungodly generally puts Orpheus in charge of the sacred – or, rather, sacrilegious – ceremonies of the underworld. Moreover, the wife of King Athamas, Ino by name, and her son Melicertes hurled themselves into the sea, of their own free will, and perished; and they were ranked among the gods in the opinion of men, just as were those other human beings belonging to that time, Castor and Pollux. The Greeks, as we know, call the mother of Melicertes Leucothea, whereas the Latin authors give her name as Matuta; but they agree in supposing her a goddess.

15. *The fall of the Argive kingdom, contemporary with the start of the reign of Picus among the Laurentines*

About that time the kingdom of the Argives ended, and was transferred to Mycenae, Agamemnon's city, and the Laurentine kingdom arose, in which Picus, son of Saturn, first received the throne. This was when the judge among the Hebrews was a woman, called Deborah; but it was the spirit of God that acted through her in this office, for she was also a prophetess, although the prophecy[49] is not clear enough for me to be able to prove its reference to Christ, without a lengthy explanation. The Laurentines, then, were by now established as a kingdom in Italy, and from those kings the Roman line of descent, after the Greeks, can be more plainly traced. However, the Assyrian kingdom still continued; and there Lamparest was the twenty-third king when Picus became the first on the Laurentine throne.

As for Saturn, the father of Picus, those who deny he was a man should observe what is the opinion of the worshippers of such gods as these. Other writers say that he reigned in Italy before his son Picus, and Virgil also says in a more familiar passage,

48. Many poems were ascribed to Orpheus in early times; Plato quotes some, and Aristotle refers to them. Clement of Alexandria gives a list of Orphic poems compiled by Epigenes, an Alexandrian scholar, and Neoplatonists quote a *Rhapsodic Theogony*, of uncertain date, which went under the name of Orpheus. A collection of oracles was attributed in classical times to the mythical singer Musaeus. Linus was the name of a mournful song with a repeated sound, *ailinon*, which was assumed to mean 'Alas, for Linus!' and stories were told to explain why Linus should be lamented. Suidas mentions Linus (with Orpheus) as a pre-Homeric poet, but there is no record of any poems attributed to him in antiquity.

49. cf. Judg. 4; 5.

A race untamed, dispersed upon the mountains
He settled, gave them laws, and chose a name,
Latium, since he upon those shores had once
Lain hid in safety. Then beneath his rule
There passed the age called 'golden'.[50]

But these are to be regarded as poetic fictions, and the story to be supported in preference is that the father of Picus was Sterces, a skilled farmer who discovered the secret of fertilizing the land with animal dung, which is called *stercus* from his name (which according to some authorities, was Stercutius). Moreover, whatever the reason for the decision to call him Saturn, this Sterces (or Stercutius) was certainly made a god for his services to agriculture. Similarly they also welcomed his son Picus into the number of such gods, and allege that he was a famous augur and warrior.[51] Picus had a son called Faunus, the second king of the Laurentines; he too is, or at any rate was, a god in their estimation. It was before the Trojan war that they accorded these divine honours to dead men.

16. *The deification of Diomede, after the fall of Troy*

Then came the fall of Troy, whose destruction is everywhere sung in poetry, and is known to every schoolboy. Its story has won outstanding fame and popularity both because of the greatness of the disaster and through the pre-eminent literary powers of the writers who recorded it. This happened during the reign of Latinus, son of Faunus, after whom the kingdom began to be called the kingdom of the Latins, the name Laurentine being dropped. When the Greek conquerors abandoned the ruins of Troy and were making their way back to their own homes they were afflicted to exhaustion by all kinds of horrible disasters; and yet some of them, too, increased the number of the gods. In fact, even Diomede[52] was turned into a god. The story

50. *Aen.*, 8, 321–5 (There is a play on *Latium* and *latuisset*, 'had lain hid').

51. Picus, an Italian agricultural deity, generally described as the first king of Italy and as a warlike hero; he was also associated with the woodpecker (*picus*), a bird sacred to Mars and important in augury. Virgil (*Aen.*, 7, 187–9) makes him the father of Faunus and grandfather of Latinus. Ovid (*Met.*, 14, 320? ff.) tells the story of his transformation into a woodpecker by Circe, whose love he rejected.

52. Legend said that Diomede, after his return from Troy, left home because of his wife's unfaithfulness and wandered to Italy, where he founded various towns in Magna Graecia, and was buried on one of the islands of Diomedes, near the Apulian coast, where he received divine or heroic honours as a founder of Greek culture in Italy; cf. Pind., *Nem.*, 10, 7. Strab., 6, 3, 9f.

goes that he was prevented from returning to his own people by a punishment divinely imposed; and the transformation of his companions into birds is not put forward as a baseless poetic fantasy;[53] it is attested as historical fact. But although supposedly a god he was not able of himself to restore his fellows to their human condition, nor yet, being a newcomer in the heavenly realm, did he obtain this boon from his King Jupiter. And yet we are assured that his temple is on the Island of Diomedea, not far from Mount Garganus in Apulia, and that those birds fly round the temple and make their abode there, displaying such wonderful devotion that they fill their beaks with water which they sprinkle on the shrine. And when Greeks, or men descended from Greek stock, arrive at that place they not only behave peaceably, they even fawn on them; on the other hand, if they catch sight of men of other races, they fly at their heads and wound them, inflicting injuries serious enough to prove fatal. For, it is said, they are adequately armed for these encounters with hard beaks of enormous size.

17. *Varro's information about the incredible transformations of human beings*

To bolster up this story Varro adduces the equally incredible tales about the notorious witch Circe, who transformed Ulysses' companions into animals, and about the Arcadians who were chosen by lot and swam across a certain lake and were there changed into wolves and lived in the desolate parts of that region in the company of wild beasts like themselves. However, if they had not eaten human flesh they used to swim back across the lake after nine years to be turned back into human beings.[54] To crown all, he expressly names a certain Demaenetus, telling a story of how he tasted the sacrifice which the Arcadians made to the god Lycaeus according to their custom, with a boy as the victim, whereupon Demaenetus was transformed into a wolf. Then in the tenth year he was restored to his proper shape; he trained as a boxer and won a prize at the Olympic games.[55] This same historian also thinks that the reason for the surname Lycaeus, given to Pan and to Jupiter[56] in Arcadia, can only be this transformation of human beings into wolves, which they supposed could only be effected by divine power. For 'wolf' in Greek is *lykos*, and

53. cf. Virg., *Aen.*, 11, 252–80; Ovid, *Met.*, 14, 455–511.
54. Plin., 8, 22.
55. This story is not found elsewhere.
56. Hdt. 4, 203. 'The hill of Zeus Lycaeus.'

the name *Lycaeus* is evidently derived from it. Varro also asserts that the Roman *Luperci*[57] took their origin from these mysteries, which were, we might say, the seed from which they developed.

18. *What are we to believe about these apparent transformations?*

Now it may well be that the readers of these accounts are waiting to hear what we have to say about them. And what can we say, except that we should 'escape from the midst of Babylon'?[58] This prophetic instruction is spiritually interpreted as meaning that we should escape from the city of this world (which is, of course, the society of wicked angels and of wicked men) advancing by the steps of faith which 'becomes active in love',[59] to take refuge in the living God. For it is obvious that the greater the power we observe in the demons, as regards this lower world, the greater the tenacity we should show in clinging to the Mediator through whom we climb from the depths to the heights. For if I were to say that we should refuse to believe these reports, there are men to be found, even today, who will assert that they have heard well-attested cases of this sort, or even that they have had first-hand experiences of them. In fact, when I was in Italy, I myself used to hear of such happenings from one district in that country. It was said that landladies conversant with these evil arts were in the habit of giving drugs in cheese to travellers, when they so wished and the opportunity offered, and by this means their guests were turned into pack-animals on the spot and were used to carry commodities of all kinds. Afterwards, when they had finished their jobs, they were restored to their original selves. And yet their minds did not become animal, but were kept rational and human. This is what Apuleius,[60] in the work bearing the title *The Golden Ass*, describes as his experience, that after taking a magic potion he became an ass, while retaining his human mind. But this may be either fact or fiction.

Stories of this kind are either untrue or at least so extraordinary that we are justified in withholding credence. And in spite of them we must believe with complete conviction that omnipotent God can do anything he pleases, by way of either punishing or of helping, while demons can effect nothing in virtue of any power belonging to their nature – since that nature is angelic by creation, though now it has

57. cf. ch. 12n.
58. Is. 48, 20.
59. Gal. 5, 6.
60. cf. Bk IV, 2n.

become wicked by their own fault – except what God permits; and his judgements are often inscrutable, but never unjust. Demons do not, of course, create real entities; if they do indeed perform any feats of the kind we are now examining, it is merely in respect of appearance that they transform beings created by the true God, to make them seem to be what they are not. And so I should not believe, on any consideration, that the body – to say nothing of the soul – can be converted into the limbs and features of animals by the craft or power of demons. Instead, I believe that a person has a phantom which in his imagination or in his dreams takes on various forms through the influence of circumstances of innumerable kinds. This phantom is not a material body, and yet with amazing speed it takes on shapes like material bodies; and it is this phantom, I hold, that can in some inexplicable fashion be presented in bodily form to the apprehension of other people, when their physical senses are asleep or in abeyance. This means that the actual bodies of the people concerned are lying somewhere else, still alive, to be sure, but with their senses suspended in lethargy far more deep and oppressive than that of sleep. Meanwhile the phantom may appear to the senses of others as embodied in the likeness of some animal; and a man may seem even to himself to be in such a state and to be carrying burdens – one may have the same experience in dreams. But if these burdens are material objects, they are carried by demons to make game of men, who observe partly the actual bodies of the burdens, partly the unreal bodies of the animals.

For instance, there was a man called Praestantius who used to tell a story of something that happened, he said, to his father. He took that magic potion in some cheese in his home, and then lay in his bed; he was apparently asleep, and yet he could not be awakened by any means. After a few days, however, he woke up, said Praestantius, as if he had been asleep, and narrated his experiences as being a dream. He had, it appeared, become a horse and with other pack animals had carried Rhaetic corn (so called because sent to Rhaetia) to the soldiers. It was discovered that this had in fact happened just as he told the story; and yet it seemed to him to have been simply a dream. Another man reported that in his own house, at night-time, before he went to bed, he saw a philosopher coming to him, a man he knew very well; and this man explained to him a number of points in Plato, which he had formerly refused to explain when asked. Now this philosopher was asked why he had done something in the other's house which he had refused to do when requested in his own home, and he said in reply, 'I did not do it; I merely dreamed that I did.'

This shows that what one man saw in his sleep was displayed to the other, while awake, by means of a phantom appearance.

These stories were told us not by inconsiderable informants whom we should think it beneath us to believe, but by persons we could not imagine telling lies to us. For that reason it seems to me that this phenomenon, which is generally talked about, and which has been recorded in literature, could have happened (assuming that it did happen) in the way I have suggested – I mean the habitual changing of human beings into wolves by Arcadian gods (or rather demons) and the feat of Circe who

> By charms transformed the comrades of Ulysses.[61]

But the birds of Diomede are said to preserve their species through successive generations, and therefore I do not believe that they came into being by the transformation of men, but that they were substituted for the men who had been spirited away, as a doe was substituted for Iphigenia, daughter of King Agamemnon.[62] For conjuring tricks of this kind could have presented no difficulty for demons who were allowed, by God's decision, to practise them; but because that maiden was afterwards found alive, it was easily realized that a doe had been substituted for her. The companions of Diomede, in contrast, suddenly disappeared from sight and did not later reappear anywhere, but were destroyed by the avenging evil angels; that is why it is supposed that they were transformed into those birds, which were secretly brought to that spot from other parts of the world where this species of bird is found, and suddenly substituted for them. While as for the story that the birds bring water in their beaks and sprinkle Diomede's temple, and that they show deference to men of Greek blood, but attack foreigners, it is not to be wondered at that the demons prompt this behaviour; for it is to their advantage to promote the belief that Diomede became a god, so that they can deceive men in this way. Their purpose is that men should worship many false gods and thus insult the one true God, and should show their devotion to dead men (who were not truly living even when they were alive) by means of temples, altars, sacrifices, and priests – all of which belong of right solely to the one true and living God.

61. Virg., *Ecl.*, 8, 70. 62. Eur. *Iph.* T., 26–30.

19. *The arrival of Aeneas in Italy at the time when Labdon was judge over the Hebrews*

At that time, after the capture and demolition of Troy, Aeneas with twenty ships, in which the survivors of the Trojans were conveyed, arrived in Italy. Latinus was then reigning there, while Mnestheus was king of Athens, Polyphides of Sicyon, Tantanes of Assyria, and Labdon was judge of the Hebrews.† Then, after the death of Latinus, Aeneas reigned for three years, while the same kings continued in the places above-mentioned, except that Pelasgus was by now on the throne of Sicyon, and Samson was judge of the Hebrews;† Samson was so amazingly strong that he has been identified with Hercules. Now the Latins made Aeneas into one of their gods,[63] since he was not seen after his death. The Sabines also enrolled their first king among the gods; he was called Sancus, or, according to some authorities, Sanctus.[64] It was in the same period that Codrus, king of Athens, concealed his identity and exposed himself to the Peloponnesians, his city's enemies, for them to kill him, and achieved his object. It is claimed that in this way he rescued his country. For the Peloponnesians had received an oracle that they would only gain the victory if they refrained from killing the Athenian king. Accordingly, he fooled them by appearing in the dress of a poor man and by provoking them to kill him in a quarrel. Hence Virgil says, 'And the quarrel provoked by Codrus.' The Athenians worshipped him too as a god, with sacrifices in his honour.[65] When Silvius was on the throne as the fourth king of the Latins (he was the son of Aeneas, not by Creusa, the mother of Ascanius, the third king of that country, but by Lavinia, daughter of Latinus, a posthumous son, as they say, to Aeneas) Oneus was ruling as twenty-ninth king of Assyria, while Melanthus was sixteenth king of Athens, and Eli the priest was judge of the Hebrews; and it was then that the kingdom of Sicyon came to an end. Tradition says that it had lasted for 959 years.

63. Ovid, *Met.*, 14, 581–608.

64. *Semo Sancus Dius Fidius*, apparently a god of sewing, of Sabine origin. He had a temple on the Quirinal.

65. Virg., *Ecl.*, 5, 11. There is no evidence that Codrus received more than a hero-cult. For this story cf. Val. Max., 5, 6.

20. *The regal succession in Israel after the period of the judges*

Soon afterwards, while the same kings were reigning in the places just mentioned, the period of the judges reached its end and the kingdom of Israel made its beginning with King Saul, in the time of the prophet Samuel. Now at that time the kings called the Silvii began to reign in Latium. The first king to be called Silvius was the son of Aeneas, and after him his successors retained this cognomen in addition to the personal names they were given, in the same way as long afterwards the successors of Caesar Augustus were surnamed Caesar. Now after the rejection of Saul and the consequent exclusion from the throne of all his descendants, David succeeded to the kingdom on Saul's death, forty years after Saul had come to power. At that time the Athenians finally dispensed with the monarchy after the death of Codrus, and began to have magistrates for the administration of their commonwealth. David also reigned forty years and after him his son Solomon was king of Israel. He founded that world-famous Temple of God in Jerusalem. In his time Alba was founded in Latium, and from that time onwards the kings began to be called 'Kings of the Albans', instead of 'Kings of the Latins', although they reigned in the same district of Latium. Solomon was succeeded by his son Rehoboam, under whom the people was divided into two kingdoms, and each part thereafter had its own succession of kings.

21. *The kings of Latium, among whom Aeneas and Aventinus were deified*

After Aeneas, who was deified, Latium had eleven kings, none of whom was made into a god. But Aventinus, the twelfth successor of Aeneas, was cut down in battle, and was buried on that mountain still called by his name; and thereafter he was added to the number of that class of gods created for themselves by men. Some authorities, it is true, have refused to record that he was killed in battle, saying instead that he disappeared, and that the mountain was not named after Aventinus, but was so called from the advent of birds (*adventu avium*). After this king the only god created in Latium was Romulus, the founder of Rome. Now between these two we find two kings, of whom the first was, to quote a verse of Virgil,

> Procus the next, the glory of Troy's race.[66]

66. *Aen.*, 6, 767.

In his time Rome was already, in a manner of speaking, in the process of being born; and so Assyria, that greatest of all empires, reached the end of her long history. For the power passed over to the Medes after nearly 1,305 years, if we reckon in the time of Belus, father of Ninus, who as the first king was content with a small dominion in that part of the world.

Procas was the king before Aemulius. Now Aemulius had made his brother Numitor's daughter, named Rhea, a Vestal Virgin; she was also called Ilia, and was the mother of Romulus. It is alleged that she conceived twins by Mars, for in this way the Romans honoured or excused her unchastity, and they adduce as proof the fact that the infants after their exposure were suckled by a she-wolf. For they hold that this species of animal belongs to Mars, and so, naturally, the she-wolf is supposed to have presented her teats to the little children simply because she recognized in them the sons of Mars, her lord. All the same, there are those who assert that when the exposed babies lay wailing they were first taken in by some unknown harlot, and that hers were the first breasts they sucked – for 'she-wolves' (*lupae*) was the name they used to give to harlots, which is why houses of ill-fame are to this day called 'wolves' dens' (*lupanaria*). Afterwards, it is said, they came into the care of a shepherd named Faustulus, and were reared by his wife Acca. And yet, if we assume that God wished to convict the man who was king, who had cruelly ordered these infants to be thrown into the water, and that God therefore decided to help the children through whom such a great city was to be founded, by having them rescued from the water by his divine intervention and then suckled by a wild animal, is there anything amazing in this supposition? Amulius was succeeded on the throne of Latium by his brother Numitor, the grandfather of Romulus; and in the first year of Numitor's reign, Rome was founded. That is why he ruled after that in company with his grandson, Romulus.

22. *Rome's foundation coincides with the end of the Assyrian kingdom, and with the reign of Hezekiah in Judah*

Not to spend time over a multitude of detail, the city of Rome was founded to be a kind of second Babylon, the daughter, as it were, of the former Babylon. It was God's design to conquer the world through her, to unite the world into the single community of the Roman commonwealth and the Roman laws, and so to impose peace throughout its length and breadth. For there were at this time powerful and valiant peoples, trained in arms, nations who would not lightly yield, whose conquest entailed enormous risks and no little devastation, with fearful hardships besides. Now at the time when the Assyrian Empire subjugated almost the whole of Asia, although this conquest was effected by war, it could be achieved without a great deal of cruel and difficult fighting, because the nations were still untrained to resist, and were not yet so numerous or so powerful. For we must remember that at the time when Ninus subdued the whole of Asia except India, not much more than a thousand years had elapsed after that great and world-wide Flood, when a mere eight souls escaped in Noah's ark. Rome, on the contrary, did not so speedily and easily subdue all those nations of the East and the West which we now see beneath her imperial sway, since her growth was a gradual process, and by the time she encountered them the nations were vigorous and warlike, in whatever direction she expanded. At the time of Rome's foundation the people of Israel had spent 718 years in the land of the promise, twenty-seven of which belong to Joshua's time, the following 329 to the period of the judges. Then, after the beginning of the monarchy in that country, 362 years had gone by. The king of Judah at this time was called Ahaz, or, according to another reckoning, it was his successor, Hezekiah. By common consent he was an excellent and extremely religious monarch, and his reign was contemporary with Romulus. Meanwhile Hoshea began to rule over the part of the Hebrew people which was called Israel.

23. *The Erythraean Sibyl and her prophecies of Christ*

It was at this same time, according to some accounts, that the Erythraean Sibyl made her predictions. Varro, we note, informs us that there were a number of Sibyls, not only one.[67] This Sibyl of Erythraea certainly recorded some utterances which are obviously concerned with Christ. I read these first in a Latin translation, in verses of bad Latinity and shaky metre, faults due, as I learned later, to the

67. *Sibyls.* The earliest of the inspired prophetesses, according to tradition, was the Erythraean Sibyl, so called either from the red soil of Marpessus, near Troy, or from Erythrae in Ionia. Her prophecies related to the Trojan war; but she is not mentioned by Homer or Herodotus. According to Varro there were ten Sibyls in all, the most famous being the Sibyl of Cumae, the reputed source of the Sibylline books kept on the Capitol. These were destroyed by fire in 83 B.C., and a collection was then made of similar documents from various places. The surviving oracles are of late Judaeo-Hellenic or Judaeo-Christian provenance, containing warnings of dreadful calamities.

incompetence of some unknown translator. This I discerned in conversations with that eminent man Flaccianus, who was, amongst other things, proconsul, a man of most ready eloquence and profound learning. We were talking about Christ, and he produced a Greek manuscript, saying that it was the poems of the Erythraean Sibyl. He showed me that in the manuscript the order of intial letters in one passage was so arranged as to form these words: *IĒSOUS CHREISTOS THEOU UIOS SŌTĒR*, the translation of which is 'Jesus Christ, the Son of God, the Saviour'. These verses, which form an acrostic giving this meaning, run as follows, in a verse translation made by someone in good Latin and sound metre;

In token of the judgement day the earth shall drip with sweat
Eternally to reign, a king shall come from heavenly seat,
Strictly to judge all flesh in power, to judge the world in might.
On this, belief and unbelief shall have our God in sight,
Uplifted with his saints on high when this world's end has come
So shall all souls in flesh attend before his throne of doom.

CHoked with thick briars and all untilled the earth now lies forlorn:
Rejected all man's idols now, his treasures turned to scorn:
Each land shall be consumed by flames that search both sea and sky,
Infernal gates of loathsome hell in fiery ruin lie.
Salvation's light shall be shed forth on saints exempt from blame:
To guilty men that day shall bring the everlasting flame.
Obscurest acts shall be revealed, his secrets each impart,
So shall God bring all thoughts to light, unlocking every heart.

THen all shall gnash their teeth, the sound of wailing shall arise,
Extinct the sun's bright ray, the dance of planets in the skies.
O'erhead the sky shall roll away, quenched be the moon's bright glow;
Uplifted shall the valleys be, the hills shall be laid low,

Until in all the world remains no eminence or height;
Into the plains subside the hills; the seas of azure bright
On a sudden cease; the earth itself shall perish, riven and rent,
Springs shall likewise be parched by fire, the streams by heat be spent.

Sadly the trumpet then shall blare, and sound its mournful strains
On high, lamenting deed of woe and mortals' varied pains.
Tartarus shows its vast abyss, as earth gapes open wide.
Enthroned sits God, and kings shall stand for judgement side by side;
Rivers of fire and brimstone stream from heaven, a fearful tide.[68]

In the Latin, these verses, translated, in a fashion, from the Greek,

68. *Oracc. Sibyll.* (ed. Geffcken) VIII, 217ff.

could not completely convey the sense of the initial letters of the original lines read in sequence; where the letter *upsilon* occupied that position in the original Latin, words could not be found which began with the equivalent letter and also suited the sense. There are three such lines, the fifth, the eighteenth and the nineteenth.[69] The result is that if one reads in sequence the initial letters of the verses, ignoring the first letters of these three lines and substituting *upsilon*, as if it were found in those places, a phrase of five words appears: Jesus Christ, the Son of God, the Saviour; but this is only when it is read as Greek instead of Latin.

There are here twenty-seven verses; and twenty-seven is the cube of three. For three times three is nine; multiply nine by three – so that the figure may add height to length and breadth – and we arrive at twenty-seven. Now if you connect the initial letters of those five Greek words, *Iêsous CHreistos THeou Uios Sôtêr* (Jesus Christ, the Son of God, the Saviour) you have the Greek word *ichthus*, which means 'fish',[70] and the allegorical meaning of this noun is Christ, because he was able to remain alive – that is, without sin – in the abyss of our mortal condition, in the depths, as it were, of the sea.

Now this Sibyl – whether the Sibyl of Erythrae or, as some are inclined to believe, of Cumae – has nothing in her whole poem, of which this is a tiny fragment, relating to the worship of false or created gods. In fact, she attacks them and their worshippers so strongly that she is evidently to be counted among those who belong to the City of God. Lactantius also inserts in his work some prophecies concerning Christ uttered by the Sibyl, though he does not state which Sibyl.[71] He quotes them separately; but I have decided that they should be set consecutively, as if the many brief statements he records made one lengthy prophecy. 'Hereafter', he says,

he will come into the wicked hands of unbelievers; and they will deal God blows with their polluted hands and spit their poisoned spittle from their unclean mouths; but he in his simplicity will offer his holy back to their strokes. And he will be silent as he receives the blows, so that no one may know that he comes as the Word, or whence he comes, so that he may speak to those in the underworld and be crowned with a crown of thorns. While for his food they have given him gall, and vinegar for his thirst; this is the

69. This does not appear in the English translation. The Latin translator did not attempt to find words beginning in U (they are rare in Latin) to preserve the acrostic.

70. One of the commonest symbols of the early Church.

71. *Div. Inst.*, 4, 18f.

table of inhospitality they will display. For you[72] yourself in your foolishness have not recognized your God when he mocked the minds of mortals; no, you even crowned him with thorns, and mixed for him the repulsive gall. But the veil of the temple will be rent; and at midday there will be the utter darkness of night for three hours. And he will fall asleep and die in truth for three days; and then he will be the first to return from the underworld and come to the light, showing to those who have been recalled the beginning of the resurrection.

Lactantius produced those Sibylline testimonies piece by piece, at various stages in his discussion, as the points he was bent on establishing seemed to require. I have made it my business to arrange the quotations in one continuous series, and to mark the breaks between passages simply by capitals – assuming that the copyists are careful not to omit them.

It should be added that some authorities state that the Erythraean Sibyl was contemporary not with Romulus, but with the Trojan War.

24. *The Seven Sages contemporary with Romulus: The deportation of Israel at this time: Romulus deified*

It is generally said that the Thales of Miletus[73] lived when Romulus was on the throne. He was one of the Seven Sages, who came after the 'theological poets' (among whom Orpheus won the greatest renown) and were called *sophoi*, which means 'wise men'. At about the same time the ten tribes, which were called Israel in the divisions of the people, were crushed by the Chaldeans and taken away to captivity in Chaldean territory.[74] Meanwhile the other two tribes, which were called by the name of Judah, remained in Judaea and had Jerusalem as the seat of their kingdom. On the death of Romulus, when he too vanished from sight, the Romans, as everybody well knows, enrolled him among the gods. This practice had so far fallen into abeyance in Cicero's time – and when it was later resumed, in the time of Caesar, it was simply a matter of flattery, not of mistaken belief – that Cicero regards it as the highest tribute to Romulus that he won this honour not in times of primitive ignorance, but in what was already an age of culture and education, even though philosophy had not yet erupted in a teeming flood of subtle and ingenious loquacity.[75]

Yet even if later periods did not establish dead men as gods, still

72. The Sibyl is addressing Judea.
73. cf. Bk VIII, 2n.
74. In 712 B.C.
75. Cic., *De Rep.*, 2, 10, 18. On the deification of Romulus cf. Bk III, 15.

they did not abandon the worship of those established by the men of old, and they continued to regard them as gods. Indeed, they went further, by increasing the allurement of empty and irreverent superstitions by means of images which the people of antiquity did not possess. This was due to the activity of foul demons at work in their hearts, deceiving them by misleading oracles as well as in other ways, so that although legends of the gods' misdeeds were not being made up in a more polished age, the existing stories were obscenely enacted in their shows as an act of homage to those false divinities.

Romulus was succeeded by Numa, who conceived the idea that the city needed the defence of a large number of gods – false gods, of course – but did not himself win the honour of enrolment in that multitude. It seems that he was reckoned to have packed heaven so tight with the hordes of divinities that he could find no room there. It is alleged that the Samian Sibyl was contemporary with Numa's reign at Rome, and with the beginning of the reign among the Hebrews of Manasseh, an impious king and, according to tradition, the murderer of the prophet Isaiah.[76]

25. *Eminent philosophers contemporary with Tarquinius Priscus, king of Rome, and Zedekiah, king of the Hebrews, the capture of Jerusalem and the destruction of the temple*

Now when Zedekiah was king of the Hebrews, and Tarquinius Priscus was reigning at Rome, as successor to Ancus Martius, the people of the Jews were led away into captivity in Babylonia,[77] after the overthrow of Jerusalem and of the famous Temple built by Solomon. For the prophets who rebuked the Jews for their acts of wickedness and impiety had foretold that this would happen to them, and especially Jeremiah, who even stated the precise number of years of the exile.[78] It was at that period that Pittacus of Mitylene, another of the Seven Sages, is said to have lived. And Eusebius writes that the other five, who are added to Thales, already mentioned, and this Pittacus, to make up the number of seven, lived at the time when the people of God were kept in captivity in Babylonia. Their names are: Solon of Athens, Chilon of Sparta, Periander of Corinth, Cleobulus of Lindus, and Bias of Priene.[79] All these 'Seven Sages' attained to

76. Tradition said that he was sawn in two (Just. Mart., *Dial.*, 120, 14).
77. 586 B.C. 78. Jer., 25, 11.
79. Plato's list (*Prot.*, 343A) gives Myson instead of Periander.

fame, after the time of the 'theological' poets, because they excelled the rest of mankind in respect of a praiseworthy quality in their way of life, and because they enshrined a number of moral precepts in short aphorisms. But they did not leave to posterity anything in the way of literary memorials, except that Solon is reported as having laid down certain laws for the Athenians; Thales was a natural scientist, and he left books containing his teachings. During the same period of the Jewish captivity Anaximander, Anaximenes and Xenophanes were also renowned as students of nature. At that time also Pythagoras flourished, and from then onwards such thinkers began to be called 'philosophers'.[80]

26. *The end of the Jewish captivity coincides with the liberation of Rome from the royal tyranny*

At the same period Cyrus, king of Persia, who was also ruling over the Chaldeans and the Assyrians, brought a considerable relaxation of the captivity of the Jews, and caused 50,000 of them to return, in order to restore the Temple.[81] But they only made a beginning, with the first foundations, and built an altar. For when their enemies raided them they were by no means strong enough to make progress with the work of building, and the task was postponed until the time of Darius. During this period occurred the events described in the Book of Judith, though the Jews, to be sure, are said to have excluded that book from their canon. Under King Darius of Persia then, on the completion of the seventy years foretold by Jeremiah the prophet, the captivity was ended and freedom restored to the Jews.[82] This was when Tarquin, the seventh king of Rome, was on the throne. After Tarquin's expulsion the Romans themselves also began to be free from the tyranny of their kings.

Up to this time the people of Israel had had prophets. Although there were many of these it is only a few whose writings are retained as canonical among the Jews and also among us. When I brought my last book to an end I promised that I would make some remarks about those prophets in this present book, and I recognize that it is now time for me to fulfil that undertaking.

80. On Anaximander and Anaximenes, cf. Bk VIII, 2. On Xenophanes, cf. Bk VII, 17n.

81. In 538 B.C. cf. Bk XVII, 23.

82. Darius came to the throne in 521 B.C. The captivity, as a compulsory exile, ended in 538.

27. *The prophets at the time of the fall of Assyria and the rise of Rome. The calling of the Gentiles foretold*

Now in order to survey the period of those prophets we must go back to a slightly earlier time. At the beginning of the book of the prophet Hosea, placed first of the twelve prophets, we find these words: 'The word of the Lord which was given to Hosea in the reigns of Uzziah, Jotham, Ahaz, and Hezekiah, kings of Judah.' Amos also writes that he prophesied in the reign of Uzziah; he adds the name of Jeroboam, king of Israel, whose reign was about the same time. Isaiah too, lists at the beginning of his book the same four kings mentioned by Hosea, and says, by way of preface, that he prophesied in their reigns. Isaiah was the son of Amos, whether of Amos the prophet just mentioned or, as is more generally supposed, another man of the same name who was not a prophet. Michah also records this period, after the reign of Uzziah, as the time of his prophecy. For he names the three following kings, named also by Hosea: Jotham, Ahaz, and Hezekiah. These men are found by their own statements to have prophesied simultaneously at this period. To them are added Jonah, also in Uzziah's reign, and Joel, when Jotham, Uzziah's successor, had by now ascended the throne. The dates of those two prophets can be found in the *Chronicle*,[83] not in their own books, since they say nothing about their times. Those times extend from Procas, king of Latium, or his predecessor Aventinus, to Romulus, now a king of Rome, or even to the opening of the reign of Numa Pompilius, his successor, seeing that Hezekiah, king of Judah, reigned up to that time. So we see that those men, two springs, as it were, of prophecy, gushed out together, at the time when the Assyrian Empire failed, and the Roman Empire started. It was obviously designed that, just as in the first period of the Assyrian Empire, Abraham made his appearance and to him were given the most explicit promises of the blessings of all nations in his descendants, so in the initial stages of the Western Babylon, during whose dominion Christ was destined to come, in whom those promises were to be fulfilled, the lips of the prophets should be opened, those prophets who in their writings as well as by their spoken words gave testimony to this great event in the future. For although there was scarcely any time from the beginning of the monarchy when the people of Israel had been deprived of prophets, those prophets had been solely for the benefit of the Israelites, with no message for the Gentiles. However, when a beginning was made of writings with a more openly prophetic

83. The *Chronicle* of Eusebius-Jerome.

import, prophecies that would be of value to the Gentile nations at some later date, the appropriate time for that beginning was when this city of Rome was being founded, which was to have dominion over the nations.

28. *The prophecies of Hosea and Amos concerned with the good news of Christ*

Now, to take the prophet Hosea, he certainly has profound things to say, but his message is difficult of penetration in proportion to its profundity. But we must select some part of his work and quote it here, in fulfilment of our promise. 'And it will happen', he says, 'that in the place where they were told: "You are not my people", they, even they, will be called "sons of the living God".'[84] The apostles also understood this as a prophetic testimony to the calling of the people of the Gentile nations, who did not previously belong to God.[85] And because the people of the Gentile nations themselves are spiritually among the children of Abraham and for that reason are correctly called Israel, he therefore goes on to say, 'And the sons of Judah and the sons of Israel will be assembled in the same place, and they will appoint for themselves one head and they shall ascend from the earth.'[86] If we were to attempt to explain this saying here and now, the flavour of its prophetic eloquence would be diluted. Nevertheless, let us call to mind that cornerstone and the two walls, one made up of Jews, the other of Gentiles;[87] and let us recognize them as 'ascending from the earth', the former under the name of 'sons of Judah' the latter under that of 'sons of Israel', and both supported 'in the same place' by the same 'one head'.

Again, the same prophet testifies that the Israelites by physical descent who now refuse to believe in Christ will afterwards believe; that is, their sons will believe – for, to be sure, those unbelievers will go 'to their own place'[88] when they die. He proclaims this when he says, 'Because the sons of Israel will dwell for many days without king, without leader, without sacrifice, without altar, without priest, without the outward ceremonies of their religion.' Who could fail to see that the Jews are now in this state? But let us listen to what he adds: 'And later the sons of Israel will return and seek the Lord their God and David their king, and they will be astonished before the Lord and his goodness in the last days.'[89] Nothing could be plainer than

84. Hos. 1, 10. 85. cf. Rom. 9, 26. 86. Hos. 1, 11.
87. cf. Eph. 2, 14; 20. 88. cf. Acts 1, 25. 89. Hos. 3, 4f.

this prophecy, since the name of King David is interpreted as signifying Christ, for, as the Apostle says, 'He came of the line of David by physical descent.'[90] This prophet foretold also that Christ's resurrection would happen on the third day, in the hidden manner suitable for such a prophecy, when he says, 'He will heal us after two days: on the third day we shall rise again.'[91] For it is in harmony with this that the Apostle says to us, 'If you have risen with Christ, look for the things that are above.'[92]

Amos also prophesies on this subject when he says, 'Prepare to call on your God, O Israel: for look, I am he that gives strength to the thunder, and creates the wind and announces to mankind their Christ.'[93] And in another place he says, 'In that day I shall raise up the tabernacle of David that has fallen down; and I shall rebuild its fallen ruins, and I shall raise up the parts destroyed, and rebuild it as it was in days of old; so that the residue of mankind may seek me out, and all the nations on whom my name is invoked. The Lord says this, and he puts it into effect.'[94]

29. *Isaiah's prophecies about Christ and his Church*

The prophet Isaiah is not in the book of the Twelve Prophets. These twelve are called 'minor' prophets because their discourses are brief in comparison with those called 'major' by reason of the lengthy volumes they composed. Among these latter is Isaiah, whom I connect with the two discussed above because they were contemporaries in prophecy. Now Isaiah in the course of his arraignment of wrong and his teaching of righteousness, among his predictions of the disasters that were to come upon the sinful people, also made many more prophecies than the others about Christ and the Church, that is, about the king and the City which he founded, so much so that by some commentators Isaiah was called an evangelist rather than a prophet.[95] But because I am determined to keep my book within bounds I shall quote here only one of many passages. Speaking, it is to be understood, in the character of God the Father, he says,

> See, my servant will understand; he will be exalted and glorified exceedingly. As many will be appalled at you, so will your appearance be deprived of glory from men and your glory be dishonoured by men. So will many nations wonder at him; and kings will keep their mouths shut: for those

90. Rom. 1, 3.
91. Hos. 6, 2.
92. Col. 3, 1.
93. Amos 4, 12f.
94. Amos 9, 11f.
95. e.g. by Jerome (*Praef. in Is.*).

who were told nothing of him will see, and those who had not heard will understand. Lord, who has believed what we have heard, and to whom has the strong arm of the Lord been revealed? We announced him in his presence as an infant, like a root in the thirsty ground. He has neither beauty nor glory. And we saw him, and he had neither looks nor grace; his appearance was without honour and inferior to that of all men. He was a man suffering punishment, one who knew how to bear infirmity. Because his face was turned away from us, he was dishonoured and not highly esteemed. He bears our sins and suffers for our sake; and we thought of him as someone in pain and punishment and affliction. But he was wounded for our wickedness and was weakened on account of our sins. The discipline which brings us peace fell on him, and by his bruises we have been healed. We have all strayed like sheep; man has strayed from his true way: and the Lord has handed him over for our sins; and he, for all his afflictions, did not open his mouth. As a sheep is led to slaughter, and as a lamb before its shearer is dumb, so he did not open his mouth. In his humiliation he was denied justice. Who shall declare his generation? For his life is taken away from the earth. Because of the iniquities of my people he was led to death. And I shall give him the wicked for his burial and the rich for his death; because he practised no iniquity and there was no deceit in his mouth. And the Lord chooses to cleanse him from suffering. If you give your life for sin, you will see a long-lived posterity; and the Lord chooses to rescue his soul from pain, to show him light and to form his understanding, to justify the righteous one who serves many well; and he himself will bear their sins. Therefore he will inherit many and divide the spoils of the mighty ones, because his soul was surrendered to death, and he was reckoned among the wicked and bore the sins of many, and was handed over for their sins.[96]

So much was said about Christ. And now let us listen to what follows, which concerns the Church: 'Rejoice', he says,

you barren woman, you who bear no children; break out into shouts, you who do not give birth. For children of the deserted woman are many, more than those of her who has a husband. Widen the space of your tent and of your hangings; fix your pegs, do not hang back; lengthen your ropes and strengthen your tent-pole, extend still to the right and the left. For your descendants will take possession of the nations, and you will people the deserted cities. Do not be afraid because you are made ashamed; do not be dismayed because you have been reproached; for you will forget your endless shame, and you will not remember the reproach of your widowhood. Because it is the Lord who made you; his name is the Lord of Hosts: and he who rescues you, the God of Israel, will be called the God of the whole earth.[97]

This must suffice. There are a number of points in it that demand

96. Is. 52, 13–53, 12 (LXX). 97. Is. 54, 1–5 (LXX).

explanation; but there are, in my judgement, enough points in the passage so plain that even our opponents are forced to recognize their meaning, though much against their will.

30. *The prophecies of Micah, Jonah and Joel connected with the new covenant*

The prophet Micah gives a picture of Christ in the image of a great mountain, when he says,

> In the last days the mountain of the Lord will be revealed, set on top of the mountains, and will be lifted up above the hills. And peoples will hasten to it, and many nations will go to it, saying, 'Come, let us go up to the mountain of the Lord, and to the house of the God of Jacob; and he will show us his way and we shall walk in his paths; because the Law will go out from Zion, and the word of the Lord from Jerusalem.' And he will judge between many peoples, and rebuke powerful nations even far off.[98]

This prophet also foretold the place of Christ's birth. 'And you, Bethlehem', he says,

> the house of Ephrata, are very small to be among the clans of Judah; yet out of you shall come forth for me one who is to be a leader over Israel. His origins are from the beginning and from the days of eternity. Therefore he will give them over, until the time when the woman in labour bears her child, and the remnant of his brothers will turn back to the sons of Israel. He will stand and look and feed his flock in the strength of the Lord, and they will be in the honour of the name of his God; for now he will be magnified even to the end of the world.[99]

The prophet Jonah, for his part, prophesied of Christ not so much by his verbal message as by some of his experiences; in fact, he prophesied more plainly in this way than if he had proclaimed Christ's death and resurrection in words. For why was he taken into the belly of the monster, and given back on the third day, except to signify that Christ would come back from the depths of hell on the third day?

All the prophecies of Joel demand much explanatory comment to throw light on the points which are connected with Christ and his Church. However, there is one passage which I shall not pass over. It is the text quoted also by the apostles, when, in fulfilment of Christ's promise, the Holy Spirit came down from above upon the assembled believers. 'It will happen', says Joel, 'after this, that I shall pour out my spirit over all mortals: and your sons and daughters will prophesy;

98. Mic. 4, 1ff. 99. Mic. 5, 2ff.

your old men will dream dreams and your young men will see visions. Indeed, at that time I shall pour out my spirit on my servants and my maidservants.'[100]

31. *The predictions about the salvation of the world in Christ found in Obadiah, Nahum, and Habbakuk*

Three of the minor prophets, Obadiah, Nahum and Habbakuk, do not tell us their dates; nor is the time of their prophecies to be found in the *Chronicle* of Eusebius and Jerome. Obadiah, it is true, is placed by them with Micah, but not in the passage where a note is given of the date when Micah is known from his own writings to have prophesied. This, I suppose, is due to the error of scribes inattentively copying the works of others. But I have not been able to find a mention of the other two in the copies of *Chronicle* in my possession. Nevertheless, since they are included in the canon, it is not right for me to pass them over.

Obadiah is the shortest of all the prophets in respect of his writings. He holds forth against Edom, that is the race of Esau, the elder of the twin sons of Isaac, grandsons of Abraham, the one who was rejected. Now if we take Edom as standing for the Gentiles, by the 'part for whole' figure of speech, we can recognize a prophecy of Christ where Obadiah says, among other things, 'Now on Mount Sion there will be salvation and there will be a holy place.' And a little later, at the end of this prophecy, 'And those who have been saved will go up from Mount Sion, to defend Mount Esau; and the kingdom will be the Lord's.[101] It is quite obvious that this was fulfilled when those saved from Mount Sion – that is, those from Judaea who believed in Christ, and in particular those recognized as apostles – went up to defend Mount Esau. How were they to defend it, except by bringing salvation, through the preaching of the gospel, to those who became believers, so that they should be rescued from the power of darkness and transferred to the kingdom of God? This is expressed by the addition of the next words: 'And the kingdom will be the Lord's.' For Mount Sion signifies Judaea, where it was predicted that there would be salvation and a holy place, which is Christ Jesus. Whereas Mount Esau is Edom, by which is signified the Church of the Gentiles; and, as I have explained, the saved from Mount Sion defended it, so that it should be a kingdom for the lord. This was obscure before the event: but what believer could fail to recognize the event?

100. Joel 2, 28f.; cf. Acts 2, 17f. 101. Obad. 17; 21.

Now the prophet Nahum says – or rather God speaks through him, saying,

> I shall abolish the carved and the moulded images, and I shall make your tomb. For look, the feet of the bringer of good news, the herald of peace, come swiftly over the mountains. Judah, celebrate your feast-days, fulfil your vows; for from now on they will not go on further, to pass into old age. It is finished, it is consumed, it is removed. He comes up who breathes in your face, snatching you away from tribulation.[102]

Who is it who will come up from the underworld and will breathe the Holy Spirit on the face of Judah, that is on the Jewish disciples? Anyone who remembers the Gospel can recall.[103] For those whose feast-days are made new, in a spiritual sense, so that they cannot pass into old age, belong to the new covenant. Moreover, it is by the gospel that the carved and the moulded images, that is, the idols of false gods, have been abolished; and we already see them consigned to oblivion, as if to the tomb. And in this once again we recognize the fulfilment of a prophecy.

As for Habbakuk, we can scarcely understand him to be speaking of anything else but the coming of Christ, who was destined to appear, when he says,

> Then the Lord answered me, saying: 'Write the vision plainly on a tablet so that he who reads these things may follow; for the vision is still awaiting its time, and it will come to reality in the end, and it will not be to no purpose. If it is slow in coming, wait for it, because it will surely come and will not be delayed.'[104]

32. *The prophecy in Habbakuk's prayer and song; an exposition*

Again, in his prayer, combined with a song,[105] to whom but the lord Christ is Habbakuk speaking when he says, 'Lord, I heard your discourse, and I was afraid: Lord, I considered your works, and I was filled with dread'? For can this represent anything but the indescribable amazement aroused by the foreknowledge of a new and sudden salvation for mankind? 'Between the two living creatures you will be recognized' can surely only mean between the two covenants, or between the two thieves, or between Moses and Elijah conversing with him on the mountain. 'When the years approach you will be known, when the time has come you will be shown' needs no ex-

102. Nah. 1, 14f.; 2, 1 (LXX).
103. John 20, 22f.
104. Hab. 2, 2f. (LXX).
105. Hab. 3 (LXX).

planation. 'When my soul is disturbed in wrath you will remember mercy' can only mean that the speaker assumes the role of the Jews, to whose nation he belonged; for when they were 'disturbed in great wrath' and were crucifying Christ, he 'remembered mercy' and said, 'Father, forgive them, because they do not know what they are doing.'[106]

'God will come from Teman, and the Holy One from the darkly shaded, thickly covered mountain.' The words, 'he will come from Teman', are taken by some translators as meaning 'from the south' or 'from the south-east', signifying midday, that is, the warmth of affection and the brightness of truth. The shaded, thickly covered mountain is indeed susceptible of a variety of interpretations; but I should be inclined to take it as standing for the profundity of the inspired Scriptures in which Christ is prophesied. There are, to be sure, many 'shaded and thickly covered' passages there, to exercise the mind of the inquirer. But Christ 'comes from' there, when he is found there by the reader who understands the meaning. 'His glory has covered the heavens, and the earth is filled with his praise' must mean the same as what is said in the psalm: 'Be exalted, O God, above the heavens, and your glory over all the earth.'[107] 'His brightness will be like the light.' Can this mean anything except that his fame will enlighten those who believe in him? 'Horns are in his hands' can only refer to the trophy of the cross. 'And he has established a steadfast love for his strength' demands no explanation.

'His word will go before his face, and it will go out on to the plain after his feet.' This can only mean that even before he came here he was fore-announced, and after he had departed hence he was proclaimed. 'He stood still, and the earth was moved' must surely mean that he stood still to help us, and the world was moved to believe. 'He looked and the nations wasted away'; that is, he had mercy, and brought the people to repentance. 'The mountains were ground down by violence'; that is, the arrogance of the proud was ground down by the might displayed in his miracles. 'The eternal hills melted away'; that is, they were brought low for a time, so that they might be raised up for eternity. 'I saw his eternal entrances in return for his labours'; that is, I observed that his labour of love was not without eternal reward. 'The tents of the Ethiopians will cower in fear, also the pavilions of the land of Midian'; that is, the nations, suddenly terrified at the news of your wonderful deeds, will form part of the Christian people, even those nations who are not under Roman rule.

106. Luke 23, 34. 107. Ps. 57, 5.

'Can it be that you are angry with the rivers, Lord, or that your fury is against the rivers, and your attack against the sea?' The meaning of this is that he does not now come to judge the world, but that the world may be saved through him.[108] 'Because you will mount your horses, and your riding will be salvation'; that is, your evangelists will convey you, and they will be guided by you, and your Gospel will be salvation for those who believe in you. 'You will surely bend your bow against sceptres, says the Lord'; that is, you will threaten even the kings of the earth with your judgement. 'The earth will be cleft by rivers'; that is, by the flowing in of the discourses of the preachers the hearts of men will be opened to acknowledge you, the men to whom it was said, 'Rend your hearts, not your clothes.'[109] What is meant by 'the peoples will see you and will grieve' except that they will be blessed by their lamentation?[110] What is meant by 'scattering the waters as you go'? Surely that as you walk, in the persons of those who bring news of you in every place, you spread the streams of doctrine on this side and that.

What is expressed by 'the abyss uttered its voice' except that the depth of the human heart has declared its decision? 'The depth of its imagination' is a kind of explanation of the previous verse, for 'depth' is the same as 'abyss'. And with 'its imagination' the words 'uttered its voice' must be supplied, meaning, as I said, 'declared its decision'. For 'imagination' is, without doubt, a vision which the heart did not keep to itself, and did not hide; it burst out with it in acknowledgement. 'The sun was raised on high, the moon halted in her course'; that is, Christ ascended to heaven, and the Church took her appointed place beneath her king. 'Your javelins will go out into the light'; that is, your words will not be issued into obscurity but into the open. 'Into the brightness of the glittering of your arms'; here we must supply 'your javelins will go'. For he had said to his friends, 'What I am telling you in the darkness, speak out in the light.'[111] 'By your threatening you will diminish the earth'; that is, you will humble men by your threats. 'And in fury you will cast down nations', because by your vengeance you will crush those who exalt themselves. 'You have gone out for the salvation of your people, so that you may save your anointed ones; you have sent death on the heads of the wicked'; there is nothing here needing explanation.

'You have raised up bonds as far as the neck'; those bonds can be taken as meaning the good bonds of wisdom so that our feet are put

108. John 3, 17.
109. Joel 2, 13.
110. cf. Matt. 5, 4.
111. Matt. 10, 27.

into its fetters, and our neck into its collar. 'You have cut through, to the amazement of his mind'; we supply 'bonds', for he has raised up the good bonds, while cutting through the evil (which are referred to when he is told, 'You have broken my bonds'[112]), and this 'to the amazement of his mind'; that is, in miraculous fashion. 'The heads of the mighty will be moved in that'; 'in that *amazement*', to be sure. 'They will open wide their mouths to bite, like a poor man eating in secret.' For there were certain members of the Jewish ruling class who came to the Lord, in admiration of his deeds and words, and in hunger for the bread of doctrine; but they ate it in secret for fear of the Jews. They are revealed as doing this in the Gospel story.[113]

'Then you drove your horses into the sea, stirring up many waters', which simply means 'many people'; for it would not have happened that some were converted through fear, while others persecuted in fury, if they had not all been stirred up. 'I watched, and my heart was appalled at the sound of the speech of my lips; and trembling entered my bones, and all my body was troubled beneath me.' He gave his attention to what he was saying, and he was terrified at his own speech, which he was pouring out in prophetic manner, and in which he discovered things that were to be. For in the disturbance of many peoples he saw the tribulations impending for the Church. Immediately he recognized himself as a member of that Church, and said, 'I shall rest in the day of tribulation', as belonging to the company of those who are 'joyful because hopeful, steadfast under tribulation',[114] 'so that I may go up to join the people of my pilgrimage', leaving, we may be sure, the wicked people, his own kin by blood, who were not on pilgrimage on this earth and were not looking for a heavenly country. 'Because the fig tree', he says, 'will not yield fruit, and there will be no produce on the vines; the labour of the olive will disappoint, and the fields afford no food. The sheep have disappeared from the pasture, and no cattle survive at the mangers.' He saw that the nation which was destined to kill Christ would lose its rich store of spiritual supplies, which he pictured allegorically, in prophetic fashion, in terms of the fertility of the land.

Now the reason why that nation suffered such an outburst of God's anger was that in their ignorance of God's way of righteousness they chose to set up their own.[115] Hence he continues, 'But *I* shall exult in the Lord; *I* shall rejoice in God my saviour. The Lord God is my strength; he will establish my feet to the end; he will set me on the

112. Ps. 116, 16. 113. cf. John 3, 2; 19, 38.
114. Rom. 12, 12. 115. cf. Rom. 10, 3.

heights, so that I may triumph with his song.' The reference is obviously to the song about which something similar is said in one of the psalms, 'He has set my feet on a rock and guided my steps; and he has put into my mouth a new song, a hymn to our God.'[116] Thus the man who triumphs with the Lord's song is one who pleases God by praising him instead of praising himself, so that 'he who is proud is proud of the Lord.'[117] Some texts, by the way, have the reading, 'I shall rejoice in God my Jesus';[118] this, in my view, is preferable to the version given by those who, in attempting to put the original phrase into Latin, have not used the actual name which for us is more welcome and more delightful to utter.

33. *The inspired prophecies of Jeremiah and Zephaniah about Christ and the calling of the Gentiles*

Jeremiah is one of the major prophets, like Isaiah, not one of the minor prophets, like the others from whose writing I have quoted a number of passages. Now Jeremiah prophesied in the reign of Josiah in Jerusalem, when Ancus Martius was on the Roman throne, and when the captivity of the Jews was already imminent. His prophetic activity extended until the fifth month of the captivity, as we discover from his writings. Zephaniah, one of the minor prophets, is linked with him, in that he himself tells us that he prophesied in the time of Josiah, though he does not say for how long. Jeremiah then, prophesied not only in the time of Ancus Martius, but also in that of Tarquinius Priscus, whom the Romans had for their fifth king. For he had already begun his reign when the captivity came about.

In a prophecy of Christ, Jeremiah says, 'The breath of our nostrils, Christ the Lord, has been taken captive in our sins',[119] thus showing, in this brief statement, that Christ is our Lord, and that he suffered for us. Again, in another place he says, 'This is my God and no other will be compared with him. He discovered the whole way of knowledge and entrusted it to Jacob his servant and Israel his beloved; after this he was seen on earth and lived among men.'[120] Some authorities attribute this testimony not to Jeremiah but to his scribe, who was called Baruch; but it is more generally held to be the work of Jeremiah.

116. Ps. 40, 2. 117. 1 Cor. 1, 31.

118. *Jesus* is Greek for *Joshua* which in Hebrew differs in only one letter from the Hebrew for 'God my saviour'; cf. Bk XVII, 18n.

119. Lam. 4, 20. 120. Bar. 3, 36.

Again, the same prophet says about Christ, 'See, the time is coming, says the Lord, when I shall raise up for David a righteous scion, who will reign as king, and will be wise, and will execute justice and righteousness on the earth. In those days Judah will be saved, and Israel dwell in confidence: and this is the name by which he will be called: "Our Righteous Lord".'[121] He spoke also about the calling of the Gentiles, which was then destined to happen and which we now see accomplished. He says, 'O Lord, my God, and my refuge in the day of disaster, to you the nations will come from the farthest part of the earth, saying: "It is true that our fathers worshipped delusive images, and in them there is no value." '[122] But the same prophet signifies that the Jews by whom he was destined to be killed would not recognize him; for he says, 'The heart is heavy in every way; and he is the man, and who recognizes him?'[123] This prophet is also the author of the passage I quoted in Book XVII,[124] concerning the new covenant, whose mediator is Christ. For, as we know, it is Jeremiah who says, 'See, the days are coming when I will ratify a new covenant for the house of Jacob', and the rest of the passage to be found there.[125]

At this point I shall put in the prophecies of Christ made by Zephaniah, a prophet contemporary with Jeremiah. They are as follows: 'Wait for me, says the Lord, in the day of my resurrection in the future. For it is my decision to assemble the nations and gather together the kingdoms.'[126] And again, 'The Lord will be full of terror for them, and he will abolish all the gods of the earth, and every man will worship him, each in his own place, all the islands of the nations.'[127] And a little later,

> At that time I shall change the language for the peoples and his posterity, so that all may call on the name of the Lord and serve him under one yoke; from the boundaries of the rivers of Ethiopia they will bring sacrifices to me. On that day you will feel no shame for all the misdeeds which you have wickedly practised against me; for I shall then take away from you the vile acts of your injustice; and you will no longer seek to make much of yourselves on my holy mountain. And I shall leave in your midst a gentle and humble people; and the remnant of Israel will reverence the name of the Lord.[128]

This is the remnant about which there is a prophecy elsewhere,

121. Jer. 23, 5f.
122. Jer. 16, 19.
123. Jer. 17, 9 (LXX).
124. Bk XVII, 3.
125. Jer. 31, 31.
126. Zeph. 3, 8.
127. Zeph. 2, 11.
128. Zeph. 3, 9–12.

quoted by the Apostle, 'Even if the number of the sons of Israel should be like the sands of the sea, only a remnant will be saved.'[129] This remnant is, of course, those of that race who have believed in Christ.

34. The prophecies of Daniel and Ezekiel which harmonize with Christ and the Church

Then again, during the actual period of the Babylonian captivity there were two other major prophets, Daniel and Ezekiel. They prophesied in the earlier part of the exile. Of these Daniel specified the time when Christ was destined to come and to suffer, by giving the number of years that were to intervene. It would be a tedious business to demonstrate this by computation, and it has been done by others before us. But Daniel has this to say on the power of Christ and on his Church,

> I saw a vision of the night, and behold, there was one coming with the clouds of heaven like a son of man; and he came to the ancient of days and was brought forward in his presence. And to him was given sovereignty, honour and kingship; and all peoples, tribes, and languages will serve him. His power is an eternal power which will not pass away, and his kingdom will not be destroyed.[130]

Ezekiel also points to Christ, in the prophetic manner, by presenting him in the person of David, because he took flesh from the line of David – and because of this 'form of a servant',[131] in which he was made man, he is called the servant of God as well as God's son. This is Ezekiel's prediction of him, in which the prophet speaks in the role of God the Father: 'I shall raise up one shepherd, my servant David, to be in charge of my flocks, to pasture them. He will pasture them and be their shepherd; while I, the Lord, shall be their God, and my servant David will be ruler among them. I, the Lord, have spoken.'[132] In another place he says,

> There will be one king ruling over them: and there will no longer be two nations, and they will no more be divided into two kingdoms; nor will they any longer be defiled with their idols and their abominations and all their sins. And I shall save them out of all their dwellings in which they have sinned, and I shall cleanse them. And they will be my people, and I shall be their God. And my servant David will be king over them, and will be the one shepherd of them all.[133]

129. Is. 10, 22; cf. Rom. 9, 27.
130. Dan. 7, 13f.
131. cf. Phil. 2, 7.
132. Ezek. 34, 23f.
133. Ezek. 37, 22ff.

35. *The predictions of the three prophets, Haggai, Zechariah, and Malachi*

There remain three minor prophets who prophesied at the end of the captivity. These are Haggai, Zechariah, and Malachi. Of these, Haggai gives the clearest prophecy of Christ and the Church, in this brief statement: 'This is what the Lord of Hosts says: "A little while now, and I shall shake the heaven and the earth, the sea and the dry land. I shall shake all nations; and then will come one who is longed for by all nations." '[134] We observe the partial fulfilment of this prophecy; we await its completion at the end of history. For he shook the heavens by the testimony of the angels and the stars when Christ became incarnate; he shook the earth by the momentous miracle involved in the virgin birth; he has shaken the sea and the dry land now that Christ is being proclaimed both in the islands and in the whole world. Thus we see that all nations are being shaken, and stirred to faith in Christ. But as soon as we come to the next statement, 'then will come one who is longed for by all nations', we have something which is still awaited, which concerns his last coming. For he had first to be loved by those who believe, so that he might be longed for by those who look for his appearance.

Zechariah says of Christ and the Church, 'Rejoice greatly, daughter of Sion! Shout for joy, daughter of Jerusalem! See, your king is coming to you, a righteous king and a saviour. He comes as a poor man, mounted on a donkey, on a colt, a donkey's foal. His power will extend from sea to sea, and from the rivers as far as the ends of the earth.'[135] We read in the Gospel of the fulfilment of this prophecy, when the Lord Christ on his journey made use of a beast of burden of this kind; and part of this prophecy is quoted there, as much of it as seemed sufficient in the context.[136] In another place the prophet addresses Christ in the spirit of prophecy, speaking about the forgiveness of sins through his blood. Here he says, 'You also, by the blood of your covenant, have rescued your prisoners from the lake in which there is no water.'[137] The question of what he meant to be understood by 'the lake' is capable of a diversity of answers. But in my opinion there is no better meaning to be put to it than that of the depths of human misery, dry, as we may call it, and sterile, where there are no streams of righteousness but only the mud of iniquity.

134. Hagg. 2, 6. 135. Zech. 9, 9f.
136. Matt., 21, 5. 137. Zech. 9, 11.

There is, to be sure, a similar reference in one of the psalms, 'He has led me out of the lake of misery, and out of the muddy clay.'[138]

Malachi gives a prophecy of the Church which we see propagated through Christ's action, when, as the mouthpiece of God, he speaks to the Jews in the most explicit terms, saying,

> I am not pleased with you, and I shall not accept an offering from your hands. For from the farthest east to the farthest west my name is honoured among the nations, and in every place sacrifice will be offered and a pure oblation; because my name is honoured among the nations, says the Lord.[139]

This sacrifice we now see being offered to God everywhere, through Christ's priesthood in the line of Melchizedech, from farthest east to farthest west; furthermore, the Jews, who were told 'I am not pleased with you and I shall not accept an offering from your hands', cannot deny that their sacrifices have ceased. This being so, why do the Jews still await another Christ? And they do this in spite of the fact that this prophecy, which they read, and which they see fulfilled, has in the person of Christ himself received its only possible fulfilment.

Then, a little later, Malachi speaks as the mouthpiece of God, and says,

> My covenant with him was a covenant of life and peace, and I granted him that he should truly fear me and stand in reverence before my name. The Law of truth was in his mouth, and guiding himself in peace he walked with me, and he converted many from wickedness; because the priest's lips will safeguard knowledge, and they will seek the Law from his mouth, since he is the angel of God Almighty.[140]

We should not be surprised that Christ Jesus is spoken of as the 'angel' of God Almighty; for just as he is called a 'servant' because of the 'form of a servant' in which he came to mankind, so he is called an 'angel' on account of the gospel which he announced to mankind. For if we translate the Greek words, 'gospel' means 'good news' and 'angel' means 'messenger'. Indeed, Malachi speaks of Christ in yet another place in these words:

> Look, I am going to send my messenger, and he will survey the road in front of me; and the Lord you are looking for will suddenly come into his temple, and the angel of the covenant whom you wish for. See, he is

138. Ps. 40, 2. 139. Mal. 1, 10. 140. Mal. 2, 5ff.

coming, says the Lord Almighty; and who will withstand the day of his coming in? And who will stand up to face his gaze?[141]

In this passage he predicts both the first and the second coming of Christ: the first, obviously, when he says, 'He will suddenly come into his temple', that is, into his physical body, to which he referred in the Gospel when he said, 'Destroy this temple, and I shall raise it up again in three days';[142] and the second in saying, 'See, he is coming, says the Lord Almighty; and who will withstand the day of his coming in? And who will stand up to face his gaze?' While as for the words 'the Lord you are looking for, and the angel of the covenant, whom you wish for', the prophet here undoubtedly indicates that even the Jews look for and wish for Christ – the Messiah – in accordance with the Scriptures which they read. But many of them have not recognized that he whom they looked for and wished for has come, because they are blinded in their hearts by their previous merits.[143]

The prophet is emphatic in his reference to a 'covenant'. He says above, 'My covenant was with him', and again, in this passage, he calls Christ 'the angel of the covenant'. Now we must undoubtedly take this to be the new covenant, in which eternal blessings are promised, not the old covenant which offered merely temporal rewards. Now the majority of mankind put a high value on such goods, and in their weakness they serve the true God for the sake of such temporal recompense; and so they are upset when they see the irreligious enjoying them in abundance. It is for this reason that the prophet is concerned to distinguish the eternal blessedness of the new covenant, which will be bestowed only on the good, from the worldly felicity of the old, which is often granted to the wicked also; and with that aim in view he says,

You have spoken harsh words about me, says the Lord. You ask: 'What have we said in your disparagement?' You have said: 'Anyone who serves God is wasting his time. What good have we got from observing his instructions, and from walking as suppliants before the face of Almighty God? And now we call the aliens happy, and all the evil-doers are restored; they have opposed God, and yet they have been preserved.' Such were the reproaches uttered by those who feared the Lord, each one to his neighbour. And the Lord noticed it and listened; and he wrote a book of remembrance in his presence for those who fear the Lord and reverence his name.[144]

141. Mal. 3, 4. 142. John 2, 19.

143. 'by their complacency about their merits'; or 'because they deserve such blindness'. The Latin is ambiguous, perhaps intentionally.

144. Mal. 3, 13–16.

That 'book of remembrance' means the New Testament.

Finally, let us listen to what follows:

> Then they will be mine, says the Lord Almighty, for my possession, on the day that I am preparing, and I shall choose them as a man chooses his son who serves him. And turn back, and you will see the difference between the righteous man and the unrighteous, between the one who serves God, and the one who does not serve him. For look, the day is coming, blazing like a furnace, and it will burn them up; and all the aliens and the evil-doers will be stubble. The day that is to come will set them on fire, says the Lord Almighty; and there will be left of them neither root nor twig. And yet for you who fear my name there will arise the sun of righteousness, and there will be healing in his wings; and you will go out leaping for joy like calves, released from their pens. And you will trample down the wicked, and they will be like ashes under your feet in the day in which I do this, says the Lord Almighty.[145]

This is the day called the Day of Judgement; and about it I shall speak, God willing, more fully in the appropriate place.

36. Esdras and the Books of the Maccabees

After these three prophets, Haggai, Zechariah and Malachi, and during the same period of the liberation of the people from the Babylonian slavery, Esdras also wrote. He has been considered a historian rather than a prophet; and that is true of the book called Esther, which describes, in praise of God, events which prove to be not far removed from this period. But Esdras may perhaps be interpreted as prophesying Christ in the passage which tells of a discussion which arose among some young men on the question about the most influential factor in events.[146] One said 'kings', another 'wine'; the third said 'women', on the ground that women generally hold sway over kings. And yet this same third man proved that truth is the victor over all things. Now if we consult the Gospel we learn that Christ is the truth.[147] From this time, after the restoration of the temple, it was not kings who ruled in Judaea, but princes, down to the time of Aristobulus.[148] The reckoning of their dates is not to be found in the sacred writings which are called 'canonical', but in other documents, which include the books of the Maccabees. These are regarded as canonical by the Church (though not by the Jews) because of the savage, the amazing sufferings endured by some of the martyrs

145. Mal. 3, 17–4, 3. 146. Esdr. 3, 1–4, 41. 147. John 14, 16.
148. Aristobulus II, the last Hasmonean ruler, 66–63 B.C.

who, before Christ's coming in his human body, contended even unto death for the cause of God's Law, and held firm under the most appalling agonies.

37. *The prophetic authority antedates the beginnings of pagan philosophy*

We can now see that the philosophers of the Gentiles were active during the period of our prophets, whose writings had already come to the knowledge of nearly all nations, though these thinkers were much more in evidence after that time. I am speaking of the philosophers who actually bore that title, for the name began with Pythagoras of Samos,[149] who first achieved eminence and recognition at the time of the release of the Jews from captivity. It follows that the other philosophers must be considerably later than the prophets. In fact, Socrates the Athenian himself, the master of all the most famous thinkers of the time, who held the highest position of authority in that branch of philosophy called moral or practical, is found placed after Esdras in the *Chronicle*. Not much later occurred the birth of Plato also, who was destined to excel by far the other disciples of Socrates.[150]

If we add to these thinkers the earlier men also, who were not yet called philosophers, namely the 'Seven Sages' and after them the natural philosophers who succeeded Thales, who followed him in their enthusiasm for research into natural phenomena, namely Anaximander, Anaximenes and Anaxagoras, and a number of others before Pythagoras first claimed the title of 'philosopher', even these men do not take precedence of our prophets, taken together, in point of temporal priority. In fact, Thales, to whom all the others were subsequent, is said to have risen to eminence in the reign of Romulus, at the time when the river of prophecy burst out from the springs of Israel in those writings which were to flow through the whole world. Thus only the great 'theological' poets, Orpheus, Linus, and Musaeus, and any others there were among the Greeks, are found to be prior to those Hebrew prophets whose writings we regard as authoritative.[151]

149. cf. Bk VIII, 2.

150. End of captivity, 538 B.C.: Pythagoras *fl. c.* 540; Socrates, 469–399; Plato, 428–349.

151. Thales *c.* 600; Anaximander *c.* 570; Anaximenes *c.* 500; Anaxagoras *c.* 460. cf. Bk VIII, 2. For the Seven Sages cf. ch. 25; on the 'theological' poets cf. ch. 15n.

But not even these poets were antecedent in date to Moses, our true theologian, who truthfully proclaimed the one true God, and whose writings now have the first place in our authorized canon. For this reason, as far as the Greeks are concerned – and it is in the Greek language that the literature of this world came to the greatest efflorescence – they have no justification for the boast that their wisdom, while not superior to our religion, in which true wisdom is to be found, at least makes up for this by being evidently more ancient Nevertheless it has to be admitted that there existed before Moses, not indeed in Greece but among foreign nations, in Egypt, for example, a considerable amount of learning which might be called the wisdom of the men concerned. Otherwise it would not be said in the holy Scriptures that Moses was 'learned in all the wisdom of the Egyptians',[152] as he assuredly was when, after his birth in Egypt, and his adoption and upbringing by Pharaoh's daughter, he had also received a liberal education. But not even the wisdom of the Egyptians could have preceded in time the wisdom of our prophets, seeing that Abraham also was a prophet. Then again, what degree of wisdom could exist in Egypt before the art of letters had been bestowed by Isis, whom the Egyptians, after her death, thought it right to worship as a great goddess?[153] Now Isis, according to tradition, was the daughter of Inachus, who became the first king of Argos at a time when we find that Abraham's grandsons had already been born.

38. *Some writings not admitted into the canon because of their great antiquity and doubtful authenticity*

But to go back to matters of far greater antiquity, our patriarch Noah certainly was living even before the great Flood; and I should be quite justified in calling him a prophet, seeing that the very ark which he built and in which he and his family escaped was a prophecy of our times.[154] Then again, Enoch, the seventh in descent from Adam, is said to have prophesied; and the authority for this is the canonical epistle of the apostle Jude.[155] But the excessive antiquity of the writings of those men has had the effect of preventing their acceptance, either by the Jews or by us, as authoritative; on account of their remoteness in time it seemed advisable to hold them suspect, for fear of advancing false claims to authenticity. For there are some writings

152. Acts 7, 22.
153. cf. ch. 3.
154. cf. Hebr. 11, 7; 1 Pet. 3, 20.
155. Jude 14.

put forward as genuine works of those authors[156] by those who without discrimination believe what they want to believe, as suits their inclination. But the purity of the canon has not admitted these works, not because the authority of these men, who God approved, is rejected, but because these documents are not believed to belong to them.

It should not, indeed, appear surprising that writings put forward under a name of such antiquity are regarded with suspicion; for in the actual history of the kings of Judah and Israel, the contents of which we believe in as historical on the authority of the same canon of Scripture, there are frequent references to matters not fully treated there which, we are told, can be found in other books written by the prophets, and in some cases the names of those prophets are not suppressed; yet these books are not found in the canon accepted by the people of God.

The reason for this omission, I confess, escapes me; except that I conceive that even those writers to whom the Holy Spirit unquestionably revealed matters which were rightly accorded religious authority, may have written sometimes as men engaged in historical research, sometimes as prophets under divine inspiration. And the two kinds of writing were so distinct that it was decided that the first kind should be attributed to the writers themselves, while the other kind was to be ascribed, as we might say, to God speaking through them. Thus one sort was concerned with the development of knowledge, the other with the establishment of religious authority; and the canon was carefully guarded as bearing this authority. Outside the canon, though works may now be issued under the names of genuine prophets, they are of no value even as adding to our supply of knowledge, since it is uncertain whether they are authentic works of the authors to whom they are ascribed. That is why no reliance is placed on them; and this is particularly true of those in which statements are found that actually contradict the reliable evidence of the canonical books, so that it is immediately apparent that they are not authentic.

39. *Hebrew a written language from the start*

Now it is not to be believed, as some people suppose, that it was only as a spoken language that Hebrew was preserved by Heber (whose name is the origin of the name 'Hebrews'[157]) and that from him it

156. e.g. Enoch; cf. Bk XV, 23. 157. cf. Bk XVI, 3.

passed on to Abraham, whereas the written language started with the Law given through Moses. We should rather believe that the recorded language, along with its literature, was safeguarded by that succession of fathers. In fact, Moses appointed men among the people to be responsible for teaching literacy, before the Hebrews had any acquaintance with the Law of God in its written form. Those men are called in Scripture *grammatoeisagogoi*,[158] which may be rendered as 'inducers – or introducers – of letters', on the ground that, in a way, they induce, or introduce, letters into the minds of learners – or rather introduce their pupils to letters.

Therefore no race should boast with empty pride of the antiquity of its wisdom, and crow over our patriarchs and prophets, in whom divine wisdom was active. For not even Egypt, whose habit it is to plume herself, falsely and idly, on the antiquity of her learning, is found to antedate the wisdom of the patriarchs with any wisdom of her own, of any quality. In fact, no one will have the hardihood to assert that the Egyptians reached a remarkable level of cultural attainment before they became familiar with reading and writing, that is, before Isis arrived and taught those accomplishments in Egypt. And indeed, as for that oft-mentioned learning of theirs, which is given the name of wisdom, what did it amount to except, in particular, astronomy and other similar branches of study which generally serve rather to exercise men's ingenuity than to enlighten their minds with genuine wisdom?

For as far as concerns philosophy, which professes to teach men something which brings them happiness, pursuits of that kind came to the fore in those countries at about the time of Mercury, who was called Trismegistus;[159] and that, to be sure, was long before the sages or philosophers of Greece, and yet after Abraham, Isaac, Jacob, and Joseph, and, in fact, after Moses himself. For inquiry reveals that it was at the time of the birth of Moses that Atlas lived,[160] the great astronomer, the brother of Prometheus, and the maternal grandfather of the elder Mercury, whose grandson was this Mercury Trismegistus.

158. Exod. 18, 21 etc. (added after the list of officers in one MS of LXX).

159. cf. Bk VIII, 23. Hermes Trismegistus, a name given by Neoplatonists and other mystical writers to the Egyptian god Thoth, the reputed author of Hellenistic religio-philosophic treatises called *Hermetica*.

160. cf. ch. 8.

40. *The baseless lies of the Egyptians about the antiquity of their learning*

It is therefore quite useless for some talkers to make unfounded claims for the antiquity of Egyptian astronomy, asserting that Egypt understood the theory of the stars more than a hundred thousand years ago. For in what books could they have recorded that number of years, seeing that they learned the art of letters from their teacher Isis not much more than two thousand years ago? That is what Varro informs us, and he is no contemptible authority on history; and besides that, his statement is consonant with the truth of the divine documents. For when we consider that 6,000 years have not yet elapsed since the first man, called Adam, why should not those people be laughed out of court, instead of being refuted, when they try to establish a chronology so different and so contrary to the truth established by investigation.

For could we rely on a better chronicler of the past than one who also foretold the future as we now see it happening before our eyes? In fact, the very disagreement of historians with one another affords us good reason for trusting, in preference to the rest, the authority who does not clash with the inspired record which we possess. Moreover, the citizens of the irreligious city, who have spread all over the world, read authors of the profoundest erudition, and see no reason for rejecting the authority of any of them; but they find them differing from one another in their treatment of events most remote from the memory of the present age, and they cannot discover whom they ought particularly to trust. In contrast, we can place our reliance on the inspired history belonging to our religion and consequently have no hesitation in treating as utterly false anything which fails to conform to it, no matter what may be the position of the other works of secular literature which, whether true or false, offer nothing of value to help us to a life of righteousness and felicity.

41. *The disagreements of philosophers and the harmony of the Scriptures*

Again, to pass on from the question of historical knowledge, the philosophers themselves – from whom we digressed to discuss these points – do not seem to have had any other aim in their laborious pursuits than to discover how we should regulate our lives towards the attainment of happiness. How is it, then, that disciples have disagreed with teachers, and fellow-disciples with one another? Must it not be because they sought the answers to these questions as men relying on human senses and human powers of reasoning?

Now it may be that there was here also the concern for self-glorification, which makes each man desire to seem wiser and cleverer than the rest and not to be a kind of retainer, pledged in loyalty to another's opinions,[161] but rather the originator of a doctrine, holding views of his own. However, I am prepared to admit that some philosophers, perhaps even the majority of them, broke away from their teachers or fellow pupils simply from the love of truth so as to fight for what they conceived to be the truth, whether they were mistaken or not. Be that as it may, what does it matter in what direction or by what way the unhappy state of man sets out on its pursuit of felicity, if it is not guided by divine authority?

It is to be noted that our authors do not disagree with one another in any way. Perish the thought! It is not for nothing that they provide the fixed and final canon of sacred literature. This agreement justifies the belief that when they wrote these books God was speaking to them, or perhaps we should say through them. And this is a belief held not by a mere handful of talkers, engaged in acrimonious discussions in schools and colleges, but by all those numerous peoples, in the countryside and in the towns, educated and uneducated alike.

The authors themselves had to be few in number, to prevent the cheapening by over-production of what ought to be precious for religious reasons; and yet not so few that there should be nothing remarkable in their agreement. For among the multitude of philosophers who have also left records of their theories by their literary labours one would have difficulty in finding any group whose opinions agreed in every particular. But to demonstrate this in the present work would take too much time. However, is there an author of any philosophical sect whatsoever, who is so completely accepted in this city of demon-worship that all the others, who have advanced different and contrary theories, are rejected?[162]

161. cf. Hor., *Ep.*, 1, 1, 14.

162. Plato, Aristotle, and the Stoics believed in one world; Anaximander and the Epicureans in innumerable worlds. Plato assumed a beginning of the world; Porphyry denied it. The pantheistic Stoics held the world to be eternal; Plato that it would come to an end. The Stoics believed in a divine intelligence controlling the world; while the Epicureans saw only the interplay of chances. Plato believed in the soul's immortality; Pythagoreans spoke of souls passing into animals. Epicureans taught that the senses must be trusted; the Sceptics of the later Academy that they are never reliable.

Did not Athens have two flourishing sects: the Epicureans, who contended that human affairs are of no concern to the gods, and the Stoics, who held the opposite opinion, and argued that human affairs are under the guidance and protection of the gods, the helpers and defenders of men? Hence I wonder why Anaxagoras[163] was put on trial for saying that the sun is a red-hot stone, and denying utterly that it is a god,[164] while in the same city Epicurus enjoyed high renown and lived in undisturbed serenity, though he not only refused to believe in the divinity of the sun or of any other heavenly body, but also contended that neither Jupiter nor any of the gods dwells in the universe in any sense, so that men's prayers and supplications may reach him.

Aristippus enjoyed a reputation at Athens, and he placed the Highest Good in physical pleasure; and there also Antisthenes maintained that man becomes happy rather by the quality of his character.[165] Here were two eminent philosophers, both followers of Socrates, who yet located the highest ideal of life in ends so different and contradictory, one of whom said that the wise man should shun politics, while the other said that it was a wise man's duty to take part in the running of his country. And each of them collected a band of disciples to support his sect.

Certainly this all went on in full view. The philosophers contended, each supporting his own opinion, with the help of their private armies, in the conspicuous and well-known porch,[166] in the gymnasia,[167] in gardens,[168] in places public and private. Some maintained that there is one world,[169] others that there are countless worlds;[170] some that this one world came into being,[171] others that it had no beginning;[172] some that it is destined to perish,[173] others that it will continue for ever;[174] some that it is controlled by a divine mind,[175] others that it is dependent on the fortuitous play of chances;[176] some that souls are immortal,[177] others that they are

163. cf. Bk VIII, 2n.

164. 'The sun is a red-hot stone, bigger than the Peloponnese.' (Diog. Laert., 2, 8).

165. cf. Bk VIII, 3n.

166. The *Stoa Poikile*, from which the Stoics took their name.

167. Aristotle taught in the Lyceum.

168. The grove of Plato's Academy and the garden of Epicurus.

169. Plato, Aristotle, Stoics.

170. Anaximander, Epicureans.

171. e.g. Plato.

172. Porphyry.

173. Plato and some Stoics.

174. Pantheistic Stoics.

175. Stoics.

176. Epicureans.

177. e.g. Plato.

mortal; of those who held that souls are immortal some alleged that they pass into animals,[178] others completely denying the possibility; while of those who held souls to be mortal, some asserted that they die soon after the death of the body, others that they live on for a shorter or a longer time, but not for ever; some setting up their final good in the body, others in the spirit, others in both, while still others added external goods to the spirit and the body; some supposing that the physical senses ought always to be trusted,[179] others that they are not always trustworthy,[180] still others maintaining that they are never to be relied on.[181]

There are all those conflicting opinions among philosophers, and there are others besides, almost beyond counting; and has any people, or senate, any government or authority in the irreligious city ever taken upon itself to adjudicate among all those diverse views, and to have some of them approved and accepted, others rejected and repudiated? Has not that city in fact held all these controversies in its embrace, without discrimination and without passing any judgement? And yet these disputants are not at variance about matters of lands, or houses, or questions of finance, but about issues which decide the misery or the happiness of our lives.

Some of their assertions, no doubt, were true; but they had equal licence for false assertions, with the inevitable result that there is every reason for giving that city the symbolic name of Babylon. For 'Babylon' means 'confusion', as we remember having said already.[182] And it is of no concern to the ruler of that city how contradictory are the mistakes that produce these quarrels, since he already has them all alike in his power, in virtue of all their irreligion, in its many forms.

In contrast, that nation, that people, that city, that commonwealth, those Israelites, to whom the utterances of God were entrusted, certainly did not lump together false and true prophets by giving them an equal sanction. Instead of this, those prophets who were in accord with each other and showed no kind of dissent were recognized and remembered as genuine authors of sacred writings. These were their philosophers, that is, lovers of wisdom, their theologians, their prophets, their teachers of integrity and piety.

Anyone who followed them in his thinking and in his manner of life was guided in his thinking and his living not by mere men, but by God who spoke through those men. If sacrilege is forbidden in these

178. Pythagoreans.

179. Epicureans, cf. Bk VIII, 5n.

180. Platonists, cf. Bk VIII, 7.

181. The sceptics of the New Academy, cf. Bk IV, 30n. Platonists, cf. Bk VIII, 7.

182. cf. Bk XVI, 4n.

writings it is God who has forbidden it. If it is said, 'You shall not commit adultery, shall not commit homicide, shall not steal', these and other like commandments have been uttered not by human mouths but by the mouthpieces of God.

Some of those philosophers, it is true, were able to perceive a certain amount of truth, among all their false notions, and they strove by laborious arguments to convince others of such truths as these: that God made this world, and himself controls it by providence, and truths about the nobility of virtue, about love of country and loyalty in friendship, about good works and all things belonging to an upright character. And yet they were ignorant of the end to which all these were to be referred and the standard by which they were to be assessed; whereas in that City of ours it was by prophetic, that is, by divine words (though conveyed by men) that they were set before the people. They were not inculcated by controversial disputations. In consequence, anyone who came to the knowledge of them dreaded to treat with scorn what was not the product of man's cleverness but the utterance of God.

42. *The Scriptures translated into Greek, by God's providence, for the benefit of the Gentiles*

Even one of the Ptolemies, kings of Egypt, was eager to become acquainted with these sacred writings and to possess them. The situation was as follows. The aggression of Alexander of Macedon, surnamed 'the Great', had won him an empire stupendous in extent but of no long duration.[183] He subdued the whole of Asia, and indeed practically the entire world, partly by force of arms, partly by terror; and among other lands of the East he entered Judaea also and acquired it.[184] Now, after his death his companions did not peaceably divide that enormous empire among themselves so as to enjoy possession of it; instead, they dissipated it by wars so as to produce general devastation. Egypt then came under the dynasty of the Ptolemies; and the first of these, the son of Lagus, deported a large number of prisoners from Judaea into Egypt.

However, his successor, another Ptolemy, surnamed Philadelphus,[185] permitted all the captives brought in by the first Ptolemy to return home as free men. In addition, he sent royal gifts to the Temple of God, and requested Eleazar, the high priest at the time, to

183. 336–323 B.C. 184. 332 B.C. 185. 285–247 B.C.

let him have a copy of the Scriptures, of which he had heard, since report proclaimed that they were certainly inspired by God. He had therefore been seized with a desire to have them in the world-famous library he had founded. The high priest sent him a copy in Hebrew, whereupon he asked for translators, and seventy-two scholars were allotted to him, six out of each of the twelve tribes, leading experts in the two languages, that is, in Greek as well as Hebrew. It is their translation that is now called, by established custom, the Septuagint.[186]

The tradition is that the agreement in the words of their versions was marvellous, amazing, and plainly inspired by God: so much so that although each of them sat in a separate place when engaged on the task – for Ptolemy decided to test their reliability in this way – they did not differ from one another in a single word, not even by a synonym conveying the same meaning; they did not even vary in the order of words. There was such a unity in their translations that it was as if there had been one translator; for in truth there was the one Spirit at work in them all. And this was the purpose of their receiving such a marvellous gift of God; that in this way the authority of those Scriptures should be emphasized, as being not human but divine – as indeed they were – and thus should benefit the Gentiles who were destined to believe in Christ. And we now see this result achieved.

43. *The authority of the Septuagint*

It is true that there have been other translators who have turned these sacred utterances from Hebrew into Greek, for example, Aquila, Symmachus, and Theodotion.[187] There is also a well-known version of unknown authorship, which is therefore called anonymously 'the fifth edition'. However the Church has accepted this Septuagint as if it were the only version; the Greek-speaking Christian peoples use it, and most of them do not know whether there is any other. From this Septuagint a translation into Latin has also been made,[188] which the

186. The full title is *Vetus Testamentum Graece iuxta Septuaginta Interpretes*. The legend of the origin of LXX is told in the *Letter of Aristeas* (second century B.C.) which is paraphrased in Joseph. *Ant.*, 12, 2, 4; 5; cf. Bk XV, 13n.

187. Aquila; cf. Bk XV, 23n.; Symmachus (late second century) translated the Old Testament into readable Greek (in contrast to Aquila); Theodotion (*fl. c.* 180) made a revision of LXX.

188. The 'Old Latin Version', or 'Versions', since there were many variants. They were all superseded by Jerome's Vulgate ('authorized version'), compiled in 404.

Latin-speaking churches retain, although our time has produced the presbyter Jerome, a man of great learning and a master of all three languages. He has translated these Scriptures into Latin not from the Greek but from the Hebrew.

Now the Jews acknowledge the reliability of the fruit of his learned labours, and maintain that the seventy translators were mistaken in many places. Nevertheless, it is the judgement of the churches of Christ that no one man should be preferred to the authority of so large a body of men chosen for this important task by Eleazar, the high priest at the time. For even supposing that there had not been obvious evidence of the presence in them of one Spirit, indubitably the Spirit of God, and that the seventy scholars had compared the words of their several translations, as men would normally do, so that what was approved by them all should stand, even so, no one translator should be given preference to them. But as so convincing a sign of God's inspiration was shown in their work, it is certain that any other reliable translator of these Scriptures from the Hebrew into any other language whatsoever will agree with the seventy translators; otherwise, if he evidently does not so agree, we must believe that the depth of prophetic meaning appears in that other version.

For the very same Spirit that was in the prophets when they uttered their messages was at work also in the seventy scholars when they translated them. And the Spirit could have said something else as well, with divine authority, as if the prophet had said both things, because it was the same Spirit that said both. The Spirit could also have said the same thing in a different way, so that even though the words were not the same, the same meaning would still shine through to those who properly understood them. He could also have omitted something, or added something, so that it might be shown in this way too that the task of translation was achieved not by the servile labour of a human bond-servant of words, but by the power of God which filled and directed the mind of the translator.

Some critics, it is true, have supposed that the Greek texts of the Septuagint version need to be corrected from the Hebrew texts. And yet they have not gone so far as to remove readings in the Septuagint which are not shown in the Hebrew. They have merely added what is found in the Hebrew but not in the Septuagint, marking those additions by putting certain signs in the forms of stars, called asterisks, at the head of those verses. Words not shown in the Hebrew but given by the Septuagint they have indicated similarly at the head of the verses by horizontal strokes, the marks used as the sign for ounces.

Many Latin texts also exhibit these signs, and they have had wide circulation.[189]

However, it is impossible, without examining both the Hebrew and the Greek texts, to discover passages not omitted or added but put in different words, whether they give another meaning, though one not conflicting with the original, or whether they can be shown to express the same meaning, though in a different way. If then we see, as we ought to see, nothing in those Scriptures except the utterances of the Spirit of God through the mouths of men, it follows that anything in the Hebrew text that is not found in that of the seventy translators is something which the Spirit of God decided not to say through the translators but through the prophets. Conversely, anything in the Septuagint that is not in the Hebrew texts is something which the same Spirit preferred to say through the translators, instead of through the prophets, thus showing that the former and the latter alike were prophets. For in the same way the Spirit spoke, as he chose, some things through Isaiah, others through Jeremiah, others through one prophet or another; or he said the same things, differently expressed, through this prophet and that. Moreover, anything that is found in both the Hebrew and the Septuagint, is something which the one same Spirit wished to say through both, but in such a way that the former gave the lead by prophesying, while the latter followed with a prophetic translation. For just as the one Spirit of peace was present in the prophets when they spoke the truth with no disagreement, so the same one Spirit was manifestly present in the scholars when without collaboration they still translated the whole in every detail as if with one mouth.

44. *The meaning of the destruction of Nineveh, where the Hebrew gives forty days, the Septuagint three*

But someone may ask, 'How am I to be sure what the prophet Jonah said to the people of Nineveh? Was it "In three days Nineveh will be overthrown" or "in forty days"?'[190] For anyone can see that the prophet sent to terrify the city with the threat of imminent destruction could not have said both. And if it was destined for destruction on the third day it certainly could not be so destined on the fortieth; if on the fortieth, certainly not on the third. So if I am asked which of these Jonah said, I suppose that it was rather what we read in the Hebrew, 'In forty days Nineveh will be overthrown.' The seventy

189. St Augustine is our only authority for this.
190. Jon. 3, 4; the Hebrew gives 40, the LXX gives 3.

translators, working so long afterwards, were surely able to say something else, yet something relevant, and conveying precisely the same meaning, though with another kind of significance. This was to warn the reader not to belittle the authority of either version, but to rise above the level of mere historical fact and to search for meanings which the historical record itself was intended to convey. Here we have, to be sure, historical events that occurred in the city of Nineveh. But they had another significance that went beyond the bounds of that city, just as it is an historical fact that the prophet himself was in the belly of the whale for three days, and yet he signified someone else, the Lord of all prophets, who was destined to be for three days in the depths of the underworld.

Therefore, if we are right in taking that city as standing in an allegorical prophecy for the Church of the Gentiles, after it had been 'overthrown' (that is, through penitence) so that it was no longer what it had been, then – since this was the result of Christ's action in the Church of the Gentiles, allegorically represented by Nineveh – it is Christ himself who is signified in respect both of the forty and of the three days. He is referred to in the forty days, because he spent forty days with his disciples after his resurrection and then ascended to heaven, in the three days because he rose again on the third day. It is as if the seventy translators were rousing from his slumbers the reader who would like to do nothing but cling to the bare historical narrative, and as if the prophets were also appealing to him to search the depths of prophecy. They are saying, in effect, 'In the forty days look for him in whom you will be able to find the three days also. You will discover the former in his ascension, the latter in his resurrection.' That is how it was possible to convey a meaning in a most convenient way by both those numbers, one being given through the mouth of the prophet Jonah, the other through the prophecy of the seventy translators, and yet both being the utterance of the self-same Spirit. I am anxious to avoid prolixity and so I shall not demonstrate this point by many instances where the seventy translators are supposed to diverge from the truth of the Hebrew text, and yet are found to be in agreement with it when they are rightly understood. Hence even I, in my small measure, follow the footsteps of the apostles, because they themselves quoted prophetic testimonies from both sources, from the Hebrew and the Septuagint; and I have assumed that both sources should be employed as authoritative, since both are one, and both are inspired by God. But now let us carry out what remains of our task, to the best of our ability.

45. *The cessation of prophecy and the adversities of the Jews after the restoration of the temple were intended as proof that it was another temple whose building had been promised by the prophets*

After the Jewish people had begun to be without prophets they deteriorated, without a shadow of doubt, at the very time, be it noted, when they expected to improve, on the restoration of the temple after the captivity in Babylon. It was in this way, we may be sure, that that people, the Jews by race, interpreted the prediction of the prophet Haggai who said, 'Great will be the glory of this latest house, above that of the first.'[191] But a little before that he had made it clear that this was said about the new covenant, where he says, in an evident promise of Christ, 'Then I shall shake all nations, and there will come one who is desired by all nations.'[192] In this passage the seventy translators gave another meaning, one appropriate to the body rather than to the head – that is to the Church rather than to Christ – in saying, with their prophetic authority, 'There will come the things which have been chosen by the Lord from all peoples'; 'the things' meaning 'the men', about whom Jesus himself said in the Gospel, 'Many are called, but few are chosen.'[193] Now it is of such chosen ones of the nations, the 'living stones',[194] that a House of God is being built, through the new covenant, far more glorious than that temple erected by King Solomon, and restored after the captivity. This explains, then, how it was that the Jewish people had no prophets from that time onwards, and was afflicted by many disasters, at the hands of foreign kings and even at the hands of the Romans; it was to prevent their imagining that this prophecy of Haggai had been fulfilled in the restoration of the temple.

Not long afterwards, in fact, the nation was subjugated on the arrival of Alexander.[195] There was, to be sure, no devastation, since they did not dare to offer any resistance, with the result that they found him peaceably inclined when they received him with the most ready submission. For all that, the glory of that house was not as great as it had been when their kings were reigning in independent sovereignty. Alexander certainly sacrificed victims in the temple of God,[196] but this was not because he had been converted to the wor-

191. Hagg. 2, 9.

192. 2, 7; cf. ch. 35; ch. 48. The Hebrew means 'desire'; LXX has a neuter plural.

193. Matt. 22, 14. 194. 1 Pet. 2, 5. 195. 332 B.C. 196. Joseph., *Ant.*, 11, 8, 5.

ship of God, but because in his irreligious folly he supposed that God was to be worshipped in company with the false gods. Later on, Ptolemy, son of Lagus, as I mentioned above, transported captives into Egypt after Alexander's death. His successor, Ptolemy Philadelphus, showed great benevolence in allowing them to return; and it is owing to him, as I related a little earlier, that we have the Scriptures in the Septuagint version.

The Jews were afterwards exhausted in the wars which are fully described in the books of the Maccabees. Then they were taken captive by Ptolemy, king of Alexandria, surnamed Epiphanes.[197] After that, they were forced to worship idols by Antiochus, king of Syria, under the stress of manifold and grievous sufferings, and the Temple itself was filled with the sacrilegious and superstitious rites of the Gentiles. In spite of this, their energetic leader Judas, surnamed Maccabeus, routed the enemy generals and purified the Temple from all the contamination of that idolatry.[198]

Not long afterwards, however, a man called Alcimus[199] was made high priest. This was unlawful, since he was not of priestly descent. Then followed a period of almost fifty years, during which the Jews knew no peace, although they were prosperous in some respects; and after this time Aristobulus[200] was the first among the Jews who, by assuming the priestly diadem became both king and high priest. Before that time, we must remember, after the return from the Babylonian captivity and the restoration of the Temple, the Jews had no kings, but commanders or leaders instead. A king, it is true, can be called a leader, because he takes the lead in ruling, and a commander because he commands the army. But it does not follow that anyone who is a commander or leader can also be called a king; and that is what this Aristobulus was.

197. Joseph, *Ant.*, 12, 3, 3.

198. The account here is confused. Palestine was part of the empire of the Ptolemies after the Battle of Ipsus, 301 B.C. Antiochus III, ruler of the Asiatic empire, tried to wrest Coele-Syria from Egypt, but was defeated at Raphia in 217 by Ptolemy IV (Philopator). In 203 the infant Ptolemy V (Epiphanes) succeeded his father. Antiochus saw his chance; Egypt was defeated in 198 and Syria, including Palestine, passed into the Empire of the Seleucids. Antiochus IV (Epiphanes) tried to stamp out Judaism in 168 B.C.; and this provoked the Maccabean rising. Jerusalem was taken from the Syrians, and the Temple was cleansed and re-dedicated in 164.

199. Leader of the pro-Syrian party in opposition to the Maccabeans.

200. Aristobulus I, 103 B.C. His father, John Hyrcanus, was the first Hasmonean king.

He was succeeded by Alexander,[201] and he also was both king and high priest; and he, as report says, was a cruel ruler to his people. After him, his wife Alexandra was queen of the Jews;[202] and from her time onwards more grievous sufferings attended them. In fact, Alexandra's sons, Aristobulus and Hyrcanus, in their struggle for the royal power, appealed to the Roman forces for help against the people of Israel – for Hyrcanus asked for Roman assistance against his brother.[203] By that time Rome had already subjugated Africa and Greece and was mistress also of a widespread dominion in other parts of the world; and yet it seemed as if she had not the strength to bear her own weight, and she had, as it were, broken herself by her own size. In fact she reached the point of serious domestic broils, and had proceeded to wars with her allies, and soon afterwards to wars between citizens, and had so diminished her strength and worn herself out that a constitutional change to a monarchy was necessary and imminent. This was the situation when Pompey, a leader of the Roman people of the highest renown, entered Judaea with an army and took the city. He opened the doors of the Temple, not with the devotion of a suppliant but by the right of a conqueror, and made his way into the Holy of Holies which only the high priest was allowed to enter; and Pompey's entrance was not in the spirit of reverence but of profanation. After confirming Hyrcanus in the high priesthood, and imposing Antipater on the subjugated nation as protector, the name then given to procurators,[204] he carried off Aristobulus as a prisoner. Henceforward the Jews also were tributaries of the Romans. At a later date Cassius[205] even plundered the Temple. Then after a few years they met with their deserts in receiving a foreigner, Herod,[206] for their king; and it was in his reign that Christ was born. For now had come the fullness of time signified by the prophetic spirit through the mouth of the patriarch Jacob, when he said, 'There shall not fail to be a prince out of Judah, nor a leader from his loins, until he comes for whom it is reserved; and he will be the expectation of the Gentiles.'[207] Thus in fact there did not fail to be a prince of the Jews up to the time of this Herod, whom they received as their first king of foreign birth. This therefore was now the time when he should come

201. Alexander Jannaeus, 102–75 B.C. He alienated the Pharisees by his military activities.

202. 75–67 B.C. Her Jewish name was Salome.

203. 64 B.C.

204. 'Procurator' was the official name. Josephus varies in his translation of the title.

205. Crassus, in fact, 53 B.C.

206. 37–4 B.C. An Idumean.

207. Gen. 49, 10.

for whom was reserved that which was promised under the new covenant, so that he should be the expectation of the Gentiles. However, it would be impossible for the Gentiles to expect his coming to exercise judgement in the splendour of his power – as we now observe them expecting it – if they did not first believe in him as he came to submit to judgement in the humility of his patient endurance.

46. The birth of our Saviour, the Word made flesh; and the dispersion of the Jews, in fulfilment of prophecy

When Herod was on the throne of Judaea, and when Caesar Augustus was emperor, after a change in the Roman constitution, and when the emperor's rule had established a world-wide peace, Christ was born, in accordance with a prophecy of earlier times,[208] in Bethlehem of Judah. He was shown in outward appearance as a human being, from a human virgin; in hidden reality he was God, from God the Father. For this is what the prophet foretold: 'See, a virgin will conceive in her womb and will bear a son, and they will call his name Emmanuel, which is translated, "God with us".'[209] Then, in order to make known the godhead in his person, he did many miracles, of which the gospel Scriptures contain as many as seemed enough to proclaim his divinity. The first of these is the great miracle of his birth; the last, his ascension into heaven with his body which had been brought to life again from the dead. But the Jews who killed him and refused to believe in him, to believe that he had to die and rise again, suffered a more wretched devastation at the hands of the Romans and were utterly uprooted from their kingdom,[210] where they had already been under the dominion of foreigners. They were dispersed all over the world – for indeed there is no part of the earth where they are not to be found – and thus by the evidence of their own Scriptures they bear witness for us that we have not fabricated the prophecies about Christ. In fact, very many of the Jews, thinking over those prophecies both before his passion and more particularly after his resurrection, have come to believe in him. About them this prediction was made: 'Even if the number of the sons of Israel shall be like the sand of the sea, it is only a remnant that will be saved.'[211] But the rest of them were blinded; and of them it was predicted: 'Let their own table prove a snare in their presence, and a retribution and a stumbling-block. Let

208. Mic. 5, 2.
209. Is. 7, 14
210. In A.D. 70.
211. Is. 10, 20.

their eyes be darkened, so that they may not see. Bend down their backs always.'[212] It follows that when the Jews do not believe in our Scriptures, their own Scriptures are fulfilled in them, while they read them with blind eyes. Unless, perhaps, someone is going to say that the Christians fabricated the prophecies of Christ which are published under the name of the Sibyl,[213] or any prophecies that there may be which are ascribed to others, which have no connection with the Jewish people. As for us, we find those prophecies sufficient which are produced from the books of our opponents; for we recognize that it is in order to give this testimony, which, in spite of themselves, they supply for our benefit by their possession and preservation of those books, that they themselves are dispersed among all nations, in whatever direction the Christian Church spreads.

In fact, there is a prophecy given before the event on this very point in the book of Psalms, which they also read. It comes in this passage: 'As for my God, his mercy will go before me; my God has shown me this in the case of my enemies. Do not slay them, lest at some time they forget your Law; scatter them by your might.'[214] God has thus shown to the Church the grace of his mercy in the case of her enemies the Jews, since, as the Apostle says, 'their failure means salvation for the Gentiles.'[215] And this is the reason for his forbearing to slay them – that is for not putting an end to their existence as Jews, although they have been conquered and oppressed by the Romans; it is for fear that they should forget the Law of God and thus fail to bear convincing witness on the point I am now dealing with. Thus it was not enough for the psalmist to say, 'Do not slay them, lest at some time they forget your Law', without adding, 'Scatter them.' For if they lived with that testimony of the Scriptures only in their own land, and not everywhere, the obvious result would be that the Church, which is everywhere, would not have them available among all nations as witnesses to the prophecies which were given beforehand concerning Christ.

47. *Were there any citizens of the heavenly City outside the race of Israel before the Christian era?*

For the same reason, if it has come, or if it ever came, to our knowledge that any foreigner (I mean by that someone not born of the race of Israel, and not given a place by that people in the canon of holy

212. Ps. 69, 22.
213. cf. ch. 23.
214. Ps. 59, 10f.
215. Rom. 11, 11.

Scripture) has written any prophecy about Christ, he can be quoted by us by way of surplus. It is not that we should stand in need of his support, if such a one failed to appear; but there is nothing far-fetched in the belief that among other peoples besides the Jews there existed men to whom this mystery was revealed, and who were compelled to go on to proclaim what they knew. It may be that they shared in the same gracious gift of God; or perhaps they did not, but were taught by evil angels; for those spirits, as we know, acknowledged Christ in his presence,[216] when the Jews did not recognize him. And I do not imagine that the Jews dare to maintain that no one has ever belonged to God apart from the Israelites, from the time when the line of Israel began, on the rejection of his elder brother. Now it is a fact that there was no other people to bear the distinctive title of the people of God; for all that, the Jews cannot deny that in other nations also there have been some men who belonged not by earthly but by heavenly fellowship to the company of the true Israelites, the citizens of the country that is above. In fact, if the Jews deny this, they are very easily proved wrong by the example of Job, that holy and amazing man. He was neither a native of Israel nor a proselyte (that is, a newly admitted member of the people of Israel). He traced his descent from the race of Edom; he was born in Edom; he died there. And such is the praise accorded him in inspired utterances that no man of his period is put on the same level as far as righteousness and devotion are concerned. And although we do not find his date in the *Chronicle*[217] we gather from the book of Job (which the Israelites received into their authoritative canon on its own merits) that he belonged to the time of the third generation after Israel.

I have no doubt that it was the design of God's providence that from this one instance we should know that there could also be those among other nations who lived by God's standards and were pleasing to God, as belonging to the spiritual Jerusalem. But it must not be believed that this was granted to anyone unless he had received a divine revelation of 'the one mediator between God and men, the man Christ Jesus'[218] whose future coming in a material body was fore-announced to the saints of antiquity, just as his coming has been announced to us as something achieved, so that one and the same faith may lead to God, through him, all who are predestined for the City of God, which is God's house and God's temple. Nevertheless, all the prophecies which are produced from non-Jewish sources concerning

216. cf. Matt. 8, 29; Mark 1, 24; Luke 4, 34.
217. The *Chronicle* of Eusebius-Jerome; cf. ch. 31.
218. 1 Tim. 2, 5.

the grace of God through Jesus Christ may be supposed to be Christian fabrications. That is why there is no surer way of refuting the 'foreigners' of whatever breed, in an argument on this subject, nothing more effective to bring them over to our side, if they are really intelligent, than to produce the inspired predictions about Christ in the texts of the Jewish Scriptures. For the expulsion of the Jews from their own home, and their dispersal throughout the world with a view to this testimony has resulted in the increase of the Church of Christ in every quarter of the globe.

48. *Haggai's prophecy of the future glory of God's house finds fulfilment in the Church of Christ*

This House of God is of greater glory than was that former house built of wood and precious stones and other costly materials and metals. Thus the prophecy of Haggai[219] was not fulfilled in the restoration of that earlier temple, for at no time after the restoration can it be shown to have had as great a glory as the temple had in Solomon's time. The truth is rather that the diminished glory of that house is demonstrated first in the cessation of prophecy, and then by great disasters of the nation itself down to the final destruction at the hands of the Romans, as witnessed by the record of events given above.[220] In contrast, this house of ours, which belongs to the new covenant, has assuredly a greater glory in that its stones are of more worth; for they are 'living stones',[221] and the building is constructed of these men who believe and who have themselves been created anew. And yet this new house was symbolized in the restoration of that temple, just because the very renewing of the temple symbolizes in a prophetic message the second covenant, the 'new covenant', as it is called. Thus, when God said, through the mouth of the prophet just mentioned, 'And I shall grant peace in that place',[222] the word 'place' is symbolic, and by it we are to understand the person whom it symbolizes. And so the re-building 'in that place' stands for the Church which was destined to be built by Christ; and the only acceptable meaning of the saying, 'I shall grant peace in this place' is, 'I shall grant peace in the place which this place symbolizes.'

The fact is that all things with symbolic meaning are seen as in some way acting the part of the things they symbolize; for instance, the Apostle says, 'That rock *was* Christ'[223] because the rock in

219. cf. Hagg. 2, 7. 220. In ch. 45. 221. 1 Pet. 2, 5.
222. Hagg. 2, 9. 223. 1 Cor. 10, 4.

question undoubtedly symbolized Christ. And so the glory of this house, the new covenant, is greater than the glory of the former house, the old covenant, and it will be seen to be even greater when it is dedicated. For then 'will come the one who is longed for by all nations',[224] as the Hebrew reads. Now his first coming was not yet longed for by all nations, for they did not know of him whom they were destined to long for, in whom they had not yet believed. Then too, in the version of the seventy translators (and their rendering is also prophetic), 'will come the chosen of the Lord from all nations'. For then, in truth, none but the elect will come, and it is of them that the Apostle says, 'Just as he has chosen us in him before the foundation of the world.'[225] Then, we may be sure, the master builder himself, who said, 'Many are called, but few are chosen',[226] is going to show us a house, built not of those who were called but came in such a way that they were thrown out of the feast,[227] but of those who have been chosen. And that house will thereafter dread no downfall, whereas at the present time when churches are made up of those, among the rest, who will be separated out as by a winnowing from on the threshing floor; and so the glory of this house is not shown in the splendour which will be seen, when all who make up the house are those who will be there for ever.

49. *The mixture of elect and reprobate in the Church*

In this wicked world, and in these evil times, the Church through her present humiliation is preparing for future exaltation. She is being trained by the stings of fear, the tortures of sorrow, the distresses of hardship, and the dangers of temptation; and she rejoices only in expectation, when her joy is wholesome. In this situation, many reprobates are mingled in the Church with the good, and both sorts are collected as it were in the dragnet of the gospel;[228] and in this world, as in a sea, both kinds swim without separation, enclosed in nets until the shore is reached. There the evil are to be divided from the good; and among the good, as it were in his temple, 'God will be all in all.'[229] In fact, we men recognize the fulfilment of the words of the speaker in the psalm, who said, 'I have made an announcement and said: "They are multiplied beyond counting." '[230] This has now been happening, ever since Christ spoke first through the mouth of John,

224. Hagg. 2, 7.
225. Eph. 1, 4.
226. Matt. 22, 14.
227. cf. Matt. 22, 11ff.
228. cf. Matt. 13, 47ff.
229. 1 Cor. 15, 28.
230. Ps. 40, 5.

his forerunner, and then by his own mouth, and said, 'Repent; for the kingdom of heaven has drawn near.'[231]

Christ chose disciples, whom he also called 'apostles'. They were men of humble birth, without position, without education, so that if there was any greatness in them or in their doings that greatness would be Christ himself present in them and acting in them. He had one among their number whom, though evil, he used for good, both to fulfil his destiny of suffering and to present to his Church a pattern of forbearance with wicked men. After sowing the seed of the holy gospel, as far as it belonged to him to sow it through his bodily presence, he suffered, he died, he rose again, showing by his suffering what we ought to undergo for the cause of truth, by his resurrection what we ought to hope for in eternity, to say nothing of the deep mystery by which his blood was shed for the remission of sins. Then he spent forty days on earth in the company of his disciples, and in their sight ascended into heaven. Ten days after that he sent the Holy Spirit he had promised; and the greatest and most unmistakable sign of the Spirit's coming to those who believed was that every one of them spoke in the languages of all nations; thus signifying that the unity of the Catholic Church would exist among all nations and would thus speak in all languages.

50. *The preaching of the Gospel made powerful through the sufferings of the preachers*

Then was fulfilled the prophecy: 'Out of Sion the law will go forth, and the word of the Lord from Jerusalem',[232] and the prediction of the Lord himself, when after his resurrection his disciples were dumbfounded and 'he opened their minds to understand the Scriptures; and he said to them: "You see that the Scriptures say that Christ was bound to suffer, and to rise again on the third day; and that in his name repentance and forgiveness of sins would be preached among all nations, starting from Jerusalem." '[233] Again, when they asked him about his last coming, he answered by saying, 'It is not for you to know the times; the Father has reserved them for his own authority. But you will receive the power of the Holy Spirit when it comes upon you, and you will be my witnesses in Jerusalem, and throughout the whole of Judaea and Samaria, and to the ends of the earth.'[234]

The Church first spread from Jerusalem, and when a great number of people in Judaea and Samaria had believed, other nations were

231. Matt. 3, 2; 4, 17.
232. Is. 2, 3.
233. Luke 24, 45ff.
234. Acts 1, 7f.

reached, the gospel being announced by those whom Christ himself had prepared like lamps, for he had trimmed them with his word and set them alight with the Holy Spirit. Now Christ had said to his disciples, 'Do not be afraid of those who kill the body, but cannot kill the soul.'[235] And to prevent their being frozen with fear they burned with the fire of love. Finally, the gospel was proclaimed throughout the whole world, not only by the disciples who had seen and heard him both before his passion and after his resurrection, but also after their death by their successors, amid terrible persecutions and the manifold tortures and deaths of martyrs. And God bore witness by signs and manifestations and varied acts of power and by the gifts of the Holy Spirit, so that the peoples of the Gentiles – believing in him who was crucified for their redemption – might reverence with Christian love the blood of the martyrs which they had shed in their diabolical fury, and so that the very kings, by whose laws the Church was being devastated, might for their salvation become subject to the name which they had ruthlessly tried to remove from the earth and might begin to persecute the false gods, in whose interests the worshippers of the true God had hitherto been persecuted.

51. *The Catholic faith actually strengthened by the heretics*

The Devil, however, seeing that the temples of demons were being abandoned, and that the human race was hastening to take the name of the Mediator who sets men free, stirred up heretics to oppose Christian doctrine – though they bore the Christian name – as if they could be retained indiscriminately in the City of God without reproof, just as the city of confusion[236] retained indifferently the philosophers who held diverse and contradictory opinions. Just so there are those in the Church of Christ who have a taste for some unhealthy and perverse notion, and who if reproved – in the hope that they may acquire a taste for what is wholesome and right – obstinately resist and refuse to correct their pestilent and deadly dogmas, and persist in defending them. These become heretics and, when they part company with the Church, they are classed among the enemies who provide discipline for her. Even so they undoubtedly benefit by their wickedness the genuine, catholic members of Christ, since God makes good use even of the wicked, and 'makes all things co-operate for good for those who love him',[237] In fact, all the enemies of the Church, however blinded

235. Matt. 10, 28. 236. 'Babylon'; cf. Bk XVI, 4n.
237. Rom. 8, 28.

by error or depraved by wickedness, train the Church in patient endurance if they are given the power of inflicting bodily harm, while if they oppose her only by their perverse notions they train her in wisdom. Moreover they train her in benevolence, or even beneficence, so that love may be shown even to enemies, whether this takes the form of persuasive teaching or of stern discipline.

Thus even the Devil, the prince of that irreligious city, when he brings his instruments to bear upon the City of God on pilgrimage in this world, is permitted to do her no harm. Without any doubt, the providence of God provides her with the consolation of prosperity so that she is not shattered by adversity, and wih the discipline of adversity so that she is not corrupted by prosperity. And he so tempers the one with the other that we recognize here the source of that saying in the psalm, 'According to the multitude of the sorrows in my heart, your consolations have gladdened my soul.'[238] Hence also the words of the Apostle, 'Rejoicing in hope, steadfast in tribulation'.[239]

For we must not imagine that there can be any time when this saying of the same teacher fails to be true, 'All who want to live a devout life in Christ suffer persecution.'[240] Because even when those who are outside do not rage and there seems to be, and really is, tranquillity, which brings great consolation, especially to the weak, even so there are always some, inside indeed there are many, who by their unprincipled behaviour torment the feelings of those who live devout lives. For such people cause the name of 'Christian' and 'Catholic' to be defamed. And the dearer this name is to those who want to live a devout life in Christ, the more they grieve that evildoers within the Church make that name less beloved than the hearts of the devout long for it to be. Besides this, when the heretics themselves are thought to have the Christian name and the sacraments, the Scriptures, and the creed, they cause great grief in the hearts of the devout. This is because many who wish to be Christians are forced to hesitate by their dissensions, and many slanderers find also among the heretics material for the defamation of the name of Christian, because these heretics too are called, in a manner of speaking, Christians. Owing to this kind of discreditable behaviour and this sort of human error, those who want to lead a devout life in Christ suffer persecution, even though they endure no physical violence or bodily torment. For they suffer this persecution not in their bodies but in their hearts. Hence the psalmist says, 'according to the multitude of sorrows in my heart' – not 'in my body'.

238. Ps. 94, 19. 239. Rom. 12, 12. 240. 2 Tim. 3, 12.

Again, the divine promises are thought of as unchangeable, and the Apostle says, 'The Lord knows his own; for those whom he foreknew he also predestined to be fashioned in the likeness of his Son.'[241] It follows that none of these can perish. That is why the psalm continues, 'Your consolations have gladdened my soul.' For the actual grief that arises in the hearts of the devout who are persecuted by the behaviour of bad Christians or false Christians is of profit to those who grieve, since it issues from a love which makes them hate the thought that these persecutors should perish or should hinder the salvation of others. Above all, great consolations appear also when they are brought out of error; and those consolations overflow the souls of the devout with a joy as great as were the pains that tormented them at the thought of their perdition.

In this manner the Church proceeds on its pilgrim way in this world, in these evil days. Its troubled course began not merely in the time of the bodily presence of Christ and the time of his apostles; it started with Abel himself, the first righteous man slain by an ungodly brother; and the pilgrimage goes on from that time right up to the end of history, with the persecutions of the world on one side, and on the other the consolations of God.

52. *The belief that after the ten persecutions that have occurred only one is still to come, in the time of Antichrist*

Accordingly, I do not imagine that we should rashly assert or believe the theory that some have entertained or still do entertain: that the Church is not going to suffer any more persecutions until the time of Antichrist, beyond the number she has already endured, namely ten.[242]

241. Rom. 8, 29.

242. The notion of ten persecutions is first found in Orosius (7, 17). It simplifies a complicated story. Christians were always liable to prosecution as members of an unlicensed sect (not a *religio licita*), and for refusal to worship the Emperor; but in general the persecutions were local and transitory. Nero's attack (64) seems to have been confined to Rome, where the Christians were made scapegoats for the great fire; the Revelation apparently refers to persecution under Domitian (81–96) for rejecting Emperor-worship. Trajan, Antoninus and the two Severi were not persecutors, but Maximinus Thrax in 235 reversed the tolerant policy of Alexander Severus. The first general persecution throughout the Empire was ordered by Decius (251); Valerian in 257 concentrated his attack on the clergy and the laymen of rank; Aurelian did not disturb the Church. Diocletian showed tolerance until 303, when he ordered the destruction of churches and the burning of Scriptures; this was followed by wholesale

On this theory the eleventh and last persecution will come from Antichrist. The first persecution they reckon to be that of Nero, the second that of Domitian, the third of Trajan, the fourth of Antoninus, the fifth of Severus, the sixth of Maximinus, the seventh of Decius, the eighth of Valerian, the ninth of Aurelian, the tenth of Diocletian and Maximian, their assumption being that the fact that there were ten plagues of Egypt, before the people of God began their exodus from that country, should be taken as signifying that the last persecution, that of Antichrist, is to be regarded as the counterpart of the eleventh plague, in which the Egyptians in their vengeful pursuit of the Hebrews, perished in the Red Sea, while the people of God passed over on dry land. In my judgement, however, those events in Egypt were not prophetic symbols of these persecutions, although those who hold this theory have shown such highly-wrought ingenuity in comparing the details in each case – but they did this not so much by prophetic inspiration as by the speculation of the human mind, which sometimes arrives at the truth, but sometimes misses the mark.

For what will the supporters of this theory have to say about the persecution in which the Lord himself was crucified? What place is this to have in their enumeration? If, however, they consider that this persecution is to be omitted from the list, on the assumption that the only instances to be reckoned are those which concern the body, and that the one in which the head was attacked and slain is to be excluded, what will they do about the one which broke out after Christ's ascension into heaven? This was in Jerusalem, where the blessed Stephen was stoned, where James the brother of John was butchered with the sword, and where the apostle Peter was imprisoned to be put to death and was rescued by an angel. Then, too, the brethren were put to flight and dispersed from Jerusalem, and Saul (who afterwards became Paul the apostle) was wreaking havoc on the Church; and Saul himself, when he was spreading the Gospel which he had persecuted, suffered the same treatment as he had inflicted, both in Judaea and among the Gentiles, wherever, with his burning enthusiasm, he proclaimed Christ. Why, then, do they decide to start with Nero, seeing that the Church in its growth reached the time of Nero amidst the most ruthless persecutions, which it would take too long to describe in full detail? But if they consider that only persecutions inflicted by

---

bloodshed, mainly due to Galerius and Maximian, which continued after Diocletian's abdication (305), especially in Syria under Maximinus Daia. Orosius ignores the severe persecution sanctioned by Marcus Aurelius in Lyons (177); Christians assumed that only bad Emperors were persecutors.

kings should be included in the list, it was a king, Herod, who inflicted the most severe persecution even after the ascension of the Lord.

Again, what answer will they give about Julian, whom they do not list among the ten? Did he not persecute the Church in forbidding the Christians to give or to receive a liberal education? Under him the elder Valentinian, who was the third emperor after him, showed himself a confessor of the Christian faith, and was deprived of his military rank. I shall pass over what Julian began to do at Antioch, and would have accomplished had it not been for one young man of unswerving faith and constancy. When many people were being arrested and taken for torture, this youth was the first to be taken, and he was tortured for a whole day, but continued singing hymns of praise while he was torn and racked. The emperor was awestricken in amazement at his bold cheerfulness, and was afraid to persecute the other victims in case he should be put to the blush with greater ignominy. Lastly, within our own memory, did not Valens, the Arian, the brother of the before-mentioned Valentinian, wreak havoc on the Catholic Church in the East in a great persecution? What a strange thing it is not to consider that the Church, as it grows and bears fruit throughout the whole world, can suffer persecution from kings among some peoples, even when it does not suffer the same among other nations! Or are we to suppose that it was not to be counted as a persecution when the king of the Goths persecuted the Christians[243] in the actual kingdom of the Goths with stupendous ferocity, since there were only Catholics there? Many of these were crowned with martyrdom, as we have heard from some of the brethren, who were boys at the time in that country, and who immediately recalled that they had witnessed these events. Then what of the recent happenings in Persia?[244] Did not persecution boil up so hotly against the Christians (if indeed it has yet calmed down) that a number of refugees from Persia fled as far as to Roman towns? When I think over events like these it seems to me that no limit can be set to the number of persecutions which the Church is bound to suffer for her training. On the other hand, it is no less rash to assert that there are to be other persecutions by kings, apart from that final persecution about which no Christian has any doubt. And so I leave the question undecided, offering no support or opposition to either side. I merely call upon both sides to renounce the audacious presumption of making any pronouncement on the question.

243. King Athamansius, in A.D. 370 (Oros., 6, 32).

244. In A.D. 420, under Isdigerdas (Thdt. *H.E.*, 5, 38).

53. *The time of the final persecution has been revealed to no human being*

That last persecution, to be sure, which will be inflicted by Antichrist, will be extinguished by Jesus himself, present in person. For the Scripture says that 'he will kill him with the breath of his mouth and annihilate him by the splendour of his coming.'[245] Here the usual question is, 'When will this happen?' But the question is completely ill-timed. For had it been in our interest to know this, who could have been a better informant than the master, God himself, when the disciples asked him? For they did not keep silent about it with him, but put the question to him in person, 'Lord, is this the time when you are going to restore the sovereignty to Israel?' But he replied, 'It is not for you to know the times which the Father has reserved for his own control.'[246] Now in fact they had not asked about the hour or the day or the year, but about the time, when they were given this answer. It is in vain, therefore, that we try to reckon and put a limit to the number of years that remain for this world, since we hear from the mouth of the Truth that it is not for us to know this. And yet some have asserted that 400, 500, or as much as 1,000 years may be completed between the Lord's ascension and his final coming. But to show how each of them supports his opinion would take too long; and in any case it is unnecessary, for they make use of human conjectures, and quote no decisive evidence from the authority of canonical Scripture. In fact, to all those who make such calculations on this subject comes the command, 'Relax your fingers, and give them a rest.'[247] And it comes from him who says, 'It is not for you to know the times, which the Father has reserved for his own control.'

But since this statement is given in the Gospel, it is not to be wondered at that the worshippers of many false gods have not been restrained by it from pretending that the length of the future duration of the Christian religion has been defined by the responses of the demons whom they worship as gods. For when those pagans saw that Christianity could not be wiped out by all those great persecutions, but on the contrary had made astonishing advances because of them, they thought up some sort of Greek verses, supposedly the effusions of a divine oracle, given to someone consulting it. In them they do indeed make Christ innocent of this alleged offence of sacrilege, but go on to

245. 2 Thess. 2, 8. 246. Acts 1, 6f.

247. The finger-counting of antiquity was a complicated and laborious process.

say that Peter used sorcery to ensure that the name of Christ should be worshipped for 365 years, and that on the completion of that number of years it should come to an immediate end.

What intelligence! What scholarship! It takes educated wits to believe such things about Christ, while refusing to believe in Christ. To believe, that is, that Peter, his disciple, did not learn magical arts from his master, yet, that though his master was innocent, his disciple was a sorcerer, and preferred that through his magical arts his master's name rather than his own should be worshipped, at the cost of great hardships and dangers to himself and at last even at the cost of shedding his own blood. If Peter the sorcerer ensured that the world should so love Christ, what had Christ done to make Peter so love him? Let them give the answer to themselves; and let them realize if they can, that by that grace from on high it came about that the world loved Christ with a view to eternal life, and by the same grace it came about that Peter loved Christ both with a view to receiving eternal life from him, and even to the extent of suffering temporal death for him. Then again, what kind of gods are those who can make this prediction but cannot avert it, who succumb to a single sorcerer and a single act of criminal magic (a child of a year old, they allege, was slain, torn to pieces, and buried with abominable ceremonies), so much so that they allowed a sect opposed to them to gather strength over such an extended period, and to survive the terrible savageries of so many great persecutions, not by resistance but by endurance, and to reach the point of overthrowing their own images, temples, ceremonies and oracles? Lastly, who was the god – it was assuredly not ours, but one of their own – who was either enticed or compelled by such a criminal act to provide that result? For it was not by using his magic on some demon, but on a god, as those verses inform us, that Peter determined this period. That is the kind of god possessed by those who do not possess Christ!

54. *The foolish pagan falsehood that limits the Christian religion to 365 years*

I might have amassed many other arguments of similar tenor, had it not been that that year has already gone by, which was foretold by a trumped-up divination and believed in by deluded idiots. In fact the 365 years were completed some time ago, starting the count from the time when the worship of Christ was established by his presence in bodily form, and by his apostles, so why should we seek any other argument to refute this falsehood? Now we need not take the time of

Christ's birth as the start of this period, because he had no disciples in his infancy and boyhood. Still, from the time when he began to have disciples, the Christian doctrine and religion undoubtedly became widely known through his bodily presence, that is, after his baptism in the river Jordan by the ministry of John. This in fact is the reason for the famous prophecy about him uttered long before, 'He will have dominion from sea to sea, and from the river as far as to the ends of the earth.'[248]

But before Christ's passion and resurrection the Christian faith had not yet reached its final formulation for all mankind. That formulation was, of course, reached at the resurrection, for this is what the apostle Paul has to say, addressing the Athenians, 'This is now the time when God gives all men everywhere notice to repent, because he has fixed a day for the judgement of the world in righteousness, by a man in whose person he has defined the faith for all mankind, by raising him from the dead.'[249] Consequently, this is a better starting-point for us to take in looking for the answer to this question; especially as it was also the time for the giving of the Holy Spirit, inasmuch as the Spirit had to be bestowed after the resurrection of Christ, in that City from which the second Law, that is, the new covenant, was due to come into operation. For the first Law, called the old covenant, came from Mount Sinai, through Moses; whereas about this second Law, which was to be given through Christ, there was a prediction which said, 'Out of Sion the Law will issue, and the word of the Lord out of Jerusalem.'[250] That is why Christ himself said that repentance had to be preached in his name among all nations, yet the start was to be made from Jerusalem.[251] Thus it was at Jerusalem that the worship of this name began, so that men believed in Jesus Christ, crucified and risen. It was there that this faith blazed up, with such remarkable beginnings that some thousands of people were converted to the name of Christ with amazing promptness. They sold their possessions to give the proceeds to the needy, and to attain to a voluntary poverty by holy resolution and burning love, and they prepared themselves, surrounded as they were by the bloodthirsty fury of the Jews, to fight for the cause of truth even unto death, and to fight not by armed force, but by the mightier power of steadfast endurance. If so much was achieved without any magical

248. Ps. 72, 8; cf. Bk XVII, 8.

249. Acts 17, 30f. (The Greek means 'by a man whom he appointed, giving an assurance of this by raising ...').

250. Is. 2, 3; cf. ch. 50.

251. cf. Luke 24, 27.

arts, why are the pagans reluctant to believe that the same result could have been attained throughout the whole world by the same divine power that effected it here?

But let us assume that Peter had already performed his act of sorcery, with this result; that at Jerusalem such great numbers of men were fired to worship the name of Christ, men who had taken him and fastened him to the cross, or had jeered at him when fastened there. If so, then that is the very year from which to start when trying to find out when the 365 years came to an end. Well, then, Christ died on the twenty-fifth of March in the consulship of the two Gemini (A.D. 29). He rose again on the third day, as the apostles proved by the evidence of their own senses. Then, after forty days, he ascended to heaven; and ten days later (that is, on the fiftieth day after his resurrection) he sent the Holy Spirit. It was then that 3,000 people believed when the apostles proclaimed Christ. It was then, therefore, that the worship of that name arose, as we believe and as the truth holds, through the effective working of the Holy Spirit, but according to the story invented – or supposed true – by the blasphemy of fools, by Peter's magic arts. Again, a little later, 5,000 people believed, after an amazing miracle, effected through the words of this same Peter, when a beggar man, so lame from his mother's womb that he was carried by others to the door of the temple to beg for alms, was cured in the name of Jesus Christ and leaped to his feet. After that the Church grew by successive additions to the number of believers.

Hence we can establish the actual day from which the year takes its start, namely the day when the Holy Spirit was sent – on the Ides of May. By reckoning the consuls from this date, the 365 years are found to be completed on the same Ides in the consulship of Honorius and Eutychianus.[252] Now in the next year, when Malius Theodorus was consul, the Christian religion should have ceased to exist, according to that oracle of the demons or fiction of men; and yet we know that at Carthage, that famous and important city – there was no need for research into what may have happened in other parts – at Carthage, Gaudentius and Jovius, the officials of the Emperor Honorius, on the eighteenth of March demolished the temples of the false gods and broke up their images. No one could fail to see how much the worship of Christ's name has increased in the space of about thirty years from that time to the present day,[253] and especially after many people had

252. A.D. 398; but 29 + 365 = 394.

253. Apparently St Augustine corrected his addition; 394 + 30 = 424, and the *City of God* was probably completed in 426.

become Christians who had formerly been kept from joining the faith by that oracular prophecy, supposing it to be genuine, and who now, after the completion of the number of years specified, saw it to be ridiculous nonsense. We, therefore, who are Christians and are called by that name, do not believe in Peter but in the one in whom Peter believed. We are edified by Peter's discourses about Christ; we are not poisoned by Peter's spells, we are not deluded by his evil arts, but we are assisted by his good offices. That same Christ, who was Peter's master in the teaching that leads to eternal life, is himself our master also.

But now at last we must bring this book to its close. In it we have brought our discussion to this point, and we have shown sufficiently, as it seemed to me, what is the development in this mortal condition of the two cities, the earthly and the Heavenly, which are mingled together from the beginning to the end of their history. One of them, the earthly city, has created for herself such false gods as she wanted, from any source she chose – even creating them out of men – in order to worship them with sacrifices. The other city, the Heavenly City on pilgrimage in this world, does not create false gods. She herself is the creation of the true God, and she herself is to be his true sacrifice. Nevertheless, both cities alike enjoy the good things, or are afflicted with the adversities of this temporal state, but with a different faith, a different expectation, a different love, until they are separated by the final judgement, and each receives her own end, of which there is no end. And those different ends of the two cities must be the next subject for our discussion.

BOOK XIX

1. *The philosophic debate on the Supreme Good and Evil*

IT is clear to me that my next task is to discuss the appointed ends of these two cities, the earthly and the heavenly. Hence I must first explain, as far as is allowed by the limits I have designed for this work, the arguments advanced by mortal men in their endeavour to create happiness for themselves amidst the unhappiness of this life. My purpose is to make clear the great difference between their hollow realities and our hope, the hope given us by God, together with the realization – that is, the true bliss – which he will give us; and to do this not merely by appealing to divine authority but also by employing such powers of reason as we can apply for the benefit of unbelievers. Now the philosophers have engaged in a great deal of complicated debate about the supreme ends of good and evil; and by concentrating their attention on this question they have tried to discover what it is that makes a man happy. For our Final Good is that for which other things are to be desired, while it is itself to be desired for its own sake. The Final Evil is that for which other things are to be shunned, while it is itself to be shunned on its own account. Thus when we now speak of the Final Good we do not mean the end of good whereby good is finished so that it does not exist, but the end whereby it is brought to final perfection and fulfilment. And by the Final Evil we do not mean the finish of evil whereby it ceases to be, but the final end to which its harmful effects eventually lead. These two ends, then, are the Supreme Good and the Supreme Evil. The search to discover these, and the quest for the attainment of the Supreme Good in this life and the avoidance of the Supreme Evil has been the object of the labours of those who have made the pursuit of wisdom their profession, amid the follies of this world. And although they have gone astray in different ways, the limits imposed by nature set bounds to their deviation from the path of truth, so that there were none who did not set the Supreme Good and the Supreme Evil in one of three locations: in the soul, or in the body, or in both. On the basis of this threefold classification into what we may call the genera of philosophic schools, Marcus Varro by careful and minute examination noted such a wide variety of opinions, in his book *On Philosophy*,[1] that by the application of certain criteria of differentiation he easily arrived at a total of 288 sects, not sects already in existence but possible schools of thought.

To demonstrate this briefly, I have to begin with the point he made in the book above mentioned, that there are four objects which men 'naturally' seek, without the help of a teacher, without the assistance of any teaching, without conscious effort, and without acquiring the art of living (we call it 'virtue', and, without any doubt, it is something which is learned[2]). Men may long for pleasure, which is a stimulation of the bodily senses that gives delight; or for repose, the state in which the person suffers no bodily distress; or for a combination of these two (which Epicurus[3] lumps together under the one name of pleasure); or, comprehensively, for the primary natural blessings[4] (among which these Epicurean pleasures are included). These last may be concerned with the body – for example, the wholeness and health of its parts and the sound condition of the whole organism; or with the mind – for example, the abilities, small or great, which are to be found among the innate endowments of human beings. Now these four – pleasure, repose, the combination of these, and the primary natural blessings – are desiderata for us in respect that either virtue (which is to be implanted later by teaching) is desirable for their sake, or they are desirable for the sake of virtue; or else both are to be desired for their own sake. Thus twelve sects are produced, since on this method of classification each of the desiderata is multiplied by three. I shall demonstrate this in one case, and then there will be no difficulty in finding it to hold good for the rest. Well then, since physical pleasure may be subordinated to virtue of mind, or preferred to it, or bracketed equal, there is threefold division of schools of thought. Now physical pleasure is subordinated to virtue when it is brought into the service of virtue. For example, it is part of the obligation involved in virtue to live for one's country and to produce sons for the sake of one's country; and neither of those duties can be fulfilled without bodily pleasure. For such pleasure is a necessary accompaniment of eating and drinking in order to live, and of sexual intercourse with a view to procreation. On the other hand, when sensual pleasure is put above virtue, it is sought for its own sake, and it is believed that virtue should be brought into its service – that is,

1. Not extant.
2. A much debated point. cf. e.g. Plat., *Men.*, 86ff; Arist., *Eth. Nic.*, 2, 1, 3.
3. cf. Bk XIV, 2.
4. 'The first things according to nature' in the Stoic phrase, cf. Cic., *De Fin.*, 2.

that the only purpose of virtue should be the achievement or maintenance of sensual pleasure. Now this is certainly an ugly way of life – it must be so when virtue is the slave of tyrant pleasure, although in this situation it is not to be called virtue. And yet this horrible degradation has some philosophers as its advocates and defenders. Again, pleasure is bracketed equal with virtue when neither is sought for the sake of the other, but both for their own sake. Hence, pleasure produces three sects, since it may be subordinated or preferred to virtue, or bracketed with it. The same holds good of repose, the combination of repose and pleasure, and the primary blessings of nature; each of those, it will be seen, gives rise to three sects. In accordance with the variations of human opinion, those three desiderata are each of them sometimes subordinated to virtue, sometimes preferred, and sometimes bracketed with it. Thus we arrive at a total of twelve sects. But this number in its turn is doubled on the application of one more differentia, namely that of social life, since any adherent of any of these sects adopts its principles either for his own sake or for the sake of his fellow-man as well, for whom he is bound to wish the same as he wishes for himself. It follows that there are twelve sects of those who suppose that some particular view should be held solely for one's own sake, and twelve others of those who decide that they should take this or that philosophical position not simply for their own sake but for the sake of others also, whose good they aim at, as well as their own. These twenty-four sects are doubled again when another differentia is brought in from the New Academy; and so we get forty-eight. For obviously each individual can hold and defend the views of any one of those schools of thought as being certain, in the same way as the Stoics defended their view that the good of man, which is to bring him happiness, consists solely in virtue of character; while another may hold any one of them, but as being uncertain, in the same way as the New Academics defended views which to them seemed not certain, indeed, but probable.[5] Thus there are twenty-four sects made up of those who consider that their views are to be adopted as certain, on account of their truth, and another twenty-four composed of those who hold that the same views should be held, though uncertain, on account of their probability. Again one adherent of any of those forty-eight sects may adopt the fashions of the general run of philosophers, while another may adopt the fashions of the Cynics,[6] and this differentia also doubles the total, giving us ninety-six. Moreover, each philosophical theory can be

5. cf. Bk IV, 30n. 6. cf. Bk XIV, 20n.

upheld and followed in one way by men who love a life of leisure, like those who neither would nor could have time for anything but the study of theoretical doctrines; in another way by those who prefer a life of business, like those who engaged in philosophizing but at the same time were concerned in national politics and the affairs of government; in yet another by those who chose a life in which the two concerns were equally combined, like those who have devoted their time alternately to learned leisure and to pressing business. On the ground of those differences the number of sects may again be trebled, to reach the total of two hundred and eighty-eight.

I have set out these points from Varro's book as briefly and clearly as I can, explaining his reasoning in my own words. Varro offers a refutation of all philosophies except one, which is the sect of his choice. He claims that this sect is the Old Academy, established by Plato and persisting down to the time of Polemo, who was, after Plato, the fourth head of the school called the Academy. This school, as Varro wants to make out, held its doctrines as certain; and by this mark he distinguishes it from that of the school of philosophy for whom everything is uncertain, the New Academy, that is, which started with Arcesilaus, the successor of Polemo. The sect of the Old Academy, in Varro's judgement, was as free from error as from doubt. Now to show in detail how the historian reaches his conclusion would take too long. Nevertheless the argument must not be completely omitted.

Varro, then, begins by setting aside all the differentiae which have multiplied the number of sects; and the reason why he holds that they should be set aside is that no difference about the Final Good is involved in them. For he considers that no sect of philosophy deserves that name unless it is distinct from the others in holding a different view of the Supreme Good and the Supreme Evil. For indeed the only purpose man has in philosophizing is the attainment of happiness; but that which makes him happy is the Supreme Good itself. Therefore the only purpose of philosophizing is the Supreme Good. It follows that a sect which has not, as a sect, its own view of the Supreme Good does not deserve the name of a sect of philosophy. Consequently, when it is asked whether a wise man should be so concerned with social life that he wants the Supreme Good, which brings man happiness, for his friend as much as for himself, and is concerned to ensure it for his friend, or whether a wise man acts as he does solely for his own happiness, then the question is not about the Ultimate Good, but about taking or not taking a partner to share in this good, and that not for the philosopher's own sake but for the sake of that partner, so that the wise man may rejoice in his companion's good as in his own. Similarly when it is asked, in connection with the New Academics, to whom everything is uncertain, whether this is the right way to regard matters which are the proper subjects of philosophy, or whether we should regard philosophical doctrines as capable of certainty – which is the conviction of other philosophers – then the question is not about what should be pursued as the Ultimate Good, but whether we should have any doubts about the truth of the very good which, as it seems, we have to pursue – or, to put it more plainly, whether the pursuit of the Ultimate Good entails the assertion by the pursuer that it is the true Ultimate Good, or the assertion that it seems true to him, although it may be false; yet in either case the object of the pursuit is precisely the same good. Then again, in the application of the differentia derived from the fashions and habits of the Cynics, the question is not about the Ultimate Good, but whether anyone who pursues what seems to him the true good, whatever it may be, which seems to him the right object of pursuit, should adopt the fashions and habits of the Cynics in his life. In actual fact there were men who won the appellation of 'Cynics' by adhering to the same fashions and habits, though they pursued different objects as Final Goods, some pursuing virtue, others pleasure. Thus whatever it is that makes the distinction between Cynics and all other philosophers, it has had no influence on the choice of the good that is to bring them happiness, and on the adherence to it. For if it did in fact make any difference in this matter, then the same kind of behaviour would necessitate the pursuit of the same end and a different way of behaving would preclude it.

2. *By this elimination Varro reaches a definition of three kinds of Ultimate Good*

Then there are the three kinds of life: the first, without being slothful, is still a life of leisure passed in the consideration of truth or the quest for it; the second is busily engaged in the world's affairs; the third is a balanced combination of the other two. Now when it is asked which of these is to be chosen for preference, here too there is involved no dispute about the Ultimate Good; the question at issue is which of those three entails difficulty in the attainment or conservation of the Supreme Good, and which assists it. For when anyone reaches the Ultimate Good it immediately brings him happiness; this is not the direct result of a life of learned leisure, or a life of public business, or a life which is an alternation of both. Certainly there can be many people living any one of those three lives and yet losing their way in the search for the Ultimate Good which brings men happiness.

Thus the question about the Supreme Good and the Supreme Evil, which is the differentiating factor in philosophical sects, is something quite different from the questions about social life, the philosophic doubt of the Academics, the clothing and feeding habits of the Cynics; or the question about the three kinds of life, the leisured, the active, and the amalgam of the two. None of those questions entails any dispute about the Ultimate Good and Evil. Accordingly, since it is by application of those four differentiae (arising from social life, from the New Academy, from the Cynics, and from the triple classification of lives) that Marcus Varro arrived at the total of 288 sects (with the possible addition of others on the same principle), he then puts aside all those, since they do not involve any question about the pursuit of the Supreme Good. For this, he says, implies that they are not genuine sects and should not be so called. Thus he returns to those twelve schools of thought which are based on the question of man's Supreme Good, whose attainment brings him happiness. Varro's purpose is to demonstrate that only one of those has the truth while all the rest are mistaken. By the elimination of the differentia based on the three types of life two-thirds of the total are subtracted, leaving ninety-six. By elimination of the differentia introduced from the Cynics the number is brought down by one half, making forty-eight. If we exclude the differentia arising from the New Academics, we are again left with one half, namely twenty-four. If we also exclude the point introduced about social life, then twelve remain, the number doubled by that differentia to make twenty-four.

Now in respect of those twelve, no reason can be advanced why they are not to be regarded as genuine sects; for it is certain that the only object of their quest is the discovery of the Ultimate Good and the Ultimate Evil (though, in fact, the discovery of the Ultimate Good immediately discloses the Ultimate Evil as its contrary). These twelve sects are produced by multiplying by three of those four desiderata of ours: pleasure, repose, the two combined, and the primary natural blessings – Varro calls these *primigenia*. The four, as we know, are sometimes each of them subordinated to virtue, so that they are considered worth aiming at not on their own account but as instrumental to virtue; sometimes they are ranked above virtue, so that virtue is supposed to be essential not on its own account, but only with a view to the attainment or conservation of those desiderata; sometimes they are bracketed equal, so that these four, as well as virtue, are believed to be proper objects of desire for their own sakes. Thus the number four is multiplied by three, and we arrive at twelve sects. Varro, however, eliminates three of the four desiderata, namely, pleasure, repose, and their combination. This is not because he disapproves of those, but because pleasure and repose are included in the *primigenia*. What need, then, is there to produce three things out of these two – two things when pleasure and repose are separate objects of pursuit, and a third by the addition of the combined pursuit? For the primary natural blessings include these, besides many other things. Thus we have three sects that, in Varro's judgement, demand careful examination, so that we may make our choice. For right reason will not allow more than one sect to be right, whether it is one of these, or is to be found elsewhere, as we shall see later. Meanwhile we must explain, as briefly and clearly as possible, how Varro selects one of these three. We must remember that these three sects arise from three views about the primary blessings of nature: that they are to be sought for the sake of virtue; that virtue is to be sought for their sake; that both virtue and the primary blessings are to be sought for their own sake.

3. *Varro's preference among the philosophical sects, based on the teaching of the Old Academy*

Varro's attempt to establish which of these three views is the true one, and the one to be adopted, proceeds as follows. To begin with, since the Ultimate Good sought for in philosophy is not the good of a tree, or a beast, or of God, but of man, he concludes that we must first ask: What is man? And in answer he gives his firm opinion that there are two elements in man's nature, body and soul; and he has not the slightest doubt that of these two constituents the soul is the better and by far the more important. But is the soul by itself the man, so that the body stands to the man as the horse to the horseman? For a horseman is not a man and a horse, but only a man; and the reason why he is called a horseman is because of a certain relation to a horse. Or is the body by itself the man, standing in some such relation to the soul as that of the cup to the drink? For it is not the cup and the drink contained in it that are together called the cup, but the cup by itself; and yet the reason for that name is the fact that it is designed to contain the drink. Or again, is it neither the soul by itself nor the body by itself that constitutes the man, but the two combined, the soul and the body being each a part of him, but the whole man consisting of both? This would be analogous to applying the term 'pair' to two horses yoked together. The offside and the nearside horse are each of them parts of the pair, but we do not call either of them, however related to the other, a pair, but only use that term of the two in combination.

Of these three possibilities Varro chooses the third; man is neither the soul alone nor the body alone, in his view; he is soul and body in combination. It follows, he says, that the Supreme Good of man, which brings him happiness, consists in the combination of goods of both his elements, of soul, that is, and body. Accordingly, he holds that the primary blessings of nature are to be desired for their own sake, as also is virtue (which is implanted by teaching), as being the art of living, the most excellent among the goods of the soul. And therefore, when this virtue (the art of the conduct of life) has received the primary natural gifts which existed without virtue, in fact were there even when as yet they were without any instruction, she herself desires all these blessings for their own sake and at the same time aims at her own increase; thus she employs them and herself at the same time, in order that she may delight in all of them and enjoy them all. This enjoyment may be greater or less in proportion as each of these goods is of greater or lesser value. Nevertheless, she rejoices in all of them, although, if necessity requires, she may scorn some of the less important with a view to the attainment or conservation of those more valuable.

Of all these goods, however, whether of soul or body, there is none at all that virtue puts above herself. For virtue makes good use both of herself and of all the other goods which bring man happiness. But if she herself is not there, then, however many goods there are, they do the possessor no good, and so are not to be called his 'goods'; for he uses these goods ill, and they cannot be of use to him. This is then the life of man which is rightly called happy – a life which enjoys virtue and the other goods of soul and body without which virtue cannot exist. But if a life enjoys any of the gifts, or many of them, which virtue can be without and still exist, it is called happier. And happiest of all if it enjoys all gifts without exception, so as to lack not even a single blessing of soul or body. Life, to be sure, is not the same thing as virtue, since not every kind of life, but only the wise conduct of life, is virtue. There can, indeed, be some sort of life without virtue; but there can be no virtue without any life at all. I could say the same of memory and reason, and any other such human characteristics. These exist before any teaching; in fact without them teaching would be quite impossible, and consequently virtue also would be impossible, since virtue is certainly developed by teaching. On the other hand, ability in running, beauty of body, outstanding physical strength and the like, can exist without virtue, just as virtue can exist without them. They are goods, for all that, and, according to these thinkers, even these goods are esteemed by virtue for their own sake, and she uses and enjoys them in a way appropriate for virtue.

The philosophers say also that this happy life is social, and for its own sake values the good of friends as its own, just as it wishes for them, for their own sake, what it wishes for itself. And 'friends' here may mean those in the same house, such as a man's wife or children, or any other members of the household; or it can mean all those in the place where a man has his home, a city, for example, and a man's friends are thus his fellow-citizens; or it can extend to the whole world, and include the nations with whom a man is joined by membership of the human society; or even to the whole universe, 'heaven and earth' as we term it, and to those whom the philosophers call gods, whom they hold to be a wise man's friends – our more familiar name for them is 'angels'. These philosophers assert that there can be no possibility of doubt about the nature of the Supreme Good and the Supreme Evil, its opposite. This, they maintain, marks the difference between themselves and those of the New Academy. And it is not of the least importance to them whether anyone who engages in philosophy adopts the Cynic dress and eating habits, or any other fashion whatsoever, in his pursuit of those ends which they hold to be the true ends. Furthermore, of the three kinds of life, the leisured, the active, and the compound of these two, they declare that they approve the third. The members of the Old Academy held and taught these views; so Varro asserts on the authority of Antiochus,[7] Cicero's master and his own, though Cicero makes out that on many points Antiochus had more in common with the Stoics than with the Old Academy. But what does that matter to us? For we ought to form our judgement on the actual facts of the case, instead of attaching importance to knowing what any particular individual thought about them.

7. Antiochus of Ascalon (*fl. c.* 80 B.C.) tried to reconcile Platonism and Stoicism, and claimed to have restored the Old Academy.

4. *The Christian view of the Supreme Good and the Supreme Evil, contrasted with that of the philosophers who found the Supreme Good in themselves*

If, therefore, we are asked what reply the City of God gives when asked about each of these points, and first what view it holds about the Ultimate Good and the Ultimate Evil, the reply will be that eternal life is the Supreme Good, and eternal death the Supreme Evil, and that to achieve the one and escape the other, we must live rightly. That is why the Scripture says, 'The just man lives on the basis of faith.'[8] For we do not yet see our good, and hence we have to seek it by believing; and it is not in our power to live rightly, unless while we believe and pray we receive help from him who has given us the faith to believe that we must be helped by him. Whereas those who have supposed that the Ultimate Good and the Ultimate Evil are to be found in this life, placing the Supreme Good in the body, or in the soul, or in both (to put it more explicitly, in pleasure, or in virtue, or in both); in repose, or in virtue, or in both; in the combination of pleasure and repose, or in virtue, or in both; in the primary gifts of nature, or in virtue, or in both – all these philosophers have wished, with amazing folly, to be happy here on earth and to achieve bliss by their own efforts. The Truth ridiculed such people through the words of the prophet: 'The Lord knows the thoughts of men'[9] – or, as the apostle Paul quotes the passage, 'The Lord knows that the thoughts of wise men are foolish.'[10]

For who is competent, however torrential the flow of his eloquence, to unfold all the miseries of this life? Cicero lamented them, as best he could, in his *Consolation* on the death of his daughter.[11] But what did his best amount to? For, to tell the truth, when, where, how can the 'primary gifts of nature', so called, be in so flourishing a state in this life that they escape being tossed about at the mercy of chance and accident? For is there any pain, the opposite of pleasure, any disturbance, the contrary of repose, that cannot befall a wise man's body? Certainly the amputation or enfeeblement of a man's limbs makes havoc of his bodily soundness; ugliness despoils his beauty, sickness his health; weakness subdues his strength, lassitude or lethargy his mobility. And is there any of these which may not assault the

8. Hab. 2, 4; Rom. 1, 17; Gal. 3, 11; Hebr. 10, 38.

9. Ps. 94, 11. 10. 1 Cor. 3, 20.

11. Only fragments remain of Cicero's *Consolatio* on the death of Tullia in 45 B.C.

wise man's physical frame? The attitudes and movements of the body, when they are graceful and harmonious, are reckoned among primary gifts of nature. But what if some illness makes the limbs shake and tremble? What if a man's spine is so curved as to bring his hands to the ground, turning the man into a virtual quadruped? Will not this destroy all beauty and grace of body whether in repose or in motion?

Then what about the primary goods, so called, of the mind itself? The two ranked first are sensation and understanding, because they lead to the apprehension and awareness of truth. But what kind of sensation is left, and how much of it, if a man becomes blind and deaf, not to mention other disabilities? And whither will reason and intelligence retire, where will they slumber, if a man is rendered insane by some disease? Crazy people say and do many incongruous things, things for the most part alien to their intentions and their characters, certainly contrary to their good intentions and characters; and when we think about their words and actions, or see them with our eyes, we can scarcely – or possibly we cannot at all – restrain our tears, if we consider their situation as it deserves to be considered. And what am I to say of those subjected to the attacks of demons? Where is their intellect hidden away under cover, while the malignant spirit employs their soul and body to work his own will? Yet is anyone quite confident that such a disaster cannot happen to a wise man in this life? Again, what sort of awareness of truth is there, how much awareness is there when we are in this material flesh, when, as we read in the truth-telling Book of Wisdom, 'The perishable body weighs down the soul, and the earthly habitation presses down the mind as it ponders many questions'?[12] Moreover, the impulse or urge towards action (if this is the right way to express what the Greeks call *hormê*), which is also counted among the primary gifts of nature, is not this impulse responsible for the gestures and actions of the insane that move our pity, that make us shudder, when sensation is perverted and reason is asleep?

Then again, what of virtue itself, which is not one of the primary gifts, since it supervenes on them later, introduced by teaching? Although it claims the topmost place among human goods, what is its activity in this world but unceasing warfare with vices, and those not external vices but internal, not other people's vices but quite clearly our own, our very own? And this is the particular struggle of that virtue called in Greek *sôphrosynê*, which is translated 'temperance'

12. Wisd. 9, 15.

– the virtue which bridles the lusts of the flesh to prevent their gaining the consent of the mind and dragging it into every kind of immorality. For it is never true, in this life, that vice does not exist, when, as the Apostle says, 'the desires of the flesh oppose the spirit'; but to this vice there is an opposing virtue, when, as the same Apostle says, 'the desires of the spirit oppose the flesh. For these two are in mutual opposition, so that you do not achieve what you want to achieve.'[13] But what in fact, do we want to achieve, when we desire to be made perfect by the Highest Good? It can, surely, only be a situation where the desires of the flesh do not oppose the spirit, and where there is in us no vice for the spirit to oppose with its desires. Now we cannot achieve this in our present life, for all our wishing. But we can at least, with God's help, see to it that we do not give way to the desires of the flesh which oppose the spirit by allowing our spirit to be overcome, and that we are not dragged to the perpetration of sin with our own consent. God forbid, then, that, so long as we are engaged in this internal strife, we should believe ourselves to have already attained that happiness, the end we desire to reach by our victory. And who has reached such a height of wisdom as to have no struggle to maintain against his lusts?

And what of that virtue called prudence? Does she not employ all her vigilance in distinguishing good from evil, so that in our pursuit of the good and our endeavour to shun the evil, no mistakes may creep in? And does not she herself thus testify that we are in the midst of evils, or rather that evils are in us? For she teaches us that it is an evil to consent in sinning, and a good to refuse to consent. But although prudence teaches us not to consent to that evil, and self-control causes us not to consent, neither prudence nor self-control removes that evil from this life. Consider the virtue of justice. The function of justice is to assign to each his due; and hence there is established in man himself a certain just order of nature, by which the soul is subordinated to God, and the body to the soul, and thus both body and soul are subordinated to God. Does not justice demonstrate, in performing this function, that she is still labouring at her task rather than resting after reaching its completion? For, we may be sure, the less the soul has God in mind in all its thinking, the less it is subordinated to God; and the more the desires of the flesh oppose the spirit, the less subordinate is the body to the soul. So long, therefore, as there is in us this weakness, this disease, this lethargy, how shall we dare to claim that we are saved? And if not saved, how shall we dare

13. Gal. 5, 17.

to assert that we are already blest with that final bliss? And then again, that virtue whose name is fortitude, however great the wisdom with which she is accompanied, bears most unmistakable witness to the fact of human ills; for it is just those ills that she is compelled to bear with patient endurance.

I am astounded at the effrontery of the Stoics in their contention that those ills are not ills at all, when they admit that if they should be so great that a wise man cannot or ought not to endure them, he is forced to put himself to death and to depart from this life.[14] Yet so great is the stupefying arrogance of those people who imagine that they find the Ultimate Good in this life and that they can attain happiness by their own efforts, that their 'wise man' (that is, the wise man as described by them in their amazing idiocy), even if he goes blind, deaf, and dumb, even if enfeebled in limb and tormented with pain, and the victim of every other kind of ill that could be mentioned or imagined, and thus is driven to do himself to death – that such a man would not blush to call that life of his, in the setting of all those ills, a life of happiness! What a life of bliss, that seeks the aid of death to end it! If this is happiness, let him continue in it! How can these circumstances fail to be evil which overcome the good of fortitude, and not only compel that same fortitude to give way to them, but to reach such a pitch of delirium as to call a life happy and in the same breath persuade a man that he should make his escape from it? Is anyone so blind as to fail to see that if it were a happy life it would not be a life to seek escape from? In fact the admission that it is a life to be escaped from is an open confession of weakness. Then what keeps the Stoics from humbling their stiff-necked pride and admitting that it is a life of misery? Was it by patient endurance that Cato took his own life?[15] Was it not rather through a lack of it? For he would not have so acted had he not been unable to endure Caesar's victory. What happened, then, to his fortitude? Why, it yielded; it succumbed. It was so thoroughly defeated that it abandoned this 'happy life'; it deserted and fled. Or was it a happy life no longer? If so, it was a wretched life. Then how can it be that those circumstances were not evil, if they made life a misery from which a man should escape?

This shows that those who acknowledged such things to be evils are talking in a more tolerable fashion; the Peripatetics, for example, and the members of the Old Academy – the sect supported by Varro. Even so, they also are guilty of a remarkable error, in contending that amid those evils, even if they are so grievous that a man who suffers them is

14. cf. Bk I, 22n. 15. cf. Bk I, 5n.

right to seek escape by self-inflicted death, life is nevertheless happy. 'Bodily torments and agonies' says Varro 'are evils, and their evil increases in proportion to their severity. And to get free of them a man should escape from this life.' What life, pray? 'This life', he replies, 'which is burdened with such great evils.' It is certainly happy, I take it, amid those same evils which lead you to say that one should escape from it? Or is your reason for calling it happy the very fact that you have permission to withdraw from these evils by death? Then what if by some divine judgement you were beset by such evils and not permitted either to die or ever to be exempt from them? Surely in that case, at any rate, you would call such a life wretched? That implies that it does not fail to be wretched simply because it is quickly abandoned, seeing that, if it were everlasting, it would be wretched, even in your judgement. And so it ought not to be regarded as free from any misery, simply because the misery is short-lived; nor – for this would be even more nonsensical – should it be called a state of bliss, simply because of the brevity of the wretchedness.

There is a mighty force in the evils which compel a man, and, according to those philosophers, even a wise man, to rob himself of his existence as a man; although they say, and say with truth, that the first and greatest utterance of nature, as we may call it, is that a man should be reconciled to himself and for that reason should naturally shun death – that he should be his own friend, in that he should emphatically desire to continue as a living being and to remain alive in this combination of body and soul, and that this should be his aim. There is a mighty force in those evils which overpower this natural feeling which makes us employ all our strength in our endeavour to avoid death – which defeat this feeling so utterly that what was shunned is now wished and longed for, and, if it cannot come to him from some other source, is inflicted on a man by himself. There is a mighty force in those evils which make Fortitude a murderer – if indeed she is still to be called fortitude when she is so utterly vanquished by those evils that she not only cannot by her endurance keep guard over the man she has undertaken to govern and protect, but is herself compelled to go so far as to kill him. The wise man ought, indeed, to endure even death with a steadfastness, but a death that comes to him from outside himself. Whereas if he is compelled, as those philosophers say, to inflict it on himself, they must surely admit that these are not only evils, but intolerable evils, when they compel him to commit this crime.

It follows from this that the life weighed down by such great and grievous ills, or at the mercy of such chances, would never be called happy, if the men who so term it, and who, when overcome by the growing weight of ills, surrender to adversity in compassing their own death – if these people would bring themselves to surrender to the truth, when overcome by sound reasoning, in their quest for the happy life, and would give up supposing that the ultimate, Supreme Good is something to be enjoyed by them in this condition of mortality. For in this state the very virtues, which are certainly the best and most useful of man's endowments here below, bear reliable witness to man's miseries in proportion to their powerful support against man's perils, hardships and sorrows. In fact, if they are genuine virtues (and genuine virtues can exist only in those in whom true godliness is present) they do not profess to have the power to ensure that the people in whom they exist will not suffer any miseries; genuine virtues are not such liars as to advance such claims. But they do claim that though human life is compelled to be wretched by all the grievous evils of this world, it is happy in the expectation of the world to come, just as, in expectation, it is saved. For how can it be happy, if it is not yet saved? This point is also made by the apostle Paul. He is speaking not about men without prudence, without steadfastness, without self-control, without justice, but about those who lived by the standards of genuine godliness, whose virtues were therefore genuine virtues, and he says, 'It is in hope that we are saved. But when hope is seen fulfilled it is hope no longer: why should a man hope for what he already sees? But if we are hoping for something we do not yet see, then it is with steadfast endurance that we await it.'[16] As, therefore, we are saved in hope, it is in hope that we have been made happy; and as we do not yet possess a present salvation, but await salvation in the future, so we do not enjoy a present happiness, but look forward to happiness in the future, and we look forward 'with steadfast endurance'. We are beset by evils, and we have to endure them steadfastly until we reach those goods where there will be everything to supply us with delight beyond the telling, and there will be nothing any longer that we are bound to endure. Such is the salvation which in the world to come will also be itself the ultimate bliss. Yet these philosophers refuse to believe in this blessedness because they do not see it; and so they attempt to fabricate for themselves an utterly delusive happiness by means of a virtue whose falsity is in proportion to its arrogance.

16. Rom. 8, 24f.

5. Social life; its value and its dangers

The philosophies hold the view that the life of the wise man should be social; and in this we support them much more heartily. For here we are, with the nineteenth book in hand on the subject of the City of God; and how could that City have made its first start, how could it have advanced along its course, how could it attain its appointed goal, if the life of the saints were not social? And yet, who would be capable of listing the number and the gravity of the ills which abound in human society amid the distresses of our mortal condition? Who would be competent to assess them? Our philosophers should listen to a character in one of their own comedies, voicing a sentiment with which all mankind agrees:

> I married a wife; and misery I found!
> Children were born; and they increased my cares.[17]

Again, think of the disorders of love, as listed in another quotation from Terence:

> Wrongs and suspicions, enmities and war—
> Then, peace again![18]

Have they not everywhere filled up the story of human experience? Are they not of frequent occurrence, even in the honourable love of friends? The story of mankind is full of them at every point; for in that story we are aware of wrongs, suspicions, enmities and war – undoubted evils, these. And even peace is a doubtful good, since we do not know the hearts of those with whom we wish to maintain peace, and even if we could know them today, we should not know what they might be like tomorrow. In fact, who are, in general, more friendly, or at any rate ought to be, than those within the walls of the same home? And yet, is anyone perfectly serene in that situation, when such grievous ills have so often arisen from the secret treachery of people within those walls? And the bitterness of these ills matches the sweetness of the peace that was reckoned genuine, when it was in fact only a very clever pretence.

This explains why some words of Cicero come so close to our hearts that we cannot but sigh when we read:

> No treachery is more insidious than that which is hidden under a pretence of loyalty, or under the name of kinship. For against an open adversary you could be on your guard and thus easily avoid him; but this

17. Ter., *Adelph.*, 5, 4, 13f. 18. *Eun.*, 1, 1, 14f.

hidden evil, within the house and family, not only arises before you are aware but even overwhelms you before you can catch sight of it and investigate it.[19]

Hence also that inspired utterance, 'A man's enemies are those of his own household',[20] is heard with deep sorrow of heart. For even if anyone is strong enough to bear these ills with equanimity, or watchful enough to guard with foresight and discretion against the contrivances of pretended friendship, nevertheless he cannot but feel grievous anguish, if he himself is a good man, at the wickedness of the traitors, when by experience he knows their utter viciousness, whether they were always evil and their goodness was a sham, or whether they suffered a change from good-nature to the malice that they now display. If, then, safety is not to be found in the home, the common refuge from the evils that befall mankind, what shall we say of the city? The larger the city, the more is its forum filled with civil lawsuits and criminal trials, even if that city be at peace, free from the alarms or – what is more frequent – the bloodshed, of sedition and civil war. It is true that cities are at times exempt from those occurrences; they are never free from the danger of them.

6. *The mistakes of human judgement, when the truth is hidden*

What of those judgements passed by men on their fellow-men, which cannot be dispensed with in cities, however much peace they enjoy? What is our feeling about them? How pitiable, how lamentable do we find them! For indeed those who pronounce judgement cannot see into the consciences of those on whom they pronounce it. And so they are often compelled to seek the truth by torturing innocent witnesses in a case which is no concern of theirs. And what about torture employed on a man in his own case? The question is whether he is guilty. He is tortured, and, even if innocent, he suffers, for a doubtful crime, a punishment about which there is no shadow of doubt and not because he is discovered to have committed it, but because it is not certain that he did not commit it. This means that the ignorance of the judge is often a calamity for the innocent. And there is something yet more intolerable, something to be bewailed, and, if it were possible, washed away by floods of tears. It is the fact that the judge tortures the accused for the sole purpose of avoiding the execution, in ignorance, of an inno-

19. Cic. *In Verr.*, 2, 1, 13. 20. Matt. 10, 36.

cent man; while his pitiable lack of knowledge leads him to put to death, tortured and innocent, the very person whom he had tortured to avoid putting the innocent to death.

Now if this accused has followed the wisdom of our philosopher friends in choosing to escape from this life rather than endure those tortures any longer, he confesses to a crime he has not committed. Then after his condemnation and execution the judge still does not know whether it was a guilty or an innocent person he has executed, after torturing him to avoid executing the innocent in ignorance. Consequently, he has tortured an innocent man to get to the truth and has killed him while still in ignorance. In view of this darkness that attends the life of human society, will our wise man take his seat on the judge's bench, or will he not have the heart to do so? Obviously, he will sit; for the claims of human society constrain him and draw him to this duty; and it is unthinkable to him that he should shirk it.

In fact, it is not to him an unthinkable horror that innocent witnesses should be tortured in cases which are no concern of theirs; or that the accused are frequently overcome by the anguish of their pain and so make false confessions and are punished despite their innocence; or that, even if not suffering capital punishment, they very often die under torture or as a result of torture; or that the prosecutors, whose motive may be a desire to benefit human society by ensuring that crimes do not go unpunished, are at times themselves condemned. The witnesses may give false evidence, the defendant himself may hold out under torture with savage resistance and refuse to confess, and the accusers may be incapable of proving the truth of their charges, however true those charges may be; and the judge, in his ignorance, may condemn them. All these serious evils our philosopher does not reckon as sins; for the wise judge does not act in this way through a will to do harm, but because ignorance is unavoidable – and yet the exigences of human society make judgement also unavoidable. Here we have what I call the wretchedness of man's situation, at any rate, even if it is not to be called the wickedness of the wise man, in his judicial capacity. Yet if it is through unavoidable ignorance and the unavoidable duty of judging that he tortures the innocent, are we to be told that it is not enough to acquit him? Must we grant him happiness as a bonus? How much more mature reflection it shows, how much more worthy of a human being it is when a man acknowledges this necessity as a mark of human wretchedness, when he hates that necessity in his own actions and when, if he has the wisdom of devotion, he cries out to God, 'Deliver me from my necessities!'[21]

7. *Human society divided by differences of language. The misery of war, even when just*

After the city or town comes the world, which the philosophers reckon as the third level of human society. They begin with the household, proceed to the city, and then arrive at the world. Now the world, being like a confluence of waters, is obviously more full of danger than the other communities by reason of its greater size. To begin with, on this level the diversity of languages separates man from man. For if two men meet, and are forced by some compelling reason not to pass on but to stay in company, then if neither knows the other's language, it is easier for dumb animals, even of different kinds, to associate together than these men, although both are human beings. For when men cannot communicate their thoughts to each other, simply because of difference of language, all the similarity of their common human nature is of no avail to unite them in fellowship. So true is this that a man would be more cheerful with his dog for company than with a foreigner. I shall be told that the Imperial City has been at pains to impose on conquered peoples not only her yoke but her language also, as a bond of peace and fellowship, so that there should be no lack of interpreters but even a profusion of them. True; but think of the cost of this achievement! Consider the scale of those wars, with all that slaughter of human beings, all the human blood that was shed!

Those wars are now past history; and yet the misery of these evils is not yet ended. For although there has been, and still is, no lack of enemies among foreign nations, against whom wars have always been waged, and are still being waged, yet the very extent of the Empire has given rise to wars of a worse kind, namely, social and civil wars, by which mankind is more lamentably disquieted either when fighting is going on in the hope of bringing hostilities eventually to a peaceful end, or when there are fears that hostilities will break out again. If I were to try to describe, with an eloquence worthy of the subject, the many and multifarious disasters, the dour and dire necessities, I could not possibly be adequate to the theme, and there would be no end to this protracted discussion. But the wise man, they say, will wage just wars. Surely, if he remembers that he is a human

21. Ps. 25, 17.

being, he will rather lament the fact that he is faced with the necessity of waging just wars; for if they were not just, he would not have to engage in them, and consequently there would be no wars for a wise man. For it is the injustice of the opposing side that lays on the wise man the duty of waging wars; and this injustice is assuredly to be deplored by a human being, since it is the injustice of human beings, even though no necessity for war should arise from it. And so everyone who reflects with sorrow on such grievous evils, in all their horror and cruelty, must acknowledge the misery of them. And yet a man who experiences such evils, or even thinks about them, without heartfelt grief, is assuredly in a far more pitiable condition, if he thinks himself happy simply because he has lost all human feeling.

8. *The friendship of good men can never be carefree, because of this life's dangers*

If we are spared that kind of ignorance, akin to madness, which is a common affliction in the wretched condition of this life, an ignorance which leads men to believe an enemy to be a friend, or a friend an enemy, what consolation have we in this human society, so replete with mistaken notions and distressing anxieties, except the unfeigned faith and mutual affections of genuine, loyal friends? Yet the more friends we have and the more dispersed they are in different places, the further and more widely extend our fears that some evil may befall them from among all the mass of evils of this present world. For not only are we troubled and anxious because they may be afflicted by famine, war, disease, or captivity, fearing that in slavery they may suffer evils beyond our powers of imagination; there is the much more bitter fear, that their friendship be changed into treachery, malice and baseness. And when such things do happen (and the more numerous our friends, the more often they happen) and the news is brought to our ears, who, except one who has this experience, can be aware of the burning sorrow that ravages our hearts? Certainly we would rather hear that our friends were dead, although this also we could not hear without grief.

For if their life brought us the consoling delights of friendship, how could it be that their death should bring us no sadness? Anyone who forbids such sadness must forbid, if he can, all friendly conversation, must lay a ban on all friendly feeling or put a stop to it, must with a ruthless insensibility break the ties of all human relationships, or else decree that they must only be engaged upon so long as they inspire no delight in a man's soul. But if this is beyond all possibility, how can it be that a man's death should not be bitter if his life is sweet to us? For this is why the grief of a heart that has not lost human feeling is a thing like some wound or ulcer, and our friendly words of consolation are the healing application. And it does not follow that there is nothing to be healed simply because the nobler a man's spirit the quicker and easier the cure.

It is true, then, that the life of mortals is afflicted, sometimes more gently, sometimes more harshly, by the death of those most dear to us, and especially the death of those whose functions are necessary for human society; and yet we should prefer to hear, or even to witness, the death of those we love, than to become aware that they have fallen from faith or from moral conflict – that is, that they have died in their very soul. The earth is full of this vast mass of evils; that is why we find this in Scripture: 'Is man's life on earth anything but temptation?'[22] And why the Lord himself says, 'Alas for the world, because of these obstacles';[23] and again, 'Because iniquity will increase beyond measure, the love of many will grow cold.'[24] The result of this situation is that when good men die who are our friends we rejoice for them; and though their death brings us sadness, we find our surer consolation in this, that they have been spared those evils by which in this life even good men are crushed or corrupted, or at least are in danger of both these disasters.

9. *The friendship of the holy angels, obscured by the deceit of demons*

Our relationship with the society of the holy angels is quite another matter. Those philosophers, we observe, who insisted that the gods are our friends[25] placed this angelic fellowship on the fourth level, as they proceeded in their scheme from the earth to the universe, intending by this method to include, in some fashion, even heaven itself. Now, with regard to the angels, we have, it is true, no manner of fear that such friends may bring us sorrow, either by their death or by their degradation. But they do not mix with us on the same familiar footing as do men – and this in itself is one of the disappointments involved in this life – and Satan, as Scripture tells us, transforms himself at times to masquerade as an angel of light,[26] to tempt those men who

22. Job 7, 1 (LXX. The Hebrew reads: 'What is man's life but warfare?').
23. Matt. 18, 7.
24. Matt. 24, 12.
25. cf. Bk IX, 23.
26. cf. 1 Cor. 11, 14.

are in need of this kind of training, or men who deserve to be thus deluded. Hence God's great mercy is needed to prevent anyone from supposing that he is enjoying the friendship of good angels when in fact it is evil demons that he has as his false friends, and when he thus suffers from the enmity of those whose harmfulness is in proportion to their cunning and deceit. In fact, where is God's great mercy needed if not by men in their most pitiable state, where they are so weighed down by ignorance that they are readily deluded by the pretences of those spirits? Now those philosophers in the ungodly city alleged that the gods were their friends; but it is quite certain that they had fallen in with these malignant demons, the powers to whom that city itself is wholly subjected, and in whose company it will suffer everlasting punishment. This is made quite clear by those beings who are worshipped in that city. It is revealed unmistakably by the sacred, or rather sacrilegious, rites by which the pagans think it right to worship them, and by the filthy shows by which they think those demons must be propitiated; and it is the demons themselves who suggest, and indeed demand, the performance of such vile obscenities.

10. *The reward of victory over temptation*

However, not even the saints and the faithful worshippers of the one true and supreme God enjoy exemption from the deceptions of the demons and from their multifarious temptations. In fact, in this situation of weakness and in these times of evil such anxiety is even not without its use in leading them to seek, with more fervent longing, that state of serenity where peace is utterly complete and assured. For there the gifts of nature, that is, the gifts bestowed on our nature by the Creator of all natures, will be not only good but also everlasting; and this applies not only to the spirit, which is healed by wisdom, but also to the body, which will be renewed by resurrection. There the virtues will not be engaged in conflict with any kind of vice or evil; they will be possessed of the reward of victory, the everlasting peace which no adversary can disturb. This is indeed the ultimate bliss, the end of ultimate fulfilment that knows no destructive end. Here in this world we are called blessed, it is true, when we enjoy peace, however little may be the peace – the peace of a good life – which can be enjoyed here. And yet such blessedness as this life affords proves to be utter misery when compared with that final bliss. And so, when we enjoy here, if we live rightly, such peace as can be the portion of mortal men under the conditions of mortality, virtue rightly uses the blessings of peace, and even when we do not possess that peace, virtue turns to a good use even the ills that man endures. But virtue is truly virtue when it refers all the good things of which it makes good use, all its achievements in making good use of good things and evil things, and when it refers itself also, to that end where our peace shall be so perfect and so great as to admit of neither improvement nor increase.

11. *The bliss of everlasting peace, which is the fulfilment of the saints*

It follows that we could say of peace, as we have said of eternal life, that it is the final fulfilment of all our goods; especially in view of what is said in a holy psalm about the City of God, the subject of this laborious discussion. These are the words: 'Praise the Lord, O Jerusalem; praise your God, O Sion: for he has strengthened the bolts of your gates; he has blessed your sons within your walls; he has made your frontiers peace.'[27] Now when the bolts of her gates have been strengthened, that means that no one will any more enter or leave that City. And this implies that we must take her 'frontiers' (or 'ends') to stand here for the peace whose finality I am trying to establish. In fact, the name of the City itself has a mystic significance, for 'Jerusalem', as I have said already, means 'vision of peace'.[28]

But the word 'peace' is freely used in application to the events of this mortal state, where there is certainly no eternal life; and so I have preferred to use the term 'eternal life' instead of 'peace' in describing the end of this City, where its Ultimate Good will be found. About this end the Apostle says, 'But now you have been set free from sin and have become the servants of God; and so you have your profit, a profit leading to sanctification, and the end is everlasting life.'[29] On the other hand, the life of the wicked may also be taken to be eternal life by those who have no familiarity with the holy Scriptures. They may follow some of the philosophers in thinking in terms of the immortality of the soul, or they may be influenced by our Christian belief in the endless punishment of the ungodly, who obviously cannot be tortured for ever without also living for ever. Consequently, in order to make it easier for everyone to understand our meaning, we have to say that the end of this City, whereby it will possess its Supreme Good,

27. Ps. 147, 12ff.
28. A fanciful etymology. 'City of Peace' is possible.
29. Rom. 6, 22.

may be called either 'peace in life everlasting' or 'life everlasting in peace'. For peace is so great a good that even in relation to the affairs of earth and of our mortal state no word ever falls more gratefully upon the ear, nothing is desired with greater longing, in fact, nothing better can be found. So if I decide to discourse about it at somewhat greater length, I shall not, I think, impose a burden on my readers, not only because I shall be speaking of the end of the City which is the subject of this work, but also because of the delightfulness of peace, which is dear to the heart of all mankind.

12. *Peace is the instinctive aim of all creatures, and is even the ultimate purpose of war*

Anyone who joins me in an examination, however slight, of human affairs, and the human nature we all share, recognizes that just as there is no man who does not wish for joy, so there is no man who does not wish for peace. Indeed, even when men choose war, their only wish is for victory; which shows that their desire in fighting is for peace with glory. For what is victory but the conquest of the opposing side? And when this is achieved, there will be peace. Even wars, then, are waged with peace as their object, even when they are waged by those who are concerned to exercise their warlike prowess, either in command or in the actual fighting. Hence it is an established fact that peace is the desired end of war. For every man is in quest of peace, even in waging war, whereas no one is in quest of war when making peace. In fact, even when men wish a present state of peace to be disturbed they do so not because they hate peace, but because they desire the present peace to be exchanged for one that suits their wishes. Thus their desire is not that there should not be peace but that it should be the kind of peace they wish for. Even in the extreme case when they have separated themselves from others by sedition, they cannot achieve their aim unless they maintain some sort of semblance of peace with their confederates in conspiracy. Moreover, even robbers, to ensure greater efficiency and security in their assaults on the peace of the rest of mankind, desire to preserve peace with their associates.

Indeed, one robber may be so unequalled in strength and so wary of having anyone to share his plans that he does not trust any associate, but plots his crimes and achieves his successes by himself, carrying off his booty after overcoming and dispatching such as he can; yet even so he maintains some kind of shadow of peace, at least with those whom he cannot kill, and from whom he wishes to conceal his activities. At the same time, he is anxious, of course, to be at peace in his own home, with his wife and children and any other members of his household; without doubt he is delighted to have them obedient to his beck and call. For if this does not happen, he is indignant; he scolds and punishes; and, if need be, he employs savage measures to impose on his household a peace which, he feels, cannot exist unless all the other elements in the same domestic society are subject to one head; and this head, in his own home, is himself. Thus, if he were offered the servitude of a larger number, of a city, maybe, or a whole nation, on the condition that they should all show the same subservience he had demanded from his household, then he would no longer lurk like a brigand in his hide-out; he would raise himself on high as a king for all to see – although the same greed and malignity would persist in him.

We see, then, that all men desire to be at peace with their own people, while wishing to impose their will upon those people's lives. For even when they wage war on others, their wish is to make those opponents their own people, if they can – to subject them, and to impose on them their own conditions of peace.

Let us, however, suppose such a man as is described in the verse of epic legends, a creature so unsociable and savage that they perhaps preferred to call him a semi-human rather than a human being. Now although his kingdom was the solitude of a dreadful cavern, and although he was so unequalled in wickedness that a name was found for him derived from that quality (he was called Cacus,[30] and *kakos* is the Greek word for 'wicked'); although he had no wife with whom to exchange endearments, no children to play with when little or to give orders to when they were a little bigger, no friends with whom to enjoy a chat, not even his father, Vulcan (he was happier than his father only in this important respect – that he did not beget another such monster as himself); although he never gave anything to anyone, but took what he wanted from anyone he could and removed, when he could, anyone he wished to remove; despite all this, in the very solitude of his cave, the floor of which, in the poet's description

> reeked ever with the blood of recent slaughter[31]

his only desire was for a peace in which no one should disturb him, and no man's violence, or the dread of it, should trouble his repose.

30. cf. Virg., *Aen.*, 8, 190–305 for the story of Cacus and Hercules.
31. Virg. *Aen.*, l. 195.

Above all, he desired to be at peace with his own body; and in so far as he achieved this, all was well with him. He gave the orders and his limbs obeyed. But his mortal nature rebelled against him because of its insatiable desires, and stirred up the civil strife of hunger, intending to dissociate the soul from the body and to exclude it; and then he sought with all possible haste to pacify that mortal nature, and to that end he ravished, murdered, and devoured. And thus, for all his monstrous savagery, his aim was still to ensure peace, for the preservation of his life, by these monstrous and savage methods. Accordingly, if he had been willing to maintain, in relation to others also, the peace he was so busily concerned to preserve in his own case and in himself, he would not have been called wicked, or a monster, or semi-human. Or if it was his outward appearance and his belching of murky flames that frightened away human companions, it may be that it was not lust for inflicting injury but the necessity of preserving his life that made him so savage. Perhaps, after all, he never existed or, more probably, he was not like the description given by poetic fantasy; for if Cacus had not been excessively blamed, Hercules would have received inadequate praise. And therefore the existence of such a man, or rather semi-human, is discredited, as are many similar poetical fictions.

We observe, then, that even the most savage beasts, from whom Cacus derived the wild-beast side of his nature (he was in fact also called a semi-beast), safeguard their own species by a kind of peace, by coition, by begetting and bearing young, by cherishing them and rearing them; even though most of them are not gregarious but solitary – not, that is, like sheep, deer, doves, starlings, and bees, but like lions, wolves, foxes, eagles and owls. What tigress does not gently purr over her cubs, and subdue her fierceness to caress them? What kite, however solitary as he hovers over his prey, does not find a mate, build a nest, help to hatch the eggs, rear the young birds, and, as we may say, preserve with the mother of his family a domestic society as peaceful as he can make it? How much more strongly is a human being drawn by the laws of his nature, so to speak, to enter upon a fellowship with all his fellow-men and to keep peace with them, as far as lies in him. For even the wicked when they go to war do so to defend the peace of their own people, and desire to make all men their own people, if they can, so that all men and all things might together be subservient to one master. And how could that happen, unless they should consent to a peace of his dictation either through love or through fear? Thus pride is a perverted imitation of God. For pride hates a fellowship of equality under God, and seeks to impose its own dominion on fellow men, in place of God's rule. This means that it hates the just peace of God, and loves its own peace of injustice. And yet it cannot help loving peace of some kind or other. For no creature's perversion is so contrary to nature as to destroy the very last vestiges of its nature.

It comes to this, then; a man who has learnt to prefer right to wrong and the rightly ordered to the perverted, sees that the peace of the unjust, compared with the peace of the just, is not worthy even of the name of peace. Yet even what is perverted must of necessity be in, or derived from, or associated with – that is, in a sense, at peace with – some part of the order of things among which it has its being or of which it consists. Otherwise it would not exist at all. For instance if anyone were to hang upside-down, this position of the body and arrangement of the limbs is undoubtedly perverted, because what should be on top, according to the dictates of nature, is underneath, and what nature intends to be underneath is on top. This perverted attitude disturbs the peace of the flesh, and causes distress for that reason. For all that, the breath is at peace with its body and is busily engaged for its preservation; that is why there is something to endure the pain. And even if the breath is finally driven from the body by its distresses, still, as long as the framework of the limbs holds together, what remains retains a kind of peace among the bodily parts; hence there is still something to hang there. And in that the earthly body pulls towards the earth, and pulls against the binding rope that holds it suspended, it tends towards the position of its own peace, and by what might be called the appeal of its weight, it demands a place where it may rest. And so even when it is by now lifeless and devoid of all sensation it does not depart from the peace of its natural position, either while possessed of it or while tending towards it. Again, if treatment with embalming fluids is applied to prevent the dissolution and disintegration of the corpse in its present shape, a kind of peace still connects the parts with one another and keeps the whole mass fixed in its earthly condition, an appropriate, and therefore a peaceable state.

On the other hand, if no preservative treatment is given, and the body is left for nature to take its course, there is for a time a kind of tumult in the corpse of exhalations disagreeable and offensive to our senses (for that is what we smell in putrefaction), which lasts until the body unites with the elements of the world as, little by little, and particle by particle, it vanishes into their peace. Nevertheless, nothing is in any way removed, in this process, from the control of the laws of the supreme Creator and Ruler who directs the peace of the whole scheme of things. For although minute animals are produced in the corpse of a larger animal, those little bodies, each and all of them, by the same law of their Creator, are subservient to their little souls in the peace that preserves their lives. And even if the flesh of dead animals is devoured by other animals, in whatever direction it is taken, with whatever substances it is united, into whatever substances it is converted and transformed, it still finds itself subject to the same laws which are diffused throughout the whole of matter for the preservation of every mortal species, establishing peace by a harmony of congruous elements.

13. *The peace of the universe maintained through all disturbances by a law of nature: the individual attains, by God's ordinance, to the state he has deserved by his free choice*

The peace of the body, we conclude, is a tempering of the component parts in duly ordered proportion; the peace of the irrational soul is a duly ordered repose of the appetites; the peace of the rational soul is the duly ordered agreement of cognition and action. The peace of body and soul is the duly ordered life and health of a living creature; peace between mortal man and God is an ordered obedience, in faith, in subjection to an everlasting law; peace between men is an ordered agreement of mind with mind; the peace of a home is the ordered agreement among those who live together about giving and obeying orders; the peace of the Heavenly City is a perfectly ordered and perfectly harmonious fellowship in the enjoyment of God, and a mutual fellowship in God; the peace of the whole universe is the tranquillity of order – and order is the arrangement of things equal and unequal in a pattern which assigns to each its proper position.

It follows that the wretched, since, in so far as they are wretched, they are obviously not in a state of peace, lack the tranquillity of order, a state in which there is no disturbance of mind. In spite of that, because their wretchedness is deserved and just, they cannot be outside the scope of order. They are not, indeed, united with the blessed; yet it is by the law of order that they are sundered from them. And when they are free from disturbance of mind, they are adjusted to their situation, with however small a degree of harmony. Thus they have amongst them some tranquillity of order, and therefore some peace. But they are still wretched just because, although they enjoy some degree of serenity and freedom from suffering, they are not in a condition where they have the right to be serene and free from pain. They are yet more wretched, however, if they are not at peace with the law by which the natural order is governed. Now when they suffer, their peace is disturbed in the part where they suffer; and yet peace still continues in the part which feels no burning pain, and where the natural frame is not broken up. Just as there is life, then, without pain, whereas there can be no pain when there is no life, so there is peace without any war, but no war without some degree of peace. This is not a consequence of war as such, but of the fact that war is waged by or within persons who are in some sense natural beings – for they could have no kind of existence without some kind of peace as the condition of their being.

There exists, then, a nature in which there is no evil, in which, indeed, no evil can exist; but there cannot exist a nature in which there is no good. Hence not even the nature of the Devil himself is evil, in so far as it is a nature; it is perversion that makes it evil. And so the Devil did not stand firm in the truth, and yet he did not escape the judgement of the truth. He did not continue in the tranquillity of order; but that did not mean that he escaped from the power of the imposer of order. The good that God imparts, which the Devil has in his nature, does not withdraw him from God's justice by which his punishment is ordained. But God, in punishing, does not chastise the good which he created, but the evil which the Devil has committed. And God does not take away all that he gave to that nature; he takes something, and yet he leaves something, so that there may be some being left to feel pain at the deprivation.

Now this pain is in itself evidence of the good that was taken away and the good that was left. In fact, if no good had been left there could have been no grief for lost good. For a sinner is in a worse state if he rejoices in the loss of righteousness; but a sinner who feels anguish, though he may gain no good from his anguish, is at least grieving at the loss of salvation. And since righteousness and salvation are both good, and the loss of any good calls for grief rather than for joy (assuming that there is no compensation for the loss in the shape of a higher good – for example, righteousness of character is a higher good than health of body), the unrighteous man's grief in his punishment is more appropriate than his rejoicing in sin. Hence, just as delight in the abandonment of good, when a man sins, is evidence of a bad will, so grief at the loss of good, when a man is punished, is evidence of a good nature. For when a man grieves at the loss of the peace of his nature, his grief arises from some remnants of that peace, which ensure that his nature is still on friendly terms with itself. Moreover, it is entirely right that in the last punishment the wicked and ungodly should bewail in their agonies the loss of their 'natural' goods, and realize that he who divested them of these goods with perfect justice is God, whom they despised when with supreme generosity he bestowed them.

God then, created all things in supreme wisdom and ordered them in perfect justice; and in establishing the mortal race of mankind as the greatest ornament of earthly things, he has given to mankind certain good things suitable to this life. These are: temporal peace, in proportion to the short span of a mortal life – the peace that consists in bodily health and soundness, and in fellowship with one's kind; and everything necessary to safeguard or recover this peace – those things, for example, which are appropriate and accessible to our senses: light, speech, air to breathe, water to drink, and whatever is suitable for the feeding and clothing of the body, for the care of the body and the adornment of the person. And all this is granted under the most equitable condition: that every mortal who uses aright such goods, goods designed to serve the peace of mortal men, shall receive goods greater in degree and superior in kind, namely, the peace of immortality, and the glory and honour appropriate to it in a life which is eternal for the enjoyment of God and of one's neighbour in God, whereas he who wrongly uses those mortal goods shall lose them, and shall not receive the blessings of eternal life.

14. *The order and law, earthly or heavenly, by which government serves the interests of human society*

We see, then, that all man's use of temporal things is related to the enjoyment of earthly peace in the earthly city; whereas in the Heavenly City it is related to the enjoyment of eternal peace. Thus, if we were irrational animals, our only aim would be the adjustment of the parts of the body in due proportion, and the quieting of the appetites – only, that is, the repose of the flesh, and an adequate supply of pleasures, so that bodily peace might promote the peace of the soul. For if bodily peace is lacking, the peace of the irrational soul is also hindered, because it cannot achieve the quieting of its appetites. But the two together promote that peace which is a mutual concord between soul and body, the peace of an ordered life and of health. For living creatures show their love of bodily peace by their avoidance of pain, and by their pursuit of pleasure to satisfy the demands of their appetites they demonstrate their love of peace of soul. In just the same way, by shunning death they indicate quite clearly how great is their love of the peace in which soul and body are harmoniously united.

But because there is in man a rational soul, he subordinates to the peace of the rational soul all that part of his nature which he shares with the beasts, so that he may engage in deliberate thought and act in accordance with this thought, so that he may thus exhibit that ordered agreement of cognition and action which we called the peace of the rational soul. For with this end in view he ought to wish to be spared the distress of pain and grief, the disturbances of desire, the dissolution of death, so that he may come to some profitable knowledge and may order his life and his moral standards in accordance with this knowledge. But he needs divine direction, which he may obey with resolution, and divine assistance that he may obey it freely, to prevent him from falling, in his enthusiasm for knowledge, a victim to some fatal error, through the weakness of the human mind. And so long as he is in this mortal body, he is a pilgrim in a foreign land, away from God; therefore he walks by faith, not by sight.[32] That is why he views all peace, of body or of soul, or of both, in relation to that peace which exists between mortal man and immortal God, so that he may exhibit an ordered obedience in faith in subjection to the everlasting Law.

Now God, our master, teaches two chief precepts, love of God and love of neighbour; and in them man finds three objects for his love: God, himself, and his neighbour; and a man who loves God is not wrong in loving himself. It follows, therefore, that he will be concerned also that his neighbour should love God, since he is told to love his neighbour as himself; and the same is true of his concern for his wife, his children, for the members of his household, and for all other men, so far as is possible. And, for the same end, he will wish his neighbour to be concerned for him, if he happens to need that concern. For this reason he will be at peace, as far as lies in him, with all men, in that peace among men, that ordered harmony; and the basis of this order is the observance of two rules: first, to do no harm to anyone, and, secondly, to help everyone whenever possible. To begin with, therefore, a man has a responsibility for his own household – obviously, both in the order of nature and in the framework of human society, he has easier and more immediate contact with them; he can exercise his concern for them. That is why the Apostle says, 'Anyone

32. cf. 2 Cor. 5, 6f.

who does not take care of his own people, especially those in his own household, is worse than an unbeliever – he is a renegade.'[33] This is where domestic peace starts, the ordered harmony about giving and obeying orders among those who live in the same house. For the orders are given by those who are concerned for the interests of others; thus the husband gives orders to the wife, parents to children, masters to servants. While those who are the objects of this concern obey orders; for example, wives obey husbands, the children obey their parents, the servants their masters. But in the household of the just man who 'lives on the basis of faith' and who is still on pilgrimage, far from that Heavenly City, even those who give orders are the servants of those whom they appear to command. For they do not give orders because of a lust for domination but from a dutiful concern for the interests of others, not with pride in taking precedence over others, but with compassion in taking care of others.

15. *Man's natural freedom; and the slavery caused by sin*

This relationship is prescribed by the order of nature, and it is in this situation that God created man. For he says, 'Let him have lordship over the fish of the sea, the birds of the sky . . . and all the reptiles that crawl on the earth.'[34] He did not wish the rational being, made in his own image, to have dominion over any but irrational creatures, not man over man, but man over the beasts. Hence the first just men were set up as shepherds of flocks, rather than as kings of men, so that in this way also God might convey the message of what was required by the order of nature, and what was demanded by the deserts of sinners – for it is understood, of course, that the condition of slavery is justly imposed on the sinner. That is why we do not hear of a slave anywhere in the Scriptures until Noah, the just man, punished his son's sin with this word;[35] and so that son deserved this name because of his misdeed, not because of his nature. The origin of the Latin word for slave, *servus*, is believed to be derived from the fact that those who by the laws of war could rightly be put to death by the conquerors, became *servi*, slaves, when they were preserved, receiving this name from their preservation.[36] But even this enslavement could not have happened, if it were not for the deserts of sin. For even when a just war is fought it is in defence of his sin that the other side is contending; and victory, even when the victory falls to the wicked, is a

33. 1 Tim. 5, 8. 34. Gen. 1, 26. 35. Gen. 9, 25.
36. A mistaken derivation generally accepted in antiquity.

humiliation visited on the conquered by divine judgement, either to correct or to punish their sins. We have a witness to this in Daniel, a man of God, who in captivity confesses to God his own sins and the sins of his people, and in devout grief testifies that they are the cause of that captivity.[37] The first cause of slavery, then, is sin, whereby man was subjected to man in the condition of bondage; and this can only happen by the judgement of God, with whom there is no injustice, and who knows how to allot different punishments according to the deserts of the offenders.

Now, as our Lord above says, 'Everyone who commits sin is sin's slave',[38] and that is why, though many devout men are slaves to unrighteous masters, yet the masters they serve are not themselves free men; 'for when a man is conquered by another he is also bound as a slave to his conqueror.'[39] And obviously it is a happier lot to be slave to a human being than to a lust; and, in fact, the most pitiless domination that devastates the hearts of men, is that exercised by this very lust for domination, to mention no others. However, in that order of peace in which men are subordinate to other men, humility is as salutary for the servants as pride is harmful to the masters. And yet by nature, in the condition in which God created man, no man is the slave either of man or of sin. But it remains true that slavery as a punishment is also ordained by that law which enjoins the preservation of the order of nature, and forbids its disturbance; in fact, if nothing had been done to contravene that law, there would have been nothing to require the discipline of slavery as a punishment. That explains also the Apostle's admonition to slaves, that they should be subject to their masters, and serve them loyally and willingly.[40] What he means is that if they cannot be set free by their masters, they themselves may thus make their slavery, in a sense, free, by serving not with the slyness of fear, but with the fidelity of affection, until all injustice disappears and all human lordship and power is annihilated, and God is all in all.[41]

16. *Equity in the relation of master and slave*

This being so, even though our righteous fathers had slaves, they so managed the peace of their households as to make a distinction between the situation of children and the condition of slaves in respect of the temporal goods of this life; and yet in the matter of the worship of

37. Dan. 9, 3–15. 38. John 8, 34. 39. 2 Pet. 2, 19.
40. cf. Eph. 6, 5. 41. 1 Cor. 15, 24; 28.

God – in whom we must place our hope of everlasting goods – they were concerned, with equal affection, for all the members of their household. This is what the order of nature prescribes, so that this is the source of the name *paterfamilias*, a name that has become so generally used that even those who exercise unjust rule rejoice to be called by this title. On the other hand, those who are genuine 'fathers of their household' are concerned for the welfare of all in their households in respect of the worship and service of God, as if they were all their children, longing and praying that they may come to the heavenly home, where it will not be a necessary duty to give orders to men, because it will no longer be a necessary duty to be concerned for the welfare of those who are already in the felicity of that immortal state. But until that home is reached, the fathers have an obligation to exercise the authority of masters greater than the duty of slaves to put up with their condition as servants.

However, if anyone in the household is, through his disobedience, an enemy to the domestic peace, he is reproved by a word, or by a blow, or any other kind of punishment that is just and legitimate, to the extent allowed by human society; but this is for the benefit of the offender, intended to readjust him to the domestic peace from which he had broken away. For just as it is not an act of kindness to help a man, when the effect of the help is to make him lose a greater good, so it is not a blameless act to spare a man, when by so doing you let him fall into a greater sin. Hence the duty of anyone who would be blameless includes not only doing no harm to anyone but also restraining a man from sin or punishing his sin, so that either the man who is chastised may be corrected by his experience, or others may be deterred by his example. Now a man's house ought to be the beginning, or rather a small component part of the city, and every beginning is directed to some end of its own kind, and every component part contributes to the completeness of the whole of which it forms a part. The implication is quite apparent, that domestic peace contributes to the peace of the city – that is, the ordered harmony of those who live together in a house in the matter of giving and obeying orders, contributes to the ordered harmony concerning authority and obedience obtaining among the citizens. Consequently it is fitting that the father of a household should take his rules from the law of the city, and govern his household in such a way that it fits in with the peace of the city.

17. *The origin of peace between the heavenly society and the earthly city, and of discord between them*

But a household of human beings whose life is not based on faith is in pursuit of an earthly peace based on the things belonging to this temporal life, and on its advantages, whereas a household of human beings whose life is based on faith looks forward to the blessings which are promised as eternal in the future, making use of earthly and temporal things like a pilgrim in a foreign land, who does not let himself be taken in by them or distracted from his course towards God, but rather treats them as supports which help him more easily to bear the burdens of 'the corruptible body which weighs heavy on the soul';[42] they must on no account be allowed to increase the load. Thus both kinds of men and both kinds of households alike make use of the things essential for this mortal life; but each has its own very different end in making use of them. So also the earthly city, whose life is not based on faith, aims at an earthly peace, and it limits the harmonious agreement of citizens concerning the giving and obeying of orders to the establishment of a kind of compromise between human wills about the things relevant to mortal life. In contrast, the Heavenly City – or rather that part of it which is on pilgrimage in this condition of mortality, and which lives on the basis of faith – must needs make use of this peace also, until this mortal state, for which this kind of peace is essential, passes away. And therefore, it leads what we may call a life of captivity in this earthly city as in a foreign land, although it has already received the promise of redemption, and the gift of the Spirit as a kind of pledge of it; and yet it does not hesitate to obey the laws of the earthly city by which those things which are designed for the support of this mortal life are regulated; and the purpose of this obedience is that, since this mortal condition is shared by both cities, a harmony may be preserved between them in things that are relevant to this condition.

But this earthly city has had some philosophers belonging to it whose theories are rejected by the teaching inspired by God. Either led astray by their own speculation or deluded by demons, these thinkers reached the belief that there are many gods who must be won over to serve human ends, and also that they have, as it were, different departments with different responsibilities attached. Thus the body is the department of one god, the mind that of another; and within the body itself, one god is in charge of the head, another of the neck and so on

42. Wisd. 9, 15.

with each of the separate members. Similarly, within the mind, one is responsible for natural ability, another for learning, another for anger, another for lust; and in the accessories of life there are separate gods over the departments of flocks, grain, wine, oil, forests, coinage, navigation, war and victory, marriage, birth, fertility, and so on.[43] The Heavenly City, in contrast, knows only one God as the object of worship, and decrees, with faithful devotion, that he only is to be served with that service which the Greeks call *latreia*, which is due to God alone. And the result of this difference has been that the Heavenly City could not have laws of religion common with the earthly city, and in defence of her religious laws she was bound to dissent from those who thought differently and to prove a burdensome nuisance to them. Thus she had to endure their anger and hatred, and the assaults of persecution; until at length that City shattered the morale of her adversaries by the terror inspired by her numbers, and by the help she continually received from God.

While this Heavenly City, therefore, is on pilgrimage in this world, she calls out citizens from all nations and so collects a society of aliens, speaking all languages. She takes no account of any difference in customs, laws, and institutions, by which earthly peace is achieved and preserved – not that she annuls or abolishes any of those, rather, she maintains them and follows them (for whatever divergences there are among the diverse nations, those institutions have one single aim – earthly peace), provided that no hindrance is presented thereby to the religion which teaches that the one supreme and true God is to be worshipped. Thus even the Heavenly City in her pilgrimage here on earth makes use of the earthly peace and defends and seeks the compromise between human wills in respect of the provisions relevant to the mortal nature of man, so far as may be permitted without detriment to true religion and piety. In fact, that City relates the earthly peace to the heavenly peace, which is so truly peaceful that it should be regarded as the only peace deserving the name, at least in respect of the rational creation; for this peace is the perfectly ordered and completely harmonious fellowship in the enjoyment of God, and of each other in God. When we arrive at that state of peace, there will be no longer a life that ends in death, but a life that is life in sure and sober truth; there will be no animal body to 'weigh down the soul' in its process of corruption; there will be a spiritual body with no cravings, a body subdued in every part to the will. This peace the Heavenly City possesses in faith while on its pilgrimage, and it lives a life of

43. cf. Bks IV, VI, VII.

righteousness, based on this faith,[44] having the attainment of that peace in view in every good action it performs in relation to God, and in relation to a neighbour, since the life of a city is inevitably a social life.

18. *The hesitations of the New Academy contrasted with the steadfast certainty of the Christian faith*

As for that characteristic which Varro produces as the distinctive mark of the New Academy,[45] the view that everything is uncertain, the City of God roundly condemns such doubt as being madness. In matters apprehended by the mind and the reason it has most certain knowledge, even if that knowledge is of small extent, on account of the 'corruptible body which weighs down the mind' – as the Apostle says, 'Our knowledge is partial.'[46] It also trusts the evidence of the senses in every matter; for the mind employs the senses through the agency of the body, and anyone who supposes that they can never be trusted is woefully mistaken. It believes also in the holy Scriptures, the old and the new, which we call canonical, whence is derived the faith which is the basis of the just man's life, the faith by which we walk on our way without doubting, in the time of our pilgrimage, in exile from the Lord. So long as this faith is sound and certain we cannot justly be reproached if we have doubts about some matters where neither sense nor reason give clear perception, where we have received no illumination from the canonical Scriptures and where we have not been given information by witnesses whom it would be irrational to distrust.

19. *The dress and behaviour of the Christian people*

It is completely irrelevant to the Heavenly City what dress is worn or what manner of life adopted by each person who follows the faith that is the way to God, provided that these do not conflict with the divine instructions. Hence, when even philosophers become Christians, they are not obliged to alter their mode of dress or their dietary habits, which offer no hindrance to religion. The only change required is in their false teachings. Thus the peculiar behaviour of the Cynics, which Varro treated as a differentia,[47] is to that city a matter of no

44. cf. Hab. 2, 4; Rom. 1, 17 etc.
45. cf. Bk IV, 30n.
46. 1 Cor. 13, 9.
47. cf. ch. 1.

importance at all, if there is nothing indecent or immoderate in that behaviour. As for the three kinds of life, the life of leisure, the life of action, and the combination of the two, anyone, to be sure, might spend his life in any of these ways without detriment to his faith, and might thus attain to the everlasting rewards. What does matter is the answers to those questions: What does a man possess as a result of his love of truth? And what does he pay out in response to the obligations of Christian love? For no one ought to be so leisured as to take no thought in that leisure for the interest of his neighbour, nor so active as to feel no need for the contemplation of God. The attraction of a life of leisure ought not to be the prospect of lazy inactivity, but the chance for the investigation and discovery of truth, on the understanding that each person makes some progress in this, and does not grudgingly withhold his discoveries from another.

In the life of action, on the other hand, what is to be treasured is not a place of honour or power in this life, since 'everything under the sun is vanity'[48] but the task itself that is achieved by means of that place of honour and that power – if that achievement is right and helpful, that is, if it serves to promote the well-being of the common people, for, as we have already argued, this well-being is according to God's intention.[49] That is why the Apostle says, 'Anyone who aspires to the episcopate aspires to an honourable *task*.'[50] He wanted to explain what 'episcopate' means; it is the name of a task, not an honour. It is, in fact, a Greek word, derived from the fact that a man who is put in authority over others 'superintends' them, that is, he has responsibility for them. For the Greek *skopos* means 'intention' (in the sense of 'direction of the attention'); and so we may, if we wish, translate *epi-skopein* as 'super-intend'. Hence a 'bishop' who has set his heart on a position of eminence rather than an opportunity for service should realize that he is no bishop. So then, no one is debarred from devoting himself to the pursuit of truth, for that involves a praiseworthy kind of leisure. But high position, although without it a people cannot be ruled, is not in itself a respectable object of ambition, even if that position be held and exercised in a manner worthy of respect. We see then that it is love of truth that looks for sanctified leisure, while it is the compulsion of love that undertakes righteous engagement in affairs. If this latter burden is not imposed on us, we should employ our freedom from business in the quest for truth and in its contemplation, while if it is laid upon us, it is to be undertaken because of the compulsion of love. Yet even in this case the delight in truth

48. Eccl. 1, 14 etc. 49. cf. ch. 14. 50. 1 Tim. 3, 1.

should not be utterly abandoned, for fear that we should lose this enjoyment and that compulsion should overwhelm us.

20. *The fellow-citizens of the saints are in this life made happy by hope*

We see, then, that the Supreme Good of the City of God is everlasting and perfect peace, which is not the peace through which men pass in their mortality, in their journey from birth to death, but that peace in which they remain in their immortal state, experiencing no adversity at all. In view of this, can anyone deny that this is the supremely blessed life, or that the present life on earth, however full it may be of the greatest possible blessings of soul and body and of external circumstances, is, in comparison, most miserable? For all that, if anyone accepts the present life in such a spirit that he uses it with the end in view of that other life on which he has set his heart with all his ardour and for which he hopes with all his confidence, such a man may without absurdity be called happy even now, though rather by future hope than in present reality. Present reality without that hope is, to be sure, a false happiness, in fact, an utter misery. For the present does not bring into play the true goods of the mind; since no wisdom is true wisdom if it does not direct its attention, in all its prudent decisions, its resolute actions, its self-control and its just dealings with others, towards that ultimate state in which God will be all in all,[51] in the assurance of eternity and the perfection of peace.

21. *Scipio's definition of a commonwealth. Was it ever a reality at Rome?*

This brings me to the place where I must fulfil, as briefly and clearly as I may, the promise I gave in the second book.[52] I there promised that I would show that there never was a Roman commonwealth answering to the definitions advanced by Scipio in Cicero's *On the Republic*. For Scipio gives a brief definition of the state, or commonwealth, as the 'weal of the people'. Now if this is a true definition there never was a Roman commonwealth, because the Roman state was never the 'weal of the people', according to Scipio's definition. For he defined a 'people' as a multitude 'united in association by a common sense of right and a community of interest'. He explains in the discussion what he means by 'a common sense of right', showing that a state cannot be maintained without justice, and where there is

51. 1 Cor. 15, 28. 52. cf. Bk II, 21.

no true justice there can be no right. For any action according to right is inevitably a just action, while no unjust action can possibly be according to right. For unjust human institutions are not to be called or supposed to be institutions of right, since even they themselves say that right is what has flowed from the fount of justice; as for the notion of justice commonly put forward by some misguided thinkers, that it is 'the interest of the strongest',[53] they hold this to be a false conception.

Therefore, where there is no true justice there can be no 'association of men united by a common sense of right', and therefore no people answering to the definition of Scipio, or Cicero. And if there is no people then there is no 'weal of the people', but some kind of a mob, not deserving the name of a people. If, therefore, a commonwealth is the 'weal of the people', and if a people does not exist where there is no 'association by a common sense of right', and there is no right where there is no justice, the irresistible conclusion is that where there is no justice there is no commonwealth. Moreover, justice is that virtue which assigns to everyone his due.[54] Then what kind of justice is it that takes a man away from the true God and subjects him to unclean demons? Is this to assign to every man his due? Or are we to say that a man is unjust when he takes an estate from a man who has bought it and hands it over to someone who has no right to it, while we give the name of just to a man who takes himself away from the Lord God who made him, and becomes the servant of malignant spirits?

There is, to be sure, in the same work, *On the Republic*, a most vigorous and powerful argument on behalf of justice against injustice. Earlier in the discussion a plea was put forward for injustice against justice, and it was alleged that a state cannot stand or be governed except by injustice, and it was posited as the strongest point in this case that it was unjust that men should be servants to other men as their masters; and yet an imperial city, the head of a great commonwealth, cannot rule its provinces except by adopting this injustice. Now it was urged in reply on the side of justice, that this situation is just, on the ground that servitude is in the interest of such men as the provincials, and that it is established for their benefit, when rightly established – that is, when unprincipled men are deprived of the freedom to do wrong with impunity. It was also asserted that the subjugated will be better off, because they were worse off before

53. cf. the argument of Thrasymachus in Plat. *Rp.* 339A–341A.
54. Aristotle's 'distributive justice' (*Eth. Nic.*, 5, 5, 2).

subjugation. In confirmation of this line of reasoning a notable illustration was adduced, ostensibly taken from nature. It was stated thus: 'How is it then that God rules man, the soul rules the body, the reason rules lust and the other perverted elements in the soul?' By this analogy it is shown plainly enough that servitude is beneficial for some men, and that servitude to God, at least, is beneficial to all.

Now in serving God the soul rightly commands the body, and in the soul itself the reason which is subject to its Lord God rightly commands the lusts and the other perverted elements. That being so, when a man does not serve God, what amount of justice are we to suppose to exist in his being? For if a soul does not serve God it cannot with any kind of justice command the body, nor can a man's reason control the vicious elements in the soul. And if there is no justice in such a man, there can be no sort of doubt that there is no justice in a gathering which consists of such men. Here, then, there is not that 'consent to the law' which makes a mob into a people, and it is 'the weal of the people' that is said to make a 'commonwealth'. As for the 'community of interest' in virtue of which, according to our definition, a gathering of men is called a 'people', is there any need for me to talk about this? Although, to be sure, if you give the matter careful thought, there are no advantages for men who live ungodly lives, the lives of all those who do not serve God, but serve demons – demons all the more blasphemous in that they desire that sacrifice be offered to them as to gods, though in fact they are most unclean spirits. However, I consider that what I have said about 'a common sense of right' is enough to make it apparent that by this definition people amongst whom there is no justice can never be said to have a commonwealth.

Now if it is said that the Romans in their commonwealth did not serve unclean spirits but good and holy gods, do we have to repeat, time and time again, the same things that we have already said often enough – in fact, more than often enough? Surely no one who has read the earlier books of this work and has reached this point can doubt that the Romans served evil and impure demons? If he can, he is either excessively dense, or unscrupulously argumentative! But, to say no more of the character of the gods the Romans worshipped with sacrifice, it is written in the Law of the true God, 'Anyone who sacrifices to gods instead of to the Lord only, will be extirpated.'[55] This shows that sacrifice to gods, whether good or bad, was against the will of him who uttered this command with so heavy a threat.

55. Exod. 22, 20.

22. *The true God, to whom alone sacrifice is due*

But it may be asked in reply, 'Who is this God you talk of, and how is it proved that he is the only one to whom the Romans owed obedience, and that they should have worshipped no god besides him?' It shows extreme blindness to ask, at this time of day, who this God is! He is the same God whose prophets foretold the events we now see happening. He is the God from whom Abraham received the message, 'In your descendants all nations will be blessed.'[56] And this promise was fulfilled in Christ, who sprang from that line by physical descent, as is acknowledged, willy nilly, even by those who have remained hostile to this name. He is the same God whose divine Spirit spoke through the lips of the men whose prophecies I have quoted in my previous books, prophecies fulfilled in the Church which we see diffused throughout the whole world. He is the God whom Varro, the greatest of Roman scholars, identifies with Jupiter; although he did not realize what he was saying. Still, I thought this worth mentioning, simply because a man of such great learning could not judge this God to be non-existent or of no worth, since he believed him to be identical with his supreme god. More important still, he is the god whom Porphyry,[57] the most learned of philosophers, although the fiercest enemy of the Christians, acknowledges to be a great god, even on the evidence of the oracles of those whom he supposes to be gods.

23. *Porphyry on the oracles about Christ given by the gods*

For Porphyry produced a book entitled *Philosophy from Oracles*,[58] a description and compilation of responses, ostensibly divine, on matters of philosophical interest, in which he says (to quote his own words, translated from the Greek), 'The following reply, in verse, was given by Apollo to one who asked what god he should propitiate in order to recall his wife from Christianity.' Then follow these words, purporting to be the utterance of Apollo:

> You might perhaps find it easier to write on water in printed characters, or fly like a bird through the air spreading light wings to the breeze, than recall to her senses an impious, polluted wife. Let her go as she pleases, persisting in her vain delusions, singing in lamentation for a god who died

56. Gen. 22, 18. 57. cf. Bk VII, 25n.

58. Extensive fragments of this work remain (J. O'Meara, *Porphyry's Philosophy from Oracles*, 1959).

in delusions, who was condemned by right-thinking judges, and killed in hideous fashion by the worst of deaths, a death bound with iron.

Then after those verses of Apollo (here given in a prose translation), Porphyry goes on to say, 'In these verses Apollo made plain the incurability of the belief of Christians, saying that the Jews uphold God more than the Christians.' See how he denigrates Christ in preferring the Jews to the Christians, when he proclaims that the Jews are upholders of God, for he expounds the verses of Apollo, where he says that Christ was slain by right-thinking judges, as if it meant that the Jews passed a just judgement and Christ deserved his punishment. What the lying prophet of Apollo said, and Porphyry believed, or what Porphyry perhaps falsely invented as the utterance of the prophet, is their affair. We shall see later how far Porphyry is consistent with himself, or rather how far he makes those oracles of his agree with one another.

Here, at any rate, he says that the Jews, as upholders of God's rights, passed a just judgement on Christ, in decreeing that he was to be tortured by the worst of deaths. And since Porphyry bears this testimony to the God of the Jews, he ought to have listened to that God when he says, 'Anyone who sacrifices to other gods, instead of to the Lord alone, will be extirpated.' However, let us come to more obvious matters, and hear Porphyry's statement about the greatness of the God of the Jews. For example, in answer to his question, 'Which is better, word (that is, reason) or law?' Apollo, says Porphyry, 'replied in these verses'. Porphyry goes on to quote the verses, from which I select the following, as sufficient: 'in God, the begetter and the king before all things, at whom heaven trembles, and earth and sea and the hidden depths of the underworld and the very divinities shudder in dread; their law is the Father whom the holy Hebrews greatly honour.'[59] In this oracle of his own god Apollo, Porphyry speaks of the God of the Hebrews as so great that the divinities themselves shudder in dread at him. Since, then, this is the God who has said, 'Anyone who sacrifices to other gods will be extirpated', it surprises me that Porphyry himself did not shudder in terror of being rooted out for offering sacrifice to other gods.

Now this philosopher has also some good things to say about Christ, when he appears to have forgotten that insult we have just spoken of, or when it seems as if the malicious remarks his gods had made were uttered in their sleep, while in their waking moments they

59. Lactantius quotes part of this oracle in Greek (*De Ira Dei*, 2, 312).

recognized his goodness and praised him as he deserved. Porphyry, in fact, says, with the air of one on the point of producing some amazing and incredible intelligence, 'What I am going to say may certainly appear startling to some. I mean the fact that the gods have pronounced Christ to have been extremely devout, and have said that he has become immortal, and that they mention him in terms of commendation; whereas the Christians, by their account, are polluted and contaminated and entangled in error; and there are many other such slanders they issue against them.' Then he proceeds to quote some of these supposed slanders of the gods against the Christians, and continues, 'On the other hand, to those who asked whether Christ was God, Hecate replied, "You know that the immortal soul goes on its way after it leaves the body; whereas when it is cut off from wisdom it wanders for ever. That soul belongs to a man of outstanding piety; this they worship because truth is a stranger to them." '[60] Then, after quoting this supposed oracle he adds his own interpretation:

Thus Hecate said that he was a most devout man, and that his soul, like the souls of the other devout men, was endowed after death with the immortality it deserved; and that Christians in their ignorance worship this soul. Moreover, to those who asked: 'Why, then was he condemned?' the goddess gave this oracular reply: 'The body, indeed, is always liable to torments that sap its strength; but the souls of the pious dwell in a heavenly abode. Now that soul of which we speak gave a fatal gift to other souls, those to whom the fates did not grant that they should possess the gifts of the gods or that they should have knowledge of immortal Jupiter; that fatal gift is entanglement in error. That is why they were hated by the gods, because, not being fated to know God or to receive gifts from the gods, they were given by this man the fatal gift of entanglement in error. For all that, he himself was devout, and, like other devout men, passed into heaven. And so you shall not slander him, but pity the insanity of men. From him comes for them a ready peril of headlong disaster.'

Is anyone so dense as to fail to realize that these oracles were either the inventions of a cunning man, a bitter enemy of the Christians, or the responses of demons devised with a like intent? For, surely, their purpose in praising Christ was to ensure that their vituperation of Christians would be accepted as truthful, so that, if possible, they might cut off the way of everlasting salvation, the way by which men and women become Christians. They feel, no doubt, that it is no hindrance to their ingenious and protean maleficence if they are believed when they praise Christ, provided that their vituperation of the Christians is also believed. Their intention is that when a man has

60. Part of the Greek is quoted in Euseb., *Dem. Ev.*, 3, 6.

believed both praise and slander they may turn him into an admirer of Christ, but an admirer who has no wish to become a Christian; and so Christ, though praised by him, will not set him free from the domination of those demons. And this is particularly true because they praise Christ in such terms that anyone who believes in the kind of Christ they proclaim does not become a genuine Christian but a Photinian heretic,[61] one who acknowledges Christ only as a man, not as God also. That is why such a man cannot be saved by him, and cannot escape or undo the snares of those lying demons.

We, on our side, can approve neither Apollo's vituperation of Christ nor Hecate's praise of him. Apollo, we remember, would have it believed that Christ was an unrighteous man, put to death, he says, by right-thinking judges; Hecate, that he was a man of supreme piety, but only a man. However, the aim of both is the same, to make men refuse to become Christians; for unless they become Christians they cannot be rescued from the power of those false gods. But our philosopher, or rather all those who believe such purported oracles against the Christians, must first, if they can, succeed in harmonizing Hecate and Apollo on the subject of Christ, so that they unite in either his condemnation or his praise. Yet even if they succeeded in this, we should none the less give a wide berth to such delusive demons, whether slanderers of Christ or admirers. And since, in fact, their god and their goddess are in disagreement, and he slanders Christ while she praises him, then surely men in general do not believe them when they vituperate the Christians, if their own thinking is sound.

Now when Porphyry – or Hecate – praises Christ, while adding that he himself gave to the Christians the fatal gift of entanglement in error, he does at the same time reveal, as he supposes, the causes of his error. But before I explain those causes in his own words, I ask first: If Christ gave this fatal gift of entanglement in error, did he do this voluntarily or involuntarily? If voluntarily, how could he be righteous? If involuntarily, how could he be blessed? But now let us listen to the causes of the error. 'There are in a certain part of the world', he says,

very small earthly spirits, subject to the authority of evil demons. The wise men of the Hebrews (and this Jesus was also one of them, as you have heard from the oracles of Apollo, quoted above) warned religious men against these evil demons and lesser spirits, and forbade them to pay

61. Photinus, bishop of Sirmium, deposed 351. He seems to have taught a kind of Sabellianism. The Photinians, his followers, were condemned at the Council of Constantinople, 381.

attention to them, telling their hearers rather to venerate the gods of heaven, but, above all, to worship God the Father. But this is what the gods also teach; and we have shown above how they advise us to turn our thoughts to God, and everywhere bid us worship him. Uninstructed and ungodly natures, however, to which fate has not granted the gifts of the gods and the knowledge of immortal Jupiter, have not listened to the gods and to inspired men; and so they have rejected all the gods, while so far from hating the forbidden demons, they offer them reverence. While pretending to worship God, they do not perform those acts by which alone God is adored. For God, as being the father of all, has indeed no lack of anything; but it is well for us when we adore him by means of justice, chastity, and other virtues, making our life itself a prayer to him by imitating him and seeking to know him. For seeking to know him purifies us, while imitation of him deifies us by bringing our disposition in line with his.

Porphyry certainly did well in thus proclaiming God the Father, and in telling of the conduct by which he is to be worshipped; and the prophetic books of the Hebrews are full of such precepts, when the life of holiness is commanded or praised. But in respect of the Christians, Porphyry's mistakes, or his calumnies, are as great as the demons (his supposed gods) could desire. He seems to assume that anyone would have difficulty in recalling the obscenities and indecencies which were performed in the theatre as acts of homage to the gods, and in observing what is read and said and heard in our churches, or what is offered to the true God, and in realizing, from this comparison, where the building up of moral character is to be found, and where its ruin. Who told him or suggested to him such a groundless and obvious lie as that the Christians revere, instead of hating, the demons whose worship was forbidden to the Hebrews? It could only have been a diabolic spirit. For in fact the God whom the wise men of the Hebrews worshipped forbids sacrifices to be offered even to the holy angels and the powers of God, those angels and powers whom we venerate and love, in this mortal pilgrimage of ours, as our completely blessed fellow citizens. He forbids this in a voice of thunder in his Law, which he gave to his Hebrew people, when he said, in words heavy with menace, 'Anyone who sacrifices to other gods will be extirpated.'[62] Now it might be supposed that this precept forbids sacrifice to those most evil demons and the earthly spirits, which Porphyry calls 'least' or 'lesser'; for even these are called 'gods' in the sacred Scriptures – of the Gentiles, that is, not in those of the Hebrews. This is made quite clear by the seventy translators in one of the psalms, where they say, 'For all

62. Exod. 22, 20.

the gods of the nations are demons.'[63] But to prevent any such supposition that sacrifice, while forbidden to those demons, was allowed to all or some of the heavenly beings, these words immediately follow: 'instead of the Lord alone', that is, 'to the Lord alone'. I say this in case anyone imagines that the words 'to the Lord alone', *Domino soli*, means 'our Lord *the sun*', to whom sacrifice is to be offered. That this is not the meaning can easily be discovered by a reference to the Greek version.

The God of the Hebrews, then, to whom this eminent philosopher gives such impressive testimony, gave to his Hebrew people the Law, written in Hebrew, a Law not obscure and unknown, but by now of wide renown among all nations. And in this Law it is written: 'Anyone who sacrifices to other gods, instead of to the Lord only, will be extirpated.' What need is there for a detailed inquiry on this subject into his Law and into his prophets? Why, the need is not for an inquiry, for the relevant passages are not hard to find or rare; all that is required is the collection and insertion in this discussion of mine of the obvious and frequent passages in which it is made as clear as daylight that the true and supreme God willed that sacrifice should be offered to no other being whatsoever, but to himself alone. Here is one statement, brief, yet certainly impressive, menacing, in fact, but with truth in the menace – a statement of the God whom the most learned of the pagans proclaims in such remarkable terms. It is a warning that must be heard, feared, and acted on, lest the disobedient be rooted out in consequence. 'Anyone who sacrifices to other gods', he says 'instead of to the Lord alone, will be extirpated.' This is not because God stands in need of anything, but because it is to our advantage to belong to him. For it is to him that the psalmist sings, in the holy Scriptures of the Hebrews, 'I have said to the Lord: "You are my God, because you have no need of my goods."'[64]

And yet it is we ourselves – we, his City – who are his best, his most glorious sacrifice. The mystic symbol of this sacrifice we celebrate in our oblations, familiar to the faithful, as we have maintained in previous books.[65] For the sacrificial victims offered by the Jews, as a foreshadowing of what was to come, were destined to come to an end. This was declared by divine oracles through the lips of the holy prophets, in resounding tones, saying that the nations from the furthest East to the furthest West would offer one sacrifice, as we now see happening. I have extracted as many of those oracles as seemed sufficient,

63. Ps. 96, 5, in the LXX.
64. Ps. 16, 2.
65. cf. esp. Bk X, 5; 6; 20.

and have already scattered them throughout this work. It follows that justice is found where God, the one supreme God, rules an obedient City according to his grace, forbidding sacrifice to any being save himself alone; and where in consequence the soul rules the body in all men who belong to this City and obey God, and the reason faithfully rules the vices in a lawful system of subordination; so that just as the individual righteous man lives on the basis of faith[66] which is active in love,[67] so the association, or people, of righteous men lives on the same basis of faith, active in love, the love with which a man loves God as God ought to be loved, and loves his neighbour as himself. But where this justice does not exist, there is certainly no 'association of men united by a common sense of right and by a community of interest'. Therefore there is no commonwealth; for where there is no 'people', there is no 'weal of the people'.

24. *An alternative definition of 'people' and 'commonwealth'*

If, on the other hand, another definition than this is found for a 'people', for example, if one should say, 'A people is the association of a multitude of rational beings united by a common agreement on the objects of their love', then it follows that to observe the character of a particular people we must examine the objects of its love. And yet, whatever those objects, if it is the association of a multitude not of animals but of rational beings, and is united by a common agreement about the objects of its love, then there is no absurdity in applying to it the title of a 'people'. And, obviously, the better the objects of this agreement, the better the people; the worse the objects of this love, the worse the people. By this definition of ours, the Roman people is a people and its estate is indubitably a commonwealth. But as for the objects of that people's love – both in the earliest times and in subsequent periods – and the morality of that people as it proceeded to bloody strife of parties and then to the social and civil wars, and corrupted and disrupted that very unity which is, as it were, the health of a people – for all this we have the witness of history; and I have had a great deal to say about it in my preceding books. And yet I shall not make that a reason for asserting that a people is not really a people or that a state is not a commonwealth, so long as there remains an association of some kind or other between a multitude of rational beings united by a common agreement on the objects of its love. How-

66. Hab. 2, 4 etc. 67. Gal. 5, 6.

ever, what I have said about the Roman people and the Roman commonwealth I must be understood to have said and felt about those of the Athenians and of any other Greeks, or of that former Babylon of the Assyrians, when they exercised imperial rule, whether on a small or a large scale, in their commonwealths – and indeed about any other nation whatsoever. For God is not the ruler of the city of the impious, because it disobeys his commandment that sacrifice should be offered to himself alone. The purpose of this law was that in that city the soul should rule over the body and reason over the vicious elements, in righteousness and faith. And because God does not rule there the general characteristic of that city is that it is devoid of true justice.

25. *True virtues impossible without true religion*

The fact is that the soul may appear to rule the body and the reason to govern the vicious elements in the most praiseworthy fashion; and yet if the soul and reason do not serve God as God himself has commanded that he should be served, then they do not in any way exercise the right kind of rule over the body and the vicious propensities. For what kind of a mistress over the body and the vices can a mind be that is ignorant of the true God and is not subjected to his rule, but instead is prostituted to the corrupting influence of vicious demons? Thus the virtues which the mind imagines it possesses, by means of which it rules the body and the vicious elements, are themselves vices rather than virtues, if the mind does not bring them into relation with God in order to achieve anything whatsoever and to maintain that achievement. For although the virtues are reckoned by some people to be genuine and honourable when they are related only to themselves and are sought for no other end, even then they are puffed up and proud, and so are to be accounted vices rather than virtues. For just as it is not something derived from the physical body itself that gives life to that body, but something above it, so it is not something that comes from man, but something above man, that makes his life blessed; and this is true not only of man but of every heavenly dominion and power whatsoever.

26. *The peace of the people alienated from God is made use of by God's People on their pilgrimage*

Thus, as the soul is the life of the physical body, so God is the blessedness of man's life. As the holy Scriptures of the Hebrews say,

'Blessed is the people, whose God is the Lord.'[68] It follows that a people alienated from that God must be wretched. Yet even such a people loves a peace of its own, which is not to be rejected; but it will not possess it in the end, because it does not make good use of it before the end. Meanwhile, however, it is important for us also that this people should possess this peace in this life, since so long as the two cities are intermingled we also make use of the peace of Babylon – although the People of God is by faith set free from Babylon, so that in the meantime they are only pilgrims in the midst of her. That is why the Apostle instructs the Church to pray for kings of that city and those in high positions, adding these words: 'that we may lead a quiet and peaceful life with all devotion and love'.[69] And when the prophet Jeremiah predicted to the ancient People of God the coming captivity, and bade them, by God's inspiration, to go obediently to Babylon, serving God even by their patient endurance, he added his own advice that prayers should be offered for Babylon, 'because in her peace is your peace'[70] – meaning, of course, the temporal peace of the meantime, which is shared by good and bad alike.

27. *The peace of God's servants, a perfect tranquillity, not experienced in this life*

In contrast, the peace which is our special possession is ours even in this life, a peace with God through faith; and it will be ours for ever, a peace with God through open vision.[71] But peace here and now, whether the peace shared by all men or our own special possession, is such that it affords a solace for our wretchedness rather than the joy of blessedness. Our righteousness itself, too, though genuine, in virtue of the genuine Ultimate Good to which it is referred, is nevertheless only such as to consist in the forgiveness of sins rather than in the perfection of virtues. The evidence for this is in the prayer of the whole City of God on pilgrimage in the world, which, as we know, cries out to God through the lips of all its members: 'Forgive us our debts, as we forgive our debtors.'[72] And this prayer is not effective for those whose 'faith, without works, is dead'[73] but only for those whose 'faith is put into action through love'.[74] For such a prayer is needed by righteous men because the reason, though subjected to God, does not

68. Ps. 144, 15.
69. 1 Tim. 2, 2.
70. Jer. 29, 7.
71. cf. 2 Cor. 5, 7.
72. Matt. 6, 12.
73. Jas. 2, 17.
74. Gal. 5, 6.

have complete command over the vices in this mortal state and in the 'corruptible body which weighs heavy on the soul'.[75] In fact, even though command be exercised over the vices it is assuredly not by any means without a conflict. And even when a man fights well and even gains the mastery by conquering and subduing such foes, still in this situation of weakness something is all too likely to creep in to cause sin, if not in hasty action, at least in a casual remark or a fleeting thought.

For this reason there is no perfect peace so long as command is exercised over the vicious propensities, because the battle is fraught with peril while those vices that resist are being reduced to submission, while those which have been overcome are not yet triumphed over in peaceful security, but are repressed under a rule still troubled by anxieties. Thus we are in the midst of these temptations, about which we find this brief saying amongst the divine oracles: 'Is a man's life on earth anything but temptation?';[76] and who can presume that his life is of such a kind that he has no need to say to God, 'Forgive us our debts', unless he is a man of overwhelming conceit, not a truly great man, but one puffed up and swollen with pride, who is with justice resisted by him who gives grace to the humble, as it says in the Scriptures, 'God resists the proud, but he gives his favour to the humble.'[77] In this life, therefore, justice in each individual exists when God rules and man obeys, when the mind rules the body and reason governs the vices even when they rebel, either by subduing them or by resisting them, while from God himself favour is sought for good deeds and pardon for offences, and thanks are duly offered to him for benefits received. But in that ultimate peace, to which this justice should be related, and for the attainment of which this justice is to be maintained, our nature will be healed by immortality and incorruption and will have no perverted elements, and nothing at all, in ourselves or any other, will be in conflict with any one of us. And so reason will not need to rule the vices, since there will be no vices, but God will hold sway over man, and the soul over the body, and in this state our delight and facility in obeying will be matched by our felicity in living and reigning. There, for each and every one, this state will be eternal, and its eternity will be assured; and for that reason the peace of this blessedness, or the blessedness of this peace, will be the Supreme Good.

75. Wisd. 9, 15. 76. Job 7, 1; cf. ch. 8n. 77. Jas. 4, 6; 1 Pet. 5, 5.

28. *The end of the wicked*

In contrast with this, however, the wretchedness of those who do not belong to this City of God will be everlasting. This is called also 'the second death', because the soul cannot be said to be alive in that state, when it is separated from the life of God, nor can the body, when it is subjected to eternal torments. And this is precisely the reason why this 'second death' will be harder to bear, because it cannot come to an end in death. But here a question arises; for just as wretchedness is the opposite of blessedness, and death of life, so war is evidently the opposite of peace. And the question is rightly asked: What war, or what kind of war, can be understood to exist in the final state of the wicked, corresponding, by way of contrast, to that peace which is proclaimed with joyful praises in the final state of the good? Now anyone who puts this question should observe what it is that is harmful and destructive in war; and he will see that it is precisely the mutual opposition and conflict of the forces engaged. What war, then, can be imagined more serious and more bitter than a struggle in which the will is so at odds with the feelings and the feelings with the will, that their hostility cannot be ended by the victory of either – a struggle in which the violence of pain is in such conflict with the nature of the body that neither can yield to the other? For in this life, when such a conflict occurs, either pain wins, and death takes away feeling, or nature conquers, and health removes the pain. But in that other life, pain continues to torment, while nature lasts to feel the pain. Neither ceases to exist, lest the punishment also should cease.

These, then, are the final states of good and evil. The first we should seek to attain, the latter we should strive to escape. And since it is through a judgement that the good will pass to the one, and the evil to the other, it is of this judgement that I shall deal, as far as God grants, in the book which follows.

BOOK XX

1. *God judges at all times; but the subject of this book is the last judgement*

I AM going to speak about the day of God's final judgement, as far as he will grant me, and to assert it in the face of the irreligious and the unbelieving; and I must start by laying down as, so to speak, the foundation of the building, the evidence of inspired Scripture. Those who refuse to believe that evidence attempt to contravert it with false and fallacious quibbles of human ingenuity, designed either to establish that what is proffered as evidence from the holy Scriptures has some different meaning or to deny altogether that it is divinely inspired. For I am of the opinion that no man on earth who understands these statements as they were uttered and believes that they were spoken by the supreme and true God through the mouths of holy souls, can fail to yield his assent to them, whether he openly acknowledges this or, because of some fault, is embarrassed and afraid to do so, or even, with an obstinacy closely akin to madness, makes every effort to defend with the utmost energy what he knows or believes to be false against what he knows or believes to be true.

Now it is a belief held by the whole Church of the true God, in private confession and also in public profession, that Christ is to come from heaven to judge both the living and the dead, and this is what we call the Last Day, the day of divine judgement – that is, the last period of time; for it is not certain for how many days this judgement will extend. But no one who reads the holy Scriptures, however inattentively, is unaware that it is the normal use of those documents to use the word 'day' for 'time'. Now when talking of the day of God's judgement, we add the word 'last' or 'final'; the reason is that God is even now judging, and he has been judging from the beginning of the human race, when he expelled the first human beings from paradise and barred them from the tree of life as perpetrators of a great sin. Yes, and even before that he undoubtedly gave judgement when he 'did not spare the angels who sinned',[1] the chief of whom, the author

1. cf. 2 Pet. 2, 4.

of his own ruin, ruined man in his envy. And it is by God's deep and just judgement[2] that the life of demons in the air of our sky and the life of men on this earth is most miserable, being full of errors and anxieties. But even if no one had sinned, it could only have been by his good and right judgement that he would have maintained in eternal blessedness the whole rational creation, as with perfect constancy it held fast to him as its Lord.

Moreover, not only does he give an all-embracing judgement on the race of demons and on the human race, condemning them to misery as the deserved retribution for the first sins of the race; he also judges the particular actions of individuals performed by the decision of their will. For the demons beg that they may not suffer torment;[3] and it is certainly not without justice that they are spared or tormented according to their particular degree of wickedness. Men also are punished by God for their deeds, often openly, always secretly, either in this life or after death, although no human being acts rightly unless he is supported by divine help, and no demon or man acts wickedly unless he is permitted by the same divine and completely just judgement. For, as the Apostle says, 'There is no injustice in God';[4] and, as he says in another place, 'His judgements are inscrutable, and his ways untraceable.'[5]

Now in this book I shall discuss, as far as God gives me power, not those first judgements, nor those judgements in the meantime, but the last judgement itself, when Christ is to come from heaven to judge the living and the dead. For that day is obviously now called the Day of Judgement in a special sense, in that no room will be left on that day for the ignorant complaint that asks why this unjust man is happy and that just man unhappy. It will then be made clear that true and complete happiness belongs to all the good, and only to them, while all the wicked, and only the wicked, are destined for deserved and supreme unhappiness.

2. *The diversity of human fortunes. God's judgement not absent, but untraceable*

In our present situation, however, we are learning to bear with equanimity the ills that even good men suffer, and at the same time not to set much store by the good things which the wicked also acquire. In this way there is salutary instruction from God, even in situations

2. cf. Bk VIII, 14.
3. cf. Matt. 8, 29.
4. Rom. 9, 4.
5. Rom. 11, 33.

where God's justice is not apparent. For we do not know by what decision of God this good man is poor, while that wicked man is rich; why this man is cheerful, though, in our opinion, his desperate moral character makes him deserve the tortures of grief, while that man, whose exemplary life convinces us that he deserves to be cheerful, is full of sorrow; why an innocent man leaves the court not merely unavenged but actually condemned, either overcome by the injustice of the judge, or overwhelmed by false evidence, while, in contrast, his criminal adversary gloats over him, as he goes away not only unpunished but even vindicated; why the impious man is hale and hearty, while the devout man pines away in weakness; why young men practise highway-robbery, and enjoy excellent health, while infants who could not have hurt anyone, even by word, are afflicted by all manner of cruel diseases; a useful member of society is snatched off by an untimely death, while one who, as it seems to us, ought never to have been born lives on long beyond the normal span; one whose record is full of crimes is exalted to high position, while another who is beyond reproach is hidden in the shadows of obscurity. Who could list or enumerate all the other examples of this kind?

Now if such cases exhibited some consistency in their very irrationality, as we may call it, if, that is, in this life (in which as the sacred psalm says, 'man is like a mere nothing, and his days pass by like a shadow'[6]) only the wicked obtained the transitory goods of this world, and only the good suffered the transitory ills, this situation could be ascribed to the just, or even the benevolent, judgement of God. Thus those who were not to attain the eternal blessings which bring true happiness would be either deluded by temporal benefits in return for their wickedness or else, by God's mercy, would be consoled by them, while those who were not to suffer eternal torments would be either afflicted by temporal ills in retribution for whatever sins, however small, they had committed, or would be trained by them to bring their virtue to perfection. But in fact, though there are good men in adversity and bad men in prosperity, which seems unjust, it remains true that, in general, bad men come to a bad end, and good men enjoy eventual success. And so the judgements of God become the more inscrutable and his ways the more untraceable.[7]

Thus we do not know by what judgement God causes these situations, or else allows them to happen; for in him there is the highest power, the highest wisdom, the highest justice, and in him there is no weakness, no unreason, no injustice. For all that, it is salutary for us to

6. Ps. 144, 4. 7. cf. Rom. 11, 33.

learn not to set great store by those things, whether good or bad, which, as we see, are common to good men and evil alike; but to seek instead those good things which are the special possession of good men, and to shun with particular care the bad things which are the distinctive property of evil men. However, when we reach that judgement of God, the time of which is in a special sense called the Day of Judgement and sometimes the Day of the Lord, then it will become plain that God's judgements are perfectly just, not only all the judgements that will then be passed, but also all the judgements passed from the beginning, and all which are to be pronounced hereafter until that judgement day. At that day too, it will become evident by what just decision of God it comes about that at this present time so many, in fact almost all, of the just judgements of God are hidden from mortal perception and understanding. However, in this matter one thing is not hidden from the faith of the devout; and that is, that what is hidden is just.

3. *Solomon on the things shared, in this life, by good and bad*

Solomon, as is well known, was the wisest king of Israel. He reigned in Jerusalem; and his book called Ecclesiastes is included by the Jews in their canon of holy Scripture. It begins with these words: ' "Vanity of vanities", the preacher said, "vanity of vanities.[8] All is vanity. What profit does a man gain for all his labour, all his toil under the sun?" ' This is the text to which he attaches the rest of his discourse, reminding us of the anxieties and errors of this life, while the passing seasons come and vanish away, this life in which there is nothing solid and stable which is retained in our possession; and in this vanity of all things under the sun he especially deplores the fact that, although wisdom excels folly as abundantly as light excels darkness, and the wise man has eyes in his head while the fool walks in darkness, nevertheless the same lot befalls all alike (meaning, of course, in this life spent 'under the sun'); and he evidently refers to those evils which, as we observe, are the common portion of good men and bad men. He also remarks that good men suffer evils, as if they themselves were evil, and evil men acquire good things, as if they themselves were good. He says, 'There is a vanity which is found on earth; the fact that there are righteous men who receive the treatment due to the ungodly;

8. cf. Eccl. 2, 13f. 'Vanity' means 'emptiness', 'futility', 'nonsense'. It seems best, failing a word to convey these shades of meaning, to retain the familiar translation.

and there are ungodly men who receive the treatment merited by the righteous. This also, I say, is vanity.'[9]

This wisest of men devoted the whole of this book to pointing out this vanity, obviously with the sole intention that we should long for that life which is not made up of vanity under this sun, but of verity under the sun's creator. Now, in this state of vanity, is it anything but a just judgement of God that man, having become like this vanity, this nothingness, should himself vanish into it? However, in the days of his vanity what matters most is whether a man resists the truth or obeys it, whether he has no part in true religion or participates in it; and this is important not in view of the acquisition of the good things of this life, or the avoidance of evils that pass away into nothingness, but in view of the future judgement, as a result of which the good will have good things and the evil will have evil things which will endure for ever. Our wise author sums it all up when he ends his book with these words: 'Fear God, and keep his commandments, because this is the whole man; for God will bring up for judgement every action in this world, wherever any has been disregarded, whether good or evil.'[10] Could he have made any statement shorter, truer, more salutary than this? 'Fear God', he says, 'and keep his commandments, because this is the whole man.' For anyone who really is anything is assuredly this – a keeper, I mean, of God's commandments – since anyone who is not this is nothing, because he remains in the likeness of vanity, which is nothingness; he is not remade in the likeness of verity, or reality. 'For every action in this world' – whatever a man does in his life here – 'whether good or evil, God will bring up for judgement, wherever any has been disregarded', that is, wherever a man in this life is seen as contemptible, and therefore is not, in fact, seen. God sees even him, and does not disregard him, nor pass him over when he pronounces judgement.

4. *Testimonies to the last judgement are to be adduced, first from the* New *Testament, then from the Old*

My intention is to produce proofs of this last judgement of God from holy Scripture, and those are to be chosen first from the books of the New Testament, afterwards from the Old. For although the Old Testament is prior in time, the New Testament is to be put before the Old in order of importance, since the Old Testament is the herald of the New. The New Testament, therefore, will be quoted first, and then the

9. Eccl. 8, 14. 10. Eccl. 12, 13f (LXX).

Old will be brought in to confirm its evidence. The Old Testament contains the Law and the Prophets, while the New has the Gospel and the apostolic writings. Now the Apostle says, 'Through the Law comes the consciousness of sin. But now God's justice has been revealed, independently of the Law, the justice to which the Law and the Prophets bear witness, the righteousness of God, through faith in Jesus Christ, for all who believe.'[11] This righteousness of God belongs to the New Testament, and it has the testimony of the old books, that is, of the Law and the Prophets. First, then, the case must be presented, and afterwards the witness must be brought in. That this order is to be observed is shown us by Jesus Christ himself, when he says, 'The scribe who is instructed in the kingdom of God is like a householder who brings out of his store-room things new and old.'[12] He did not say 'old and new', which he obviously would have said had he not preferred to observe the order of value rather than the order of time.

5. Statements of the Lord and Saviour about God's judgement at the end of the world

Thus, in rebuking the cities which had not believed although he had performed works of power in them, the Saviour himself says, 'But I tell you, it will be an easier time for Tyre and Sidon in the day of judgement, than for you.'[13] And a little later, addressing another city: 'Mark my words, it will be an easier time for the land of Sodom on the day of judgement, than for you.'[14] Here he is most explicitly predicting that a day of judgement is to come. And he says in another passage:

> The men of Nineveh will rise up in the judgement with this generation, and they will condemn it; because they repented at the preaching of Jonah, and look, something more than Jonah is here. The Queen of the South will rise up in the judgement with this generation, and will condemn it; because she came from the ends of the earth to hear Solomon's wisdom, and look, something more than Solomon is here.[15]

In this passage we learn two things: that there is a judgement to come; and that it will coincide with the resurrection of the dead. For when he said this about the men of Nineveh and about the Queen of the South, he was undoubtedly speaking about the dead; and yet he said that they would 'rise up' at the day of judgement. And in saying 'they

11. Rom. 3, 20ff. 12. Matt. 13, 52. 13. Matt. 11, 22.
14. Matt. 11, 24. 15. Matt. 12, 41f.

will condemn' he did not mean that they themselves would pass judgement; he means that the comparison of others with them would lead to the merited condemnation of the others.

Again, in another context, when speaking about the present intermixture of good men and wicked, and their subsequent separation (which will, of course, happen at the day of judgement) he brought in the comparison of the wheat sown and the tares sown later. This he explains to his disciples as follows:

> The sower of the good seed is the Son of Man; the field is the world; the good seed stands for the sons of the kingdom; but the tares are the sons of the Evil One; the enemy, who sowed them is the Devil; the harvest is the consummation of the age, and the reapers are the angels. So, just as the tares are collected and burned in the fire, that is what will happen at the consummation of the age. The Son of Man will send his angels, and they will collect from his kingdom all stumbling-blocks, and those whose deeds are wicked, and will consign them to a burning furnace: there will be weeping there, and grinding of teeth. Then the righteous will shine as bright as the sun in the kingdom of their Father. He who has ears, let him listen.[16]

In this passage he did not, it is true, use the term 'judgement', or 'day of judgement'; but he gave a much clearer account of it in describing the details, and foretold that it would happen at the end of the age.

Similarly, he said to his disciples, 'Mark my words; in the renewal of all things, when the Son of Man has taken his seat on his throne of majesty, you who have followed me will also sit on twelve thrones, as judges of the twelve tribes of Israel.'[17] We learn from this that Jesus will judge, with his disciples. That is why he says to the Jews, in another place, 'If I cast out devils by Beelzebub, by whom do your own people cast them out? Therefore they will be your judges.'[18] Now we are not to imagine that there will be only twelve men associated with him as judges, simply because he says that they will sit on twelve thrones. For by the number twelve is symbolized a kind of universal character in the multitude of those judging. For the numbers three and four are parts of seven; and seven is a customary symbol of universality. And the product of three and four is twelve, for three fours are twelve, as are four threes; and there may be other explanations of the number twelve which would give the same significance. Otherwise, since we are told that Matthias was appointed an apostle in the place of the traitor Judas,[19] there will be no throne

16. Matt. 13, 37–43. 17. Matt. 19, 28. 18. Matt. 12, 27.

19. cf. Acts 1, 25f. On the significance of numbers cf. Bk XI, 30f; XV, 20; XVII, 4; ch. 7.

of judgement for the Apostle Paul who 'laboured more than all of them'.[20] Yet Paul undoubtedly shows that he belongs to the number of the judges, with the other saints, when he says, 'Are you unaware that we shall sit in judgement on angels?'[21] The same consideration applies to the number twelve in reference to those who are to be judged. For the statement about being 'judges of the twelve tribes of Israel' does not mean that the tribe of Levi, the thirteenth tribe, is therefore not to be judged by them; or that only that people is to be judged and not the rest of the nations as well. And when Christ says, 'in the renewal' he means, without any doubt, the resurrection of the dead to be understood by that word 'renewal'; for our flesh will be renewed by being made exempt from decay, just as our soul is renewed by faith.

I pass over a large number of passages which seem to refer to the last judgement, but turn out to be ambiguous on careful examination, or to have more relevance to some other subject. They may refer, for example, to the coming of the Saviour in the sense that he comes throughout this present age in the person of his Church, that is in his members, part by part and little by little, since the whole Church is his body; or the reference may be to the destruction of the earthly Jerusalem. For when he speaks of that destruction he generally uses language suitable to describing the end of the world and the last great day of judgement; so that the two events cannot possibly be distinguished except by comparing the parallel statements on this subject in the three evangelists, Matthew, Mark and Luke. For one sets out certain points more obscurely, another more plainly; and this comparison is needed to make it clear where statements referring to the same subject begin. I have been at pains to follow this procedure in a letter I wrote to Hesychius of blessed memory, bishop of Salona, a letter entitled 'On the End of the World.'[22]

I shall now go on to quote the statements in the Gospel according to Matthew about the separation of the good and the evil by the instant and ultimate judgement of Christ.

When the Son of Man comes in his majesty; and all the angels with him, he will sit on his throne of majesty; and all the nations will be gathered before him. Then he will separate them from one another, like a shepherd separating the sheep from the goats, and he will place the sheep on his

20. 1 Cor. 15, 10. 21. 1 Cor. 6, 2f.

22. *Ep.*, 199, the second of two letters written to Hesychius, bishop of Salona (Split, in Dalmatia), in answer to a query about the apocalyptic chronology in Dan. 9, 24ff.

right, and the goats on his left. Then the King will say to those on his right: 'Come, you that have my Father's blessing, take possession of the kingdom prepared for you from the creation of the world. For when I was hungry, you gave me food; when I was thirsty, you gave me drink; when I was a stranger, you took me in; when I was naked, you clothed me; when I was ill, you came to my help; when I was in prison, you came to see me.' Then the righteous will reply: 'Lord, when did we see you hungry, and fed you; or thirsty, and gave you drink; a stranger, and we took you in; naked, and we clothed you? When did we see you ill or in prison, and came to see you?' And the King will answer: 'This is what I tell you: Whenever you did this for one of my brothers, even the least important, you did it to me.' Then he will say to those on the left: 'Out of my sight, you accursed, into the eternal fire, made ready for the Devil and his angels.'

Then he gives a list of what they have *not* done, corresponding to the list of what those on the right *have* done. And when they make the corresponding reply by asking when they saw him in need of these things, he replies that what was not done to the humblest of his brothers was not done to him. He concludes the discourse with the words: 'Then those will go into everlasting punishment while the just go into everlasting life.'[23]

Now the evangelist John gives an account of a very explicit prediction by Jesus that the judgement would happen at the resurrection of the dead. For he said first, 'For the Father does not judge anyone, but has given all judgement to the Son, so that all men may honour the Son, just as they honour the Father. Anyone who denies honour to the Son denies it also to the Father who sent him.' Then he immediately added: 'Mark my words carefully: I am telling you that he who listens to my words and puts his faith in him who sent me possesses eternal life, and does not come up for judgement, but has passed over from death to life.'[24] Observe that he said here that the faithful will not come up for judgement. Then how will they be separated from the evil by judgement and stand on his right hand, unless in this passage he used 'judgement' for 'condemnation'? For that is the kind of judgement into which those people will not come who hear his words and put their faith in the one who sent him.

6. *The first resurrection, and the second*

Jesus then goes on to say, 'Mark my words carefully: I am telling you that a time is coming, in fact it has already come, when the dead will

23. Matt. 25, 34–45. 24. John 5, 22–24.

hear the voice of the Son of God, and those who hear shall live. For as the Father has life in himself, so has the Son, by the Father's gift.'[25] He is not yet speaking of the second resurrection, that is, the resurrection of the body, which is to come at the end of the world, but about the first, which is here and now. It is, in fact, to distinguish the two that he says, 'The time is coming, in fact it is already come.' This resurrection, however, is not the resurrection of the body, but of the soul. For souls also have their own death, in the shape of irreligion and sin, the death died by those referred to by the Lord when he says, 'Let the dead bury their own dead',[26] that is, 'Let those who are dead in soul bury those who are dead in body.' Thus he is speaking of those who are dead in soul, because of irreligion and wickedness, when he says, 'The time is coming, in fact it has already come, when the dead will hear the voice of the Son of God, and those who hear shall live.' By 'those who hear' he means 'those who obey and believe, and who persevere to the end'. And he does not here make any distinction between the good and the evil. For it is good for all to hear his voice, and to come to life by passing over from the death of irreligion to the life of devotion.

It is of this death that the apostle Paul is speaking when he says, 'Therefore all mankind has died; and he died for all, so that men, when they are alive, should not live for themselves henceforth, but should live for him who for their sake died and rose again.'[27] So all men are dead in sin, without any exception at all, whether that sin is original sin or voluntary sin – in addition to that – commited either in ignorance of what is right, or by failing to do what is known to be right. And for all these dead, there died the one man truly alive, that is, the one who had no sin at all. And his purpose was that those who are alive through the forgiveness of sins should henceforth live not for themselves but for him who died for all mankind, on account of our sins, and rose again for our justification[28] so that we may put our faith in him who justifies the irreligious,[29] and being brought from irreligion to righteousness – brought as if from death to life – might thus be able to take part in the first resurrection which is here and now. For in this first resurrection only those take part who will be blessed for eternity, whereas in the second, about which Jesus is soon to speak, he will teach us that the blessed and the wretched alike take part. The one is the resurrection of mercy, the other the resurrection

25. John 5, 25f. 26. Matt. 8, 22. 27. 2 Cor. 5, 14f.
28. cf. Rom. 4, 25. 29. cf. Rom. 4, 5.

of judgement. That is the meaning of the verse in the psalm, 'I will sing to you, Lord, of mercy and of judgement.'[30]

Jesus goes on to speak of this judgement, in saying, 'And he has given him authority to pass judgement, because he is the Son of Man.' Here he is showing that he will come to judge in the body in which he came to be judged; that is the point of saying 'because he is the Son of Man'. Then he adds the words relevant to our present topic: 'Do not be surprised at this, that the time is coming when all who are in the grave will hear his voice and will come out; those who have done right will rise to life, those who have done wrong will rise for judgement.'[31] This is 'judgement' in the sense in which he used the word a little before, meaning 'condemnation', when he said, 'He who listens to my words, and puts his faith in him who sent me, has everlasting life, and will not come up for judgement, but has passed over from death to life.' This means that by taking part in the first resurrection, which effects the passage from death to life, he will not come up for condemnation, which is what he means by the term 'judgement', as he does also in this other place, where he says, 'Those who have done wrong will rise for judgement.' And so anyone who does not wish to be condemned in the second resurrection must rise up in the first. For 'the time is coming, in fact it has already come, when the dead will hear the voice of the Son of God, and those who hear will live', that is, they will not come into condemnation, the 'second death', as it is called. Into this death, after the second resurrection, the resurrection of bodies which is to come, they will be hurled who do not rise up in the first resurrection, the resurrection of souls. 'For the time is coming' (and here he does not say 'and in fact it has come already' because it is to be at the end of the world, that is, at the last and greatest judgement of God) 'when all who are in the grave will hear his voice and will come out.' He does not say, as in the first resurrection, 'and those who hear it will live'. For not all will live, that is, not all will have that life which, because it is a life of bliss, is the only life truly worthy of the name. For obviously they could not, without life of some sort, hear and come forth from the grave in the resurrection of the body.

Now he tells us in the next verse why they will not all live. 'Those who have done right', he says, 'will rise to life' – they are those who are to live – 'but those who have done wrong will rise for judgement' – they are those who are not to live, because they are to die the second death. They have, in fact, done wrong because their life has been wicked. And their life has been wicked because in the first resur-

30. Ps. 101, 1. 31. John 5, 27–9.

rection, the resurrection of souls which is here and now, they have not risen to a new life, or they did once so rise, but have not continued in that new life to the end. There are thus two rebirths, of which I have already spoken above: one according to faith, which comes here and now through baptism, and the other in the body, a rebirth which will come in its freedom from decay and death, as a result of the great and last judgement. Similarly, there are two resurrections: the first, the resurrection of the soul, which is here and now, and prevents us from coming to the second death; and the second, which is not now, but is to come at the end of the world. This is not the resurrection of the soul but of the body, and by means of the last judgement it will consign many to the second death, and bring others to the life that knows no death.

7. The two resurrections, and the millennium. The descriptions of John in the Apocalypse, and their interpretation

The evangelist John also spoke about those two resurrections in the book called the Apocalypse; but he spoke in such a way that the first of them has been misunderstood by some of our people and, besides this, has even been turned into ridiculous fables. Now this is what the apostle John says in the book just mentioned:

> Then I saw an angel descending from heaven, holding in his hand the key of the abyss and a chain. He seized the dragon, that serpent of old, whose other names are the Devil, and Satan; and he chained him up for a thousand years; and he threw him into the abyss, and shut it up and sealed it over him, so that he could no more lead astray the nations until the thousand years should be ended. After that he must be let loose for a short time.
>
> Then I saw thrones, and those who sat on them; and judgement was given. And the souls of those slain because of their witness to Jesus and because of the word of God, and those who had not worshipped the beast and its image, or received its mark on their forehead or hand, these reigned with Jesus for a thousand years. But the rest of the dead did not come to life until the end of the thousand years. This is the first resurrection. Blessed and holy is the man who shares in this first resurrection. Over them the second death has no power; but they will be priests of God and of Christ, and will reign with him for the thousand years.[32]

Now some people have assumed, in view of this passage, that the

32. Rev. 20 1–6.

first resurrection will be a bodily resurrection. They have been particularly excited, among other reasons, by the actual number of a thousand years, taking it as appropriate that there should be a kind of Sabbath for the saints for all that time, a holy rest, that is, after the labours of the six thousand years since man's creation, when in retribution for his great sin he was expelled from paradise into the troubles of this mortal condition. Scripture says, 'With the Lord, one day is like a thousand years and a thousand years like one day',[33] and, on this assumption, there follows, after the completion of six thousand years – six of these 'days' – a kind of seventh day of Sabbath rest for the final thousand years, with the saints rising again, obviously to celebrate this Sabbath.

This notion would be in some degree tolerable if it were believed that in that Sabbath some delights of a spiritual character were to be available for the saints because of the presence of the Lord. I also entertained this notion at one time. But in fact those people assert that those who have risen again will spend their rest in the most unrestrained material feasts, in which there will be so much to eat and drink that not only will those supplies keep within no bounds of moderation but will also exceed the limits even of incredibility. But this can only be believed by materialists; and those with spiritual interests give the name 'Chiliasts' to the believers in this picture, a term which we can translate by a word derived from the equivalent Latin, 'Millenarians'. It would take too long to refute them in detail; we ought instead to show how this scriptural passage is to be taken.

Now the Lord Jesus Christ himself says, 'No one can get into the house of a strong man and carry off his property, without first tying up the strong man.'[34] By the 'strong man' he intends us to understand the Devil, because the Devil had the power to take the human race into captivity. The 'property' that Christ was to carry off represents those whom the Devil held in his possession; but they were to become Christ's faithful followers. It was to tie up this 'strong man' that the angel, in the apostle's vision in the Apocalypse, was 'descending from heaven, holding in his hand the key of the abyss and a chain'. And 'he seized the dragon', he says, 'that serpent of old, whose other names are the Devil, and Satan, and he chained him up for a thousand years.' That means that he put a check and a bridle on his power to lead astray and to hold in possession those who were to be set free.

Now the thousand years, as it seems to me, can be interpreted in

33. 2 Pet. 3, 8. 34. Matt. 12, 29.

two ways. It may indicate that this event happens in the last thousand years, that is, in the sixth millennium, the sixth day, as it were, of which the latter stretches are now passing, and a Sabbath is to follow that has no evening, the rest, that is to say, of the saints, which has no end. Thus our author used the term 'a thousand years' to denote the last part of this millennium – or 'day' – which remained before the end of the world, employing the figure of speech by which the whole stands for the part. Alternatively, he may have intended the thousand years to stand for the whole period of this world's history, signifying the entirety of time by a perfect number. For, of course, the number 1,000 is the cube of 10, since 10 multiplied by 10 is 100, a square but plane figure; but to give height to the figure and make it solid 100 is again multiplied by 10, and we get 1,000. Moreover, it seems that 100 is sometimes used to stand for totality; for example, the Lord promised anyone who left all his possessions and followed him that he would 'receive a hundredfold in this world',[35] and we may say that the Apostle is explaining this when he speaks of 'seeming to have nothing, and yet possessing everything',[36] because at an earlier time it has been said that 'the entire world is included in the wealth of a man of faith.'[37] If this is so, how much more does 1,000 represent totality, being the square of 10 converted into a solid figure! Hence when we read in the psalm, 'He has always remembered his covenant, the word which he gave to a thousand generations',[38] there is no better interpretation of those words than by taking 'a thousand generations' as signifying 'all generations'.

'And he threw him', says John, 'into the abyss', meaning, clearly, that he cast the Devil into the abyss; and 'the abyss' symbolizes the innumerable multitude of the impious, in whose hearts there is a great depth of malignity against the Church of God. Not that the Devil was not in them before; but the reason why he is said to be thrown there is that when he is excluded from believers he starts to have a greater hold on the irreligious. For any person is more securely in the Devil's possession when he is not only estranged from God but goes on to conceive a gratuitous hatred for God's servants. 'And he shut it up', it continues, 'and sealed it over him, so that he could no more lead astray the nations until the thousand years should be ended.' 'Shut it up' means that 'the angel put a ban on the Devil, so that he could not come out', he was forbidden to pass the barrier – to 'transgress'. While the addition of 'and sealed it' seems to me to signify that God wished it

35. Matt. 19, 29. On significant numbers cf. ch. 5, and references there.
36. 2 Cor. 6, 10. 37. Prov. 17, 6 (LXX). 38. Ps. 105, 8.

to be kept a secret who belongs to the Devil's party, and who does not. For in this world, to be sure, this is kept a secret, since it is uncertain whether he who seems to be standing firm is destined to fall and whether he who seems to lie fallen is destined to rise again.

Now because he is bound and shut up by this ban the Devil is prohibited and inhibited from leading astray the nations which belonged to Christ but were in time past led astray by him or held in his grip. For God chose those nations before the foundation of the world, to 'rescue them from the power of darkness and transfer them to the kingdom of his beloved Son', as the Apostle says.[39] For there is no one among the faithful who is not aware that the Devil even now leads nations astray and drags them off with him into eternal punishment; but not those peoples destined for everlasting life. No one should be disturbed by the fact that the Devil often leads astray even those who have already been reborn in Christ and are walking in the ways of God. For 'the Lord knows those who belong to him';[40] and the Devil leads none of them astray into eternal condemnation. For the Lord knows them, as God knows (from whom nothing is hidden, not even any of the things yet to be) not as a man knows; for a man sees another man as he is at that time (if indeed he really sees him, when he does not see his heart), but he does not see what kind of a man even he himself is to become in the future. This, then, is the purpose for which the Devil is bound and shut up in the abyss; so that he may no longer lead astray the nations of which the Church is made up, nations whom he led astray and held in his grip before they were a Church. For what is said is not 'that he should not lead anyone astray' but 'that he should not lead *the nations* astray', by which the writer undoubtedly meant the Church to be understood; 'until the end of the thousand years', that is, either what remains of the sixth day (which consists of one thousand years), or all the years to come which will complete the history of the world.

As for the words, 'so that he should no longer lead astray the nations until the thousand years should be ended', this statement is not to be taken as implying that he will afterwards lead astray only those nations of which the predestined Church is composed, which he had formerly been prevented from seducing by the fact that he was bound and shut up in the abyss. But there are two possibilities: either the saying employs that mode of expression which is found with some frequency in Scripture, as for example in the psalm which says, 'So

39. Eph. 1, 4.   40. 2 Tim. 2, 19.

our eyes are fixed on the Lord our God until he has mercy upon us',[41] which does not mean that when God has shown mercy the eyes of his servants will cease to be fixed on him; or else the true sequence of the sentence is, 'And he shut it up and sealed it over him until the end of the thousand years'; and the significance of the interpolated clause, 'so that he should not lead the nations astray', is not to be understood from its place in the sentence, but separately; in fact, as if it were added at the end. Thus the whole sentence would run, 'And he shut it up and sealed it above him until the thousand years should be ended, so that he could no longer lead the nations astray'; that is, the reason why he shut him up until the thousand years should be ended, was to prevent him from leading the nations astray.

8. *The binding and unloosing of the Devil*

'After this', the narrative continues, 'the Devil must be unloosed for a short time.' Now if the binding and shutting up of the Devil means that he cannot lead the Church astray, will his unloosing mean that he can do so again? God forbid! For he will never seduce that Church which was predestined and chosen before the foundation of the world, the Church of which it is said that 'the Lord knows those who belong to him.' And yet there will be a Church on earth at that time also when the Devil is due to be unloosed, just as there has been a Church on earth from the time of the world's foundation, and as there will always be, represented by its members as each new generation succeeds the generation that passes away. In fact, a little after this John says that when the Devil has been unloosed he will lead nations astray throughout the world and draw them into waging war on the Church, and that the number of the Church's enemies will be as the sands of the sea. 'And they went up', he says, 'over the breadth of the land, and surrounded the camp of the saints and the beloved city; and fire came down on them from heaven and devoured them. And the Devil, who seduced them, was thrown into the lake of fire and sulphur, where the beast and the false prophet are; and they will be tormented day and night for ever.'[42]

Now this refers to the last judgement; but I thought it should be quoted at this point for a particular reason: to prevent anyone from supposing that in the short time when the Devil will be let loose there will be no Church on this earth, either because he will find no Church here when he is unloosed or because he will have annihilated it by all

41. Ps. 123, 2. 42. Rev. 20, 9f.

kinds of persecutions. And so the Devil is bound throughout the whole period embraced by the Apocalypse, that is, from the first coming of Christ to the end of the world, which will be Christ's second coming, and the meaning of the binding is not that he ceases to seduce the Church during that interval called 'the thousand years', as is shown by the fact that when unloosed he is evidently not destined to lead it astray. For assuredly if his binding meant that he is unable, or not allowed, to lead it astray, his unloosing can only mean that he is now able, or permitted, to do so. But God forbid that this should be the case! Instead, what the binding of the Devil means is that he is not permitted to exert his whole power of temptation either by force or by guile to seduce men to his side by violent compulsion or fraudulent delusion. For if he were permitted for so long a time, a time when so many were so insecure, he would overthrow very many of the faithful or prevent very many from believing, and those would be the kind of men to whom God did not will that this should happen. It was to prevent his achieving this that he was bound.

But the Devil will be unloosed when the 'short time' comes; for we are told that he is going to rage with all his strength, and with the strength of his supporters for three years and six months.[43] And yet those against whom he has to wage war will be the kind of people who cannot be conquered by his great attack and all his stratagems. But if he had never been unloosed his malign power would not have been so clearly seen, and the endurance of the Holy City would never have been so clearly proved in its utter faithfulness; above all it would not have been so manifest what good use the Omnipotent was to make of the Devil's great wickedness. The Omnipotent did not debar him altogether from putting the saints to the test; but he threw out the Devil from their inner man, the seat of belief in God, so that they might profit from his outward assault. And he tied him up among those who belong to his party, lest by pouring out his malice and exercising it to the utmost of his power he should hinder or break down the faith of countless weak persons, by whom the Church was to be filled up and multiplied, destroying the faith of some who already believed, hindering the faith of others who were on the point of believing. In the end the Omnipotent will unloose him, so that the City of God may behold how powerful a foe it has overcome, to the immense glory of its Redeemer, its Helper, its Deliverer. What are we, to be sure, in comparison with the saints and believers of the future, seeing that so mighty an adversary will be let loose against them,

43. cf. Rev. 12, 12; 11, 2; 12, 6; 13, 5.

whereas we have the greatest peril in our struggle with him although he is bound? And yet there is no doubt that even during this period of time there have been, and there are today, some soldiers of Christ so wise and brave that even if they were living in this mortal condition at the time when the Devil is to be unloosed, they would take the most prudent precautions against his stratagems, and withstand his assaults with the utmost steadfastness.

Now this binding of the Devil was not only effected at the time when the Church began to spread beyond the land of Judaea into other nations, at various times; it is happening even now, and will continue to happen until the end of the age, when he is to be unloosed. For even now men are being converted to the faith from the unbelief in which the Devil held them in his power, and without doubt they will go on being converted to the end of the age; and this 'strong man' is obviously being bound in the case of every man who is snatched away from him, as part of his property. And the abyss in which he is confined is not done away with when those are dead who were alive at the time when he was first shut up; others have taken their place, as new generations are born, and they go on being replaced until this age comes to an end. These are men who hate the Christians, and in the dark depths of their hearts the Devil is shut up every day, as in an abyss. On the other hand, it is a matter of some question whether during those last three years and six months, when the Devil is unloosed and will be raging with all his strength, anyone will join the faith who has not previously been of the faith. For if the 'property of the strong man' is snatched away even when the strong man is unloosed, that would be inconsistent with the statement that no one 'enters the house of a strong man to take off his property, without first tying up the strong man'.[44] It seems, therefore, that this statement forces us to suppose that in that period, brief though it is, no one will join the people of Christ, but the Devil will do battle with those who are found to be already Christians; and although some of them will be defeated and will follow the Devil, they will not be people belonging to the predestined number of the sons of God. For it is not for nothing that the same apostle John who wrote this Apocalypse says of some people, in his epistle, that 'they went out from our company, but they did not really belong to us; if they had belonged to us, they would have stayed with us.'[45]

But what happens to the little ones? For it would be too incredible to suppose that at that time there will be no infant children of Chris-

44. Matt. 12, 9. 45. 1 John 2, 19.

tians, already born, who will be caught unbaptized, or that none will be born during that very period; or that if there are such, they will not somehow or other be brought by their parents to the 'washing of rebirth'.[46] And yet if this happens, how are those pieces of 'property' to be snatched away from the Devil when he is unloosed, seeing that 'no one enters his house, to take off his property, without first binding him'? But in fact we must in preference believe that there will be instances both of people falling away from the Church and of new members being added, even in that period. We may be sure that there will be sufficient courage shown by parents in seeking baptism for their little ones and by those who come to believe for the first time in that period to give them victory over that 'strong man', even though he is not bound – that is, even though he plots with all his tricks and attacks with all his strength, those people will have the vigilance to be aware of him and the endurance to withstand him, and so his 'property' will be snatched from him even though he is not bound.

That will not mean that the statement in the Gospel will be proved false, that no one 'enters the house of a strong man, to take off his property, without first binding the strong man'. For the truth of the statement is seen in the observance of this order: first comes the binding of the strong man, then the seizure of his property; and this is followed by such a multiplication of the Church among all nations far and wide, by the accession of both strong and weak, that as a result of a robust confidence in things divinely predicted and fulfilled, the Church is strong enough to carry off the Devil's property even though he has been unloosed. It is indeed true that we have to admit that 'since wickedness abounds, the love of many people grows cold',[47] and that those who are not entered in the book of life will give way in large numbers before the unexampled magnitude of the persecutions and deceptions of the Devil, now unloosed; it is equally true that we must suppose that the good whom that time shall find faithful will prevail over the Devil. And besides those there are some who up to that time have been outside the Church, who will then, with the help of God's grace, and by the study of the Scriptures (in which is foretold, besides other things, the very end which they now perceive approaching) become more resolute to believe what they did not believe before, and strong enough to overcome the Devil, even when unloosed. If this is what will happen, then the binding of the Devil must be said to come first, so that there may follow the seizure of his goods, both when he is bound and when he is unloosed; for this is the

46. Tit. 3, 5. 47. cf. Matt. 24, 12.

meaning of the words, 'Who will enter the house of a strong man, to take away his property, without first binding the strong man?'

9. *The nature of the kingdom of the saints, lasting a thousand years; and its difference from the eternal kingdom*

In the meantime, while the Devil is bound for a thousand years, the saints reign with Christ, also for a thousand years; which are without doubt to be taken in the same sense, and as denoting the same period, that is, the period beginning with Christ's first coming. We must certainly rule out any reference to that kingdom which he is to speak of at the end of the world, in the words, 'Come, you that have my Father's blessing, take possession of the kingdom prepared for you';[48] and so, even now, although in some other and far inferior way, his saints must be reigning with him, the saints to whom he says, 'See, I am always with you, right up to the end of the world';[49] for otherwise the Church could surely not be called his kingdom, or the kingdom of heaven. For it is obviously in this period that the scribe is 'instructed in the kingdom of God', the scribe, whom we mentioned above, who 'brings out of his store things new and old'.[50] And it is from the Church that the reapers are to collect the tares which the Lord allowed to grow together with the wheat until the harvest, as he explains when he says, 'The harvest is the end of the world, and the reapers are the angels. And so, just as the tares are collected and burned in the fire, that is what will happen at the consummation of the age. The Son of Man will send his angels, and they will collect from his kingdom all stumbling-blocks.'[51] Can he here be speaking of a kingdom where there are no stumbling-blocks? If not, then they must be collected from this kingdom which is the Church in this world.

Moreover, Christ says, 'Anyone who breaks one of the least of those commandments, and teaches other people, will be called the least in the kingdom of heaven, whereas anyone who keeps the commandments, and teaches others to do the same, will be called great in the kingdom of heaven.'[52] He speaks of both men as being in the kingdom of heaven, the man who does not keep the commandments which he teaches (for the meaning of 'to break' is 'not to observe', 'not to carry out') and the man who carries them out, and teaches others to do the same; but he calls one 'least' and the other 'great'. And immedi-

48. Matt. 25, 34.
49. Matt. 28, 20.
50. Matt. 13, 52.
51. Matt. 13, 39ff.
52 Matt. 5, 19.

ately he goes on to add, 'For I tell you that unless your righteousness far exceeds that of the scribes and Pharisees', that is, of those who break what they teach (for he says of the scribes and Pharisees in another place, 'For they talk, but they do not practise'[53]) – unless 'your righteousness far exceeds theirs', that is, unless you do not break, but instead carry out, what you teach, 'you will not enter the kingdom of heaven.'

So then we must understand the kingdom of heaven in one sense as a kingdom in which both are included, the man who breaks what he teaches, and the man who practises it, though one is the least and the other is great in the kingdom, while in another sense it is a kingdom into which there enters only the man who practises what he teaches. Thus where both are to be found we have the Church as it now is; but where only the one kind will be found, there is the Church as it will be, when no evil person will be included. It follows that the Church even now is the kingdom of Christ and the kingdom of heaven. And so even now his saints reign with him, though not in the same way as they will then reign; and yet the tares do not reign with him, although they are growing in the Church side by side with the wheat. For those people reign with Christ who do what the Apostle speaks of when he says, 'If you have risen again with Christ, show a taste for the higher wisdom, where Christ is seated at God's right hand; let your aspirations rise to that higher realm, and do not confine them to this earthly sphere.'[54] Of such people he also says that 'their true home is in heaven.'[55] Ultimately, those people reign with him who are in his kingdom in such a way that they themselves *are* his kingdom. But in what way can those people be the kingdom of Christ who, to mention nothing else, although they are included in it until the collection and removal of all stumbling-blocks at the end of the world, are nevertheless seeking their own interests in that kingdom, and not the interests of Jesus Christ?[56]

It is therefore of this kingdom at war, in which conflict still rages with the enemy, that the Apocalypse is speaking in the passage we are considering. In this kingdom sometimes there is fighting against vices that attack us, though sometimes they submit to being ruled, until that kingdom of perfect peace comes where the King will reign without opposition. And so the passage is also concerned with the first resurrection, which is now in being. For the apostle first says that the Devil is bound for a thousand years, and afterwards unloosed for a

53. Matt. 23, 3. 54. Col. 3, 1f.
55. Phil. 3, 20. 56. cf. Phil. 2, 21.

short time; and then he gives a summary of what the Church does during those thousand years, or what is done in it, when he says, 'I saw thrones, and those who sat on them, and judgement was given.'[57] This must not be supposed to refer to the last judgement. The thrones are to be interpreted as the seats of the authorities by whom the Church is now governed, and those sitting on them as the authorities themselves. And it seems clear that the best interpretation of the judgement given is that referred to in the words: 'Whatever you bind on earth will be bound in heaven; and whatever you loose on earth will be loosed in heaven.'[58] Hence the Apostle says, 'What have I to do with judging those outside? As for those inside, surely you yourselves judge their cases?'[59] And the Apocalypse continues, 'The souls of those who were slain because of their witness to Jesus and because of the word of God', and we take this with the words that follow later: 'reigned with Jesus for a thousand years'.[60] These are, clearly, the souls of the martyrs, their bodies being not yet restored to them.

For the souls of the pious dead are not separated from the Church, which is even now the kingdom of Christ. Otherwise they would not be commemorated at the altar of God at the time of the partaking of the body of Christ, nor would it be of any avail to have recourse to the Church's baptism in time of peril, for fear that this life should end without baptism, nor to have recourse to reconciliation at such time, if it happens that one is separated from this body under penance or through one's own bad conscience. Why are such steps taken, unless it is because the faithful are still members of this body, even when they have departed this life? And therefore their souls, even though not yet with their bodies, already reign with him while those thousand years are running their course. That is why we read, in another place in the same book: 'Blessed are the dead who die in the Lord. Yes, indeed, says the Spirit, from henceforth they may rest from their toils: for their deeds go with them.'[61] And so the Church now begins to reign with Christ among the living and the dead. For 'this is the reason', says the apostle, 'why Christ died, that he might be Lord of both the living and the dead.'[62] But this reign after death belongs especially to those who struggled on truth's behalf even to death; and that is why it is only the souls of the martyrs that are mentioned in the Apocalypse. Nevertheless we take the part as implying the whole,

57. Rev. 20, 4. 58. Matt. 18, 18. 59. 1 Cor. 5, 12.
60. Rev. 20, 4. 61. Rev. 14, 13. 62. Rom. 14, 9.

and interpret it as meaning that the rest of the dead also belong to the Church, which is the kingdom of Christ.

The narrative continues, 'And any who had not worshipped the beast or his image or received his mark on their foreheads or their hands',[63] and we ought to understand this as referring to the living and the dead alike. The next question, what this beast stands for, needs more careful investigation; it would not, however, be repugnant to the true faith to understand the beast to represent the godless city itself, and the people of the unbelievers, contrasted with the people of the faith and the City of God. 'His image', to be sure, seems to me to stand for 'his pretence', the pretence shown, that is, in those people who profess the faith but live the lives of unbelievers. For they put up a show of being what they are not, and they are called Christians, not because of a truthful representation of Christianity, but because of an illusory resemblance to it. For it is not only the open enemies of the name of Christ and his most glorious City who belong to this beast; there are also the tares which are to be gathered at the end of the world and taken from Christ's kingdom, that is, from the Church. And who else can be meant by 'those who do not worship the beast or his image' except those who follow the instruction of the apostle by not 'taking the yoke with the unbelievers'?[64] For 'do not worship' means 'do not consent', 'are not subordinate to'. And 'do not receive his mark' refers to the sign of guilt, 'on their foreheads' because of their profession, 'on their hands' because of their activities. Those who have no part in those evil practices, therefore, whether they are still alive in the mortal body, or have departed this life, are reigning even now with Christ, in a way appropriate to this period, during all the intervening time, symbolized by the number of the years – a thousand.

'The rest of them', it says, 'did not come to life.'[65] For 'the time has already come when the dead hear the voice of the Son of God, and those who hear shall live.'[66] The rest of them, it follows, will not live. But the next words in the Apocalypse, 'until the thousand years are ended', must be taken to imply that they did not come to life when they should have done so, that is, by passing over from death to life. That is why, when the day comes on which the resurrection of the body also is effected, they will come out of the grave not to life but for judge-

63. Rev. 20, 4.

64. cf. 2 Cor. 6, 14. The Apocalypse, in fact, is speaking of the Emperor's image.

65. Rev. 20, 5.

66. John 5, 25; cf. ch. 6.

ment, to the condemnation, that is, which is called the second death. For anyone who has not come to life until the end of the thousand years – anyone, that is, who during the whole of that period when the first resurrection is going on has not heard the voice of the Son of God, and passed over from death to life – will pass, at the second resurrection, the resurrection of the body, into the second death, with his body. For John goes on to add, 'This is the first resurrection. Blessed and holy is the man who has a part in this first resurrection',[67] that is, who participates in it. Now the man who participates in it is the man who not only comes to life again from the death of sin, but continues in this condition of new life. 'Over them', says the Apocalypse, 'the second death has no power.' This implies that death has power over the rest, who were described earlier as 'those who did not come to life until the end of the thousand years'.[68] For in all that period of time, which John calls 'a thousand years', however long the life of any of those people in the body during that time, they did not come to life again from the death in which their impiety held them. This coming to life again would have made them sharers in the first resurrection; and then the second death would have had no power over them.

10. *The notion that resurrection has reference only to the body, not to the soul*

Some people have the idea that 'resurrection' can only mean the resurrection of the body, and they maintain that this first resurrection also will be that of the body. For, they say, only what can fall can rise again; now bodies fall when they die, in fact, corpses are called *cadavera* from the fact that they fall (*cadendo*). Consequently, they say, there cannot be a resurrection of souls, only of bodies. But what have they to say in reply to the Apostle, who speaks of such a resurrection? For when he says, 'If you have risen with Christ, show a taste for the higher wisdom',[69] he was surely addressing those who had risen again in the 'inner man', not the outer. He expresses the same thought elsewhere in different words, when he says, 'So that, just as Christ rose again from the dead in the glory of the Father, we also may walk in a new way of life.'[70] The same idea underlies this saying, 'Awake, you sleeper, and arise from the dead, and Christ will shine on you.'[71]

67. Rev. 20, 6. 68. Rev. 20, 5. 69. Col. 3, 1f.
70. Rom. 6, 4. 71. Eph. 5, 14.

Now as for their statement that only those who fall can rise, and their consequent assumption that resurrection refers only to bodies, why do they not listen to such sayings as, 'Do not depart from him, for fear you may fall',[72] and, 'in relation to his own Master he stands or falls',[73] and, 'Anyone who thinks he is standing firm should beware in case he may fall'?[74] For the fall that we should beware of is, I imagine, the fall of the soul, not that of the body. If, therefore, resurrection is of things that fall, and if souls also fall, then assuredly it is to be admitted that souls rise again.

One further point on this passage: the statement that 'death has no power over them' is followed by these words: 'But they will be priests of God and of Christ, and will reign with him for a thousand years.'[75] This clearly does not mean only the bishops and presbyters, who are now called by the distinctive name of 'priests' in the Church; but just as we call all Christians 'Christs' in virtue of their sacramental anointing (*chrisma*) so we call them all 'priests' because they are members of the one Priest. And the apostle Peter says of them that they are 'a holy people, a royal priesthood'.[76] It is to be observed that in this passage John conveys the suggestion, though briefly and in passing, that Christ is God, when he says, 'priests of God and Christ', that is of the Father and the Son, although it was in respect of the 'form of a servant'[77] and as Son of Man that Christ was 'made a priest for ever in the line of Melchisedech'.[78] This is a point I have mentioned more than once in this work.[79]

11. *Gog and Magog, the agents of the Devil's persecution towards the end of the world*

'And when the thousand years are over' the narrative continues, 'Satan will be unloosed from his prison, and will go out to lead astray the nations in the four corners of the earth, and he will draw them into war; these are Gog and Magog, and their number is like the sands of the sea.'[80] He leads them astray, we see, so that he can draw them into war. For he has been leading them astray before this, by all means at his command, using multifarious kinds of evil. But 'he will go out' means 'he will burst out of his lair of hatred into open persecution'. This, in fact, will be the last persecution, when the last judgement is

72. Ecclus. 2, 7. 73. Rom. 14, 4. 74. 1 Cor. 10, 12.
75. Rev. 20, 6. 76. 1 Pet. 2, 9. 77. Phil. 2, 7.
78. cf. Ps. 110, 4; Hebr. 7, 17–21.
79. cf. Bk XVI, 22; XVII, 17–20.
80. Rev. 20, 7f.

imminent, and this persecution will be suffered throughout the whole world by the holy Church, the universal City of Christ being persecuted by the universal city of the Devil, each at the height of its power on earth. For the nations called Gog and Magog are not to be taken as standing for some barbarian peoples, whose home is in some particular part of the earth, whether the Getae and the Massagetae (as some have guessed on account of the initials of their names), or some other peoples of foreign race, outside Roman sway. It is indicated, in fact, that they exist all over the world, when the first statement about 'nations in the four corners of the earth' is followed by the remark that those nations are Gog and Magog. I find that the names mean: Gog, 'a roof'; Magog, 'from the roof',[81] or, as we might say, the house and the one who proceeds from the house.

These, then, are the nations in which, according to our interpretation given above,[82] the Devil is shut up, as it were, in an abyss; and the Devil himself is, in a way, one who rushes out and proceeds from them; as they are 'the roof', he is the one who proceeds 'from the roof'. If, on the other hand, we refer both names to the nations, instead of applying one to them and the other to the Devil, then they will be 'the roof' because the ancient enemy is shut up in them and, in a sense, covered by them; and they will also be 'from the roof' when they burst out from covert into overt hatred. As for the words, 'and they went up over the breadth of the earth and surrounded the camp of the saints and the beloved city',[83] this clearly does not mean that they have come, or will come, to one place, as if the camp of the saints and the beloved City are to be in some one place. For these are simply the Church of Christ spread all over the world. It follows that wherever the Church is at that time, and it will be among all the nations – which is the meaning of 'over the breadth of the earth' – there the camp of the saints will be, and there God's beloved City. There it will be surrounded by all its enemies – for they also will be present along with that City, among all nations – in the savagery of that persecution. That is, the City will be hemmed in, hard pressed, shut up, in the straits of tribulation, yet it will not abandon its warfare, which is here called 'the camp'.

12. *The fire that consumed Gog and Magog: and the fire of the last punishment*

'And fire came down from heaven and devoured them.' This must not be supposed to describe the last punishment, which is to come with

81. Impossible etymologies. 82. cf. ch. 7. 83. Rev. 20, 9; cf. ch. 8.

the sentence, 'Out of my sight, accursed ones, into the eternal fire.'[84] For then, to be sure, they themselves are to be flung into the fire, instead of having fire coming down from heaven upon them. This fire from heaven, in fact, is rightly taken to mean the firmness of the saints, which will keep them from giving way to those who rage against them and from carrying out the wishes of these opponents. For the heaven is the 'firmament' through whose 'firmness' these attackers will be tormented with blazing zeal, since they will be unable to draw the saints of Christ to the part of Antichrist. This zeal will be the fire that devours them, and it will be 'from God', since it is by the gift of God that the saints are made invincible, and that is what torments their enemies. For while 'zeal' has a good sense in 'the zeal of your house has consumed me',[85] it has an opposite sense in 'Zeal has taken hold of the uninstructed people, and now fire will consume those opponents.'[86] Notice the phrase 'and now', which clearly rules out a reference to the last judgement. Alternatively, the fire that comes down from heaven and devours them may mean the blow that is to be dealt to persecutors of the Church when Christ comes and finds them alive in the earth and when he kills the Antichrist with the breath of his mouth.[87] But even so this will not be the final punishment of the impious; that last punishment is the punishment they are to undergo after the resurrection of the body.

13. *The relation of the persecution of Antichrist to the thousand years*

This last persecution, which is to be inflicted by Antichrist, will last for three years and six months; I have already stated this, and it is also laid down earlier in the Apocalypse, and in the book of the prophet Daniel.[88] Brief though this time is, it is a proper matter for debate whether it is included in the thousand years during which the Devil is said to be bound, while the saints reign with Christ, or whether this short space is to be added, as an extra period. For if we say that it is within the thousand years, then it will be seen that the reign of the saints with Christ is not coextensive with the binding of the Devil, but lasts a longer time. For the saints will surely reign with their King even in that persecution, in fact, especially at that time, when they will overcome all its great evils, at a time when the Devil is no longer bound, and so can persecute them with all his might. How is it, then,

84. Matt. 25, 41. 85. Ps. 69, 9. 86. Is. 26, 11 (LXX).
87. cf. 2 Thess. 2. 8. 88. cf. ch. 8; Dan. 12, 7.

that Scripture limits both the Devil's binding and the reign of the saints to the same period of the thousand years, if the Devil's binding is to come to an end three years and six months before the end of the thousand-year reign of the saints with Christ?

On the other hand, if we say that this brief space of persecution is not to be reckoned in with the thousand years, but added to them instead, then the statements of the narrative can be understood in their literal sense. First comes the statement, 'The priests of God and of Christ will reign with him for a thousand years.' This is followed by, 'And when the thousand years are ended, Satan will be unloosed from his prison.'[89] Taken in this way, the meaning is that the reign of the saints and the imprisonment of the Devil are to end at the same time. Then the time of the persecution belongs, we believe, neither to the reign of the saints nor to the imprisonment of Satan – both lasting a thousand years – but is to be reckoned as an additional period. But on this supposition we shall be forced to admit that the saints will not reign with Christ in that time of persecution. Yet who would dare to say that his members will not reign with him at that time when they will cleave to him most closely and strongly and at a time when the fiercer the assault of war the greater the glory of refusal to yield, and the richer the martyr's crown?

Alternatively, if they are not to be accounted as destined to reign, because of the tribulations they are to endure, it will follow that in earlier times also, during those thousand years, all the saints who suffered tribulation must not be accounted as having been reigning with Christ during the actual time of their tribulation. Accordingly, those whose souls the author of the Apocalypse writes that he beheld, those who were 'killed because of their witness to Jesus and because of the word of God',[90] did not reign with Christ when they were suffering persecutions, and they themselves were not the kingdom of Christ, although Christ possessed them in a pre-eminent sense. Now this, to be sure, is utterly absurd, a conclusion to be repudiated at all costs. In fact, it is certain that the victorious souls of the glorious martyrs, at least, after overcoming all their sufferings and after the end of all their hardships, reigned with Christ, when they had laid down their mortal members; and they are still reigning, until the thousand years are ended, so that they may go on reigning when they have received their bodies, which will then be immortal.

Thus, during those three and a half years, the souls of those slain for their witness to Christ, both those which had already left their

89. Rev. 20, 6f. 90. Rev. 6, 9.

bodies and those which are destined to leave them in the last persecution, will reign with him until this mortal age is ended and we pass over to that kingdom where there will be no death. Hence the reign of the saints with Christ will last for more years than the Devil's imprisonment in chains, because they will reign with their King, God's Son, during the three and a half years also when the Devil is no longer bound. The conclusion is, then, that when we hear these words: 'The priests of God and of Christ will reign with him for a thousand years; and when the thousand years are ended Satan will be unloosed from his prison', we should take it in one of two ways: either the thousand years of the reign of the saints is not ended, but the imprisonment of the Devil in chains is at an end, so that both sides have their thousand years, that is, their particular totality of years, though the length of the periods differs, the reign of the saints being longer, while the imprisonment of the Devil is shorter in duration; or else, since three years and six months is a very short space of time, it may be assumed that it does not require taking into account, whether it appears to diminish the Devil's bondage or to increase the length of the reign of the saints. This is like the question of the four hundred years which I discussed in the sixteenth book of this work;[91] for there were rather more than four hundred, and yet they were given in round numbers as four hundred. There are many similar forms of expression to be found in the sacred writings, if one looks out for them.

14. *The condemnation of the Devil and his followers; and a summary account of the resurrection of the body and the final judgement*

This mention of the last persecution is followed by a brief epitome of all that is still to be suffered by the opposing city, together with its leader, at the last judgement. 'Then the Devil, their seducer, was flung into the lake of fire and sulphur, into which the beast and the false prophet had been cast. And they will be tormented day and night for ever.'[92] The correct interpretation of 'the beast', is, as I said earlier,[93] the ungodly city itself; while its 'false prophet' stands either for Antichrist, or for that 'image', that is that pretence, about which I spoke in that passage. After this, the author gives a summary account of the last judgement itself, which will take place at the resurrection

91. Bk XVI, 24. 92. Rev. 20, 10. 93. ch. 9.

of the dead, that is, of the body, describing how it was revealed to him. 'Then I saw a great white throne, and the One who sat on it: from his presence heaven and earth fled, and no place was left for them.'[94] He does not say, 'I saw a great white throne, and the One who sat on it, *and* from his presence heaven and earth fled', because this had not yet happened, that is, it did not happen before judgement had been passed on the living and the dead. What he says is that he saw sitting on the throne the One from whose presence heaven and earth fled – but that happens afterwards. For after the judgement has been accomplished this heaven and this earth will, of course, cease to be, when a new heaven and a new earth will come into being. For it is by a transformation of the physical universe, not by its annihilation, that this world will pass away. Hence the Apostle's statement, 'The form of this world is passing away, and I want you to be spared anxiety.'[95] It is, then, the outward form, not the substance, that passes.

Now when John has described his vision of One sitting on a throne, from whose presence heaven and earth fled – a vision to be fulfilled hereafter – he continues, 'Then I saw the dead, great and small; and the books were opened. Then another book was opened, the book of the life of every man; and the dead were judged according to their deeds, on the record in those books.'[96] He speaks of 'books opened' and 'a book', and he did not omit to describe what kind of a book this was: it was 'the book of every man's life'. The 'books' mentioned first must therefore be taken as the sacred books, old and new, which were opened to show what commandments God had given in them, with orders that they should be fulfilled, while the other book, the book of every man's life, was to show which of these commandments each man had fulfilled or failed to fulfil. If this book is imagined as a material volume, who could estimate its size or length? How long would it take to read a book containing the whole life of every person? Or are we to suppose that there will be the same number of angels present as men, and that each man will listen to the account of his life being read by the angel assigned to him? If so, there will not be one book for all, but one for each person. However, the scriptural passage intends us to take it as one book, since it says, 'Another book was opened.' Consequently, we must understand this to mean a kind of divine power which will ensure that all the actions, good or bad, of every individual will be recalled to mind and presented to the mind's view with miraculous speed, so that each man's knowledge will accuse or excuse his

94. Rev. 20, 11. 95. 1 Cor. 7, 31f. 96. Rev. 20, 12.

conscience,[97] and thus each and all will be judged simultaneously. This divine power is no doubt called a 'book' because it ensures the recollection of the facts, and those facts are, as we may say, 'read' in this process.

Then, to make it clear who the dead are, the small and the great, who are to be judged, the author recapitulates[98], as if going back to make a point which he had omitted, or rather postponed. 'The sea gave up the dead that were in it, and Death and Hades gave back the dead which they had in their keeping.'[99] This, beyond any doubt, took place before the judgement of the dead; and yet the judgement is described first. This is what I meant by saying that the author went back, by way of recapitulation, to make a point which he had left out. But after that he keeps to the order of events; and to make that order clear, he repeats in its own place, and here more appropriately, what he has already said about the dead who were judged. For after saying, 'The sea gave up the dead that were in it, and death and Hades gave back the dead that they had in their keeping', he straightway adds what he has stated a little before: 'And they were judged, each of them on the record of his actions.' This is the same as he has said above: 'The dead were judged on the record of their actions.'

15. *The meaning of the dead given up by the sea, and by Death and Hades*

Now who are meant by the dead who were in the sea, and whom the sea gave up? It cannot be meant that those who die in the sea are not in Hades; or that their bodies are preserved in the sea; or – a still more absurd suggestion – that the sea had in its keeping the good dead, while Hades had the wicked. Who could entertain such a notion? Some people, however, make the very reasonable assumption that in this context the sea stands for this age. On this assumption, when the author wanted to express symbolically the fact that judgement is to be passed on those whom Christ will find on earth still in the bodily frame, at the same time as on those who are to rise again, he called them 'the dead', including in that category the good, of whom it is said, 'You are dead, and your lives are hidden with Christ in God', as well as the wicked, of whom it is said: 'Let the dead bury their dead.'[100] There is also another reason for calling them dead, the fact that they wear mortal bodies; which is why the Apostle says, 'The

97. cf. Rom. 2, 15.
98. cf. Bk XVI, 5; 15.
99. Rev. 20, 13.
100. Col. 3, 3; Matt. 8, 33.

body, to be sure, is dead because of sin: but the spirit is life because we have been justified';[101] thus pointing out that in a man who is alive and still in the bodily frame there is a body which is dead and a spirit which is life. He did not say, we notice, that the body is 'mortal', but that it is 'dead', although a little later he describes the same bodies as 'mortal', which is the more usual description. We conclude, then, that 'the sea gave up the dead who were in it' means that this age gave up all who belonged to it, because they had not yet died.

'And Death and Hades gave back the dead whom they had in their keeping.' The sea 'gave them *up*', because these people presented themselves in the condition in which they were found, whereas Death and Hades 'gave them *back*', because they recalled them to the life from which they had departed. And it may be that there was good reason for finding it insufficient to say 'Death' *or* 'Hades', and for using both terms: 'Death', perhaps, with reference to the good, who could suffer only death, and not hell as well; 'Hades' with reference to the wicked, who suffer punishment also in hell. For if there seems no absurdity in the belief that the holy men of old, who held a faith in the Christ who was still to come, dwelt in regions far removed from the torments of the ungodly, but still in the nether world, until Christ's blood and his descent to those regions should rescue them from that place, then surely from that time onwards the good believers, now redeemed by the shedding of his blood as their ransom, have no experience at all of Hades, as they wait to receive back their bodies and to receive the good things they deserve.

The statement that 'they were judged, each of them on the record of their actions', is followed by a brief description of the manner of the judgement: 'Then Death and Hades were flung into the lake of fire', these terms signifying the Devil (as responsible for death and the pains of hell) and, together with him, the whole society of the demons. This has, in fact, already been said more explicitly, in the anticipatory statement that 'the Devil, their seducer, was flung into the lake of fire and sulphur.' And the somewhat obscure additional clause, 'into which the beast and the false prophet had been cast', is here replaced by the more explicit statement: 'Then those whose names were not found in the book of life were flung into the lake of fire.' This 'book' is not an aid to God's memory, to prevent him from making a mistake through forgetfulness! What is symbolized is the predestination of those to whom eternal life will be given. For God is not unaware of their existence, so that he has to refer to the book to know about

101. Rom. 8, 10.

them. The fact is that his foreknowledge of them, which is infallible, is itself the book of life in which they are written, that is, they are known beforehand.

16. *The new heaven and the new earth*

Having ended his prophecy of the future judgement of the wicked, the author has now to treat also of the good. And so, after his brief development of the Lord's statement that 'these will go into everlasting punishment' he proceeds to the development of the connected statement that 'the righteous will go into eternal life.'[102] John goes on to say, 'Then I saw a new heaven and a new earth. For the first heaven and the first earth have vanished, and there is no longer any sea.'[103] This will come to pass in the order already described by anticipation, where he has said that he saw One sitting on a throne, and heaven and earth vanished from his presence.[104] For after judgement has been passed on those who are not recorded in the book of life and they have been flung into the lake of fire (a fire whose nature and whose situation in the world or the universe is, I conceive, known to no one, unless perhaps the Spirit of God has revealed it to someone) then the form of this world will pass away in a blazing up of the fires of the world, just as the Deluge was caused by the overflowing of the waters of the world. Thus in that blazing up, as I call it, of the fires of the world, the qualities of the corruptible elements which were appropriate for our corruptible bodies will utterly perish in the burning, and our substance itself will acquire the qualities which will be suited, by a miraculous transformation, to our immortal bodies, with the obvious purpose of furnishing the world, now renewed for the better, with a fitting population of human beings, renewed for the better even in their flesh.

As for the statement that 'there is no longer any sea', I should find it hard to say whether it is dried up by the intense heat, or whether the sea also is to be changed for the better. We are indeed told that there is to be a new heaven and a new earth; but I do not recall having anywhere read anything about a new sea, unless it is what is found in the same book, the description of 'what seemed a sea of glass, like crystal'.[105] But the author was not speaking in that place about the end of the world, nor does he appear to have meant the sea in the literal sense, but 'what seemed a sea'. In fact, just as the prophetic style of

102. Matt. 25, 46.
103. Rev. 21, 1.
104. Rev. 20, 11; cf. ch. 14.
105. Rev. 4, 6; 15, 2.

speech is apt to mingle metaphorical with literal expressions and so, as it were, to veil the meaning, similarly it may be that the words, 'there is no longer any sea', referred to the 'sea' about which he had just said that 'the sea gave up the dead that were in its keeping'. For from that time the rough weather and the storms of this age will cease to exist; and 'the sea' is used as an allegory of this stormy age.

17. *The unending glory of the Church after the end*

Then I saw the great City, the new Jerusalem, coming down out of heaven from God, made ready like a new bride adorned for her husband. And I heard a great voice from the throne, saying: 'See, the dwelling of God with men; and he will dwell among them, and they will be his people, and God himself will be with them. And he will wipe away every tear from their eyes; death shall be no more, and there will be no mourning or crying, nor any pain; for the old order of things has passed away.' And the One who sat on the throne said: 'See, I am making all things new.'[106]

This City is said to come down from heaven because the grace by which God created it is heavenly. That is why he says to it, through the mouth of Isaiah, 'I, your creator, am the Lord.'[107] This City has been coming down from heaven since its beginning, from the time when its citizens began to increase in number as they have continued to increase throughout the period of this present age, by the grace of God which comes from above by means of the 'washing of rebirth'[108] in the Holy Spirit sent down from heaven. But through the judgement of God, which will be the last judgement, administered by his Son Jesus Christ, the splendour of that City will be made apparent, by God's gift. So great will be that splendour, and so new, that no traces of age will remain, since even our bodies will pass from their old corruption and mortality into incorruption and immortality.[109]

Now it would show excessive effrontery, as it seems to me, to take this as referring to the period in which the City reigns with its King for a thousand years. For our author says quite explicitly, 'God will wipe away every tear from their eyes; and death will be no more, and there will be no mourning or crying, nor any more pain.' And who could be so absurd, so crazed with a love for perverse argument, as to have the hardihood to maintain that in the midst of the troubles of this mortal state not only the holy people but every individual saint who lives this life, or will live it, or has lived it, has no tears and no

106. Rev. 20, 2–5. 107. Is. 45, 8 (LXX).
108. Tit. 3, 5. 109. cf. 1 Cor. 15, 53f.

sorrows in this life? The truth is rather that the more holy a man is, and the deeper his longing for holiness, the more abundant is his weeping when he prays. Do we not hear the voice of a citizen of the Jerusalem above in such utterances as these: 'My tears have been my only food, day and night', and: 'Every night I shall soak my bed and drench my couch with my tears', and: 'My groaning is not hidden from you', and: 'My sorrow was renewed'?[110] Are we really to suppose that those people are not God's children who 'groan, in oppression because they do not wish to be stripped, but rather to have the new clothing put on, so that this mortal element may be absorbed by life'?[111] Or those who, though 'having the first-fruits of the Spirit, are groaning inwardly while they await their adoption, the setting free of their body'?[112] And was not the apostle Paul a citizen of Jerusalem above, and was he not all the more a citizen when he felt deep sadness and continual grief in his heart for the Israelites, his brothers in the physical sense?[113]

Moreover, when will 'death be no more' in that city? Surely only when it will be said, 'Death, where is your strife? Death, where is your sting? The sting of death is sin.'[114] Without doubt there will be no more sin when it will be asked: 'Where is it?' But in our present state it is not some weak citizen of that City, but our author, John himself, who cries out in his epistle, 'If we say that we are without sin, we are fooling ourselves and we are remote from the truth.'[115]

Now in this book called the Apocalypse there are, to be sure, many obscure statements, designed to exercise the mind of the reader; and there are few statements there whose clarity enables us to track down the meaning of the rest, at the price of some effort. This is principally because our author repeats the same things in many ways, so that he appears to be speaking of different matters, though in fact he is found on examination to be treating of the same subjects in different terms. But there is nothing like this in the statement that 'God will wipe away every tear from their eyes, and death will be no more, and there will be no more sorrow or crying, nor will there be any more pain.' The reference here to the world to come, to immortality and the eternity of the saints, is as clear as day; for then, and only then, will those painful things cease to be. So clear is it that if we suppose the state-

110. Ps. 42, 3; 6, 6; 38, 9; 39, 2. 111. cf. 2 Cor. 5, 2ff.

112. Rom. 8, 23. 113. Rom 9, 2ff.

114. 1 Cor. 15, 55f. (St Augustine's text must have read *neikos*, 'strife', for *nîkos*, 'victory').

115. 1 John 1, 8.

ments to be obscure we must not expect to find any clarity in our reading of the holy Scriptures.

18. *The statements of Peter about the last judgement*

Now let us see what the apostle Peter also has written about this judgement. 'In the last days,' he says,

there will come those who scoff and who live for the indulgence of their own desires; and they will say: 'Where is the promise of his coming? Our fathers have gone to their rest, but from then onwards everything has gone on just as it has been from the beginning of creation.' For they choose to ignore the fact that there were heaven and earth in days of old, created (by God's word) of water and with water: by means of which the world of that time was flooded by water and perished. But the heavens and earth that now exist have been kept in store (again by God's word) to be reserved for the fire until the day of judgement, the day of the destruction of the ungodly. But there is one thing, dear brothers, that you must not fail to notice: that with the Lord one day is like a thousand years, and a thousand years like one day. The Lord is not slow in fulfilling his promise, as some people imagine; but he is patient for your sake, because it is not his will that anyone should be lost, but that all should be turned to repentance. But the day of the Lord will come, unexpectedly, as a thief comes; and on that day the heavens will pass away in a mighty rush, and the elements will blaze up into disintegration, and the earth and all things on the earth will be burnt up. And since all things are to perish, consider what kind of people you ought to be. You must live lives of holiness, looking for the day of the Lord and hastening towards its coming; that day which will set the heavens on fire, for their disintegration, and melt the elements with the heat of the flames. Nevertheless, we remember his promise, and we look forward to new heavens and a new earth, in which righteousness makes her abode.[116]

He has said nothing here about the resurrection of the dead, but he certainly has enough to say about the destruction of this world. Moreover, in mentioning the Deluge that happened in time gone by, he seems to be warning us, in a way, of the extent of the destruction which, as we are to believe, will come upon the world at the end of this age. For he says that the world which then existed was destroyed, and not only the cirle of the earth but the heavens also, which we are undoubtedly to take as standing for the heavens of this lower air, for that part, that tract of the sky, which the waters overwhelmed in their rising. Thus it was the whole, or almost the whole, of the windy air –

116. 2 Pet. 3, 3–13.

Peter calls it 'heaven', or rather 'the heavens'. but he surely means the lower parts, not the highest parts where the sun, moon, and stars are stationed – it was this air that was converted into a liquid state and in this way perished along with the earth, whose former aspect was certainly wiped out by the deluge. 'But the heavens and earth that now exist have been kept in store, again by God's word, to be reserved for the fire until the day of judgement, the day of the destruction of the ungodly.' Accordingly, the heavens and the earth, that is, the world which replaced the world destroyed by the Deluge, was stored away from that water, and is itself reserved for the last fire, until the day of judgement, the day of the destruction of the ungodly. For he does not hesitate to say that there will be a destruction of men also through this mighty transformation; and yet their substance will remain, although in eternal pains.

Now perhaps someone will ask this question: If the world is to blaze up, after the judgement, until it is replaced by a new heaven and a new earth, where will the saints be in the actual time of the conflagration, since they will have bodies and therefore must be in some material place? We can reply that they will be in the higher regions to which the flames of that fire will not rise, in the same way as the waters of the Flood did not rise to that level. For they will have bodies of such a nature that they may be in whatever place they choose. But in any case they will have become immortal and exempt from decay and so they will not have much fear of the fire of that conflagration, seeing that the corruptible and mortal bodies of the three men could remain alive and unharmed in the burning furnace.[117]

19. *Paul's statements in his epistle to the Thessalonians about the appearance of Antichrist, preceding the Day of the Lord*

I am aware that there are many statements in the Gospels and the Epistles about this last divine judgement which I have to pass over, for fear this volume might run on to an excessive length. But I must not on any account pass over what the apostle Paul writes to the Thessalonians.

I beg you, my brothers, by the coming of our Lord Jesus Christ and of our gathering to him, that you do not let yourselves be disturbed in mind or terrified, either by some 'inspired' utterance or statement or some letter purporting to be from us, giving it out that the Day of the Lord is at hand.

117. cf. Dan. 3, 13–27.

Do not let anyone lead you astray in any way. For that day cannot come without being preceded by the coming of the Apostate[118] and the revelation of the Man of Sin, the Son of Perdition, who is the Adversary. He exalts himself over everything that is called god or is the object of worship, so that he even seats himself in the temple of God, displaying himself as if he were a god. Do you not remember that I told you this when I was still with you? And you know what now restrains him, so that he will be revealed only at the right time. For the secret power of wickedness is already at work; only let him who now restrains, restrain him until he is removed from the scene. Then that wicked one will be revealed, and the Lord Jesus will kill him with the breath of his mouth, and will annihilate him by the radiance of his coming. But the coming of the wicked one is in accordance with Satan's way of working, accompanied by every kind of miracle and sign and by lying portents, and all manner of deception that wickedness can use on those who are on the way to destruction, because they did not welcome the love of truth so that they might be saved. That is why God will subject them to the influence of delusion, so that they may believe a lie, and may all be brought to judgement, all who did not believe the truth, but gave their support to wickedness.[119]

No one can doubt that Paul is here speaking of Antichrist, telling us that the day of judgement (which he calls the Day of the Lord) will not come without the prior coming of a figure whom he calls the Apostate, meaning, of course, an apostate from the Lord God. And if this appellation can rightly be attached to all the ungodly, how much more to him! There is, however, some uncertainty about the 'temple' in which he is to take his seat. Is it in the ruins of the Temple built by King Solomon, or actually in a church? For the Apostle would not say 'the temple of God' if he meant the temple of some idol or demon. For that reason some people would have it that Antichrist means here not the leader himself but what we may call his whole body, the multitude, that is, of those who belong to him, together with himself, their leader. And they suppose that then it would be more correct to say, following the original Greek, that he 'takes his seat *as* the temple of God', instead of '*in* the temple of God', purporting to be himself God's temple, that is, the Church: in the same way as we say, 'He sits as a friend', meaning 'like a friend' – there are customary expressions in this form.

As for the statement, 'and you know what now restrains him' – that is, what is stopping him, what is the cause of his delay – 'so that he will be revealed only at the right time', Paul did not choose to speak explicitly, because, as he says, they knew it. And that is why we who

118. Gk, 'the apostasy'. 119. 2 Thess. 2, 1–12.

have not their knowledge, are anxious to arrive at the Apostle's meaning; but we find ourselves unable to do so, for all our efforts, especially as his next statement makes the meaning still more obscure. For what does he mean by saying, 'For the secret power of wickedness is already at work; only let him who now restrains, restrain him until he is removed from the scene, and then the wicked one will be revealed'? I admit that the meaning of this completely escapes me. For all that, I shall not refrain from mentioning some guesses at the meaning which I have been able to hear or read.

Some people suppose those words to refer to the Roman imperial power, and they think that the reason for Paul's reluctance to write more explicitly was the fear of incurring a charge of slander, in wishing ill to the Roman Empire when it was hoped that it would last for ever. On this assumption 'the secret power of wickedness already at work' would be intended as a reference to Nero, whose actions already seemed like those of Antichrist. Hence there are people who suggest that Nero is to rise again and become Antichrist, while others suppose that he was not killed, but withdrawn instead so that he might be supposed killed[120] and that he is still alive and in concealment in the vigour of the age he had reached at the time of his supposed death, until 'he will be revealed at the right time for him' and restored to his throne. For myself I am much astonished at the great presumption of those who venture such guesses.

On the other hand, when the Apostle says, 'Only let him who now restrains, restrain until he is removed from the scene', there is no incongruity in believing this to refer to the Roman imperial power, saying, in effect, 'Let him who now reigns, reign until he is removed from the scene', that is, until taken away. 'Then the wicked one will be revealed': there is no doubt that this means Antichrist. However, there are others who think that 'you know what restrains' and 'the secret power of wickedness' refer only to the evil people and the pretended Christians who are in the Church, until they reach such a number as to constitute a great people for Antichrist; this, they hold, is 'the secret power of wickedness' because it is, evidently, concealed. And they suppose the Apostle to be exhorting the faithful to hold on with perseverance to the faith they hold. In their view, he is saying, 'Only let him who holds hold on, until he is removed from the scene', meaning 'until the secret power of wickedness, now concealed, departs

120. Tacitus mentions this belief as prevalent in the East in A.D. 69 (*Hist.*, 2, 8); and Suetonius says that a conviction of Nero's imminent return to take vengeance persisted for a long time (*Nero*, 57).

from the Church'. They also find a reference to this 'secret power' in what John the evangelist says in his epistle: 'My children, it is the last hour! You have been told that Antichrist is to come, and now many antichrists have appeared; which is how we recognize that this is the last hour. They went out from among us, but they did not belong to us; if they had belonged, they would surely have stayed with us.'[121] So in that hour which John calls 'the last hour', before the end, many heretics went out from the company of the Church; similarly, on this interpretation, at the actual time of the end there will go forth from the Church all who do not belong to Christ but to that last Antichrist, and it is then that he will be revealed.

Thus there are different interpretations of the obscure words of the Apostle, put forward by different commentators. But the general meaning of what he said is not doubtful. Christ will not come to judge the living and the dead without the prior coming of his adversary, Antichrist, to seduce those who are dead in soul – although their seduction depends on the judgement of God, which is now concealed. For, as it is said, 'The coming of the wicked one is in accordance with Satan's way of working, accompanied by every kind of miracle and sign and by lying portents, and all manner of deception that wickedness can use on those on the way to destruction.' It is, in fact, at that time that Satan will be unloosed, and by the agency of that Antichrist he will carry on his work with every kind of miracle of his, marvellously, yes, but mendaciously. It is a continual matter of debate whether these are called 'signs and lying portents' because he is going to deceive mortal senses by illusions, by appearing to do what he does not really perform, or because, while they are genuine prodigies, their effect will be to draw men into falsehood, in that people will believe that they could only have been achieved by the power of God, being unaware of the strength of the Devil, and especially his strength when he has received such power as he never before enjoyed. For when fire fell from heaven and wiped out, in one sweep, all the large household and the numerous flocks of holy Job, and a whirlwind rushed down and overthrew his house and slew his children,[122] those were no illusions; and yet they were the work of Satan, to whom God had given this power.

Now the reason for the description, 'signs and lying portents', will become more evident when they happen. But whatever the reason, those who are led astray by those signs and wonders will be those who deserve to be led astray, 'because', in the Apostle's words, 'they did not

121. John 2, 18f. 122. cf. Job 1, 16–19.

welcome the love of truth so that they might be saved.' And the Apostle had no hesitation in adding, 'for this reason God will subject them to the influence of delusion, so that they may believe a lie.' God, that is, will 'subject them to that influence' in the sense that, by a just decision of his own, he will allow the Devil to perform those feats, although the Devil performs them with a wicked and malignant design. 'That they may all be brought to judgement', he says, 'all who did not believe the truth, but gave their support to wickedness.' Thus they will be led astray after being judged, and after being led astray they will be judged. But when they have been judged they will be led astray by those judgements of God, secretly just, and justly secret, that judgement he has never ceased to exercise since the first sin of rational creatures; and after being led astray they will be judged by that last and open judgement administered by Jesus Christ, who is to judge with perfect justice, though it was with utter injustice that he himself was judged.

20. *Paul's teaching in the First Epistle to the Thessalonians about the resurrection of the dead*

In this passage the Apostle says nothing about the resurrection of the dead. However, in his first epistle to the same Thessalonians he writes as follows:

> We do not want you to be ignorant, brothers, about those who have fallen asleep; we want to prevent your sorrowing like the rest of mankind, who are without hope. We believe that Jesus died and rose again; if so, through Jesus, God will likewise bring, along with Jesus, those who have fallen asleep in his faith. For we have this to say to you as the word of the Lord: that we who are left alive until the coming of the Lord shall not precede those who have fallen asleep. For the Lord himself will descend from heaven at the word of command, at the sound of the archangel's voice, and the trumpet-call of God; and the Christian dead will rise first, then we who are left alive shall be caught up, along with them, in the clouds, to meet Christ in the air. Thus we shall always be with the Lord.[123]

The Apostle's words show with the utmost clarity that there will be a resurrection of the dead when Christ comes; and assuredly the purpose of his coming will be to judge the living and the dead.

But it is continually being asked whether those whom Christ is to find living in this world (represented in the Apostle's picture by himself and his contemporaries) are never to die at all, or whether in that precise moment of time when they are caught up in the clouds, along

123. 1 Thess. 4, 13–17.

with those rising again, to meet Christ in the air, they will pass with marvellous speed through death to immortality. For it must not be said that it is impossible for them to die and to come to life again in that space of time when they are being carried on high through the air. We are not to take the statement that 'we shall always be with the Lord', as meaning that we are to remain for ever in the air with the Lord. He himself will assuredly not remain there; he will pass through as he comes. The meeting with him, we may be sure, will take place as he comes, not while he lingers there; and we 'shall be with the Lord' in the sense that we shall have immortal bodies and so we shall be with him everywhere. The Apostle himself seems to demand that we should take his words in this sense; that is, we should take it that those whom the Lord will find alive here will undergo death and receive immortality in that brief space of time. He confirms this interpretation when he says, 'In Christ all men will be brought to life', and by his statement in another passage, dealing directly with the resurrection of the body: 'The seed you sow does not come to life unless it first dies.'[124]

If so, how can those whom Christ finds alive here come to life in him by receiving immortality, without dying, when we see that this was the point of the saying that 'the seed you sow does not come to life unless it first dies'? Or if it is not correct to speak of human bodies as being 'sown' unless they in some way return to the earth at death (as in the sentence divinely pronounced on the transgressor, the father of mankind: 'Earth you are, and to earth you will go'[125]) then we have to admit that those whom Christ, at his coming, will find not yet parted from the body, are not covered by the words of the Apostle and of Genesis – being caught up in the clouds they are certainly not sown, since they neither go to the earth nor return to it, whether they experience no death at all or die for a short space in the air.

But there is yet another saying of the Apostle that comes to mind; it is what he said to the Corinthians on the subject of the resurrection of the body. 'We shall all rise again', he says, or according to other manuscripts, 'We shall all sleep.'[126] Since, then, the resurrection cannot happen without a preceding death and we can only interpret sleep in this passage as meaning death, how can it be that 'all' sleep and rise again, if so many whom Christ is to find in the body will neither sleep nor rise again? If, then, we believe that the saints who

124. 1 Cor. 15, 22; 36. 125. Gen. 3, 19.

126. 1 Cor. 15, 51. There are several variant readings in this verse; but the better MSS read, 'We shall not all sleep.'

are found alive at Christ's coming and are caught up to meet him will part from their bodies in that same snatching up and will straightway return to those bodies, now immortal – if we assume this, we shall encounter no difficulties in the words of the Apostle, either when he says, 'The seed you sow does not come to life unless it first dies', or when he says: 'We shall all rise again', or, 'We shall all sleep.' For they also will not be brought to life again unless they first die, however momentarily, and so they will not be debarred from resurrection, which for them is preceded by a sleep – an extremely short sleep, it is true, yet still a sleep. If it comes to that, why should we think it incredible that all those many bodies are, in a fashion, 'sown' in the air, where they come to life again straightway, a life exempt from death and decay? After all, we believe the explicit statement of the Apostle, that the resurrection will happen 'in the twinkling of an eye',[127] and that the dust of corpses of remote antiquity will return with such ease and with a speed beyond all reckoning to limbs which are to live a life without ending.

We are not even to conclude that those saints are to be exempt from the sentence pronounced on man, 'You are earth, and to earth you will go', on the assumption that their bodies, when they die, will not fall back to earth, but just as they will die in the actual process of being caught up, so they will also rise again while they are being borne up into the air. 'To earth you will go' means, we may be sure, 'On losing your life you will go back to what you were before you received life', that is, 'when the breath of life has left you you will be what you were before you received that breath' (for, as we know, it was into a face of earth that God 'breathed the breath of life' when 'man was made a living soul'). It is tantamount to saying, 'You are animated earth, which you were not before: you will be inanimate earth, as you were before.' This is the condition of all the bodies of the dead, even before they begin to putrify, and it will be the condition of the bodies of those saints, if they die, wherever they die, when they are deprived of life, only to receive it again straightway. Thus they will 'go to earth' because from being living men they will become earth, in the same way as what becomes ashes 'turns to ashes', what becomes decrepit 'goes into decrepitude', what was clay and becomes a jar 'turns into a jar' – there are thousands of similar expressions. How this is to happen is something we can now only vaguely imagine with the poor little powers of our reason; but then, when it happens, we shall be able to understand. It is certainly our duty, if we wish to be

127. 1 Cor. 15, 22.

Christians, to believe that there will be a resurrection of the dead, and a resurrection in the flesh, when Christ comes to judge the living and the dead; it does not follow that our faith in this subject is vain just because we are unable to comprehend perfectly how this is to come about.

Our present obligation, however, is to show, as we promised above,[128] what the ancient prophetical books foretold about this last judgement of God, as far as shall seem sufficient; and, in my opinion, it will not be necessary to treat them with any great length of exposition, if the reader will be at pains to make use of the help we have already furnished.

21. *Isaiah on the resurrection, and on the judgement of retribution*

The prophet Isaiah says, 'The dead will rise again, and those who were in the graves will rise again, and all who are in the earth will rejoice; for the dew which comes from you is health for them; but the earth of the ungodly will fall.'[129] All the earlier part of this passage is concerned with the resurrection of the blessed. But the words, 'the earth of the ungodly will fall', are correctly interpreted to mean that the downfall of condemnation will involve the bodies of the ungodly. And if we should decide to go on to a more attentive and detailed examination of what is said about the resurrection of the good we must refer to the first resurrection the statement that 'the dead will rise again', while the words that follow, 'and those who were in the graves will rise again', must be referred to the second resurrection. Now if we look for a reference to those saints whom the Lord is to find alive here, the next statement may be appropriately assigned to them: 'And all who are in the earth will rejoice; for the dew which comes from you is health for them.' 'Health' in this passage we may correctly interpret as 'immortality'; for health in the fullest sense is health which is not continually restored by food – by daily medicines, as it were.

In the same fashion, after first giving hope to the good about the day of judgement, the same prophet then proceeds to strike terror into the wicked. He says,

> This is what the Lord says: 'See, I am turning towards them like a river of peace, and like a torrent that inundates the glory of the nations. Their sons will be carried on the shoulders and will be comforted on the knees. Like a

128. cf. ch. 4. 129. Is. 26, 19 (LXX).

son whom his mother comforts so I will comfort you. And in Jerusalem you will be comforted, and you will see, and your heart will rejoice, and your bones will rise up like the grass. And the hand of the Lord will be known to his worshippers, and he will threaten the insolent. For see, the Lord will come like a fire, and his chariot like a tempest, to wreak vengeance in his indignation and devastation with the flames of fire. For by the fire of the Lord all the earth will be judged and all mankind by his sword. Many will be wounded by the Lord.[130]

In his promise to the good we should undoubtedly understand the 'river of peace' as meaning the overflowing abundance of his peace, and there could be no greater peace than that. With this peace we shall, assuredly, be refreshed in the end as if with water. We have in fact spoken of this in the previous book, and spoken to overflowing! This is the river which he says he will direct towards those to whom he promises bliss so great that we may understand that all things in that region of felicity, that region in the heavens, are fully supplied by this river. But because the peace of incorruption and immorality will flow thence upon earthly bodies also, he says that he will 'direct' (or 'turn down') this river so that it may flow, as it were, from the realms above even to the lower regions and may put men on the same footing as the angels.

By 'Jerusalem', moreover, we must understand not the Jerusalem who is enslaved along with her children, but our free mother, the Jerusalem which, according to the Apostle, is eternal in the heavens.[131] There, after the hardships of our anxieties and worries in this mortal state we shall be comforted like little children carried on the mother's shoulders and nursed in her lap. For that unaccustomed bliss will lift us up, untrained and immature as we are, and support us with tenderest caresses. There 'we shall see, and our heart will rejoice.' The prophet does not expressly say what it is that we shall see; but what can it be but God? For thus the promise of the Gospel will be fulfilled in us, where it says, 'Blessed are the pure in heart, for they will see God.'[132] And we shall see all those things which we do not see now; but even now, because we believe, we imagine them, up to the poor capacity of our human minds; though our idea of them falls incomparably short of the reality. 'And you will see', says the prophet, 'and your heart will rejoice.' Here, you believe; there, you will see.

However, for fear that we should suppose, because he says, 'Your heart will rejoice', that the blessings of that Jerusalem belong exclus-

130. Is. 66, 12–16. 131. cf. Gal. 4, 26. 132. Matt. 5, 8.

ively to the spirit, he goes on to say, 'And your bones will rise up like the grass', thus touching on the resurrection of the body, as if repairing an omission; for this resurrection will not happen *after* we have seen: we shall see after it has taken place. He has, in fact, spoken earlier about the new heaven and the new earth in the course of his description of the things promised to the saints at the end, often repeated in many different images. 'There will be a new heaven and a new earth; and they will not remember the former heaven and earth, and the memory of them will not come to their mind; but they will find joy and gladness in the new creation. See, I shall make Jerusalem a gladness and my people a joy; and I shall be glad in Jerusalem and rejoice in my people; and no more will there be heard in her the voice of weeping'[133], and the rest of the promises which some people try to refer to that life in the body during those thousand years. For metaphorical and literal expressions are intermingled, in the prophetic manner, so that a sober attentiveness may arrive at the spiritual meaning by a painstaking effort which is both useful and salutary; whereas the indolence of the flesh and the slowness of an uninstructed and untrained mind is content with the superficial, literal meaning and thinks that no inner meaning is to be sought. These remarks must suffice for the prophetic utterances in Scripture which precede the passsage under discussion.

To return to the passage from which we digressed: when the prophet says, 'and your bones will rise up like the grass', he is certainly describing the resurrection of the body, but he goes on to show that it is only the resurrection of the good that he is now speaking of. He does this by adding, 'and the hand of the Lord will be known to his worshippers.' This must surely mean the hand of one who distinguishes his worshippers from his despisers. He refers to the latter in the words that follow without a break. 'And he will threaten the insolent', he says, or, as another translator renders it, 'the unbelieving'. At that time he will not threaten them: the words that are now spoken in menace will then be fulfilled in practice. 'For see', he says, 'the Lord will come like a fire, and his chariots like a tempest, to execute vengeance in his indignation and devastation with the flames of fire. For by the fire of the Lord all the earth will be judged, and all mankind by his sword. Many will be wounded by the Lord.' 'Fire', 'whirlwind', 'sword', all stand for the punishment of judgement; for the prophet says that the Lord himself will come as a fire, to those, of course, to whom his coming is to bring punishment. But the 'chariots' (the word

133. Is. 65. 17ff.

used is plural) we appropriately take as standing for the ministering angels. As for the statement that the whole earth and all mankind are judged by the fire and the sword of the Lord, we must understand the reference here to be not to the spiritual and holy but to the earthly and carnal, such people as are described as 'having worldly wisdom' and 'carnally minded', which is 'death'; the people generally called 'flesh' by the Lord, when he says, 'My spirit will not always remain in those men, because they are flesh.'[134]

The 'wound' referred to in the next statement, 'Many will be wounded by the Lord', is the 'wound' by which the second death will be effected. Now it is possible, to be sure, to take 'fire', 'sword' and 'wound' in a good sense. For the Lord said that he wanted 'to send fire on the earth'; and the divided tongues 'appeared to them to be flames of fire' when the Holy Spirit came; and 'I have not come', said the Lord, 'to send peace on earth, but a sword.' And Scripture says that the word of God is a two-edged sword, because of its double edge, the two testaments; and in the Song of Songs the holy Church says that she is wounded by love, shot, as it were, by love's arrow.[135] But in the context of our passage, when we hear or read that the Lord is to come as an avenger, it is obvious how these words are to be understood.

Then, after a brief mention of those who will be destroyed in this judgement, where the sinners and the ungodly are symbolized by those who did not abstain from the foods forbidden by the old Law,[136] the prophet gives a summary account of the grace of the new covenant from the first coming of the Saviour to the last judgement, which is our present subject. Thus he brings his discourse to an end. For he tells us that the Lord says that he is coming to assemble all the nations, and that they are to come and see his glory. 'For', as the Apostle says, 'all men have sinned and lack the glory of God.'[137] And the Lord says that he will leave signs on them – evidently in order that they may be amazed at them and come to believe in him; and that he will send out from their number men who have been saved, dispatching them to various peoples and to far-off islands, which have not heard his name or seen his glory; and that they will proclaim his glory among the nations and will bring in the brothers of those whom the prophet was addressing, that is, brothers in the faith of the chosen Israelites under God the Father; and that they will bring

134. Phil. 3, 19; Rom. 8, 6; Gen. 6, 3.
135. Luke 12, 49; Acts 2, 3; Matt. 10, 34; Hebr. 4, 12; S. of S. 2, 5.
136. cf. Is. 66, 17. 137. Is. 66, 19; Rom. 3, 23.

from all the nations a gift for the Lord on beasts of burden and on vehicles (these 'beasts' and 'vehicles' are rightly interpreted as symbolizing the divine assistance by the two types of God's ministers, angelic and human) bringing their gift to the Holy City of Jerusalem, which is now spread throughout the world in the persons of the faithful people of God.[138] For where men receive divine assistance, that is where men believe; and where they believe, that is where they come.

Then the Lord compares these newcomers to the children of Israel offering him their sacrifices in his house with psalms, as the Church now does everywhere. And he promises that he will accept some of them to be his priests and Levites;[139] and we now see that fulfilled in the same degree. For now we do not see priests and Levites chosen from a clan, related by flesh and blood, which was the rule according to descent from Aaron, but, as was rightly established under the new covenant (where the chief priest, 'in the line of Melchizedech',[140] is Christ) each man is chosen in accordance with the merit bestowed on him by God's grace. They are not to be valued merely for that title, which unworthy men often acquire, but for something which is not common to good men and bad, namely holiness.

After speaking of that unmistakable and well-known mercy of God, which is even now bestowed on the Church, the Lord gives a promise of the final states which will be reached when the final judgement has separated the good and the wicked. He speaks through the mouth of the prophet (or the prophet speaks as representing the Lord) and says,

> For as the new heaven and the new earth will remain before me, says the Lord, so will your race and your name remain, and month will follow month, and Sabbath will follow Sabbath. All mankind will come into my presence to worship in Jerusalem, says the Lord. And they will go out and will see the limbs of human beings who have rebelled against me. Their worm will not die, their fire will not be put out, and they will be a spectacle for all mankind.[141]

This was the point at which the prophet ended his book, the point at which the world will come to an end. Some people, it is true, have given the translation 'corpses of men'[142] instead of 'limbs of human beings', meaning by 'corpses' the visible punishment of the body, although the word 'corpse' is normally used only of lifeless flesh, whereas those bodies will be alive, since otherwise they could not feel

138. Is. 66, 19f. 139. Is. 66, 21. 140. Ps. 110, 4.
141. Is. 66, 22ff. 142. The reading of the Vulgate.

any torments; unless perhaps those bodies also may without absurdity be called 'corpses' on the ground that they are the bodies of dead men, that is, of men who will fall into the second death – hence the words I have quoted above from the same prophet: 'But the earth of the ungodly will fall.'[143] Yet who could fail to see that *cadavera* ('corpses') are so called from falling (*cadendo*)?[144] At the same time, it is obvious that those translators used 'men' to convey the same meaning as 'human beings'. For no one is likely to assert that women who transgress will not incur that punishment! The fact is that both sexes are included under the more important sex, especially as that was the sex from which woman was created. But the point of the greatest relevance to our subject is that the words 'all flesh will come' refer also to the good, for God's People will be made up of men of every race – though not all mankind will be there, since many will be enduring punishment. In fact (and this is the point I was establishing) 'flesh' is the word used in reference to the good as well as the bad, and 'limbs' or 'corpses' in reference to the wicked; and this makes it plain that the judgement by which the good and the wicked are separated into their appropriate final states will certainly follow the resurrection of the body, and thus our faith in this resurrection is strengthened by the use of these terms to describe the facts.

22. *The saints' knowledge of the punishment of the wicked*

But how is it that the good will 'go out' to see the punishment of the wicked? Are we to imagine that they are to leave their blessed abodes by a bodily movement and to proceed to the region of punishment, so that they may view the torments of the wicked in bodily presence? Certainly not. It is by their knowledge that they will 'go out'; and the expression conveys the idea that those who are being tormented will be outside. That is also why the Lord calls that region 'outer darkness', in contrast to the 'entrance', referred to when the good servant was told to 'enter into the joy of your Lord'.[145] The intention of this expression is to prevent any notion that the wicked enter in so that they may be known, and to insist that the good go out to them in virtue of the knowledge which will make them recognize the wicked for what they are; they will be aware of the situation outside. Those who are undergoing punishment will not know what is happening inside, in the joy of the Lord; whereas those who are in that joy will

143. Is. 26, 19, (LXX). 144. cf. ch. 10.
145. Matt. 25, 30; 21; 23.

know what is happening outside, in the 'outer darkness'. That is the reason for saying 'they will go out'; those who are 'outside', in relation to the good, will assuredly not be hidden from the good. For if the prophets were able to know those things before they had happened, because God was present, in however small a degree, in the minds of those mortals, how can the immortal saints fail to know what has already happened, at the time when 'God will be all in all'?[146]

The 'seed', then, and the 'name' will stand fast in that blessed condition of the saints – the seed mentioned by John when he says, 'his seed remains in him', and the name referred to in another message delivered by Isaiah: 'I will give them an everlasting name.'[147] 'Month will follow month, Sabbath will follow Sabbath' is as much as to say, 'Moon after moon, rest after rest'. And the good will have both 'moon' and 'rest' when they pass from these old shadows of time into the new lights of eternity.

In the punishment of the wicked, on the other hand, the unquenchable fire and the undying worm are differently explained by different authorities. Some people, in fact, refer both to the body; others refer both to the soul. Yet others refer the fire to the body in the literal sense, and the worm to the soul in the metaphorical sense, and this interpretation seems more credible. But there is no time to discuss this difference at the moment; for the subject I have undertaken to deal with in this book is the last judgement, which effects the separation between the good and the wicked; their actual rewards and punishments have to be discussed in greater detail at another time.

23. *Daniel's prophecies about Antichrist, the judgement, and the reign of the saints*

Daniel prophesies about the last judgement in such a way as to predict also the prior coming of Antichrist, and to continue his narrative as far as the eternal reign of the saints. He begins with his prophetic vision of the four beasts, symbolizing four kingdoms, and the fourth of these is overcome by a king who is recognized as Antichrist. This is followed by the eternal reign of the Son of Man, who is understood to be Christ; and then Daniel says, 'As for me, Daniel, my spirit shuddered in my dwelling, and the visions of my head disturbed me. And I approached one of the bystanders, and asked him the truth about all those things; and he told me the truth.'[148]

Daniel then tells what he heard from him of whom he had inquired about all those matters, putting it as if it were the bystander giving

146. 1 Cor. 15, 28. 147. 1 John 3, 9; Is. 56, 5. 148. Dan. 7, 15f.

explanation to him. 'These four beasts: four kingdoms will arise on earth, which will be removed; and the saints of the Most High will receive the kingdom and will possess it for ever, for ever and ever. Then I enquired carefully', he says,

about the fourth beast, which was different from every other beast, far more terrible, with iron teeth and bronze claws, chewing and crushing to pieces and trampling underfoot what remained. And I asked about the ten horns on his head, and about the other horn which came up and struck down three of the former horns; this horn had eyes and a mouth uttering great boasts, and it looked bigger than the rest of them. I watched it making war on the saints, and getting the better of them, until the Ancient One came and gave the kingdom to the saints of the Most High, when the time came for the saints to take possession of the kingdom.[149]

This, says Daniel, is the question he asked. And he goes on to give the reply he received. 'Then he said' (that is, the man questioned gave this reply),

The fourth beast is the fourth kingdom which will be on the earth. It will prevail over all kingdoms: and it will devour the whole earth, and trample on it and destroy it. And the ten horns: ten kings will arise. And after them will arise another who will surpass in wickedness all who preceded him. He will humble three kings, and will speak insulting words against the Most High; and he will harass the saints of the Most High, and will conceive the notion of changing times and laws. And power will be given into his hand for a time and times and half a time. Then a court will sit, and they will take away his sovereignty, to be destroyed and finally brought to nothing. Then the kingdom and the power and the might of all the kings under the whole heaven will be given to the saints of the Most High. His kingdom is an everlasting kingdom, and all principalities will serve and obey him.

'Here', says Daniel, 'the discourse ended. As for me, Daniel, my thoughts greatly disturbed me, and my appearance was altered. But I kept those words to myself.'

Some commentators have interpreted those four kingdoms as the Assyrians, the Persians, the Macedonians, and the Romans. Those who would like to know how appropriate this interpretation is should read the commentary on Daniel by the presbyter Jerome, a most learned and detailed study. Yet anyone who reads the passage in Daniel, even if half-asleep, cannot conceivably doubt that the reign of Antichrist is to be endured, if only for a brief space of time, with its bitter savagery against the Church, until by the final judgement of God the saints receive their everlasting kingdom. It is, we know, abun-

149. Dan. 7, 23–8.

dantly clear, from the number of days given in a later passage,[150] that 'a time and times and half a time' stand for 'a year, two years, and half a year' – three and a half years, though in the Scriptures this is often given in months. For although 'times' in Latin looks like an indefinite expression, the original word is dual, a form not found in Latin: but Greek has the dual form, and so, it is said,[151] does Hebrew. Hence 'times' means here 'two times'. I confess, indeed, that I fear we may be mistaken in respect of the ten kings whom Antichrist, as it seems, is to find, who are ostensibly ten men; I am afraid, that is, that Antichrist may come unexpectedly, seeing that there are not as many kings as that in existence in the Roman world. But it may be suggested that the number ten signifies the total number of kings after whom he is to come, in the same way as totality is frequently signified by a thousand, or a hundred, or seven,[152] or by several other numbers – there is no need to give a list of them here.

There is another passage in Daniel which runs as follows:

> Then there will be a time of distress unparalleled from the first beginning of mankind on the earth until that time. When that time comes all your people will be preserved who are found recorded in the book. And many of those who are sleeping in the heaped-up earth will rise up, some to eternal life, some to shame and eternal disgrace. Then those who understand will shine like the brightness of the vault of heaven, and many of the just will shine like the stars for all eternity.[153]

This passage closely resembles the statement in the Gospel quoted earlier,[154] at least in regard to the resurrection of the dead. For those who are described there as being 'in the graves' are here described as 'in the heaped-up earth', or, as others translate it, 'in the dust of the earth'; and as it is said there that 'they will come out', so here 'they will rise up'; there it says that 'those whose actions have been good will come out to the resurrection of life, but those whose actions have been evil, to the resurrection of judgement', and in this passage, similarly, 'some to eternal life, some to shame and eternal disgrace'. And it must not be regarded as a discrepancy that the Gospel mentions '*all* who are in the graves', while the prophet, instead of saying 'all', says '*many* of those who are sleeping in the heaped-up earth'. For Scripture often puts 'many' for 'all'. For example, it was said to Abraham: 'I have appointed you as the father of *many* nations', but, in another place, 'In your descendants *all* nations will be blessed.'[155]

150. Dan. 12, 11. 151. It is true.
152. cf. ch. 5; ch. 7; and Bk XI, 31f.; XV, 20; XVII, 4.
153. Dan. 12, 1–3. 154. John 5, 28f; cf. ch. 6.
155. Gen. 17, 5; 22, 18.

On the subject of the resurrection thus described the prophet Daniel receives a personal message a little later on, when he is told, 'You also come and rest: for there is still a day before the completion of the consummation, and you will rest, and will rise again to receive your share at the end of time.'[156]

24. *Prophecies in the psalms about the end of the world and the last judgement*

The psalms contain many references to the last judgement, most of them being brief statements made in passing. But I shall certainly not fail to mention the most explicit statement in the psalms about the end of this world. 'In the beginning you founded the world, Lord, and the heavens are the work of your hands. They will perish, but you endure; and they will all grow old like a piece of clothing, and you will change them like a garment, and they will be changed. But you are always the same, and your years will never end.'[157] Why is it that though Porphyry praises the devotion of the Hebrews in their worship of a God who is great and true and terrible even to the divine powers,[158] he charges the Christians with supreme folly in asserting that this world is doomed to perish? He supports the charge with quotations from the oracles of his gods. But observe this statement from the sacred Scriptures of the Hebrews. It is addressed to the God whom even the divinities themselves regard with dread; and it says, 'The heavens are the work of your hands; they will perish.'

Now, are we to suppose that the world will not perish, when the heavens perish? For the heavens are the higher and the more secure part of the world. If this statement is displeasing to Jupiter, on whose oracle, as being of higher authority, the philosopher bases his attack on the credulity of Christians, why does he not make the same attack on the wisdom of the Hebrews, as being folly? For it is in their religious literature that the statement is found. Moreover if Porphyry so much approves of this Hebrew wisdom that he proclaims its merits by the utterances of his gods, as well as with his own voice, and if the statement that the heavens are doomed to perish occurs in that wisdom, why does his delusion reach such a pitch of futility as to cry out against this tenet of the Christian faith? Why condemn, along with the rest of that faith, or even above the rest, the belief that the world is to perish, which is necessarily entailed by the belief that the heavens will pass away? It is true that in the sacred books, which are

156. Dan. 12, 13. 157. Ps. 102, 25ff. 158. cf. Bk XIX, 23.

the special property of us Christians, and are not shared by us with the Hebrews, that is, in the Gospels and the apostolic writings, one finds such statements as: 'The form of this world is transitory'; 'The world is passing away'; 'Heaven and earth will pass away.'[159] But I regard 'transitory' and 'pass away' as somewhat milder expressions than 'perish'.

In the epistle of the apostle Peter, also, in which it is said that the world which then existed perished under the Flood of water, it is quite clear what part of the world is signified by the whole, and to what extent it is said to have perished, and what heavens were kept in store, to be reserved for the fire until the day of judgement and of the destruction of wicked men.[160] Then he says, a little later, 'The day of the Lord will come unexpectedly, as a thief comes; and on that day the heavens will pass away in a mighty rush, and the elements will blaze up into disintegration, and the earth and all things on the earth will be burnt up'; and he adds, 'Since all things are to perish, consider what kind of people you ought to be.'[161] Now these heavens which are doomed to perish may be taken to be the heavens which are, according to Peter, 'kept in store, to be reserved for the fire', and the elements which are to 'blaze up' may be taken to be those stormy, turbulent elements in this lowest section of the world, in which, he says, those same heavens are kept in store, while the higher heavens, in whose vault the stars are stationed, remain unharmed and continue in their own inviolate condition. In fact, even the scriptural statement that 'the stars are to fall from heaven'[162] – leaving aside the fact that it can much more plausibly be taken in another sense – demonstrates rather that the heavens are going to remain, if the stars are indeed to fall from them! For either this expression is metaphorical (the more probable interpretation) or else it describes something which will occur in this lowest heaven, albeit an event certainly more amazing than any phenomenon of these days. Something of this kind is that star in Virgil that

> Trailing its torch coursed with bright light through heaven

and 'hid itself in the forest of Ida'.[163]

What I have quoted from the psalm, on the other hand, seems to leave none of the heavens outside the scope of this future destruction. For it says, 'The heavens are the work of your hands; they will perish.' And as none of them is outside the scope of God's work, so none of

159. 1 Cor. 7, 31; 1 John 2, 17; Matt. 24, 35.
160. 2 Pet. 3, 6f.
161. 2 Pet. 3, 10f.
162. Matt. 24, 29.
163. *Aen.*, 2, 694; 696.

them is withdrawn from the scope of the destruction. And yet our philosophers will not deign to support the piety of the Hebrews approved by the oracles of their gods, by quoting the expressions of the apostle Peter, whom they bitterly hate. They might, at least, avoid the supposition that it is the whole of the world that is to perish, by the argument that in the psalmist's statement, 'they shall perish', the whole stands for the part, because it is only the lowest heavens that are to perish. This would be in line with the apostle's use of 'the whole for the part' in his epistle, where he says that the world perished in the Flood, whereas in fact it was only the lowest part of it that perished, along with its own region of the heavens. But since, as I said, they will not condescend to approve Peter's view, and to ascribe to the final conflagration only so much effect as we attribute to the Deluge – for they maintain that waters or flames could never wipe out the whole human race – their only course is to declare that the reason why their gods praised the wisdom of the Hebrews is that the gods had failed to read that particular psalm!

Again, in the forty-ninth psalm we see a reference to the last judgement of God in these verses: 'God will come in manifest presence; he will not be silent. Fire will blaze before him; and around him will be a mighty tempest. He will summon the heaven above, and the earth, to judge among his people. Assemble his righteous ones before him, who put his covenant above sacrifices.'[164] This we take as describing our Lord Jesus Christ, whose coming from heaven we await, to judge the living and the dead. For he will come in manifest presence, to execute just judgement on the just and the unjust – he who first came secretly, to be judged unjustly by the unjust. He, I repeat, 'will come in manifest presence; he will not be silent'; this means that he will make his presence known by the voice of his judgement, he who when he first came in secret was silent before his judge, when he 'was brought like a sheep to be slaughtered, and was speechless like a lamb in the presence of the shearer', as we read in Isaiah's prophecy of him,[165] and as we see in the fulfilment of that prophecy in the Gospel story. As for the fire and the tempest, I have already said how those are to be understood when I treated of a similar passage in the prophecy of Isaiah. And as for 'he will summon the heavens above', the saints and the just are properly called 'heaven', and so this doubtless means what the apostle is describing when he says, 'We shall be caught up

164. Ps. 50 (49 in LXX), 3ff.
165. cf. Is. 53, 7; Matt. 26, 62f.; 27, 12, 14; John 19, 9.

along with them in the clouds into the air, to meet Christ.'[166] For, if we take the superficial meaning, what is meant by the summoning of heaven 'above', as if it could be anywhere else than 'above'? And as for the words following, 'and the earth, to judge among his people', if we take this with 'he will summon', that is, 'he will summon the earth also', instead of connecting it also with 'above', this seems to give a meaning in harmony with sound faith, in that 'heaven' is taken to mean those who will be associated with Christ in judging, while 'earth' means those who are to be judged. Thus we are to take 'will summon the heaven above' as meaning 'he will summon the angels in the high exalted realms, and with them he will descend to execute judgement'; then 'and he will summon the earth' will mean 'summon the men on earth to submit to judgement'. But if we have to take both 'he will summon' and 'above' with 'and the earth', the meaning will be: 'He will summon the heaven above, and the earth above'; and in that case it is best, I think, to understand it as describing all those who will be caught up into the air to meet Christ, but 'heaven' will refer to their souls and 'earth' to their bodies.

Then 'to judge among his people' can surely only mean that he will separate by his judgement the good from the wicked, the 'sheep' from the 'goats'. Then he turns to speak to the angels: 'Assemble his righteous ones before him', for a matter of such importance must needs be carried out by the ministry of the angels. If we ask further who those 'righteous ones' are whom the angels are to assemble, we have the answer in 'those who put his covenant above sacrifices'. This is the whole life of the righteous, to put the covenant of God above sacrifices. For either it is the deeds of mercy which are 'above sacrifices', that is are to be preferred to sacrifices, in harmony with God's declaration that he 'desires mercy rather than sacrifice';[167] or, if 'above sacrifices' is taken to mean '*in* sacrifices' in the same way as something which certainly happens *in* the world is said to be done '*upon* earth', then in that case it is just those deeds of mercy that are undoubtedly the sacrifices which are pleasing to God – a point which I recollect having made in the tenth book of this work;[168] and in those deeds of mercy the righteous 'set up God's covenant' because they do them in view of the promises contained in the new covenant. Hence, when his righteous ones have been assembled and stationed on his right hand in the last judgement, Christ will undoubtedly say to them, 'Come, you that have my Father's blessing, take possession of the kingdom prepared for you from the foundation of the world. For I

166. 1 Thess. 4, 17; cf. ch. 20. 167. Hos. 6, 6. 168. cf. Bk x, 6.

was hungry, and you gave me food to eat'[169] and so on – a public statement of the good deeds of the good, and the everlasting rewards which will be given them by the last sentence pronounced by the Judge.

25. *The prophecy of Malachi about the last judgement and the purifying punishments*

The prophet Malachiel or Malachi (who is also called 'Angel') is thought by some to be Ezra the priest (Jerome says that this was an opinion held by the Hebrews[170]), who was the author of some other works[171] received in the canon. He gives a prophecy of the last judgement in the following passage:

> See, he comes, says the Lord Almighty! And who will withstand the day of his coming, and who will be able to endure to look him in the face? For he comes like a refiner's fire and like a fuller's herb; and he will sit, refining and purifying as it were gold and silver. And he will purify the sons of Levi, and will pour them out like gold and silver. Then they will offer to the Lord sacrifices in righteousness, and the sacrifice of Judah and Jerusalem will be pleasing to the Lord, as in the days of old and in years gone by. And I shall come to you in judgement, and I shall be a swift witness against sorcerers, and against adulterers, and against those who swear in my name falsely, and those who defraud the worker of his wages, and use their power to oppress the widows and maltreat the orphans and pervert judgement against the stranger, and have no fear of me, says the Lord Almighty. For I am the Lord your God; and I do not change.[172]

From these words it seems quite evident that in the judgement the punishments of some are to be purificatory. For how else are we to understand this passage: 'Who will withstand the day of his coming, and who will be able to look him in the face? For he comes like a refiner's fire and like a fuller's herb; and he will sit, refining and purifying as it were silver and gold. And he will purify the sons of Levi, and will pour them out like gold and silver'? Isaiah also says something in the same strain, 'The Lord will wash the stains of the sons and daughters of Sion, and will cleanse the blood from the midst of them by the breath of judgement and the breath of burning.'[173] Now perhaps we might say that they are cleansed from their stains and purified in a certain sense when the wicked are separated from

169. Matt. 25, 34.
170. Hier., *Praef. in Mal.* The 'other works' are Ezra and Nehemiah.
171. Ezra and Nehemiah.
172. Mal. 3, 1–6. 173. Is. 4, 4.

them by the penal judgement, and when the segregation and condemnation of the wicked effects the purgation of the rest, because thereafter they are going to live free from any contamination by such people. But Malachi says, 'And he will purify the sons of Levi, and will pour them out like gold and silver; and then they will offer to the Lord sacrifices in righteousness, and the sacrifice of Judah and Jerusalem will be pleasing to the Lord'; and in these words he is obviously pointing out that those who have been cleansed will then be pleasing to the Lord in respect of their sacrifices of righteousness; and that implies that they themselves will be cleansed from their own unrighteousness which rendered them displeasing to God. Moreover, they themselves, after their cleansing, will be sacrificial offerings in their complete and perfect righteousness; for what offerings do such people make which is more acceptable to God than the offering of themselves? However, the more searching examination of the question of purificatory punishment must be postponed to another time.

As for 'the sons of Levi', and 'Judah', and 'Jerusalem', we ought to take those as standing for the Church of God itself, assembled not only from the Hebrews but from other nations also. And we should understand not the Church in its present state, when 'if we say that we have no sin we are fooling ourselves and we are strangers to the truth',[174] but the Church as it will be then, purified by the last judgement as a threshing-floor by the winnowing wind, and when those who need such purification have been so cleansed by fire that there will be no one at all who has to offer sacrifice for his sins. For all who offer such sacrifice are assuredly in a state of sin, and it is for their sins that they make their offering, so that when God has accepted their offering their sins may then be forgiven.

26. *The sacrifices 'pleasing to the Lord' to be offered by the holy people*

Now it was because God wished to make it plain that his City will not at that time continue to observe the custom of sacrifice that he said that the sons of Levi would offer sacrifices 'in righteousness'; for that implies that they will not offer in sin, and consequently not *for* sin. Thus we can understand what is meant by the statement that follows: 'Then the sacrifice of Judah and Jerusalem will be pleasing to the Lord as in the days of old and in the years gone by.' We realize that it is in vain that the Jews promise themselves a return of the past times of

174. 1 John 1, 8.

their sacrifices according to the Law of the old covenant. For it was not in righteousness but in sin that they then offered sacrifices; for at that time it was chiefly and primarily for sins that they offered them, so much so that the priest himself (whom we are certainly bound to suppose to have been more righteous than the rest of the people) used to make offering, in accordance with God's commandment, for his own sins first, and then for the sins of the people. That is why we are now obliged to explain the meaning of 'as in the days of old and in the years gone by'. This may perhaps recall the time when the first human beings were in paradise. For at that time, when they were pure and untouched by any taint or stain of sin, they offered themselves to God as the most unpolluted sacrifices. But after they had been expelled from paradise because of their transgression and when human nature had been condemned in their persons, thenceforth 'no one is free from stain', as the Scripture says, 'not even an infant who has lived but one day on the earth';[175] no one, that is, except the one Mediator, and any who have received the baptism of rebirth and who are still in early infancy.

But it may be replied that one may rightly claim that 'sacrifices in righteousness' are offered by those who offer in faith, 'since the righteous man lives on the basis of faith'[176] And yet a righteous man 'deceives himself if he says that he has no sin', and therefore he does not say so, simply because he lives on the basis of faith. And in any case, is anyone really going to assert that this time of faith is to be put on the same level as that final state when those who offer sacrifices in righteousness will be cleansed by the fire of the last judgement? For this reason, since we must believe that after such a cleansing the righteous will have no sin, then assuredly that time, as far as the freedom from sin is concerned, is comparable only with that time when the first human beings lived in paradise, before their transgression, in the felicity of utter innocence. This then, is the correct interpretation of 'as in the days of old, and as in the years gone by'.

Isaiah also, after giving the promise of a new heaven and a new earth, proceeds to give some allegorical and enigmatic descriptions of the bliss of the saints; but my concern to avoid prolixity forbids me to attempt an adequate explanation of all of them. However, they include this statement: 'As the days of the tree of life will be the days of my people';[177] and anyone who has the slightest knowledge of the holy Scriptures cannot fail to know where God planted the tree of life, from the fruit of which the first human beings were debarred when

175. Job 14, 4. 176. Rom. 1, 17. 177. Is. 65, 22.

their own wickedness expelled them from paradise and a fiery guard of terror was set round that tree.

Now it may be contended that the 'days of the tree of life', mentioned by the prophet Isaiah, stand for the present days of the Church of Christ, and that Christ himself is prophetically called 'the tree of life', because he is himself the Wisdom of God, of which Solomon says, 'Wisdom is a tree of life to those who embrace her.'[178] It may further be maintained that those first human beings did not spend 'years' in that paradise, in fact they were expelled from it so quickly that they did not produce a child there; and therefore, it may be said, that time cannot be meant by the words 'as in the days of old and in the years gone by'. If this argument is advanced, I pass over the question, to avoid the necessity of a discussion of every detail, which would be a lengthy business, in order to establish one point with the support of incontestable truth.

In fact I notice another meaning to prevent our supposing that it was the return of the 'days of old and years gone by' of carnal sacrifices that was promised us, as a great privilege, by the prophet. For the sacrificial victims, demanded by old Law, were unblemished specimens of each class of animal, without any defect whatsoever; and they symbolized holy men, without any sin at all, and only one such man has ever been found, and that man was Christ. Now at the judgement those who are worthy of such purification are to be purified even by fire; and after that there will be found in all the saints no sin at all; and in this condition they will offer themselves in righteousness, so that such victims will be unblemished and without any defect. And thus they will certainly be 'as in the days of old and in the years gone by' when the purest sacrificial victims were offered as a foreshadowing of this reality. For then there will be in the immortal flesh and mind of the saints this purity which was prefigured in the bodies of those sacrificial animals.

Then, turning to those who deserve not cleansing but condemnation, the prophecy continues: 'And I shall come to you in judgement, and I shall be a swift witness against sorcerers, and against adulterers' and so on; and, after a list of crimes deserving condemnation, it proceeds: 'For I am the Lord your God; and I do not change.' He says that he himself will be a 'witness' because in his judgement he has no need of other witnesses; and he will be 'swift' either because he is to come suddenly, and his judgement, which seemed so slow in coming, will be exceedingly swift in its unexpected

178. Prov. 3, 18.

coming; or else because he will convict men's consciences without any lengthy speech. 'For in the thoughts of the wicked man', as the Scripture says, 'inquiry will be made'; and the Apostle says, 'Their thoughts will present the case against them and the case for them, on the day when God will judge the secrets of human hearts, according to my Gospel, through Jesus Christ.'[179] In this way also we must understand that the Lord will be a 'swift witness', since he is going to recall to man's memory, without delay, the evidence which will serve to convict and punish man's conscience.

27. *The separation of good and bad, making evident the distinction established at the last judgement*

There is another passage from this prophet on the subject of the last judgement; and I have already quoted it in the eighteenth book,[180] when dealing with another topic.

> They will be mine, says the Lord Almighty, on the day when I take them into my possession; and I shall choose them as a man chooses his son who serves him. And I shall turn, and you will see the difference between a righteous and a wicked man, between a man who serves God and a man who does not serve him. For see, the day is coming, blazing like a furnace; and it will burn them up; and all the foreigners and the evil-doers will be stubble. The day that is to come will set them on fire, says the Lord Almighty, and there will be left in them neither branch nor twig. And there will arise for you who fear my name the sun of righteousness, and healing will be in his wings. You will go out, leaping for joy like calves released from their pens; and you will trample on the wicked, and they will be like ashes under your feet, says the Lord Almighty.[181]

This wide gulf between rewards and punishments, the rift that sunders the righteous from the unrighteous, is something we do not discern beneath the light of this sun in the futility of this life; but when it is revealed in the clear light beneath that sun of righteousness at the manifestation of that other life, then beyond doubt there will be a judgement such as there has never been.

28. *The Law of Moses is to be spiritually interpreted*

Malachi's next verse, 'Remember the Law of Moses my servant, which I delivered to him in Horeb for all Israel',[182] is opportune in re-

179. Wisd. 1, 9; Rom. 2, 15f. 180. Bk XVIII, 35.

181. Mal. 3, 17–4, 3. (For 'I shall turn', Hebrew, LXX and Vulgate have 'Turn yourselves'. So has St Augustine in XVIII, 35).

182. Mal. 4. 4.

calling precepts and judgements, following as it does the declaration of the great distinction that is to be made between those who keep the Law and those who treat it with contempt. At the same time, the prophet's intention is that men should learn to understand the Law in a spiritual manner, and find Christ in that Law; for Christ by his judgement is to effect the separation of the good from the wicked. It is, in fact, not for nothing that the same Lord says to the Jews, 'If you believed Moses you would also believe me; for it was about me that Moses wrote.'[183] Now it was surely by taking the Law in a material construction and by failure to realize that its earthly promises are symbols of heavenly realities that the people rushed to make complaints, even daring to say, 'A man who serves God is a fool. What good does it do us that we have kept his commandments, and have walked as suppliants in the sight of the Lord Almighty? Now we call blessed those who are estranged from God; and all those whose actions are wicked are prospering.'[184]

By these words of theirs the prophet was in a sense driven to give warning of the last judgement, when the wicked will not enjoy even illusory bliss, but will be shown in their unmistakable wretchedness, whereas the good will not suffer any misery, not even temporal unhappiness, but will enjoy a manifest and everlasting felicity. The prophet has indeed quoted earlier some similar complaints of those people: 'Everyone who behaves wickedly is good in the eyes of the Lord; such people have his approval.'[185] They were brought, I say, to such complaints against God by taking the Law of Moses in a material sense. For this reason also the writer of the seventy-second psalm says that his feet were almost shaken and his steps unsteady – in fact, so unsteady that he stumbled – because he was jealous of the sinners, observing them at peace; so that he said, among other things, 'How can God know about this? Is the Most High aware of it?' And he said also, 'Is it really to no purpose that I have kept my heart righteous and washed my hands among the innocent?' But in the end he finds the solution to this difficult problem, which arises when the good appear to be wretched and the wicked seem happy; and he says, 'This difficulty is beyond me, until I enter the sanctuary of God and understand the last things.'[186] For in the last judgement, we may be sure, things will not be like this; indeed, in the obvious wretchedness of the wicked and the obvious felicity of the righteous a state of things very different from the present situation will be revealed.

183. John 5, 46. 184. Mal. 3, 14f. 185. Mal. 2, 17.
186. Ps. 73 (72 in LXX) 3; 11; 13; 16f.

29. *The coming of Elijah before the judgement, for the conversion of the Jews*

Malachi thus admonishes his people to remember the Law of Moses, for he foresaw that for a long time yet they would not interpret it spiritually, as they ought to have done; and he continues, 'See, I shall send you Elijah the Tishbite, before the great and splendid Day of the Lord; and he will turn the heart of the father to the son and the heart of a man to his neighbour, so that in my coming I may not utterly shake the earth.'[187] The belief that in the final period before the judgement this great and wonderful prophet Elijah will expound the Law to the Jews, and that through his activity the Jews are destined to believe in our Christ, this is a very frequent subject in the conversation of believers, and a frequent thought in their hearts. The expectation that he will come before the coming of the Saviour in judgement is certainly not without good reason, since there is good reason for the belief that he is still alive; for he was carried up from the world of men in a fiery chariot, as holy Scripture testifies most explicitly.[188] Well then, when he comes, he will explain in a spiritual sense the Law which the Jews now take in a material sense, and by so doing he will 'turn the heart of the father toward the son', that is, the hearts of the fathers towards the children – for the seventy translators have used the singular for the plural. The meaning, then, is that the sons, that is, the Jews, will interpret the Law as their fathers – that is, the prophets, including Moses himself – interpreted it. For it is thus that the heart of the fathers will be turned towards the children when the understanding of the fathers is brought to the understanding of the children. And 'the hearts of the children will be turned to the fathers' when children share the views of their fathers. The Septuagint here says, 'the heart of a man to his neighbour' – for fathers and sons are the closest of neighbours.

However, another and a more attractive meaning can be found in the words of the seventy translators, who translated in the manner of prophets.[189] This meaning is that Elijah is to turn the heart of God the Father towards the Son, not, of course, by causing the Father to love the Son, but by teaching men that the Father loves the Son, so that the Jews also, who first hated the Son, will love this same Son, who is our Christ. For now, in the thought of the Jews, God keeps his heart turned away from our Christ, for that is what they suppose. And so in their thought God's heart will be turned towards the Son when they themselves have their hearts turned by conversion, and

187. Mal. 4, 5f. 188. 2 Kings 2, 11. 189. cf. Bk XVIII, 43.

have learnt of the love of the Father for the Son. The next words, 'and the heart of a man to his neighbour' – that is, Elijah will also turn the heart of a man to his neighbour – are surely best understood as meaning the turning of a man's heart to the man Christ. For though Christ is our God 'in the form of God', he condescended to take 'the form of a servant'[190] and so to become our neighbour. This then, is what Elijah will achieve 'so that, in my coming, I may not utterly shake the earth'. For 'the earth' stands for those whose wisdom is earthly, as to this day is the wisdom of the Jews, who are Jews only in the racial sense. It is from this defect that those complaints against God have arisen, when people say, 'The wicked have God's approval' and 'The man who serves God is a fool.'[191]

30. *The Old Testament prophecies of judgement give no explicit mention of Christ. But some passages, where God is the speaker, make it clear that he is identified with Christ*

There are many other passages of holy Scripture witnessing to the last judgement of God, and to collect them all would be an excessively lengthy task. It must suffice that I have proved that judgement to have been foretold by both the Old and the New Testaments. What is not so explicitly expressed in the Old Testament as in the New is that this judgement is to be administered by Christ, that is, that Christ is to come from heaven as judge; and the reason for this uncertainty is that when in the Old Testament the Lord God says that he is going to come, or when it is said of him that he will come, it does not immediately follow that Christ is meant; for the Lord God means the Father or the Son or the Holy Spirit. But this is a question which we must not leave without examining the evidence. In the first place we have to show how Jesus Christ speaks in the prophetic books in the character of the Lord God, and yet it is abundantly clear that Jesus Christ is speaking; so that in other places also when this is not immediately apparent, and yet it is said that the Lord God is come for that last judgement, it may be understood that Jesus Christ is meant.

There is a passage in the prophet Isaiah which clearly demonstrates the point I am making. For God says, through the mouth of the prophet,

> Listen to me, Jacob, Israel whom I call. I am the first, and I am for all eternity. My hand laid the foundations of the earth, and my right hand

190 cf. Phil. 2, 7. 191. Mal. 2, 17; 3, 14; cf. ch. 28.

established the heaven. I shall call them, and they will stand together, and they will all be assembled and will listen. Who has announced this to him? It is for love of you that I have performed your will upon Babylon, so that I might remove the offspring of the Chaldeans. I have spoken, and I have called him. I brought him hither and prospered his plans. Draw near to me and listen to this. From the beginning I have not spoken to you in secret; when these things were happening, I was there. And now the Lord God has sent me; and so has his Spirit.[192]

It is certainly Christ himself who is speaking; yet it would not be understood to be Jesus Christ, had he not added, 'And now the Lord God has sent me; and so has his Spirit.' For he said this 'in the form of a servant', using here a past tense to describe a future event, a usage we find in the same prophet when he says, 'He was led[193] like a lamb to be slaughtered', not 'he will be led', thus employing a past tense for an event in the future. And prophecy continually uses this mode of speaking.

There is another passage, in Zechariah, which plainly shows the Almighty sending the Almighty; and who can these be except God the Father sending God the Son? The passage runs, 'This is what the Lord Almighty says: "After glory he has sent me to the nations who despoiled you; for whoever has touched you is as if he touched the pupil of his eye. See, I shall raise my hand over them, and they will be plunder for those who had been their slaves; and you will know that the Lord Almighty has sent me." '[194] Observe that the Lord Almighty says that he was sent by the Lord Almighty. Who would dare to take these words as representing anything but an utterance of Christ, speaking, obviously, to 'the lost sheep of the house of Israel', for he says in the Gospel, 'I have been sent only to the lost sheep of the house of Israel.'[195] And here he compares them to the pupil of God's eye because of God's special feeling of affection for them; the apostles themselves were sheep of this kind. But after the glory, that is, of course, after his resurrection (for before the resurrection, as the evangelist says, 'Jesus was not yet glorified'[196]) he was sent to the Gentiles also in the persons of his apostles, and so the saying in the psalm was fulfilled: 'You will rescue me from the opposition of the people, you will set me at the head of the Gentiles.'[197] The result was that those who had despoiled the Israelites, those by whom the Israelites had been enslaved when they were subject to the Gentiles, were not

192. Is. 48, 12–16.
193. Is. 53, 7. LXX has the past tense.
194. Zech. 2, 8f.
195. Matt. 15, 24.
196. John 7, 39.
197. Ps. 18, 43.

merely to be despoiled in their turn in the same way; they were to become themselves the spoil of the Israelites. This, in fact, is what Christ promised to his disciples in saying, 'I shall make you fishers of men', and to one of them, 'From now on you will be catching men.'[198] Thus they did indeed become spoil, but for their good, as property snatched from that 'strong man', a strong man bound with greater strength.[199]

Similarly, the Lord speaks through the same prophet and says,

> When that day comes, I shall seek to remove all the nations who come against Jerusalem; and I shall pour out over the house of David and over the inhabitants of Jerusalem the spirit of grace and mercy. Then they will look at me because they have gloated over me; and they will mourn for him as if for one very dear, and they will grieve as men grieve for an only son.[200]

Now can we think that it is in the power of anyone but God to remove all the nations hostile to the holy city of Jerusalem and all who 'come against her', that is, are opposed to her, or, as others translate it, 'come over her', that is, to subject her to themselves? And 'to pour out over the house of David and the inhabitants of that city the spirit of grace and mercy'? This is without doubt an act of God, and the words are spoken, through the prophet, in the person of God; and yet Christ demonstrates that he is the God who achieves this great act, those divine acts, by adding, 'Then they will look at me because they gloated over me, and they will mourn for him as for one very dear, and they will grieve as men grieve for an only son.'

For on that day even the Jews will certainly repent, even those Jews who are to receive 'the spirit of grace and mercy'. They will repent that they gloated over Christ in his suffering, when they look at him as he comes in his majesty, and recognize him as the one who formerly came in humility, whom they mocked at in the persons of their parents; however, those parents themselves, who committed that great impiety, will rise again and see him, but now for their punishment, no longer for their correction. And so it is not the parents who are to be taken as meant in the passage when it says, 'and I shall pour out upon the House of David and the inhabitants of Jerusalem the spirit of grace and mercy: and they will look at me because they gloated over me'; it is, nevertheless, those who come from their stock that are meant, those who are to believe at that time through the work of

198. Matt. 4, 19; Luke 5, 10.
199. Matt. 12, 29; cf. ch. 7.
200. Zech. 12, 9f.

Elijah. But just as we say to the Jews, 'You put Christ to death', although it was their parents who did this, so they will grieve for having in a sense done themselves what was actually done by those from whose stock they have descended. Thus, although they have received the spirit of grace and mercy and, being now members of the faith, will not be condemned along with their impious parents, they will nevertheless grieve as if they themselves had done what was done by their parents. They will grieve, therefore, not because they feel guilty of this crime, but because they feel the emotions of true religion.

It is true that where the Septuagint has 'they will look at me because they gloated over me', a translation directly from the Hebrew gives 'they will look on me whom they pierced'; and this yields a more explicit description of the crucified Christ. And yet the 'gloating' which the seventy translators preferred to give as their rendering was in evidence in the whole of his passion. For they did in fact gloat over Christ when he was arrested, when he was bound, when he was judged, when he was clothed with humiliating garments as an insult, and was crowned with thorns; when he was struck on the head with a reed, and received homage on bended knees in mockery; when he carried his cross, and when in the end he hung upon that cross. Thus it is not by following one translation only but by joining together both translations, by reading 'pierced' as well as 'gloated', that we recognize here in greater detail the reality of the Lord's passion.

So when we read in the prophetic books that God is to come to execute the last judgement we are bound to take it that Christ is meant, even though there is no other indication of him, simply because it is the judgement; because, although the Father will judge, it is through the coming of the Son of Man that he will execute judgement. For the Father himself in his own manifest presence 'judges no one; he has entrusted all judgement to the Son'.[201] And the Son will be manifested as man for his execution of judgement, just as it was as a man that he was judged. For can anyone else than Christ be meant when God speaks in similar terms through Isaiah, using the name of Jacob and Israel, from whose line Christ received his body? This is what the Scripture says:

Jacob is my servant; I shall lift him up: Israel is my chosen one; my Spirit has taken him to himself. I have given my Spirit to him; he will bring forth judgement for the nations. He will not cry out, nor will he cease to speak,

201. John 5, 22.

and his voice will not be heard outside. He will not break a crushed reed, and he will not quench a smoking wick; but he will bring forth judgement in truth. He will shine and will not be broken down, until he establishes judgement on the earth. In his name the nations will put their hope.[202]

In the Hebrew the names 'Jacob' and 'Israel' are not found, but simply 'my servant'. Doubtless the seventy translators wished to warn the reader of the full meaning to be given to this phrase, to point out, that is, the reference to 'the form of a servant' in which the Most High showed himself in utter humility; and so, to signify him, they put in the name of the man from whose line Christ took that 'form of a servant'.[203]

'The Holy Spirit was given' to him, as was shown by the appearance of a dove, according to the testimony of the evangelist.[204] He 'brought forth judgement to the nations', because he foretold the judgement to come which had been hidden from them. In his gentleness 'he did not cry out', and yet 'he did not cease to speak' in his proclamation of the truth; but his voice was not, and is not, 'heard outside' because he is not obeyed by those who are outside and are cut off from his body. And it was the Jews themselves that 'he did not break', or 'quench', those persecutors of his, who are likened to a 'crushed reed' which has lost its perfection, and a 'smoking wick' which has lost its light; he did not break or quench them, because he spared them, since he had not yet come to judge them but to be judged by them. He certainly 'brought forth judgement in truth' by predicting to them the judgement, when they were to be punished if they persisted in their malignity. His face 'shone' on the mountain;[205] his fame shone in the whole world. He is not 'broken', or crushed, because neither in his own person nor in his Church has he yielded to his persecutors so as to cease to be. And so that event has not happened of which his enemies have spoken, or still speak, when they say, 'When will he die and his name perish?'[206] – nor will it happen before 'he establishes judgement on the earth'.

Here it is, then, made manifest, the hidden thing for which we were looking. This, in fact, is the last judgement which he will establish on the earth when he himself comes from heaven. And we now see fulfilled the last words of the prophecy about him: 'In his name the nations will put their hope.' This, at least, cannot be denied; and its truth should lead to a belief in that statement which *is* shamelessly denied. For who would have expected an event which even those who

202. Is. 42, 1–4 (LXX). 203. Phil. 2, 7. 204. Matt. 3, 16.
205. Matt. 17, 1f. 206. Ps. 41, 5.

still refuse to believe in Christ now see in process, along with us, and because they are unable to deny it, they 'gnash their teeth and waste away'?[207] Who would have expected that the nations would put their hope in the name of Christ, at the time when he was arrested, bound, scourged, ridiculed, crucified; when even his disciples had lost the hope in him which they had by then begun to have? The hope that was then held scarcely by the one thief on the cross is now held by nations scattered far and wide, who are signed with the sign of that very cross on which he died, so that they may not die for ever.

There is no one therefore who denies or doubts that the last judgement, as it is foretold in holy Scripture, is to be executed by Jesus Christ, unless it is someone who, with an unbelievable kind of animosity or blindness, does not believe in those sacred writings, which have by now demonstrated their truth to the whole world. And so in that judgement, or in connection with that judgement, we have learnt that those events are to come about: Elijah the Tishbite will come; Jews will accept the faith; Antichrist will persecute; Christ will judge; the dead will rise again; the good and the evil will be separated; the earth will be destroyed in the flames and then will be renewed. All those events, we must believe, will come about; but in what way, and in what order they will come, actual experience will then teach us with a finality surpassing anything our human understanding is now capable of attaining. However, I consider that these events are destined to come about in the order I have given.

Two books relating to our task remain for the fulfilment, with God's help, of my promises. One of them will treat of the punishment of the wicked; the other of the felicity of the righteous. In them, as God shall grant, I will in particular refute the human arguments which some wretched creatures gnaw over, pluming themselves on their own wisdom, in disparagement of the divine predictions and prophecies, while they despise, as false and laughable, the wholesome nourishment of the faith. Those, on the other hand, who are wise by God's standards hold to the truth and the omnipotence of God as the strongest proof of things which seem incredible to men, and yet are included in the holy Scriptures, whose truth has already been vindicated in so many ways. Such people are convinced that God could not conceivably have lied in the Scriptures, and that he can do what to the unbeliever is impossible.

207. Ps. 112, 10.

BOOK XXI

1. *The punishment of the condemned to be treated before the bliss of the saints*

NOW that both those cities, God's City and the Devil's, have reached their appointed ends, through the judgement of Jesus Christ our Lord – the judge of the living and the dead – we must proceed to a more careful discussion of the kind of punishment which is in store for the Devil, and for all those of his party; and, with the help of God, I shall discharge this task in the present book, to the best of my power. The reason for preferring this order, and dealing afterwards with the felicity of the saints, is that both the saints and the damned will be united with their bodies, and it seems more incredible that bodies should endure in eternal torments than that they should continue, without pain, in everlasting bliss. It follows that when I have shown that this eternal punishment ought not to be thought incredible, this will be a great help to me by making it much easier to believe that the bodily immortality of the saints is to be exempt from any kind of distress. And this order is not repugnant to the holy Scriptures; for there we find sometimes the bliss of the saints put first, as in: 'those whose actions have been good will come from the graves to the resurrection of life; those whose deeds have been wicked, to the resurrection of judgement'; whereas sometimes it is put second, as in the following: 'The Son of Man will send his angels, and they will gather out of his kingdom all the stumbling-blocks and consign them to a blazing furnace of fire: there will be weeping and gnashing of teeth. Then the righteous will shine like the sun in the kingdom of their Father';[1] and as in this statement: 'So those will go to eternal punishment; but the righteous will go into life eternal.'[2] In the prophets also it will be found on examination that now the one order is observed, now the other; it would take too long to list the instances, and I have already given my reason for the order I have adopted.

1. John 5, 29; Matt. 13, 41. 2. Matt. 25, 46.

2. *Can a material body be exempt from destruction by fire?*

What evidence can I produce to convince the unbelievers that it is possible for human bodies, possessed of soul and life, not only to escape disintegration by death but even to persist in the torments of everlasting fires? For these unbelievers refuse to allow us to ascribe this to the power of the Almighty, and they demand that we persuade them by producing some instance of it. We may reply that there are examples of animals which are undoubtedly subject to decay, because they are mortal, which nevertheless can live in the middle of a fire; and that there is also a species of worm to be found in the gushing springs of hot baths. These are too hot for anyone to put a hand in with impunity, whereas the worms not only live in it without damage but are unable to exist elsewhere. But the incredulous either refuse to believe this if we are unable to give a demonstration, or, if we are able to give concrete proof of our statements before their eyes, or to establish the facts by means of qualified witnesses, they maintain with unshaken scepticism that the phenomena are insufficient as a precedent for the matter in question. They argue that these animals do not live for ever, and that they live in those temperatures without feeling pain; in fact, they say, they thrive in elements to which their nature is adapted, which are not to them a means of torment. We are asked to suppose that it is not more incredible that creatures should thrive in such an environment than that they should be tortured in it! For it is amazing that any creature should be in pain in the fire and yet should continue to live; but it is more astonishing that it should live in the fire without feeling pain. But if the latter is believed to be a fact, why should the former be incredible?

3. *Can a physical body endure eternal pain?*

But, they urge, there is no body which can suffer pain and at the same time can be incapable of dying. How do we know this? Who can be sure whether it is or is not in their bodies that demons are suffering when they confess that they are tormented with great pain? If it is replied that there is certainly no solid and visible body (or, to put it in a word, no *flesh*) which can suffer and yet cannot die, is this not merely to make an assertion grounded only on human inference from the experience of the physical senses? For men have acquaintance solely with *mortal* flesh, and so they judge anything to be utterly impossible that does not fall within their experience, and on this assumption they base their reasoning. Yet what sort of logic is it to make pain a proof of death when it is in fact the evidence of life! For although the question is whether eternal life in pain is possible, nevertheless one thing is certain, that anything which feels pain is alive, and no pain can exist except in a living thing. Thus it is inevitable that a sufferer should be alive, but it is not inevitable that pain should kill the sufferer, because pain does not in every case kill bodies liable to death and undoubtedly destined for death. The reason why some pain can cause death is that the soul is connected with this body of ours in such a way that it succumbs and departs from the body under pressure from extreme pain. In our bodily frame, in fact, the connection of the limbs and the vital parts is so weak that it cannot endure the violent assault of extreme, or even considerable pain. But in the life hereafter the soul and the body will be connected in such a way that just as the bond that links them will not be unloosed by any passage of time, however long, so it will not be able to be broken by any pain. Accordingly, even though there now exists no physical body of such a kind as to be capable of suffering pain while being incapable of dying, there will then be flesh of such a kind as does not now exist, just as there will also be a death of such a kind as does not now exist. For death will not then be non-existent but everlasting, seeing that the soul will not be able to live, because deprived of God, nor yet to be released from bodily suffering by dying. The first death drives the soul from the body against her will; the second death holds the soul in the body against her will. But both these deaths have this in common, that the soul suffers against her will from her connection with the body.

Now these opponents of ours observe that there now exists no kind of physical body which is capable of pain but incapable of death; what they fail to observe is that there is something which is by nature more important than the body, namely, the soul. The soul gives life to the body by its presence, and rules the body; and this soul itself can suffer pain, while being incapable of death. Here we have found something which feels pain and yet is immortal. This property, which now, as we know, belongs to the souls of all men, will at that time belong to the bodies of the damned. If we consider more carefully, we see that pain, which is said to be connected with the body, is in fact more closely connected with the soul. For pain is really an experience of the soul, not of the body, even when the cause of pain is presented to the soul by the body – when pain is felt in the part where the body is hurt. Thus, just as we speak of bodies 'feeling' and 'living', although it is the soul that gives feeling and life to the body; so also we talk of bodies 'suffering pain' although there can be no pain in the body unless it comes from the soul. And so the soul feels pain along with the body in that part of the body where something occurs to cause pain; and the soul feels pain by itself, although it is in the body, when it is saddened by some cause, even an invisible cause, while the body is unaffected. The soul also suffers when it is not enshrined in a body; for there can be no doubt that the rich man was suffering when he said, 'I am tortured in these flames.'[3] The body, in contrast, does not suffer pain when divorced from the soul, nor, when it is united with the soul, does it suffer independently of the soul. If therefore it would be right to take the fact of pain as an argument for death, on the ground that the possibility of pain entails the possibility of death, death would then be connected with the soul rather than with the body, inasmuch as pain is particularly connected with the soul. Since, however, the soul has more capacity for pain, but is incapable of death, what force is there in the contention that the bodies of the damned, because they will exist in pain, must for that reason be supposed to be destined to die? The Platonists, it is true, asserted that the soul's capacity for fear, desire, pain, and joy derives from the structure of earthly bodies that are bound for death; that is why Virgil says, 'Hence' – that is, from the earthly, bodily parts that are doomed to die –

Hence the soul's fear, desire, sorrow, and joy.[4]

But we have proved to those philosophers in the twelfth book of this work that, on their own showing, souls when purified from every stain contracted from the body are possessed of a fatal longing which makes them begin to desire to return to their bodies. Now the possibility of desire automatically entails the possibility of pain; for frustrated desire, when it either fails to attain its object or loses it after the attainment, turns into pain. The conclusion is that if the soul, which is the principal if not the only subject of the experience of pain, nevertheless has some kind of immortality of its own, appropriate to its mode of being, the fact that the bodies of the damned will feel pain does not entail that they will be capable of dying. Above all, if bodies are responsible for the suffering of the soul, why is it that they can impose suffering on the soul but not death, unless the fact is that it does not follow that what produces pain must also produce death? Then why is it incredible that the fire can impose pain but not death on those bodies, in the same way as the bodies themselves make the souls suffer pain without thereby compelling the death of the souls?

3. Luke 16, 24. 4. *Aen.*, 6, 733.

This shows that the fact of pain is not a cogent proof of future death.

4. *Instances in nature showing that bodies can live under conditions of torture*

We are told by writers who have carefully studied the natural history of animals that the salamander lives in fire;[5] and there are some mountains in Sicily which are a seething mass of flames and yet remain entire; they have been in this state from immemorial antiquity up to the present time and are likely so to continue. This being so, we have in them sufficiently reliable evidence that not everything which burns is destroyed; and the soul gives us warrant for thinking that not everything which is susceptible to pain is capable also of death. Then why are instances still demanded of us to establish that there is nothing incredible in our teaching that the bodies of human beings condemned to eternal punishment by fire do not lose their soul, but burn without loss of substance and feel pain without ceasing to be? For in that future state the substance of our bodies will have a quality bestowed by him who has bestowed on so many different things the marvellous and various properties which we observe without amazement simply because they are so many. For who but the Creator of all things gave to the peacock the power of resisting putrefaction after death? I had heard of this property and had thought it incredible, until one day at Carthage I was served with a roast peacock, and I gave orders that what seemed a sufficient quantity of meat should be cut from the breast and kept. After an interval of some days, long enough to have ensured the putrefaction of any other kind of cooked meat, this was brought out and presented to me; and I found it had no offensive smell. It was then put back in store, and after more than thirty days it was found to be in the same condition; and there was no change in a year's time except that the flesh was somewhat dry and shrivelled. Who has given to chaff the power of cooling, so that it will keep snow covered with chaff from melting, or the power of heating, so that it will ripen green apples?

Then there is fire itself. Who can explain its marvels? It is itself bright; but it blackens everything that is burnt in it; its colour is beautiful; and yet it discolours everything that it embraces and licks

5. cf. Bk XII, 4. In antiquity the salamander was reputed a fire-extinguisher (Plin. 10, 67). The belief that it lived in fire is later than Pliny. Aristotle believed that some creatures could live in fire (*Hist. An.*, 5, 19).

with its flames, and from a bright living coal produces the filthiest charcoal. And yet this kind of transformation is no hard and fast rule; for by a contrary process stones baked in a glowing fire are themselves turned to a shining white, and although the fire is red rather than white, while the stones become white, still whiteness has the same affinity with light as blackness with darkness. Thus when the fire burns in the wood to bake the stones, it has contrary effects in similar substances. For stones and pieces of wood are different, but not contrary, as are white and black; and fire produces whiteness in stones but blackness in wood; it is bright, and it gives brightness to stones but it darkens the wood, although it would have no effect on the former if it were not alive in the latter. Again, is it not remarkable that charcoal is so brittle that it can be broken with the lightest blow, can easily be ground to powder; and yet it is so durable that it cannot be broken down by moisture, cannot be destroyed by age – so much so that it is customary to put charcoal under boundary marks when they are set up, to refute any litigant who might come forward at any time in the remote future and maintain that a stone fixed in earth was not a boundary stone?[6] What is it that makes charcoal capable of enduring so long when buried in damp earth, where timber would rot? Surely it can only be fire, the great destroyer of all substances!

Let us consider the marvels of lime. Apart from the fact that it grows white by the action of fire which makes other things dirty (I have said enough about that already), it also in some most mysterious way takes fire into itself from the fire, and it stores the fire inside the mass of lime, which is cold to the touch, so secretly that it does not present itself to our senses in any way at all, but, when it has been discovered by experiment, it is known to be asleep within the mass even when there is no evidence of its presence. That is why we call it 'quicklime', living lime, as if the fire hidden within it were the invisible soul of a visible body. But the really wonderful thing is that when it is quenched, it is kindled! For to get rid of its hidden fire, water is poured on it, or it is plunged into water, and then it grows hot, though it was cold before; and that is the effect of water, which cools all other substances when they are hot. And so, as that lump of lime expires, so to speak, the fire hidden in it makes its appearance at its departure; and thereafter the lime is so cold in death, as it were, that if water is applied to it it will not blaze up, and what was called 'quick-

6. This is obscure. Diogenes Laertius (2, 103) says that charcoal was put under the foundations of the temple of Artemis at Ephesus to give stability; cf. Plin., 36, 14.

lime' is now called 'quenched' or 'killed' lime. Could anything be added to make this marvel more astounding? Yes, there is something more. If you use oil, instead of water, the lime does not grow hot, whether oil is poured on the lime or the lime is plunged in the oil! And yet oil is fuel of fire, and water is not! If we had read about this marvel, or had heard it related of some Indian stone which could not come into our experience, we should certainly dismiss it as a falsehood; or at least we should be vastly astonished. But things which come before our eyes in everyday experience are little reckoned of, not because they are less remarkable in nature but simply because of their continual occurrence – so much so that we have ceased to marvel at many of the marvels of India itself (a part of the world so remote from us) which it has proved possible to bring into our experience.

Many people among us possess diamonds, especially our jewellers and goldsmiths; and the diamond is a stone which, so we are told, neither steel nor fire nor any other force can prevail over, except goat's blood.[7] But do we suppose that those who possess diamonds and are familiar with them are as astonished at the diamond's properties as were those to whom those powers were first displayed? Those who have not seen those powers demonstrated may perhaps not believe in them; or if they do believe, they marvel at something beyond their experience. If they happen to become acquainted with the diamond, they are indeed for a time filled with amazement at something unfamiliar; but daily familiarity gradually blunts the edge of wonder. We know that the loadstone has an astonishing power to attract iron; and when I first saw this phenomenon I was utterly amazed. I saw, I most certainly saw, an iron ring snatched up and held aloft by a stone! And then it seemed as if the stone had given its own power to the iron which it had snatched up, and made it a joint property; for this first ring was applied to another ring, which it lifted aloft; and the second ring clung to the first just as the first ring clung to the stone; in the same way a third ring was added, then a fourth; and in the end there was a kind of chain of rings hanging, the rings not being joined together internally, by the interlinking of their circles, but adhering to each other from outside. Who could fail to be astounded at this property of the stone, which was not merely inherent in it but also passed on through so many objects suspended from it, and bound them together by invisible connections?

But much more astonishing than this is an experiment with the loadstone which I learnt about from my brother and fellow-bishop,

7. Plin., 20, 1; 28, 9.

Severus of Milevis. He told me that he had seen Bathanarius, sometime count of Africa, when the bishop was at dinner at his house, produce a loadstone and hold it beneath a silver dish on which he placed a piece of iron. Then he moved his hand, with the stone in it, underneath the dish and the iron moved about on the dish, following his movements; and there was no effect on the dish in between, while the stone was being drawn by the man backwards and forwards underneath at extremely rapid speed, and the iron was rushing to and fro on top under the influence of the stone. I have described something that I myself witnessed, and I have reported something which I was told by someone else, but someone I believed as thoroughly as if I had witnessed the scene myself. I will now add something which I have read about this loadstone: that when a diamond is placed next to it, the stone does not draw any iron; and if it has already drawn iron to itself, it lets it go as soon as the diamond approaches.[8] These stones are imported from India; and if by this time we have become acquainted with them and have ceased to marvel, how much more will this be true of those who export them to us, if these stones are quite common with them. Perhaps they regard them as we regard lime, whose remarkable property of growing hot in water, which normally quenches fire, while not becoming hot in oil, which usually kindles fire, we do not wonder at because it is such an everyday matter.

5. *Many things are to be believed though not susceptible of rational proof*

In spite of all this, the unbelievers demand a rational proof from us when we proclaim the miracles of God in the past and his marvellous works that are still to come, which we cannot present to the experience of the unbelievers. And since we cannot supply this rational proof of those matters (for they are beyond the powers of the human mind) the unbelievers assume that our statements are false, whereas they themselves ought to supply a rational explanation of all those amazing phenomena which we observe, or at any rate are able to observe. And if they see that this is beyond man's capacity, they should admit that the fact that a rational explanation cannot be given for something does not mean that it could not have happened in the past, or that it could not happen in the future, seeing that there are these things in the present which are equally insusceptible of rational ex-

8. The magnet is described in Plin., 20, 1; the neutralizing power of the diamond in Plin. 28, 9.

planation. And so I shall not proceed to give a list of the very many marvels which are not matters of past history, but still are existing in various places; anyone who has the will and the opportunity of going to those places may go to find out whether they are truly reported. I shall mention just a few of them.

We are told that the salt of Agrigentum in Sicily melts when put in the fire as if in water: when put in water it crackles as if in the fire. The Garamantes have a spring so cold in the day that it is undrinkable, and so hot at night as to be untouchable. There is another remarkable spring, in Epirus; like other springs it extinguishes a lighted torch which is plunged into it: but unlike the other springs, it rekindles an extinguished torch. The asbestos of Arcadia gets its name from the fact that, once kindled, it cannot be put out.[9] There is a kind of fig-tree in Egypt whose wood has the unique property of sinking in water instead of floating; and, what is more astonishing, when it has been for some time at the bottom of the water it rises again to appear on the surface, when it ought to have become sodden and so heavier through the weight of water. In the land of Sodom there are apples that grow and come to an appearance of ripeness; but if you test them by biting into them or by pressing them they burst open and disappear into dust and ashes.[10] The pyrites stone of Persia, if pressed hard, burns the hand that holds it (that is why it is called 'the fire stone', from *pyr*, the Greek for 'fire'). In Persia there is also another stone, selenite, with a white inner part which waxes and wanes with the moon. In Cappadocia the mares conceive with the wind, but their foals live for only three years at most. Tylon, an island of India, has this superiority over other countries, that none of the trees which grow there is ever stripped of its covering of foliage.[11]

These and other innumerable marvels are to be found not in the records of things past and done but in the accounts of places in the present world. It would take too long to pursue them all, and I have other business in hand; but the unbelievers should give a rational account of them, if they can, since they refuse to believe the inspired Scriptures. They say that they refuse to believe in the divine inspiration of the Scriptures just because of the incredible statements contained in them, such as the matter on which I am now engaged.

9. These wonders are related in Plin., 31, 7; 5, 5; 2, 103; 37, 10; 13, 7.

10. Tac. *Hist.*, 3, 7; Joseph., *Bell. Iud.*, 4, 8, 4. Pliny, strangely enough, does not mention the legendary, and proverbial, 'Dead Sea fruit'.

11. On the first three phenomena cf. Plin., 37, 11; 37, 10; 8, 42. Pliny mentions Tylon as well wooded, without describing the trees as all evergreen.

For reason, in their contention, utterly forbids us to suppose that flesh can burn without being consumed; that it can feel pain, and yet not die. Rational thinkers they are, to be sure, of great ability! They can give a rational explanation of all those phenomena universally agreed to be marvellous! Then let them rationalize these few examples which I have quoted; for, without a shadow of doubt, if they had been unaware of their existence, and we had said that they were to happen in the future, they would have been much less ready to believe in them than they are to believe us when we speak about the coming judgement. In fact, would any of them believe us if, instead of saying that there will be living bodies of men which are destined to burn and feel pain for ever, without ever dying, we had said that in a future age there would be salt which fire would cause to dissolve as if in water, whereas water would cause it to crackle as if in fire; or that there would be a spring whose water became so hot in the cool of the night as to be untouchable, and so cold in the heat of the day as to be undrinkable; or that there would be a stone whose heat would burn the hand of anyone who squeezed it, or another stone which when set on fire could not be extinguished by any means; or if we spoke of any of the other wonders which I considered worth mentioning just now, passing over countless other marvels? If we had said that those wonders were to happen in that age which is still to come and if those sceptics had replied, 'If you want us to believe all this, give us a rational explanation in each case', we should have admitted our inability to do so, simply because the feeble reasoning powers of mortal minds are defeated by these, as by other similar wonderful works of God. And yet we should have maintained that our rational belief was unshaken, that the Almighty does not act irrationally in cases where the feeble human mind cannot give a rational explanation; and that in many matters, certainly, we are uncertain of God's will; and yet one thing is utterly certain, that nothing that he wills is impossible for him, for we cannot believe that God is impotent, or that God is a liar. Nevertheless, though those unbelievers cavil at our faith and demand rational explanations, what reply have they when faced with those marvels, for which the human reason can supply no explanation, but which certainly exist and seem to contradict the rational order of nature? If we said that they were to occur in the future, a rational explanation would be demanded from us by the unbelievers just as they demand it for those events which we do assert as destined to happen in the future. Accordingly, since the fact that, in the case of those works of God, the reasoning powers of the human heart and mind are baffled does not mean that such marvels do not exist, so we must not infer that those future events will not occur simply because the human mind cannot supply a rational explanation of them, any more than of the others.

6. Not *all marvels are natural: many are devised by man's ingenuity, many by the craft of demons*

At this point, it may be, our opponents will answer, 'Of course, all those marvels have no reality: we do not believe a word of them. The tales about them, and the records of them, are all lies.' And they may go on to add their arguments, and say, 'If those tales are to be believed, then you should also believe the story, told in the same source, that there was, and still is, a shrine of Venus, with a lampstand in it, and in the lampstand a lamp which burns under the open sky so steadily that no storm of wind or rain could ever put it out;[12] and hence, like the stone you mentioned, it is called the *Lychnos asbestos*, 'the inextinguishable lamp'. It is quite possible that they will make this objection, and their purpose will be to confront us with a dilemma: if we say that this story is not to be believed, we shall weaken the authority of the records of marvels we quoted, whereas if we admit its credibility, we shall be supporting the power of the pagan gods. But, as I said in the eighteenth book of this work,[13] we are not obliged to believe everything contained in the historical records of the pagans, since their chroniclers, as Varro declares, seem to be at pains to differ from one another – apparently of set purpose! But we are free to believe, if we so choose, those reports which are not in conflict with the books which, as we have no doubt, we are obliged to believe. Now in the matter of these marvels we may content ourselves with those which we can find in our own experience and those for which there is no difficulty in finding adequate evidence. These should be sufficient for our purpose, to persuade the unbelievers of those events which are to come. As for this shrine of Venus and its 'inextinguishable lamp', not only does it fail to constrict us in our argument; it actually opens up a wider field for us. For we can add to that inextinguishable lamp a host of other marvels of human and of magical origin – that is, miracles of the demon's black arts performed by men, and miracles performed by the demons themselves. If we choose to deny the reality of

12. Pliny has a story of a shrine of Venus at Paphos 'on whose *altar* the rain never falls' (2, 96).

13. Bk XVIII, 18.

these, we shall ourselves be in conflict with the truth of the sacred books in which we believe. Thus either human ingenuity has devised in that inextinguishable lamp some contrivance based on the asbestos stone; or else it was contrived by magic art to give men something to marvel at in that shrine; or perhaps some demon presented himself there under the name of Venus with such effect that this prodigy was displayed to the public there and continued there for so many years. For the demons are enticed to take up their abodes by the action of created beings, created not by them, but by God; they are attracted by a wide variety of baits, proportionate to the wide variety of demons, not by food, as animals are enticed, but as spirits they are allured by tokens – designed to suit their different tastes – in the shape of various kinds of stones, plants, pieces of wood, animals, spells and ceremonies.

The demons, for their part, seek to ensure that they will be so enticed by men; and they do this by first misleading human beings by their subtle cleverness, either by breathing a secret poison into their hearts, or even by appearing to them in the deceptive guise of friends, making a few of them disciples of their own, and teachers of very many others. For it would be impossible for men to discover, without previous instruction from the demons themselves, the different likes and aversions of the various demons, the names by which they are to be invoked or compelled to do man's will. Hence comes the first appearance of the magic arts and their practitioners. But their most effective hold upon the hearts of mortals (and it is in the possession of them that they especially glory) is gained when they transform themselves into angels of light.[14]

We see then that their activities are very numerous, and the more we acknowledge the marvel of them the more careful we should be to avoid them. And yet those activities actually prove a help to us towards the achievement of our present task. For if the foul demons have such power, how much greater is the power of the holy angels, and how much greater than all of them is the power of God, who has given even the angels themselves the ability to work such great miracles.

Thus God's created beings can, by the use of human arts, effect so many marvels, which they call *mêchanêmata* (contrivances), of a nature so astounding that those unfamiliar with them would suppose them to be the works of God himself. That is how in one of the temples an image of iron hung suspended in mid-air between two

14. cf. 2 Cor. 11, 14.

loadstones of the required size, fastened, one in the floor, the other in the roof, suggesting to those who did not know what was above and beneath the image that it hung there by an exercise of divine power;[15] and we have already said that something of this sort may have been effected by some craftsman in the case of the well-known 'Lamp of Venus' by the use of the asbestos stone. And it seems that the demons can raise the operations of the magicians (our Scriptures call them 'sorcerers' and 'enchanters') to such a pitch of efficiency that Virgil, that famous poet, thought himself to be in harmony with the general sense of mankind when he wrote these lines about a woman who was a great mistress of that kind of art:

> She promises with spells to soothe man's mind,
> If she so will, or to inflict harsh sorrow;
> To stop the flow of rivers, turn the stars
> Back on their course. She will arouse the spirits
> That haunt the night; and you will feel the earth
> Groaning beneath your feet, and from the mountains
> Behold the trees descending to the plain.[16]

Now, if all this be true, how much more has God the power to achieve things incredible to the unbeliever but easy to his omnipotence, seeing that he himself endowed stones and other substances with their wonderful properties, and that he it is who bestowed on man the wit to employ those properties in marvellous ways, and gave to the angels a nature with powers surpassing those of all living creatures on earth. And all this he did with a power whose wonder exceeds all wonders taken together, with a wisdom shown in the wonders he performs, in those which he orders, in those which he permits; and the use he makes of his creation is as wonderful as the act of creation itself.

7. *The omnipotence of the Creator is the ground of belief in marvels*

Then why should not God have power to make the bodies of the dead rise again, and the bodies of the damned to suffer torment in the everlasting fire, since he made the world so full of innumerable marvels in the sky, on the earth, in the air, and in the water – although the world itself is beyond doubt a marvel greater and more wonderful than all the wonders with which it is filled? But these rationalists with whom, or rather against whom, we are now engaged, also believe in the existence of God, by whom the world was made; and

15. Plin., 34, 14. 16. *Aen.*, 4, 487ff., describing a Libyan priestess.

they believe in gods created by him, through whose agency he governs the world; and either they do not deny or else they go further and openly proclaim that there are powers in the universe which effect marvels, whether produced spontaneously or obtained by the performance of some kind of rite or ceremony, or even achieved by magic arts.

And yet, when we put before them an instance of some wonderful property displayed by other substances which are neither rational living creatures nor spirits endowed with any kind of reason (the kind of thing of which I have mentioned a few instances), then their usual reply is, 'This is the force of nature; this is their natural quality; these are the special properties of their natural substances.' This, then, is the complete rational explanation! This explains why flame makes the salt of Agrigentum fluid, while water makes it crackle – because that is its nature! And yet this appears to be in fact contrary to nature; for nature has given to salt the property of dissolving in water, and to fire, and not to water, the property of drying. 'Ah yes', they say, 'but it is the natural property of this particular salt to display these contrary effects.' Very good. Then this is the rational explanation offered in the case of the spring of Garamantum, where the same source is cold in the daytime and boiling hot at night, both properties causing distress to those who touch; and it applies also to that other spring which is cold to the touch and, like other springs, extinguishes a burning torch, and yet, unlike other springs, and miraculously, it also rekindles the torch it has put out; and to the asbestos stone, which has no fire of its own, and yet, when it has received fire, blazes so fiercely with a fire not its own that it cannot be quenched; and to other marvels besides which it would be tedious to go over. Although they may seem to display an inherent property which is unexampled and contrary to nature, the only rational explanation that is offered is, 'That is their nature'! A good short answer, to be sure! A sufficient reason, indeed!

But since God is the author of all natures, why do they object to our supplying a stronger reason? For when they refuse to believe something, alleging its impossibility, and demand that we supply a rational explanation, we reply that the explanation is the will of Almighty God. For God is certainly called 'Almighty' for one reason only; that he has the power to do whatever he wills, and he has the power to create so many things which would be reckoned obviously impossible, if they were not displayed to our senses or else reported by witnesses who have always proved reliable; and this applies not only to phenomena very unfamiliar to us but even to the most familiar instances I have quoted. As for the accounts which have no supporting evidence beyond the statements of the authors of the books in which we read them, and which are written by authors not instructed by divine inspiration and therefore susceptible, perhaps, to human delusion, it is open to anyone to withhold belief from them, and no one can justly be blamed for so doing.

For myself, indeed, I do not wish all the instances I have quoted to be believed without question; I myself do not believe them all implicitly, in the sense of having no doubt at all in my mind, apart from those of which I have had personal experience, or which can easily be put to the proof by anyone at all. Examples of these are: the fact that lime grows hot in water, and remains cold in oil; that the loadstone by some insensible power of suction attracts iron, though it will not stir a straw; that the flesh of a peacock does not putrefy, whereas Plato's body decayed; that chaff is cool, in the sense that it keeps snow from melting, and warm, in the sense that it brings apples to ripeness; that a bright fire bakes stones to a shining whiteness appropriate to its own brilliance, while it burns most things to a dusky hue quite contrary to that brilliance. There is a similar paradox in the fact that dark stains are spread from shining oil, and likewise dark lines are imprinted by gleaming silver, and that in some substances blazing fire effects a reversal of their qualities: beautiful woods become unsightly, durable timber becomes brittle, and timber liable to rot is made resistant to decay.

I have personal knowledge of these facts, some of which are known to all, others to most people; and there are a great many other such facts which it would be tedious to insert in this book. However, with regard to the instances I quoted from my reading and not from my own experience, I have not been able to find any reliable witnesses to establish the truth of these stories, except for the report about the spring in which burning torches are extinguished and then relit, and the account of the apples of Sodom, which look ripe on the outside but inside are full of smoke. In fact in the case of that spring I have not found any witnesses to declare that they have seen it in Epirus, but I have encountered people who know a similar fountain in Gaul, not far from Grenoble. The apples of Sodom, on the other hand, are attested not only in literary sources worthy of credence, but also by many who talk of them from personal experience; and so I cannot doubt the truth of the report.

As for the other stories, my position is that I have decided that I should neither affirm nor deny their truth; but I have quoted them along with the others for the very reason that I have read them in authorities from the side of our antagonists. My purpose here is to demonstrate the kind of marvels recorded in profusion in pagan literature and generally believed by our opponents, although no rational explanation is offered, whereas the same people cannot bring themselves to believe us, even though rational grounds are produced, when we say that Almighty God is to perform an act which lies outside their experience and contravenes the evidence of their senses. For what better reason or more valid ground could be given in such matters than when the assertion that the Almighty can achieve this result and the statement that he is going to achieve it is supported by the written evidence that he has foretold this achievement, evidence contained in books in which he foretold many other acts which he is proved to have performed? He will certainly effect what are supposed to be impossibilities, because he has foretold that he will do so; for in the past he has fulfilled his promises and has thus ensured belief in things that passed belief, even from nations that refused belief.

8. *A change of some property in a substance is not contrary to nature*

However, our opponents may retort, their refusal to believe in our assertion that human bodies are destined to burn for ever and that these bodies will never die is based on this consideration: that we know that the nature of human bodies has been very differently constituted; and hence it is impossible here to advance the explanation offered in respect of those natural marvels we have mentioned. It cannot in this case be said that 'this is a natural power' or 'this is a natural property of this substance'; for in fact we are aware that this is *not* a natural property of human bodies.

Now we have an answer to this, based on our sacred books, namely, that this human flesh of ours was differently constituted before man's sin; I mean that it was possible for this flesh never to suffer death. That condition changed after man's sin, and man's flesh became what it has always been known to be in this distressful situation of mortality, so that it cannot hold on to life for ever; by the same token, at the resurrection of the dead it will be differently constituted from the flesh as it is known to us. But our opponents do not believe in those books of ours, in which we read the description of man's condition when he lived in paradise and learn how remote he was from the inevitability of death. For if they believed them, then of course we should not be engaged with them in a laborious debate about the punishment of the damned. As it is, then, we shall have to produce some evidence from the writings of the most learned of their own authors, to show that it is possible for a particular substance to acquire a character different from that which has become familiar in experience as belonging to the definition of its nature.

There is a passage in Marcus Varro's book entitled *On the Race of the Roman People* which I will quote in the author's own words:

> A wonderful portent appeared in the sky. Castor[17] writes that in the well-known star Venus, called Vesperugo by Plautus, and Hesperus by Homer[18] (who speaks of it as 'most beautiful'), a remarkable portent appeared. The star actually changed its colour, its size, its shape, and its course; a thing which had never happened before, and has never happened again. This occurred in the reign of King Ogygus,[19] according to the famous mathematicians Adrastus of Cyzicus and Dion of Neapolis.

Now Varro would certainly not have called this phenomenon a portent if it had not seemed contrary to nature; in fact we say, as a matter of course, that all portents are contrary to nature. But they are not. For how can an event be contrary to nature when it happens by the will of God, since the will of the great Creator assuredly *is* the nature of every created thing? A portent, therefore, does not occur contrary to nature, but contrary to what is known of nature.

Now who can count the enormous number of portents which are included in pagan histories? But at the moment we must confine our attention to what is relevant to the matter in hand. Is there anything so firmly regulated by the author of the nature of the sky and the earth as the orderly course of the stars? Is there anything so securely established by unvarying laws? And yet, when it so pleased him who rules his own creation with supreme dominion and power, the star renowned beyond all other stars for size and splendour altered its size, its shape and, still more wonderful, the decreed order of its course. On that occasion this star certainly upset the rules of the astrologers, if any of those rules were by then in existence. For astrologers have their written rules according to which they compute, by calculations thought to be infallible, the past and future movements of the stars: and in reliance on those rules they have been bold enough

17. A grammarian and chronicle of the first century B.C. often cited by Eusebius.

18 Plaut., *Amph.*, 1, 1, 119; Hom., *Od.*, 22, 318.

19. cf. Bk XVIII. 8.

to assert that what happened then to Lucifer never happened before and has never happened afterwards.

We, on the other hand, have read in our sacred books that even the sun itself stood still, when that holy man Joshua asked this boon from the Lord God, until the battle on which he was engaged came to a victorious end;[20] and that it turned back in its course, to signify by this prodigy, as an adjunct to God's promise, the addition of fifteen years to the life of King Hezekiah.[21] But when the pagans believe in the reality of such miracles as those, which were granted to the merits of the saints, they ascribe them to magic arts. Hence the line which I quoted earlier from Virgil:

> To stop the flow of rivers, turn the stars
> Back on their course.[22]

For in fact we read in our sacred books that a river stood still and its waters flowed upstream and downstream when, under the leadership of the above-mentioned Joshua, the People of God made their way across, and that the same thing happened when Elijah the prophet crossed over, followed by his disciple Elisha.[23] And I have just mentioned that the greatest of stars turned back on its course in the reign of Hezekiah. But the behaviour of Lucifer as recorded by Varro is not there said to have occurred in response to a petition from any human being.

Those unbelievers therefore must not throw dust in their own eyes in this matter of the knowledge of nature, and assume that it is not possible for something to occur in any substance through the exercise of divine power, which conflicts with the property of that substance as known to them in their own human experience. And yet the natural phenomena known to all men are no less wonderful, and would be a source of astonishment to all who observe them, if it were not man's habit to restrict his wonder at miracles to the rarities. For example, could anyone fail to see, on rational consideration, how marvellous it is that, despite the countless numbers of mankind, and despite the great similarity among men through their possession of a common nature, each individual has his unique individual appearance? The truth is that if there were not this underlying similarity man could not be distinguished as a separate species from the other animals, while at the same time, without those individual differences, one man could not be distinguished from another. Thus we acknowledge that

20. cf. Josh. 10, 13.
21. cf. Is. 38, 8.
22. *Aen.*, 4, 489.
23. Josh. 3, 16; 2 Kings 2, 8; 14.

men are alike, and equally we discover that they are different. Now it is the observation of the differences between men that should arouse our wonder; for the likeness would seem to be normal, as something demanded by our common nature. And yet because it is rarities that arouse wonder, we are much more astonished when we find two people so alike that we are always, or very frequently, making mistakes when we try to distinguish them.

But it may be that our friends do not believe the story reported, as I said, by Varro, although he is one of their authorities, and the most learned authority at that; or else they are less impressed by the alleged incident because the star did not continue for long out of its accustomed course, but soon returned to its orbit. Here then is another instance for them, something which can be demonstrated at the present day, and something which, I imagine, should suffice to warn them that when they have observed some characteristics in the constitution of any substance in nature, and have made themselves familiar with it, they ought not to put limitations on God as a result of this, and assume that he cannot alter it and change it into something very different from what they have known of it. The land of Sodom was once, as we know, not as it is today. It once presented an appearance like that of other countries, and was as rich and fertile as any, if not more so; in fact in the inspired narrative it is compared to God's paradise.[24] But after it was smitten from heaven – a fact confirmed by pagan records also,[25] and the evidence can today be seen by visitors to those parts – it became and still remains a place of horror, a portent of soot and ashes, and its apples present a delusive appearance of ripeness on their surface, but inside they hold nothing but dust. Note that the land was not always like this, and yet it is like this today. See how its nature was changed, by the Creator of all natures, into this disgusting condition, so different from what it was. What a miracle of transformation! It was a long time before this fate came to it; and it has long continued in that sorry state.

So, just as it was not impossible for God to set in being natures according to his will, so it is afterwards not impossible for him to change those natures which he has set in being, in whatever way he chooses. Hence the enormous crop of marvels, which we call 'monsters', 'signs', 'portents', or 'prodigies'; if I chose to recall them and mention them all, would there ever be an end to this work? The name 'monster', we are told, evidently comes from *monstrare*, 'to show', because they show by signifying something; 'sign' (*ostentum*) comes

24. cf. Gen. 13, 10. 25. cf. Tac., *Hist.*, 5, 7.

from *ostendere*, 'to point out', 'portent' from *portendere*, 'to portend', that is, 'to show beforehand' (*praeostendere*), and 'prodigy' from *porro dicere*, 'to foretell the future'. Those who divine by such signs are often at fault in the predictions they base on them; or they may give true forecasts, under the influence of evil spirits, whose aim it is to entangle in the toils of baneful superstition the minds of such human beings who deserve that kind of punishment; or else in the course of their many predictions they may from time to time hit upon some truth. How all this comes about, it is up to these interpreters to decide!

Now these signs are, apparently, contrary to nature and they are called 'unnatural'; and the Apostle uses the same human way of speaking when he talks of the wild olive being 'unnaturally' grafted on to the cultivated tree, and sharing in the richness of the garden olive. For us, however, they have a message. These 'monsters', 'signs', 'portents', and 'prodigies', as they are called, ought to 'show' us, to 'point out' to us, to 'portend' and 'foretell', that God is to do what he prophesied that he would do with the bodies of the dead, with no difficulty to hinder him, no law of nature to debar him from so doing. And how he has foretold this, I have, I think, sufficiently shown in my previous book, by extracting from the Old and the New Testament not indeed all the passages relevant to the topic, but what I judged to be enough for the purpose of this work.

9. *The nature of eternal punishment*

Therefore what God said through the mouth of his prophet, about the eternal punishment of the damned, will come true; it will most certainly come true that 'their worm will never die and their fire will not go out.'[26] Our Lord Jesus himself took care to emphasize this with even greater vehemence when he spoke of the bodily parts which cause a man to go wrong, making them stand for the people whom a man loves as he loves his own right hand. He bids him cut them off: 'It is better for you to go into life maimed' he says, 'than to keep both hands and go to hell, into the inextinguishable fire, where their worm never dies and their fire does not go out.' Similarly, he says of the foot: 'It is better for you to go lame into eternal life than to keep both feet and be consigned to hell, to the inextinguishable fire, where their worm never dies, and their fire does not go out.' He says the same about the eye: 'It is better for you to enter the kingdom of God with

26. Is. 66, 24.

one eye, than to keep both eyes and be consigned to the hell of fire, where their worm never dies and their fire does not go out.'[27] He did not find it irksome to repeat the same form of words three times in the same passage. Who could fail to be appalled at this repetition, this vehement emphasis on that punishment, uttered from his divine lips?

Now as for this fire and this worm, there are some who want to make both of them refer to the pains of the soul, not of the body. They say that those whose penitence is too late, and therefore ineffectual, those who have thus been separated from God, are burnt in the fire of the soul's sorrow and pain; and therefore, they maintain, 'fire' is quite appropriately used as a symbol for that burning pain. That is why the Apostle says, 'If anyone is led astray, do I not *burn* with indignation?'[28] They suppose that the 'worm' is to be taken in the same way; for, they say, the Scripture says, 'Like the moth in a garment, or the worm in timber, so does sorrow torment the heart of a man.'[29] Those, on the other hand, who feel sure that in that punishment there will be pain of both soul and body declare that the body is burnt by the fire while the soul is, in a sense, gnawed by the 'worm' of sorrow. This is a more plausible suggestion, inasmuch as it is obviously absurd to suppose that in that state either soul or body will be exempt from pain. And yet for my part I should be more ready to ascribe both of them to the body than neither of them, and to assume that the scriptural statement is silent about the pain of the soul for this reason, that, although it is not stated, it is taken as implied that when the body is thus in pain, the soul also will be tortured with unavailing remorse. For in the Old Testament we have this saying, 'The punishment of the flesh of the wicked is the fire and the worm';[30] which could be put more briefly as 'the punishment of the wicked'. The reason for the addition of 'the flesh' can surely only be that both the fire and the worm will be punishments of the body. Or it may be that the writer chose to say 'the punishment of the flesh' because what will be punished in a man is his wickedness in having lived a life of fleshly sensuality; for that is the reason why he will come to the second death, which is what the Apostle means when he says, 'If you live on the level of fleshly sensuality, you will die.'[31]

Well then, each one of us must choose as he thinks fit between those interpretations. He may ascribe the fire to the body, and the worm to the mind, the former literally and the latter metaphorically; or he may attribute both, in the literal sense, to the body. For in any

27. Mark 9, 42ff. 28. 2 Cor. 11, 29. 29. Prov. 25, 20.
30. Ecclus. 7, 17. 31. Rom. 8, 13.

case I have sufficiently argued that it is possible for living creatures to remain alive in the fire, being burnt without being consumed, feeling pain without incurring death; and this by means of a miracle of the omnipotent Creator. Anyone who says that this is impossible for the Creator does not realize who is responsible for whatever marvels he finds in the whole of the world of nature. It is, in fact, God himself who has created all that is wonderful in this world, the great miracles and the minor marvels which I have mentioned; and he has included them all in that unique wonder, that miracle of miracles, the world itself.

Then let each one choose the alternative he prefers; he may think either that the worm, along with the fire, refers, in the literal sense, to the bodily punishment, or that it refers to the punishment of the soul, the word being used by a transference of sense from the material to the immaterial. Which of these is the true explanation will be all too swiftly revealed by the actual event, when the knowledge of the saints will be such as to need no experience to teach them the truth about those pains; that wisdom, which will then be full and perfect, will then suffice by itself for them to know this also – for 'now our knowledge is partial', until perfection comes.[32] The important thing is that we should never believe that those bodies are to be such as to feel no anguish in the fire.

10. *If the fire of hell is material fire, can it affect immaterial demons?*

At this point we are confronted with another question: If this fire is not to be immaterial, like the pain of the soul, but material fire, inflicting pain by contact, so that bodies can be tortured by it, then how will there be punishment in it for the evil spirits? It is obviously the same fire which will be used for the punishment of the demons as well as human beings; for Christ says, 'Out of my sight, you accursed, into the eternal fire, which is prepared *for the Devil and his angels*.'[33] Now it may well be that demons have a kind of body of their own, as learned men have thought, composed of the thick moist air of this atmosphere whose pressure we feel when the wind is blowing. If an element of this sort could not be affected by fire it would not burn us when it has been heated in the baths; for it is first burned so that it can burn, and it passes on an experience it undergoes.

If, however, anyone maintains that demons have no bodies at all,

32. cf. 1 Cor. 13, 9. 33. Matt. 25, 41.

there is no need for us to toil at a laborious inquiry into the question, or to engage in any contentious debate. Why, in fact, should we not say that immaterial spirits can be tormented by the pain of material fire in a way which is real, however amazing, seeing that the spirit of man, which without doubt is immaterial also, can at this present time be shut up within the framework of a material body, and that it will be possible at the judgement for them to be bound to their bodies with an indissoluble connection? And so, even if they have no bodies, the spirits of the demons, or rather the demons who are spirits, will be in contact with material fires for their torment, though they themselves are immaterial. This will not mean that the fires with which they are in contact will, because of this conjunction, receive spirit and so become living beings, composed of body and spirit. As I said, this contact will be in a wondrous manner that cannot be described; and the spirits, instead of giving life to the fire, will receive their punishment from the fire. There is a different manner of contact of spirit with body, which produces a living being; and that conjunction is utterly amazing and beyond our powers of comprehension. I am speaking of man himself.

I should indeed have said that the spirits are destined to burn, without possessing any material body, just as the rich man was on fire in Hades when he said, 'I am tortured in those flames';[34] this is what I should have said, if I had not observed that the appropriate reply would be that the flames in the parable were of the same kind as the eyes which the rich man 'raised and saw Lazarus', and the tongue on which he longed for a drop of water to be poured, and the finger of Lazarus which he suggested as the instrument of that boon – and yet these characters were souls without bodies. Thus the flames burning the rich man and the little drop of water he craved were of the same nature as visions seen in dreams, or in an ecstasy, when people perceive entities which are immaterial and yet display the likeness of material realities. For even when the subject himself appears in such visions (in spirit, not in body), he sees himself there so like his own bodily appearance as to be completely indistinguishable from it. But in fact that hell, which is also called 'the lake of fire and sulphur',[35] will be a material fire and will torture the bodies of the damned, whether the bodies of human beings and also of demons – the solid bodies of human beings, the demons' bodies of air – or the body together with the spirit in the case of human beings, but in the case of demons the spirits without bodies – those spirits being in contact with

34. Luke 16, 24. 35. Rev. 20, 9.

the fire for their punishment, not for the imparting of life to material fire. The fire will assuredly be one and the same for both classes of the damned, as the Truth has told us.

11. *The proportion between the offence and the punishment in respect of time*

Now some of those adversaries against whose attacks we are defending the City of God may consider it unjust that in retribution for sins which, however serious, were certainly committed in a short space of time, each person should be condemned to eternal punishment; as if the justice of any law at any time consisted in its concern that the length of the punishment of the offender should be equal to the length of time of the offence! Cicero[36] tells us that there were eight types of punishment provided in the laws: fines, imprisonment, flogging, equivalent damages, deprivation, exile, death, and slavery. Now can any of those be confined within the brief space of time that would correspond to the swiftness of the misdeed, so that the punishment should be effected in the few moments that it takes to arrest the offender? Perhaps the fourth punishment, but no other. For 'equivalent damages' is the procedure by which the offender suffers what he has inflicted, as prescribed in the law of 'an eye for an eye, a tooth for a tooth'.[37] It is in fact possible for a man to lose an eye by this severe act of vengeance, in as short a time as it took him to put out the other man's eye by his heinous crime. But, to take another case, if it is thought reasonable that a man should be flogged for kissing another man's wife, then surely the action of a moment is punished by a flogging whose pain lasts a matter of hours. There is no comparison between the durations; and a fleeting pleasure is punished by a lasting pain. Then again, what of imprisonment? Are we to suppose that each offender is to be judged to deserve imprisonment for as long a time as it took to commit the offence for which he is confined? In fact, a slave is very justly punished by a term of years in fetters when he has attacked his master with a passing word or has inflicted on him a blow that is over in a swift second. While as for fines, deprivations, exile, and slavery, these are generally imposed without any prospect of pardon or relaxation; and in that case, do they not appear like eternal punishments by the standard of this mortal life? The only reason why they cannot be everlasting is that this life, in which this punishment is inflicted, is itself not extended

36. Not in *De Legibus*, or in any extant work.

37. Exod. 21, 24.

into eternity. Yet the offences which are punished by the longest possible retribution are committed in the shortest possible time; and no one has ever stood up to advance the proposal that the torments of the guilty should be limited to the time taken to commit homicide, adultery, sacrilege, or any of those crimes whose enormity is to be measured not by the length of time they take, but by the magnitude of their wickedness and impiety.

As for the criminal who suffers capital punishment for some grave offence, do the laws estimate his punishment according to the time that it takes to kill him, which is very short, and ignore the fact that he is removed for ever from the company of the living? Thus the removal of men from this mortal community by the punishment of the first death answers to their removal from that Immortal City by the punishment of the second death. For just as the laws of the former city have no power to recall to that community one who has been put to death, so, when a man has been condemned to the second death, the laws of that other City cannot call him back to life eternal. What becomes then, they ask, of the truth of Christ's saying, 'With whatever measure you deal out to others, it will be dealt to you in return',[38] if temporal sin is punished with eternal pains? But they do not observe that 'the same measure' has reference not to the equality of the *time* of the retribution, but to the equivalence of evil, in that one who does evil will have evil done to him; although the statement may be taken as referring directly to the subject about which the Lord was speaking at the time, the subject of judgement and condemnation. In that case if a man who judges unjustly and condemns unjustly is justly judged and condemned, he receives 'in the same measure' even though what he receives is not what he gave. He did something by a judicial act and it is by a judicial act that something is done to him; and yet what he did in condemning was an act of injustice, whereas it is an act of justice that he suffers by being condemned.

12. *The magnitude of the first transgression, making liable to eternal punishment all who are outside the Saviour's grace*

Now the reason why eternal punishment appears harsh and unjust to human sensibilities, is that in this feeble condition of those sensibilities under their condition of mortality man lacks the sensibility of the highest and purest wisdom, the sense which should enable him to feel the gravity of the wickedness in the first act of disobedience.

38. Luke 6, 38.

For the more intimate the first man's enjoyment of God, the greater his impiety in abandoning God. By so doing he merited eternal evil, in that he destroyed in himself a good that might have been eternal. In consequence, the whole of mankind is a 'condemned lump'; for he who committed the first sin was punished, and along with him all the stock which had its roots in him. The result is that there is no escape for anyone from this justly deserved punishment, except by merciful and undeserved grace; and mankind is divided between those in whom the power of merciful grace is demonstrated, and those in whom is shown the might of just retribution. Neither of those could be displayed in respect of all mankind; for if all had remained condemned to the punishment entailed by just condemnation, then God's merciful grace would not have been seen at work in anyone; on the other hand, if all had been transferred from darkness into light, the truth of God's vengeance would not have been made evident. Now there are many more condemned by vengeance than are released by mercy; and the reason for this is that it should in this way be made plain what was the due of all mankind. For if this due punishment were imposed on all, no one would have the right to criticize the justice of God in that retribution; but the fact that so many are released from it is the ground for heart-felt thanksgiving for the free bounty of our Deliverer.

13. *The false notion that punishment after death is merely for purification*

Now the Platonists[39], while refusing to believe that any sins go unpunished, hold that all punishments are directed towards purification, whether they are punishments inflicted by human laws or those imposed by divine decree, and whether the latter are suffered in this life, or after death, when someone is spared in this life, or when his affliction does not result in his correction. This belief is expressed in the passage in Virgil, where he first speaks of earthly bodies and their mortal parts, and says of men's souls that

> Hence come desire and fear, gladness and sorrow,
> They look not up to heaven, but lie confined
> In darkness and the sightless dungeon's gloom.

and then goes on immediately:

> Yet at their last light, when the life departs,

39. e.g. Plot., *Enn.* 3, 2, 41.

(that is when this mortal life leaves them at their last day)

> Even then they are not freed from woe and pain;
> The body's plagues do not vanish utterly.
> For many evils, hardening deep within
> Must needs grow rooted there in wondrous wise.
> Therefore they suffer chastisement of pain,
> Paying the price of ancient sin. And some
> Are hung suspended in the idle winds;
> Others are washed from guilt beneath the surge
> Of the vast deep; in others the infection
> Is burned away by fire.[40]

Those who hold this view will have it that the only punishments after death are those intended to purify, so that souls may be cleansed from any infection contracted by contact with the earth by purifying pains inflicted by one of the elements superior to the earth, which are air, fire and water. The air is meant by the phrase 'suspended in the winds', the water, by 'the vast deep', while the fire is expressly named in 'is burned away by fire'. On our part we acknowledge that even in this mortal life there are indeed some purificatory punishments; but penalties inflicted on those whose life is not improved thereby or is even made worse, are not purificatory. Punishments are a means of purification only to those who are disciplined and corrected by them. All other punishments, whether temporal or eternal, are imposed on every person in accordance with the treatment he is to receive from God's providence; they are imposed either in retribution for sins, whether past sins or sins in which the person so chastised is still living, or else they serve to exercise and to display the virtues of the good; and they are administered through the agency of men, or of angels, whether good or evil angels. It must be observed that when any man suffers any harm through the wickedness or the mistake of another, then that other human being commits a sin in doing some harm to another man either through ignorance or through ill-will; God commits no sin in allowing this wrong to happen by his decision, which is just, albeit inscrutable. As for temporal pains, some people suffer them in this life only, others after death, others both in this life and in the other;[41] yet all this precedes that last and strictest judgement. However, not all men who endure temporal pains after death come into those eternal punishments, which are to come after that judgement. Some, in fact, will receive forgiveness in the world to come

40. *Aen.* 6, 733ff. 41. cf. ch. 26.

for what is not forgiven in this, as I have said above, so that they may not be punished with the eternal chastisement of the world to come.

14. *The temporal pains of this life, to which the human condition is subject*

But there are very few who undergo no punishments in this life, and suffer them only after death. However, I myself have known and heard of some who up to the decrepitude of old age never experienced as much as the mildest of fevers, whose whole life has been undisturbed; and yet the whole of man's life is pain, because the whole of it is temptation, as the holy Scriptures proclaim. For Scripture says, 'Is human life on the earth anything but temptation?'[42] Folly and ignorance are in themselves no small punishment, and it is rightly considered that they should at all costs be avoided – so much so that children are compelled, by dint of painful punishments, either to learn a craft or to acquire a literary education. And the process of learning with its attendant punishment is so painful that children not infrequently prefer to endure the punishments designed to compel them to learn, rather than to submit to the process of learning. In fact is there anyone who, faced with the choice between death and a second childhood, would not shrink in dread from the latter prospect and elect to die? Infancy, indeed, starts this life not with smiles but with tears; and this is, in a way, an unconscious prophecy of the troubles on which it is entering. It is said that Zoroaster was the only human being who smiled when he was born,[43] and yet that portent of a smile boded no good for him. For he was, so they say, the inventor of magic arts;[44] and yet those arts did not avail him anything, not even in respect of the insubstantial felicity of this present life; for he was king of Bactria, but he was overcome in war by Ninus, king of Assyria.[45] It is altogether inevitable that those words of Scripture should prove true, 'A heavy yoke is laid on Adam's sons, from the day they issue from their mother's womb until the day when they go for burial to the mother of all things.'[46] So true is this that even the infants who are set free, by the washing of rebirth, from the fetters of original sin (which was the only sin that bound them) still endure

42. Job, 7, 1 (LXX) SC; cf. Bk XIX, 8n. 43. cf. Plin., 7, 15. 44. Plin. 30, 2.

45. Euseb-Hier., *Chron.*, 1, 20, 13. Modern scholars suggest a sixth-century date for Zoroaster (Zarathustra) whose teaching became the dominant religion of Persia under the Sassanids (A.D. 211–640).

46. Ecclus. 40, 1.

many afflictions, and some of them even suffer from time to time the assaults of malignant spirits. And yet we must never think that these sufferings can do them real harm, even if they grow so severe as to cut off the soul from the body, so that they bring this life to an end at that tender age.

15. *The whole of God's redeeming work has reference to the world to come*

Nevertheless in the 'heavy yoke laid on Adam's sons, from the day they issue from their mother's womb until the day they go for burial to the mother of all things' even this evil is found to be marvellous in its effect, in that it induces us to live soberly and to realize that because of the first and supremely grave sin, committed in paradise, this life has been made a life of punishment for us, and that all the provisions of the new covenant refer only to our new inheritance in the world to come. In this world we are given an earnest of that inheritance, and we shall at the appointed time come into the inheritance of which this is a pledge; but at present we go on our way in hope, and we make progress from day to day as we 'put to death the evil actions of the body by the power of the Spirit'. For 'God knows those who belong to him', and 'all those who are led by God's Spirit are the sons of God';[47] but they are sons by grace, not by nature; for God's only Son by nature was made the Son of Man for us by compassion, so that we who by nature are sons of men might become sons of God through him by grace. He, as we know, while continuing changeless, took our nature to himself from us so that in that nature he might take us to himself; and while retaining his divinity he became partaker of our weakness. His purpose was that we should be changed for the better, and by participation in his immortality and his righteousness should lose our condition of sinfulness and mortality, and should retain the good that he did while in our nature, perfected by the supreme good in the goodness of his nature. For just as we have descended to this evil state through one man who sinned, so through one man[48] (who is also God) who justifies us we shall ascend to that height of goodness. And yet no one should be confident that he has passed over from the one state to the other, until he has arrived where there will be no more temptation – until he has achieved that peace which is his aim in the many varied struggles of this present warfare, in which 'the desires of the body oppose the spirit, and the spirit fights against the body's

47. Rom. 8, 13; 2 Tim. 2, 19; Rom. 8, 14. 48. cf. Rom. 5, 12.

desires.'[49] Now this war would never have been if human nature had, by free choice, persisted in that right condition in which it was created. As it is, however, human nature has refused to keep that peace with God in happiness; and so in its unhappiness it is at war with itself. And yet this evil state is better than the earlier condition of this life; for it is better to struggle against vices than to be free from conflict under their domination. Better war with the hope of everlasting peace than slavery without any thought of liberation. Our desire is, indeed, to be free even of this war; and by the fire of divine love we are set on fire with longing to attain that orderly peace where the lower elements may be subdued to the higher in a stability that can never be shaken. But even if (perish the thought!) there were no hope of attaining this great good, we ought none the less to prefer to continue in this state of conflict, with all its troubles, than to allow our vices to have dominion over us by ceasing to resist.

16. *The laws of grace which govern every stage in the life of the regenerate*

But so great is God's mercy towards the 'vessels of mercy which he has designed for glory'[50] that although in infancy, the first age of man, the child is under the control of bodily desires and offers no resistance to them; nevertheless, if the child has received the sacrament of our Mediator, then even if his life ends at this age, he has assuredly been 'transferred from the power of darkness'[51] into the kingdom of Christ, and not only is he not destined for everlasting pains but he will not even undergo any purifying torments after death. The same holds true for the second age, which we call childhood, when reason has not yet undertaken the battle against the lower nature, and when, in general, the child is dominated by all kinds of vicious pleasures, because although he now has the power of speech, his undeveloped mind is not yet capable of understanding the commandments. For this spiritual rebirth is by itself enough to ensure that the baptized will not be debarred from felicity by the evil contracted, along with death, in physical birth. But when the child arrives at years of discretion, when he can now understand the commandments and can be subject to the rule of the Law, then he must take up the struggle against evil impulses, and fight vigorously, to avoid being led into sins which will bring damnation. And if those impulses have not yet grown strong and their victory has not become habitual, then they are more easily

49. Gal. 5, 17. 50. Rom. 9, 23. 51. Col. 1, 13.

overcome, and they yield to the victor; but if they have grown accustomed to conquest and command, victory over them is difficult, and costs great hardship. And this warfare is not waged with genuinely whole-hearted purpose, unless the motive is the love of true righteousness, which comes through faith in Christ. For if the Law is there with its commands, but the Spirit with its help is absent, the very prohibition of the sin increases the craving for sin, and when that craving wins the day, the guilt of transgression is added to the evil impulses. Not infrequently, to be sure, the obvious vices are overcome by vices so masked that they are reputed virtues; and the king of those is pride, an exalted self-satisfaction which brings a disastrous fall. Then, and only then, must those evil impulses be reckoned as defeated, when they are defeated by the love of God, which none but God himself can give; and he gives it only through 'the mediator between God and men, the man Christ Jesus',[52] who was made partaker of our mortality to make us partakers of his divinity. Very few are so lucky as to avoid committing some sin worthy of damnation after they have entered on adolescence, either a moral offence or breach of the Law or some false opinion showing a criminal impiety; very few young men succeed in overcoming, with the abundant help of the Spirit, everything which could gain the mastery over them through the temptations of sensual pleasure. Very many, however, when they have accepted the authority of the commandments, are first vanquished by overpowering impulses of evil, and become transgressors of the Law, then they have recourse to the help of his grace, so that with this assistance they may win the victory by bitter penitence and more strenuous warfare, when they have first subjected their mind to God and have thus put their mind in command of their sensual desires.

It follows that anyone who desires to escape everlasting pains needs not only to be baptized but also to be justified in Christ, and thus to pass from the Devil to Christ. But he should not imagine that any pains will be purificatory, except those that precede that ultimate and terrible judgement. However it is certainly not to be denied that the eternal fire itself will be proportionate to the deserts of the wicked, which differ though all alike are evil; and for some it will be milder, for others more severe, whether the fire itself will vary in its power and heat in proportion to the punishment of each sinner, or whether its heat will be everywhere the same but the pain will be felt in different degrees.

52. 1 Tim. 2, 5.

17. *The opinion that punishment will not last for ever*

I am aware that I now have to engage in a debate, devoid of rancour, with those compassionate Christians who refuse to believe that the punishment of hell will be everlasting either in the case of all those men whom the completely just Judge accounts deserving of that chastisement, or at least in the case of some of them; they hold that they are to be set free after fixed limits of time have been passed, the periods being longer or shorter in proportion to the magnitude of their offences. On this subject the most compassionate of all was Origen, who believed that the Devil himself and his angels will be rescued from their torments and brought into the company of the holy angels, after the more severe and more lasting chastisements appropriate to their deserts.[53] But the Church has rejected Origen's teaching,[54] and not without good reason, on account of this opinion and a number of others, in particular his theory of the incessant alternations of misery and bliss, the endless shuttling to and fro between those states at predetermined epochs. For in fact he lost even the appearance of compassion in that he assigned to the saints genuine misery, by which they paid their penalties, and false bliss, in which they could not experience the joy of everlasting good in genuine security – I mean that they could not be certain of it without any apprehension.

Very different, however, is the error, promoted by tenderness of heart and human compassion, of those who suppose that the miseries of those condemned by that judgement will be temporal, whereas the felicity of all men, who are released after a shorter or longer period, will be everlasting. Now if this opinion is good and true, just because it is compassionate, then it will be the better and the truer the more compassionate it is. Then let the fountain of compassion be deepened and enlarged until it extends as far as the evil angels, who must be set free, although, of course, after many ages, and ages of any length that can be imagined! Why should this fountain flow as far as the whole of human kind, and then dry up as soon as it reaches the angels? And yet our friends cannot bring themselves to stretch out further in their compassion until they reach the liberation of the Devil himself! Nevertheless, if anyone could bring himself to go so far he would outdo them in compassion! For all that, his error would manifestly

53. cf. Orig. *De Princ.* 1, 6, 3; 3, 6, 5. Gregory of Nyssa held a similar view; cf. *Oratio Catechetica* 26.

54. At a council at Alexandria, A.D. 400, whose condemnation of Origen was accepted by Pope Anastasius I. cf. Bk XI, 23n.

surpass all errors in its perversity, its wrong-headed contradiction of the express words of God, by the same margin as, in his own estimation, his belief surpasses all other opinions in its clemency.

18. *The opinion that all men are to be saved from damnation by the intercession of the saints*

There are even some people, as I know from having met them and talked with them, who give the appearance of reverencing the holy Scriptures and yet lead reprehensible lives; when such people plead their own case they attribute to God a tenderness towards the human race much more lavish than that ascribed to him by those I have just mentioned. They admit, indeed, that the divine predictions about the wicked and the unbelievers are true, in that this is the fate they deserve; but they maintain that when it comes to the judgement, mercy is destined to carry the day. For God, they say, will in his mercy grant them the prayers and intercessions of his saints; because if the saints prayed for them when they experienced their enmity, how much more will they intercede for them when they see them prostrated in humble supplication!

It is indeed incredible, they urge, that the saints should lose their tender feelings of compassion at a time when they have reached the fulfilment of perfect sanctity – incredible that whereas they prayed for their enemies in the past, when they themselves were not yet sinless, they should not now pray for their suppliants, when they themselves have entered on a state of sinlessness. Are we really to suppose that God will not listen to his children, all these beloved children, at a time when they have come to such a degree of holiness that he will find no hindrance to their entreaty?

There is a passage in the psalms which is quoted as evidence by those who allow the infidel and the ungodly to be released from all ills, though after a long period of torment; but our present tender-hearted ones claim it even more as evidence for their contention. It runs, 'Will God really forget to be merciful? Will he in his wrath restrain his compassion?'[55] His wrath, they say, means the infliction of eternal punishment, by his sentence, on all who are unworthy of everlasting bliss. But if God allows a long punishment, or even if he permits any punishment at all, then obviously he will be 'restraining his compassion', so that this can happen; and the psalmist says that he will not do this. For he does not say, 'Will God in his anger really restrain

55. Ps. 77, 9.

his compassion *for long?*' and so he implies that God will not restrain his compassion at all.

Now those who hold this view will have it that the threat of God's judgement is not a lying threat, although in fact he is not going to condemn anyone, in the same way as we cannot say that it was a lying threat when God said that he was about to destroy the city of Nineveh.[56] For then, they say, he did not fulfil his threat, although he foretold the fall of Nineveh unconditionally. He did not say, 'Nineveh will be overthrown, *unless the people repent and amend their ways*'; he put in no such additional clause when he announced the coming destruction of that city. But they regard that threat as being truthful for this reason: that God predicted something that the Ninevites truly deserved to suffer, although he was not to bring it about. He spared them, to be sure, they say, but of course he was well aware that they would repent; and yet he predicted the coming destruction, absolutely and definitely. This then, they contend, was true in respect of the truth of his sternness, because they deserved it; but it was not true in consideration of his mercy, which he did not restrain in his wrath; and so he spared the suppliants the punishment with which he had threatened the unruly. Well then, they argue, if on this occasion he spared the Ninevites, when he was bound to disappoint his holy prophet by so doing, how much more will he spare those sinners, at their pitiful supplication, at a time when all his saints will be begging him to spare them!

This is the surmise they cherish; and they suppose that the reason for the silence of holy Scripture on this point is to ensure that many people should amend their lives for fear of lengthy or even everlasting pains, and that thus there should be people capable of praying for those who have not amended. And yet, in their opinion, the inspired oracles have not been completely silent on the point. For example, consider this quotation: 'How great, Lord, is your kindness, which you have kept secret for those who fear you.'[57] Surely, they say, the point of this is that we should understand that the great kindness of God has been hidden and kept secret to keep men in fear? They also quote the Apostle's saying that 'God has confined all men in unbelief, so that he may have compassion on all',[58] and they go on to say that what he intended to convey by this was that no one will be condemned by God.

And yet even the people who hold this view do not stretch their conjecture to include the liberation of the Devil and his angels, or

56. cf. Jon. 3, 4. 57. Ps. 31, 20. 58. Rom. 11, 32.

even their exemption from damnation. They are in fact moved by a human compassion which is concerned only for human beings; and in particular they are pleading their own cause, promising themselves a delusive impunity for their own disreputable lives by supposing an all-embracing mercy of God towards the human race. And for that reason they are surpassed in their preaching of God's mercy by those who promise this impunity even to the prince of the demons and to his satellites.

19. *The opinion that even heretics will escape punishment through participation in the Body of Christ*

Similarly, there are others who promise freedom from eternal chastisement not indeed to all men as such, but only to those who have been washed in Christ's baptism, who are partakers of his body, whatever may have been the manner of their life, in whatever heresy or impiety they have been involved. They base this belief on the saying of Jesus, 'This is the bread which comes down from heaven; and so anyone who has eaten of this bread will not die. I am the living bread which has come down from heaven.'[59] It follows, they say, that such people must needs be rescued from eternal death, and eventually be brought to eternal life.

20. *The belief that salvation is confined to Catholics, who will be pardoned in spite of crimes and errors*

Again, there are others who do not promise this exemption to all who have received the sacrament of his body, but restrict it to Catholics, however evil their lives, because they have eaten the Body of Christ not only in the sacramental sign but in reality, because they have been established in that Body of Christ, of which the Apostle says, 'We are many; but we are one loaf, one Body.'[60] And so they may fall into some kind of heresy or even into pagan idolatry; and yet, simply because in the Body of Christ, the Catholic Church, they have received Christ's baptism and have eaten Christ's Body, they will not die eternally, but will in the end attain to life everlasting; and all their irreligion, whatever its degree of gravity, will not be enough to make their punishment eternal; it can only increase the length and severity of their chastisement.

59. John 6, 50f. 60. 1 Cor. 10. 17.

21. *The belief that all who hold the Catholic faith are to be saved, however evil their lives*

There are some who quote, 'The man who stands firm to the end will be saved';[61] and make this the basis for their assurance that those who continue in the Catholic Church, and only those, will attain salvation, however evil their lives; they are to be saved through fire, to be sure, thanks to the foundation of which the Apostle speaks. 'No one,' he says,

can lay any other foundation than the one that has already been laid, that is Jesus Christ. For if anyone builds on that foundation in gold, silver, precious stones, or in timber, hay, or straw, the work done by each man will be revealed. For the day will bring it to light. The day will be revealed in fire, and the fire will test the quality of each man's work. If a man's work on that foundation stands up to the test, he will get his reward; if it is burnt down he will have to bear the loss; and yet he will be saved himself, like a man who has come through fire.[62]

Therefore, they say, the Catholic Christian, whatever the quality of his life, has Christ for his foundation, which no heresy, cut off from Christ's Body, can have. And simply for that reason the Catholic Christian, even if he has lived an evil life, will, they suppose, be saved, just like the builders in timber, hay, or straw; like them, he will be saved 'through fire', that is, he will be set free after the pains of that fire which at the last judgement will be the instrument of punishment for the wicked.

22. *The suggestion that offences committed amongst works of mercy will not be called into condemnation*

I have discovered that some people hold that the only sinners who will burn in an eternity of punishment are those who omit to perform works of mercy as a fitting atonement for their sins. They base this belief on the saying of the apostle James, that 'the judgement will be merciless on one who has shown no mercy.'[63] It follows, they say, that anyone who has shown mercy, even though he has not changed his behaviour for the better, but has lived a life of crime and sin even in the midst of his works of mercy, will be treated with compassion at the judgement, so that either he will escape condemnation to any chastisement, or he will be released after a time, short or prolonged, from the punishment to which he is condemned. That is why, they hold, the

61. Matt. 24, 13. 62. 1 Cor. 3, 11ff. 63. Jas. 2, 13.

Judge of the living and the dead chose to describe himself as speaking only about works of mercy performed or neglected when he addressed those on the right, to whom he was to grant everlasting life, and also those on the left whom he was to condemn to everlasting punishment.[64]

They also quote the daily petition in the Lord's prayer as being relevant to this: 'Forgive us our debts, as we forgive our debtors.' For anyone who forgives another who has sinned against him, undoubtedly performs a work of mercy in pardoning the sin. And the Lord himself expresses approval of such an action when he says, 'For if you forgive your fellow-men their sins, your Father will also forgive your sins; on the other hand, if you do not forgive your fellow-men, your Father in heaven will not forgive you.'[65] Thus the saying of the apostle James that 'judgement will be merciless on one who has shown no mercy' has reference to works of mercy of this kind; and observe, they say, that the Lord did not say 'great sins' or 'small sins' but, 'Your Father will forgive your sins, if you forgive your fellow-men.' Relying on this, they hold that even those who live unprincipled lives until their dying day have all their sins forgiven every day, whatever their character or their magnitude, just as this prayer itself is repeated every day, provided only that they observe this condition, namely, that they forgive, from the bottom of their heart, those who have injured them by any kind of offence, when they ask pardon.

When I have replied to all these suggestions, with God's help, this book will reach its end.

23. *Refutation of those who extend salvation to the devils*

First we must seek to discover why it is that the Church has been unable to tolerate the suggestion that promises purification even to the Devil after pains of great severity and long duration, or even holds out hope of his free pardon. It was not that all those holy men, learned in the Scriptures of both estaments, grudged to angels, of whatever kind or in whatever numbers, the attainment of cleansing and of bliss in the Kingdom of Heaven, after chastisements of whatever kind and of whatever magnitude. It was rather that they saw that the sentence of the Lord could not be evacuated of meaning or deprived of its force; the sentence, I mean, that he, on his own prediction, was to pronounce in these words: 'Out of my sight, accursed ones, into the eternal fire

64. cf. Matt. 25, 34ff. 65. Matt. 6, 14ff.

which is prepared for the Devil and his angels'[66] – a clear indication that the Devil and his angels are to burn in eternal fire.

The same holds good for this statement in the Apocalypse: 'The Devil, who seduced them, was consigned to the lake of fire and sulphur, into which the beast and the false prophet had been cast; and they will be tortured day and night for ever and ever.'[67] 'Eternal' in the first passage is expressed in the second by 'for ever and ever', and those words have only one meaning in scriptural usage: the exclusion of any temporal end. And this is why there cannot conceivably be found any reason better founded or more evident for the fixed and immutable conviction of true religion that the Devil and his angels will never attain to justification and to the life of the saints. There can be, I say, no stronger reason than this: that the Scriptures, which never deceive, say that God has not spared them, that in fact he has already condemned them to be thrust into the prison of nether darkness, committed for safe keeping there and for their punishment at the last judgement[68] when the eternal fire will receive them, in which they will be tortured for ever and ever.

This being so, how can all men, or even any men, be exempted from this eternity of punishment without the immediate weakening of the faith whereby we believe that the chastisement of the demons is to be everlasting? For if all or any of those 'accursed ones' will not be for ever in the fire, those who are to be told to get 'out of my sight, into the eternal fire which is prepared for the Devil and his angels', is there any reason for believing that the Devil and his angels will be in that fire for ever? Is it suggested that God's sentence pronounced on all the wicked, angels as well as men, will be true in the case of angels, but false in respect of human beings? If so, then human surmise will prove more valid than the utterance of God! But since this cannot be, our friends who long to get rid of eternal punishment should cease to argue against God, and should instead obey God's commandments, while there is still time.

Moreover, is it not folly to assume that eternal punishment signifies a fire lasting a long time, while believing that eternal life is life without end? For Christ, in the very same passage, included both punishment and life in one and the same sentence when he said, 'So those people will go into eternal punishment, while the righteous will go into eternal life.'[69] If both are 'eternal', it follows necessarily that either both are to be taken as long-lasting but finite, or both as endless

66. Matt. 25, 41. 67. Rev. 20, 10f.
68. cf. 2 Pet. 2, 4. 69. Matt. 25, 46.

and perpetual. The phrases 'eternal punishment' and 'eternal life' are parallel and it would be absurd to use them in one and the same sentence to mean: 'Eternal life will be infinite, while eternal punishment will have an end.' Hence, because the eternal life of the saints will be endless, the eternal punishment also, for those condemned to it, will assuredly have no end.

24. *Refutation of the view that the guilty will be spared through the intercession of the saints*

The same consideration suffices to refute those who in their own defence attempt to oppose God's words with what purports to be a higher degree of compassion, making out that God's words are true in the sense that men deserve to suffer what he has said they will suffer, not in the sense that they are in fact to suffer it. For he will grant them, they say, the prayers of his saints, who will even then be praying for their enemies, and praying all the more because they are now, to be sure, more holy, and their supplication is more effective and more worthy of God's hearing since by this time they have no sin whatsoever. How can they help praying, in their entire sanctity, with their prayers of utter purity and complete compassion, prayers with the power to obtain every request – how can they help praying even for those angels for whom the eternal fire has been prepared, beseeching God to soften his sentence and alter it for the better, and to part those sufferers from that fire? And will there by any chance be anyone who will go so far as to assume that something more than this will happen? I mean, will anyone assert that the holy angels also will join with the holy men (who will then be 'on the same footing as the angels of God') in prayer for the angels, as well as the human beings, who are to be condemned? That they will entreat God that through his compassion these angels may not suffer what they deserved to suffer in accordance with his truth? No one of sound faith has ever said this, or will ever say it. Otherwise there is no reason why the Church should not pray even now for the Devil and his angels, seeing that God has bidden her to pray for her enemies!

In fact the reason which now prevents the Church from praying for the evil angels, whom she knows to be her enemies, is the same reason which will then prevent her at that time of judgement from praying, however perfect her holiness, for the human beings who are to be tormented in eternal fire. Her reason for praying now for her enemies among mankind is that there is time for fruitful penitence. For what she chiefly prays for on their behalf is surely 'that God', in the Apostle's words, 'may grant them penitence, and that they may come to their senses and escape from the snare of the Devil, by whom they have been trapped and are held at his pleasure'.[70] In fact, if the Church had such certain information about people as to know who were already predestined, although still under the conditions of this life, to go into the eternal fire with the Devil, then the Church would pray as little for them as it does for him. But she has not this certainty about anyone; therefore she prays for all her enemies, her human enemies, that is, while they are in the bodily state; but that does not mean that her prayers for all of them are heard and answered. In fact her prayers are heard only when she prays for those who, although they oppose the Church, are predestined to salvation so that the Church's prayers for them are answered and they are made sons of the Church. But if any of them keep their heart impenitent up to their dying day, if they are not transformed from enemies into friends, are we to suppose that the Church still prays for them, that is, for the spirits of such men when they have departed this life? Of course not! And this is simply because anyone who has not been transferred to the side of Christ while he lives in the body is thereafter reckoned as belonging to the Devil's party.

The reason then for not offering prayer at the time of judgement for those human beings who are consigned for punishment to the eternal fire is the same as the reason for not praying now for the evil angels. And likewise there is the same reason for praying at this time for human beings who are infidel and irreligious, and yet refusing to pray for them when they are departed. For the prayer of the Church itself, or even the prayer of devout individuals, is heard and answered on behalf of some of the departed, but only on behalf of those who have been reborn in Christ and whose life in the body has not been so evil that they are judged unworthy of such mercy, and yet not so good that they are seen to have no need of it. Likewise, after the resurrection of the dead there will still be some on whom mercy will be bestowed, after punishment suffered by the souls of the dead, so that they will not be consigned to the eternal fire. For it could not truthfully be said of some people that they will be forgiven neither in this age nor in the age to come,[71] unless there were some who receive forgiveness in the age to come though not in this age.

Nevertheless, this is what has been said by the Judge of the living and the dead: 'Come, you that have my Father's blessing; take pos-

70. 2 Tim. 2, 25f. 71. Matt. 12, 32.

session of the kingdom prepared for you from the foundation of the world'; and to the others, in contrast: 'Out of my sight, you accursed ones, into the eternal fire, which is prepared for the Devil and his angels'; and, 'these will go to eternal punishment, while the righteous will go to eternal life.'[72] In view of this, it is excessively presumptuous to assert that there will be eternal punishment for none of those who, so God has said, will go to punishment which will be eternal, and by the persuasion of this presumptuous notion to produce despair, or at least doubt, about the eternity of the future life itself.

No one, therefore, should take this verse of the psalm: 'Will God really forget to show mercy? Will he in his wrath restrain his compassion?'[73] and interpret it in such a way as to suggest the notion that God's sentence is true in respect of the good, but false in respect of the wicked, or true in respect of good human beings and evil angels, but false in respect of evil human beings. In fact, this verse of the psalm refers to the 'vessels of mercy' and the 'sons of the promise',[74] one of whom was the prophet himself; and he first says, 'Will God really "forget to show mercy", in making his sun shine on the good and bad and then immediately continues, 'Then I said: Now I have begun; this is an alteration of the right hand of God Most High.' Here, obviously, he has explained what he meant by, 'Will God in his wrath restrain his compassion?' For this mortal life is itself part of God's wrath, this life in which 'man becomes like a piece of futility; his days pass by like shadows.'[75] Yet even in this manifestation of his anger God does not 'forget to show mercy', in making his sun shine on the good and bad alike and sending rain on the righteous and the unrighteous,[76] and in this way he does not in wrath restrain his compassion. And this is particularly true in what the psalmist expresses by saying, 'Now I have begun; this is an alteration of the right hand of God Most High.' For in this life, a life full of troubles, which is a manifestation of God's wrath, God changes the 'vessels of mercy' into a better state (although his wrath still continues in the misery of this condition of decay) because even in his wrath he does not restrain his compassion.

Since, then, the truth of this inspired song is fully shown in this way, it is not necessary to take it as relevant to that situation where those who do not belong to the City of God will be punished by everlasting chastisement. But those who are determined to extend the scope of statement in the psalm to make it apply to the torments of the wicked, should even so take it in this sense; that while the wrath

72. Matt. 25, 34; 41; 46. 73. Ps. 77, 9; 10 (LXX). 74. Rom. 9, 23; Gal. 4, 28.
75. Ps. 144, 4. 76. Matt. 5, 45.

of God persists (and its persistence in that eternal punishment is foretold) God does not 'in his wrath restrain his compassion' in that he causes those sinners to be tormented with less fierceness in the punishment than they deserve. It is not that they escape those punishments altogether nor even that the punishments eventually come to an end; but their sufferings are milder and lighter than their deserts. In this way the wrath of God will continue, and yet he will not in that wrath of his restrain his compassion. But it must not be supposed that I support this view because I do not contradict it.

But as for those who suppose that such sayings as 'Out of my sight, you accursed, into the eternal fire', 'these will go to everlasting punishment', 'they will be tormented for ever', 'their worm never dies and the fire will not be put out',[77] and others in the same strain, are uttered more by way of threat than as presentations of literal truth, such interpreters are rebutted and refuted not so much by me as by the evidence of Scripture itself, which is quite explicit and copious on the point. The Ninevites, to be sure, repented in this life, and their repentance was fruitful;[78] they sowed, we might say, in the field in which God wishes the seed to be 'sown in tears' so that the crop may later be 'reaped with joy'.[79] And yet who will deny that God's prediction was fulfilled in them? Any man who fails to notice how God overthrows not only in anger but also in mercy. For sinners are 'overthrown' in two different ways: either as the men of Sodom were overthrown, where it is men who are punished for their sins; or in the manner of Nineveh, where it is the sins of men that are destroyed by their repentance. Thus what God predicted came about: the Nineveh which was wicked was overthrown, and a good Nineveh was built, which did not exist before. For a city is overthrown by a collapse of morality, even though the walls and buildings are still standing. And so although the prophet was bitterly disappointed because the event did not happen, whose coming he had prophesied and the men of Nineveh had in consequence feared, nevertheless the event came about that God had predicted in his foreknowledge, since he who foretold it knew how it was to be fulfilled to better purpose.

However, if those exponents of a perverse compassion would care to know the reference of the verse which says, 'How great is the abundance of your sweet kindness, Lord, which you have kept hidden for those who fear you', they should read what follows: 'You have brought it to fulfilment for those who put their hope in you.'[80] Now

77. Matt. 25, 41; 46; Rev. 20, 10; Is. 66, 24; Mark 9, 48.
78. Jon. 3, 7ff.
79. Ps. 126, 5.
80. Ps. 31, 19.

what is meant by 'you have kept it hidden for those who fear you', and 'you have brought it to fulfilment for those who put their hope in you'? Surely it can only mean that God's righteousness is not sweet to those who wish 'to establish their own righteousness'[81] which depends on the Law. It is not sweet to them because they do not know it; they have not tasted it. For they put their hope in themselves, and not in God; and that is why the abundance of God's sweet kindness is concealed from them; because they fear God, it is true, but with that servile fear which is not found in love, since 'perfect love drives out fear'.[82]

Therefore it is for those who put their hope in him that he brings to fulfilment his kindness, by inspiring his own love in them so that when they boast, with holy fear (not the fear which is driven out by love, but the fear which lasts for ever and ever), they will be 'boasting in the Lord'.[83] This righteousness of God, which is the gift of grace without regard to merits, is unknown to those who wish to establish a righteousness of their own, and for that reason have not subjected themselves to the righteousness of God, which is Christ. It is in this righteousness that the abundant kindness of God is found; hence the psalm says, 'Taste and see how sweet the Lord is.'[84] This sweetness we do indeed taste in our pilgrimage, but we do not have our fill of it; instead, we 'hunger and thirst' for it, so that we may have our fill hereafter, when 'we shall see him as he is'; and then the scriptural saying will be fulfilled: 'I shall be satisfied, when your glory is made manifest.'[85] Thus Christ 'brings to fulfilment the great abundance of his kindness for those who put their hope in him'.

Furthermore, assuming that God 'keeps hidden for those who fear him' this kindness of his (as these people imagine it) which he is to show in not condemning the wicked – keeping it hidden so that men may be unaware of it and therefore may live rightly for fear of damnation, and so that there may be those who will pray for people who do not live aright – on this assumption, how does God 'bring it to fulfilment for those who put their hope in him', seeing that (according to this dream of theirs) this kindness is going to prevent him from condemning those who do *not* put their hope in him? The upshot is that we should seek the kindness which he fulfils for those who put their hope in him, not the kindness which he is supposed to fulfil for those who scorn and blaspheme him. And so a man looks in vain, after he has quitted this mortal body, for something which he has not troubled to obtain while in the body.

81. Rom. 10, 3. 82. 1 John 4, 18. 83. 1 Cor. 1, 30f.
84. Ps. 34, 8. 85. Matt. 5, 6; 1 John 3, 2; Ps. 17, 15.

There is also that statement of the Apostle, 'God has confined them all in unbelief, so that he may show mercy to them all.' Now the meaning of this is not that God is not going to condemn anyone; the purpose of the statement is made clear by what was said just before. For the Apostle was speaking to the Gentiles about the Jews who were destined to believe later; as we know, he wrote his epistles to Gentiles who were already believers. And this is what he says, 'Just as you at one time did not believe in God, but you have now obtained mercy through their refusal to believe; so now, in the face of the mercy you enjoy, they have refused to believe, so that they also may obtain mercy.'[86] He then adds the statement on which our friends, in their error, base their complacency: 'For God has confined them all in unbelief, so that he may show mercy on them all.' And by 'all' he can only mean those of whom he is speaking, as much as to say, 'You and them.' God, then, has confined in unbelief both Gentiles and Jews, those whom he 'foreknew and predestined to become true likenesses of his Son';[87] and his purpose in this was that they should become ashamed, in their repentance, of the bitterness of their unbelief, and should turn to the sweetness of God's mercy. And so they would cry out, in the words of the psalm, 'How great is the abundance of your kindness, Lord, which you have kept secret for those who fear you; but you have brought it to fulfilment for those who put their hope' – not in themselves but – 'in you!'[88] So we see that God has mercy on all the 'vessels of mercy'; but what is meant by 'all'? It must mean all those from among the Gentiles as well as all those of the Jews whom he predestined, called, justified, and glorified.[89] He will not spare all men; but none of these will incur his condemnation.

25. *Refutation of the suggestions that the sacraments will save from eternal punishment heretics of evil life, lapsed Catholics, or Catholics of evil life*

We must now answer those who exclude from their promise of freedom from the eternal fire not only the Devil and his angels (as also do those tender hearts we have just been considering) but also all mankind apart from those who have been washed by Christ's baptism and have been made partakers of his body and blood. To these they promise salvation, irrespective of their manner of life, whatever their heresy or impiety. But they are contradicted by the Apostle, when he says,

86. Rom. 11, 30ff.
87. Rom 8, 29.
88. Ps. 31, 19.
89. Rom. 8, 30.

'The results of sensuality are obvious: fornication, indecency, sexual promiscuity; idolatry and sorcery; feuds, quarrels, jealousy, animosity, disputes, factions, envy; drunkenness, orgies and things of that kind. I warn you now, as I warned you before; those who behave in this way will not inherit the Kingdom of God.'[90] The Apostle's judgement is certainly at fault here, if such people will be set free, no matter after how long a time, and will inherit the Kingdom of God! However it is not a fault, and they certainly will not inherit that kingdom. And if they will never enter into that inheritance, they will be kept in eternal punishment; for there is no intermediate place where anyone who is not established in that kingdom may exist without punishment.

On this question it is right that we should ask what interpretation is to be given to the following saying of the Lord Jesus, 'This is the bread which comes down from heaven, so that a man may eat it, and never die. I am the living bread which has come down from heaven. Anyone who eats this bread will live for ever'.[91] The people whom I am answering at the moment have filched their interpretation of this passage from others whom I now have to answer. These others do not promise this liberation to all who enjoy the sacraments of baptism and of the Body of Christ; they restrict it to the Catholics,[92] however unworthy their lives, because, they say, the Catholics have eaten the body of Christ not only in the outward sacrament, but in reality, since they, of course, are established in his Body, the Body of which the Apostle says, 'We are many; but we are one loaf, and one body.'[93] Thus he who is in the unity of Christ's Body, that is, the structure composed of Christians who are members of Christ, whose body the faithful habitually take when they communicate at the altar – such a man may be said in truth to eat the body of Christ and to drink Christ's blood. It follows that heretics and schismatics, being separated from the unity of this Body, are able to take the same sacrament; but it is not for their profit. No, indeed; it is for their harm. It will result for them in a heavier punishment rather than in their liberation, even a delayed liberation. For it is obvious that they are not in that 'bond of peace'[94] which is expressed in this sacrament.

And yet even those who are right on this point, that a person who is not in the Body of Christ cannot be said to eat Christ's body, are wrong in promising eventual liberation from the fire of eternal punishment to those who have lapsed from the unity of that Body into

90. Gal. 5, 19ff. 91. John 6, 50ff. 92. ch. 21.
93. 1 Cor. 10, 17. 94. Eph. 4, 3.

heresy, or even into the superstition of the pagan world. They are wrong, in the first place because they have failed to notice, as they should have done, how intolerable it would be, how utterly remote from sound doctrine, that many, and indeed almost all, of those who have left the Church to start impious heresies and have become heresiarchs, should be in a better position than those who never became Catholics because they had fallen into the snares of those heretics. But this would follow, if the heresiarchs are granted freedom from everlasting punishment by the fact that they have been baptized in the Catholic Church and that at the beginning they received the sacrament of the Body of Christ in the true Body of Christ, whereas in fact a deserter of the faith, and one who from a deserter has turned into an opponent, is surely worse than one who has not deserted the faith because he has never possessed it. And they are wrong, in the second place, because they, like those others, are opposed by the Apostle in the words already quoted, when after the list of the results of sensuality he gives the warning that 'those who behave in this way will never inherit the Kingdom of God.'[95]

Hence those people who continue to the end of their lives in the fellowship of the Catholic Church have no reason to feel secure, if their moral behaviour is disreputable and deserving of condemnation. They should base no security on consideration of the statement in Scripture that 'the man who perseveres right up to the end will be saved',[96] while by the wickedness of their lives they desert Christ, who is their righteousness of life, either by fornication or by committing other criminal indecencies of sensuality which the Apostle was unwilling even to name; or by abandoning themselves to depraved self-indulgence; or by doing any of the things about which he says, 'Those who behave in this way will not inherit the kingdom of God.' And for that reason, those who behave in that way will inevitably be in eternal punishment, seeing that it will be impossible for them to be in the Kingdom of God. For in persevering in such conduct to their life's end they are not to be said to have persevered in Christ right up to the end, because to persevere in Christ means to persevere in faith in him; now this faith, in the Apostle's definition, 'is active in love', and 'love', as he says in another place, 'is never active in wrong'.[97] It also follows that those people cannot be said to eat Christ's body, since they are not to be reckoned among the members of Christ. Apart from anything else, they cannot at the same time be members of Christ and

95. Gal. 5, 21. 96. Matt. 10, 22.
97. Gal. 5, 6; 1 Cor. 13, 4; cf. Rom 13, 10.

members of a harlot.[98] Above all, Christ himself says, 'Anyone who eats my flesh and drinks my blood lives in me, and I live in him.'[99] And thus he shows what it is to eat Christ's body and to drink his blood not just in the outward sacrament but in the reality; it is to live in Christ so that Christ lives in the believer. For in this statement he is saying, in effect, 'Anyone who does not live in me, anyone in whom I do not live, must not say or suppose that he eats my body or drinks my blood.' And so those who are not members of Christ do not live in Christ; and those who make themselves members of a harlot are not members of Christ, unless by repentance they abandon that evil state and return by reconciliation to the other state of good.

26. *The meaning of having Christ as the 'foundation'; and of 'saved by fire'*

Yes, but Catholic Christians, they say, have Christ for their foundation, and they have not departed from unity with him, even if they have built on this foundation a life of any degree of badness, 'wood', it may be called, 'or hay, or straw'.[100] And so that right faith, which makes Christ the foundation, will avail to save them eventually from that eternal fire albeit with some loss, since the structure built on it will be burnt up. These people can have a short answer from the apostle James: 'If anyone claims that he has faith, and does not show it in his actions, how can his faith avail to save him?'[101] Well then, they say, who is it that the apostle Paul means when he says, 'But the man himself will be saved, but like a man saved from fire'? Very good; let us join forces to discover who it is. But one thing is beyond doubt: it is not the kind of man they are talking about. For then we should be starting a dispute between the statements of the two apostles, if one of them is taken as saying, 'Even if someone's actions are evil, his faith will save him, through fire', while the other says, 'If a man does not show his faith in his actions, how can his faith avail to save him?'

Now we shall discover who can be saved 'through fire', if we start by discovering what it means to have Christ as one's foundation. To get at the meaning as quickly as possible from the metaphor itself: the foundation precedes any of the building; and so if anyone has Christ in his heart in the sense that he puts no earthly and temporal thing before Christ – not even those which are lawful and permitted – that man has Christ as his foundation. If he does put such things before

98. cf. 1 Cor. 6, 15. 99. John 6, 56.
100. 1 Cor. 3, 12ff. 101. Jas. 2, 14.

Christ, then even if he appears to hold the Christian faith, Christ is not the foundation in him, since for him Christ takes second place. And if he thinks nothing of the saving commandments and acts unlawfully, he is all the more convicted of putting Christ last instead of first, when he has relegated him to secondary importance as a source of command or permission, and has slighted his commands or his permission in choosing to gratify his sensuality by immoral acts. And so, if a Christian loves a harlot and 'becomes one body with her by linking himself to her',[102] he no longer has Christ for his foundation, whereas if a man loves his wife, assuming that he loves her according to Christ's standards,[103] then who can doubt that he has Christ as his foundation? But if he loves her in the way of the world, with a sensual love, with an unhealthy lust, in the manner of 'the pagans who are ignorant of God', even this the Apostle allows by way of indulgence, or rather Christ does so through his apostle.[104] It is possible, then, for such a man to have Christ as his foundation. For provided that he does not put any such sensual pleasure before the claims of Christ, then although he builds in 'wood, hay, and straw', Christ is the foundation, and for that reason he will be saved 'through fire'. For pleasures of this kind and the earthly sort of love, which because of the bond of marriage do not incur damnation, will nevertheless be burnt up by the fire of tribulation; and bereavement and any other calamities which put an end to such pleasures are all connected with this 'fire'. And in this way the building will bring loss to the builder in that he will not keep what he has built on the foundation and he will be tormented by the loss of the enjoyment that certainly gave him delight. Yet he will be saved 'through fire' in virtue of that foundation, because if a persecutor had given him the choice between having that enjoyment and having Christ, he would have chosen Christ in preference to those delights.

Now listen to the Apostle describing a man who builds gold, silver, precious stones, on this foundation. 'The unmarried man', he says, 'gives his thoughts to the Lord's affairs; his aim is to please the Lord'; and then describing the builder in wood, hay and straw, 'The married man, in contrast, concentrates on worldly matters; his concern is how to please his wife', and so 'The work of each builder will be revealed; for the day' (the day of tribulation, of course) 'will show it up, since it will be revealed in fire.'[105] ('Fire' is his name for this tribulation, as in another place, where we read, 'The furnace tests the vessels of the

102. 1 Cor. 6, 16.
103. cf. Eph. 5, 25.
104. 1 Thess. 4, 5; cf. 1 Cor. 7, 5f.
105. 1 Cor. 7, 32f; 3, 13.

potter, and the trial of tribulation tests righteous men.'[106]) 'And the fire will test the quality of each man's work. If a man's work on the foundation stands' (and it is a man's thoughts on the Lord's affairs, his aim to please God, that give this permanence) 'he will get his wages' (that is, he will receive his reward from the object of his concern); 'if anyone's work is burnt down, he will suffer loss' (since he will no longer have what he was so fond of), 'but the man himself will be saved' (because tribulation could never remove him from the firm base of that foundation) 'but it will be as a man is saved from a fire' (for he must feel burning pain at the loss of what entranced him when he possessed it). There, then, you have this 'fire', as it seems to me, which enriches the one and impoverishes the other; it tests both, while it condemns neither.

On the other hand, we may be inclined to take this fire as being that referred to by the Lord when he says to those on the left, 'Out of my sight, you accursed, into the eternal fire',[107] so that among the accursed, it is believed, are the builders in wood, hay, and straw on that foundation, and they will be released from that fire, after a period imposed on them in retribution for their ill deserts, through the merits of that good foundation. But what view shall we take, on this assumption, about those on the right, to whom it will be said, 'Come, you that have my Father's blessing; inherit the kingdom prepared for you'? Must they not be the builders in gold, silver and precious stones on that foundation? But, on this interpretation, both groups, on the right and on the left, are to be consigned to that fire; for, as we see, both groups are to be tested by that fire, of which it is said, 'The day will show it up, since it will be revealed in the fire, and the fire will test the quality of each man's work.'[108] So the fire will test in both cases, and in consequence a man's work will not be destroyed if his structure stands up under the fire, and he will get his wages, whereas the man whose work is burnt down will suffer loss.

If this is true, that fire is obviously not the eternal fire; for into the eternal fire only those on the left will be sent by the last, the irrevocable, condemnation, while the fire in the present passage tests those on the right as well. But for some the result of that test will be that the structure erected by them on Christ, the foundation, will prove to be such as will not be burnt up and destroyed by the fire. For others there will be a different result; the fire will set on fire their superstructure, and this will mean loss for them; but they will be saved, because they have retained Christ as their firmly laid foundation, with a love ex-

106. Ecclus. 27, 5. 107. Matt. 25, 41. 108. 1 Cor. 3, 13.

ceeding their other loves. Moreover, if they are saved, then of course they will take their stand on the right, and will hear, along with the others, this command: 'Come, you who have my Father's blessing, inherit the kingdom prepared for you.' They will not stand on the left, where those will be standing who will not be saved, and who will therefore hear the words, 'Out of my sight, you accursed, into the eternal fire.' And from that fire no one will be saved, because all those on the left will go into eternal punishment, 'where their worm never dies, and the fire is never put out';[109] and in that fire they will be tortured day and night for ever and ever.

As for the interval between the death of this present body and the coming of that Day, the day of condemnation and reward which is to be after the general resurrection of the body, it may be alleged that during this interval the spirits of the departed suffer this sort of fire, though it is not felt by those whose ways of living and loving have not been such, in their life in the body, as to have produced 'wood, hay, and straw' to be burnt down by the fire. Others, on this theory, feel that fire, because they carry about with them 'buildings' of this sort; and such people experience the 'fire' of transitory tribulation which reduces these 'buildings' to ashes. For these structures belong to this world, although they receive pardon, and do not entail damnation; and the fire may be experienced perhaps only after this life, or both in this life and hereafter, or in this life only and not hereafter.

Now I am not concerned to refute this suggestion, because it may well be true. It is indeed possible that the actual death of the body may form part of this tribulation. This death came into being through the perpetration of the first sin; and it may be that the period which follows death brings to each one an experience suited to the 'building' he has erected. The same is true of the persecutions in which the martyrs won their crowns, and which brought suffering to all Christian people; these attacks 'test' both kinds of 'structure', like a fire. Some 'buildings' are destroyed, along with the builders, if Christ is not discovered to be their foundation; others are destroyed, but without the builders, if Christ is so discovered, for 'the builders themselves will be saved' although 'with loss'. But other 'buildings' are not destroyed, because they prove to be of such quality as to last for ever.

There will also be tribulation at the end of this world's history, in the time of Antichrist; and it will be such a tribulation as has never been before. How many buildings will there be then to be tested by

109. Is. 66, 24; Mark 9, 48.

that fire! Some will be of gold, some of straw, built upon the best of foundations, which is Christ Jesus, and so the fire will test both kinds of building, and to the one sort of people it will bring joy, to the others it will bring loss; but it will destroy neither sort in whom it finds those buildings, because of this stable foundation. But anyone who puts any loved objects before Christ does not have Christ for his foundation. I am not speaking only of a man's wife, when he treats her as a means of sensual pleasure in carnal copulation; I am referring also to those relationships of natural affection where there is no question of such sensual indulgence. If a man loves any member of his family, with a human being's instinctive affection, in such a way as to put Christ second, then Christ is not his foundation, and for that reason such a man will not be 'saved by fire', because it will be impossible for him to be with the Saviour. Indeed Christ made a most explicit statement on this point when he said, 'Anyone who loves his father or his mother more than me is not worthy of me; and anyone who loves a son or a daughter more than me is not worthy of me.'[110] On the other hand, anyone who loves those close relations in this instinctive way, without putting them in front of the Lord Christ, anyone who would prefer to be deprived of them rather than to lose Christ, if he were brought to the test of this dilemma, such a man will be 'saved through fire', because the loss of those loved ones will cause him burning pain in proportion to the closeness of his attachment to them. But we may add that anyone who loves father or mother, sons or daughters according to the standards of Christ, so that he is concerned that they may inherit Christ's kingdom and be united to Christ, or anyone who loves them for the fact that they are members of Christ; it is impossible that such affection should prove to be something that has to be destroyed along with the 'wood, hay and straw'. This will, beyond dispute, be reckoned as part of the structure of 'gold, silver, and precious stone'. For if a man loves others entirely for Christ's sake, how can he love them more than Christ?

27. *Refutation of the argument that works of mercy will atone for persistent wickedness*

It remains for us to reply to the contention that the only people to burn in eternal fire are those who have omitted to perform works of mercy to counterbalance their sins. This contention is based on the saying of the apostle James, 'Judgement will be merciless on those who have shown no mercy.'[111] It follows, they say, that anyone who does

110. Matt. 10, 37. 111. Jas. 2, 13.

show mercy, even though he has not amended his dissolute behaviour, but has lived a life of depravity and corruption along with his works of mercy, will meet with mercy at the judgement, so that either he will escape damnation altogether or else he will be set free after some time from the punishment to which he is condemned at the last judgement. And that, they suppose, is the reason why Christ will separate those on the right from those on the left by this sole criterion, their performance or their neglect of works of mercy; and the former he will bring into his kingdom, the latter he will consign to eternal punishment. They hold that their daily sins, which they never cease to commit, can be forgiven on account of their acts of mercy, whatever the nature and the magnitude of these sins; and in support of that belief they try to call in as their witness the prayer which the Lord himself taught us. There is never a day, they say, on which the Christian does not repeat this prayer; by the same token, there is no daily sin, whatever its nature, which is not forgiven through that prayer, when we say, 'Forgive us our debts', provided that we are careful to fulfil the following clause: 'as we forgive our debtors'. For the Lord, they urge, does not say, 'If you forgive other men their sins, your Father will forgive your trivial daily offences'; he says, 'He will forgive you your sins.'[112] Therefore whatever the nature of those sins, whatever their magnitude, even though they are committed every day, and though a man does not amend his life and abandon those sins, nevertheless those sins, they claim, can be forgiven through the mercy shown in not refusing forgiveness to others.

Those people are indeed right in warning us that acts of mercy should be performed *in adequate proportion* to our sins; for if they had said that any kind of acts of mercy could obtain mercy for daily sins and even for great sins, sins of any magnitude, and for a life of habitual crime, they would see that they were saying something absurd and ridiculous. For on this principle they would be forced to admit the possibility that a man of great wealth could atone for homicide, adultery and every crime in the calendar by laying out a shilling a day in works of charity. Now such an assertion would be utterly absurd and insane; but, that being granted, if we inquire what are the acts of mercy in adequate proportion to sins that Christ's forerunner spoke of when he said: 'Produce fruits *appropriate* to repentance',[113] we shall find, without a shadow of doubt, that they are *not* produced by those who disfigure their lives, to the day of their death, by the perpetration of daily offences. In the first place, such people when they rob others

112. Matt. 6, 12; 14. 113. Matt. 3, 8.

of their property take far more in plunder than they give in charity; and yet by bestowing a minute proportion of this plunder on the poor they suppose that they are feeding Christ. So much so that in their belief they have bought, or rather are buying each day, a licence from him for their misdeeds, they proceed in their fancied impunity to commit all the grave offences that ensure their damnation. And yet if they had distributed all their goods to the needy members of Christ in atonement for just one sin, this could not have been of any service to them, if they had not abandoned such practices by the acquisition of the 'love which does no evil'.[114] Therefore, anyone who would perform acts of mercy in adequate proportion to his sins should begin with himself in their performance. For it is wrong not to do to oneself what one does to one's neighbour, since we have heard God saying, 'You shall love your neighbour as yourself'; and we have been told to 'have compassion on your own soul by pleasing God'.[115] If anyone does not show this mercy to his own soul, that is, by pleasing God, how can he be said to perform acts of mercy in adequate proportion to his sins? There is another text in Scripture to the same effect: 'If a man is mean to himself, to whom will he be generous?'[116] Now works of mercy assist our prayers; and we must certainly take careful note when we read these words, 'My son you have sinned: do not go on to sin again; and pray for mercy for your past sins, that they may be forgiven.'[117] Works of mercy, then, are to be performed for this end, that when we entreat forgiveness for past offences, our prayers may be heard, and not that we should continue in our evil courses in the confidence of having acquired, by our acts of charity, a licence to sin.

Moreover, when the Lord foretold that he would put the performance of acts of charity to the account of those on the right, and their omission to the account of those on the left, his intention was to show what power such acts have to cancel former offences, but not to give perpetual impunity for sins. For if men refuse to abandon the practice of crimes and to amend their lives, they cannot be said to perform acts of mercy. In fact, when Christ says, 'When you failed to do this to one of the least of these, you failed to do it to me',[118] he makes it clear that they do not do it even when they suppose that they are doing it. For if they gave food to a hungry Christian, as being a Christian, they certainly would not deprive themselves of the food of righteousness, which is Christ himself, since God is not concerned

114. cf. 1 Cor. 13, 4. 115. Lev. 19, 18; cf. Matt. 22, 39; Ecclus. 30, 24.
116. Ecclus. 14, 5. 117. Ecclus. 21, 1. 118. Matt. 25, 45.

about the recipient of a gift, but about its motive. Anyone who loves Christ in a Christian gives help to that Christian with the intention of coming closer to Christ, not of escaping from Christ unpunished. For the more one loves what Christ disapproves the more one abandons Christ. For what does the fact of baptism profit anyone if he is not made righteous? Christ said, it is true, that 'unless a man is reborn by means of water and the Spirit, he will not enter the Kingdom of God'; but did he not also say, 'Unless your righteousness far exceeds that of the Scribes and Pharisees, you will not enter the Kingdom of Heaven'?[119] Why is it that many people rush to be baptized through fear inspired by the first saying, but not so many are concerned to be made righteous? People are not scared, it seems, by the second warning.

Thus in the same way that a man does not say to his brother. 'You fool!' when he says it in hostility to his brother's sins, not to his brother as brother (for in the latter case he would be liable to the fire of hell);[120] so, on the other side, when a man gives charitable aid to a Christian it is not to a Christian that he gives it if he does not love Christ in that Christian. But no one can love Christ if he shrinks from being made righteous in Christ. Now if anyone is caught in the offence of saying 'You fool!' to his brother, saying it, that is, in wrongful abuse, not with the intention of restraining his brother from sin, it is utterly inadequate for him to attempt atonement by acts of charity, unless he combines this with the healing process of reconciliation. This is prescribed in the passage which follows in the same place: 'If you are bringing an offering to the altar and there recall that your brother has a cause for grievance against you; leave your offering there before the altar; go and be reconciled to your brother first, and then come and offer your gift.' In the same way it is futile to perform acts of charity, whatever their scale, while continuing in criminal habits.

Our daily prayer, which Jesus himself taught us (hence it is called the Lord's Prayer) does indeed cancel our daily sins, when we say, each day, 'Forgive us our debts' and when the following clause, 'as we forgive our debtors', is not only said but also put into practice. But this clause is said because sins are committed, not in order that we should commit sins because it is said. For by this clause in the prayer our Saviour wished to make it known that however righteous our life in the darkness and weakness of our present condition, we are never without sins and we are bound to pray for their forgiveness and

119. John 3, 5; Matt. 5, 20. 120. Matt. 5, 22.

to pardon those who do us wrong, so that we ourselves may receive pardon. And so, when the Lord said, 'If you forgive your fellow men their sins, your Father will also forgive yours', his intention was not that this prayer should give us confidence to commit daily crimes with supposed impunity, either because our power frees us from the fear of the laws of man or because our craftiness enables us to deceive our fellows. His purpose was that we should learn by this prayer not to imagine ourselves to be sinless, even if we are not liable to any criminal charges. God gave the same warning to the priests of the old law in the instructions about sacrifice, when he ordered them to offer sacrifice first for their own sins, and then for the sins of the people.[121]

We should notice carefully the precise words of our great Master and Lord. For he does not say, 'If you forgive your fellow-men their sins, your Father will forgive your sins *of any kind whatever*.' What he says is, '*Your* sins'. Now remember, he was teaching a prayer to be said daily; and he was speaking, of course, to disciples, who were justified. 'Your sins' therefore, can only mean 'the sins from which even you cannot be free, though you have been justified and sanctified'. Now those people who try to find in this prayer an excuse for committing crimes every day, assert that the Lord did not say 'trivial sins' but 'your sins', and that this proves that he meant to include great sins. We, on the other hand, take into account here the kind of people he was addressing, and when we hear the words, 'your sins', we are bound to assume it means only minor sins, because people of that kind did not commit major offences.

Furthermore, those more grievous sins, which have to be abandoned with a thorough amendment of life, are not forgiven to those who use this prayer unless the condition is fulfilled that they 'forgive their debtors'. For the smallest sins, which occur even in the lives of the righteous, are not forgiven except under this condition; then how much more certain it is that those involved in a multitude of major crimes can never obtain pardon, even though they have already ceased to commit them, if they inexorably refuse to forgive others the various wrongs they have done them. For the Lord says, 'If you do not forgive your fellow-men, your Father will not forgive you.' And the words of the apostle James are to the same effect, when he says that 'judgement will be merciless to those who have shown no mercy.'[122] And here, surely, that servant is bound to come to mind, whose master forgave him a debt of ten thousand talents, but afterwards demanded their repayment because the servant on his part had not

121. Lev. 16, 6. 122. Jas. 2, 13.

shown compassion to his fellow-servants who owed him a hundred denarii.[123] And so it is in those who are 'sons of the promise' and 'vessels of mercy' that the saying holds good which comes immediately after in the letter of the same apostle. He says, 'Mercy exults over judgement.'[124] For those righteous ones have lived such holy lives that they receive 'into everlasting dwellings' other people as well, who have 'made them their friends by means of the worldly wealth of unrighteousness';[125] and they have attained this righteousness because they have been delivered by the compassion of him who justifies the wicked by reckoning the reward on the basis not of debt but of grace.[126] The Apostle himself is, as we know, among that number; for he says, 'I have been granted mercy, so that I might be faithful.'[127]

On the other hand, those who are 'received' by those justified souls 'into everlasting dwellings' are not, it must be admitted, endowed with the moral character that would make it possible for their manner of life to be enough to fit them for deliverance without the intercession of the saints; and therefore even more in them does 'mercy exult over justice'. For all that, it must not be thought that any thorough criminal, if he has made no change in his life to make it good, or even more tolerable, can be received into 'eternal dwellings', although he has been of service to the saints 'by means of the worldly wealth of unrighteousness' that is, with his money or other resources, which were ill-gained. And even if they are honestly come by, they are not the true riches, but only what unrighteousness counts as riches; for such a man does not know what the true riches are, those riches which are enjoyed in abundance by those who receive others 'into eternal dwellings'.

There must therefore be a kind of life which is not so evil that generosity in charity cannot help those who live in that way towards the attainment of the Kingdom of Heaven, and yet not so good that it is in itself sufficient for the achievement of that supreme felicity, if such people do not meet with compassion through the merits of those whose friendship they have won. (I always find it surprising that we can discover in Virgil an expression of the same thought as is uttered in those words of our Lord, 'Win friends for yourselves by means of the worldly wealth of unrighteousness, so that they on their part may receive you into the eternal dwellings'; and in the very similar saying, 'Anyone who welcomes a prophet because he is a prophet will have a

123. cf. Matt. 18, 23ff. 124. Gal. 4, 28; Rom. 9, 23; Jas. 2, 13.
125. Luke 16, 9. 126. cf. Rom. 4, 4. 127. 1 Cor. 7, 25.

prophet's reward: and anyone who welcomes a righteous man because he is a righteous man will receive a righteous man's reward'.[128] Now when Virgil describes the Elysian fields, where, as the pagans think, the souls of the blessed dwell, he places there not only those who have been able to reach that abode by reasons of their own merits; he adds that there are found there

Those whose high deserts
Made others mindful of them.[129]

He means those who have deserved well of others, and by so doing have made those others 'mindful of them'. It is, in fact, just as if these people had said the words frequently on the lips of a Christian when he commends himself to some saint, and says, 'Remember me', and seeks to ensure this remembrance by deserving well of that holy man.)

But what that kind of life may be is a question most difficult to answer; and it would be most perilous to define what those sins are which in themselves prevent attainment to the kingdom of God while admitting of pardon through the merits of holy friends. I myself, at least, have given much thought to the latter question without having been able to reach a conclusion. And it may well be that the answer is kept a secret for fear that the knowledge might blunt men's zeal to make progress towards the avoidance of all kinds of sin. For if it were known what those sins were, or at any rate what kind of sins they were, for whose forgiveness the intercession of the righteous should be sought and hoped for, even while the sins still continued, and while they were not removed in an advance to a higher standard of life, then human beings in their sloth would allow themselves to be involved in them with supposed impunity, and they would not be concerned to free themselves from such entanglements by any virtuous endeavour. Their sole quest would be to gain freedom from punishment through the merits of others, whose friendship they had won by generous acts of charity, made possible by 'the worldly wealth of unrighteousness'. As it is, however, so long as men do not know the limits within which wrong-doing is venial, even if persevered in, then, beyond dispute, more active zeal is shown for improvement of life by means of prayer and effort, and there is no slackening in concern to 'win friends by the use of the worldly wealth of unrighteousness'.

But whether this liberation is attained through a man's own prayers or through the intercession of saints, its effect is that the person

128. Luke 16, 9; Matt. 10, 41. 129. *Aen.*, 6, 664.

concerned is not consigned to eternal fire; it is not that after being consigned there he is released after a long or a short period. Now there are some people who suppose that the scriptural passage about the 'thirty-fold, sixty-fold, a hundred-fold'[130] crop from a good soil is to be taken as meaning that the saints liberate others according to their different merits, some giving freedom to thirty, some to sixty, some to a hundred; but even those people generally assume that this will happen at the day of judgement, not after the judgement. Apropos of this speculation, someone made a very shrewd remark when he observed how people most perversely assured themselves of impunity, on the assumption that everyone could in this way be included among those exempt from damnation. He is said to have remarked, 'We should be better employed in taking care to lead good lives, so as to join the number of the future intercessors for others' salvation.' For otherwise there may be so few of them that they will soon have used up their thirty, or sixty, or a hundred, and a great many will be left unredeemed, without the possibility of rescue from punishment by the intercession of the saints; and among the disappointed may be found any of those people who are so rashly and irresponsibly promising themselves the prospect of benefiting by some other person's 'crop'.

This may suffice for my reply to those who while not slighting the authority of the sacred Scriptures, which we have as our common possession, nevertheless interpret them wrongly and suppose that what is to happen will be not what the Scriptures speak of, but what they themselves would like to happen. Well, we have given this reply; and now, as we promised, we bring this book to an end.

130. Matt. 13, 8.

BOOK XXII

1. *The creation of angels and men*

As I promised in the last book, this final book of the whole work will contain a discussion of the eternal bliss of the City of God. This City is not called 'eternal' in the sense that it continues its life throughout many ages, and yet is to come to an end at last, but in the sense of the scriptural saying, that 'his kingdom will have no end.'[1] Nor will this City present a mere semblance of perpetuity by generations arising to succeed generations as they die; as happens in a tree clothed with perennial foliage, where the same greenness seems to persist, the appearance of thick growth being preserved as leaves decay and fall to be replaced by new. But in this City all the citizens will be immortal, for human beings also will obtain that which the angels have never lost. This will be effected by God, the founder of that City; for he has promised it, and he cannot lie; and to confirm his promise he has done many things that he has promised, and many that he has not promised.

For it is he who made the world, filled with all good things, things accessible to sense, and those perceived by the understanding; and in the world his greatest work was the creation of spirits, to whom he gave intelligence, making them capable of contemplating him, able to apprehend him; and he bound them together in one fellowship, which we call the Holy and Heavenly City, in which God himself is for those spirits the means of their life and their felicity, is, as it were, their common life and food. He has bestowed on these intellectual natures the power of free choice, which enabled them, if they so chose, to desert God, that is, to abandon their felicity, with misery to follow immediately. He foreknew that some of the angels, in their pride, would wish to be self-sufficient for their own felicity, and hence would forsake their true good; and yet he did not deprive them of this power, judging it an act of greater power and greater goodness to bring good even out of evil than to exclude the existence of evil. There would not, in fact, have been any evil at all, had not that nature which was capable of change (although good and created by the supreme God

1. 1 Luke 1, 33.

who is also the changeless good, who made all things good) produced evil for itself by sinning. This sin is itself the evidence that proves that the nature was created good; for if it had not itself been a great good, although not equal to the Creator, then assuredly this apostasy from God, as from their light, could not have been their evil. We may find an analogy in blindness. Blindness is a defect of the eye, and that in itself indicates that the eye was created for seeing; and thus even by its own defect it is shown to be more excellent than the other parts of the body as being capable of perceiving light, since that is why it is a defect in the eye to be deprived of light. In the same way the nature which enjoyed God proves that it was created excellent by that very defect, by the fact that it is wretched simply because it does not enjoy God.

Now God inflicted on the apostate angels, for their self-chosen fall, the just punishment of everlasting misery, while to the others, who continued in that highest good, he gave the certainty of their endless continuance therein, as the reward for that continuance. And God made man also upright, with the same power of free choice, an animal of earth, yet worthy of heaven if he adhered to the author of his being, but, by the same token, destined, if he abandoned God, for a misery appropriate to his kind of nature. Now God foreknew that man would sin by breaking God's Law through his apostasy from God; and yet, as in the case of the angels, God did not deprive man of the power of free choice, foreseeing, at the same time, the good that he was to bring out of man's evil. For out of this mortal progeny, so rightly and justly condemned, God by his grace is gathering a people so great that from them he may fill the place of the fallen angels and restore their number. And thus that beloved Heavenly City will not be deprived of its full number of citizens; it may perhaps rejoice in a still more abundant population.

2. *The eternal and unchangeable will of God*

Evil men do many things contrary to the will of God; but so great is his wisdom, and so great his power, that all things which seem to oppose his will tend towards those results or ends which he himself has foreknown as good and just. For this reason, when God is said to 'change his will', as, for example, when 'he becomes angry' with those people to whom 'he was lenient', it is the people who change, rather than God; and they find him, in a sense, 'changed' in their experience. Similarly, to people with inflammation of the eyes the sun 'changes' and turns, in a sense, from mild to harsh, from a source of pleasure to a cause of irritation, whereas in fact the sun remains in itself exactly as it was before. God's activity in the heart of those who obey his commandments is also called God's will, the activity of which the Apostle speaks when he says, 'It is God who produces in you both the will ...';[2] in the same way, the 'righteousness of God' means not only the quality whereby God himself is righteous, but also the quality that God produces in a man who is justified by him. So also we speak of 'God's Law' when it is really the Law for mankind, given by God. For Jesus was certainly speaking to men when he said, 'It is written in your Law', whereas in another place we read that 'the Law of God is in his heart.'[3] Thus in accordance with this will which God is said to produce in men, God also is said to will what he does not will himself but makes his followers will; just as God is said to know what he makes the ignorant know. For instance, when the Apostle says, 'Now that you have come to know God, or rather, now that you have become known to him',[4] it is utterly wrong to suppose that God came to know them at that time; they were known to him before the foundation of the world.[5] God is said to have come to know them at that time because it was then that he brought it about that he should be known by them. I remember having discussed those turns of speech before, in previous books.[6] It is in accordance with this use of the phrase 'God's will', whereby we say that God wills what he causes others to will, who are ignorant of the future, that God 'wills' many things which he himself does not effect.

God's saints, for example, with a holy will inspired by him, will that many things should happen, which do not in fact happen; as when they pray for others with holy devotion, and God does not give effect to their prayers, although he has produced in them, by his Holy Spirit, this will to pray. For this reason, when holy men will and pray, according to God's teaching, that a particular person may be saved, we may say, by this mode of speech, that 'God wills it and does not effect it', in the sense that we say that God wills something when he makes others will it. But according to his own will, which, along with his foreknowledge, is eternal, God assuredly made all things in heaven and earth; he has made whatever he willed to make, and not only things past and things present. He has already made things that are yet to be. However, before the time comes when he has willed that something should come to be which he has foreknown and planned before all time began, we

2. Phil. 2, 13. 3. John 8, 17; Ps. 36, 31. 4. Gal. 4, 9.
5. cf. 1 Pet. 1, 20. 6. Bk XI, 8; XIV, 11; XV, 25; XVI, 6.

say, 'It will happen when God wills.' This does not mean that God will then have a new will which he did not have before; but that something will then come about which has been prepared from all eternity in his unchanging will.

3. *The promise of eternal bliss for the saints and perpetual punishment for the wicked*

Therefore (to omit many other points) as we now see fulfilled in Christ the promise given to Abraham, 'In your posterity all nations will be blessed';[7] so there will be fulfilment of what God promised to the same posterity, when he says through the mouth of the prophet, 'Those who were in the tombs will rise again', and

> There will be a new heaven, and a new earth; and men will not remember the past, and it will not come to their minds. But they will find gladness and exultation in her. See, I shall make Jerusalem to be exultation and her people to be gladness; and I shall exult in Jerusalem and I shall be glad in my people. No more will the sound of weeping be heard in her.[8]

And by the lips of another prophet we are told what God said to him: 'At that time all your people will be saved, all who will be found recorded in the book. And many of those who sleep in the dust' (or, in another translation, 'the mound') 'of the earth will rise up, some to go to eternal life, while the others go to reproach and eternal shame.' And in another place we have this message from the same prophet, 'The saints of God Most High will receive the kingdom; and they will possess it for ever and ever'; and, a little later: 'His kingdom is an everlasting kingdom.'[9] There are other passages on the same subject which I quoted in the twentieth book,[10] and other prophecies, found in the Holy Scriptures, which I have not quoted. All those will come about, just as those things have already come about which the unbelievers thought would never happen. For it is the same God who promised both the latter and the former; and he is the God before whom the pagan divinities shrink in terror, on the witness of Porphyry,[11] the most renowned of the pagan philosophers.

7. Gen. 22, 18. 8. Is. 26, 19; 65, 17ff. 9. Dan. 12, 1f.; 7, 18; 7, 27.
10. Bk XX, 21. 11. cf. Bk XIX, 23.

4. *A reply to the worldly-wise, who suppose it impossible for earthly bodies to be transferred to heaven*

Some scholars and philosophers, it is true, defy the force of this great authority which, in fulfilment of its own prediction, made so long ago, has converted all kinds of men to believe in this state of bliss and to hope for it; for they flatter themselves on presenting a shrewd argument against the resurrection of the body when they quote a passage from the third book of Cicero's *On the Commonwealth*. For while asserting that Hercules and Romulus were deified human beings, he has this to say: 'Their bodies were not taken up into heaven, indeed Nature would not allow what comes of the earth to dwell anywhere but on the earth.'[12]

Such is the impressive reasoning of the wise; but 'God knows their thoughts, how futile they are.'[13] For suppose that we were merely souls, that is, spirits without bodies, and if while we lived in heaven we knew nothing of earthly creatures, and we were told that what was in store for us was that we were going to be linked with earthly bodies by some miraculous bond, to give life to those bodies. Would we not refuse to believe it? Would we not find a much stronger argument against it in saying that Nature does not allow an incorporeal substance to be bound by a corporeal tie? And yet the world is full of souls animating these earthly physical frames, combined and bound up with them in a mysterious fashion. Why then, if it is the will of the same God who made this living creature, cannot an earthly body be raised up to a heavenly body, if the soul, which belongs to a more exalted order of being than any body, even a heavenly body, could be linked with an earthly body? Are we to say that so inconsiderable an earthly particle could hold within itself something superior to a heavenly body, something that gives to that particle sensibility and life, and yet heaven will disdain to receive it when it feels and lives, or will not be able to sustain it when received although it owes its sensibility and its life to a substance superior to any celestial body? The reason why this does not happen now is that the time has not yet come when he has decided that it should happen, he who created this present state of things, which has been cheapened by familiarity, but which is in fact much more wonderful than that translation which our philosophers find incredible. Why, in fact, are we not more violently amazed that immaterial souls, superior to celestial bodies, are bound within earthly bodies, than that bodies, although earthly, should be

12. Cic. *De Rep.*, 3, 28. 13. Ps. 94, 11.

exalted to abodes which are material, albeit heavenly? It can only be that the former is a matter of common observation, and we ourselves are so constituted, whereas we are not in the latter state and it is something we have never yet observed. For it is beyond dispute that on sober and rational consideration the interweaving of material with immaterial substances proves to be a greater miracle of divine power than the conjunction of the material with the material, different though they may be in that the one is heavenly and the other terrestrial.

5. *The resurrection of the flesh, which some refuse to believe, despite its general acceptance*

This may once have been incredible; but see, the whole world has now come to believe that the earthly body of Christ has been taken up into heaven. Learned and unlearned alike have now come to believe in the resurrection of his flesh and his ascension to the realms on high, and only a very few among learned and unlearned still remain in stupefied incredulity. If what the world believes is credible, the unbelievers should notice how stupid they are! If it is incredible, then surely it is even more incredible that so incredible a thing should be so credited! So we have two incredible things, the resurrection of our body to eternity, and the world's credence in this incredibility, both of them foretold by God before either of them came to pass.[14]

One of the two incredibilities we already observe to have happened; the world credits what had been incredible. Why then should we despair of the one remaining? It has come to pass that the world now believes what was incredible; why should it not likewise come to pass (though the world, in the same way as before, believes this incredible) that the world should believe a thing which is now so incredible? Especially as both those incredibilities (one of which we see fulfilled, while we believe the other) are predicted in the same Sciptures by which the world has been brought to believe. And indeed the actual manner in which the world came to this belief turns out to be even more incredible.

There were just a few men, the merest handful, untrained in the liberal arts, completely uneducated, as far as pagan philosophy is concerned, with no knowledge of literature, no equipment in logic, no trappings of rhetoric. And Christ sent them out as fishermen with the nets of faith into the sea of this world; and in this way he caught all

14. cf. Matt. 26, 13.

those fish of every kind, including – more wonderful, because rarer – even some of the philosophers themselves. And so, if you please (or rather, because you ought to be pleased), let us add a third incredibility to the two others.

Here then we have those incredibilities; and yet they happened. It is incredible that Christ rose in the flesh and with his flesh ascended into heaven. It is incredible that the world believed so incredible an event; and it is incredible that men of no birth, no standing, no learning, and so few of them, should have been able to persuade, so effectively, the whole world, including the learned men. The first of those three incredibilities our opponents refuse to believe; the second they are compelled to observe; and unless they believe the third, they cannot account for the second. The resurrection of Christ, and his ascension into heaven with the flesh in which he rose again, is by now proclaimed and believed throughout the world; if it is incredible, how is it that it is believed throughout the world? If many people, people of noble birth, of high position, of profound learning, had said that they had witnessed it and had been at pains to spread the news of what they had witnessed, it would be no marvel, if the world believed them; it would be crass obstinacy in our opponents to refuse belief. If, and this is the truth, the world has believed a few men, of obscure birth, of no importance and of no learning, who assert in speech and writing that they have witnessed this event, why do a few men show this perverse obstinacy in continued refusal to believe the believing world? The world has believed a tiny number of men of low birth, low position, with no academic qualifications; and it has believed them just because in the persons of such insignificant witnesses the power of God exercised a much more wonderful persuasion. What I mean is that those who persuaded men of this truth did so by utterances which on their lips were turned into miracles, rather than mere words. For those who had not witnessed Christ's resurrection in the flesh, and his ascension into heaven in that same flesh, believed the report of those who told what they had seen, who not only spoke of it, but displayed miraculous signs. In fact, people who were known to have only one language, or two at most, were suddenly heard speaking miraculously in the languages of all nations;[15] a man lame from birth stood up, sound and strong after forty years, cured at their word in the name of Christ; cloths taken from their persons had power to heal the sick; a countless number of sufferers from various diseases were stationed along the road by which the disciples were to pass, so that as they passed their

15. Acts 2.

shadows might pass over the sufferers and, as a rule, the sick were restored to health;[16] and many other amazing acts were performed by the disciples in Christ's name; indeed, even the dead were restored to life. All this was observed by those who had not witnessed Christ's resurrection.

Now if these people admit that those things happened as they are recorded, then here we have all those incredibilities to add to our first three. And in order to make credible that one incredible event, Christ's resurrection and ascension, as it is reported, we heap up all this evidence for a multitude of incredible events; and yet we still cannot turn them from their hair-raising obstinacy and bring them to believe. Nevertheless, if they do not even believe that those miracles were effected through Christ's apostles, to ensure belief in their proclamation of Christ's resurrection and ascension, then this one overpowering miracle is enough for us – that the whole world has come to believe in it without any miracles at all!

6. *The Romans made Romulus a god because they loved him: the Church loved Christ because it believed him to be God*

Let us also call to mind on this topic the surprise expressed by Cicero at the reputed divinity of Romulus. I shall quote the actual words.

> What is remarkable in the case of Romulus is that all the others who have been turned from human beings into Gods, lived in the less advanced ages of mankind, so that a pious fraud was an easier enterprise since uneducated people were readily induced to believe it. But the age of Romulus was less than six centuries ago, when literacy and education was already well established and the errors of primitive times had been entirely removed from a society of developing culture.

And a little later he has this to say, to the same effect, still on the subject of Romulus,

> Hence it can be gathered that Homer lived a great many years before Romulus. Men were educated by the time of Romulus, and it was an age of some culture; as a result, there was scarcely any opportunity for the spread of legend. For a primitive age is receptive of fables, which, indeed, often show a degree of skill in their invention; whereas a more cultivated age is especially ready to mock at this kind of thing, and rejects any story which defies possibility.[17]

16. Acts 3, 1–10; 19, 10; 5, 15. 17. Cic., *De Rep.* 2, 10.

Now Marcus Tullius Cicero was among the most learned and eloquent of all mankind, and his reason for saying that the belief in the divinity of Romulus is surprising is that it grew up in times of enlightenment, when false fables did not meet a ready reception. And yet who ever believed in the divinity of Romulus except Rome, and that when Rome was small and at the beginning of her history? Thereafter it was inevitable that posterity should preserve the tradition handed down from earlier times, and the community, as we say, drank in this superstition with its mother's milk. Then the city grew in power and attained a great empire; and from this height of power she diffused, from that higher level, as it were, this belief among the other nations, whom she dominated. Those nations professed this belief, without indeed believing it, to avoid giving offence to the city to whom they were enslaved, in the matter of that city's founder. They would have given offence by differing from Rome about the title of Romulus; for Rome's belief in his divinity did not spring from a love of error but from an error of love. In contrast, although Christ is the founder of the eternal Heavenly City, that City's belief in Christ as God does not arise from her foundation by him; the truth is that her foundation arises from her belief in Christ as God. Rome worshipped her founder as a god after she had been built and dedicated; but this Heavenly Jerusalem put Christ as the foundation of her faith, so that she might be built and dedicated. Rome believed Romulus to be a god because she loved him; the Heavenly City loved Christ because she believed him to be God. Thus Rome had already an object of her love, which she could readily turn from a loved object into a final good, falsely believed in; correspondingly, our City had already an object of her belief, so that she might not rashly love a false good but with true faith might set her affection on the true good. For apart from all those great miracles which persuaded her that Christ is God, there were also the preceding prophecies, divinely inspired and completely worthy of belief, which are no longer believed as destined for future fulfilment in Christ, as they were believed by the fathers, but are shown to have been fulfilled in him. About Romulus, in contrast, we are told and we read that he founded Rome and that he reigned there. This is what happened; it was not prophesied before it happened. While in the story of his reception among the gods the documents record a belief rather than communicate a fact, for there are no miraculous signs to confirm that this really happened to him. There is, to be sure, that she-wolf, which is thought to have been a notable portent; but is it a portent of a quality or a magnitude to demonstrate his divinity? Even assuming that this she-wolf was really a wild beast, and not a harlot,[18] the portent was shared by both brothers; and yet the other brother is not regarded as a god. And has anyone ever been forbidden to assert that Romulus or Hercules, or other similar men are gods, and yet has preferred to die rather than to refrain from asserting it? Again, would any nation worship Romulus among its gods, were it not forced to do so by fear of Roman power? On the other hand, could anyone count the multitude who have chosen to die the most cruel, the most brutal death conceivable, rather than deny the divinity of Christ?

Moreover, even the slightest fear of the indignation which, they felt, might be aroused in Roman minds if the worship of Romulus was omitted, drove some of the communities subject to Roman authority to offer him divine honours; but the fear of the heaviest punishments of all kinds, very different from the slight fear of hurting Roman feelings, and even the fear of death itself, the most terrible of all fears, could not restrain a multitude of martyrs throughout the world from worshipping Christ as God and, what is more, from proclaiming him as God. And yet in those times of persecution the City of Christ never fought against her wicked persecutors for her temporal preservation, even though while still on pilgrimage in this world she had on her side whole armies of mighty peoples; instead, she refrained from fighting back, to ensure her eternal salvation. Her people were bound, imprisoned, scourged, tortured, burned, butchered, massacred – and they multiplied. For them there was but one way to fight for their safety and that was to hold safety in contempt for their Saviour's sake.

I know that Cicero argues (if I am not mistaken it is in the third book of his, *On the Commonwealth*) that the ideal city never takes up arms except in defence of its faith or its safety.[19] He shows in another passage what he means by 'for its safety', what kind of 'safety' he intends to be undestood·

From the pains which even the most insensitive feel, such as want and exile, imprisonment and scourging, private individuals often make their escape, since the swift escape of death is available; for a community on the other hand, the death which seems to free the individual from his pain, is itself a punishment. For a community must be constituted with a view to its eternal continuance. And so death is never natural to a commonwealth, as it is to a man. For a man death is not only inevitable but very often even desirable; whereas when a city is destroyed, wiped out, extinguished,

18. cf. Livy 1, 4, and Bk XVIII, 21. 'She-wolf' was in Rome a cant term for 'prostitute'.

19. Not in any extant part of *De Rep.*

it is (to compare small with great) as if the whole of this world should collapse and perish.[20]

The reason for Cicero's statement is that, like the Platonists,[21] he held that the world was imperishable. It is certain, therefore, that he wished a city to take up arms in defence of that safety which ensures its continuance as a city in this world, as he says, for eternity, although this permanence is maintained as the individual members die and are replaced by new births, just as the thick foliage of the olive, the laurel, and other perennial trees is maintained by the fall and renewal of the leaves. As Cicero says, death often rescues individual men from pain, instead of being a disaster to them; but the death of a whole community is always a disaster. Hence it is a fair question whether the Saguntines[22] acted rightly when they would rather have their whole city perish than break the faith which bound them to the Roman commonwealth itself, a decision for which they are praised by all the citizens of the earthly commonwealth. But I do not see how they could comply with Cicero's argument, in which it is said that war should never be engaged on, except in defence either of faith or safety. For we are not told which of the two is to have the preference, if both faith and safety run jointly into the same danger, so that the one cannot be preserved without the loss of the other. For it is obvious that if the Saguntines had chosen safety they must have abandoned faith; if faith had been kept they must certainly have relinquished their safety – which is what happened.

But the safety of the City of God is such that it can be possessed, or rather acquired, only with faith and through faith; and when faith is once lost no one can attain to that safety, or salvation. That thought in a steadfast and resolute heart made so many and such noble martyrs; not one such martyr was inspired, or could have been inspired, by Romulus, when he was believed to be a god.

7. *The world's belief in Christ was due to the power of God, not to human persuasion*

However, it is utterly absurd to mention the false divinity of Romulus when we are speaking of Christ. And yet if Romulus lived almost six hundred years before Cicero, and that age, it is said, was so highly educated that it rejected any impossible story, how much more in the time of Cicero, six hundred years later, and still more in the reigns of

20. Cic., *De Rep.* 3, 23. 21. cf. Bk VIII, 6. 22. cf. Bk VIII, 20.

Augustus and Tiberius – which were undoubtedly more enlightened times – would the human mind have been unable to tolerate the notion of Christ's physical resurrection and his ascension to heaven! Men would have laughed it out of court; they would have shut their ears and their hearts against the idea, had not the possibility and the actuality of these events been demonstrated by the divine power of truth itself or rather by the truth of the divine power, with confirmation by miraculous signs. And so, in spite of all the opposition and all the terror of so many great persecutions, Christians held with unswerving faith to the belief in the previous resurrection of Christ, in the coming resurrection to the new age of all mankind, and in the immortality of the body. And this belief was fearlessly proclaimed; and was to produce a more plentiful harvest throughout the world when the blood of martyrs was the seed sown.[23] For the preceding proclamations of the prophets were read, the demonstrations of power pointed the same way, and truth, new to experience though not contrary to reason, exercised its persuasion, until the world which had persecuted in frenzy now followed in faith.

8. *Miracles, performed to make the world believe, have not ceased now that the world does believe*

Why, it is asked, do no miracles occur nowadays, such as occurred (you maintain) in former times? I could reply that they were necessary then, before the world came to believe, in order to win the world's belief. Anyone who still looks for portents, to make him believe, is himself the greatest portent, in refusing to believe when all the world believes. But the purpose of the question is to discourage belief in the occurrence of those miracles in the past. How is it then that Christ is now hymned everywhere, with such profound faith, as having been taken up to heaven in bodily form? How is it that in enlightened times, when every impossibility was rejected with scorn, the world believed excessively miraculous incredibilities without the confirmation of any miracles at all? Are our opponents going to say that they were credible, and were credited for that reason? Then why do they themselves not believe them?

Here then, in brief, is my dilemma. Either the incredible event which was not seen was confirmed by other incredible things, which nevertheless occurred and were seen, or else the event is so credible as

23. This celebrated metaphor appears first in Tertullian (*Apol.*, 21; 50.): 'We become more numerous as a result of your frequent reapings. The blood of Christians is seed.'

to need no miracles to support it – and then it proves our opponents' excessive incredulity. I pose this dilemma, with apology, to refute this extreme foolishness. In fact, many miracles have occurred, as we cannot deny, to testify to that one supreme miracle of salvation, the miracle of Christ's ascension into heaven in the flesh in which he rose from the dead. Those miracles are all recorded, as we know, in the Scriptures, which never lie. There we are told what happened and the belief they were intended to support. They have become known in order to promote faith; they have become more widely known through the faith which they promoted. The accounts are read among the nations, so that the people may believe; but they would never have been read, had they not been believed. And in fact, even now miracles are being performed in Christ's name either by his sacrament, or by the prayers or the memorials of his saints, but they do not enjoy the blaze of publicity which would spread their fame with a glory to equal that of those earlier marvels.

The canon of holy Scripture, which had to be defined, ensured that those earlier miracles should be read everywhere, and should stick in the memory of the people everywhere, whereas the more recent examples, wherever they occur, are scarcely known to the whole community there, or even throughout the particular neighbourhood. Even there only a very few know about them in most instances, and all the rest are quite unaware, especially if it is a city of any great size; and when the story comes to other places and other people it is not confirmed by sufficient authority to ensure ready or even hesitating acceptance, although faithful Christians pass the news on to others of the faithful.

A miracle that happened at Milan while I was there, when a blind man had his sight restored, succeeded in becoming more widely known because Milan is an important city, and because the emperor was there at the time. A great crowd had gathered to see the bodies of the martyrs Protasius and Gervasius, and the miracle took place before all those witnesses.[24] Those bodies had been lost and nothing at

24. Nothing is known of the twin martyrs; but the discovery of their bodies in 386, after a divine message to St Ambrose, and their enshrinement, with the attendant miracles, made a vivid episode in the struggle at Milan between the bishop and the Arian Empress Justina, mother of Valentinian II, the emperor here mentioned. This must explain the wide spread of their cult, and the popularity of Gervase (but not, apparently, of Protase) in church dedications and as a Christian name, especially in France. Gibbon tells the story in the twenty-seventh chapter of *The Decline and Fall of the Roman Empire*. The original sources, besides the present chapter, are: Ambr., *Ep.*, 22; Aug., *Conf.*, 9, 7; *Serm.*, 286; 318.

all was known about them; but their hiding-place was revealed in a dream to Ambrose, bishop of Milan, and they were discovered. It was there that the darkness, in which the blind man had lived so long, was dispelled; and he saw the light of day.

In contrast with this, there are surely only a very few at Carthage who know about the healing of Innocentius, sometime counsellor of the vice-prefecture. But I was present as an eye-witness; for when I came with my brother Alypius[25] from overseas, when we were not yet ordained though already servants of God, Innocentius entertained us, and we were staying in his house at the time. The counsellor was a most devout man, and it was a very religous household. He was under treatment for fistulas, having a number of them intertwined in the rectum, and others more deep-seated. The surgeons had operated on some and were now proceeding with medical treatment; but the patient had suffered long-lasting and acute pain in the operation. Now there still remained one ulcer which had escaped the notice of the medical men, and it was so deeply hidden that they could not get at it, since it would require to be opened up by an incision. Finally all the ulcers were healed which were open for treatment, but this one only still remained and on it they spent their pains to no purpose. The patient was suspicious of the delay, and grew extremely apprehensive at the prospect of a second operation. Another medical man, a member of his household, had predicted this possibility. The others had not allowed him in as a witness of the first operation, so that he might at least observe their procedure; and Innocentius angrily dismissed him from the house, and could scarcely be brought to allow him back. But now the patient burst out with the question, 'Are you going to operate again? That fellow whom you barred from the operation, am I to have him saying "I told you so"?' They laughed at the other as a physician of no experience, and soothed the patient with fair words and promises. Days passed, and all their efforts proved ineffective. Still the physicians stuck to their reassurances, undertaking to close the fistula by medical treatment, without using the knife. Then they called in another doctor, an old man called Ammonius who enjoyed a considerable reputation in his profession, and after his examination he gave the same assurance as the medical attendants and predicted a favourable result from their skill and devotion.

The patient's confidence was restored by this authoritative prognosis, and he jeered with facetious cheerfulness at his household phys-

25. Bishop of Thagaste; the boyhood and lifelong friend of St Augustine. He is often mentioned in the *Confessions*.

ician, who had prophesied a second operation to come, and he assumed himself already cured. To cut a long story short, after a considerable time spent to no effect, the doctors, exhausted and embarrassed, had to admit that no cure was possible without further use of the knife. The patient was aghast; he turned deadly pale, distraught with the extremity of terror. When he had recovered his wits and was able to speak, he ordered them to be off and never come near him again. Then, tired out with weeping, he could think of no other course, in his present straits, but to send for a doctor of Alexandria who at that time had the reputation of a surgeon of genius, and to let him perform the operation which Innocentius in his anger had forbidden the others to attempt. The surgeon came; but when the artist in him observed in the scars the quality of the work done by the others, he acted like an honest man and persuaded the patient that it would be better that the doctors who had worked so hard on his case (as he saw, with admiration, from his examination) should have the satisfaction of completing the cure. He added that a cure was really impossible without another operation; and that it would be against his principles to take the crowning honour of all their work from those whose supreme artistry, conscientious pains, and attention to detail, he admired when he inspected the scars. They were accordingly re-instated in the confidence of Innocentius, and it was decided that the Alexandrian should stand by while the others made an incision to open up the fistula, which by now, as all agreed, was otherwise incurable. The operation was put off until the next day. But when the physicians had departed, the lamentations of the master of the house aroused such grief in the household that it resembled the mourning at a funeral; and we had difficulty in getting it under control.

Now there were some holy men who used to visit the sufferer every day, Saturninus of blessed memory, at that time bishop of Uzalis, Gulosus, a presbyter of the church of Carthage, and the deacons of that church; among those (and the only one of them still on earth) was Aurelius, now a bishop and a man to be mentioned by me with due respect. I have often recalled with him 'the wonderful works of God', and we have often spoken of this event, for I discovered that he had a vivid recollection of what I am now describing. When those holy men were paying Innocentius their customary evening visit on the day in question, he asked them, with piteous tears, to be good enough to come in the morning to be present at his death, instead of at his suffering. For his previous torments had so unnerved him that he felt sure that he was destined to perish under the surgeon's hands. The others tried to reassure him, and urged him to trust in God, and submit to God's will like a man. Then we betook ourselves to prayers; and when we knelt down, in the usual way, and bent towards the ground, Innocentius hurled himself forward, as if someone had pushed him flat on his face; and he began to pray. It is beyond the power of words to express the manner of his prayer, his passion, his agitation, his flood of tears, his groans, and the sobs which shook his whole frame and almost stifled his breath. Whether the others were praying, whether they could take their attention from him, I could not tell; for my part, I was utterly unable to utter a prayer; all I could do was to say this brief sentence in my heart, 'Lord, what prayers of your people do you hear, if you do not hear these?' For it seemed to me that he could go no further, unless it was to breathe his last in prayer. We rose from our knees and, after receiving the bishop's blessing, we left, the sick man entreating his visitors to come back in the morning, while they bade him be of good heart. The dreaded morning dawned; the servants of God arrived as they had promised; the surgeons entered. All preparations had been made which that fateful hour demanded; the fearful instruments were produced, while we all sat there in dumbfounded suspense. Those of the visitors whose authority was greatest tried to raise the patient's drooping spirits with words of encouragement, while his body was being laid in position ready for the work of the surgeon. The bandages were untied; the place was bared. The surgeon examined it, and knife in hand ready for the incision, he searched for the fistula that was to be cut. He inspected it closely; felt it with his fingers; then he examined it in every way – he found it firmly cicatrized. The rejoicing that followed, the thanksgiving to God, the merciful and almighty, which poured from every mouth with tears of happiness – all this I have not the words to express. The scene can be better imagined than described.

In the same city there was a woman named Innocentia, a woman of great devotion and of high standing in that community. She suffered from a cancer of the breast, a condition, according to the physicians, incurable by the medical treatment. Therefore the general practice is to cut out the cancer, removing from the body the part which harbours the growth; or else they use no treatment at all, in order to prolong the life of the sufferer to some extent, although death, even if somewhat delayed, is the inevitable result of the complaint. This latter course, they say, follows the advice of Hippocrates. Innocentia was told all this by her doctor, a well-qualified man and a close friend of the family; and she turned for help to God alone, in prayer. When

Easter was approaching she was instructed in a dream to watch on the women's side at the baptistery and ask the first newly-baptized woman who met her to sign the affected place with the sign of Christ. This she did; and she was immediately restored to health. The physician who had advised her not to attempt any treatment, if she wished to prolong her life somewhat, examined her and found her completely cured, though when he had made the same examination previously he had recognized her condition. Naturally, he questioned her closely about the treatment she had used, being eager, we may well suppose, to discover a medicine which would prove Hippocrates wrong in his dictum. When he had heard her account of what had happened, his voice and his expression suggested, we are told, that he thought little of it, so much so that she was afraid that he might make some insulting remark about Christ. But he replied with an air of humorous solemnity: 'Why, I thought you were going to tell me something remarkable!' And when she looked horrified at this, he hastily added, 'What was so extraordinary in Christ's healing a cancer, when he once raised to life a man four days dead?'

Now when I heard of this event I was indignant that so astounding a miracle, performed in so important a city, and on a person far from obscure, should have been kept secret like this; and I thought it right to admonish her and to speak to her with some sharpness on the matter. She replied that she had not kept silence about it; and I then inquired of the matrons who happened to be her most intimate friends at the time, asking if they had known about it. They replied that they were quite unaware of it. 'Look here', I then said to her, 'How can you say you are not keeping it quiet, seeing that those who are so close to you have heard nothing of it?' The result of my brief question was that she related to her friends the whole sequence of events, just as it happened, and they listened in great amazement and gave praise to God.

There was also a physician in the same city who suffered from the gout. He had given in his name for baptism, and the night before he was to receive that sacrament he had a dream in which a number of curly-haired negro boys, whom he took to be demons, forbade him to be baptized that year. He refused to obey them, and they then stamped on his foot, causing him the acutest pain, worse than he had ever experienced before. But he went on with his purpose and in getting the better of his opponents was all the more resolved not to postpone his washing in the bath of rebirth, as he had vowed; and in his baptism he was there and then not only relieved of the pain, which had been unwontedly excruciating, but was completely free from the gout from then onwards, never suffering any pain in his feet for the rest of a long life. And yet, does anyone know this man's story? I know it, at any rate, and so do a very few of the brethren to whom it succeeded in reaching.

There was a sometime stage-player of Curubis,[26] who was cured at baptism not only of paralysis but also of a serious hernia. He came up from the font of rebirth free from both distressing conditions, as if there had never been anything physically wrong with him. Yet did anyone know of this outside Curubis, except a very few who chanced to hear about it in various places? For my part, when I heard the story I succeeded in getting him sent to Carthage, on the orders of the holy Bishop Aurelius,[27] although I had already been told about his case by people whose word I could take without hesitation.

We have in our neighbourhood an ex-tribune named Hesperius. He has a small estate called Zubedi, in the district of Fussala. He discovered, from the harm inflicted on his livestock and his servants, that his house was suffering the destructive attacks of malignant spirits; and in my absence he begged my presbyters that one of them should go to his place to overcome the demons by prayer. One of them went, and offered there the sacrifice of Christ, praying with all his might that this molestation should cease. God straightway took pity, and the trouble came to an end. Now Hesperius had received from a friend a sample of sacred earth taken from Jerusalem, where Christ was buried and rose again on the third day. He had hung it up in his bedroom, to ward off any evil from his own person. But when his house had been purified from this infestation he wondered what should be done with the earth, since, from motives of reverence, he did not want to keep it in his bedroom any longer. Now, as it happened, I was in the neighbourhood, with a colleague of mine, Maximinus, bishop of the church at Sinitis. Hesperius asked us to come to his house; and we went. He told us the whole story; and then he begged us to have the sacred earth buried somewhere, and a place of prayer established on the spot, so that Christians might assemble there to celebrate the worship of God. We had no objection, and the proposal was put into effect. Now there was in that place a young rustic suffering from paralysis. When he heard what had happened he begged his parents to carry him to that sacred spot, and be quick about it. He was carried there; he prayed; and he left the place cured, on his own legs.

26. A town near Carthage; Cyprian lived there in exile.

27. St Aurelius, Bishop of Carthage, *c.* 391–*c.* 430. Four of St Augustine's surviving letters were written to him. He presided over a number of councils.

There is a house called Victoriana, less than thirty miles from Hippo Regius. In that house there is a relic of Protasius and Gervasius, the martyrs of Milan. To this place was brought a youth who had come into contact with a demon when he was washing a horse in the river at the height of summer. When he lay there at Victoriana, at the point of death, and indeed looking very like a corpse, the lady of the house came in with her maidservants, accompanied by some other devout souls, for the customary evening hymns and prayers; and they began to sing a hymn. The youth was shaken out of his coma by their voices, as if by a sudden shock; and with a terrifying roar he seized hold of the altar, clutching it as if tied to it or stuck to it, not daring to move, or else without the power of movement. Then with a mighty shriek the demon begged for mercy, and confessed when and where and how it made its way into the young man. Finally it declared that it would depart from him, and named the various limbs and parts which, so it threatened, it would maim as it left them; and while saying this, it withdrew from the man. But one of his eyes slipped down to his jaw, hanging by a small vein from the socket, as from its root, and the whole centre of the eye, which had been dark, became white. Now there were many people present, for others had run up to the place, summoned by his cries, and had prostrated themselves in prayer for him; and when they saw this sight, although they rejoiced to see him standing there in his right mind, they grieved for the loss of his eye, and advised that a doctor should be sent for. Then his brother-in-law, who had brought him there, said, 'God, who put the demon to flight, has power to restore his eye, at the prayers of the saints.' He then replaced, as best he could, the eye which had slipped out and was dangling there; he bound it with a napkin, and said that he thought that the bandage should not be untied until a week's time. Those instructions were followed, and the eye was found to be completely healed. There were many other cures at this place, which it would take too long to describe.

I know of a virgin at Hippo who was quickly cured of demon-possession after anointing herself with oil in which were mixed the tears of a presbyter, shed while he was praying for her. I also know of a bishop who prayed once for a young man whom he had never seen, and the young man was immediately dispossessed of a demon. There was an old man here in Hippo called Florentius, a poor, devout person, who made his living by tailoring. He lost his cloak and had no money to buy another; and so he went to the shrine of the Twenty Martyrs, whose memory is cherished in our part of the world, and prayed in a loud voice that he might get some clothing. His prayer was heard by some young men who happened to be there; they laughed at him, and when he went away they followed him, teasing him by pretending that he had asked the martyrs for fifty pennies, to buy some clothes. He was walking on without a word when he saw a fish, just cast up by the sea, panting on the shore. With the encouragement and support of the bystanders he picked it up, and took it to a delicatessen store kept by a cook called Cattosus, a good Christian, to whom he sold the fish for three hundred pence, after telling him what had happened. He planned to buy some wool with the money, so that his wife could do her best to produce the material for a garment. But when Cattosus was cutting up the fish he found a gold ring in its stomach, and his feeling of sympathy and his fear of a bad conscience compelled him to hand the ring over to Florentius, saying as he did so, 'Look at this! That's how the Twenty Martyrs have given you clothes!'

When the relics of the glorious martyr Stephen arrived at Aquae Tibilitanae, brought by Bishop Praejectus, there was an immense gathering of people who flocked to the place. Among them was a blind woman, who begged to be led to the bishop as he carried the relics. The bishop gave her some flowers which he was carrying; she took them, put them to her eyes – and immediately her sight was restored. To the amazement of the bystanders she went on ahead, overjoyed, finding her own way and no longer needing a guide. The relics of this martyr were deposited in the castle of Siniti, near the colony of Hippo; and they were carried by Lucullus, bishop of that place, with the people going in front and following him. Now the bishop had been troubled for a long time with a fistula, and he was waiting for an operation by his medical attendant, a close friend of his. But it was suddenly healed by the carrying of that sacred burden; in fact no trace of the trouble could be found in him afterwards.

Eucharius is a presbyter from Spain, living at Calama. He had been suffering from the stone for a long time; but he was cured by the relics of the same martyr, which were brought to him by Bishop Possidius. Later on he was stricken with another disease; the illness grew worse; he was laid out for dead, and his thumbs were already tied together. But the presbyter's tunic was sent to the martyr's shrine; it was brought back and put on his body as he lay there; and by the aid of the martyr the presbyter revived.

In the same place lived a man of high rank in his order, named Martialis. He was by now advanced in years and showed great hostility to the Christian religion. He had, for all that, a daughter who was a believer, and a son-in-law who had been baptized that year. When Martialis fell ill, his daughter and her husband besought him with many tears to become a Christian; but he flatly refused and sent them away in a fury of indignation. His son-in-law then decided to go to the shrine of St Stephen and to pray there with all his might for Martialis that God would bring him to a better frame of mind, so that he should not put off believing in Christ. He carried out his resolve with tumultuous groans and tears, with ardent devotion and sincere affection. On his departure he took some of the flowers from the altar, those nearest to hand, and after nightfall he put them at the head of the sick man. Then they all went to sleep. And what should happen but that before daylight Martialis called out for someone to run to fetch the bishop! Now the bishop happened at the time to be staying with me at Hippo. And so, when Martialis learnt that the bishop was away, he asked the presbyters to come. They came; he said that he believed, and he was baptized, to the general amazement and delight. For as long as he lived after that these words were always on his lips, 'Christ, receive my spirit', although he did not know that those were the last words of the blessed Stephen, when he was stoned to death by the Jews. Those were also the last words of Martialis; for he died not long after this. The same martyr was responsible for the cure at that place of two citizens and one stranger, all suffering from the gout. The citizens were well aware of the course to take when they were in pain; but the stranger learnt of it by revelation; and when he had followed that course, his pain was immediately relieved.

Andurus is the name of an estate where there is a church containing a shrine of the martyr Stephen. A little boy was playing there in the square when the oxen drawing a cart got out of control; the child was crushed by a wheel and lay there convulsed, at the point of death. His mother snatched him up and placed him in the shrine, and he not only revived but showed no sign of injury.

There was a holy woman living on a neighbouring manor which is called Caspaliana. She was seriously ill, and when her life was despaired of, her robe was taken to the shrine at Andurus; but before it came back, she was dead. However, her parents covered the corpse with the garment; she breathed again, and was restored to life and health.

At Hippo, a Syrian called Bassus was praying at the shrine of this martyr for his daughter, who was dangerously ill; and he had brought with him one of her garments. Then some boys come running to bring him the news that she was dead. But since he was at prayer his friends intercepted the boys, and stopped them from telling him, for fear that he would begin wailing in the streets. When he arrived back at his house he found it resounding with the lamentations of his household; but he had brought with him his daughter's garment; he laid it on her, and she was restored to life.

Again, in the same city of ours, the son of a banker, Irenaeus, fell ill and died. His lifeless body was laid out, and preparations for burial were in train amid wailing and lamentation, when one of the friends who were offering words of consolation put in the suggestion that the body should be anointed with St Stephen's oil. This was done, and the boy revived. Then there was an ex-tribune in our city called Eleusinus whose little son sickened and passed away. His father took the little body and laid it on the shrine of the martyrs which is in his suburb; he poured out his prayers there, accompanied by many tears; then he lifted up the boy, and found him alive.

Now what am I to do? I am constrained by my promise to complete this work, a promise which must be fulfilled; and that means that I cannot relate all the stories of miracles that I know. But I have no doubt that many of my Christian friends, on reading what I have written, will be grieved that I have omitted so much that is quite as familiar to them as to me. I must here and now ask them to forgive me, and to consider what a lengthy and laborious task it would be to give a complete account; and, after all, it is something which the purpose of this work does not oblige me to attempt. In fact, if I decided to record merely the miracles of healing, to say nothing of other marvels, which were performed at Calama and at Hippo through this martyr, the glorious St Stephen, the record would fill many books; and even then it would not be a complete collection, but would contain only those described in the documents issued for reading in public. I have been concerned that such accounts should be published because I saw that signs of divine power like those of older days were frequently occurring in modern times too, and I felt that they should not pass into oblivion, unnoticed by the people in general. It is not yet two years since the shrine we have been speaking of was established at Hippo and, to my certain knowledge, many miracles have occurred there which are not recorded in the published documents; and nearly seventy of these documents have been produced, at the time of writing. The shrine at Calama is of more ancient foundation, and the records are issued more frequently, so that they far outnumber those of Hippo.

Uzalis is a colony near Utica; and we have learnt of many miracles performed there through the same martyr, whose shrine was established by Bishop Evodius a long time before ours at Hippo. But it is not the custom there to publish pamphlets about them; or rather it was not the custom, for it may be that they have started to do so. For there was a lady of high rank, named Petronilla, who at this shrine had been miraculously cured of a serious and chronic illness which had defied all medical treatment; and when I was there I strongly urged her, with the consent of the bishop above mentioned, to have the story published for reading to the people; and she complied with ready obedience. There was one passage in her tale which I cannot refrain from mentioning here, although I am compelled to hurry on to matters of urgent importance for this work.

She says that she was persuaded by a Jew to thread a ring in a girdle of hair and wear this girdle next to her skin, under all her clothes; this ring had, under its jewel, a stone found in the kidneys of an ox. She had this alleged remedy tied round her when she started for the martyr's shrine; and after leaving Carthage she had stopped at a house of hers by the river Bagrada. Setting out from there to complete her journey she was surprised to see the ring lying on the ground in front of her feet. She tested the girdle of hair, to which it had been attached, and found it firmly tied, just as it had been, with all its knots completely intact. She therefore supposed that the ring had snapped and jumped off. But when she found that the ring also was completely intact she assumed she had been given, in this amazing occurrence, a kind of pledge of her coming cure; and she untied the girdle and threw it, together with the ring, into the stream. This may not be credible to those who also refuse to believe that the Lord Jesus was born without the loss of his mother's virginity, and that he entered a room to meet his disciples when the doors were shut. But they should investigate this story, and if they find it true, they should believe those other accounts. The lady in question is of high position, of noble birth, nobly married, and she lives in Carthage. The importance of the city, and of the person concerned will not allow the facts to evade detection. Certainly the martyr himself, whose intervention restored the lady to health, believed in the son of a mother who remained a virgin; in one who entered through closed doors to join his disciples; above all (and this is the purpose of all that I am saying) in one who ascended into heaven in the flesh in which he had risen from the dead. And the reason why these great works are performed through this martyr is that he laid down his life for the faith he held.

Thus even at this present time the same God who effected the miracles we read of is at work in the performance of many miracles by what agents he chooses and by what means he chooses for their performance. But these modern miracles are not so widely known; nor have they been pounded into the memory by frequent reading, as gravel is pounded into a path, to make sure that they do not pass out of the mind. At Hippo we have started the practice of reading to the people the accounts of those who receive such blessings. But even where this care is taken those who are present hear the story only once; and many of the people are not present. The result is that after some days those who were there do not keep in their minds what they have heard; and scarcely anyone can be found who is able to tell the story he heard to one whom he knows to have been absent.

There was one miracle performed in our city, no more significant than those I have recounted, but so widely famed that I should imagine no one from Hippo failed to witness it or at least to hear about it, and no one could have forgotten it. There were seven brothers and three sisters from Caesarea in Cappadocia, of respectable standing in their community, whose mother had recently been left destitute by the death of their father. She had been badly treated by her children, and in her bitter indignation had laid a curse on them. As a result, the divine chastisement came upon them, and they were all afflicted with a frightful trembling of the limbs. Being unable to bear the stares of their fellow-citizens, aroused by their distressing appearance, they took to wandering wherever the whim suggested, and in this way they visited almost every part of the Roman world. Two of them came to our part of the world, a brother and sister, Paulus and Palladia; they were known in many other places, and reports of their wretched plight had spread far and wide. They arrived at Hippo about a fortnight before Easter; and they attended church every day, visiting the shrine there of the glorious martyr Stephen, and praying that God would now be appeased and restore them to their former health. There, as wherever they went, they drew the gaze of the whole city. There were a number of people who had seen them elsewhere and knew the cause of their tremors, and they told the story to others whenever they had the chance.

Easter arrived, and on the morning of that very Sunday, when a crowded congregation had already assembled. the young man, as he prayed, was holding on to the grating of the holy shrine containing the martyr's relics. Suddenly he fell flat on his face and lay there as if asleep; and yet he was no longer trembling as he usually did even in his sleep. Those present were astonished; some of them were panic-stricken, others were filled with pity; and when they made as if to lift the man up, some people stopped them and said that they should instead wait and see what happened. Then, suddenly, he got up; he was not trembling. He had been cured, and he was standing there, completely recovered, meeting the stares of the congregation.

Who could then refrain from giving praise to God? The whole church was filled in every corner with shouts of thanksgiving. They ran with the news to where I was sitting, ready for the procession. They came rushing one after another, each one telling me, as if it were fresh news, what I had been told by the one before. I was joyfully offering my private thanks to God when the young man himself came in with many others and bent down at my knees, then straightened himself to receive my kiss. Then we went out to join the congregation. The church was packed, and it rang with the shouts of joy: 'Thanks be to God! God be praised!' The cries came from all sides; not a mouth was silent. I greeted the people; they replied with shouts expressing even greater fervour. At last silence was restored and the appointed lessons from holy Scripture were read.

Then when we reached the place for my sermon I simply said a few words appropriate to the occasion and the joy and happiness of the event; for I thought it better to give them a chance to hear, or rather to ponder in their hearts, what might be called the eloquence of God in a work of divine power. The man had breakfast with us and gave a detailed account of the whole tragic history of himself, his brothers, his sisters, and his mother. And so on the following day after the sermon I promised that an official record of his story would be issued for public reading. This promise was fulfilled three days after Easter Sunday, when I made the brother and sister stand on the steps of the bishop's throne, just below the level from which I addressed the congregation, while the narrative was read.

The whole congregation, men and women alike, fixed their gaze on the pair, the brother standing without any untoward movement, the sister trembling in every limb. Those who had not seen the effect of the divine mercy in him now observed it from seeing his sister. They realized what they had to give thanks for in his case, and what they had to pray for on her behalf. Meanwhile, at the conclusion of the reading, I instructed both of them to withdraw from the sight of the people; and then I had just begun to discuss the whole case in some detail. Then, while I was speaking, what should be heard but the sound of fresh cries of thanksgiving from the martyr's shrine! The people who had been listening to my address turned in that direction and began to flock to the spot.

The explanation was that when the girl had descended from the step where she was standing, she went over to the martyr's shrine to pray. As soon as she touched the grating, she, as her brother had done, fell down as if asleep and got up cured. And so while I was asking what had happened and what had occasioned the joyful uproar, they returned with her into the basilica where I was, bringing her back from the martyr's shrine in perfect health.

Then indeed there arose such a clamour of wonder, such a continuous shouting, mingled with tears, that it seemed impossible that it should ever end. The girl was brought back to the place where just now she had stood trembling. Those who had grieved that she had remained so different from her brother now rejoiced to see her so like him. They perceived that they had not yet poured out their prayers for her, and yet already their first intention of goodwill for her had been so quickly answered. They rejoiced in the praises of God with wordless cries, with such a noise that my ears could scarcely endure it. Now was there anything in their hearts as they rejoiced except the same faith in Christ for which Stephen shed his blood?

9. *The miracles performed by the martyrs in Christ's name bear witness to their faith in Christ*

What do these miracles attest but the faith which proclaims that Christ rose in the flesh and ascended into heaven with the flesh? For the martyrs were all martyrs, that is witnesses, to this faith. It was in bearing witness to this faith that the martyrs endured the bitter enmity and the savage cruelty of the world; and they overcame the world not by resisting but by dying. For this faith they died; and they can now obtain these blessings from the Lord, for whose name they were slain. For this faith their wonderful endurance went before, so that all this power might follow in these wonderful works. Now if the resurrection to eternal life has not already taken place in the person of Christ, or if it is not to come in the future, in accordance with the prophecies of Christ, or in accordance with prophecies given before that by the prophets who announced the coming of Christ, how is it that the martyrs, who were slain for the faith that proclaims this resurrection, have the power to work such marvels? For God may himself perform them by himself, through that wonderful operation of his power whereby, being eternal, he is active in temporal events; or he may effect them through the agency of his servants; and when he effects them by his servants he may do this through the spirits of the martyrs, as he also acts through men who are still in the bodily state; or he may effect all those wonders through the service of the angels, the invisible, immaterial, unchangeable agents of his commands, in which case the acts said to be done by the martyrs are in fact done in answer to their prayers, not through their direct activity. Or it may be that some miracles are effected in these ways, others by different methods which are quite beyond mortal comprehension. Be that as it may, they all testify to the faith in which the resurrection to eternal life is proclaimed.

10. *The superiority of the martyrs over the demons, and the difference between their miracles*

At this point we shall probably be told that the pagan gods have performed some miracles. Well then, it is all to the good, if the pagans are ready to put their gods on the same level as our dead men. Are they going to admit that they have gods who are merely men deified after death, like Hercules, like Romulus, like many others whom they suppose to have been received into the ranks of the gods? For us, however, the martyrs are not gods, because we know one only God, who is the God both of us and of our martyrs. And apart from that, the miracles allegedly performed in the pagan temples are not worthy of comparison with those performed at the shrines of our martyrs. And even if there seems to be any similarity, their gods are outdone by our martyrs, as Pharaoh's magicians were by Moses.[28] Moreover, the pagan marvels were the work of demons, in the arrogance of their foul pride which made them ambitious to be the gods of the pagans, whereas the Christian miracles are the work of martyrs, or rather they are the work of God, with the co-operation of the martyrs or in response to their prayers; and the purpose of those miracles is the advancement of that faith by which we believe, not that the martyrs are our gods, but that we and they have the same God. It comes to this: the pagans have built temples for their gods, they have set up altars, established priesthoods and offered sacrifices, whereas we Christians construct, in honour of our martyrs, not temples, as if to gods, but memorial shrines, as to men who are dead, but whose spirits are living with God. We do not in those shrines raise altars on which to sacrifice to the martyrs, but to the one God, who is the martyrs' God and ours; and at this sacrifice the martyrs are *named*, in their own place and in the appointed order, as men of God who have overcome the world in

28. cf. Exod. 8.

the confession of his name. They are not *invoked* by the priest who offers the sacrifice. For, of course, he is offering the sacrifice to God, not to the martyrs (although he offers it at their shrine) because he is God's priest, not theirs. Indeed, the sacrifice itself is the Body of Christ, which is not offered to them, because they themselves are that Body.

This being so, which of these are more credible, as workers of miracles? Those whose desire it is to be reckoned gods by those for whom they perform these works? Or those who do something that excites wonder, in order to promote belief in God, which is what Christ also is? Those who have chosen that their ceremonies shall be acts of disgrace?[29] Or those who do not choose that ceremonies in their honour should sing their praises but that the whole act, in which they are truly praised, should advance the glory of him in whom they are praised? For, to be sure, it is in the Lord that their souls are praised.[30] Let us then believe in those latter, since they speak the truth, as well as performing wonders. In fact, it was for speaking the truth that they suffered; and because of this they have the power to perform miracles. And among all the truths they speak this is the most important: that Christ rose from the dead and first displayed the immortality of the resurrection in his own body, and promised that it would come to us at the beginning of the new age or (which is the same) at the end of this world.

11. *An answer to the Platonists' contention that an earthly body cannot exist in heaven*

Now those rational thinkers ('whose thoughts God knows to be foolishness'[31]) argue against this great gift of God, the resurrection of the body; and they base their argument on the weights of the elements. They have learnt, to be sure, from their master, Plato, that the two greatest bodies of the universe, at the opposite extremes of the universe, are linked and connected by two intermediary elements, air and water.[32] Then, they say, starting from this earth at the bottom and working upwards, the next element is the water, above that the air, and above that, finally, the sky; and it therefore follows that an earthly body cannot exist in heaven; for each element is balanced by its own weight, so that each keeps to its own place. Here you see the

29. cf. Bk II, 8. 30. cf. Ps. 34, 3 (LXX).
31. Ps. 94, 11. 32. Plat. *Tim.*, 32A.

kind of arguments that human weakness, swayed by folly, opposes to the divine omnipotence. How is it that there are so many earthly bodies in the air, although air is the third element from earth? God has given to the birds, with their earthly bodies, the ability to be borne aloft in the air because of the lightness of their feathers and wings; are we to suppose that he will not be able to give to the bodies of men, now made immortal, the quality which will enable them to live even in the highest heaven? On the Platonists' argument the earthly animals which are unable to fly – a category which includes human beings – ought to live under the earth, just as the fishes, the water animals, live under the water. How is it then that an earthly animal lives his life not just as one remove from earth, that is, in water, but in the third element, the air? Why is it that although he belongs to the earth, he is immediately choked if he is forced to try to sustain life in the next element above the earth and yet he succeeds in living in the third? Are the elements out of order here? Or is the fault not in the natural world but in the arguments of the Platonists? I forbear quoting the point I have already made in the thirteenth book,[33] about the many heavy earthly substances, lead for example, which may be given a form by a craftsman to enable them to float in water. Are we, I asked there, to deny the Almighty Artist the power to give the human body a quality which will enable it to be borne up to heaven and to exist there?

This much is certain: if the Platonists think over what I said in that former passage, they cannot find any answer to it, in terms of that 'order of the elements', about which they are so confident. For even if, in the ascending scale, earth is first, water second, air third, heaven fourth, still, the substance of the soul is above them all. Aristotle calls it 'the fifth material substance',[34] whereas Plato calls it immaterial. If it were the fifth it would certainly be above the others; but if it is immaterial it is much more superior to all material things. Then what is it doing in an earthly body? It is the most rarefied of substances; what is it doing in this gross mass? It is the lightest; what is it doing in this heavy weight? It is the swiftest; how does it consort with this sluggishness? Must we suppose that it has not the power to ensure, in virtue of its extraordinary quality of nature, that the body belonging to it shall be raised up to heaven? In our present state the natural substance of earthly bodies is able to keep the soul on the earthly level;

33. Bk XIII, 18.

34. cf. Cic., *Tusc Disp.* 1, 27, 65: 'A kind of fifth nature'; Arist., *De An.* 2, 2, 414A: 'The soul is not a body; but it belongs to a body and exists in a body.'

will not the soul eventually have the power to raise the earthly body to a higher realm?

And now if we turn to examine the miracles of paganism, the achievements of their gods which they oppose to those of our martyrs, we shall find that those achievements support our side, and supply us with invaluable assistance. In fact, among their greater miracles is the one recorded by Varro concerning a Vestal Virgin who had come under suspicion of unchastity and was in danger of her life. The story goes that she filled a sieve with water from the Tiber, and carried it to her judges without spilling a drop. Now who was it that kept that weight of water in the sieve? Who was it who prevented the water from pouring out on to the ground from all those gaping holes? The reply will be, 'Some god, or some demon.' If a god, are we to think him a greater deity than the God who made the world? If a demon, is he to be supposed more powerful than an angel, the servant of the God who made the world? If then a lesser god, or angel or demon had the power to suspend a weight of the liquid element in such a way that the natural properties of water appeared to be changed, is it conceivable that Almighty God, the creator of all the elements, will not have the power to annul the heavy weight of an earthly body, to enable the revived body to live in the same element in which God has chosen that the reviving spirit should dwell?

Moreover, these philosophers make air the middle element, with water below and fire above it. How is it then that we often find it between water and water, and between water and earth? What do they make of watery clouds, and the fact that the intermediate air is found between those clouds and the sea? Assuming this classification of elements by weight, how is it that violent torrents, filled with water, which flow on earth under the lower air, begin by being suspended in the clouds above the lower air? Above all, how is it that the air is intermediate between the height of heaven and the dry expanses of earth, wherever the world stretches, if its appointed place is between sky and water, just as water is stationed between air and earth?

Finally, granted this established order of the elements, expounded by Plato, in which the two extremes, fire and earth, are connected by two intermediaries, air and water, with fire located in the sky, while earth is at the bottom as a kind of foundation for the world, and therefore earth cannot be in the sky; granted this, how is it that fire itself can exist on the earth? According to this scheme, to be sure, these two elements, earth and fire, ought to be in their proper places, the lowest level and the highest; and then, if they refuse to allow a place in the highest sphere for the element which belongs to the lowest level, then equally the highest element can have no place in the lowliest region. The Platonists suppose that not a particle of earth can exist in heaven, now or at any future time; by the same token we ought not to see any particle of fire on earth. But in fact there is fire not only on earth but inside the earth, so much so that the tops of mountains belch out fire. And, apart from this, we see that fire exists on earth for the uses of mankind; and we observe that it is derived from the earth, since it is produced from timber and from stones, which are, beyond dispute, earthly material substances. Ah, but that elemental fire (they object) is calm, pure, harmless, everlasting; this fire of ours is turbulent, smoky, at once destructive and destructible. And yet it does not destroy the mountains in which it blazes continually, nor the hollows in the earth. But let us agree that our fire is different from that pure element, and is adapted for an existence on earth; then why will they not let us believe that the natural substance of earthly bodies may eventually be made indestructible and thus will be adapted for heaven, just as fire is made destructible and adapted for this earth of ours?

The conclusion is that the Platonist's arguments for the classification of the elements by weight cannot set limits on the power of Almighty God so that he cannot make our bodies capable even of a dwelling in the heavens.

12. *A reply to the calumnies with which unbelievers pour scorn on the Christian belief in resurrection*

It is the habit of the pagans to subject our belief in a bodily resurrection to a scrupulous examination and to ridicule it with such questions as, 'What about abortions? Will they rise again?' and (seeing that the Lord says, 'Make no mistake, not one hair on your head will perish'[35]) they ask, 'Will all bodies be the same height and size? Or will there be different shapes and sizes? And if they are all the same, what about abortive births? If they rise again, how will they have the bulk they never had in this world? If abortions do not rise, because they were not born, but slipped, then the same question is transferred to little children. 'How can they attain the size which they have not reached when they die at that early age?' Now we are not going to say that those infants will not rise again; for they are capable not only of being born, but also of being reborn. The unbelievers then ask, 'What

35. Luke 21, 18.

will be the exact height and size of the resurrected body?' And if all men are destined to be as tall and as big as the largest and tallest men that ever were on earth, then, they ask, not only in respect of infants, but about the majority of mankind, 'How are they to have added to them what they lacked here, if each one receives precisely what he possessed here?' On the other hand if we take the words of the Apostle, that we shall all attain 'to the stature of the full maturity of Christ',[36] and his other statement about being 'predestined to be shaped into the likeness of his Son';[37] and if we are to take this to mean that all human beings who will be in his kingdom will have bodies of the same size and shape as Christ's body, then, say the pagans, 'many people will need a reduction in size and height of body; and then what happens to that promise that "not a hair will perish", if such a great amount of the actual body is to be removed?' And indeed, in this matter of hair, one might ask whether all that the barber has cut off is to be restored! And if so, the ugliness of the sight would be enough to horrify anyone! And what of the fingernails? It seems to follow of necessity that all that has been removed in manicure must be replaced! And then what happens to the body's comeliness, which ought surely to be greater, in that immortal condition, than it could be in the state of decay? And yet, if all this is not restored, it follows that it will perish; and then, they say, what about that assurance that 'not a hair will perish'? They produce similar arguments about fatness and thinness. If all are to be equal then obviously there will not be some thin ones and some fat ones. Then some will need an addition, others a subtraction; and in that case there will not be a restoration of the former body as it was. Sometimes it will receive what was not there before; sometimes it will lose what it formerly possessed.

Our opponents then pass on to the actual decay and dissolution of bodies. Some in part are turned into dust, and in part evaporate into the air; some people are consumed by wild beasts, others by fire; others again perish by shipwreck or meet some other watery end, and their flesh decays and dissolves. These considerations influence these thinkers in no small degree, and they cannot believe that all such bodies can be collected and restored to their integrity. They then make play with deformities and defects, either accidental or congenital; they talk with a mixture of horror and derision about monstrous births, asking what kind of resurrection is in store for such unpleasantness. If we reply that nothing of this kind will reappear in the resurrected body, then flatter themselves that they will rebut our answer by quoting the

36. Eph. 4, 13. 37. Rom. 8, 29.

marks of the wounds, since we give it out that Christ rose from the dead with those marks on his body. But among all those posers the most difficult question they confront us with is this: 'When someone's body has been eaten by another man, who turns to cannibalism on the compulsion of hunger, into whose body will it return?' For it has been converted into the flesh of the man who has been nourished by such food, and it has supplied the losses which the emaciation of hunger had produced. Is it then to be returned to the man whose body it had been originally? Or to the man whose flesh it became? The reason for their inquiry is to throw scorn on the belief in the resurrection; and what they themselves offer to the human soul is either the promise of an alternation of genuine unhappiness and false felicity – the prospect offered by Plato – or, with Porphyry, the assurance of an eventual end to misery, with no return to that state, after passing through repeated changes of body;[38] but this end does not come with the possession of an immortal body, but by the escape from any kind of body.

13. *The problem of abortive births*

To all these points, apparently contradictory to my position, which the opposing party has deployed against me, I shall reply, if God in his mercy supports my efforts. As for abortions, which have been alive in the mother's womb but have died there, I cannot bring myself either to affirm or deny that they will share in the resurrection. And yet, if they are not excluded from the number of the dead, I cannot see how they can be excluded from the resurrection of the dead. For either it is not all the dead that will rise again, and there will be some souls eternally without bodies, although they had human bodies, even if only in the mother's womb, or else all human souls will receive again the bodies which they had, when those bodies rise again, wherever the bodies they left lived and died. And in the latter case I do not see how I can say that all those who died in the mother's womb have no share in the resurrection of the dead. But whichever of these views be held, what I am now going to say about newly born infants is to be taken as applying also to abortions, if they take part in the resurrection.

14. *The question whether infants at the resurrection will have the body they would have had at maturity*

As for little children, I can only say that they will not rise again

38. cf. Plat., *Rp.*, 619D; *Phaedr.*, 249A: cf. Bk X, 29; 30; Bk XII, 27.

with the tiny bodies they had when they died. By a marvellous and instantaneous act of God they will gain that maturity they would have attained by the slow lapse of time. For we may be sure that in the Lord's statement that 'not a hair of your head will perish' he promises that what was already there would not be lacking; but that does not deny that what was lacking will be supplied. Now the infant at death lacked its perfect bodily development; even a perfect infant, to be sure, has not the perfection of full bodily development – it has not attained the limit of its potential stature.

All human beings possess that limit of perfection, in that they are conceived and born with it. But they have it in potentiality, not in its material realization, in the same way as all parts of the body are already latent in the seed, although a number of them are still lacking even at birth, the teeth, for instance, and other such details. There is thus, it seems, a kind of pattern already imposed potentially on the material substance of the individual, set out, one might say, like the pattern on a loom; and thus what does not yet exist, or rather what is there but hidden, will come into being, or rather will appear, in the course of time. And so in respect of this pattern or potentiality an infant can be said to be short or tall in that he is destined to be the one or the other.

In view of this pattern we evidently have no need to fear any loss of body at the resurrection. Even if there were a destined equality of all bodies, so that all would attain the stature of giants, to ensure that those who were tallest in this life should not have their stature diminished (for such a loss would contravene the promise of Christ that 'not a hair will perish'); even so, as we are well aware, it could not be beyond the resources of the Creator, who made everything from nothing, to make the additions that he, the Supreme Artist, knew to be required.

15. *Will all resurrected bodies attain the stature of the Lord's body?*

However, Christ himself undoubtedly rose again with the same bodily stature as he had when he died; and we are forbidden to suggest that when the time comes for the general resurrection his body will attain a size that it did not have when he appeared to the disciples in the form that was so familiar to them; the idea being that he should equal the height of the tallest of mankind. Now if we insist that all the larger people must have their bodies reduced to the same size as Christ's body, then a great deal will 'perish' from the bodies of many, although Christ has promised that 'not one hair will perish'. It remains, therefore, that each person will be given the stature which he had in his prime, even though he was an old man when he died, or, if he died before maturity, the stature he would have attained. As for the Apostle's statement about 'stature of the full maturity of Christ',[39] this is either to be taken in a different sense, namely that Christ's 'full stature' is reached when, with Christ as the head, all the members of his body come to maturity, represented by the peoples who accept the Christian faith; or else, if the words refer to the bodily resurrection, we must take them to mean that the bodies of the dead will rise neither younger nor older than Christ. They will be of the same age, the same prime of life, which Christ, as we know, had reached. For the most learned authorities of this world define the age of human maturity as being about thirty years; they say that after that period of life a man begins to go downhill towards middle age and senility. And that is why, on this interpretation, the Apostle speaks not of 'the full bodily stature' but 'the stature of the full maturity' of Christ.

16. *The meaning of 'shaped into the likeness of God's Son'*

Now St Paul talks of being 'predestined to be shaped into the likeness of God's son'.[40] This can be taken as referring to the inner man. The Apostle says elsewhere, 'Don't model yourselves on the world's pattern. You have a new outlook; remodel yourselves accordingly.'[41] When we remodel ourselves to avoid being modelled on the world's pattern, then we are shaped into the likeness of God's son. We can also take it in this way: that as Christ was made like us in the condition of mortality, so we will be made like him in the condition of immortality. This obviously has reference to the resurrection of the body. But if these words are meant to instruct us also about the form of the resurrected body, then this likeness to Christ is to be understood (like the 'stature') of the age, not the size of that body.

Thus all human beings will rise again with a body of the same size as they had, or would have had, in the prime of life. And yet, to be sure, it would be no disadvantage even if the form of that body were that of an infant or an old man; for in the resurrection no weakness will remain, either of mind or body. And so, if anyone maintains that every person will rise again with the same kind of body that he had

39. Eph. 4, 13. 40. Rom. 8, 29. 41. Rom. 12. 2.

when he departed this life, we need not go to great lengths to contravert this position.

17. *Will women retain their sex in the resurrected body?*

Because of these sayings, 'Until we reach the perfection of manhood, the stature of the full maturity of Christ',[42] and 'Being shaped into the likeness of God's Son',[43] some people suppose that women will not keep their sex at the resurrection; but, they say, they will all rise again as men, since God made man out of clay, and woman out of man. For my part, I feel that theirs is the more sensible opinion who have no doubt that there will be both sexes in the resurrection. For in that life there will be no sexual lust, which is the cause of shame. For the first human beings, before their sin, 'were naked, the man and the woman, and they were not ashamed'.[44]

Thus while all defects will be removed from those bodies, their essential nature will be preserved. Now a woman's sex is not a defect; it is natural. And in the resurrection it will be free of the necessity of intercourse and childbirth. However, the female organs will not subserve their former use; they will be part of a new beauty, which will not excite the lust of the beholder – there will be no lust in that life – but will arouse the praises of God for his wisdom and compassion, in that he not only created out of nothing but freed from corruption that which he had created.

Now in creating woman at the outset of the human race, by taking a rib from the side of the sleeping man, the Creator must have intended, by this act, a prophecy of Christ and his Church. The sleep of that man clearly stood for the death of Christ; and Christ's side, as he hung lifeless on the cross, was pierced by a lance. And from the wound there flowed blood and water,[45] which we recognize as the sacraments by which the Church is built up. This, in fact, is the precise word used in Scripture of woman's creation; it says not that God 'formed', or 'fashioned' a woman but that 'he built it (the rib) up into a woman'.[46] Hence the Apostle also speaks of the 'building up' of the Body of Christ, which is the Church.[47] The woman, then, is the creation of God, just as is the man; but her creation out of man emphasizes the idea of the unity between them; and in the manner of that creation there is, as I have said, a foreshadowing of Christ and his Church.

42. Eph. 4, 13; Rom. 8, 29. 43. Rom. 8, 29. 44. Gen. 2, 21.
45. John 19, 34. 46. Gen. 2, 22. 47. Eph. 4, 12.

Thus he who established the two sexes will restore them both. And indeed, Jesus was questioned by the Sadducees, who denied the resurrection; and they asked to which of seven brothers a wife would belong, to whom they had all been married (since each of them wished to produce descendants for his dead predecessor, according to the Law's instructions); and Jesus replied, 'You are on the wrong track, because you do not understand the Scriptures, or the power of God.' And though he might have said, 'The woman you are asking about will not be a woman; she will be a man', he did not say this. What he said was, 'For in the resurrected life men and women do not marry; they are like the angels of God in heaven.'[48] That is, they are like them in immortality and felicity, not in body; nor are they like them in their resurrection, since the angels, being unable to die, need no resurrection. Thus Christ denies the existence of marriage in the resurrected life; he does not deny the existence of women in heaven. If he had foreknown that there would be no female sex in that life he could quickly and easily have disposed of the Sadducees' question by saying as much, whereas in fact he expressly stated that there would be both sexes, when he said, 'they are not married', referring to woman, and 'they do not marry wives', referring to men. It follows that there will be in that life those who in this life normally marry, and those who are taken in marriage; but they will not do so in heaven.

18. *Christ, the perfect man; and the Church, his Body and his fulfilment*

To proceed: St Paul speaks about the attainment of perfect manhood by all, and we should notice the whole context of this saying.

The one who descended is the very same as the one who rose up above all the heavens to fill all things. And his gift to some was that they should be apostles; others were to be prophets; others, evangelists; others, pastors and teachers; so that the saints should together make a complete unity in the activity of service, for the building up of the Body of Christ; until we all arrive at unity in the faith and in our knowledge of God's Son, and reach the perfection of manhood, the stature of the perfect maturity of Christ. Then we shall no longer be children, or tossed to and fro and carried off our feet by every passing wind of doctrine, as the playthings of human cleverness in the devising of deception. Instead, we shall practise the truth in love and thus we shall grow up in Christ in every way; and Christ is the head, through whom the whole Body is fitted and joined together, with strength

48. Matt. 22, 29f.

supplied through every joint, while each separate part performs its orderly function. Thus the body develops towards the building up of its complete structure, in love.[49]

Here we see what is meant by the 'perfection of manhood', the union of head and body, which consists of all the members, and they will be completed in due time. Meanwhile the members are being added to this body every day, while the Church is being built up. And this Church is addressed in the words, 'You are the Body of Christ, each of you being a separate part'; and in another place we read, 'on behalf of his Body, that is, the Church';[50] and again, 'We are many; but we are one loaf, one Body.'[51] And about the building up of this Body, St Paul says in the present passage, 'to make a complete unity in the activity of service, for the building up of the Body of Christ',[52] then adding the words which concern us at the moment, 'until we all arrive at unity in the faith and in our knowledge of God's Son, and reach the perfection of manhood, the stature of the perfect maturity of Christ' and so on. Then he explains how we are to understand 'stature' here and the Body to which it refers, when he says, 'Thus we shall grow up in Christ in every way; and Christ is the head through whom the whole Body is fitted and joined together, with strength supplied through every joint, while each separate part performs its orderly function.'

Thus there is a measure, an orderly function, of each separate part, and, correspondingly, a measure, or stature, of the whole body, which consists of all its parts. And this is the 'stature of fulfilment' in the phrase, 'the stature of the perfect maturity of Christ'. This fulfilment, or maturity, is mentioned also in the place where St Paul says of the Church, 'And he (God) has made him (Christ) the supreme head of the Church, which is his Body, the fulfilment of him who reaches complete fulfilment in the whole creation.'[53]

If, however, this passage is to be referred to the form of the resurrected body, what is there to prevent our supposing that the mention of 'man' implies 'woman' also, *vir* being used here for *homo* ('human being')? There is a similar use in the verse, 'Blessed is the man (*vir*) who fears the Lord',[54] which obviously includes the women who fear him.

49. Eph. 4, 10ff. 50. 1 Cor. 12, 27. 51. 1 Cor. 10, 17.
52. Eph. 1, 22f. 53. Eph. 1, 22f. 54. Ps 112, 1.

19. *The perfection of the resurrected body*

Now what reply am I to make about the hair and the nails? If we take it that the promise, 'not a hair will perish', means that there will be no deformity in the body, it follows at once that any constituents which would produce deformity if uncontrolled will go to make up the whole bulk of the body, but they will not be in places where they would disfigure the proportions of the parts. There is an analogy in pottery. If clay is used to make a pot, and then the material is brought back to the original lump to make a completely fresh start, it is not essential that the piece of clay which formed the handle should make the handle in the second attempt; and the same with the bottom of the pot, and so on. All that is required is that the whole pot should be re-made out of the whole lump, that is, that all the clay should go back into the whole pot, with nothing left over.

Now the hair has been cut, and the nails have been pared, again and again. And if the restoration of what has been cut would disfigure the body, then it will not be restored. But that does not mean that anything will 'perish' from the person at the resurrection. Such constituents will be returned to the same body, to take their place in its structure, undergoing a change of substance to make them suitable for the parts in which they are used. And yet, in fact, when the Lord said, 'Not one hair of your head will perish',[55] he can be understood to refer to the number of hairs, not to length of the hair. This more plausible interpretation is supported by the statement elsewhere that 'all the hairs of your head are numbered.'[56] What I mean by saying this is not that I think that anything will perish which is present in any body as belonging to the essential nature of that body; but that anything in that nature that is deformed – and, of course, the sole purpose of the deformity is to give yet another proof of the penal condition of mortals in this life – anything of this kind will be restored in such a way as to remove the deformity while preserving the substance intact. An artist who has for some reason produced an ugly statue can recast it and make it beautiful, removing the ugliness without any loss of the material substance. And if there was any displeasing excess in some parts of the first figure, anything out of proportion to the rest, he does not have to cut it off or throw away any part of the whole; he can simply moisten the whole of the material and remix it, without producing any ugliness or diminishing the quantity of material. If a human artist can do this, what are we to think of

55. Luke 21, 18. 56. Luke 12, 7.

the Almighty Artist? Can he not remove all the deformities of the human body, not only the familiar ones but also the rare and the monstrous, such as are in keeping with the miseries of this life, but are utterly incongruous with the future felicity of the saints? Can he not get rid of them, just as the unpleasant products of the waste matter of the body, ugly though natural, are removed without any loss of substance in the body?

This means that fat people and thin people have no need to fear that at the resurrection they will be the kind of people they would not have chosen to be in this life, if they had had the chance. For all physical beauty depends on a harmony between the parts of the body, combined with an attractive complexion. When there is not this harmony and proportion the appearance is displeasing, either because of distortion, or because of some excess or deficiency. Thus there will be no ugliness, which is caused by such disharmony, when distortions have been corrected and unpleasing deficiencies supplied from resources known to the Creator, and unprepossessing excesses reduced without loss of essential substance. Moreover, imagine the beauty of the complexion, when 'the righteous will shine like the sun in their Father's kingdom'.[57] In the Body of Christ, after his resurrection, this splendour, we must believe, was hidden from the eyes of the disciples; it was not lacking in that body, but the weak eyes of human beings could not have borne to look upon it, and at that time it was essential that his disciples should direct their gaze on him, so that they might recognize him. That was the purpose of his showing the scars of his wounds for them to touch, and of his taking food and drink; it was not that he needed nourishment but that he had the power to take it. Now it sometimes happens that something which is present is still not seen by people who see other things that are there, as that lustre of Christ's Body was there, as I said, but unseen by those who saw other details of the scene. This condition is called in Greek *aorâsia* ('sightlessness') which in the book of Genesis is represented in our translation by *caecitas*, ('blindness') since the translators could not find an adequate Latin equivalent. This is what happened to the men of Sodom, when they were looking for the door of the righteous Lot, and failed to find it.[58] If their condition had been true blindness, preventing them from seeing anything, they would have looked for guides to lead them back home, not for a door to give them entrance to a house.

Now we feel such extraordinary affection for the blessed martyrs that

57. Matt. 13, 43. 58. Gen. 19, 11.

in the kingdom of God we want to see on their bodies the scars of the wounds which they suffered for Christ's name; and see them perhaps we shall. For in those wounds there will be no deformity, but only dignity, and the beauty of their valour will shine out, a beauty *in* the body and yet not *of* the body. And if the martyrs have had any limbs cut off, any parts removed, they will not lack those parts at the resurrection; for they have been told that 'not a hair of your head will perish.' But if it will be right that in that new age the marks of glorious wounds should remain in those immortal bodies, for all to see, then scars of the blows or the cuts will also be visible in places where limbs were hacked off, although the parts have not been lost, but restored. And so the defects which have thus been caused in the body will no longer be there, in that new life; and yet, to be sure, those proofs of valour are not to be accounted defects, or to be called by that name.

20. *The restoration of the whole body at the resurrection, no matter how its parts have been dispersed*

As for bodies that have been consumed by wild beasts, or by fire, or those parts that have disintegrated into dust and ashes, or those parts that have dissolved into moisture, or have evaporated into the air, it is unthinkable that the Creator should lack the power to revive them all and restore them to life. It is inconceivable that any nook or cranny of the natural world, though it may hold those bodies concealed from our detection, could elude the notice or evade the power of the Creator of all things. Cicero, the great pagan author, attempted to define God, as well as he could; and this is what he says: 'A kind of Mind, free and unconstrained, remote from any materiality and mortality, conscious of all things, and moving all things, endowed with everlasting movement.'[59] This is what Cicero found in the teaching of the great philosophers. And so, to speak in their terms, what can be hidden from one who knows everything? What can escape irrevocably from the power of one who moves the universe?

And now we must offer a solution to the problem that seems the most difficult of all, the question to whom a body will be restored at the resurrection when it has become part of the body of another living man. Suppose that someone under compulsion of the last straits of starvation eats human corpses. This terrible thing has happened. as we know from the testimony of ancient history and even from the

59. Cic., *Tusc. Disp.*, 1, 27, 66.

unhappy experiences of our own times.[60] Now surely no one is going to maintain, with any show of truth or reason, that the whole of a body so eaten passes straight through the intestinal tract without any change or conversion into flesh of the eater? The former emaciation of the eater and its subsequent disappearance are sufficient indication that physical deficiencies are supplied by such nutriment. But what I have just said by way of premise should be enough to untie this knot.

Any flesh that starvation stripped from the hungry man evidently exhaled into the air, and the Creator, as I said, has power to bring it back from the air. And so that other flesh will be restored to the man in whom it first began to be human flesh. We must reckon the other man to have borrowed it; and like borrowed money, it has to be given back to the place from which it was taken. And this man's flesh, which starvation had stripped from him, will be restored to him by the one who can bring back even what has been exhaled into the air. Indeed, even if that flesh had completely disappeared, and none of its material had remained in any cranny of the natural world, the Almighty would reproduce it from what source he chose. But seeing that the Truth stated that 'not a hair of your head will perish', it would be absurd of us to imagine that so much flesh could disappear completely when it has been eaten away and destroyed by starvation, whereas a man's hair cannot so disappear.

When all these arguments have been examined and weighed to the best of our ability, we reach this conclusion: that in the resurrection of the body for eternal life the body will have the size and dimensions which it had attained, or was to attain, at maturity, according to the design implanted in the body of each person, with its appropriate beauty preserved also in the proportions of all the parts. If, in order to preserve this beauty, something has been taken from a part displeasing by excessive size, and if this is dispersed throughout the whole body, in such a way that this material is not lost, while the congruence of the parts is kept, then there is no absurdity in believing that there may be some addition to the stature of the body as a result of this, provided that the material is so distributed in all parts as to preserve the beauty of the whole, which would be spoilt if it were concentrated disproportionately in one place.

On the other hand, if it is maintained that every person is to rise again with the precise stature he had when he departed this life, there is no occasion for violent opposition to such an opinion, provided only

60. During Alaric's siege of Rome, A.D. 409–10; cf. Hier., *Ep.*, 127, 12.

that all ugliness must disappear, all weakness, all sluggishness, all corruption, and anything else that is inconsistent with that kingdom in which the sons of the resurrection and of the promise[61] will be equal to the angels of God, in felicity if not in body or in age.

21. *The new and spiritual body of the saints*

Thus all that has perished from the living body, or from the corpse after death, will be restored. And with it will arise all that remains in the grave, changed from the old animal body into a new spiritual body, clothed in incorruptibility and immortality. Even if because of some serious accident, or through the savagery of the enemy, it has been ground utterly into dust and scattered, as far as may be, to the winds or in the waters, so that it has ceased to be an entity in any particular place, even so it cannot possibly be withdrawn from the power of the Almighty Creator, and 'not a hair of its head will perish.' The spiritual flesh will thus be subject to the spirit, but it will be flesh, not spirit, just as the carnal spirit was subject to the flesh, and yet was spirit, not flesh.

We have some experience of this situation in the distorted condition of our state of punishment. For Paul was speaking to people who were carnal in respect of the spirit, not merely in respect of the flesh, when he said, 'I could not speak to you as spiritual people; I had to treat you as carnal.'[62] Man in this life is called spiritual, though still remaining carnal, and though he is still aware of 'another law in his body, battling against the law of his reason'.[63] But he will be spiritual even in body, when the same flesh rises again and the words of Scripture are fulfilled, in that what 'is sown as an animal body is raised as a spiritual body'.[64] But what will be the grace of that spiritual body, and the extent of that grace, is something of which we have had as yet no experience; and I am afraid that it would be rash to offer any description of it.

And yet we cannot keep silent about the joy of our hope, because of the praise due to God; and it was from the bottom of a heart on fire with holy love that these words came: 'Lord, I have loved the beauty of your house.'[65] And so, with God's help, we may do our best to conjecture from the blessings which God showers on good and bad alike in this life of trouble, how great will be the joy which of course we cannot adequately describe, because it is beyond our present experi-

61. Luke 20, 37; Gal. 4, 28. 62. 1 Cor. 3, 1. 63. Rom. 7, 23.
64. 1 Cor. 15, 44. 65. Ps. 26, 8.

ence. For I pass over the joy of man's first-created innocence, the blessed life of that pair in the fertility of paradise, because this was so short; it did not last long enough to be felt by their children. But who can fully describe all the evidence of God's goodness towards mankind, even in this life that we know, in which we now are, in which we suffer temptations, or rather a life which is a continual temptation,[66] however far we may advance in goodness, all the time that we are in it?

22. *The miseries to which the first sins has exposed mankind, relief from which comes only through Christ's grace*

As for that first origin of mankind, this present life of ours (if a state full of so much grievous misery can be called a life) is evidence that all the mortal descendants of the first man came under condemnation. Such is the clear evidence of that terrifying abyss of ignorance, as it may be called, which is the source of all error, in whose gloomy depths all the sons of Adam are engulfed, so that man cannot be rescued from it without toil, sorrow and fear. What else is the message of all the evils of humanity? The love of futile and harmful satisfactions, with its results: carking anxieties, agitations of mind, disappointments, fears, frenzied joys, quarrels, disputes, wars, treacheries, hatreds, enmities, deceits, flattery, fraud, theft, rapine, perfidy, pride, ambition, envy, murder, parricide, cruelty, savagery, villainy, lust, promiscuity, indecency, unchastity, fornication, adultery, incest, unnatural vice in men and women (disgusting acts too filthy to be named), sacrilege, collusion, false witness, unjust judgement, violence, robbery, and all other such evils which do not immediately come to mind, although they never cease to beset this life of man – all these evils belong to man in his wickedness, and they all spring from that root of error and perverted affection which every son of Adam brings with him at his birth. For who is not aware of the vast ignorance of the truth (which is abundantly seen in infancy) and the wealth of futile desires (which begins to be obvious in boyhood) which accompanies a man on his entrance into this world, so that if man were left to live as he chose and act as he pleased he would fall into all, or most, of those crimes and sins which I have mentioned – and others which I was not able to mention.

But the divine governance does not altogether abandon man in his condemnation, and God does not in his anger restrain his com-

66. cf. Job 7, 1 (LXX); cf. Bk XIX, 8n.

passion[67] and so his prohibitions and instructions keep watch in the feelings of mankind against those dark influences which were in us at birth, and resist their assaults; and yet those commandments bring us plenty of trouble and sorrow. For what is the meaning of the manifold fears which we use on little children to keep their foolishness in order? What is the purpose of the pedagogue, the schoolmaster, the stick, the strap, the birch, and all the means of discipline? By such means, as holy Scripture teaches,[68] the flanks of a beloved child must be beaten, for fear he may grow up untamed, and become so hardened that he is almost, or even completely, beyond discipline. What is the point of these punishments, but to overcome ignorance and to bridle corrupt desire – the evils we bring with us into this world? How is it that what we learn with toil we forget with ease? That it is hard to learn, but easy to be in ignorance? That activity goes against the grain, while indolence is second nature? Is it not clear from this into what a state our spoilt nature sinks readily and promptly, as it were by its own weight? Is it not plain how much help it needs for its reclamation? Sloth, indolence, idleness, indifference – those are the vices which make us shun all toil. For toil, even when profitable for us, is in itself a punishment.

But apart from the punishments of childhood, without which the young cannot learn the lessons their elders wish them to be taught (although what the elders wish is scarcely ever for the child's advantage), there are the pains which trouble all mankind. How many of those there are, and how oppressive, which are not directed to the punishment of the wickedness and lawlessness of evil man, but are part of our common condition of wretchedness! Who can discuss them all in a discourse? Who can grasp them all in his thought? Think of the fears of disaster, and the actual disasters, occasioned by bereavement and mourning, by material losses and by judicial condemnation, by the deceits and lies of men, by false suspicion, by all the violent acts and crimes of others! Men are plundered by their fellowmen and taken captive, they are chained and imprisoned, exiled and tortured, limbs are cut off and organs of sense destroyed, bodies are brutally misused to gratify the obscene lust of the oppressor, and many such horrors are of frequent occurrence. Then there are the fears of the dreaded calamities from non-human sources; and they are past counting: the dread of the extremes of heat and cold; of storm tempest, and flood; of thunder and lightning, hail and thunderbolt; of earthquakes and upheavals; the terror of being crushed by falling

67. Ps. 77, 10. 68. Ecclus. 30, 12.

buildings, of attacks by animals, in panic or in malice; of the bites of wild beasts, which may only be painful, but may sometimes be fatal, as in the rabies which is caught from an infected dog, so that an animal normally tame and affectionate to its master sometimes causes more panic and terror than a lion or poisonous snake, and the effect on anyone who happens to be infected by its bite is to make him the object of greater dread to parents, wife, or children than any wild beast. Think of the perils of seafarers and the perils of travellers by land! Anyone walking anywhere is liable to sudden accidents. A man was returning home from the forum, with nothing wrong with his legs; he fell and broke his leg; the injury cost him his life. One would suppose the sitting posture to be perfectly safe. And yet the priest Eli fell from the chair where he was sitting, and died.[69] Then there are the apprehensions of farmers for their crops (apprehensions, indeed, shared by all men): all the accidents of the weather and the soil, and the dangers from animal pests. They, however, generally feel secure when once their crops are collected and stored. And yet I know of cases where an excellent harvest has been swept out of barns and ruined by a sudden flood, when men have had to take to flight.

Moreover, can anyone have confidence in his innocence for protection against the myriad and multifarious assaults of demons? Indeed, to warn us against such confidence, even little children who have been baptized (and what could be more innocent?) are often troubled by demons so that by God's permission of their sufferings it may be made especially clear to us that this life is a calamity to be deplored, while the other life is the felicity for which we should long. Again, there are the evils that arise from the body, in the shape of diseases; and there are so many of them that all the books of the physicians cannot contain them all. And in many of those, indeed in almost all of them, the treatment and the medicines are themselves instruments of torture, so that patients are rescued from a painful end by a painful cure. Moreover, is it not a fact that excessive heat has brought men to such extremity of thirst that they have drunk human urine, and even their own? Has not famine brought men to such a pitch of hunger that they have not been able to refrain from eating human flesh? And not only the flesh of men found dead but of men killed by them for this purpose, and not only unknown strangers; mothers have even eaten their sons, when the frenzied cravings for food brought them to this incredible cruelty. Again, even sleep, whose other name is rest, is often rendered so restless by visions in dreams,

69. 1 Sam. 4, 18.

disquieted beyond the power of words to describe, disturbed by terrors, horrible albeit insubstantial, presented and, as it were, displayed in sleep so vividly that we are unable to distinguish vision from reality; and thus the soul and all the senses are thrown into confusion. Think also of the delusive visions by which in some diseases and as the result of some drugs the patient is even more pitiably disturbed while awake; indeed, so multifarious is the trickery practised by malignant demons that by such visions they often deceive men in perfect health, so that if they cannot seduce the subjects to their side, they may at least play tricks on them, for the sole delight of imposing false impressions in whatever way they can.

From this life of misery, a kind of hell on earth, there is no liberation save through the grace of Christ our Saviour, our God and our Lord. His name is Jesus; and Jesus, we know, means Saviour. And, above all, it is his grace which will save us from a worse life, or rather death, after this life; and that death will be everlasting. Now it is true that there are many consolations, many alleviations in this life, administered by holy things and by holy men; and yet those boons are not always granted to those who ask, and for this reason: that men should not go to religion for such benefits, since the motive for religion should be rather that other life, which will be completely free of all such ills. And if this grace helps the more deserving amid those miseries, the purpose is that a man's heart should display courage under those afflictions in proportion to its faith. And to this end, according to the learned of this world, philosophy also is of value, the true philosophy, that is, which the gods, says Cicero, have granted only to a few; 'No greater gift', he says, 'has been given, or could have been given by the gods to mankind.'[70] It is noteworthy that even our pagan adversaries are in some fashion compelled to admit their dependence on divine grace for their philosophy, not for philosophy of any kind, but for the true philosophy. Moreover, if true philosophy, the sole defence against the miseries of this life, is divinely given only to a few, it becomes very clear from this that the human race has been condemned to the punishment of those afflictions. But just as this, on the pagan's admission, is the greatest gift of heaven, so we must believe that it is given by no other god but the one God to whom even the worshippers of many gods ascribe a position of pre-eminence.

70. Cic., *Acad. Post.*, 1, 2, 7.

23. *The afflictions peculiar to the righteous*

Apart from the sufferings in this life which are the common lot of good and evil alike, the righteous have some troubles peculiarly their own, in their warfare against evil propensities, and in the temptations and perils in which those battles involve them. For the flesh never ceases to have 'desires which resist the spirit' and vice versa, so that 'we do not do what we would like to do',[71] though this conflict is sometimes fierce, sometimes comparatively slack. We would wish to annihilate all evil desires; but what we have to do is, with divine help, to employ our best efforts in the subjection of those desires to our will by refusing to consent to them; we must be on guard with unfailing vigilance, to make sure that we are not deluded by plausible suggestions, or deceived by clever talk, or immersed in the darkness of error, for fear that we may believe evil to be good, or good evil, that fear may distract us from doing our duty, that 'the sun' may 'set on our anger',[72] that hostility may provoke us into returning evil for evil,[73] that dishonourable or immoderate sadness may overwhelm us, that an unthankful heart make us sluggish in doing acts of kindness, that a clear conscience become wearied by malicious gossip, while our ill-founded suspicion of others leads us astray or others' false suspicion of us breaks our spirits. We must watch against the danger that 'sin may hold sway in our mortal body', to make us obey its cravings, so that we may 'offer our bodies to sin as the instruments of wickedness';[74] that our eyes may be the servants of our desires, that longing for revenge may overcome us, that our vision and our imagination may dwell on wrongful delights, that we may listen with pleasure to shameful and indecent talk, that our liking and not God's Law may govern our actions; that in this conflict, so full of toil and danger, we should expect to win the victory in our own strength, or ascribe a victory, when won, to our own strength, instead of attributing it to the grace of him, who, as the Apostle says, 'gives us the victory through our Lord Jesus Christ; let us thank God for it';[75] as he says, in another place, 'From all these trials we emerge triumphant, through the strength of him who loved us.'[76]

For all that, we must be aware that however valiantly we battle in the fight against evil propensities, and even if we win the battle and subdue the enemy, as long as we are in this body we shall always have reason to say to God, 'Forgive us our debts.'[77] But in that kingdom,

71. Gal. 5, 17. 72. Eph. 4, 26. 73. Rom. 12, 17. 74. Rom. 6, 12f.
75. 1 Cor. 15, 57. 76. Rom. 8, 37. 77. Matt. 6, 12.

where we shall live for ever, with immortal bodies, there will be no battles to be fought, and no debts to be forgiven; nor would there have been in this life, if our nature had kept the innocence in which it was first created. And so we see that this conflict of ours in which we stand in peril, and from which we long to be set free by a final victory, is bound up with the miseries of this life, which we know by experience, by the evidence of all those heavy afflictions, to be a life under condemnation.

24. *The good things of which this life is full, even though it is subject to condemnation*

The wretched condition of humanity in this life is the punishment for sin, and we praise God's justice in that punishment. And yet his goodness has filled even this misery with innumerable blessings of all kinds; and those blessings we must now consider. First there is that blessing conferred on man before his sin, when God said, 'Increase and multiply, and fill the earth.'[78] Even after man's sin God refused to revoke that blessing, and the fruitfulness thus given remained in the race of man, despite the condemnation. The fault of the first sin could not abolish the marvellous power of seed, and the even more wonderful power by which seed produces seed, a power which is inherent and, we might say, interwoven in human bodies; this power remained although through that sin the inevitability of death was imposed upon us. And in that stream, as it were, of propagation run two currents: the evil derived from the first parent, and also the blessing bestowed by the Creator. In the original evil there are two elements, the sin and the punishment; and in the original good two other elements, propagation and conformation (the identity of species). Now I have already said enough, for my present purpose, about the two evils, the sin which arises from our own recklessness, and the punishment, which comes from God's judgement. My intention now is to treat the blessings which God has bestowed, and still bestows, even on the corrupted and condemned state of mankind. For even in condemning him God did not deprive man of all the good he had given; had he done so, man would have simply ceased to exist. Nor did God remove man from his power, even when he made him subject to the Devil by way of punishment; for God has not put even the Devil outside his dominion. He who supremely exists gives to the Devil himself his natural subsistence, since whatever exists owes its existence to God.

78. Gen. 1, 28.

Those two goods, then, as I have said, flow as it were from the fountain of God's goodness even into a nature corrupted by sin and condemned to punishment. The first of them, propagation, God conferred by his blessing in the course of those first creative works from which he rested on the seventh day, while the second, conformation, he still gives in his continued activity up to this day. In fact, if God were to withdraw his effective power from the world, his creatures could not make progress, to attain their prescribed development and complete their span of life; in fact they could not even continue in the state in which they were created. Therefore God created man with the added power of propagation, so that he could beget other human beings, conveying also to those offspring the possibility, not the necessity, of propagation. True, God did remove this power from certain individuals, at his pleasure, making them infertile; but he did not deprive the whole race of this gift, when once it had been conferred on the first pair by that blessing on mankind. This reproductive power, then, was not removed by man's sin; 'man, placed in a position of honour is brought to the level of the beasts',[79] and he breeds like the beasts. And yet there is still the spark, as it were, of that reason in virtue of which he was made in the image of God; that spark has not been utterly put out.

Now if conformation to type were not preserved in that reproduction, the line of propagation would not keep to its specific forms and modes of being. Furthermore, even if human beings had not cohabited, and God had decided nevertheless to fill the world with mankind, he could have created all human beings, as he created the first man, without the mating of the sexes, whereas without God's creative power the mating could not produce offspring. And so we may apply to this physical reproduction what the Apostle says about spiritual creation, and the fashioning of man in religion and righteousness. St Paul says, 'It is not the planter, or the waterer, that is important: it is God, for he gives the growth.'[80] Similarly we can say in this context, 'It is not the act of mating, or the insemination, that matters; it is God who gives the form. It is not the mother, who conceives, carries, bears and feeds, that matters; it is God, for he gives the growth.'

For it is through God's creative activity which continues to this day that the seeds display themselves and evolve as it were from secret and invisible folds into the visible forms of this beauty which appear to our eyes. It is God who effects that miraculous combination of an immaterial with a material substance, with the former in command, the

79. Ps. 49, 12; 20. 80. 1 Cor. 3, 7.

latter in subjection; God unites them to make a living creature. This is a work of such wonder and grandeur as to astound the mind that seriously considers it, and to evoke praise to the Creator; and this is true not only as that work is observed in man, a rational being and on that account of more excellence and greater worth than all other creatures, but even in the case of the tiniest fly. It is God who has given man his mind. In the infant the reason and intelligence in the mind is, in a way, dormant, apparently non-existent; but, of course, it has to be aroused and developed with increasing years. And thus the mind becomes capable of knowledge and learning, ready for the perception of truth, and able to love the good. This capacity enables the mind to absorb wisdom, to acquire the virtues of prudence, fortitude, temperance, and justice, to equip man for the struggle against error and all the evil propensities inherent in man's nature, so that he may overcome them because his heart is set only on that Supreme and Unchanging Good. Man may indeed fail in this; yet, even so, what a great and marvellous good is this capacity for such good, a capacity divinely implanted in a rational nature!

Who can adequately describe, or even imagine, the work of the Almighty? There is, first, this capacity for the good life, the ability to attain eternal felicity, by those arts which are called virtues, which are given solely by the grace of God in Christ to the children of the promise and of the kingdom.[81] And besides this there are all the important arts discovered and developed by human genius, some for necessary uses, others simply for pleasure. Man shows remarkable powers of mind and reason in the satisfaction of his aims, even though they may be unnecessary, or even dangerous and harmful; and those powers are evidence of the blessings he enjoys in his natural powers which enable him to discover, to learn, and to practise those arts. Think of the wonderful inventions of clothing and building, the astounding achievements of human industry! Think of man's progress in agriculture and navigation; of the variety, in conception and accomplishment, man has shown in pottery, in sculpture, in painting; the marvels in theatrical spectacles, in which man's contrivances in design and production have excited wonder in the spectators and incredulity in the minds of those who heard of them; all his ingenious devices for the capturing, killing, or taming of wild animals. Then there are all the weapons against his fellow-man in the shape of prisons, arms, and engines of war; all the medical resources for preserving or restoring health; all the seasonings or spices to gratify his

81. Gal. 4, 28; Matt. 8, 12.

palate or to tickle his appetite. Consider the multitudinous variety of the means of information and persuasion, among which the spoken and written word has the first place; the enjoyment afforded to the mind by the trappings of eloquence and the rich diversity of poetry; the delight given to the ears by the instruments of music and the melodies of all kinds that man has discovered. Consider man's skill in geometry and arithmetic, his intelligence shown in plotting the positions and courses of the stars. How abundant is man's stock of knowledge of natural phenomena! It is beyond description, especially if one should choose to dwell upon particulars, instead of heaping all together in a general mass. Finally, the brilliant wit shown by philosophers and heretics in defending their very errors and falsehoods is something which beggars imagination! It must be remembered that we are now speaking of the natural abilities of the human mind, the chief ornament of this mortal life, without reference to the faith or to the way of truth, by which man attains to the life eternal.

Since the creator of this nature, with all its powers, is, we know, the true and supreme God, and since he governs all that he has made, exercising supreme power and supreme justice, then assuredly that nature would never have fallen into this wretchedness, would never have been destined to proceed from those miseries into eternal woes (except for some, who will be set free), had it not been for the overwhelming gravity of that first sin committed by the first man, the father of the whole human race.

Moreover, even in the body, which is something we have in common with the brute creation – which is in fact weaker than the bodies of any of the lower animals – even here what evidence we find of the goodness of God, of the providence of the mighty Creator! Are not the sense organs and the other parts of that body so arranged, and the form and shape and size of the whole body so designed as to show that it was created as the servant to the rational soul? For example: we observe how the irrational animals generally have their faces turned towards the ground; but man's posture is erect, facing towards the sky, to admonish him to fix his thoughts on heavenly things. Then the marvellous mobility with which his tongue and hands are endowed is so appropriate, so adapted for speaking and writing and for the accomplishment of a multitude of arts and crafts. And is not this sufficient indication that a body of this kind was designed as an adjunct to the soul? And does it not show the character of the soul it serves? And even if we take out of account the necessary functions of the parts, there is a harmonious congruence between them, a beauty in their equality and correspondence, so much so that one would be at a loss to say whether utility or beauty is the major consideration in their creation.

This would be more apparent to us if we were aware of the precise proportions in which the components are combined and fitted together; and it may be that human wit could discover these proportions, if it set itself to the task, in the exterior parts which are clearly visible. As for the parts which are hidden from view, like the complex system of veins, sinews and internal organs, the secrets of the vital parts, the proportions of these are beyond discovery. Even though some surgeons, anatomists they are called, have ruthlessly applied themselves to the carving up of dead bodies, even though they have cut into the bodies of dying men to make their examinations, and have probed into all the secrets of the human body, with little regard for humanity, in order to assist their diagnosis, to locate the trouble and find a method of cure – even after all that, no man could ever find, no man has ever dared to try to find, those proportions of which I am speaking, by which the whole body, within and without, is arranged as a system of mutual adaptation. The Greeks call this adaptation 'harmony', on the analogy of a musical instrument; and if we were aware of it, we should find in the internal organs also, which make no display of beauty, a rational loveliness so delightful as to be preferred to all that give pleasure to the eyes in the outward form – preferred, that is, in the judgement of the mind, of which the eyes are instruments. There are some details in the body which are there simply for aesthetic reasons, and for no practical purpose – for example, the nipples on a man's chest, and the beard on his face, the latter being clearly for a masculine ornament, not for protection. This is shown by the fact that women's faces are hairless, and since women are the weaker sex, it would surely be more appropriate for them to be given such a protection. Now if it is true (and it is scarcely a matter of debate) that there is no visible part of the body which is merely adapted to its function without being also of aesthetic value, there are also parts which have only aesthetic value without any practical purpose. Hence it can, I think, readily be inferred that in the design of the human body dignity was a more important consideration than utility. For practical needs are, of course, transitory; and a time will come when we shall enjoy one another's beauty for itself alone, without any lust. And this above all is a motive for the praise of the Creator, to whom the psalm says, 'You have clothed yourself in praise and beauty.'[82]

82. Ps. 104, 1 (LXX).

Then there is the beauty and utility of the natural creation, which the divine generosity has bestowed on man, for him to behold and to take into use, even though mankind has been condemned and cast out from paradise into the hardships and miseries of this life. How could any description do justice to all these blessings? The manifold diversity of beauty in sky and earth and sea; the abundance of light, and its miraculous loveliness, in sun and moon and stars; the dark shades of woods, the colour and fragrance of flowers; the multitudinous varieties of birds, with their songs and their bright plumage; the countless different species of living creatures of all shapes and sizes, amongst whom it is the smallest in bulk that moves our greatest wonder – for we are more astonished at the activities of the tiny ants and bees than at the immense bulk of whales. Then there is the mighty spectacle of the sea itself, putting on its changing colours like different garments, now green, with all the many varied shades, now purple, now blue. Moreover, what a delightful sight it is when stormy, giving added pleasure to the spectator because of the agreeable thought that he is not a sailor tossed and heaved about on it![83] Think too of the abundant supply of food everywhere to satisfy our hunger, the variety of flavours to suit our pampered taste, lavishly distributed by the riches of nature, not produced by the skill and labour of cooks! Think, too, of all the resources for the preservation of health, or for its restoration, the welcome alternation of day and night, the soothing coolness of the breezes, all the material for clothing provided by plants and animals. Who could give a complete list of all these natural blessings?

I have here made a kind of compressed pile of blessings. If I decided to take them singly, to unwrap each one, as it were, and examine it, with all the detailed blessings contained within it, what a time it would take! And these are all the consolations of mankind under condemnation, not the rewards of the blessed. What then will those rewards be, if the consolations are so many and so wonderful? What will God give to those whom he has predestined to life, if he has given all these to those predestined to death? What blessings in that life of happiness will he provide for those for whom in this life of wretchedness he willed that his only-begotten Son should endure such sufferings, even unto death? That is why the Apostle speaks of those predestined to that kingdom in those words: 'God did not spare his own Son, but gave him up on behalf of us all. Then is it not certain that with this gift he will give us all he has to give?'[84] When this promise

83. cf. Lucr. 2, 1ff. 84. Rom. 8, 23.

is fulfilled, what shall we be? What will be our condition? What blessings are we to receive in that kingdom, seeing that in Christ's death for us we have already received such a pledge! What will man's spirit be like when it is free from any kind of imperfection, when there are no evil tendencies for man to be subject to, or to yield to, or to fight against – however praiseworthy such a struggle may be; when the spirit of man is made perfect in undisturbed peace and goodness!

How complete, how lovely, how certain will be the knowledge of all things, a knowledge without error, entailing no toil! For there we shall drink of God's Wisdom at its very source, with supreme felicity and without any difficulty. How wonderful will be that body which will be completely subdued to the spirit, will receive from the spirit all that it needs for its life, and will need no other nourishment! It will not be animal; it will be a spiritual body, possessing the substance of flesh, but untainted by any carnal corruption.

25. *The obstinacy of those who deny the resurrection of the body*

Now there is no dispute between us and the well-known philosophers about the blessings that the soul will enjoy in perfect felicity after this life. But they quarrel with us about the resurrection of the body; in fact they strenuously deny it. And yet the increase of believers has left very few who deny this resurrection. Many have come to believe, learned as well as unlearned, the wise of this world as well as the simple. They have turned with faithful hearts to Christ, who has proved, by his resurrection, the truth of what seems absurd to this obstinate few. The world has come to believe in what God foretold would happen; and God foretold also that the world would believe in it. And, of course, it was not the witchcraft of Peter[85] that compelled God to make this prediction so long before, to win the praise of believers. For he is the God before whom the pagan divinities themselves shrink in dread. Such, at least, is the admission of Porphyry,[86] who is concerned to prove this by the oracles of those goods of his. I have mentioned this several times already; but I think it worthwhile to remind the reader once again. Porphyry in fact goes so far in his praise of our God as to call him Father, and King. It would be intolerable to understand his prediction in the sense desired by those who have not joined the world in believing what God predicted that the world would come to believe. Surely it is better to take it in the sense in which the

85. cf Bk XVIII, 53f. 86. cf. Bk XIX, 22; XX, 24.

world believes it, as it had been predicted so long before that the world would come to believe, and not in the sense, or nonsense, suggested by a mere handful, who refuse to join the world in believing it in the way predicted.

Now they may say that we must interpret this belief in another way, on the ground that if they said the scriptural evidence was nonsense they would be offering an insult to the God whom they commend so highly. But surely they insult him as much, if not more, if they say that the Scriptures are to be understood otherwise than the world has believed them; for God himself approved the belief that the world would come to hold; he promised this belief, and he has fulfilled that promise. Are we to suppose that God cannot effect the resurrection of the body to eternal life? Or is it that we must not believe that he will do so, on the ground that it would be an evil thing, something unworthy of God? As for God's omnipotence, which he shows in the performance of so many great marvels, I have said a great deal about this already. But if our friends want to discover something that the Almighty cannot do, here they have it: *God cannot lie*. And so let us believe that he will do what he *can* do by refusing to believe that he does what he *cannot* do. Thus, by refusing to believe that God can lie, our philosophers may reach the belief that he will do what he has promised to do; and let them believe it in the sense in which the world has come to believe it, since God foretold that the world would believe; he approved that the world should hold this belief; he promised that the world would believe; and by now he has shown that the world has come to believe.

And how can these dissentients show that this resurrection is an evil thing? There will be no corruption there, and corruption is the evil of the body. The question of order of the elements I have already discussed; and I have said enough about other conjectural theories put forward by human ingenuity. As for the swiftness of movement to be expected in an incorruptible body, and of the immortal condition of the body, and its incorruptible superiority to the state of perfectly balanced health in this present body, these points I have, I believe, established adequately in my thirteenth book.[87] Those who have not read those earlier passages, or who wish to refresh their memory, may refer back to what I have said there.

87. Bk XIII, 18.

26. *Porphyry's contention, that souls in bliss can have no contact with a body, is refuted by Plato*

Our philosophers quote Porphyry as saying that if the soul is to be in bliss it must be free of all contact with a body; and so, according to them, it is of no use for us to say that the body is to be incorruptible, seeing that the soul will not be blessed unless it escapes altogether from anything material. Now I have already dealt with this objection, as far as was required, in the thirteenth book; and here I will call attention to one point only. Plato, the master of all those philosophers, must correct his own writings, if this is true. For Plato says that those gods of theirs have been shut up in heavenly bodies; and so, if Porphyry is right, Plato must say that those gods will escape from their bodies, that is, that they will die, in order to attain to bliss. And yet God, their creator, promised them immortality, that they would dwell for ever in those same bodies in order to assure them of their felicity. And this was not because of something in their nature, but because of his all-powerful design. In the same passage Plato also refutes the contention that the resurrection of the body is incredible simply because it is impossible. In fact, God, the uncreated, is represented in Plato as saying quite explicitly to the gods created by him that he is going to do something impossible; this is when he promises them immortality. This is what he says, in Plato's narrative: 'Because you have come into being, you cannot be immortal and indissoluble; and yet you will never suffer dissolution, nor will the fate of death ever destroy you. For that fate will not prevail over my purpose, which is a bond for your perpetuity, a more powerful bond than those by which you are bound together.'[88] No one, unless he is deaf as well as daft, could have any doubt, on hearing these words, that the creator God, according to Plato, promised the gods of his creation that he would do an impossibility. For in saying, 'It is true that you cannot be immortal, but by my will you shall be immortal', he is saying, in effect, 'By my act you will become something which is impossible.'

And so he who, in Plato, promised to perform this impossibility, will raise up the flesh so that it will be incorruptible, immortal, and spiritual. Why do these objectors still cry out that what God has promised is impossible, when the world has believed in God's promise, as it was promised that the world would believe, and when we cry out that it is God who will do this; and God does impossible things, as even Plato himself declares?

88. cf. Bk XIII, 16f; Plat., *Tim.*, 41Af.

It follows that what is needed for the soul's life of bliss is not the escape from any kind of body but the possession of an imperishable body. And what imperishable body could be more fitting for their joy than the body in which, when it was perishable, they endured their sorrow? For in that condition they will not experience that 'dread lust' of which Virgil (following Plato) speaks, that makes them

once more desire
To take a mortal body.[89]

I mean that in this state they will feel no desire to return to a mortal body, when they will possess the body to which they desire to return, and possess it in such a way as never to relinquish that possession, never to be parted from that body by any death even for a brief moment.

27. *The contradictions between Plato and Porphyry. If they yielded to one another in these they would not be far from the truth*

Plato and Porphyry each made certain statements which might have brought them both to become Christians if they had exchanged them with one another. Plato said that souls could not exist for ever in a bodiless state; for that is why he said that the souls even of the wise will return into bodies again, after no matter how long a time. Porphyry, on his side, said that the soul completely purified will never return to the evils of this world after it has gone back to the Father. Thus, if Plato had communicated to Porphyry the truth he had seen, namely that even the souls of the just and wise, after complete purification, will return to human bodies, and if Porphyry, on his part, had communicated to Plato the truth that he had seen, that holy souls will never return to the miseries of the perishable body;[90] if, that is, those were not beliefs peculiar to each of them, but held jointly by both, then, I imagine, they would see that it followed that souls would return to bodies, and would receive the kind of bodies in which they might live in bliss and immortality. For even holy souls, according to Plato, will return to human bodies, while Porphyry maintains that holy souls will not return to the evils of this world. Let Porphyry, then, join Plato in saying, 'They will return to bodies'; and let Plato say, with Porphyry, 'They will not return to evils.' Then let them

89. Virg., *Aen.*, 6, 751; cf. Plat., *Phaedr.*, 249A; *Rp.*, X, 619f.
90. cf. Bk XIII, 16; XXII, 12.

agree that they will return to the kind of bodies in which they will suffer no evils. Such bodies can only be those which God promises when he says that blessed souls will live for ever with their own flesh. As far as I can see, they would both readily grant so much to us; I mean that, having admitted that the souls of saints will return to immortal bodies, they would allow them to return to their own bodies, the bodies in which they endured the ills of this life, the bodies in which they had worshipped God with faithful devotion so that they might be delivered from these miseries.

28. *How Plato, Labeo, or even Varro might have brought themselves to a true faith in the resurrection, if their opinions had combined into a unified statement*

A number of our people have a great affection for Plato because of the unique charm of his style, and because of a number of points on which he had a true insight; and for that reason they say that his view about the resurrection of the dead was something like ours. Cicero, however, in touching on this in his work *On the Commonwealth*,[91] asserts that Plato was speaking in fun and not intending a statement of truth. For he tells of a man who came to life again and gave an account of some experiences which agreed with Plato's arguments.[92] Labeo[93] also says that there were two men who died on the same day, and they met at a cross-roads, and were afterwards commanded to return to their bodies; and they determined that they would live together in friendship, and they did so, until they afterwards died again. Now these authors have told stories of a bodily resurrection taking place, of a kind such as happened with those whom we know to have been restored to this life, but not in the sense that they did not die again. But Marcus Varro records a more marvellous matter in his book *On the Race of the Roman People*. I have thought it best to quote his own words:

> Some 'genethliacs' (casters of nativities) have laid it down that for men who are to be born again there is what the Greeks call *palingenesia* ('another birth'); and this, according to them, takes place after four hundred and forty years. Its effect is to bring again into conjunction the same body and the same soul which were formerly united in a human being.

Now there is something of importance said here by Varro, or by his 'genethliacs', whoever they were; for he records their opinion without

91. Probably in De Rep. 6 (of which only fragments remain).
92. Plat., *Rp.*, 614Bff (The vision of Er). 93. cf. Bk II, 11.

revealing their names. The theory is false, to be sure, because in fact, when the souls have once returned to the bodies in which they were formerly clothed, they are never to leave them thereafter; and yet this theory overthrows and destroys many of the arguments for the impossibility of the resurrection, the subject on which our opponents are continually harping. For those who hold, or have held, this theory cannot suppose it impossible that corpses which have disintegrated into the atmosphere, into dust, into ashes, into fluids, into the bodies of animals, or even of men, who devoured them – that such bodies should return to their former state.

Therefore Plato and Porphyry, or rather their admirers now living, agree with us in believing that even holy souls will return to bodies (as Plato says), but that they will not return to any evils (as Porphyry says). Now it follows from these premises that the soul will receive the kind of body in which it can live for ever in felicity, without any evil; and this is the teaching of the Christian faith. Then all they have to do is to add, from Varro, the doctrine that the soul returns to the same body as before; and then the whole difficulty about the resurrection of the flesh will be solved for them.

29. *The kind of vision with which the saints will see God, in the world to come*

Now let us see, as far as the Lord deigns to help us to see, what the saints will be doing in their immortal and spiritual bodies, when the flesh will no longer be living 'according to the flesh' but 'according to the spirit'. And yet, to tell the truth, I do not know what will be the nature of that activity, or rather of that rest and leisure. I have never seen it with my physical sight; and if I were to say that I had seen it with my mind – with my intellect – what is the human understanding, in capacity or in quality, to comprehend such unique perfection? For there will be that 'peace of God which', as the Apostle says, 'is beyond all understanding'.[94] It surpasses our understanding; there can be no doubt of that. If it surpasses the understanding even of the angels, so that St Paul in saying 'all understanding' does not make an exception of them, we must then take him as meaning that the peace of God, the peace that God himself enjoys, cannot be known by the angels, still less by us men, in the way that God experiences it. And so 'beyond understanding' means, without doubt, 'beyond all understanding except his own'.

94. Phil. 4, 7.

But we, in our measure, are made partakers of his peace; and so we know the perfection of peace in ourselves, peace among ourselves, and peace with God, according to our standard of perfection. Likewise the angels know it, in their measure. But human beings in their present state know it in a far lower degree, however highly developed may be their intellectual powers. We must remember what a great man it was who said, 'Our knowledge is partial, and our prophesying is partial, until perfection comes', and, 'We now see a dim reflection in a mirror; but then we shall see face to face.'[95] This is how the holy angels see already, those who are called *our* angels, because we have been rescued from the power of darkness, we have received the pledge of the Spirit, and have been transferred to the kingdom of Christ, and so we already begin to belong to those angls with whom we shall share the possession of that holy and most delightful City of God, about which I have already written all these books. Thus those angels of God are also *our* angels, in the same way as the Christ of God is *our* Christ. They are God's angels because they have not abandoned God; they are our angels because they have begun to have us as their fellow-citizens. And the Lord Jesus said, 'Take care not to despise any of these little ones; for I tell you that their angels in heaven always see the face of my Father who is in heaven.'[96] Therefore we also shall see as they see already; but we do not as yet see like this. That is why the Apostle says, as I have already quoted, 'Now we see a puzzling reflection in a mirror; but then we shall see face to face.' And so this vision is reserved for us as the reward of faith; and the apostle John speaks of the vision in these words: 'When he is fully revealed, we shall be like him, because we shall see him as he is.'[97] Now we must take 'the face' of God as meaning his revelation and not the part of the body such as we have and to which we give that name.

Hence, if I am asked what will be the activity of the saints in that spiritual body, I cannot say that I see now; I can only say that I believe, as it says in the psalm, 'I believed, and therefore I spoke.'[98] And so I say that the saints will see God *in* the body; but whether they will see *through* the eyes of the body, in the same way as we now see the sun, moon, stars, sea and earth and all things on the earth – that is no easy question. It is, for example, hard to say that the saints will then have bodies of such a kind that they will not be able to shut and open their eyes at will; and yet it is more difficult to say that anyone who shuts his eyes there will not see God.

95. 1 Cor. 13, 9ff. 96. Matt. 18, 10.
97. 1 John 3, 2. 98. Ps 116, 10.

Now, the prophet Elisha, though not physically present, saw his servant Gehazi receiving the gifts from Naaman the Syrian, whom the prophet had healed from leprosy, while the wicked servant assumed that he had not been observed, since his master was not there to see. How much more then in that spiritual body will the saints see everything, not only if they close their eyes, but even when they are not present in the body! For that will be the time of the perfection of which the Apostle speaks when he says, 'Our knowledge is partial and our prophesying is partial; but when perfection comes then all that is incomplete will disappear.' St Paul then tries to find an analogy to express the difference between this life and the life that is to come, and not only the present life of ordinary people but even the life of those endowed with special sanctity. And he says,

> When I was a child, I used to think like a child, to speak like a child, to reason like a child: but now that I have become a man I have put childish habits behind me. Now we see a puzzling reflection in a mirror; but then we shall see face to face. The knowledge I now have is partial; but then I shall know as clearly as I am known.[99]

Thus the prophetic power of men of wonderful powers in this life is as childhood to maturity, in comparison with the knowledge enjoyed in that life to come. And yet even in the conditions of this life Elisha saw his servant receiving those gifts, although he himself was not there. We must conclude then that when perfection has come, when 'the corruptible body no longer weighs down the soul',[100] but when the body, freed from corruption, offers no hindrance to the soul, the saints will certainly need no bodily eyes to see what is there to be seen, since Elisha did not need them to see his servant when he himself was not present.

According to the Septuagint translation, the prophet said to Gehazi, 'Did not my heart go with you, when the man turned back from his chariot to meet you, and you took the money. . . .' But Jerome's translation from the Hebrew is, 'Was not my heart there present, when the man returned from his chariot to meet you?'[101] It was therefore in his heart that the prophet saw what happened, as he himself said, with the miraculous assistance, as no one doubts, of the divine power. But how much more richly will all abound in that gift, when God will be all in all![102] Nevertheless, those physical eyes also will have their own function and the spirit will make use of them through the spiritual body. For the prophet did not need those bodily

99. 1 Cor. 13, 9f. 100. Wisd. 9, 10.
101. 2 Kings 5, 26. 102. 1 Cor. 15, 28.

organs to see his absent servant; but that did not mean that he did not use them to see things at hand, although he could have seen them by the spirit even if he had closed his eyes, in the same way as he saw things not present, when he was not in any physical relationship with them. So we must never think of saying that the saints in that life will not see God if their eyes are shut; for they will always see him in the spirit.

But the puzzle is, whether they will also see by means of the bodily eyes when they have them open. For if even those spiritual eyes will in this way have no more power in the spiritual body than the eyes which we now have, then without doubt it will not be possible to see God by their means. Therefore they will be possessed of a very different power, if that immaterial nature is to be seen by their means – that nature which is not confined to any space but is everywhere in its wholeness. For we say that God is in heaven and earth (as he himself says, through his prophet: 'I fill heaven and earth'[103]); but that does not mean that we are to say that he has part of himself in heaven and part in earth. He is wholly in heaven, wholly in earth, and that not at different times but simultaneously; and this cannot be true of a material substance. Therefore the power of those eyes will be extraordinary in its potency – not in the sense of being a sharper eyesight than that possessed, they say, by snakes and eagles (for however keen-sighted those animals may be, they can see only material things) – but in the sense of having the ability to see the immaterial. And it may be that this extraordinary power of sight was given for a time even in this mortal body to the eyes of the holy man Job, when he says to God, 'I heard you before by the hearing of the ear, but now my eye sees you. Therefore I am sunk in self-contempt and consumed with self-despair. I am dust and ashes in my own esteem.'[104] Although there is nothing here to forbid its interpretation in the sense of the 'eye of the heart' referred to by the Apostle when he speaks of having 'the eyes of the heart enlightened'.[105] But no Christian doubts that it is with those eyes of the heart, or mind, that God will be seen, when he is seen. For every Christian accepts with faith the truth of the saying of God, his teacher, 'Blessed are the pure in heart, because they will see God.'[106]

But the point in question is whether God will be seen also with physical eyes in that future life. Now we have the scriptural statement that 'all flesh will see the salvation of God';[107] but this need

103. Jer. 23, 24. 104. Job 42, 5f. 105. Eph. 1, 18.
106. Matt. 5, 8. 107. Luke 3, 6.

present no difficulty; it can be taken to mean that 'everyone will see the Christ of God', and he certainly has been seen in physical form, and he will be so seen when he comes to judge the living and the dead. And that he is the salvation of God is shown by the testimony of many scriptural passages; but the clearest of testimony is given in the words of the venerable old man Simeon, who took the infant Christ into his arms and said, 'Now, Lord, you are releasing your servant in peace, according to your promise, because my eyes have seen *your salvation*.'[108] And the words of Job, as given in a version based directly on the Hebrew, 'and I shall see God in my flesh',[109] were undoubtedly prophetic of the resurrection of the flesh. And yet he does not say, '*by means of* my flesh I shall see God.' Indeed, even if he had so put it, he could have been taken to mean 'I shall see Christ, my God, who will be seen in flesh and through the medium of flesh.' As it is, we may take it to mean, 'I shall be in the flesh, when I shall see God.'

As for the Apostle's phrase, 'face to face',[110] that does not compel us to believe that we shall see God by means of this corporal face, with its corporal eyes. We shall see God by the spirit without any interruption. For if there was not also a 'face' of the inner man the same Apostle would not say, 'But we, gazing at the glory of the Lord with face unveiled, are transformed into the same image from glory to glory, as it were by the Spirit of the Lord.'[111] And we can give no other interpretation to the verse of the psalm which says, 'Approach him and be enlightened; and your faces will not be ashamed.'[112] For it is by faith that we approach God, and faith is a matter of mind and heart, not of the physical body. And yet we do not know what new qualities the spiritual body will have, for we are speaking of something beyond our experience. And so, when there are some things which are beyond our understanding, and on which the authority of holy Scripture offers no assistance, then we must needs be in the state described in the Book of Wisdom, in these words: 'The thoughts of men are timorous and our foresight is uncertain.'[113]

Now the philosophers maintain that 'intelligible' things are seen by the mind's vision, and 'sensible' things, that is, material things, are apprehended by the bodily senses, whereas the mind, they say, cannot observe intelligible things by means of the body, nor material things by its own unaided activity. If this reasoning could be established as certain, then indeed it would entail the certainty that God cannot be

108. Luke 2, 29f. 109. Job 19, 26. 110. 1 Cor. 13, 12.
111. 2 Cor. 3, 18. 112. Ps. 34, 6. 113. Wisd. 9, 14.

seen at all by the eyes of the body, even of a spiritual body. But in fact this reasoning is shown up as ridiculous both by reason itself and by the authority of the prophets. For who could be so estranged from the truth as to dare to assert that God is ignorant of material things? But does it follow that for such knowledge he must have a body, so as to attain this knowledge by means of bodily eyes? Again, the story of the prophet Elisha, which we were discussing just now, shows quite clearly that material things can be apprehended by the spirit, without the help of the bodily organs. For when the servant Gehazi took the presents, that was certainly a material happening; yet the prophet saw it by the spirit, not by the bodily sense. It is agreed, then, that material things are apprehended by the spirit; why should there not likewise be such a mighty power in a spiritual body that the spirit may be perceived by such a body? For God is Spirit.[114] Moreover, everyone is aware of his own life, the life with which he is now alive in the body, the life which makes those earthly members grow, and makes them living; everyone is aware of this life not by means of the eyes of the body but through the inward sense. However, the lives of others, although invisible, he sees by means of the body. For how do we distinguish living bodies from non-living except by observing bodies and lives simultaneously? We cannot see the lives except by means of the body and yet we do not observe with bodily eyes the lives apart from the bodies.

For such reasons it is possible, it is indeed most probable, that we shall then see the physical bodies of the new heaven and the new earth in such a fashion as to observe God in utter clarity and distinctness, seeing him present everywhere and governing the whole material scheme of things by means of the bodies we shall then inhabit and the bodies we shall see wherever we turn our eyes. It will not be as it is now, when the invisible realities of God are apprehended and observed through the material things of his creation, and are partially apprehended by means of a puzzling reflection in a mirror. Rather in that new age the faith, by which we believe, will have a greater reality for us than the appearance of material things which we see with our bodily eyes. Now in this present life we are in contact with fellow-beings who are alive and display the motions of life; and as soon as we see them we do not *believe* them to be alive, we *observe* the fact. We could not observe their life without their bodies; but we see it in them, without any possibility of doubt, through their bodies. Similarly, in the future life, wherever we turn the spiritual eyes of our bodies we

114. John 4, 23.

shall discern, by means of our bodies, the incorporeal God directing the whole universe.

God then will be seen by those eyes in virtue of their possession (in this transformed condition) of something of an intellectual quality, a power to discern things of an immaterial nature. Yet it is difficult, if not impossible, to support this suggestion by any evidence of passages in holy Scripture. An alternative suggestion is easier to understand: perhaps God will be known to us and visible to us in the sense that he will be spiritually perceived by each one of us in each one of us, perceived in one another, perceived by each in himself; he will be seen in the new heaven and the new earth, in the whole creation as it then will be; he will be seen in every body by means of bodies, wherever the eyes of the spiritual body are directed with their penetrating gaze.

The thoughts of our minds will lie open to mutual observation; and the words of the Apostle will be fulfilled; for he said, 'Pass no premature judgements', adding immediately, 'until the Lord comes. For he will light up what is hidden in darkness and will reveal the thoughts of the heart. And then each one will have his praise from God.'[115]

30. *The eternal felicity of the City of God in its perpetual Sabbath*

How great will be that felicity, where there will be no evil, where no good will be withheld, where there will be leisure for the praises of God, who will be all in all![116] What other occupation could there be, in a state where there will be no inactivity of idleness, and yet no toil constrained by want? I can think of none. And this is the picture suggested to my mind by the sacred canticle, when I read or hear the words, 'Blessed are those who dwell in your house; they will praise you for ever and ever!'[117]

All the limbs and organs of the body, no longer subject to decay, the parts which we now see assigned to various essential functions, will then be freed from all such constraint, since full, secure, certain and eternal felicity will have displaced necessity; and all those parts will contribute to the praise of God. For even those elements in the bodily harmony of which I have already spoken, the harmonies which, in our present state, are hidden, will then be hidden no longer. Dispersed internally and externally throughout the whole body, and combined with other great and marvellous things that will then be revealed, they will kindle our rational minds to the praise of the great

115. 1 Cor. 4, 5. 116. 1 Cor. 15, 28. 117. Ps. 84, 5.

Artist by the delight afforded by a beauty that satisfies the reason.

I am not rash enough to attempt to describe what the movements of such bodies will be in that life, for it is quite beyond my power of imagination. However, everything there will be lovely in its form, and lovely in motion and in rest, for anything that is not lovely will be excluded. And we may be sure that where the spirit wills there the body will straightway be; and the spirit will never will anything but what is to bring new beauty to the spirit and the body.

There will be true glory, where no one will be praised in error or in flattery; there will be true honour, where it is denied to none who is worthy, and bestowed on none who is unworthy. And honour will not be courted by any unworthy claimant, for none but the worthy can gain admission there. There will be true peace, where none will suffer attack from within himself nor from any foe outside.

The reward of virtue will be God himself, who gave the virtue, together with the promise of himself, the best and greatest of all possible promises. For what did he mean when he said, in the words of the prophet, 'I shall be their God, and they will be my people'?[118] Did he not mean, 'I shall be the source of their satisfaction; I shall be everything that men can honourably desire: life, health, food, wealth, glory, honour, peace and every blessing'? For that is also the correct interpretation of the Apostle's words, 'so that God may be all in all'.[119] He will be the goal of all our longings; and we shall see him for ever; we shall love him without satiety; we shall praise him without wearying. This will be the duty, the delight, the activity of all, shared by all who share the life of eternity.

But what will be the grades of honour and glory here, appropriate to degrees of merit? Who is capable of imagining them, not to speak of describing them? But there will be such distinctions; of that there can be no doubt. And here also that blessed City will find in itself a great blessing, in that no inferior will feel envy of his superior, any more than the other angels are envious of the archangels. No one will wish to be what it has not been granted him to be; and yet he will be bound in the closest bond of peaceful harmony with one to whom it has been granted; just as in the body the finger does not wish to be the eye, since both members are included in the harmonious organization of the whole body. And so although one will have a gift inferior to another, he will have also the compensatory gift of contentment with what he has.

Now the fact that they will be unable to delight in sin does not

118. Lev. 26, 12. 119. 1 Cor. 15, 28.

entail that they will have no free will. In fact, the will will be the freer in that it is freed from a delight in sin and immovably fixed in a delight in not sinning. The first freedom of will, given to man when he was created upright at the beginning, was an ability not to sin, combined with the possibility of sinning. But this last freedom will be more potent, for it will bring the impossibility of sinning; yet this also will be the result of God's gift, not of some inherent quality of nature. For to be a partaker of God is not the same thing as to be God; the inability to sin belongs to God's nature, while he who partakes of God's nature receives the impossibility of sinning as a gift from God. Moreover, the stages of the divine gift had to be preserved. Free will was given first, with the ability not to sin; and the last gift was the inability to sin. The first freedom was designed for acquiring merit; the last was concerned with the reception of a reward. But because human nature sinned when it had the power to sin it is set free by a more abundant gift of grace so that it may be brought to that condition of liberty in which it is incapable of sin.

For the first immortality, which Adam lost by sinning, was the ability to avoid death; the final immortality will be the inability to die and in the same way, the first free will is the ability to avoid sin. For as man cannot lose the will to happiness, so he will not be able to lose the will to piety and justice. By sinning we lose our hold on piety and happiness; and yet in losing our happiness we do not lose the will to happiness. Certainly God himself cannot sin; are we therefore to say that God has no free will?

In the Heavenly City then, there will be freedom of will. It will be one and the same freedom in all, and indivisible in the separate individuals. It will be freed from all evil and filled with all good, enjoying unfailingly the delight of eternal joys, forgetting all offences, forgetting all punishments. Yet it will not forget its own liberation, nor be ungrateful to its liberator. It will remember even its past evils as far as intellectual knowledge is concerned; but it will utterly forget them as far as sense experience is concerned. For the highly trained physician is acquainted with almost all diseases, as far as they can be known in theory, while he is ignorant of most of them in respect of personal experience, since he has not suffered from them.

Thus, knowledge of evil is of two kinds: one in which it is accessible to apprehension by the mind, the other in which it is a matter of direct experience. Similarly, vices are known in one way through the teaching of the wise, and in another way in the evil life of the fools. There are two corresponding ways of forgetting evil. The learned scholar's way of forgetting is different from that of one who has experienced suffering. The scholar forgets by neglecting his studies; the sufferer, by escaping from his misery. The saints will have no sensible recollection of past evils; theirs will be the second kind of forgetfulness by which they will be set free from them all, and they will be completely erased from their feelings.

Yet such is the power of knowledge – and it will be very great in the saints – that it will prevent not only their own past misery but also the eternal misery of the damned from disappearing from memory. Otherwise, if they were to lose the knowledge of their past misery how will they, as the psalm says, 'sing the mercies of the Lord for all eternity'?[120] Nothing will give more joy to that City than this song to the glory of the grace of Christ by whose blood we have been set free. There that precept will find fulfilment: 'Be still, and know that I am God.'[121] That will truly be the greatest of Sabbaths; a Sabbath that has no evening, the Sabbath that the Lord approved at the beginning of creation, where it says, 'God rested on the seventh day from all his works, which he had been doing; and *God blessed the seventh day* and made it holy, because on that day he rested from all his works, which God had begun to do.'[122]

We ourselves shall become that seventh day, when we have been replenished and restored by his blessing and sanctification. There we shall have leisure to be still, and we shall see that he is God, whereas we wished to be that ourselves when we fell away from him, after listening to the Seducer saying, 'You will be like gods.' Then we abandoned the true God, by whose creative help we should have become gods, but by participating in him, not by deserting him. For what have we done without him? We have 'fallen away in his anger'.[123] But now restored by him and perfected by his greater grace we shall be still and at leisure for eternity, seeing that he is God, and being filled by him when he will be all in all.[124]

For all our good works, when they are understood as being his works, not ours, are then reckoned to us for the attainment of that Sabbath rest. If we ascribe them to ourselves they will be 'servile work', and it is said that, on the Sabbath, 'You shall do no servile work.'[125] Hence the message by the mouth of the prophet Ezekiel: 'I gave them my Sabbaths as a sign between me and them; so that they might know that I am the Lord, and that I sanctify them.'[126] This we

120. Ps. 89, 2. 121. Ps. 46, 11. 122. Gen. 2, 2f. 123. Ps. 90 (LXX).
124. 1 Cor. 15, 28. 125. Deut. 5, 14. 126. Ezek. 20, 12.

shall then know perfectly, when we are perfectly at rest, and in stillness see perfectly that he is God.

Now if the epochs of history are reckoned as 'days', following the apparent temporal scheme of Scripture, this Sabbath period will emerge more clearly as the seventh of those epochs. The first 'day' is the first period, from Adam to the Flood; the second from the Flood to Abraham. Those correspond not by equality in the passage of time, but in respect of the number of generations, for there are found to be ten generations in each of those periods.

From that time, in the scheme of the evangelist Matthew, there are three epochs, which take us down to the coming of Christ; one from Abraham to David, a second from David to the Exile in Babylon, and the third extending to the coming of Christ in the flesh. Thus we have a total of five periods. We are now in the sixth epoch, but that cannot be measured by the number of generations, because it is said, 'It is not for you to know the dates: the Father has decided those by his own authority.'[127] After this present age God will rest, as it were, on the seventh day, and he will cause us, who are the seventh day, to find our rest in him.

However, it would be a long task to go on to discuss each of those epochs in detail. The important thing is that the seventh will be our Sabbath, whose end will not be an evening, but the Lord's Day, an eighth day, as it were, which is to last for ever, a day consecrated by the resurrection of Christ, foreshadowing the eternal rest not only of the spirit but of the body also. There we shall be still and see; we shall see and we shall love; we shall love and we shall praise. Behold what will be, in the end, without end! For what is our end but to reach that kingdom which has no end?

*

And now, as I think, I have discharged my debt, with the completion, by God's help, of this huge work. It may be too much for some, too little for others. Of both these groups I ask forgiveness. But of those for whom it is enough I make this request: that they do not thank me, but join with me in rendering thanks to God. Amen. Amen.

127. Acts 1, 7.

Index